MW01025455

"As any seminary instructor will tell you, finding a good introductory textbook on the Old Testament is no easy task. Some are too critical while others are too general. Some are too conservative while others are too progressive. Some are too comparative while others are too insular. Some are too historical while others are too theologically oriented, often with little or no regard for the literary-historical context of the text itself. Rick Hess, however, has truly found a 'golden mean' with this new introduction. Students, teachers, pastors, and anyone else interested in the Word of God will love it."

—**Michael S. Moore**, Fuller Theological Seminary

"An intelligent introduction accessible to the neophyte while engaging the more experienced Old Testament reader. Hess ably balances the needs of seminarians and graduate students in a 'rich and multifaceted' exposition of the Old Testament. This is a go-to volume for thoughtful entry to not only the Old Testament but also the disciplines of its study. With attention to interpretive voices through time and surveys of interpretive methods behind, in, and in front of the text, this book is the work of a senior scholar engaged thoughtfully and passionately in the study and teaching of the Old Testament."

—**Lissa M. Wray Beal**, Providence Theological Seminary

"This new introduction to the Old Testament offers a brief outline and overview of each book, considers the history of its interpretation, and provides an analysis of its major themes within the context of the broader biblical canon. It represents an impressive synthesis of the dimensions of modern biblical study identified in its title: the historical, the theological, and the critical."

—**Iain Provan**, Regent College

"Hess has provided a comprehensive introduction to the study of the Old Testament that covers a wide range of scholarship, including his own careful analysis of every Old Testament book. He writes on the subject with remarkable erudition and clarity, making the work accessible and comprehensible to a broad audience. This book is an invaluable resource for any serious student of the Bible. I highly recommend it."

—**Carol M. Kaminski**, Gordon-Conwell Theological Seminary

"An accessible yet informed introduction to the Old Testament. Hess orients readers to a breadth of approaches from ancient to modern without losing sight of the content of Scripture and its theological message for today."

—**Mark J. Boda**, McMaster Divinity College and McMaster University

THE OLD TESTAMENT

A Historical, Theological, and Critical Introduction

RICHARD S. HESS

B
Baker Academic
a division of Baker Publishing Group
Grand Rapids, Michigan

© 2016 by Richard S. Hess

Published by Baker Academic
a division of Baker Publishing Group
P.O. Box 6287, Grand Rapids, MI 49516-6287
www.bakeracademic.com

Printed in the United States of America

All rights reserved. No part of this publication may be reproduced, stored in a retrieval system, or transmitted in any form or by any means—for example, electronic, photocopy, recording—without the prior written permission of the publisher. The only exception is brief quotations in printed reviews.

Library of Congress Cataloging-in-Publication Data
Names: Hess, Richard S., author.
Title: The Old Testament : a historical, theological, and critical introduction / Richard S. Hess.
Description: Grand Rapids, MI : Baker Publishing Group, 2016. | Includes bibliographical references and index.
Identifiers: LCCN 2016024916 | ISBN 9780801037146 (cloth)
Subjects: LCSH: Bible. Old Testament—Introductions. | Bible. Old Testament—Criticism, interpretaiton, etc.
Classification: LCC BS1140.3 .H47 2016 | DDC 221.6/1—dc23
LC record available at https://lccn.loc.gov/2016024916

Unless otherwise indicated, Scripture quotations are from the New Revised Standard Version of the Bible, copyright © 1989, by the Division of Christian Education of the National Council of the Churches of Christ in the United States of America. Used by permission. All rights reserved.

Quotations labeled NIV are from the Holy Bible, New International Version®. NIV®. Copyright © 1973, 1978, 1984, 2011 by Biblica, Inc.™ Used by permission of Zondervan. All rights reserved worldwide. www.zondervan.com

In quoting NRSV and NIV, Yahweh often replaces Lord.

16 17 18 19 20 21 22 7 6 5 4 3 2 1

To Nathan, Cameryn, Miriam, Taylor, Rachel, Abigail, and Kelton,
God's gifts to their grandparents.
May they each learn to love the Old Testament,
and may they each come to know the One
whom the Old Testament reveals.

CONTENTS

PREFACE

The story of this book began shortly after the publication of *Israelite Religions*. Jim Kinney, vice president for Baker Publishing Group, asked me to consider writing a survey of the Old Testament that could be used in seminaries and graduate schools. At the time it seemed to be a daunting task. Various events and circumstances intervened during the years that followed to slow the completion of this work. However, I found that the process gave me an opportunity for a closer review of the vast literature. I benefited from many new works that added to my understanding of the subjects addressed and that have enriched the volume greatly.

This book is designed to meet the needs of the broad variety of students who come to study the Old Testament at a seminary or at a graduate level. It does not presume a deep knowledge of the Scriptures, although I wrote it with the intent to inform any serious reader. It is written in a world different from the days when I attended seminary as a student. I review the text and its criticism as well as offer an evaluation of critics and their theories. There is theological reflection on each Old Testament book along with consideration of the value in teaching each one. However, there are also sections on how each book and its message fit into the larger canon of the Old and New Testaments. I provide reviews of the history of interpretation, especially as the text was studied and preached in the synagogue and in the church through the centuries. There is an examination of the literary aspects of each text that extends beyond traditional form criticism and includes modern and postmodern approaches. Here as well I attempt to go beyond my own limitations and at an introductory level to reflect the manner in which the text has come to mean something in areas of gender, globalization, and various (post)modern ideologies. In this manner an attempt is made to respect and touch on many of the newer approaches to the interpretation of the Old Testament or Hebrew Bible for today.

I thank Jim Kinney and Baker Academic for supporting this work and for their patience through the process of writing it. I am also grateful for the students in my classes at Denver Seminary, from whom I have learned much and whose reading of some of this book in manuscript form assisted in enhancing its value. My colleagues in the department, M. Daniel ("Danny") Carroll R., Hélène Dallaire, and now Knut Heim, have taught me much, and I thank them. The interest and encouragement of Provost Randy MacFarland, President Mark Young, and Chancellor Gordon MacDonald meant a great deal as I worked away over the years. I also wish to thank Matt Hollomon for his eagerness to proofread much of the manuscript. May God bless each of these in their life, family, and work. There are many other colleagues and fellow students of these ancient books whom I cannot list here, yet my gratitude goes to each who has influenced me in so many ways. I, of course, take full responsibility for the contents of this work.

Most of all I extend my appreciation to my family. Our children and their spouses—Fraser and Elizabeth Hess, Greig and Jenna Hess, and Fiona and David Glas—all mean more to me than I can express. Every day I give God thanks for them and for their own wonderful children, to whom this book is dedicated. More than to anyone else, I express my deepest thanks to my wonderful wife, Rev. Dr. Jean Hess. Through these years she has been a source of encouragement and joy. She has challenged and invited me to learn more about myself and to begin to understand what married life means as God created it. At our 316 Celtic Christian Church, where Jean serves as lead pastor and I assist, we have walked the good road of ministry together. As fellow pilgrims in Celtic Christianity, we have sung and prayed to God and visited the ancient sites of this academic and mission movement of old. In 2013 I was delighted to see a further physical and spiritual expression of this in the revised publication of Jean's *Journey to the Manger with St. Patrick and Friends: A Six-Week Celtic Advent Devotional*. It is within this ancient life of Christianity and its values of creation, mission, fellowship, and outreach to those in need that we have come to find an integration of the Old Testament with the faith of the ages and with our own lives. It is out of these many influences and blessings that I offer this study for the glory of God and for the edification of those who seek to understand better the inheritance of faith.

Visit www.bakeracademic.com/professors
to access study aids
and instructor materials
for this textbook.

ABBREVIATIONS

General, Versions, and Ancient Sources

AD	Anno Domini
Ant.	*Jewish Antiquities*, by Josephus
ASV	American Standard Version
AT	Alpha Text (of LXX)
b.	Babylonian Talmud
B. Bat.	*Baba Batra*
BC	before Christ
BHK	*Biblia Hebraica*. Edited by Rudolph Kittel. Leipzig: Hinrichs, 1905–6
BHQ	*Biblia Hebraica Quinta*. Edited by Adrian Schenker et al. Stuttgart: Deutsche Bibelgesellschaft, 2004–
BHS	*Biblia Hebraica Stuttgartensia*. Edited by Karl Elliger and Wilhelm Rudolph. Stuttgart: Deutsche Bibelgellschaft, 1983
ca.	circa, around, approximately
cf.	*confer*, compare
chap(s).	chapter(s)
col(s).	column(s)
D	Deuteronomist source
E	Elohist source
e.g.	*exempli gratia*, for example
esp.	especially
ESV	English Standard Version
etc.	*et cetera*, and the rest of the same kind
fl.	*floruit*, flourished
frg.	fragment
HCSB	Holman Christian Standard Bible
Heb.	Hebrew
Hist.	*Histories*, by Herodotus
idem	the same (author)
i.e.	*id est*, that is
J	Jahwist or Yahwist source
KJV	King James Version
lit.	literally
LXX	Septuagint, OT in Greek plus the Apocrypha
m.	Mishnah
mg.	marginal reading/note
MT	Masoretic Text (Hebrew Bible) and its verse numbers
NASB	New American Standard Bible
NIV	New International Version
NJPS	*The Tanakh: The New Jewish Publication Society Translation* (1985)
NKJV	New King James Version
NLT	New Living Translation

no(s).	number(s)
NRSV	New Revised Standard Version
NT	New Testament
OT	Old Testament, Hebrew Bible
p(p).	page(s)
P	Priestly source
pl.	plural
4QMMT	a sample Dead Sea Scroll, this found in Cave 4 near Qumran
rev.	revised
RSH	translation by Richard S. Hess
RSV	Revised Stand Version
TLB	The Living Bible
v(v).	verse(s)
vol(s).	volume(s)
vs.	versus
×	times a term appears

Journals and Series

AB	Anchor Bible and Anchor Yale Bible
ABD	*Anchor Bible Dictionary*. Edited by David Noel Freedman. 6 vols. Garden City, NY: Doubleday, 1992
ABR	*Australian Biblical Review*
ABRL	Anchor Bible Reference Library
ACCS	Ancient Christian Commentary on Scripture
ALASP	Abhandlungen zur Literatur Alt-Syrien-Palästinas und Mesopotamiens
ANET	*Ancient Near Eastern Texts Relating to the Old Testament*. Edited by James Pritchard. 3rd ed. Princeton: Princeton University Press, 1969
AOAT	Alter Orient und Altes Testament
AOTC	Apollos Old Testament Commentary
ARM	Archives royales de Mari
ASOR	American Schools of Oriental Research
AT	Alalakh Text, numbering follows Donald J. Wiseman, *The Alalakh Tablets*. Occasional Publications of the British Institute of Archaeology at Ankara 2. London: British Institute of Archaeology, 1953
BA	*Biblical Archaeologist*
BAR	*Biblical Archaeology Review*
BASOR	*Bulletin of the American Schools of Oriental Research*
BBR	*Bulletin for Biblical Research*
BBRSup	Bulletin for Biblical Research Supplement
BCOTWP	Baker Commentary on the Old Testament: Wisdom and Psalms
BETL	Bibliotheca ephemeridum theologicarum lovaniensium
Bib	*Biblica*
BibInt	*Biblical Interpretation*
BK	*Bibel und Kirche*
BKAT	Biblischer Kommentar, Altes Testament
BLS	Bible and Literature Series
BN	*Biblische Notizen*
BR	*Bible Review*
BT	*The Bible Translator*
BTB	*Biblical Theology Bulletin*
BZAW	Beihefte zur Zeitschrift für die alttestamentliche Wissenschaft
CahRB	Cahiers de la Revue biblique
CB	Coniectanea biblica: Old Testament Series
CBC	Cambridge Bible Commentary
CBQ	*Catholic Biblical Quarterly*
ConC	Continental Commentaries

COS	*The Context of Scripture*. Edited by William W. Hallo and K. Lawson Younger Jr. 3 vols. Leiden: Brill, 1997–2002
CurRes	*Currents in Research in Biblical Studies*
DJ	*Denver Journal: An Online Review of Current Biblical and Theological Studies*
DJD	Discoveries in the Judaean Desert
DOTHB	*Dictionary of the Old Testament: Historical Books*. Edited by Bill T. Arnold and Hugh G. M. Williamson. Downers Grove, IL: InterVarsity; Leicester: InterVarsity, 2005
DOTP	*Dictionary of the Old Testament: Prophets*. Edited by Mark J. Boda and Gordon J. McConville. Downers Grove, IL: IVP Academic; Nottingham, UK: InterVarsity, 2012
DOTWPW	*Dictionary of the Old Testament: Wisdom, Poetry and Writings*. Edited by Tremper Longman III and Peter Enns. Downers Grove, IL: IVP Academic; Nottingham, UK: Inter-Varsity, 2008
DRev	*The Downside Review*
DTIB	*Dictionary for Theological Interpretation of the Bible*. Edited by Kevin J. Vanhoozer, Craig G. Bartholomew, Daniel J. Treier, and N. T. Wright. London: SPCK; Grand Rapids: Baker Academic, 2005
EA	El Amarna letter
ECC	Eerdmans Critical Commentary
ErIsr	*Eretz Israel*
FAT	Forschungen zum Alten Testament
FCB	Feminist Companion to the Bible
FOTL	Forms of Old Testament Literature
HAR	*Hebrew Annual Review*
HAT	Handbuch zum Alten Testament
HCOT	Historical Commentary on the Old Testament
HS	*Hebrew Studies*
HSM	Harvard Semitic Monographs
HSS	Harvard Semitic Studies
HTS	Harvard Theological Studies
HUCA	*Hebrew Union College Annual*
IBC	Interpretation: A Bible Commentary for Teaching and Preaching
ICC	International Critical Commentary
IEJ	*Israel Exploration Journal*
Int	*Interpretation*
JAAR	*Journal of the American Academy of Religion*
JAOS	*Journal of the American Oriental Society*
JATS	*Journal of the Adventist Theological Society*
JBL	*Journal of Biblical Literature*
JBS	Jerusalem Biblical Studies
JCS	*Journal of Cuneiform Studies*
JETS	*Journal of the Evangelical Theological Society*
JJS	*Journal of Jewish Studies*
JNES	*Journal of Near Eastern Studies*
JPSBC	Jewish Publication Society Bible Commentary
JPSTC	Jewish Publication Society Torah Commentary
JSem	*Journal for Semitics*
JSNTSup	Journal for the Study of the New Testament: Supplement Series

JSOT	*Journal for the Study of the Old Testament*
JSOTSup	Journal for the Study of the Old Testament: Supplement Series
JTT	*Journal of Translation and Textlinguistics*
KBANT	Kommentare und Beiträge zum Alten und Neuen Testament
KEL	Kregel Exegetical Library
KHC	Kurzer Hand-Commentar zum Alten Testament
KTU	*The Cuneiform Alphabetic Texts from Ugarit, Ras Ibn Hani and Other Places*. Edited by Manfried Dietrich, Oswald Loretz, and Joaquín Sanmartín. 3rd, enlarged ed. AOAT 360/1. Münster: Ugarit-Verlag, 2013
LHBOTS	Library of Hebrew Bible/Old Testament Studies
LNTS	Library of New Testament Studies
LOT	Literature of the Old Testament
Ma	*Maarav*
MCI	Modern Critical Interpretations
NAC	New American Commentary
NCB	New Century Bible
NCBC	New Cambridge Bible Commentary
NEA	*Near Eastern Archaeology*
NIBC	New International Biblical Commentary
NICNT	New International Commentary on the New Testament
NICOT	New International Commentary on the Old Testament
NIVAC	New International Version Application Commentary
NSBT	New Studies in Biblical Theology
OBO	Orbis biblicus et orientalis
OEBB	*The Oxford Encyclopedia of the Books of the Bible*. Edited by Michael D. Coogan. 2 vols. Oxford: Oxford University Press, 2011
OLA	Orientalia lovaniensia analecta
OTE	*Old Testament Essays*
OTG	Old Testament Guides
OTL	Old Testament Library
OTS	Oudtestamentische studiën
PEQ	*Palestine Exploration Quarterly*
RB	*Revue biblique*
RCSOT	Reformation Commentary on Scripture: Old Testament
RGG	*Die Religion in Geschichte und Gegenwart*. Edited by K. Galling. 6 vols. 3rd ed. Tübingen: Mohr Siebeck, 1957–65
RS	Ras Shamra
RSR	*Religious Studies Review*
SAA	State Archives of Assyria
SBA	Stuttgarter biblische Aufsatzbände
SBL	Society of Biblical Literature
SBLDS	Society of Biblical Literature Dissertation Series
SBLSCS	Society of Biblical Literature Septuagint and Cognate Studies
SBLWAW	Society of Biblical Literature Writings from the Ancient World
SBS	Stuttgarter Bibelstudien
SBT	Studies in Biblical Theology
SBTS	Sources for Biblical and Theological Study
SCS	Septuagint Commentary Series
SEL	*Studi epigrafici e linguistici*
SHANE	Studies in the History of the Ancient Near East

SHBC — Smyth & Helwys Bible Commentary
SJOT — *Scandinavian Journal of the Old Testament*
SOTBT — Studies in Old Testament Biblical Theology
SSN — Studia semitica neerlandica
STDJ — Studies on the Texts of the Desert of Judah
TA — *Tel Aviv*
TCLA — Texts from Christian Late Antiquity
TDOT — *Theological Dictionary of the Old Testament*. Edited by G. Johannes Bottterweck, Helmer Ringgren, and Heinz-Josef Fabry. Translated by J. T. Willis, D. E. Green, and D. W. Stott. 15 vols. Grand Rapids: Eerdmans, 1974–2006
Them — *Themelios*
TOTC — Tyndale Old Testament Commentary
TynBul — *Tyndale Bulletin*
UBL — Ugaritisch-biblische Literatur
UF — *Ugarit-Forschungen*
VT — *Vetus Testamentum*
VTSup — Vetus Testamentum Supplements
WBC — Word Biblical Commentary
WUNT — Wissenschaftliche Untersuchungen zum Neuen Testament
ZA — *Zeitschrift für Assyriologie*
ZABR — *Zeitschrift für altorientalische und biblische Rechtsgeschichte*
ZAW — *Zeitschrift für die alttestamentliche Wissenschaft*
ZDPV — *Zeitschrift des deutschen Palästina-Vereins*
ZIBBCOT — *Zondervan Illustrated Bible Backgrounds Commentary: Old Testament*. Edited by John H. Walton. 5 vols. Grand Rapids: Zondervan, 2009

INTRODUCTION

The Old Testament just seems old! What value does it have for someone living in the twenty-first century, thousands of years after the last book was written? Can it speak to us today? What message does it still hold? In fact, what is the Old Testament, and how do we begin to understand it? We will look at these questions as we journey through the Old Testament, its interpretation, and its teaching.

The purpose of this introduction is threefold: (1) to explain the definition and structure of the Old Testament, (2) to provide essential guidance regarding the composition and manuscript evidence of the Old Testament, and (3) to orient readers to the study of the Old Testament, surveying the interpretive methods explored in the following chapters of this work. Along the way this book will consider the makeup of the Old Testament, examine the Old Testament's claims about its special place, consider what can be known about how it came into existence as a book, review the most important early manuscripts that constitute the Old Testament, and discuss the study of the Old Testament as a prelude to the remainder of this introductory survey.

Definition and Structure of the Old Testament

What is the Old Testament? At its simplest level this term comprises two words, an adjective and a noun. An internet search shows it as a name applied to a heavy metal band and a 1983 movie. Dictionaries explain that the noun derives from the Latin *testamentum*, meaning "a will," as in "last will and testament." An older use of the term understood it as a covenant. The first occurrence of the word for "covenant" in the Bible (Heb. *bĕrît*) appears in Genesis 6:18. There God establishes his covenant with Noah and his family when they enter the ark. God promises to deliver them. The word occurs again after Noah exits the ark, in Genesis 9:9–17. Here God promises never to destroy the earth again and presents the rainbow as the sign of this covenant. From the beginning the covenant establishes a relationship between God and humanity, one of preservation and salvation. For this reason the term "covenant" or "testament" signifies a document that describes such a relationship and brings salvation to humanity.

The adjective that describes this testament or covenant is "old." The term "old testament," or "old covenant," does not appear in the Old Testament itself. It occurs in 2 Corinthians 3:14 in the New Testament, where it takes on a sense in which a veil obscures the significance of the Old Testament until Jesus Christ removes it. The term "new covenant" does appear in the Old Testament. In Jeremiah 31:31 God promises that he will establish a new covenant in the future. Hebrews 8:6–13; 9:15; and 12:24 identify this new covenant with the work of Jesus. At the Last Supper, Jesus takes the cup and identifies it and its contents: "This cup is the new covenant in my blood" (Luke 22:20; cf. 1 Cor. 11:25). The old covenant, therefore, precedes the new covenant. For this reason some have used terms such as "Older Testament" or "First Testament" in place of "Old Testament." Nevertheless, the term "Old Testament" remains popular. From its perspective, it presupposes the New Testament that is to come in the future.

For this reason some argue that the term "Hebrew Bible" serves a greater ecumenical purpose. It is the common Jewish designation of the same texts of Scripture as the Protestant Old Testament. The term "Hebrew" may refer to the language in which most of the text is written, or it may refer to the Hebrew people, synonymous with the Jewish people in contemporary nomenclature. However, the use of the term "Old Testament" does not denigrate other traditions. Instead, it affirms the role of these texts in the Scriptures of Christian traditions. Indeed, the term has long been so popular that it takes the role of a proper name used in a wide variety of scholarly and lay contexts.

The component parts of the Old Testament include thirty-nine books. In the medieval and modern Hebrew Bibles and in Judaism today, these books comprise three sections. The first section, the Torah, consists of Genesis, Exodus, Leviticus, Numbers, and Deuteronomy. The second section is the Prophets, referred to in Hebrew as Nevi'im (or Nebi'im). This includes the Former Prophets, which are the history books of Joshua, Judges, 1–2 Samuel, and 1–2 Kings, and the Latter Prophets, which are Isaiah, Jeremiah, Ezekiel, and the twelve Minor Prophets. The third section is the Writings, or the Ketuvim (or Ketubim). These books are ordered thus: Job, Psalms, Proverbs, Ruth, Esther, Lamentations, Song of Songs (also called the Song of Solomon), Ecclesiastes, Daniel, Ezra, Nehemiah, and 1–2 Chronicles. Together these three divisions—Torah, Nevi'im, Ketuvim—are sometimes known by the acronym TaNaK (or Tanakh).

This ordering of books diverges from the Christian tradition, where Ruth follows Judges. Then 1–2 Chronicles, Ezra, Nehemiah, and Esther appear after 2 Kings—thus a core of historical books comes between the Torah and the poetic books. The Latter Prophets are moved to the end of the Old Testament. This volume follows this order, as do all of the Protestant Christian traditions (and the Roman Catholic tradition, if one omits the apocryphal additions, which some call deuterocanonical). The books may be divided into four major groups. The first is identical to the Jewish division, the Pentateuch or Torah, consisting of Genesis through Deuteronomy. The second section includes the Historical Books, from Joshua to Esther. The third division is that of the poetic books, beginning with Job and Psalms and extending through the Song of Songs. The last section is the prophetic books, made up of the Major Prophets and the Minor Prophets. The Major Prophets extend from Isaiah to Daniel, while the Minor Prophets include the Twelve that begin with Hosea and end with Malachi.

The Jewish canon and the Protestant Christian canon are not the only two examples of the manner in which books are ordered in the Old Testament. However, they have become the dominant means of organization. We begin with individual writings and scrolls. By the third or fourth century AD, what we know of as the Old Testament appears. These were collections of scrolls. Since the whole Old Testament had grown and could not be contained within a single scroll, it was distributed across many scrolls. For this reason the fixed order of the Old Testament canon did not appear until later, when manuscripts were bound in a codex (see the sidebar "The Codex").

The Codex

A codex is similar to the modern book form. The term "codex" (pl. "codices") is from the Latin *caudex*, which refers to a block of wood sawed into tablets and fastened at one edge—the earliest form of the codex. Later the leaves of the codex were of papyrus (cf. "paper") or parchment or vellum, often bound within wooden covers. Manuscript pages were folded in half and sewn into quires (like signatures in modern books), and quires were bound to one another. Beginning in the first century AD and gaining popularity during the second and third centuries, the codex came to be favored by Christians. With this format, it was eventually possible to collect the entire Bible (OT and NT, for the Christian church) into a single volume of a codex, such as the well-known early complete Bibles: Codex Vaticanus, Codex Sinaiticus, and Codex Alexandrinus (see "Uncial Greek Manuscripts" in the discussion of textual criticism).

Composition and Manuscript Evidence of the Old Testament

Canon

Contents of the Old Testament

Without the canon there can be no Bible.[1] So what is the canon of the Old Testament, and how did it come into existence? The term "canon" has come to include the sense of any official body of media or literature. With reference to the Bible it indicates those books or portions of Scripture that are regarded as inspired and thus carry an authority as God's Word. The specific issues of inspiration and authority address concerns appropriate to the various theologies of Christian traditions. Believers want to understand the formation of the text as authoritative Scripture. Jewish and Protestant faiths recognize an identical set of books as the Old Testament, or the Hebrew Bible. The Roman Catholic Church adds Tobit, Judith, 1–2 Maccabees, Wisdom (of Solomon), Sirach (also called Sira, Ben Sira, or Ecclesiasticus), Baruch, and Additions to Daniel and to Esther. This additional literature is called the deuterocanonical ("second canon") books or the Apocrypha ("hidden"). The Eastern Orthodox canon of the Old Testament includes additional books, as is also true of some Oriental churches. For example, the Coptic Church recognizes *1 Enoch* as a book of Scripture. Moving in the opposite direction, the ancient Samaritans focused on the Torah alone as their canon.

Early Testimony to the Old Testament Canon

The origins of a concept of canon for the Old Testament remain lost to history. However, Deuteronomy 4:2 and 12:32 demonstrate that even in biblical times the writers and readers drew a line between what they thought of as Scripture and what they did not. These texts forbid the addition or subtraction of anything that does not belong to what was originally revealed. The prologue of Sirach, from the second century BC, refers to "the Law and the Prophets and the other books of our ancestors." Philo of Alexandria, writing in the early decades of the first century AD, described psalms and laws and oracles delivered through the mouths of prophets (*Contemplative Life* 25). Thus some of the earliest Jewish literature witnesses to an awareness of Scripture and a threefold division of those sacred texts. While the New Testament bears witness to this sort of structure (Luke 24:44), both Jesus's words and those of other Gospel writers also attest to a twofold form: the Law and the Prophets (Matt. 7:12; 22:40; Luke 16:16; Acts 13:15; Rom. 3:21).

Further witnesses to the Old Testament canon also emerged by the first century AD, especially with regard to the number of books (or scrolls) that

1. For discussion of this topic and for further bibliography, see, e.g., McDonald, *Biblical Canon*; idem, *Formation of the Bible*. Among the many other works discussing this subject, see esp. Wegner, *From Texts to Translations*.

writers ascribed to the sacred collection. In 2 Esdras (*4 Ezra*), which is often attributed to this period, Ezra is instructed to "make public" twenty-four books (14:44–46). More frequently the number twenty-two is mentioned: in the first century, by Josephus (*Against Apion* 1.39); in the late second century, by Origen (cited by Eusebius, *Ecclesiastical History* 2.25); and late in the fourth century, by Jerome (*Preface to Commentary on Samuel and Kings*). Such numbers presume the twelve Minor Prophets as a single book; the twofold divisions of Samuel, Kings, and Chronicles each taken as a single work; and other joinings of some books (e.g., Ezra–Nehemiah).

Later Jewish tradition (*b. Gittin* 56a–b) remembers a rabbinic council at Jamnia (Yavneh) sometime after the fall of Jerusalem in AD 70. References to a discussion possibly in this context appear as early as the Mishnah (*Yadayim* 3.5), compiled at the end of the second century. If the reference there to books that "defile the hands" implies those in the canon of the Hebrew Bible, then it affirms the continued inclusion of some challenged books such as Ecclesiastes and the Song of Songs.[2] Whether such a council actually occurred, the presence of discussion regarding these books, and perhaps Esther, is attested in this period in Judaism. There is, however, no explicit indication that authoritative sources denied these works canonicity. The only question was whether these works should continue to enjoy status as books that may be considered canonical. Both the memory of the discussion from this period and the unified witness of later Judaism attest that they did have this status.

Within early Christianity one of the first and most important witnesses is that of Melito bishop of Sardis (ca. AD 170). He journeyed to Palestine and returned with a canon that can be understood as equal to the Hebrew one, except for Esther.[3] The absence of Esther may have been his own decision since its pro-Jewish position has been a target for many Christians with anti-Semitic tendencies over the centuries.[4] However, this is not the only possibility.

Judean Desert Manuscripts

The Dead Sea Scrolls have received such prominent attention that a whole volume could be devoted to surveying the study of what they tell us about the Old Testament canon. These texts, found in the caves near Khirbet Qumran, were copied between about 250 BC and AD 70. The collection represents more than nine hundred scrolls, many preserved only in fragmentary form. Although Psalms is not the only biblical book under consideration, much

2. See discussion of and challenges to this by J. Lewis, "Jamnia Revisited."

3. Understanding Jeremiah to include Lamentations, Esdras to included Ezra and Nehemiah, and the Proverbs and Wisdom of Solomon to describe the book of Proverbs. The earliest source is the fourth-century church historian and bishop of Caesarea, Eusebius (*Ecclesiastical History* 4.26).

4. Cf. Bush, "Book of Esther." For an alternative suggestion, see "Name, Text, and Outline" for Esther (below).

has been made of the variety of orders and contents among multiple copies of the Psalms.[5] It is evident that some scrolls include psalms that are in addition to what is found in the Masoretic Text of the Psalms, the text on which all modern English translations of the Old Testament and Hebrew Bible are based.[6] Further, this variety of psalms occurs at times in a sequence different from the book of Psalms in the Masoretic Text.[7] Nevertheless, the Masada copy of the Psalms (from between about 50 BC and AD 72) follows the Masoretic Text closely.[8] And how were other books regarded? Some scholars have argued that texts such as *1 Enoch* and *Jubilees* were treated as canonical while Chronicles was not.[9] However, they cannot point to criteria that explicitly establish a canonical collection that includes these books.

Other evidence gives caution against the current, widespread assumption that the Old Testament canon was in flux in the first century AD. One text that counters this skepticism is 4QMMT (4Q398 frg. 10), which refers to "the book of Moses and the books of the prophets and David." This alludes to the threefold division of the canon of the Hebrew Bible found in contemporary Jewish writers, as already noted. While it does not establish the identification of the specific books in those categories, it does recognize categories of books within the canon.

Another concern has to do with the contents of the books themselves and the extent to which they were in flux. By one count about 40 percent of the biblical manuscripts traced to the caves of Qumran are proto-Masoretic.[10] This proto-Masoretic text, which lies behind the Masoretic text, was not selected at random by some later scholar choosing from multiple textual traditions. If that is the case, then perhaps the same may be said for the books included in the Masoretic Text. The same is true of all twenty-five non-Qumran biblical manuscripts and manuscript fragments copied between about 50 BC and AD 150 and found in two other Judean Desert sites: Masada and the Bar Kokhba caves.[11] They are all proto-Masoretic texts (see further "Hebrew Manuscripts" under the discussion of textual criticism, below).[12]

Apocrypha

Although the formation of many of the canons lies beyond the limits of this work, the question remains as to why there are two canons of the Old

5. Ulrich, "Text of the Hebrew Scriptures."
6. This includes all of those who regard the Hebrew texts of the OT as of primary importance.
7. See "Name, Text, and Outline" for Psalms (below).
8. For more on the Masada manuscripts, see the sidebar "Masada" (below).
9. Cf., e.g., Crawford, "'Rewritten' Bible," 1.
10. So Tov, "History and Significance," 64.
11. Tov, *Textual Criticism*, 29.
12. These are sometimes designated as precursors. A precursor is a manuscript lying in the textual tradition that leads directly to the later manuscripts in that tradition. In this case, the MT is that textual tradition.

The Origins of the Septuagint

The abbreviation for the Septuagint is LXX, the Roman numeral for seventy, reflecting the number of translators (also reported as 72) who worked on rendering the Hebrew Torah into Greek. This tradition appears in its earliest extant form in the Greek *Letter of Aristeas*. From clues within the letter itself, scholars have determined its likely origin to be in the second century BC. However, the letter purports to have as its author a witness to this translation in Alexandria during the reign of Ptolemy II, in about 275 BC. Later scholars embellished this tradition, emphasizing the miraculous nature of the agreement among the translators that created the Septuagint and thus trying to demonstrate its divine inspiration.

If Ptolemy II was a patron (and perhaps founder) of the celebrated library of Alexandria, it is reasonable that he, perhaps encouraged by the large Jewish community in Alexandria, would have sought a Greek translation of the most sacred books of Jewish Scripture. That he might have called a large body of scholars from Jerusalem to undertake this effort is also reasonable. Whether pairs of scholars were placed in separate huts for a specific amount of time and produced identical translations of the same Torah passages, as later tradition recounts, is not as self-evident. However, the Jews of Alexandria and in many cities around the Mediterranean (and beyond) spoke Greek as their first language. They would surely have received this translation well. The entire Hebrew Bible was rendered into Greek likely by the end of the third century BC or soon afterward.

Testament/Hebrew Bible that appear in mainstream Christianity and Judaism. As noted above, Protestant Christianity and Judaism hold to a canon of thirty-nine books. Roman Catholicism, however, bears witness to these books as well as to additional ones (the Apocrypha) as part of its canon (as deuterocanonical). The discussion surrounding these books is complex, with much disagreement.[13] What this work presents is a possible model for understanding the background of the different canons.

The Apocrypha appears in the earliest Bibles of the Greek translation of the Old Testament, called the Septuagint (LXX; see the sidebar "The Origins of the Septuagint"). The "books" of this time were scrolls, and a single translation of the Septuagint would have been written on perhaps two dozen such scrolls, so it is likely that these would have been assembled in collections of some sort, such as in the library of Alexandria, the meeting place of the Jews of Alexandria, or elsewhere. As additional Jewish literature was written

13. See the essays in McDonald and Sanders, *Canon Debate*. Cf. also Kraft, "Para-mania."

in Greek or translated into Greek, the best of this would have naturally been written in other scrolls placed with those of Scripture. As the codex format gained popularity in the second or third centuries, particularly among Christians (see the sidebar "The Codex," above), in the Greek-speaking communities, where the Septuagint continued to be regarded as the Holy Scriptures, it became natural for all these valued scrolls that had been gathered to be copied into a single codex. The Septuagint thus came to incorporate the apocryphal books as well as the earlier collection of thirty-nine translated books of the Hebrew Bible. As described below, the earliest complete Bibles known today are codices (pl. of codex) of the Greek Old Testament and New Testament that date from the fourth century AD. They include apocryphal books and, in some cases, additional literature from outside the canon, which became accepted along with the books of the Old and New Testaments. Gradually the role of these additional texts as Scripture was accepted by the communities who preserved them.

However, among the Hebrew-reading Jews, the canon of the Bible remained the thirty-nine books in the Hebrew Bible. This priority of the Hebrew canon influenced the religious world of Jesus in first-century Galilee. It is likely that Jesus, during his ministry, and the disciples (especially before AD 70) used this canon. Therefore, it is not surprising that Paul, writing in Greek, should credit the Jews with the identification and preservation of the "oracles of God" in Romans 3:1–2.

A Model for Canon Formation of the Hebrew Bible

A possible model for the formation of the Hebrew canon may be suggested here in broad outline. Deuteronomy 31:26 records that the "book of the law" (presumably Deuteronomy or a text similar to it) was to be placed in the most holy place of the tabernacle.[14] As the Word of God was being written, it continued to be collected and preserved in the Jerusalem temple, where it could be read and copied by others who were interested in its contents. By 586 BC copies would have been taken by the exiles out of the country, while other copies may have been hidden near Jerusalem. Even if copies were not already present at Jerusalem, Ezra returned with the books of the Law (the Pentateuch). He and others may have brought back various books of the

14. Timothy H. Lim, in *The Formation of the Jewish Canon*, asserts that the absence of explicit evidence for a collection of sacred texts in the Jerusalem temple proves that there was no such collection. He dates the Jewish formation of the canon to the second or third century AD. Michael L. Satlow, in *How the Bible Became Holy*, finds the first evidence of a canon in fourth-century-AD Christianity. David M. Carr, in *The Formation of the Hebrew Bible*, who studies more closely the Israelite educational system (beginning in the early Iron Age) as the context for the emergence of the biblical Scriptures, allows for a Hasmonean context for significant formation of the Old Testament, reaching back into the early centuries BC. These discussions demonstrate the paucity of evidence and the variety of reconstructions possible.

Bible to Jerusalem. In any case, a collection in the temple allowed the priesthood to regulate what they considered as Scripture and what they did not. At some point prophecy was regarded as having ceased, and the final scrolls came into the collection.[15] After that, as far as the sources attest,[16] no further scrolls were added to the Hebrew Bible as preserved in the Jerusalem temple. As noted above, these were the thirty-nine books that came to be known as the Old Testament. The rabbis recognized the authority of these texts after the fall of Jerusalem in AD 70.

Text and Textual Criticism

For any ancient text, such as the Bible, that was preserved and transmitted in manuscript (that is, hand-copied) form over a number of years, any two copies of the same text potentially differ in any given word or phrase. These differences are called variant readings. Textual criticism studies these differences and tries to understand how they came into being. Thus textual criticism consists of two parts: (1) the identification of manuscripts and their readings, and (2) the decisions and the reasonings (or mistakes) behind them to explain how the variant readings were obtained. The first part is a massive undertaking, given the thousands of manuscripts and the variants that they contain. The second part is both a science and an art: scholars disagree in the theory and method of the work and in the practical application of it for any given variant.

Textual Traditions

Because the subject of textual traditions is so important for establishing what the ancient text actually contained, it should be the first topic addressed for any text within the Old Testament. A full discussion lies beyond this book.[17] Space allows only for a review of the major textual traditions and the manuscripts represented by them. A textual tradition is a collection of manuscripts whose readings, although varying in some details, possess a general uniformity in their overall witness to a common text from which they were all copied. Textual traditions are often described as families of manuscripts. A textual tradition cannot be held in one's hand, but a manuscript can be so held, since a manuscript is an individual and tangible witness to that text.

15. Thus 1 Macc. 4:46, "until a prophet should come," suggests the absence of prophecy.

16. These sources include 1 and 2 Maccabees, as well as sources cited above that attest to major divisions and the number of books in the Hebrew Scriptures.

17. See (in English), e.g., Brotzman, *Old Testament Textual Criticism*; Deist, *Witnesses to the Old Testament*; Hess, "Textual Criticism (Old Testament)"; Jobes and Silva, *Invitation to the Septuagint*; Tov, *Text-Critical Use of the Septuagint*; idem, *Textual Criticism*; Wegner, *From Texts to Translations*; Würthwein, *Text of the Old Testament*.

The two largest general textual traditions for the Old Testament are those of the Septuagint (LXX) and of the Masoretic Text (MT). Greek manuscripts often represent the former, and Hebrew manuscripts tend to make up the latter. There are exceptions to this, however. The following catalog considers the major early witnesses to the Old Testament in terms of the known manuscripts and also looks at what textual traditions they represent. First we look at the Hebrew manuscripts of the Old Testament, and then we consider the Greek and other important ancient translations.

Hebrew Manuscripts

The earliest manuscript of any recognizable part of the Old Testament is a text of part of Numbers 6:24–26 found incised on two small silver scrolls discovered in 1979 during the excavation of Judean burial sites at Ketef Hinnom, immediately southwest of the city of David in Jerusalem. This text is too brief to make a definite connection with a particular tradition. However, it is a form of the blessing of Aaron as well as possibly Deuteronomy 7:9.[18] Because biblical texts would have been written on perishable materials such as papyrus or vellum (animal skin), these silver-inscribed scrolls are the only ancient biblical texts preserved in the settled areas of Judah and Israel, thus the earliest such texts.[19] Although they were discovered in a burial context that dates from the years immediately before the destruction of Jerusalem in 586 BC, it is likely that the actual composition of these silver manuscripts should be assigned an earlier date, in the seventh century BC.

Subsequent to this, the earliest dated manuscripts derive from the Dead Sea Scrolls (see above). The composition of these texts began around 250 BC and continued as late as the destruction of the site of Qumran, around AD 68. The textual traditions represented by several hundred biblical manuscripts are mixed. As noted above, at one point Emanuel Tov estimated that 40 percent of the biblical manuscripts closely follow the proto-Masoretic text.[20] However, another Hebrew textual tradition that developed, the Samaritan, finds representation among several manuscripts.[21] There are other unidentified textual traditions, or possibly creative renderings of the biblical text for other purposes (see, for example, the mention of pesher, below), as well as those related to the Bible only in a thematic fashion.[22] Among the most important Dead Sea Scrolls for textual criticism are the Hebrew fragments

18. Waaler, "Revised Date?"

19. Barkay et al., "Challenges of Ketef Hinnom"; idem, "Amulets from Ketef Hinnom."

20. Tov, "History and Significance," 64.

21. Notably 4QpaleoExod[m] (4Q22) and 4QNum[b] (4Q27).

22. The *Reworked Pentateuch* (4Q158) exemplifies a creative rendering of the biblical text, while Pseudo-Ezekiel and Pseudo-Daniel exemplify resemblances to the original books that are only thematic. Cf. Crawford, "'Rewritten' Bible."

Masada

South of Qumran, along the western shore of the Dead Sea, lies Masada, an outcropping of land with steep ascents from all directions. Here Herod the Great established an elaborate palace system as a retreat from the cares of Judea in the first century BC. Seventy years later, when the Judean war against Rome broke out, about a thousand Jewish zealots came to this site and lived there until AD 73; then, after the armies of Rome destroyed Jerusalem, the Romans laid siege to Masada. They built a massive siege ramp (still visible) and prepared to attack the site; the Jewish historian Josephus reports that, rather than fall into enemy hands, the community committed suicide (except for two women and five children, who hid in a cistern and survived). The Romans discovered the synagogue the Jews had made for their worship. But the biblical scrolls that the Jews brought with them remained buried until discovered in the twentieth century.

of Samuel (4QSam), whose readings remain closer to the Septuagintal textual tradition.[23]

If the proto-Masoretic text was the dominant text type during this time (see the discussion of canon, above), then how does one explain the other textual traditions among some of the Qumran manuscripts? There is an assumption that the Qumran discoveries have identified variant text types rather than variant purposes to which biblical texts might be used. Yet more could be made of how the Masada scrolls conform to the Masoretic Text, although these scrolls would arguably be closest to what Judaism of the first century recognized as the authoritative Hebrew text. They were brought from Jerusalem, possibly from the temple. The Masada Jewish community consisted of zealots whose political conviction to have an independent Judea could have led them to derive their biblical manuscripts from the exemplars in the Jerusalem temple, a form of the biblical text that Judaism most widely held and revered (see the sidebar "Masada"). However, the Qumran community represented a sectarian form of Judaism that had split away from the mainstream and formed its own group. Their manuscripts include copies of Scripture, but also paraphrases, pesher interpretations (explaining Scripture to fit current events), so-called parabiblical texts, and texts considerably different from the biblical materials on which they were based.[24] Various purposes for texts (e.g., liturgical, ideological) might have dictated selection of text traditions other than that accepted by the Jerusalem temple and motivated alteration

23. Cross et al., *Qumran Cave 4*.
24. See the review by Crawford, "'Rewritten' Bible."

of the wording to conform to the Qumran way of life. In light of this, taking all sources into consideration and weighing rather than counting variants, the dominant text type in the first century AD remains the proto-Masoretic Hebrew text.[25]

The Qumran and other manuscript evidence from around the Dead Sea did not suffer destruction, thanks to the dry climate and the remote and hidden locations of the manuscripts. The same has been true of manuscripts discovered in Egypt. The Nash Papyrus of the Decalogue and that of Deuteronomy 6:4–7 both date from the second century BC. Discovered in the nineteenth century, prior to the finding of the Dead Sea Scrolls, and (like the Dead Sea Scrolls) dated based on paleography (the study of handwriting and the shapes of the letters), these texts represented the earliest witness to the Old Testament.

The biblical manuscripts from Masada, excavated by Yigael Yadin and others in the mid-twentieth century, and from the caves of Bar Kokhba a century later, as well as from the desert site of Murabbaʿat (also of the second century AD), all witness to the proto-Masoretic textual tradition. The same tradition was found in the synagogue in the oldest part of Cairo. There, in 1896, renovations uncovered a room that proved to be an ancient genizah, a storehouse for sacred texts that contain the divine name of God. The Cairo Genizah has yielded about three hundred thousand fragments, including biblical manuscripts from as early as the fifth century AD.

A small fragment of the Hebrew Bible, possibly related to the Cairo Genizah collection, surfaced in Beirut in 1972, known as the Ashkar-Gilson manuscript number 2. It has been compared with another partial text, known as the London Manuscript, as having been written by the same person. Paul Sanders argues that both the Ashkar-Gilson manuscript and the London manuscript derive from the same Torah scroll and that it has been dated to the seventh or eighth century AD.[26] Together these unvocalized fragments contain parts of Exodus 9–16 and preserve a text identical to that used by the Masoretes. The structure, including the "brickwork" formatting of the poem in Exodus 15 (identical to the Masoretic Text), demonstrates that the Masoretes accurately copied earlier manuscripts.

Masoretic Text

The Masoretes themselves consisted of a few families who copied biblical manuscripts that were sold to synagogues. They flourished around AD 780–930, with their center in Tiberias, on the western shore of the Sea of Galilee. Most important for copying accurate texts was the Ben Asher family. The Aleppo Codex, thought to have been lost in the anti-Jewish riots of 1947, resurfaced and was purchased by the Israeli government. It may represent the finest example of the Masoretic tradition. Dating from AD 900–950, it reflects

25. Gentry, "Text of the Old Testament."
26. P. Sanders, "Missing Link."

the Masoretes' innovation of adding vowel letters to the consonantal text, plus accent marks and detailed notes, all designed to ensure accurate copying and reading of the entire Hebrew Bible. Codex Cairensis (from Cairo) dates from AD 895, and the Petersburg Codex of the Prophets dates from AD 916.

The addition of vowel letters provided the first complete edition of the Hebrew Bible that preserved both the consonantal text (as had the earlier manuscripts) and the oral tradition of pronouncing the Hebrew text. The former is called the *Kethib*, "that which is written." The latter is known as the *Qere*, "that which is read (out loud)." The two usually agree, but there are some important differences. For example, the divine name is written consonantly as *yhwh*. However, it is pronounced as *adonai*, "lord." Traditionally, this was done to preserve the sanctity of the name of God. However, other differences between the *Kethib* and the *Qere* indicate variations in how a text is understood and interpreted.

One of the most important and accurate exemplars in the Masoretic tradition is Codex Leningradensis (L), which dates from AD 1008 and is preserved in the Hermitage Museum in St. Petersburg. It is the standard for all United Bible Societies editions of the Hebrew Bible (e.g., *BHK*, *BHS*, and *BHQ* [first published in fascicles, 2004–]). While many of the earlier manuscripts in the proto-Masoretic tradition attest to the high degree of accuracy in the Masoretic copying of manuscripts, special note should be made of two texts that are important for Christian theology: Isaiah and the opening chapters of Genesis. Among the manuscripts from Qumran, 1QIsa[a] is remarkably close to the Isaiah of L, and 1QIsa[b] is even closer; although it is separated from L by more than one thousand years, only five complete words are added and six words are missing in a text that contains parts or all of forty-six chapters of Isaiah. Also, 4QGen[b] is identical to Genesis 1:1–4:11 in L. Thus the earliest Qumran finds dating from the third century BC bear evidence, among other things, of a tradition of the exact copying of texts belonging to the Masoretic family, that is, of proto-Masoretic texts. Where the manuscripts can be checked, this evidence suggests a tradition of precise copying of the biblical text.

Samaritan Manuscripts

A second Hebrew text tradition is that preserved by the Samaritans. Although not as important in terms of accuracy, it remains a witness to the early biblical text. The text was edited according to Samaritan theological interests. Manuscripts date from as early as the eleventh century AD, although a few manuscripts that date perhaps a millennium earlier from Qumran preserve this text tradition.

Greek Manuscripts

The Septuagintal textual tradition, while represented in a few Hebrew manuscripts at Qumran, remains primarily attested in Greek manuscripts and their translations. Some papyri and vellum Septuagint manuscripts from Egypt were discovered in the past century and include pentateuchal texts dating as early as the second century BC. The Qumran Septuagint Greek manuscripts of Leviticus, 4QLXXLev^{a} and 4QpapLXXLev^{b}, both date to the first century BC, and both preserve a text probably closer to the Old Greek (i.e., the first Greek translation) than to the later codices listed below. The 4QLXXLev^{a} manuscript is slightly freer than the later texts and seems to be revised toward the Masoretic Text.[27]

The Chester Beatty papyri, now preserved in the Chester Beatty Library in Dublin, were first announced in 1931. Discovered in a Coptic graveyard at or near the Fayum district of Egypt, these papyri include fragments of most of the Septuagint books of the Old Testament. Their dating is between the late second and fourth centuries AD, with most having been copied in the third century. Especially important is the text of Daniel (Papyri 967 and 968), which preserves the earliest and only witness of the Old Greek translation of this book, before its witness in later Hexaplaric manuscripts.[28]

An important Greek manuscript from the early second century AD is the scroll of the twelve Minor Prophets found at Naḥal Ḥever (8ḤevXIIgr). Although written in Greek, it is closer to the Masoretic textual tradition.

Hexapla

The Christian biblical scholar Origen, who lived in Caesarea and died ca. AD 253, undertook a major work in the final decades of his life. Copying the entire Old Testament in six columns (and at times eight), he produced the Hexapla. The first column contained the Hebrew (proto-MT), before vowel points and accents were inserted. The second column, with each verse corresponding to that in the first column, presented the Hebrew text in Greek transliteration. This provided the first known written text that attests the vocalization of the Hebrew text, using the Greek vowels. The third column held the Greek translation of Aquila, generally believed to be a convert to Judaism who produced the work around AD 130. The fourth column had the Greek translation of Symmachus, also believed to be a convert to Judaism, who produced the work around AD 170. The fifth column contained the Septuagint as Origen knew it. The sixth and final column presented the Greek translation credited to Theodotion, another convert to Judaism, usually dated to the second century AD. However, the New Testament and other early Greek references to the Bible preserve Theodotionic readings, which suggest that at least some of the sixth column of the Hexapla may predate the second century AD.

Jerome claims to have visited Caesarea around AD 400 and to have seen the original Hexapla. However, the work was not preserved in its entirety. Today fragmentary citations by later scholars witness to it as does a translation into

27. Tov, *Textual Criticism*, 132.
28. Ibid., 133.

Syriac some centuries later, known as the Syro-Hexapla. Where it is preserved, Origen's fifth column is a valuable witness to the early Septuagint. Although he edited the text he had received, Origen made notations every time he added or omitted any text. Unfortunately, the problems with the preservation of this text have included inaccurate copying of these notes. Thus it is not always certain what was original and what was added by Origen.

Uncial Greek Manuscripts

Most important are the uncial manuscripts of the Septuagint, preserved in a particular style of Greek writing, using uncial (primarily uppercase, or capital) letters. These are in the form of books, or codices, and provide the earliest extant copies of the entire Old Testament and of the entire Bible (OT and NT). The earliest of these codices is likely the fourth-century-AD Codex Vaticanus (B), preserved in the Vatican Library from at least as early as the fifteenth century. This codex, originating in either Egypt or Palestine (probably Caesarea), preserves the best complete Septuagint manuscript. It forms the basis for some of the most widely used later and modern editions and translations of the Septuagint, as well as the Septuagint Commentary Series (SCS). The latter provides a full text, translation, and commentary on the literary aspects of many biblical books in this codex.[29] Eusebius of Caesarea recounts how Constantine, when he united the Roman Empire under the official religion of Christianity in AD 325, commanded that fifty (Greek) Bibles be prepared to be distributed among the new churches being built in the East. Codex Vaticanus may have been one of those created for this purpose (*Life of Constantine* 4.37), although others argue that it originated somewhat later in the fourth century.

A second fourth-century uncial is Codex Sinaiticus (abbreviated S or א). This codex is generally thought to be slightly later than B; however, the two often agree and thus bear witness to the Old Greek. Even so, S has been further influenced by other Greek translation traditions and is not thought to have a text that reflects the earlier Septuagint as clearly as B. Codex Sinaiticus was found by Constantin von Tischendorf (1815–74) at Saint Catherine's Monastery in the southern Sinai Peninsula (at the base of Jebel Musa, the traditional site of Mount Sinai). When he departed from the monastery in 1859, he took the manuscript with him. His own claim that he discovered the text in a wastepaper basket was contradicted by the monks, who have maintained that Tischendorf borrowed the codex and never returned it. Today the British Library houses it.

The third-most important uncial is Codex Alexandrinus (A), dating from the fifth century AD. Scholars observe its tendency to harmonize conflicting

29. Published by Brill and edited by S. E. Porter, R. S. Hess, and J. Jarick; 13 volumes appeared by January 2015. Where the original Codex Vaticanus is not attested, as in much of Genesis, other textual evidence is incorporated.

passages. The Hexapla influenced A more than the other uncials, so that at times the codex follows the Hexaplaric tradition without variation.[30] Today it rests beside S in the British Library in London.

Greek Text Editions

The minuscule manuscripts (written with lowercase, cursive letters) date from the ninth to the sixteenth centuries AD. They are conveniently referenced in the major critical editions of the Septuagint: the earlier Cambridge edition and the more recent Göttingen Septuagint. Both use an eclectic text—the editor chooses the best reading from among the variants to assemble a new text.[31] The other variants are then listed in a detailed critical apparatus. Neither series is complete, although the Göttingen Septuagint continues to publish volumes.

Aramaic and Syriac Manuscripts

The third-most important language for Old Testament textual witnesses is Aramaic. This divides into two groups: Jewish Aramaic texts in Hebrew script and Christian Aramaic texts in the Syriac language and script. The Jewish Aramaic texts are best represented in the targums, which are homiletic paraphrases of biblical texts and refer to the biblical text. The Aramaic word "targum" (cf. Ezra 4:7 MT) refers to the rendering of a text in a particular language. While citizens of Judah (i.e., Yehud), in the Persian period and for centuries afterward, spoke and read Aramaic, their Bible was written in Hebrew. This required a translation of the biblical text, one that could be accompanied by an exposition of a passage's teaching and its application for the listeners. The earliest targum manuscripts date from the medieval period. Their contents render the date of authorship difficult; some scholars argue that the targums preserve traditions of interpretation extending to the early Christian or pre-Christian period. The Palestinian targums likely date between the beginning of Palestinian rabbinic literature and the Palestinian Talmud, in the first half of the first millennium AD.[32] The remaining Jewish targums also likely date from this period.[33] Thus the references to the Hebrew Bible provide valuable attestations as to the text used in the Holy Land and outside it by Jewish people in the early first millennium AD.

Christian Aramaic, known as Syriac, developed separate letter forms for the alphabet and evolved into different dialects. The Syriac translation of the Bible became known as the Peshitta. Some argue that the translation of the Bible into Syriac began as early as the second century AD, when Syriac-speaking

30. Tov, *Textual Criticism*, 133.

31. This is in contrast to a diplomatic text, which follows the text of a specific manuscript and notes variants from that text in the critical apparatus. This is the method used in *BHS* and *BHQ*, which follows the text of L.

32. Flesher and Chilton, *Targums*, 151–66.

33. Ibid., 169–264.

Edessa became the first kingdom to adopt Christianity as the official religion. This would suggest the text had a Christian origin and transmission. Nevertheless, some scholars have identified Jewish exegetical tendencies in the Torah. The earliest manuscripts date from the fifth century AD. The text lies in the proto-Masoretic tradition, although more divergent (i.e., with more variants) than the targums. Some books show affinities with the Septuagint, either in its exegetical interests or, as with Proverbs, in the translation itself.[34]

Latin Manuscripts

Latin translations of the Bible predate the church father Jerome, the translator of the Vulgate. These Old Latin fragments provide valuable witness to a text form as found in 1–2 Samuel and 1–2 Kings in some Greek versions. The so-called Lucianic version[35] provides examples of correction toward the proto-Masoretic text but also an early textual tradition distinct in places from the Septuagint and from the proto-Masoretic text. Between AD 390 and 405, Jerome produced a Latin translation of the entire Bible, which became known as the Vulgate. He based his translation on the proto-Masoretic Hebrew text, and his Vulgate is best placed in this textual tradition. However, it often finds influence from the Septuagint of his era.

Conclusion

Other early versions include Coptic, Ethiopic (Geʿez), Armenian, and Arabic translations. However, the major textual traditions of the Septuagint and Masoretic Text remain dominant in the early versions. Whereas the Septuagint provides a vast variety of variants and numerous streams within its textual tradition, the Masoretic Text preserves a more uniform text that, in some of the examples cited above, continued unchanged for more than a thousand years.

The Study of the Old Testament

Finding the Right Tools

The study of the Old Testament can lead one into a dizzying variety of modern approaches. It is not the purpose of this book to describe them all. There are many useful tools for guidance in the study of the Old Testament. An important resource is a good up-to-date bibliography, such as the online (free access) "Annotated Old Testament Bibliography" produced by H. Dallaire, K. Heim, Daniel Carroll R., and R. S. Hess. This is regularly updated

34. Tov, *Textual Criticism*, 151–52.

35. The term "Lucianic recension" is more often used and better describes the textual tradition.

and can be accessed by going to the Denver Seminary website.[36] Scrolling through this bibliography, one will find recommendations on books for a wide variety of Old Testament areas: introductions; series; theology; histories of Israel; archaeology; atlases; translations of collections of ancient Near Eastern texts; ancient Near Eastern histories; Hebrew lexicons; biblical-theological dictionaries; concordances; Hebrew grammars; Old Testament canon/textual criticism; sociological and anthropological studies; feminist, minority, and third world approaches; literary approaches; Israelite religion; messianic Judaism; and commentaries by Bible book.

The last section gives the titles of about a dozen recommended English-language exegetical commentaries for each book of the Old Testament, listed in order according to the Protestant canon. Every suggested book in all sections of the bibliography includes a brief annotation describing its value. Many of the readers (approximately two thousand hits monthly) who access the *Denver Journal* find the Old Testament and New Testament bibliographies to be useful in their study of the Bible, whether for personal enrichment or for the purposes of teaching or preaching from the Bible in various parts of the world.

Where Do Readers Go from Here?

The remaining chapters of this book provide an introduction to the study of the Old Testament as well as a survey of the contents of these books. The present student population entering many seminaries, divinity schools, and graduate programs in biblical studies represents great diversity in terms of preparation for the study of the Old Testament. Some have had little or no exposure to this part of the Bible. Others may have taken several undergraduate courses on the subject or come with a strong church education. The philosophy behind the organization and contents of this book assumes that a seminary course, for example, might include students from across this spectrum. Therefore, we try to accommodate readers with a variety of backgrounds. In addition, the areas that the study of the Old Testament regularly engages have expanded in the past decades. It was once thought sufficient to discuss the major critical approaches and consider key theological insights and contributions related to the text of the Old Testament. Although these remain relevant, they are no longer sufficient for an introduction to the Old Testament if they ignore methods of Bible study that reflect the globalization of the discipline as well as the emergence of new literary, canonical, and history-of-interpretation approaches. Although a book of this length cannot adequately address every area of interest, it can introduce readers to these

36. At the Denver Seminary website (http://www.denverseminary.edu), go to the "Resources" menu of the homepage. This takes you to the *Denver Journal* (http://www.denverseminary.edu/resources/denver-journal/), where you can access the current volume. The first entry in that volume is the "Annotated Old Testament Bibliography" for the current year.

subjects and at least some of their major trajectories, which will prepare them for further study.

In light of this perspective, the present work uses the following outline to guide the discussion of every book of the Old Testament. Each chapter will have four major divisions, beginning with **Name, Text, and Outline.** Beyond giving the name of the book, most studies will examine the rationale for the name and, in the case of the prophetic books and others such as Ruth and Esther, the significance of that name in ancient Israelite society. This section will also consider the text of the book. Are there any special problems with the Masoretic Text here? What value might the Septuagint provide, as well as other versions? Was the book always included in the canon without question, or did disputes arise regarding its role? Where relevant, each chapter will consider these questions. Finally, a brief outline of the book will be given. Usually this introduction favors a broad survey of the major content divisions, while recognizing that no outline is definitive.

The second major division, **Overview**, briefly summarizes the biblical book. Although everyone who takes the time to read an introduction such as this work will likely have read the biblical text itself, it is helpful to review the contents of the biblical book. This may help readers to better understand some important elements that they may have overlooked or misunderstood. It also assists those not acquainted with the style of various books of the Old Testament by summarizing these ancient texts in contemporary language.

The third major division, **Reading**, surveys methods of interpretation in six major categories: premodern readings, higher criticism, literary readings, gender and ideological criticism, ancient Near Eastern context, and canonical context.

The section on "Premodern Readings" allows the contemporary inquirer to consider how various readers of past centuries and millennia understood the biblical book and some of its features. Occasional interpretations of the twentieth and twenty-first centuries, especially when these are artistic presentations that have had wide public impact, are also included. While the discussion is broadly based, some preference will be given to Jewish and Christian interpretations. Occasionally expressions of the biblical book in art and literature will also be included here (or sometimes in the "Literary Readings" below). In this way this section introduces the reader to what some designate the "History of Interpretation" and the "*Rezeptionsgeschichte*." The former emphasizes the manner in which the text has been understood, especially in terms of theology and teaching for communities of faith. The latter focuses on the impact that the text has had on various forms of media and culture. Many see substantial overlap between the two.

A section on "Higher Criticism" will review major critical approaches devoted to the interpretation of the book. (For the Pentateuch, the first five books of the OT, the discussion on higher criticism is divided into two categories: "Source Criticism" and "Tradition History.") Areas of source, form, redaction, and tradition criticism will be considered where appropriate. The classic and more recent expressions of critical study will be surveyed and evaluated in terms of contributions and problems to the study of the biblical text. Here, as much as in any other section, this work considers classic issues of authorship, date, provenance (origin), and life setting of the book. As will quickly be apparent, there is not always an obvious or easy answer to these questions.

The following section, "Literary Readings," surveys literary approaches to the book. Issues of genres or literary forms will play a role in many of these sections. However, even more basic will be a review of some of the most important elements for understanding and reading the text as a piece of literature. Although the "Higher Criticism" section may emphasize the division of the book into discrete parts, this "Literary Readings" section focuses on the unity of the text and how the component parts work together to convey key messages for the themes. Character development, literary devices, word pictures, and other elements also play a role for some books of the Bible.

The section "Gender and Ideological Criticism" moves the reader onto the global stage by examining the role that this text or parts of it play in addressing some concerns of justice and equality among various peoples. By sometimes looking at specific global readings and at readings by women as well as men, it may be possible to widen the dimensions of elements of the text that readers may have overlooked or downplayed, due to preconceived assumptions.

The "Ancient Near Eastern Context" of each book will address some of the traditional historical and cultural questions about the meaning of the text in the original context in which it was written. What role and meaning did the text have for those who first read or listened to its message? While looking at elements of this subject that have been around for decades and have provided for the interpretation of the biblical book and the means of addressing some of the key questions of its historical value and role, this introduction will also reflect on some of the more important discoveries and analyses of the past twenty years or more that have at times effected a small revolution in understanding the words or parts of a biblical book.

A final section on reading methodology considers the "Canonical Context." In this area the reader will reflect on some of the key passages and themes that may have begun or found development in this Old Testament book and how they were developed elsewhere in the Old Testament. Further, the New Testament often moved forward and utilized some of the key texts to build its presentation of the new covenant and to interpret the role and teaching of Jesus. With this section, readers come full circle, returning to the earlier interpretations and approaches to this biblical book and its contribution to understanding who God is and our relationship with the divine, with one another, and with the world in which we all live.

This then leads to the fourth major division, **Theological Perspectives.** In this area, readers encounter some of the major themes found in the biblical book. This involves a survey of issues and questions regarding elements that may appear out of place, ethical matters related to what values may be taught, and reflections on what are the most important ideas that the original author(s) intended to convey to future generations.[37] The beginnings of a biblical theology emerge here, with much more to be explored and developed from the selection of key theological and ethical teachings.

The survey of each book then concludes with a brief list of commentaries and related books that the reader might find helpful for further study. These are annotated to assist with the selection of some of the best recent literature in biblical interpretation.

Having reviewed the makeup and text of the Old Testament, and considered the manner in which this book is laid out as a means to access the Old Testament, we can begin opening the pages of the ancient Scriptures and consider how they testify to God at work in a world long ago and how this may speak to our lives today.

37. For a general survey of ethics, see Otto, *Theologische Ethik*; Parry, *Old Testament and Christian Ethics*. More recent work may be accessed in Hess, "Because of the Wickedness of These Nations."

PART 1

PENTATEUCH

We all like quick summaries of books we are studying. The first five books of the Bible provide that for the Old Testament and the Bible as a whole. Here we find all the later types of Old Testament literature, and we learn about the main characters of the book: God and the people he created. We also read about what will happen in the ages to come. It's all here at the beginning.

All forms of the Old Testament and of the Christian and Jewish Bibles begin with the same first five books, known as the Pentateuch: Genesis, Exodus, Leviticus, Numbers, and Deuteronomy. These are composed mainly of narratives and legal texts. They tell a story that begins with God's creation of the world and moves forward to humans and their sin. Sin grows greater until violence is everywhere and threatens to destroy humanity and God's creation. God sends a flood to destroy the earth but preserves alive the one righteous man and his family. They repopulate the earth. Their descendants try to make a tower to reach heaven, but divine intervention scatters them across the world. From these events God chooses a single man, Abraham, and his family to find a new basis for relationship. God longs to bless the world through this family. In a miraculous manner, God gives Abraham and his wife, Sarah, a son, Isaac. Isaac and his wife, Rebekah, continue the line of promise. One of their sons, Jacob, tricks his father so that he receives the blessing; he flees to find and build a family for himself. At his return to the land that God has promised to Abraham and his family, Jacob receives a new name, Israel, which will become the name of his descendants and of God's chosen people. The entire family is led to Egypt by means of one of Jacob's younger sons, Joseph.

Over several centuries there, Jacob's sons and their families become a populous nation. Defeating the schemes of the current pharaoh (king of Egypt) to kill all the male infants of the Israelites, Moses's mother preserves her son, who grows up in Pharaoh's household before fleeing eastward into the desert. Sometime later God calls Moses to return and to demand that Pharaoh release the Israelites he has enslaved. The God of Israel reveals his name as Yahweh, translated in many English Bibles as "the LORD." Pharaoh refuses the request, and ten plagues follow. At the last plague, the death of all the Egyptian first-born, Pharaoh relents, and the Israelites begin their escape. Soon changing his mind, Pharaoh has Egyptian chariotry pursue Israel and trap them at the Red (Reed) Sea.[1] There God miraculously parts the sea, Israel escapes, and the waters cover the Egyptian army. In the desert, God miraculously provides for Israel. At Mount Sinai they receive God's covenant and feast with him. There also they break the covenant by worshiping the gold calf. Moses intercedes for Israel, and God reveals his mercy and forgiveness by allowing Israel to live and by continuing to journey with them to the promised land. The laws given at Mount Sinai guide Israel in how they should worship God, how they should relate to other Israelites, and how they should live in the world and alongside the surrounding nations. God calls Israel to be holy as he is holy.

The Israelites continue their journey through the desert but fail a variety of tests where they must trust God rather than complain or challenge divinely appointed authority. The major failure occurs when the nation refuses to enter the land and occupy it. As a result, God condemns the adults to spend the rest of their lives in the desert, unable to enter the land. In the decades that follow, that generation gradually dies, and a new generation comes again to the border of the land of promise. There Moses, who has led these people for forty years, gives a final speech, in which he reviews the need to remain faithful to God. He provides many laws that form examples of principles by which Israel can live faithfully in the land they are about to enter.

In general, the biblical text itself does not indicate who wrote these books. However, the role of Moses is so significant that Jesus and New Testament writers will call the whole corpus "Moses" (Luke 16:29; Acts 6:11, 14). Further, Deuteronomy 31:9 ascribes authorship of "this law" to Moses, and later Old Testament texts identify the law given in the Pentateuch as "the law of Moses" (Josh. 23:6; 1 Kings 2:3; Dan. 9:11, 13; etc.).

Those who regard Moses as a historical figure date him to the latter half of the second millennium BC. Some put him in the fifteenth century; others, such as this author, place him in the thirteenth century BC.

These texts remain the key starting point for the whole of the Bible. They provide the essential understanding of the biblical view of creation, sin, the belief in a single loving and holy God, and the need of God's people for redemption and a life of love and holiness so that they may enjoy the blessings of a covenant relationship with God.

1. For a discussion of the name of this sea, see "Ancient Near Eastern Context" for Exodus.

1

GENESIS

Few texts in the world have been read by as many people as the book of Genesis, especially the beginning chapters. Here we learn God's role in the creation of the world, humanity's failures from the beginning, and the grand hope through which all nations will know God's blessing.

Name, Text, and Outline

The name Genesis (Heb. *bĕrēʾšît*; Greek [LXX] most commonly *genesis*) is the title found in the Septuagint. It carries the meaning "beginnings." The original Hebrew text used the first word of the scroll as the name for the book, following a practice that occurs throughout the Pentateuch and also among other ancient Near Eastern literature.

The Masoretic Text of Genesis does not have significant textual problems. As Susan Brayford has shown, the Septuagint differs in some points, creating an overall literary emphasis distinct from that of the Masoretic Hebrew, but rarely significant in its variation.[1]

OUTLINE

1. The Primeval Age (1:1–11:32)
   - A. Creation: The First Toledot[2] (Family History) (1:1–2:25)
     1. Of the Cosmos (1:1–2:4a)
     2. Of the Human Home (2:4b–25)

1. Brayford, *Genesis*.
2. See the discussion of *tôlĕdôt* ("genealogies") in "Literary Readings" below.

B. The Fall and Its Consequences (3:1–24)
C. Cain and Abel (4:1–16)
D. From Cain to Noah: The Second Toledot (4:17–5:32)
E. The Flood (6:1–8:22)
F. God's Covenant with Noah (9:1–29)
G. From Noah to Abram: The Third Toledot (10:1–11:32)

II. The Ancestral Age (12:1–50:26)
A. Abraham (12:1–25:18)
B. Isaac (25:19–26; 26:1–35)
C. Jacob (25:27–34; 27:1–35:29)
D. Esau (36:1–43)
E. Judah (38:1–30)
F. Joseph (37:1–36; 39:1–50:26)

Overview of Genesis

The most important point about the structure of Genesis is that it has two major divisions. The first section, up to the end of chapter 11, describes events and people from creation to the Tower of Babel. The second division develops the story of Abram and his family and culminates in the accounts of Jacob (also called Israel) and Joseph (Gen. 12–50). The book, almost entirely narrative, is written so that the second part continues where the first part leaves off.

The work begins with the story of the world's creation, told in two parts. The first part (1:1–2:4a) describes the creation of the whole cosmos in the form of a weeklong period. The emphasis of this story is on God (called Elohim [*'ĕlōhîm*]) as the creator of the abundant life that fills the three environments created and separated in the first three days: the sky, the sea, and the dry land. After the birds, fish, and land animals appear in days 4–6, the creation culminates in the formation of humanity, male and female, who appear in the image of God. God then ceases work on the seventh day, the Sabbath. In this manner, the created order has built into it a weekly day of rest, and the whole of creation moves forward to climax in this final day of rest.

The second story of creation (2:4b–25) outlines the creation of the man as well as his home, his work, and his companion.[3] The emphasis of this story is on God (here called by the personal name Yahweh [Lord in most English versions], as well as the title Elohim, thus Yahweh Elohim) as the creator of humanity. "The Lord God" places the man in an environment that was previously unproductive and without life. Man works the garden, into which God places trees and a verdant abundance of life, symbolized by the great waters of four rivers. Here the man names the animals, in the sense

3. Hess, "Splitting."

of identifying their function and purpose. The failure to find "someone like himself" is the outcome of viewing the animals for this purpose (naming or classifying them according to function). His partner is found when God creates the woman from his side. The ideal picture at the end of Genesis 2 is a harmony of relationships.[4] All of this is shattered in chapter 3 with the deception and the decision to disobey God. The resulting fear and recriminations reflect the loss of harmony between the man and the woman and also with God. The judgments of 3:14–19 identify each of the participants and describe how their alienation from each other and from the land will result in many difficulties in life. The punishment, in which the man and woman are driven from the garden, means that they will no longer enjoy the close relationship with God that they had from the beginning.

Genesis 4 describes the further alienation of the human race from God and from one another. Fratricide, with Cain killing Abel, leads to multiple and murderous acts of vengeance by his descendant Lamech.[5] The substitute line of Seth (Gen. 5) eventuates in the one who is promised to bring comfort, Noah (5:29). Nevertheless, the great corruption of humanity as expressed in their violence leads to the divine judgment of the flood, from which Noah and his family alone are saved (Gen. 6). The flood destroys all life except those in Noah's ark, whom God remembers (8:1) and so preserves. After the flood, God promises never to send such worldwide destruction again but requires from humanity respect for human life and an end to the violence of earlier times. Nevertheless, Noah's drunkenness leads to immorality and the loss of the pristine world after the flood. Chapter 10 represents the Bible's great statement of the unity and equality of all peoples. Here all the known nations of the world are portrayed as descended from one family, and thus all possess the image of God (9:6).

The Tower of Babel in 11:1–9 provides Genesis 1–11's third key example in which humanity tries to overstep its divinely ordained limits to grasp hold of and become like God—whether in eating the fruit of the forbidden tree (3:1–13), in permitting intermarriage with the sons of God so as to extend human life (6:1–3), or in making a name for oneself that would endure (11:1–9). In each case, God thwarts human plans. In the last example, the line of Noah's son Shem moves forward until the time of Abram.

Genesis 12 begins a new section of the book. Created in the image of God, humanity has constantly desired to thwart this image and become like God. Now God chooses to focus on a single segment of the human race rather than on all the created people. He singles out Abram and calls him out from the civilized world and his family's secure business in Haran. Abram is to take his wife, Sarai, and their immediate family and journey to the unknown

4. Hess, "Genesis 1–3."
5. Hauser, "Genesis 2–3."

land of Canaan, a backward and dangerous place. God commands this in 12:1–3 and promises Abram a covenant consisting of the threefold promise: (1) land, though at this stage it is couched only in the form of the land that God promises to show Abram; (2) seed, meaning descendants, a great nation and a great name promised to Abram in contrast to the builders of Babel, who sought to make a name for themselves apart from God; and (3) becoming an instrument of universal blessing to all humankind. Although the latter promise has the most powerful relevance for Christians (who find the universal blessing in Jesus Christ, the Messiah and descendant of Abraham), the first two are essential for the latter promise to be realized. Land and seed will become the most important means to this great end of blessing for all.

The remainder of the story of Abram (renamed Abraham in 17:5, as Sarai is renamed Sarah in 17:15) tells of a series of tests for Abraham's faith. As he passes many of these tests, the promises are expanded and become more and more significant. Finally, in Genesis 22 he encounters the greatest test of all. In previous chapters, Abraham has been promised a son and heir. However, he and Sarah are old. So he tries other means of obtaining a son: adopting his loyal servant Eliezer, and later fathering the child Ishmael through Sarah's female slave Hagar. Neither of these fulfills God's purposes, however, and in the end God's word comes true so that Abraham and Sarah have the child of promise, Isaac. Yet God commands Abraham to sacrifice his son Isaac on Mount Moriah. Abraham's ready obedience (though God interrupts the deed and saves Isaac) culminates in the greatest extension of the covenant so that now Abraham's descendants will even possess the cities of their enemies and thus control the whole of the promised land, including the fortified defenses (22:17–18). Throughout his life, Abraham builds altars throughout the promised land as a testimony to God's ownership of it (12:6–8; 13:18), and he purchases a small parcel of land as a burial plot for his wife and family (25:10; 49:29–30). It remains for those who come after him to realize the promise of the land.

Isaac appears in Genesis primarily as the son of Abraham and as the father of Jacob and Esau. Jacob follows Isaac and is characterized as a trickster who convinces his twin (though elder) brother, Esau, to sell his birthright and then tricks his father into giving him the blessing of inheritance that should have belonged to Esau. Jacob flees to his relative Laban in their ancestral home of Haran in northeastern Aram (= Harran in northern Mesopotamia, now in Turkey and just north of Syria). Jacob finds wives here, just as Abraham's servant had journeyed here to find a wife for Isaac. Jacob works seven years for Laban in order to marry Laban's daughter Rachel. However, Laban deceives Jacob at his wedding, and Jacob finds that he has married Rachel's older sister, Leah. He agrees to work for Laban for another seven years in order to marry Rachel. From Leah and Rachel, and from their female slaves Zilpah and Bilhah, are born the twelve sons who become the biblical ancestors to the tribes of

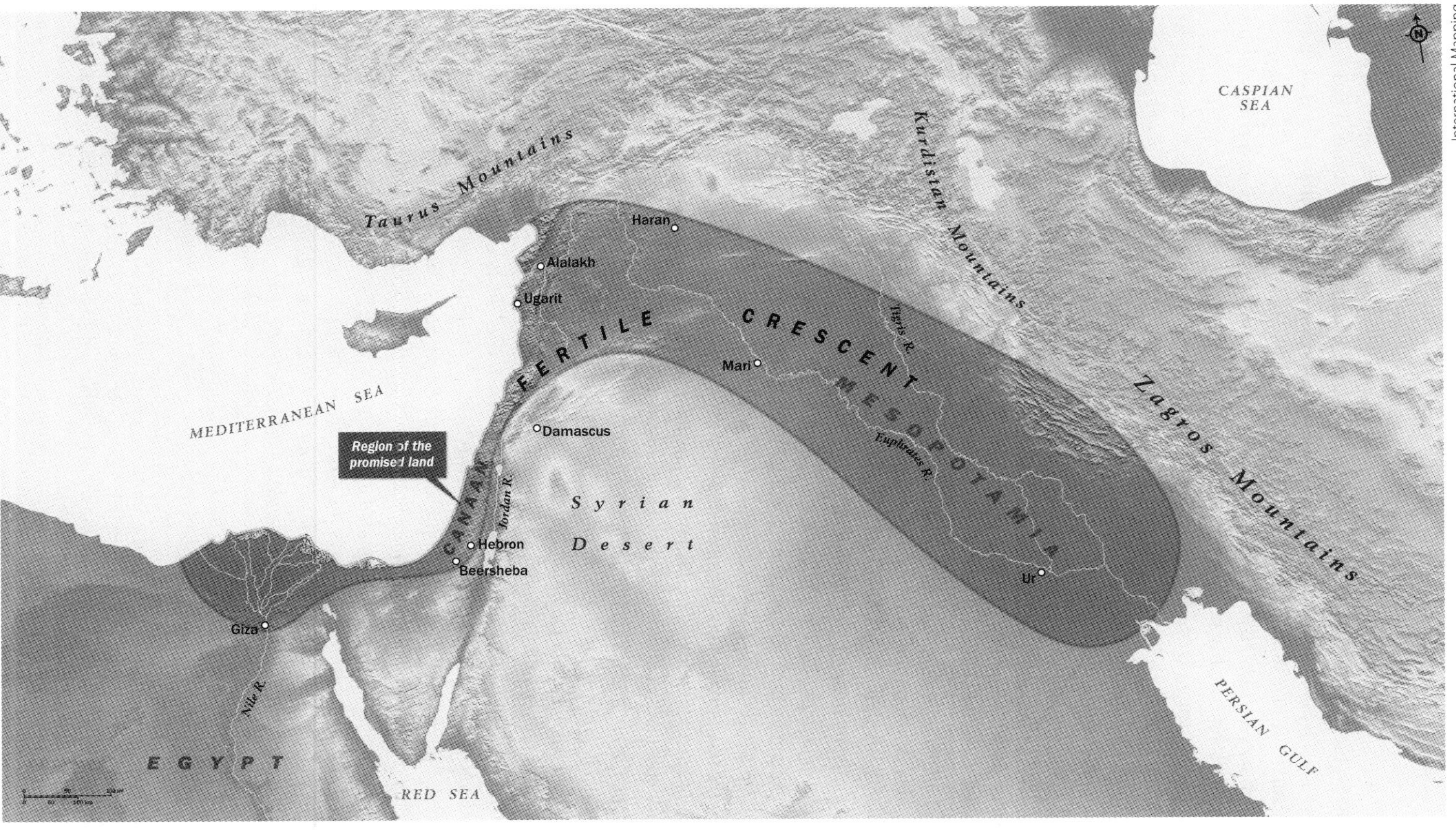

International Mapping

The Fertile Crescent

Israel. Jacob works twenty years for Laban, and God prospers him in all he does. God directs Jacob to leave Laban and return to the promised land. On his way, Laban catches up with him and makes a treaty so that Jacob and his family do not make claims to the lands of Laban, and vice versa. Jacob then prepares to meet his brother, Esau, who has acquired property and power of his own. Before doing so and before entering the land of promise, however, Jacob spends a night by himself on the north bank of the Jabbok River—just as he was alone when he left this land. There he wrestles with a man. As is so often the case in these events (cf. Gen. 19), Jacob's confrontation with a man morphs into a confrontation with God. It is here that Jacob is given the name Israel, "because you have struggled with God and with humans and have overcome" (32:28 NIV). His meeting with Esau becomes a joyful reunion (33:1–16): the brothers bless each other. Esau returns to his homeland of Seir, or Edom, to the south, while Jacob makes his way westward to Shechem; there Jacob builds an altar, as did Abraham when he first came into the land (33:20; cf. 12:6).

In chapter 34, Shechem, son of Hamor (Hamor is king of the city of Shechem), rapes Jacob's daughter Dinah. Her brothers wreak vengeance on Shechem and all the males of the city: after the men accept and undergo circumcision, Jacob's sons attack and murder them. Jacob accuses his sons of bringing trouble on him and all of his family. Jacob is then led by God to move south and leave the area and the threat of revenge for this deed (Gen. 35). First, Jacob has his family put away all the "teraphim" (cf. 31:19, 34–35 ASV; probably ancestral images, "household gods") and other religious paraphernalia that they have brought from Haran. Just as Abraham before him, Jacob, having received divine protection, moves south to Bethel and there builds an altar to God. He journeys farther south to Hebron, where he is reunited with his father, Isaac, before Isaac's death (35:27–29). As so often in the structure of Genesis, there first appears the line of the brother(s) that does not continue in the text (Cain in Gen. 4; the Table of Nations[6] in Gen. 10; Ishmael in Gen. 25), followed by the line of promise and the stories of those descendants. Here Esau's line is found in chapter 36, preceding the stories concerning Joseph and the other descendants of Jacob in chapters 37–50.

Genesis 37 sets the stage for the story of how Joseph, loved by his father and betrayed by his jealous half brothers, is sold into slavery and taken to Egypt.[7] Joseph demonstrates his role as a wisdom figure who fits the advice of Proverbs and other such sources of guidance. He refuses the advances of

6. This is the designation often used for Gen. 10, where the nations of the world (known to the author) are identified and related to the lines of the sons of Noah.

7. The dynamics of family life are seen nowhere more clearly than in the stories of Israel's ancestors in Gen. 12–50. Indeed, the problems created by dysfunctional families, especially with stepchildren and half brothers and half sisters, occur to a unique degree in these chapters. If one wishes to study the life of the family in the Bible, one cannot do better than to begin with these narratives. See Wenham, "Family."

his master's wife (Gen. 39:7–20; cf. Prov. 7:6–27). Joseph interprets dreams (Gen. 40–41; cf. Dan. 2–7), and he rises to the level of second in rank to the king (cf. Prov. 22:29).

From this background Joseph is able to provide for his family, although at first he does not reveal who he is when they come to buy Egyptian grain (Gen. 43–44). Instead, he tests his brothers and reveals himself only when he brings them to the great distress of having to trade their youngest brother, Benjamin (who is favored by their father), in exchange for the grain necessary for their family to live. When Joseph reveals himself, his office and favor with the pharaoh become the means by which Joseph's father and brothers and all of their families are preserved, as they come to Egypt and live there. Genesis 49 records Jacob's poetic last words, in which he blesses each of his sons and predicts the future of the tribes of Israel. The last chapter describes the return to Canaan to bury Jacob, anticipating the return of all Israel to the land (50:1–14). It also summarizes the rest of Joseph's life and his death, with the promise that the descendants of Israel would someday return his body to that promised land (50:20–26; anticipating Exod. 13:19). This final chapter also defines the life of Joseph as characterized by a mature and loving attitude toward his brothers. With their father dead, Joseph's brothers worry that Joseph will take vengeance for what they did to him so long ago. Instead, Joseph forgives them. Again, his role as a sage enables Joseph to understand the greater significance of how God could use the brothers' evil intention for good (50:19–20 RSH): "Don't be afraid. Am I in God's place? You planned evil for me, but God planned good so that this day he might preserve alive many people." Through this confession believers are reminded of the ongoing work of God's covenant with Abraham, that through him and his offspring the many nations of the world would be blessed (12:1–3).

Reading Genesis

Premodern Readings

Many books have addressed aspects of this subject. Here there is room for only a few observations. In Christianity and Judaism the earliest known attribution of authorship of the Pentateuch ascribed a substantial amount of it to Moses. Although he did not claim to live during the events of Genesis, he was credited with composing the text largely in the form available now. From the beginning, the church and synagogue interpreted the texts of creation literally, but they also tended to find in the text metaphorical and other symbolic meanings in support of their own philosophical understandings of the beginning of the world. The stories of Abraham, Isaac, Jacob, and Joseph provided moral lessons for living a faithful life before God. Historical questions were not raised or challenged.

By the mid-first millennium AD, both rabbinic and Christian exegetes identified similar motifs and shared methods of argument, however much their theological and exegetical conclusions differed.[8] Josephus and Philo, as well as pseudepigraphic writings, influenced both traditions. The church fathers attributed their exegetical approaches to Jewish traditions. Nevertheless, early Christian and Jewish interpretations diverged. On the one hand, both traditions saw the rejection of Hagar and Ishmael by Abraham and Sarah ultimately in a positive light, as part of God's will. In reading the Joseph story, Christians and Jews also shared common views of slavery. On the other hand, a text such as Genesis 49:8–12 became a prediction of Jesus as the Messiah in Christian circles, while in rabbinic tradition it predicted a messiah yet to come who would usher in a new age for Israel.

During the Enlightenment (from the late seventeenth century until the end of the eighteenth century) the book of Genesis became the primary connection between the historical time of the later texts and the events of creation and its immediate and subsequent events. This understanding encouraged scientists such as Isaac Newton to attempt to calculate the age of the earth and the date of creation. From such attempts emerged the Anglican archbishop Ussher's famous dating of the beginning of the world at 4004 BC.

Source Criticism

The emergence of source criticism is often traced to the work of the French physician Jean Astruc, who in 1753 hypothesized that the two creation stories in Genesis 1 and 2 represent two different literary sources.[9] The doublet of two stories about the same event, the different divine names,[10] and the different theological emphases (transcendent creator of the cosmos in chap. 1 versus the immanent creator of humanity in the second story) all contributed to the identification of different sources in Genesis and the Pentateuch. Julius Wellhausen's 1878 *Prolegomena to the History of the Religion of Israel* gave a definitive form to the theory. He hypothesized four sources, all composed later than the traditional time of the latest events of Genesis or of their author. These were written at various times and reflected various concerns in the history of ancient Israel.

The earliest document was "J," after the divine name of God (Yahweh) as spelled in German with an initial *J*. It was written in the court of David or one of his successors and reflects concerns with legitimizing the monarchy and David's dynasty. It originally comprised a continuous record of history from creation to the time of David, ending in the Pentateuch with the death of

8. Grypeou and Spurling, *Genesis in Late Antiquity*, 437–44.

9. For this and the following discussion, see the summary in Hess, *Israelite Religions*, 45–59.

10. Elohim (*'ĕlōhîm*) in Gen. 1; Yahweh Elohim in Gen. 2:4–3:24; see the "Overview of Genesis" above.

Moses. The second creation story (Gen. 2:4–25), with its form of a standard Hebrew narrative and its use of Yahweh in the divine name, is claimed as an example of a J narrative, in Wellhausen's analysis.

The second document, "E," was so called due to its connection with the divine name Elohim. It reflects concerns of the eighth century BC and the northern kingdom of Jeroboam II at that time. Prophetic emphases and northern sites dominate the literature ascribed to E, as does the concern for intermediaries between God and the chosen people. The story of Jacob at Bethel (Gen. 28:10–22), with its location at a northern cult center (Bethel), is said to contain E narrative materials.[11]

The third document, "D," was composed during the reign of Josiah and is often related to the scroll discovered in the process of cleansing the temple around 622 BC (2 Kings 22). This text is similar to the book of Deuteronomy and thus emphasizes the covenant with God and the sense in which all life is to be lived under the divine reign. No area is absent from divine interest and concern. Covenant references that occur in Genesis 9, 15, and 17 may contain D materials.

The last document, "P," was designated as such due to its connection with the priestly school of the postexilic period (after 539 BC), when those returning to Jerusalem set up a theocratic kingdom within the Persian Empire, where priests held local political power. These priests ascribed the origins of their powers and prerogatives to Moses. The concerns of P are sacrifices, genealogies, division between clean and unclean, the Sabbath, and the varied legislation of the priestly school as found especially in Leviticus. Genesis 1:1–2:4 emphasizes the Sabbath day and distinctions in creation and so is usually regarded as from the P source.

All these texts were originally understood as a series of separate documents that were written and then added to one another. In more than a century since Wellhausen, variations on these sources have been proposed. Some have added more sources. Others have combined J and E, or dated P before the exile. More common has been the tendency to see in source criticism what was actually a series of redactions or theological editings of the text. Many would argue that D took over more and more prominence as the primary redactor that ordered and affected all that had appeared earlier. A popular approach among many critical scholars has been the dating of the Pentateuch's formation in the Persian and Hellenistic periods.[12]

Yet this very tendency toward rearrangement affected the monolithic nature of the hypothesis. In addition, many archaeological discoveries have now

11. Here and elsewhere, the terms "cult" and "cult center" refer to evidence of religious activities. The term "cult" is used without any pejorative implications as to the religion that may have been practiced.

12. For example, see many of the studies in Federico Giuntoli and Konrad Schmid, eds., *The Post-Priestly Pentateuch*.

challenged assumptions about the use of criteria for identifying and dating sources that derive from nineteenth-century ways of looking at the world. For example, the much earlier (fifteenth–twelfth centuries BC) Hittite suzerain-vassal treaties give evidence of a remarkable similarity to the outline of Deuteronomy 1–28. There is also the manner in which recently published texts from thirteenth-century-BC Emar have demonstrated the antiquity of practices (priestly anointing) and of literary forms (detailed multimonth ritual calendars) traditionally assigned to postexilic P authors. Add to this the archaic name forms, grammatical spellings and morphology, and aspects of the cultural world of Genesis that fit best in the second millennium BC (or sometimes the early second millennium), and one has some strong arguments to regard this material as something more than an invention of the Israelite monarchy and postexilic world of the first millennium BC. Finally, there is the question of the logic of literary formation. As will be seen, more recent literary analysis of the text of Genesis and the entire Pentateuch has found alternative explanations for the duplications of stories, the different names of God, and the variety of theological emphases. There is no longer only the option of distinct literary sources. For present-day scholars, who are further removed from the philosophies of the Enlightenment and nineteenth-century Europe, it is possible to question assumptions about creating criteria intended to identify sources.

Nevertheless, there has emerged a Neo-Documentarian school represented by scholars such as Joel Baden.[13] He and others affirm the basic documents of the traditional documentary hypothesis in terms of distinct literary compositions joined by a single editor, retaining, for example, separate J and E sources. These scholars separate the literary form of the documents from the question of the date of their composition. Their interest is in the literary composition of the Pentateuch.

The source-critical approach remains a useful tool for the literary analysis of Genesis and the Pentateuch as a whole. Assertions to maintain elements of the Documentary Hypothesis will continue. However, one does not need to accept the older or more recent forms of the theory to appreciate the emphases on narrative, law, and ceremonial and priestly matters that form important strands for understanding these first biblical books.

Tradition History

A second critical approach also played a key role in the interpretation of Genesis, especially in the twentieth century.[14] This method emerged from the discovery and decipherment of ancient Near Eastern texts that contained stories and forms similar to those in Genesis, such as creation and flood ac-

13. Baden, *Composition of the Pentateuch*; idem, *J, E, and the Redaction of the Pentateuch*.
14. D. Knight, *Rediscovering the Traditions*.

counts. The result was an attempt to identify traditions, often oral but also written, that were passed on across cultures and through time. Hermann Gunkel is usually considered the one who began this approach.[15] He influenced Albrecht Alt and Martin Noth, whose work laid the foundations for much of the later interpretation of the Pentateuch (and the OT) in Germany and beyond. Related approaches emerged in Scandinavia and in the United States, where the emphasis on the passing on of oral literatures was studied in light of the early Ugaritic poetic myths from the thirteenth century BC.

Of special interest for Genesis was the manner in which Alt studied the religion of the ancestors in Genesis 12–36 (and the old poem of Gen. 49). He hypothesized that originally multiple deities were worshiped by the ancestors of the tribes of Israel.[16] The tribes themselves may not originally have been related but may have constituted different entities whose founders—such as Abraham, Isaac, Esau, and Jacob—were not originally in the same family. Only late in the history of the traditions was there a need to bring together these tribal leaders. Instead, terms such as "the Fear of Isaac" (Gen. 31:42) and "the Mighty One of Jacob" (49:24) were the names of tribal gods, originally perhaps human ancestors of each of the tribes. When the nation of Israel became unified, it brought together these names, as well as those of local Canaanite deities (forms of names of the god El, such as El Elyon in Jerusalem, El Bethel at Bethel, El Berit at Shechem, etc.), and subsumed them under the one God, who was given these names and titles. This combination of traditions remains speculative. Aside from the biblical usage of the names as now known, there is no evidence for an early identity to any of these deities.[17]

More recent studies have argued that these traditions played a significant role and may even have originated in the exilic and postexilic periods. Israel was deported across the Euphrates and settled in the Babylonian Empire in 586 BC and was only permitted to return to the promised land after the establishment of the Persian Empire and the edicts allowing for their return (after 539 BC). Likewise, the writers of Genesis from that late period wished to portray Israel's ancestors as coming from the area of Babylon and establishing their claim to the promised land of Canaan. The Genesis stories were invented or developed from old traditions, it is claimed, to encourage Israel to become like its fictional ancestors and return and rebuild in the land of Canaan. This, combined with a Persian-period interest in codifying laws throughout their empire, led to the authorization of the composition of Genesis and the entire Pentateuch as now preserved.[18]

15. Gunkel, *Legends of Genesis*.

16. Alt, "God of the Fathers."

17. See its continued popularity in McCarter, "The Patriarchal Age."

18. For the original theory, see Frei, "Zentralgewalt." See also Albertz, *Israelite Religion*, 2:138–39; Blenkinsopp, *Pentateuch*, 120, 156, 171, 238; Blum, *Studien*, 345–60; Carr, *Reading the Fractures of Genesis*, 312–35; Rendtorff, "Chronicles"; J. W. Watts, *Reading the Law*, 137–44.

This reconstruction fails to convince because there is little social and religious resemblance between the world of Genesis 12–36 and that of the postexilic returnees. Abraham, Isaac, Jacob, and their families get along with their Canaanite neighbors and make covenant rather than war with them (Gen. 12, 13, 20, 26, etc.). The postexilic world preached a policy of separation and described ongoing conflict with neighbors (cf. Nehemiah). Further, there is no awareness of religious conflict between the one God of Abram and his family and other deities around Canaan. This is completely different from the separation of the postexilic community from the surrounding communities and their religious practices. Finally, Abraham and his successors sacrifice throughout the land of Canaan; they know nothing of practices such as Sabbath observance, priestly lines, temple worship, and distinctions between clean and unclean animals. All this formed an essential part of the postexilic community's worship at only one altar in the Jerusalem sanctuary. If postexilic writers were redacting (or creating) the traditions of Genesis to conform to and promote the interests of the ruling postexilic priesthood, they surely could have done a better job.[19]

There are also important linguistic arguments for dating this priestly (see "Source Criticism," above) material before the exile (pre-586 BC).[20] Among other evidence, there is the view that much of the legal material fits this earlier period better. In addition, there is linguistic evidence in the use of vocabulary and expressions that appear in the postexilic period and yet have also been observed in the language of preexilic texts.[21]

Literary Readings

There are many literary approaches to the biblical text of Genesis. The stories of Abraham, Jacob, and Joseph are among the most popular. Their literary analysis has revealed a large number of important insights into the study of the materials. Indeed, the study of literary aspects of the Genesis narratives has formed some of the foundational work for the literary study of Hebrew biblical material as a whole.[22] In particular, the repetition of key

19. See Moberly, *Genesis 12–50*; idem, *Old Testament*.

20. Above all, see Kaufmann, *Religion of Israel*, 175–200. For the legal contexts, see Haran, "Priestly Source"; Friedman, *Who Wrote the Bible?*; Milgrom, *Leviticus*, 3–12; Weinfeld, *Place of the Law*.

21. For the foundation of this research, see Hurvitz, *Transition Period*; idem, *Linguistic Study*; idem, "Dating the Priestly"; idem, "Continuity and Change"; Kofoed, "Using Linguistic Differences." Behind this work lies the theory of Kutscher, *History of the Hebrew Language*, esp. 81–84. For criticism of this view, see the essay in Young, *Biblical Hebrew*, 150–275; and the response in M. Smith, *Priestly Vision*, 292–93. As Smith notes, the linguistic arguments have remained unaddressed by many of the scholars holding to a postexilic date.

22. See such basic works as Alter, *Art of Biblical Narrative*; Amit, *Reading Biblical Narratives*; Bar-Efrat, *Narrative Art*; Fokkelman, *Reading Biblical Narrative*; Gunn and Fewell, *Narrative in the Hebrew Bible*; Sternberg, *Poetics of Biblical Narrative*.

words and phrases, the development of plot, the practice of "gapping" (omitting expected details in the narrative) at significant moments, the emphasis on the external action more than the inward attitudes, and the use of structural markers—all contribute toward the interest and intent of the stories as they have been preserved. There is an obvious difference between the narratives of Abraham, as found in Genesis 12–25, and those of Isaac and especially of Joseph. Although there are threads of continuity, the Abrahamic material tends to provide discrete units that can be divided by chapters. The later ancestor stories sometimes do this, but more often the stories are connected so that they are essential to the overall plot (as with Jacob) or they form part of a larger story (as with Joseph).

Genesis 1–11 presents its own challenges. Here the overall role of the genealogies as a structuring principle is more prominent than in the rest of Genesis. Thus the *tôlĕdôt*, or "genealogies," appear in pairs: Cain (4:17–24) followed by Seth (4:25–5:23), and the Table of Nations (Gen. 10) followed by Shem (11:10–32). The first occurrence of *tôlĕdôt* appears in 2:4, where the account of the creation of the heavens and the earth is given this name. No genealogy is present (or possible since people are created only late into the events), so it may be that the week of seven days defines the *tôlĕdôt*, where each day builds logically on the previous day to create life. Interestingly, at the beginning of Genesis there are two creation accounts, just as there are genealogical doublets later in these chapters (as noted above). This suggests an intentional structuring. Indeed, more can be said. In each case a general genealogy is followed by a more specific or detailed account. Thus Genesis 1 describes the more general creation of the cosmos; then 2:4b–25 identifies the specific creation of the man and his environment. Genesis 4 outlines Cain's line and comments on various aspects of culture. Genesis 5 focuses on Seth's line and is concerned specifically with religious matters (e.g., Enoch walking with God and Lamech's boast). Genesis 10 identifies all peoples of the known world, while Genesis 11 focuses on the line of promise that moves from Shem to Abram and then onward to the covenant and the story of Abram's life and line.[23]

Finally, note should be made of the personal names that appear throughout Genesis and function as wordplay to integrate and emphasize the narratives.[24] Eve's name looks like a form of the Hebrew root "to live," with the sense "to give life," related to her role as the one who will bear children and bring life into the world (3:16, 20). Adam (*ʾādām*) is related to the word for "ground," *ʾădāmâ*, as the ground from which the man is taken and to which he returns, and as that which it is his responsibility to maintain (2:7, 15; 3:17–19).

23. Hess, "Genesis 1–2 in Its Literary Context."
24. Hess, *Studies in the Personal Names*.

The name of Noah sounds like a Hebrew root for "rest, comfort." It appears in the prophecy of his father, Lamech (5:29). Like Noah, many names are explained in the text and connected to words that sound like the name. So there is Israel, who "struggled" with God (32:28); Jacob, who "took hold

Literary Aspects of Genesis 3

The first verse of Genesis 3 introduces the character of the snake with an emphasis that unusually puts his name first. There is also Hebrew wordplay on the snake's "craftiness," *ʿārûm*, and the similar-sounding description of the couple, one verse before, as "naked," *ʿărûmmîm*. These two rare words portend how the craftiness of the serpent will overturn the innocence of the couple as represented by their nudity.

A close comparison between the references to God's words in Genesis 2:16–17 demonstrates how the snake repeatedly denies those words. In Hebrew this involves a word-for-word quotation of the statement with the addition of the negative in the front. Thus in 2:16 God says literally, "From every tree of the garden you may indeed eat." In 3:1 the snake says, "Not will you eat from every tree of the garden!" or "You will *not* eat from every tree of the garden!" The same occurs in the denial of death in 3:4.

By contrast, the woman's quotation of 2:16–17 is much closer to God's words. Nevertheless, she does change the wording to avoid the name of the forbidden tree, replacing it with "the tree that is in the middle of the garden." Since many trees could be described as "in the middle of the garden," this tends to make the command appear arbitrary. The statement that God has prohibited them from touching the fruit is also an addition, since this was never stated. It is true that one does not normally touch fruit unless one wishes to eat it, but the effect here is to make the divine command appear arbitrary and the punishment out of proportion: death for touching fruit! The "tree of the knowledge of good and evil" is much debated but seems to be connected with moral knowledge of right and wrong. If so, then the point of the prohibition may not have been permanent but rather for a time, until the couple achieved a level of ethical understanding that prepared them to partake. In any case, the eating of the fruit by the woman and the man who was with her (all the time, presumably) in verse 6 is filled with verbs that suggest quick and decisive action when the decision is reached.

The sequence of characters in 3:1–6, snake-woman-man, is reversed in the divine interrogation of verses 9–13. This is reversed again, back to snake-woman-man, in the judgments of verses 14–19, suggesting a literary device (more than a chiasm, rather a kind of oscillation), moving back and forth to address all the characters involved in an equal manner.

of" his brother's heel at their birth (25:26); and Joseph, whose name refers to how God "added" another son (30:24). Other names do not sound or look like the roots to which they are supposedly connected, such as Abraham, who is the father of "a multitude" (*hămôn*, 17:5). More significant are names whose connection with similar-sounding Hebrew roots is not explicit in the text but may implicitly suggest something that the author wished to communicate. Thus the collection of names in the second half of the genealogy of Shem includes many names similar to place names in northern Syria, such as Serug, Nahor, Terah, and perhaps Haran (11:20–32). All of this may be related to the original homeland region of Abram's family on the Balikh River plain and those related plains whose rivers join the Euphrates. The name of Sarah, Hebrew for "princess," clearly relates to her role as the mother of many kings and leaders of nations (17:15–16).

Gender and Ideological Criticism

Genesis, with its numerous narratives of families and especially the descriptions of female characters (Sarah, Hagar, Rebekah, Leah, and Rachel), contains opportunities to explore the significance of women in these stories and to portray their roles as figures of influence and importance (e.g., Sarah's influence on Abraham concerning the fate of Hagar and Ishmael in Gen. 16, 21). At the same time there are recurrent themes of the woman as sexually and socially stereotyped, whether as the prostitute (Tamar in Gen. 38), as the seductress (Potiphar's wife in 39:7–20), as the mother (Jacob's wives and concubines in 29:31–35:20), or as the pawn shared for the purposes of favorable treatment with leaders in Egypt and Gerar (Gen. 12, 20, 26). Thus the cultural context provides both positive and negative roles for women and men and their relationships.

The application of other ideologies is vast and to some extent governed by the interests and cultures of those engaged in writing the analyses. For Genesis 12–36, a general picture of a small family surviving in an alien world and environment emerges. Abram, Isaac, and Jacob are at the mercy of the Canaanite rulers in the land where they are guests and never really citizens. The same is also true for Jacob when he returns to his grandfather's homeland in Haran (28:10). This is, however, contrasted with the picture of Abram the warrior, who subdues an international coalition of kings and their armies in Genesis 14. Further, to avoid any indebtedness, he is able to reject the gifts offered by the king of Sodom, and he chooses his ally in the form of Melchizedek, king of Salem. Thus political power remains relative in these chapters of Genesis. Abraham and his successors position their families for their maximum advantage in relation to their neighbors. Much more detail is provided in the story of Joseph. Here God is at work behind the scenes to reverse the seemingly hopeless fortune of a naïve youth sold into slavery by his brothers, betrayed

The Atrahasis Epic

Eighteenth-century-BC Old Babylonian Epic of Atrahasis

Although the most famous creation story from Babylonia is *Enuma Elish*, it is actually late, dating from the seventh century BC in the form in which it was first discovered and still preserved today. The work is strongly influenced by a desire to demonstrate that Marduk, Babylon's chief god, was also the leading deity of the heavenly court. An earlier and largely preserved account comes from Mesopotamia and is called the Atrahasis Epic. It includes a story of creation but also has a description of the flood and of a succession of kings who ruled on earth. In this manner it represents Genesis 1–11 more closely than any of the other creation accounts discovered so far. Nevertheless, the differences between Genesis and Atrahasis are profound. For example, the one God of the Bible evaluates and judges according to moral norms, but the Atrahasis pantheon decides on a flood due to overpopulation and perhaps the noise created by so great an abundance of humanity.

One interesting note in the Atrahasis account concerns the creation of humanity. Here the woman is mentioned first, and then man appears. Scholars recognize that Old Babylonia (around the time of its famous king and lawgiver Hammurabi [eighteenth century BC]) was no less patriarchal than Israel and the rest of the ancient Near East. Thus there is no basis in this account, or presumably in the Genesis account, for a sequence of woman-man or man-woman suggesting anything about hierarchy.

by his master's wife, and imprisoned without expectation of release. Joseph's ascent from a prisoner to second in command of the most powerful nation on earth exemplifies both the manner in which Abram's descendants become instruments of international blessing (12:2–3) and the manner in which the God of the family of Abraham is able to reverse the fates of nations and of the world, to honor those whom God has chosen and blessed.

The picture of Genesis 1–11 stands out in terms of these approaches. From an alternative, feminist perspective, the role of women in the first three chapters of the Bible remains the focus of controversy in the Old Testament. Questions of the order of the creation of the man followed by the woman, of the apparent submission of the woman in 3:16, and of the man's naming (and therefore exerting authority over) the woman in 3:20—these issues represent only peaks of the iceberg in the frigid waters of hierarchy that dominate many schools of thought in evangelicalism and other perspectives.[25] Even 1:26–28 is read as "whispering" male headship because the word for "humanity," *ʾādām*, can mean "man," as it does in chapter 2. However, none of these arguments are irrefutable.

First, with reference to the order of creation, ancient Near Eastern examples from patriarchal cultures describe the first human couple by mentioning the woman before the man (see the sidebar "The Atrahasis Epic"). However, this says nothing about the authority of the woman over the man (or vice versa) in those cultures. The same may be assumed in Genesis, so that the burden of proof lies with those who wish to demonstrate a hierarchy on the basis of creation order. Second, the rulership of the man over the woman in Genesis 3:16 is at best a prophecy of the dominant patriarchalism that would come to exist at times in Israel and elsewhere in the world. It is no more a statement of the divine will than is the use of weed killer a means of thwarting the divine will because weeds are "prophesied" in the next three verses. Third, the naming of someone is no more an exertion of power over them than is the West Semitic naming of gods and goddesses an exertion of authority over these beings (whom the Canaanites and other neighbors of Israel worshiped). Naming is rather an insight into the nature and role of a person or thing in the world. Finally, because a word such as *ʾādām* can be defined as A ("man") or B ("humanity, Homo sapiens") does not mean that where context requires it to be defined as B (as in 1:26–28), it must also carry the "baggage" of the meaning A (as in Gen. 2–3).

Other ideological concerns appear in Genesis 1–11. Vegetarianism is clearly the original ideal (1:29–30), while meat eating comes later and appears as a concession (9:3).[26] More generally, ecological concerns dominate these texts, beginning with the image of God expressed by humanity's rulership over creation (1:26–28). Whether in taking care of the garden of Eden or in naming (and so classifying) the animals (2:8, 15, 19–20), the role of humanity's rulership is understood as a continuation of the creation process that God began, with its emphasis on the enrichment and value of all forms of life.[27] The flood of Genesis 6 is attributed to multiplication of violence on the earth; the flood destroys all forms of created life except what is saved in the ark (6:11–13). Even with the concession to humanity for the killing of animals, it is given only with the command that all life, human and animal, is a sacred gift from God

25. E.g., David Clines's feminist but "irredeemably patriarchal" reading of this material. See the discussion in Hess, "Genesis 1–3," for this reference and those in the paragraph.

26. Or a solution to lack of available food in the world and so a means to prevent famine, esp. in light of the concerns for food in the lives of Abraham, Jacob, and Joseph. See Birch et al., *Theological Introduction*, 56.

27. Hess, "Genesis 1–3," 81–82.

and that the killing of such life is a matter requiring a special consideration. Humanity is to remember this by honoring the blood of all animals (9:4–5).

Such violence also impacts other human life. Human culture and society cannot control this: the culturally rich line of Cain begins with fratricide and ends with a vision of multiple acts of murderous violence (4:1–24). The Tower of Babel narrative provides a critique of the state apart from divine control (11:1–9).[28] The absolute value of human life, created in God's image, is affirmed by the prohibition of murder; there can be no payment for murder other than with the life of the murderer (9:6).

Well known is the imperialistic and exegetically incorrect attitude that affirmed racial slavery in nineteenth-century America on the basis of Noah's curse of Canaan in Genesis 9:25–27. Although Genesis 10 connects Canaan's father with inhabitants of Africa, there is no curse on Ham, only on Canaan. It is ironic that this misinterpretation overlooked the power of the unique text of Genesis 10. This Table of Nations identifies all peoples of the known world as fundamentally equal before God. All share a common ancestry and possess the image of God. Grounds for prejudice and inequality are excluded.

Ancient Near Eastern Context

It was the nineteenth-century discovery and translation of some Akkadian (the language of Babylonia and Assyria) texts, whose content resembled the creation and flood stories of Genesis, that brought to light the question of the relationship of the Bible and the ancient Near East. Although Continental thought of around 1900 emphasized the dependence of the Bible on Babylonian myths, American scholarship of the mid-twentieth century found a common heritage in the two. However, there never was a close relationship between the creation stories of Genesis 1–2 and any ancient Near Eastern accounts. Babylonian myths such as *Enuma Elish* describe how the chief god of Babylon, Marduk, battled the sweet-water goddess Tiamat, defeated her, and thereby became leader of the pantheon. Marduk created the world from her body. Closer in form and content are the flood stories, such as that contained as part of the larger Gilgamesh Epic. Even here, however, the reason for the flood had more to do with the nuisance that the large population and/or noise of humanity had become to the divine world. There is no sense of a moral reason for the flood, as in Genesis 6. Nevertheless, the similarities of detail suggest a common origin for these narratives. Indeed, the much earlier (eighteenth century BC) Old Babylonian Atrahasis Epic combines a creation and a flood account, along with other elements found in Genesis 1–11, to create the closest parallel to Genesis in terms of the sequence of materials (see the sidebar "The Atrahasis Epic"). This seems unlikely to be

28. Among the many cultural critiques of this phenomenon, see Schaeffer, *Death in the City*.

coincidence and reflects a common and early West Semitic origin for this material and its order.

Seventh-century-BC fragment of the Gilgamesh Epic

The Babylonian epics, such as *Enuma Elish*, integrate the creation account with a struggle, Marduk versus Tiamat. Closer to Israel is the city of Ugarit (near the Mediterranean coast of Syria), where the Baal cycle of myths relates the conflict between the storm-god Marduk and the sea-god Yam. However, there is no description of the creation of anything. The Ugaritic myth has Yam struggling, yet without any creation, but Genesis 1 has an account of creation without any struggle. In this way Genesis differs from both the Babylonian and Ugaritic accounts.[29]

It has been noticed that, while the world of Genesis 2 (esp. the names of the rivers Euphrates and Tigris) relates to Mesopotamia (modern northern Syria and Iraq), Genesis 3 pictures a world similar to the one encountered by early Israel where it first settled in the central hill country of Palestine.[30] Thus the picture is more complex than one of simply sharing traditions with neighboring cultures. Just as the religious portrayal of a single God is unique to the Bible, the biblical creation account, genealogies and king lists, flood stories, and even a story about the Tower of Babel and the creation of many languages have no precise parallel with those found elsewhere in the ancient Near East; rather, they share some elements but then go their own ways. For example, the preflood part of the Sumerian King List also provides long lives for its rulers, comparable to the long-lived members of the line of Seth in Genesis 5. However, the Sumerian King List gives the royal reigns of each ruler in terms of tens of thousands of years, rather than the hundreds of years ascribed to figures in the Bible. Other king lists associate a cultural hero or sage with each of the antediluvian kings, and they ascribe a specific achievement to each of these.[31] The Bible provides a separate list of such cultural achievements that it connects with the line of Cain (Gen. 4:17–24). As already observed, the Bible also places that line under divine judgment for the proliferation of violence. Some have tried to connect biblical figures such as Nimrod (10:8–12) with historical Mesopotamian kings such as Sargon of Akkad or Tulkulti-Ninurta, or architecture such as the Tower of Babel

29. See Tsumura, "Doctrine of Creation," 11.
30. See Meyers, *Discovering Eve*; idem, *Rediscovering Eve*; Hess "Genesis 1–2."
31. Hess, "Genealogies."

Chronological Divisions for the Ancient Near East

Early Bronze Age (EB)	ca. 3300–2000 BC
Middle Bronze Age (MB)	ca. 2000–1550 BC
Middle Bronze Age IIA	ca. 1850–1750 BC
Middle Bronze Age IIB	ca. 1750–1650 BC
Middle Bronze Age IIC	ca. 1650–1550 BC
Late Bronze Age (LB)	ca. 1550–1200 BC
Late Bronze Age IA	ca. 1550–1450 BC
Late Bronze Age IB	ca. 1450–1400 BC
Late Bronze Age IIA	ca. 1400–1300 BC
Late Bronze Age IIB (LBIII)	ca. 1300–1200 BC
Iron Age	ca. 1200–586 BC
Iron IA	ca. 1200–1100 BC
Iron IB	ca. 1100–1000 BC
Iron IIA	ca. 1000–900 BC
Iron IIB	ca. 900–700 BC
Iron IIC	ca. 700–586 BC
Neo-Babylonian	586–539 BC
Persian	539–332 BC
Hellenistic	332–53 BC

Note: I recognize and am pleased to affirm the legitimacy of the usage of BCE in place of BC and of CE in place of AD. I have chosen to use the traditional and widely recognized rubrics without disrespect to the use of BCE and CE.

(11:1–9) with ancient Mesopotamian monuments; yet this enterprise remains speculative, and there are no historical anchors before the time of Abram.[32]

The story of Abram and his family in Genesis 12–36 begins in Mesopotamia. The evidence locates his family in northeastern Aram (in northern Mesopotamia, just north of present-day Syria), in an area that was the center of West Semitic culture in the early second millennium BC. And indeed, although there are many problems with the details of biblical chronology, the preexodus context of these narratives invites a date in the second millennium BC. Although some (e.g., Benjamin Mazar) found an original context for these accounts in the Late Bronze Age (1550–1200 BC), some of the most influential American Old Testament scholars of the twentieth century, such as Cyrus Gordon and William F. Albright, argued that these narratives agree well with the customs of the Middle Bronze Age, thus from sometime early in the second

32. For Sargon of Akkad, see Knohl, "Nimrod"; for Tulkulti-Ninurta, see von Soden, "Nimrod."

Map of South Canaan from Genesis 12

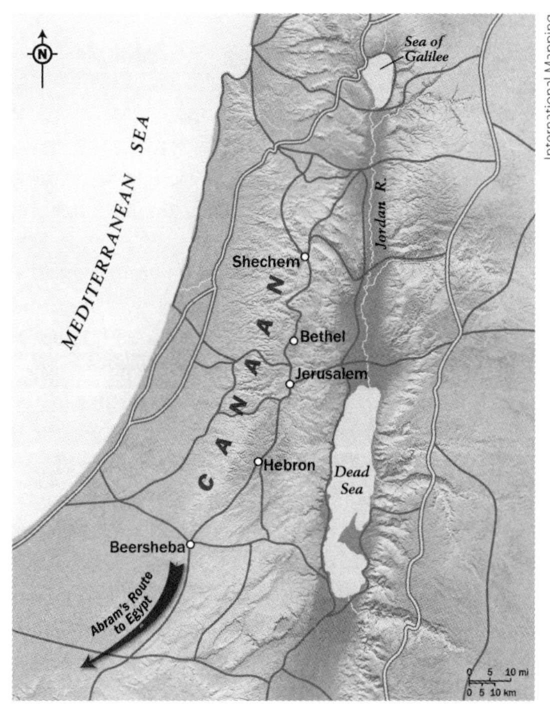

International Mapping

millennium BC (ca. 2000–1550 BC).[33] They based this conclusion primarily on the discovery and publication of archives from the Middle and Late Bronze Age of the West Semitic world, such as those from Amarna, Ugarit, Mari, Nuzi, and Alalakh. Many customs found in Genesis also appear in these texts, such as marrying one's sister, using concubines and their children to preserve inheritance, adoption, land grants, and marriage customs. Soon after Albright's death in 1971, John Van Seters and Thomas L. Thompson published studies challenging these conclusions.[34] They argued that equally significant parallels can be found in the first millennium BC and so the connections with these archives are insignificant. While this is certainly true in some cases, the extreme position has led some to overlook the fact that nowhere is there such a concentration of similarities within a single region and time as in the texts from Middle Bronze Age Alalakh and Mari, and from Late Bronze Age Nuzi. The same is true of the personal names of many of the figures from this early period. Their composition with the *y*-prefix matches the forms of biblical names such as Jacob, Isaac, and Joseph. It was not that examples could not be found later. Rather, it was the significantly larger percentage that came only from this early period.[35]

Less noticed has been the continued publication of the thousands of letters from eighteenth-century-BC Mari. The English translation of hundreds of these letters by Wolfgang Heimpel and the additional study of many unpublished texts by Daniel Fleming have resulted in waves of new parallels that

33. See B. Mazar, *Early Biblical Period*; Albright, "Abram the Hebrew"; Gordon, "Abraham of Ur."

34. See Van Seters, *Abraham in History*; T. Thompson, *Historicity*.

35. Kitchen, *Reliability*, 341–43; Hess, "Alalakh 5"; idem, "The Bible and Alalakh."

Alalakh

The site of Tell Atchana (the modern name for the ancient site of Alalakh) lies in southern Turkey and dominates the Hatay Plain, where ancient and modern farming has reaped a rich harvest. West of Aleppo (ancient Halab) and north of Ugarit, this inland kingdom had strata of occupation, the most important of which for textual sources were Levels IV and VII. Level IV includes the fifteenth through fourteenth centuries BC, beginning with the earlier reign of Idrimi, whose famous story of his rise to power (an early example of historiography in the West Semitic world) is written across his statue in Akkadian. Level VII includes the other major collection of cuneiform tablets, from the eighteenth century BC.

Texts from Tell Atchana have a number of cultural similarities with Genesis.[a] AT 52 (Level VII; *COS* 3.99B:249–50), which records the sale of a town, uses the word for "good" (*ṭa-a-ab*), cognate to Hebrew "good" (*ṭôb*), with the sense of satisfaction regarding the results of the agreement. This term appears in Genesis 1:4, 10, 12, 18, 21, 25, and 31 for God's evaluation of the results of creation. AT 93 (*COS* 3.101C:252; Niedorf, *Die mittelbabylonischen Rechtsurkunden*, 284–88), another Level IV text, provides for a second wife if the first does not give birth after seven years. Compare how Jacob worked for seven years before marrying one of Laban's daughters (Gen. 29:15–35). Finally, AT 7 (*COS* 3.129:282) from Level VII is worth considering. This text provides for the division of inherited property between a brother and a sister. The brother is given the right to select his share first. Compare Genesis 13, where Abram and Lot divide the land. There Abram willingly gives Lot the choice of the share he wants.

[a] For additional examples of cultural similarities, see Hess, "B. Contracts"; idem, "E. Wills."

provide a further cultural context for the Genesis narratives.[36] Thus among the letters are examples of animals being killed while parties are making a treaty (Gen. 15; this also occurs in a roughly contemporary Alalakh land grant), the term "everlasting covenant" (Gen. 9:16; 17:7, 13, 19), and disputes over water rights (Gen. 26).[37] Further research has revealed connections with Genesis that had not previously been developed. For example, it had long been noted that Genesis 14 is unique in the accounts of Abram in that he is involved in fighting an international coalition of kings. Ancient Near Eastern scholars have stated that only in the Middle Bronze Age, and at no later time, could such a coalition have come together and crossed the Fertile Crescent from as

36. Heimpel, *Letters*; Fleming, "Genesis in History." See also Sasson, *From the Mari Archives*.
37. Hess, "Alalakh 1."

Mari

Rama/Wikimedia Commons

Eighteenth-century-BC fresco from the palace at Mari showing King Zimri Lim in the context of his divine choice as king

The ancient site of Mari is located along the west bank of the Euphrates River at the point where it bends to flow eastward. Today it is near Syria's border with Iraq, on the Syrian side. Thousands of cuneiform tablets from about the eighteenth century BC have been excavated and are still being published. Hundreds of these are letters between the king and other officials and leaders. They reveal what appears to be the final two or three years in the life of independent Mari. Most of the citizens bear names composed of elements that are West Semitic. The language(s) represented by these names are called Amorite, similar to the language spoken by the family of Abram.

In addition to some of the parallels with customs in the Bible, the letters reveal tribal confederations all around the city. They demonstrate that the tribes and the city-state of Mari were not two separate societies that somehow got along. Rather, the occupants of the city and of the tribal groups were made up of members of the same family. Just as in Genesis 37, where Jacob remains settled with some members of his extended family but sends most of his sons to take the flocks to pasture some sixty miles away from home for long periods of time, the same events are repeated many times at Mari, where families could be separated in this manner by hundreds of miles for similar lengths of time.[a]

[a] Fleming, "From Joseph to David," 84–86.

far east as Elam into the West Semitic world. Now the Mari texts attest to just such incursions by Elam into Mari territory and possibly beyond. At no later time in ancient Near Eastern history are armies from an independent Elam roaming into the West Semitic world. Another interesting correspondence comes from the two tribal coalitions that were involved with Mari to the extent that leaders of these tribal coalitions could also become kings of Mari. One of these two groups was the Binu-Yamina, equivalent in Hebrew to the name Benjamin, the only son of Jacob named by Jacob (Gen. 35:18).

The religious center for this tribal coalition was Haran, the ancestral home of Abram and the same region where Jacob and Laban moved about with their flocks and herds (11:31–32; 12:4–5; 28:10; 29:4).

The Joseph story also fits well in the early or middle second millennium BC. Details such as the pharaoh's birthday (Gen. 40:20), the sale price of Joseph (37:28), his investiture (41:42–43), the rise to power of a Semite such as Joseph (41:40), mummification of Joseph's body and its placement in a coffin (50:26), and his Egyptian name (41:45)—all of these have their parallels and fit well in mid-second-millennium-BC Egypt.

Specific arguments against the antiquity and authenticity of the materials in Genesis have not changed significantly over the years.[38] They revolve around the domestication of camels (12:16; 24:10–63; 30:43; 31:17, 34; 32:7, 15; 37:25), which is thought not to have occurred until 1100 BC; the mention of the Philistines (Gen. 26), who do not appear outside the Bible before the thirteenth century BC; and the mention of other peoples and places, such as Edom (32:3; 36:1; passim), often thought not to have existed before the first millennium BC. However, written (as well as nonwritten) evidence suggesting the use and domestication of camels is found earlier.[39] The "Philistines" could be a general reference to Aegean peoples by a writer composing in a later period. Edomite tribes are attested in thirteenth-century-BC Egyptian papyri, and their earlier existence is not impossible.

The study of the ancient Near East, especially the archives of the West Semitic world from the Middle and Late Bronze Ages, remains essential to properly understanding the world and context of the book of Genesis.

Canonical Context

Since Genesis is the first book of the Torah and of the whole Bible, it is not surprising that this work should be formative for many developments. It is assumed for almost everything that follows in the Old Testament and becomes an essential theological underpinning for the New Testament. Some thirty verses from Genesis are quoted in the New Testament.[40]

The creation itself is recalled in later texts that compare and contrast with Genesis (e.g., Job 38–39; Isa. 40–45; John 1; Col. 1). Adam is known elsewhere in the Old Testament (Hosea 6:7), and his sin becomes essential to the theology of Romans (5:14) and 1 Corinthians (15:22, 45), providing a foil for Jesus Christ, the second Adam. Eve does not appear again in the Old

38. Hess, review of *Bible Unearthed*.

39. For twenty-first/twentieth-century-BC Ur and elsewhere, see Steinkeller, "Camels in Ur III Babylonia?"; Heide ("Domestication of the Camel," 358) identifies the two-humped Bactrian camel as early as the mid-third millennium BC, in an animal list from Fara.

40. Menken and Moyise, *Genesis in the New Testament*, 1. See the chapters in their volume for detailed study of each part of the NT and its use of Genesis.

Testament but in the New Testament becomes a symbol of susceptibility to deception (2 Cor. 11:3) and a secondary figure in the creation order (1 Tim. 2:13, although it is not clear whether this is apostolic teaching about a peculiar problem in the local church).[41]

The figure of Abraham appears more frequently, at least 108 times beyond Genesis in the Old Testament and New Testament. The emphasis on the promise that God gave to Abraham (Gen. 12:1–3) becomes a key aspect of these occurrences. However, he is also remembered in the New Testament as the great exemplar of faith (Rom. 4:12–16; Gal. 3:8–14; Heb. 11:8–19; cf. Gen. 15:6). Sarah becomes a model of God's miraculous work and a symbol of faithful obedience (Isa. 51:2; Rom. 9:9; Heb. 11:11; 1 Pet. 3:6). Hagar, however, comes to symbolize physical Israel, which remains in slavery because it has not recognized Jesus as the Messiah (Gal. 4:24–25). Jacob occurs hundreds of times as the synonym for the people of Israel. His second name, Israel, also appears frequently, as do the twelve sons of Jacob, especially as found in their tribal territories. Jacob's favored wife, Rachel, becomes a symbol of sorrow at the judgment and the slaughter of the innocents (Jer. 31:15; Matt. 2:18).

The stories of Genesis anticipate the law and its regulations. For example, the incest accounts regarding Noah and especially Lot prepare the reader to understand the importance of the laws on this subject in Leviticus 18 and 20. The covenant with Noah in Genesis 9 remains in force for the non-Israelite peoples of the world. Its high valuation of all human life provides the basis for having justice and respecting natural law, as found in Amos 1–2 and Romans 1. It also may function to justify the requirements placed on the gentile Christians in Acts 15. The paradigm of Abraham's act of faith (Gen. 15:6) and the promise by God to him and his descendants of land, seed, and becoming an instrument of universal blessing (Gen. 12:1–3) become the basis for the acquisition of the land in Joshua and its occupation by the people of Israel in Judges and 1–2 Samuel. This gift of land returns as both a promise and a warning (of losing the land) throughout the monarchy and in the prophets. The New Testament transfers the promise of Abraham's seed to Christ and the church (Gal. 3:16, 19, 29).

The narrative of Genesis also provides a canonical context. It traces Israel and all people back to a common source, created in the image of God. It traces all life and creation itself back to the good word of God. It then proceeds to narrow its attention to the descendants of Adam and the line of Noah to Abram. And from Abram it focuses on the family of his grandson Jacob and their journey to Egypt and life there. As Genesis closes, the reader knows that the promises have not yet been realized and that Israel's life in

41. On the roles of Eve and Adam, see Clines, "What Does Eve Do to Help?"; Hess, "Genesis 1–3." For an understanding of 1 Tim. 2:9–13 in its specific first-century Ephesian context, see Hoag, *Wealth in Ancient Ephesus*, 61–99.

Egypt is temporary and must come to an end. Thus the stage is set for the events of Exodus.

Theological Perspectives of Genesis

Loving God

Readers meet God in Genesis 1 as Elohim, a title for a supremely powerful deity that here emphasizes God as creator of the cosmos.[42] God is unitary, as demonstrated by the singular verbs where Elohim, a word that appears to be a plural in Hebrew, is the subject. Yet there seems to be a complexity as God's self-deliberation results in making humanity "in our image" in Genesis 1:26. The plural at the beginning of the verse could reflect the divine council that accompanies Elohim (cf. Isa. 6; Job 1–2; Ps. 82). However, there is no evidence that "our image" is the image of that council. Rather, it is always understood as exclusively the image of God. This and the "spirit of God" in Genesis 1:2 suggest something more complex and multifaceted than the unitary monad of some philosophers. This is hardly the full-blown Trinity of the early church, but it does anticipate something more.

God alone is portrayed as "in the beginning" in the first verse of the Bible. While the second verse may well picture a poetic way of describing nothing (or more precisely, no life), creation out of nothing (*creatio ex nihilo*) is not stated in so many words.[43] That doctrine is more clearly found in Isaiah 40–45 and in the New Testament. However, throughout the Bible only God "creates" (Heb. *bārāʾ*), and this doctrine makes sense of the story of creation. Further, Genesis 1:1–3 is best understood in light of *creatio ex nihilo*. Thus verse 1 is a summary statement of what follows. Verse 2 represents a description of the setting for the action of creation that begins in verse 3. Hence the "formless and empty" earth of verse 2 (NIV) identifies a situation that is not yet, an abstract way of describing a lack or emptiness. The waters of verse 2 are not the "seas" of verse 10 but part of the "earth" that is about to be created. Thus the spirit of God hovers as a picture of God's preparation to act.[44]

God's creation is described as "good" (1:4, 10, 12, 18, 21, 25, 31), a word that in treaty language emphasizes loyalty and agreement. Here it emphasizes the moral quality of divine goodness that is placed into the created order. It also affirms that creation is in perfect harmony with God, responding to the

42. Hess, "Creator of Heaven and Earth."

43. Yet see the use of the repeated expression "according to its kind" (NKJV). In light of Ezek. 47:10 and other evidence, Neville ("Differentiation") argues that it should be translated "all kinds; every kind" and understood as describing how God created everything, and thus there was nothing that was already in existence.

44. See Tsumura, *Creation and Destruction*; and the summary and update, idem, "Doctrine of Creation."

divine creative word exactly as intended. After all is created, the superlative "very good" affirms that all is just as God intended. God has built goodness into the world and, despite all the brokenness and suffering, will bring this world to a good end. God has likewise built into the world the climactic day of the Sabbath as a time of rest. While Israel observes this in the weekly Sabbath, both Old Testament and New Testament prophecies look forward to the end of human history, when God will provide a Sabbath rest for all the people of God (see Heb. 4).

God creates the world (days 1–3: the dominant term here is that he "separates" what is mixed) in Genesis 1 so that it can form the background for the creation of life in days 4–6. Every sphere of existence (sky, seas, and land) is filled with life, and this life is given both power and divine authority to reproduce and to fill the earth. While this serves as a polemic against Canaanite and other rituals to promote reproduction (plants and animals have this capacity within themselves), its chief concern is to further God's initial creation of life.

The manifestation of God's image in men and women is made explicit in the unique responsibility to rule the earth and all creation (1:26–28). As proposed above, the man begins to exert this role in chapter 2, where he takes care of the garden (2:15) and names or classifies the animals (2:19–20). This image is marred by the willful sin of humanity but nevertheless reaffirmed in 5:1–3 and 9:6. Genesis 1–11 provides examples of how humanity fails to fulfill its charge to reflect God's will on earth by living out the image of God. Genesis 12 begins the story of how God chooses one family from all the earth and attempts to guide them into the divine will for God's image to be affirmed. The first five books of the Bible (the Pentateuch) contain specifics of the divine will. The remainder of the Old Testament relates the story of how Israel tried to realize this image despite repeated failures. The New Testament teaches that Jesus Christ came as the truest image of God (Col. 1:15). His proclamation of the kingdom of God in the Gospels constitutes an attempt to continue to reflect this image in the ongoing life of the church and Christianity up to the present day.

The sin of Genesis 3 brings to an end the perfect harmony of the Creator and creation. This result is due to the desire of the woman and man to choose to become like God (3:5–7). This same motivation leads to God's condemnation of the human race in 6:1–7. There the sons of God (Angels? See 2 Pet. 2:4; Jude 6) and daughters of humanity copulate, perhaps in order to reproduce human offspring that, like God, will live forever. The same sort of concern inspires the Tower of Babel, where its builders say, "Let us make a name for ourselves" (Gen. 11:4). In every case, God thwarts the plans of sin, on a worldwide scale in Genesis 1–11 and then more locally in the remainder of the book.

It is beginning with the second creation story in Genesis 2:4b–25 that the personal name of God appears: Yahweh (old English Bibles used Jehovah;

most modern versions style it as Lord, with small capitals for the last three letters). God is personally concerned with the man and with his companion, the woman. The garden of Eden—with its gold and precious stones, its water and tree of life, its caretaker, and its function to provide a place for God to meet with humanity—implies its role as a prototypical sanctuary. It anticipates similar items in the tabernacle of Exodus and the temple of 1 Kings. Sin leads to the shedding of animal blood as a means to cover the effects of the resulting shame (Gen. 3:21), and to banishment from the garden "temple" (3:23–24). The same will be true of Israel's sin. It will also end in banishment from Jerusalem and its temple. The next generation of the first family begins the practice of sacrifice as a means to worship God (4:3–4). Despite the terrible end of this first attempt to worship God (with Cain's murder of Abel), altars and sacrifices continue to be used for this purpose by Noah, Abraham, Isaac, and Jacob (8:20; 12:7–8; 13:18; 22:9; 26:25; 33:20; 35:1–7). For Abraham and his offspring, it becomes a means of claiming the promises of the land for themselves and their families and descendants. It may be for this reason that their altars are built only in the promised land.

A second great theological theme running parallel to sacrifices and altars is that of covenant. God desires to establish and define a relationship with people, beginning with Eden. When sin destroys the ideal harmony of that relationship, God establishes a covenant with Noah, who is "righteous" (Gen. 6:9) amid a wicked generation. Thus God rescues Noah and his family from the judgment of the flood and uses the first occurrence of "covenant" (Heb. *bĕrît*) to promise salvation (6:18). That term recurs in 9:9–17, where God promises never again to destroy the earth with a flood. God also creates a covenant with Abram in 12:1–3. That promise of land, seed, and becoming a blessing to others is not called a covenant until the scene where Abram divides the animals and God appears in a vision (15:18). Just as the sign of the rainbow confirms God's covenant with Noah and his successors in the human family, so the sign of circumcision confirms the covenant with Abraham and his successors (Gen. 17). That relationship is confirmed again to Isaac and to Jacob, although the term for "covenant" does not appear for God's defined relationship with them (however, the term for "promise" does occur in 21:1–2 and 28:15). Thus the covenant becomes a means by which God defines a relationship of salvation and promise to creation, to humanity, and to a chosen people.

Loving Others

The stories of Genesis have much to say about the life of the family and its value. Their focus on families illustrates the essential role this group plays in any society. The jealousies and rivalries, although common to most families, seem magnified through the practice of polygyny. Indeed, although the text does not forbid this practice, so little good and so much trouble comes from it that the narratives stand as a warning to avoid it as contrary to the monogamous ideal of Genesis 2:24.

The role of sexual morality is not overtly emphasized. However, when both Abraham and Isaac are ready to compromise the honor of their wives for their own personal interests (Gen. 12, 20, 26), God intervenes, and the Egyptian and Philistine leaders confess and obey God's word. Of similar concern are the acts of incest that the language of 9:20–27 suggests lie behind Noah's cursing of Canaan, and that recurs with Lot and his daughters in 19:30–38. In both examples the narrative tacitly draws a connection between alcohol consumption and sexual immorality.

The account of Sodom and its same-sex interests in Genesis 19 does not speak only to the issue of sexual morality but also to the matter of hospitality. As righteous Abraham entertains and shows hospitality to the messengers from God, unrighteous Sodom seeks to abuse them without regard for the universal values of hospitality and grace toward outsiders. This issue of accepting the outsider appears repeatedly (1) while Abraham and his family live as aliens in a land that is not truly their own (although it is promised to them), (2) in the story of Jacob as he lives with Laban in northern Mesopotamia and remains at Laban's mercy until he is shown that he may leave (31:11–13), and (3) while Joseph (and later Jacob's entire family) is a guest of the pharaoh in Egypt, all the while blessing the pharaoh. This touches on the larger theme of justice toward others. Abram seeks justice for his nephew Lot and then for Sarah's maidservant Hagar (see Gen. 13, 14, 16, 19, 21). Jacob wants justice for the slain people of Shechem, despite the original crime of rape (Gen. 34).[45] Joseph seeks justice for his family when they come to live in Egypt (Gen. 46–47) and, in a classic text, denies that he can stand in the place of God to judge (and punish) his siblings after their father's death (50:19–21). This statement precisely parallels the words of his father (Jacob) to his mother (Rachel) when she was unable to have children (30:2).

Throughout Genesis 12–50, the three main characters symbolize the great and abiding virtues of 1 Corinthians 13:13. Abraham is the man of faith who acts on God's words without question, even when that means sacrificing his only son (Gen. 22). Jacob is the character who most clearly evidences hope, as he hopes for his children despite their hatred for one another, and God hopes for Jacob despite his role as a trickster. Behind this hope are the attitude and actions of divine grace upon one who does not appear to deserve it. Finally, as Genesis 50 (esp. v. 19) demonstrates, Joseph's life is characterized by love and forgiveness for his brothers and for all who mistreated him on his divinely ordained path to second in command over Egypt. Behind this, as well, are the love and forgiveness of God toward Joseph's boasts of rulership over his

45. Parry, *Old Testament and Christian Ethics.*

brothers and his father (Gen. 37). Through the hardship of his trials, Joseph matures into the model of love with which Genesis concludes.

Key Commentaries and Studies

Arnold, Bill T. *Genesis*. NCBC. Cambridge: Cambridge University Press, 2009. Best review of most current materials for exegesis. Many helpful insights.

Brayford, Susan. *Genesis*. SCS. Leiden: Brill, 2007. Important for the study of the LXX translation of the text.

Gunkel, Hermann. *The Legends of Genesis*. Translated by W. H. Carruth. New York: Schocken, 1901. Key for early comparative studies.

Hess, Richard S., and David T. Tsumura, eds. *"I Studied Inscriptions from before the Flood": Ancient Near Eastern, Linguistic and Literary Approaches to Genesis 1–11*. SBTS 4. Winona Lake, IN: Eisenbrauns, 1994. Current review of important recent studies.

Hess, Richard S., Philip Satterthwaite, and Gordon Wenham, eds. *He Swore an Oath: Biblical Themes from Genesis 12–50*. 2nd ed. Carlisle, UK: Paternoster; Grand Rapids: Baker, 1994. Wide-ranging essays on the interpretation of these texts.

Mathews, Kenneth A. *Genesis*. Vol. 1, *1–11:26*. Vol. 2, *11:27–50:26*. NAC 1A–1B. Nashville: Broadman & Holman, 1996–2005. Thorough exegesis and interaction with research.

Rad, Gerhard von. *Genesis: A Commentary*. Translated by John H. Marks. OTL. Philadelphia: Westminster, 1972. Classic theological interpretation from a higher-critical perspective.

Smith, Mark S. *The Priestly Vision of Genesis 1*. Minneapolis: Fortress, 2010. Thorough study of critical scholarship on the first chapter of Genesis (1:1–2:4a).

Waltke, Bruce K., with Cathi J. Fredricks. *Genesis: A Commentary*. Grand Rapids: Zondervan, 2001. Clear translation and interpretation; strong theological exegesis.

Wenham, Gordon. *Genesis*. Vol. 1, *1–15*. Vol. 2, *16–50*. WBC 1–2. Waco: Word, 1987–94. Best detailed evangelical commentary for exegesis.

2

EXODUS

The book of Exodus describes the deliverance of God's people from Egypt. Many modern preachers of liberation use the exodus as a model for their proclamation. How much of this is legitimate? Is the exodus a matter of faith or of politics, or both?

Name, Text, and Outline

The name Exodus derives from the title of this scroll in the Septuagint. It means "exit, way out." The Hebrew name is *šĕmôt*, literally, "names." In keeping with the practice noted for Genesis, this scroll is named by the first important word. In this case *šĕmôt* is the second word of the book, the first word being the less significant "these (are)."

As with Genesis, the Masoretic Hebrew text possesses few uncertainties regarding its content. The Septuagint translators struggled with archaic language (Exod. 15), foreign terms (Egyptian expressions in the opening chapters), and architectural descriptions (Exod. 25–31, 35–40). The second account of the tabernacle, in which its construction is described, is shorter than in the Masoretic Text. Chapters 12–23 take on characteristics of the later rabbinic exegesis. Other than in some of the descriptions of the tabernacle construction, the Hebrew text on which the Septuagint translation is based did not differ substantially from the consonantal Hebrew of the Masoretic Text.[1]

1. Gurtner, *Exodus*, 13.

OUTLINE

I. The Midwives (1:1–22)
II. Moses's Preparation (2:1–4:31)
  A. Birth and Early Egyptian Life (2:1–14)
  B. Midian and Call (2:15–4:31)
III. Confrontation with Pharaoh (5:1–11:10)
  A. First Meeting with Pharaoh and Further Oppressions (5:1–21)
  B. Return to God and God's Name Revealed as Redeemer (5:22–7:7)
  C. The Plagues (7:8–11:10)
IV. The Passover (12:1–13:19)
V. The Exodus and Reed Sea Crossing (13:20–15:21)
VI. The Journey to Mount Sinai (15:22–18:27)
VII. Sinai and the Covenant (19:1–24:17)
VIII. First Forty Days: Tabernacle and Sabbath Preserve the Sinai Experience (24:18–31:18)
IX. Second Forty Days: The Gold Calf and the New Set of Tablets (32:1–34:35)
X. The Construction of the Tabernacle (35:1–40:38)

Overview of Exodus

The story of Exodus begins with Israel outside the land of promise, just as Genesis 12 begins with Abram and his family outside that land. However, at the beginning of this book they are in Egypt rather than in Haran. They are no longer a single family but the beginnings of a nation that has grown large (Exod. 1:7). Even so, the appearance on Egypt's throne of a pharaoh who does not remember Joseph and all that he did for Egypt and for an earlier pharaoh (1:8) signals trouble. This pharaoh understands Israel in purely political terms as those who are not Egyptians and whose number will threaten Egypt's existence, especially if an enemy causes the pharaoh to commit Egyptian forces and thereby reveal vulnerability in the land (1:9–10). Rather than expel Israel, Pharaoh chooses to enslave them in order to build store cities for his wealth. No matter how hard and bitter Pharaoh makes their existence, they increase in number. So Pharaoh tries another plan. He instructs the two Israelite midwives to kill all the male babies as soon as they are born. However, the midwives deceive Pharaoh by reporting that the Israelite women give birth before the midwives arrive. So they protect the baby boys. Pharaoh then commands the Egyptians to kill any boy who is born to the Israelites (1:22).

Into such a world, Moses is born. The story of Exodus 1 reveals the character of this pharaoh as a brutal and paranoid leader. He does not respect the value of innocent human life, despite this divine teaching to all people (Gen. 9:6). If Pharaoh and the people of Egypt try to kill the male babies of Israel, who are innocent, they may rightly expect that their own male children may someday face the same fate. In contrast, Israel appears free of any wrong and blessed by God with increasing numbers. Not only does this fulfill the divine promise to Abraham of numerous offspring (Gen. 13:16; 15:5; 26:4), but it also recalls Jacob's increase in numbers and wealth despite Laban's attempt to take advantage of him in another foreign land (Gen. 29–31).

This background sets the stage for Israel's birth as a nation amid an international political struggle as the leadership and people of their host country are set to fight against that birth. So the narrative demonstrates how Israel is repeatedly brought to the brink of failure and extinction, and then pulled out of it at the last minute by God's grace. Exodus 2 demonstrates how, already at his birth, Moses faces possible death and the end of God's plan to use him as a deliverer. Moses, however, escapes murder by the Egyptians when his mother puts him in a basket in the Nile. Pharaoh's daughter discovers him and raises him as her own. His biological mother becomes his nurse, thus providing her a presence alongside her son.

Exodus 2 continues with Moses as a young adult who witnesses a fellow Israelite beaten by an Egyptian and who responds by murdering the Egyptian. Threatened with the death penalty by Pharaoh, Moses flees to the land of Midian, where he gets married and begets a son. So Moses takes on the life of a shepherd (3:1) with security and satisfaction, far removed from the troubles of Egypt. Here a new threat emerges: Will Moses's good life prevent him from returning and taking on the responsibility of a deliverer? Even the death of the pharaoh who sought Moses's life does not move him. Exodus 3–4 describes God's appearance to Moses from a burning bush on Mount Horeb, "the mountain of God." There God shocks Moses into listening to the cries of Israel in their oppression. Despite Moses's protest that he has no power to persuade, God gives him the power to work miracles. His brother Aaron will speak for him (4:14–15). In 4:21–26, God describes Israel as his son, who is threatened by Pharaoh and his obstinacy. The incident with God seeking to kill Moses's son fits in this context as the manner in which Moses learns what it means to have one's son threatened by another.

In the following chapters, Moses tries to convince Pharaoh to release the Israelites. However, Pharaoh refuses. God promises to harden Pharaoh's heart (4:21; 7:3) and then proceeds to allow Pharaoh to harden his own heart and so to refuse Moses's requests (cf. 8:15, 32; 9:12, 34; 10:1, 20, 27; 11:10). The mightiest ruler on earth refuses to allow Israel to become a free nation before God. Each plague that God sends further hardens Pharaoh's heart so that he increases his oppression against Israel. Finally, the tenth plague comes. This brings about the death of every firstborn male in Egypt, including the firstborn of Pharaoh; only the Israelites and those who celebrate the Passover are exempt (Exod. 12–13). Pharaoh finally relents and expels Israel (13:17 reports it indirectly, as though it is a consequence of God's acts rather than any sort of beneficence on the part of Pharaoh).

But this is not the end of Pharaoh's threat to Israel. Exodus 14:1–15:21 reports how Pharaoh soon changes his mind and sends earth's most powerful army after this ragtag band of freed slaves. However, he cannot destroy God's people. Israel is delivered by the miraculous parting of the waters of the sea, in which Pharaoh's chariotry then drowns.

The next threat to Israel's existence comes from nature: thirst and famine. God provides manna in the wilderness and water from a rock (15:22–17:7). At the same time there is the danger of becoming lost in the desert. How will Israel survive this threat? From the beginning of their journey, Israel is led by God's pillars of cloud and fire (13:21–22). Victory over the Amalekites

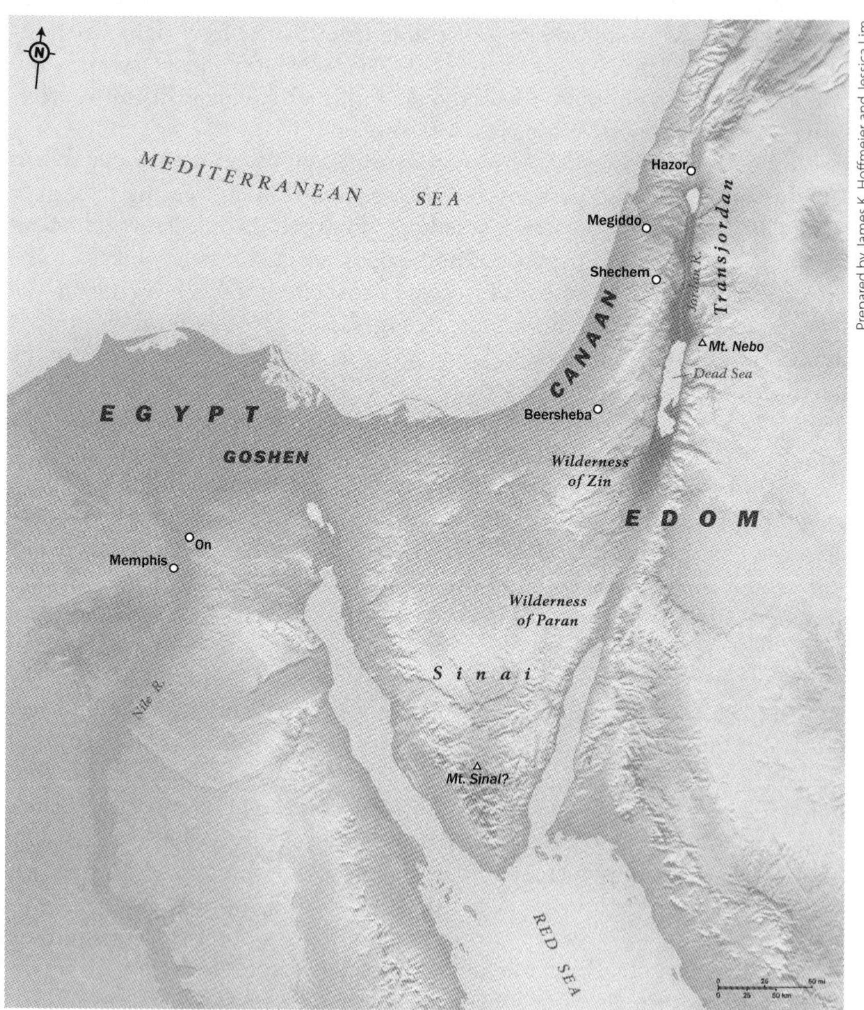

Map of Egypt and Canaan at the time of Joseph

(17:8–16) and the organization of a system of judicial administration (Exod. 18) represent the ongoing means to exist.

The people reach the mountain of God. Mount Sinai (also called Horeb) is a holy mountain where the presence of God will appear. God is hidden behind the special effects of cloud, thunder, and lightning. Here the covenant teaches Israel what it means to be holy as God is holy (Exod. 19). Moses ascends the mountain and receives the covenant, first in terms of the summary of the Decalogue (20:1–17) and then in terms of an expanded collection of civil and religious laws (20:22–23:33), referred to as the "Book/Scroll of the Covenant" (24:7). In a religious ceremony the people of Israel twice affirm their willingness to accept this covenant (24:3, 7; cf. 19:8). Israel's leaders seal and celebrate this commitment and relationship with blood and with a divine feast with God on the mountain (24:8–11).

There follows the laws (1) for the construction of the tabernacle, a portable sanctuary with its accoutrements and priestly adornments, and (2) for the observance of the Sabbath (25:1–31:18). The tabernacle and the Sabbath provide ongoing means for Israel to know God's presence.

While Moses delays on the mountain with God, the people seek their own means of securing the ongoing presence of God. In Exodus 32 they construct an image of a gold calf, which they worship as the god who brought them out of Egypt. As they have feasted with God, they also eat and drink before this image. In Exodus, this forms the last and most pernicious threat to Israel's existence. Israel is threatened from within by its own sin. It breaks its covenant with God. The order of the law is shattered by the disorder of the people's rebellion. Sons of Levites stop this worship with the killing of three thousand participants, and as a reward they receive the temple service (described as a blessing in 32:29). This and a divinely sent plague punish those involved in the false worship.

God reaffirms the covenant relationship in both word and image with Moses (Exod. 33–34) and then with Israel (Exod. 35–40). With Moses, the confirmation comes through divine self-revelation (image) and through a reiteration of the words of the covenant (word). With Israel, it involves the observance of the Sabbath (word) and the construction of the tabernacle (an image of his presence among Israel, if not of God himself).

Reading Exodus

Premodern Readings[2]

The great story of Israel's birth has always captured the imagination of Jews and Christians, enjoying many retellings and dramatizations through

2. This largely summarizes the greater detail found in Childs, *Book of Exodus*, and esp. his "History of Exegesis" sections through the commentary. See also Crawford, "Exodus in the Dead

the ages. The early commentators saw the emphasis on Israel's great increase in population as a fulfillment of Genesis 1:28 and of the promise to Abraham (noted above). The lies of the midwives became the medieval focal point for discussions on the legitimacy of lying. God's self-revelation in Exodus 3 constitutes Jesus Christ for most Christian theologians in church history. For the philosophers, the divine self-revelation of 3:14 expresses an identity tied up with ontology and the basis of all existence. The connection of the plagues and divine judgment remains a key theme through the history of interpretation. In addition, much is made of the number ten, often relating it to the Decalogue and the manner in which Egypt violated all the commands of God.

More than any other text, the narrative of the exodus from Egypt and the Passover gave the people of God a connection to the original event through word and sign. In Judaism, the celebration of the Passover itself is traced back to this text, in which the act of redemption and its significance are placed in the context of an annual celebration from its beginning (Exod. 12). The theme of God's remembrance and choice of his people occurs already in the literature of Israel's exile and the intertestamental period.[3] In Christianity, this celebration led into the Last Supper and the significance of Jesus's own redemption, to be remembered in word and deed in the celebration of Holy Communion. In both, the meal and its accompanying words become the means of participating in the historic act of God's redemption and the means of looking to the future and to the full salvation of God's people with the coming/return of the Messiah.

From the earliest interpreters, the great miracle of the Red (Reed) Sea's parting and Israel's deliverance is either allegorized into something glorifying wisdom and condemning passion (Philo and Wisdom of Solomon) or rationalized into something akin to an event in the life of Alexander the Great (Josephus). In this great event, early Judaism's midrashic interpretation finds fulfillment of the Genesis promise to the ancestors. More specifically, the provision of manna is God's response to Abraham's act of feeding the divine messengers when they visit him (Gen. 18). In the water of the Red Sea, patristic interpreters found judgment and a baptism providing salvation from that judgment. Spurred on by Jesus's own explanation in John 6, in the manna they also saw the eucharistic bread. The visit of Jethro (Exod. 18) became an

Sea Scrolls"; Greenspoon, "Textual and Translation Issues in Greek Exodus"; Lund, "Exodus in Syriac"; Everson, "The *Vetus Latina* and the Vulgate"; Chilton, "The Exodus Theology of the Palestinian Targumim"; Sterling, "The People of the Covenant or the People of God"; Spilsbury, "Exodus in Josephus"; Doering, "The Reception of the Book of Exodus"; Elowsky, "Exodus in the Fathers"; and Visotzky, "Exodus in Rabbinic Interpretation." All of these appear in Dozeman, Evans, and Lohr, eds., *The Book of Exodus*. See also Briggs and Lohr, *A Theological Introduction to the Pentateuch*.

3. Macatangay, "Election by Allusion."

illustration of the use of profane knowledge in the service of God. More than any other figure of the Old Testament, Moses, through his deeds and words and through images of him (drawn especially from Exodus), influenced the founding and history of the United States.[4]

The giving of the Decalogue and the text itself formed the foundation for the understanding of biblical law in both Judaism and Christianity. In Judaism, it became the fountainhead for the whole study of Torah. In Christianity, it remained the point of departure for the classic distinction between the moral, civil, and ceremonial laws. Each generation applied the text to the concerns of its day while maintaining that the law has universal application for all times and cultures.

The remainder of the book is dominated by the laws of the Book of the Covenant and by the tabernacle as it is described and then constructed. In Judaism, these became key texts, studied as a means to understand God's principles of justice and the means to approach God in proper worship. In Christianity, the interpretation of these texts is often short-circuited by focusing on this material as somehow prefiguring Jesus Christ. The inadequacy of these provisions (the need for something more than the laws alone) is attested in their failure to prevent the worship of the gold calf.

Source Criticism

The study of the sources continued into the book of Exodus.[5] Here it divided the text verse by verse into remarkably detailed and speculative separate literary texts. For example, even a moderate source critic such as Brevard Childs had no trouble in identifying and isolating all four sources as represented in Exodus 12 and 13 (P in 12:1–20, 28, 40–51; 13:1–2; J in 12:21–23, 27b, 29–34, 37–39; D in 12:24–27a; 13:3–16; E in 12:35–36).[6] Thus J keeps the narratives of the plagues and the Passover independent of each other. For example, in the plagues no special sign separates Israel and Egypt, but in the Passover account blood divides the two nations. In the plagues narrative the focus is on Yahweh's battle with Pharaoh, whereas in the Passover account God uses the angel of death as an intermediary. The source theory goes on to argue that P harmonizes the two parts of J.

From this perspective, the legal collections represent separate items added from outside the sources themselves. Thus, on the one hand, the Decalogue, the Book of the Covenant, and the so-called Ritual Decalogue of Exodus 34 all have their origin separate from the traditional literary sources. These beginnings are often associated with tradition history. On the other hand, the

4. Feiler, *America's Prophet*.

5. For an introduction to the study of sources for the Pentateuch, see "Source Criticism" for Genesis.

6. Childs, *Book of Exodus*, 184–95.

P source dominates the latter part of the scroll, emphasizing the construction of the tabernacle, the high-priestly garments, and the Sabbath.

Despite criticism of this view,[7] David P. Wright has persuasively compared the overall legal collection of the Covenant Code (Exod. 20:22–23:33) with that of the Code of Hammurabi from the eighteenth century BC.[8] However, Wright believes that the authors of the Covenant Code borrowed from later copies of Hammurabi's Code in the first millennium BC. Behind this lies the assumption that there was no legal tradition before this time in the West Semitic world. However, the discovery of a fragmentary law collection at the northern Israelite site of Hazor, dating from within a century or two of the composition of the laws of Hammurabi, has challenged these assumptions.[9] It is clear that a legal tradition with laws whose form and content resemble those of Hammurabi did exist in the land of Israel during the second millennium BC. Thus a legal collection such as the Covenant Code, or the collections in Leviticus and Deuteronomy, have a precedent in southern Canaan in written jurisprudence of the West Semitic world.

Tradition History

The Moses stories of Exodus have been widely compared with other ancient accounts. The story of the hero who is miraculously delivered from death as a child has numerous parallels, beginning with the legend behind the birth and early childhood of the third-millennium-BC Assyrian king Sargon of Akkad.[10] There is also a Hittite myth about a queen who sends her infant sons in baskets to the sea (*COS* 1.71:181–82).[11] The sixteenth/fifteenth-century-BC autobiography of Idrimi of Alalakh tells how this king was thrust away from his people and then returned to deliver them and to rule over them (*COS* 1.148:479–80). Various elements of this motif match the experience of Moses.

Three questions of tradition history may be considered here in the study of Exodus: the explanation of the plagues, the origin of the Passover, and the background to the laws in the Pentateuch. Tradition history of the Pentateuch, as noted in the chapter on Genesis, is the study of traditions, usually oral, that lie behind the written text as now preserved. Another discipline, form criticism, closely resembles this approach, as it looks at the smallest units making up the stories and seeks to classify them according to their literary structure. It then considers the social setting in which such materials may have

7. See Wells, "Covenant Code."

8. D. Wright, "Laws of Hammurabi"; idem, *Inventing God's Law*. See also the sidebar "Hammurabi's Laws and Values."

9. Horowitz, Oshima, and Vukosavović, "Hazor 18."

10. B. Lewis, *Sargon Legend*.

11. Hoffner, *Hittite Myths*.

emerged. This can include such a matter as the plague of the frogs, which may have been inserted to explain why there are so many frogs in Egypt (one of the signs continuing "to this day" in Jer. 32:20). However, this is not what the text itself claims. As many frogs as there are in Egypt, the plague creates so many more. Alternatively, the focus of the text may be on a religious custom. For example, there is the mysterious comment in Exodus 4:24–26, where Zipporah circumcises Moses's son to prevent God from killing "him" (whether "him" refers to Moses or to his son is unclear). Some see here an original account about a demonic attack where the demon was later replaced by God in the story. Others suggest God's anger for Moses's son not being circumcised. Perhaps there is a relationship with the bloodguilt of Moses's earlier murder of an Egyptian.[12] Or it may simply be connected to God's earlier statement in the same chapter about Israel as his firstborn son. Perhaps God wishes to teach Moses experientially about what it means to have a beloved child threatened; this is done at the crucial time of Moses's return to the people of Israel, who were already identified by male circumcision (Gen. 17). As is apparent from this brief treatment, much discussion on these matters remains highly speculative. The more it can be supported by connection to the biblical text or by other ancient Near Eastern comparative sources, the stronger the case may be.

A good example of this is found in the plagues. Some have seen behind them a purely rationalistic explanation. The transformation of the Nile into a river of blood is related to red clay in the river, which appears at the beginning of the summer. Then the plague of frogs would result as these creatures leave the river, which became unable to support life.[13] In recent years the plague of darkness (and also the soot or ash of Exod. 9:8–9) has been connected to the volcanic eruption of the Aegean island of Thera (Santorini). This seismic event affected the whole eastern Mediterranean. However, this explosion has been dated to the seventeenth century BC, much earlier than the biblical text would allow as a date for the events.

A second approach to the plagues relates them to various Egyptian deities.[14] From the time of the early Christian scholar Origen, some have connected the plague on the cattle with the Egyptian worship of animals. It would certainly seem most appropriate for the plague of darkness. If the most powerful temple in Egypt was that dedicated to Amon-Re, the sun-god, then this second-to-last plague challenges the power of Egypt's chief god. The last plague, the death of the firstborn, recalls the repeated claims by the pharaoh in Egyptian texts to be the source and giver of life to all people. Again, this would challenge such a claim. Some scholars, such as William Propp, review the larger religious

12. For these and other views, see Propp, *Exodus*, 233–43. See also Exod. 2:11–15.
13. Kitchen, *Reliability*, 249–52.
14. Hoffmeier, *Israel in Egypt*, 146–53.

Plagues and Egyptian Deities

Although the account of Exodus 7–12 makes no explicit connection between the plagues and their challenge to the deities of Egypt, there are many deities whose mastery of the various areas that the plagues touch would be called into question. This is especially true of the last two plagues. The darkness dismisses the power of the most powerful deity in Egypt and the greatest temple. The death of the firstborn directly challenges the pharaoh's power as a god and as the giver of life to all of Egypt.

Plague 1 (7:15–25), Nile changed to blood: The Nile was deified as Hapi, the source of Egypt's water. Red was the color of Hapi's enemy and murderer, Seth.[a]

Plague 2 (8:1–6), frogs: Heqat, with a frog's head, was in control of the multiplication of frogs, thought to symbolize prosperity.

Plagues 3–4 (8:16–24), gnats and flies (mosquitoes?): Khepher, the flying beetle, was supposed to be a god of resurrection.

Plague 5 (9:1–7), pestilence on domesticated animals: There was a bull cult of Apis. Other deities such as Re and Ptah could be symbolized as bulls.

Plague 6 (9:8–12), boils or smallpox: Sekhmet and Amon-Re were reckoned as healer deities.

Plague 7 (9:13–35), hail: Compare beliefs about Nut (sky), Shu (supported the sky), and Tefnut (moisture).

Plague 8 (10:1–20), locusts: Senehem supposedly protected against pests, as did other deities.

Plague 9 (10:21–29), darkness: Amen-Re was the sun-god, and the pharaoh was honored as the "Son of Re."

Plague 10 (Exod. 11–12), death of firstborn: This plague directly challenges Pharaoh, who claims to give life to the people of Egypt.[b]

[a] Kitchen, *Reliability*, 253, and for plagues 2 and 9.

[b] See Hort, "Plagues of Egypt"; Currid, *Ancient Egypt*, 109–13; Hoffmeier, *Israel in Egypt*, 146–53.

and especially mythological literature of the ancient Near East in order to demonstrate the presence of each of these plagues as common motifs of judgment or divine wrath.[15] However, the biblical text does not try to connect the plagues to either natural causes or myths. Rather, the plagues manifest the power of the God of Moses and of Israel.

As noted above (under "Source Criticism"), the Passover was a focus of attention for source-critical theory. It also raised the question as to where

15. Propp, *Exodus*, 347–52.

the different parts of the celebration originated. In his source-critical publication of 1878, Julius Wellhausen addresses this issue, suggesting that the Feast of Unleavened Bread was originally an agricultural feast separate from the Passover and its roasting of the lamb.[16] These two were combined only in the time of Josiah (ca. 622 BC), hundreds of years after the exodus events.

Other scholars also argue that the Passover developed separately from the Feast of Unleavened Bread.[17] Instead of a settled agricultural context (as for the Feast of Unleavened Bread), the Passover originated in a sacrificial ritual of nomads as they prepared to migrate to arable summer pastures. In the spring, the nomads sacrificed a young animal, a lamb, before their movement. Blood from this sacrifice was smeared on the tent posts to ward off evil spirits. Eventually Israelites attached this ritual to the exodus from Egypt and then to the Feast of Unleavened Bread.

However, there are problems with this interpretation. First, it is entirely speculative, without evidence from settled or nomadic peoples.[18] Second, as T. Desmond Alexander has observed, wherever the Passover is mentioned in the Pentateuch, the Feast of Unleavened Bread also appears.[19] So the biblical text provides no evidence for this distinction. Third, the diets of pastoralists are not exclusively carnivorous, nor are the eating habits of settled people only vegetarian. Pastoralists eat bread and villagers eat meat.[20] Finally, as a comparable spring festival from the time of Moses, the thirteenth-century-BC *zukru* festival is attested in texts from Emar and contemporary with the time when one might date Moses and the exodus.[21] *Zukru* derives from the Semitic root *zkr*, "to remember," used also of the Passover in Exodus 12:14 and Leviticus 23:24. It began on the fifteenth day of the first month and lasted seven days, just like the Passover and the Feast of Unleavened Bread. Also like the Passover, twilight was a critical time, a lamb was roasted, and distinctive bread and herbs were eaten. In this early period, this was a festival of a settled people, combining the major elements of the Passover. Thus interpretations of the Passover as a late combination of a nomadic festival where meat was used, and an agricultural festival where bread was eaten, lack warrant. As with Emar's *zukru* festival, so Israel's Passover and Feast of Unleavened Bread were joined from the beginning, and both festivals focused on the people's great god (Dagon at Emar, and Yahweh for Israel).

16. Wellhausen, *Prolegomena*, 99–108.
17. Rost, "Weidewechsel."
18. Van Seters, "Place of the Yahwist."
19. Alexander, "Passover Sacrifice."
20. Propp, *Exodus*, 428–29.
21. For a study of the Emar texts, see Fleming, *Time at Emar*. For comparisons between this Emar festival and the Passover, see Fleming, "Break in the Line"; idem, "Israelite Festival Calendar"; and Hess, "Multi-Month Ritual Calendars."

The third major area of study of oral tradition in Exodus relates to the question of the origins of the various laws. Albrecht Alt divided the laws into two major groups, according to the form of the law.[22] On the one hand were the casuistic, or case, laws, which envisioned specific situations and applied legal consequences. On the other hand were the apodictic commands, which were not restricted to specific situations. The latter included the sort of civil laws that occur in the Decalogue: "Do not kill! Do not commit adultery! Do not steal!" (Exod. 20:13–15 RSH). These commands are short and easily remembered. They fit the theory of nomadic law, where tribes orally pass on the laws and preserve them through memory rather than write them down. The case law, however, fits the picture of Canaanite cities, where precedents are established and legal decisions are recorded rather than transmitted orally. However, this theory is not supported by the evidence. To the contrary, other legal collections (including those appearing as treaty stipulations) contain examples of both kinds of laws.[23]

Literary Readings

Literary approaches abound with relation to any narrative context. This is especially true of the dramatic story of Moses. For this reason, a variety of interpretations have found their way into popular art forms, including famous movies such as *The Ten Commandments* (1956) and the popular animation *Prince of Egypt* (1998).[24] However, literary studies have been sensitive to the repetition of similar terms and ideas, and to the apparent contradictions in the text. For example, there is the question as to how God can say that this is the first revelation of his name Yahweh (Exod. 6:3) when the name occurs repeatedly in Genesis, where in 4:26 it is specifically stated that people began to call on the name of Yahweh.[25] This suggests that the name Yahweh was not used by Abraham, Isaac, and Jacob in Genesis but that it was written in by the author wherever there was an emphasis on the personal revelation of God and so also on the use of his personal name. It may also imply that God's revelation of the name Yahweh was a revelation in Exodus of God as the Creator and Redeemer of his people.

A second literary concern arises with attempts to put together all the activity at Mount Sinai into a coherent and chronological order. This has not proved to be easy. Many commentators suggest a variety of sources to explain the relationship. However, studies of Hebrew narratives as well as sensitivities to

22. Alt, "Origins of Israelite Law."

23. Apodictic laws are less frequent in ancient Near Eastern legal collections, and the same is true of their appearance in biblical law collections in comparison with casuistic laws. See Sparks, *Ancient Texts*, 417.

24. Culbertson and Wainwright, *The Bible in/and Popular Culture.*

25. Hess, *Israelite Religions*, 172–75.

© Baker Publishing Group and Dr. James C. Martin

Jebel Musa, traditional site of Mount Sinai in the southern Sinai Peninsula

the theological emphases have suggested means of explaining these problems without resorting to separate sources.[26]

The legal collections themselves raise literary questions as to the reason for their structure. This is already established by the Decalogue, where a comprehensive law code begins and ends with religious considerations as to how to best love and worship God. The Decalogue is framed by religious emphases, as Moses receives the law directly from the presence of God. The first half of the Decalogue also describes how to relate to God (Exod. 20:3–12). Compare the Book of the Covenant (20:22–23:33), also framed by religious considerations. Further, the opening section presents laws on how to build an altar (20:22–26), alongside the rights of Hebrew slaves (21:1–11). Homiletically, these two sets of laws describe both of the areas in which Israel is most likely to go astray, in relation to loving God (i.e., worship with sacrifice on the altar rather than with images) and loving neighbors (i.e., the treatment of the most vulnerable members of society). Exodus 21:12 begins the general civil law that applies to all Israel. Its first laws deal with murder, just as the second half of the Decalogue (20:13–17) begins with the prohibition of murder. The Decalogue follows with a law connected with marriage (adultery), which has the same sequence in the Book of the Covenant, where 21:22 refers to a couple in a marriage relationship. As the prohibition against theft follows in the Decalogue, the laws concerning theft also follow in the Covenant Code

26. See, e.g., Moberly, *At the Mountain of God*; idem, *Genesis 12–50*; idem, *Old Testament*. For an alternative view using sources, see Schwartz, "Priestly Account."

(22:1–4). Finally, laws related to honesty follow both in the Decalogue and in 22:7–17. There is an overall literary sequence in the civil law in which the most important laws deal with murder and the absolute value of human life, whether slave or free.[27] Such a priority, as reflected in the first position of the laws, is not found in other ancient Near Eastern legal collections.[28]

Gender and Ideological Criticism

Analysis of the narratives dealing with women includes those who function to deliver Israel, such as the midwives of Exodus 1, and those who lead in the worship and praise of God after the great deliverance at the Red Sea (15:20–21). In the latter case, the role of Miriam as a prophetess and leader of Israel in worship plays a significant part in Israel's understanding of itself before God. While Miriam's status as sister of Aaron (and Moses) may give her a special position, the text makes the point that the women follow Miriam in the musical performance. The special role of women in musical performance begins here in Israel and will remain significant in the nation's early history.

Ideological studies on Exodus continue to focus on the event of the exodus. For liberation theology, this became the paradigmatic event in the Old Testament and in the entire Christian canon. The narratives of the escape from Egypt and freedom for the Israelites have become a major Hebrew Bible source for liberation theology. It is clear that the liberation of the people from Egyptian servitude is an important theme in this book. However, the people do not cease to be servants. More accurately, Old Testament theologians such as Terence Fretheim and Walter Brueggemann agree in recognizing a transfer of loyalty: from Egypt to Yahweh.[29] Furthermore, they reject any artificial dualism between the theological and the political in the text. Yahweh's demands on Israel are those of a political lord over a vassal. God rejects Pharaoh because he refuses to recognize Yahweh's sovereignty over Egypt and Israel. Thus God calls for the release of Israel so that they may worship God rather than Pharaoh. This is both a theological and a political challenge. Israel's worship of its God serves as both a religious activity and a political one, for it explicitly places the God of Israel in a superior position to Pharaoh. Pharaoh's rejection of Moses's request (Exod. 5:2), "I do not know Yahweh," is a rejection of God's authority. In diplomatic language, to "know" God or any superior is to recognize their lordship. Where the state becomes god, there is no difference between the two arenas of human activity.

27. Kaufman, "Second Table."

28. See the Ur-Nammu, Lipit-Ishtar, Hammurabi, Middle Assyrian, and Hittite legal collections; the Hittite law comes closer to the biblical priorities than any others do. For more on these collections, see the sidebar "Hammurabi's Laws and Values."

29. Fretheim, *Exodus*; Brueggemann, "Pharaoh as Vassal."

Further, the earlier discussion on the Decalogue and the Book of the Covenant brings into focus the social emphasis of the Israelites. In the social realm of the Decalogue, the prohibition on murder comes first, just as it does after the introductory section of the Book of the Covenant, beginning at Exodus 21:12. This establishes the absolute value of human life: nothing is more important in Israel. The capital nature of the offense also emphasizes that justice will not accept anything less than a human life in exchange for

Hammurabi's Laws and Values

Half a dozen ancient Near Eastern legal collections come from the period between the twenty-first century BC and the eleventh century BC. Few, if any, appear after that time. Among them are Ur-Nammu, Lipit-Ishtar, Eshnunna, Hammurabi, Middle Assyrian, and Hittite laws.[a] The law collection of Hammurabi was best preserved and often copied.[b] It was probably not used in lawcourts.[c] Rather, it demonstrates how just and fair King Hammurabi was.[d] Its propaganda was designed to convince the citizens of his land that the king practiced justice. Other legal collections may or may not have been composed for this reason.

It is likely that the structure of the Book of the Covenant intentionally follows that of the laws of Hammurabi.[e] However, this is not the same as sharing the value system reflected in Old Babylonian law. Hammurabi's laws do not begin in the same way as the social laws of the Decalogue or those of the Book of the Covenant. These begin with prohibitions of murder and recognize the value of the person without regard for the class of the individual. The laws of Hammurabi begin with matters of false accusation, witchcraft, jurisprudence; then, starting with law 6, the laws deal with temple theft and other property and business matters. These laws preserve the status quo and favor those who have wealth and power. This is contrary to the equality described in many of the biblical laws and to the priority given to the poor and vulnerable.

[a] For a summary and translation of each of these legal collections, practice texts, and later Neo-Babylonian laws that emulated Hammurabi's laws, see Roth, *Law Collections*. For a bibliographic review of relevant publications and their relation to the Hebrew Bible, see Sparks, *Ancient Texts*, 417–34.

[b] For text, translation, and commentary, see Richardson, *Hammurabi's Laws*.

[c] See Landsberger, "Babylonischen Termini."

[d] See J. Finkelstein, "Ammisaduqa's Edict"; idem, "Late Old Babylonian Copy"; idem, "Some Recent Studies"; F. Kraus, *Königliche Verfügungen*, 114–20. Many of these laws come from court cases and were transmitted through scribal schools. See Petschow, "Zur Systematik"; Westbrook, "Biblical and Cuneiform Law Codes"; Otto, "Aspects of Legal Reforms."

[e] D. Wright, "Laws of Hammurabi"; idem, *Inventing God's Law*. See the criticism of Wells, "Covenant Code"; and the response of D. Wright, *Inventing God's Law*.

the life taken. No silver or gold or any created thing can provide equal payment for the cost of a human life, created in God's image. The prohibition against adultery emphasizes marriage and the family that may result as the foundation to Israelite society. It is second in importance after the worth of the individual human life. Finally, the prohibition against theft emphasizes the value of private property (neither government property nor temple property is envisioned in the Decalogue, which deals with individuals and families). It is legitimate but tertiary in importance, after human life and family.

Ancient Near Eastern Context

It is not uncommon for contemporary critical studies of Exodus to downplay or deny outright the historicity of the exodus event. However, in addition to all the evidence cited here in favor of its historicity, questions remain: If there had been no oppression and exodus, why would any Israelite authors invent such a humiliating origin for their people?[30] If the Israelites were indigenous to Canaan and never came from Egypt, how did this story come to form the beginning of the nation's founding epic?[31]

Conservative scholars, who accept the historicity of the exodus, debate when the event took place. The two major dates tend to be either the fifteenth or thirteenth century BC. For the former, the date of 1447 BC is arrived at on the basis of a perceived absolute date of 480 years before the fourth year of Solomon's reign, as defined by 1 Kings 6:1. Those who champion the thirteenth century BC doubt that it is necessary to interpret 1 Kings 6:1 as a literal 480 years. They cite God's speech in Genesis 15, where 400 years appear to be equated with four generations (vv. 13, 16). The thirteenth-century date has a variety of archaeological and textual evidence to support it, as noted by Egyptologists such as Kenneth Kitchen and James Hoffmeier.[32] Items related to Egypt and the wilderness are of prime interest here.

Only for the thirteenth century BC is it attested that the pharaoh of Egypt had his capital in the eastern Delta region. This is important if Moses and Aaron visited Pharaoh and returned on the same day to Pithom and Ramesses, to speak with their fellow Israelites. The site of Qantir (also called Tell el-Dabʿa) was likely the Pi-Ramesses mentioned in the thirteenth-century Egyptian records as a place with a stable that could accommodate five hundred horses, along with large granaries, and as identical to the biblical memory of the place named "Rameses" (Exod. 1:11). This site was named Ramesses for

30. For much of the following, see Hoffmeier, *Israel in Egypt*; idem, *Ancient Israel in Sinai*; idem, "Exodus and Wilderness Narratives"; Kitchen, *Reliability*, 241–312; Hoffmeier, Millard, and Rendsburg, *"Did I Not Bring Israel Out of Egypt?"* (with a variety of articles providing groundwork for historical value to the traditions of the exodus); Davies, "Was There an Exodus?"

31. See Sarna and Shanks, "Israel in Egypt," 45.

32. See sources by Kitchen and by Hoffmeier cited in the notes above.

© Baker Publishing Group and Dr. James C. Martin courtesy of the The Egyptian Ministry of Antiquities

King Ramesses II as warrior (thirteenth century BC)

the first time in the thirteenth century and ceased to exist after the eleventh century BC. Tell el-Dabʿa, with its non-Egyptian culture, could have been the residence of people such as Israelites. It had been occupied in the eighteenth century but was then abandoned and rebuilt only in the thirteenth century BC. It is huge in area and provides architectural and pottery evidence of a non-Egyptian West Semitic culture, like that of the Israelites and the Canaanites.

As a pharaoh of the exodus, Ramesses II of the thirteenth century would make an ideal candidate. He was vain and self-focused, a borderline megalomaniac, some say. His eldest son did not succeed him. The Papyri Anastasi (III, V, and VI) contain records from the thirteenth century BC that establish a tight control of the eastern borders, with daily records of all crossings. In one account two slaves escape from Egypt but are hunted, caught, and returned. In another account an Edomite tribe requests admittance during a drought. In the wilderness of the Israeli Negev, the thirteenth-century-BC Hathor shrine in the Timna Valley provides the only archaeological example in the region of a tent sanctuary like the biblical tabernacle (see the sidebar "Timna Valley Shrine").

Specific and distinct elements in the Exodus account point to an authentic Egyptian background. Moses's birth in Exodus 2:1–10 (esp. v. 3) uses a number of authentic Egyptian words: basket, bulrushes (papyrus), pitch, reeds, river, and brink. Moses's experience in the royal court nurseries, as a "child of the nursery," is attested of other Semites of high rank in the pharaoh's court. There are tomb scenes of prisoners making bricks for Egyptian temples from around 1450 BC. At Deir el Medina (west of Thebes), laborers were given

Timna Valley Shrine

In modern Israel the Timna Valley lies about eighteen miles north of the city of Eilat, a harbor on the Gulf of Aqaba. The valley is rich in metal deposits, as witnessed both by the reddish hues of the landscape and by the saucer depressions that betray the existence of thousands of old mine shafts filled in by sand. Copper was mined and refined in this area. In the twelfth century BC it may well have been the Egyptian site of Atiqa, mentioned in Papyrus Harris as a source of this metal for Ramesses III. In the midst of the valley, situated beside a cliff face, are the remains of a cult center excavated by Benno Rothenberg in the 1960s.[a] Marked off by a rectangular wall of low stones, the site had a paved area in its center and a drainage channel therefrom, presumably to carry off the blood of animal sacrifices. On the rock face above the site, an Egyptian image connects the shrine with the goddess Hathor. The excavator found quantities of red and yellow cloth, which suggested the presence of a tent over the shrine, the only example found in the region that could relate to the tent shrine of Israel as described in Exodus. At the site they also found an image of a bronze serpent, recalling the account of Numbers 21:4–9. Some have associated the miners and those who worshiped at the cult site with the Midianites.

[a] Rothenberg, *Timna*; Hess, "The Southern Desert."

special religious holidays from work in order "to worship their god," either as a group or individually "making offering." For the plagues, see the discussion under "Tradition History" (above).

As Hoffmeier reports, paleo-geomorphological studies of the border region between Egypt and the Sinai Peninsula reveal a great deal more moisture three millennia before the present. Artificial canals connected lakes and marshes. All these bodies of water served as part of the natural border to the east. The name Red Sea comes from the Hebrew *yam sûp* (or *sûf*, Exod. 13:18), with *sûp* borrowed directly from the Egyptian *ṯwf*, "reed." The Greek translation of Exodus in the Septuagint did not know this and tried the translation "red." However, the original sense was "Reed Sea," one that contains reeds and marshy areas, however deep many of the lakes may have been.

In addition to the already-mentioned evidence for a tent shrine in the Timna Valley of the Negev, further evidence from this period may be suggested. Much of the language describing the tabernacle and God's appearance has parallels in West Semitic religious texts of eighteenth-century-BC Mari and thirteenth-century-BC Ugarit.[33] The description of the sacred

33. Fleming, "Mari's Large Public Tent."

tabernacle in Exodus resembles wooden structures that protected the dead pharaoh's sarcophagus in New Kingdom tombs such as that of the famous King Tut(ankhamen). These decorated, gold-overlaid, and linen-covered wood frames and solid structures resemble the construction techniques of the account in Exodus 25–40.

To this may be added structures of similar proportions and two rooms (cf. the holy place and the holy of holies) such as the pictures of the war tent of Ramesses II at Abu Simbel.[34] This architecture ceased after 1200 BC, when military camps took on an oval form. Ramesses's war camp consisted of a rectangular courtyard within the larger rectangular camp; a rectangular reception tent (parallel to the tabernacle's holy place); and the adjacent square pharaoh's chamber with two winged deities (Horus) flanking the pharaoh's cartouche (similar to Israel's holy of holies and the two cherubim). Besides attesting to the authenticity and antiquity of the tabernacle, such a comparison reinforces the sense in which the camp of Israel was understood as on a war footing. Their God Yahweh was a warrior deity, leading his people in victorious battle (cf. Exod. 15).

Canonical Context

The connection between Moses and the New Testament Redeemer begins in Matthew, with another king's attempt to end the life of Jesus by murdering all the male babies (Matt. 2:16–18). As with Moses, the Gospel narrative soon follows with a flight from the country and a subsequent return after the death of the king (Exod. 2:23–25; Matt. 2:19–21). The Gospel writer thus casts the coming of Jesus in the same paradigm as the coming of the Old Testament "redeemer," Moses (Acts 7:35 ESV). The passage about Moses's murder of an Egyptian and the insolent response of one of the Hebrew people even appears in Stephen's speech (7:23–35) as an example of Jewish rejection of their redeemer, followed nevertheless by God's call to Moses. This story occurs again in Hebrews 11:24–28 as a model of the world's rejection of Christ and his followers. God's self-revelation to Moses as identical to the God of the ancestors (in Genesis) forms the background for Jesus's claim that God is a God of the living (Matt. 22:32). As the whole redemptive purpose of God for Israel is revealed in the divine name Yahweh (Exod. 6:2–13), so the whole redemptive purpose of God for the world is revealed in the name and person of Jesus Christ in the Gospel of John. The hardening of Pharaoh's heart appears in Romans 9:17–18 as a means to affirm God's freedom to act toward people for good or for evil. The plague tradition in Exodus differs from that in Joel 2, Isaiah 13, and elsewhere in the Prophets in that it has no eschatological emphasis. Nevertheless, its rehearsal in Psalms 78 and 105

34. Kitchen, "The Desert Tabernacle."

anticipates the remarkably similar set of plagues described in Revelation 16, where the seven vials or bowls appear. Whether or not these were mediated through apocalyptic traditions such as those found in *1 Enoch*, they attest to the appearance of this severe judgment on the unrepentant, coming at the beginning and the end of the history of God's people.

As observed above, the Passover has ongoing significance for the people of God. With the days of Unleavened Bread, it forms an essential part of the biblical calendars that describe the annual festivals to be remembered (Exod. 23; Lev. 23; Num. 28–29; Deut. 16). Its celebration positively expresses the faithfulness of the good kings Hezekiah and Josiah (2 Kings 23; 2 Chron. 30, 35). It is part of the faithfulness of the returned exiles (Ezra 6:19–20) and anticipated with the future restoration of the temple (Ezek. 45:21). Joshua and Israel celebrate it when they enter the promised land, and with its meals they eat of the firstfruits of that land (Josh. 5:10–11). In the Gospels it becomes the focus for Jesus's Last Supper, where mention of the lamb at the meal is omitted in anticipation of his own sacrifice on the cross (Matt. 26; Mark 14; Luke 22; John 12–19).

First Corinthians 10 provides the most explicit description of the deliverance, comparing it to a baptism. Here Paul emphasizes the failure of Israel to remain faithful, leading to their death in the wilderness despite all that God had done for them. Paul thus warns Christians to avoid temptation and sin. In John 6:31–58 Jesus compares himself to the manna that Israel ate in the wilderness as a gift from God, providing true nourishment.

The Decalogue of Exodus 20 is repeated in detail in Deuteronomy 5. It thus forms a unique survey of the law. This is important enough to be repeated with the law itself. The effect is to emphasize the centrality of this law and to prepare the way for commands concerned with loving God (the first half) and loving one's neighbor (the second half). The commands, especially those of exclusive loyalty and devotion to God, continue to be repeated by the prophets and others long after that first generation has died. They remain an issue into the New Testament, where each of them is repeated in one way or another. The only exception is the Sabbath, and that is for a very good reason. As this first command to observe the Sabbath connected it closely with God's historic act of redemption in the exodus, so the New Testament would connect the meeting and worship of the Christian church with God's historic act of redemption through the death of Jesus Christ and his resurrection, which occurred on a Sunday.

The Book of the Covenant contains a variety of laws, some of which are further developed in the legal collections of Leviticus and Deuteronomy. In the New Testament, Jesus consciously develops the lex talionis, "eye for eye," statement of Exodus 21:24 (cf. Lev. 24:20; Deut. 19:21) in Matthew 5:38, where he introduces the personal law of forgiveness and love as superseding all attempts at otherwise controlling vengeance.

The tabernacle recurs as the place of sacrifice in Leviticus, the center of the Israelite camp in Numbers, and the temporary house of God for the ark in the promised land (1–2 Samuel; 1–2 Chronicles). It anticipates the temple of Solomon in 1 Kings 6–9. In Stephen's speech (Acts 7:44–45), it becomes a type of the heavenly sanctuary. A similar theme develops in Hebrews 8–9, where the tabernacle prefigures the coming of Christ.

Aaron's gold calf (Exod. 32:1–35) anticipates the purification offering for the priestly ordination, which is to be a living calf (Lev. 9:2–8). It is recalled in Deuteronomy 9:16 and 21 as the symbol of the people's sin and the object of Moses's wrath when he destroys it. (See plate 1 in the gallery for an example of a bronze calf.)

The final chapters (35–40) of Exodus describe the construction of the tabernacle. This leads naturally into Leviticus, where the sacrifices for sin and other purposes are described and where the priests who oversee the sacrifices are installed.[35]

Theological Perspectives of Exodus

Key to the first part of Exodus is the manner in which God delights in turning the impossibilities of the people of God into opportunities for divine grace to work. Despite what appears to be certain death and destruction, God works against the powers of darkness (cf. Eph. 6:10–12) to manifest salvation and deliverance. In this context the divine self-revelation of God is more than of his own existence (Exod. 3:14). It is an invitation to trust the one who is constantly with the ancestors, with Moses and Israel, and with the people of God today. The revelation of the name of Yahweh in Exodus 6:2–13 forms an expression of God as the powerful Redeemer who fulfills the promised covenant.

It is in this context that it is best to understand the lies of the midwives (see under "Premodern Readings," above). Such ruses appear in the narratives of early Israel (see Rahab in Josh. 2) as illustrations of a means to deal with situations where the powerful exploit the weak and the latter have only their wits as recourse. This is not to condone lies (the text does not pass judgment) but to recognize the value of preserving God's people and to make use of these sorts of ruses to preserve that mission and life within a fallen world that threatens them.

The miraculous signs of the plagues (contrasted with the miraculous preservation of Israel) serve as challenges for faith. Each one calls its observers to a point of decision for or against faith in God (as in Egypt, Exod. 9:20–21). They cannot return to the point before the sign. Instead, they either move

35. See Evans, "Exodus in the New Testament."

closer to God or further away. In this context, the hardening of Pharaoh's heart becomes a way to describe Pharaoh's own turning away from God.[36]

The role of the exodus itself is the focus of the narrative of this biblical book. It declares God's historic act of redemption. Yet by reporting this event in the context of commands as to how it is to be celebrated in the future, Exodus immediately ties this event to the participation of all the faithful of every generation, commemorating the act of redemption. It is remembered and celebrated as foundational to what it means to be Israel, the people of God.

The crossing of the Red Sea becomes the means by which Israel receives the amazing grace of God, who delights to demonstrate his power and deliverance after every other way of escape is blocked. God invites Israel to respond in faith and thus to find salvation. The divine provision of the manna teaches Israel the need to receive from God day by day. Faith is a daily walk with God and not a one-time event.

The Ten Commandments form the single most important set of laws in the Bible. The first half emphasizes the means to love God: negatively, by not honoring any other deities or trying to define and control God by creating an image of the Deity; positively, by allowing but restricting the use of the divine name and observing one day in every seven to remember that God redeemed Israel.[37] Children must honor their parents, with the presumption that this is directed first to adult sons and daughters who would take care of their parents and also honor them by following their faith in God. With its emphasis on honoring parents, who stand in the place of God (note that the word "honor" is used regularly of that which is given to God), and on the family relationship, this command hinges the commands to love God and those in the second half of the Decalogue concerned with the love of one's neighbor. In the latter, murder, adultery, and theft present an intentional order and priority, where the value of human life is placed highest of all. False witness is judicial perjury; such transgression guarantees chaos and injustice. Finally, the prohibition on coveting focuses on the reason for breaking all the other commands, the desire of the heart directed toward the creature rather than the Creator.

Ethically, there are important principles that the book of Exodus teaches. God's concern for the poor and oppressed is established as he delivers through the exodus, overthrowing the might and power represented by the pharaoh and his army. This same concern is to be expressed for the weak and powerless in Israelite society, especially the slaves and the visitors. All are to stop

36. See McAffee, "Heart of Pharaoh." His linguistic analysis of the terms and verbal forms used suggests that God carried through something that he predicted Pharaoh would possess and in fact did. The hardening of Pharaoh's heart is connected with God's responses to Pharaoh's refusal to let the people go.

37. For the important theme of rest here and throughout the book, see Brueggemann, "The God Who Gives Rest."

work on the Sabbath. The slave laws guarantee rights to those of the lowest class, something not found in other ancient Near Eastern legal texts. Because the value of human life is absolute, no master can get away with a mere fine if he intentionally kills a slave. Life must be given for life. Private property is valued and preserved, but it does not supersede the value of human life or that of the family and the marriage covenant. The civil law of the Book of the Covenant is enveloped within religious legislation: at the beginning is the altar law (20:22–26) and at the end are the prohibition on worshiping the gods of the Canaanites and the promise of God's defeat of Israel's enemy (23:27–33). This bracketing demonstrates the priority of one's relationship with God and how it affects all the ethical and other choices of life.

Israel's twofold decision to accept the Book of the Covenant, saying yes after each of the two times it is asked (24:3, 7), affirms that this is a free decision on the nation's part. The Israelite leaders' subsequent feast with God (24:11) demonstrates an ideal of communion expected again in the messianic banquet and here celebrated before Israel has opportunity to sin. Eating and drinking before the gold calf is a form of worship and communion that contrasts with the actions of chapter 24. It also explains the just punishment of drinking water mixed with the ground-up gold calf (32:6, 20). Punishment of death accompanies the breaking of the covenant in this blatant fashion (32:26–35). Moses's intercession pleases God so that there is not a permanent breach between God and this people (Exod. 33). God's decision to forgive Israel and be forbearing is part of the divine character of mercy (34:6–7). So Moses receives another set of laws on stone tablets, laws demanding separation from the nations and the gods of Canaan, and instead celebration of the Sabbath and of the calendar of feasts.

Although Exodus 35–40 describes the tabernacle as a place where the holy God will meet with Moses and the high priests, these chapters do more than repeat Exodus 25–30. The tabernacle does continue to be a place where God will travel with the Israelites and bless them, yet it of necessity becomes something more. Sin has broken the close fellowship. The tabernacle will serve to deal with the sin and provide forgiveness for the people. Thus the tabernacle provides more than a means for God's continuing presence to travel with Israel when they leave Mount Sinai. It is also the means by which Israel will find its way back to God after sin.

So what remains important for the Christian with respect to the Old Testament law? First, the laws reflect the ideals of God and thus enable the study of them to understand something of God's character and of how the Creator designed the world and human society. Second, the decisions of the Jerusalem Council in Acts 15 do not eliminate any responsibility to live a holy life before God. Although the specifics of the Old Testament law are not carried over into the new covenant, the council does affirm laws prohibiting the consumption of food offered to idols, blood, and meat sacrificed to idols, as well as involvement in sexual immorality. As with the beginning of the Book of the Covenant (Exod. 20:22–21:11), it is arguable that love for God and for one another in the areas where Israel was most likely to go astray remain the concerns of the Jerusalem Council for New Testament Christians. Christians are no longer under the cultic regulations of the Sinai covenant, nor are they a physical people united by ethnicity (Eph. 2) and connected with the land. Therefore, laws addressed to the agrarian society of ancient Israel do not necessarily have direct relevance for Christians. Nevertheless, the principles behind each of the laws remain, providing the exemplary element.

Key Commentaries and Studies

Childs, Brevard S. *The Book of Exodus: A Critical, Theological Commentary*. OTL. Philadelphia: Westminster, 1974. The application of the canonical approach to a higher-critical commentary.

Durham, John I. *Exodus*. WBC 3. Waco: Word, 1987. Follows the method of Childs.

Garrett, Duane A. *A Commentary on Exodus*. KEL. Grand Rapids: Kregel, 2014. A strong exegetical commentary on the Hebrew texts, with well-reasoned insights.

Horowitz, Wayne, Takayoshi Oshima, and Filip Vukosavović. "Hazor 18: Fragments of a Cuneiform Law Collection from Hazor." *IEJ* 62 (2012): 158–76. Contains legal texts from southern Canaan dating from the second millennium BC.

Meyers, Carol L. *Exodus*. NCBC. Cambridge: Cambridge University Press, 2005. Anthropological analysis of the ritual texts and compositional issues in the narratives.

Propp, William H. *Exodus: A New Translation with Introduction and Commentary*. Vol. 1, *1–18*. Vol. 2, *19–40*. AB 2–2A. New York: Doubleday, 1999–2006. Thorough exegetical study.

Stuart, Douglas K. *Exodus*. NAC 2. Nashville: Broadman & Holman, 2006. Important evangelical commentary with valuable exegetical insights.

3

LEVITICUS

Animal sacrifice might seem strange to us. Doesn't it prove that God hates animals? As we study Leviticus, we can see that God's love and blood sacrifice are not irreconcilable but provide the necessary means for God to live with his people and to love them.

Name, Text, and Outline

The name Leviticus derives from the Greek (LXX) name for the book. It is odd because Leviticus is not addressed particularly to the tribe of Levi, nor is it primarily concerned with the distinctiveness of this group, pertaining to their tabernacle service. In Leviticus "the Levites" are mentioned only in 25:32–33. As with the preceding books, the Hebrew name for Leviticus derives from the first word, *wayyiqrāʾ*, "he called."

The Masoretic Text of Leviticus preserves a readable text without major problems of interpretation. The Septuagint differs at some points, to create an overall literary emphasis distinct from that of the Masoretic Hebrew, with various renderings of some special terms and a freedom to create new ways to render the technical sacrificial language.

OUTLINE

I. Sacrifices and Offerings (1:1–7:38)
   A. Handbook for the People (1:1–6:7 [5:26 MT])
   B. Guidelines for the Priests (6:8 [6:1 MT]–7:38)
II. Ordination of the Priests (8:1–10:20)

- III. Laws of Unclean Animals and People (11:1–15:33)
  - A. Food (11:1–47)
  - B. Childbirth (12:1–8)
  - C. Skin Diseases and Mildew (13:1–14:57)
  - D. Bodily Discharges (15:1–33)
- IV. Day of Atonement (16:1–34)
- V. The Holiness Code (17:1–26:46)
  - A. Blood (17:1–16)
  - B. Holiness of People (18:1–22:33)
    1. Sex (18:1–30)
    2. Israel (19:1–37)
    3. Sex and Family Matters (20:1–27)
    4. Priests (21:1–22:33)
  - C. Holiness of Time (23:1–44)
  - D. Holiness of Place (24:1–25:55)
    1. Sanctuary (24:1–9)
    2. Blasphemer (24:10–23)
    3. Land (25:1–55)
  - E. Blessings and Curses (26:1–46)
- VI. Vows and Things Dedicated (27:1–34)

Overview of Leviticus

The scroll of Leviticus begins with a consideration of the sacrifices. Thus 1:1–6:7 (5:26 MT) reviews the burnt offering, the grain offering, the fellowship offering, the purification offering, and the reparation offering. As the opening verses of the book indicate, these instructions are directed to all the people of Israel. They describe the procedure and purpose of the offerings as well as (for the animal sacrifices) who is to offer what type of offerings, according to social and economic status. A shorter summary of the offerings follows (6:8 [6:1 MT]–7:38) in this order: burnt offering, grain offering, purification offering, reparation offering, fellowship offering. This especially focuses on who receives the food of the offerings, beginning with what is given entirely to God (the burnt offering) and ending with what is divided between God, the priest, and the offerer (the fellowship offering). In between, the food of the offering is shared by God and the priests. Because the priests receive a share of most of the offerings, it is thought that this section addresses priestly concerns (cf. 7:35–36).

Leviticus 8–10 describes the ordination or installation of the priests. In chapter 8 Moses leads in the action done to and for the priests. In chapter 9 the priests inaugurate their work with sacrifices for themselves and for Israel. In chapter 10 two sons of Aaron offer a "strange fire" (KJV) that brings on the wrath of God for violation of the holy place. They instantly die, and their father Aaron receives a warning not to mourn for them. This introduces further instructions for how the priests must keep themselves holy and concludes with the final actions related to the priestly consecration.

The consecration of the priests introduces laws distinguishing what is clean and unclean. The text identifies which animals are clean and which are unclean (Lev. 11). It considers childbirth, skin diseases, and mildew (Lev. 12–14) as well as bodily discharges (Lev. 15).

The instructions concerning sacrifices and priests, as well as what renders one unclean in the sight of God, prepare for the enactment of the Day of Atonement (Lev. 16). On one day each year the priest makes atonement for himself and for Israel through purification and burnt offerings, as well as through the action of sending a goat into the wilderness bearing the sins of Israel.

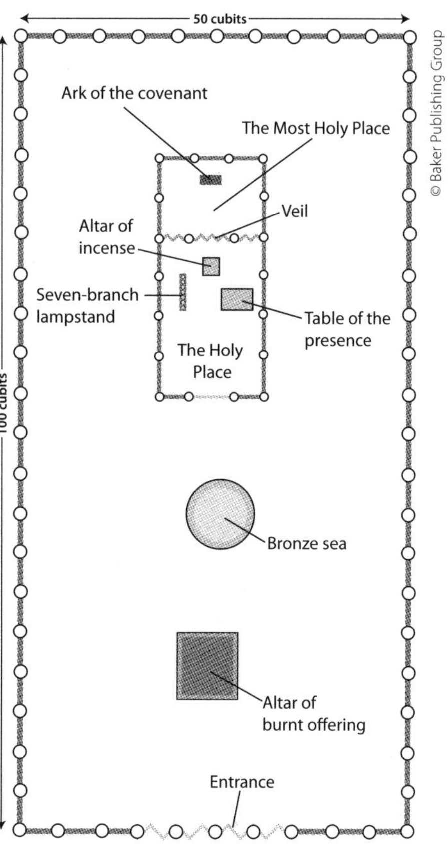

© Baker Publishing Group

Diagram of the tabernacle

The following ten chapters (17–26), sometimes called the Holiness Code, address various matters of how Israel and the priests should act to maintain their holy relationship with God. The concern for the proper handling of blood, which forms a unique symbol of physical life given by God, heads this section (Lev. 17). There follows the concern for holiness among the people of God. Chapters 18 and 20 repeat material related to incest and larger family concerns. They also frame Leviticus 19, which summarizes both ceremonial and ethical aspects of the law. Leviticus 21–22 considers priestly purity and the question of who may eat which offerings. Chapter 23 discusses the holiness of Israel in relation to time as it focuses on the Sabbath and the annual festivals. Leviticus 24:1–9 gives directions on maintaining the holiness of the tent of meeting (or tabernacle) with lamps and bread, and 25:1–55 presents legislation for maintaining the holiness of the entire land, with Sabbatical years and the redemption of property. In between is a narrative about the identification and punishment of the blasphemer, who blasphemes God's name and so pollutes the tent and the land (24:10–23).

Introduced by a brief reminder in areas where Israel is likely to go astray (idolatry, Sabbath keeping, and the purity of the sanctuary; 26:1–2), the Holiness Code comes to an end with blessings for obedience (26:3–13), curses for disobedience (26:14–39), and statements of God's faithfulness, along with encouragement to repent (26:40–46). The final chapter serves as an addendum that discusses vows, tithes, and the dedication of property, things, and people to God (27:1–34).

Reading Leviticus

Premodern Readings

In Judaism, the Mishnah devotes many of its sections to the literal interpretation of the sacrifices and other cultic matters addressed in Leviticus. This literal interpretation is further expanded by the Jerusalem and Babylonian Talmuds. Both rabbinic Judaism and the Karaite movement continued this sort of explanation, with the latter sometimes blending the midrashic component of the traditions. The medieval sages dominated the interpretive traditions of the Torah and devoted no small efforts to a literal interpretation.[1]

Christian interpreters established a tradition of allegorical interpretation that did not end with the Reformation but continued across the spectrum of confessions. It remains dominant in many devotional commentaries. However, from as early as the Reformation, with scholars such as John Calvin, and continuing into the later periods through much of the twentieth century, a parallel stream of christological interpretation diverged from mere allegory. It drew on the rich rabbinic traditions and studied much of the text on a more literal level before arguing for a fulfillment in Jesus Christ often determined as much by the New Testament Epistle to the Hebrews as by anything else. While Carl Friedrich Keil may be the best known in this Protestant tradition, Andrew Bonar and Samuel H. Kellogg also represent serious attempts to understand the text on a literal level.[2]

1. The sages, listed with the century in which their major work was done, are as follows: Saadiah ben Joseph Gaon (tenth cent.), Rashi (Solomon ben Isaac, eleventh cent.), Rashbam (Samuel ben Meir, twelfth cent.), Ibn Ezra (Abraham, twelfth cent.), Bekhor Shor (Joseph ben Isaac, twelfth cent.), Radak (David Ḳimḥi, thirteenth cent.), Ramban (Moses ben Naḥman, thirteenth cent.), Aaron ben Joseph ha-Rofe (wrote a commentary on the Pentateuch, *Sepher ha-Mibḥar*, ca. 1300), Aaron ben Elijah (a Karaite who wrote *Keter Torah*, fourteenth cent.), Abravanel (Isaac ben Judah, fifteenth cent.), Sforno (Obadiah ben Jacob, sixteenth cent.), and Naphtali Herz Wessely (eighteenth cent.). See Milgrom, *Leviticus*, 63–66.

2. Keil, *Third Book of Moses*; Bonar, *Leviticus*; Kellogg, *Book of Leviticus*.

However, it was not in the arena of commentary writing that the study of Leviticus entered into modern critical scholarship, but rather from examining the history of ancient religion and the important role played by the Israelite cult as described in Leviticus.

Source Criticism

If there is one book in the Pentateuch that most characterizes the Priestly (P) document, it is Leviticus.[3] Its discussion of sacrifices, priests, clean and unclean, and rituals places the first sixteen chapters in the center of the texts concerned with priestly matters. It was Julius Wellhausen who moved the P document to the final position of the four major documents in the chronological sequence of their composition.[4] He positioned it in the postexilic period as the evolutionary model took control of nineteenth-century scholarship and demanded that the complex rituals of Leviticus be placed chronologically late, at the end of a long process that increasingly separated people from God through the use of priestly intermediaries and the various ritual paraphernalia.

Yet temple and ritual records from Egypt and Mesopotamia challenge these assumptions. Already in the second millennium BC, both cultures demonstrate the presence of complex cultic rites that vitiate any argument that Israel's cult necessarily reflects a relatively late development of the first millennium. The appearance of rituals in the Hittite texts discovered in modern-day Turkey and at ancient Ugarit, on the Mediterranean coast of Syria, has increased an understanding of the ritual context in the second millennium BC. In all these societies, complex rituals were in place and practiced before Israel became a nation. The effect of all this is to call into question the assumption that the rituals and ceremonies found in the scroll of Leviticus must be late due to their detail and complexity. Indeed, comparisons with early and nearby societies suggest a simplification of ceremony in Leviticus. The picture is one in which the biblical approach appears to take familiar forms to simplify them, and to use them to explain the distinctive relationship between the one God of Israel and his people.

The ancient site of Emar, along the Euphrates in northern Syria, yielded a new form of extrabiblical religious texts as scholars began to publish and to study them in the late twentieth century. Like Israel and Ugarit, this culture was also West Semitic and contemporary. Unlike Ugarit, Emar shared with Israel a primarily agrarian inland culture in which the king was not involved in every major ritual. As publication has continued, it has forced a reconsideration of some long-held assumptions about the origins of the priestly texts. A good example can be found in Leviticus 8:30. The chief priest is

3. For an introduction to P and source criticism of the Pentateuch, see "Source Criticism" for Genesis.

4. Wellhausen, *Prolegomena*.

Emar Anointing Text

The site of Emar (modern Tell Meskene) lies along the Euphrates River about sixty miles east of Aleppo. It was inhabited during the third and second millennia, coming to an end around 1170 BC. From the 1970s onward, excavators have uncovered hundreds of cuneiform tablets. Along with those appearing on the black market, the number of tablets approaches twelve hundred. Among these, text 369 is especially important since it describes the installation ceremony for the high priestess. Along with Leviticus 8–10, these two represent the only West Semitic rituals for the ordination of members of the priesthood. In this case the woman is chosen by lot and anointed for her role as priestess of the chief deity, the weather-god (Baal is the common name for this deity in southern Canaan and the Bible). As in the Leviticus account, the event lasts seven days, and various sacrifices are offered to the deity. The king and the royal household are notably absent in this ritual. The activities include a series of processions. The text begins as follows:[a]

> The ritual tablets of the high priestess of Emar's storm-god.
>
> When Emar's citizens raise the high priestess for the storm-god, they take lots from NINURTA's temple, and they seize them before the storm-god. The daughter of any Emar citizen may be designated. On that day they take good oil from both the palace and NINKUR's temple. They place it on her head. They offer a sheep, a jar, and a portion of wine.
>
> . . . On the second day there is the shaving of the priestess. . . . Before the evening they take good oil from NINKUR's temple and from the palace. At the gate of the storm-god the diviner pours it on the head of the high priestess.

[a] Hess, *Israelite Religions*, 115.

anointed with oil and blood. Martin Noth represents the traditional critical view that this act of anointing passed to the high priest only in the postexilic period, when there was no longer a king, who himself had previously been anointed.[5] Under the Persian Empire, the high priest was the leader of the Jewish community in Jerusalem and the closest thing to a king. So the act of anointing the priest began late. It was derived from and intended to replace the anointing of the king. However, this rite of anointing priestly figures with oil is attested already in thirteenth-century-BC Emar, as is also true of the act of anointing with blood.[6] Studies of cultic texts at Emar, as well as texts of the Hittites and their Hurrian neighbors (all of the second millennium BC), have become important sources for appreciating the antiquity of various traditions in Leviticus.

5. Noth, *Leviticus*, 38.
6. Fleming, "Biblical Tradition of Anointing," 410.

The Ketef Hinnom Silver Scrolls

Discovered in the tombs at Ketef Hinnom in Jerusalem were two texts dated to the mid-seventh century BC. They contain part of the priestly blessing from Numbers 6:24–26. A priestly blessing should be P and thus postexilic. Some have tried to find here an example of an earlier tradition incorporated into a later P source. However, the excavator, Gabriel Barkay, believes that the blessing in the biblical text is earlier than the forms of this blessing that occur at Ketef Hinnom.[a] Other P terms appear on these texts, such as the word for "redeemer" (*kî bô gō'ēl*, "for in him is redeeming/redeemer").[b] Erik Waaler also argues that Deuteronomy 7:9 is found on the first text (the first of two small silver scrolls) as a "quotation" in which seventeen of the twenty Hebrew letters are identical (the first three are different).[c] He observes that both biblical texts match the letters found in both the Masoretic Text and in the two Ketef Hinnom texts. Thus these are best understood as written copies of the biblical text that suggest a standardized and recognized text on which one could draw.

a. Barkay, "Priestly Benediction," 177.
b. Ibid., 179.
c. Waaler, "Revised Date?," 49–51.

Tradition History

The traditions behind the legal collections of Israel have been seen as emerging out of a variety of circumstances. More recently, scholars have argued that the biblical law collections are idealized and theological in their purpose. They cannot be traced to any historical origin or background where they were applied to a society. However, several elements in the legal collections provide parallels with the culturally related laws of the Hittites from the fourteenth to the thirteenth centuries BC.[7] These elements thus exhibit a remarkable preservation of principles behind legal collections that some would say have been edited and redacted beyond recognition. They include distinctions between clean and unclean animals, double compensation for items stolen from someone else, and reduction of fines between earlier and later editions of the same law.

Leviticus 11 and Deuteronomy 14 contain lists of clean and unclean animals. The clean animals may be eaten by Israelites. The unclean animals may not. The Hittite laws also include clean and unclean animals. Harry Hoffner reports that the clean animals seem to be those that the Hittites were closest to in their daily lives. The same may be said of Israelite practice:

7. Hess, review of *Laws of the Hittites*.

> In ancient Israelite law the "clean" land animals which were permitted for eating and sacrifice were the ox, the sheep and the goat, animals which had the longest history of domestic association with the early Israelites going back to their semi-nomadic period. The pig, being an animal normally kept by settled (non-nomadic) peoples, appeared relatively late in Israelite domestic experience and was therefore never included among the "clean" animals. The horse and the camel also were relatively late entrants in the Israelite domesticated animal scene. Somewhat the same logic can be applied to the Hittite animal world. Animals such as the ox, sheep and pig were kept by the Hittites and their ancestors long before the horse and mule were introduced.[8]

Of all the unclean animals, the pig is the best known (Lev. 11:7; Deut. 14:8). It is not to be eaten, nor is any part of its carcass to be touched by an Israelite. From Israel's earliest settlement (ca. 1200 BC by the dating chosen here), archaeological excavations of many sites in the highlands of Palestine (where Israel settled) have confirmed the absence of evidence for the consumption of pork. This contrasts with contemporary settlements in the lowlands, especially those of the Philistines, where pork was eaten.

The principle of double compensation appears in Exodus 22:4, 7, 9 (22:3, 6, 8 MT), where all property thefts require repayment of twice the original value. The presumably later law of Leviticus 5:16 stipulates a repayment at 20 percent above the original value. While this law occurs in a different context, there does seem to be a significant reduction in the penalty for theft. For an example of multiple compensation in Hittite law, see the requirement of twelve sheep for a stolen ewe.[9] Further, the Hittite laws contain fines that distinguish between what is required "earlier" and what is required by a new edition of the same laws. The later fines always reduce the amount demanded, and that reduction can be as much as 70 percent, close to the reduction from Exodus to Leviticus.[10]

Whatever traditions lay behind the Levitical laws as now preserved, in various cases the existing evidence witnesses to a great antiquity to these laws within the context of ancient Near Eastern jurisprudence.

Literary Readings

Fundamental to literary readings are the vocabulary and style. Avi Hurvitz studied these and found vocabulary peculiar to the priestly material of Leviticus that one would expect to find instead in the late book of Ezekiel and in undoubtedly postexilic writings.[11] However, in Ezekiel and in other

8. Hoffner, *Laws of the Hittites*, 224.
9. Hittite law 69. See Hoffner, *Laws of the Hittites*, 78.
10. Hoffner, *Laws of the Hittites*, 3–5.
11. Hurvitz, *Transition Period*; idem, "Dating the Priestly."

postexilic writings, these terms are missing and sometimes replaced with different, later expressions.

Leviticus 23 contains a cultic calendar similar to four other calendars in the Pentateuch. However, only here (and in the calendar of Num. 28–29) do the festivals appear in great detail. This sort of repetition of Israel's cultic calendar has allowed critics to examine, contrast, and discuss development in a manner not found with other legal texts. For example, Leviticus 23:7–8 prescribes offerings but does not detail the contents, which do appear in Numbers 28:19–24. Therefore, it seemed appropriate to assume that the writer of Leviticus 23 must have been aware of the text of Numbers 28 and that Leviticus 23 otherwise represents one of the latest texts containing Israel's cultic calendar.

Outside the Bible, there is only one other West Semitic multimonth cultic calendar, one at thirtieth-century-BC Emar. Comparisons between Leviticus 23 and the Emar calendar have demonstrated parallels of structure and content in general and specific matters. For example, it has long been thought that Leviticus 23:39–41 is a later editorial expansion of verses 34–36. Both describe the Feast of Tabernacles, occurring on the same days of the same month. However, each section uses a different name for the feast and provides different (though not contradictory) details as to how it should be celebrated. Exactly the same phenomenon appears in the Emar cultic calendar. Side by side in that text are two descriptions of two festivals that are to be celebrated on the same days of the same month. Each has a different designation, and each has different (though not contradictory) details as to how it should be celebrated. Thus the mere fact that there are two descriptions of festivals at the same time in Leviticus 23 is not in itself sufficient to demonstrate later editorial additions, no matter how unusual that may appear to modern sensibilities. If supposed duplications and insertions can be shown to have already existed as part of a single, integral, and similar text of the thirteenth century BC, what does this say about the literary history of Leviticus 23? If this unity occurs in the one text where it can be tested with a parallel West Semitic source, what does this say about the application of the same methods of editorial dissection to other chapters in Leviticus?[12] All assumptions deserve reexamination with a predisposition for crediting greater unity in the text as now preserved.

Another area of literary focus is the sequence of the sacrifices in Leviticus 1–9. Leviticus 1:1–6:7 is intended for an audience that also includes laity (see 1:1–2). As Anson Rainey observes, this section is made up of sacrifices that provide a pleasing aroma (the burnt offering, the grain offering, the fellowship offering; 1:3–3:17), followed by those that pertain exclusively to forgiveness of sin (the purification offering, the reparation offering; 4:1–6:7 [5:26 MT]).[13] In the first section the burnt offering is directed to God to express total

12. Hess, "Multi-Month Ritual Calendars"; Babcock, *Sacred Ritual.*

13. Rainey, "Order of Sacrifices."

dedication, and the grain offering is always associated with the burnt offering. In the second part, sins primarily against God are dealt with first (purification offering), followed by those affecting other people (reparation offering). This is a useful explanation. However, Leviticus 4:31 also describes the burning of a purification offering as an "aroma pleasing to the LORD" (NIV). While this appears only once, it serves to link this offering with those of Leviticus 1–3 as well as to introduce the purification offerings in Leviticus 4–6.

In the second section (6:8 [6:1 MT]–7:38), the order of sacrifices is identical to the order in the first six chapters, with one exception. The fellowship offering is reserved until last. This section is administrative, in contrast to the first description of the sacrifices in Leviticus.[14] This structure is concerned with who receives the offerings and the relative frequency of the offerings. God alone receives the burnt offering. Along with the Deity, the priests receive parts of the grain, purification, and reparation offerings. God, the priest, and also the offerer receive from the fellowship offering. In terms of the frequency of the offerings, a comparison with Numbers 28–29 reveals that the burnt offerings outnumber the purification offerings. The third section, Leviticus 8–9, deals with the actual sequence in which the sacrifices are presented in ordination and in many other ceremonies (see also Lev. 14–15; 2 Chron. 29:20–36; Ezek. 43:18–27): purification offering, burnt offering, fellowship offering.

A larger consideration is the structure of Leviticus as a whole. Mary Douglas has found a chiasm in the book:[15]

Things and persons consecrated to the Lord (Lev. 1–9)
  The holy place defiled (Lev. 10)
    Blemish, leprosy (Lev. 11–15)
      Atonement for tabernacle (Lev. 16) and summary (Lev. 17)
        Sex, Molech (Lev. 18)
          Midturn: Equity between people (Lev. 19)
        Sex, Molech (Lev. 20)
      Blemish, leprosy (Lev. 21–22)
    Holy times, Day of Atonement (23)
  The Name defiled (Lev. 24)
Things and persons belonging to the Lord (Lev. 25)
Ending: Equity between God and people (Lev. 26; see Lev. 19)
Latch: Redeeming things and persons consecrated or belonging to the Lord (Lev. 27)

Another way to study the literary structure of the whole book is to identify repetitive words and phrases in the book of Leviticus. Wilfried Warning counts

14. Ibid., 487–93.
15. Douglas, "Forbidden Animals," 11.

occurrences of these and how they link sections together as well as the manner in which especially the seventh and twelfth occurrences play an important role.[16] This approach argues for an original stylistic unity to the Hebrew text. It, along with the other points above, calls into question many facile assumptions about the fragmentation of the text as from multiple editorial hands.

Gender and Ideological Criticism

Many approaches and issues regarding women and men may be addressed in these texts. Two are considered here: Why is the priesthood limited to males? Why does the woman who gives birth remain unclean twice as long if the baby is a female? Neither of these questions is easy to answer since both are tied into the anthropology of systems of cult and law that modern scholars cannot fully understand on the basis of the present evidence. In terms of what can be deduced (see below), some reasons may be suggested. However, these do not provide the final answer, which may be more fundamental to the roles involved.

For example, the issue of the male priesthood may be distinctive to ancient Israel in Canaanite and West Semitic culture. The one other priestly installation ritual attested, at Emar from the thirteenth century BC, envisions the induction of a priestess. Important female priests were active in cults at Ebla, Mari, and elsewhere in the West Semitic world of the Bronze Age. Was the selection of male priests a rejection of a practice associated with the worship of other gods? It is possible, but these neighboring religions also made use of male priests and officials. There is no explicit reason given for the limitation of the priesthood to males. It may be reflected in the uncleanness of male emissions and female menstruation. The monthly menstrual cycle results in about a week of uncleanness on each occasion (Lev. 15:19). This would significantly reduce the amount of time that a woman could function in a priestly role. In contrast, male emissions create a situation of uncleanness for the remainder of the day (15:16).

Leviticus 12 records the matters of uncleanness regarding childbirth. If a woman bears a daughter, she remains unclean for twice as long as for bearing a son. While the offerings are the same for either a boy or a girl, there is a clear difference in the period of uncleanness. Again, no explicit reason is given. Some have suggested that the newborn girl may herself be susceptible to a discharge and that this would therefore double the period of uncleanness. This may or may not be true, but no other reason presents itself. What is clear in all these examples is that the semen and blood that do not generate life, and even that which accompanies the birth of new life, renders the people involved as unclean. In some sense the wholeness of the body is compromised, and

16. Warning, *Literary Artistry in Leviticus.*

these precious life-giving substances are not entirely used for their intended purpose. Thus lack of wholeness is associated with uncleanness.

The study of ideology in Leviticus includes a focus on the method by which the ancient priesthood of Israel constructed the world around its own understanding of reality. The use of models from anthropology has allowed readers to peer into that world and try to gauge its interest in establishing boundaries between things clean and unclean, sacred and profane. Perhaps more than anyone else working in this area, Douglas has contributed significantly to the study of Leviticus. In several works she has sought to understand the essential components of the holy and sacred in ancient Israel.[17] Because her theories explain the structure of the biblical cult and rituals as presented in the text, they do not depend on a particular critical reconstruction of Leviticus.

Leviticus 11 is a good example to be considered. The principles by which Israelites can determine whether an animal is clean or unclean are clearly set forth in this text. However, reasons for distinguishing these animals are never discussed in the Bible. Anthropological explanations have proved helpful, particularly those elaborated by Douglas. Her earlier work developed the view that an animal's status is determined by its locomotion. Following Genesis 1 and the division of the world into three areas—land, water, and sky—it is concluded that clean animals use means of locomotion corresponding to the sphere of their existence: land animals walk, fish swim, and birds fly.[18] Where there is another method of locomotion, and particularly where animals do not remain in one of the three spheres but cross from one area to another, the animal is unclean. Although this interpretation explains many animals, it does not explain them all. Another approach is to declare as unclean the animals that eat dead creatures and their blood[19] plus insects that bite or otherwise destroy the products of culture.[20] Again, this does not explain all parts of the classification.

Douglas also distinguished between "unclean" and "abomination" as used in Leviticus.[21] In particular, Leviticus 11 identifies the land animals as "unclean" (Heb. *ṭāmēʾ*) and those that "teem" or "swarm" in the sky and in the waters as an "abomination" (Heb. *šeqeṣ*). However, as Douglas observes, even in this text the terms are used interchangeably, and Deuteronomy 14 clearly mixes them. Therefore the distinction is not as important as the principle of God's protection of animal life. By forbidding not only the eating of these animals

17. Douglas, *Purity and Danger*; idem, "Forbidden Animals"; idem, "Sacred Contagion"; idem, *Leviticus as Literature*.

18. Douglas, *Purity and Danger*, 55–58.

19. Moskala, *Laws of Clean*.

20. Such as moths. See M. Carroll, "One More Time." Douglas ("Forbidden Animals" and "Sacred Contagion") also relates uncleanness with animals whose appearance seems unbalanced or lacking. See under "Tradition History" (above) for the pig.

21. Douglas, *Leviticus as Literature*, 134–75.

but also the touching of their carcasses, God has effectively declared any such use of them off-limits to Israel. Especially the animals that swarm or teem have no place on Israel's menu. These symbolize the great (re)productivity of God's creation of life and their obedience to his command to multiply and increase. Instead, a restricted group of animals may serve the purpose of food. In particular, these are animals that sojourn with Israel and are designated as sacrificial substitutes for the people of the nation (see above).

Readers also consider the larger issue regarding the structure of the sacred and the profane as understood in Leviticus (as well as Exodus and Numbers) in terms of place, people, and animals. The most holy place (holy of holies) in the tabernacle provides the unique center of the divine life of God among his people. In that space are the most expensive precious metals and stones, the best fabrics, the special aromas of unique incense, and the most skillfully made decorations. It also receives the most legal details governing its construction, transportation, and who may and may not enter it (and under what circumstances). The camp of Israel is also a holy place, where the divine life of God resides. It also has regulations regarding who may live there and what may be done there. However, since the divine life is not present with the same intensity as in the tabernacle, the regulations for the camp are not as strict, nor are the laws regarding the positioning of the tribes and their general life so detailed. In third position is the space outside the camp of Israel, a place where this special divine life of God is not necessarily found in any consistent manner. It is therefore the place of the absence of life and order. Instead, death and chaos characterize this place. Very few (if any) rules govern this wild land or wilderness. Thus corpses are to be removed from the camp and buried there.

In terms of people, the role of the high priest is the most restricted of any in the Bible. Specifics about whom he may marry, what he may eat, what he may wear, and even the prohibition concerning mourning for his dead relatives—all of these are given and applied to an extent not found elsewhere in the Pentateuch. Yet the high priest alone has the privilege of entering into the most holy place and directly experiencing the divine life. He also wears clothing of greater value than any other person. All of this defines a figure who, along with his fellow priests and their families, has the greatest privileges but also the most severe restrictions. The call to a special holiness corresponds to the special blessings of this office. Israelites and those who live among them also have a series of rules about what they may eat, whom they may marry, and what they may wear. However, their lives are not as strictly governed as those of the priests and especially of the high priest. Outside the people of God are the nations. These have far fewer limitations or rules placed on them. They are expected to look to Israel as a nation of priests (Exod. 19:6), just as Israel looks to its own priests.

Corresponding to these three places and three groups of people are the animals. As a special group of very limited varieties, the sacrificial animals relate to the priests. Like the priests, they must have no deformities or any part of their bodies missing. Here wholeness of form corresponds to holiness of function. The clean animals alone are allowed within the camp of Israel and can be used for food. As the priests are a subset of the Israelites, so the sacrificial animals are a subset of the clean animals. These may be used for food and for clothing. As with the other nations outside Israel, so the unclean animals are separate from the clean animals. In a real sense God protects these unclean animals by rendering them off-limits to Israel. Thus there is an implicit ecology in which a large section of the natural world is not available to be exploited by Israel for its own purposes. More than any other texts in the ancient world, chapters such as Leviticus 11 and Deuteronomy 14 describe a unique concern for the welfare of the animal kingdom. Even if the animals closest to Israel (which the people would be most likely to have an affection for and least likely to destroy wantonly) remain liable to being consumed by Israelites, great numbers of species are effectively protected by this legislation.[22]

Ancient Near Eastern Context

The book of Leviticus exhibits many parallels with ancient Near Eastern culture. Most of these come from texts of the Late Bronze Age (ca. 1550–1200 BC), such as from Ugarit, Nuzi, and Egypt and the Middle Assyrian laws. Even closer is the cultural milieu of the Hittites. However, no closer cultural context can compare to the ritual texts of the thirteenth-century-BC city of Emar in northern Aram/Syria. This latter comparison has already been mentioned in terms of the priestly installation rituals and the cultic calendar, with its festivals. In terms of cultures other than Emar, ritual, legal, administrative, and other texts exhibit parallels on all levels with the text of Leviticus. Thus the late second millennium BC remains the closest cultural environment for the traditions and institutions described in Leviticus.

In the late 1920s the discovery of the ancient city of Ugarit on the Mediterranean coast of Syria, along with its many thirteenth-century-BC religious texts written in its distinctive West Semitic language and script, revolutionized ideas concerning Israelite religion. Ugarit religion, like that of the surrounding civilizations of Babylonia, Assyria, and the Hittites, represents a far more complex sacrificial system and cult in general than that found in the pages of the Old Testament. By comparison, Leviticus minimizes the details

22. The role of care for the land and for the animal world is explicit in the laws of Leviticus and Deuteronomy. Crop rotation and fallowing the soil, as well as protecting fruit trees, combine with explicit laws concerning humane treatment of animals and procedures for slaughtering them with a minimum of pain. These sharply contrast with and indict many modern practices of mining, factory farming, and horrific animal brutality to (often falsely) minimize the cost of meat. See Richter, "Environmental Law."

Feldstein/Wikimedia Commons

Ruins of the thirteenth-century-BC city of Ugarit

of sacrificial procedure and especially the many steps involved as well as the groups of animals required to keep the divine world satisfied. This simplification represents the opposite of what has been proposed. Rather than Leviticus providing evidence of the evolution of the sacrificial elements into late and complex descriptions, Ugarit is already complex, and Israel is simple by contrast. Thus the sacrificial system in Israel does not provide evidence of a late and highly developed system. It is almost as though the theology surrounding the Israelite sacrifices sought to maximize the significance of each of them but to minimize the details necessary to perform the rituals.

With this important distinction in mind, it is also significant to notice the similarities between Israel and Ugarit as well as other neighboring cultures. The basic term for a sacrifice is *zebaḥ* in Hebrew, which is similar to *ḏbḥ* in Ugaritic. Again, the *tĕnûpâ* ("elevation/wave offering") in Hebrew resembles the similar *šnpt* in Ugaritic. The same is true of the Hebrew *ʿôlâ* ("burnt offering") and *šĕlāmîm* ("fellowship/peace offering"). These terms also appear in Ugaritic. However, their purposes seem to be focused more on offerings designed to attract the deity to the temple and to greet the deity on arrival at the temple.[23] These purposes are not mentioned in the Bible for the same offerings.

23. Levine, "*Lpny YHWH*."

Ugaritic Rituals

The site of modern Ras Shamra was ancient Ugarit, a city-state in the second millennium BC. Its location near the Mediterranean coast of modern Syria gave it dominance in international trade. Thousands of cuneiform tablets were found from the thirteenth century BC, many of them written with the alphabetic script whose thirty characters express the West Semitic language of Ugaritic. Although Ugarit succumbed to various forces in the early twelfth century BC, these texts demonstrate a close affinity with aspects of Hebrew language and poetry, as well as the culture of Israel and the religions of Canaan. The ritual tablets, which detail sacrifices for the gods, provide a contrast with those of Israel. They are far more complicated and detailed. Emphasis is placed on a variety of meat and other sacrifices to be made to deities. The many deities named suggest an extensive pantheon. The king and royal house participated in many of the sacrifices, to the extent that the king took on many priestly functions. The overall picture of the dozens of ritual texts suggests greater detail and complexity than that reflected in Leviticus. In contrast to the tendency of a previous generation of critical scholarship, this evidence suggests that the rituals of Leviticus are not at the end of centuries of complex and arcane evolution but are a simplification of what is known about the rituals of surrounding cultures (such as Ugarit) in the earliest period of Israel's history as a people.

The same is true of similarities between aspects of Israel's theology of sacrifice and the rationale of its neighbors. The sense in which evil and sin are transferred from the offerer to the animal sacrifice is found in Israel and in Hittite rituals. The related idea that animal sacrifice can atone for (or forgive) moral and religious guilt (and possibly also sins against various groups in society) occurs in Israel and at Ugarit.[24] The distinction between clean and unclean animals in terms of their use and particularly for special sacrifices and rituals occurs as well in a treaty text from eighteenth-century-BC Mari.[25] Finally, scholars compare the calendar and special festivals. This is especially true of the *zukru* festival, found at thirteenth-century-BC Emar (see "Tradition History" for Exodus). Like the Passover and Unleavened Bread festival, this one also occurs on the fourteenth day of the month and is focused on the family rather than on the royal household. Like the Sabbatical year (Lev. 25:1–7), it takes place every seventh year.[26]

24. Moor and Sanders, "Ugaritic Expiation Ritual."
25. Malamat, "Note on the Ritual."
26. Fleming, *Installation*, 229–55.

On the sexual prohibitions of Leviticus 18 and 20 and comparative ancient Near Eastern practices, see below under "Theological Perspectives of Leviticus." Leviticus 18:21 and 20:2–5 also ban the worship of Molech through the sacrifice of children. This ban implies that child sacrifice did take place. The Egyptian relief of Merneptah's attack on the (then) Canaanite city of Ashkelon in the late thirteenth century BC may imply human sacrifice as smaller figures (children) are held over the walls of the city, perhaps in an attempt to sacrifice them so as to appease the gods. At Carthage, whose Punic culture continued the Canaanite (= Phoenician) culture that Israel encountered much earlier, six centuries of burials attest to children cremated at the high place where the gods were worshiped in such a manner. In Spain, the huge altar of Pozo Moro, also Phoenician, includes a scene of a god consuming anthropomorphic figures at a festival, suggesting the sacrifice of humans to the deity.[27]

Debt slaves in Israel could work to reduce the principal of their debt (Lev. 25:39–45), in contrast to Babylonia and Assyria, where only the interest accruing on the debt could be worked off through the labor of indentured servants. The debt owed on the principal would normally remain. Furthermore, the debt slave in Israel, unlike elsewhere, had the expectation of release after a specified period of time.

The tithe of produce and animals was required for the temple (Lev. 27:30–33; Deut. 14:22–29). This was compulsory, just as similar tithes in early Mesopotamia had been. This tax recognizes God's ownership of all that Israel has been given; the tithe is required as a token recognizing that fact.

Canonical Context

Leviticus represents a series of laws given at Mount Sinai concerning cult and how to live a holy life before a holy God. In the book of Exodus, God redeems Israel at the Red Sea and leads them to Mount Sinai, where they willingly receive the covenant and, in the innocence of their new relationship with God, feast with him (Exod. 24:1–11). The tabernacle and the Sabbath become the means by which God will continue to live with his people in a special way (Exod. 25–31). However, Israel sins by making and worshiping the gold calf. Nevertheless, they live and complete the construction of the tabernacle (Exod. 32–40). This prepares for the instructions concerning the sacrifices that are to take place in the tabernacle. Their details are defined in Leviticus 1–7. These include means to obtain atonement for the sins that the Israelites have committed. Leviticus 1–7 also makes provisions for the people of God to express worship and praise to God through sacrifices of various sorts. Leviticus 8–10 then provides the personnel to administer these sacrifices before God by means of the ordination of the priesthood.

27. Hess, *Israelite Religions*, 101–2, 326–27.

Chapters 11–15 form the basis for understanding the boundaries between what is clean and what is unclean, as found in key aspects of life. This serves as the background for the Day of Atonement, whose ritual is described in detail in Leviticus 16 and forms the basis for understanding the forgiveness of sins before God in the Old Testament, just as it anticipates the coming of Christ and his perfect atonement in the New Testament (above all, in the Epistle to the Hebrews). The remaining chapters of Leviticus deal with specific aspects of holiness before God, beginning with the special role of blood (Lev. 17) and continuing through a variety of concerns. Some of the earlier laws, such as the Decalogue, are repeated in these chapters, especially Leviticus 19:3–12. Leviticus 19, lying at the heart of the regulations for holiness, is developed throughout the biblical text.[28] These laws provide the means for living that the Israelites will have at their disposal when they break camp in Numbers and proceed to the promised land. The later indictment for the nation's sin and lack of faithfulness will be all the stronger since Israel already has this revelation that enables a means to approach God and find forgiveness where sin has been committed. Israel also possesses this law as a guide to train the people in the ways of faithfulness and holiness before a holy God.

This law and its distinctions form the basis for understanding all further mention of the various sacrifices, especially the purification (sin) offering, the burnt offering, and the fellowship (peace) offering. The tension between the perfunctory offering of sacrifices and the sense of loyalty toward God is continually a matter of concern in the Old Testament, beginning with Samuel's indictment of Saul (1 Sam. 15:22) and continuing through the prophets to Malachi (1:13; 2:3). Yet Samuel himself offers sacrifices, as does every high priest after him. For the New Testament and above all the writer of Hebrews (esp. chap. 10), Christ has served as both the sinless priest and the perfect blood sacrifice and thus fulfilled all that the sacrificial system anticipated. He was a priest after the order of Melchizedek (cf. Gen. 14), who did not need to offer a purification offering for himself (since he was sinless) and needed to sacrifice only once for the sins of the world. Beyond this, the sacrificial system provides the foundation for understanding the life of discipleship in the New Testament (see the next section).

Theological Perspectives of Leviticus

The key areas of sin, sacrifice, and holiness need to be considered. In terms of sin, there are the sacrifices for sin. These expiatory sacrifices include the purification, reparation, and guilt offerings (Lev. 4–7). They concern the following

28. For its discussion in Deut. 10:12–11:1; Zech. 7:8–14; 8:14–17; Matt. 5:21–48; Rom 13:8–14; Eph. 4–6; 1 Thessalonians; 1 Pet. 1:13–14; and the literature at Qumran, see Kim, *Holiness and Perfection*.

types of wrongdoings: the ritual impurity (Heb. *ṭumĕʾâ*), the defiant sin (*pešaʿ*), the nondefiant sin (*ḥaṭṭāʾt*), and the culpability resulting from sin (*ʿāwōn*). All occur in Leviticus 16, where the Day of Atonement/Purification purges the first three (16:16) from the sanctuary; removes the second, third, and fourth from the camp (16:21); and cleanses the people of the nondefiant sin (16:30, 34).[29] During the rest of the year, Leviticus 4–5 allows for the removal of all but the defiant sin from the people. The impurity of the sin can transfer to the sanctuary, so it too must be cleansed. Culpability for sin is taken up by the priests (only the priests bear this, never the sanctuary). The Day of Atonement deals with these.

The question of the "defiant sin" and its removal remains. This sin includes Molech worship (Lev. 20:3) and nonrepentant corpse contamination (Num. 19:13, 20) in the laws of the Pentateuch. God forgives this sin (Exod. 34:7; Num. 14:18; Pss. 32:1; 51:3; 65:3 [65:4 MT]; Isa. 43:25; etc.) by bearing it himself.[30] God's justice provides a means for dealing with sin and its guilt without denying it or showing favoritism. The divine mercy of God maintains a relationship with his people despite their lapses. This demonstrates God's holiness, which provides a means by which sinful Israel can enjoy fellowship with a holy God through the forgiveness of their sins. The purification offering, also called the sin offering, provides for the forgiveness of sins. The burnt offering also has an aspect of atonement, but it can and does serve other purposes.

The guilt offering or reparation offering involves the forgiveness of specific sins, including cheating God (through the sanctuary and priesthood) or swindling one's neighbor. These atoning sacrifices include a portion of the meat that is burned to God and another portion that is to be eaten by the priests. That the priests eat part of the offering for sin, something not found elsewhere, may eliminate any magical element from the theology of such sacrifices. That is to say, the meat of the blood sacrifice does not somehow contain the sins of the offerer. Instead, the sacrifice symbolizes and in some sense is received by God as sufficient to make atonement for those sins.

In addition to the atoning purposes of sacrifices and offerings, Israel also uses them to respond to God for all of his gifts. The burnt offerings and grain offerings especially serve as means of dedication to God. In the offerings of the firstfruits, they recognize God's gift of all that Israel enjoys. Like the Sabbath, in which Israel returns to God one day in seven as a token of God's gift of all the time that each Israelite enjoys during his or her lifetime, so in these offerings the people of God return to God a token of all that he has given them in sustenance. They recognize God as God, not only spiritually and intellectually, but also in a material way. Thus they recognize the integration of the spiritual and physical. They actualize their faith and worship.

29. Gane, "Moral Evils."
30. Ibid.

Old Testament Law and the Christian Today

While some have suggested that the Old Testament law remains incumbent or an ideal for Christians to follow, this has not been the attitude in most of Christianity. On the one hand, there has been the tendency to allegorize the law and to make it symbolic of Jesus Christ and his work. On the other hand, there has been the attempt to divide the law into three parts: ceremonial, religious, and civil. The religious law, as seen in the first half of the Decalogue and in instruction regarding the worship of God alone, is thought to remain in effect for Christians. The civil law is thought to be culturally conditioned for the society of ancient Israel and not necessarily valid for today, although principles of justice and mercy that lie behind this law remain. The ceremonial law is thought to have been fulfilled in Jesus Christ's sacrificial death and resurrection and therefore no longer of any validity in itself. Rather, Christ's sacrifice points to the fulfillment of the ceremonial law and thus this law disappears after the reality comes that this law foreshadows. In general, this method of interpretation has worked well for many in the church. However, it has the tendency to denigrate the value of the ceremonial law, the tabernacle, the sacrifices, and the priesthood, as well as distinguishing things that are clean or unclean. Not only has this led to a lack of full appreciation of Christian discipleship, as noted here; it has also led to a misunderstanding of blood as the symbol of life and its essential role in understanding the nature of redemption.[a]

[a] Hess, *Israelite Religions*, 195–97. Cf. also Crüsemann, *The Torah*.

The burnt offering is the only blood sacrifice in which everything edible is consumed on the altar. As the offerers place their hands on this offering, they sense that they are dedicating everything to God. Fellowship (peace) offerings provide communion with God.[31] These offerings alone involve dividing the meat into parts offered to God, parts reserved for the priests, and parts to be enjoyed by the offerers (and possibly their families) in fellowship with God.

The sequence of purification offering, burnt offering, and fellowship offering occurs (partially or completely) in the ordination of the priests (Lev. 8–9), in the Day of Atonement rituals (Lev. 16), and elsewhere. It describes the essential order for the sinner's approach to God: repentance and forgiveness, (re)dedication, fellowship. Paul and other apostles who wrote the New Testament epistles developed this essential order and teaching of the sacrificial system and applied it to the path of Christian discipleship. They did not invent

31. Jenson, *Graded Holiness*; idem, "Levitical Sacrificial System"; Wenham, "Theology of Old Testament Sacrifice."

the importance of the Christian life as characterized by confession of sin, dedication to God, and continued fellowship with God. Instead, they knew of it from these offerings and their sequence as revealed for the first time in Leviticus. Thus in addition to a background for Christ's own redemption and its significance, the sacrificial system was appropriated as a paradigm for all true Christian discipleship.

Holiness is the fundamental aspect of God (Lev. 10:3) that renders him different and apart from the world that he has created. God calls his people to holiness so that they too may be different from the world and like himself (11:44, 45; 19:2; 20:7–8). God can make his people holy (12:8; 20:8; 21:8, 15; 22:9, 32). As already noted, the sacrifices and offerings teach Israel how to be God's holy people (2:3, 10; 6:17, 25, 29; 7:1, 6; 10:12, 17), as do holy places (6:16, 26, 27, 30; 10:13; 16:2). In addition, God designates special aspects of holiness to people (6:18; 21:6–8) and to objects (5:15–16). The priests are responsible for teaching the people what is holy (10:10). Violation of this holiness through sin demands death as a punishment in the presence of a holy God, who cannot tolerate sin. This is why atonement offerings normally require blood sacrifice, as the only means sufficient to pay the terrible price of sin. The people of God as a whole form a holy community, just as individually they are called to preserve holiness in their daily lives, by what they eat, what they wear, and how they act toward one another. This anticipates 1 Peter 2:4–12, where Christians are built into a holy house in which Christ has become the chief cornerstone. The holiness of the tabernacle and the physical purification of Israel correspond to the holiness of the church as the body of Christ and the moral and ethical purity of Christians.

As noted in "Literary Readings," above, the command to love others (Lev. 19:18) holds a central position in the central chaper of the book of Leviticus and in the Holiness Code's legislation of chapters 17–26. Surrounding it in chapter 19, one finds repeated many of the instructions from the Decalogue (Exod. 20; Deut. 5) as well as practical concerns, such as preserving parts of the harvest for those who are poor (Lev. 19:10; 23:22). Leaving a remnant of the harvest was known elsewhere in the ancient Near East as a means to provide for the poor. However, the addition of the "foreigner visiting (residing for a limited time) in the land" (RSH; Heb. *gēr*) is unique to Israel (19:10, 33). In this way, concern for the needs of others reaches beyond one's own family, friends, and village to include the whole of humanity.

Leviticus 18 and 20 focus on matters of holiness especially in terms of sexual unions that cross boundaries considered unclean. The greatest detail is devoted to incest prohibitions. As Leviticus 18:1–5 says, Egypt and Canaan practiced or tolerated forms of incest, adultery, same-sex relations, and bestiality. The biblical texts (Gen. 19:5–8; 39; Ezek. 16:26; 23:3, 19–20) and Egyptian myths impute practices to gods and goddesses that were also known in the society. The city-state of Ugarit lay close to the land of Canaan, and its texts describe

Canaanite practices such as Baal's copulation with a heifer and El's explicit sexual involvement with two goddesses who are referred to as his daughters. Other cultures, such as Hittite, found these connections abhorrent. Thus the Bible correctly distinguishes Egyptian and Canaanite customs from those of other ancient Near Eastern peoples. Certain other nations possessed laws against various forms of incest and bestiality. Some Hittite and Babylonian incest laws are identical to those in Leviticus; yet other laws make distinctions between slave and free, suggesting that being in a different social class determines the ethics.

The controversial prohibition against same-sex relations appears in Leviticus 18:22 and again in 20:13. Its occurrence immediately after the prohibition of Molech worship (with its sacrifice of children) in 18:21 and immediately before the prohibition against bestiality in 18:23 (which, as noted above, was connected with some of the Canaanite gods) suggests that this practice may also have been associated with worship of other deities. In any case, in both occurrences, it alone is specifically marked as "detestable" (Heb. *tô'ēbâ*). This strong term occurs elsewhere in Leviticus (20:13) only as a summary judgment for all the forbidden practices in Leviticus 18 (esp. vv. 22–30). Its specific marking of these acts may lie behind Paul's development of it in Romans 1:26–28, as a distinctive sign of moral compromise.

As stated above, holiness for Israel includes the value placed on human and animal life (Lev. 17), and setting aside specific people (21:1–22:16), foods (22:17–33), times (23:1–44), and places (24:1–25:34) to God. Addenda at the end emphasize the value to be placed on those most vulnerable, the slaves of society (given rights only in Israel), in 25:35–55. Blessings and curses provide motivation for faithfulness as well as the importance of consequences for one's actions (Lev. 26). Finally, notes on the vows made to God complete the book (27:1–34) and emphasize the importance that God places on human words and on adhering to truthfulness.

Key Commentaries and Studies

Douglas, Mary. *Purity and Danger.* London: Routledge & Keegan Paul, 1966. Most important application of anthropology to Israelite cultic and ceremonial laws.

Hartley, John E. *Leviticus.* WBC 4. Waco: Word, 1992. Detailed exegesis.

Hess, Richard S. "Leviticus." Pages 563–826 in vol. 1 of *The Expositor's Bible Commentary.* Edited by T. Longman III and D. E. Garland. Rev. ed. Grand Rapids: Zondervan, 2008. Up-to-date evangelical survey.

Keil, Carl Friedrich. *The Third Book of Moses.* Vol. 2 of *The Pentateuch.* Edited by C. F. Keil and F. Delitzsch. Translated by James Martin. 1862. Repr., Grand Rapids: Eerdmans, 1975. A classic conservative guide for biblical theology.

Kellogg, Samuel H. *The Book of Leviticus.* 3rd ed. 1899. Repr., Minneapolis: Klock & Klock, 1978. Most valuable nineteenth-century work for application to Christian faith.

Milgrom, Jacob. *Leviticus: A New Translation with Introduction and Commentary.* Vol. 1, *1–16*. Vol. 2, *17–22*. Vol. 3, *23–27*. AB 3, 3A–3B. New York: Doubleday, 1991–2001. The fruits of a lifetime of work, incorporating all major areas of study of the book of Leviticus.

Wenham, Gordon J. *The Book of Leviticus*. NICOT. Grand Rapids: Eerdmans, 1979. Application of anthropology to categories of holiness, with evangelical emphasis on theological application.

4

NUMBERS

Our lives are filled with small decisions. As we make them, we exercise our faith in—or opposition to—God. Small steps prepare us for the big decisions in life. This is the story of Numbers. As Israel began its journey from Mount Sinai, it faced smaller tests along the way. Sadly, its repeated failures did not prepare it to face the greater test at Kadesh Barnea. Nevertheless, God's grace appeared in the form of a bronze serpent that provided life for those who believed. We too face tests as well as the opportunity to find God's grace.

Name, Text, and Outline

"Numbers" is the English translation of the Greek (LXX) title, *Arithmoi*. The Hebrew title, *bĕmidbar*, "in the wilderness (of Sinai)," is the fifth word on the scroll, following "Yahweh spoke to Moses." The Masoretic Hebrew text remains reliable here, as is the case across the first five books of the Bible. The Septuagint is a somewhat literal rendering; yet it selects from a variety of choices for translating the same Hebrew words, to fit the immediate context in which they appear.

OUTLINE

1. Mount Sinai (1:1–10:36)
   - A. Census of Tribes and Families (1:1–4:49)
   - B. Cultic Matters (5:1–9:23)
   - C. Breaking Camp (10:1–36)

II. The Journey (11:1–21:35)
  A. Three Rebellions (11:1–12:16)
  B. Report of the Spies and Result (13:1–14:45)
  C. Cultic Matters for All Israel (15:1–41)
  D. Priestly and Levitical Matters (16:1–19:22)
  E. Final Rebellions and Journey to Moab (20:1–21:35)
III. Plains of Moab (22:1–32:42)
  A. Balak and Balaam (22:1–24:25)
  B. Baal of Peor (25:1–18)
  C. Census of Tribes and Families (26:1–65)
  D. Inheritance and Succession (27:1–23)
  E. Cultic Calendar (28:1–29:40 [30:1 MT])
  F. Vows (30:1–16 [30:2–17 MT])
  G. Battles and Settlement (31:1–32:42)
IV. Summary of the Journey and Its Goal (33:1–36:13)
  A. Review of Itinerary (33:1–49)
  B. Command to Take the Promised Land (33:50–56)
  C. Boundaries and Allotments (34:1–29)
  D. Priestly and Levitical Towns and Murder (35:1–34)
  E. Daughters of Zelophehad and Inheritance Rights (36:1–13)

Overview of Numbers

The book of Numbers contains a mixture of narrative and law that sometimes seems difficult to follow. It clearly includes the story of Israel's departure from Mount Sinai, their journey, and their arrival on the plains of Moab, as well as an overall summary and look to the future. However, the contents do not merely describe a series of events. There are ceremonial and priestly laws at the beginning (Num. 5–9), in the middle (15 and 19), and at the end (27–30, 35–36) of this scroll. Before proceeding, it may be best to describe the overall story and its legal "interruptions."

The scroll begins with a divine command from Yahweh at the tent of meeting in the desert of Sinai. Moses and Aaron are to take a census of all the tribes of Israel in terms of the men who are of age to fight. These are then positioned for the march and for camping in relation to the tabernacle. The tribe of Levi and Aaron's priestly family within that tribe are numbered and named separately. They have the responsibility for the tabernacle and all of its property. Except for the Levites, the tribal census is identified with military service (1:3): all the men in Israel who are twenty years and older and able to serve in the armed forces. Numbers pictures Israel in battle formation on its journey to the promised land. If this is true, then the military leader is Yahweh, Israel's God. The Levites, and especially the priests, serve as his personal attendants.

While still at Mount Sinai, Israel receives additional laws concerned with ritual purity and with offerings. A test for marital fidelity maintains the fundamental social unit in the nation (Num. 5). Laws concerning the Nazirites anticipate their roles as especially dedicated to God and as military and political leaders (6:1–21). The priestly blessing of Aaron prepares Israel to go to war (6:22–27). The tribal offerings provide a response from each tribe for Aaron's blessing of the families and as a means to support the tabernacle service (Num. 7). The Levites as a tribe are offered to Yahweh in place of the firstborn of the other tribes of Israel so that they may devote their lives to the work of the tent of meeting, or tabernacle (Num. 8 in contrast to Exod. 13:2). The celebration of the Passover, and providing a second celebration for those unclean at the time of the first, signals preparation of the people

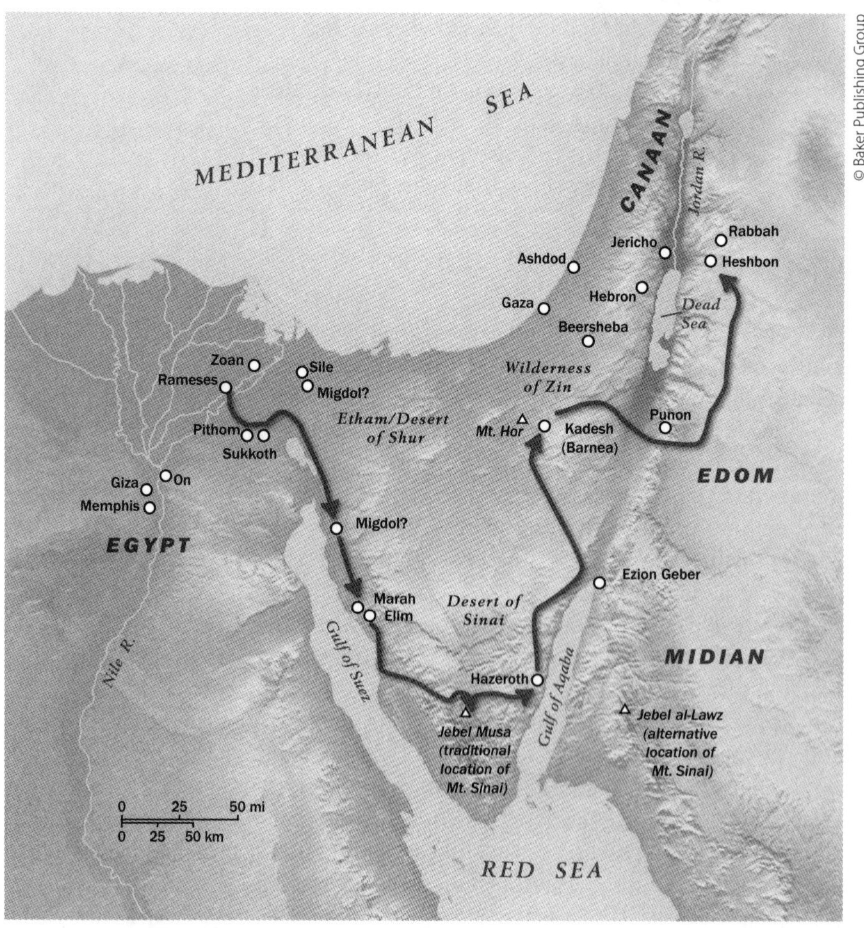

© Baker Publishing Group

Likely route of the exodus

The Number 603,550

In modern translations the figure 603,550 appears in Numbers 1:46 as the census count of all the fighting men of Israel before they depart from Mount Sinai. It has led to the view that about two million Israelites left Egypt and wandered through the desert. The problems with that number crossing a body of water, being fed with quails, leaving no trace in the desert, and finding a place to gather at the base of the mountain, and other such matters have been explored elsewhere. If one accepts the God of Israel as the Creator of the universe, then these problems are not really the issue. More to the point is the question of whether the pharaoh could enslave so many when his own country's population was no match, or that the Israelites would fear entering a country where they would outnumber the inhabitants by perhaps forty to one. Even more problematic is a text such as Numbers 3:43, where the number of firstborn males is 22,273. Simple division results in each mother in Israel bearing an average of 27 of the male warriors. Although ancient texts with numbers are notoriously difficult and no solution is perfect, perhaps it is better to understand the word translated "thousand" (Heb. *ʾelep*) as having the meaning "clan, squad" (see Judg. 6:15). This meaning is possible and can be used in military contexts. So understood, the number would be 603 squads (and perhaps 550 warriors who were not assigned to squads at that time). Since a squad could include a much smaller number of soldiers than a thousand, the actual number of Israelite warriors intended by the biblical text could have been much fewer, in the thousands or tens of thousands.

for a military mission (Num. 9:1–14), just as it did at the time of the exodus (Exod. 12–15) and as it would in the following generation when they enter the land and prepare for battle (Josh. 5). The leadership of Yahweh appears in a cloud that covers the tabernacle. When it moves, it signals that Israel is to move (Num. 9:15–23). Numbers 10 describes how the Israelites break camp in an orderly fashion and move forward from the region of Mount Sinai.

The main part of the scroll of Numbers reviews the journey from Sinai to the plains of Moab. As when Israel left Egypt, the story begins with three accounts of complaint about the conditions and includes God's response and judgment: the general hardship (11:1–3), the lack of meat (11:4–35), and the question of Moses's worthiness for leadership (Num. 12). Numbers 13–14 focuses on the central event of this journey: sending spies into the promised land, their divided report, the decision of Israel not to enter the land, God's judgment that they will all die in the desert, and then the failed attempt by Israel to march into that land. As happened after Israel's sin with the gold calf (Exod. 32) and the priestly sin with the "strange fire" (Lev. 10 KJV), so this sin is followed by laws about ceremonial and priestly matters: offerings and unintentional sins,[1] and the example of one who breaks the Sabbath.[2]

Another rebellion against the authority of the leadership, this time against Aaron as well as Moses, breaks out in Numbers 16–17. Next are further laws about Levites (Num. 18), the offering of the red heifer (19:1–10), and the treatment of dead bodies (19:11–22). Again, the main narrative picks up after this discourse on law. A further rebellion over water (20:1–13) introduces the divine chastisement of Moses. Following that is Edom's refusal to allow Israel to pass through its land (20:14–21), Aaron's death (20:22–29), the defeat of the king of Arad (21:1–3), and the final rebellion in the wilderness, where Israel complains, God sends fiery serpents, and Moses is instructed to erect a bronze serpent to stop the plague (21:4–9). The remainder of Numbers 21 summarizes the travel to Moab and Israel's important victories over Sihon king of Heshbon and Og king of Bashan.

The arrival on the plains of Moab introduces the story of the foreign prophet Balaam and his inability to curse Israel despite Balak's hiring of him (Num. 22–24). Four times Balaam blesses Israel. Despite the blessing on Israel, the people sin by employing orgiastic rituals to worship Baal of Peor (Num. 25). As with the earlier census that followed the gold calf incident (Exod. 32; Num. 1), this national sin is followed by a census (Num. 26), laws relating to inheritance and succession (Num. 27), the calendar of festivals (Num. 28–29), and vows (Num. 30). Israel has victory over Balak and his allies in some final battles. Next is the settlement of two and a half tribes east of the Jordan River in the recently acquired land (Num. 31–32).

The story of Numbers ends with a review of the journey (Num. 33:1–49) and a command to enter and occupy the promised land (33:50–56). This latter point is developed with a definition of the borders of Canaan and the allotments to be given to the tribes (Num. 34). The scroll ends with decisions regarding Levitical towns, towns of refuge and their purpose, and the inheritance of daughters (e.g., of Zelophehad; see Num. 35–36).

Reading Numbers

Premodern Readings

The stories of Numbers became popular examples for moral direction in Christian discussion of this book. The early chapters serve as a means to

1. Numbers 15:1–31, with the note (in vv. 30–31) that no offering is possible for intentional sins such as Israel committed when it refused to trust God to lead it into the promised land.

2. Numbers 15:32–36 is an example of a violation amid legal regulations, just as in Lev. 24:11–23.

discuss the ordering of God's people. Much of the itinerary occupied the attention of biblical cartographers. The midsection of the book provided a means to illustrate God's promised blessings with the magnificent foods that the spies brought out of Canaan while also providing opportunity to probe the failings of human nature in the bitter complaints and lack of belief that God will accomplish what he has promised. Study of the Balaam stories focused on the prophecies, especially the "star" and "scepter" of Numbers 24:17 that had already been applied to a coming Messiah in the period before and during the earthly life of Jesus Christ. It remained a key text identifying the Messiah as a member of the tribe of Judah. The later texts of Numbers were used as further evidence of Israel's sin with Baal of Peor and as the solemn fulfillment of the judgment that the entire generation (except Joshua and Caleb) would die in the wilderness. So the warning was there for Christians to remain faithful, seeing Israel's experience as a lesson for themselves (1 Cor. 10:6–11).

For Judaism, this section of the Torah resumes a focus on a narrative that has been replaced by legal stipulations since the arrival at Mount Sinai in Exodus 19. However, the interweaving of law with narrative provides an ideal opportunity to explore both and to bring them together in a manner not found elsewhere in the Torah. As a result, texts such as *Midrash Rabbah* and *Sifre Numbers* abound in integrating stories about Israel with its structure and order. Some texts, such as the priestly blessing of Numbers 6:24–26, became ongoing expressions of a yearning for peace and well-being by the community. The budding of Aaron's staff (17:8) became the origin of the scepter that every king of David's line continued to hold while the Old Testament monarchy endured in Jerusalem. Other interpretations stress the ambiguity of human characters in the light of God's holiness. Thus, although Miriam faces punishment for questioning Moses's authority, her merit also provides Israel with a well of water that follows them through the wilderness. Balaam may be the archetypal wicked hater of Israel and the Jews. However, he is also a great philosopher and a prophet of God.

Source Criticism

Source criticism has long seen in the book of Numbers a mixture of texts not so easily identified primarily with a single source, as in much of the remainder of the Pentateuch. Here instead the combination of narrative and law, as well as specific vocabulary, invites the recognition of two primary sources. The one is characterized by a combination of both the Yahwist and the Elohist, often cited in the commentaries simply as JE. More clearly than in the material from the first three books of the Bible, the JE texts of Numbers envision as their goal the occupation of the promised land. The other primary source connects with the Priestly (P) source and is found in those items inherently connected with priestly matters: purity and other holiness legislation, ordering of the tribes, blessing, and so forth.

However, the evidence related to the book of Numbers has raised more questions about these conclusions in the later twentieth century than perhaps from any other single piece of evidence. Two key textual discoveries have raised important questions about this matter. First, there is the 1979 discovery of the two small silver scrolls in a Judean burial cave on the western shoulder of the Hinnom Valley (hence the name Ketef Hinnom, "shoulder of the Hinnom"), lying immediately west of the biblical city of Jerusalem.[3] When unrolled, these scrolls reveal part of the text of Aaron's blessing, Numbers 6:24–26, as well as some other writing (perhaps from Deuteronomy).[4] Analysis of the writing style used to create the letters (paleography) concluded that they had been written around 650 BC. Thus this quintessential priestly text, the blessing of the high priest, is dated to a period before the time of the exile. So it predates the writing of the Priestly corpus, according to most views. It supports the origins of the Priestly source at a time before the exile and establishes the fact that such biblical texts were known and used in the mid-seventh century BC in Judah.

The other textual discovery was finding the Balaam Inscription at Tell Deir ʿAllā, located in the Jordan Valley east of the Jordan River.[5] Some of the writing on the plaster fragments that decorated one of a cult center's rooms describes visions of Balaam son of Beor. The text, dating from the eighth century BC, demonstrates that Balaam was known as a seer or prophet at this time within and outside Israel. Thus, where it can be tested, the evidence suggests that source-critical conclusions ascribing the creation of this material to the postexilic period must be modified.

Tradition History

Given the diversity of the material written in the book of Numbers, it is perhaps to be expected that the focus would be on separate chapters and the traditions reflected by one related group of stories or another (e.g., census, Korah's rebellions, Balaam stories, sending of the spies and their report, Miriam, Sihon and Og). The origin of these as independents units of tradition has gradually given way to recognizing their ideological purpose in an ancient context. So it is now thought that the text of Numbers was brought together at the end of Judah's independent history, during the reign of Josiah

3. See the sidebar "The Ketef Hinnom Silver Scrolls" in chap. 3 and comments of the excavator, Barkay, "Priestly Benediction"; as well as published editions of the texts in Barkay et al., "Challenges of Ketef Hinnom"; idem, "Amulets from Ketef Hinnom." For more on these texts, see also "Source Criticism" for Leviticus.

4. See Waaler, "Revised Date."

5. Hackett, *The Balaam Text*.

Balaam Inscription

The site of Tell Deir ʿAllā is situated in the Jordan Valley, east of the river and in modern Jordan. Excavation at the site, which some connect with the Sukkoth of Judges 8:5–14, has revealed a room containing many pieces of plaster fallen to the ground. Dating from about the eighth century BC, this plaster contains traces of red and black ink that, when reconstructed into two combinations, reveals a text written in a language distinctive to the site. However, its close relationship to both Hebrew and Aramaic allows for a reading of the text as a vision that Balaam son of Beor had. The text mentions the presence of Balaam in the divine assembly of El, where he encounters the Shaddayin (perhaps related to the divine title El Shaddai), or divine court. It describes a vision in which the world is turned upside down and expected events of nature do not happen. The evidence suggests that at this site, not necessarily related to orthodox Israelite believers in Yahweh, Balaam as a seer and prophet was a legendary figure in the eighth century BC.

(or later), and ultimately written as now presented by priestly editors (redactors) in the postexilic period. Thus Adriane Leveen observes the emphasis on the Levites and priests in ordering and maintaining the people of God.[6] Among the people themselves, she finds many examples of their lack of faith and failure to remember what God has done for them in bringing them as far as they have come. In all, there is a mirroring of the concerns of priestly authority and the danger of failing to follow the word of God as is found in the priestly theocracy among the returnees in Jerusalem of the Persian period. The warning to a people who had witnessed so much of God's power and then apparently so quickly forgotten it is compounded by their utter disappearance, abandoned to judgment in the desert. For a people for whom gravesites and memorials are so important (cf. Miriam's grave, Num. 20:1), the disappearance of an entire generation in the desert is a testament to the terrible judgment for their lack of faith in God's promises (Num. 14). It is the gentile Balaam who redirects the people's attention away from their focus on and complaints about their wilderness problems (Num. 20–21) to the blessings of the future and the favor of God (Num. 22–24). The Baal of Peor incident seems to reaffirm the people's faithlessness in contrast to Balaam's truthfulness (Num. 25). However, the traditions of another census, itinerary, description of the promised land, and new set of laws (Num. 26–36) affirm that God has not forgotten Israel. In the same manner, the redactor wishes to emphasize that

6. Leveen, *Memory and Tradition*.

God has not forgotten his people in the tiny Persian-controlled province so many centuries later. And indeed, while one may question the assumptions of explicit postexilic redactions, readers cannot fail to see a pattern established in which the faithfulness of God, despite the faithlessness of God's people, forms a recurring theme that continues into the New Testament era and beyond.

Literary Readings

The scenes of Numbers have invited a great deal of reflection on their literary organization. On the one hand, there are correspondences between the events of the wilderness journey from Egypt to Sinai and those that form the journey in Numbers from Sinai to Kadesh Barnea. On the other hand, there are the two parallel descriptions of (1) the journey from Mount Sinai to Kadesh Barnea, and then (2) the journey from there to the plains of Moab. Although the specific points of division are debated, it is generally agreed that the overall structure of the book divides naturally into three parts. The first ten chapters describe the preparations for the march while Israel remains at Mount Sinai. Chapters 11–21 reflect on the time in the wilderness and at Kadesh and then the journey to the plains of Moab. The third section begins with the Balaam story and leads through to the final chapters of the book that summarize the whole.

Gordon Wenham characterizes each of the three journeys in Exodus and Numbers by certain recurring elements, although they do not always adhere to the same order in the text:[7]

Event	Exodus: from Egypt to Sinai	Numbers: from Sinai to Kadesh Barnea	Numbers: from Kadesh Barnea to Moab
Victory songs	15:1–18	10:35–36	21:14–15
Miriam	15:20–21	12:1–15	20:1
People complain	15:23–24	11:1	20:2–5, 13
Moses intercedes	15:25	11:2, 11–15	20:6, 10
Miraculous food	16:1–35	11:4–35	
Miraculous water	17:1–7		20:2–13

The reader will observe that, in addition to the echoes of Exodus that appear in Numbers, the chart demonstrates the manner in which these elements recur at the beginning and end of the wilderness wanderings in Numbers itself. Thus each time Israel sets forth into the desert, whether from Egypt, Mount Sinai, or Kadesh Barnea, a series of events occurs. As already noticed, the first ten chapters of Numbers and the final eleven chapters (Num. 26–36)

7. Wenham, *Numbers* (1997), 17.

parallel one another in their contents: census, breaking camp/itinerary, and religious laws.

The literary context of the central part of the book may be organized around seven rebellions that take place:[8]

1. People *complain* about their misfortune, and God sends *fire*. Moses intercedes (Num. 11:1–2).
2. People *want meat*, and God sends *quails and a plague* (11:4–34).
3. Miriam and Aaron *question Moses's* authority, and Miriam becomes leprous for seven days (12:1–15).
4. People follow the *spies' majority report* and are condemned to *wander in the desert* for forty years until that generation dies (13:1–14:38).
5. Korah leads a *rebellion*, and there is subsequent murmuring against his death. The *earth swallows Korah, and a plague* follows (16:1–50).
6. People *want water*, and Moses *strikes a rock* (20:1–13).
7. People *complain* about food and water. God sends *fiery serpents.* Moses makes a bronze serpent and sets it on a pole, and *those who gaze on it live* (21:4–9).

Of special interest in this literary structure is its chiastic form. In the first and last rebellions, the people complain about their lot in the desert, and God sends some form of fire as a punishment. In both cases, Moses's explicit intercession on their behalf occurs, as does a means of salvation. In rebellions 2 and 6, the people desire a specific food or drink, and God provides it. However, there is also a judgment, whether against the people in the form of a plague, or against Moses in the decision that he will not enter the promised land. Rebellions 3 and 5 are directed against leadership, whether that of Moses or of Aaron. In both cases the result is death, whether as a symbol (leprosy) or in reality (with Korah and his followers). At the center of a chiasm lies its focus and the most important point. This is the people's decision to follow the report of the ten spies and not to trust God to give them the land. The punishment of wandering the wilderness and death affects the whole generation, a far more terrible result than any of the other punishments in the rebellions.

Gender and Ideological Criticism

Although the book of Numbers raises many issues and opportunities for interpretation in these areas, frequent questions about the role of women arise regarding the section concerning the suspected adulteress in Numbers 5

8. Cf. ibid., 50–54.

and the choice of Miriam for the punishment in chapter 12. Numbers 5:11–31 addresses a situation in which a husband suspects his wife of adultery. He takes her to the tabernacle, where she swears an oath before God that she is innocent. Then she drinks a mixture of water and soil from the floor of the tabernacle, along with the ink from the text of a scroll bearing curses. If she is innocent, there is no bad effect from this drink. But if she is guilty, the area of her body connected with the bearing of children is affected, and she will be unable to bear children. A question arises: Why is there no similar law for the husband suspected by his wife? The answer may lie in the possibility that there was such a law. It is something readers might expect while looking at the context. The law that immediately precedes this one, in 5:5–10, explicitly applies to both men and women. The same is true for the law of the Nazirite that immediately follows this law, in 6:1–21. Thus readers may presume that, like these other laws, this one may also have been balanced by a counterpart for the female who suspected her husband of adultery. If so, the failure to explicitly mention this may be due to the "default male" nature of the laws.

Compare the Decalogue and the command in Exodus 20:17 (Deut. 5:21): "You shall not covet your neighbor's wife." This law seems to apply only to the male. Nevertheless, the Decalogue is understood by most to apply to both male and female. Where there is a distinction between genders, the law applicable to the male is explicitly stated. The same may be true here. There is, of course, a view that adultery was a crime that only the female could commit. This is thought to be the case because the female was considered the property of the male, and thus adultery was a kind of theft, a conclusion drawn from the study of the Mesopotamian legal collections and decisions.[9] However, this is nowhere explicit in the biblical text. Indeed, one may argue, the unique tradition that understands every male and female as possessing the image of God (something normally limited to kings in neighboring cultures) might also ascribe equal value to both sexes in this matter. Finally, it should also be recognized that the accusation and the test for adultery could be done in private. The law does not envision a public forum as it would if it were to indicate a requirement of additional witnesses.

The other concern, that of Miriam's leprosy, needs to be approached in both the context of the Pentateuch and in terms of the meaning and significance of this disease. Miriam, sister of Moses and Aaron, has led Israel in celebration of the victory at the Red Sea (Exod. 15:20–21). Her death and burial are also recorded in Numbers 20:1. In Numbers 12 she joins with Aaron in questioning Moses's authority, explicitly his marriage to an African (Cushite). This issue is addressed by God's own intervention (12:1–10), in which Miriam becomes leprous for seven days. Why was not

9. Van der Toorn, *Sin and Sanction*.

Aaron punished as well? Readers are not told, but there are several points to keep in mind.

As the main priest, Aaron offered sacrifice on behalf of Israel. The punishment of leprosy would preclude his priestly duties and render Israel even more vulnerable to God's judgment and punishment. There is also the nature of leprosy itself. The traditional understanding of leprosy in the Old Testament as Hansen's disease is incorrect. Archaeological evidence does not attest to the presence of this sort of leprosy in the Middle East before the time of Alexander's return from India, in the late fourth century BC. Instead, this leprosy is best understood as a form of psoriasis. Thus Miriam has this temporary condition. Why does this require her exclusion from the camp? The answer lies in the holiness of God, who cannot tolerate death or even signs of death. Psoriasis looks like dead skin (and often is). Its connection with this symbol of death renders the victim unclean and requires removal from the camp. Thus the punishment is temporary.

Further, Miriam may have led her brother Aaron in this protest. Numbers 12:1 mentions her first as acting subject and then Aaron second. The verb, "speak (against)," is a feminine singular, highlighting Miriam's role. Unlike Aaron, Miriam is identified as a prophet (Exod. 15:20). In light of Moses's desire for all of God's people to be prophets (Num. 11:29), this story may witness to a conflict where God demonstrates that Moses's authority is superior to all prophetic activity, even that of his sister.[10]

Other ideological concerns remain, especially the slaughter of Israelite enemies, as in Numbers 31. Midianites are killed apparently because they are either soldiers or have engaged in the orgiastic worship of Baal of Peor (involving women who have slept with men; 31:7, 16–18). The remaining young girls are preserved alive. The command to kill all the boys recalls the decision of Pharaoh in Exodus to kill all firstborn males, as well as the death of every firstborn in Egypt (the tenth plague). So understood, these horrors define the elimination of a people and their ability to fight back, in the present and in the future. However, there may be indications of other survivors and a different understanding of the text. Although verse 17 may lead one to conclude that all males (boys as well as men) are killed, and only young girls are preserved, verses 35, 40, 46, and 47 refer to a large number of "persons" who remain alive and are made into slaves for Israel. These verses do not describe the survivors of Midian as only women but include terms that lead one to understand that men likewise survived. This requires a more careful reading of the text than is often done. It may be that only those directly involved in the battle (i.e., warriors) or in leading Israel into immorality (and thus the "boys" would be more mature and not young children) were held responsible and executed at God's command.

10. Hamor, *Women's Divination in Biblical Literature*, 61–81.

Ancient Near Eastern Context

There is a vast array of material that can be related to both the literature of the wilderness wandering and the actual reality of the wilderness itself. In terms of comparative literature, there is no satisfactory identification of the overall text of Numbers with a genre or similar style in the ancient Near East. So much is happening in the book that readers have more success in

Instruction for the Royal Bodyguard

During much of the Late Bronze Age (1550–1200 BC) the Hittite Empire reached across most of what is modern Turkey. Through its surrogate in Carchemish, the empire controlled parts of northern Syria. The language, written in syllabic cuneiform like Assyrian and Babylonian, was not Semitic but Indo-European. Indeed, Hittite is the earliest attested Indo-European language. Although the culture might seem removed from that of ancient Israel, there were many similarities. There was the Hittite treaty form and its close relationship to Deuteronomy (see the chapter on Deuteronomy, below), and Hittite similarities with many of the cultic forms and laws of Leviticus.[a] A genre of literature not found elsewhere in the ancient Near East was instruction or protocol texts. These were manuals for border commanders, the royal bodyguard, and others with explicit instructions about how to perform their tasks. An example is the Instruction for the Royal Bodyguard, where these appear in the opening section of the first of a series of tablets containing instruction.[b]

Column 1, lines 1–6:

> [first line missing] . . . (When) the guards (go) up (to the palace), they [march] in front of the gatekeepers (and) sweepers. They enter and take their stand at the door of the courtyard, with their eyes turned outwards, so that they cover one courtyard of the palace. Then they (sweepers) sweep.

Column 2, lines 32–38 (regarding the cart in which the king travels to court):

> When the guards march, two guards are walking in front and hold spears; and they are lined up. [To their] left marches a palace attendant and holds a lituus; and he, too, is lined up with the two gu[ard]s (so that) the three (of them) are lined up together. The guards and the palace attendants march in three files: two files of guards and one file of palace attendants. But they march one IKU {a measure of distance} behind(?) the cart.

[a] Milgrom, *Leviticus*—and the many addenda comparing Hittite rituals.
[b] Güterbock and Hout, *Hittite Instruction*, 5.

Stephen C. Meyers

Artist's re-creation of Ramesses II's military camp based on thirteenth-century-BC reliefs of the Battle of Kadesh at Abu Simbel

identifying specific sections. In the census list of chapters 1–4, some find parallels with administrative lists containing personal names that are found in Late Bronze Age texts from Alalakh, Ugarit, and elsewhere. However, none of those texts are organized along kinship lines. Closer for comparison is the Hittite Instruction for the Royal Bodyguard and the pictorial representation of the war camp of the pharaoh Ramesses II. Neither of these are census lists, but both describe the king and his soldiers arrayed around him in a specific order.

The Hittite Instruction describes the positioning of the king's guards when the king is in the palace, when he travels, and when he is holding court.[11] Details are given as to where they should stand, the order in which they should march, how they should take care of the king, and various shouts and other audible noises that announce the departure and the approach of the king. All of this corresponds to Numbers 1–4 and 9–10, where the presence of God, symbolized by the ark of the covenant, substitutes for the king. In a similar manner these chapters outline the position of the tribes around the ark and the sequence when marching. They also provide detailed instructions about who should carry what implements related to the ark. Further, they indicate the audible signals and songs that accompany the beginning and conclusion of the march for each day. In this manner the texts serve similar purposes. For Israel, they suggest its role as an honor guard for their God, the King who leads them and who fights for them.

The pictorial representation of the war camp of Pharaoh Ramesses II at Abu Simbel has many correspondences to the camp of Israel as detailed in

11. Güterbock and Hout, *Hittite Instruction*.

Numbers 1–4 and 9–10.[12] Here as well, the tent of the pharaoh, divided into two parts (one part for audiences and one part for private quarters), lies in the center of the rectangular camp, with the soldiers camped around it. There are clear demarcations between where the camp ends and where the surrounding wilderness begins. All of this corresponds to the tabernacle of the Pentateuch, which is also divided into two parts, the holy place and the most holy place.[13] It also has the tribes of Israel camped around it in a large rectangular encampment. This form of an Egyptian war camp is found only in the second millennium BC, and not later. Its similarities to the Israelite camp as pictured in Numbers suggest that the latter envisioned a martial purpose: the entire camp was on a military footing.

The location of Mount Sinai and the routes to there and from there have been the source of much discussion. A northern route, near the Mediterranean, seems unlikely. It is explicitly refuted in Exodus 13:17. Archaeologically, such a route would have provided the shortest way to Canaan but would have been guarded by Egyptian forts and their garrisons. A route through the middle of the Sinai Peninsula is possible and would provide the most direct access to Mount Sinai if it is to be located in northwestern Saudi Arabia at a mountain such as Jebel el-Lawz. However, the limestone rock of Et-Tih, which covers the central Sinai, provides little evidence of water sources such as Israel would have needed and at times God miraculously provided.

Those most familiar with the Egyptian sources and the topography of the Sinai opt for the southern route.[14] They locate Mount Sinai either at the traditional site of Jebel Musa, identified as such since the fourth century AD, or at one of the other possible mountains in the southern part of the peninsula that would allow for a group of people to assemble beneath it. Routes about 140–180 miles in length go north to ʿAin el-Qudeirat, the traditional site of Kadesh Barnea. This would not be a difficult journey to cover in eleven days (Deut. 1:2). There are oases along the way that can be related to the sites named in Numbers 11, 20–21, and 33.

The site of Kadesh Barnea betrays no occupation at the time when Israel should have been there. However, this is not surprising for a nomadic people who did not remain long at this site. Their thirty-eight years of wandering included a great deal of time spent in the region east and south of Kadesh Barnea, what today is referred to as the Israeli Negev (as opposed to the biblical Negev, which was limited to the region around the Beersheba Valley).

Thus the events of Numbers 13:1–21:12 took place largely in this region. It is one that has abundant natural resources, especially copper. This was mined throughout ancient times in the Timna Valley west of the Arabah,

12. Homan, "Divine Warrior."

13. "Holy of holies" is the literal translation of the Hebrew and used in that language to express the superlative (as in the title Song of Songs).

14. Kitchen, *Reliability*; Hoffmeier, *Israel in Egypt*.

Thirteenth-century-BC bronze serpent from Timna Valley "Midianite temple" in the Negev

© Baker Publishing Group and Dr. James C. Martin. The Eretz Israel Museum

and in the Wadi Feinan, the Edomite lowlands east of the Arabah. Commerce used this region for conveying trade goods, especially spices from the horn of Africa (Somalia, Eritrea, and Djibouti) and modern Yemen to the south (the Queen of Sheba's likely home). At the northern tip of the Gulf of Aqaba, where the modern port cities of Eilat and Aqaba are situated, goods would be transported either northwest to the Mediterranean ports or directly north along the Arabah to the Dead Sea and from there to countries such as Judah, Israel, Moab, Ammon, and so forth.

In addition, this region has left considerable evidence of religious monuments. Most important are the standing stones or biblical mazzebot (*maṣṣēbôt*, "[sacred] pillars"; Exod. 34:13; Lev. 26:1; Deut. 7:5; 12:3). These mazzebot appear at some thirty sites in the southern Negev, with some that can be dated by carbon 14 to more than ten millennia before the present.[15] They may appear in groups of seven, ten, or more; libations were poured in front of them so as to venerate the deities, ancestors, or whatever the uncut stones represent. Some mark tombs of venerated individuals, while other tombs are marked by piles of stones, a kind of ancient billboard visible from paths on which pilgrims might have journeyed. Mazzebot also appear in open sanctuaries, where a low double or triple wall of stones marks off a rectangle in the desert. With its corners facing the points of the compass, more than twenty of these open-air sanctuaries occur in pairs. Often one corner of the sacred space is further marked off by stones and apparently functioned as a holy of holies.

In the copper-rich Timna Valley, the Hathor temple was found (see the sidebar "Timna Valley Shrine" in the chapter on Exodus). This was essentially an open-air sanctuary used by the miners, perhaps Midianites, and occupied by the Egyptians in the thirteenth and twelfth centuries BC. They portrayed the Egyptian deity Hathor on the cliff above the site and thus syncretized this "high place." As noted, quantities of red and yellow cloth found there indicate a tent shrine, the only one in the area from any period of time that resembles the biblical tabernacle in this sense. Also found at this site was a bronze image of a snake, which evokes the story of Numbers 21:1–9 and the construction of a bronze serpent there.

All of this is more than mere general background to the biblical story. It brings to mind the biblical story of Baal of Peor (Num. 23:28; 25:3) and the religious activities there. Thus the text reminds readers that Israel did not

15. Avner, "Mazzebot Sites."

need to wait until it entered Canaan to encounter the challenges of religions not devoted to Yahweh alone. Further, items such as the uncut stones of the Israelite altar (Exod. 20:24–26) most closely resemble the unhewn stones used for religious purposes in the Negev. Canaanites and others in the settled lands to the north and west dressed their stones for altars, temples, and so forth. Sacred spaces remind readers of Mount Sinai (Exod. 19:12) and the tabernacle itself. Mazzebot or stones of special significance have already been used by Jacob at Bethel and Moses at Mount Sinai, and will be used again when Israel enters the promised land (Gen. 31:45; 35:14; Exod. 24:4; Josh. 4; 24:26). As for Moses before them —and Elijah, John the Baptist, Jesus, and Christian saints of later times—the desert would be a place to encounter God in a special way. Even the Hathor sanctuary in the Timna Valley could be a source for the tentlike structure of the tabernacle and for the theme of the bronze serpent in the desert.

Much has been made of the mention of the king of Arad in Numbers 21:1–3 and that the traditional site of Arad was not inhabited at this time (i.e., the Late Bronze and Early Iron Ages). That site was a major center in the third millennium BC, one of the largest cities from the Early Bronze Age in the southern Levant. Perhaps the name of the city lived on in the region and the chieftain ("king") of the local area continued to use it. On similar issues about the existence of Edom, see "Ancient Near Eastern Context" for Genesis (above). The figure of Balaam son of Beor is remembered in an eighth-century-BC site in the Jordan Valley, Tell Deir ʿAllā. See further under "Source Criticism" (above).

Canonical Context

Numbers 1:1–10:10 is set at Mount Sinai. There is an alternation of the prescriptive laws and descriptive narratives. However, the narrative is not simply a historical chronology.[16] Thus Numbers 7 describes the gifts each tribe brings at the consecration of the tabernacle, an event that was completed at the end of the book of Exodus. This is also true of Numbers 9:15–16, whereas 9:17–23 describes the events following Israel's departure from Mount Sinai and chronologically following 10:10. The text reaches out beyond the temporal limits of its initial and final verses and both precedes and anticipates events. However, throughout its presentation it consistently emphasizes aspects of holiness and separation from that which is unclean or sinful. The numbering and organization of the camp in the first four chapters parallel the numbering and organization of the creation during the first three days of Genesis 1:3–13. The uncleanness caused by disease and by marital unfaithfulness appears in Numbers 5, along with the consequences that would separate such a person from the camp. Numbers 6 considers the special holiness and separation

16. Childs, *Introduction*, 195.

that the Nazirite is to possess. The gifts for the dedication of the tabernacle in Numbers 7 set aside property and sacrificial offerings from each tribe and thus render the tribe holy and acceptable before God. The following chapter describes the setting apart or consecration of the Levites and their service before God. Chapter 9 considers uncleanness in the camp due to dead bodies and the option to celebrate the Passover a month later for certain Israelites who may be unclean at the time of that holiday. Numbers 9:15–23 describes the presence of God indicated by a cloud at the tabernacle; this presence will provide divine leadership for the people. As the lamps provide holy light in 8:1–4, so the trumpets provide holiness for what is heard in 10:1–10. These media bring holy guidance for the people.

Numbers 10:11–21:34 describes the journey from Mount Sinai to the plains of Moab. The connections with the narratives of Exodus and the overall chiastic structure have been noted in the "Literary Readings" section. This all underlines the repeated violation of the holy by Israelites. The laws in chapters 15–19 return to a concern for all Israel's holiness (Num. 15) as well as the holiness of the priests and Levites (Num. 16–19). The regulations are set for all the generations, a theme repeated in chapters 15, 18, and 19. These laws provide further means of restoration for Israel so that the holiness of God does not harm or destroy the people. Later texts remember the desert as an example of Israel's sin in testing God and his judgment (Pss. 78:17, 19, 40; 95:8; 106:14, 32; Ezek. 20:13–36; Amos 2:10; Heb. 3:8, 17), as well as God's gracious provision (Ps. 78:15; Hosea 13:5; Amos 2:10; Acts 7:36–44). Above all, 1 Corinthians 10:1–13 declares the stories of the wilderness wanderings to be examples for Christians to avoid idolatry, immorality, and grumbling, thereby to understand that they are not subject to greater temptation to sin than those who have lived earlier. Yet God's grace will provide a way, as Numbers 21:1–9 illustrates. The bronze snake symbolizes the sin and rebellion of the people. They are called to turn their eyes in faith and thereby to find salvation and healing from the snakebites. So Jesus uses this imagery in John 3:14–15 as a description of his own death on the cross. People are invited to turn from sin to gaze on the one who has become sin so that Christians might believe in his atoning death and know salvation and healing.

Numbers 22:1–36:13 describes the events of defeating Sihon and Og east of the Jordan Valley. In this, the text anticipates the greater victories in the book of Joshua. Again, the narrative is interwoven with the legal elements. The story of Balak and Balaam (Num. 22–24) is remembered not only in the next generation (Josh. 24:9–10) but also in Micah 6:5 and Nehemiah 13:2, where God is praised for turning this intended occasion for cursing into one of blessing. In the New Testament, 2 Peter 2:15 and Revelation 2:14 accuse Balaam of greed and of leading Israel into sinful rituals linked with Baal of Peor (Num. 25; 31:16). This latter sin served as a warning to later generations of Israelites so that they might avoid idolatry (Ps. 106:28; Hosea 9:10). As noted previously, the emphasis on the census and numbering (Num. 26) returns to concerns of holiness in ordering Israel, as was the case at the beginning of the book. The incidents of inheritance rights through Zelophehad's daughters frame this final section of laws at Numbers 26:33; 27:1–11 and at Numbers 36:1–13. In doing so, it affirms the holiness of all Israel, both women and men, and the right of the blessing of inheritance as given to women as well as men.

Theological Perspectives of Numbers

As with the canonical context, the theology of Numbers focuses on the holiness of God. It does so in three ways: God's instruction to Israel as to what it means to be holy; Israel's rebellions, which stand in contrast to the holiness; and God's judgment against Israel coupled with his mercy to preserve the nation and to provide a future generation with the opportunity to choose life.

In this respect Numbers 1–10 focuses on the holiness to which Israel is called while yet at Mount Sinai. The previous event in which all Israel has participated is the worship of the gold calf (Exod. 32). The previous event in which the priests have participated is the offering of "strange fire" and the subsequent death of the two sons of Aaron, who presented that fire (Lev. 10 KJV). The Day of Atonement (Lev. 16) has been a means for God to accept the blood of animals and forgive Israel for these infractions. As noticed above, the ordering of the people and the holiness legislation in the opening section of Numbers reflect the order and holiness of God. They prepare the people to follow God, who leads them as the great warrior victorious over his enemies (Exod. 15). However, the rebellions of the people that extend over the next eleven chapters of the scroll of Numbers outline a steadfast refusal of Israel to achieve their call to holiness. Nowhere is this seen more clearly than in Numbers 13–14. Despite all that God has done for Israel and the demonstrations of his power, they refuse to believe that he can give them victory over the Canaanites and the Amorites in the promised land. Their refusal to believe seals their fate. That generation will never enter the land. Like Adam, they will die for their sin—not at once, but in the natural processes of life over the next generation (Rom. 6:23). Even here, God does not destroy all the people. In his mercy, he provides for the descendants of this rebellious generation, so that they will know of his blessing. And so he leads them onward. But God also gives Israel and its spiritual leadership more teachings as to how they may live in conformity with his will and know his forgiveness (Num. 15–19).

Numbers 22–24 illustrates God's protection of his people, just as in their other military victories against their enemies. Here, however, their enemy Balak tries to fight them through magical means rather than by force of arms. He hires a prophet to curse them. The blessings that proceed from Balaam's mouth demonstrate God's power over the spiritual forces of the world. Not only does Balaam fail, but also his blessings encourage Israel. However, what he cannot do through spiritual power, the king of Moab achieves by enticing them to join Midian in orgiastic worship of Baal of Peor. Such a local nature spirit is credited for the region's fertility. This Baal's veneration becomes another means for Israel to ignore the provision of God and to seek food and prosperity from sources that God has condemned. It is ironic that the last event of the old generation of Israel before the census of chapter 25, the one that prepares for the new generation about to enter the land of promise, parallels their first act in Exodus 32, the direct violation of the first and second commands of the Ten Commandments and God's covenant. Here as well a plague results as a consequence of the sin. Yet the real mercy is that God spares Israel and the new generation to go forward.

Numbers 27–36 is framed by the discussion of the inheritance of Zelophehad's daughters. All this affirms the holiness of God and how it calls his people to be set apart unto him in their land. Thus behind the holiness of the land lies that of the family units, whether they are extended families, clans, or tribes. The unity of all Israel as a holy people before God involves Moses's appointment of a successor (27:12–23). The sanctity of time and possessions can be found in the special calendar of Numbers 28–29, with its emphasis on the offerings. The laws on vows (Num. 30) preserve the sanctity within the family as a holy and ordered people who come before God. What is dedicated to God from battle appears in Numbers 31. The special disposition of the land east of the Jordan is described in Numbers 32 so that it is rendered holy before God as a place for his people to live. Even the wanderings in the wilderness are remembered as part of God's plan for Israel; thus Numbers 33 begins with the report that the people have been led by Moses and Aaron and that Moses "wrote down" their itinerary "by command of the Lord" (v. 2; see v. 38). The boundaries of the promised land in Numbers 34, like the Levitical and priestly cities and the discussion of how to avoid judgment on the land for murder, all set apart the land as holy to God. Thus the land and the people and families who live in it are given to God. The absolute value of human life (Gen. 9:5–6) requires that any blood shed through murder finds atonement by the taking of the life of the murderer. Otherwise the land is no longer holy but becomes polluted by this uncleanness.

Some of the key ethical points of this book repeat or anticipate what appears elsewhere. Thus the issues of the challenge to divinely ordained leadership and the question of the apparently blood-filled extermination of Israel's enemies will occur again, especially in the books of Joshua, Judges, Samuel, and Kings. The question of gender roles in the examination of the suspected adulteress and in the leprosy of Miriam is addressed above under "Gender and Ideological Criticism." The matter of the inheritance of the land, as illustrated in the allotments of Numbers 34 and 35, and in the rights of Zelophehad's daughters (Num. 27 and 36), reflects the Israelites' ethical behavior in the land as God's requirement in the covenant. God gives the land to Israel in response to their faithfulness. Land is the major source of family security and of wealth generation in the ancient world. Thus its preservation in each family is essential for Israel's security and each family's well-being. The guarantee of this for every family, including those without sons (e.g., Zelophehad), provides a certification of God's faithfulness to each and every family, his demonstration of covenantal love to them for a thousand generations (Exod. 20:6; Deut. 5:10). And it is this connection with God's love that turns readers back to consider the major concerns of Numbers, those dealing with a holy God's love and provision for his people, even when they do not regard him well.

Key Commentaries and Studies

Ashley, Timothy R. *The Book of Numbers*. NICOT. Grand Rapids: Eerdmans, 1993. Evangelical focus on the final form of the text and on its translation.

Budd, Philip J. *Numbers*. WBC 5. Waco: Word, 1984. Detailed study with full discussion of critical issues.

Cole, R. Dennis. *Numbers*. NAC 3B. Nashville: Broadman & Holman, 2000. Evangelical study with excellent survey of the realia and the historical and literary aspects.

Levine, Baruch A. *Numbers: A New Translation with Introduction and Commentary*. Vol. 1, *1–20*. Vol. 2, *21–36*. AB 4–4A. Garden City, NY: Doubleday, 1993–2000. Most thorough study of the text and its background.

Milgrom, Jacob. *Numbers*. JPSTC. New York: Jewish Publication Society, 1990. Study of the Hebrew text with appreciation of the book's historical value.

Wenham, Gordon J. *Numbers*. OTG. Sheffield: Sheffield Academic, 1997. Best introduction to the book.

———. *Numbers: An Introduction and Commentary*. TOTC. Leicester, UK: Inter-Varsity; Downers Grove, IL: InterVarsity, 1981. Evangelical commentary, outstanding on literary perspectives.

5

DEUTERONOMY

How much of one's life is important to God? In the book of Deuteronomy, the revelation of God touches on every area of the lives of the ancient Israelites. This provides a means of integrating individual lives into families and society, an integration that challenges the fragmentation of the person in our own culture.

Name, Text, and Outline

The name Deuteronomy comes from the Greek (LXX) name for the scroll, with the meaning of "a second law." This expression appears in the Greek translation of Deuteronomy only as a copy of a law made by the king (Deut. 17:18; cf. Josh. 8:32). As the title of the book, the term comments on the second occasion of the giving of the law, a generation after the first time at Mount Sinai. The Hebrew name, (*had*)*dĕbārîm*, "(the) words," makes use of the second word in the scroll, which appears in the phrase "These are the words." The Masoretic Text of Deuteronomy has a well-preserved text, with little need for emendation in order to understand it. The Septuagint provides a literal translation into Greek, with less stylistic smoothness than Genesis and Exodus. It betrays signs of the Hellenistic cultural context and includes expansions similar to those in the Dead Sea Scrolls.

OUTLINE

I. Title and Preamble (1:1–5)
II. Historical Review (1:6–3:29)

- A. Horeb/Sinai (1:6–18)
- B. Kadesh Barnea (1:19–46)
- C. Edom/Seir, Moab, Ammon (2:1–25)
- D. Sihon and Og (2:26–3:11)
- E. East of the Jordan (3:12–29)

III. General Laws of Loyalty (4:1–11:32)
- A. Introduction (4:1–49)
- B. Ten Commandments (5:1–33)
- C. Love of God in the Promised Land (6:1–25)
- D. Possession of the Promised Land (7:1–26)
- E. Wilderness and Sinai (8:1–10:22)
- F. Possession of the Promised Land (11:1–32)

IV. Detailed Laws (12:1–26:19)
- A. Right Worship: Physical World (12:1–14:29)
- B. Right Worship: Time (15:1–16:17)
- C. Authorities (16:18–18:22)
- D. Killing (19:1–22:8)
- E. Improper Relationships (22:9–23:18 [23:19 MT])
- F. Private Property (28:19 [23:20 MT]–24:22)
- G. Balanced Relationships (25:1–19)
- H. Firstfruits (26:1–15)
- I. Conclusion (26:16–19)

V. Curses and Blessings (27:1–28:68)

VI. General Laws of Loyalty (29:1 [28:69 MT]–31:30)

VII. Psalms of Praise and Prophecy (32:1–33:29)

VIII. Death of Moses (34:1–12)

Overview of Deuteronomy

The scroll of Deuteronomy continues the story of Israel's journey after arriving at the last stage of travel east of the Jordan River. As a nation they are assembled to receive the words of Moses at the end of his life. That message (or series of messages) is presented as Deuteronomy. After introducing the speaker, Moses, who proclaims the words of Israel's God (1:6), the first three chapters focus on a review of Israel's journey from leaving Mount Sinai to arriving at their present location. Moses reviews the choice of representatives to assist him in leading the people. Next is the story of the mission and report of Israel's twelve spies, sent from Kadesh Barnea to search out the promised land. Moses recounts Israel's history of a lack of faith. He speaks of God's judgment that their generation will not enter the land. Their abortive attempt then to take that land, despite the divine warning, ends in ignominious defeat. Their journey continues southward, and then to the east and north as they bypass the Edomites and Moabites. However, God gives Israel victory over Sihon king of Heshbon and Og king of Bashan. Israel acquires their territory, and Moses gives Reuben, Gad, and half the tribe of Manasseh this land for their possession. Eventually God confirms that Moses will not enter the promised land but that Joshua will lead the people to possess it. This historical review emphasizes God's faithfulness to Israel, sometimes even in the midst of their disobedience.

The next major section, chapters 4–11, turns to consider general admonitions to Israel to remain loyal to God. Its introduction encourages obedience to the merciful God of Israel and yet also warns that disobedience brings consequences. This prepares for the summary of the law as found in the Ten Commandments, repeated in Deuteronomy 5 with minor changes from Exodus 20. The command to love God and to educate one's children in this covenant follows in Deuteronomy 6, most famously in the Shema of verses 4–9 (so called because the first word in v. 4 is *šĕmaʿ*, "Hear!"). Deuteronomy 7 warns against any association with the Canaanites and their religious practices. Chapter 8 emphasizes God's care for the nation in the desert and warns of forgetting about God when enjoying the blessings of the promised land. Deuteronomy 9 and 10 contrast Moses's intercession before God with Israel's sin of worshiping the gold calf and of continually complaining throughout their trek in the desert. Chapter 11 summarizes the general admonitions of the preceding section and sets before Israel a curse and a blessing that they must choose.

Deuteronomy 12–26, the central section of the scroll, provides specific legislation for living in the promised land, where Israel is now headed. The laws are many and diverse. Although a general order may be discerned, apparently miscellaneous laws are inserted here and there in the text. A close study reveals that these are often connected to the larger context by related words or similar-sounding terms. Nevertheless, the concern here is to outline the major divisions.

As with other major law collections in the Pentateuch (Exod. 20:1–17; 20:22–23:33; Lev. 17–26), religious laws precede the civil laws. Broadly outlined, the religious laws include those concerned with the physical realia (Deut. 12–14) and those focused on the temporal (Deut. 15–16). As with the beginning of the Book of the Covenant (Exod. 20:22–26), the religious laws start with regulations concerning an altar chosen by God (Deut. 12) and continue by looking at wrong worship (Deut. 13), right worship in terms of clean food (14:1–21), and tithes (14:22–29). The temporal dimension of the religious instruction includes Sabbatical years (Deut. 15) and festivals (Deut. 16).

The first area of civil laws considers the roles and responsibilities of those who are in positions of authority and influence: judges (16:18–17:13), kings (17:14–20), priests (18:1–8), and prophets (18:9–22). These represent individuals who stand in the place of God as rulers and judges over the people and who proclaim and interpret the word of God with power. After such life-and-death decision makers naturally follow laws that deal with the taking of human life: homicide, including matters of theft and false witness (Deut. 19); warfare (Deut. 20) and other laws relating to killing and war (Deut. 21); and (the converse) protecting the lives of animals and people (22:1–8).

© Baker Publishing Group and Dr. James C. Martin

Ninth-century-BC "calendar" of the agricultural year found at Gezer

Next are matters of improper or unclean relationships: plant and animal mixtures (22:9–12), sexual relations (22:13–23:1 [23:2 MT]), relations with other nations (23:2–8 [23:3–9 MT]), sex and military matters (23:9–16 [23:10–17 MT]), and cult prostitutes (23:17–18 [23:18–19 MT]). Much of Deuteronomy 23 and 24 considers the subject of private property and issues that may arise: lending (23:19–20 [23:20–21 MT]), vows (23:21–23 [23:22–24 MT]), gleaning (23:24–25 [23:25–26 MT]), collusion (24:1–4), honeymoons (24:5), millstones (24:6), kidnapping (24:7), disease (24:8–9), and debts and the poor (24:10–22). Deuteronomy 25 considers various items that describe balanced relationships. These include the limits of corporal punishment, allowing an ox to eat from the grain it threshes, levirate marriage, fair fights, just weights and balances, and justice for what Amalek did toward Israel. Chapter 26 turns to the offerings of the firstfruits and tithes in the promised land, along with the confession of God's redemption of Israel. Verses 16–19 conclude the chapter and the legal section by calling for obedience and promising divine favor.

Deuteronomy 27 describes the ceremony of covenant renewal that Israel is to perform at Mount Ebal, in the promised land, including a series of curses for those who violate the basic laws of justice for the neighbor. This is followed by lists of curses and blessings for disobedience and obedience toward the law (Deut. 28). General laws of loyalty and the results of obedience and disobedience then appear (Deut. 29–31). Moses concludes Deuteronomy and his life with psalms of praise toward God and prophecy regarding Israel's future (Deut. 32–33). The great leader of Israel then dies and is succeeded by Joshua (Deut. 34).

Although some specific laws are connected with Moses's earlier composition (Exod. 24:4), Deuteronomy is the first work that appears to be attributed in large part to a human author (or at least someone recording what God has said; Deut. 10:4; 31:9, 22).

Reading Deuteronomy

Premodern Readings

Deuteronomy played a key role in Judaism in the time of Jesus. For Philo of Alexandria, the laws provided allegorical resources for understanding the philosophical world in which he wrote. However, they also served as Moses's final testament. In the Gospels, Jesus cites Deuteronomy more than any book of the Pentateuch. The Dead Sea Scrolls also cite this book more than they do the other four. Deuteronomy formed one of the chief sources of law and its discussion in the rabbinic literature of Judaism. Indeed, the command to recite the Shema (Deut. 6:4–9) and the question as to when in the evening (and morning) it should be recited occupy the first legal discussion at the beginning of the Mishnah. This is the earliest compendium of legal discussion, traditionally related to the end of the second century AD. In the early church, texts such as the Ten Commandments (Deut. 5) aroused interest; however, the legal nature of Deuteronomy contrasted with the gospel of grace and the freedom from the law that were understood to be part of the new covenant as introduced by Jesus Christ. Nevertheless, the ninth-century British king Alfred the Great exemplifies the use of Deuteronomy (as well as Exod. 20–23) as a basis for the formulation of one of the earliest surviving English legal collections.

The Reformation, with its emphasis on the canonical Scriptures in their original context and meaning, brought about a renewed interest in the book of Deuteronomy. In his commentary on this legal material Martin Luther saw the value of the state as led by God to create and preserve order in the world. John Calvin emphasized the role of the law as a schoolmaster to lead sinners to understand their need for grace and for Jesus Christ (Gal. 3:24).[1]

Source Criticism

Ever since the work of W. M. L. de Wette in 1806, Deuteronomy, in some manner, has been connected with the book of the law found in the temple by Hilkiah in 2 Kings 22–23 and involved in Josiah's reformation.[2] Early in

1. See the similarities and differences of the two reformers in Höpfl, *Luther and Calvin on Secular Authority.*

2. This argument actually appears in a footnote of de Wette's sixteen-page doctoral dissertation, which attempted to prove that Deuteronomy was written later than the rest of the Pentateuch. See Rogerson, *W. M. L. de Wette*, 39–42; de Wette, *Dissertation critica qua Deuteronomium.*

critical thought, a form of Deuteronomy was considered to have been planted in the temple so as to be found by those renovating it and thereby to inaugurate Josiah's work of closing the high places and centralizing worship in Jerusalem. More recently, however, Deuteronomy has come to be understood as a work promoting the reforms begun by the king. Drawing on the concept of the covenant and other expressions as found in the eighth-century-BC writings of Hosea, source critics theorized a northern Israelite influence as a result of scribes going south at the time of the destruction of the northern kingdom around 722 BC.

Following earlier source critics, Julius Wellhausen located the Deuteronomistic source (D) as a seventh-century document and determined that this source included and affected previous texts in the Pentateuch.[3] Its emphasis on the kingdom of God as affecting every area of life and on the covenant as God's means of relating to his people easily connected with the reforms of Josiah.

In the middle of the twentieth century, the German critic Martin Noth proposed the theory of the Deuteronomistic History, in which the narratives of Joshua, Judges, Samuel, and Kings were attributed to one editor living at the end of the monarchy.[4] This editor sought to explain the fall of Jerusalem as a result of Israel's failure to worship its God alone. According to Noth, this history began with the summary of the preconquest story as found in Deuteronomy's first four chapters. Chapters 5–11 then provided the general introduction to the specific legal collection of chapters 12–26.

Tradition History

Gerhard von Rad related the book of Deuteronomy to an original covenant document designed to provide a religious and military union for Israel's twelve tribes.[5] This view emphasized the paraenetic use of the laws in Deuteronomy. They were designed to teach Israel concerning its life and faithfulness to God.

Recent years have seen an emphasis on the redactional nature of the Deuteronomistic source late in the history of the monarchy.[6] This has had an effect on the understanding of Deuteronomy. Less emphasis has been placed on its origins earlier in the monarchy, and more has been placed on multiple editions of the book that emerged later in the seventh, sixth, and fifth centuries BC. Although theories about different editions of Deuteronomy used to be based on its alternation between singular and plural forms of address (both in the second person), this has not enjoyed as much emphasis recently. This

3. Wellhausen, *Prolegomena*.

4. Noth, *The Deuteronomistic History*.

5. Von Rad called this union an amphictyony; see his *Deuteronomy*, the 1966 translation of the 1964 original.

6. Vogt, *Deuteronomic Theology*.

is because such alternations appear in treaties of the West Semitic world and in other West Semitic literature.[7] Instead, the emphasis is now placed on multiple introductions and conclusions. The former begin at Deuteronomy 1:1; 4:44, 45; then the latter can be found starting at 28:68; 29:28; and 34:10–12. As exemplified by Thomas Römer and Karel van der Toorn, the preexilic scroll of Deuteronomy began with the Shema (6:4–9) and concluded with the legal section at the end of chapter 26.[8] Some of the blessings and curses of Deuteronomy 28 were also included. The second edition appeared during the Babylonian exile. According to van der Toorn, it began at 4:44 and ended at 29:28. It also expanded the curses of chapter 28 to include a "prophecy" of Israel going into exile (a pseudoprophecy of exile, which had already occurred at the time it was written). According to Römer, it included parts of Deuteronomy 1–4, especially the descriptions of Israel's expectation of God's promise of the land, something Israel did not have after the Babylonians captured and destroyed it. In the same manner the verses of Deuteronomy 34, in which Moses is denied admittance into the land, would have been added at this time. Van der Toorn adds a second exilic edition, appearing at the end of that time, which included these texts. He refers to a final edition, appearing after Israel's return from exile (after 537 BC), as the wisdom edition, in which chapters 4 and 30 were added since they envision national conversion (4:29–31) and return from exile (30:1–10). It also includes additions to Deuteronomy 19–25, especially sections that provide reasons for the laws. In this edition Römer places 6:6–9, which he sees as a command to turn every private home into a temple by writing the words of the law at its entrance. And so Deuteronomy's redactional layers reflect the movement from a religion based on a centralized temple and a covenant with God to one emphasizing the written word.

These attempts to deconstruct Deuteronomy into several redactional layers and to locate them in the history of Israel during the mid-first millennium BC need to be examined in light of the evidence discussed below in "Ancient Near Eastern Context."

Literary Readings

An appropriate understanding of the literary form of Deuteronomy depends on the correct identification of the work in terms of its overall literary form. This form derives from a combination of the recognized ancient Near Eastern form of suzerain-vassal treaty (hereafter, vassal treaty) and addresses or sermons exhorting faithfulness toward God. The sermonic nature of the text is especially clear in chapters 4–11, with their general appeals to loyalty

7. See, e.g., the Aramaic Sefire treaties in the still-useful edition of Fitzmyer, *Aramaic Inscriptions*.

8. Römer, *Deuteronomistic History*; van der Toorn, *Scribal Culture*.

toward God and their narrative reminiscences of events in Israel's past illustrating these elements. Evidence is also strong in the legislation of chapters 12–26, especially in the second half of those chapters, where many reasons are given to explain various laws. However, the stronger and more visible connection with a literary form has been the identification of the vassal treaty as found in many dozens of examples throughout the ancient Near East. More on the background and fuller significance appears in "Ancient Near Eastern Context" (below).

Certain primary elements compose this important treaty form and are significant for the pattern of Deuteronomy. The structure and contents of chapters 1–31 of the book may be said to represent that of ancient Near Eastern treaties, especially those of the Hittites from around the thirteenth century BC. The treaty structure can be divided into six parts, each represented in the Deuteronomy text:

Treaty	Deuteronomy
1. Title/Preamble	1:1–5 or 6 (God with Moses as mediator)
2. Historical Prologue	1:6–3:29
3a. Basic Commands	4:1–11:32
3b. Detailed Laws	12:1–26:19
4a. Deposit of Text	31:24–26
4b. Public Reading	31:10–13
5. Witnesses	30:19; 31:19, 21, 26, 28
6a. Blessings	28:1–14
6b. Curses	28:15–68

The title or preamble identifies the overlord or great king who has the power to make and enforce the treaty. In the case of Deuteronomy, this role is filled by God, who is Israel's suzerain. However, Moses also appears as God's mouthpiece.

The historical prologue forms what can be understood as a second introduction and therefore may begin to explain the appearance of multiple introductions to the book of Deuteronomy. This material recounts the relations between the overlord and that vassal, sometimes going back two or more generations in time. The purpose is not merely to provide a history lesson. Rather, the overlord uses this part of the treaty to recall how often he has been loyal to the vassal and how the loyalty of the vassal (and his predecessors) has paid off for the vassal. The effect is to provide motivation for the vassal to accept the present treaty because he (no "she" is recorded in this role among the Hittites) has seen how this has benefited him and his ancestors, not only personally but especially with the promise that the dynasty of the vassal ruler will remain in place and be guaranteed by the power of the overlord. In a similar manner,

God reminds Israel of their times of faithfulness and unfaithfulness in the previous generation. Faithfulness has led to success and blessing. Unfaithfulness has resulted in the opposite. So now God challenges Israel to remain faithful so that the present generation, about to enter the promised land, may occupy it and enjoy it in security and prosperity.

© Baker Publishing Group and Dr. James C. Martin. Turkish Ministry of Antiquities.

Hittite vassal treaty between King Tudhaliya IV and Kurunta of Tarhuntassa (thirteenth century BC)

The commands, both the general stipulations and the specific ones, provide the means for the vassal to demonstrate loyalty in a variety of circumstances. For example, virtually every unbroken example of this part of the treaty includes an extradition clause. If any enemy of the overlord escapes to the vassal's country, the vassal must catch that enemy and return him to the overlord. This and other laws are designed to demonstrate loyalty on the part of the vassal. These stipulations are not limited to what is often thought of as political or military concerns. One Hittite treaty includes clauses forbidding various types of sexual relations with relatives and women of the palace.[9] For Israel, the "basic commands" include repeated demands for loyalty on the part of the vassal: Israel is commanded to recognize that their God is the only God and hence not to worship other deities. The second half of this section includes many detailed stipulations. A significant literary aspect of these specific laws is their arrangement (see "Theological Perspectives of Deuteronomy," below).

Unlike points 1–3, 5, and 6, the fourth area of the treaty is not always found in Hittite vassal treaties. Nevertheless, it is very important. As with Deuteronomy 31:24–26, so the Hittite vassal treaties with this clause call for the treaty to be placed in the major temple of the vassal state. This deposit accomplished more than recognizing the sanctity of the document. It stored the tablet or (in the case of Deuteronomy) scroll in the safest place in the country. The temples, with their accumulated wealth and recognized divine connection, were given the most security of any buildings in the country. Their holiness, as expressions of the very identity of the state itself,

9. Beckman, *Hittite Diplomatic Texts*, 27–28.

also provided a taboo against any who would contemplate breaking in and stealing the documents found there. Thus the covenant with God and Israel was deposited in the holiest and safest place possible in the country. This guaranteed that no one could steal the text or alter it in any way, thereby preserving its integrity. The clause regarding public reading ensured that those responsible for observing the treaty would themselves hear the original version. Again, this prevented anyone in the society from altering the

Ancient Near Eastern Treaties

The number of extant treaties from Egypt, Syria, Mesopotamia, and Anatolia in the ancient Near East approaches one hundred.[a] Some, such as the treaty between the Hittite king Ḫattušiliš III and the pharaoh Ramesses II, are parity treaties. A parity treaty defines relations between two independent political entities that recognize the equal status of each. In this thirteenth-century-BC document, drawn up following the Battle of Qadesh (or Kadesh; ca. 1274 BC) between the two powers, the Hittites and Egyptians recognize the futility of continued war and seek to identify a common border and a mutually beneficial relationship. Most treaties, however, are asymmetrical in their relations: one side represents the superior power, and the other side represents the inferior and dependent state. The former is called the suzerain and the latter the vassal. In such a case the treaty defines a relationship that is largely dictated by the suzerain and accepted by the vassal as the consequence of being a conquered state.

By the accidents of archaeology, there are two main groups of such vassal treaties. The earliest date from the fourteenth and thirteenth centuries BC and have mostly been found in the Hittite capital of Ḫattuša.[b] They represent the Hittite kings as the superior powers, dictating terms to vassal states throughout the regions of modern-day Turkey and Syria. They are mostly written in the Hittite language and cuneiform script. The later group of vassal treaties dates from the eighth and seventh centuries BC. They were administered by the Neo-Assyrian kings, who were based in the region of modern-day eastern Iraq and gradually conquered weaker states to the west, especially in Iraq and Syria. Their treaties were written in either the Assyrian cuneiform language and script[c] or the Aramaic language and script (as with the Sefire treaties).[d] At different times in its history, arguably, ancient Israel was influenced by both groups of treaties.

[a] For a comprehensive study of virtually all these documents, see Kitchen and Lawrence, *Treaty, Law and Covenant*.

[b] Beckman, *Hittite Diplomatic Texts*.

[c] Parpola and Watanabe, *Neo-Assyrian Treaties*.

[d] See Fitzmyer, *Aramaic Inscriptions*.

meaning or intent of the work. It meant that all the people who are vassals (here, all Israel) would periodically hear the covenant read directly from the original document itself.

In the various countries of the ancient Near East, the witnesses included the major gods and goddesses in the pantheons of both the vassal and the overlord. This list was intended to invoke these deities to enforce the observance of the treaty by the vassal. Observance would lead the gods to bless the vassal and the land of the vassal(s). Disobedience would result in divine curses on the land and the dynasty of the vassal(s). Because Israel worshiped only one deity and because that deity was one of the two parties in the covenant (the overlord), there was no corresponding god list. However, the text does call on witnesses in Deuteronomy 30:19; 31:19, 21, 26, and 28. Deuteronomy 31:19 mentions a song, perhaps the poem of chapter 32, and most likely something that the people could easily learn and remember as a means to instruct and encourage them to faithfulness. A second witness is the book of the law, probably something similar to Deuteronomy itself. This instructs the people on how to be faithful and indicts them for their lack of faithfulness. Finally, heaven and earth are called as witnesses. These two also appear in some of the Hittite vassal treaties as witnesses. Their significance is likely tied up with showering water on the earth so that the land may give forth its fertility in agricultural produce.

The blessings and curses of Deuteronomy 28 correspond to similar curses and blessings that occur in the Hittite vassal treaties. There are blessings for obedience and curses for disobedience, and both relate to the continuation of the dynasty and the family of the king. In Deuteronomy, fertility is also a theme. However, it is tied in with God's direct ownership of the land. In both the treaties and Deuteronomy, some of the curses are mirror images of the blessings, and vice versa. Therefore, this concluding section provides a demonstration as to how the divine realm will enforce loyal obedience to the covenant.

In this manner most of the text of Deuteronomy can be divided into parts that correspond to the vassal treaty. This medium of revelation constitutes a means by which God reveals to Israel his intent to have and to define a relationship.

Gender and Ideological Criticism

Throughout the greater part of the book of Deuteronomy, there is a direct application of the laws and the larger covenant to both men and women (4:16; 15:12; 17:2, 5; 22:5; 23:17; 24:1; 29:18). Deuteronomy 22:13–29 includes laws related to rape and consensual sex outside of marriage. All adulterous unions are punishable by death on the part of both participants. However, for other sexual relations, with a woman already engaged to be married, there is leniency for the woman if the act takes place outside of a town or context where her screams of protest cannot be heard. Sex between a man and a woman who are not married or engaged results in the requirement that the man pay the father of the woman an expensive bridal price (50 shekels of silver) and that he marry her, with no possibility of divorce. While there are different ways to understand these cases, in many instances the huge price of the fine would place the man in debt servitude to the father of the woman for years and thus under the control of the offended family. The right of divorce is assumed in Deuteronomy 24:1–4. There, however, it concerns the question of the woman who is divorced from her first husband; marries a second husband, who then divorces her; and then wishes to remarry her first husband. This is forbidden. Although one could envision a variety of possible reasons for this set of actions, one likely eventuality has to do with collusion in which the original couple scheme to acquire the wealth of the second husband through this system of divorce and remarriage. Thus while the possibility of divorce is envisioned, it is not endorsed, nor is it to be used for the personal acquisition of wealth.

Because of the critical tradition of connecting Deuteronomy with the reforms of Josiah, the laws or parts of them are often interpreted as means by which the rulers of Israel gained centralized power and control of the religious establishment. This assumes a late development of monotheism and a political purpose behind its origins and many of the laws in the book of Deuteronomy. Although there is no easy way by which to prove this interpretation or to disprove it, there remains the widespread acceptance of this text from its appearance during the time of Josiah. Judah as a whole (or at least a significant number of its citizens) recognized a work that echoed ancient traditions in their religious heritage.

Furthermore, the view that closing or destroying the high places would provide an increase in power seems illogical. Power and control are exercised through the distribution of means of control throughout the land. Thus although centralization might be part of amassing power, it makes no sense simply to eliminate a natural means of controlling the populace (via destroying the high places) and not to replace it with something similar in local areas throughout Israel.

The concern for social justice among those poor and least able to defend themselves is also present in a powerful and repeated way in Deuteronomy. Traditionally, the poor and vulnerable are individuals who do not have connections to major families in the kingdom and thus cannot appeal to relatives for aid and support in times of need, such as the orphan, the widow, and the stranger who is living in the land but who has no family ties nearby. Texts regarding justice and equal rights for such people occur repeatedly in Deuteronomy (5:14–15; 10:18–19; 14:21, 28–29; 15:12–15; 16:9–15; 23:7, 15–16; 24:7, 14–15, 17–22; 26:12–13).

Ancient Near Eastern Context

When two countries in the ancient world went to war, they would often end their conflict by drawing up a treaty. There is nothing unusual about this since it has happened throughout human history and continues to take place to the present day. These treaties can be divided into two groups (see the sidebar "Ancient Near Eastern Treaties").

The example of the thirteenth-century-BC parity treaty between the Hittites and the Egyptians is especially interesting because both the Egyptian and the Hittite treaties, as well as the descriptions by each sovereign, are available in their respective countries. The Egyptian pharaoh, Ramesses II, claimed a victory in his own accounts of the battle. However, both the Hittite records and the treaty itself demonstrate the stalemate that resulted and the parity between the two. Although every writer may have biases (sometimes called ideological predispositions), it is possible to discern the differences between those whose bias distorts their report so that it is not accurate, and those who can portray an event with historical credibility.[10] Not every bias distorts to the same extent, nor is every record utterly unreliable to the historian. It is valuable to keep this in mind when studying biblical history and to develop skills as to how to discern what is of value and what is not.

The second type of treaty was the vassal treaty, already described above. This treaty resulted from the demonstration of a clear superiority of one of the warring factions. Essentially it allowed the victor to dictate terms to the loser. The treaty would be renewed during critical times, such as the beginning of a new ruler's reign. It defined a relationship and supported that connection through specific demands that the vassal was expected to fulfill.

From the ancient Near East, more than ninety separate treaties have been discovered and dated to between 2500 and 600 BC.[11] Most are vassal treaties. Most also fall into two groups: (1) those connected with the Hittites and dating from about the fourteenth and thirteenth centuries BC; and (2) those connected with the Neo-Assyrian period and dating between the ninth and seventh centuries BC. Each of these groups of vassal treaties has a specific form. The form of the earlier set of Hittite treaties includes the elements mentioned above in "Literary Readings." The pattern of the later set is similar to the form of the Hittite treaties. However, neither a historical prologue nor a blessings section is found in the treaties from the first millennium BC. The absence of these two elements bears witness to the distinctive nature of the later treaties.[12] Apparently less value was placed in motivating vassals to obedience through

10. See Liverani, *Prestige and Interest*.

11. Kitchen, *Reliability*, 283–89; Kitchen and Lawrence, *Treaty, Law and Covenant*.

12. Kitchen (*Reliability*, 290–91) systematically surveys all the attempts to find these elements in the later treaties and concludes that there is no evidence for the claims of other scholars that first-millennium-BC vassal treaties possess clear evidence for either historical prologues or blessings.

historical reflections on how well such a relationship can work. There also seems to have been less concern with the promise of rewards: the threats among the curses became longer, more numerous, and more colorful.

It is therefore of great interest to compare this treaty structure with that found in the book of Deuteronomy as well as in other biblical covenants such as the Ten Commandments (Exod. 20; Deut. 5), the Book of the Covenant (Exod. 20:22–23:33), and the covenant renewal of Joshua 24. In all these cases, but especially in Deuteronomy, a structure identical to the Hittite vassal treaty can be identified. Unlike the late treaties, the book of Deuteronomy contains both the section on the history of the relations between the two parties and a set of blessings as well as curses. This is a remarkable parallel and attests to a structure known elsewhere only (but with many attestations) in the fourteenth and thirteenth centuries BC. Many vassal treaties also exist from the first millennium BC, but none with this structure. On the basis of such a formal parallel, it is very beneficial for modern scholars to study the Hittite treaties.

Desiring to identify the formation of the book of Deuteronomy with the seventh-century period of Josiah's reforms, scholars have tried to argue for a later origin to the structure of Deuteronomy. Some deny any connection of this biblical covenant with the treaties of the ancient Near East.[13] However, such a denial flies in the face of the remarkable parallels of structure.

Some argue that there is no social context for the origin of a covenant document for Israel in the late second millennium BC.[14] This vague objection must deal with the generally accepted presence of Israel in Palestine by the late thirteenth century BC and with the archaeological evidence for a somewhat egalitarian culture of highland villages. On the one hand, this egalitarianism would eliminate the need for a hierarchical contract between the inhabitants. On the other hand, it could more easily envision such a vassal treaty/covenant with a God who is worshiped in a context that promotes concerns of social justice (see "Ancient Near Eastern Context" for Judges).

Since Israel was located in a cultural climate influenced by the region of the Hittites to the north and by other cultural conventions of its day, it is not inconceivable that this international vassal treaty form (preserved by the accidents of archaeology primarily among the Hittites) could have been known to some of these early Israelites who had access to neighboring cultures. Accepting the biblical claim of an early date for this covenant is a matter of faith, but the parallels with the second-millennium-BC vassal treaty structure is a matter of comparative literary study.

A more widely accepted objection has been the attempt to find literary parallels between Deuteronomy and the later treaties of the Neo-Assyrian period.[15]

13. Nicholson, *God and His People*.

14. Römer, *Deuteronomistic History*, 74–75.

15. See Otto, "Aspects of Legal Reforms"; idem, "Ursprünge der Bundestheologie."

One early attempt to identify a blessing in a broken section of an Aramaic treaty from Sefire rests on the reconstruction of a single word containing three letters and found following a series of curses. Clearly, this could easily prove to be another curse if the full text were available. More widely accepted has been the attempt of Eckhard Otto and H. U. Steymans to study the curses of Deuteronomy and compare them with curses of similar content and form in the seventh-century-BC vassal treaty of the Assyrian king Esarhaddon.[16] If the wording can be shown to be so close, it must certainly demonstrate a connection with these later treaties rather than earlier ones.

First of all, readers need to recognize that the overall structure of the text of Deuteronomy is the focus of the present discussion. There is no attempt to argue that every verse of every section is proved to come from the second millennium BC. Indeed, it can be argued that the prose of the book reflects an updating in the latter part of the Judean monarchy (eighth through early sixth centuries BC). If this is the case, then a covenant document thought to describe an ongoing relationship between God and Israel might be expected to have been glossed and further defined, keeping with the spirit of the original text. Nevertheless, the emphasis on the words (Deut. 11:18; 31:1, 28) of Moses and the warnings neither to add nor subtract from what is commanded (4:2; 12:32) give one pause before opting for large additions.

A second concern has been the nature of the parallels. Markus Zehnder has demonstrated that the degree of explicit verbal similarity between Esarhaddon's treaty and Deuteronomy 28 is overdrawn; Joshua Berman has considered the same for the laws concerning those who advise turning to other gods in Deuteronomy 13.[17] The wording is different. Further, the scope, purpose, and extant copies of the vassal treaty of Esarhaddon make it unlikely that the Judean scribes would have had access to this document or would have been inclined to use it when the Neo-Assyrian Empire was declining (i.e., the era of King Josiah). Finally, there is no clear dependence of Deuteronomy on Esarhaddon's treaty: virtually all categories of Deuteronomy's contents under consideration appear in Hittite treaties and other documents of the ancient Near East in the second millennium BC. At most, here in Esarhaddon's treaty is evidence of some shared literary traditions. However, Berman demonstrates closer connections between the Hittite vassal treaty and Deuteronomy 13, in terms of content and form, than can be found in comparison with later Neo-Assyrian treaties such as that of Esarhaddon.

So in conclusion, the single most important connection of Deuteronomy to the ancient Near Eastern context is its close relationship to the structure of the Hittite vassal treaties, a structure that changed after the twelfth century BC

16. In addition to the previous footnote, see Steymans, *Deuteronomium 28*. This theory enjoys ongoing support. See Römer, *Deuteronomistic History*, 74–78; idem, *Invention of God*, 203–4.

17. See Zehnder, "Building on Stone? . . . I"; idem, "Building on Stone? . . . II"; Berman, "CTH 133." See also Kitchen, *Reliability*, 292–94.

and is not attested elsewhere except in the covenant of Deuteronomy, as well as the covenants in Exodus and Joshua. Connections such as those between the curses of Deuteronomy 28 and the vassal treaty of Esarhaddon do not demonstrate more than common traditions of expression that can be found in many ancient texts extending over far-reaching geographical and chronological vistas, and going back to the second-millennium-BC Hittite treaties.

Canonical Context

Deuteronomy serves as a final will and testament of Moses to all Israel. Numbers 20:12 makes clear that Moses will not enter the promised land with Israel (see Deut. 1:37). Therefore the introduction of Deuteronomy (1:1–5) situates the events of this book as lying at the end of Israel's time of forty years in the wilderness (Num. 14:33–34). The historical summary of the first four chapters situates Israel's identity and constitution as a people of God at Mount Sinai. It rehearses the manner in which God has led the people through the wilderness, despite their rebellion, and the way in which he has fought for them against their enemies. Corresponding to this review of the events recorded in Exodus and Numbers, Deuteronomy 8 emphasizes God's provision for Israel in the wilderness over the forty years. Chapters 9 and 10 juxtapose this positive view with the sins at Mount Sinai as well as those rebellions on the way to the promised land. This serves as a contrast to the laws God gave Moses. Deuteronomy 11:1–7 returns to the events of the oppression in and deliverance from Egypt, recorded in the first half of the book of Exodus. Deuteronomy 11 summarizes these lessons in the life of Israel and applies them to the land that Israel will begin to possess (see the book of Joshua). In the land as well, Israel will learn about the blessings of prosperity for faithfulness and ultimately about the curses for unfaithfulness—a theme that reaches its fullest exposition in Deuteronomy 28 and also governs the story of Judges, 1–2 Samuel, and 1–2 Kings, as well as many of the psalms and prophetic books.

In the New Testament, Jesus refers to texts from Deuteronomy in some of the key moments of his life. This begins with his temptation in "the wilderness": after Jesus fasts for forty days, the devil invites him to change stones into bread. His refusal to do so is accompanied by the quotation from Deuteronomy 8:3. There God explains the purpose for this wilderness wandering: to teach the people that they will live not only by eating bread but also by the power of God's Word. The forty years of Israel's wandering and its analysis in Deuteronomy 8 become the template for understanding the purpose of Jesus's own preparation and ministry in Matthew 4:4 and Luke 4:4. The example of Israel's wilderness experience provides the model for the people of God, teaching how they need to live by faith, apart from guarantees of material possessions.

The Ten Commandments in the Laws of Deuteronomy

Deuteronomy includes the rehearsal and development of many of the earlier laws in the book of Exodus, especially those in chapters 20–24. In Deuteronomy 5:6–21, the Ten Commandments of Exodus 20:1–17 receive the closest and most complete repetition of any set of laws in the Pentateuch. This also forms the basis for the overall structure of the laws of Deuteronomy 6–25, joined together both by similar ideas and by literary devices such as catchwords and phrases:[a]

1–2 Have no other gods, no image worship (Deut. 6:1–12:28).
3 Don't misuse God's name (Deut. 13:1–14:27).
4 Observe Sabbaths (and festivals) (Deut. 15:1–16:17).
5 Obey parents (and authority figures) (Deut. 16:18–18:22).
6 Don't kill (Deut. 19:1–22:8).
7 Don't commit adultery (Deut. 22:9–23:18 [23:19 MT]).
8 Don't steal (Deut. 23:19 [23:20 MT]–24:7).
9 Don't lie and cheat (Deut. 24:8–25:4).
10 Don't covet (Deut. 25:5–16).

If the laws of Deuteronomy do follow the structure of the Decalogue, then they represent a development of these laws and are presented as the full and final exposition of the earlier laws given at Mount Sinai.

[a] Kaufman, "Structure of the Deuteronomic Law," adapted.

Jesus again refers to Deuteronomy, this time 6:16, where God forbids others to test him. God provides the example of Massah, one of the places in Exodus 17 where Israel complained and thereby tested whether God could provide for their needs. Jesus uses it as the response to another temptation, in which the devil invites him to toss himself down from the Temple Mount and be rescued by angels. This demonstrates the refusal to force God's hand as Israel did and anticipates the crucifixion, where Jesus again refuses to allow his own well-being to supersede God's plan. In both examples, Deuteronomy calls people to faith and faithfulness so that they neither expect God to do what they want nor complain at the first sign of difficulty.

In the Epistles the book of Deuteronomy becomes the symbol of the law, the "embodiment of knowledge and truth" (Rom. 2:20). In Romans, Paul writes that this covenant testifies against Israel—in that it has not fulfilled the covenant. Nevertheless, this brings about God's plan through the ages to benefit the whole world. Paul concludes his warning against the boasting of the Jews, who possess the law, with a reference to the "circumcision . . . of the heart" (Rom. 2:29), a theme that frames the laws of Deuteronomy. Thus, according to Deuteronomy 10:16, God commands all Israel, "Circumcise your heart, and stiffen your neck no longer" (NASB). For Israel, this occurs when it opens itself to the law and recognizes the law as part of God's ongoing plan for Israel.

Yet, as Paul reflects and as the writer of Deuteronomy knew, this would be an impossible task for Israel. So at the end of the laws, Deuteronomy 28 portrays many more judgments against the people of God for their failure than it does blessings for their obedience. These culminate in the exile, in which the covenant blessing of the land is removed from Israel. It becomes a people in exile who are in danger of losing their identity. Deuteronomy 29 begins a kind of second treaty/covenant text at the end of the first treaty/covenant. Again it begins with the titular part (Deut. 29:1–2a [28:69–29:1a MT]). The remainder of the chapter appears as a second historical prologue. However, this time it begins briefly in the past, focuses on the personal decision of Israelites in the present generation, and moves forward to consider the consequences of disobedience. This will be Israel's history. However, the reader of these events now stands on the other side of the exile and sees this judgment.

Such a reader was the apostle Paul, who recognized that the covenant did not lead directly and permanently to the blessings for Israel and for the world. Instead, the sin of Israel brought the judgments. Yet, as Deuteronomy 29:22–29 (29:21–28 MT) demonstrates, even this terrible outcome becomes a means of understanding for both the nations of the world and future generations of Israel beyond the exile. It is to this hope that Paul turns in Romans 10:1–13 as he recalls the words of Deuteronomy 30. Israel has been saved in the exodus experience, and each generation appropriates that in their hearts by faith. The sign of that faith, the circumcision of their hearts in Deuteronomy 10:16, was adherence to the covenant laws. However, the failure of this circumcision and the consequent judgments did not end this faith.

In the life, death, and resurrection of Jesus Christ, now proclaimed as Lord, Paul sees the one Israelite who fulfills the law and makes a way for Israel and for all the nations of the world to find the fulfillment of God's plan. Israel's sin becomes a means for God to act. So the circumcision of the heart in Romans 2:29, reflecting on the command in Deuteronomy 10:16, now through Christ becomes the fulfillment of Deuteronomy 30:6, that "the Lord your God will circumcise your heart so that you may love the Lord your God with all your heart and with all your soul, and so you will have life" (RSH; cf. NRSV).

What God commanded, his grace now makes available. And so it is indeed not "too difficult" (Deut. 30:11 NIV), because what God commands, he now has done through Jesus Christ: Israel and the world need no longer search for the one who is the Messiah, the Christ (whether they realize it or not), neither in the heavens above nor in the earth beneath (Deut. 30:12–14; Rom. 10:6–8). Instead, God's promised circumcision now comes through Jesus Christ, whose obedience moves God's plan for the covenant to its conclusion. In place of the laws and stipulations, there is the gracious act of God, who will give the blessing of life to Israel (Deut. 30:15–20), to enable its people to live fully in the covenant. Paul summarizes this in his exhortation to confess with the mouth and believe in the heart that God has raised the Messiah Jesus from the dead (Rom. 10:9–10).[18] More on the significance of the covenant follows in the next section.

Theological Perspectives of Deuteronomy

The importance of Deuteronomy can be found in three key areas: the significance of the covenant, the meaning and impact of the Ten Commandments, and the foundations of Israelite and Jewish belief as attested in the Shema of 6:4–9. These are perhaps the most important examples of the great theological teachings of this book.

The Covenant

The meaning and application of Deuteronomy as covenant and law builds on the section above, dealing with the canonical context. First, however, readers need to step back and reflect on the nature of the covenant as presented in Deuteronomy. As argued above, there is a close relationship of structure and various aspects of content with the vassal treaty form as found among the Hittites of the second millennium BC. If this is true, and if in some sense Deuteronomy is a product of divine inspiration, then here is an example of the attempt to put the words of God into a known medium of the day. However, the medium is not overtly religious, like a sacrificial text or hymn of praise. Rather, this medium originates in the political world.

It is the genius of Deuteronomy's author to transform the medium and thereby introduce a new means of relationship between a god and his people. All the nations had their chief gods, and in some cases there was talk of some sort of relationship between the god and the community or nation. But only in Israel was this expressed in the detail and public proclamation of a treaty form. What Israel's God demanded and promised was not limited or unknown but rather the explicit promise of an ongoing relationship with his people that they could understand and that God would make possible for them to share in if only they would remain faithful to him. This is an example of a cultural transformation of media, something readers will see again in other contexts of the Old Testament (e.g., the Psalms, the Proverbs, and the Prophets). Its illustration here demonstrates the model of "Christ transforming culture," as expressed so well in Richard Niebuhr's *Christ and Culture*. Ancient cultural

18. See McConville, *Grace in the End*; N. T. Wright, *Justification*.

Treaty and Covenant Vocabulary

Many of the covenant terms share a meaning similar to their usage in the context of treaty. Thus "love" (Deut. 6:5) requires faithfulness, that which is exclusively owed to the overlord. To love God is to be faithful to him.[a] Correspondingly, to hate someone is to become disloyal toward that person. The servant (9:27) is a person who owes exclusive loyalty toward his or her overlord. Israel is God's servant so long as it recognizes exclusive loyalty toward God. "To know" is to recognize this committed relationship. Israel knows God, and God knows Israel so long as this relationship of loyalty remains (7:9; 11:2; 13:3). The "special" (KJV) or "treasured possession" that God recognizes in his choice of Israel also has parallels in treaty language (7:6). Here the Hebrew *sĕgullâ* is related to Akkadian *sikiltu*, used by kings to describe their unique relationship to God. In both the biblical and ancient Near Eastern contexts, it refers to a relationship not determined by blood, but rather one that resembles the adopted son or daughter. This means that God has freely and graciously accepted Israel into a special and intimate relationship.

[a] Moran, "Love of God."

forms were adopted and adapted to meet the theological concerns of the author. In place of a treaty between an overlord and a vassal state, the covenant defined God as Israel's overlord, and Israel was given its responsibilities in a context that it could understand and appropriate.

In the vassal treaty, Hittite overlords emphasize their mercy toward the vassals and their families; so also in the covenant, God emphasizes his mercy toward Israel to forgive (Deut. 4:31). Within the covenant relationship, there is provision for forgiveness through the sacrificial system. As with the treaty, so the covenant ends only through persistent disobedience that mocks the commitment at the heart of the covenant.[19] Such a personal nature to the covenant, coupled with individual responsibility, led directly to the hope of a prophet such as Jeremiah (Jer. 31) for a new covenant written directly on the hearts of the people.

This suggests that the covenant should not be understood as legalism, a means to earn favor with God (and salvation) by obedience. The establishment of the relationship with God, or the primary salvation experience, occurred through the exodus of Israel from Egypt. The nation crossed the Red Sea in safety while God destroyed the enemy army that was intent on destroying Israel as a nation. The laws of the covenant define and provide a means to live

19. Knoppers, "Ancient Near Eastern Royal Grants," 686.

out the already-existing relationship. Since the Hebrew view of the person is that of integrated body and spirit, then that which is believed spiritually and intellectually must be actualized in the form of a life lived in faithfulness to God's covenant.

The Ten Commandments

As noted, the Ten Commandments provide an outline for the remainder of the legal stipulations (see the sidebar "The Ten Commandments in the Laws of Deuteronomy"). For this reason it is worthwhile to consider their structure and application as recorded in Deuteronomy 5:6–21. The "Ten Words," or Decalogue, begin with a formula of self-identification: "I am Yahweh your God, who brought you out of the land of Egypt, out of the house of slaves." In this way God identifies himself by using his personal name and claiming that Israel should recognize him as "your God." The basis for this claim lies in the historic act of redemption that God has enacted in the exodus and by which he freed the people of Israel from slavery.

God is known in a manner different from other deities. Other gods and goddesses also have names, but they are recognized by their forms and images, by their dress and the symbols they may hold in their hands (weapons or other devices important in their myths). Only the God of Israel identifies himself by claiming a people for himself on the basis of a miraculous event that he has performed at a specific point in history. Further, he addresses this to the generation after the one that has actually experienced the exodus. In so doing, it becomes available to every subsequent generation that identifies with that first generation and so participates in the exodus as well. This occurs especially in the celebration of the Sabbath (see below) and in the annual event of the Passover.

This formula identifies Egypt as the "house of slaves." In this manner the special significance of Israel's experience before its redemption is remembered. Israel longed to be free from that difficult and hostile life, and God's redemption released the nation from bondage. The servitude has a religious dimension insofar as it means that Israel served the pharaoh, but then they were freed to serve their true God. It also has a social dimension in that Israel's experience with slavery should enable it to act graciously toward the weak and vulnerable in its own society. Never again should anyone experience oppression and suffering as Israel did.

Verse 7 prohibits the recognition (and presumably the worship) of any god other than Yahweh. This is categorical and exclusive of other competing deities among the nations that Israel will destroy, as well as among those that may be its allies. The implications of this suggest an allegiance to the nation of Israel and to its covenant, as opposed to alliance with any other nation and its god(s). God is not just first but also alone worthy of devotion.

Verses 8–10 prohibit the construction of images of God, especially Israel's God. This is closely tied with verse 7. The reason behind this may be found in Deuteronomy 4:15–20 (v. 15, "You saw no form on the day Yahweh spoke to you at Horeb from the midst of the fire" [RSH]). No rival human witness is acceptable, nor is any attempt to transform the worship of the living God

Deuteronomy 5:6–21

[6]I am Yahweh your God, who brought you out of the land of Egypt, out of the
house of slaves.
[7]Don't have other gods before me. [8]Don't make for yourself images of
anything that is in the sky above, on the earth beneath, or in the waters
under the earth. [9]Don't bow down to them, and don't serve them, because I,
Yahweh your God, am a jealous god who visits the sin of the parents on the
children of the third and fourth (generations) of those who hate me. [10]How-
ever, I show my faithful love to a thousand (generations) of those who love
me and who keep my commands.
[11]Don't mention the name of Yahweh your God for no good reason, because Yahweh will not consider innocent anyone who mentions his name
for no good reason.
[12]Observe the Sabbath to keep it holy, just as Yahweh your God commanded you. [13]Work for six days, and do all your business. [14]However, the
seventh day belongs to Yahweh your God. Don't do any business (then). This
applies to you, to your son and daughter, to your male and female slaves, to
your ox, your donkey, and to all your livestock, and to the foreigner within
your gates. In this way your male and female slave will rest, just like you.
[15]Remember how you were slaves in the land of Egypt and how Yahweh
your God brought you out of there with a strong hand and an outstretched
arm. For this reason Yahweh your God has commanded you to treat the Sabbath day in this way.
[16]Respect your father and mother just as Yahweh your God has commanded you, so that your days may be as long as possible and so that you
may have a good life on the land that Yahweh your God is about to give to
you.
[17]Don't murder!
[18]Don't commit adultery!
[19]Don't steal!
[20]Don't lie under oath to your neighbor!
[21]Don't covet your neighbor's wife! Don't desire your neighbor's house,
his land, his male and female slaves, his oxen and donkeys, or anything that
belongs to your neighbor. (RSH)

into an attachment to a particular object, institution, or routine. The areas from which images may not be drawn parallel those of Genesis 1: the sky, the sea, and the dry land. These are the fundamental categorical divisions of the ancient Israelite worldview.

The "jealousy" of God can also be used to describe the manner in which God is zealous for his honor as a holy God and as God alone. To "hate God" is an expression drawn in part from treaty language to describe disloyalty to God. Correspondingly, to "love God" implies faithfulness and obedience to him. Why does God extend a warning of punishment to the third and fourth generations? Why not extend it to the second, the fifth, or some other generations? The third and fourth generations refer to the grandchildren and great-grandchildren of the one who "hates" God. Such people must know that their beliefs and actions will affect their family as long as they might live, even to their grandchildren and great-grandchildren. Thus the effect on their family remains throughout the lifetime of the faithless Israelites, but not forever.

The reference to God's acts of "showing love" to a thousand implies the superabundance of divine grace on the families of those who remain faithful. Note that this expression, the verb "to do, make" followed by the Hebrew *ḥesed*, "covenantal love, loyalty," is at the heart of the prayer of Abraham's servant who seeks a wife for Abraham's son Isaac (Gen. 24:12–14). It forms part of Rahab's plea for the salvation of her family (Josh. 2:12). In a similar manner here, God promises to bless the family of the faithful person and to preserve and prosper it.

Verse 11 prohibits any misuse of the name of Yahweh. God did not reveal himself in a material form, but he did reveal his personal name. In this way he made his name and thus himself vulnerable to misuse. What sort of misuse does this expression envision? In addition to swearing, this could include any misappropriation of the name for purposes of magic or taking oaths. As with the second commandment, this one refuses to set up a rival to the true God in any form, including that of an image, whether physical or verbal. There is no secret ceremony or hidden knowledge (such as God's name) that only a select few know. It is entirely a matter of risking a personal relationship and the openness of a prescribed public cult and of a name available to everyone. Such regulation is necessary since the spoken word is the one way in which God can be represented. For this reason, denial of this name and of the God it represents does not bode well for anyone, even such powerful figures as the pharaoh (Exod. 5:2) and the Assyrian king Sennacherib (2 Kings 19:20–37 = Isa. 37:22–38).

The previous commands describe how God is *not* to be worshiped; verses 12–15 provide the positive guidance as to how God *is* to be worshiped. The "Sabbath" is a term probably originating in a word meaning "to cease." Certainly the cessation of normal activity is part of Sabbath observance.

However, in the text the sanctifying of the Sabbath carries with it a positive function as well, "to make holy."

In Exodus 20:11 the basis for the Sabbath is tied to the creation of the world in six days, followed by God's rest on the seventh. Thus the Sabbath observance becomes a reflection of the created order. In Deuteronomy, the reason for the Sabbath is attached to God's deliverance of Israel from Egypt. In the Dead Sea Scrolls (4QDeut), the text combines both reasons at this point, clearly a conflation of both Deuteronomy and Exodus.[20] More surprising is that the Masoretic Text of both Deuteronomy and Exodus have not conflated the reasons but have preserved them separately.[21]

The Sabbath, as the setting aside of one day out of every seven to worship God, was considered to be unique to ancient Israel. Although the Akkadian *šappatu* (a word possibly related to Hebrew *šabbāt*) defined the fifteenth day of a month, it is unclear that this had any religious significance or relationship to the Israelite Sabbath. However, an Old Akkadian (third-millennium-BC) text relating to rituals at the temple of the sun-god honored at Sippar in Babylonia mentions liturgical activities to be carried out at the temple on the eighth and fifteenth days of every month as well as possibly on the first day.[22] This, and other rituals like it, provide the closest similarity to a Sabbath outside of the Bible and before Judaism. However, none of this resembles the biblical Sabbath, where the emphasis is on the people and their rest rather than the service of the temple.

Here in Deuteronomy, an additional phrase (v. 14) mandates rest for Israel's slaves. Beyond this, Sabbath sanctification includes remembering that Israel itself was once in servitude and that Yahweh delivered Israel therefrom in Egypt. Thus after commands prohibiting improper worship of Israel's God, this one allows for a particular type of worship, one that remembers God's deliverance and seeks to provide for those who are still in slavery.

Sabbath is connected with the sanctification of time, just as sacrifice is related to the sanctification of the world. In each case part of the whole is given back to the Creator in recognition of his prior ownership. This is the key idea behind the Sabbath law, and arguably it continues to be a valid priority. It thus is not a matter of a specific rule concerning observance of one day in seven in a special way. Instead, it is a recognition that God is the Lord of time, and therefore we as believers should acknowledge this and return to God the first and best part of the "time" that he has given to us. This can be done by setting aside one day, such as Sunday, in a special way to God.

20. See S. White, "All Souls Deuteronomy."

21. This suggests the care with which they were copied. It also raises questions about the value of the Dead Sea Scrolls for OT textual criticism. One cannot assume that these texts preserve better readings.

22. Maul, "Gottesdienst."

Verse 16 commands each listener to honor his or her parents. The expression used here is the sort of honoring that is sometimes offered to God (likewise for the different verb in the parallel in Lev. 19:3). This means that there is basis for the view that, in a society ordered according to the will of God, the parents stand in the place of God in relation to their children. Therefore, this command also serves to connect the preceding four, which deal with the divine realm, with the five that follow, all of which deal with the realm of human society. On the material level, this concern for the respect of parents has parallels in contemporary Babylonian society, where a man faced prison for beating his parents. Thus the concept of honor here has economic implications, such as responsibility to foster well-being and supply food and clothing.

At the fifteenth-century-BC site of Nuzi in northeastern Iraq, a childless couple could "adopt" an adult heir, who would take care of them in exchange for the inheritance upon their death. Burial practices and offerings for the dead might be included in the responsibilities of an obedient child in the ancient world. The chief heir, probably the eldest son, would inherit the land, which constituted the chief inheritance of the family and was the location of the burial plot.[23] So there is the connection between this command and the reference to the land (inheritance) that God has given. Socially, the honoring of parents becomes the model for all hierarchies, both those in the family and those in society.

On a covenant level there is the sense in which the parents are responsible to model and teach the beliefs and ways of the covenant to their children. As they do this, the children learn about and follow their parents in their faith. Thus the parents pass their faith on from one generation to the next. In this manner they experience the blessings of the covenant, which preeminently emphasize security and prosperity in the land that God has given as an inheritance to each family, and so generation after generation lives for many ages in the land of promise. The implication is that the first and primary recipients of this command are the adult Israelites. Of course, this applies to the children and to the entire community, but as with the other commands, the first and primary addressees are the adults in the community.

Verse 17 forbids murder. This does not include prohibition of participating in war or levying a prescribed death penalty, both of which are permitted, according to Deuteronomy 20 and 21. It does emphasize the worth of the person as created in the image of God, something that the text of Genesis 9:5–6 requires. The only adequate exchange for taking human life in personal anger or revenge requires that the life of the guilty party be given. Even killing in warfare was regarded as rendering one unclean in the ancient Near East.

23. For children's responsibilities to their parents, see Hess, "'Because of the Wickedness of These Nations.'"

Bathing rituals for weapons and for warriors are mentioned.[24] However, the biblical text draws a clear line between the intentional taking of innocent life and the killing that occurs through warfare.

This is the first of the commands that is exclusively concerned with social relationships. As already noted, it is not randomly placed. It represents the primary and absolute value of human life.

In verse 18 adultery is forbidden. In this situation at least one of the parties involved is married. In some ways this is the worst of all sexual offenses because it involves the breaking of a covenantal marriage commitment. Therefore, the punishment is capital.

In the Bible and ancient Near Eastern world, adultery was understood as sexual intercourse between a man and the wife of another man, without the permission of the husband.[25] In the Bible, the husband has the right to demand punishment or not, but he cannot punish the other man without punishing his own wife at least as severely (so as to prevent collusion and entrapment). In the ancient Near East, adultery was conceived at least in part as an offense between the two men. Nevertheless, in both Mesopotamia and in the Bible, male promiscuity and adultery were regarded as shameful and causing defilement.[26]

In the Bible, adultery also breaks an agreed-upon contract between two parties. Since this contract is the basis for the formation of the family, the foundation of social order, it symbolizes all contracts and warns against tampering with them. Therefore, the prohibition of adultery seeks to preserve both the family order and the larger order of society. In the social laws, violation of this prohibition is second in rank only to the destruction of human life.

Verse 19 prohibits theft. Since the earlier offenses of murder and adultery are capital ones, the expectation is that this too should be a capital offense. Therefore, some have seen here a particular kind of theft: kidnapping. This may be involved, but the wording of the text does not require it. On the one hand, given the context of the relative set of values found here and elsewhere in the law codes of the Bible, and in contrast with other codes of the ancient Near East, readers do better to see here a prohibition of theft in general. On the other hand, kidnapping violates a specific covenant bond between people in society, the mention of which fits well with the Decalogue's context in the covenant of Deuteronomy. Private property is acceptable in the biblical faith. However, it is not more important than human life or the marriage relationship. Thus all material possessions are relativized before these greater values.

24. Riley, "Does Yhwh Get His Hands Dirty?"

25. Westbrook, "Adultery." However, it is nowhere explicit in the Bible that men cannot be guilty of adultery as well. See Prov. 6:32, where a man is warned against committing adultery with someone else's wife.

26. Van der Toorn, *Sin and Sanction*.

In verse 20 false witness is prohibited. In the Decalogue, this serves to establish some order in running courts and making inquiry into crimes. It is therefore primarily concerned with judicial perjury. At the same time, the covenantal interest means that what is involved here is keeping covenant with one's own word, involving a concern to portray truth and reality without slanting it to one's own benefit, and also a concern that the word of a person be reliable.

Verse 21 forbids coveting. Although there has been much discussion on this command, the Hebrew describes a desire for what is not one's own. As Peter Craigie emphasizes, this is the heart of self-interest's exposure that permeates the second half of the Decalogue.[27] The breaking of many of the other commands begins with the violation of this command in the heart. It is the one command that cannot be prosecuted in a court, but it lies at the base of many violations. The first verb for "covet" suggests an emotion that leads to action. The second verb (v. 22) focuses on the emotions.

The order of people and things to be coveted is different in Exodus and in Deuteronomy. In Deuteronomy, the first item coveted is the neighbor's wife. This receives a separate clause. It is best explained by understanding that the Exodus passage is interested in emphasizing the property concerns at this point, but Deuteronomy continues to specify the neighbor's covenantal relationship: the most binding relationship is with one's spouse (and family), and secondarily with one's household and its members.

The Shema

The first three verses of Deuteronomy 6 follow the Decalogue of chapter 5 and its concluding instructions from God that he will give the laws to teach the people (v. 31). These laws are designed for life in the promised land (6:1), to be lived by all generations of Israel (v. 2). They provide success, increase in numbers, and a fruitful land (v. 3). In order to achieve this, there follows the most important of the commands, appearing at the head of the instructions that begin in 6:4.

Deuteronomy 6:4 9 begins with the Hebrew word *šĕma'*. As with the books of the Pentateuch, where the first important word forms the Hebrew title, so here the text that follows is called the Shema. This word is a command: "Hear!" The command to hear is more than the exercise of an auditory facility. Hearing in the Bible is closely connected with assent, obedience, and action. Those who hear should prepare to obey. The second word, "Israel," identifies the intended audience. This is not limited to the Israel that stands before Moses, preparing to cross over the Jordan to the promised land. It includes all later generations who, when they read this scroll of Deuteronomy and recite the Shema, again stand before Moses and hear the divine words.

27. Craigie, *Deuteronomy*.

Deuteronomy 6:4–9

4Hear, O Israel! Yahweh our God, Yahweh is one.

5Love Yahweh your God with all of your heart, with all of your soul, and with all of your ability.

6Let these words that I command you today be on your heart.

7Teach them to your children while you are living in your home, while you are traveling on the road, as you lie down, and as you get up.

8Bind them as a sign on your hand and make them into a marker on your forehead.

9Write them on the doorframe of your home and on your gates. (RSH)

The phrase that follows constitutes four words in Hebrew, literally, "Yahweh–our God–Yahweh–one." The personal name of God occurs twice. Along with this covenant name, there appears the confession that this Deity is Israel's God. He does not belong to one Israelite and not another, but he belongs to all who confess him and his covenant. Thus here he is not "my God" but "our God." The four words come to a climax with the final declaration: "Yahweh is one." Oneness carries with it the sense of the single Deity as opposed to the several or many gods who were worshiped by every other nation in the ancient Near East.[28] This excludes religious pluralism as an option for Israel. The Israelites cannot and must not recognize multiple gods as legitimate or confess other equally legitimate ways to know the Sovereign Creator. Furthermore, the combining of Yahweh with other gods and their characteristics, a phenomenon known as syncretism and very popular in the ancient world, is excluded by the confession that Yahweh is absolutely unique.

Oneness also implies a simplicity of will. There is only one set of commands, one force guiding the world and Israel. Thus there is no contradiction in commands, nor is there need to worry which deity should be appeased. This is not to suggest that God is not complex in his manner and forms of revelation. However, it does imply that there is no further court of appeal, and there is no option in terms of the instructions that follow.

In Deuteronomy 6:5, "love" forms the second command after the one to hear. As already mentioned, in a covenantal context this implies the necessity of loyal obedience. It also suggests that there can be a means of expressing and possessing a relationship with the God of Israel.[29] There is no evidence that the meaning of the term "love" was limited to treaty language. In its Old Testament context, it could involve helping or being beneficial to some-

28. Cf. Block, "How Many Is God?"
29. Moran, "Love of God."

one, such as the neighbor. "Love!" implies not only obedience (the meaning of the term in the treaty language: faithfulness to the covenant) but also the engagement of the whole person in relation to the divine, resembling the parent-child relationship. This becomes clear in the description of the various aspects of the human that follow, elements that constitute the loving and loyal person.[30]

The "heart" is the Hebrew term *lēb* (*lēbāb*). It constitutes the mind or reason, which directs the rest of the person. The term appears to describe the physical heart in 1 Samuel 25:37–38 and in Jeremiah 4:19, where it may identify a heart attack. It can describe feelings, not often, but certainly in Proverbs 14:30; 15:13; and 17:22. The term can be used for wish, desire, and longing, such as in Psalm 21:2 and Numbers 15:39. Elsewhere, especially in 1 Kings 3:9–12, the heart is the center of the mind and reason. The mind and emotions affect the decisions of the will toward obedience, as here, in Deuteronomy 8:2, and with Ezekiel's concern to get a new heart in 18:31. This term also describes the heart of God, as in Hosea 11:8–9: "How can I give you up, O Ephraim! . . . My heart turns over within me, my compassion is mightily kindled. I will not execute my fierce anger. . . . For I am God and not man" (RSH). This refers to the overthrow of God's deliberate decision. God's unqualified mercy turns against his decision for judgment. God's heart, or his free resolve of love, turns against his decision of anger. Without knowledge of the heart of God, a person's real situation is incomprehensible, as is the sacrifice of God's Son.

The second term, often translated as "soul," is the Hebrew *nepeš*. It identifies the life desire of the person. Genesis 2:7 understands it as a combination of flesh (dust) and spirit (breath). Physically, it can refer to the throat, as in Isaiah 5:14 and Psalm 105:18. However, it most frequently describes desire, especially the desire for life, as in Deuteronomy 23:24 (23:25 MT) and Proverbs 16:26. This can describe the life situation of the person (Exod. 23:9) and the source of life, identified with the sanctity of blood in Leviticus 17:11. The command in Deuteronomy 6:5 thus means that one should carry all one's longing desire into love for God. As a corollary, it also implies that God meets the deepest desires of the person. The *nepeš* is the element of the person that desires life, seeks it out, and experiences it. It is the vitality of the person. In itself it is not sufficient, but it is always needy and desiring. At the root of this desire, God meets the person, whether in the covenant of the Old Testament or the New Testament.

The word usually translated as "strength" is Hebrew *mĕʾōd*. It seems tied closely with the physical strength of the person and so enables the performance of tasks prescribed by God's will.

30. Westermann, *Anthropology and the Old Testament*; Di Vito, "Old Testament Anthropology."

Thus the person is described as loving God through the totality of a decision of the mind and will, a direction of the desires, and a physical affirmation in the performance of what is required. The corresponding implications are that God's word does appeal to reason and understanding, that obeying it fulfills the most basic human desires/needs, and that accomplishing this does not lie beyond a person's ability.

Verses 6–9 go on to apply this command and its understanding to education. There is a specific concern to understand the will of God (v. 6), keeping his words on the heart and the mind, where they can be understood as one meditates on them, fostering the will where the decision can be made to obey. The first verb in verse 7, "repeat," requires the passing on of the commands to the next generation. It is done, not in a particular school, but at all times in the course of life, and throughout the day. The hand and forehead of verse 8 suggest the strength and identity (Ezek. 9:4) of the person. In verse 9 the house and (city) gates represent the family and society. Many temples and cultic objects in Palestine were placed at the gates of the city. In this manner the visitor entering the gate would immediately know who guarded and was responsible for that population. So Israel is to identify its God, not through an image, but through the divine instruction of God's word.

This education is to take place everywhere, through the whole life of the person, and permeate into every family and the whole of society. Education defined the roles a person played in society and thereby determined the identity of the person. In Judaism in the Old Testament period, in Jesus's time, and right up to the present, this passage has remained central. In many traditions, these words or other parts of the law of God are written down and the texts are attached to doorposts, or at times of prayer they are bound in phylacteries on the forehead and on the arms. But beyond this, here is the basis for the extraordinary value placed on education. In Christianity, too often the facile rejection of these chapters as legalistic has meant overlooking the important basis that they serve for teaching about who people are.

The love of God is the first prerequisite for the giving of the covenant. God must love the people to whom the covenant relationship is offered, and the people must choose to love God in accepting the covenant. The expression of love for God and the continued relationship with God involves the exertion of the mind and will as well as the attitude of openness that allows the divine to meet the most basic needs and desires of the person. The covenant of God separates the people who accept it from the rest of the world. It does not allow for acceptance or incorporation of other gods and goddesses. It does not allow the people of God to accept any involvement with these other groups who worship other gods. The uniqueness of God and the demand for exclusive worship are results of the holiness of God.

Key Commentaries and Studies

Christensen, Duane L. *Deuteronomy*. Vol. 1, *1:1–21:9*. Rev. ed. Vol. 2, *21:10–34:12*. WBC 6A–B. Waco: Word, 2001–2. Analyzes Deuteronomy as a poem composed of five concentric units. Important evangelical exegesis.

Craigie, Peter C. *The Book of Deuteronomy*. NICOT. Grand Rapids: Eerdmans, 1976. Clearly written evangelical, exegetical study making use of the comparative ancient Near Eastern materials.

McConville, J. Gordon. *Deuteronomy*. AOTC 5. Leicester, UK: Apollos; Downers Grove, IL: InterVarsity, 2002. Evangelical theological source.

———. *Grace in the End: A Study in Deuteronomistic Theology*. SBT. Carlisle, UK: Paternoster, 1993. Useful summary of theology.

Miller, Patrick D. *Deuteronomy*. IBC. Louisville: John Knox, 1990. Theological application in the context of comparative ancient Near Eastern materials.

Nelson, Richard D. *Deuteronomy: A Commentary*. OTL. Louisville: Westminster John Knox, 2002. Critical and exegetical.

Rad, Gerhard von. *Deuteronomy: A Commentary*. Translated by Dorothea Barton. OTL. Philadelphia: Westminster, 1966. Classic theological study.

Richter, Sandra L. "Environmental Law in Deuteronomy: One Lens on a Biblical Theology of Creation Care." *BBR* 20 (2010): 355–76. An ecological perspective for Deuteronomy.

Thompson, John A. *Deuteronomy: An Introduction and Commentary*. TOTC. Leicester, UK: Inter-Varsity; Downers Grove, IL: InterVarsity, 1974. Evangelical and strong on ancient Near Eastern backgrounds.

Wright, Christopher J. H. *Deuteronomy*. NIBC. Peabody, MA: Hendrickson, 1996. Evangelical, with emphasis on ethics and theology.

PART 2

HISTORICAL BOOKS

The Historical Books include Joshua, Judges, Ruth, 1–2 Samuel, 1–2 Kings, 1–2 Chronicles, Ezra, Nehemiah, and Esther. The only explicit indicators of authorship are in the book of Nehemiah, with its first-person notes. Jewish tradition assigns the book of Judges and some of 1–2 Samuel to Samuel; 1–2 Kings reached their completion in the exile or afterward. Sources are mentioned in these books (as already in Josh. 10) but no specific authors. Rabbinic tradition also assigns 1–2 Chronicles to Ezra, in addition to the book that bears his name. These traditions come via texts written much later, so it is difficult to know the degree of certainty that readers should give to them.

The Historical Books are more or less in chronological order, from the death of Moses until and including Israel's experiences in the Persian Empire. The story begins with Israel crossing the Jordan River under the leadership of Joshua, successor to Moses. With Yahweh's help, the Israelites fight and overcome the strongholds of Jericho and Ai, as well as the gathered Canaanite armies of the southern and northern coalitions. There follows Joshua's allotment of the Holy Land to the tribes of Israel and their clans. Close to his death, Joshua renews the covenant that God made with Israel at the time of Moses. In the following generations, God raises up judges, who deliver the nation, or parts of it, from their oppressors. As Israel turns away from God and worships other gods, the God of Israel then punishes his people by allowing another nation to subdue and abuse them. The people repent of their sin of choosing to worship other gods and call on God for salvation. He takes

KINGS OF ISRAEL AND JUDAH

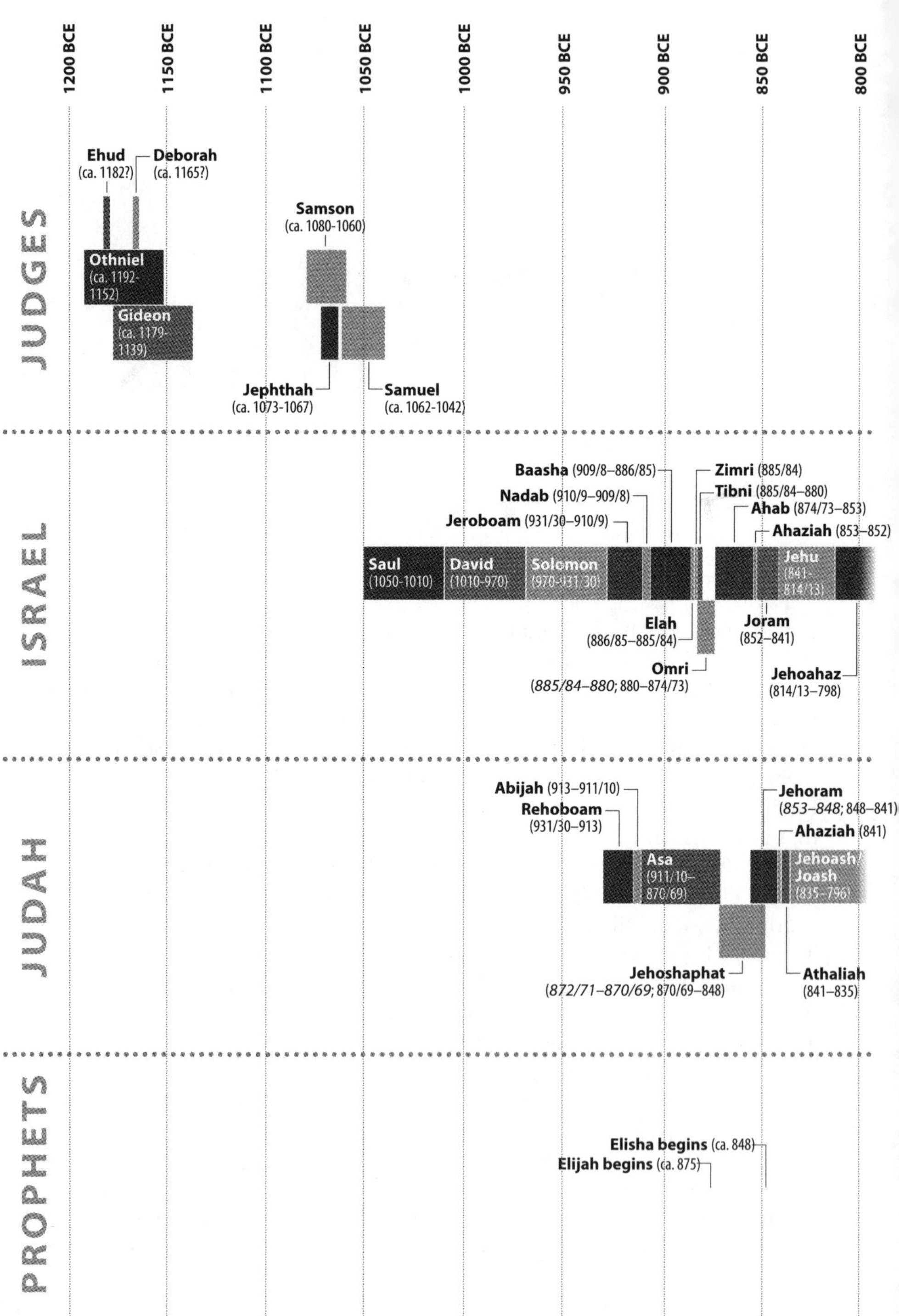

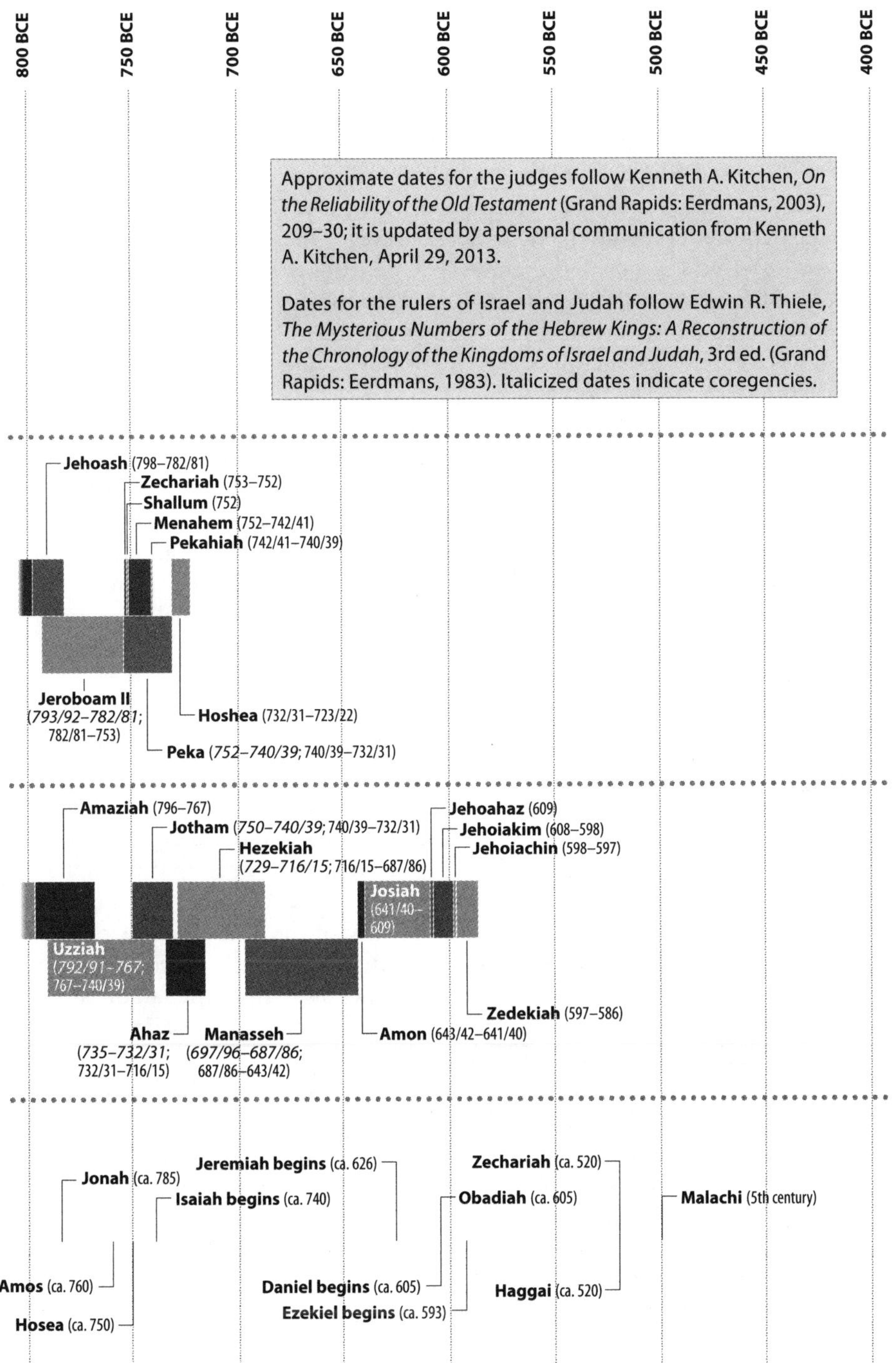

© Baker Publishing Group

pity on them and sends judges to deliver them. Israel again enjoys peace and prosperity, but with the death of each deliverer, they return to the worship of other gods. The cycle continues like this but spirals downward into civil war, where the tribe of Benjamin is almost wiped out. The story of Ruth provides a contrast of peace and love in place of war and killing. God is still at work in Israel, bringing Ruth, a foreigner from Moab, to faith in him and to love and marry Boaz in Bethlehem. Ruth becomes one of the ancestors of King David.

The last judge is the prophet Samuel, who guides Israel to fight against their chief foreign enemy, the Philistines. However, the people demand a king, as the other nations around them have. God leads Samuel and Israel in the choice of Saul, who directs the army to fight the enemies of Israel. But he proves disobedient, and God chooses David of Bethlehem to lead Israel in Saul's place. Saul resists this, seeks to kill David, and ultimately dies on the battlefield, defeated by the Philistines. David now becomes king, first over the southern kingdom of Judah, and then over all Israel. He rules from Jerusalem and defeats Israel's enemies, creating an empire that stretches from Egypt to the Euphrates River. However, he has his servant Uriah killed in order to marry Uriah's wife, Bathsheba. God condemns this, and the sin brings strife into David's household. David's kingdom passes to his son Solomon, who requests wisdom from God to lead the people. God grants this, and Solomon builds a magnificent temple dedicated to the God of Israel. However, influenced by his many foreign wives, Solomon sins by turning from God to worship foreign gods.

In 731 BC, God removes the northern kingdom from the control of Solomon's son Rehoboam. The northern kingdom, Israel, has a series of dynasties that turn from God and encourage the people to worship away from Jerusalem and the temple there. The worst of these kings is Ahab, who marries Jezebel, a princess from the Canaanite city of Tyre. She tries to replace the Lord with the false god Baal as the national deity of Israel. God raises up the prophet Elijah, who defeats her plans. His successor, Elisha, continues to represent the worship of the true God in Israel while most of the kings lead the people astray. The final generation includes great material accomplishments by King Jeroboam II, but his death is only a few decades away from the fall of Israel to the Assyrians (722 BC) as judgment for their failure to worship the true God of Israel (who had given them this land in the first place).

Meanwhile, in the southern kingdom of Judah, more kings worship the true God at his temple in Jerusalem and seek to be faithful to him. Jehoshaphat extends Judah's strength in the ninth century BC. In 701 BC Hezekiah faithfully withstands the Assyrian army, which destroyed the northern kingdom two decades earlier. Eighty years later, in 622 BC, the young king Josiah reforms the nation under the guidance of the book of the law, likely the text of Deuteronomy found while the temple was being cleaned in preparation for its rededication and use. Nevertheless, the following kings do not seek the Lord

© Baker Publishing Group and Dr. James C. Martin

Relief (ca. 730–727 BC) of Tiglath-pileser III attacking a city. Tiglath-pileser III was one of the foreign kings who conquered the kings of Israel.

with their whole heart. In 587/586 BC the Babylonian army enters Jerusalem, destroys the temple, and deports a portion of the population.

One of the last Judean rulers who was deported to Babylon was King Jehoiachin. By the end of 2 Kings (25:27–30) he is portrayed as eating at the Babylonian king's table. This note gives hope that all is not lost and that the story of God's work with his people may move forward. In 539 BC, King Cyrus of Persia enters Babylon and brings all the lands of that empire under the dominion of the Persian Empire. A grandson of Jehoiachin returns with others to rebuild the temple in Jerusalem and to reestablish God's rule there. The challenges of this small group in Jerusalem continue over the next century as the governor Nehemiah and the scribe Ezra come from Persia to Jerusalem. Nehemiah oversees the rebuilding of the walls, despite opposition from surrounding states and local rulers. He insists that the people take care of one another and that they avoid marriage entanglements with those outside the community of faith (unlike Solomon). Ezra reads the law of the Pentateuch before the people in the midst of Jerusalem. He brings them back to faithful observance of God's covenant. Far away from Jerusalem, in the halls of power at the capital of the Persian Empire, the faithful Jew Esther weds King Xerxes and becomes queen. She overcomes the threat of genocide to deliver God's people from destruction. This becomes celebrated annually in the Feast of Purim.

Thus the history of Israel repeatedly emphasizes the importance of the wholehearted dedication of God's people to his covenant and especially to the worship of God alone.

6

JOSHUA

Perhaps the greatest challenge to belief in Israel's (and Christianity's) God is his apparent brutality in commanding the destruction of the Canaanites. Nowhere does this issue come into sharper focus than in the book of Joshua.

Name, Text, and Outline

The name of the book of Joshua is the same in both the Hebrew and Greek texts. "Joshua" (Heb. *yĕhôšua'*) refers to its chief human character, Joshua son of Nun, who appears throughout the work. The Masoretic Text of Joshua diverges from that of the Septuagint in several places. Various details of the allotments in chapters 16 and 18–19 disagree. The towns of refuge listed in Joshua 20:4–6 are not found in the Septuagint. The last five verses of Joshua (24:29–33) follow a different order in the Septuagint. Like the parallel text of Judges 2:6–9, the Septuagint of Joshua places the notice of Israelite faithfulness before Joshua's death. In the Septuagint Joshua concludes with a more extended passage parallel to Judges 3:12, 14. Most significant, the text regarding the building of the altar in 8:30–35 of the Masoretic Text follows 9:1–2 in the Septuagint. This may or may not be related to the two fragments of Joshua from the Dead Sea Scrolls, 4QJosh[a] and 4QJosh[b].[1] In particular, 4QJosh[a] positions Joshua 8:34–35 before a paragraph otherwise unattested and then continues the text with Joshua 5:2–7 and selections from chapters 6–10. Minor differences, such as the use of the name Achar for Achan in Joshua 7

1. Tov, "4QJosh[b]"; Greenspoon, "Qumran Fragments."

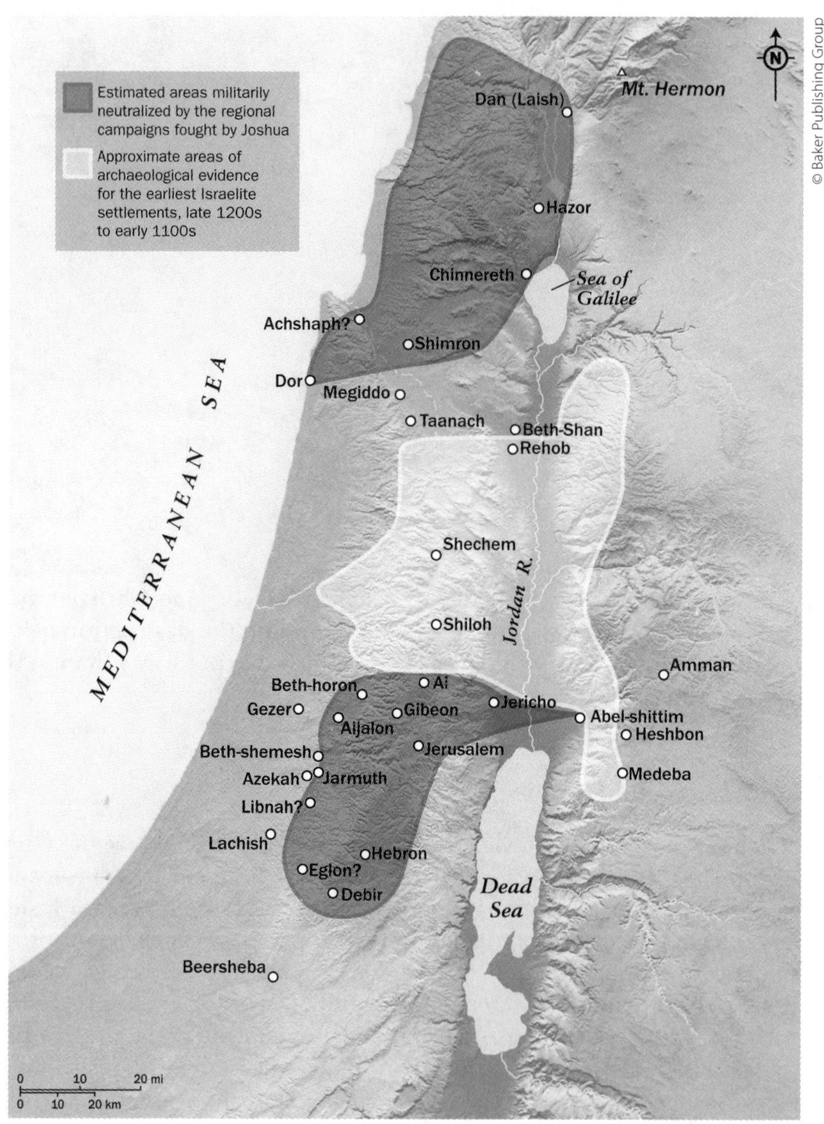

Map of major places in the book of Joshua

(cf. MT, NRSV: Achan in 7:1, 18–20; Achor in 7:24, 26; Achar in 1 Chron. 2:7), add to the impression of a different text attested by the Septuagint, in contrast to the Masoretic Text.[2] Nevertheless, the Masoretic Text appears internally consistent in its ordering of the text. It also remains closer to ancient parallels in the names it records.

2. Hess, "Achan."

OUTLINE

I. The Battles of Israel (1:1–12:24)
   A. Joshua as Leader (1:1–18)
   B. Rahab as Leader of Her People (2:1–24)
   C. Israel Enters the Promised Land (3:1–5:12)
   D. Israel Defeats Its Enemies (5:13–11:11)
      1. Jericho (5:13–6:27)
      2. Ai (7:1–8:29)
      3. Ebal: Covenant Renewal (8:30–35)
      4. Gibeon: The Exception (9:1–27)
      5. Southern Coalition (10:1–43)
      6. Northern Coalition (11:1–11)
   E. Summary (11:12–12:24)
II. The Allotments of Israel (13:1–21:45)
   A. Remaining Land (13:1–7)
   B. Tribes East of the Jordan River (13:8–33)
   C. Judah (14:1–15:63)
   D. Joseph Tribes (16:1–17:18)
   E. Remaining Allotments (18:1–19:51)
   F. Towns of Refuge (20:1–9)
   G. Levitical Towns (21:1–42)
   H. Conclusion (21:43–45)
III. Worship in the Land (22:1–24:33)
   A. Disputed Altar (22:1–34)
   B. Joshua's Addresses (23:1–24:27)
   C. The Settlement (24:28–33)

Overview of Joshua

The book of Joshua begins after the death of Moses with the need for a replacement of leadership. The first five verses of the work outline the book with commands as to what Joshua and Israel must do. The emphasis shifts to God's promise to remain with Joshua and Israel as a means to enable the leader to meditate on and to obey God's word. As Joshua charges Israel to prepare to cross the Jordan in three days, so he challenges the tribes east of the Jordan River to remain loyal even though they already possess their land.

The second chapter of Joshua addresses the role of Rahab as a figure who represents the Canaanites. She leads her family in her faithful confession of God and his historic acts of redemption, as well as in providing salvation for the spies and thus for her family. Chapters 3 and 4 describe how God provides a miracle for this generation to cross the Jordan on dry ground, just as the previous generation crossed the Red Sea. After entering the promised land, they circumcise their men and celebrate the Passover by eating the firstfruits of the barley harvest (Josh. 5). Joshua's confrontation with the commander of the Lord of Hosts turns into instructions that God gives for securing Jericho's submission. The remainder of chapter 6 describes Israel's obedience to those instructions in marching around Jericho for seven days before the collapse of the walls and the victory of Israel. The preservation of Rahab and her family balances and interweaves with this story. Chapter 7 describes the first assault on the next target, Ai. This fails because of the unfaithfulness of Achan, who did not destroy all the remains of Jericho but kept some valuables for himself. He remains quiet about this violation of God's commands until he is identified by lot as the culprit. The Israelites need to deal with this sin before they can hope for God's help in their struggles in the land. Thus they put to death Achan and all his family, who might well have known of the stolen items hidden under their tent.

The second assault on the fortress of Ai succeeds (Josh. 8). Joshua uses a ploy in which he leads the army at Ai out of their fort and then has a prepared ambush consisting of Israelites who come from behind the Ai army and squeeze the enemy force. The result is the destruction of the Ai army and the execution of its king. This opens the route for Israel into the central hill country of the promised land. Joshua 8:30–35 records how this access enables Joshua to assemble Israel at Mount Ebal, just north of Shechem. There he leads the people in a renewal of their dedication to God.

With these victories the fame of Israel becomes even better known in the region. The leaders west of the Jordan River make plans to defeat and destroy the people of God (9:1–2). However, the citizens of Gibeon (north of Jerusalem and south of Bethel) decide to try a ruse of their own. Believing that Israel will not make a peace treaty with anyone in the promised land, they pretend to come to God's people from a far and distant land, outside Palestine. With worn clothes and moldy food, they persuade Israel to accept their word and to make a peace treaty. Israel fails to bring this matter before God and so errs in its judgment. With the treaty concluded, Israel learns of the Gibeonite ruse but is now bound by oaths of loyalty to protect this people. So they make the best of a bad situation. Led by Joshua, the people agree to allow the Gibeonites to continue to live but require them to serve as woodcutters and water carriers for God's holy place.

When the Canaanite (or Amorite) king of Jerusalem learns what his neighbors have done, he organizes a coalition of the leading powers in southern Palestine to defeat and destroy Gibeon (Josh. 10). However, Gibeon appeals to Israel to come to its aid. A nightlong march allows the Israelites to surprise the Amorite army. With divinely sent miracles, such as the casting of hailstones on the enemy and what may be the lengthening of the day, God fights for Israel and kills more of the enemy than do the Israelites themselves. They seem to follow God's work west into the Beth Horon pass and then south and east in an arc that encompasses the major fortified centers of the south. In a repetitive style reminiscent of ancient Near Eastern conquest accounts, Israel comes to fortified center after fortified center and reduces each one to rubble. The effect is to eliminate all resistance across the region. As a sign of victory, Israel hangs the enemy kings who led the attack.

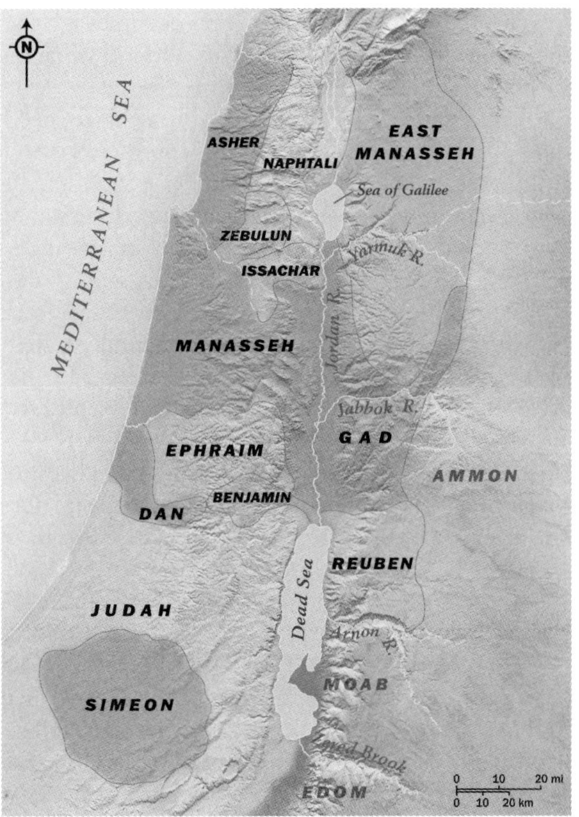

Areas of the tribal allotments

International Mapping

Joshua 11 recounts the battle with the coalition of northern enemies. This is led by the mighty city of Hazor, leader throughout southern Canaan in size and strength. The northern campaign quickly turns into a rout in which Israel pursues the Canaanites around the Galilee and destroys their forces. They also demolish and burn the city fortress of Hazor. This victory and all the victories of the Israelite army over their enemies east and west of the Jordan River are summarized in Joshua 12.

Joshua 13–19 outlines the land not yet attacked (13:1–7) and then devotes great detail to defining the places allotted to each tribe of Israel. Joshua 13:8–33 reviews those tribal lands of Reuben, Gad, and the half-tribe of Manasseh east of the Jordan River. These are described primarily in terms of regions. Chapters 14 and 15 consider the southern allotment of the tribe of Judah, first according to its boundaries and then by describing regions within the tribes according to their towns. Joshua 14 and 15:13–19 interweave narratives from Caleb's family into the allotment of Judah. In chapter 14 Caleb testifies of his faithfulness to God from the previous generation when, as one of the twelve sent to spy out the land of Canaan, he counseled that Israel could indeed take the land and defeat its enemies. In the section on Caleb in the following chapter, this hero drives out three Anakites who occupied Hebron and then gives his daughter to Othniel, who occupies nearby Kiriath-sepher. He then gives them springs connected with the land when his daughter requests them for herself and her husband.

Chapters 16 and 17 recount the allotments to the "Joseph" tribes of Ephraim and half of Manasseh (the sons of Joseph in Genesis). This forms the center of the northern part of Israel, in the hill country where the nation first settles. All the remaining tribal allotments are addressed in Joshua 18–19. This section concludes with Joshua's personal inheritance and his future burial site (19:49–50).

Chapter 20 summarizes the towns of refuge, scattered throughout the allotments, to which one who has accidentally killed another person may flee in order to avoid a vendetta from the dead person's family. Chapter 21 concludes the allotments by outlining the forty-eight towns scattered throughout the tribes that are to be given to the Levite tribe. The Levites receive no land inheritance because they are to devote their lives to serving God's sacrificial system and to assisting Israel in the service of and obedience to God. Thus these towns form a return gift from Israel to God. As the people were first given all the towns by God, now they set aside some of these towns for divine service.

The final three chapters begin with a dispute concerning an altar near the Jordan constructed by the tribes east of the Jordan in their own land (22:10–11). This creates concern from the tribes west of the Jordan that their fellow Israelites might violate God's covenant by sacrificing outside the promised land (west of the Jordan River). However, the tribes east of the Jordan avoid a civil war when they affirm that they do not intend to perform sacrifices on the altar but rather intend to use it as a memorial and a reminder that they are part of the nation and faith west of the Jordan. Chapters 23–24 form two sermons given by Joshua at the end of his life. His purpose is to exhort all Israel to continue to remain faithful to God and his covenant for all their lives and for the lives of future generations. The people affirm their intent to serve God alone. The final verses in the book, 24:28–33, record the faithfulness of Israel throughout the remainder of Joshua's life. They conclude with the deaths and burials of Joshua and of Eleazar the high priest.

Reading Joshua

Premodern Readings

The book of Joshua was received in the synagogue as an application of the teachings of the Torah and as a source of midrashic interpretation for the guidance of one's life. Thus the example of Achan proves that the confession of one's sin when facing capital punishment provides atonement for a believing Jew despite the nature of the crime. Joshua promises Achan that the Lord will bring trouble on him "today," but not in the life to come. There he will be received as a member of the covenant (*m. Sanhedrin* 6.2). In the early church, Joshua became a foreshadowing of Jesus Christ through types of Christ, as seen in the commander of the Lord's army (Josh. 5:13–15) and in the very name of Joshua himself, a name that is identical to Jesus in the Greek Bible (Eusebius, *Preparation for the Gospel* 1.3.3–4).

It was especially in the Renaissance that interest in historical claims led to understanding the picture of the book of Joshua in historical terms. The book itself reflects a culture and life different from that of the Middle Ages; however, explanations for events in the past could be understood by using analogies with the present. Thus the historicity of the Bible, and of Joshua in particular, became an accepted assumption at the time of the Reformation. A literal interpretation of the text was assumed. The destruction of the Canaanites, beginning with the victory over the inhabitants of Jericho, occupied both an optimistic and Romantic place in the stories of heroes and successes among the Old Testament people of God, as well as the front stage for Enlightenment luminaries who attacked the God of the Old Testament as cruel and vindictive. Thus the focus of interpretation of the book of Joshua remained on the narratives of the first half.

From these premodern readings, two dominant thematic directions emerged. One remained in the sphere of popular theology. It saw Joshua as a type of Christ and the conquest of the Canaanites as a metaphor for the Christian life as one of victory over sin when accompanied by a strong faith in Christ. The second dominant stream examined the ethics of the Israelite invasion and found them wanting. How could a loving God endorse the deaths of so many innocent women and children? This ethical concern was and remains a primary cause for doubt and rejection concerning the God of the Bible.

Higher Criticism[3]

Earlier critical studies of the book of Joshua extended the sources of the Pentateuch into this work. Some argued that it was part of an original Hexateuch that included the Pentateuch plus Joshua. However, it was felt that Joshua was removed from the other five scrolls due to its political implications as a claim to Israelite sovereignty over the promised land. The recognition of this close connection was based on the flow of narrative from the final chapter of Deuteronomy into the first chapter of Joshua and from similarities of vocabulary and theology that the two books share.

In 1943 Martin Noth introduced the term and theory of "Deuteronomistic History."[4] He suggested that an editor living at the end of the monarchy (sixth century BC) had access to historical records in Jerusalem and put together a

3. See summaries in Richter, *Deuteronomistic History*; idem, "Deuteronomistic History"; and Römer, *Deuteronomistic History*.

4. Noth, *Deuteronomistic History*.

work that comprised the narrative sections at the beginning and end of Deuteronomy, as well as the scrolls of Joshua, Judges, 1–2 Samuel, and 1–2 Kings. The name Deuteronomistic (also called Deuteronomist)[5] derives from the book of Deuteronomy and the supposed D source, both of which related to the history theologically and perhaps in terms of having the same authors or editors. The language of covenant, as found in Deuteronomy, also occurs in these books. Indeed, Noth argued that the entire purpose of the story was to explain how God could allow his temple and his city to be destroyed by the Babylonians in 587/586 BC. This was due to the unfaithfulness of the people and their leaders, who turned from the covenant of Deuteronomy and worshiped other gods. The notes and speeches placed in the Historical Books formed the basis for this primary theme, which can be traced throughout the work.

The evaluation of Joshua and the Deuteronomistic History is based on various claims. It is indeed "Deuteronomistic" if the term means that it preserves a similar theological perspective and language as that found in Deuteronomy. Daniel Block has demonstrated that the ideas and even the expressions that characterized the national theology (or ideology) were preserved for centuries in similar literature in the ancient Near East.[6] Another concept, God placing his name on Jerusalem, is not a late hypostatic idea of some sort of "name theology," as some have argued. Instead, it represents an ancient idea expressed throughout the Semitic world already in the second millennium BC.[7]

However, the mere editing of existing and ancient records is often not the primary concern of the theory of the Deuteronomistic History. Instead, the emphasis is placed on the bias, distortion, and wholesale invention of the history. This was coupled with controversy about when this happened and how many editors put the work together substantially as now extant. Thus Frank Moore Cross of Harvard University and his student Richard Nelson argued for two editors.[8] One editor composed the Deuteronomistic History in Josiah's time to advocate that king's religious movement and to centralize power against those who were opponents of a single God who could be worshiped in a single place, Jerusalem. A second editor added the conclusion to 2 Kings after the exile.

John Van Seters, however, argued for Noth's single editor in the exile (mid-sixth century BC) but called into question any historical value to the

5. Some (but not all) scholars distinguish these terms so that "Deuteronomistic" refers to the work of Deuteronomy while "Deuteronomist" refers to the history as discussed here. Others distinguish between them so that "Deuteronomistic" refers to the historical work whereas "Deuteronomist" refers to its author. This work will try to be clear from the context as to what reference is envisioned.

6. Block, *Gods of the Nations*.

7. Richter, *Deuteronomistic History*.

8. Cross, *Canaanite Myth*; Nelson, *Double Redaction*.

Deuteronomistic History, especially the early part.[9] Nevertheless, substantial parts of this history were missing at the time of its initial composition and were added later. Steven L. McKenzie agreed with the theory of a single redactor (or editor) but set the time of this writer as immediately after the fall of Jerusalem in 586 BC.[10] In what has been called the Göttingen school, Rudolph Smend and others, such as Walter Dietrich, argued for multiple exilic and postexilic redactional layers.[11] This has led in three directions: the abandonment of any hope for a unified Deuteronomistic History,[12] the identification of the Deuteronomist(s) with a Greek conception of history that by definition eliminates the miraculous as nonhistorical,[13] and the distinction of biblical historical writing as based on narrative sequence rather than the rejection of the miraculous.[14]

To these trajectories should be added the view of Iain Provan, for whom the Deuteronomistic History's primary concern was with the abolition of the high places.[15] This would include only 1–2 Samuel, and 1 Kings through 2 Kings 18–19, stopping at the end of the reign of Hezekiah. The latter part of 2 Kings and Joshua and Judges were added later. With Norbert Lohfink's theory that the first part of the Deuteronomistic History (Deut. 1–Josh. 22) was a conquest account invented during the reign of King Josiah to justify his desire to expand his kingdom, students come back to a focus on Josiah.[16] For this reason, Thomas Römer has provided a recent synthesis, with a three-stage development to the Deuteronomistic History: a Neo-Assyrian redaction focused in the seventh century (around the reign of Josiah, 641–609 BC), a Neo-Babylonian redaction focused on the exile (586–539 BC), and a Persian redaction focused on the following century.[17]

In all the discussion regarding the historical worth of the Deuteronomistic History, the book of Joshua has always received the least value. It is considered largely a piece of propaganda. Yet such assessments often betray a lack of understanding regarding the text. It is true that Joshua itself makes no claim as to when or by whom it was written. Linguistically, the Hebrew text fits well within the period of the late monarchy (ca. seventh century BC). Similar to the other books of the Deuteronomistic History, it could be the product of one or several editors. However, where the text can be examined regarding the dating behind its traditions, there are distinctive elements, such as the

9. Van Seters, *In Search of History*.
10. McKenzie, *Trouble with Kings*.
11. Smend, "Gesetz"; Dietrich, "Martin Noth."
12. Knauf, "Does (DtrH) Exist?"
13. Van Seters, *In Search of History*.
14. L. Stone, "Revival of Narrative."
15. Provan, *Hezekiah*.
16. Lohfink, "Kerygmata."
17. Römer, *Deuteronomistic History*. For a detailed review that challenges some of the historical assumptions made by Römer, see Hess, "New Generation?"

personal names, that cannot be explained as later than the tenth century BC and indeed fit best no later than the twelfth century BC.[18]

Literary Readings

Foundational work in the literary analysis of Joshua began in the last two decades of the twentieth century.[19] Early work recognized the apparent contradiction between claims of a complete conquest of the whole land (Josh. 10:42; 11:16, 23; 21:43–45; 23:14) and admission that some towns and regions were not conquered (11:19, 22; 13:1–7; 14:12; 15:14–17, 63; 16:10; 17:12–13, 16; 19:47; 23:5–13). This apparent contradiction was expanded on by Daniel Hawk, who identified two contradictory threads of narrative and editorial comment running through the book.[20] Thus chapter 1 contains assertions of complete obedience. Yet by the end of the chapter, this is tempered by Joshua's challenge to the Transjordanian tribes as to whether they will be fully obedient (vv. 12–15). Chapter 2 seems to illustrate the disobedience of the spies in that they make a covenant with an enemy Canaanite, Rahab. While 11:16–23 appears to emphasize complete conquest of the land, verses 19 and 22 state that only partial conquest actually took place. For Hawk, chapters 13–22 begin with an orderly allotment, illustrated by Judah in chapters 14–15, but then disintegrate into partial (or no) town lists and partial (or no) border descriptions by the time the last tribes are described in chapters 18–19. Chapters 22–24 provide ambiguities about the Transjordanian tribes and about the faithfulness of Israel that remain unresolved at the end of the book. From a literary perspective, Hawk feels that these contradictions reflect different purposes in the literary strategy of the author, of God, of Joshua, and of the reader.

However, none of these arguments stand up under close scrutiny. The Transjordanian tribal statement in 1:16–18 serves as a loyalty oath and lacks any implicit threat toward Joshua. Rather, the tribes pray that he may obey and remain loyal to God. The covenant with Rahab is in keeping with the purpose of the spies.[21] The differences in the tribal descriptions may reflect as much a question of the actual history of these tribes and the information available to the author when compiling the book as they do any sort of "contradiction."

18. See Hess, "Non-Israelite Personal Names." For further evidence, see "Ancient Near Eastern Context," below; Hess, *Joshua* (1996), 26–31 (2008 repr., 27–33); and much more evidence in Hess, "Joshua."

19. See the earlier reviews by Hess: "Studies in the Book of Joshua"; and *Joshua* (1996), 35–42 (2008 repr., 39–45). Also see "Ancient Near Eastern Context," below.

20. Hawk, *Every Promise Fulfilled*.

21. The term for spies in Josh. 2:1 is *mĕraggĕlîm*. In 2 Sam. 15:10 it describes those who disseminate information and seek to rally people to their side. So in Josh. 2 it identifies these "spies" as those who will make known the plan of God to those they find who are loyal to God, such as Rahab.

Indeed, Judah is best preserved, as the largest allotment and the one whose tribe remained independent longest in Israelite history. At least some of the uncertainties in the final chapters anticipate the widespread abandonment of faith by the Israelites in the following generation. The issue of the complete versus partial conquest of the land returns readers to the original literary puzzle of the book. Behind this lie many observations that could be made, but only two will be proffered here.

First, a text such as Joshua 11:16–23 is less a collection of alternating literary strategies, much less contradictions, and more an example of ancient rhetorical forms. A careful reading of this text contrasts the regions with some peoples. Thus every region of the land is visited by Joshua and defeated. However, not all the peoples are slain. The Gibeonites (v. 19) and some of the Anakites (v. 22) survive. The text does not see this as a contradiction (or different reading strategies), and neither should readers.

Second, popular interpretations of Joshua assume a conquest and then read into the text that this is what is being described. However, the "taking" of the land involves the dismantling of the forts and fortress towns that stand in the way of Israel's initial settlement in part of the land and the defeat of armies that oppose the nation. Although an allotment of the land is made in chapters 13–19, there is no command to occupy this land immediately. Rather, the picture, especially as it emerges in 17:14–18, is one of initial settlement in the hill country, central in the land, with occasional settlement in a few other areas (see 14:6–15).

Gordon Mitchell emphasizes contradictions in the book of Joshua in order to identify ideological tendencies.[22] This approach begins with the command to exterminate all Canaanites versus the reality of preserving Rahab's family and the Gibeonites. It continues with the theme of rest in the land that Mitchell identifies, especially in chapters 13–21. All of this is seen in the historical and social context of the postexilic period, when Joshua was written, according to Mitchell. However, the issue of preserving some Canaanites is not a contradiction, especially if they are seen as becoming Israelites by their confession of faith or other means. Rest is a theme but not the final theme of Joshua. Otherwise, it is difficult to understand the readiness of the tribes to go to war in chapter 22 and the warnings and danger signs in chapter 24 that are explicitly connected with the unfaithfulness of the judges' generation and its ongoing battles.

Others stress various elements of literary study. Thus Magnus Ottosson, for example, stresses the value of rulership in the book.[23] He sees some literary form to the tribal allotments and suggests that the more towns named (as with Judah), the more highly regarded is the tribe. Nicolai Winther-Nielsen turns

22. Mitchell, *Together in the Land*.
23. Ottosson, *Josuaboken*.

his attention to linguistic analysis.[24] Using functional discourse grammar, he finds a thematic unity to the book of Joshua that is announced by the opening five verses. He also solves some of the traditional problems in the book by using this method. For example, it suggests that there is one, not two, crossings of the Jordan in chapters 3–4, and a single memorial pile of stones that Joshua erects in memory of the incident.

Moshe Weinfeld compares Greek and later classical traditions of land settlement and occupation with Joshua.[25] He identifies the following similarities: (1) confirmation by oracles, (2) building monuments and altars (with sacrifice), (3) casting lots to allocate the land, (4) laws given by a god, and (5) both a leader/founder and a priest.

Other literary approaches explored are in the areas of ideology[26] and of ancient Near Eastern studies (see below).

Gender and Ideological Criticism

In Joshua 2 and 6, Rahab dominates the narratives. She appears in Joshua as the Canaanite woman who protects the spies and delivers her family from destruction. On the one hand, her story seems unnecessary to the larger account of Joshua. If she were not in the account, it would not suffer any major loss of plot. However, theologically and thematically, Rahab plays a key role. As Joshua is introduced in chapter 1 as the faithful servant of God who leads his people to victory and security in the land God has given them, so Rahab appears as a faithful servant of God who leads her people (in this case, her family) to salvation and security in the land that God has now given them. For this reason, and with her confession of faith, Rahab represents a heroic example to future generations. She is remembered in this manner in the New Testament, where she receives a place in the line of Jesus (Matt. 1:5) and a unique spot in the great chapter of faith (Heb. 11:31), and is considered an example of one who lived righteously (James 2:25).

So it may be surprising that the first thing told to readers about Rahab is that she is a prostitute. However, this role never emerges as prominent. Rather, as is known from roughly contemporary sources, this occupation was expected of a woman who runs an inn, such as Rahab apparently does. This would explain its attraction for "spies," who were not only gathering information but also looking to find supporters of their cause (as with the same word in 2 Sam. 15:10).[27] Thus an inn might not be a surprising place for them to enter, where they could survey the region's population for support.

24. Winther-Nielsen, *Functional Discourse Grammar*.

25. Weinfeld, *Promise of the Land*, 22–51.

26. Rowlett, *Rhetoric of Violence*.

27. For an inn to be at a strategic crossroads such as Jericho is not surprising, as such seems to appear later, in Jesus's parable of the Good Samaritan (Luke 10:30–34). See also note 21.

Rahab and the Ancient Texts

The story of an innkeeper with an inn on the wall and of fugitives who escape and are sought for three days is not unique to Joshua 2. Already in the eighth century the Laws of Hammurabi (law 109) warn of a female innkeeper in whose residence criminals congregate. If she does not seize them and turn them over to the authorities, she is to be put to death. From the Hittite Instructions to the Border Garrisons, of the fourteenth and thirteenth centuries BC, there is the prohibition against using part of the city wall for an inn (§24). In another part of the instructions, an enemy is to be followed for three days, just as with the spies in Joshua 2:16, 22. The name of Rahab is found as part of a longer name in texts from the Canaanite city of Taanach in the fourteenth century BC. There a man by the name of *e-lu-ra-hé-ba* lived. His name means, "The god (El) has enlarged (the womb)." It is a name confessing and giving thanks for a successful birth.[a]

[a] See Wiseman, "Rahab"; *COS* 1.84:221–25; Hess, "Non-Israelite Personal Names."

The well-known narrative of Rahab's hiding of the spies (2:2–8) has several elements that are duplicated, a sign of their special importance. The purpose of the Israelites "to spy out the land" (2:2 NIV) is told to Jericho's leader, who sends his agents to demand that Rahab turn them over, using the same phrase (2:3). This emphasizes how dangerous it is for Rahab to hide the spies. She will forfeit her life if discovered. That Rahab has hidden the spies occurs twice (2:4, 6), as does the location of her hiding them, on the roof (2:6, 8). These verses stress the personal risk that Rahab takes on herself to guarantee the safety of the Israelites. Since the roof is the inmost part of her house, it may also symbolize how she holds back nothing but opens to them every part of what is hers.

Her twofold denial, "I don't know where they came from" and "I don't know where they went" (2:4, 5 RSH), emphasizes her lack of cooperation with the agents and thus enhances the riskiness of her commitment to the spies. Regarding the ethics of this, one may ask what Rahab could have said. If she had told the truth, she would have betrayed those to whom she had committed herself. If she had remained silent, she would have aroused suspicion. As with the midwives of Exodus (see "Theological Perspectives of Exodus"), so here as well the lie or ruse forms a response of the powerless to the powerful.

Joshua 2:7 repeats the point from verse 5 that the gate of Jericho is shut. A town gate symbolizes the whole town (see "Theological Perspectives of Deuteronomy"; Deut. 6:9). This is the character of Jericho. Its gate and walls stand as a barrier and opposition to the advance of God's kingdom, as seen in the ark of the covenant, which symbolizes God, and in the people of God.

The closure of the gate means the resistance of all Jericho (as in 6:1) and its opposition. For this reason the collapse of the walls in 6:20 perfectly counterbalances this gate that in 2:5, 7 (cf. 6:1) is closed. This also means that the spies cannot exit the way they have entered and thus become even more dependent on Rahab. And so Rahab's open window becomes the solution to the closed gate. It symbolizes the openness of Rahab and her family to Israel and Israel's God, just as the closed gate symbolizes Jericho's resistance.

Rahab's confession begins in 2:9 and, along with her statement of what she wants from the spies, constitutes one of the longest prose monologues by a woman in the Hebrew Bible. She begins with "I know" so as to intentionally contrast with her earlier statements, "I don't know." She no longer holds allegiance to the agents of Jericho's king and so distances herself with her two false statements. However, Rahab trusts the spies and will tell them the truth, what she knows. As verses 9–11 develop in their confession of faith, Rahab's "I know" corresponds to the "credo" (lit., "I believe") that begins the creedal confessions of Latin Christianity.

The actual confession has a chiastic structure, with special importance attached to its beginning and end, and especially to its middle. The first and last verses affirm the authority and power of Yahweh to accomplish what he has promised to his people.

A The LORD has given this land to you.
  B A great fear of you has fallen on us.
  B All who live in this country are melting in fear because of you. (v. 9b)
    C We have heard. . . .
      D (v. 10)
    C′ We have heard. . . .
  B′ Our hearts sank. . . .
  B′ Everyone's courage failed because of you.
A′ The LORD your God is God in heaven above and on the earth below. (v. 11 RSH)

Rahab begins and ends with asserting God's control of all and how that includes a divine gift to Israel of the land. At the center of this construction lies verse 10, where Rahab recalls the exodus and divine miracle at the Red Sea and how God has enabled the defeat of Sihon and Og. This represents the great victories at the beginning and end of the wilderness journey. In verse 11 the references to hearts melting and courage failing draw directly on the prophecy in the Song of the Sea in Exodus 15, where verses 15–16 use these same terms that Rahab does here when they predict how the Canaanites will respond. This has come to pass. At the heart of the confession are the historic acts of God's redemption of his people. Thus the foundation of Rahab's faith lies in God's historic act that has redeemed the people of Israel. In few other places in the Old Testament is the connection of faith in and confession of God's historic work so clear as it is here. As an illustration of the similarity of God's work in both Testaments, it is as if Rahab has read Romans 10:9.

The remainder of Rahab's role in the message of Joshua and here in chapter 2 can be distilled in three points. First, the text demonstrates the character of Rahab when in verse 13 she pleads for her family. She lists all of her relatives but nowhere mentions herself explicitly. Her focus is on her family's well-being more than her own. Her risk of life is for them, not for herself.

A second point occurs in what the spies require of her: not to tell the Jericho agents about the spies' escape, to gather all her family into her house, and to put a scarlet thread in her window. Although one sees the logic in bringing the family together and in using some sort of marker, these requirements cannot but remind the reader of the Passover that will be celebrated by Israel in Joshua 5, after the crossing of the Jordan River. Like Israel, Rahab will draw all of her family into a single home. At Passover, Israel kills a lamb and places blood on the doorposts; here Rahab takes a red thread and places it at her window. This window forms the access between Israel and Rahab and represents the door by which, with the people of God, she celebrates the founding act of redemption.

A third point occurs in Joshua 2:24, when the spies report to Joshua. They quote Rahab's words in 2:9 and 11 concerning God's gift of the land and the Canaanites' fear. The spies tell Joshua about the faith of Rahab rather than the strength of the enemy. This is the opposite of the spies' majority report in Numbers 13:31–33 and of the report of the spies in Joshua 7:3. Both emphasize the strength or weakness of the opposition. However, in both cases the result is a defeat for Israel. Only when the spies trust in God as Rahab trusts in God do they find success.

Finally, the salvation of Rahab and her family is a story interwoven with the narrative of the destruction of Jericho. In Joshua 6:16–25, the narrative intentionally alternates between these two events. Further, a word count in the original Hebrew of these verses reveals 102 words devoted to the destruction of Jericho and nearly as many, 86 words, devoted to Rahab's rescue. For the author of this account, the salvation of Rahab and her family is as important as the destruction of Jericho.

For more than thirty-five years, ideologies of peace and warfare have been at the forefront in the study of the book of Joshua.[28] In 1979 Norman Gottwald published his monumental work, *The Tribes of Yahweh*, in which he argues that the nation emerged out of a conflict between (1) leaders of Canaanite towns and cities and (2) peasants who worked for them. The peasants launched a revolt that led to their victory, a revolt interpreted by Gottwald using a

28. Cf. Dever, *Who Were the Early Israelites?*; Hawkins, *How Israel Became a People.*

Marxist model. They fled to the hill country and set up egalitarian villages that became known as Israel. Of the many problems with trying to find this event in the biblical records (as Gottwald argues can be done),[29] K. Lawson Younger Jr. identifies probably the most significant.[30] The battle accounts in the book of Joshua, especially those in chapters 9–12, possess a style and structure (Younger's "transmission code") like those of all the other ancient Near Eastern empires (Hittite, Egyptian, Assyrian, Babylonian, etc.). Why use such an imperial style of communication if one is trying to argue for the opposite (a revolt against imperial powers)?

At the opposite end of the ideological (and chronological spectrum) is the attempt to identify (in Joshua) a propaganda piece for Josiah. Following Nelson's identification of these two figures, Lori Rowlett studies the propaganda of terror used by the Neo-Assyrian kings, both verbally in their annals and pictorially in their palace reliefs.[31] She argues that this was taken over and used by the scribes of Josiah in examples such as the defeat and execution of the southern coalition kings in Joshua 10:25–28. Joshua invites the Israelites to place their feet on the necks of the five kings. He executes the kings, hangs their bodies on five trees until the evening, and then buries them in a cave. This activity, witnessed only by the victorious army of Israel, can hardly be compared to the flaying, impaling, and heaping up of corpses common in the brutal portrayals of the Neo-Assyrian kings such as Assurnasirpal II. Further, these depictions were meant to be seen and heard by the potential enemies, both soldiers and civilians, not by the victorious army.[32]

Nevertheless, the picture of Joshua as leading a group of religious fanatics bent on butchering children and innocents remains and is a major point used in the negative apologetics that portray Yahweh as a monster. However, a careful reading of the text of Joshua reveals little that supports this view and a lot that does not. See further below, "Theological Perspectives of Joshua."

Ancient Near Eastern Context

The ancient Near Eastern background of the book of Joshua is vast. One could argue that much of the archaeology of Palestine in the first half of the twentieth century (and before that time) was dedicated to finding the sites and destructions described in the book of Joshua. This has continued, especially with questions raised by more popular forms of archaeology, such as the question of an altar on Mount Ebal and its connection with Joshua 8:30–35 and Joshua 24.

29. Cf. also Coote and Whitelam, *The Emergence of Early Israel.*

30. Younger, *Ancient Conquest Accounts.*

31. Nelson, "Josiah"; Rowlett, *Rhetoric of Violence*; Liverani, "The Ideology of the Assyrian Empire."

32. Hess, "War."

Given the vast amount of materials and issues involved, here the focus is on two questions that dominate every discussion of the study of Joshua: How did Israel become a people? In the light of comparative ancient Near Eastern studies, what is the literary form of the whole book of Joshua?

The theories of how Israel emerged in Canaan may be divided into five views: conquest, peaceful infiltration, peasant revolt, sedentarization, and ecological/economic factors. The oldest and longest-held view is that of the conquest. This is the traditional, literal reading of the book of Joshua: the Israelites came into the land from outside, attacking and destroying town

Mount Ebal Installation

On Mount Ebal there is only one archaeological site dated within centuries before or after the period suggested by Israel's first appearance. It is an installation on the third-highest peak. There are two phases, dated by pottery and scarabs to the latter part of the thirteenth century and the first part of the twelfth century BC. According to the excavator, Adam Zertal, the first phase involved little more than an ashpit; the second phase included a stone structure around the ashpit, variously identified as an altar, a watchtower, or a farm.[a] On the basis of the remaining structure and the animal bones (cattle, sheep, and deer bones mostly; no pig bones or donkey bones), Zertal has suggested a cultic purpose. While this remains uncertain and unproved, it is also the explanation that best fits the evidence. Any connection with Joshua 8:30–35 is disputed.

Ralph K. Hawkins

Mount Ebal installation

[a] Cf. the summary of Hawkins, *The Iron Age I Structure on Mt. Ebal.*

Archaeology of Jericho and Ai

Jericho is associated with Tell es-Sultan, a site in the Jordan Valley. It lies about seventeen miles east of Jerusalem, a route that includes nearly three-quarters of a mile descent into the Jordan Valley (from 2,400 feet above sea level to 1,200 feet below sea level), at one of the lowest spots on earth. The site lies on historic crossroads, including a major north–south route from the Galilee and an east–west route across the Jordan River. Three routes lead into the Benjaminite territory to the west: to Jerusalem, to Bethel, and to a point farther north in the hill country. Following earlier excavations, John Garstang worked at the site in the 1930s, and Kathleen Kenyon went back to excavate in the 1950s. An Italian team led by Lorenzo Nigro and Nicolo Marchetti revisited the site in the late 1990s. In reviewing the evidence from the Kenyon excavations, most ceramic archaeologists who have examined the evidence from the site agree that there is minimal evidence for occupation at the site during the Late Bronze Age and the early Iron Age (ca. 1550–1000 BC), suggesting that the accounts of Joshua 2 and 6 have no basis in reality. However, if the site was a small fort, then there would be little evidence remaining of occupation, and any remaining pottery would be the cruder ware that is not diagnostic in the way that the pottery of elite classes would be. Also, little remains on the site postdating the Middle Bronze Age (ca. eighteenth century BC).

Like the site of Jericho, Ai (usually identified with et-Tell, east of Beitin) lacks archaeological evidence for occupation during the time of the conquest. This is true whether one accepts an early date or a late date for the exodus. Walls remain from the third millennium BC and, as with Jericho, could have been reused for purposes of a makeshift fort. Of interest is the Israelite village that was discovered at the site from the twelfth century. It is one of the hundreds that have been identified as appearing at this time in the hill country. The contours of the site also fit the description of the ambush and main battle in Joshua 7.

after town. It serves the traditional view of history as a record of wars and battles. Such a view is supported by a simple reading of the book of Joshua and by a destruction level at Hazor that the excavators ascribe to the thirteenth century BC, when the present author dates Israel's exodus from Egypt and entrance into the promised land. Joshua 11:13 says that, among all the towns that Israel defeated (presumably after Jericho and Ai, which were burned, according to the text), only Hazor was burned. This might also explain the absence of burn layers (a primary means of detecting the destruction of a town) at other sites mentioned in Joshua. Yet for the site of Jericho and the

© Baker Publishing Group and Dr. James C. Martin

Jericho excavations: even the layer at the top is too early for Joshua's Jericho

traditional site of Ai (et-Tell), the absence of evidence of occupation during the Late Bronze Age and the early Iron Age argues against this view (see the sidebar "Archaeology of Jericho and Ai"). If they were not inhabited, they could not have been defeated, and these premier examples of the conquests of Joshua disappear.

The second theory assumes that the Israelites were originally and always nomadic peoples from east of the Jordan River. As has been the case for millennia, these tribal groups would journey westward across the Jordan River to find pastures for their flocks. This is what happened in the case of early Israel. The effect was to produce a gradual migration of tribes over one or more generations. This theory was developed in the early twentieth century by Albrecht Alt. In the context one can see this view as sharing a common understanding with European history: tribal groups typically migrate from the east to occupy land. This theory finds more recent proponents among scholars such as Anson Rainey, who argues, among other things, that the origins of the Hebrew language have closer affinities with West Semitic dialects from inland than from those along the Mediterranean coast.[33] Yet this proposal has been criticized as failing to explain violent destruction levels at Hazor and possibly elsewhere. However, occasional battles are not fatal flaws to the overall argument.

The third theory, that of Norman Gottwald, has already been discussed in the above section "Gender and Ideological Criticism." It was developed by an American scholar profoundly affected by his protests of US involvement in the Vietnam War. While this theory has not enjoyed lasting popularity in the West (although it continues to be championed in various two-thirds world readings of the biblical texts), it represents one of the earliest attempts to argue that

33. See Rainey, "Whence Came the Israelites?"; idem, "Inside, Outside"; idem, "Shasu or Habiru."

the Israelites originated not from outside Canaan but from within the land. The theory that the Israelites were originally Canaanites has now been more widely accepted and finds advocates in the remaining views.

A fourth perspective was developed by the Israeli scholar Israel Finkelstein. It emerges out of his own study of the site surveys of the West Bank after its occupation by Israel following the Six-Day War of 1967. His 1988 publication of *The Archaeology of the Israelite Settlement* marked a change in the understanding of the hill country of Palestine. For the first time, survey evidence demonstrated a dramatic shift in settlement patterns, from a few fortified centers in the thirteenth century to several hundred villages around and after 1200 BC.

For Israel Finkelstein, this was evidence that the Israelites had been pastoral peoples who migrated across the hill country in the Late Bronze Age (1550–1200 BC) and then, perhaps for various reasons, shifted to permanent settlements in the form of villages. The evidence for their earlier presence are the cemeteries at sites like Dothan and Jericho, where the cities were either uninhabited or had too small of a population present to produce the number of burials. Israel Finkelstein pointed to the cyclical nature of this activity; in earlier times and as recently as the Middle Bronze Age (ca. 2000–1550 BC), sedentarized groups had lived in settled communities in the hill country. They would then revert to pastoral nomadism before "resedentarizing," as they did around 1200 BC.

A significant criticism of this view has been the lack of evidence for a sufficiently large population in the hill country to fill out the numbers needed to live in all the settlements. Another issue has been the assumption that no one (or very few) came from outside Palestine to settle in the hill country.[34] This is difficult to prove, especially in light of the linguistic and archaeological evidence for cultural influence and population presence from northern Syria in the Late Bronze Age and later.

The fifth theory is more accurately described as a collection of views that ascribe importance to political, economic, and ecological factors. They explain the reason behind the settlement of people in the hill-country villages, coming from collapsing urban centers of Canaan, from "resedentarizing" pastoralists (à la Israel Finkelstein), and possibly from outside Palestine. In this region the major political change occurred with the disintegration of the Egyptian New Kingdom. It may have peaked again under Pharaoh Merneptah in the final decade of the thirteenth century BC, but it waned in the following decades and disappeared by the middle of the twelfth century BC. As it did so, the threat of taxation, corvée labor, and oppressive policies diminished. The highlands provided an inviting home for those wishing to have nothing

34. See Hess, "Hurrians"; idem, "Cultural Aspects"; Rainey, "Whence Came the Israelites?"; idem, "Inside, Outside."

Merneptah Stele

Pharaoh Merneptah was the leader of Egypt at the end of the thirteenth century BC. Merneptah was the last pharaoh of the New Kingdom empire to make successful expeditions to Palestine. In 1209 BC he erected a stele commemorating his successful campaigns in Africa as well as southern Canaan in the preceding years. The final lines of the stele (or stela) mention successes in Palestine against the Canaanite towns of Ashkelon, Gezer, and Yanaom (this latter town is probably located across the Jordan River in modern-day Jordan). Located geographically between the first two and the third towns is the name of a people group (not a region or a town, as indicated by the determinative signs in front of the three towns) named Israel. This is the first and only extrabiblical mention of Israel in the second millennium BC. It suggests the presence of a people group named Israel appearing for the first time in a region in Palestine, probably in or around the hill country.

© Baker Publishing Group and Dr. James C. Martin

Stele of Pharaoh Merneptah's campaigns (ca. 1209 BC), where Israel is mentioned in the highlighted portion three lines from the bottom

to do with the bureaucratic centralization of power in the Canaanite cities and their Egyptian masters.

The ecological factors are more difficult to identify, although some claim to see a significant warming and drying trend across the Mediterranean region around 1200 BC.[35] Whatever the case, the groups of Aegean-based peoples, known as the Sea Peoples to Ramesses III and other Egyptians, were on the move at this time. These immigrants were seeking a place for their families to live. Settling on the eastern Mediterranean coast, they were dominated by a group known as the *plst*, who gave their name to Philistia, then to Palestine in the south, and to a similarly named entity for a time in the Hatay region to the north, in the region of the later city of Antioch. At the same time, and perhaps for similar reasons of food and security, a group known as the Israelites settled in the hill country of southern Canaan.

Which of these models is the historical truth, and which formed the background for the period described in the book of Joshua? It is difficult to draw

35. T. Thompson, *Early History*.

absolute conclusions. The biblical record emphasizes theological motivations and focuses on confessions and acts of faith in Yahweh, God of Israel. Even so, the textual tradition suggests that the events of Joshua 1–12 took place in a period of about five years.[36] That would account for a fraction of the time envisioned by the second through fifth models. There could have been a "conquest," as reflected in the archaeological record of thirteenth-century Hazor. This could have been followed by a gradual settlement of the land, as the second model suggests.[37] Whether other disgruntled Canaanites joined Israel (see Judg. 2:10–13 for assimilation in the following generations), Rahab and her family as well as the Gibeonites are remembered as among the first to become Israelite of those who were already in the land (Josh. 6:25; 11:19). The ecological and larger political factors could have been present but did not draw the attention of those who preserved the traditions of Joshua and wrote the account. Thus the evidence suggests a diversity of human and environmental factors.[38]

A second area of impact on the book of Joshua has emerged from the study of ancient Near Eastern texts and their similarities with scenes and descriptions in the book. For example, there are the ancient Near Eastern annals and other battle accounts and those in Joshua 9–12,[39] the administrative town lists and treaty boundary descriptions and the allotment accounts of Joshua 13–19,[40] and the vassal-treaty structure of Joshua 24:1–27.[41]

Missing from these discussions is any consideration of the work as a whole. Is it to be seen as a piece of propaganda, largely invented by scribes working according to the desires of King Josiah in 622 BC? Is there something more tangible? One can notice the second-millennium context for descriptions surrounding the Jericho story, personal and people-group names, items stolen by Achan, boundary lists, the vassal-treaty structure of Joshua 24, and other items.[42] All of these argue for an antiquity and an authenticity to the book of Joshua as set within the late second millennium BC, perhaps around 1200 BC. Attempts

36. See Josh. 14:7–10; Joshua tells Israel he was forty when sent from Kadesh Barnea as one of the spies, before the forty years of wilderness wandering. In Josh. 14 he is eighty-five, set after the events of Josh. 1–12.

37. The language of the allotments of Josh. 13–19 does not require settlement at the same time. Early settlement west of the Jordan River is suggested for the area around Hebron (14:6–15; 15:13–19) and the central hill country of Ephraim and Manasseh (17:14–18). This latter region is exactly the center where the explosion of villages in Palestine occurs ca. 1200 BC.

38. See further discussion of the models in Hess, "Early Israel"; and of the archaeological and anthropological evidence in Faust, *Israel's Ethnogenesis*. For the broader background to the study of Israel's history, see Hess, "Introduction."

39. See Hess, "Mayarzana"; and the comprehensive work of Younger, *Ancient Conquest Accounts*.

40. See Hess, "Asking Historical Questions;"; idem, "Late Bronze Age"; idem, "Typology."

41. See Hess, *Joshua* (1996), 30–31, 49–51, 299–309 (2008 repr., 33, 54–55, 329–40).

42. See the summary in ibid. (1996), 26–31 (2008 repr., 27–33); Hess, "West Semitic Texts."

to argue for later fabrication due to an absence of the mention of Egypt in the book of Joshua, coming from a time the Egyptian New Kingdom was present in Canaan, fall down when compared with contemporary literature from Canaan.[43]

The remaining comparative literature addresses the whole book or all the substantial elements of the work. Its overall form is as a land grant. There are many such grants from the ancient Near East. The closest comparison with the book of Joshua arguably lies with the eighteenth-century-BC grant of the city of Alalakh and its environs from Abbael, king of Aleppo, to Yarim-Lim, who assisted him in his battles.[44] The similarity in form may be observed in the following:

Common Element	Alalakh Text (AT 456)[a]	Joshua
Narrative background, circumstances leading to the gift	lines 1–30	1:1–12:24
Allotment, naming specific towns and recipients	lines 31–39a	13:1–21:45
Question of sacrifice as part of the gift	lines 39b–42	22:1–34[b]
Repeated stipulations for loyalty, with warnings for disloyalty	lines 43–50a and (repeated in) lines 50b–62	23:1–16 and (repeated in) 24:1–15
Witnesses and oaths reinforce the agreement	lines 68–76[c]	24:16–33

[a] *COS* 2.137:369–70.

[b] This chapter identifies the incorrect method of sacrifice, where the Transjordanian tribes alone might be involved. The actual role of the correct form of sacrifice permeates the text of Joshua, occurring explicitly at 8:30–35 and 24:1–15. In the Alalakh text, sacrifice as part of the grant is described here as taking place.

[c] Lines 63–67 are badly broken.

Of course, one text such as this does not establish a particular genre. Yet within the wider diversity of land grants, the text most closely resembling the structure of the book of Joshua was written not in the seventh century BC but more that a thousand years earlier in the eighteenth century (Alalakh, above).

Canonical Context

The book of Joshua follows the death of Moses, as recorded in the verses immediately preceding this book (Deut. 34). It introduces the figure of Joshua son of Nun as the leader of Israel and successor of Moses.[45] He first appears in

43. Hess, "Joshua and Egypt."

44. This section follows Hess, "Book of Joshua as a Land Grant"; idem, "Joshua," 9–13. See these for details regarding the similarities. The Alalakh text is AT 456 (*COS* 2.137:369–70); idem, "Alalakh 1."

45. These twin roles can also be compared to Solomon in relation to David. Cf. Schäfer-Lichtenberger, *Josua und Salomo*.

Exodus 17:9–14, where he leads the army to defeat the Amalekites while Moses holds up his hands in prayer. Joshua becomes Moses's assistant, ascending the holy mountain with him in 24:13, and thereby avoiding the indulgence of Israel in the worship of the gold calf (Exod. 32). Although he is intimate with God in the tent of meeting (33:11), he receives Moses's rebuke for wishing to control the spread of God's spirit that occurs in the prophesying throughout the camp (Num. 11). Yet Joshua and Caleb are the two spies who believe that God has given them the land (Num. 13–14). Therefore, Joshua is commissioned as Moses's successor before Moses dies (Num. 27; Deut. 3; 31; 34:9).

Beyond the connecting-bridge texts of Judges 2:7–8, 21–23 (and the genealogical listing of 1 Chron. 7:27), Joshua is mentioned again in the Old Testament only in reference to his curse on Jericho and its fulfillment (1 Kings 16:34) and in reference to a Passover in the time of Nehemiah that had no comparison since the days of Joshua (Neh. 8:17). In speaking of the Sabbath rest for the people of God, Hebrews 4:8 observes that Joshua's action of leading the people into the promised land did not completely fulfill that prophecy. Instead, it is still available to believers who depend on Jesus as their high priest.

The other figure who lives on in the canon is that of Rahab of Jericho. As noted above, she appears again only in the New Testament.[46] There she is part of the line of the Messiah, Jesus Christ (Matt. 1:5), a heroine of faith who welcomes (and protects) the spies (Heb. 11:31), and a righteous figure for the same reason (James 2:25).

The taking of the promised land, so essential to the whole book of Joshua, is prophesied to Abraham (Gen. 12:1–7; 13:15–17; 15:7, 18; 17:8; 24:7; 28:4), and to Jacob (Gen. 28:13; 35:12; 48:4). Genesis 35:12 includes a reference to the divine promise of this land to Isaac as well. So it is that in Genesis 28:13; 35:12; and 48:3–4 the promised land is a promise that is made to Abraham, Isaac, and Jacob but is fulfilled only with the generation of Joshua. This promise is repeated many times in the Bible. It gains special prominence in 1 Kings 8; 1 Chronicles 11:10; 2 Chronicles 6:25, 31; Nehemiah 9:15, 23, 35–36; Psalm 105:11. It becomes the basis for a return to the land and a restoration of all the earlier blessings (Isa. 9:1–2; Jer. 30:3; 32:22; 35:15; Ezek. 20:6, 15, 28; 20:42; 28:25; 36:28; 37:25; Amos 9:15; Matt. 4:15–16; Acts 7:3–5; 13:19). In both Stephen's speech (Acts 7:45) and Paul's first recorded message on his first missionary journey, at Pisidian Antioch (Acts 13:19), the speakers emphasize the defeat of the enemies in the land and the divine gift of that land to Israel. This theme becomes the basis for God's guarantee of his promises, which leads to their fulfillment in Jesus Christ, whom God raised from the dead.

46. Rahab of Jericho must be distinguished from the sea monster Rahab in Job 9:13; 26:12; Pss. 87:4; 89:10 (89:11 MT); Isa. 30:7; 51:9. The name of the latter figure is spelled differently in the Hebrew text.

Theological Perspectives of Joshua

In our survey of this complex book, many theological and ethical themes have already been cited. Here, two points need to be in focus. First, the first chapter of Joshua should be seen as a summary of the whole of the book, both in terms of its content and insofar as key themes of theology and leadership are concerned. Second, the perennial issue of Joshua and genocide must be considered. To what extent does the text indicate that the wars of Joshua were genocidal in their intent and scope?

Joshua 1: The Vision and Actions of Leadership

Joshua 1 provides an introduction that traces many of the major theological and ethical themes of the book.[47] The chapter can be divided into three parts: the divine promises and responsibilities to Joshua and Israel (vv. 1–9), Joshua's assumption of leadership (vv. 10–12), and the Transjordanian tribes as Joshua's first test of leadership (vv. 13–18).

The first five verses of Joshua 1 serve as the "vision of leadership" for Joshua and for Israel. Verse 1 begins with a need for leadership. It forms a transition that joins with the last chapter of Deuteronomy. The term "servant of the LORD," used as an epithet of Moses, appears for the first time in Deuteronomy 34:5, literally on the previous page of the Bible. The book of Joshua applies it to Moses fourteen times. It becomes an epithet of Joshua for the first time at his death in Joshua 24:29. The term is more generally used of the people of God until Jesus references it in John 15:15 at the Last Supper. There he describes how he will address his disciples no longer as servants but as friends. Thus he raises the level of relationship and intimacy. Yet the apostle Paul will joyfully express this submission as a "slave of Christ" (Rom. 1:1 NRSV mg.; 1 Cor. 7:22; Eph. 6:6).

The background of Joshua son of Nun has already been outlined. For this figure, leadership begins with a call from God, recognized by others (such as Moses, who appointed him general to fight Israel's first battle in the wilderness). It then develops through the experiences of a disciplined life.

Verse 2 begins with the divine command to enter the land. This summarizes Joshua 1–5. The additional note that Moses has died indicates once again that there is a need for leadership. Because Moses has died, Joshua can now lead. The verb "cross over" (Heb. *ʿābar*) is a key word in chapters 1–5. It is repeated and interwoven into these chapters in a manner that ties numerous activities with the overall purpose of this text, crossing the Jordan River. Another key term is "all" (Heb. *kōl*), as found in "all Israel." The unity of Israel is key for its success. Whenever Israel is united, it cannot lose. Whenever it is divided, it cannot win. The unity of God's people

47. For the following, see esp. Hess, *Joshua* (1996), 67–80 (2008 repr., 73–88).

remains key for the success of its mission. So Jesus prays in his high-priestly prayer, in John 17:21.

The command to receive the land in Joshua 1:3 summarizes Joshua 6–12. The land is a gift from God. Just as the people receive the covenant from God and are called to be obedient, so the gift of the land represents God's "part" in the covenant agreement. Deuteronomy 34:4 describes how God made the promise of the land to Moses. This seems to be the literary reference here, despite the normal reference to the land promised to the ancestors (as in Genesis; see "Canonical Context," above). The connection here to Moses serves to affirm that everything Moses has received by way of promises from God, Joshua now receives. He is fully the successor of Moses. As with salvation in the New Testament, so the gift of land in Joshua is a free gift, where God does the work and his people accept it.

Joshua 1:4 reflects on the occupation of the land and thus summarizes chapters 13–22. The "desert," or "wilderness" (Heb. *midbār*), describes the hill country of the south. The same term is used in Joshua 8:15, 20 and 12:8 to describe this region. "The Lebanon" (Semitic for "white") represents the range of mountains that includes Canaan. "The river" is the Euphrates, where the northeastern end of the region of Canaan terminates. The "land of the Hittites" includes Egypt's name for the region of northern Canaan. The Mediterranean Sea is the western border of Canaan. Thus the land of Canaan, as understood by the Old Testament (Gen. 10:19; Num. 13:17, 21–22; 34:3–12), is identical to this land as understood in the Egyptian records of the second millennium BC and to the promised land of the Bible.

Next, Joshua 1:5 looks forward to life in the promised land. The expression "all the days of your life" directs the reader to the final chapters of the book and the last days of the life of Joshua. With chapters 23 and 24, this theme closes the book of Joshua. In this way 1:2–5 constitutes a table of contents that summarizes the major themes and purposes of the book.

Of special importance here is the promise of God's presence. As God was fully present with Moses, so also he will be with Joshua. No one will be able to "stand before" Joshua, as Israel "stands before" God in Joshua 24:1 (RSH). As the Gibeonites plead with Israel not to "leave" them and break their treaty (10:6), so God will not "leave" Joshua, nor will he "forsake" the newly appointed leaders, unlike the soldiers of Ai, who "forsook" their fort (8:17).

The theme of God's presence is key to the second half of the divine address in 1:5–9. It forms an envelope, beginning the section here in verse 5 and concluding it in verse 9. God has given Joshua and Israel the mission in the first half of the speech. Now he promises Joshua success by reiterating his promise. The presence of God forms the basis for all successful missions. It is found here at the beginning of Israel's greatest success in its long history. It recurs in the New Testament in the Great Commission (Matt. 28:18–20; cf.

Mark 16:15; Acts 1:8). Just as God sent Joshua with a mission, Jesus sends his disciples on a mission to evangelize the world. With that charge Jesus also promises his presence through to the end of the age. As in the case of Joshua, Christian leadership also begins with a need and a vision given by God. It is God's presence in that mission that guarantees success.

Joshua 1:5–11 turns to the challenge of leadership. The first part, verses 5–9, continues God's address. Thus verse 5 forms a literary "hinge," completing what precedes it and introducing the new theme of Joshua's obedience. This is commanded three times, in the phrase "Be strong and courageous" (vv. 6, 7, 9). As in Deuteronomy 31:6, this command follows the promise of divine presence in Joshua 1:5. The phrase "Be strong and courageous" is used of calling to divine mission and a great task. With these words, Joshua exhorts Israel to continue their rout of the southern coalition (10:25). It occurs in David's charge to Solomon to build the temple (1 Chron. 28:20), and Hezekiah uses it to rally Jerusalem in what seems like a hopeless cause against the Assyrians (2 Chron. 32:7). Here as well, God's presence leads to mission and a challenge for courage in facing obstacles.

The law of Moses is also mentioned three times in Joshua 1:7–8 (including the oblique reference to "everything written in it"). The emphatic "Be strong and very courageous" is attached to that law. God promises success and prosperity for those who meditate on and obey the law of Moses. This reminds Bible students of the charge to Timothy to study and obey God's Word (1 Tim. 4:11–14). Nevertheless, more is going on here, as can be seen by examining the chiastic structure of 1:5–9 (RSH):

- A I will be with you; I will never leave you nor forsake you.
  - B Be strong and courageous. . . . Be strong and very courageous.
    - C Be careful to obey all the law my servant Moses gave you; do not turn from it to the right or to the left, that you may be successful wherever you go.
      - D Do not let this book of the law depart from your mouth: meditate on it day and night
    - C′ so that you may be careful to do everything written in it. Then you will be prosperous and successful.
  - B′ Be strong and courageous. Do not be terrified; do not be discouraged,
- A′ for the Lord your God will be with you wherever you go.

By focusing on the outer frame or envelope that promises divine presence and on the CDC′ point about the book of the law, which is mentioned three times, readers recognize that Joshua will succeed not because he obeys God's instruction but because God will be present with Joshua to enable him to obey God's instruction. God enables his leaders to be obedient and to remain faithful to him. It is accomplished not in human strength but through God's mighty power (see Rom. 5–6).

With the end of God's speech, the matter turns to Joshua. The death of Moses has created a leadership vacuum and an unstable time between leaders. Although Joshua has been publicly appointed by Moses, the question remains whether the tribes will accept his leadership. In Joshua 1:10–11, Joshua acts decisively, as he will do repeatedly in the book, in order to put the divine mission into effect. Thus "Joshua ordered" (NIV) the officers of the people to take the message of preparation through the camp to Israel. The officers of the people identify a group who at one time served as the foremen in Egypt and bore the brunt of the pharaoh's demands that the people make more bricks and gather their own straw (Exod. 5:6–19). Some of these officers are appointed judges (Deut. 1:15; 16:18). They are the ones authorized to pronounce exception clauses for those excluded from military service, and they appoint military leaders (Deut. 20:5–9). They function as a secular counterpart to the priests and form the administrative staff of Joshua.

As God has spoken to Joshua, he speaks to Israel (through his delegated officers) in Joshua 1:11. The words are different, but the goal (crossing) is identical. The command "Go through the camp" uses the same verb as 1:2 (*ʿābar*, "cross"). The verb will recur to describe crossing over the Jordan. This verb connects all the actions of Joshua and the people with this single idea of crossing the Jordan and entering the promised land. The opportunity to provision themselves recalls the first crossing of the Reed Sea, where the people had no time and took unleavened bread. Here there will be sufficient preparation for this crossing of a body of water. The three days correspond to the amount of time that the spies will spend around Jericho in chapter 2. The expression "cross the Jordan . . . the land the LORD your God is giving you" echoes words in verse 2. As God has instructed Joshua, so he instructs the people. Here the instruction is applied to Israel, not just to Joshua. Thus the leader obeys the divine commands to prepare the people for crossing.

At first it may appear odd that 1:12–18 follows the monumental appointment of Joshua and the sharing of the mission with him and with Israel. However, the interchange in these verses focuses on the greatest challenge to Joshua's leadership in Israel. The tribes of Reuben, Gad, and half of Manasseh have requested and received their allotments east of the Jordan River. The agreement has been made by Moses. However, Joshua's leadership will focus on the land west of the Jordan. Since the Transjordanian tribes already have their land (east of the Jordan), why would they have any interest in following Joshua west and risking their lives for no personal gain? In all Israel, Joshua's leadership is most precarious with these tribes. If he is not recognized by them, their rejection will divide the nation. Joshua's leadership and the unity of Israel are threatened. Nevertheless, Joshua initiates a meeting with these tribes. He illustrates that a good leader must be able to identify the crucial problems and threats to the mission. Among these, the most important is the unity of the people.

In response to this challenge, Joshua quotes Deuteronomy 3:18–20, almost word for word. In doing so, Joshua plays his trump card: the quotation of Moses when he gave the Transjordanian tribes their land becomes the means to appeal for their support west of the Jordan. Thus Joshua argues that if these tribes accept the gift from the authority of Moses, they must also accept his charge. Only in this way will they find divine rest. He models how a good leader must know and use God's Word and must be prepared to point the people to the true rest that they seek.

In Joshua 1:16–18 the Transjordanian tribes recognize Joshua's leadership over a united Israel. Verse 16 and the first half of verse 17 form an oath of loyalty. There are three statements, each one beginning with "all" (Heb. *kōl*), using the verbs "command," "send," and "hear/obey." The first two phrases promise complete loyalty in all actions: "Everything you command us we will do, and everywhere you send us we will go." The third connects Joshua's leadership with Moses, just as God did: "Just as we obeyed Moses in everything, so we will obey you." As seems to have been the case elsewhere when a new leader began ruling over Canaan, so here an oath of loyalty is made to the new leader. All tribes may have taken such an oath, but the Bible records only the ones least likely to agree to it. The emphasis is on unity.

Given this context, it is difficult to interpret the syntax of the final part of verse 17 as a veiled threat meaning, "We will serve you only as long as God is with you." More likely, following this oath of complete loyalty, these Transjordanian tribes express a wish or prayer: "May God be with you just as he was with Moses."

This blessing on Joshua is followed by a curse on his enemies (and thus on the enemies of all Israel, including the Transjordanian tribes). It also begins with "all" (*kōl*), emphasizing the unity of the tribes with their leader. The verb "rebel" (Heb. *mārad*) is used of Israel's rebellion at Kadesh Barnea (Num. 14:9), of the nation's past history (Deut. 9:7, 24; 31:27), and of the rebellious son (21:18–21). All of these end in the punishment of death. The same is true here. The final exhortation to be strong and courageous continues the theme of the words God spoke to Joshua. The Israelites recognize his role as undisputed leader of Israel.

Joshua models a leader who uses God-given gifts to achieve the ideal of a people united in following God. This affirms the importance of unity and the serious problems of division (cf. John 17:20–23; 1 Cor. 3). When Israel follows God and Joshua in this united manner, Israel wins its battles. When it does not, it fails. This is the same unity and loyalty that will enable the people to accept the divisions and allotments that they are each given, that will encourage them to set aside towns of refuge and towns for the Levites (thus giving back to God something he gave to them), and that will motivate them to confess their covenantal loyalty to God at the end of Joshua's life.

Joshua and Genocide

The picture of Joshua leading the Israelites under divine command to brutally murder innocent noncombatants, including children, women, and old men, is one that has been used again and again to discourage belief in Yahweh, the God of the Old and New Testaments.[48] How can a God of love command such slaughter? It is the thesis of this section that, while the holiness of God is absolute, the reality portrayed by the book of Joshua is significantly different from that often suggested by skeptics.

First, there is no question that God commands the complete overthrow and destruction of all towns and armies that oppose him and his people as they enter the land. This is clear in Deuteronomy 20:16–18. It is called the *ḥērem*, the complete dedication to God of what is already his creation but has turned against him. In a sense, all willful sin before a holy God is theft of his creation and deserves no less a punishment than death (Ezek. 18:14, 20). And all have sinned (Rom. 3:23; 5:12). However, God's mercy is no less alive in the Old Testament than in the New Testament. Even in the book of Joshua, there is little evidence for the "slaughter of the innocents" (see below).

In the accounts of Jericho and Ai, Joshua and the Israelites are actually attacking forts rather than population centers (see the sidebar "Archaeology of Jericho and Ai"). Further, these were probably not large centers but smaller forts whose garrisons may have numbered about a hundred, more or less.[49] Because so much space is devoted to the descriptions of the events at Jericho and Ai, there has been a natural assumption that these were major population centers. However, this is nowhere stated, unlike Gibeon (Josh. 10:2) and Hazor (11:10), which are both identified as large cities. The word for "city" (Heb. *ʿîr*) can mean a population center of any size, such as a hamlet or village (e.g., Bethlehem, 1 Sam. 20:6), or a fort or citadel within a larger town or city, as with Ammonite Rabbah (2 Sam. 12:26) or Zion of Jerusalem (2 Sam. 5:7, 9). Similarly, regarding the "king" of Jericho and Ai, the Hebrew *melek* does not need to refer to an independent sovereign but, as with the related *malik* in the fourteenth-century-BC Amarna letters from this region, may refer to someone appointed to oversee a place.[50] The term "Ai" (appearing

48. For the following, see esp. Hess, "War," 24–32; idem, "Jericho and Ai."

49. On the use of "thousand" (Heb. *ʾelep*) in military contexts with the sense of a squad (and so fewer than a thousand, as in Josh. 8:12, 25), see the sidebar "The Number 603,550" in the chapter on Numbers.

50. See the discussion in Hess, *Joshua* (1996), 138 (2008 repr., 152). Grabbe ("Comfortable Theory") criticizes me for not explaining this in my discussion of Ai in *Joshua*. He never notes that I make the point and present the evidence from Akkadian in the earlier discussion on

with a definite article in the MT) means "the Ruin" and may further suggest the reuse of the site as a fort. If this interpretation is correct, then the only civilians present in Jericho or Ai would have been Rahab and her family, who managed the local inn. They would have been the exceptions, not the rule.

What, then, are readers to make of the references that Joshua and Israel killed everyone, "men and women," in Jericho (Josh. 6:21) and Ai (8:25)? Literally, the expression in both places is the same, "from man and until woman."[51] This expression occurs elsewhere six times, referring to Amalek (1 Sam. 15:3, without the *waw*), to Nob (1 Sam. 15:3), to Jerusalem under David (2 Sam. 6:19 = 1 Chron. 16:3), to Jerusalem during Ezra's time (Neh. 8:2), and to Israel (2 Chron. 15:13). It is always preceded by "all" (Heb. *kōl*) and thus appears to be stereotypical for describing everyone, whether there are actually women, children, or (in the case of Jericho and Ai) noncombatants present.[52] If these are set ways of saying "everyone," then they imply nothing about the presence of noncombatants, who are otherwise not mentioned or named in the stories in Joshua.

Finally, it should be noted that the Israelite army walked around Jericho for seven days before it attacked (Josh. 6:2–15). One of the Hebrew roots describing this "march" (*nqp*) occurs in Psalm 48:13 as a description of inspecting the walls of Jerusalem. So the army of Israel circled Jericho to see whether anyone would provide an opening for them to enter. Mercy was extended for each of the six days as this march took place. Here, at Ai, and in the battles with the southern and northern armies (below), the key issue was whether the "kings" and their forces believed that the God of Joshua and Israel had brought them to this land. Their failure to believe formed a central rationale for the battles that occurred.[53]

When readers turn to the other major battles, those against the southern coalition in Joshua 10 and the northern coalition in chapter 11, a similar situation appears. Both battles began with an attack on an ally of Israel (Gibeon, 10:3–5) or an attack on Israel itself (11:1–5). That the towns are described as destroyed (10:28–39; 11:11, 14) but not burned (11:13) may suggest that parts of walls were dismantled and the capacity to resist was minimized.

The absence of any mention of noncombatants implies that they likely did not remain in the towns as "sitting targets," with their armies decimated and

---

Jericho, and therefore I assume that the same linguistic argument can apply to the same word two chapters later. Yet this forms the centerpiece of his article and criticism. See now further evidence in Hess, "Jericho and Ai," 39–41.

51. Heb. *mēʾîš wĕʿad-ʾiššâ*. Joshua 6:21 adds "from young and until old," using the same syntax.

52. Hess, "Jericho and Ai," 39. Only in 1 Sam. 22:19, reporting Saul's extermination of the inhabitants of Nob, are children (and any noncombatants) explicitly mentioned. Does this mean that, when using this phrase, it was felt necessary to mention noncombatants if they were involved?

53. Stone, "Ethical and Apologetic Tendencies."

their leaders captured and killed. The average peasant might well be expected to have fled. It is possible that some left Canaan, which was the original point of dispossessing the Canaanites of their land.[54]

However, it is more likely that many of the Canaanites hid in the wild regions and terrain around their towns. In Deuteronomy 20 the Israelites were told to destroy the fortified towns, not to chase Canaanites out of hiding places everywhere in the land. Indeed, the failure to remove the Canaanites from the land means that they remained in the land to lead the Israelites away from God (Josh. 13:13; Judg. 2:10–13). If they had all been killed, this would not have been possible.

In sum, the major battles were defensive. There was no genocide of Canaanites recorded in the book of Joshua. The Canaanites remained in all regions of the land (Judg. 1) and intermarried with the Israelites in the following generations. The *ḥērem*, the complete dedication to God of what is already his creation but has turned against him, was directed against the armies with their religious and political leaders who controlled the fortified centers of power, the "cities" of Deuteronomy 20. These were centers of oppression for most of the inhabitants of Canaan and the location of the great temples to the false gods of the land.

Key Commentaries and Studies

Auld, A. Graeme. *Joshua: Jesus Son of Nauē in Codex Vaticanus*. SCS. Leiden: Brill, 2005. Translation of and commentary on an important LXX text of Joshua.

Butler, T. *Joshua 1–12* and *Joshua 13–24*. 2 vols. WBC 7A and 7B. Second edition. Grand Rapids: Zondervan, 2014. Emphasis on the full range of literary-critical, historical, and critical aspects of the text as a Deuteronomistic work.

Dallaire, Hélène. "Joshua." Pages 815–1042 in T. Longman III and D. E. Garland, eds., *The Expositor's Bible Commentary Revised Edition 2: Numbers–Ruth*. Grand Rapids: Zondervan, 2012. Reader-friendly, up-to-date, evangelical interpretation.

Dozeman, Thomas B. *Joshua 1–12: A New Translation with Introduction and Commentary*. AB 6B. New Haven: Yale University Press, 2015. Thorough review of methods and exegetical approaches with many key insights on texts and issues.

Finkelstein, Israel. *The Archaeology of the Israelite Settlement*. Jerusalem: Israel Exploration Society, 1988. Breakthrough study analyzing the evidence of settlement patterns at the beginning of Israel's appearance in Canaan.

Hess, Richard S. *Joshua: An Introduction and Commentary*. TOTC. Downers Grove, IL: InterVarsity, 1996. Repr., Downers Grove, IL: IVP Academic, 2008. First commentary to incorporate settlement evidence and make use of various types of literary analysis.

Nelson, Richard D. *Joshua: A Commentary*. OTL. Louisville: Westminster John Knox, 1997. Joshua set in the context of the Deuteronomistic redaction.

54. The verbal form for "drive out" is the Hiphil stem of the root *yrš*, as in Josh. 3:10; 13:13; 23:5, 9, 13.

Römer, Thomas. *The So-Called Deuteronomistic History: A Sociological, Historical and Literary Introduction.* New York: T&T Clark, 2007. Survey of new directions in the theory of the Deuteronomistic History.

Younger, K. Lawson, Jr. *Ancient Conquest Accounts: A Study in Ancient Near Eastern and Biblical History Writing.* JSOTSup 98. Sheffield: Sheffield Academic, 1990. Key analysis of "conquest" narratives in the light of ancient Near Eastern comparative literature.

7

JUDGES

If Samson is the superhero of the Old Testament, then the stories about Samson must have represented some of the most exciting accounts for generations of Israelites. The message of the book of Judges, however, has less to do with superpowers and more to do with whether Israel will choose to follow God.

Name, Text, and Outline

The name of the book is Judges in both the Hebrew and Greek traditions. It refers to the main human characters of the book, who dominate the stories in chapters 2–16. The Masoretic Text of Judges is largely reliable. This text preserves some older Hebrew; indeed, the poem of chapter 5 may preserve some of the oldest Hebrew in the Bible. The Septuagint has different versions of this book in its major manuscripts and textual traditions (see also Daniel and Esther). Thus Codex Alexandrinus preserves a text based on the corrections of Origen as found in the Hexapla. Codex Vaticanus is part of the *kaige* collection of manuscripts and texts that give evidence of corrections back to the Hebrew. Although these preserve some original readings, a text closer to the original Septuagint may remain in the Lucianic (or Antiochene) recension of the Greek and in Old Latin manuscripts.

Among the Dead Sea Scrolls, the most significant manuscript is 4QJudg[a], a fragment of chapter 6 that omits verses 7–10. This first-century-BC fragment has led some to conclude that it preserves a pre-Deuteronomistic text because many would see the omitted verses as Deuteronomistic additions. However, verses 7 and 11 both begin with the same two letters, and that might suggest a haplography in which a copyist skipped the paragraph of verses 7–10. There is also the larger question of the genre and purpose of the fragment at Qumran, which are impossible to determine.

OUTLINE

I. After Joshua (1:1–3:6)
   A. Land (1:1–36)
   B. Religion (2:1–3:6)
II. Judges (3:7–16:31)
   A. Othniel (3:7–11)
   B. Ehud (3:12–30)
   C. Shamgar (3:31)
   D. Deborah (4:1–5:31)
   E. Gideon (6:1–8:35)
   F. Interlude: Abimelech (9:1–57)
   G. Tola (10:1–2)
   H. Jair (10:3–5)
   I. Sin and Judgment (10:6–18)
   J. Jephthah (11:1–12:7)
   K. Ibzan (12:8–10)
   L. Elon (12:11–12)
   M. Abdon (12:13–15)
   N. Samson (13:1–16:31)
III. Land without Leaders (17:1–21:24)
   A. Migration of Dan (17:1–18:31)
   B. Rape of the Levite's Concubine (19:1–30)
   C. Civil War against Benjamin (20:1–48)
   D. Repopulating Benjamin (21:1–24)
IV. Evaluation (21:25)

Overview of Judges

The book of Judges is composed almost entirely of narrative. The first chapter examines the occupation of different regions that have not been described in Joshua. Judah captures Bezek, the region of Arad, and Hebron. Ephraim and Manasseh take Bethel. However, the second half of the chapter lists towns and areas that remain in Canaanite hands, though at times under the supervision of Israelites (1:28, 35). In chapter 2, God's messenger accuses the people of disobeying God by allowing altars of other deities to remain. He promises that the other nations will continue to be thorns in the side of Israel. As Joshua dies and the elders of his generation pass away, the people turn to worship the gods of the surrounding nations. God becomes enraged at this and turns them over to their enemies, who defeat them. God gives them judges, who deliver them, but Israel soon turns away to worship other gods. This happens repeatedly and forms the basis for the stories of the judges that follow.

The first oppression comes from Cushan-rishathaim king of Aram-naharaim ("of the Two Rivers," Tigris and Euphrates, northeast of Israel), who has subjected Israel for eight years. The nephew of Caleb, Othniel, delivers Israel (3:7–11). Eglon of Moab is the second threat to Israel. He joins with the

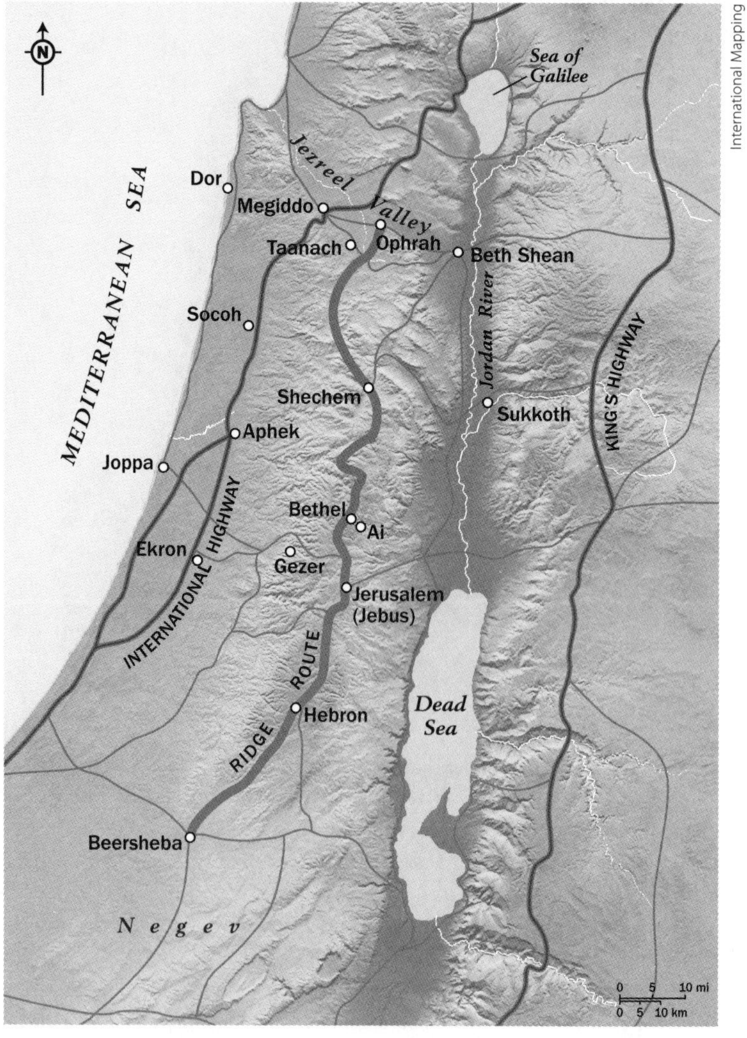

International Mapping

Important places from Judges 1–12

Ammonites and Amalekites and captures the region of "the city of palms."[1] Ehud from the tribe of Benjamin tricks his way into a private audience with Eglon, where he assassinates him. He rallies the land of Ephraim, and Ephraim follows him to attack Moab and bring it under subjection to Israel (3:12–30). Shamgar "son of Anath" is noted in one verse (3:31) and credited with killing six hundred Philistines with a cattle prod.

Judges 4–5 recounts the remarkable story of the prophetess Deborah, who leads the troops of Israel along with Barak. Together they defeat Jabin king of Hazor, who controls the key Jezreel Valley in northern Israel. Jabin is able to marshal nine hundred iron chariots to fight Israel. The Canaanite general Sisera and his chariots are routed by Barak and his soldiers, who descend Mount Tabor. Sisera flees and finds the tent of Jael, who invites him in, gives him something to drink, and kills him while he sleeps. The poem of chapter 5 celebrates this victory, re-creating scenes among the allies and the enemy.

In Judges 6 God hands Israel over to the Midianites for seven years. The Israelites lose most of their crops and their livestock. After warning Israel of its sin, the angel of the Lord appears to Gideon in his village of Ophrah and calls him to lead Israel against Midian. Gideon destroys his father's altar to Baal in the night but is discovered. His father defends him and suggests that Baal himself should come against Gideon if he has offended the god. This is the background of Gideon's name Jerubbaal, "Let Baal contend" (6:32). Gideon summons all of northern Israel for battle. Before he leads them against Midian, Gideon tests God with a fleece. First, it becomes wet in the morning while the ground is dry. Then it becomes dry while the ground is wet. After receiving the two signs from God, Gideon leads the troops to the spring of Harod, south of the Midianite camp in the Jezreel Valley.

In chapter 7, at God's instruction Gideon twice reduces the number of Israelites who will fight. First Gideon invites all who are afraid to go home. Then he has the remaining men drink water: those who lap (lift) it with their hands, "as a dog laps" water, are allowed to stay. The remaining three hundred approach the Midianite camp at night, blowing trumpets, breaking jars, shouting, and waving torches. The enemy flees, with Israel pursuing and destroying them and their leaders. In Judges 8 the rout becomes a complete victory for Gideon and his army. Now the issue turns to the aftermath of the battle. The tribe of Ephraim has aided Gideon, so they receive the glory of killing the Midianite leaders. But the Transjordanian towns of Succoth and Penuel would not even give Gideon's army food, so their leaders are executed and their defenses are destroyed. The same happens with the enemy. Israel wants Gideon for their king. He refuses but uses the plunder to make an ephod of gold, which becomes an object of worship.

1. That is, Jericho, as in 2 Chron. 28:15. This seems to describe a parallel entrance into Canaan like that of Josh. 1–6, but in this case it is the work of the enemies of Israel.

After Gideon's death, his son Abimelech, who is half Canaanite by Gideon's concubine in Shechem, rallies Shechem to his side (Judg. 9). Shechem gives him money. Abimelech hires a group of mercenaries, who help him murder all seventy of his brothers. Only one survives, Jotham. When Abimelech is crowned king in Shechem, Jotham warns the people of retribution for their part in killing the brothers. Abimelech rules Israel for three years before the citizens of Shechem turn against him. In the ensuing battle the people of Shechem are burned to death in their own temple. Abimelech, however, is killed at Thebez, when a woman drops part of a millstone from the tower roof onto his head. Thus Jotham's curse comes true.

The first five verses of Judges 10 describe how Tola of Issachar and Jair of Gilead judge Israel for more than four decades. The remainder of the chapter describes the wickedness of Israel in its worship of other gods, God's judgment on Israel by sending the Ammonites and Philistines, and Israel's cry to God for deliverance. Chapter 11 introduces Jephthah, a Transjordanian from Gilead. The son of a prostitute and rejected by his half brothers, he lives in another land and gathers around him a gang of men with nothing to lose.

When the Ammonites oppress Jephthah's hometown and the region around it, the leaders beg him to return and lead them against Ammon. He agrees to this. After negotiations with Ammon fail, he defeats the enemy and frees Gilead from its control. However, he has taken an oath to God to sacrifice whomever or whatever he meets first on his return home. His daughter and only child comes to meet him, and this causes him grief as he has to fulfill his vow. Nevertheless, she mourns her virginity and begins a practice that continues in Israel: women mourning Jephthah's daughter for four days each year. A straightforward reading of the words of the passage suggest that Jephthah kills his daughter to fulfill the vow. Jephthah then takes revenge on the tribe of Ephraim for not assisting in the battle (12:1–7). He defeats their army, which has crossed (eastward) into Gilead. Survivors who try to cross the Jordan River (westward) back to Ephraim are identified by the manner in which they pronounce the word "Shibboleth." Their accent gives them away and leads to their deaths.

Ibzan, Elon, and Abdon (12:8–15) are three minor judges in the sense that little is known about them. Ibzan comes from Bethlehem, but it is not clear whether this is in the north or the south. If the former, then all three come from the region of the Galilee or (in the case of Abdon) Ephraim. Together they judge Israel for twenty-five years.

There follows four chapters (96 verses) on Samson, more attention than that given to any other judge. The story begins with a long (40 years of) Philistine oppression. Manoah and his wife live in the region of the tribe of Dan, near the frontier with the Philistines. An angel appears first to the wife and then to both wife and husband. The angel promises that the wife, who has been sterile, will have a child. The child is to be dedicated to the Lord

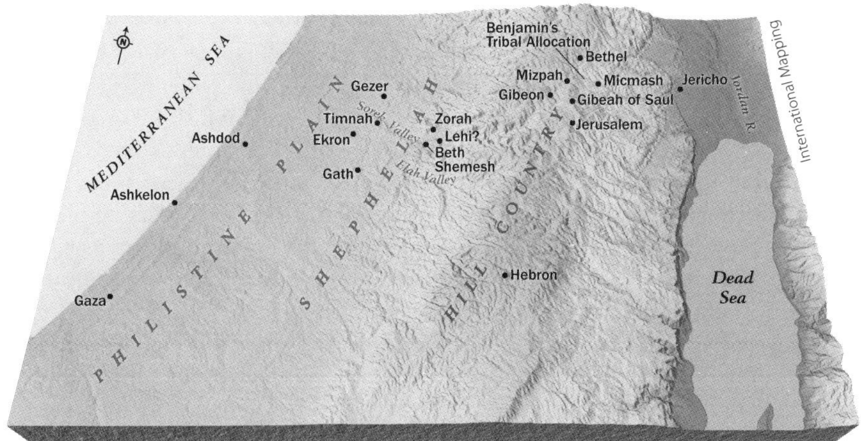

Places of Samson's exploits

and be a Nazirite. So the woman should not drink alcohol or eat anything unclean, from conception onward. They prepare a goat as a burnt offering for the Lord, and the angel ascends in the fire of the offering. Chapter 13 ends with the birth and growing up of Samson.

Samson makes an initial connection with a Philistine woman in Timnah (Judg. 14). He asks his parents to arrange the marriage for him. It is all part of God's plan to find an occasion to fight the Philistines. At the wedding feast Samson proposes a riddle to his thirty Philistine companions and promises them festal garments if they can solve the riddle. It has to do with his earlier killing of a lion and the honey that he found later in the animal's carcass. The wedding attendants threaten Samson's wife and family in order to discover the answer. She weeps before Samson throughout the weeklong feast until he tells her the answer. When he learns that he has been tricked, he goes to Ashkelon, kills thirty men there, takes their clothes, and gives them to the wedding attendants to fulfill his promise.

The violence escalates in Judges 15. When Samson learns that his wife has been given to another man, he ties torches to the tails of foxes and burns the Philistine fields and vineyards. The Philistines then incinerate Samson's former wife and her father. Samson retaliates and kills many Philistines. They respond by drawing up in battle formation against Judah. The Judeans go to Samson and arrange to bind him and to hand him over to the Philistines. When he is near the Philistines, he breaks his bonds and kills a thousand of them with a donkey's jawbone. After becoming thirsty, he cries to God and is given a spring of water from which to drink. The chapter concludes with a note that he judges Israel for twenty years.

Samson's exploits continue in chapter 16. At Gaza, where he visits a prostitute, Samson foils the plot of the Philistines by leaving in the middle of the night and taking the city gate with him. The final woman who comes into his life is Delilah. He loves her, but she agrees to sell the secret of his strength to the Philistines. She persuades him to tell her what the secret is. However, the first two times he lies, and her attempts at entrapment fail. Nevertheless, Delilah wears him down to the point where he tells her of the secret related to his hair. She arranges to have his head shaved while he sleeps. The Philistines capture him, blind him, and take him to Gaza, where they chain him in Dagon's temple. There his hair begins to grow and his strength returns. He destroys the temple, killing the rulers and many others partying in it, and dies with them. He is buried in his father's tomb.

Chapter 17 leaves the stories of the judges and enters into a final set of tales where almost no one has a name and where the characters are all Israelites. Only Micah is named. He appears in Judges 17–18, where he returns money he has taken from his mother. She dedicates the silver to the Lord to make an image, which is placed in Micah's house. Micah has a shrine with images and an ephod. He appoints one of his sons as priest. There appears on the scene a Levite from Bethlehem in Judah. He comes north to Micah's house in Ephraim, where Micah hires him to be his priest.

Chapter 18 gives attention to the tribe of Dan, which cannot prevent Philistine incursions into their land (in the hill country 15 miles west of Jebusite Jerusalem) and sends some scouts to find another place to live. On the way through Ephraim, they stop at Micah's house and meet a Levite "priest," who promises them success. Further north, they identify the town of Laish, located in a fertile area and vulnerable to attack. The tribe of Dan agrees with the scouts' assessment of Laish: six hundred men and their families migrate 130 miles northward. On their way they take the Levite as their priest and steal all the images and the ephod of Micah. They slaughter the inhabitants of Laish and burn their city, which they rename Dan (just south of Mount Hermon). At the end of the story (18:30) readers learn that the Levite is a grandson of Moses and that he and his descendants continue to serve as priests for Dan until the destruction of the northern kingdom.

The story of Judges 19 also concerns a Levite living in Ephraim (Is it the same Levite as in Judg. 18, before he travels to Dan?) who has a concubine whom he has acquired from Bethlehem in Judah. The concubine becomes unfaithful and returns to her father's house in Bethlehem, where the Levite searches for her four months later. There her father entertains them four days before the Levite insists on leaving to return to his home with the woman. As they leave late in the day, they pass Jebusite Jerusalem when it is getting dark. The Levite's servant begs to spend the night there, but the Levite insists on continuing north to the Israelite town of Gibeah. There no one takes them into their home. However, an old Ephraimite man persuades them to spend the night in his house. Shortly after that, men from Gibeah come to the house and demand to have sex with the Levite. The old man refuses and offers them his virgin daughter and the concubine. When they continue their demands, the Levite gives them his concubine, whom they abuse until dawn, when she collapses on the doorstep. There the Levite finds her and throws her body on his donkey. When he arrives home, he cuts her body into twelve parts and sends them throughout Israel.

In chapter 20, the Israelites gather an army against Gibeah and its tribe, Benjamin. They demand the men of Gibeah who committed this sin, but Benjamin refuses to surrender them. Israel's armies are beaten back in the first two battles, leading them to pray, fast, and sacrifice to the Lord. On the third attack they use a ruse similar to that used at Ai in Joshua 8. They are victorious over their fellow Benjaminites. They massacre almost the whole tribe, leaving only six hundred men alive. Chapter 21 appears to show mercy for the remaining Benjaminite males. Although the Israelites have sworn not to give any of their daughters in marriage to Benjamin, this does not apply to the people of Jabesh-gilead, who had stayed away. Therefore, the Israelites send a force to wipe out the inhabitants of Jabesh-gilead but to preserve any virgins. There are four hundred women who are given to the Benjaminites. But there remain men without wives. The Israelites therefore allow the remaining Benjaminites to kidnap women during the annual festival of the Lord at Shiloh, when the young women dance.

The book ends with a repeated refrain: There was no king for Israel at that time (cf. 17:6; 18:1; 19:1), and so everyone did what they thought was right (21:25).

Reading Judges

Premodern Readings[2]

Outside of the Hebrew Bible, the earliest references to the judges occur in Ben Sira (Sirach, second century BC), who describes the judges as those who resisted idolatry (46:11–12). In these characters Judaism found many illustrations of a religion that was lived out in difficult conditions. It shared with Christianity an admiration for the courage and faithfulness of some of the judges.

In early Christianity, Irenaeus found symbolic significance in the stories of the judges. The jawbone that Samson uses to kill Philistines is the body of Christ.[3] However, after Samson's fornication the spirit of God does not come upon Samson. Origen also allegorized the stories.[4] He saw in God's handing Is-

2. For sources and further discussion, see Sasson, *Judges 1–12*, 15–20; Mobley, "Judges," 527–30.

3. Roberts and Rambaut, *The Writings of Irenaeus*, 178 §41.

4. Dively Lauro, *Origen: Homilies on Judges*.

rael over to enemies such as Cushan-rishathaim an example of divine handing over of the proud to the enemy so that they might experience healing through humiliation. Othniel represents an archangel who delivers the people of God. The kings called together in Deborah's song (Judg. 5:3) are Christians called together because of Christ's reign among them. The boy who leads Samson to the pillars is John the Baptist. The two pillars are the two covenants. Others, such as Clement of Alexandria (*Stromata* book 1, chap. 21), attempted to use the book for a chronological reconstruction of the period. Tertullian saw the book as a series of illustrations of how God uses enemy nations to discipline Israel. Ambrose (*De viduis* chap. 8, §§42–47) composed a remarkable text extolling Deborah as a great leader of men, as one chosen and used by God. There was a fascination with the allegorical identification of Gideon's fleece. For Jerome, it is the Lamb of God moistened by the dew of heaven and reaching throughout the world.[5] Augustine (*Quaestiones in Heptateuchum* 7.49.6) used both allegory and literal interpretations: for Jephthah's vow, Judges 11:30–40 teaches that Jephthah does indeed sacrifice his daughter despite divine prohibition of human sacrifice, so God is displeased with this. The dominant interpretation by Christian theologians through the first millennium remained allegorical.

Martin Luther used the stories as illustrations.[6] God's sending forth of the armies from other nations against Israel was designed to teach Israel just as the divine sending of troubles teaches people to have faith. The great commentary on Judges following the Reformation was that of Richard Rogers, who in 1615 read the book and its leading characters through the lens of Hebrews 11, as positive examples of faith.[7] In the eighteenth century, Jonathan Edwards discussed Jephthah's vow as one source for principles on the making of solemn vows. For Matthew Henry, the Jephthah vow was indeed a sacrifice of his daughter, but exactly what sort remains unstated.[8] For John Wesley it was not a human sacrifice but devotion to perpetual virginity.[9] Carl Friedrich Keil's commentary from the nineteenth century remains within this tradition of accepting a more literal dimension to the stories and their implications.[10]

Higher Criticism

The modern and critical interpretation of the book of Judges understands it as part of the Deuteronomistic History.[11] A major theme of Judges is that everyone does what is right in his or her own eyes: this also characterizes approaches to the book of Judges. For Martin Noth, the Deuteronomist used

5. Cain, *Jerome's Epitaph on Paula*, 259 §10.8.
6. See Moore, *Judges*, xvii–l.
7. Rogers, *A Commentary on Judges.*
8. Henry, *Matthew Henry's Commentary in One Volume.*
9. Wesley, *Explanatory Notes upon the Old Testament.*
10. Keil, *Joshua, Judges, Ruth*, 388–95.
11. For this, see "Higher Criticism" for Joshua. For what follows, see Butler, *Judges*, xliii–li.

two sources for much of the book of Judges: a collection of hero stories and a list of those who were the minor judges.[12] He combined these, noting that Jephthah appeared in both and that therefore they were related. It is generally agreed that Deuteronomistic language is scarce in the book. Some, such as Moshe Weinfeld, have argued that many of the narratives begin with one or two Deuteronomistic words or phrases.[13] Others find no evidence for Deuteronomistic language in the book.[14]

Rudolf Smend and others who followed him have argued for multiple Deuteronomistic layers.[15] In particular, Smend finds an exilic "nomistic" redaction, with emphasis on the law (in Judges this appears in the beginning at 1:17–2:5; 2:17, 20–21, 23). Uwe Becker sees a more basic work expanded by this redactor and then given its final shape by a postexilic priestly redaction.[16] This last redaction views the judges' enterprise as a failure and looks to the monarchy for hope.

John Van Seters reverses the process and argues that the Pentateuch was written as an introduction to the Deuteronomistic History.[17] Most of the stories of the judges developed out of unrelated folk legends that the Deuteronomist strung together with an artificial chronology. It was created as background to the history of the kings, with the introduction added by the priestly editor.

But this needs to be balanced by an opposite set of opinions that reject large-scale identifiable Deuteronomistic materials in Judges. Frederick Greenspahn already anticipated Robert Miller by arguing that, except for the general opposition to idolatry, there is little in the book that can be identified as Deuteronomistic.[18] From a different perspective, Philip R. Davies maintains that the whole enterprise should be abandoned.[19] Richard Coggins observes that three entities are Deuteronomistic and that these are confused in the discussion about books such as Judges: the book of Deuteronomy, the putting together of the story's sequence, and a theological (ideological) movement.[20] Without careful delineation of these three, the discussion is counterproductive.

A. Graeme Auld sees the opening chapters of Judges as later than and dependent on a Deuteronomist.[21] Ingrid Hjelm pushes the book as late as the Hasmonean activities of the second century BC.[22] For Thomas Römer, exilic authors used an earlier collection of stories, added Othniel, and created the

12. Noth, *Überlieferungsgeschichtliche Studien*.
13. Weinfeld, *Deuteronomy*.
14. See, e.g., R. Miller, "Deuteronomistic Theology."
15. Smend, "Gesetz."
16. Becker, "Endredaktionelle Kontextvernetzungen."
17. Van Seters, "Deuteronomist from Joshua to Samuel."
18. Greenspahn, "Theology of the Framework"; cf. R. Miller, "Deuteronomistic Theology."
19. P. Davies, *In Search*.
20. Coggins, "What Does 'Deuteronomistic' Mean?"
21. Auld, *Kings without Privilege*.
22. Hjelm, *Jerusalem's Rise*.

basic text of Judges.[23] Judges 2:1–20 was added in the postexilic period. Susan Niditch argues for three "voices": an early epic-bardic voice, preserved most clearly in the poem of Deborah (Judg. 5); a theological voice, concerned with covenant and with Deuteronomism in the seventh to sixth centuries BC; and a Persian or Hellenistic humanist voice, which rejects the vagaries of power found in these accounts and anticipates the need for the monarchy.[24]

Over against this tendency, Nicolai Winther-Nielsen has applied pragmatic linguistics to argue that the author(s) intended here an authentic account of reality.[25] In his commentary, Daniel Block assumes that the text is early and that its contents are historical.[26] Increasingly, the book of Judges is seen primarily as a literary work, either with a historical outline and reality,[27] or with just a few incidental historical realities that remain in the development of the narratives.[28] It may well be that linguistic arguments provide one of the few anchors in trying to relate this material to some sort of reality. This, along with the literary readings that follow, provides a depth to the book that roots it in realities without ignoring its position within the larger picture of the Deuteronomistic History.

The book of Judges makes no claim as to its authorship. Elements in it (see "Ancient Near Eastern Context") attest to an authentic witness from Iron Age I (1200–1000 BC). As in Joshua, the Hebrew language of the prose sections identifies a composition written well into the monarchy. The note at Judges 18:30 suggests an awareness of the exile of the northern kingdom (ca. 722 BC). Beyond this, statements about the appearance of the work as now preserved remain speculative.

Literary Readings

As much and more than any ancient work (within or outside the Bible), the book of Judges has benefited from the remarkable development of appreciation for the literary nature of the Bible; here "literary" means the modern approach of reading a text to appreciate its meaning and intent as it has been handed down to us, rather than trying to identify written sources or oral traditions that may (or may not) lie behind the present text. The literary nature of the stories of Judges and of the book as a whole has been the subject of intense study. Although the book of Judges has also been of great interest in the discussion of the history of ancient Israel, literary patterns in a book do not allow conclusions about whether a work is historical.[29]

23. Römer, *Deuteronomistic History*.
24. Niditch, *Judges*.
25. Winther-Nielsen, "Fact, Fiction."
26. Block, *Judges, Ruth*.
27. Butler, *Judges*, lxx–lxxii.
28. Sasson, *Judges 1–12*, xi (comment of John Collins on Sasson's work).
29. Contra Åhlström, *History of Ancient Palestine*, 375.

This is true of the pattern found in many of the judges and identified already in chapter 2 of the book: Israelite apostasy, divinely sent oppression, frequent repentance, and deliverance led by a judge.[30] Israel, or a portion of the people, would remain faithful to God for some years (sometimes until the death of the judge) and then revert to the worship of other deities. This pattern has long been noticed, but it is also true that the pattern breaks down as the stories of the judges proceed.[31]

Othniel, the first judge (Judg. 3:7–11), is identified as the nephew of Caleb, from the generation of the wilderness wandering, in chapter 1 (vv. 11–15). Othniel conforms closely with the ideal pattern of the judges:[32] he simply succeeds in defeating the enemy, with no details. Ehud works apart from Yahweh's explicit involvement in the text. Nevertheless, he is faithful in his work as a judge and succeeds in assassinating the enemy leader and in rallying Israel to fight. Shamgar is the first judge to fight the Philistines (3:31). Yet both his non-Hebrew name and his association with the Canaanite goddess of war (Anat) raise questions about his dedication to Yahweh.[33]

Deborah represents the figure of an honored woman and leader in Israel, in contrast to the treatment of women in the final chapters. Even so, in the story of the greatest battles in Judges—with the northern coalition of Canaanites, led by the most powerful city, Hazor—not all of the tribes respond to the call of Deborah and Barak to aid them.

Gideon has divine assurance but also reveals much doubt. In the end he creates a gold ephod with the gold of those who seek to honor him, and this object becomes a focus of false worship.[34] Although Gideon mouths an unwillingness to become king, his son does proclaim himself king and instigates war and bloodshed.

Jephthah's account does not reveal much intervention from Yahweh, and he may wind up killing a member of his own family, something that foreshadows the slaughter of a whole tribe of Israel in the later chapters.[35]

30. Kitchen (*Reliability*, 217) attests to the same pattern operating on a personal level in the thirteenth/twelfth century in Egypt: A well-known votive inscription (Berlin 20377) from 1260 BC, left by the draftsman Nebre on behalf of his son Nakhtamun, recounts how the son disobeyed the god Amun and was punished with an illness that almost killed him. Nebre made supplications to the deity, and Amun delivered Nakhtamun.

31. See Polzin, *Deuteronomy, Joshua, Judges*; Gunn, "Joshua and Judges"; Webb, *Book of Judges*; Exum, "Centre Cannot Hold."

32. See Schneider, *Judges*, 40.

33. Schneider (ibid., 56) observes that the goddess Anat's name appears in the name Shamgar ben Anat (Judg. 3:31) and thus anticipates the female characters Deborah and Jael.

34. On the leadership of Gideon and the following judges, see Assis, *Self-Interest or Communal Interest*.

35. The sacrifice of Jephthah's daughter has been taken by many modern interpreters as a human sacrifice, although this is an assumption that is not explicitly stated in the text. See the comment of Campbell, "Storyteller's Role," 439: "The gift of the spirit is demeaned by a foolish vow."

Judges 5 as a Victory Poem

In a book that is otherwise mostly prose, there appears this lengthy poem in Judges 5. It is widely regarded as one of the most ancient pieces of writing (not updated grammatically as prose is more likely to have been) in the Old Testament. Judges 5 has been used as a source for reconstructing the society and history of the period.[a] Although both Deborah and Barak are mentioned in 5:1, the verb "to sing" is feminine and singular, suggesting a preeminence to Deborah regarding this song. It celebrates the military victory of Israel over Canaan, and it follows a prose account of the event in chapter 4. In this way it corresponds to the poem celebrating the victory of Israel over Egypt in Exodus 15, which also follows a prose account in chapter 14. Some have suggested that the prose account was added much later and therefore is a theological interpretation that is less trustworthy as a historical source. However, roughly contemporary with these events is the poetic victory poem of the thirteenth-century-BC Assyrian king Tukulti-Ninurta I. Prose Assyrian annals of events in Assyrian history also date from the thirteenth and twelfth centuries BC. The same phenomenon seems to occur in the thirteenth-century Battle of Qadesh, as recorded by the Egyptian pharaoh Ramesses II. A lengthy poem and a prose text of significant detail both record the event.[b] There was not a question of either poetry or prose in recording events. The two could appear at the same time.

[a] Stager, "Song of Deborah."
[b] For translation, see *COS* 2.5:32–40.

Samson delivers but does not affect complete deliverance from Israel's enemies, the Philistines. His work is compromised by his involvement with Philistine women. In the end his mission and his gift of strength are compromised.

Samson has been explored in a variety of ways, such as literary characterization. Niditch describes him as a culture hero, a trickster, and a bandit.[36] She suggests that the conflict between Israel and the Philistines, as seen in Samson and his enemies, is portrayed as a clash between nature and culture, between "us" and "them," and between rebel and establishment. Parallels have been noticed between events in the Samson stories and events in the epics of Homer (e.g., telling riddles, strength in hair, Samson as a Hercules figure).[37] Samson spends most of his time between two radically different cultures.

There are also parallels between Samson and the Hebrew culture. Note the similarities with the narratives of Saul: received Yahweh's spirit, fought

36. Niditch, "Samson as Culture Hero."
37. Stager, "When Canaanites."

Philistines, committed suicide.[38] There is also the matter of Samson's name, based on the Hebrew word for "sun." John Day observes his association with the place Beth-shemesh ("house/temple of the sun"), the focus on hair, which (as with Hercules's later portraits) can be a symbol of the sun's rays, and the similarity with Psalm 19:5 (19:6 MT): the sun "like a strong man runs its course with joy."[39] Day also notices that the second part of the name Delilah[40] sounds like Hebrew *laylâ*, "night." Perhaps Samson's stories evoke images of the Canaanite sun-god, but if so, in Samson's case they seem to provide a polemic about the impotence of that deity.

In Judges 17–21 there is an absence of judges.[41] The enemy has become internal, within Israel itself. There is the brutal rape and murder of the Levite's companion. This is avenged by much greater killing (of Benjaminite women) and forcibly taking four hundred virgins from Jabesh-gilead.[42] Is God guilty here? Or is it possible to see God as willing to work with his people even if this means allowing them to fall into the errors of their ways? The book demonstrates the failure of premonarchic tribal Israel to rule itself, just as Samuel and Kings will demonstrate the failure of monarchic Israel to do the same thing in a manner faithful to God.

Don Michael Hudson notices the anonymity of the characters in these final chapters.[43] He suggests that (1) each character typifies all Israel in its evil and violence and that (2) namelessness represents the alienation and ultimate annihilation of the people of Israel. Philip Satterthwaite identifies large-scale patterns in which chapters 17–18 and 19–21 both begin with individuals and broaden to include tribes.[44] The evils of Judges 17–21 prefigure the same sorts of sins under the monarchy, demonstrating that neither form of government by itself is sufficient to guarantee goodness.[45]

38. Brooks, "Saul and the Samson Narrative."

39. Day, "Ugarit and the Bible," 47.

40. Schneider, *Judges*, 231–32, identifies Delilah as Micah's mother in Judg. 17. Both Judg. 16:5 and 17:3 are connected with "eleven hundred shekels of silver" (NIV).

41. These chapters also appear to be out of chronological order. See Rainey and Notley, *Sacred Bridge*, 142: Rainey suggests that these events occurred in the early part of the period of the judges.

42. See Exum, "Centre Cannot Hold."

43. Hudson, "Land of Epithets."

44. Satterthwaite ("No King") determines that this alternation describes the sickness that permeates all of Israelite society. Threefold repetitions occur in the war against Benjamin (Judg. 20), the artificial nature of the cult objects in the Danite shrine (Judg. 18), and the oath forbidding intermarriage with the Benjaminites (Judg. 21). All of these stress different aspects of the biblical text's theology: the terrible civil war is intensified, the Danite shrine is shown to be false, and the oath against the Benjaminites is altered and violated while a semblance of it is maintained.

45. In this light McConville (*Grace in the End*, 110) notices the contrast between Josh. 18:1, where the central sanctuary (cf. Deut. 12) is established at Shiloh, and Judg. 18:31, where the unity of worship is called into question.

Gender and Ideological Criticism

For the book of Judges, the discussion of gender is important. There is a wide variety of roles and responsibilities for women that is explicit in the text of Judges. Achsah negotiates inheritance rights (as did the daughters of Zelophehad before her, doing so with Moses). The mother of Micah has resources to cast an image of precious metal. Jael functions as an assassin. Deborah is a political and military leader of a tribal coalition.[46] Indeed, the period of the judges, and especially the story of Deborah (Judg. 4–5), "generated a piece of literature that imagined a woman as being a significant actor in the military functioning of her society."[47] The lives of women as discovered through both texts and archaeology are playing roles of increasing significance in the interpretation of these Old Testament texts and others that often describe the history of Israel.[48]

In brief, it seems that in early Israel, around the time of the judges, social roles were not stratified, and outsiders as well as members of both genders could take on a variety of roles. This recurs somewhat at the end of the monarchy (cf. Huldah the prophetess), but it is not so prevalent during most of the monarchy (David to Josiah), when women's roles were traditionally domestic and appear in the texts and archaeology in terms of bread making and weaving, in addition to childbearing and child rearing.[49]

From a literary standpoint, Tammi Joy Schneider has observed how the book of Judges portrays a worsening treatment of women that parallels

46. The presence of a female general in the military world of ancient Israel is not confined to the story of Deborah. As in the Bible, it was not common, but that does not mean it was unknown. In the eighteenth-century-BC West Semitic city of Mari are records of a female general commanding ten thousand troops. See Heimpel, *Letters*, 101, 478, 484–85, 552.

47. See S. Ackerman, "Digging Up Deborah," 177. Van Wolde ("Yāʿēl") compares Deborah and Jael, noting that particularly with Jael the feminine role is reversed as wordplay in the text stresses the masculine aspects of her activity as an outsider. Her name is also marked masculine (without the characteristic feminine ending, -*â*), and her actions toward Sisera are particularly masculine. Block ("Why Deborah's Different") regards her as Yahweh's representative, who operates when priests are absent to determine the divine will. For C. Smith ("Biblical Perspectives"), Deborah and other women represent a wielding of power in various ways, where no one in Israel has absolute power except God. Smith (ibid., 102) writes:

> In both the Old and New Testaments, the structures of power within society give less power to women, and yet women are shown as wielding power in various ways, from the searching after knowledge of Eve, and the sexual power used by Delilah in the entrapment of Samson, to the military power of Deborah and the use of force by Jael (Judg. 4.17–22). Men are not always more powerful than women, and the Bible deals with this in various ways, from the approving (Rahab, Jael, Deborah), through the relatively neutral or ambivalent (Delilah, Bathsheba), to the downright disapproving (Jezebel).

48. A good introduction to the OT and archaeology and women can be found in the survey by S. Ackerman, "Digging Up Deborah." Meyers ("Engendering Syro-Palestinian Archaeology") reviews current anthropological and archaeological strategies on this subject.

49. Yet bread making and weaving may be associated with various religious cults in Israel.

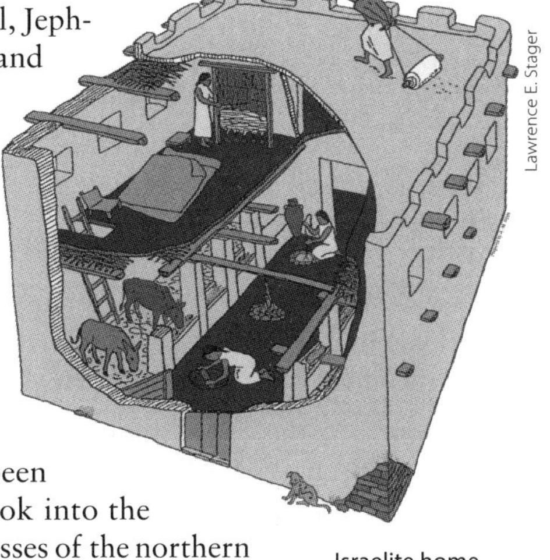
Lawrence E. Stager

Israelite home

Israel's fortunes.[50] See the figures of Jael, Jephthah's daughter, the raped concubine, and the women of Jabesh-gilead and of Shiloh. There is evidence of intermarriage with non-Israelite peoples, such as seen in the name of Shamgar.[51] There is also an increasingly negative emphasis on foreign women, prostitution, and rape, as with Sisera's mother, Jephthah's mother, Samson's women, and the raped concubine.

Although many ideological interpretations have appeared, there has been general acceptance for dating the book into the monarchy and emphasizing the weaknesses of the northern kingdom of Israel in contrast to Judah in the south.[52] For Marc Brettler, the book of Judges represents a work of propaganda written by those in Judah and Jerusalem to claim the success of the south over the north.[53] Thus 1:1–2:10 forms a prologue in which Judah is the most heroic tribe. All the others are weaker. In 2:11–16:31 the judges appear first from Judah (Othniel) and then from the northern tribes. As the story moves north, the judges become more flawed. Judges 17–18 is a polemic against the later worship at Dan by northerners (1 Kings 12:29–30). Judges 19 parallels the story of Sodom and Gomorrah in Genesis 19. The whole of chapters 19–21 is an anti-Saul polemic, one written against the tribe of Benjamin, from which Saul came. Thus Saul was not to be chosen, but rather David of Judah and his successors.

50. Schneider, *Judges*.

51. Shamgar's title, "son of Anat," names a Canaanite goddess of war and may refer to a warrior group to which he belongs: the title occurs on arrowheads of the period and elsewhere. His personal name is not Hebrew or even West Semitic. See Rainey and Notley, *Sacred Bridge*, 136–37; Hess, "Arrowheads."

52. See, e.g., Amit, *Book of Judges*, whose literary study concludes that the story is about the south's perspective of the northern kingdom's demise ca. 722 BC. The cycles are held together both by the implicit and explicit "signs" that signal God's presence with Israel and by an increasing failure in the form of leadership provided by the judges. In Judg. 1:1–2:5, the period of the "elders" already anticipates that of the judges, introduced by 2:11–3:6 (and connected by 2:6–10). Throughout the book there is progression toward anarchy, culminating in the final episodes of Judg. 17–21, which themselves are a deliberate equation of events from the early days of the judges (Judg. 17–18, the Micah episode) with those of the end of the period (Judg. 19–21, the civil war against Benjamin). The solution of the monarchy was not understood as ideal, a message contained in the Abimelech episode at the center of the narratives (8:29–9:57), but a necessary and better alternative to the failure of the period of the judges. See also Sweeney, "Davidic Polemics"; Polliack, "Review of *The Book of Judges: The Art of Editing* by Y. Amir."

53. Brettler, "Book of Judges."

There are problems with this interpretation. It is not the only explanation for these claims of the text. Other equally probable views provide different interpretations.[54] Also, some judges, such as Samson, do not fit this scheme so well. They spend time in Judah as well as in the north. A third point regards the civil war against the Benjaminites at the end of the book. This tribe was not alone in being considered evil. The Israelites who opposed them were guilty of expanding the punishment to the whole tribe. An anti-Saul polemic is an oversimplification.

Ancient Near Eastern Context

Following the chronology already discussed for Exodus and Joshua, it seems appropriate to place the period of the judges in the twelfth and part of the eleventh centuries BC. Archaeologically, the events of Judges 18 have been related to the destruction of Tel Dan level VIIA, around 1200 BC. The Canaanite town was replaced by a smaller habitation that used vessels of local manufacture.

The period of the judges may be characterized by several major cultural elements.[55] First, major Canaanite towns continued in the land into the twelfth century and Iron Age I (ca. 1200–1000 BC). At Lachish, to the west of Jerusalem, a ewer from about 1220 BC provides depictions of ibexes flanking a tree that Ruth Hestrin has identified as symbolic of Asherah, a goddess also found portrayed in Egypt and in the north at Ugarit.[56]

At Shechem (Tell Balatah) amid the hill country, Lawrence Stager has identified the main fortress sanctuary there with the temple of El/Baal-berith destroyed by Abimelech (Judg. 9:4, 46).[57] This fortress was destroyed in about 1100 BC. (See plate 2 in the gallery.)

Figurines and cuneiform texts from Shechem tentatively suggest that the Baal-berith of Judges 8:33 (cf. 6:25–27) was an epithet, "Lord of the covenant," of the god El Berith, who functioned as a divine witness of treaties

54. For example, Becker (*Richterzeit*) has also found a thematic emphasis on kingship but understands it in terms of an original redaction opposed to kingship, and then a later Deuteronomistic redaction (= edition) that tried to justify kingship as a necessary outcome of the judges period. The addition of the opening chapters is an example of this later editing, an idea also suggested by McCarter ("Origins of Israelite Religion") and Lindars (*Judges 1–5*). Lindars sees Judg. 1:1–2:5 as added to define the book of Judges as a separate unit, while the earlier 2:6–3:6 was the original Deuteronomist introduction to this section of the Deuteronomistic History, continuing on from Joshua. Further, O'Connell (*Rhetoric of the Book of Judges*) cogently argues that the writing of much of the book of Judges fits best in the early period of David's reign, before his capture of Jerusalem. Such a period can just as likely explain the selection and presentation of events as later times.

55. On many aspects of the life of early Israel, see King and Stager, *Life in Biblical Israel*.

56. Hestrin, "Understanding Asherah."

57. Stager, "Shechem Temple."

and covenants made on behalf of the city.[58] Labaya of the Amarna letters and Abimelech both recruited local thugs for their own security and to intimidate others to do their will.[59] Labaya was likely murdered, as was Abimelech. While these events may be repeated in many places and times, it is worth noting that at Shechem two major stories of leaders repeat this motif.

A second social phenomenon is the villages in the central hill country of southern Canaan that increased dramatically in number during this period.[60] Between Jerusalem in the south and the Jezreel Valley in the north, there is a dramatic change in settlement pattern around 1200 BC. At this time, and perhaps related to Israel as mentioned in the Merneptah Stele (1209 BC; see the sidebar "Merneptah Stele" in the chapter on Joshua) and in Judges, the occupation ceases to be confined to a few fortified centers and any nomadic groups present. Instead, it spreads out in the appearance of about three hundred villages throughout this region. This is the clearest evidence for the settlement of Israel in the tribal areas of Benjamin, Ephraim, and Manasseh.[61]

However, this settlement culture of villages does not remain. Around 1050 BC there is a reduction in the number of villages in the central hill country. In part this could be due to further Israelite settlement elsewhere. Even so, during the period that biblical chronology assigns to Saul and David, the population begins to concentrate in urban centers. Thus the evidence of the excavations of Iron Age I (1200–1000 BC) sites supports the centralization of population with the rise of the monarchy.[62]

Third, there is a general absence of archaeological evidence for religious sites in the hill country. Unlike in the preceding Late Bronze Age towns and contemporary ones (such as Shechem), temples and shrines are absent from these sites. Other than at the already-mentioned and controversial Mount Ebal site (see the sidebar "Mount Ebal Installation" in the chapter on Joshua), the major piece of evidence for religious elements can be found at the Bull site four miles east of Dothan. The bronze bull may be an image of Baal similar to the one destroyed by Gideon in Judges 6:27.[63] Compare the (village) altar to Baal in 6:25–26 and Gideon's later ephod (8:27), as well as the ephod, teraphim, and image of 17:4–5.[64]

Other sites may reveal the occasional standing stone or bench. The meager remains testify to the simplicity of the culture of the hill-country villages where early Israel seems to have first settled. They lived in small, oval-shaped sites with coarse pots and silos, leaving little evidence of imports or specially

58. T. Lewis, "Identity and Function."
59. Rainey and Notley, *Sacred Bridge*, 140; L. G. Stone, "Early Israel," 159.
60. See "Ancient Near Eastern Context" for Joshua.
61. I. Finkelstein, *Archaeology of the Israelite Settlement*; cf. Josh. 17:14–18.
62. See Faust, "Abandonment, Urbanization."
63. See Bloch-Smith and Nakhai, "Landscape," 76–77.
64. See Callaway and Miller, "Settlement in Canaan," 86.

Abecedaries

The development of an alphabetic script took place among the West Semitic peoples (including the Israelites and the Canaanites) in the second millennium BC. The writing of this script first appears in Egypt and at sites in the western Sinai. Indeed, the script (though not the language) involves borrowing from Egyptian hieroglyphs. The largest number of texts written in an alphabetic script at this time date from the thirteenth century BC at Ugarit (see the sidebar "Ugaritic Rituals" in the chapter on Leviticus). At the same time, texts from Ugarit and elsewhere also contain abecedaries, practice alphabets in which each letter of the alphabet is written in an accepted sequence. The ʿIzbet Sartah abecedary is the earliest one in Palestine (eleventh century BC) that uses a script whose descendants include the Hebrew script of the monarchy. A second abecedary was found at Tel Zayit, southwest of Jerusalem, dating from the tenth century BC, the period that the Bible attributes to Solomon and his immediate successors. Such a sequence of the letters of the alphabet, called an acrostic, also occurs in Lamentations and in a number of psalms. This alphabetization is a means of describing the law of God as including everything—from A to Z. In these cases each verse begins with the next letter of the alphabet. The best-known example is Psalm 119, where verses 1–8 each begin with the first letter of the alphabet, verses 9–16 each begin with the second letter, and so on. Psalm 119 is a reflection on God's torah or covenant.

decorated wares. There is no evidence of monumental buildings or of centralized authority. There was thus no king in early Israel, no standing army, and no bureaucracy for controlling peasants and collecting taxes.[65] Israel subsisted by means of agriculture and pastoralism.

Fourth, the development of writing with an alphabetic script (as is the case with biblical Hebrew) is attested from centuries before Israel appears in the Holy Land and on through the period of Israel in the land.[66] At an Israelite village from the period of the judges, an abecedary on a pottery fragment was discovered (see the sidebar "Abecedaries"). The site for the abecedary was ʿIzbet Sartah, possibly the Ebenezer in 1 Samuel 4:1. This evidence suggests that people were learning to read and write at this period in the area traditionally assigned to ancient Israel. Perhaps the story of Judges 8:14 is not so preposterous if an average youth could at least write the names of people he knew.

65. See Dever, *What Did?*, 113.

66. See the list in Hess, "Literacy in Iron Age Israel," 83–87; and further bibliography in Misgav, Garfinkel, and Ganor, "Ostracon," 246–47.

From an archaeological perspective, the assumptions that every ethnic group must have a distinct archaeologically observable culture are not well founded. Elizabeth Bloch-Smith argues that an easier means to identify cultural distinctives is by looking at what is unique in Israelite culture in relation to a clearly distinctive group such as the Philistines.[67] She finds that having small beards, practicing circumcision, and banning pork are indicators by which Israelites may have distinguished themselves from the Philistines.[68] This has been taken further by Avraham Faust,[69] who argues that in the twelfth century BC, Israel distinguished itself from the surrounding wealth-loving, security-conscious, and hierarchical Canaanites by living in poor, simple, undefended villages, where the architecture and and other archaeological finds reveal an egalitarian ethos. During the eleventh century, Faust states, Israel distinguished itself from its new threat, the Philistines, by means of circumcision and pork avoidance. This may be true, but it is clear that some practices, such as pork avoidance, are already attested in twelfth-century Israelite villages and thus cannot be explained as originating for this reason in the eleventh century.

Beyond these general observations, there have been many specific connections with the judges, of which four examples may be suggested here. One of the most challenging identifications appears at the beginning of the book. The first judge, Othniel, fights an enemy, Cushan-rishathaim king of Aram (Judg. 3:9–11), who has often been identified as fictional since the name means "Dark doubly wicked one."[70] Kenneth Kitchen proposes that the second part of the name is a wordplay.[71] "Rishathaim" may be two words meaning "head/leader of Athaim." Athaim has not yet been identified. This would parallel Cushan's second title, king of Aram. Aram appears in Egyptian sources in the fourteenth and thirteenth centuries.[72] It is a region in north-central Syria, which was gradually lost from the control of the Assyrians Tukulti-Ninurti I (1245–1208 BC) and his successors and taken over by the Ahlamu (= Aramaeans).[73] As has been observed, the extrabiblical evidence suggests that the names are historical and authentic to the period of the judges, rather than fabricated.[74]

67. Bloch-Smith, "Israelite Ethnicity in Iron I."

68. See also Millard, "Amorites and Israelites," who compares these practices with the Amorites, who appear in Syria and Mesopotamia at the beginning of the second millennium BC, according to contemporary texts. Yet this new people group leaves no distinctive pottery or architecture.

69. See Faust, *Israel's Ethnogenesis*; idem, "How Did Israel Become a People?"

70. Aram relates to the homeland of the Israelites. Cushan is associated with the Midianites in Hab. 3:7. See Rainey and Notley, *Sacred Bridge*, 136.

71. Kitchen, *Reliability*, 211–12.

72. Mentioned by Amenophis III and the Merneptah Stele.

73. Younger, "The Late Bronze Age."

74. See Garsiel, "Homiletic Name-Derivations"; Hess, "Israelite Identity"; idem, "Name Game."

Names in the Book of Judges

As is true elsewhere in the Old Testament (e.g., Genesis), personal names in the book of Judges often have a Hebrew etymology and mean something related to the name bearer.[a] Thus the name Gideon derives from the root meaning "hew, hack, cut down" and characterizes his destruction of the altar to Baal. His father refers to the meaning of the name Jerubbaal, "Let Baal contend," which is another name by which Gideon is known (Judg. 6:28–32). There are examples of this form of name in the ancient Near East. Perhaps two centuries earlier the leader of Byblos had a name with the same initial element, Rib-Adda (or Rib-Hadda), meaning "[The god] Haddu contends."

Most of the names in Judges have Hebrew or West Semitic roots.[b] For example, the name Deborah, understood by some as related to a root meaning "bee," may arguably derive from a verbal root meaning "to lead," as appropriate for her role. Others, such as Barak ("lightning"), Jael ("mountain goat"), Heber ("friend, clan"), Eglon ("calf"), and Samson ("sun" [see above]) have names that contain elements common to personal names of West Semitic peoples in the second millennium BC (but less often or not at all in the first millennium BC). As mentioned, the judge Shamgar probably does not have a West Semitic (or Hebrew) name. It may be Hurrian, from a second-millennium-BC people from northern Syria whose culture influenced Palestine at that time. The Canaanite general Sisera has a name that is not West Semitic but is otherwise unknown.

[a] Garsiel, "Homiletic Name-Derivations"; Lindars, *Judges 1–5*.
[b] See Hess, "Israelite Identity"; idem, "Name Game."

A second connection has to do with the style of writing. Winther-Nielsen advocates an awareness of the contexts and varieties of discourse types (e.g., conversations, exposition, listing, storytelling) as all found in Judges and as demonstrating what looks much more like a reporting on past history rather than fiction. He states that pragmatic analysis of the language and text of the narrative must precede questions of history and theology.[75]

Third, the major Galilee battles of "the Waters of Merom" (Josh. 11) and especially of Deborah (Judg. 4–5) may have been conflicts having in part to do with trade routes and resources, the former in Upper Galilee and the latter in Lower Galilee.[76] Although a king Jabin is connected with Hazor in both accounts, they are distinguished. Joshua's Jabin I is always called "king of Hazor," as is the leader of Hazor in the Amarna letters (fourteenth century).

75. Winther-Nielsen, "Fact, Fiction," 77.
76. Gal, *Lower Galilee during the Iron Age*, 88–90; Rainey and Notley, *Sacred Bridge*, 137.

© Baker Publishing Group and Dr. James C. Martin

Sheltered remains of Late Bronze Age palace at Hazor that Joshua may have destroyed

However, with the defeat of Jabin I, the fortified center of Hazor was destroyed, and Jabin II may have ruled from another center while retaining a nominal presence in the much-diminished site of Hazor. Interestingly, his general, Sisera, comes not from Hazor but from Haresheth-ha-goiim, the plain east of Megiddo near Taanach.[77] While Jabin II is called "King Jabin of Canaan, who reigned in Hazor" (4:2), and once "King Jabin of Hazor" (4:17), he is twice referred to as "King Jabin of Canaan" (4:23–24); so he kept the title over the kingdom of Hazor but used the wider term more frequently.[78]

Fourth, Amihai Mazar's recent excavations at Beth-shan have revealed a violent destruction of the city by fire at this time.[79] Mazar suggests that this could be related to the Midianite invasion and Gideon's response. The oppression of the agricultural villagers by Midianite camel nomads in the Gideon story was repeated in the same area of Lower Galilee during the nineteenth century when Ottoman imperial rule was weak.[80]

Canonical Context

The book of Judges begins with a direct link to its predecessor, Joshua, when Judges 2:8–9 repeats the notes in Joshua 24:29–30, concerning the death

77. See Rainey and Notley, *Sacred Bridge*, 137–38: according to Rainey, in poetic language Judg. 5:4–5, 20–21 suggests that a rainstorm turned the Kishon Brook into a flood of water and mud, bogging down the Canaanite chariots and causing the crews to dismount and flee.

78. See Kitchen (*Reliability*, 184–85, 213) for a summary of other fourteenth or thirteenth-century ancient Near Eastern examples where, at different times in history, two or more rulers over the same city-state or country possessed the same name: Niqmadu and Ammishtamru at Ugarit; Suppiluliumas, Mursilis, and Tudhaliya among the Hittites; and Ramesses in Egypt.

79. See A. Mazar, "Beth Shean in the Iron Age."

80. Rainey and Notley, *Sacred Bridge*, 139.

and burial of Joshua. This is not only intended as a link in the chronological sequence; it also provides a contrast for what follows and the characteristics of the two generations. Whereas Joshua 24:31 (and the remaining two verses of the book) emphasizes how Israel has followed God during the generation of Joshua, Judges 2:10–13 emphasizes how the generation that begins the period of the judges does not know Israel's God or what he has done for Israel. They therefore turn their backs on him and worship the Baals.

A major contrast lies between the text of Joshua, especially chapters 1–12, and the first chapter of Judges. Whereas Joshua emphasizes a systematic defeat of the Canaanites throughout the land and victory in every part, Judges 1 portrays a haphazard conquest of some Canaanite cities, with gaps remaining. However, Joshua's perspective is different from that of Judges. Joshua stresses the faithful leadership of its chief human character. On the one hand, Joshua 1–12 prepares for the allotment of the land in chapters 13–19, therefore emphasizing God's gift of the whole land. In addition, phrases such as "all Israel" and "all the land" may be rhetorical devices to generalize Israel's success rather than literal head counts or measurements of the land of southern Canaan.[81] On the other hand, Judges 1 emphasizes the lack of a complete conquest of the land (something already noted in Joshua) in order to prepare the reader for following chapters that address the enemies faced by later generations of Israelites.

Later biblical texts remember the "days of the judges" as the time of Ruth (Ruth 1:1), as days of Passover celebration (2 Kings 23:22), and as a time of God's provision for Israel (Acts 13:20). In Hebrews 11:32–33, Gideon, Barak, Samson, and Jephthah are listed as heroes of faith in God, along with David, Samuel, and the prophets. An earlier text, 1 Samuel 12:11, records another group of judges (Jerubbaal [Gideon], Barak, and Jephthah, along with Samuel) who are remembered as divinely sent deliverers. In 2 Samuel 11:21, Abimelech, the son of Gideon, is remembered in terms of his death as part of Joab's explanation for the strategy leading to Uriah's death. Otherwise, there is not much in terms of explicit reference to this work.

Nevertheless, canonically Judges fulfills the important role of bridging the gap between the generation of Moses and Joshua and the entrance into the land and the generation in which the first kings of Israel arise.

Theological Perspectives of Judges

The basic purpose of the book of Judges becomes evident in chapter 2. As noticed above, the book tries to record and interpret the events that follow the death of Joshua. His leadership is not repeated for this coming generation.

81. For comparable expressions in neighboring cultures, see Younger, *Ancient Conquest Accounts*, 241–54.

Israel does not devote itself to a single human figure or to a single deity. Instead, the unity of the previous period dissolves, first in a search for other gods and goddesses to worship, then in petty conflicts scattered here and there across the land, and finally in civil war itself. In a very earthy manner, the direct association between human character and actions and divine engagement takes place. In this world in which everyone does what is right in his or her own eyes (Judg. 17:6; 21:25), the focus falls on human challenges and tragedies.

As the tribes are only partially successful in their battles in Judges 1, so it seems that this remains true throughout the whole work. No one can be certain that any enemy is ever completely defeated. If the Aramaeans and Canaanites do not reappear, the Philistines and Midianites do. Even the others are not completely gone: later they are seen in Israel's history, as readers of Judges know all too well. By the end of the book, the enemy has become Israel itself. Israel fights a civil war and nearly destroys a tribe. The cost of failure in battle and of division among the peoples appears to reach a zenith.

If the judges seem less and less successful in war, the treatment of the people follows the same downhill pattern. As seen above, women receive worse and worse treatment as the book progresses. The same may be said of people in general. The initial emphasis (with Othniel, Ehud, Deborah, and Gideon) is on the killing of armies, generals, and kings who seek to destroy Israel. However, the second part of the book (Jephthah and his daughter, Samson and Philistines, Dan and the city of Dan, and Israel and the tribe of Benjamin) turns to the slaughter of innocent victims, whether among the enemy or, more often, within Israel itself.

Some see this as an indictment of the period before kingship, and as a means by which the writer (living during the monarchy) looks forward to the coming of the Davidic king. Indeed, the emphasis on the absence of a king does appear, but it is found in the final chapters, which also lack judges (Judg. 17:6; 18:1; 19:1; 21:25). It is true that in all three major sections of the book, there is a downward spiral. The tribe of Judah seems to have success, but in the first section the other tribes fail to achieve a complete conquest (1:1–3:6). Further, the second half of this section summarizes the general failure of Israel to take the land and to worship Yahweh alone.

The downward spiral of the second section has already been recognized in "Literary Readings." The final section (17:1–21:25) further illustrates this. If this is the picture that the book seeks to communicate, then what does it say about kingship and governance? It may cause the reader to look forward to the ideal kingship of David, but the warnings in 1 Samuel and the failures of kingship in both the northern and southern kingdoms hardly portray this as an ideal. One may speak of an ideal king, the messiah, who is still to come, but surely that message finds a more persuasive context in the traditional prophetic books than it does in Judges. After all, this book does not even mention a coming king. The kings it does portray—whether the grotesque

Eglon, the brutal Jabin, or the murderous Abimelech—are hardly figures that in any way anticipate something positive.

It seems that the focus of the indictment recurring at the end of the book is not just that there was no king but also that people did what was right in their own eyes. There is a contrast between this expression and the phrase that evaluates a king nine times in Kings and seven times in Chronicles: "He did what was right in the eyes of the LORD."[82] The focus is not on judges or kings themselves. Rather, the critique of the book of Judges emphasizes the failure of individuals and groups among God's people to follow his covenant and walk in his ways; instead, they follow their own desires and concerns. This is the point of the initial statements in Judges 2:11–3:6. Following the deaths of Joshua and the leaders of a generation that has chosen to follow God and his covenant, there arises a generation that does not make this choice. The cycles of the judges prefigure the kings. Those who choose for God succeed; those who focus on their own desires (worshiping other gods) fail in their personal lives and achieve any success only at a great cost to themselves and to Israel. This parallels many of the kings in Jerusalem. That the whole period of the judges gradually spirals downward and collapses may be compared to both the northern and southern kingdoms of Israel and Judah. They also spiral downward until, as with the final chapters of Judges, the continuing survival of Israel is in doubt.

The book of Judges prefigures many of the writing prophets. As the people of God choose other gods and goddesses in this early period, so the prophets indict their descendants for making the same wrong choices. God identifies and preserves a faithful remnant but, as with the judges, withdraws his protection from the people as a whole. In this way the book of Judges continues the theological teaching of loyalty to God's covenant, something seen in the first generation of Israel, who received the covenant, and found in every generation after that.

From an archaeological perspective, there is an idealism to this period. It is a time of egalitarian villages, where the houses are of about the same size. People are not wealthy, but it seems that everyone lives at about the same level and that the highland villages are not subject to taxation and oppression by kings and other leaders. Nevertheless, in examining the text of Judges, readers see that this sort of idealism does not guarantee security and well-being for the people. The text portrays one of the most insecure and violent times in the history of Israel. Although there are successes (e.g., Deborah and Barak) and there is also a memory of peace and happiness (in the book of Ruth), the overall message is clear. Personal and corporate covenantal faith in Yahweh,

82. First Kings 15:5, 11; 22:43; 2 Kings 12:2; 14:3; 15:3, 34; 18:3; 22:2; 2 Chron. 20:32; 24:2; 25:2; 26:4; 27:2; 29:2; 34:2. To this list one may add the reference to Ahaz, that he did not do what was right in the eyes of Yahweh (2 Kings 16:2 = 2 Chron. 28:1), and 1 Kings 14:8, where God speaks in the first person about David having done "what was right in my eyes."

rather than in political or economic circumstances, brings divine blessing and prosperity. From these stories of the early generations of Israel in the land, the later generations had this guidance in the book of Judges. Israel's failure in later centuries was not inevitable but rather the consequence of its own decisions about its loyalty to God.

Key Commentaries and Studies

Block, Daniel I. *Judges, Ruth*. NAC 6. Nashville: Broadman & Holman, 1999. Thorough evangelical study with careful exegesis.

Butler, Trent. *Judges*. WBC 8. Nashville: Nelson, 2009. Most complete and current study of the book of Judges. Evangelical in orientation.

Chisholm, Robert B., Jr. *A Commentary on Judges and Ruth*. Kregel Exegetical Library. Grand Rapids: Kregel, 2013. Valuable historical, exegetical, and theological insights from an evangelical perspective.

Niditch, Susan. *Judges: A Commentary*. OTL. Louisville: Westminster John Knox, 2008. A folklorist approach to the interpretation of Judges, with emphasis on the traditions behind the work.

Sasson, Jack M. *Judges 1–12: A New Translation with Introduction and Commentary*. AB 6D. New Haven: Yale, 2014. The best commentary on the exegesis and its context in Early Iron Age Israel and the ancient Near East.

Webb, Barry G. *The Book of Judges*. NICOT. Grand Rapids: Eerdmans, 2012. Careful evangelical literary analysis of the Hebrew text.

Younger, K. Lawson, Jr. *Judges and Ruth*. NIVAC. Grand Rapids: Zondervan, 2002. A masterful study of the historical context and rhetorical forms and structures; evangelical.

8

RUTH

After reading Judges, you might be tempted to think that nothing of value could come from this period. But the book of Ruth provides a balance to that view as it sets its beautiful love story in those violent times, demonstrating that in every age God is at work.

Name, Text, and Outline

The name of Ruth identifies the chief human character of the book. This title occurs in both the Hebrew and Greek texts. The text is well preserved in the Masoretic tradition. Fragments among the Dead Sea Scrolls witness to this preservation. The Septuagint text differs in no major way from the Hebrew, although Elimelech becomes Abimelech. The Peshitta and the Old Latin texts that remain tend to avoid references to Ruth "uncovering" at the threshing floor (Ruth 3:4, 7). The Peshitta is also a freer translation, perhaps homiletical.

OUTLINE

I. Naomi Leaves with a Family and Returns with Ruth (1:1–22)
II. Ruth Gleans in the Fields of Boaz, Who Provides for Her (2:1–23)
III. Ruth and Boaz Meet at the Threshing Floor (3:1–18)
IV. Boaz Provides for Ruth by Arranging to Marry Her (4:1–12)
V. Naomi Has a New Family (4:13–17)
VI. The Place of the New Family in the Line from Perez to David (4:18–22)

Overview of Ruth

The story begins with an explicit connection to the period of the judges (Ruth 1:1). At that time Elimelech lives in Bethlehem of Judah with his wife, Naomi, and his two sons, Mahlon and Chilion. They depart to live in Moab due to a famine in their homeland (1:1, 6). There Elimelech dies. The sons both marry Moabite women, but Mahlon and Chilion also die. At this point news comes that there is food in Bethlehem, and so Naomi prepares to return to her homeland. She counsels her daughters-in-law to return to their family homes. After some protest, Orpah follows her advice. Ruth, however, swears to follow Naomi and join her people and her God (1:16–17). Naomi and Ruth journey to Bethlehem and arrive in the spring, at the beginning of the barley harvest.

Ruth goes out into the barley fields to glean some food for her and Naomi to live. She finds herself gleaning in a field owned by Elimelech's relative Boaz (2:1–3). When Boaz arrives, he inquires as to the identity of Ruth. Boaz speaks to her and asks her not to glean elsewhere but to stay where he will protect and provide for her. He blesses her for leaving her Moabite family and taking care of Naomi. Boaz provides Ruth with bread and roasted grain, and he instructs his workers to assist her. When evening comes and she is threshing the sheaves, an ephah of barley remains. That is ten to twenty liters, or about a week's worth of food for the two women.

© Baker Publishing Group and Dr. James C. Martin

Looking east across the Jordan Valley toward the Moab Plateau region

When she brings the barley back to Naomi and tells her what happened, Naomi explains the identity of Boaz as a close relative, a "kinsman redeemer" (2:20 RSH). At Naomi's behest, Ruth returns to the field of Boaz and continues to glean there. At the time of winnowing, Naomi instructs Ruth to go to the threshing floor and wait in secret until Boaz has finished eating and drinking and goes to lie down for the night. Then she must "uncover his feet" and lie down (3:4). Ruth agrees to this. When she uncovers his feet, he awakens and learns of her identity and her wish for him to act as "kinsman redeemer" (3:9 RSH). Boaz agrees but observes that there is a closer kinsman. He promises to negotiate with this person and, if the kinsman is unwilling to redeem Ruth and Naomi and the family property, Boaz will do it. He gives her some barley and sends her back to Naomi in secret. Naomi assures Ruth that Boaz will follow through on his words (3:18).

Boaz arrives at the town gate, where he assembles ten elders and meets with the closer kinsman. He describes how Naomi is selling some land that Elimelech owned, and how the kinsman has the right of first choice when it comes to purchasing the land. The kinsman agrees to redeem it (4:4). At this point, Boaz asserts that the kinsman also acquires Naomi and Ruth, with whom he must follow through the custom of continuing the name of the dead. At this the kinsman refuses because such an action would endanger his own household and inheritance. He gives Boaz the legal right to redeem Ruth and Naomi according to custom, by removing his sandal and passing it to Boaz (4:7–8). Boaz then concludes the legal transaction by announcing it publicly before the elders. The elders affirm the decision and bless Boaz.

Boaz marries Ruth, and they bear a son. This leads the women of Bethlehem to bless Naomi, bless her kinsman redeemer Boaz, and name the son Obed. He will become the grandfather of David. The book of Ruth concludes with a genealogy whose line places Boaz as seventh and David as tenth and last in the line.

Reading Ruth

Premodern Readings

One of the earliest Jewish interpretations of Ruth appears in the Aramaic *Targum Ruth*. From this time there is already a tradition that connects Pentecost with the giving of the law at Mount Sinai. Ruth is one of the five Megilloth, or Scrolls, along with Ecclesiastes, Lamentations, Song of Songs, and Esther. Each scroll is read at one of the major annual Jewish special days. Ruth is read at Pentecost. Thus the connection with the giving of the law allows for interpretation connected with it. Mahlon and Chilion die because they marry Moabites, and that violates the law. Ruth represents a proselyte who is blessed by God as she follows God faithfully and leaves behind her former life.

In these readings, Boaz is a righteous judge whose prayers end the famine (Ruth 1:6), who prophesies that Ruth will be the ancestress of kings and prophets, and who is a model of self-control with Ruth at the threshing floor.[1] *Ruth Rabbah*, another early Jewish text, follows these same themes. Elimelech becomes an evil, wealthy landowner who leaves his home during famine, rather than help those in need. Ruth contrasts as a convert to Judaism.

In early Christianity, focus on the interpretation of Ruth first appeared around AD 200. The writers interpreted Ruth allegorically.[2] Hippolytus of Rome identifies the water that Ruth shares with the workers (2:9) with baptism. Origen finds a symbol of the church in Ruth. She represents the non-Jews who convert to Christianity. Ambrose describes how Boaz chooses Ruth because of the virtues he sees in her.

Medieval and Reformation Christians continued to examine some of the more perplexing issues of this small biblical book: the sexuality and what went on at the threshing floor, the question of the sandal ceremony, and the overall purpose of the book. Martin Luther follows earlier interpreters in stressing how Ruth portrays a foreigner coming to the covenant.[3] Christologically, Luther sees in Ruth lying at Boaz's feet the soul lying down at the humanity of Christ and then being covered by his righteousness. Notes in the sixteenth-century Geneva Bible find in Ruth a model of patient endurance of earthly problems until God brings deliverance. In the seventeenth century, John Bunyan rendered the story of Ruth into a poem.

Christian interpreters were more inclined to borrow from Jewish approaches to uncover solutions to these hermeneutical issues.[4] Both Jewish and Christian exegetes continued to see the importance of the genealogy's role as a means of tying this book to the line of David and the Davidic covenant. The implications for the Messiah were also important, and in Christianity the connection with Jesus Christ played a key role, as seen already in Matthew 1:5.

Higher Criticism

The shorter nature of this story, as well as its physical separation from the Pentateuch and the Deuteronomistic History and the source and redaction issues reflected in these works, has caused critical studies regarding the work to focus on three major questions: the form or genre of the work, its unity, and the purpose that the work was originally intended to serve.

The form of the work continues to be discussed and debated. Hermann Gunkel began the modern study of forms and traditions at the beginning of the nineteenth century. For him, the story of Ruth goes back to an Egyptian

1. Nielsen, *Ruth*, 18.
2. Giannarelli, "The Book of Ruth," 12–15.
3. Luther, *Ruth*.
4. See L. Smith, *Medieval Exegesis*.

fairy tale that evolved into the account of Judah and Tamar (Gen. 38), and an earlier account where Naomi bore a child and heir after the death of Elimelech. Later, Ruth was added. This and similar approaches represent highly speculative accounts that have not convinced many scholars. Neither fertility myths nor the coalescing of multiple stories seems likely, given the simplicity and unity of the account as now preserved. Attribution to oral tales has been made by some, while others question the lack of sufficient formulas and of the sort of story pattern that would be expected for an oral background.

Daniel Block clarifies the distinctions between a tale, a short story, and a novella since they are often used in literary contexts.[5] Generally, the particular classification depends on length, where the tale is the shortest and the novella is the longest. However, a literary distinction exists between the short story, where the character of the main actors and speakers is revealed, and the novella, where the characters develop. Although a few may see some development of Naomi's character between chapters 1 and 4, this is arguably more a matter of how her character is revealed under changing circumstances. In any case, the figures of Ruth and Boaz do not demonstrate character development but rather have their characters revealed through their circumstances and interactions. The work is therefore best classified as a short story.

Much of the unity of the book is self-evident from the nature of the narrative. While one cannot prove beyond all doubt that the book of Ruth is not a combination of two or more earlier narratives, this becomes less persuasive the more readers appreciate the depth of the story's plot and how each verse of the narrative contributes to it. The great degree of unity in the story as it stands makes the search for a unity behind this account of no significance for its present interpretation.

The most important question regarding unity concerns the genealogy that appears as an artificial addition onto the end of the book (Ruth 4:18–22). This forms the strongest evidence that, at least in this case, the book is a composite in which a genealogy of David was added at its end. On the one hand, the answer to this question is bound together with the issue of the overall purpose of the book. On the other hand, there is the basic question of the literary form of this sort of genealogy. For example, the largest set of genealogies in the Bible can be found in 1 Chronicles 1–9. Brief notes and stories occur throughout this text. They illustrate that a genealogy does not need to exist by itself, with nothing else attached to it. Closer in resemblance to the linear genealogy of ten generations, as found in Ruth, are those of Seth and Shem in Genesis 5:1–32 and 11:10–28. Both occur with that combination of short stories and genealogies that appears in Genesis 1–11. Thus the genealogy of Genesis 5 is clearly attached to Genesis 4 and the story of Cain and Abel. The death of Abel and the rebellion of Cain create the need for a new line,

5. Block, "Ruth 1," 677.

that of Seth. The same is true in Genesis 11, where the end of the flood and the words of Noah in chapter 9 prepare for the Table of Nations in chapter 10, which anticipates the line of Shem by describing its earliest generations. Each of these genealogies also anticipates what follows. Genesis 5 ends with Noah, who survives the flood of chapters 6–9. Genesis 11 ends with Abram, who receives the promise and journeys to the land of promise in chapter 12. So Ruth ends with the coming of David, whose life is described in 1–2 Samuel.

It is less common for genealogies to have no connection with narrative in the Bible than it is for them to be connected, as in the book of Ruth. Nor is this limited to the biblical record. For the West Semitic background of this style, see "Ancient Near Eastern Context" below.

The third area asks the question of the purpose of Ruth. Answering this anticipates some of the theological discussion below (as well as the literary and ideological observations). However, three points of purpose within the historical context of ancient Israel are key in considering the question of the date and authorship of the book.

The first purpose deals with the ideal portrayals of the characters. Ruth models the foreign convert to the covenant who pledges absolute loyalty to Naomi, her family, and her faith. Ruth lives that out through the chapters. Boaz is the just and generous Israelite farmer who goes beyond the letter of the law to allow gleaners in his field (Lev. 19:9; 23:22) by taking care of their needs and protecting them. Further, his love for Ruth brings him to negotiate for his right to marry her (but only within the context of the community's law and custom) and to follow through with this concern by providing fully for her and for her mother-in-law. Naomi demonstrates a figure who will persevere despite the bereavements and hardships she has known. She is a fighter who will not surrender despite the loss of husband and children. Even in her bitterness (as later in her joy), she confesses the sovereignty of God and submits to his will (Ruth 1:20–21).

These examples of righteous characters become models for Israel to emulate. Faithfulness to the covenant in bad circumstances as well as in good times remains the way God's people are called to live. The same is true of a generosity and graciousness that characterizes Boaz, who accepts and loves the foreigner Ruth. And this is the second purpose—the acceptance of foreigners into Israel who convert to the faith and honor God and the laws and customs of God's people. People can and do come from outside the faith and may find acceptance into the covenant that God has provided. When this happens, they leave behind the customs and beliefs of their former land, and they find gracious reception and hospitality in a new home, with a new faith and way of life.

The third arena of purpose explains the genealogy at the end of the book. It is to explain how Ruth of Moab and Boaz of Bethlehem go far beyond becoming another Israelite couple during the period of the judges. They form part of the ancestry of King David and thus participate in all that God's plan will bring through his covenant with David's household and lineage.

In the context of these three purposes, when and where would the story of Ruth as preserved best fit? It has long been commented that the postexilic period would suit the genealogy, given the priestly interest in genealogy at that time. This book could also be seen as an alternative message to the people of that time. Move beyond your exclusive attitudes of banning mixed marriages and the like! Accept all peoples who come in faith! Of course, such messages may also occur in preexilic times with such texts as the seventh-century-BC Old Hebrew inscription at Ein Gedi, where Yahweh is described as ruler of the nations. And indeed, the importance of the Davidic line for the identity of the monarchy can hardly be minimized. Thus a preexilic context would fit as well. Indeed, the same era that remembered how David sent his family to safety in Moab when he was threatened (1 Sam. 22:3–4) may also provide a context for the acceptance of a woman of Moab into Israel and into his family line. There is no reason to doubt that this literary world could lie in the court of David as easily as it could among the postexilic priests. And how much more powerful a message this would provide if successive generations during the monarchy, as well as those who lived after the exile, could hear and appreciate the messages found here.

As an addendum to this discussion, students may assess the linguistic arguments for this dating. In particular, there are the supposed Aramaisms that have been used to demonstrate a later postexilic date. However, scholars' knowledge of Hebrew and Aramaic in Palestine throughout the first millennium BC is and probably always will be partial. Conclusions drawn from this sort of argumentation require additional evidence. And even if one could prove a particular date on the basis of these terms, it would not preclude an earlier composition that was updated, something possible with other parts of the Hebrew Bible and a phenomenon known to have occurred in datable Egyptian texts. A related problem may be one of gender incongruence, something that occurs in a number of texts in the Bible dominated by feminine characters. A variety of explanations have been hypothesized for this; however, the comparative evidence points to similarities with such forms in the thirteenth-century Ugaritic texts.[6]

Literary Readings

There is much discussion of the literary form and structure of this beautiful love story. The opening two verses set the historical context (the time of the judges) and provide an introduction to the names and setting of what appears to be the story of the movement of a Judean family to Moab. The

6. Hubbard, *Book of Ruth*, 4. For a full discussion of the problem and the evidence, see Ratner, "Gender Problems." For a possibly related issue with the third-person feminine singular pronoun in the Pentateuch, see Hess, "Adam, Father, He."

whole family is introduced in the first four verses, although by the time the wives join, Naomi has become a widow. Verses 3 and 5 establish the problem. All the men in the family have died, and there are no heirs. From this point the key elements in the story take place in the form of dialogue. In the first chapter, Naomi's speech appears in eight of the twenty-two verses. It introduces Ruth's statement of commitment in verses 16–17 and responds to the question of the women of Bethlehem. The question is two words in the Hebrew, and then Naomi's response comprises twenty-eight words. She is the dominant speaker; this has led some to ascribe to her the role of chief character in the book. However, in chapter 1 it is Ruth who defies Naomi's wishes. Ruth does so only to commit herself completely to her mother-in-law. Nevertheless, she will make this one decision to control her own destiny.

In chapter 2, Ruth is the first to speak, and again she directs her own fate. She asks permission to glean in the fields. Naomi gives her permission, but the idea comes from Ruth. Boaz is introduced as one who greets his workers, so that the first words that come from his mouth are "Yahweh be with you": he acknowledges his God in the first word from his mouth. The blessing from Yahweh that comes from the mouths of the workers assumes that they also believe as Boaz does and that they are in harmony with their boss. Further, the theme of harmony permeates the conversation between Boaz and Ruth. By the time he speaks with her, Boaz already knows a great deal about her, more than she may suspect.

On the one hand, far from accusing her of being a foreigner with no rights, Boaz praises her for taking care of a fellow Israelite, Naomi (a woman he could be expected to have some responsibility for as a kinsman). Ruth, on the other hand, does not challenge him as owner of the land or demand rights and privileges. She gratefully accepts his gracious gifts and acknowledges her low standing, even with respect to his servant girls. The effect is one of mutual blessing. The physical part of the blessing, however, is all on the side of Ruth. She receives a quantity of grain far in excess of what a day of gleaning might produce. When Naomi sees this, she dominates the conversation with Ruth. Ruth merely reports what Boaz has said (2:21) while Naomi interprets the events.

The first four verses of chapter 3 again contain Naomi's words. She instructs Ruth in some detail about preparing herself and going to the threshing floor. Ruth responds with obedience (3:5). The scene where Boaz eats and drinks at the threshing floor, and then lies down sated, is not incidental. It represents a major literary theme, that of food and both its absence and its abundance. Famine is what began the story. Naomi's family left Judah because there was no food. When the food returned, so did Naomi. The need for food is what sent Ruth out to glean. Boaz, with his abundance of food, represents the character who does not hoard but graciously gives to those in need. His gifts do not diminish him. He still has an abundance to eat and drink with friends and, later in this chapter, to give to Ruth as a promissory gift for her and Naomi.

Boaz's concern to protect the privacy of the meeting (3:14) may be to respect Ruth's reputation. However, in the context it is more likely to avoid any gossip that might reach the ears of the nearer kinsman and diminish the surprise of Boaz's proposal and the change of mind. The final three verses of the chapter again present Naomi as the dominant speaker, predicting the next steps that Boaz will take.

The final chapter is dominated by the negotiation between Boaz and the nearer kinsman. Although it is debated just how it happens, Boaz does overturn the initial decision of the kinsman to redeem the land of Elimelech. His decision is connected with the introduction of Ruth into the picture. The kinsman will not marry Ruth and take care of Naomi. However good or bad the motivation for the kinsman to refuse Ruth, it provides one more example of the loss of a possible male member of Naomi's family who would provide grandchildren for her. This time the loss is a means to a better end, one that clears the way so that Boaz can now marry Ruth.

In the center of the book, Boaz and Ruth bless one another (Ruth 2–3). In the beginning, Ruth blesses Naomi with her commitment. Naomi, however, does not seem to recognize this for all that it implies. Here in chapter 4 the elders of Bethlehem bless Boaz and clear the way for him to marry. Following this scene the women of Bethlehem bless Naomi at the birth of her grandchild. In contrast to chapter 1, they speak more than Naomi and pronounce their good wishes. They also name the child (4:17). Although not attested elsewhere in the Bible, this sort of custom is known in other cultures around the world. Their act of naming is an act of insight into the significance of the child or of his birth. Obed is a shortened form of Obadiah, meaning "one who serves Yahweh." The naming practice here, as elsewhere, is not an act of authority over the baby but one of discernment. They understand that this child will serve the Lord, and because of that service, great things will come.

As though to demonstrate the truthfulness of their naming, 4:18–22 provides a genealogy of David that demonstrates how important Boaz and Ruth are to the coming of the king of promise, David. The genealogy is crafted so that Boaz is in the seventh position and David is the tenth name. These are the key slots in a genealogy of ten generations. Compare the line of Seth in Genesis 5. There Enoch, who went straight to heaven without tasting death, is in position seven, and Noah is in the tenth and final position.

Gender and Ideological Criticism

An interesting example of the many gendered approaches to Ruth is that of Ellen Van Wolde.[7] She studies the intertextual connection between the story

7. Van Wolde, "Texts in Dialogue." For other treatments comparing these two stories, see Brenner, "Naomi and Ruth"; Fewell and Gunn, *Compromising Redemption*.

of Judah and Tamar in Genesis 38 and that of Ruth—a connection explicitly made in Ruth 4:12, where the elders of Bethlehem relate Ruth and Boaz to this couple in their blessing of Naomi's family. Both Ruth and Genesis 38 begin with a note about the period of time when the story occurs, and both have someone leaving their country to go to a foreign land. The foreign women, Ruth and Tamar, are absent at both the beginning and at the end of the accounts.

In these frames Van Wolde finds the theme of the ongoing life of the descendants of Judah. The foreign women facilitate the process. Both stories portray something of levirate marriage. Both ascribe to Yahweh's intent the deaths of the original husbands at the beginning of the stories. After the deaths of the sons/husbands, both Judah and Naomi (the two people responsible for Tamar and Ruth) advise them to return to their birth homes. Both Tamar and Ruth wait for a time and then carry out a plan to involve an older male relative by preparing their appearance in a special way and meeting the man in a public place. They seek to continue the line of their dead husbands. Both succeed.

There are other areas for comparison. However, one point of discussion has to do with Naomi's instruction to Ruth to approach Boaz alone on the threshing floor at night and to "uncover" at "(the place of?) his feet." She complies (Ruth 3:4, 7). Some have observed that "feet" can be a euphemism for the male sex organs (as can "hand"). However, that would make the act very explicit in a cultural context that would view it negatively (as least in terms of the pentateuchal law and the approved practices seen elsewhere). Indeed, the picture would then seem to assume a marriage rather than propose one.

For Van Wolde, Ruth uncovers herself: she takes off her clothes and lies at his feet.[8] Generally for male and evangelical commentators, Ruth uncovers Boaz's feet, a symbol of her desire to be accepted by him.[9] Nevertheless, Van Wolde's argument seems to lie with the view that the expression for "feet" must mean "place of the feet." Taken literally, it would make no sense to say that Ruth uncovers the place of Boaz's feet. Nevertheless, the one occurrence of this term for "feet" outside of Ruth is in Daniel 10:6. There it is used alongside the common terms for body, face, eyes, and arms. Thus in the only other occurrence of this term, it can and does mean simply "feet," rather than "place of feet."

Robert Hubbard seems most likely correct when he finds here some custom that moderns no longer have insight into, or a means of chilling Boaz so that he would awake and find Ruth at his feet.[10] Van Wolde seems correct in arguing against any overt sexual acts. It would render nonsense of their dialogue and much of the fourth chapter, where formal arrangements for a marriage take place. Ruth 4:13 becomes especially awkward because it describes the subse-

8. Van Wolde, "Texts in Dialogue"; and for Nielsen, *Ruth*, 72.

9. Hubbard, *Book of Ruth*, 203–5; Bush, *Ruth, Esther*, 153; Younger, *Judges and Ruth*, 459.

10. Hubbard, *Book of Ruth*, 203–5.

quent marriage, which is then followed by sexual relations and the conception and birth of a child.

Ideologically, the story of Ruth has been used by both sides of the immigration debate. On the one hand, M. Daniel Carroll R. has well expressed this story as a premier example of many that describe how a non-Israelite is welcomed into the land and family of Israel.[11] On the other hand, James K. Hoffmeier asserts that Ruth effectively becomes a full Israelite in the process of her becoming part of the genealogy of David.[12] Ruth's statement to Naomi (1:16–17) is as close as one can get to a legal declaration of renunciation of her heritage and people and her full embracing of Naomi's people (Israel) and religion (Yahweh). Comparable statements in the ancient Near East as recorded in written documents are used to establish legal marriages, adoptions, and divorces.[13] In allusively mentioning Naomi's "daughter-in-law," 4:15 illustrates how the women of Bethlehem praise Ruth but also how her name disappears from the text at the end of the story.[14] Is this some sort of downplaying of her role, or an invitation to identify with Ruth in a positive manner—as the anonymity at the end of Judges may create the same effect, but there serve as a warning?

Finally, readers may consider the position of an African woman scholar in a South African context. Madipoane Masenya (ngwana' Mphahlele) argues that one of the most astonishing points of the narrative is the manner in which the young widow Ruth binds herself to the old mother-in-law Naomi. The effect of this is to render a value to female relationships, despite the overall male-centered nature of the society. This means one should recognize that marriage is not essential for God to work, but that God can and does work through human agents, regardless of such matters: "If we as individuals and participants in structures of power become willing agents and take upon ourselves the responsibility to transform our hopeless situations, we, like Ruth and Naomi, can trust God to make us rise above those circumstances."[15]

Ancient Near Eastern Context

The pastoral setting of Ruth has many elements that invite exploration in re-creating the scene of the ancient Near East. The village life of the earliest presence of Israel as a people in the Holy Land is attested both in the Bible

11. Carroll R., *Christians at the Border*.

12. See Hoffmeier, *Immigration Crisis*, 103–7. For the broader perspective of foreigners in the ancient Near East, see the examples and categories of Beckman, "Foreigners."

13. They also occur among Jews as early as the late fifth-century-BC legal documents from Elephantine.

14. Van Wolde, "Texts in Dialogue."

15. Masenya, "Ruth," 91. See also Siquans, "Foreignness and Poverty in the Book of Ruth."

The Town Gate

At the time of the judges, most Israelite villages were not fortified, and so the reference to the "city gate" in Ruth may have been symbolic or more likely referred to the main road or path as it entered the population center. At the northern extent of Israel, the city of Dan provides the best example of a gate, although from the later period of the monarchy. At this site one could see an outer courtyard, where several clusters of standing stones were identified. Inside the first gate were turns in the path, for security, and side chambers, such as at the city gates of Gezer, Megiddo, and Hazor. In one larger area could be found a bench where the elders could sit when pronouncing judgments on legal cases. Next to the bench was what appears to be a raised spot for a canopied chair or throne. Probably the king sat here when he came to pronounce judgment. Farther along the path is a second gate, which allows access behind the main city wall. In the outer court and here and there along the path through the gates are several collections of standing stones, used to venerate local deities or spirits, or for some other purpose. Because everyone who entered or exited the town would pass through the gate, it formed the public square and the central marketplace for exchanging goods and meeting people.

and in the numerous villages that appear in the early twelfth century BC.[16] Bethlehem was one of the southernmost villages of the central hill country inhabited by Israel.

Ruth 1:1 sets the historical and cultural context at the time of the judges. Yet readers of the book of Judges come away with a very different picture of the era. It is one of violence and destruction, not peace and love, as in Ruth. It is a time of fighting one's neighbors rather than accepting them into the covenant. Since the story of Ruth takes place during the March–April period of the barley harvest, there is much here to connect with the special customs of the threshing floor, the city gate, and property transactions in general. All of these may have varied from one culture to another, as in smaller ways from one town to another.

Two examples of ancient Near Eastern texts support items that are peculiar or at least important to the book of Ruth: (1) a mixed genre of prose and genealogy, and (2) the levirate marriage. The presence of genealogies mixed with prose texts, especially stories, has already been noticed in terms of the evidence from the Bible. Genesis 1–11 is an especially good example (see under "Higher Criticism," above). Similar genealogies with prose notes were also seen in the king lists of Babylon, Assyria, and other sources.

16. See "Ancient Near Eastern Context" for both Joshua and Judges.

Of special interest is a source from the culturally and chronologically nearby world of the Ugaritic texts. Ugarit was a city on the Syrian coast of the Mediterranean Sea. The texts discussed here date from the thirteenth century BC. There is only the main text, involving the royal spirits of the departed kings.[17] This text, now analyzed in light of a related Akkadian King List from Ugarit, contains a list of up to nearly fifty kings of Ugarit on one side. They have died and become divinized in the minds of the creator and first readers of this tablet. The other side of the Ugaritic tablet contains a prose or poetic text that identifies some musical instruments and appears to include the poetic repetition of some lines. If this is a ritual, it is to be connected with the king list on the other side. In the case of Ruth, a list leading to King David appears at the end of the book. However, the remainder of the work consists of the story. Like the Ugaritic text, it appears to be a work of art. However, its purpose is not to benefit dead leaders, but just the opposite. It praises the least of the people of Judah and the small town of Bethlehem. It glorifies the widow from Moab and recounts how, by the grace of God, she found a place in the line of the chosen kings of Judah.

A second example has to do with the levirate marriage custom (marriage to a brother-in-law, brother of the husband who died). Deuteronomy 25:5–10 establishes the law to guarantee that each family would have an heir and that the inheritance of land would remain in the family. It requires that, if a married man dies childless, and his widow remains alive and capable of bearing children, the brother of the dead man marry the widow and give the inheritance of the dead man to any male heir from that union. Naomi envisions this, but as an unrealistic possibility, in Ruth 1:11–13. Something like this appears to take place in 4:1–13. However, neither Boaz nor the nearer kinsman are brothers of Mahlon, the dead husband of Ruth. Further, Ruth does not participate in the sandal ceremony, nor are the particular actions with the sandal performed in Ruth 4 envisioned in the laws of Deuteronomy 25.

However, while this is not precisely the levirate law of Deuteronomy, it may be an extension of that law in accordance with already-established customs. Levirate laws similar to those known in Israel did exist elsewhere in the ancient Near East. In the Anatolian kingdom of the Hittites, whose laws might be dated to the fourteenth and thirteenth centuries BC, law 193 reads: "If a man has a wife, and the man dies, his brother shall take his widow as wife. (If the brother dies,) his father shall take her. When afterwards his father dies, his (i.e., the father's) brother shall take the woman whom he had."[18]

This law envisions a further extension of the biblical levirate law, to include the father (cf. Gen. 38, Judah and Tamar) and even additional male

17. See Pardee (*Ritual and Cult at Ugarit*, 195–210) for introduction to, translation of, and notes on Ugaritic text RS 24.257 as well as the related Akkadian King List of Ugarit, RS 94.2518.

18. Hoffner, *Laws of the Hittites*, 152.

family members. Indeed, the enforcement of this law appears to have been applied by one Hittite king to a vassal king, in instructing him to take his daughter who had been widowed and to give her in marriage to the dead man's brother.[19]

Canonical Context

Much has already been discussed regarding the canonical context. For the connections with Judah and Tamar in Genesis 38, see "Gender and Ideological Criticism" (above). The single occurrence of "Ruth" in the New Testament also coincides with the occurrence of "Tamar." Both appear in the genealogy of Jesus in Matthew 1:3, 5. They introduce one of Matthew's messages, that the gospel of Jesus Christ is for all nations of the world, for men and women, and for all peoples, regardless of their social condition.

The connection of Ruth with the levirate laws of Deuteronomy 25 has already been identified. The same is true of the genealogy and the obvious connection of the succeeding period with David and the emergence of the Davidic dynasty.

This small book has a distinctive position in the Hebrew and Greek Scriptures. The usual position in the Hebrew Masoretic Text places Ruth in the third part of the canon, the Writings. There it follows Proverbs and begins the Megilloth, the smaller Scrolls (Ruth, Esther, Ecclesiastes, Lamentations, and Song of Songs). In Ruth 3:11, after Ruth awakens Boaz at the threshing floor, Boaz describes her as a "woman of noble character" (Heb. *ʾēšet ḥayil*). This term occurs elsewhere only in Proverbs 12:4 and 31:10. Chapter 31 is the last chapter of the book of Proverbs and immediately precedes Ruth in the Hebrew canonical order. It has long been noticed that the wife of noble character, as described in Proverbs 31, may be a foreshadowing of the woman of noble character after whom the book of Ruth is named.

The dominant order in the Septuagint manuscripts, as also found in the Christian Old Testament, has the book of Ruth following Judges. Set in the period of the judges (Ruth 1:1), this book balances the violence and brutality of the age. The peaceful and pastoral love story demonstrates a very different picture from that seen in the preceding book. In contrast to the final chapters of the book of Judges, where the names of the characters disappear and anonymity and loss of identity pervade the account, the book of Ruth begins with a flurry of personal names as the book focuses on identity, personal character, and relationships. The book of Judges, especially in the final chapters, demonstrates how the Israelites abandon their faith. On the contrary, the book of Ruth illustrates how a woman of Moab comes to true

19. Section 29 of the treaty between Suppiluliuma I of Hatti and Huqqana of Hayasa. See Beckman, *Hittite Diplomatic Texts*, 28.

faith. In both accounts, God is at work behind the scenes. However, in Ruth the picture is one that has the grace of God working for good.

Theological Perspectives of Ruth

In the book of Ruth, God is without doubt confessed as the key figure at work. The personal name Yahweh occurs some seventeen times. Yahweh appears twice as part of the narratives: in 1:6, where Yahweh gives his people food; and in 4:13, where Yahweh enables conception and the birth of a child for Boaz and Ruth. Arguably, these are the events that set the story in motion and that bring it to its climax. Thus God is sovereign over all the events of the story.

Otherwise, Yahweh's name appears regularly on the lips of all the major characters and the groups of men and women who address Boaz and Ruth in chapter 4. They attribute to him bad and most often good circumstances. They use his name in greetings and blessings. There is no evidence of false use or misuse of the name. Instead, their confession of Israel's God ennobles the characters as they share a common faith and view of the world and how it works. Yahweh reigns in Bethlehem, and its citizens openly confess their belief that every area of their lives depends on his goodness and mercy.

It is this image of God's gracious work and loving-kindness toward all peoples that lies behind the story of Ruth. Although the Hebrew term *ḥesed* is not found in Ruth, it characterizes the entire narrative. God is there, both in the explicit events and dialogue where all that is good is attributed to Yahweh, and in the palpable sense of God's work behind the scenes to bring to pass his plans of good for Naomi, Ruth, and Boaz—and his salvation of his people through the birth of David's grandfather and beginning the messianic line.

The characters as gracious models of faith, hope, and love have already been discussed in "Literary Readings" (above), as well as in "Gender and Ideological Criticism." See also "Premodern Readings" and "Canonical Context" for the role of this book and its characters in the greater plan of God's kingdom.

Key Commentaries and Studies

Block, Daniel I. *Judges, Ruth*. NAC 6. Nashville: Broadman & Holman, 1999. This is an excellent, evangelical, detailed commentary.

Bush, Frederic W. *Ruth, Esther.* WBC 9. Dallas: Word, 1996. This commentary represents the work of a scholar of ancient languages and of the biblical backgrounds of the second millennium BC.

Hubbard, Robert L., Jr. *The Book of Ruth*. NICOT. Grand Rapids: Eerdmans, 1988. This balanced, evangelical study represents strengths in form criticism and the examination of the broad range of scholarship.

Nielsen, Kirsten. *Ruth: A Commentary.* OTL. Louisville: Westminster John Knox, 1997. Rhetorical and intertextual specialties in this work that is sensitive to feminist concerns.

Sasson, Jack M. *Ruth: A New Translation with a Philological Commentary and a Formalist-Folklorist Interpretation*. 2nd ed. Sheffield: Sheffield Academic, 1989. Written by an ancient Near Eastern specialist.

Schipper, Jeremy. *Ruth: A New Translation with Introduction and Commentary*. AB 7D. New Haven: Yale University Press, 2016. An up-to-date resource for a concise survey of interpretations and informed exegetical insights.

Younger, K. Lawson, Jr. *Judges and Ruth*. NIVAC. Grand Rapids: Zondervan, 2002. Careful literary analysis, thorough understanding of the background, and an evangelical perspective.

9

1–2 SAMUEL

A question to keep in mind when reading 1–2 Samuel is, Who is most likely to succeed? Is it the tall, handsome Saul, whom all the people admire? Or is it the barren Hannah? Is it David, least among his many brothers and pursued by the murderous King Saul? In these chapters we see God's unexpected choices and purposes.

Name, Text, and Outline

The name of the Hebrew book, Samuel (*šĕmûʾēl*), is also the name of the chief human character in the first part of 1 Samuel. While the books themselves are silent on their authorship and date, the Talmud records the rabbinic tradition that 1 Samuel 1–24 was written by Samuel and that Nathan and Gad wrote the rest of the work (*b. B. Bat.* 14b–15a; drawing on 1 Chron. 29:29). The text divides into two scrolls or books, 1 and 2 Samuel. This probably reflects the size of the work, which was better accommodated by two scrolls. The Septuagint uses the term "Kingdoms" (or "Reigns") for these books and for those of 1–2 Kings. Thus there are four Kingdoms books that correspond to 1–2 Samuel and 1–2 Kings.

The Masoretic Hebrew text of 1–2 Samuel is widely recognized as the most problematic of all the Hebrew books of the Old Testament. Even so, it can largely be read as it stands, with the intent of the text understood. This is especially true if one is able to repoint the consonantal text and accept

Addition to 1 Samuel 11

The Dead Sea Scrolls text 4QSam[a] includes, at the beginning of 1 Samuel 11, an explanation for the Ammonite war and their demand to blind the citizens of Jabesh-gilead. The NRSV is convinced of its authenticity and provides the following translation:

> Now Nahash, king of the Ammonites, had been grievously oppressing the Gadites and the Reubenites. He would gouge out the right eye of each of them and would not grant Israel a deliverer. No one was left of the Israelites across the Jordan whose right eye Nahash, king of the Ammonites, had not gouged out. But there were seven thousand men who had escaped from the Ammonites and had entered Jabesh-gilead.
>
> 11:1 About a month later, . . .

This addition is not attested in a Septuagint, Masoretic Text, or other manuscript. As David T. Tsumura observes, there is nothing in the text that could "trigger" any haplography that might explain how a scribe overlooked this text and skipped from the end of chapter 10 to what is now the first verse of chapter 11.[a] Further, Nahash is never called "king" in 1 Samuel 11 as he is in this fragment in both cases where the king is named. Thus, despite the assumptions of some scholars, including the translators of 1 Samuel 11 for the NRSV, there are good reasons to suspect 4QSam[a] as containing an addition to the original text, rather than serving as the authentic and sole witness to it.

[a] Tsumura, *First Book of Samuel*, 302–3.

alternative possibilities that these interpretations suggest.[1] The Septuagint and texts among the Dead Sea Scrolls (4QSam[a] and 4QSam[c]) attest to a significantly shorter account of the David and Goliath story (1 Sam. 17–18); they do not have 1 Samuel 2:8–9a but include a longer text similar to Jeremiah 9:22–23.[2] The scrolls also add a paragraph of background information at the beginning of 1 Samuel 11 and the story of the siege of Jabesh-gilead. These and other variants are matched in the Dead Sea Scrolls manuscripts.

To this complexity should be added the question of the Lucianic recension of these books as preserved in Septuagint manuscripts (b, o, c_2, e_2). Sometimes referred to as Antiochene, this manuscript tradition attests to an early and distinct *Vorlage* (original Hebrew text translated into Greek and Latin) that was, in its later history, corrected toward the Masoretic Text. The Lucianic text

1. See, e.g., Tsumura, *First Book of Samuel*, 2–10, who proposes phonetic spellings and idiomatic expressions.
2. Dines, *Septuagint*, 17.

is separate from the Septuagint tradition and an important witness for possibly early and original readings among the textual witnesses to 1–4 Kingdoms.

Thus the textual traditions that witness to 1–2 Samuel are complex and vary from their earliest period. There is no agreement in scholarship as to which of these manuscripts preserves the most-original readings. A full study of investigations into the textual history of Samuel lies beyond this introduction. We will look at the Masoretic Text and some significant variants with the Septuagint and Lucianic recensions that are relevant.

OUTLINE

- I. Hannah's Story (1 Sam. 1:1–2:11)
  - A. Hannah Desires a Child and God's Gift (1:1–28)
  - B. Hannah Praises (2:1–10)
  - C. Transition to Samuel's Story (2:11)
- II. Samuel's Story (2:12–8:22)
  - A. Eli's Sons and Samuel (2:12–36)
  - B. Call of Samuel (3:1–21)
  - C. Israel without Samuel (4:1–7:2)
    - 1. Israel's Loss in Battle and the Capture of the Ark (4:1–22)
    - 2. The Ark Defeats the Philistines, Who Return It (5:1–7:2)
  - D. Samuel's Ministry (7:3–8:3)
  - E. Israel Demands a King (8:4–22)
- III. Saul's Story (9:1–15:35)
  - A. Samuel Anoints Saul as King Privately (9:1–10:1)
  - B. Saul Publicly Recognized as King (10:2–27)
  - C. Saul Defeats the Ammonites (11:1–15)
  - D. Samuel Addresses Israel (12:1–25)
  - E. Saul Reigns (13:1–14:52)
  - F. Saul Rejected as King (15:1–35)
- IV. David Rises (1 Sam. 16:1–2 Sam. 1:27)
  - A. Samuel Anoints David (1 Sam. 16:1–13)
  - B. David Heals Saul (16:14–23)
  - C. David and Goliath (17:1–54)
  - D. David Becomes Involved in Saul's Family (17:55–18:28)
  - E. Saul Seeks to Kill David (18:29–20:42)
  - F. David Escapes Saul in Judah (21:1–26:25)
  - G. David Fights with the Philistines (27:1–30:31)
  - H. Saul and Jonathan Killed (31:1–13)
  - I. David Eulogizes Saul (2 Sam. 1:1–27)
- V. David's Story (2 Sam. 2:1–20:26)
  - A. David Reigns in Hebron (2:1–4:12)
  - B. David Reigns in Jerusalem (5:1–7:29)
    - 1. Jerusalem Captured (5:1–25)
    - 2. The Ark Brought to Jerusalem (6:1–23)

3. God Promises David His Kingship (7:1–29)
C. David Campaigns from Jerusalem (8:1–10:19)
D. David, Bathsheba, and the Result (11:1–14:33)
E. Absalom Rebels and the Result (15:1–20:3)
F. Sheba Revolts (20:4–26)

VI. Appendices (21:1–24:25)
A. Saul's Family (21:1–14)
B. Philistine Heroes (21:15–22)
C. Thanksgiving Psalm (22:1–51)
D. David's "Last Words" (23:1–7)
E. Israelite Heroes (23:8–39)
F. The Census and the Result (24:1–25)

Overview of 1 and 2 Samuel

First and Second Samuel are the story of early Israel and how it moves from the time of the judges to the monarchy. The many details require a longer overview. The account begins with Hannah, who is one of two wives of Elkanah, residing in the central region of Israel, in the land of Ephraim. Hannah is most loved by Elkanah, but she is barren. Her rival wife, who has children, torments Hannah. At an annual sacrifice to the Lord in Shiloh, Hannah prays to have a son. She promises God she will dedicate him to the Lord's service as a Nazirite. Thinking that Hannah is drunk, the priest Eli tells her to become sober. She protests that she is not drunk but praying quietly to God. So Eli blesses her that God might give Hannah her request. Hannah becomes pregnant and gives birth to Samuel. When she has weaned him, she brings him to the annual sacrifice, where Hannah dedicates Samuel to God. She gives him to Eli to be a servant of God at the tabernacle in Shiloh.

Hannah praises God with a psalm (1 Sam. 2:1–10), describing how God takes the humble and poor and raises them to positions of honor. The psalm ends with praise for God strengthening his king and exalting his anointed ("messiah"). Eli's sons, however, do not exemplify devotion to God. They take whatever meat and fat parts they want from the offerings that belong to the Lord, and they have sex with the women who serve at the tabernacle. Meanwhile Hannah visits Samuel each year and brings him a new robe to wear. So Hannah is blessed with more children, but a prophet condemns Eli, promising the loss of his sons and their replacement by someone outside his family.

Samuel serves God and receives his call (1 Sam. 3). At night God calls him by name three times. Only the third time does he realize what is happening (that it isn't Eli calling him). God promises that he will bless Samuel as much as he will punish the sons of Eli. As Samuel grows, the Lord continues to minister through him, and all Israel recognizes that the boy is a prophet.

In 1 Samuel 4, the Philistines are at war with Israel. They occupy Aphek, near the coast, while the Israelites hold Ebenezer, farther inland. When the Philistines win a battle, Israel decides they will apply the full power of their God: they bring the ark of the covenant from Shiloh, with the two sons of Eli. The Philistines' fear when they hear Israel's army welcoming the ark empowers them to defeat Israel decisively. The ark is captured, and many Israelites are killed, including Eli's two sons. On hearing the news, Eli falls backward off his chair and dies of a broken neck. His grandson is born at the same time and receives the name Ichabod, meaning, "Where is the glory?" (NLT) or "There is no glory" (TLB).

The Philistines place the ark in their temple to the god Dagon at Ashdod (1 Sam. 5). However, the ark remains standing in the temple while the image of Dagon falls on its face and breaks. So they move the ark to the Philistine city of Gath and then to Ekron. At each town God afflicts the Philistines with tumors of some sort. The priests and diviners among the Philistines have them send the ark, along with a guilt offering of five gold tumors and five gold rats, down the road to the Israelites at Beth-shemesh (1 Sam. 6). When they arrive on a cart drawn by two cows, the Israelites use the wood of the cart to offer a burnt offering of the cows to the Lord. However, seventy citizens of Beth-shemesh die because they look into the ark. The survivors send a message to Kiriath-jearim to accept the ark. They do so at the house of Abinadab, where his son Eleazar guards it for twenty years (1 Sam. 7:1–2). There follows a time of national confession and repentance at Mizpah. There Samuel leads the Israelites, and there the Philistines attack. God fights for Israel and throws the Philistines into panic so that neither they nor the Amorites trouble Israel for the lifetime of Samuel. Samuel's work as a judge is centered in the hill country around Mizpah and Bethel. Ramah is his home, where he has an altar. In 1 Samuel 8, Samuel has appointed his two sons as leaders in Beersheba. They are dishonest, however. So the people ask Samuel to appoint a king for them like the other nations. God states that they are rejecting his kingship and then authorizes Samuel to explain what this would mean for Israel. A king would take their sons and daughters for his own purposes. Nevertheless, they continue to want a king.

Kish, father of Saul of Benjamin, has lost some donkeys (1 Sam. 9). Saul and a servant go in search of them. They come to Zuph, where the servant knows of Samuel, who might be able to tell them where the donkeys have gone. God has told Samuel that Saul is coming, whom Samuel is to anoint as leader over Israel, to deliver Israel from the Philistines. When Samuel recognizes Saul, who is taller than other Israelites, God prompts Samuel, and he identifies himself as the seer. He directs Saul to the place of sacrifice and of a special meal with thirty invited guests. Samuel places Saul at the head of the dining table and gives him a special portion of meat. Saul stays with Samuel overnight. The next day Samuel sends Saul's party ahead but meets

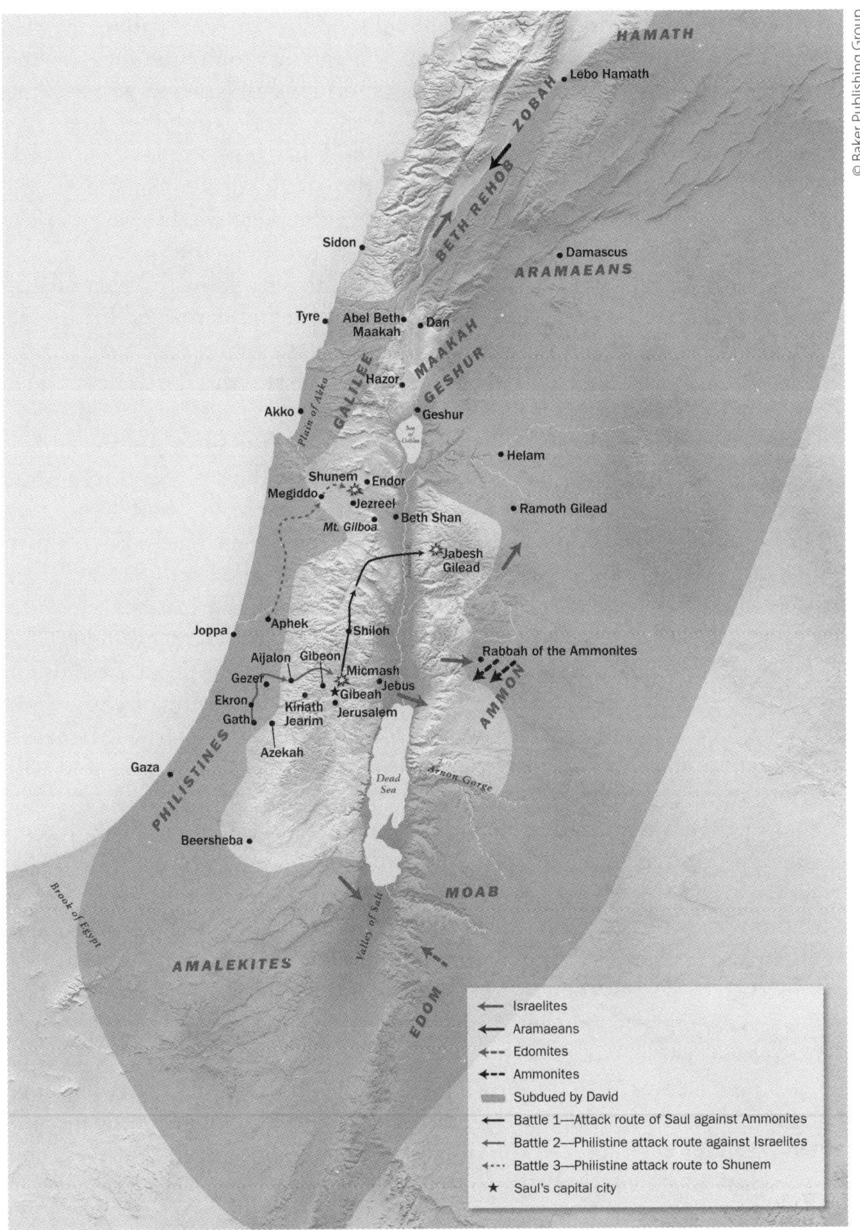

© Baker Publishing Group

Events from the time of Saul

privately with Saul. Samuel then pours oil on Saul's head and recognizes his leadership over Israel (1 Sam. 10). Samuel predicts that Saul will meet three groups on his return home: the first bringing the donkeys, the second bringing food, and and the third prophesying. Saul meets all three. He joins the last group as the spirit of the Lord comes on him and he prophesies, much to the surprise of those who know him. Samuel summons all Israel to worship the Lord at Mizpah. There he reports God's words as indicating that Israel has rejected God. They want a king who will now be chosen before the Lord. Progressing from tribe to clan to family in the casting of lots, Saul is chosen but is not around. He is found hiding among the baggage. However, when all Israel sees how tall he is and hears Samuel pronouncing him as chosen by the Lord, they accept him as king. Samuel also explains the meaning of kingship and writes its description on a scroll, which is deposited before the Lord. Some accept Saul, but others despise him.

The Ammonites lay siege to the Israelite town of Jabesh-gilead (1 Sam. 11). They demand the right to gouge out the right eye of every man in the city. The citizens appeal to Israel. When Saul hears of it, the spirit of God comes on him: he takes his oxen, cuts them up, and sends their pieces throughout Israel as a summons to assemble an army. Saul leads this army, and they defeat the Ammonites. The people are led by Samuel to confirm Saul's kingship at Gilgal and to celebrate with fellowship offerings to the Lord. Samuel then delivers his last attested address to all Israel (1 Sam. 12). He testifies how God has done so much for Israel despite their many sins, which have brought judgment. Now they have rejected God's kingship. To make his point, he calls on God to send a thunderstorm despite the season of late spring or early summer, when it does not rain. This event strikes fear into the hearts of Israel as they repent and ask Samuel to pray for them. He says he will pray and will continue to teach them.

Out of the army assembled against Ammon, Saul retains three thousand soldiers for himself and a thousand for his son Jonathan (1 Sam. 13). When Jonathan attacks the Philistine outpost at Geba, the result brings the Philistines with thousands of chariots near where Saul is camped. Israel is fearful, and many in Saul's army begin to abandon him. He waits for a week as Samuel has instructed. When Samuel does not arrive, Saul himself chooses to sacrifice to God. As soon as he finishes, Samuel appears and criticizes him. He states that Saul has lost a lasting kingdom and that God has chosen someone else. When Samuel leaves Saul, the king has about six hundred warriors remaining. The Philistines, meanwhile, are sending raiding parties all around Saul and cutting through the center of the Israelite settlement in the hill country. They also control all the blacksmiths so that only Saul and Jonathan have proper weapons among all of Israel.

In 1 Samuel 14 Jonathan and his armor bearer succeed in showing themselves to some Philistines, who challenge them. The Israelite duo then climb up and kill twenty Philistines. At this point a panic breaks out among the Philistines. Saul then sends his army after the Philistines, and they chase them from Israel. However, Saul makes a rash vow that no one can eat anything until the battle is ended. So the Israelites are tired and hungry during their pursuit, and they do not enjoy as great a victory as they might. Jonathan, unaware of the vow, eats some honey and renews his strength. However, at the end of the day Saul must control the army, which seizes the Philistine cattle and begins eating them raw. Saul builds an altar for butchering the animals properly. However, God does not respond to his requests about what to do next with the Philistines. Suspecting that someone has disregarded his vow, Saul uses the Urim and Thummim to identify the culprit. When Jonathan is identified, the Israelite army intervenes and prevents his execution. Saul is successful in battles against Israel's enemies throughout his reign.

God commands the extermination of the Amalekites, whose ancestors ambushed innocent Israelites in their first generation of wandering in the wilderness, after leaving Egypt (1 Sam. 15). With due warning to any who fear Israel and its God, Saul and the Israelites attack Amalek and leave no one alive except their king and the best of their flocks. Samuel brings God's judgment on Saul for disobeying the command to kill everyone, including the king of the Amalekites: "To obey is better than sacrifice, and to heed is better than the fat of rams" (15:22b). Here God rejects more than a dynasty for Saul; God also rejects Saul's kingship. Saul then begs for Samuel's (and God's) forgiveness and catches hold of Samuel's robe when he turns to leave, but to no avail. Samuel puts the Amalekite king to death and then leaves Saul, never to see him again.

God tells Samuel to stop mourning for Saul (1 Sam. 16). The Lord sends him to Bethlehem to anoint a son of Jesse. Going under the ruse of performing a sacrifice, Samuel arrives in Bethlehem. He calls for Jesse and has each of his sons pass by. But God does not accept any of them until the last, David, is called from his job of tending the flock. Samuel anoints him with oil before his brothers. When the spirit of the Lord departs from Saul and an evil spirit begins to trouble him, David is called to play his lyre for the king and calm him.

The famous story of David and Goliath appears in 1 Samuel 17. Saul and Israel's army are intimidated by the Philistine champion Goliath, who stands some nine feet in height. Jesse sends his son David to deliver food to his brothers on Israel's battle line and to learn how the battle is faring. While there, David learns of Goliath and offers to Saul that he will meet the Philistine in battle. Saul agrees and sends David. David downs Goliath with a stone from his sling. He kills him with his own sword and cuts off his head. The Philistines panic and flee, with Israel in pursuit. At the end of the story, David is presented to Saul. At this point the people begin to praise David more than Saul (1 Sam. 18), making Saul jealous. Yet David succeeds in every battle, becomes a close friend of the king's son and successor Jonathan, and is married to Saul's daughter after collecting double the number of Philistine foreskins Saul demands as a bride-price. Saul intends this bride-price to bring an end to David, believing that the Philistines will kill him. When it does not happen,

Saul tells Jonathan and his court to kill David (1 Sam. 19). But Jonathan, who loves David, warns him. He persuades his father, the king, of David's loyalty and value. But later an evil spirit seizes Saul, and he tries to pin David to the wall with his spear. David escapes the palace and goes into hiding. Michal, Saul's daughter and David's wife, assists David in his escape. He flees north to Samuel at Ramah. Saul sends several squads to capture David, but each one fails and joins in the ecstatic prophesying there. When Saul goes, the same thing happens to him.

Jonathan does not believe that his father really wants to kill David (1 Sam. 20). He makes an agreement with David to give him a signal on the day after a Feast of the New Moon that Saul holds and at which David is expected to be present. Jonathan is to give an excuse when Saul inquires about David, that he has a family engagement. If Saul accepts the excuse, then Jonathan is right and David is safe. If Saul becomes enraged, then David must flee. The latter occurs, and Jonathan signals this to David. The two part as sworn friends. David flees to Nob, where he obtains Goliath's sword from the priests there (1 Sam. 21). Then he tries to find refuge with the Philistine king of Gath, but when David is recognized by the servants as an enemy and pretends to be insane, the king refuses him. From there, David journeys with his family and other supporters to Moab (1 Sam. 22) while Saul exterminates the priesthood and people at Nob for assisting David. David then continues his journeys to Judah, to fight the Philistines at Keilah and to spend a brief time at Ziph (1 Sam. 23), and to En Gedi. In the En Gedi region David is able to kill Saul in a cave but does not (1 Sam. 24). As a result, Saul considers David more worthy than himself.

David sends his men to request provision from Nabal after they have protected his shepherds. Nabal refuses, but his wife gives David and his men food and drink. Nabal dies, and his widow becomes David's wife (1 Sam. 25). At another place in the desert of Ziph, David and his men again have Saul in their power while he sleeps. However, they only take evidence of their presence, which demonstrates to Saul how loyal David is (1 Sam. 26).

Fearing for his life, David flees again to the Philistine city of Gath, where the king, Achish, gives him a town. From there he conducts raids against Israel's enemies while telling Achish he is fighting enemies of the Philistines (1 Sam. 27).

As the Philistines gather for a major battle, Saul, fearful for his life, consults a medium (1 Sam. 28). Although he has banished mediums from Israel, when God does not respond to his queries he finds a woman who conjures up a form of the dead Samuel. Samuel then reaffirms God's judgment and promises that Saul and his sons will die in the battle the following day. As that day approaches, the Philistines do not allow David and his army to fight for them (1 Sam. 29), so David's group returns to the land of the Philistines. When they arrive at Ziglag, David finds that it has been sacked by Amalekite

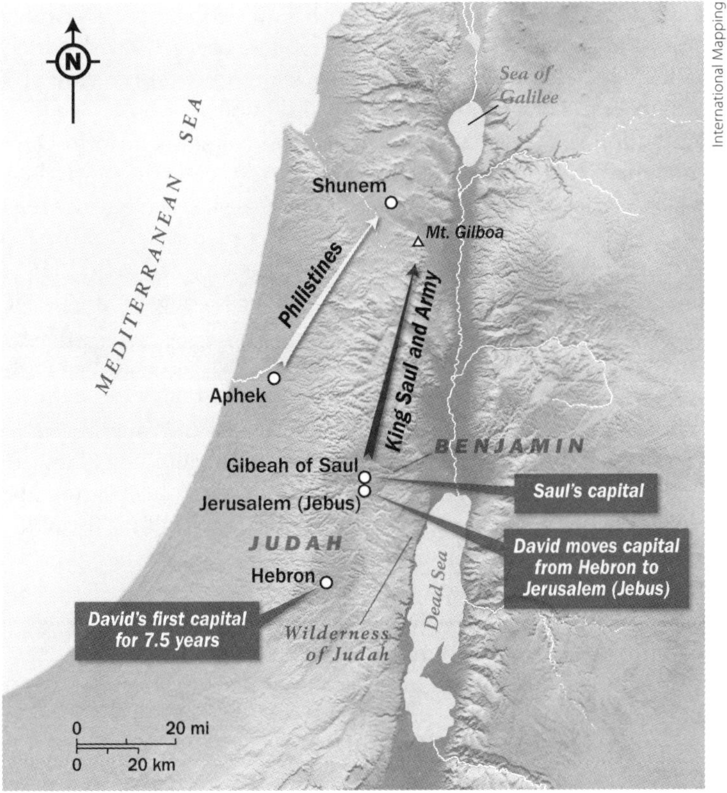

Saul's last battle

raiders (1 Sam. 30). He goes after them, defeats them, and retrieves all the plunder. This he shares with all his men as well as friends in Judah. Meanwhile, the Philistines defeat Israel at Mount Gilboa (1 Sam. 31). They kill Saul's sons and then wound Saul, who kills himself rather than fall into Philistine hands. The Philistines display the bodies of Saul and his sons on the walls of Beth-shan, but agents from Jabesh-gilead come by night, retrieve the bodies, and give the remains a burial in their hometown.

David's reception of the report of Saul's death, his execution of the Amalekite who claims to have killed Saul, and his eulogy over the glories of Saul and Jonathan begin 2 Samuel. After inquiring of the Lord, David is led to Hebron, where the citizens of Judah anoint him king (2 Sam. 2). Abner the general takes Saul's son Ishbosheth and establishes him as king over Israel in Mahanaim, east of the Jordan River. Joab, who is David's general, meets Abner and his men at the pool of Gibeon. They begin a battle, in which Abner kills Joab's brother Asahel. Finally, Abner calls it off, and they depart. However, nearly four hundred die, most of them Benjaminites who side with Abner.

Ishbosheth accuses Abner of sleeping with Saul's concubine, so Abner begins negotiations to join David and to bring all Israel over to David's side (2 Sam. 3). Before it can be completed, Joab pulls aside Abner at the gate of Hebron and murders him. David condemns Joab and publicly mourns Abner's death. Two Benjaminites assassinate Ishbosheth and bring his head to David, who condemns them and executes them for the deed (2 Sam. 4). With their leader and his general dead, the elders of all the tribes of Israel come to Hebron and appoint David as their king (2 Sam. 5). He then proceeds to capture Jerusalem and make its fortress his own, renamed as "the city of David" (5:7). Twice the Philistines come to attack David, and twice he defeats them, according to the Lord's counsel.

David brings the ark from Abinadab's house, where it has been for twenty years, to Jerusalem (2 Sam. 6). At first he gets only as far as the house of Obed-Edom because the Lord strikes down Uzzah for reaching out his hand to steady the ark. However, when David hears how God has blessed Obed-Edom, he decides to move it to Jerusalem, with much celebration and dancing. While David gives cakes to all who celebrate with him, his wife Michal despises him for dancing half naked and tells him so. As a final note, we are told that she never has a child.

David is settled in a large palace in Jerusalem and longs to build a "house" or temple for the Lord (2 Sam. 7). The prophet Nathan gives assent at first, but then in a dream God reveals that David is not to build a "house" for him. Instead, God will build a "house" or dynasty for David. David's son will build God's house, and his offspring will always reign in Jerusalem over the people of God. David expresses humility and praise when Nathan tells him of this.

In every direction, David has victory over and subdues the nations (2 Sam. 8). He sets up his administration. He also seeks to do good for the descendants of Saul and Jonathan, specifically, Mephibosheth, who is to eat at the royal table and to own the lands that Saul owned. David seeks peace with the Ammonites, but they humiliate

© Baker Publishing Group and Dr. James C. Martin

Idrimi, king of fifteenth-century-BC Alalakh, whose story of gaining the crown demonstrates how narratives similar to that of David's becoming king were written even before the biblical king

his emissaries (2 Sam. 10), so he fights them and their Aramaean allies, and he defeats them.

David does not go to war in the spring but sends Joab with his army to defeat Ammon and lay siege to its capital, Rabbah (2 Sam. 11). He spies Bathsheba bathing and calls her to his palace, where he has sex with her, despite knowing that she is the wife of Uriah the Hittite, who is at the time away in the battle. When she becomes pregnant, David brings back Uriah under other pretenses and encourages him to sleep with his wife. He refuses, despite David's best efforts. So David sends him back to the battle with sealed instructions for Joab to position Uriah so that he will be killed in the battle. After this happens, Bathsheba mourns for him and then moves into David's palace. The Lord sends Nathan to David with the story of a rich man who took a poor man's only and much-loved lamb to serve a guest (2 Sam. 12). David sentences the rich man to death, and Nathan responds, "You are the man!" So God judges David by promising that violence will remain in his house and by causing Bathsheba's son to die in infancy. The couple have a second son, whom they name Solomon, but Nathan names him Jedidiah, "Loved by the LORD." David completes the conquest of Rabbah and the Ammonites.

Second Samuel 13 turns to consider the next generation of David's family as God's judgment against David begins to be realized. In the first account, David's son Amnon desires his half sister Tamar. He tricks her in to coming to his room and then rapes her. Afterward he despises her and sends her away. She flees to her brother Absalom. David learns of the incident and becomes angry but does nothing else. Two years later, when Absalom and his half brothers are away from Jerusalem, Amnon becomes drunk, and Absalom's men kill him. The matter is reported to David, but Absalom flees to his mother's family in Geshur (east of the Sea of Galilee) and remains there for three years. Joab knows that David longs for Absalom's return (2 Sam. 14). He brings a wise woman from Tekoa and has her tell a story about how one of her sons has killed the other in a quarrel and now her clan demands his blood. However, she does not want to lose both sons. David agrees to protect him, and she points out that this is similar to his own situation with Absalom. David realizes that Joab is behind this and has Joab bring Absalom back to Jerusalem. He does not see Absalom for an additional two years, however, until Absalom convinces Joab to persuade David to meet with him.

Despite their reconciliation, Absalom conceives a plot to win the hearts of the people of Israel over to him by meeting them at the city gate and supporting their claims to justice (2 Sam. 15). After four years he requests permission to go to Hebron. While he is there with hundreds of supporters, messengers throughout the country proclaim Absalom as king. After hearing this, David flees Jerusalem. He sends back two priests, Zadok and Abiathar, and a loyal friend Hushai, whom he instructs to play the part of a traitor against David and a counselor to Absalom. While David proceeds to the Jordan River, he is blessed by Ziba but cursed by Shimei of Saul's house (2 Sam. 16). Meanwhile, Absalom enters Jerusalem, where his trusted counselor Ahithophel advises him to sleep with David's concubines who remain in the palace. He does this in a public demonstration of his claim to kingship. Ahithophel recommends that Absalom pursue David immediately, while Hushai recommends that all Israel first be gathered and then they should go after him with overwhelming force (2 Sam. 17). Absalom follows Hushai's advice, and this allows David to escape east of the Jordan River to Mahanaim, where he receives further aid and support. Ahithophel kills himself because his advice was rejected. The battle that follows is won by David's men (2 Sam. 18). He stays behind but orders his generals not to treat Absalom badly. However, when Absalom's hair becomes caught in a tree and he is left hanging, Joab kills the prince. This is reported to David, who weeps for him. Joab hears of David's mourning and confronts him with the challenge that he should encourage his army or they will all desert (2 Sam. 19). David does this and then begins his return to Jerusalem. Many come with him either to confirm their loyalty or to claim it.

However, Sheba of Benjamin initiates another revolt against David (2 Sam. 20). Israel joins in this while Judah remains loyal to David. The troops loyal to David muster at Gibeon, under the leadership of Joab. David has promised the generalship to Amasa. When Amasa arrives with his contingent, Joab pretends to greet him and then stabs and eviscerates him. All Judah follows Joab, who pursues Sheba to Abel of Beth-maacah, near the northern limit of Israel. They are about to tear down the wall of the city when a wise woman negotiates with Joab and persuades the citizens to trade the head of Sheba for the security of Abel of Beth-maacah.

In 2 Samuel 21, David ends a famine of three years by appeasing the Gibeonites and handing over seven of Saul's descendants so that the Gibeonites might take vengeance on them for the vengeance Saul took on Gibeon. David then gives their bones, as well as those of Saul and Jonathan (brought from Jabesh-gilead), an honored burial in the tomb of Saul's father, Kish. The chapter ends with four incidents where individual Israelites defeat champions of the Philistines. David has become too old to go to war.

Second Samuel 22 forms a psalm where David describes his dangers and praises God for his deliverance. In 2 Samuel 23, David's "last words" include observations about ruling God's people in righteousness and about avoiding evil men. There follows a summary with the names of David's mighty warriors and their deeds. In the final chapter (2 Sam. 24) David insists on numbering the armies of Judah and of Israel, despite the protests of his generals. When he does so, he is convicted, and God gives him the choice of three judgments: famine, flight from enemies, or a plague. The plague ensues with the deaths of seventy thousand. Where the plague stops, at the threshing floor of Araunah the Jebusite, is a place that David purchases so he can sacrifice burnt and fellowship offerings.

Reading 1 and 2 Samuel

Premodern Readings

The earliest interpretations divide between those that use 1–2 Samuel as a historical source to recount the history of early Israel and those that find in David especially a model or harbinger of some aspect of God's plan and blessing. The former can be found in Josephus's *Jewish Antiquities*, which follows a historical analysis, not unlike that already established in 1–2 Chronicles. The latter can be seen in Sirach 47:4–5, where David's killing of Goliath focuses on his calling on God to deliver his people. The same is true of Samuel in Sirach 46:16–17. Ben Sira regards Samuel as a prophet (46:15); in early Christianity, this role develops much more for David. There his words and writings are seen as prophetic from the inception of the church (Acts 2:29–31).

In the history of Christian interpretation 1–2 Samuel has been read largely through an allegorical method that emphasizes David as a Christ figure. Thus his life prefigures the coming of Jesus, his work, suffering, and death, and his exaltation and promised return to rule. For Augustine, Saul as the enemy of David can represent the Jews, who sought to put Jesus Christ to death.[3] Saul becomes an embodiment of Satan's plan on earth to persecute the church, as in the work of Nicholas of Lyra (ca. 1200).[4]

The Reformation emphasized the historical background and the theological intent of the text. Alongside this method, the interest in the kingdom of God brought about by Jesus Christ found its anticipation in the kingdom of David. The promises to David became a key means of realizing the fulfillment of the reign of Jesus Christ in the New Testament and in his ongoing kingdom of the church. Some Reformation interpretations saw Saul as representative of the dead law, and so his persecution of David (and murder of the priests of Nob) could be likened to the persecution of Reformation clergy by civil authorities.

Those who continue to work with the books of Samuel in their canonical form find a congenial source of many narratives and characters that can serve as a means to moralize and preach lessons for life. Those who avoid this approach still find the accounts to preserve much in the way of theological and ethical instruction. Thus William Blaikie's volumes on the books of Samuel preserve many worthy insights, often of a devotional nature but always drawn from the substance of the biblical text. For example, consider his reflection on God's promise to David for an eternal dynasty in 2 Samuel 7:

> But in refusing him that request, He makes over to him mercies of far higher reach and importance. He refuses his immediate request only to grant to him far above all that he was able to ask or think. And how often does God do so!

3. Augustine, *De civitate dei* 17.6.
4. Gunn, *Fate of King Saul*, 23.

> How often, when His people are worrying and perplexing themselves about their prayers not being answered, is God answering them in a far richer way! Glimpses of this we see occasionally, but the full revelation of it remains for the future. You pray to the degree of agony for the preservation of a beloved life; it is not granted; God appears deaf to your cry; a year or two after, things happen that would have broken your friend's heart or driven reason from its throne; you understand now why God did not fulfill your petition. Oh for the spirit of trust that shall never charge God foolishly! Oh for the faith that does not make haste, but waits patiently for the Lord,—waits for the explanation that shall come in the end, at the revelation of Jesus Christ![5]

Higher Criticism

Due to his interest in sources for the biblical texts, Julius Wellhausen proposed an earlier promonarchic source in 1 Samuel in conflict with a later, postexilic, antimonarchic source.[6] In so doing, he identified one of the key issues in the analysis of this book, the question of its relation to the monarchy. Some texts appear to be positive and others negative. The issue remains a vital crux. He also carried forward the assumptions of source criticism that the text incorporates two or more originally independent witnesses of the same events or stories.

In opposition to the extension of the Documentary Hypothesis (or some mutation of the same) into the Historical Books, and especially that of Samuel, stands the work of Leonhard Rost, *Succession to the Throne of David*. Rost, writing in 1926, identified separate documents compiled to create 1–2 Samuel. Although these have their own individual developments of literary traditions, they do not represent sources covering the same events but from different perspectives. Instead, they represent separate events connected in historical or narrative sequence: the Ark Narrative (most of 1 Sam. 4:1b–7:1; 2 Sam. 6), the History of the Rise of David (1 Sam. 16:14–2 Sam. 5), and the Succession Narrative (2 Sam. 9–20; 1 Kings 1–2). The Ark Narrative describes the loss of the ark of the covenant to the Philistines and its return, ultimately leading to the procession to Jerusalem, led by David. The History of the Rise of David narrates how David becomes king even though he is not chosen by Saul to be that king's successor. In particular, it argues that David does nothing to harm or kill Saul or his son Jonathan. The Succession Narrative has been understood to describe how Solomon becomes David's successor even though he is not the firstborn or even preeminent in the birth order of David's many children.

Martin Noth's theory of a single editor creating the Deuteronomistic History finds the books of Samuel to lie at the heart of this collection (see

5. Blaikie, *Second Book of Samuel*, 104.
6. Wellhausen, *Der Text der Bücher Samuelis*.

"Higher Criticism" for Joshua).[7] However, Noth identifies few items in the story of Saul or that of David as distinctive Deuteronomistic additions. Yet Noth follows Wellhausen's promonarchic and antimonarchic divisions for 1 Samuel 7–13 (referring to them as traditions rather than sources). Like the theory of Wellhausen, that of Noth rests on the assumption that one can clearly delineate which texts are promonarchic and which are antimonarchic; however, the passages are not so easily divided into two opposing collections.

Most commentators and researchers have used Rost's theory as a starting point for further research. However, there is little agreement here. Is this material contrived, as when Michal despises David in 2 Samuel 6? Are the texts literary artistry (pure entertainment) or political propaganda?[8] To what extent is the focus of the various discrete narratives in 2 Samuel really on the question of who will succeed David? To what extent does the succession lie with God's relationship to David and his household? Writing in 1979, Brevard Childs was correct in observing, "A deep-seated confusion in methodology still obtains, especially regarding the level on which one reads the material and the intention of the final shaping of the tradition. The result is that the options become almost endless, with little prospect of adjudicating between rival theories."[9]

The last decades have seen a collapse of any agreement other than on a general starting point for theories that makes use of these three literary pieces as key collections in the discussion. Even here, however, there is no agreement as to the beginning and end of these pieces and their particular contents. Further, the Ark Narrative itself occupies part of a larger narrative in 1 Samuel 1–7 (and beyond) and is connected to its surrounding context in a manner that suggests an overall integrity. For example, Samuel's leadership in the victory of Israel over the Philistines in chapter 7 directly contrasts with the defeat of the sons of Eli and their battle with the Philistines in chapter 4.[10] Yet this is a fulfillment of the divine judgment against the sons of Eli and of the divine election and call of Samuel in chapters 2–3.

Traditional critical approaches have faced challenges to their methods by intensive literary studies of the narratives and by a rising historical skepticism that grew at the end of the twentieth century and the beginning of the twenty-first century. As a result, many scholars have concluded that, while the Ark Narrative may preserve some earlier traditions originating in the northern kingdom (Israel), its present construction with the departure of the glory from Israel (1 Sam. 4:21) is best seen as coincident with or later than the destruction of the Jerusalem temple by the Babylonians in 587/586 BC.

7. Noth, *Deuteronomistic History*.

8. For entertainment, see Gunn, *Fate of King Saul*; for political propaganda, see Whybray, *Succession Narrative*.

9. Childs, *Introduction*, 271.

10. Polzin, *1 Samuel*.

For Thomas Römer, the History of the Rise of David reflects elements of the Assyrian threat to Jerusalem in the seventh century, while the Succession Narrative includes intrigues that would have been known to its readers in the events surrounding the succession of Assyrian kings such as Esarhaddon in the mid-seventh century BC.[11]

For other scholars, the negative presentation of Saul and his rivalry with the Gibeonites is seen as largely a creation of the Persian-period struggles between the community in Jerusalem and rivals to the north.[12] However, others question whether this is a reworking of earlier traditions.[13] In the end, the multifaceted nature of the literature allows for application to many times and places. To be persuasive, the critical theories themselves must fall back on literary analysis and historical reconstruction. In order to establish controls for better understanding the meaning and message of 1–2 Samuel, at this point it is necessary to consider the literary readings and the ancient Near Eastern backgrounds.

Literary Readings

The beginning of literary readings of larger segments of 1–2 Samuel, as opposed to devotional and premodern commentaries that stress theological lessons (but nevertheless provide important and often similar literary approaches), can be traced to the 1978 and 1980 publications by David Gunn. These are worthy of some discussion because they represent a foundation on which others have built, a foundation reaching beyond the study of 1–2 Samuel. Indeed, in terms of an exemplary methodology, one scholar has identified Gunn's 1980 *The Fate of King Saul* as "one of the most important works in biblical studies written in the past decade, especially for scholars interested in applying literary criticism to biblical narrative."[14]

Gunn's 1978 *The Story of King David: Genre and Interpretation* introduces the reader and student of the Bible to modern literary interpretation of a sizable text of biblical literature that extends through the books of Samuel and into the opening chapters of 1 Kings. For Gunn, the reading of such an account should first be approached on the assumption that it was written as a work of art for purposes of entertainment.[15] Gunn suggests that David's story is built out of and patterned on traditional motifs. There is the love-hate relationship between David and his general Joab (and Joab's brothers), the judgment-eliciting parables presented in a deceptive manner by Nathan and the wise woman of Tekoa (2 Sam. 12 and 14), the woman who brings death

11. Römer, *Deuteronomistic History*, 91–97.
12. Edelman, "Did Saulide-Davidide Rivalry?"
13. Römer, *Deuteronomistic History*.
14. J. Ackerman, review of *Fate of King Saul*, 438.
15. Gunn, *Story of King David*, 38.

between two men (cf. Rizpah, Bathsheba, Tamar, Abishag), the woman who hides spies (2 Sam. 17), the two messengers (2 Sam. 18), and the letter that brings the bearer's death (2 Sam. 11). Gunn devotes some space to discussing the historical traditions and the impact of oral origins on the account, arguing that content and elements such as repetition, vocabulary, and inclusio (beginning and ending with the same or a similar phrase) place 2 Samuel 2–4 alongside 2 Samuel 9–1 Kings 2 as part of this story. However, Gunn rejects the view that the main theme is who will succeed David as king (i.e., Solomon). Rather, the events all focus in one way or another on David and his story. That story involves both the private and public life of David and the manner in which these intertwine and affect each other. Thus David's weak response to Amnon's rape of his half sister echoes David's own issues when it comes to sexual ethics and anticipates his weak response to the vengeance of Absalom as well as the full-blown coup that emerges in the following chapters. In another manner, David's wife Michal is the daughter of Saul and thus harbors the potential of an heir who would bring together both houses. Her barrenness guarantees that such a public joining of dynasties never takes place.

Gunn finds a theme of seizure that runs through much of this story. David seizes Bathsheba. As noted, Amnon seizes Tamar in rape. Absalom seizes Amnon in murder. Absalom then attempts to seize his father's kingdom. However, this is thwarted by the opposite of seizing. David does not hold on to the kingdom, leaving Jerusalem and fleeing east of the Jordan River. The effect is to allow freedom to everything and everyone, including Absalom. In the end, however, those who bind themselves to David (such as Hushai) become instrumental in the decisions that Absalom makes. If Ziba is not given the same freedom as Absalom, perhaps this has more to do with the intense love that David feels for his fallen son. It is surely an irony that the end of David's life sees the kingdom seized by Bathsheba, whom he originally seized—thereby beginning the story. She gives it to her son Solomon, whose qualification for it seems to be that he knows better how to seize it than does his rival, Adonijah.

In Gunn's second book, *The Fate of King Saul*, he discusses the life and death of Saul as described in 1 Samuel 8:1–2 Samuel 2:7. Here the rejection of Saul is seen as rather unfair. Early initiative that is rewarded results in condemnation later when he sacrifices after waiting a week for Samuel (1 Sam. 13). The people's repentance is accepted in 1 Samuel 12, but Saul's is rejected in chapter 15. For Gunn, Saul is convicted on a technicality, and Samuel has no interest in allowing him to explain his actions. Samuel remains in complete control as he warns the people that the success of their kingdom and king rests on their decision to follow God in everything. Indeed, Saul's difficult situation develops into a contrast between the rejected and ill-fated Saul and the blessed David, who can do nothing wrong. When Jonathan gives David his robe and armor and he accepts them, it powerfully contrasts with Saul's tearing of Samuel's robe and David's refusal to wear Saul's armor to fight Goliath. Thus David receives from Jonathan what he cannot receive from Saul.

This brief summary exemplifies a foundational literary approach toward the books of Samuel. From the large number of contributions that have appeared in the decades since, whether as individual studies of specific parts of Samuel or as commentaries on one or both books of Samuel, the research has regularly appealed to Gunn in terms of agreeing with, disagreeing with, or amending his approach and conclusions. The implications of this approach have extended across the spectrum into the categories that follow.

Gender and Ideological Criticism

The female roles in the books of Samuel have an important place from the first chapter. As Athalya Brenner explains, Hannah and Nehusta the mother of Jehoiachin, who accompanies Jehoiachin to Babylon in 2 Kings 24:8–17, create an inclusio (envelope) for the four historical books.[16] Yet the appearance of female figures at the beginning and end of a book can also be found in other texts (e.g., Proverbs) and is not unique here. The role of women in Samuel places a distinctive value on motherhood. Not only is the queen mother given a special status (see "Gender and Ideological Criticism" for 1–2 Kings) but women are also given identities and define themselves in becoming (or not becoming) mothers. For example, there is the king's daughter, Michal, daughter of Saul and David's wife, who saves David's life when pursued by her father and later stands up to David for dancing in what she considers an inappropriate manner; her story abruptly comes to an end with the report that she "had no child to the day of her death" (2 Sam. 6:23).

The role of Hannah as Samuel's mother is unique as a woman who strikes a bargain with God. The self-centered attempt by Elkanah to console her for her barrenness in 1 Samuel 1:8 (called accusatory and abusive, borne of a desire to blame someone for the barrenness[17]) leaves for Hannah no opportunity to truly share her feelings and rather leads to the response of moving away from Elkanah after an appropriate period (finishing the meal) and finding a quiet and separate place to pour out her soul to God.[18] Nevertheless, the role of Hannah is unusual as a woman with a prominence of focus in the biblical narrative.[19] She not only has a name, but it appears fourteen times more than the name of almost any other Old Testament woman except Miriam or the matriarchs (Sarah, Rebekah, Rachel, and Leah). Further, she is the subject of a verb three times as often as she is the object, and she engages in dialogue with more people in 1 Samuel 1 than anyone else. Thus she has

16. Brenner, "Introduction," 13–16.
17. L. Klein, "Hannah."
18. Cf. Amit, "Am I Not More Devoted?"
19. Meyers, "Hannah and Her Sacrifice."

a prominence that plays a significant literary role in the story of the book. Hannah's barrenness and abuse by her rival find a solution as she encounters Yahweh and gives birth to Samuel, who will himself take a defeated and abused Israel and give it victory (1 Sam. 4–7). Yet just as Hannah surrenders Samuel to the tabernacle service while continuing to support him (2:19), so Samuel will surrender his role of leader to the kingship of Saul while continuing to support the nation (12:23–25). Just as important is the manner in which Hannah's private prayer and concerns have a profound public effect on the whole of the nation. Similarly, Saul's private rivalry with David and the even greater private lusts and intrigues of David and his household will all have an effect on the public lives of these kings and on the public fate of the nation of Israel.

In the context of the issue of gender, there is the question of the original ideology and intent of the text and especially of the original historical context. The Bathsheba incident of 2 Samuel 11–12 provides a particular example in which the female figure and the king's desire for her appear to bring about the undoing of the dynasty. Yet this must be placed within the context of the West Semitic concept of the warrior and especially that found in the predecessors of Israel, the tribal confederations of the Amorites at Mari in the eighteenth century BC. Daniel Bodi uses illustrations from Akkadian texts to provide examples of how a Mari king instructs his lazy son in the art of warfare and leadership.[20] He extols the virtues of leading his army into battle and crudely mocks his son for sitting at home and for occupying his time with his wives. Bodi observes a shift at Mari and in David's Israel from the nomadic ideal of a tribal leader and warrior to a settled ruler who lives in a city and a palace, rather than a tent. When this occurs at Mari, it is marked by, among other things, the acquisition of a harem, which can include hundreds of women.[21] To acquire another's harem is a sign of political power and dominance over the defeated ruler, as can be seen with Absalom's acquisition of his father's harem. This transition compares well with David's decision to leave the fighting to his general Joab as well as his involvement with Bathsheba. In these activities he moves from the tribal and nomadic warrior ideal to the settled and often despised (at least by the warriors) ruler in a palace. This picture contrasts with David during the time of Saul, when he lives in a tent, is at the forefront of the battles, and acquires the wives of Nabal and others. It also corresponds to Absalom's already-mentioned acquisition of David's harem and to Solomon's much larger harem.[22]

20. Bodi, *Demise of the Warlord*.

21. For an important critique of the use of the term "harem," see Bharj and Hagerty, "A Postcolonial Feminist Critique."

22. Even such a huge harem is not impossible in light of the numbers of women mentioned in the Mari texts and the manner in which Solomon would have acquired the harems of his father, David, and of the various rulers that he conquered.

Interest in the David and Bathsheba story plays an important role in Gerald West's discussion of reading the text of Samuel with South African women and others.[23] The women see the relationship with David in 2 Samuel 11 as one in which Bathsheba is raped. They identify with this text as well as with the story of Tamar in 2 Samuel 13. Her rape and the responses of her father and brothers are points of identification for those who have been abused and find similar realities in the biblical text. Neither is this the only point of relationship West finds between southern African cultures and the books of Samuel. West lists some twenty-six specific points.[24] A few may be listed from 1 Samuel 1–7:

- polygamous family and its rivalries (1:2–6)
- eating sacrificed meat (1:4)
- barrenness and the yearning for a male child (1:10–11)
- dedication of a child to an office in life (1:22)
- abuse of privilege by children of leaders and the disappointment (2:12–17)
- recognition of a new leader by other tribes (2:20)
- prophet's warning to leaders (2:27–36)
- conflict with neighboring tribes (4:1–7:14)
- local deities (5:1–2)
- importance of cattle to the community (6:7)
- slaughtering an animal to communicate with a deity or ancestor (7:9)

Although West emphasizes the use of the Bible in denying traditional and tribal religions, and the value of 1–2 Samuel in legitimating this, it seems less clear that the books of Samuel actually do accept consultation with the dead. Even a controversial text such as 1 Samuel 28 remains at best ambiguous regarding the nature of the Samuel figure and any sense of approval of this by the narrator. Nevertheless, in many ways the cultural world of 1–2 Samuel legitimately connects better with much of the world's majority population than with the twenty-first-century Western world.

Ancient Near Eastern Context

There are many areas of ancient Near Eastern studies that impact 1–2 Samuel. Some of these have already been identified. Three areas will be considered here as they impact the important background behind the text of Samuel. To a great extent these have been determined by the ongoing discussion of scholarship as it has challenged an Iron Age I (1200–1000 BC) context for the traditions that lie behind the written documents as now extant. Some

23. G. West, "1 and 2 Samuel."
24. Ibid., 94.

aspects of this have already been discussed (see the preceding section and the Mari background to David the warrior). Here is consideration of issues that represent the broad backgrounds and areas of research impacting 1–2 Samuel and also address some key historical questions: the rise of the monarchy under Saul and David, the literary context behind the History of the Rise of David, and the archaeological and textual evidence for the kingdom of David.

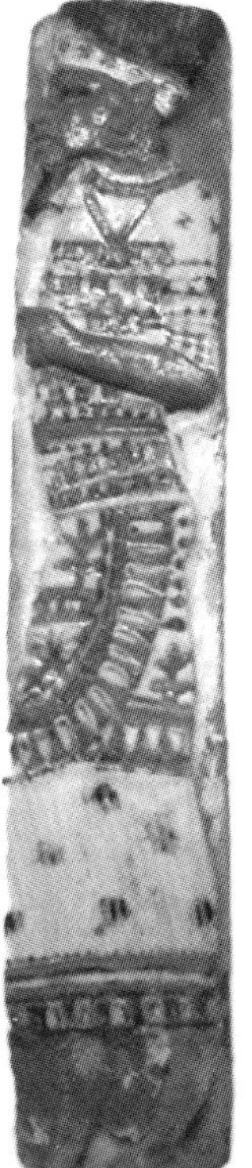

Captmondo/Wikimedia Commons

Egyptian tiles portraying Canaanites

Rise of the Monarchy

The question regarding the rise of the monarchy has received a great deal of attention. Earlier sociopolitical theories held to different emphases of a cluster of influences that gave rise to the monarchy. For some, the development of technologies in the hill country—such as terraces, plastered water cisterns, and the use of iron—led to agricultural surpluses there and thus to an economic elite in Israel, thereby attracting Philistine aggression.[25] For others, increase in population led to increased competition with the Philistines and others over the limited resources.

A sociological approach was advocated by Neils Lemche.[26] The emergence of different classes in Israel led to tribal chieftains who unified the tribal elements as a "protector of the dependent lower classes" and as an elected "brother" of the wealthy. The tribal chief's own interests in a dynasty and further expansion of personal power led to a separation from the wealthier classes. Due to the individualistic and autonomous nature of tribal societies (cf. Judges), when confronted with a centralized state such as the Philistines, Israel must either centralize itself in order to survive or face dissolution and integration into the other state. Saul's chieftainship was unable to marshal sufficient resources to overcome the Philistine threat. It gave way to David's kingship, one that utilized more resources, through his ability to ignore the tribal system, and eventually to unite all of Canaan.

25. See, e.g., Gottwald, *Tribes of Yahweh*.
26. Lemche, "Israel."

For Thomas L. Thompson, Saul, David, and Solomon never existed.[27] The population of the hill country was too sparse (1) to create any economic threat to the lowlanders at this time (whom Thompson does not believe were Philistines) and (2) to allow for any sort of kingdom at Jerusalem to form before the eighth and seventh centuries BC. However, Thompson does not address the following matters: (1) Israel Finkelstein and others do postulate a larger population in the hill country, which continues to grow with new surveys, so that William Dever, in conjunction with Finkelstein, can posit a population as high as one hundred thousand.[28] (2) The destruction of Shiloh was violent. (3) There was settlement exactly where the early monarchy is first placed and the events of Samuel occur—in the tribal area of Benjamin (Saul's tribe), at Jerusalem and Hebron, and near Bethlehem. (4) Common archaeological forms (e.g., multichamber gates) at Gezer, Megiddo, and Hazor all point to what Dever identifies as the "most significant single criterion for defining 'statehood'": centralization of power.[29]

The most important evidence related to the question of the rise of the Israelite monarchy comes from the settlement data that has appeared as a result of surveys completed by Israeli archaeologists in the late twentieth century, above all those collected and published by Finkelstein based on work done in the hill country after 1967. The results reveal increasing sedentarization of pastoral groups in the central hill country, in about 1200–1000 BC, which led to movement westward onto the western slopes of Samaria and the Judean hills. This area required a specialized horticultural economy to flourish, one that led to increased flow of goods between regions, with increased public administration and social stratification. The horticultural produce tempted the Philistines on the plain, where such products were not available. In the south, Israelite expansion into the Beersheba basin in the eleventh century, with a center at Tel Masos (Hormah?), gained them control of trade routes, especially with Saul's victory over Amalek (1 Sam. 15). Israelite administrative systems existed in the hill country and to the south by the mid-eleventh century, so the shift to central administration was not so drastic. Settlement in the Judean hill country almost doubled in the approximate period 1050–900 BC.[30] Pressure from Amalek, Ammon, and especially the Philistines created the catalyst for the rise of the monarchy. The reappearance of a dominant "Philistine" material culture in the late eleventh century in the western Jezreel Valley may attest to the biblical victory over Saul at Gilboa (1 Sam. 31).[31] Benjamin suffered most from the pressures of the Philistines. As a result the tribal area of Benjamin became the natural center from which the Israelite

27. T. Thompson, *Early History*; see also P. Davies, *In Search*.

28. I. Finkelstein, *Archaeology of the Israelite Settlement*; Dever, *What Did?*, 127.

29. Dever, *What Did?*, 126.

30. Ofer, "Hill Country," 102; Rainey, "Stones for Bread," 141.

31. Raban, "Philistines."

resistance would come. It would also form the core of the centralized leadership that emerged with Saul. Zvi Gal finds several settlement shifts in the Jezreel and Beth-shan Valleys.[32] In the eleventh century there was a short period of village occupation in the valleys while the Canaanite cities continued to exist. He relates this to the Sea Peoples. This was followed by the destruction of these cities and the end of this occupation. New occupation in Eastern Lower Galilee, the Jezreel Valley, and the Beth-shan Valley took place in the tenth century. Gal relates this to the Israelite occupation.

Literary Context of the History of the Rise of David

The History of the Rise of David describes how David became king even though he was not in any line of succession to Israel's throne. The biblical text argues that David's predecessor was impious and therefore rejected by God as king. It suggests that Saul and his own choice as successor, his son Jonathan, were killed in battle by their enemies. The biblical text repeatedly makes the point that David was always loyal to Saul and never sought to seize the kingdom from him. Indeed, David had several opportunities to kill Saul but refused to do so. This was true to such an extent that Saul blessed David for what he had done and proclaimed David's righteousness. Jonathan was close to David and recognized his legitimacy as the chosen successor to Saul. Indeed, again and again David is portrayed as blessed by God, chosen by him to be Israel's king, and successful in all his battles and other endeavors. When Saul and Jonathan are killed in battle, David is physically away from the scene and has no role in their deaths. He eulogizes them and seeks to do good to Saul's descendants, especially those in the line of Jonathan, such as his son Mephibosheth. The precise beginning and end of this History of the Rise of David is disputed, but it clearly begins somewhere in 1 Samuel 15–16, where David is recognized by the prophet Samuel, is anointed king, and begins his time of service in the palace of Saul. It must come to an end after the deaths of Saul and Jonathan (1 Sam. 31) and their eulogy (2 Sam. 1), and also after the end of the reign of Ishbosheth, son of Saul and claimant to his throne in the north of Israel (2 Sam. 4). The ending may be somewhere in 2 Samuel 5, when David is made king over all Israel; 2 Samuel 6, where he establishes Jerusalem as his capital; or 2 Samuel 7:1, with its note that David is settled in his palace and that the Lord has given him rest from his enemies.

The Apology of Ḫattušiliš III is a thirteenth-century-BC document written by the king of the Hittites, who seeks to justify his position as king despite the fact that he was not in the line of succession to the throne. He was a member of the royal family but had two older brothers. Since the work of Herbert Wolf, there has been an awareness that this document holds many

32. Gal, "Period of the Israelite Settlement," 114; Bloch-Smith and Nakhai, "Landscape," 83.

similarities with the History of the Rise of David.[33] Both represent lengthy presentations of the rise of a figure to become ruler of his people despite not being the obvious choice, according to the principles of succession. Both portray their protagonists as chosen by their gods and as acting righteously, while their predecessor becomes jealous of them and acts in an unrighteous manner. Various specifics occur—such as the foretelling of kingship for the David figure, the son of the Saul figure following him and ruling for seven years until the David figure succeeds, the use of witchcraft, the success of the David figure in establishing his kingdom over the surrounding nations, and a final section dealing with the building up of the temple of the deity who supported "David." Indeed, even some minor incidents, such as the manner in which Ḫattušiliš claims to have single-handedly defeated the "one who runs in front" of an enemy army and thereby to have sent that army fleeing, compare with the story of David and Goliath in 1 Samuel 17.[34] One does not need to see a genre with these two documents being the only extant examples. Rather, this represents the production of literature that reflects similar concerns and has many parallels. The History of the Rise of David may not directly borrow from this work, but it clearly shares many features, and one can see evidence in both for a complete document authored within a lifetime of the events and without large-scale editing and redaction subsequent to its production.

The Kingdom of David

The question of the evidence for David's kingdom can be divided into the two broad areas of written and material evidence. First, the written evidence is significant. The partial stele (or stela) discovered in July 1993 at a city gate at northern Israelite Dan has been dated to the mid-ninth century BC (see the sidebar "Tel Dan Stele").[35] Two additional fragments were found later.[36] The stele's mention of the "house of David" provides the earliest certain reference to David outside the Bible. It also demonstrates the importance of David, for the expression "house of *X*" is regularly used of dynasties with the figure named being the founder of that dynasty. Thus it suggests the existence of an important dynasty in Palestine in the ninth century, whose founder was David. It suggests that Israel and Judah were well-established states in the ninth century. Despite attempts to find other explanations for this name, Gary Knoppers states that no place name or deity named David or Dod has yet been identified; hence, the inscription "does point to David as a historical figure."[37]

33. Wolf, *Apology of Ḫattušiliš*; Tadmor, "Autobiographical Apology."
34. Hoffner, "Hittite Analogy."
35. Biran and Naveh, "Aramaic Stele Fragment."
36. Biran and Naveh, "Tel Dan Inscription."
37. Knoppers, "Vanishing Solomon," 38–39.

Tel Dan Stele

The text of the Tel Dan Stele is clear, although broken. The English translation provided here follows that of Aḥituv (and Rainey):[a]

1. [. . .] and cut (a treaty) [. . .]
2. [. . . -'e]l my father went up [against him when] he was fighting in Abe[l?]
3. And my father lay down, he went to his [ancestors (place of) eternity]. And the king of I[s-
4. rael entered previously in the land of my father. [And] Hadad made me myself king.
5. And Hadad went in front of me, [and] I departed from [the] seven [cities]
6. of my kingdom, and I slew [seven]ty kings, who harnessed thous[sands of cha-]
7. riots and thousands of horsemen/horses. And [was killed Jo]ram son of [Ahab]
8. king of Israel, and [was] killed [Aḥaz]yahu son of [Jehoram, ki-]
9. ng of the House of David. And I set [their cities into ruin and turned]
10. their land into [desolation. And I slew all of it and I settled there]
11. other [people]. As to the te[mple, I devoted it. And Jehu son of Omri ru-]
12. led over Is[rael . . . . . . and I laid]
13. siege upon [. . .]

[a] Aḥituv, *Echoes from the Past*, 468; see also Schniedewind, "The Tel Dan Stele."

The discovery of this name on the Tel Dan Stele encouraged André Lemaire to affirm his suggestion that the same "house of David" also appears in the ninth-century Moabite Stele, where King Mesha of Moab celebrates his victory over the northern kingdom (Israel) and mentions the capture of Horonen, possessed by the house of David.[38] Kenneth Kitchen also finds the name in the place name "the heights of *Dwt*" on the Egyptian itinerary of Shishak I from 925 BC.[39] Citing examples where an Egyptian *t* transcribed a Semitic *d* in various proper names, as well as other Asiatic "David's" (e.g., *Twti* and *Tt-w't*), along with a sixth-century Ethiopic rendering of King David in the same manner (*Dwt*; a naming tradition that continues to the present among Christian Amharic speakers), Kitchen argues convincingly for the south Judean

38. Lemaire, "House of David"; idem, "Dynastie davidique"; cf. Kitchen, *Reliability*, 452.
39. Kitchen, "Possible Mention of David"; idem, *Reliability*, 93, 453.

Eighth-century-BC inscription from Dan describing how the Aramean king warred with Israel and with the "house of David"

© Baker Publishing Group and Dr. James C. M

tenth-century place name, the heights of David, as the earliest extrabiblical reference to the founder of Judah's dynasty.

Textually, the lack of evidence from the time of David and Solomon has led to charges that these figures did not exist or at most were minor and local rulers. Yet the period of David and Solomon's rule is one of weakness in both Egypt and Mesopotamia, the two primary sources for extrabiblical records. Therefore one might not expect the existence of records. Kitchen observes that at this time the kings of Egypt ruled from Memphis and the Delta, where all historical records have perished.[40] Contemporary records from southern Egypt contain no historical information. There are no historical inscriptions of any kind from Egypt that mention Palestine or any of its states between Ramesses III (ca. 1184–1153) and Shishak I (ca. 945–924 BC).[41] The first mention of an Israelite or Judean king in Mesopotamian records is that of Ahab in the mid-ninth century BC, during the encounter of Shalmaneser III with him at the Battle of Qarqar (853 BC). This was a period of Assyrian resurgence.

Alan Millard has observed that the absence of inscriptions from otherwise well-known rulers is not unique to David and Solomon.[42] Not a single monumental inscription has been found from the Hasmonean dynasty or from Herod's kingdom during his reign. However, there is increasing evidence for written records from early Israel, even though all papyrus and vellum documents, on which most writing was done and virtually all writing of any length, perished in the climate of Jerusalem and most of Israel (except for the very dry Judean desert, where the earliest records are the Dead Sea Scrolls of the second century BC and one Iron Age document that contains no historical information). John Holladay's observation regarding "intense scribal activity" that existed is given in evidence by Phoenician sarcophagi, arrowheads, and the 'Izbet Sartah abecedary (an eleventh-century text found at a village, indicating interest in learning to read and write even

40. Kitchen, "How We Know," 32–37.

41. Kitchen, *Reliability*, 156.

42. Millard, "Knowledge of Writing," 215.

Khirbet Qeiyafa inscription (tenth century BC), probably from the period of the united monarchy

Khirbet Qeiyafa, a tenth-century-BC fort, perhaps biblical Shaaraim ("two gates")

Michael Netzer/Wikimedia Commons//
Skyview Photography Ltd/Wikimedia Commons

there, far from urban and political centers; see the sidebar "Abecedaries" in the chapter on Judges).[43] To these should now be added the two Khirbet Qeiyafa inscriptions and a short Jerusalem inscription. The first consists of five lines (or more) of text found at a fort on the border between Israel and Philistia, overlooking the Elah Valley and dating from the time of David, in the early tenth century BC. Whether it is a letter, a legal document, a list of names, or something else, its inconsistent style suggests that more persons than trained scribes did write documents of some length (and could also read them).[44] The second, briefer inscription contains the name Esh-Baal. This name is known from the Bible, where it identifies a member of Saul's family (1 Chron. 8:33; 9:39).[45] The Jerusalem inscription also dates from the tenth century BC, although five or six letters have been disputed as to their reading and interpretation.[46]

Knoppers observes that it is methodologically incorrect to infer an "impoverishment of culture" due to an absence of archaeological evidence.[47] On this basis the postexilic period should also be a time of cultural and textual absence. Yet this is the very time when most scholars date the major production of much of the biblical materials. The Amarna Age (fourteenth century BC) was capable of producing written documents of a literary style, and there is no reason to doubt that tenth-century Jerusalem was any less populated or likely to produce written texts.[48] Nuzi, which has produced more than 6,500

43. J. Holladay, "Kingdoms of Israel and Judah," 381.
44. Cf. Misgav, Garfinkel, and Ganor, "Ostracon"; Millard, "Ostracon."
45. Cf. Garfinkel et al., "ʾIšbaʿal Inscription."
46. Mazar, Ben-Shlomo, and Aḥituv, "Inscribed Pithos"; Galil, "*ʾyyn ḥlqʾ*."
47. Knoppers, "Vanishing Solomon," 40–42.
48. Na'aman, "Trowel vs. the Text."

texts from the Late Bronze Age, is a site whose population was estimated at two thousand—not that different from the size of Jerusalem.

Nadav Na'aman offers comparative arguments for the presence of a scribal center in tenth-century Jerusalem and for the rise of David.[49] First, by comparing private libraries in Egypt and Assyria, and the work of the historians Manetho and Berossus, Na'aman concludes that Jerusalem could have preserved a similar library. Second, the textually attested and sudden rise of other figures such as Yahdun-Lim, Shamshi-Addu, and Zimri-Lim suggests that it would be possible for a figure like David to quickly build a kingdom and for it to disappear just as quickly. Kitchen observes that the "mini-empire" of David and Solomon may be compared with roughly contemporary mini-empires of Tabal in southeast Anatolia, Carchemish to the east of Tabal, and Aram-Zobah.[50] All of these flourished between 1200 and 900 BC, the only period when such mini-empires could. Those of Tabal and Carchemish are attested in contemporary Luwian inscriptions.

Much more could be said about the background of David's kingdom in terms of contemporary written sources from outside the Bible. The interspersing of historical records of battles with religious notes is common in ancient texts. Thus 2 Samuel 8 is thematic rather than chronological. Reports of conquest interspersed with statements that Yahweh saved David and that David made temple donations (8:10–11) are similar to Egyptian pharaoh accounts of the Late Bronze Age and to the annals of Tiglath-pileser I.[51] Stylistic features of this may be compared with royal Mesopotamian inscriptions, suggesting that 2 Samuel 8 could have been originally written as a monumental inscription.[52]

Of greater significance is the promise of an eternal dynasty to David in 2 Samuel 7. This should not be seen as a late interpolation of Deuteronomistic language to justify the reign of Josiah or for some postexilic purposes. Moshe Weinfeld compares the Davidic covenants (and those with Abraham in Gen. 12–18) with Neo-Assyrian land grants and especially with the earlier (1500–1200 BC) Hittite grants in which the most prominent items bestowed by the Hittite king on Syrian vassals were land and the right of the reigning sovereign to preserve his dynasty.[53] The following are examples of ideas similar to those found in 2 Samuel.

> A treaty between a Hittite king and Ulmi-Teshub includes the statement, "If one of your descendants sins, the king will prosecute him at his court. Then when he is found guilty, . . . if he deserves death, he will die. But

49. Na'aman, "Contribution of the Amarna Letters"; idem, "Sources and Composition," 180–83; idem, "Cow Town or Royal Capital?"

50. Kitchen, "How We Know," 37, 58; idem, "Controlling Role"; idem, *Reliability*, 99–100.

51. Halpern, "Construction of the Davidic State," 54–55.

52. R. Good, "2 Samuel 8."

53. Weinfeld, *Promise of the Land*, 236–47.

nobody will take away from the descendant of Ulmi-Teshub either his house or his land in order to give it to a descendant of somebody else."[54] A similar expression is found in a will from Nuzi.

A bilingual inscription of the Hittite king Ḫattušiliš I includes a testament, "Behold, I declared for you the young Labarna: He shall sit on the throne. I, the king, called him my son." Thus the concept of sonship, as Weinfeld observes, has nothing to do with a mythology where a god "adopts" a human king into divinity as his son. This was the view of some biblical scholars in the past. Instead, it is part of the legitimating process in which the king establishes a dynasty. Also at Nuzi, adoption contracts call someone "son" in order to establish the rights and privileges of the one chosen.

Many other verbal parallels with ancient Near Eastern documents of various types can be found. Gary Knoppers successfully challenges the argument that 2 Samuel 7 must be based on a land-grant document in terms of structure, verbal parallelism, and the unconditional nature of the divine promise in 2 Samuel 7 versus the conditional nature of most royal grants.[55] The biblical documents draw from a variety of sources, according to their own needs and purposes.

© Baker Publishing Group and Dr. James C. Martin
Neo-Hittite musical group (from the period of Israel's monarchy)

Much could be said about the matter of material archaeology and the sites mentioned in 1–2 Samuel that have been investigated. A great deal of controversy exists about the dating of some of these sites. However, in recent years much of the debate has returned to the archaeology of Jerusalem, which can be summarized briefly here. Jane Cahill, the archaeologist entrusted with the publication of Yigael Shiloh's excavations at the city of David, eastern slope, reconstructs the evidence as follows.[56] In the earlier Middle Bronze II period (1800–1550 BC), there existed a large fortification wall midway up the east slope (the only side excavated), twin towers guarding the Gihon Spring water source, a pool from the spring that reached through an extension of the access tunnel to Warren's Shaft (itself a natural "hole" discovered later; related to 2 Sam. 5:8), a

54. Knoppers, "Ancient Near Eastern Royal Grants," 682.

55. Ibid.

56. Cahill, "Time of the United Monarchy"; idem, "David and Solomon's Time."

High/Low Chronology—Archaeology and Dating

At many archaeological sites periods of occupation are distinguished by layers or strata of remains, indicated by a Roman numeral. The larger the numeral, the earlier the layer or stratum. Israel Finkelstein and Neal Asher Silberman argue that the traditional layers at major excavated sites in ancient Israel that had been dated to the tenth century and the time of David and Solomon should be moved into the ninth century and the era of Omri and Ahab.[a] Pharaoh Shishak records a destruction of major sites in 925 BC, and that includes the following archaeological levels dated to the late tenth century BC: Megiddo VA/IVB, Taanach IIB, Beth-shan Upper V, and Gezer VII. Also likely, though not mentioned on what is preserved of Shishak's account, are Hazor IX, Tel Abu Hawan III, Tell Keisan VIIIA, Tel Mevorakh VII, Tel Michal, Tel Qasile VIII, Tel Batash IV, Tell el-Hama, Tell es-Saidiyeh XI, and Tell Mazar.[b]

[a] Finkelstein and Silberman, *David and Solomon*.
[b] See Dever, *What Did?*, 135.

second water shaft that carried water from the spring along the eastern slope to water the Kidron Valley, and the stepped-stone structure including both the infrastructure and the external structure. This 120-foot-high structure held a major fortress that was the "fortress of Zion," which David encountered in 2 Samuel 5:7–9 (NIV). The Amarna letters from Jerusalem indicate that occupation of this site and its structure continued from the fourteenth century BC until the time of David. The Iron Age I (1200–1000 BC) continued use of all the items from the earlier Middle Bronze Age.

Earlier excavations of the tenth-century-BC period from the time of David revealed at least two houses built right into the stepped-stone structure. Their dressed masonry and continued usage suggest wealthy and powerful owners. At the same time, outside the wall were houses built with thinner walls and of fieldstones, indicating poorer people and the presence of social stratification at this time. Cahill notes that the ability to build into and thereby remove some of the stepped-stone structure suggests that the major government and religious buildings of this period were moved from that structure northward to the present Temple Mount.[57] Nevertheless, the stepped-stone structure was one of the largest buildings, if not the largest, in Palestine in the twelfth to tenth centuries BC. The pottery evidence points to an Iron I date.

Eilat Mazar's excavation revealed a lengthy wall south of the Jerusalem Temple Mount and north of the "stepped structure."[58] It could support a

57. Cahill, "David and Solomon's Time."
58. E. Mazar, "King David's Palace?"

High/Low Chronology and Taanach

Daniel Master argues as follows: Gezer VIII is monumental in architecture, with nothing similar preceding or outside the central area.[a] This suggests a shift to a regional administrative center. The same is true of Stratum X of Hazor, which follows a poor stratum (XI) and becomes a well-planned administrative center with a six-chambered gate and a casemate wall. The Egyptian fragment at Beth-shan and Shishak's record at Karnak indicate that he did destroy Megiddo, and that must be either the massive destruction of Stratum VI or the limited one of Stratum VA/IVB. Master contends that Taanach is the best source of absolute chronology because only one stratum could have been destroyed by Shishak: IIB. This is a better anchor than Israel Finkelstein's Jezreel, which has no contemporary textual support or a reliable sequence of floors. Following Walter Rast, Master notes that Taanach IIB is the same as Megiddo VA/IVB and Gezer VIII.[b] This contradicts Finkelstein's attempt to date Hazor XII–XI to the late eleventh century and the construction of Hazor X to the Omrides in the early ninth century.[c] If Megiddo VA/IVB was destroyed by Shishak in 925 BC, then Megiddo VIA, two strata before this level, could hardly be later than the twelfth/eleventh century. Since Hazor XII/XI's pottery is best equated with Megiddo VIB and especially VIA,[d] this level of Hazor, even if both strata XII and XI are identical, can easily be dated to the twelfth century and describe an occupation of the site of Hazor not long after the destruction of Hazor XIII in the thirteenth century BC.

[a] Master, "State Formation Theory."
[b] Rast, *Taanach I*.
[c] Finkelstein, Ussishkin, and Halpern, *Megiddo III*.
[d] According to ibid., 236.

multistoried structure and reflects an unusually large building, with elite Phoenician wares, uncommon to a small inland village; all this points to a center of rule and power that reflects a capital city whose influence extends beyond the immediately surrounding region.

There is the charge that Jerusalem was too small and insignificant to be the capital of an empire and that the land of Palestine in the tenth century was largely uninhabited. Israel Finkelstein, with the assistance of Neil Silberman, has popularized this understanding by combining a view of Jerusalem as a small village with the redating of traditionally tenth-century (Solomon's time) structures to the ninth century (Ahab's time).[59] This ignores Mazar's excavations, dates the pottery (the main source of evidence for dating) in a

59. Finkelstein and Silberman, *David and Solomon*.

way unacceptable to most archaeologists, and remains speculative.[60] Kitchen makes a comparison with the sixteenth/fifteenth-century capital of Egypt, Thebes, during the time of the creation of its New Kingdom empire.[61] It was also a small village or town.

Canonical Context

The connection of 1–2 Samuel with what precedes in the Bible can be found in references to Samuel and his sons as judges (1 Sam. 7:15; 8:1) and the continuation of a village-based society with no centralized control or leadership into the first part of the books of Samuel. Indeed, the presence of the ark of the covenant, so prominent as a symbol of God's presence with his people, continues its role as found in the Pentateuch and in Joshua. It will appear in the opening chapters of 1 Kings as well. However, after its deposit in the temple in 1 Kings 8, its physical existence is not attested again in the story of Israel's history, with the exception of a brief mention in 2 Chronicles 35:3 and Jeremiah 3:16. While some might see as irregularities in the involvement of Samuel as a priest (though not from the tribe of Levi, much less from the line of Aaron) or of Uriah the Hittite as a prominent soldier, such irregularities resemble more closely the greater flexibility of the period of the judges, where roles were not so fixed as they would become in later generations after the monarchy's establishment.

Samuel appears in later Israel: he is remembered as one who celebrated the Passover correctly (2 Chron. 35:18), called on God's name (Ps. 99:6), and interceded on behalf of Israel (Jer. 15:1). Samuel's role as a righteous prophet is remembered in the New Testament (Acts 3:24; 13:20; Heb. 11:32). Shiloh is remembered as a place abandoned by God as a result of the sins of Eli and his sons, who took the ark from there (1 Sam. 4; Ps. 78:60). Shiloh's destruction (not recorded in the Bible, but archaeologically attested by an Iron Age I ash layer at the site) becomes a model for what will happen to the temple in Jerusalem in Jeremiah's prophecies (Jer. 7:12–14; 26:6, 9).

First Chronicles 10 mentions Saul in detail, but only in terms of his death and what happens to the corpses of Saul and Jonathan. Verse 13 explicitly states that Saul died due to his unfaithfulness and mentions both his disobedience to God's word and his consultation of a medium. His name appears in the Hebrew titles to five Psalms, always as the enemy of David.

David, his dynasty, and the eternal covenant that God made with him become the chief treasure that the books of Samuel bestow on the remainder

60. See Coogan, "Assessing David and Solomon." I. Finkelstein ("Large Stone Structure") contends that the early dating is confined to at best half a room. But Faust ("Large Stone Structure"; idem, "Did Eilat Mazar Find?") states that he misses much of the data, including the massive W20, which is abutted by the Iron I layer. Faust believes the building was built earlier (Jebusite) but continued to be used by David as a palace.

61. Kitchen, *Reliability*, 154.

of the Bible. The end of David's life as described in 1 Kings 1–2 is the chief connection between 1–2 Samuel and the book that follows. However, he appears in 1 Kings as a weak and dying king, quite the opposite of his character even as it is described at the end of 2 Samuel. The Historical Books, especially 1–2 Kings, evaluate the later kings in David's dynasty in light of David as a model (1 Kings 15:3, 11; 2 Kings 14:3; 18:3; 22:2). The "house of David" becomes a term to describe his dynasty (2 Kings 17:21). While 1 Chronicles reviews many of the events involving David in 1–2 Samuel, it adds an emphasis on the role he plays in setting up an administration and especially in establishing the people necessary for worship in the temple that his son will build. In the fifth century BC, the books of Ezra and Nehemiah describe how the worship in Jerusalem is reconstituted and continued with groups and direction similar to what was instituted by David (Ezra 3:10; 8:2, 20; Neh. 12:24, 36–46).

Of course, the name of David appears dozens of times in the titles of psalms dedicated to him. In the texts of the psalms, David appears in the second half of the Psalter as one chosen by God (Ps. 78:70) and promised an eternal covenant in which there would always be a ruler in Jerusalem who was his descendant (89:20, 35–37, 49; 132:11–12). The prophets also speak of the dynasty of David (Isa. 7:2, 13; 22:22), its loss as a result of God's judgment of his people (Jer. 22:30; 36:30), and its resurrection and greater, future glory (Jer. 33:17–26; Ezek. 37:24–25; Hosea 3:5; Zech. 12:7–13:1).

In the Gospels of the New Testament, the themes of 1–2 Samuel are connected preeminently with David and Jesus as the son of David (Matt. 1:1). Mary's hymn of praise, or Magnificat (Luke 1:46–55), is modeled on Hannah's prayer in 1 Samuel 2. Recorded in the three Synoptic Gospels, Jesus asks the Jewish leaders about the title of Psalm 110 (Matt. 22:41–46; Mark 12:35–37; Luke 20:41–44). By leaving open the question as to whom David addressed as "lord," Jesus invites identification with himself as one greater than David. Through quoting the Psalms, the book of Acts (1:16; 2:25, 34; 4:25; 13:34) repeatedly remembers David's word in speeches designed to persuade others of the work and person of Jesus Christ. Paul appears to refer to similar matters in Romans 4:6 and 11:9, as does the author of Hebrews (4:7). Jesus is connected with the "key of David" in Revelation 3:7, where he bears the title "the Root (and Offspring) of David" (5:5; 22:16; cf. 3:7). In the New Testament, these connections are messianic, designed to find in Christ Jesus the fulfillment of what was prophesied for and by David in the Old Testament.

Theological Perspectives of 1 and 2 Samuel

Many theological themes have already been discussed. See above especially in the sections "Higher Criticism," "Literary Readings," "Gender and Ideological

Criticism," and "Canonical Context." In general the direction of the books and their theological themes are voiced in the speeches and dialogues. Already in the first chapter with the story of Hannah, there is the sense of God at work behind the scenes to overturn the expected possessors of power and to give to the poor and weak the blessings that they seek. Hannah's prayer in 1 Samuel 2:1–10 anticipates everything that will follow: the joy of the blessed, the holiness and sovereignty of God, divine protection for those who wait on God, the humbling of the proud and lifting of the poor and needy from the ash heap, and the confession that God judges and chooses whom he will for kingship.

Samuel

Samuel is the last of the judges and the first of the prophetic figures who will represent God's word and will to the king. God overcomes the laxity and corruption of the priesthood of Eli's time by appointing a young man whose ability to hear his voice and respond begins his career. Samuel himself is not perfect and faces corruption among his own sons, but not before the sons of Eli literally attempt to "put God in a box" and take him with them to the battlefield. God's sovereignty assumes freedom, and so he will not be manipulated. The defeat of Israel, the deaths of their priests, and the loss of the symbol of Israel's God are proofs not of Yahweh's lack of power but of his own sovereign decision to punish those among his people who have presumed on divine holiness and used what God has given them for their own benefit rather than to worship and praise him. Thus the Philistines are mistaken to assume that Yahweh is now under their own god's control. The opposite proves to be true, and so the Philistines learn that God will not be mocked, when he sends plagues on them. In the end their own religious leaders recognize the need to honor Israel's God, to give him sacrifices for their sin and guilt, and to allow Yahweh the freedom to return to his people. "While Israel's own religious and political institutions are failing, the Philistines are learning that Yahweh is indeed king, and that God is capable of protecting Israel from all harm."[62]

It is not in the clarity of a battle strategy that Israel will win its wars but in the cries to God and sacrifices to him by a priest such as Samuel. Then God fights for Israel in 1 Samuel 7, where the book's single example of divinely miraculous aid in warfare comes with loud thunder and panic among the enemy. The faithful circuit of Samuel's ministry (1 Sam. 7:15–17) is a benediction on the judgeship of Samuel and on the peace that comes from faithfulness to God and true repentance, rather than a particular form of government.

62. B. Arnold, "Samuel, Books of," 872.

Israel's demand for a king in 1 Samuel 8 becomes a rejection of the leadership of the Lord, Yahweh, who created and redeemed Israel at the beginning (1 Sam. 8:7–9). The protocols by which a king will rule are presented by Samuel in 1 Samuel 8:11–18 and form a checklist for Solomon and later kings, to expose their oppression of the people. So it is that on Solomon's death, the people are eager to separate from a regime that their predecessors had so desperately sought from God and his agent.

Saul

The kingship of Saul contrasts with the earlier judgeships since it will involve rulership over all Israel and will anticipate the promise of a dynasty. Initially, Samuel appoints Saul as a *nāgîd* and tells him that God has designated him for this position as "ruler" (1 Sam. 10:1). The title *melek*, "king," is proclaimed by the people toward Saul in 1 Samuel 10:24, confirmed by them in 11:15, and only indirectly affirmed by Samuel, first of all in 12:1–2. Indeed, in his early wars Saul appears as a tribal military leader for whom kingship is at best a part-time activity. When the Ammonite threat is conveyed to Saul, he is pictured as returning with his oxen from plowing (1 Sam. 11:5). Indeed, the theme of humility and God's choice of those who are not in a position of prominence seems to continue through the early years of Saul. However, it does not remain.

Saul's need to appeal to the tribes in 1 Samuel 11 for help in order to fight the Ammonites suggests that he does not have any significant standing army available to him. While this will change as the years progress, there is no evidence for a larger administration of the sort that David possesses (cf. 2 Sam. 21 and 23), much less one like Solomon will have.

Much has been made of God's rejection of Saul. Clearly Samuel pronounces that divine rejection. Certainly there is an expectation for Saul to follow God's guidance despite public opinion, private misgivings, or the attraction of political moves. In 1 Samuel, Saul's failure in this regard becomes the author's reason for Saul's rejection.[63] Saul cannot find any response from God for his requests. God is silent and does not answer Saul, neither earlier in his battles (1 Sam. 14:37) nor at the last one (28:6). If Saul is condemned for acting as a priest (13:4–15), why is this not the case with David and Solomon when they sacrifice for Israel? In the end it seems as though the difference has more to do with the heart than with outward actions. As Mark George has observed, David is a man after Yahweh's own heart because of his continual practice of inquiring of God and then declaring his trust in God.[64] These actions stand in contrast to Saul's par-

63. Edelman, *King Saul*.
64. George, "Yhwh's Own Heart," 457.

ticular concern for cultic observance and his failure to inquire continually of Yahweh.

David

In addition to the earlier observations on David, the heart of the theology of David in 1–2 Samuel lies close to the question of kingship. Gordon McConville observes how recent scholarship stresses that the people want a monarchy but actually receive more than they bargain for.[65] He further argues that Deuteronomy places limitations on the powers of the king and that the Deuteronomistic History demonstrates the failure of the monarchy. For McConville, the "appendix" of 2 Samuel 21–24 forms an important conclusion to the story of David. It demonstrates that like Saul (21:1–14), David (24:1–5) fails, and so the dynastic promise of 2 Samuel 7 cannot "really be the vehicle of permanent blessing for Israel."[66]

However, this does not mean that the theology of kingship results in a universally negative verdict from God.[67] The kingship is indeed structured with foreign elements that enter from outside Israel. Yes, Yahwism has always incorporated foreign elements and made use of them, by transforming them. The books of Samuel do not hide the base, human motivations of the characters, and especially the kings, including David. However, God can work in spite of people's sinful desires. The period of Joshua and Judges was no less brutal than that of the monarchy.

Kingship is first introduced and criticized with the reign of Saul. In 1 Samuel 8 Yahweh seems more willing to grant a king than Samuel does. Certainly there are positive reflections in 1 Samuel 9–11. Some of the unhappiness in Samuel comes from his own feeling of rejection (1 Sam. 8:7). David is after God's heart (1 Sam. 13:14) and is promised an eternal dynasty (2 Sam. 7). In this context there seems little that can go wrong. Yet the sins of the deception and murder of Uriah and of adultery with Bathsheba leave a condemnation on the dynasty of ongoing violence (2 Sam. 12:10). Thus even the most positive of kingships has serious blemishes.

It is this uncertainty regarding kingship—indeed, this ambiguity with the one who begins the line of the messiahs who reign in Jerusalem and will reign yet again—that marks kingship as both a blessing and a curse. Yet this confluence of positive and negative evaluations demonstrates that no system of human government will be perfect. Every form is flawed, and perhaps it is for this reason that God's observation about Israel's rejection of him (1 Sam. 8:7) is never revoked. Yet in the finely balanced presentation of kingship, there lies an even more profound balance. There is little in the text that presents the

65. McConville, *Grace in the End*.
66. Ibid., 118.
67. Roberts, "In Defense of the Monarchy."

overt miracles of God as influencing the outcome of human events. In this amazing and powerful narrative, the presence of God is undoubted, but it is not overt in the type of dramatic miracles that have accompanied Israel in the pentateuchal accounts of the exodus and wilderness wanderings. There is no better explanation of this than that given by Gerhard von Rad in his *Old Testament Theology*, an explanation that once again returns to a key theological theme of 1–2 Samuel, that of God's sovereignty in the course of human events:

> This view of history marks the change to a completely new concept of Jahweh's action within it. For the old narrators Jahweh's control of history was principally seen in miracles, in the *charisma* of a leader, in catastrophes, or other signal manifestations of his power: above all it was tied to sacral institutions (the holy war, the Ark, etc.). But now the whole thing was completely changed. Nowhere is there a miracle, and nowhere in the events a sacral point, something like a sacred middle-point, from which the great historical impulses issue. The causal chain of human events is closed without a break—nowhere does the narrator keep a place open where the divine action can interact with the earthly history. And we should look in vain here for a sacred core to which the turbulent events are explicitly or implicitly related. The sphere in which this history moves is completely secular, and the forces in play derive solely from men who are far from allowing themselves to be directed by special religious influences. But the reason why the historian no longer had need of all the traditional means of portrayal (miracles, etc.) was that his concept of the nature of the divine guidance of history was completely different. Jahweh's control takes in all that happens. It does not let itself be seen intermittently in holy miracles; it is as good as hidden from the natural eye: but it continuously permeates all departments of life, public and private, religious and secular alike. The special field where this control of history operates is the human heart, whose impulses and resolves Jahweh in sovereign fashion makes subservient to his plan for history.[68]

Key Commentaries and Studies

Arnold, Bill T. *1 and 2 Samuel*. NIVAC. Grand Rapids: Zondervan, 2003. Excellent study of the text as a historical source, with literary analysis and application.

Brueggemann, Walter. *First and Second Samuel*. IBC. Louisville: Westminster John Knox, 1990. Strong on literary analysis and ideological interpretation.

Klein, Ralph W. *1 Samuel*. 2nd ed. WBC 10. Nashville: Nelson, 2008. Useful critical analysis of the interpretation of 1 Samuel.

Long, V. Philips, ed. *Israel's Past in Present Research: Essays on Ancient Israelite Historiography*. SBTS 7. Winona Lake, IN: Eisenbrauns, 1999. Key collection of essays on the writing of OT historical texts, with emphasis on the integration of literary and historical texts.

68. Von Rad, *Old Testament Theology*, 1:315–16.

McCarter, P. Kyle, Jr. *I and II Samuel: A New Translation with Introduction, Notes, and Commentary.* Vol. 1, *I Samuel.* Vol. 2, *II Samuel.* AB 8–9. Garden City, NY: Doubleday, 1980–84. First and still most significant attestation and application of the relevant Dead Sea Scrolls and versions to the text of Samuel.

Tsumura, David Toshio. *The First Book of Samuel.* NICOT. Grand Rapids: Eerdmans, 2007. Strongest analysis of the Hebrew syntax of the MT.

10

1–2 KINGS

From David's last days to the end of Jerusalem's independence, 1–2 Kings lays out the heart of ancient Israel's story. Is it really all about kings and their times, or is it about God and faithfulness to him?

Name, Text, and Outline

The name Kings is a literal translation of the Hebrew term *mĕlākîm*. For the Greek (LXX) name, Kingdoms or Reigns, see "Name, Text, and Outline" for 1–2 Samuel. In the case of 1–2 Kings, the Septuagint lists these as 3–4 Kingdoms, continuing the story of the two books of Samuel. From an early period the Kings text was divided into two scrolls, and that led to the distinction of the two parts. The name reflects the contents as it describes the monarchy, from that of David (at the end of his life) until the destruction of the southern kingdom (Judah) and the immediate aftermath. The Talmud (*b. B. Bat.* 15a) ascribes the authorship of the book to the prophet Jeremiah. Indeed, Jeremiah and Kings resemble each other in their theological language of the covenant and faithfulness to God. However, the Bible nowhere identifies the specific author(s) of 1–2 Kings.

Next to Jeremiah and the books of Samuel, the books of Kings have the greatest differences between the Masoretic Text and the Septuagint, more than those occurring in any other book in the Old Testament. For many scholars of the Septuagint, much of 3 and 4 Kingdoms is represented in the *kaige* translation and revision of the Old Greek of Kings. The Old Greek text may appear in a group of manuscripts (b, o, c_2, e_2) identified as Antiochian or (proto-)Lucianic. This Old Greek text is believed by some to translate a

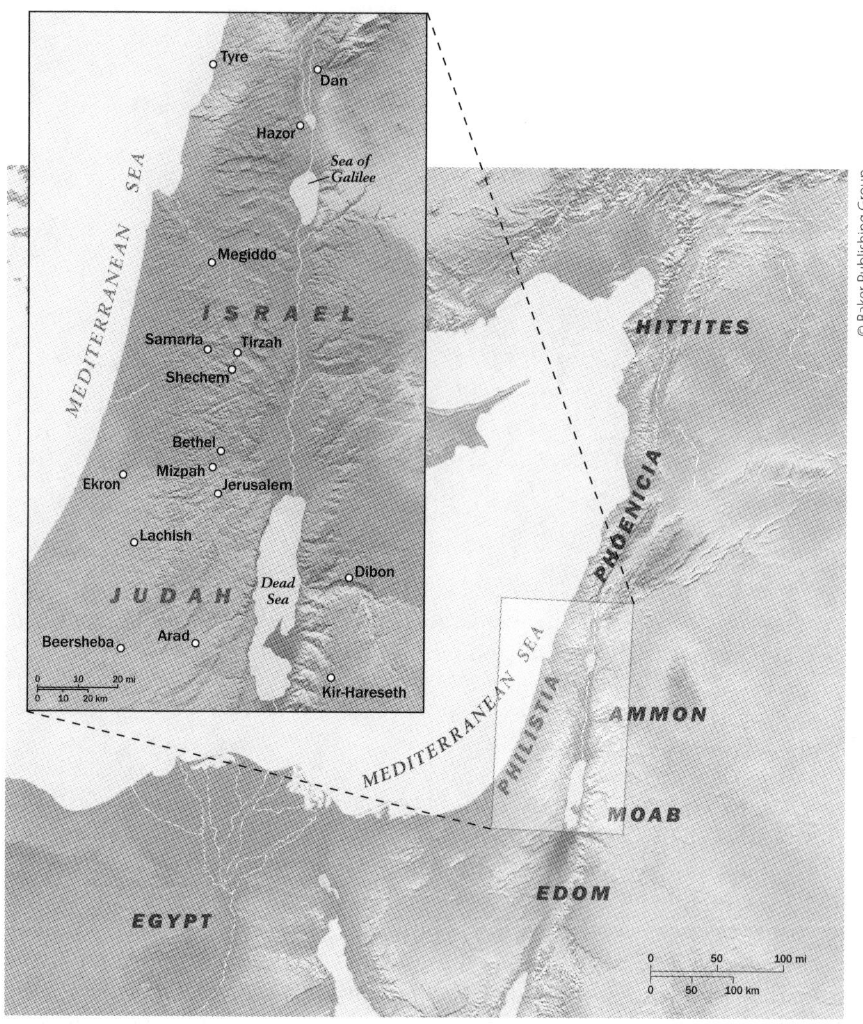

© Baker Publishing Group

Kingdoms and regions in the time of David

Hebrew text that predates the Masoretic Text as it is now extant in its earliest manuscripts. So a question arises: Is the Septuagint of 3–4 Kingdoms a midrashic development of the Masoretic Text, or does it provide a window into a pre-Masoretic text? This is not an issue about whether the Septuagint might correct some corrupt parts of the Masoretic Text, as may be the case for 1–2 Samuel. Rather, the Masoretic Text largely reads well and has no need of "correction." The issue here is whether the substantially different text represented by the Septuagint is a translation of a more ancient Hebrew text that

Temple Construction Text

The Luwian text of King Katuwas was excavated by Leonard Woolley at Carchemish (now in southern Turkey, near Syria) in 1911–14. Sometime after its discovery, it was largely destroyed. Fragments remain at the Anatolian Civilizations Museum in Ankara and at the British Museum. It was written in the late tenth or early ninth century BC, within a generation of the life of Solomon. The text that deals with the construction of the temple is brief, but the importance is the sequence of events as described there. It begins with the temple (§§11–12), next turns to the gates to which the inscription is attached (§13), and then turns back to the construction of the temple, which is described as going on (§14) while Katuwas further enhances the gates with the inscribed orthostats (upright stones) and other structures (§§15–16). This parallel sequence, in which the construction of the temple is ongoing in tandem with other structures, occurs in the Masoretic Text of 1 Kings 6–7. First, there is the construction of the temple in 1 Kings 6. Then 1 Kings 7:1–12 turns to the building of palaces and other nontemple structures. Only after that does 1 Kings 7:13–51 turn its attention back to the temple and consider its furnishings. Thus the contemporary Luwian text parallels the Masoretic Text of 1 Kings 6–7 in its sequence, but is not in the order of either the Septuagint or Josephus.[a]

[a] See Hess, "Katuwas and the Masoretic Text."

is closer to the original.[1] If the latter is true, then it is the Masoretic Text that contains the midrash, or additions to the original text in the form of stories and explanations designed to aid the reader in understanding the original.[2]

However, it is not necessarily the case that the Greek translation is based on a Hebrew text substantially different from what came to be the Masoretic Text. Thus a recent study has examined major differences in the sequence of Masoretic and Septuagint texts in 1 Kings 2–11.[3] Through a detailed examination of these sequence shifts and a review of the variety of critical and contextual matters related to the discussion of each text, it is possible to analyze the arguments from all sides of the question. The conclusion is that the Masoretic Text regularly preserves a text that is less well ordered and less systematic in its idealization of Solomon. Therefore it has had less editorial work done to create a more pious and wise Solomon in the eyes of

1. An original Hebrew text from which a translation—such as the Septuagint—has been derived is called a Vorlage.

2. Schenker, *Septante et texte massorétique*.

3. Cf. Van Keulen, *Solomonic Narrative*.

later readers. Indeed, in at least one case—the order of the construction of the temple, the other palaces in Jerusalem, and their decorations—the order of the Masoretic Text can be supported by contemporary building accounts in the ancient Near East (see the sidebar "Temple Construction Text").[4] Thus the Masoretic Text consistently preserves an older text of Kings. This does not settle the debate, but it does demonstrate that a greater antiquity for the Septuagint cannot be assumed and that the Masoretic Text remains a plausible starting point for the study of the original text of 1–2 Kings.

OUTLINE

I. United Monarchy (1 Kings 1:1–12:24)
  A. David's Old Age (1:1–4)
  B. Adonijah (1:5–27)
  C. Solomon Becomes King (1:28–53)
  D. David's Charge to Solomon (2:1–9)
  E. David's Death (2:10–12)
  F. Solomon's Reign (2:13–11:43)
    1. Vengeance (2:13–46)
    2. Request for Wisdom (3:1–15)
    3. Wise Judgment (3:16–28)
    4. Administration (4:1–34 [5:14 MT])
    5. Construction of the Temple (5:1 [5:15 MT]–6:38)
    6. Solomon's Palaces (7:1–12)
    7. Temple Furnishings (7:13–51)
    8. Temple Dedication (8:1–66)
    9. God's Final Appearance to Solomon (9:1–9)
    10. Administration (9:10–28)
    11. Queen of Sheba (10:1–13)
    12. Wealth (10:14–29)
    13. Wives (11:1–13)
    14. Enemies (11:14–40)
    15. Death (11:41–43)
  G. Division of the Kingdom (12:1–24)
II. The Early Years: Jeroboam I to Zimri (12:25–16:20)
  A. Jeroboam I (12:25–14:20)
  B. Rehoboam (14:21–31)
  C. Abijah/Abijam (15:1–8)
  D. Asa (15:9–24)
  E. Nadab (15:25–32)
  F. Baasha (15:33–16:7)
  G. Elah (16:8–14)
  H. Zimri (16:15–20)

4. Hess, "Katuwas and the Masoretic Text."

- III. The Omride Dynasty (1 Kings 16:21–2 Kings 10:17)
  - A. Omri (1 Kings 16:21–28)
  - B. Ahab Becomes King (16:29–34)
  - C. Elijah (17:1–18:15)
  - D. Mount Carmel Contest (18:16–46)
  - E. Mount Horeb (19:1–18)
  - F. Elisha's Appointment (19:19–21)
  - G. Ben-hadad (20:1–43)
  - H. Naboth and His Ancestral Vineyard (21:1–29)
  - I. Ahab's Last Battle and Death (22:1–40)
  - J. Jehoshaphat (22:41–50 [22:51 MT])
  - K. Ahaziah (1 Kings 22:51 [22:52 MT]–2 Kings 1:18)
  - L. Elijah's Ascent (2 Kings 2:1–18)
  - M. Elisha's Work (2:19–25)
  - N. War with Moab (3:1–27)
  - O. Elisha's Work (4:1–8:15)
  - P. Jehoram (8:16–24)
  - Q. Ahaziah (8:25–29)
  - R. Jehu and the End of Ahab's Family (9:1–10:17)
- IV. Jehu to the End of the Northern Kingdom (10:18–17:41)
  - A. Jehu (10:18–36)
  - B. Athaliah (11:1–20)
  - C. Joash (11:21–12:21 [12:1–22])
  - D. Jehoahaz (13:1–9)
  - E. Jehoash (13:10–25)
  - F. Amaziah (14:1–22)
  - G. Jeroboam II (14:23–29)
  - H. Azariah (15:1–7)
  - I. Zechariah (15:8–12)
  - J. Shallum (15:13–16)
  - K. Menahem (15:17–22)
  - L. Pekahiah (15:23–26)
  - M. Pekah (15:27–31)
  - N. Jotham (15:32–38)
  - O. Ahaz (16:1–20)
  - P. Hoshea (17:1–6)
  - Q. Israel's Downfall Explained (17:7–23)
  - R. Samaria Resettled (17:24–41)
- V. Hezekiah (18:1–20:21)
  - A. Faithfulness (18:1–16)
  - B. Assyrian Threat (18:17–37)
  - C. Cry to God (19:1–19)
  - D. Salvation (19:20–37)
  - E. Illness (20:1–11)
  - F. Babylon (20:12–19)

G. Death (20:20–21)

VI. The Last Kings of Judah (21:1–25:21)
   A. Manasseh (21:1–18)
   B. Amon (21:19–26)
   C. Josiah (22:1–23:30)
   D. Jehoahaz (23:31–35)
   E. Jehoiakim (23:36–24:7)
   F. Jehoiachin (24:8–17)
   G. Zedekiah (24:18–25:21)

VII. Babylonian Rule (25:22–30)

Overview of 1 and 2 Kings

As with 1 and 2 Samuel, the overview will survey many of the details of these books. First Kings 1 begins with the last days of David, the chief human protagonist of the preceding work of 2 Samuel. David has reached a stage in life where he has trouble staying warm. So a woman, Abishag, is found to provide warmth for him. Juxtaposed with David's age and weakness is the decision of David's son Adonijah to gather allies such as Joab and Abiathar. While they meet together to recognize Adonijah's claim to kingship, Nathan arranges with Bathsheba, Solomon's mother, to come before David and speak of a promise that David has made to anoint Solomon as his successor. David declares this and appoints Zadok, Nathan, Benaiah, and their supporters to proclaim Solomon king at the Gihon Spring. When Adonijah and his party learn of this, their alliance falls apart. The supporters go their way while Adonijah flees to grasp hold of the horns of the altar. Solomon promises that Adonijah will not be hurt if he acts properly, and Solomon sends Adonijah home.

David's final words to Solomon include a command to follow Yahweh and to take vengeance on Joab and Shimei (1 Kings 2). After David's death, Adonijah meets with Bathsheba and asks her to intercede with Solomon so that Adonijah may have Abishag as his wife. When Bathsheba asks Solomon for David's nurse, Solomon erupts in fury at a request that would give Adonijah a claim on David's legacy. Solomon sends Benaiah to execute Adonijah. Solomon then expels Abiathar the priest, who supported Adonijah, from Jerusalem. Joab seeks refuge at the horns of the altar. After an unsuccessful attempt to have Joab leave the altar willingly, Solomon charges Benaiah to kill him at the altar. Solomon appoints Benaiah as general of the army and Zadok as priest. He puts Shimei under voluntary arrest in Jerusalem. However, after a few years Shimei leaves Jerusalem. Solomon learns of this and has Benaiah execute Shimei also.

First Kings 3 begins with a note about Solomon's marriage to the daughter of the pharaoh of Egypt. It focuses on Solomon's journey to the high place of Gibeon and his sacrifice of a thousand burnt offerings. God appears to

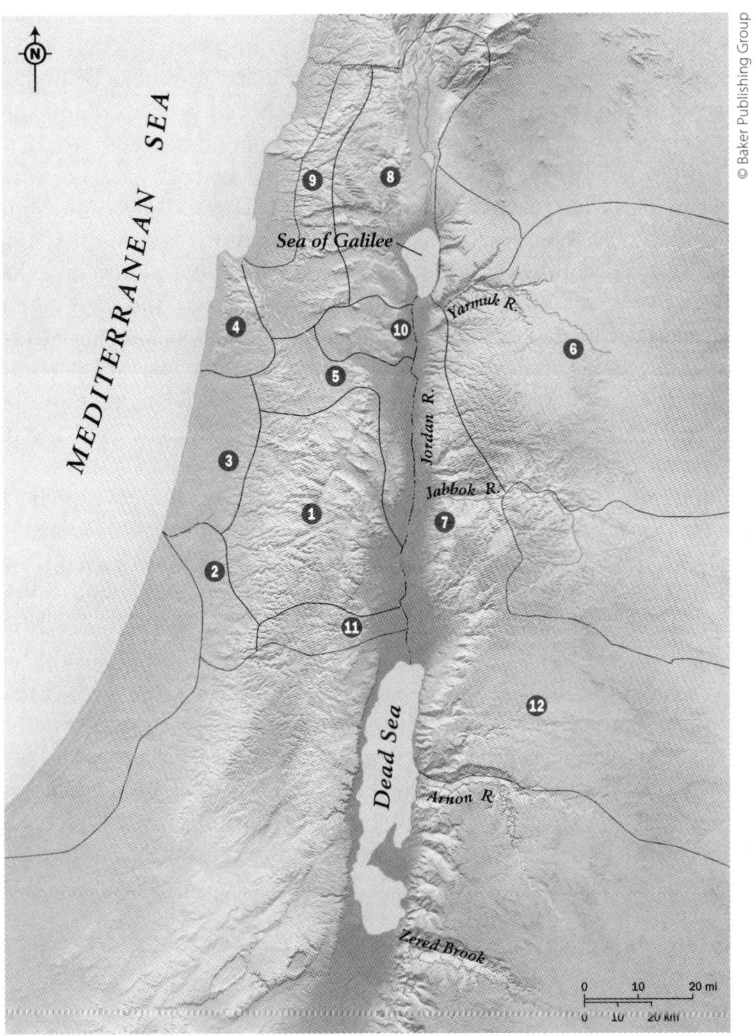

© Baker Publishing Group

Solomon's districts

Solomon in a dream there and asks what Solomon wants as king. Solomon requests a "listening heart" (3:9 RSH) to make wise judgments and to distinguish between good and evil. God is delighted at this and grants it along with promises of wealth, long life, and success against Solomon's enemies. The story of the two prostitutes and the surviving baby illustrates this wisdom. Solomon listens to the two carefully and decides to order the baby cut in half because he understands that in this case it will reveal the false claimant and the true mother. This leads to his fame as just and wise.

Solomon appoints officials to his administration and divides Israel into twelve districts, over which he appoints twelve governors (1 Kings 4). Several paragraphs describe the vast area he rules, the large number of people, his great wealth, and the areas of his wisdom. In this context Solomon contacts Hiram king of Tyre to supply cedar and pinewood and expert woodcutters, while gathering huge numbers of his own people as work gangs to cut stone and to move it and the wood to Jerusalem (1 Kings 5). Solomon builds a temple ninety feet long, thirty feet wide, and forty-five feet high (1 Kings 6). He adds latticed windows, side rooms, cedar paneling, plenty of gold, and doors of olive wood covered with gold. Solomon then builds several palaces in Jerusalem, using cedar and stone (1 Kings 7). He has another Hiram, an artisan, build the capitals on the columns, along with all sorts of decorations. He makes the great "Sea" of cast metal held up by twelve metal bulls, as well as bronze stands and basins and all the objects of gold to be used and placed in the temple.

Solomon then has the priests carry in the ark of Yahweh's covenant (1 Kings 8). He recalls Yahweh's promise to David and the expectation that David's son will build a temple. Solomon's prayer considers that not even this great temple that he has built, nor the heavens and the earth, can contain Yahweh. Instead, Solomon focuses on what it means for Yahweh's name to be at the temple: people can turn toward the temple and pray to the God that it represents, and God will hear and respond. Solomon asks that such turning to God will be true of himself, of Israel, and even of foreigners. Further, he prays that God will respond when people look toward this place and pray for victory against their enemies and for forgiveness of their sin. He blesses God for keeping his word and for bringing about the fulfillment of his promises. The people celebrate for two weeks while Solomon sacrifices thousands of burnt offerings, grain offerings, and fellowship offerings.

Again God meets with Solomon as he has at Gibeon (1 Kings 9). He promises Solomon blessings if he remains faithful. However, he warns Solomon that sin will lead to Israel's departure from their land and to the end of the temple. Solomon pays Hiram king of Tyre with some towns near their mutual border, although Hiram is not pleased with them. Solomon fortifies Jerusalem, along with his cities of Hazor, Megiddo, and Gezer, as well as other storage cities. The non-Israelites in his kingdom are enrolled in forced labor to complete his projects. The Israelites, however, he appoints as leaders and officials. He sacrifices burnt and fellowship offerings, burns incense to Yahweh, and builds a fleet on the Red Sea with a crew supplied by Hiram. They bring him much gold of Ophir. The queen of Sheba visits Solomon and praises him and God for his wealth and wisdom. She gives him gold, spices, and gems (1 Kings 10). He gives her whatever she wants. Everything in Solomon's palaces and the temple is of gold. His throne is ivory, and all the world brings tribute to Solomon in order to learn from his wisdom.

© Baker Publishing Group. Illustration by Shaun Venish.

Artist's reconstruction of Solomon's temple

Solomon acquires hundreds of wives and concubines (1 Kings 11). They represent other nations and their deities. So in his old age, Solomon worships these other gods. God comes to him a third time and pronounces judgment for this sin. Solomon's successor will not rule over all Israel but will rule over only two tribes. So Hadad of Edom and Rezon of Damascus begin to take away the empire that Solomon has ruled. Jeroboam, his officer in charge of the work gang of Ephraim and Manasseh, is approached by Ahijah the prophet, who promises him ten tribes of Israel and a dynasty like David's, if he remains faithful to God. Jeroboam has to flee to Egypt because Solomon tries to kill him.

After this Solomon dies. He is followed on the throne by his son Rehoboam. Under the influence of young men, friends his own age, Rehoboam refuses to lighten the workload that his father has placed on the northern tribes, when they meet with him at Shechem (1 Kings 12). The Israelites of the north abandon him and kill his officer, Adoram, whom he has put in charge of the work gang. Jeroboam returns from Egypt and is proclaimed king by the northern tribes. Although Rehoboam assembles a Judean army to try to win back his kingdom, a prophet warns them not to fight against Israel in the north. So they abandon the battle plans. Jeroboam establishes his capitals at Shechem and also at Penuel, east of the Jordan River. He sets up gold calves as images for worship at Bethel in the south and Dan in the north of his kingdom. Jeroboam also appoints his own priests, builds high places, and establishes a special holy day for worship. A Judean prophet comes to Bethel and condemns the altar and Jeroboam (1 Kings 13), prophesying the coming of King Josiah, who will desecrate the false altar with human bones. Jeroboam tries to seize him but his hand withers. He invites the prophet to stay, but the prophet refuses, having been warned by God not to eat or drink anything in the north. Nevertheless, an old prophet in Bethel persuades him to eat and drink with him. When the Judean prophet tries to return to his home, he is killed by a lion. Jeroboam continues his sin.

When Abijah, son of Jeroboam, becomes sick, the king sends his wife in disguise to the prophet Ahijah, who has been warned by God and told to condemn Jeroboam for his sin, to predict Abijah's death when the queen returns, and to prophesy the violent end of Jeroboam's dynasty (1 Kings 14). After reigning for a total of twenty-two years, Jeroboam dies.

In Judah, Rehoboam rules for seventeen years. Judah builds more high places, appoints false religious officials, and worships other gods. Shishak king of Egypt attacks Jerusalem and removes all the treasure from the city. Abijah/Abijam (NIV, LXX/NRSV, MT) follows Rehoboam and continues the sins of his father (1 Kings 15). As his father has fought Jeroboam, so does Abijam. Asa follows Abijam and rules forty-one years in Jerusalem. He does what is right before Yahweh, removing the false cultic officials; putting away images of

Richard S. Hess

Platform for the gold calf at Dan

other gods, including the one his mother has made for the goddess Asherah; and returning the holy things to Yahweh's temple. He fights Baasha, Israel's king. Asa bribes officials as well as Ben-hadad, ruler of Damascus. Ben-hadad attacks Israel and occupies its northern towns. Asa dismantles the fortifications of Baasha. In his old age, Asa becomes diseased in his feet and dies.

In Israel, Jeroboam is succeeded by Nadab, who does evil, as his father did. Baasha of Issachar attacks and kills Nadab and then wipes out the whole family of Jeroboam. However, Baasha follows the evil ways of Jeroboam throughout his lifetime. Yahweh condemns Baasha for all his sin by speaking through the prophet Jehu (1 Kings 16). Elah son of Baasha follows his father but is killed by Zimri, the officer in charge of Elah's chariots. Zimri takes the throne and kills all of Baasha's household. Only a week after he becomes ruler, however, Zimri dies at his own hand, after the army has instead declared Omri king over Israel. There is civil war in Israel, but Omri wins the struggle and establishes his capital at Samaria. He worships images and angers Yahweh. Ahab his son follows him in the thirty-eighth year of Asa king of Judah. He marries Jezebel, daughter of the Sidonian king. Ahab builds an altar to Baal in the temple that he has built to the god. Ahab also makes an Asherah tree and does more evil than all the kings who have preceded him.

It is at this time that Elijah prophesies that it will not rain in Israel (1 Kings 17). Elijah flees to Kerith, where God takes care of him, and then to Zarephath near Sidon, where a widow, who receives a miraculous provision of oil and flour, takes care of him. Her son becomes ill and dies, but Elijah prays to God, and the boy's life is restored.

Ahab and his officer Obadiah go throughout Israel in search of grass for their animals. Elijah comes to Obadiah, who fears God and protects his true prophets, and sends him to tell Ahab that Elijah will meet him. When Elijah meets Ahab, he calls Ahab's prophets of Baal to a contest on Mount Carmel. Elijah challenges the 450 prophets to call on their god to bring fire down on the altar and devour the sacrifice of a bull. They try but fail. Then Elijah builds an altar, pours water over it, and calls on God to send down fire on the bull. The fire falls from God. Israel sees this and confesses that Yahweh is God. Elijah kills the prophets of Baal. After this comes a great rainstorm.

Threatened with death by Jezebel, Elijah becomes discouraged and heads south (1 Kings 19). Going into the desert for a day, he longs for death. An angel wakes him and gives him food to eat and something to drink. He comes to Mount Horeb and spends the night in a cave. Yahweh asks him why he is there, and so Elijah speaks of how Israel has turned against God. With an almost inaudible voice, God charges him to anoint Hazael as the next king of Damascus and Jehu as the next king over Israel. Finally, he is to anoint Elisha as his own successor. God has preserved seven thousand in Israel who do not worship Baal but remain loyal. Elijah returns and meets Elisha, who follows and serves him.

Ben-hadad, king of Aram, brings together his allies and makes war on Israel (1 Kings 20). Aided by prophets who encourage the Israelite army, Ahab defeats Ben-hadad twice in battles in the hills and on the plains. In the second victory, he captures Ben-hadad, who promises Ahab markets in Damascus and the restoration of all the north of Israel that Ben-hadad's father has seized. So Ahab makes a treaty with him and releases him. A prophet has a friend wound him and then disguises himself with a bandage. He delivers a message to Ahab that God will demand his life and people because Ahab has allowed Ben-hadad and his people to live.

At Jezreel, Naboth owns a vineyard next to Ahab's palace, a vineyard that Ahab desperately wants (1 Kings 21). However, Naboth will not sell the land that has been given by God to his ancestors. When Jezebel hears of this, she arranges for two liars to accuse Naboth publicly of cursing God and the king. They do this, and the people put Naboth to death. Ahab then takes possession of Naboth's vineyard. Elijah pronounces judgment on Ahab and his family: they will all die and not be buried. Some, such as Jezebel, will face additional humiliation. Ahab then humbles himself, and so God promises that this will not happen until after Ahab's own death.

Jehoshaphat, king of Judah, consults the king of Israel about war with the Aramaeans (1 Kings 22). They agree, but Jehoshaphat wishes to hear from all the prophets. Micaiah the prophet declares, like the other court prophets, that the two kings will be successful. However, he is being sarcastic and eventually warns that the masters of the armies will not return to their homes in peace. Micaiah relates a vision in which Yahweh is on his throne and asks for one of his court to put a lying spirit into the mouths of the prophets. Ahab imprisons Micaiah, but he does not change his message. In the battle Ahab disguises himself, but a stray arrow pierces his armor. He dies in the evening and is buried in Samaria. They wash the chariot of his blood, and dogs lick it, just as Elijah has prophesied.

Jehoshaphat rules in Jerusalem for twenty-five years, but he does not tear down the high places. However, he does rid the lands of cultic officials who follow other gods. He also builds a fleet to travel to Ophir for gold. However, it is destroyed while still in port.

Ahaziah succeeds his father, Ahab, and does evil just as Ahab and Jezebel have done, worshiping Baal. When Ahaziah falls through the window of his upper room, he inquires of the god Baal-zebub of Ekron whether he will live (2 Kings 1). God gives Elijah a message that Ahaziah will die due to his lack of trust in Yahweh. Ahaziah sends fifty men to apprehend Elijah, who calls down fire that consumes them. This happens twice. The third time, however, the commander of the fifty men begs Elijah to spare them. Elijah is told by God to go with the men. He confronts Ahaziah with the news of his fate, and it happens just as Elijah has said. Joram his brother becomes king because Ahaziah has no son.

The time comes for Elijah to leave this world (2 Kings 2). Elisha goes with him to Jericho, where the two cross over on dry ground because the waters divide when Elijah strikes them with his cloak. Elijah invites Elisha to ask for something, and he requests double the spirit of Elijah. Suddenly a fiery chariot and horses divide them, and Elijah is swept to heaven in their storm. Only Elijah's coat is left, and Elisha takes it. The "sons of the prophets" in Jericho say they will send fifty strong men to search for Elijah. Elisha does not want them to go, but they persuade him, and so the fifty search for three days but find nothing. Elisha miraculously freshens the bitter waters at Jericho. On his way to Bethel, a gang of youths approaches him and mocks him. He curses them, and two bears tear at forty-two of the youths.

Joram rules Israel for twelve years (2 Kings 3). He does evil in God's sight as Jeroboam did, even though he removes the standing stone dedicated to Baal. Mesha king of Moab has given Israel the wool of a hundred thousand rams as an annual tribute. When Ahab dies, Moab revolts. Joram joins with Jehoshaphat of Judah and Edom's king to fight Moab. Along the way Elijah promises them provisions and victory over Moab. As the battle is going against Moab's king, the Moabite leader takes a fighting force and tries to break through to the king of Edom. Being unsuccessful, he takes "his" son (likely the son of the king of Edom) and offers him as a sacrifice on the walls of the city. The coalition breaks apart, and Israel returns home.

For the wife of a prophet's son, Elisha miraculously provides a large supply of oil so that she can sell it and pay off her debts (2 Kings 4). A wealthy woman at Shunem arranges an upper room in her house as a place where Elisha can stay as he passes by on his journeys. Elisha promises her a son, and one is born to her a year later. However, the son becomes ill and dies. When the woman tells Elisha, he sends his servant Gehazi to place his staff on the child, but that does nothing. So Elisha goes and lies over the child. The boy revives, and the mother receives him. Elisha also takes a pot of poisonous food and makes it edible with flour. At another time he takes twenty loaves of bread and a sack of grain to feed a hundred men and has leftovers.

An Aramaean general named Naaman contracts leprosy (2 Kings 5). His wife has an Israelite slave girl who tells her mistress about Elisha, a prophet in Samaria who can cure Naaman. The Aramaean king hears of this, so he sends Naaman with gifts and a request to Israel's king to heal Naaman. The Israelite king reads the request as an excuse to go to war. But Elisha learns of it and says that Naaman may visit him. Elisha sends a messenger to Naaman, instructing him to wash seven times in the Jordan River, and he will be clean. At first, Naaman is angry, but his servants persuade him to follow Elisha's word. After he has bathed seven times, his flesh is restored. Naaman attempts to give gifts to Elisha, who refuses them. He requests two mule-loads of earth so that he can sacrifice and worship the Lord on Israelite "land." After he departs from Elisha, Naaman is tracked by Elisha's servant, Gehazi. Gehazi lies to Naaman about Elisha's desire for some silver and garments. Naaman happily gives Gehazi what he has requested and departs. When Gehazi returns to Elisha, he denies having gone to see Naaman, and so Elisha sends leprosy on Gehazi and his descendants.

Elisha gives permission for a new building on the campus where the sons of the prophets live (2 Kings 6). They cut down some trees, but an ax flies into the nearby water. Elisha throws a piece of wood at the spot, and the axhead floats.

The Aramaean king moves around in Israel to try to surprise and capture the king of Israel. Each time, however, Elisha warns the Israelite king. This infuriates the Aramaean king, and so he sends an army of horses and chariots to surround the city of Dothan, where Elisha is. As they approach, Elisha prays, and they are blinded. Then he leads them into the capital city of Samaria and advises the king to give them food and water and allow them to return home. The king does this, and that stops the Aramaean raiding parties.

Ben-hadad's siege of Samaria leads to a severe famine where mothers cannibalize their own sons. The king blames Elisha and swears that he will execute him. Elisha, who is at his own home, foresees the king's intention before the king himself arrives to carry out the execution. Elisha prophesies that twenty-four hours from the moment of his speaking, wheat flour and barley will be readily available in Samaria (2 Kings 7). The officer who is with the king expresses doubt that this can happen, and Elisha says he will see but not eat from the abundance. In despair, four lepers leave Samaria and go over to the Aramaean camp in hopes of obtaining mercy from them. However, Yahweh has caused the Aramaeans to hear the sound of a powerful army in the night, and they have all fled, leaving their food and belongings. After taking their share of food and booty, the lepers return to Samaria with the good news. The king checks out their story by sending messengers to follow the trail of debris that the Aramaeans have left. Then the people of Samaria go to the Aramaean camp and take all the food and drink they want. The officer who has questioned Elisha's prophecy is trampled in the city gate and dies.

Elisha warns the woman whose son he has made alive that a famine is coming and will remain for seven years (2 Kings 8). She moves away until the end of that time and then returns and seeks an audience with the king, to retrieve her house and property. Gehazi is just telling the king about her story when she arrives, and so the king gives the woman everything that belongs to her.

Elisha goes to Damascus, where Ben-hadad, the Aramaean king, is ill. Ben-hadad sends Hazael with a gift to inquire of Elisha as to his fate. Elisha says he will die and Hazael will succeed him and do evil to Israel. Hazael returns to Ben-hadad but says that the king will live. The next day Hazael smothers Ben-hadad in his bed, and Hazael becomes king.

In Judah, Jehoram succeeds his father, Jehoshaphat, as king. He rules eight years and follows the wicked ways of his father-in-law, Ahab. During his time Judah loses control of Edom and of Libnah. Jehoram's son Ahaziah follows his father but reigns only one year. When his uncle Joram is beaten by the Aramaeans and is suffering from his wounds at Jezreel, Ahaziah goes to visit him. The fight against the Aramaeans is taking place at Ramoth-gilead. Elisha sends one of the sons of the prophets there to anoint Jehu as the next king of Israel (2 Kings 9). He anoints him king and commands him to kill all who remain of the house of Ahab. The anointing is done in secret, but when his officers learn of it, they proclaim Jehu as king. Jehu takes his chariot and races to Jezreel. Joram sees him coming and sends messengers, but they all join Jehu. When Joram takes his chariot, he meets Jehu at Naboth's vineyard. Jehu condemns him for following the sorceries of his mother, Jezebel. When Joram turns his chariot and tries to escape, Jehu shoots him in the back. King Ahaziah of Judah, who is a grandson of Ahab, sees this happening and flees in his chariot. However, Jehu's men shoot Ahaziah in his chariot, and he dies at Megiddo.

At Jezreel, Jehu encounters Jezebel looking out a window from an upper floor. He calls her eunuchs to his service, and they toss her out the window so that she dies, and dogs eat her remains. Jehu then sends letters to the administrators at Samaria to gather the sons of Ahab and make one of them king so that they can fight for their claim to kingship (2 Kings 10). However, the officials negotiate with Jehu and slaughter the seventy princes of Ahab. They send their heads in baskets to Jehu. At Jezreel, Jehu kills everyone else associated with Ahab and his dynasty. On his way to Samaria, Jehu encounters forty close kin of King Ahaziah of Judah. He has them executed. Jehu then commands all priests and officiants of Baal to come to the capital and to worship Baal at his temple. He gathers them all and has his soldiers kill every one of them. He makes the temple into a latrine. However, Jehu does not do away with the gold calves that Jeroboam has set up in Bethel and Dan. God promises him that his descendants will rule Israel until the fourth generation. During Jehu's reign, King Hazael of the Aramaeans captures Gilead and Bashan, east of the Jordan Valley.

With King Ahaziah of Judah's death, Athaliah, his mother and the daughter of Ahab and Jezebel, seeks to kill the entire dynasty of David in Jerusalem and to declare herself ruler (2 Kings 11). However, the sister of Ahaziah hides Joash, one of Ahaziah's sons. After seven years the priest Jehoiada brings together the leaders loyal to Joash and makes them guard the prince. Then they bring out Joash into the public and proclaim him king. When Athaliah sees the public acclamation, she cries, "Treason! Treason!" They seize and execute her at a distance from the temple. They destroy the temple of Baal, grind its images to dust, and execute the priest.

At the age of seven, Joash begins his forty-year reign in Jerusalem (2 Kings 12). He does not remove the high places but otherwise follows God and seeks to repair the temple. The money that has been freely given by the people is used to pay the carpenters and masons to repair the temple. When King Hazael of the Aramaeans comes against Judah and threatens Jerusalem, Joash takes all the money that has been collected and everything in the treasuries and turns it over to Hazael, who then withdraws.

Hazael and his son Ben-hadad oppress the northern kingdom (Israel) throughout the reign of Jehoahaz, son of Jehu. God provides a savior for Israel so that the people can live as before. However, Jehoahaz's army is reduced in size and power. Jehoahaz's son Jehoash follows him and does evil like his father. As Elisha lies dying, Jehoash comes to visit him. Elisha has him shoot an arrow and strike the other arrows on the ground. When Jehoash does so three times and stops, Elisha becomes angry and says that if he would have struck the ground five or six times, Israel would have finished off the Aramaean threat. As it is, he will defeat the Aramaeans three times. This happens during battles with Ben-hadad, son of Hazael. Elisha's death leads to a final miracle. When a burial party is attacked by some Moabite gangs, they toss the corpse into Elisha's grave. When it touches Elisha's bones, the dead body revives.

Amaziah becomes king in Judah and puts to death those who have assassinated his father, Joash (2 Kings 14). He defeats the Edomites and seeks an alliance with King Jehoash of Israel. Jehoash will not agree, and Israel and Judah fight at Beth-shemesh. Jehoash takes Amaziah captive and marches to Jerusalem, where he tears down a large section of the city walls and takes away all the remainder of the gold and silver left in the temple.

Azariah (= Uzziah in 2 Chron. 26:1) follows Amaziah as king of Judah and rebuilds Elath.

Jeroboam II begins ruling Israel in Amaziah's fifteenth year and reigns for forty-one years. He does evil in Yahweh's eyes, following in the sins of Jeroboam I. Under this leader, Israel regains land as far north as Lebo-hamath and as far south as the Sea of the Arabah (Dead Sea), as Jonah has prophesied (14:25). Jeroboam II controls Damascus and Hamath.

Azariah becomes king of Judah in Jeroboam II's twenty-seventh year and reigns for fifty-two years (2 Kings 15). He does what is right, like his father, but he does not remove the high places. He becomes a leper and needs to live in a separate house while his son Jotham takes care of the daily governing tasks.

In the northern kingdom, Zechariah follows his father, Jeroboam II, but is assassinated by Shallum after six months. So the line of Jehu sees four generations as kings over Israel. Shallum is killed by Menahem after only a month. Menahem attacks Tiphsah (perhaps Tappuah [15:16 RSV], near Tirzah), ripping open pregnant women in the process. He follows in the sins of Jeroboam I. Menahem has to deal with the Assyrian king Tiglath-pileser III. Menahem taxes Israel, especially the wealthy class, and pays the Assyrian a thousand talents of silver. Pekahiah succeeds his father, Menahem. He reigns for two years and then is assassinated by his officer Pekah. During Pekah's twenty-year reign, Tiglath-pileser attacks and annexes the Galilee region, with

Chart of the Kings

Israel	Judah	Aram	Assyria
Jeroboam (931/30–910/9)	Rehoboam (931/30–913)		
	Abijah (913–911/10)		
Nadab (910/9–909/8)	Asa (911/10–870/69)		Adad-nirari II (911–891)
Baasha (909/8–886/85)			Tukulti-Ninurta II (890–884)
Elah (886/85–885/84)		Bar-hadad I (885–870)	Assurnasirpal II (883–859)
Zimri (885/84)			
Tibni (885/84–880)			
Omri (*885/84–880*; 880–874/73)			
Ahab (874/73–853)	Jehoshaphat (*872/71–870/69*; 870/69–848)	Hadadezer (870–842)	Shalmaneser III (858–824)
Ahaziah (853–852)	Jehoram (*853–848*; 848–841)		
Joram (852–841)	Ahaziah (841)		
Jehu (841–814/13)	Athaliah (841–835)	Hazael (841–806)	Shamshi-Adad V (823–811)
Jehoahaz (814/13–798)	Jehoash/Joash (835–796)		Adad-nirari III (810–783)
Jehoash (798–782/81)	Amaziah (796–767)		
Jeroboam II (*793/92–782/81*; 782/81–753)	Uzziah (*792/91–767*; 767–740/39)		Tiglath-pileser III (744–727)
Zechariah (753–752)			
Shallum (752)			
Menahem (752–742/41)	Jotham (*750–740/39*; 740/39–732/31)		
Pekahiah (742/41–740/39)			
Pekah (*752–740/39*; 740/39–732/31)	Ahaz (*735–732/31*; 732/31–716/15)		Shalmaneser V (727–722)
Hoshea (732/31–723/22)			Sargon II (722–705)
	Hezekiah (*729–716/15*; 716/15–687/86)		Sennacherib (705–681)
	Manasseh (*697/96–687/86*; 687/86–643/42)		
	Amon (643/42–641/40)		

Israel	Judah	Aram	Assyria
	Josiah (641/40–609)		
	Jehoahaz (609)		
	Jehoiakim (608–598)		
	Jehoiachin (598–597)		
	Zedekiah (597–586)		

Overlapping reigns and coregencies appear in italics. Dates for Judean and Israelite kings are from Edwin R. Thiele, *The Mysterious Numbers of the Hebrew Kings: A Reconstruction of the Chronology of the Kingdoms of Israel and Judah*, 3rd ed. (Grand Rapids: Eerdmans, 1983), 217.

its cities, and he deports the Israelites there to Assyria. Hoshea assassinates Pekah and becomes king.

In Judah, Jotham succeeds his father, Ahaziah (= Uzziah), in the second year of Pekah and rules Judah for sixteen years. Jotham also follows God, as Uzziah has done, but he does not remove the high places. At that time Rezin of the Aramaeans and Pekah of Samaria begin to attack Judah. Ahaz succeeds his father, Jotham, and reigns for twenty years (2 Kings 16). He sacrifices on the high places and does what is wrong before God, to the point of sacrificing his son. Rezin and Pekah attack Ahaz in Jerusalem but cannot defeat him, although Rezin does capture Elath. Ahaz requests help from King Tiglath-pileser III of Assyria, who annexes Damascus and kills Rezin. In Damascus, Ahaz meets Tiglath-pileser. He copies the (likely) Assyrian altar there and follows Assyrian practices in sacrifices and in redesigning features in the Jerusalem temple. The king of Assyria attacks Samaria and Hoshea, who is ruling there (2 Kings 17; see the sidebar "The Fall of Samaria"). He besieges the capital for three years. Samaria falls, and its inhabitants are deported to other Assyrian provinces.

Second Kings 17:7–23 summarizes the sins of Israel that have provoked God to allow the Assyrians to deport them from the land. Worshiping and burning incense at high places, making images of Asherah and Baal, sacrificing their sons and daughters, and following the sins of Jeroboam—all these deeds by Israelites have led to their judgment. Verses 24–41 describe how the region of Samaria is repopulated with peoples from all around the ancient Near East. Although a priest from Samaria is returned to the land to teach the people concerning the worship of Yahweh, they do not listen and instead continue to worship and serve other gods.

Hezekiah succeeds his father, Ahaz, as king in Jerusalem (2 Kings 18). He follows Yahweh and destroys the high places and all the images and sacred stones and trees. Sennacherib, king of Assyria, attacks Judah. Hezekiah gives him all of his silver and gold to leave Judah alone. The king of Assyria sends his officers to Jerusalem. The officers of Hezekiah meet them. Sennacherib's officers state that Yahweh has told Sennacherib to attack Judah. Then they

The Fall of Samaria

It was likely Shalmaneser V who began the siege of Samaria. By this time only the capital city and the surrounding countryside remained independent of the Assyrians. The siege lasted three years, from 725 onward. At its beginning King Hoshea was likely taken prisoner. At its end, in 722 BC, Shalmaneser V died, but Samaria fell. Nevertheless, the city survived into the first years of King Sargon II of Assyria. As Hoshea formerly sought an alliance with Egypt, so now Samaria joined a coalition led by the king of Hamath in Syria. In 720 BC the Assyrian army made its way southward and arrived in Samaria. The following recount the scene, in Anson Rainey's translation:[a]

> The city of Samaria I besieged and I conquered. 27,290 people who resided in it I took as booty. I conscripted fifty chariots from them and the rest I had instructed in their proper behaviour. My eunuch I appointed over them, and I imposed on them the tribute like the previous king. (Great Display Inscription II, 23–25)
>
> [The Sa]marians who conspired with a [hostile] king to not render servitude [and to not re]nder tribute, opened hostilities. In the strength of the great gods, my [lor]ds, I engaged them. [2]7,280 people with their char[iots] and the deities, their helpers, I counted as spoil. Two hundred chariots for [my] roy[al] contingent I conscripted from among them. The rest of them I settled within the land of Assyria. The city of Samaria I resettled and made it greater than before. People of the lands conquered by my own hands I installed there. My eunuch I appointed over them as governor and I reckoned them as people of Assyria. (Nimrud Prism, Fragment D, 25–41)

[a] Rainey and Notley, *Sacred Bridge*, 234–35; see also Younger, "Fall of Samaria." The inscriptions cited here are those of King Sargon II of Assyria.

shout to the people who are standing nearby not to listen to Hezekiah but to surrender and live. No other nation has withstood Assyria, they boast. The people remain silent according to the command of King Hezekiah. The delegation reports to Hezekiah. Isaiah the prophet says that Sennacherib will hear news that will take him back to his own country, where he will die violently. After that, Sennacherib withdraws from his siege of Lachish to fight Egypt. However, he sends a letter to Hezekiah, challenging him not to believe in Yahweh's promise of deliverance. No other gods effect deliverance for their communities, Sennacherib claims. Hezekiah takes the correspondence to the temple and spreads it before Yahweh. He prays and expresses faith that God can rescue so that his kingdom might know that Yahweh alone is God. Isaiah sends a message that Yahweh will not stand for these insults from the Assyrian king. Sennacherib will not come to Jerusalem; he will go home.

This happens: the angel of Yahweh fights for Israel and kills 185,000 Assyrian soldiers. When Sennacherib returns home, his sons murder him while he is worshiping his god.

Hezekiah becomes ill, and Isaiah tells him that he will die. Hezekiah begs for more years, and so God grants it by having Isaiah prepare a fig poultice and administer it. When Hezekiah asks for a sign that God will heal him, Isaiah says that God will make the sundial go in reverse for "ten steps." This happens, and Hezekiah recovers. The king of Babylon sends messengers to Hezekiah with a gift, urging him to join an alliance against Assyria. Hezekiah agrees and shows the messengers all of his treasures, arms, and fortifications. Isaiah prophesies that everything that Hezekiah has shown the messengers will be taken by the Babylonians, and all of Hezekiah's descendants will go into exile and serve the king of Babylon.

Manasseh follows Hezekiah and reigns fifty-five years (2 Kings 21). He does evil, building high places, altars to Baal, Asherah images, and altars to the host of heaven in the temple of Jerusalem. He sacrifices his own son and practices sorcery. Manasseh leads Judah into greater sin than the people whom God expelled from the land when he gave it to Israel. So God speaks through the prophets, promising the destruction of Jerusalem and the expulsion of Judah from the land. Amon follows Manasseh, his father, and reigns for two years, doing evil. His officials assassinate him in his palace, and then they themselves are killed. Josiah, son of Amon, becomes king.

Josiah reigns thirty-one years (2 Kings 22). He does what is upright. In his eighteenth year he orders the repair of the temple. In the process Hilkiah the priest finds the scroll of the law. When it is read to the king, he tears his clothes and seeks forgiveness for disobeying what is written in the scroll and what was not earlier known. Hilkiah goes to Huldah the female prophet, who says that God is bringing judgment against Judah. Yet because of Josiah's repentance, he himself will not see the judgment.

Josiah calls together all the people of Judah and reads them the scroll of the covenant found in the temple (2 Kings 23). He destroys everything associated with Baal and Asherah in Jerusalem, Judah, and as far north as Bethel and beyond, throughout Samaria. Josiah desecrates the place of child sacrifice in the Hinnom Valley. He does away with the shrines in every city and with horses and chariots dedicated to the sun. Josiah removes the altars that Manasseh has built. He destroys all the images and temples built to other gods and goddesses east of Jerusalem. Josiah dies when Pharaoh Necho II has him killed at Megiddo.

Josiah's son Jehoahaz succeeds him and reigns for three months. Pharaoh Necho imprisons him, but not before the pharaoh has taxed the land of Judah. Necho then appoints another son of Josiah as ruler, Jehoiakim. Jehoiakim taxes Israel to pay tribute to Necho. Like his ancestors, Jehoiakim does evil in the eyes of Yahweh and pours out the blood of the innocent (2 Kings 24).

Jehoiakim submits to King Nebuchadnezzar of Babylon and then rebels after three years. After eleven years of rule, Jehoiakim dies. His son Jehoiachin rules for three months. Nebuchadnezzar's army attacks Jerusalem. In 597 BC Jehoiachin is taken prisoner and deported, along with his mother and all the elite of the land. Nebuchadnezzar appoints a son of Josiah, Zedekiah, as king over Jerusalem and Judah.

Zedekiah rebels against the king of Babylon. Nebuchadnezzar attacks Jerusalem and builds a siege wall around it (2 Kings 25). The city suffers famine. As the Babylonians are entering the city, its defenders are fleeing toward the Jordan Valley. The Babylonians seize Zedekiah at Jericho and bring him to Nebuchadnezzar. His sons are killed, and he is blinded and led in chains to Babylon. The Babylonians burn the temple and all of Jerusalem. They deport the survivors, leaving only the poorest of the land. They carry away to Babylon all the remaining vessels, articles, and valuable items from the temple. The leading priests and officials are brought before Nebuchadnezzar and put to death. So Judah goes into exile.

Nebuchadnezzar appoints Gedaliah as governor over the land and those who have remained there. Gedaliah sets up his offices in Mizpah. After a few months Ishmael assassinates Gedaliah and his officials. At that point all the people flee to Egypt.

Second Kings concludes with a note concerning King Jehoiachin of Judah in exile. Thirty-seven years into his exile, Jehoiachin is released from prison and seated with other kings who eat before Evil-merodach, king of Babylon.

Reading 1 and 2 Kings

Premodern Readings

Philo of Alexandria (*Confusion of Tongues* 149) set the tone for the interpretation of 1–2 Kings when he observed that the evaluations accompanying the lives of each of the kings of Israel and Judah ("did evil in the eyes of the Lord," "did not turn away from the sins of Jeroboam son of Nebat," "trusted in the Lord," etc.) represent, in the case of the positive evaluations, those souls made immortal by their virtues.[5] Josephus (*Ant.* 1.14) follows in this direction: he observes that these books teach the reader about the importance of conformity to God's will. Those who do so succeed, while those who don't surely fail.

The patristic period saw an emphasis on various figures in 1–2 Kings as types who foreshadow Christ and his bringing of salvation.[6] These types could be found in the election, judgments, and construction projects of Solomon

5. Provan, *1 and 2 Kings* (OTG), 25.
6. Conti and Pilara, *1–2 Kings*, xviii.

as well as in the lives and deeds of the prophets Elijah and Elisha. The early Christian interpreters also found evidence of moral teaching in Ahab, the prophet of 1 Kings 13, Jehu, and Josiah. By comparison, other events and teachings in the books of Kings were ignored. Thus neither the Latin nor the Greek fathers produced full commentaries on the books, although the Venerable Bede (ca. 672–735) authored an extensive commentary on the temple of Solomon, specifying how various parts of the construction foreshadow the doctrine of Christ and the New Testament as a whole.[7] There is also the work of Theodoret of Cyrus (ca. 393–457), which includes comments on difficult sections of the Historical Books. This provides a more literal interpretation of the text, with concise references to typological aspects related to Christ. Only in the Syriac writings do scholars find early commentary on 1–2 Kings, attributed to Ephrem the Syrian (ca. 306–373), but likely written a century after him. There is an extended discussion of Elijah and Elisha as well as allegorical and typological exegesis. Jacob of Serug (ca. 451–521) composed homilies, presented as metrical poems, that deal with events such as the judgment of Solomon, Elijah, and Elisha.[8] By the ninth century, the Syriac father Isho‘dad of Merv and the Latin writers Rabanus Maurus and Walafrid(ius) Strabo were writing commentaries on the whole of 1–2 Kings. Isho‘dad follows in the literal tradition resembling Theodoret but with original typological and allegorical notes as well. Rabanus and Walafridius continue the typological approach of Bede into the medieval period, where it remains influential in the West.

An example of the more literal approach, although tied to a theological interpretation, may be found in the explanation of Isho‘dad of Merv regarding the 1 Kings 22 account of the lying spirit that God sends from his council to lead Ahab into battle:

> The "spirit" who "came forward and stood [before the Lord]" is an angel and not an evil spirit, namely, Satan, as certain [authors] suggest. In fact, why would an evil spirit stand before the Lord? On the contrary, this spirit is Michael, the leader of the people. It is he who says in his zeal, "I will entice him," that is, "Allow me to leave and abandon the prophets of lies, instead of hindering them, as I have done many times, in order to stop and prevent their false prophecies. As a consequence, the destiny of Ahab will be according to what justice requires, because he will obey [his false prophets] with all his heart if I do not prevent this." (*Books of Sessions*, 1 Kings 22:20)[9]

The rabbinic and later Reformation interpretations advanced the literal approach, while at the same time appreciating the moral analysis reflected

7. Ibid., xxiv.
8. Kaufman, *Judgment of Solomon*; idem, *Homily on Elijah*; idem, *Homily on Elisha*.
9. Conti and Pilara, *1–2 Kings*, 136.

Ephrem on 2 Kings 2:20

In 2 Kings 2 the story of the tearing of youths or children by the bears (2:20) is explained by Ephrem the Syrian:

> It seems that the impudence of the children resulted from the teaching of their parents, because they were iniquitous and hostile to Elijah and all his disciples. And we may also think that they had been sent by their masters to repeat what they had learned. The word proclaimed according to Elisha by the disciples of Elijah, their fellow citizens, with regard to the ascension of their master grieved the people of Bethel a great deal. That is why, I suppose, those children did not only mention his baldness but also found further insults, which they said before him to outrage his fame, so that nobody might believe his word, if he repeated in Bethel what he had told and about which he had convinced many people in Jericho. In fact, they had meditated on this evil thought and said, "This is the reason for his coming." Now, Elisha, even though he was upset by the effrontery of the children, was much more enraged by the craftiness and the iniquities of their parents, and he corrected both by a harsh and terrible sentence: he punished the former, so that they might not add to their iniquity by growing up to adulthood; the latter, so that they might be corrected and cease from their wickedness. He, who had blessed the children of Jericho and benefited them to the highest degree for their faith, because, after seeing that they had divided the Jordan through his word, they had said that the spirit of Elijah rested on Elisha, decreed this bitter sentence against the people of Bethel. Indeed, the people of Bethel did not believe, when they heard from children of prophets who were in their city, the news of the ascension of Elijah.[a]

[a] Conti and Pilara, *1–2 Kings*, 149.

in the evaluations of the kings and of the kingdoms. For an example of the literal approach of the rabbinic tradition (with its sensitivity to the grammar of the Hebrew text), Radak (Rav David Ḳimḥi) comments on 2 Kings 3:26–27 and the sacrifice of the king's son. Radak suggests that the king of Moab did not sacrifice his own son; rather, the Moabite ruler captured the son of the king of Edom. When the Edomite ruler saw his own son put to death by the Moabites, he turned against the Israelite coalition, who did not protect him. Further, the condemnation of Amos 2:1 describes the burning of the remains of the Edomite prince.[10]

Anson Rainey observes that the view that the Edomite prince was already a prisoner of Moab has no support in the text, but the view that the Moabites tried to break through the allies at the place of the Edomite army and failed, though not without taking captive the Edomite prince, fits well this narrative.

10. Rainey in Rainey and Notley, *Sacred Bridge*, 205.

Higher Criticism

The books of Kings lie at the heart of the Deuteronomistic History and its discussion. This history, defined as Deuteronomy through 2 Kings, reaches its fulfillment in 1–2 Kings, where the understanding and implications of the covenant document of Deuteronomy are fully realized. Connections between Deuteronomy and the Historical Books that follow can be traced back to Spinoza (ca. 1670).[11] It was W. M. L. de Wette who in 1806 proposed that the book or scroll of the law, described as found during Josiah's (ca. 622 BC) renovation of the temple in Jerusalem and as leading to the reforms during his reign (2 Kings 22–23), should be identified with Deuteronomy.[12] However, it was thought that this was itself a story created during the time of Josiah or later, with the intent of justifying a new set of practices during the late seventh century, not with the intent of reforming existing practice back to the covenant of an earlier period.

The pre–Martin Noth era of studies can be divided into three groups of critics. First, there were those who extended the source criticism of the Pentateuch (see "Source Criticism" for Genesis) into the Historical Books as far as 1–2 Kings. They ascribed similar sources to these books, although they recognized Deuteronomistic redactions to create the final form now known. Second, some argued that Kings and the other books originated as individual units but underwent Deuteronomistic redactions to bring them into their present forms. A third group was influenced by form criticism and sought to explain 1–2 Kings in terms of independent forms that were brought together and then redacted. However, these forms do not necessarily have any relationship to the traditional pentateuchal sources.

It was from this last category that Noth developed his understanding of the Deuteronomistic History as extending from Deuteronomy to 2 Kings, as the work of a single editor, as constructed from preexisting materials, and as unrelated to the J, E, and P sources.[13] Rather, the editor, working shortly after the last event of 2 Kings, that of Jehoiachin's release from prison in Babylon in about 562 BC, compiled sources, beginning with the laws of Deuteronomy, and related them by similar vocabulary and a chronological scheme. Most importantly, speeches, beginning with that of Moses in Deuteronomy 1–3; prayers, such as Solomon's dedication of the temple in 1 Kings 8; and reflections, such as 2 Kings 17, where the explanation is given for the fall of the northern kingdom, tie together the sources and provide for an understanding of the central thesis of the whole work. The point is to explain how the people of God and the line of Davidic kings came to an end, with the destruction of

11. For this and what follows, see esp. the summary of Richter, "Deuteronomistic History." See also "Higher Criticism" for Joshua.

12. de Wette, *Dissertation critica qua Deuteronomium*.

13. Noth, *Überlieferungsgeschichtliche Studien*.

the temple and the deportation of the inhabitants of the land, and how this came about because of the wholesale rejection of the demand that Yahweh alone be worshiped in his temple and without images. This rejection and the accompanying divine judgment took place despite the verbal warnings of the prophets and despite the series of punishments that God inflicted on the people, culminating with the destruction of the northern kingdom and then the destruction of the southern kingdom, Judah and Jerusalem. It was the ultimate result of the prophecy-followed-by-fulfillment scheme that dominates the structure of the Deuteronomistic History.

Although Noth did not identify any early parallels with this type of history writing, John Van Seters has argued that Herodotus and Thucydides in the fifth century BC composed this same type of historical narrative.[14] They also introduced and integrated their understanding of history by the use of speeches placed in the mouths of key figures at turning points in the narratives. Gerhard von Rad found in the Deuteronomistic History a message that includes hope as well as judgment.[15] The release of Jehoiachin at the end of 2 Kings looks forward to the return from the exile and the rehabilitation of the Davidic line of kings. Hans W. Wolff agreed and described other passages in 1–2 Kings (and elsewhere) that indicate this hope.[16] This led to his proposal of further redactional activity in the books. In America, Frank Moore Cross developed the theory of two redactions to the Deuteronomistic History, one that was preexilic and one that was postexilic.[17] In Germany, Rudolf Smend suggested three redactions.[18]

Cross argued (with others, such as D. J. McCarthy) that the oracle of 2 Samuel 7 must be considered an essential part of the Deuteronomistic History.[19] It defines an unconditional blessing on David of an eternal dynasty. Thus the first editor of the Deuteronomistic History lived in the time of Josiah and saw his reformation as a fulfillment of the blessings of God on the kingdom of Judah. This writer contrasts the northern kingdom, which has followed the sins of Jeroboam I (a theme repeatedly stressed in the evaluations of the kings of the north), with the southern kingdom, where the divine promises to David (a corresponding theme mentioned in the evaluation of Judean kings) remain. Thus the evaluation of the northern kingdom's destruction, with no hope of return (2 Kings 17), contrasts with finding the book of the covenant and the reformation in the southern kingdom under Josiah (2 Kings 22). The first redactor, living at the time of Josiah, saw the fulfillment of God's dynastic promise with Josiah in the south. This is the reason for the exten-

14. Van Seters, *In Search of History*.
15. Von Rad, *Old Testament Theology*.
16. Wolff, "Kerygma of the Deuteronomic Historical Work."
17. Cross, *Canaanite Myth*.
18. Smend, "Gesetz."
19. See McCarthy, "II Samuel 7."

sive description of Josiah's reign and for the access to and use of annalistic sources to write the Deuteronomistic History. The second redactor, writing in the exile, added the final chapters to 2 Kings and inserted notes throughout the Deuteronomistic History referring to the inevitability of divine judgment and the warnings to the line of David. Students of Cross have continued this interpretation, although they have understood the covenant of 2 Samuel 7 as conditional from the beginning.[20]

Smend developed what came to be known as the Göttingen school of interpretation.[21] He saw the core of the Deuteronomistic History as compiled in the early period of the exile, with at least two later redactions. The last of these redactors emphasized the law and its obedience. The presence of foreign peoples within the promised land demonstrated that the covenant was broken and the law not followed. Walter Dietrich argued for a prophetic redactor who had added the prophetic narratives and was responsible for the prophecy-followed-by-fulfillment structure of the Deuteronomistic History.[22] Criticisms of this approach have focused on the ill-defined dates of the redactions and on the difficulty in identifying a continuous original narrative on which the later redactors worked.

Further developments in the late twentieth century went in multiple directions.[23] There were those who examined the role of centralizing the worship of Yahweh, as suggested in Deuteronomy 12, and its impact on the whole of the Deuteronomistic History.[24] On a structural level, the notices of evaluation and reigns of each of the kings were examined to propose a third major redaction, ending with the reign of Hezekiah, although dating later, or even composed by a second Deuteronomistic Historian, and not a redactor.[25] However, Van Seters argued that even the sources identified in the books of Kings cannot be trusted as actual sources.[26] They perhaps are fictitious constructions. In contrast, Baruch Halpern argued for the substantial historicity of these sources and returned to a view not unlike that of Noth, in which the author(s) constructed the history in a manner that sought to make sense of the events.[27] By the end of the twentieth century, scholars could express doubt as to whether the Deuteronomistic History was a convincing explanation of the construction of 1–2 Kings. On the one hand, the theory extended far beyond its original corpus so that a Deuteronomistic redaction was found

20. See, e.g., Nelson, *Double Redaction.*

21. Smend, "Gesetz."

22. Dietrich, "Martin Noth."

23. Richter, "Deuteronomistic History," 225–27.

24. So Weinfeld, *Deuteronomy.* The debate continues on syntactic grounds; e.g., Greenspahn, "Deuteronomy and Centralization"; and B. Arnold, "Deuteronomy 12."

25. On the later dating, see Provan, *Hezekiah*; on a second Deuteronomistic Historian, see Peckham, *Deuteronomistic History.*

26. Van Seters, *In Search of History.*

27. Halpern, *First Historians.*

everywhere in the Bible. On the other hand, the certainty of its character and the boundaries of its presence were no longer assured in any meaningful way.

Thomas Römer proposed his own three-stage development to the Deuteronomistic History: a Neo-Assyrian redaction focused in the seventh century (around the reign of Josiah, 641–609 BC), a Neo-Babylonian redaction focused on the exile (586–539 BC), and a Persian redaction focused on the following century.[28] Issues with this sort of historical reconstruction include problems with interpretations of specific historical data as well as broad generalizations about the formation of the documents themselves.[29] Nevertheless, it is significant that his approach turns away from purely postexilic work and finds material in earlier layers that reaches back well into the divided monarchy of Israel and Judah. The same is true of the 2007 work of Marvin Sweeney.[30] He begins with the exilic edition of 1–2 Kings, works back from there, and identifies four literary layers: Josiah in the late seventh century BC, Hezekiah in the late eighth century, Jehu and his dynasty in the early eighth century, and Solomon in the late tenth century. The latter includes much of 1–2 Samuel as well as 1 Kings 1–10. Research and reconstructions will continue; yet for the dominant biblical view of Israel's history, how to construct the literary history of this central work remains a matter of ongoing debate.

Literary Readings

A literary emphasis on the books of Kings, like that of the other Historical Books, is natural, given the dominance of narratives that tell the story. While literary studies are to be expected, they are also important for an appropriate understanding of the books. In one sense the story has already been told in the "Overview of 1 and 2 Kings." However, the abundant literary approaches to 1–2 Kings seek to go beyond the mere rehearsing of the story. In such studies, scholars wish to emphasize the purpose of these narratives and the manner in which the writers achieve that purpose. In the process one may ask what role or significance might be attributed to unexpected notes or emphases, or even the positioning of narratives where they presently are. For example, why does the book begin with a presentation of the aging King David, his difficulties, and finally his death? The death of the chief character of a work might be expected to come at the end, not at the beginning. Indeed, the so-called Succession Narrative normally encompasses most of 2 Samuel and the first two chapters of 1 Kings.[31] So why begin with the last days of David? In particular, what sort of book opens with an explanation about

28. Römer, *Deuteronomistic History*.

29. For a critical evaluation of the work and of this approach, see Hess, "New Generation?"

30. Sweeney, *I and II Kings*, 3–32.

31. For a discussion of the Succession Narrative and its strengths and weaknesses, see "Higher Criticism" and "Ancient Near Eastern Context" for 1–2 Samuel.

how the king cannot keep warm and acquires the most beautiful woman throughout the land to keep him warm at night? On the one hand, these opening four verses anticipate the need for a successor that the following text will address, and they introduce the figure of Abishag, who will play the key role in providing Solomon with an excuse to end the life of his onetime rival, Adonijah. On the other hand, this brief text anticipates the story of the books of Kings. Significant phrases found elsewhere in the Bible and especially in 1–2 Kings include these: "old and advancing in years," "keeping warm," "young virgin," and "he did not know (her)." Together they point to the king's impotence; more broadly they present David as foreshadowing the history of Israel in the books of Kings, the threat of David's dynasty failing to continue in Jerusalem.[32]

One of the major stories is that of Hezekiah in his confrontation with the Assyrian king Sennacherib.[33] The account of 2 Kings 18:14–16 appears to portray Hezekiah paying off Sennacherib with gold and the Assyrians consequently withdrawing from Judah. However, 2 Kings 18:17–19:37 seems to portray a different set of events: Sennacherib threatens Hezekiah, and the king turns to God, who miraculously delivers him. Thus scholars have posited two separate sources that the ancient editor allowed to stand alongside each other. However, it is a common style of Hebrew narrative to introduce the story with a summary statement that telescopes the beginning and end of the events into a single brief description. Thus the events recorded in 18:17–19:37 took place after the Assyrians attacked Judah. The departure of Sennacherib was accompanied by a payment from Hezekiah that is described in 18:14–16. Understood in this manner, the brief summary provides the appearance of what happened from an outside perspective. In contrast, the longer account probes into the spiritual realities and the power of God.

Iain Provan has contributed important literary readings of 1–2 Kings.[34] He defines the overall plot of the book as "the attempt that Israel makes under its monarchy (or more often, does not make) to live as the people of God in the promised land, and how God deals with his people in their success and failure."[35] He observes how this plot progresses and especially the manner in which it is signaled sequentially by the regnal formulas that evaluate each king of the northern kingdom (Israel) and of the southern kingdom (Judah). To illustrate the literary approach, Provan introduces the questions surrounding the evaluative chapter, 2 Kings 17, giving notice of the exile of Samaria and the theological reason for it.[36] He sees the apparent contradiction in the

32. Hess, "David and Abishag."

33. Hess, "Hezekiah and Sennacherib."

34. See Provan, *1 and 2 Kings* (OTG), 1–6, for an introduction; the entire commentary for an example of a literary approach, and esp. 27–44.

35. Ibid., 27.

36. Ibid., 28–29, 36–40.

observations that the people of the land worship the Lord (vv. 32–33), but then they do not worship him (v. 34), and then they do (v. 41).

There is also the question of why the repetition of 2 Kings 17:1–6 and 18:9–12. And there is the question of how the formulas describing the reigns of the kings work. The formulas for the last four kings of Judah have an abbreviated form that is identical for each of them, but different from the earlier kings. Is this the sign of a later addition to the book? These problems do have literary solutions. First, the worship of other gods, even when done alongside that of Yahweh, was not acceptable and could not be performed in conjunction with true worship (17:37–38). Therefore, in Samaria there was no correct worship of the true and sole God. These verses describe actions and rituals but not heartfelt worship. The issue of the repetition of 17:1–6 in 18:9–12 is not a matter of multiple sources. Rather, the summary in 2 Kings 18 reminds the reader of the threatening environment in which Hezekiah finds himself, one in which the more powerful northern kingdom was brought to an end by this mighty force of Assyria. It also highlights the sin of the northern kingdom that resulted in this punishment, just as the faith of Hezekiah results in Judah's miraculous deliverance. Further, the last king of the north was Hoshea, whose name means "salvation" and who receives the comment that, while he was evil, he was not as evil as his predecessors. Thus this comparatively "righteous" king was not able to rescue Israel due to its sins. Would the reforms of Hezekiah come in time to see the salvation of Judah? Regarding the repetition of the regnal formulas for the last four kings of Judah, Provan follows Richard Nelson to find in this repetition an iterative style that emphasizes the repeated disobedience of these final kings, one that leads to the judgment of God.[37]

Gender and Ideological Criticism

The many women who appear in 1–2 Kings occupy a variety of positions. In most cases, as with their male counterparts, the positions are among the peasants and commoners, whose major concern is daily survival. For example, many of the women mentioned in the Elijah and Elisha stories occupy this level of society. However, some women, especially the wealthy woman who provides a room for Elisha in her house at Shunem and whose son Elisha revives (2 Kings 4), play an important role in the story. The same is true of the Israelite prisoner-of-war slave in Damascus who informs Naaman of the possibility of healing through Elisha (2 Kings 5). Nevertheless, the society of the monarchy was more stratified than the preceding period of the judges. Many positions of power and influence were held by Israelites and Judeans who passed them down from father to son. For those outside these families, whether men or women,

37. See Nelson, *First and Second Kings*.

Phoenician ivory portraying woman at the window

there was little opportunity to rise through the ranks to attain high offices. A beautiful woman such as Abishag (1 Kings 1) could take on a position of nursing the aged King David, but there is no indication of any further influence that she possessed. The role of prophet could include a woman such as Huldah in Jerusalem, who responded to Josiah's concerns (2 Kings 22).

Other than these occasional glimpses, the major role that women occupied in the books of 1–2 Kings was that of queen mother.[38] The mother of the king (Heb. *gĕbîrâ*) is named for every Judean king except Jehoram (2 Kings 8:16–18) and Ahaz (16:2–3). There is much debate as to the degree to which this was an official office, as among the Hittites, where the queen mother (*tawananna*) had both political and priestly office, or whether, as in other countries, it was an unofficial position. While queenship was normally the consequence of marriage to the king, the nature of polygyny meant that not every royal wife held this role. Rather, it was often those who were the most ambitious and clever who managed to arrange for their sons to succeed their husband as king. In some cases, the same woman held this role over multiple administrations. Thus Maakah, daughter of Abishalom and wife of Rehoboam (who may have married her as part of his attempt to reunite the northern kingdom with Judah), was the queen mother under her son Abijam and her grandson Asa (1 Kings 15).[39] Asa's removal of her Asherah cult figure (or symbol) and his deposition of her from being queen mother may have signaled an end to the aspirations of a whole group of followers who from the time of Solomon had promoted a greater accommodation with other deities. There is no doubt that some, especially Jezebel in the north and to a lesser extent Athaliah in the south, attracted groups of followers and formed factions within their kingdoms. For this reason, and the significant roles played by Jezebel and Athaliah, queen mothers have been understood as negative figures in Israel. Yet this was not necessarily the case. Nehushta seems to have

38. For summaries of the evidence, see esp. Ben-Barak, "Status and Right"; Marsman, *Women in Ugarit and Israel*, 345–70, esp. 360–68.

39. Cf. Spanier, "Queen Mother."

worn a crown alongside her son Jehoiachin, and to have accompanied him (as second in command) into exile in Babylon (Jer. 13:18; 2 Kings 24:8–15).

Bathsheba's story illustrates many roles of the queen mother in 1 Kings 1–2. She is responsible, with Nathan the prophet, for reminding David of his promise to make her son Solomon the next in line to the throne. Through her intercession, Solomon is crowned king. Adonijah later approaches her after his loss of any claim to kingship. He seeks to marry Abishag. While there is much ambiguity in how this should be understood (Does he wish to acquire a [non]concubine of David as his wife to establish a claim to kingship? Or does he see this as a safe request to maintain status in the Jerusalem court because she is technically not a concubine?), he approaches the queen mother Bathsheba, who can intercede for him. When Bathsheba agrees (Again, is this because she sees no challenge to her son's throne in this matter? Or is it because she sees the danger it would be for Solomon and wishes to eliminate Adonijah once and for all?) to intercede, she approaches her son. King Solomon bows before her, gives her a throne on his right (the place of honor; 1 Kings 2:19), and promises not to refuse her request. This demonstrates the power and influence that the queen mother exercised with the king. It also explains why her role as an intercessor was so important. At thirteenth-century-BC Ugarit, many letters are preserved that are addressed to the queen mother. Again and again, individuals write her to request her to intercede on their behalf to the king for particular concerns. The same was true in Israel, where a queen mother such as Bathsheba could be involved in the selection of the heir to her husband and could function as a chief adviser to her son the king.

Given the fascinating narratives that compose so much of 1–2 Kings, it is not surprising that they remain a rich source for the development of narrative theologies throughout the world. Of special interest and concern, however, is the ideological development of interpretations of these texts from ancient history and their application to the ongoing politics of the Middle East. This begins with an approach that developed in the last decade of the twentieth century and continues in its influence until the present. Thomas L. Thompson, Philip R. Davies, and Neils Lemche have declared that there was no history of Israel as described in the Bible, that instead it was a creation of later scribes for ideological purposes of their own.[40] Most clearly expressed by Thompson in his 1992 work *Early History of the Israelite People*, there was no united monarchy, nor was there a David or Solomon. The states of Judah in the south and Israel in the north did not exist before the eighth century BC. By that time the Assyrians began attacking this region of the world and deporting its

40. T. Thompson, *Early History*; idem, "Neo-Albrightian School?"; idem, *Mythic Past*; idem, *Messiah Myth*; P. Davies, *In Search*; idem, *Origins*; idem, *Memories*; Lemche, *Israelites in History*; idem, *Prelude to Israel's Past*; idem, *Early Israel*.

peoples. They resettled other groups in the region. Not only did this occur in the region of Samaria (as 2 Kings 17 reports), it also occurred everywhere in the north and then in the southern kingdom (Judah). By the time of the Persian period and the resettlement of these lands, the people who arrived and lived there in the following centuries bore no ethnic relationship to those present during the earlier centuries. Thus the construction of biblical history as it appears in the Hebrew Bible or Old Testament is the product of scribes working in the later Persian or Hellenistic Ages. It is a fictitious re-creation of an imagined past, designed to give an identity to the Jewish people who lived in Palestine at the end of the first millennium BC.

While it is true that this reconstruction does not appear in the later works of Philip R. Davies and Neils Lemche, it remains the foundation of this approach, and some of its elements have influenced ideologies beyond the scholarly discussions. The 1996 study of Keith W. Whitelam (*The Invention of Ancient Israel: The Silencing of Palestinian History*) takes this analysis a step further and accuses the dominant Western (esp. Israeli and American) tradition of biblical scholarship over the past two centuries of pro-Zionist, pro-Israelite, and anti-Palestinian bias. The interest of biblical scholarship has been to support the claims of the Bible and thereby to support the existence of the State of Israel and oppose the claims of the Palestinians. Given this logical development of the proposed historical model, it is not surprising that Thompson's work has been translated into Arabic and is read by students in universities of the Arabic-speaking world. The ideological nature of these claims of Thompson and others, as well as the fundamental problems with their wholesale rejection of historical claims in the Bible, have been widely discussed and analyzed.[41] Nevertheless, their profound effect on the volatile political world of the Middle East has been observed and critiqued by William Dever:

> Earlier, the *Jerusalem Post* (October 11, 1997) had already broken the story of "Historical Battleground," documenting how the newly-constituted Palestine Authority in the West Bank had begun to use archaeology to establish *its* claim to the land, even issuing revisionist elementary school textbooks to augment the "arsenal of historical weaponry." This was followed by a much more detailed and explicit report by Netty Gross of a clash between Israeli and Palestinian archaeologists at a symposium in Gaza on "Who Got Here First, and Does It Matter?"; "Demolishing David," *Jerusalem Report* (September 11, 2000).

41. See "Ancient Near Eastern Context" for 1–2 Samuel and for 1–2 Kings. Some useful critiques can be found in Dever, *What Did?*; Provan, "Ideologies, Literary and Critical"; Hess, "Recent Studies." Among the many other studies are four collections of essays that grew out of conferences devoted to the study of historical Israel: Long, Baker, and Wenham, *Old Testament History*; Hoffmeier and Millard, *Biblical Archaeology*; Block, *Israel*; and Hess, Klingbeil, and Ray, *Israelite History*.

> Whitelam should be pleased; he and other meddling revisionists have succeeded in undoing the efforts of two generations of Palestinian archaeologists—of *all* nationalities and persuasions—to keep Middle Eastern nationalism and religious fanaticism out of archaeology.[42]

Ancient Near Eastern Context

Over the past century thousands of scholarly articles and monographs have probably appeared on every possible element found in the texts of 1–2 Kings, detailing the extrabiblical literary and archaeological evidence that might in some manner address the text. It will be necessary to limit discussion here to the most important and relevant materials. The writing prophets Hosea, Amos, Micah, and Isaiah are all set in the time of key historical events in the eighth century BC; the other prophets worked in the seventh and sixth centuries and in the postexilic period. Thus the ancient Near Eastern context from the eighth century onward offers significant historical connections between the relevant prophetic books and 1–2 Kings (as well as 1–2 Chronicles). Therefore, after some general comments, the material addressed here will be limited to the earlier period, before the writing prophets, especially the Solomonic period.

The kings of Israel and Judah who appear in 1–2 Kings are named in the ninth century BC by the Tel Dan Stele and the Mesha of Moab Stele of the same general period. The former mentions [Jo]ram, [Ahaz]yahu, and David (see the sidebar "Tel Dan Stele" in the chapter on 1–2 Samuel). The Mesha Stele mentions Omri. Other West Semitic ostraca, seals, bullae, and inscriptions mention additional kings and names of figures known from 1–2 Kings.[43] Of the eleven kings of Israel and Judah mentioned in the Neo-Assyrian records, every king correlates with the Assyrian kings and with the chronological sequence suggested in the books of Kings. Wilfred Lambert provides examples of relating the biblical narratives to the Assyrian records and the culture they represent.[44] And the author does not find difficulty with the preservation of the biblical records through the Babylonian destruction of Jerusalem and the deportation of Judeans in the exile. Whether through individuals concealing small scrolls on their person or (like Jeremiah and Baruch) remaining in the land, the records are preserved.

The study of tenth-century Israel during the kingship of Solomon (ca. 971–931 BC) considers the administration and especially the temple in the light of surrounding cultures and evidence. The governing administration for the

42. Dever, *What Did?*, 294n78.

43. See Lemaire ("Hebrew and West Semitic Inscriptions") for a sequential list of relevant inscriptions from around the ancient Near East and a summary of their connections with the books of Kings and other historical witnesses from the Bible.

44. Lambert, "Mesopotamian Sources."

twelve tribes under Solomon ignored the tribal territories and instead used a system of provinces, each with its own governor. This is attested by the archival document preserved in 1 Kings 4:7–19, whose formal similarities to administrative texts from Late Bronze Age (1550–1200 BC) Alalakh and Ugarit suggest an authentic antiquity to the document.[45] Even the supposed anomalies (e.g., various notes inserted in the list and the unnamed governor who is last on the list) have direct parallels with other administrative documents recovered from the second-millennium-BC West Semitic city-states of Alalakh and Ugarit. The list describes twelve administrative districts, each of which was responsible for a monthly provision of the royal house, or 8 percent of the total.[46] The monthly requirements of flour (19,800 liters daily) could be met from 424 acres of fields from each district, requiring a total of about 8 square miles of land (1 Kings 4:22).[47]

Solomon received gifts of 120 talents of gold from Hiram of Tyre and the same from the queen of Sheba; tribute and taxes totaling 666 gold talents came to him annually (1 Kings 9:14; 10:10, 14). Compare these amounts to Metten II of Tyre (ca. 730 BC), who paid 150 talents of gold to Tiglath-pileser III. Sargon II gave 154 talents of gold to the gods. In the fifteenth century BC, the Egyptian pharaoh Thutmose III gave over 200 talents of gold to the god Amun at Thebes. Above all, Pharaoh Osorkon I—the successor of Shishak, who plundered Jerusalem after Solomon's death—gave 383 tons of gold to the temples of Egypt, equal to sixteen–seventeen years of Solomon's annual revenue. Was it from Shishak's raid on Jerusalem that Osorkon's father obtained the gold?[48]

Solomon is recorded as having built the temple and other buildings in Jerusalem. Solomon's construction of the temple united all the people in the effort of its construction and in rendering Jerusalem and its God as the recognized center of the greatest empire of its time, with the greatest God, who therefore

45. See Hess, "Form and Structure"; followed by Rainey, "Stones for Bread," 147–48. In addition to the literary form, the names on the list betray evidence of an early text: five of the eleven governors have their name in the form of "son of X" or "ben-X." This name form appears early in the monarchy and gradually disappears. It suggests the kin-based society of the early Israelite period (as do the Ahi- names, i.e., "[my] brother is . . ."). Further, the name of one of the fathers of a governor, Ahilud, is found on a twelfth-century jar handle at Raddanah, near Ramallah. The "Hanan" of Elon-beth-hanan ("oaktree of the house of Hanan") in 1 Kings 4:9 occurs on a thirteenth/twelfth-century-BC ostracon and a tenth-century gaming board, both from nearby Beth-shemesh, as well as on a tenth-century bowl fragment from Timnah, five miles away (Dever, *What Did?*, 143; Kitchen, *Reliability*, 132). As to the fifteen place names, all but two can be identified with known sites. See Dever, *What Did?*, 138–42.

46. This would have supplemented the draft for military and other purposes of two thousand per tribe each month, as based on the practice of David (2 Sam. 24:2; 1 Chron. 21:1–5; 27:1–15, 23–24). The northern levy was of *ʾîš-yiśrāʾēl* (2 Sam. 10:17) and the southern of *ʾîš-yĕhûdâ* (2 Sam. 20:4–8). Cf. Yadin, "Army Reserves," 356–58; Zevit, *Religions of Ancient Israel*, 637.

47. Kitchen, *Reliability*, 133.

48. Ibid., 133–34, 454.

Mesha of Moab Stele

This stele, dating from the second half of the ninth century BC, was discovered by F. A. Klein in 1868. It was smashed, but not before a papier-mâché copy was made of it. That copy and the original are preserved in the Louvre Museum in Paris. The text includes the earliest mention of Omri, Mesha, Yahweh, and the Moabite god Chemosh outside the Bible. Translation of relevant sections from the Moabite include:[a]

> I am Mesha, son of Chemosh[yat], king of Moab, the Dibonite. My father ruled over Moab thirty years, and I ruled after my father. I made this high place for Chemosh at Qarḥoh,—a high pl[ace of sal]vation—because he delivered me from all the kings, and because he showed me [victory] over all my enemies.
>
> Omri ruled over Israel. He oppressed Moab for a long time, because Chemosh was angry at his land. His son succeeded him. He also said, "I will oppress Moab!" In my days he said . . . I saw [victory] over him and his household. Israel has utterly perished forever. Omri has possessed all the land of Madeba [= Medeba]. He had already resided there during his time and half his son's time, forty years. But Chemosh restored it in my days. . . .
>
> The people of Gad had settled in the land of ʿAṭarot from of old, and the king of Israel had fortified ʿAṭarot for them. Nevertheless, I fought against the town, and seized it. I killed all the people from the city, as a satisfaction [offering] for Chemosh and Moab. I brought back from there the hearth[?] of [its] *dwd*[?]. I dragged it before Chemosh in Qiryat. I settled in it the men of Sharon and those of Maḥarat.
>
> Then Chemosh said to me: "Go, seize Nebo from Israel." So I went by night. I fought against it from the break of dawn until noon. I seized it. I killed all: 7,000 warriors, foreign men, women [warriors?], foreign women, and "wombs" [slave women?]. I devoted it to Ashtar Chemosh. I took from there the altar hearth of Yahweh. I dragged them before Chemosh.
>
> The king of Israel fortified Yahaz. He resided there when he fought against me. Chemosh drove him out before me. I took 200 men from Moab, all its leaders. I went up against Yahaz. I seized it in order to add [it] to Dibon. . . .
>
> Regarding Horonaim, the house of David resided in it. . . . Chemosh said to me: "Go down, fight against Horonaim." So I went down . . . and Chemosh [rest]ored it in my days.

[a] Hess, *Israelite Religions*, 275.

lived in the greatest temple.[49] Its description is that of long-room Syrian styles of temples, with a close parallel at ʿAin Dara in north Syria. There the tenth-century-BC temple possessed three rooms, two pillars at the entrance, features such as recessed and latticed windows, and a multistory set of rooms built

49. Cf. Meyers, "David as Temple Builder"; Strange, "Theology and Politics," 24–29—but here his attempt to ascribe a divine kingship to Solomon is speculative.

around three sides of the temple.[50] Even closer in size are the two long-room temples at Tell Tayinat, west of ʿAin Dara and not far from the classical city of Antioch on the Orontes. (See plate 3 in the gallery.) These temples come close to the proportions of Solomon's. They had three parts to their structure and two columns at the entrance. There is even the presence of a treaty along with other texts and valuables deposited in the most holy place.[51]

Victor Hurowitz discusses the architecture of Solomon's temple in light of what is known about other ancient Near Eastern temples and palaces.[52] Hurowitz concludes that the temple of Solomon was decorated with floral patterns to symbolize the garden that often surrounded temples and palaces; that the pillars Yachin and Boaz represented the trees of life and knowledge as in the garden of Eden; that the lion and cattle decorations symbolized the peaceful coexistence of wild and tame animals; that the cedarwood represented the Lebanon mountains, where the deity was often said to reside; and that the common location of divine palaces by a sea and at the confluence of rivers was represented by the bronze sea and the water basins.[53] Dever concurs, adding ashlar masonry, wooden beams alternating with stone at every third course, carved wooden panels placed over the masonry, and decorations of cherubs, lions, and palm trees.[54] Note Dever's comment: "We now have direct Bronze and Iron Age parallels for *every single feature* of the 'Solomonic temple' as described in the Hebrew Bible; and the best parallels come from, and only from, the Canaanite-Phoenician world of the 15th–9th centuries."[55]

The Forest of Lebanon hall (1 Kings 7:2; 10:17, 21) was built 150 by 75 feet, where some 32 pillars produced three aisles with three double doors at either end. Five hundred (200 large and 300 small) gold shields decorated the hall. In the fourteenth century BC at Amarna in Egypt, Pharaoh Akhenaton's palace hall had 527 pillars in a hall of 380 by 240 feet. To the north in the thirteenth century, the Hittite king received people in a hall of 100 square feet, with 25 wooden pillars and architraves. Solomonic-sized halls are found at Kition in the ninth century and Urartu in the eighth/seventh centuries BC. In 714 BC, Sargon II looted gold shields from an Urartian temple, and such adorned the temple of Zeus at Olympia. Solomon's complex of loosely attached royal

50. See Monson, "Temple of Solomon"; idem, "The New ʿAin Dara Temple"; Kitchen, *Reliability*, 123–27. Kitchen compares the architecture with second-millennium-BC temples in Egypt and at Ḫattuša, Ekalte, Ebla, Alalakh, and Hazor. In many of these temples, with storerooms built around three sides, the storage space was often larger than the area of the sacred structure itself.

51. Hurowitz, "Solomon's Temple in Context."

52. Hurowitz, "Inside Solomon's Temple," 37.

53. Hurowitz ("Inside Solomon's Temple," 33) suggests that the animals depicted God's power and dominion in creation, and the cherubim represented his retinue and guard. See also Kitchen, *Reliability*, 128–31.

54. Dever, *What Did?*, 145–57.

55. Ibid., 145.

buildings also occurs in Ḫattuša, Ebla, and Alalakh of the third and second millennia and at Tell Tayinat, Hamath, and Zinjirli in the first millennium BC. Solomon's gold throne and table service (1 Kings 10:18–21) may be compared with Pharaoh Amenophis (Amenhotep) III of Egypt, who sent Kadashman-Enlil I of Babylon some beds of gold and ten chairs of ebony overlaid with gold (EA 5). Compare also Pharaoh Tutankhamen's gold-overlaid throne, footstool, and bed, as well as golden table services (or vessels) in the graves of Assyrian queens of the ninth and eighth centuries.[56]

According to Peter Machinist, the way in which the realia of Solomon's kingdom were used is a justification for the Israelite appropriation of Canaanite culture.[57] Psalm 29 appropriates attributes for Yahweh that had been given to Baal. The building projects in the Canaanite center of Jerusalem and especially the construction of the temple on the basis of Canaanite forms—these were all arguments that Yahweh had conquered the Canaanite deities. Machinist compares a similar situation in Mesopotamia a century or two earlier in which literature and architecture were used in Assyria to demonstrate its conquest and appropriation of Babylonia and its culture.

Hurowitz compares temple-building accounts from ancient Mesopotamia, from Ugarit, and from the Bible.[58] At least five elements occur in all the accounts: (1) a reason to build or restore a temple that includes a divine command or consent; (2) preparations for the construction; (3) description of the construction process and of the result; (4) dedication of the structure; (5) prayers for blessings on the temple and its builder; and sometimes (6) conditional curses and blessings to the future ruler who will be called on to rebuild the temple. Each of these categories is applied to the appropriate section of 1 Kings 5–9, and the structures of both the nonbiblical account and the biblical one are found to be identical. The closest single account to 1 Kings 5–9 is that of the twelfth/eleventh-century Assyrian king Tiglath-pileser I.[59]

Formally, Solomon's prayer of dedication in 1 Kings 8 may resemble other prayers of dedication by Assyrian and Babylonian rulers. In all of these, concerns for dynastic stability and the answering of prayers predominate. However, with the Mesopotamian rulers, it is assumed that the deity will answer because of the new home that is built for it. In 1 Kings, the temple is not assumed to be a "home" for the Deity. Nor does Solomon assume he

56. Damerji and Kamil, *Gräber assyrischer Königinnen*, 23–32, 40–52, etc.

57. Machinist, "Literature as Politics."

58. Hurowitz, *I Have Built You*. Cf. Cross, "The Priestly Tabernacle," for a different perspective.

59. The same comparisons can be made with the building of the second temple in Zech. 4:6–10. Cf. Laato, "Zachariah 4,6b–10a." Van Seters ("Solomon's Temple") disputes the parallels as general and vague, but he does not provide the sort of detailed examination that Hurowitz (*I Have Built You*) undertakes, both of the varieties of literature and of the study of the texts themselves. Yet he is accurate in his observation that, when it comes to the written text, the perspective is not that of the king but that of the historian (Van Seters, 55).

can "buy" God's favor. Instead, Solomon appeals to the word of God, in the forms of the divine promise to David and of the covenant made with Israel. Thus an ancient Near Eastern form is followed, but its content is transformed by a wholly unique biblical theology.

Canonical Context

It has been noted how well 1 Kings 1–2 concludes the life story of David that is detailed in 1–2 Samuel, and especially how these final chapters bring to a conclusion the story of who will succeed David. As David himself appears at the end of his life, many of the events in 1 Kings 2 bring to a completion stories of injustice and accusation against David as carried out by various members of his court and kingdom.

As various elements of Solomon's life and words can be compared with texts of Proverbs and other Wisdom literature, the life of Jeroboam I (1 Kings 12) offers a closer comparison with that of Moses as he leads the Israelites from oppression. Jeroboam also spends time in Egypt at Pharaoh's court. Yet in this story the oppression is the result not of Pharaoh but of Israel's own king, Rehoboam. Verbal and conceptual ties lead to the release of Israel through Jeroboam, despite his earlier role as in charge of the corvée of Israel. This redeemer of Israel then models the worst parts of Aaron as he constructs the gold calves and leads Israel to worship them.[60] So the words to introduce those gold calves in 1 Kings 12:28 follow almost exactly the words of Exodus 32:4.

Many texts of 1–2 Kings are repeated and developed in 1–2 Chronicles. Additional key periods of faith and failure have their parallels elsewhere in the Hebrew Bible. The reign of Hezekiah and his fight against Sennacherib, as well as his sickness, Isaiah's words and deeds, and the Babylonian envoys all have parallels in Isaiah (2 Kings 18:13–20:19 is found in Isa. 36:1–39:8). The same is true of the end of Judah and Jerusalem at the hands of the Babylonian invaders (2 Kings 24:18–25:30 occurs at Jer. 52:1–34). Indeed, Provan notes that the final words of the prophet Micaiah in 1 Kings 22:28 parallel the opening words of the book of the prophet Micah (1:2).[61] Writing prophets such as Isaiah (2 Kings 19–20) and Jeremiah (2 Kings 23:31; 24:18) appear in 2 Kings.[62]

The New Testament makes few specific references to 1–2 Kings. At one point Jesus refers to God's sending of Elijah to a non-Israelite widow in Sidon (Luke 4:26). Otherwise, there are a few references to the life and death of David and Solomon in speeches in Acts (7:47; 13:36) and to the ark and temple in Revelation (11:19; 16:1, 7; 15:8). However, the specific reference to Elijah in Jesus's words highlights the repeated descriptions of Jesus's miracles and

60. Provan, *1 and 2 Kings* (OTG), 42.

61. Ibid., 41.

62. The names Obadiah, Zephaniah, and Zechariah also occur in 1–2 Kings, but they are probably not connected with the writing prophets themselves. See also Jonah in 2 Kings 14:25.

other works that are modeled on the deeds of Elijah and Elisha as described in 1–2 Kings. Again and again the works of Jesus point to his ministry in the tradition and power of the prophets of the Old Testament, their ministry both to God's people and to the world in general, and their critique of the political and religious power brokers of the larger community of God's people.

Theological Perspectives of 1 and 2 Kings

Many of the key theological messages of 1–2 Kings are summarized in the previous sections. Decline comes due to the lack of faith in Yahweh among both the leaders and the people. Evaluations are keyed to whether one follows the ways of Jeroboam I or the ways of David and Yahweh's covenant with him. Writers recognize how 1–2 Kings provides a foundation for the geopolitical world of the Middle East and the current existence of the State of Israel (from 1948). The temple of Solomon is a proclamation of Yahweh's power, presence, and sovereignty over the Israelite kingdom and the world. The model prophets Elijah and Elisha serve as a background and pattern for the mission and ministry of Jesus (and his followers). These themes represent the purpose and place of 1–2 Kings within the biblical revelation.

The theological foundation of these books lies in the confession that Yahweh the Lord is alone God.[63] There is no other god, and no other should be worshiped. Beginning with Solomon, every king of the north and south is evaluated in terms of the manner in which they recognize this fact and respond to it, promoting the worship of other gods or reforming their worship and that of the people so that Yahweh alone is honored. All kings of the north fail to a greater or lesser extent. In the southern kingdom, some kings also fail. However, figures like Hezekiah and Josiah are commended for their faith. This contrast comes to a focus at the fall of the northern kingdom (Israel) in 2 Kings 17. There the kings of the north, with all their wealth and military power, are unable to resist the power of Assyria; the northern kingdom collapses, like all the other nations before it. This is due to their worship of other gods, just like those nations. In direct contrast is the story of Hezekiah of Judah, a weaker and poorer country. It also is threatened by Sennacherib (2 Kings 18–19), who boasts of his superiority and claims that Yahweh lies to Judah when he tells them that they will succeed or that Yahweh is any different from the other gods whose nations have fallen. Hezekiah takes this to God. The response through the prophet Isaiah is that the Assyrians will not attack or destroy Jerusalem. Indeed, the Assyrian army will depart, and their king will face a violent death. This all comes to pass. The contrast with the northern kingdom could not be more dramatic and more telling. Everything

63. Hess, "Kings, Books of."

depends on faith in the one God, Yahweh, and on living according to that faith. Nothing depends on strength of arms or wealth.

In addition to the kings, the prophets, especially Elijah and Elisha, demonstrate that the matter of faith and a personal relationship with God are the responsibility of each person. Faith in God and the willingness to step out and to live in that faith bring life, whether food in the midst of famine, healing where there is no recourse, hope instead of despair, and even life from the dead. Refusal to accept Yahweh and his word brings famine amid plenty, sickness instead of wealth, despair, and ultimately (sometimes quickly and suddenly) death. The challenge to believe is decisive for all people, and the prophets drive that message home again and again, just as Jesus Christ would in his ministry, teaching, and death and resurrection.

Alongside this is the promise to David that a descendant of his will forever rule from Jerusalem. This covenant, made in 2 Samuel 7, includes the condition that each ruler will be subject to God's chastisement to the degree that he fails to follow him. As mentioned under "Literary Readings," David represents a quick snapshot of the challenge that Israel faces throughout the books of Kings. David's physical weakness and death, which begin 1 Kings, parallel the spiritual malaise of Solomon's reign, one that begins so well with the promise of a "listening heart" (3:9 RSH) and yet ends with the loss of the whole kingdom except for two tribes. Thus Israel will make this journey as a physical nation, people, and leadership, and as a spiritual entity that again and again turns away from God to worship other gods. Yet the promise of the Davidic kingship, of the messiah, does not vanish. It remains when David decides who will succeed him. It continues when most of the kingdom revolts against Rehoboam, and again and again as nations and peoples gather to destroy the line of David. Athaliah almost succeeds in destroying the entire line: only Joash remains, a small child hidden away in the temple. Yet the line continues. Again, Pekah and Rezin seek to attack Ahaz and replace him and his family with their own choice. A generation later the world's most powerful king tries to do the same thing to Hezekiah. Yet the line remains. So it is at the end of 2 Kings, when Zedekiah is put to death along with his sons. The author turns to his predecessor, Jehoiachin, who remains alive in Babylon. His is the royal line that will continue; through him the messiah will come who will fulfill all the expectations of the prophets and the best kings and the most faithful citizens of God's land and people.

Climactically, here is the great prayer found in Solomon's dedication of the temple, as described in 1 Kings 8. This text has recently been studied and summarized by Christopher J. H. Wright.[64] The beginning of this prayer is a confession of praise to Yahweh for keeping the promises that he made to David (8:14–21). Implicit here is the point that God will continue to keep

64. C. Wright, *Mission of God's People*, 132–36.

his promise. As argued above, 1–2 Kings demonstrates this faithfulness of God through the generations of the monarchy. Solomon goes on to beg that, when sin and punishment come, God may hear a penitent person or nation and the temple may be a symbol of this and of the forgiveness and restoration (8:25–40). Before turning back to the concerns for which Israel might pray toward the temple, Solomon makes a remarkable request in 8:41–43. This concerns the foreigner who has heard something of Yahweh but does not belong to God's people. Solomon asks that when this foreigner prays to Yahweh, directing his attention to the temple, God may grant the foreigner whatever he or she may request. The motive that Solomon gives for this is so that all peoples on earth may know the name of God and fear him, so that they may know that God's name is found at this temple. Thus Solomon's prayer, at its center, looks beyond Israel and sees a greater purpose for all that God has done. It is a matter of mission. The temple and Solomon's prayer envision a greater purpose in which God's promise to Abram (Gen. 12:1–3), that all nations of the world will be blessed through Abram's line, comes closer to fulfillment. Solomon therefore prays that Yahweh may be known throughout the world and that Yahweh's response to the cries and prayers of even unbelievers toward him might be respected.

After again reviewing the needs of the people and asking God to respond to Israel, Solomon concludes in 1 Kings 8:60–61. He connects the role of the mission and purpose of God's universal plan ("so that all the earth's peoples may know that Yahweh is God and that there is no other god" [RSH]) irrevocably with the need for the people of God to live a life of faith and discipleship ("Let your hearts be completely dedicated to Yahweh our God by walking in his statutes and keeping his commands, just as you are doing today" [RSH]). Thus the ethics of the life of God's people becomes the means by which the witness of God to the world is made known and the basis for enabling God to work through his people, to bless them and to bless all those who turn to him.

Key Commentaries and Studies

Arnold, Bill T., and Richard S. Hess, eds. *Ancient Israel's History: An Introduction to Issues and Sources.* Grand Rapids: Baker Academic, 2014. Most useful and current survey of the evidence and controversies regarding Israelite history. For the period of 1 and 2 Kings see especially Steven M. Ortiz, "7. United Monarchy: Archaeology and Literary Sources," 227–61; James K. Mead, "8. The Biblical Prophets in Historiography," 262–85; Kyle Greenwood, "9. Late Tenth- and Ninth-Century Issues: Ahab Underplayed? Jehoshaphat Overplayed?," 286–318; Sandra Richter, "10. Eighth-Century Issues: The World of Jeroboam II, the Fall of Samaria, and the Reign of Hezekiah," 319–49; Brad E. Kelle, "11. Judah in the Seventh Century: From the Aftermath of Sennacherib's Invasion to the Beginning of Jehoiakim's Rebellion," 350–82; Peter van der Veen, "12. Sixth-Century Issues: The Fall of Jerusalem, the Exile, and the Return," 383–405.

Cogan, Mordechai. *I Kings*. AB 10. New York: Doubleday, 2000. The starting point for any study of the historical and archaeological background to the text.

Cogan, Mordechai, and Hayim Tadmor. *II Kings*. AB 11. New York: Doubleday, 1988. One of the best presentations of the historical and archaeological background.

Provan, Iain W. *1 and 2 Kings*. NIBC. Peabody, MA: Hendrickson, 1995. Sensitive literary reading of the text with an awareness of the critical issues and of the theological significance.

Rainey, Anson F., and R. Steven Notley. *The Sacred Bridge: Carta's Atlas of the Biblical World*. Jerusalem: Carta, 2006. Most useful for a synthesis of the historical and geographical witnesses to the events of 1–2 Kings.

Sweeney, Marvin A. *I and II Kings: A Commentary*. OTL. Louisville: Westminster John Knox, 2007. A master of form-critical and historical exegesis examines the text; an essential reference tool for the study of these biblical books.

11

1–2 CHRONICLES

Who reads Chronicles? These often neglected books describe the worship of God in the temple and in the history of Old Testament Israel. But there's much more. Beginning with Adam in the first verse, the promise emerges of God's plan for all the world to know him.

Name, Text, and Outline

The name Chronicles is a translation of the Hebrew *dibrê hayyāmîm*. The Greek name, *paraleipomenōn*, carries the sense of "those things that remain (are left over)." Without doubt compiled no earlier than the Persian period, the text makes no claim as to who wrote it, but it does identify many sources. The Babylonian Talmud (*B. Bat.* 15a) indicates that Ezra wrote the work. This derives from an awareness of similarities between 1–2 Chronicles and Ezra–Nehemiah.

The Septuagint text of 1–2 Chronicles does not differ greatly from the Masoretic Text. However, the Septuagint does preserve a free translation, one that tends to render the Hebrew into Greek phrase by phrase rather than word for word. There is minimal attestation of 1–2 Chronicles among the Dead Sea Scrolls fragments. In terms of the Hebrew text, it is readable as it stands, and there is little need for textual criticism for these purposes. The larger issue is the comparison of the Greek (LXX) of Chronicles where Chronicles agrees with the other texts of the Bible, especially 1–2 Kings. Thus four potential witnesses of this period are preserved: the Hebrew and Greek of Chronicles, and the Hebrew and Greek of the parallel text in Kings (or elsewhere). Issues regarding these "synoptic" texts concern the origin and development of the texts and their traditions.[1]

1. Tov, *Textual Criticism*, 143, 321.

OUTLINE

I. The Family of God's People (1 Chron. 1:1–9:34)
  A. From Adam to Israel (1:1–2:2)
  B. Judah (2:3–4:23)
    1. Judah (2:3–55)
    2. David (3:1–24)
    3. Judah (4:1–23)
  C. Simeon (4:24–43)
  D. Transjordan (5:1–26)
    1. Reuben (5:1–10)
    2. Gad (5:11–17)
    3. Occupation of the Transjordan (5:18–22)
    4. Half of Manasseh (5:23–26)
  E. Levi (6:1–81 [5:27–6:66 MT])
    1. Priests and Levites (6:1–53 [5:27–6:38 MT])
    2. Levitical Cities (6:54–81 [6:39–66 MT])
  F. Northern Israel (7:1–9:1a)
    1. Issachar (7:1–5)
    2. Benjamin (7:6–12)
    3. Naphtali (7:13)
    4. Manasseh (7:14–19)
    5. Ephraim (7:20–29)
    6. Asher (7:30–40)
    7. Benjamin (8:1–9:1a)
  G. Returnees and Responsibilities (9:1b–34)

II. David (9:35–29:30)
  A. Saul's Death (9:35–10:14)
    1. Saul's Genealogy (9:35–44)
    2. Mount Gilboa (10:1–14)
  B. David's Rise (11:1–12:40)
    1. David Made King (11:1–3)
    2. Capture of Jerusalem (11:4–9)
    3. David's Mighty Warriors (11:10–47)
    4. David's Other Warriors (12:1–40 [12:41 MT])
  C. David's Reign—God in Jerusalem (13:1–17:27)
    1. The Ark Leaves Kiriath-jearim (13:1–14)
    2. David at Home (14:1–7)
    3. David Defeats the Enemy Philistines (14:8–17)
    4. The Ark Comes to Jerusalem (15:1–16:3)
    5. Worship of God (16:4–43)
    6. God's Eternal Covenant with David (17:1–15)
    7. David's Praise for the Covenant (17:16–27)
  D. David's Military Career (18:1–21:17)
    1. Summary of Conquests (18:1–13)
    2. David's Officers (18:14–17)

        3. Ammon (19:1–20:3)
        4. Philistia (20:4–8)
        5. Military Census and Judgment (21:1–17)
    E. David's Cultic Activities (21:18–26:32)
        1. Identification of the Place for the Temple (21:18–22:1)
        2. David's Preparations for the Temple (22:2–19)
        3. Levite and Priest Census (23:1–5)
        4. Divisions of Families (23:6–23)
        5. Levite Responsibilities (23:24–32)
        6. Divisions of Priestly Houses (24:1–19)
        7. Remaining Levites (24:20–31)
        8. Divisions of Prophets and Musicians (25:1–31)
        9. Divisions of Gatekeepers (26:1–19)
        10. Divisions of Those Responsible for Cultic Matters (26:20–32)
    F. David's Military and Civil Administration (27:1–34)
        1. Divisions of the Military (27:1–15)
        2. Divisions of the Tribal Leaders (27:16–22)
        3. Military Census and Judgment Summary (27:23–24)
        4. Overseers (27:25–34)
    G. David's Final Works and Words (28:1–29:30)
        1. David's Charge to Solomon for the Temple (28:1–21)
        2. David's Charge to the Leadership and Temple Gifts (29:1–9)
        3. David's Leadership in Worship and Praise (29:10–20)
        4. Solomon Becomes King (29:21–25)
        5. David's Death (29:26–30)
III. Solomon (2 Chron. 1:1–9:31)
    A. Solomon's Request for Wisdom (1:1–17)
    B. Solomon's Preparations for Temple Building (2:1–18 [1:18–2:17 MT])
    C. Construction of the Temple (3:1–17)
    D. Addition of Temple Furnishings (4:1–5:1)
    E. Placement of the Ark in the Temple (5:2–14)
    F. Solomon's Address to Israel (6:1–11)
    G. Solomon's Prayer of Dedication (6:12–42)
    H. Solomon's Sacrifices and Celebration (7:1–10)
    I. Yahweh's Appearance to Solomon (7:11–22)
    J. Solomon's Buildings and Defenses (8:1–18)
    K. Solomon and the Queen of Sheba (9:1–12)
    L. Solomon's Wealth (9:13–28)
    M. Solomon's Death (9:29–31)
IV. Kings of Judah (10:1–36:19)
    A. Rehoboam (10:1–12:16)
        1. Division of the Kingdom (10:1–11:4)
        2. Rehoboam's Kingdom Established (11:5–23)
        3. Shishak's Attack (12:1–12)
        4. Rehoboam's Death (12:13–16)

- B. Abijah (13:1–14:1 [13:23 MT])
- C. Asa (14:2 [14:1 MT]–16:14)
  1. Reform and Military Success (14:2 [14:1 MT]–15:19)
  2. War against Israel (16:1–10)
  3. Asa's Death (16:11–14)
- D. Jehoshaphat (17:1–21:1)
  1. Reform and Organization (17:1–19)
  2. Ahab (18:1–19:3)
  3. Judicial Reform (19:4–11)
  4. Victory over Moab, Ammon, and Edom (20:1–30)
  5. Jehoshaphat's Death (20:31–21:1)
- E. Jehoram (21:2–20)
- F. Ahaziah (22:1–9)
- G. Athaliah (22:10–23:21)
  1. Coup (22:10–12)
  2. Revolt (23:1–21)
- H. Joash (24:1–27)
- I. Amaziah (25:1–28)
- J. Uzziah (26:1–23)
- K. Jotham (27:1–9)
- L. Ahaz (28:1–27)
- M. Hezekiah (29:1–32:33)
  1. Temple Reform (29:1–36)
  2. Passover Celebration (30:1–27)
  3. Temple Gifts and Service (31:1–21)
  4. Assyrian Invasion (32:1–23)
  5. Hezekiah's Reign and Death (32:24–33)
- N. Manasseh (33:1–20)
- O. Amon (33:21–25)
- P. Josiah (34:1–35:27)
  1. Reform (34:1–13)
  2. Finding the Book of the Law of Yahweh (34:14–33)
  3. Passover Celebration (35:1–19)
  4. Josiah's Death (35:20–27)
- Q. Jehoahaz (36:1–4)
- R. Jehoiakim (36:5–8)
- S. Jehoiachin (36:9–10)
- T. Zedekiah (36:11–14)
- U. Babylonian Destruction (36:15–19)

V. Exile and Return (36:20–23)

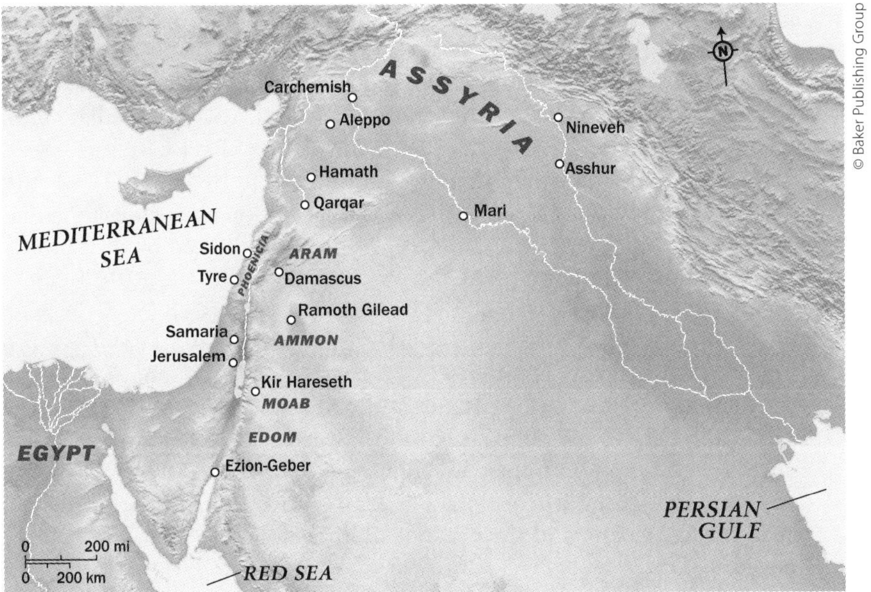

© Baker Publishing Group

The early period of the monarchy

Overview of 1 and 2 Chronicles

The books begin with a set of genealogies. First Chronicles 1:1–4 summarizes the line from Adam to Noah (Gen. 5:1–32) and adds the names of Noah's sons. The offspring of Noah in verses 5–16 summarizes the descendants of Japheth (vv. 5–7) and Ham (vv. 8–16) as found in the Table of Nations in Genesis 10:2–20. The line of Shem (1 Chron. 1:17–23) is found in Genesis (10:21–31), with the full line reaching to Abram (1 Chron. 1:17–27) occurring in summary form in Genesis 11:10–27. First Chronicles 1:28 lists the two sons of Abraham: Isaac and Ishmael. There follows the lines of Abraham's wives and concubines: Hagar (1 Chron. 1:29–31 = Gen. 25:12–16),[2] Keturah (1 Chron. 1:32–33 = Gen. 25:1–4), and Sarah (1 Chron. 1:34). Esau, grandson of Abraham and Sarah, has descendants listed in 1 Chronicles 1:35–37 (= Gen. 36:10–14) and verses 38–42 (= Gen. 36:20–28), with an additional list of rulers in verses 43–54 (= Gen. 36:31–43).

First Chronicles 2 considers the sons and descendants of Jacob, also called Israel. The sons of Israel are listed in 2:1–2 (= Gen. 35:23–26), followed by Judah (1 Chron. 2:3–4 summarizes Gen. 38:1–30; some of 1 Chron. 2:5–9

2. The use of the "equal" (=) sign here and throughout this overview indicates synoptic texts found elsewhere in the OT. It is not meant to suggest a word-for-word identity between Chronicles and the other passage (yet that is often the case) but notes a substantial identity between two (or more) passages.

occurs in Ruth 4:18–19; Josh. 7:1). First Chronicles 2 goes on to list descendants of three brothers, sons of Hezron from the line of Judah: Ram (2:10–17), Caleb (2:18–24) and his clans (2:42–55), and Jerahmeel (2:25–41).

Through Ram comes the line that leads to David. David's immediate family appears in 1 Chronicles 3:1–9 (= 2 Sam. 3:2–5; 5:14–16; 1 Chron. 14:4–7). Next comes the line of David through the monarchy (1 Chron. 3:10–16), into the exile, and beyond (3:17–24). The Chronicler then provides the other families and descendants of Judah (4:1–23). This is followed by the families and descendants of Simeon (4:24–43; vv. 28–33 = Josh. 19:2–10), Reuben (1 Chron. 5:1–10), Gad (5:11–22), the half-tribe of Manasseh (5:23–26), and Levi (6:1–30), followed by sections on Levitical temple workers (6:31–53) and on the Levitical towns (6:54–81 = Josh. 21:4–39), Issachar (1 Chron. 7:1–5), Benjamin (7:6–12), Naphtali (7:13), Manasseh (7:14–19), Ephraim (7:20–29), and Asher (7:30–40). There follows the family of Benjamin, leading to King Saul and then on to his descendants (1 Chron. 8:1–39), concluding with a summary of all the genealogies of Israel (9:1a). A listing of those who returned from the exile and their responsibilities follows (9:1b–34; vv. 1–17 = Neh. 11:3–19).

The genealogy of Saul (1 Chron. 9:35–44 = 8:28–38) and his death in the battle with the Philistines at Mount Gilboa (10:1–14; vv. 1–12 summarize 1 Sam. 31:1–13; 2 Sam. 1:4–12) provide the prelude to the life of David, which constitutes the remainder of 1 Chronicles. All Israel anoints David king at Hebron (1 Chron. 11:1–3 = 2 Sam. 5:1–3), whence he advances on Jerusalem and—through the bravery of Joab, who becomes his general—takes it for his personal city and capital of his kingdom (1 Chron. 11:4–9 = 2 Sam. 5:6–10). Next is a list of David's mighty warriors and some notes on great deeds that some of them did (1 Chron. 11:10–47; vv. 10–41 = 2 Sam. 23:8–39). First Chronicles 12:1–40 records many of the other warriors who joined his ranks and some of their great deeds. Important matters regarding the establishment of temple worship by David and the preservation of his dynasty follow. This begins with moving the ark of God from Kiriath-jearim closer to Jerusalem (1 Chron. 13:1–14 = 2 Sam. 6:1–11). David builds his palace with assistance from Hiram (1 Chron. 14:1–7 = 2 Sam. 5:11–16) and accumulates more wives and children. In two battles against the Philistines, at Baal-perazim and initially at Gibeon, David leads his army to defeat them (1 Chron. 14:8–17 = 2 Sam. 5:17–25). A carefully organized procession led by David celebrates the movement of the ark into a tent in Jerusalem (1 Chron. 15:1–16:3, summarized in 2 Sam. 6:12–19). After appointing Levites, led by Asaph, to process before the ark and make music, David proclaims a worship psalm that combines sections of three psalms as now preserved (1 Chron. 16:4–36; thus 16:8–22, 23–33, 34–36 = Pss. 105:1–15; 96:1–13; 106:1, 47–48). David appoints Asaph and others to take care of the ark in Jerusalem, and Zadok and other priests to minister at the tabernacle at the high place in Gibeon (1 Chron. 16:37–43). Next

© Baker Publishing Group and Dr. James C. Martin

City of David stepped structure believed to support royal palace and buildings during the monarchy

is the story of Nathan and the eternal dynasty that God promises to David (1 Chron. 17:1–15 = 2 Sam. 7:1–17). After this, David expresses praise and thanksgiving to God (1 Chron. 17:16–27 = 2 Sam. 7:18–29).

David's many military victories, especially those over the Aramaeans to his north, are summarized (1 Chron. 18:1–13 = 2 Sam. 8:1–14) and followed by a list of his officers (1 Chron. 18:14–17 = 2 Sam. 8:15–18). The humiliation of David's messengers by King Hanun of the Ammonites leads to battle with Ammon and its ally, Aram, and the defeat of both enemies (1 Chron. 19:1–19 = 2 Sam. 10:1–19; 1 Chron. 20:1–3 = 2 Sam. 11:1; 12:29–31). Various warriors defeat heroes of the Philistines (1 Chron. 20:4–8 = 2 Sam. 21:15–22). Satan incites David to take a census of Israel (1 Chron. 21:1–17 = 2 Sam. 24:1–17). God condemns this and gives David a choice of three punishments. David chooses a plague against Israel. The plague stops, and the angel who has brought it stands at the threshing floor of Araunah the Jebusite (see the sidebar "Araunah the Jebusite"). The angel of Yahweh orders David to build an altar right there. David buys the threshing floor and offers sacrifice. He determines that the temple shall be built on that spot (1 Chron. 21:18–22:1). David collects materials to build the temple and charges his son Solomon with the construction (22:2–19).

First Chronicles 23 portrays David as old and making the final preparations for the worship in the temple. He takes a census of the Levites, who are to assist the priests with temple functions (23:1–5). He divides the Levites according to their families from the three sons of Levi—Gershon, Kohath, and Merari—and he assigns to them various tasks (23:6–32). The priests also have their divisions and responsibilities, determined by lot (24:1–19). There are other members of the tribe of Levi who are also divided (24:20–31). David chooses sons of Asaph, Jeduthun, and Heman for various duties to perform music in the temple (25:1–31). These are also drawn by lot. Further divisions are made for gatekeepers and those in charge of the treasuries of the house of God (26:1–32). Twelve military divisions rotate, so that one division is

Araunah the Jebusite

Araunah the Jebusite appears in 2 Samuel 24:16–24 and in 1 Chronicles 21:15–25 as the owner of the threshing floor that David purchases and where the temple will be built. It is marked as the place where the angel who has brought the plague against Israel is stopped. During the decades before Israel arrived in Canaan, or earlier, Jebusites—like other smaller groups of inhabitants, such as Horites, Hivites, Perizzites, and Girgashites—may have migrated from farther north, in what now are modern Syria and Turkey. Their origin and occupation of Jerusalem evoke the name of the fourteen-century-BC leader of Jerusalem (in the Amarna letters) Abdi-Heba; the second part of the name refers to a north Syrian goddess. The name of Araunah is not Semitic (Hebrew is a Semitic language) and is spelled differently in Samuel and Chronicles, suggesting lack of clarity about it. However, its etymology has also been related to the Hurrian peoples who were centered in northern Syria in the mid-second millennium BC but disappeared after the tenth century. It may be related to the Hurrian word for "lord, master," *ewri*. If so, the name may suggest a title of some sort of leadership or special status in Jerusalem before its conquest by David. The owner of the highest point of Jerusalem at that time, and what is today the Temple Mount, might be expected to be an influential figure in pre-Israelite Jerusalem.

on duty only one month each year (27:1–15). There are also tribal officers (27:16–24) and administrative overseers of various properties of the king (27:25–34). Before all the leadership of Israel, David charges his son Solomon to follow Yahweh and to build the temple according to the plans that he has made (28:1–21). David gives additional treasures for building the temple, and Israel's leadership follows his example (29:1–9). Then he leads the assembly and praises God in his prayer, dedicating all that has been given (29:10–20). Sacrifices are made, and Solomon becomes king (29:21–25). David dies after a reign of forty years (29:26–28 = 1 Kings 2:10–12). A final note in 1 Chronicles points the reader to the records of Samuel the seer, Nathan the prophet, and Gad the seer for further information regarding David's reign (29:29–30).

Second Chronicles begins with a note on Solomon's establishment of his throne (1:1). This is followed by the account of his visit to the high place at Gibeon, where the tabernacle that was built and carried about in the wilderness is found (1:2–13 = 1 Kings 3:4–15). The bronze altar of Bezalel lies in front of it. There Solomon sacrifices, and then God appears to him at night. Solomon requests wisdom and knowledge, and God promises it along with all the other wealth, riches, and honor that he does not request. The text describes Solomon's military might in chariots, his wealth, and his international trade in chariots (2 Chron. 1:14–17 = 1 Kings 10:26–29 = 2 Chron. 9:25–28). Solomon then requests King Hiram[3] of Tyre to provide a skilled artisan; cedar, pine, and algum wood; and promises wheat, barley, wine, and oil in exchange (2 Chron. 2:1–18 = 1 Kings 5:1–16). Hiram agrees. With detail, the text describes construction of the temple (2 Chron. 3:1–14 = 1 Kings 6:1–29), followed by the altar, molten sea, basins, gold lampstands, pots, shovels, and temple decorations (2 Chron. 4:1–5:1, where 4:2–6 and 4:10–5:1 = 1 Kings 7:23–26, 38–51). After this, Solomon brings together a great crowd and leads a grand procession to bring the altar from its tent in Jerusalem to its place in the inner sanctuary. He concludes by reminding the people that this city is where God has shown David that he has chosen him to rule and his son to build the temple for his Name (2 Chron. 5:2–6:11 = 1 Kings 8:1–21). Solomon turns toward the altar and makes his great prayer of dedication, praising God as one who cannot be contained by such a temple and asking that it be a center to which both Israelites and foreigners (2 Chron. 6:32–33), all who face in its direction and cry to God for a variety of needs, may be heard, and God may respond favorably (2 Chron. 6:12–40 = 1 Kings 8:22–53). Solomon concludes with a psalm text asking God to come with the ark into its resting place and to accept the king and successor of David (2 Chron. 6:41–42 = Ps. 132:8–10). At that point fire comes from heaven to consume the burnt offering and sacrifices, and the glory of Yahweh fills the temple, causing all Israel to worship and then to celebrate for seven days, accompanied by many sacrifices (2 Chron. 7:1–10 = 1 Kings 8:62–66). God appears once again to Solomon, bringing a promise of blessing for obedience yet also a warning of judgment and exile for disobedience (2 Chron. 7:11–22 = 1 Kings 9:1–9).

Solomon fortifies his cities, conscripts non-Israelites for his building projects, appoints Israelites as military and civil leaders, builds a special palace for Pharaoh's daughter as his wife, orders the rotation of offerings and sacrifices at the temple, and builds a fleet that brings back gold from Ophir (2 Chron. 8:1–18 = 1 Kings 9:10–28). The queen of Sheba visits Solomon, sees his works and wisdom, praises him and his God, and trades many spices and gems (2 Chron. 9:1–12 = 1 Kings 10:1–13). The story of Solomon draws to a close with details about the gold he receives, his gold shields and cups, his ivory throne, and the other wealth and wisdom that he possesses (2 Chron. 9:13–28 = 1 Kings 10:14–29; 2 Chron. 9:25–28 = 2 Chron. 1:14–17). After sources are cited for more information, in the records of Nathan the prophet, the prophecy of Ahijah the Shilonite, and the visions of Iddo the seer, Solomon's death and burial are reported (2 Chron. 9:29–31 = 1 Kings 11:41–43). He has reigned forty years.

3. The Hebrew here is Huram, a transliteration of the Masoretic Text. However, the identical figure in 1 Kings is Hiram. The original name is Hiram, not Huram, which must be a copyist error.

Solomon's son Rehoboam succeeds him. Following the advice of his young friends and counselors (and not that of the older counselors), he tells the people of the northern tribes of his kingdom that he will increase the demands he places on them (2 Chron. 10:1–11:4 = 1 Kings 12:1–4). This leads to the division of the kingdom. Rehoboam fortifies cities throughout Judah and places his own priests to serve before goat and calf images on the high places. The faithful priests, Levites, and Judeans come to Jerusalem to worship (2 Chron. 11:5–17). Among Rehoboam's eighteen wives (and sixty concubines), he loves Maacah daughter of Absalom, who bears him Abijah to be his successor (2 Chron. 11:18–22; Abijam in 2 Kings 14:31). In Rehoboam's fifth year, Pharaoh Shishak of Egypt attacks Jerusalem with a large and powerful African army (2 Chron. 12:1–16; vv. 9–16 = 1 Kings 14:21, 25–31). Shishak takes all the gold and treasures of the temple and palace. Because Rehoboam and the Judean people repent before the Lord when the prophet Shemaiah says that God will abandon them to Shishak in punishment for abandoning God, they are not destroyed. Rehoboam reigns seventeen years, fights continuously with Jeroboam of Israel, and at his death passes on the kingdom to his son Abijah.

During Abijah's reign, a battle takes place with Jeroboam of Israel (2 Chron. 13:1–14:1, where 13:1–2 + 13:22–14:1 = 1 Kings 15:1–2, 6–8). Abijah announces to Israel that they have forsaken Yahweh's priests, the sons of Aaron, and have appointed their own, whereas the true priests serve Yahweh in the true temple service in Jerusalem. Jeroboam meanwhile tries to send part of his army around to the rear of Abijah's army. However, the Judeans cry to Yahweh, who gives them victory so that Jeroboam does not regain power during Abijah's reign.

Abijah is succeeded by his son Asa, who is described as a good king (2 Chron. 14:2–16:14; 14:2–3 = 1 Kings 15:11–12; 2 Chron. 15:16–19 = 1 Kings 15:13–16; 2 Chron. 16:1–6 + 16:11–17:1 = 1 Kings 15:17–24). In an attack by Zerah the Cushite (MT), Asa calls on Yahweh, who strikes down the Cushites. Encouraged by the prophecy of Azariah, Asa removes all the images and repairs Yahweh's altar. All Judah and Benjamin assemble in Jerusalem and sacrifice to Yahweh. They commit themselves to God, and he gives them peace on every side. Asa removes Maacah his grandmother from her position as queen mother, and he destroys her Asherah image. He seeks the help of Ben-hadad of Damascus when Baasha of Israel threatens Judah, but Hanani the seer condemns him for not trusting in God. Asa becomes diseased in his feet but does not seek help from Yahweh. He dies after forty-one years of rule.

Jehoshaphat the son of Asa succeeds him (2 Chron. 17:1–19). Like his father, Jehoshaphat begins by removing the high places and images of other gods. In his third year he sends officers and Levites throughout Judah to teach the book of the law in all the towns. Judeans, Philistines, and Arabs bring

Jehoshaphat tribute. He has much wealth and a powerful army that guards all of Judah. However, Jehoshaphat allies with Ahab of Samaria to fight the king of Aram for Ramoth-gilead (2 Chron. 18:1–34 = 1 Kings 22:1–36). Micaiah the prophet of Yahweh speaks a warning against Ahab's court prophets and does not endorse the battle. Ahab is killed, but Jehoshaphat escapes. The seer Jehu son of Hanani condemns Jehoshaphat for his alliance with Ahab but commends him for purifying Judah of idolatrous worship. Jehoshaphat appoints judges throughout the fortified cities of Judah with the instructions to judge with justice because they are judging for Yahweh, not for any human (2 Chron. 19:4–11). Levites and elders are appointed to administer the law throughout Judah. A great army from Moab, Ammon, and elsewhere comes to fight Judah (2 Chron. 20:1–30). Jehoshaphat proclaims a fast, is joined by many Judeans, and at the temple praises Yahweh and prays for guidance. The spirit of Yahweh comes to Jahaziel a descendant of Asaph, who promises Jehoshaphat that God will fight for them. The Judeans march out to the desert of Tekoa, singing and praising God. Yahweh throws the attackers into confusion, leading them to kill one another. When the Judeans arrive, no one is alive. They plunder the dead for three days and then spend a day praising God. The land has peace. Jehoshaphat does much good during his reign of twenty-five years, but he does not remove the high places. When he builds a fleet of ships with King Ahaziah of Israel, who has done evil, God wrecks the fleet (2 Chron. 20:31–21:1 = 1 Kings 22:41–50).

Jehoram, firstborn of Jehoshaphat, becomes the next king of Judah (2 Chron. 21:2–20; vv. 5–10, 20 = 2 Kings 8:16–24). Jehoram kills all of his brothers and follows the evil ways of the kings of Israel. He marries Ahab's daughter. He loses control of Edom and of Libnah. Elijah sends him a letter describing the wrongs he has done and warning that God's judgment will come with the loss of his family and a disease of his own intestines. Jehoram's family (except for his youngest son, Ahaziah) and goods are taken by an invasion of Philistines and Arabs. A disease of the bowels afflicts him for more than a year until he dies in great pain, after eight years of rule. His people make no fire for him as they have done for the other kings of Judah.

Ahaziah follows Jehoram and does evil as Ahab has done in the north, like Jehoram his father (2 Chron. 22:1–9 = 2 Kings 8:25–29; 9:21–29). After reigning only a year, Ahaziah dies at the hand of Jehu while visiting King Joram of Israel, whom Jehu also kills. Athaliah, mother of Ahaziah and daughter of Ahab and Jezebel, then tries to wipe out all that remains of the house of Judah (2 Chron. 22:10–23:21 = 2 Kings 11:1–21). Only Joash son of Ahaziah is rescued, and he is hidden in the temple by his aunt, the wife of the high priest Jehoiada. After six years Jehoiada brings together the military, religious, and civil leadership of Judah and makes a covenant with God. They proceed with a revolt that leads to the death of Athaliah and the installation of Joash as king of Judah.

Joash reigns forty years (2 Chron. 24:1–27; 24:1–14 = 2 Kings 12:1–16; 2 Chron. 24:23–27 = 2 Kings 12:17–21). Joash and Jehoiada encourage the people to give the tithe Moses has commanded so that it can be used to repair the temple and its objects, and the people respond generously. Jehoiada dies at 130 years of age. After his death the officials lead Joash to abandon the worship of Yahweh and to worship with Asherah images. Yahweh's spirit comes to Zechariah son of Jehoiada the priest, and he warns the people. But Joash and the people stone Zechariah, and he dies while asking God to call the people to account. The Aramaeans come against Judah and defeat their much larger army. Joash is wounded and then murdered by his officials.

Amaziah son of Joash reigns for twenty-nine years, following Yahweh, but not completely (2 Chron. 25:1–28; 25:1–4 = 2 Kings 14:1–6; 2 Chron. 25:11–12 = 2 Kings 14:7; 2 Chron. 25:17–28 = 2 Kings 14:8–20). He executes those who have assassinated his father. Amaziah has a great victory against Edom, but he brings Edomite gods back and sacrifices to them. For this a prophet condemns him. Therefore, King Jehoash of Israel captures Amaziah, breaks down six hundred feet of the wall around Jerusalem, and removes all the gold and silver items in the temple. Amaziah lives fifteen years after the death of Jehoash. After Amaziah turns away from the Lord, he flees Jerusalem to escape conspiracy but is assassinated in Lachish.

Uzziah son of Amaziah is sixteen years old when he becomes king, and he reigns fifty-two years (2 Chron. 26:1–23; 26:1–4 = 2 Kings 14:21–22 + 15:1–3; 2 Chron. 26:21–23 = 2 Kings 15:5–7). In his early years he is instructed by Zechariah and so follows Yahweh. Uzziah restores the port of Elath. He defeats the Philistines, the Arabs, and the Meunites. He is wealthy, with much livestock. Uzziah builds many defenses and a large and strong army. However, in his pride he offers incense in the temple. The priests confront him, and he becomes leprous. Uzziah remains leprous until his death and lives in a separate house. Isaiah records the other events of his reign.

Jotham becomes king after his father, Uzziah (2 Chron. 27:1–9; vv. 1–4, 7–9 = 2 Kings 15:32–38). He reigns for sixteen years and follows Yahweh. He fortifies Jerusalem, builds towns and forts in the Judean hills, and defeats the Ammonites. Jotham's son Ahaz succeeds him and reigns for sixteen years (2 Chron. 28:1–27 = 2 Kings 16:1–20). Ahaz worships Baal, sacrifices his sons in fire, and orders sacrifices on the high places. The Aramaean king defeats him and takes many Judeans captive. King Pekah of Israel also kills many Judeans and takes their families into captivity. However, the prophet Oded warns the northerners, and so they return the prisoners of war to their homeland. Ahaz seeks help from Tiglath-pileser III of Assyria and offers him tribute, but Ahaz receives no assistance. (See plate 4 in the gallery for an image of Tiglath-pileser III.) The Edomites and Philistines take prisoners and towns from Ahaz. He sacrifices to Aramaean gods, closes the temple of Yahweh, and sets up altars and high places throughout Jerusalem and in every town in Judah.

© Baker Publishing Group and Dr. James C. Martin

Judean fort at Arad, top half showing remains of outer court with fieldstone altar, second court to the left, and holy of holies niche with steps farther to the left

Hezekiah son of Ahaz succeeds his father and rules for twenty-nine years; he does what is right, just as David has done (2 Chron. 29:1–32:33; 29:1–2 = 2 Kings 18:2–3). In the first month of his reign, Hezekiah opens and restores the temple. He directs the priests and Levites to purify themselves and then to consecrate the temple. With a huge number of burnt offerings, he quickly reestablishes the service of the temple. Hezekiah sends word throughout Judah and in the north up to Dan, calling the faithful to come to Jerusalem to celebrate the Passover. They have to do this in the second month, rather than the first, because not enough priests have been consecrated in time for the first month. The people come, destroy all the non-Yahweh altars and places of worship in and around Jerusalem, celebrate the Passover for two weeks instead of one, and then go throughout Judah and eliminate all the high places as well as their sacred stones and poles. Some of the northerners have not purified themselves, yet eat of the Passover meal. Nevertheless, Hezekiah prays for them, and Yahweh accepts their worship and heals them. Hezekiah commands the Judeans to bring their offerings, and there are so many that the priests and Levites in Jerusalem have plenty to spare (2 Chron. 31:20–21 = 2 Kings 18:5–7). So they enroll all those born in the proper lines who live anywhere in Judah and give them shares of food.

King Sennacherib of Assyria invades Judah. Hezekiah has water sources outside the city blocked off, repairs his defenses, and encourages his people with the belief that Yahweh will fight for Judah. The Assyrian belittles Yahweh as unable to rescue his people. Hezekiah and Isaiah pray to Yahweh, who destroys the Assyrian army, has Sennacherib killed by his own sons back in his temple in Assyria, and exalts the reputation of Hezekiah among the other nations (2 Chron. 32:9–19 = 2 Kings 18:17–35 = Isa. 36:2–20; 2 Chron. 32:20–23 = 2 Kings 19:35–37 = Isa. 37:36–38). Hezekiah becomes ill, but Yahweh heals him. Hezekiah becomes proud but repents; he becomes very wealthy and builds the water channel to bring the Gihon Spring over to the west side of the city of David. God tests him with Babylonian envoys (2 Chron. 32:24–33 = 2 Kings 20:1–21 = Isa. 38:1–8; 39:1–8). When Hezekiah dies, the people honor him.

Zev Radovan/www.BibleLandPictures.com
Seal impression with part of the name of Hezekiah

Manasseh son of Hezekiah reigns fifty-five years in Jerusalem and does what is evil (2 Chron. 33:1–20; 33:1–9 = 2 Kings 21:1–9; 2 Chron. 33:18–20 = 2 Kings 21:17–18). He worships Baal, sacrifices his sons in fire, and orders sacrifices on the high places. In the temple he builds altars to worship the stars of heaven. He leads the Judeans into greater evil than the Canaanites, whom they have replaced. The king of Assyria puts a hook in Manasseh's nose and takes him to Babylon, where he repents and turns back to Yahweh (see the sidebar "Manasseh in Babylon"). Manasseh then returns to Judah and rebuilds its walls and defenses. He gets rid of the foreign gods and images and restores the altar and temple, renewing its offerings. Manasseh's son Amon succeeds him but rules only two years, doing evil in Yahweh's eyes (2 Chron. 33:21–25 = 2 Kings 21:19–24). The court officials conspire against Amon and assassinate him. Then the people of the land kill all the plotters.

Amon's son Josiah reigns thirty-one years in Jerusalem and does what is right, according to the ways of David (2 Chron. 34:1–35:27). He destroys all the high places and images of other gods and goddesses. In his eighteenth year he begins to purify the land and the temple, using the money collected from the offerings of the people (2 Chron. 34:1–2 = 2 Kings 22:1–2; 2 Chron. 34:3–7 = 2 Kings 23:4–20; 2 Chron. 34:8–13 = 2 Kings 22:3–7). Hilkiah the priest finds the book of the law and reads it to Josiah; Huldah the prophetess promises that judgment will come but not during Josiah's reign, because he has repented (2 Chron. 34:14–28 = 2 Kings 22:18–20). Josiah has the book of the covenant read to everyone in Jerusalem, and they all pledge themselves to follow it (2 Chron. 34:29–32 = 2 Kings 23:1–3). Josiah celebrates a Passover for all the people, sacrificing thirty thousand sheep and goats; no such Passover has been seen in Israel since the days of Samuel (2 Chron. 35:1, 18–19 =

Manasseh in Babylon

The record of Manasseh's evil acts against Yahweh are well known and recorded in both 2 Kings 21:1–9, 16–18 and 2 Chronicles 33:1–20. The resulting prophetic condemnation as the cause célèbre for the downfall of Judah appears in detail in 2 Kings 21:10–15 but is mentioned only briefly in 2 Chronicles 33:10. The Chronicler alone mentions the Assyrian king's deportation of Manasseh to Babylon, where he held Manasseh as a prisoner for a time, until the Assyrian allowed Manasseh to return to Jerusalem near the end of his life. Chronicles also describes Manasseh's repentance in Babylon.

Many scholars have doubted the historicity of this account. They find it unlikely that the Assyrian king would take Manasseh in chains to Babylon, the capital of the Babylonian Empire, rather than to one of the Assyrian capitals. They see this as a dramatic gesture by the Chronicler to portray Manasseh as a prototype of Judah, who will be deported to Babylon, repent there, return to Jerusalem, and restore the temple. However, this can be understood in the context of Judean and Assyrian geopolitics.

A generation earlier, in 701 BC, the Assyrian king was unable to take Jerusalem, as recorded in Chronicles, Kings, and Isaiah (2 Chron. 32:9–19 = 2 Kings 18:17–35 = Isa. 36:2–20; 2 Chron. 32:20–23 = 2 Kings 19:35–37 = Isa. 37:36–38). Although Jerusalem survived, Judah was devastated. To deal with economic disaster, Manasseh opened markets with the Phoenicians and others and diplomatically recognized their gods in Jerusalem. Not only did this compromise anger Yahweh's prophets; it was also understood as an alliance against the Assyrian king Assurbanipal. The chief instigator of this coalition in rebellion against the Assyrian king was the king of Babylon, whom Assurbanipal destroyed in 648 BC. At that point the Assyrian king brought Manasseh and other allies before him in Babylon. Manasseh's repentance before God coincides with the favorable treatment he received from the Assyrian king, who allowed him to return from Babylon to Jerusalem and to rebuild. Manasseh's later reforms, which pleased the Chronicler, also represent the cutting of ties with the Phoenicians and others who continued to plot against Assurbanipal.[a]

[a] See Rainey, "Manasseh, King of Judah."

2 Kings 23:21–23).[4] Josiah goes to meet Pharaoh Neco of Egypt in battle at Megiddo's plain. Josiah is shot by archers and returns to Jerusalem, where he dies (2 Chron. 35:20–27 = 2 Kings 23:28–30). Jeremiah composes laments

4. Also 2 Chron. 35:1–36:23 is found paraphrased in 1 Esd. 1:1–55.

for Josiah that appear in the Book of Laments and are still sung to this day. Jehoahaz son of Josiah follows him as king.

Jehoahaz reigns for three months (2 Chron. 36:1–4 = 2 Kings 23:31–34). Pharaoh Neco imprisons him and takes him to Egypt, but not before Neco taxes the land of Judah. Neco then appoints Jehoiakim, another son of Josiah, as ruler. Like his brother, Jehoiakim does evil in the eyes of Yahweh (2 Chron. 36:5–8 = 2 Kings 23:36–24:6). After eleven years of rule, Jehoiakim dies. Jehoiakim's son Jehoiachin rules for three months (2 Chron. 36:9–10 = 2 Kings 24:8–17). Nebuchadnezzar's army attacks Jerusalem, and Jehoiachin is taken prisoner and deported, along with items from the temple. Nebuchadnezzar appoints a son of Josiah, Zedekiah, as king over Jerusalem and Judah.

Zedekiah does evil in the eyes of Yahweh and does not humble himself before Jeremiah the prophet (2 Chron. 36:11–19 = 2 Kings 24:18–25:9 = Jer. 52:1–13). Zedekiah also withholds tribute and thus rebels against the king of Babylon, who has made him take an oath of loyalty. Zedekiah becomes stiff-necked and hardens his heart against God, and all the people become more and more unfaithful.

The people will not listen to God or his prophets (2 Chron. 36:14–16 summarizes 2 Kings 25:1–21 = Jer. 52:4–27). Nebuchadnezzar attacks Jerusalem, kills many people, and takes into exile in Babylon those who escape the sword, along with the treasures of the temple. So the land enjoys its Sabbath rest for seventy years, and the word of Yahweh through Jeremiah is fulfilled (2 Chron. 36:21 = Jer. 25:11–12; 29:10). In his first year of rule, Cyrus king of Persia issues a proclamation allowing the people to return and rebuild the temple in Jerusalem (2 Chron. 36:22–23 = Ezra 1:1–3).

Reading 1 and 2 Chronicles

Premodern Readings

The history of the interpretation of 1–2 Chronicles began early, with 1 Esdras, which paraphrases the last two chapters of 2 Chronicles. Elsewhere, the early versions and Josephus combine the works of Kings and Chronicles, as well as other sources that coincide with the texts of Chronicles, and demonstrate an awareness of these related texts. That the Bible reader has already encountered so many of the passages in 1–2 Chronicles in earlier parts of the Bible means that the work of Chronicles has received less comment than where those texts first appear. This is true whether one follows the Jewish (Masoretic) or Christian (largely Septuagint) order of the canon. In addition, the genealogies of the first nine chapters of 1 Chronicles provide little opportunity for commentary or elaboration. Nevertheless, many of the names lists, especially in the first two or three chapters, do have narratives associated with them in other biblical books. Thus commentators of the past focused on the passages where the stories were. Here as well, the books of Chronicles remain derivative and secondary, receiving less interest and attention.

For sample interpretations of most of 1–2 Chronicles, the reader should consult the earlier "Premodern Readings" for 1–2 Samuel and especially for 1–2 Kings. Where comments were made on distinctive sections of Chronicles, the commentators gave their attention to typological and moral interpretation of the events and people described. They considered David to be a ruler and saint and used his deeds in these books to identify elements to be imitated. Solomon as well was considered as one to be emulated, especially in his capacity as a sage. Later kings were also thought of as moral examples.

So Basil the Great comments on Jehoshaphat, whom the prophet of God condemns for his alliance with Ahab (2 Chron. 19:3), yet concerning whom the prophet declares, "Some good is found in you":

> If you see your neighbor committing sin, take care not to dwell exclusively on his sin, but think of the many things he has done and continues to do rightly. Many times, by examining the whole and not taking the part only into account, you will find that he is better than you. God does not examine humans according to the part, for he says, "I come to gather together their works and thoughts." Furthermore, when he rebuked Jehoshaphat for a sin committed in an unguarded moment, he mentioned also the good he had done, saying, "But good works are found in you." (*On Humility*)[5]

The importance of Manasseh's repentance and forgiveness in 2 Chronicles 33 became an important theme, beginning with the Prayer of Manasseh (in the Apocrypha), which attests to the type of repentance involved for one so wicked. John Chrysostom comments as well, in his *Letter to the Fallen*:

> [Manasseh,] having become more ungodly than all who were before him, when he afterwards repented was ranked among the friends of God. Now if, looking to the magnitude of his own iniquities, he had despaired of restoration and repentance, he would have missed all that he afterwards obtained; but as it was, looking to the boundlessness of God's tender mercy instead of the enormity of his transgressions, and having broken in two the bonds of the devil, he rose up and contended with him and finished the good course.[6]

Higher Criticism

Martin Noth identified the Deuteronomistic History in his *Überlieferungsgeschichtliche Studien* in the middle of the twentieth century.[7] He went

5. Conti and Pilara, *1–2 Kings*, 283.

6. Ibid., 299.

7. See further discussion in "Source Criticism" for Deuteronomy and "Higher Criticism" for Joshua and 1–2 Kings.

on to discuss the Chronicler's History, which he assumed to be a unified work consisting of 1–2 Chronicles along with Ezra and Nehemiah. The question of the relationship between Chronicles and Ezra and Nehemiah is ancient (see above, "Name, Text, and Outline"). There is no simple answer to it.[8] Sara Japhet and Hugh Williamson argue that, linguistically, common authorship of the two sets of books is not so evident, either due to the use of different technical terms and other features or due to the sharing of expressions of late biblical Hebrew found in other writings of the period as well.[9] However, David Talshir has argued that the closeness in style and phrasing between Chronicles and Ezra–Nehemiah is significantly more than that between Chronicles and Esther, for example.[10]

It is clear that there are similar theological emphases, such as worship, temple, and law. There is a general absence of emphasis on the exodus and conquest. However, that is not the same thing as saying that the two works are identical. Chronicles preserves a much broader view of Israel, inclusive of all sorts of people. Ezra and Nehemiah have a greater exclusivity; they are not interested in bringing the north back to a relationship with Jerusalem and Yahweh (as the Chronicler is). Nevertheless, Ezra 1–3 flows naturally from the end of 2 Chronicles. For this reason, it is likely that there was an awareness of similar sources and ideas between the two, but it is unlikely that the same person composed the whole work.

The questions of authorship and date are not easily answered for the books of Chronicles by themselves. It is not self-evident whether one or several authors and editors wrote, or whether a school composed the work. Clearly, the more one emphasizes the authorship of Chronicles in this manner, the more it separates the work from Ezra–Nehemiah. As for the dating, if Ezra intentionally begins at the end of 2 Chronicles, and if it follows the model of Solomon's temple in its own reconstruction of the temple after the return from the exile, then Chronicles belongs before its successor. If that is the case, then a date in the fifth century BC is not too early.

The sources that the Chronicler used have not been clearly identified, and source criticism itself remains a subjective enterprise when applied to these books. Sources are cited for a variety of reasons that may include the validation of a character or evaluation, the referencing of additional resources not included in the text of Chronicles, and theological rationale. The Chronicler does not appear to cite sources when he is using canonical biblical sources.

In contrast, the use of existing texts that are found elsewhere in the Bible, especially 1–2 Samuel and 1–2 Kings, has occasioned much discussion. The studies have gone in three broad directions: those who deny a dependency

8. The following summarizes Knoppers, *I Chronicles 1–9*, 66–137.

9. Japhet, "Supposed Common Authorship"; idem, *Ideology of the Book of Chronicles*, 7–15; Williamson, *Israel in the Books of Chronicles*, 37–59.

10. Talshir, "Linguistic Relationship."

of Chronicles on Kings, those who assume dependency and catalog various types, and those who seek to understand this relationship in light of ancient categories and techniques of borrowing and copying found elsewhere in the ancient and classical world.

A. Graeme Auld's *Kings without Privilege* provides an example of the thesis that the material common to Samuel and Kings and to Chronicles reflects a shared source that was used by the authors of both accounts. Chronicles did not adapt the text of Samuel and Kings. Samuel and Kings do not preserve the original source. Instead, the biblical texts are themselves derivative from a common source. Auld here has demonstrated that many of the literary arguments used to support the traditional hypothesis—that 1–2 Chronicles depends on 1–2 Samuel and 1–2 Kings—are reversible. An important element of this argument depends on the assumption that the Lucianic or Antiochene (Greek) Text is more original than the Masoretic (Heb.) Text. On the problems with this view, see "Name, Text, and Outline" for 1–2 Samuel and 1–2 Kings.

The second approach is exemplified in Martin Selman's *1 Chronicles*, where he categorizes the different biblical texts that appear to copy other texts according to the methods they use.[11] First, Selman observes that certain materials in 1–2 Samuel and 1–2 Kings are omitted. For example, the vicissitudes of David's personal and family life do not occur in Chronicles. Much of the material regarding the northern kingdom (Israel) has disappeared. Part of this is due to the assumption by the Chronicler that the reader shares with the author a knowledge of Samuel and Kings. Therefore, it is not necessary to repeat this material. Part also depends on the Chronicler's focus toward what will endure beyond the exile.

Selman's second category includes summaries of what is not important to the Chronicler. David's military victories are brought together and summarized in 1 Chronicles 18–20. Solomon's exploits beyond his construction of the temple are not detailed.

Selman's third area identifies changes that are those small alterations that carry significant implications. Thus in the dynastic promise of God to David, "Your house and your kingdom" (referring to David) become "my house and my kingdom" (2 Sam. 7:16 vs. 1 Chron. 17:14). Again, in the division of the kingdom under Rehoboam, there are added references to "Israel" as the citizenry of the southern kingdom (not just the northern) to emphasize the manner in which this divided what was to be true Israel (1 Kings 12:16–19 vs. 2 Chron. 10:16–19).

There are, fourth, large expansions in Chronicles. Thus the eight chapters of 1 Chronicles 22–29 detail David's preparations for the construction of the temple with many appointments of priests, Levites, musicians, and so forth. This is nowhere found in the books of Samuel or Kings. Only a few

11. Selman, *1 Chronicles*, 34–42.

notes about David's instruction to Solomon to bring justice to his enemies appear in 1 Kings 2:1–9. Better known are the cases where the repentance and subsequent faithfulness of Rehoboam (2 Chron. 11–12), Abijah (13:1–14:1), and, above all, Manasseh (2 Chron. 33) are highlighted in Chronicles and completely ignored in the parallel passages of 1–2 Kings.

While similar methods are used by the Chronicler in referring to other parts of the Old Testament, the preferred approach is by allusion (more often than direct quotation). Thus Selman identifies numerous allusions in David's census of 1 Chronicles 21, in addition to the references to 2 Samuel 11–12 and 24: the destroying angel of the Passover (1 Chron. 21:15–20, 27; cf. Exod. 12:23), Abraham's purchase of burial grounds (1 Chron. 21:22–26; cf. Gen. 23), Gideon's encounter with an angel (1 Chron. 21:20–25; cf. Judg. 6:11–24), and fire from heaven (1 Chron. 21:26; cf. Lev. 9:24).[12] There is also the use of a character or object as a paradigm or pattern. Thus the tabernacle of Exodus 25 and 35–39 becomes a pattern in terms of its form and the order of its construction for Solomon's temple (1 Chron. 28–29; 2 Chron. 3–4). God's glory appears at the dedication (2 Chron. 5:13–14 and Exod. 40:34–35).

The third approach to the sources behind Chronicles categorizes the text of Chronicles in terms of known or acknowledged techniques for appropriating other texts. In this matter Gary Knoppers examines the midrashic method of early Judaism, the "rewritten Bible" technique ascribed to some texts of the Dead Sea Scrolls, the use of canonical or inner-biblical exegesis within the Old Testament itself, and the various terms used by classical writers to identify plagiarism, parody, and epitomization.[13] He finds that none of these are entirely satisfactory. These types of mimesis are to be expected, given the context of the Bible and the context of the ancient world (ancient Near Eastern or classical). Knoppers argues that the techniques of imitation and reuse of older works suggests a respect and admiration for the earlier biblical material and yet a new creation that would lead readers to view the earlier writings in a new light; further, what results is a different work, a new creation of older and new materials combined in a creative manner to address concerns and needs unique to the time and culture in which and for which the Chronicler was writing.

Literary Readings

The books of Chronicles do not appear as a favorite set of books for their literary study. Part of this is due to the manner in which they repeat what has already been written elsewhere. For this reason there seems to be little in the narratives about which to comment. A second reason has to do

12. Ibid., 40.

13. Knoppers, "Synoptic Problem?"; idem, *I Chronicles 1–9*, 118–37. The Hebrew term "midrash" (*midrāš*) actually occurs in 2 Chron. 13:22 and 24:27.

with how the first major section, 1 Chronicles 1–9, constitutes list after list of personal names, with very little that can be concluded regarding literary forms. Nevertheless, even this opening section provides a strong literary message. As recognized in other studies, the purpose of ancient genealogies was to establish identity and status by relating those named to one another. Here the connection begins with Adam, the first human and ancestor of the entire human race. It continues through all those connected with the ancient line that led to Abraham and then to Jacob/Israel and all the descendants. Thus the author portrays the entire people of Israel as the people of God, who are related to one another diachronically as well as synchronically. They possess a common heritage and identity. While the role of the kings of Judah as part of the divinely ordained house of David is given significance, so is the line of high priests and the many divisions of those who serve in the temple. This gives a value and importance to the many who serve in the Jerusalem temple after the exile, in the era when 1–2 Chronicles was written.

With the emphasis that this work places on temple worship, it is not surprising that this emphasis is a key part of the narratives attached to David and to Solomon. Saul, Israel's first king, needs only to die to set the stage for the kingship of David. Even though David lives in the pretemple era and does not participate directly in building the temple, lengthy sections of Chronicles are devoted to the preparations that he makes in bringing together the natural resources and the people of Israel for the construction and functioning of the temple. He charges Solomon with completing the task, and Solomon undertakes this: the preponderance of text devoted to his reign is concerned with the temple and his prayer of dedication.

The succeeding kings are evaluated by, among other things, the manner in which they support and encourage worship at the temple. While many of the events of their reigns are also found in 1–2 Kings, there are distinctive elements in 1–2 Chronicles that generate an emphasis on the temple and Jerusalem. For example, King Jehoshaphat undertakes judicial reform as part of his reign; the key emphasis is on teaching the torah, the law of Yahweh, so that all Judah will know God's will and follow it. This is accompanied by the appointment of judges, who are admonished to judge all people with fairness (2 Chron. 19:4–11). There immediately follows a vast coalition of enemies to the east and south who come together to destroy Judah (2 Chron. 20).

Jehoshaphat brings together the people of Judah in order to fast and pray to God at the temple. There he reminds God of all that he has done for Judah and how the enemies attack in an unprovoked manner. The king calls on God to judge the enemies. The spirit of Yahweh then comes upon Jahaziel, a Levite and descendant of the special line of Asaph, so key in the worship of God in the temple, according to the Chronicler. Yahweh promises that he will fight for Judah and that their role will be to witness it (as at the Red Sea in Exod. 14–15). After worshiping and praising God some more, the Judeans leave early in the morning. Jehoshaphat encourages them with promises that Yahweh will be with them and then appoints men to sing praises to the holiness of Yahweh as they march. God sets his own ambushes against the enemy army, throwing them into confusion so that they turn on and destroy one another. When the Judeans arrive, they find only corpses and plunder, enough of the latter that it takes three days to gather it. They regather on the fourth day and march back to Jerusalem, praising God with psalms and musical instruments. Their journey ends where it has begun, at the temple. When Judah's neighbors hear of this, the fear of Yahweh comes on them, and no one dares to challenge Jehoshaphat the rest of his life.

As Knoppers observes, this entire story is set in a literary form characteristic of the battles that Yahweh fights against Israel's opponents.[14] Its origins go back to the first battles against Egypt (Exod. 14–15), and it continues throughout the nation's history. The Jerusalem temple is a symbol of not only the nation at worship before God but also the beginning and end of God's greatest battles on behalf of his people. This literary form, like the book of which it is a part, provides a theological message for the postexilic community, who would be the first to read and hear the book. The God who created and redeemed Israel from its enemy at the exodus from Egypt is the same God to whom Jehoshaphat can pray and from whom he can receive the same sort of victory from overwhelming numbers of enemies. This is the same God to whom the present community can pray at the temple in Jerusalem, the same God who can act again to preserve and protect them from their enemies.

Gender and Ideological Criticism

As in the above observations, many of the narratives in 1–2 Chronicles are found elsewhere. This is true of virtually every genealogy and story that addresses gender, whether Timna and Tamar in the first chapter, or Bathsheba, Athaliah, and Huldah in the later chapters. It is, however, significant that women appear throughout the two books. The effect is to place them in a similar position as that found in the other narrative books of the Old Testament. Both genders remain an essential part of Israel's history and worship.

The same observations may be made regarding ideological interpretations. Nevertheless, as mentioned above, the presence of genealogies in the first nine chapters and of distinctive narratives not found in 1–2 Kings or elsewhere provides opportunity for an ideological approach reflecting circumstances not unlike those of the small postexilic Jerusalem community, surrounded by the threats of a much larger empire of which they were a part. Thus Fook-Kong Wong describes the situation of the Chinese Christians in Hong Kong

14. Knoppers, "Jerusalem at War."

in the years following the transfer of the colony back to mainland control.[15] The genealogies of the first nine chapters of 1 Chronicles provide an identity for the Jewish returnees in Jerusalem. Such a need existed in the Hong Kong that Wong describes. The turbulent times involved the loss of honor from providing for one's family. There was an increasing alienation between family members. The vast genealogy of Chronicles reminds Chinese Christians of the need to connect again with family and with their Christian family. It reminds the reader of the great importance of the people of God as a family of God, dependent on one another for encouragement, respect, support, and the mutual connections that give believers new life.

For many righteous kings of Judah, the same is true of the additions to their narratives. Again and again, these unique accounts describe how God miraculously intervenes to save his people from the elimination of their king and nation. As seen in the story of Jehoshaphat in 2 Chronicles 20, to cite but one example, the willingness to surrender all to God in faith, worship, and praise allows him to work and bring about victory, where none is reasonably expected. Wherever there is the threat of materialism, as Wong finds in Hong Kong, or anything else that would tempt one to shift focus from absolute reliance on God alone, this must be resisted in order to allow God to work.

Ancient Near Eastern Context

The first nine chapters of 1 Chronicles represent a distinct set of genealogies. Elsewhere in the Bible most genealogies tend to follow a fixed form and constitute a single line. Thus Genesis 5 begins with Adam and ends with Noah, where each generation has a single person named in the father-to-son sequence. The same occurs on the line from Shem to Abram in Genesis 11:10–26. Except at the beginning and the end of the lines, there are few notes to interrupt the repetitive nature of the account. Of the two examples mentioned here, there is only one deviation in the middle of a genealogy. That is the account of Enoch in Genesis 5:22–24. Otherwise there are no notes.

First Chronicles 1–9 is different. It is far larger, more complex, and more varied than the other genealogies in the Bible. While parts of it are linear, other sections include brothers and sisters, wives and mothers, and people whose relationship is not always clearly defined. There are many more notes scattered throughout the work. The occupations of individuals become more important, not least the lines of kings and high priests.

Comparisons with ancient Near Eastern king lists, the customary genre to compare with genealogies of more than three or four generations in the Bible, also should be made.[16] These are lists of kings and occasionally priests. They

15. Wong, "1 and 2 Chronicles."

16. See further on this material in Hess, "Genealogies."

include primarily names, sometimes with indications of the lengths of their reigns. Little or no relational or kinship information is passed along between the names. The one exception is the recurring emphasis on sonship in some of the genealogies. This is a clue as to a major difference between most ancient Near Eastern king lists and most biblical genealogies, including those of 1 Chronicles. If they don't actually move back in time, they do emphasize the past with the references to "son of" that may recur. The Sumerian King List and other Babylonian and Assyrian royal genealogies argue for the legitimacy of the king as in the proper succession of predecessors who are traced back to the beginning or earliest known times of the kingdom. The picture is different with the biblical genealogies, including those of 1 Chronicles 1–9. Here the emphasis is on the larger family of Israel and its connection with the family of humanity. This is clear in the first chapter, where everything begins with Adam. While lists of kings and priests do appear, they are always within the context of the larger family. Beginning with David, the kings of Judah constitute a single dynasty and therefore a single family. This resembles the Assyrian King List, which constitutes a single dynasty. The same is true of the line of high priests as well as the lists of temple personnel, musicians, and others. The overall picture is one of a great family united and worshiping God generation after generation, from the creation until the Chronicler's present day. Thus 1 Chronicles 1–9 looks back in time to the grand heritage of Israel, yet it also looks forward in time to the ongoing worship and praise of the one eternal God. In this manner there is a difference from the other ancient Near Eastern genealogies, which are primarily concerned with the past and the legitimacy it can offer to the present. While that is present in Chronicles, it is not primary. That concern is to teach the generations that are alive of who they are (their heritage) and especially of where they are going. It therefore serves as an identity for the whole postexilic nation centered in Jerusalem around the temple.

A second area of comparison with this unique element in Chronicles is the larger structure of the genealogies within the book. While these texts have notes and elaborations within them, they also form a conscious introduction to the remainder of the book. Some of the implications have already been discussed in the preceding paragraphs. However, the overall structure of a large section made up entirely of names in genealogical form, followed by narrative in the second part, is unique within the biblical canon. Thus the genealogies consist of 407 verses, while the remainder of 1–2 Chronicles includes 1,357 verses. So the genealogies are about 30 percent of the total. The same is true of the two ancient king lists that remain closest to the West Semitic culture of the biblical world: the Hammurabi Dynasty King List and the Ugarit King List. The Hammurabi Dynasty King List (*COS* 1.134:461–63) includes nineteen names, followed by the kings of the First Dynasty of Babylon (the Hammurabi Dynasty, ca. 1894–1595 BC), and then a list of other royal houses. The description that follows demonstrates that this tablet was written for a funerary cult in which the spirits of the dead were given offerings. Their names were also recited. The point here is that there is a genealogical element as well as a prose element to the tablet, indicating that the two were combined for religious purposes. The Ugaritic King List (*COS* 1.104:356–57) provides a list of the kings of that Late Bronze Age city (ca. 1550–1170 BC) in chronological order. A note of divinity in front of each name suggests that (1) the king was deified after his death or (2) the reference is to the personal god of the king. In any case, the list of rulers on one side of the cuneiform tablet is then supplemented by a psalm on the other side that describes how music performed with tambourines and flutes was dedicated to a god with the epithet "the Pleasant One" (Ugaritic *nʿm*). Like the structure of Chronicles, both texts include a genealogy with a description that connects it to religious, cultic, and musical functions. Thus these genealogies provide examples of how worship was associated with genealogies more than a millennium before the composition of 1–2 Chronicles.

A final note regarding the genealogies turns the focus away from ancient Near Eastern comparisons and looks at the early example of a Greek genealogy, that of the Greek Catalog of Women.[17] This work is preserved in fragments. It seems to be set in its final form sometime in the sixth century BC. The catalog begins with an age in which male gods produced offspring through female mortals. It claims that this took place before the Trojan War. As the lines are followed after that war, the focus moves to a separation of the demigods from mortals and how this provided the background for the names of towns and regions in the Greek-speaking world and beyond. This genealogy and that of 1 Chronicles 1–9 are not only connected by their close proximity in time and their interest in reflecting more than kings. Like the Chronicles list, the Greek Catalog includes more than one name for each generation. It also includes names that are connected with regions, such as tribes and even towns, like those found in the offspring of Manasseh. There individual names become connected with towns in the region. However, the genealogies of the Greek Catalog include other groups of people, even mythical ones. Further, they suggest an origin of the different peoples from various unions of different deities and mortal families. So there is no commonality to all humanity. This remains unlike the genealogies of 1 Chronicles 1–9, where Israel, like all peoples (cf. Gen. 10), comes from the common origins of Adam and the line through Noah. This basic equality is fundamental, even in texts such as 1–2 Chronicles that prize the pedigrees of priests, kings, Levites, and others. Despite this, they remain part of all humanity, not an exclusive, privileged race. The priesthood serves Israel, who seeks to represent the true worship of

17. Further discussion can be found in ibid., 69–71. For the publication of the Greek Catalog, see M. West, *Hesiodic Catalogue of Women*.

God in the world. For this reason, as in 1 Kings 8, when Solomon dedicates the temple with his prayer, that prayer includes a concern for non-Israelites and foreigners, that in praying toward the temple they might find the true God, who answers prayers (2 Chron. 6:32–33). Thus both sets of genealogies provide distinctives that serve to introduce some of the most important values for the Greek and Jewish peoples.

Beyond this, one may point to the additional detail that Chronicles provides regarding the materials that David obtains in preparation for building the temple. Although Victor Hurowitz views much of this as "midrashic," a review of the Mesopotamian and Hittite temple-building accounts suggests that such material has parallels in the ancient world and should not be understood necessarily as a later addition.[18] This includes the identification of the site for the temple as well as David's preparations and the divisions of the work and temple service (1 Chron. 21:18–26:32). See "Ancient Near Eastern Context" for 1–2 Kings.

Canonical Context

Many of the major canonical references elsewhere in the Hebrew Bible (and in 1 Esdras of the Apocrypha) have been noticed in the "Overview of 1 and 2 Chronicles" (above). The diversity of quotations, elaborations, reworkings, and other methods of utilizing existing biblical texts, as well as influencing other texts, has been observed in "Literary Readings" (above). The Chronicler has created a book that tells the story of Israel in a special way and in doing so develops sources found elsewhere in the Old Testament.

The genealogies of 1 Chronicles 1–9 anticipate summaries and an extension of the line of Adam through Abraham and David in Matthew 1:1–17 and Luke 3:23–38. Otherwise, there are virtually no direct references to Chronicles in the New Testament, at least none where the text has not already been cited in an earlier biblical book. An exception occurs in 2 Chronicles 20:7, where Jehoshaphat prays for deliverance from the great enemies that threaten Judah and Jerusalem. He recalls God's great deeds of the past on behalf of his people. This includes the gift of the land "forever to the descendants of your friend Abraham." James 2:23 recalls this epithet of Abraham as "the friend of God" in using his life and faith as an illustration of the importance of actions that are in accord with one's words and beliefs.

Theological Perspectives of 1 and 2 Chronicles

Much of the theological content has already been considered in the above discussions, especially regarding "Higher Criticism" and "Literary Readings."

18. Hurowitz, *I Have Built You*, 25, 106–7.

Here it is important to add three key emphases that should be considered as part of the book's message: Israel united as a worshiping community, the temple as the place for meeting God on earth, and the personal work of God in the lives of key figures to bring about repentance and restoration.

The emphasis on all Israel begins with the genealogies (see "Ancient Near Eastern Context," above). The many names stress the presence of pre-Israel, going back to Adam and continuing in each generation of the history of the world until Jacob/Israel and his children. A cascade of names follows, in which the tribes and their representatives are named, beginning with Judah and the line of David, and focusing on the priests and Levites and their cities amid the tribal genealogies. First Chronicles 9 concludes the genealogies with a list of the returnees from exile, creating the effect of bringing the people of God, generation by generation, from the beginning until the present day. The stories of David and Solomon stress the presence of all Israel from the time David becomes king (1 Chron. 11:1–3) and through the movement of the ark, the defeat of enemies with Israel's army, the promise of an eternal covenant with David to rule over the house of Israel, the preparations for the temple, the divisions of the military and civil administration, and David's charge to Solomon before all the people. The many names of heroic warriors, of priests and temple personnel, and of administrative officials reinforce the presence of the whole nation and its representatives working and bearing witness together. This powerful picture of the unity of God's people continues into 2 Chronicles and Solomon's administration in the first nine chapters. The sacrifices that begin his reign, the final preparations and construction of the temple, the sacrifices and prayers of dedication, and the glorious wealth and fame of his kingdom all define and engage the whole nation of Israel. As already observed, the division of the kingdom is marked by a recognition that this divides the people into Israelites in the north and in the south (2 Chron. 10:1–11:4). This division, however, will not be healed by the wars of Abijah and Asa (2 Chron. 12–16), or by alliances with wicked kings of the north (18:1–19:3). Such compromise can endanger the existence of Judah as a community that worships Yahweh (22:10–23:21) and requires faithful stewards to hide, preserve, and fight for the rightful king in the line of David. If all Israel is to be united, it must be in the proper worship before God, as the great Passover of Hezekiah (2 Chron. 30) and the even greater one of Josiah (35:1–19) illustrate. As the final years of the kingdom of Judah appear to constrict the land and numbers of Israel, until finally the remaining people are taken and scattered, so the proclamation of Cyrus at the end of the book (36:23) identifies "whoever among you from all of his people whom Yahweh their God is with, let them [lit., "him"] go up" (RSH). The conclusion thus envisions the return and reunion of all Israel in Jerusalem, centered on the temple.

The centrality of the temple in 1–2 Chronicles forms one of the most obvious themes to the reader of these books. The genealogies of the first part of

Chronicles anticipate the nature and function of the temple by naming the line of priests and the Levites who served in Jerusalem, and in other priestly centers throughout the country (1 Chron. 6:1–81). The temple's location in Jerusalem and specifically at the threshing floor of Araunah (11:4–9; 21:18–22:1), the movement of the ark to Jerusalem (13:1–14; 15:1–16:3), the worship of God (16:4–43), the preparations for building the temple (22:2–19), and the appointments of priests, Levites, and other temple personnel (23:1–26:32)—all these provide the background for David's charge to Solomon (1 Chron. 28), his charge to the leadership (29:1–9), and his last recorded time of worship and praise (29:10–20). Solomon continues the preparations for the temple and then constructs it (2 Chron. 2–3). Further temple furnishings (4:1–5:1), the placement of the ark in the temple (5:2–14), Solomon's address and prayer of dedication (6:1–42), and his sacrifices and celebration (7:1–10)—these all, at the center of 1–2 Chronicles, continue to provide focus on the temple. As Solomon's prayer and the subsequent promises by Yahweh indicate, the temple has become the symbol of God's presence so that all who respect it and revere it will receive God's blessing.

Thus the sin of Rehoboam in turning from God results in Shishak's invasion and the stripping of the wealth of the temple (2 Chron. 12:1–12). Nearly half of the 256 occurrences of "house of Yahweh" in the Old Testament appear in 1–2 Chronicles. Of these, more than sixty-five appearances may be found in the final chapters of 2 Chronicles, those that begin with Rehoboam and continue through the remainder of the book. It is Jehoshaphat's prayer from the temple courts that brings about God's promise of a miraculous victory (20:1–30). It is Hezekiah's temple gifts and service (2 Chron. 31) that follow the Passover at the temple and precede the miraculous deliverance of Judah and the temple from the Assyrian king (32:1–23). It is the cleaning and repair of the temple that leads to the discovery of the book of the law and the reform and Passover celebration of Josiah (34:1–35:19). At the end of the monarchy, the Babylonian destruction is capped by the burning of the temple and the theft of the temple treasures (36:18–19). Finally, the focus of Cyrus's edict is on the reconstruction of the temple in Jerusalem (36:23). From beginning to end, Chronicles remains concerned with the temple. More than in Samuel or Kings, this structure symbolizes Israel worshiping God in Chronicles. It is from this worship that the people of God derive their strength and witness for ministry and mission to the world in which they find themselves. It is to this worship that the people of God turn to find the relationship for which the human race, beginning with Adam, was created.

The third area of theological interest is that of repentance and restoration. This concern has been misunderstood as a focus on the immediate retribution. However, it seems that the repeated engagement of people with God is less interested in how quickly the cause leads to the effect than it is in the

Achan and Achar

First Chronicles 2:7 incidentally refers to "Achar, bringer of trouble to Israel when he violated the ban" (RSH). This refers to the events of Joshua 7, where he is called Achan. At the conquest of Jericho, Achan/Achar took some valuables from Jericho even though God had commanded that everything should be destroyed or otherwise dedicated to him. As a result, God did not allow Israel to win its battle against Ai. When Joshua learned of the sin, Achan's guilt was identified by lot. He and his family (Did they know of these valuables hidden in their tent and remain quiet?) were executed after he confessed his sin. The note in Chronicles illustrates the tendency of this genealogy, like others, to insert notes as items of information that further identify the nature and purpose of the genealogy.

Another feature here is the wordplay that allows for an alteration of the name itself. In the Hebrew of Joshua 7, the name Achan appears. However, in the Septuagint of Joshua and of 1 Chronicles 2, the name Achar is used. The Masoretic Hebrew of 1 Chronicles 2 agrees with the Septuagint and reads Achar. While there is not much difference between an "n" and an "r" in Hebrew writing, the consistent spelling of this name makes it unlikely to be due to a scribe mistaking one character for the other. Achan is not related to any known Hebrew root or other name. However, this name, or an identically sounding form, does appear in the second-millennium West Semitic town of Alalakh, today in southern Turkey.

"Achar," on the contrary, is a term that is never used elsewhere as a personal name. Nevertheless, it has a good Hebrew root meaning "to bring trouble." The use of "Achar" in 1 Chronicles 2:7 (MT, LXX) creates a wordplay: "Achar who *achared* Israel." Thus the name as it appears in 1 Chronicles serves the wordplay as a nickname. Such alteration exemplifies one small picture of the Chronicler's skill in a distinctive interpretation of the history of Israel in the genealogies.[a]

[a] See Hess, "Achan."

extent to which conversion takes place.[19] Even in the genealogies, the notes reflect the warning of a figure such as Achar (1 Chron. 2:7; wordplay meaning "trouble," for Achan in Josh. 7) and the reversal of bad things in the figure of Jabez (1 Chron. 4:9–10). His name, meaning "pain," was reversed into blessing by his faithful prayer.

The notes about David's warriors reflect their devotion to their king (1 Chron. 11:10–12:40), just as David himself focuses on his love and devotion

19. Throntveit, "Chronicles," 130; Kelly, *Retribution and Eschatology*.

toward God and the eternal covenant that results (1 Chron. 13–17). The promise, however, depends on the faithfulness of each of his offspring. David seeks God in 1 Chronicles, and Solomon does the same in 2 Chronicles, above all in the construction of the temple, as already mentioned. Yahweh's appearance and promise and warning to Solomon form the heart of the message of the books. Nowhere is this more true than in 2 Chronicles 7:14:

> If my people who are called by my name
> will humble themselves,
> will pray,
> will seek my face,
> will turn from their evil ways;
> then
> I will hear from heaven,
> will forgive their sin,
> and will heal their land. (RSH)

This forms the key for the people of God. In emphasizing the fulfillment of this promise, the kings of the line of Judah are presented in a more positive light than they appear in the books of Kings. Abijah's speech to the north denouncing their abandonment of God's place of worship and priesthood leads to Judah's victory over Israel, despite being outflanked and outnumbered (2 Chron. 13:1–20). Jehoshaphat's prayer to God, reminding God of his faithfulness, leads to the famous victory against the huge eastern army in 2 Chronicles 20. Again, the victories of Hezekiah and Josiah are directly connected with their faithful lives. More dramatic than any, however, is the repentance of Manasseh after a life of unsurpassed wickedness in 2 Chronicles 33:1–20. His repentance in exile and his return and restoration of the true worship of God anticipate the experience of Judah: its wickedness, its going to Babylon in exile, and its repentance and return to Jerusalem, where the temple is rebuilt and a new opportunity for proper worship of God is renewed. So Cyrus's offer for the people of God to return to Jerusalem and rebuild concludes the books of Chronicles (2 Chron. 36:23) with the final word—actually, a command: "Let them go up!" Repentance and the gracious restoration of divine favor continue to be the principle by which the people of God live in a sinful world.

Key Commentaries and Studies

Japhet, Sara. *I and II Chronicles: A Commentary.* OTL. Louisville: Westminster John Knox, 1993. An innovative and unique commentary that presents a theologically and exegetically holistic reading.

Kelly, Brian E. *Retribution and Eschatology in Chronicles.* JSOTSup 211. Sheffield: Sheffield Academic, 1996. A convincing challenge to the "immediate retribution" reading of Chronicles, focusing on its message of hope and restoration.

Knoppers, Gary N. *I Chronicles: A New Translation with Introduction and Commentary*. Vol. 1, *1–9*. Vol. 2, *10–29*. AB 12–12A. New York: Doubleday, 2003–4. The most thorough and critically aware work, with an appreciation of the historical and exegetical context.

Selman, Martin J. *1 Chronicles: An Introduction and Commentary.* TOTC. Leicester, UK: Inter-Varsity; Downers Grove, IL: InterVarsity, 1994.

———. *2 Chronicles: An Introduction and Commentary.* TOTC. Leicester, UK: Inter-Varsity; Downers Grove, IL: InterVarsity, 1994. These two volumes provide an important evangelical theological appreciation of the text.

Williamson, Hugh G. M. *1 and 2 Chronicles.* NCB. Grand Rapids: Eerdmans, 1982. A key work, positioning the book in a theological, critical, and historical context.

12

EZRA AND NEHEMIAH

How do you rebuild on ancient foundations that have been destroyed? Ezra and Nehemiah describe the rebuilding of a people and city who are threatened with destruction by both outer and inner challenges to their survival.

Name, Text, and Outline

Ezra and Nehemiah are named after two major human characters in Jerusalem of the mid-fifth century BC. Ezra was the scribe who returned to Jerusalem with a copy of the Torah and the power to enforce it on the community there. Nehemiah was the royal cupbearer who had two terms as governor in Jerusalem and rebuilt the walls of the city. Ezra derives from the Hebrew and Aramaic root *ʿzr*, meaning "help, assist." It is a shortened form of a longer name, with either a form of God or Yahweh added. Nehemiah consists of two elements, *nḥm* followed by Yahw(eh), "Yahweh comforted."

The book of Nehemiah contains first-person memoirs that claim authorship by Nehemiah. The Babylonian Talmud (*B. Bat.* 15a) holds that Ezra composed the two books as now extant. There has been little agreement beyond these testimonies. Various scholars have identified either the Chronicler or Ezra as the author of both books, while others argue for two distinct authors, such as Ezra and Nehemiah.

The Masoretic Text of the Hebrew and Aramaic is relatively well preserved for both books. The duplicated list in Ezra 2 and Nehemiah 7 contains differences that may reflect common scribal errors in copying numbers and letters that appear similar. Three fragments of Ezra (4QEzra) 4:2–11; 5:17; and 6:1–5 are all that remain of either book among the Dead Sea Scrolls.

The time of Ezra and Nehemiah

The Septuagint preserves the two books as a single work, 2 Esdras, while the Latin Vulgate identifies 1 Esdras with Ezra and 2 Esdras with Nehemiah. The Septuagint also preserves a book named 1 Esdras in its tradition (3 Esdras in the Vulgate). This work contains a paraphrase of 2 Chronicles 35–36, all of Ezra, and Nehemiah 7:73–8:12. It also adds a tale about Darius's bodyguards not found in the Masoretic Text. There is no targum to Ezra or Nehemiah. Apart from Daniel, Ezra is the only book containing significant sections in Aramaic: 4:8–6:18 and 7:12–26.

As in the Septuagint, the Masoretic Text also regards Ezra and Nehemiah as a single work. However, the early Christian canonical attestation of Melito of Sardis (ca. AD 170) recognizes two books. The division was recognized by Origen and codified by Jerome in his Vulgate translation.

OUTLINE

I. Return from Exile and Rebuilding the Temple (Ezra 1:1–6:22)
   A. Return of the Exiles (1:1–11)
      1. Proclamation of Cyrus (1:1–4)
      2. Return under Sheshbazzar (1:5–11)
   B. List of Returnees (2:1–70)
   C. Early Rebuilding (3:1–13)
      1. Altar (3:1–3)
      2. Feast of Tabernacles (3:4–6)
      3. Foundation of the Temple (3:7–13)
   D. Opposition (4:1–23)
      1. Reign of Cyrus (4:1–5)
      2. Reign of Xerxes (4:6)
      3. Reign of Artaxerxes (4:7–23)
   E. Temple Completed (4:24–6:22)
      1. Reign of Darius (4:24)
      2. Haggai and Zechariah (5:1–2)
      3. Opposition and Darius's Order (5:3–6:12)
      4. Completion and Dedication (6:13–18)
      5. Passover (6:19–22)

II. Ezra (7:1–10:44)
   A. Return to Jerusalem (7:1–8:36)
   B. Foreign Wives (9:1–10:44)

III. Nehemiah's First Governorship in Jerusalem: Security (Neh. 1:1–7:4)
   A. News and Nehemiah's Response (1:1–11)
   B. Royal Permission and Journey (2:1–10)
   C. Inspection and Encouragement (2:11–20)
   D. List of Wall Builders (3:1–32)
   E. Opposition of Sanballat and Tobiah (4:1–23 [3:33–4:17 MT])
   F. Nehemiah Cares for the Poor (5:1–19)
   G. Further Opposition (6:1–14)
   H. Completion of the Wall and External Threats (6:15–19)
   I. Dealing with the Threats (7:1–4)

IV. Nehemiah's First Governorship in Jerusalem: Social and Religious Order (7:5–12:47)
   A. List of Returnees (7:5–73a)
   B. Ezra's Preaching and Reform (7:73b–10:39)
      1. Preaching the Torah (7:73b–8:12)
      2. Feast of Tabernacles (8:13–18)

        3. Fasting and Prayer (9:1–37)
        4. Agreement and Signatories (9:38–10:29 [10:1–30 MT])
        5. Provisions to Maintain the Temple (10:30–39 [10:31–40 MT])
    C. Residents to Live in Jerusalem and in Towns (11:1–36)
        1. Jerusalem (11:1–24)
        2. Neighboring Towns (11:25–36)
    D. Priests and Levites (12:1–26)
    E. Dedication of the Wall (12:27–43)
    F. Temple Service (12:44–47)
V. Nehemiah's Second Governorship in Jerusalem (13:1–31)
    A. Problems (13:1–5)
    B. Return (13:6–7)
    C. Reforms (13:8–31)

Overview of Ezra and Nehemiah

Ezra begins with the proclamation of Cyrus in his first year, which fulfills the word of Yahweh spoken by Jeremiah. King Cyrus of the Persian Empire recognizes that Yahweh is God and has given him the dominion. God has also appointed Cyrus to build his temple in Jerusalem. Therefore Cyrus commands any of God's people who so desire to go up to Jerusalem and the remainder to assist with support. Led by Sheshbazzar, those who return to Jerusalem bring with them articles of the temple that were seized by Nebuchadnezzar, who destroyed the earlier temple. Some 5,400 items of gold and silver were removed and taken. Ezra 2 (= Neh. 7) provides a list of all of those who first return to Jerusalem according to their families. In addition to Israelites in general, there are priests, Levites, musicians, gatekeepers, temple servants, and civil officials who can trace their connection to the officers of Solomon, and others. The first concern of the returnees is to build an altar where, from the first day of the seventh month (September/October), the priests begin to offer the daily sacrifices that are demanded by God (Ezra 3).

The people lay the foundation of the temple and proceed to praise God and to worship him. There are great shouts of joy mixed in with the weeping of those who are older and remember the past glory of the earlier temple. In Ezra 4 the enemies of the people of God come to Jerusalem and offer to assist. However, the Jews will not allow that. So the attacks on Jerusalem begin as letters written during the reigns of the Persian kings Xerxes (Ahasuerus) and Artaxerxes I. The latter's research confirms the rebellious nature of Jerusalem, and so he orders temple construction to be halted.

During the reign of Darius, the temple construction had been stopped. At the encouragement of the prophets Haggai and Zechariah, the people

© Ritmeyer Archaeological Design

Replica of the second temple as renovated by Herod

resume the construction. The regional government objects and sends a letter to Darius, informing him that the people in Jerusalem claim to have permission from Cyrus to reconstruct the destroyed temple (Ezra 5). Darius investigates the matter and concludes that his predecessor Cyrus indeed authorized the rebuilding. So he orders it to go forward without interference and with support from the royal treasury (Ezra 6). With the encouragement of the prophets Haggai and Zechariah, the temple is completed in Darius's sixth year. The priests and Levites are installed in their temple service, and the Passover is celebrated.

Ezra, of the priestly line of Aaron, arrives at Jerusalem in the reign of King Artaxerxes I of Persia (Ezra 7). In the seventh year of Artaxerxes I, Ezra brings the law of Moses, authority and resources from the Persian king, and priests and Levites. The king orders Ezra to teach all the people of the region concerning the law of Yahweh and to punish whoever does not obey. Following a list of those who accompany him (Ezra 8), Ezra describes how he assembles those who make the journey in Babylon. They fast and pray for a safe journey since they are traveling without armed escort from the Persians. God graciously grants them a safe journey in their four months of travel through the summer. They sacrifice burnt offerings when they arrive. The leaders inform Ezra of the intermarriages that Jews have made with other people around them (Ezra 9). When Ezra hears this, he tears his hair and beard, and also his

© Baker Publishing Group and Dr. James C. Martin

Part of the wall in Jerusalem dating back to Nehemiah

tunic and robe. He sits appalled at the sin and confesses it before God. Others gather around him and begin weeping (Ezra 10). Ezra continues to fast and proclaim a convocation of all who live in Judah and Benjamin. They gather, hear his charge against them, consider his challenge for them to separate themselves from foreign wives, and agree to do so. By the first day of the first month, the elders have decided all the cases involved, in terms of both the foreign wives and the children involved.

Nehemiah's book begins with one of his friends informing him of the vulnerable state of Jerusalem, with its wall broken. Nehemiah fasts and prays, confessing the sins of his people and asking that he might receive a favorable reply from his request to the king. As cupbearer for Artaxerxes I, Nehemiah gives him his wine, but the king notices his sad face and asks for an explanation (Neh. 2). Nehemiah speaks to the king, prays again to God, and asks the king for permission to go to Jerusalem and to rebuild it. The king grants his request for passports, an armed escort, and access to the timber and resources necessary to rebuild the walls. When Nehemiah arrives, he tours the walls at night and then asks the Jewish leaders of Jerusalem to assist him. They agree, yet their neighbors (Sanballat, Tobiah, and Geshem) mock them. Nehemiah 3 describes the work squads and where along the wall they labor to repair it. When mockery from those neighbors does not stop their work, the enemies of the Jews plot to attack them suddenly and kill them (Neh. 4). However, Nehemiah stations half the men with weapons as guards day and night. They work on the wall from first light until the stars appear. They always keep their weapons with them.

Nehemiah 5 records the concerns of the poor among the people of God. The wealthy are charging their brothers and sisters interest so that they cannot earn enough to eat and have to sell family members into debt slavery. When Nehemiah hears this, he brings the nobles and officials together and makes them take an oath not to charge interest but to return what they have so extorted. They do as they have promised. Nehemiah himself does not take the governor's portion or tax from the people. Nevertheless, he feeds some 150 fellow Jews as well as visitors at his table. He does this for the twelve years of his governorship.

Sanballat and Geshem try to lure Nehemiah into an ambush in the valley of Ono (Neh. 6:1–14). He suspects them and says he cannot leave the wall-building project. Four times they try this, and each time he refuses. Sanballat tries to intimidate Nehemiah by threatening to tell Artaxerxes that he is plotting a revolt. Nehemiah will not be intimidated. His enemies hire Shemaiah to try to convince him to hide in the temple, an act that would discredit Nehemiah before the Jews. Nehemiah refuses. Tobiah uses the nobles in Jerusalem who are obligated to him to intimidate Nehemiah, but the letters and plots fail. The walls are completed, and loyal gatekeepers and officials are appointed to keep them barred each day until the sun is hot (6:15–7:4).

Nehemiah finds the list of the original returnees and reproduces it (Neh. 7:6–73 = Ezra 2:1–70). In the seventh month, Ezra, the teacher of the law, brings out the book of the law of Moses (Neh. 8). On the first day all the Israelites gather at the Water Gate, and Ezra reads from the book from daybreak until noon. He stands on a wooden platform above the people. The Levites read from the book of the law and explain or translate it. Ezra and Nehemiah instruct the people to consecrate the day and to celebrate with food and drink. They celebrate the Feast of Tabernacles in a festival that is as great as any since Israel first entered the land under Joshua. For seven days, Ezra reads from the book of the law, and on the eighth day they hold an assembly.

The people of Israel gather again at the same place on the twenty-fourth day of the same month (Neh. 9). Wearing sackcloth and with fasting and weeping, they confess their sins and the sins of their ancestors. The prayer rehearses the great deeds of God as creator of the world, redeemer of Israel, and their lawgiver and protector. The sins of the people are also rehearsed, from the gold-calf rebellion through the times of the judges and kings. Israel has not listened to the prophets and has abandoned the God who blessed them with the land. So their descendants have become slaves and oppressed in the same land. Therefore, the people enter a renewed covenant with God. Those who so agree are named (Neh. 10) along with specifics about the laws they will obey. This includes the abandonment of intermarriages with those of mixed ancestry ("the peoples of the land," 10:28–31), the maintenance of the Sabbath for all, and the giving of tithes, offerings, and firstfruits. In order to repopulate Jerusalem and maintain its security, the leaders and a tenth of the remaining people are chosen to live there (Neh. 11). The names of leaders, gatekeepers, and other officials follow. The towns where the Jewish people live throughout Judah and Benjamin are described. The text lists names of priests and Levites who have first returned from exile, as well as later generations to the time of Nehemiah and Ezra (Neh. 12). At the dedication of the walls of Jerusalem, the leaders and two choirs position themselves on those walls and offer God praise and worship. Gifts, firstfruits, and tithes are gathered into the storehouses for the portions of the priests, musicians, gatekeepers, and Levites.

After some time away from Jerusalem to serve Artaxerxes, king of Babylon, Nehemiah returns (Neh. 13). When he comes to Jerusalem, he finds Tobiah living in a temple storeroom. Nehemiah removes all Tobiah's possessions and purifies the room. He brings the Levites and musicians back from the fields where they have been working because they are not receiving their assigned portions. Nehemiah rebukes the officials, and Judah again brings offerings to the temple. He also closes Jerusalem during the Sabbath so that no business can be conducted. He eliminates the mixed marriages that have been reintroduced. He purifies the priests and Levites.

Nehemiah closes his book with a refrain that is repeated throughout his book: "Remember me with favor, my God" (13:31 NIV).

Reading Ezra and Nehemiah

Premodern Readings

The use of Ezra–Nehemiah in the pre-Christian writings of 1–2 Esdras has been mentioned (see "Name, Text, and Outline," above). Judaism credits Ezra with establishing the Great Assembly, a group of scholars who passed on the Torah and the traditions of the faith until the emergence of the Sanhedrin. This was the authoritative body on matters of Jewish law. They established the practice of Torah reading, the Amidah prayer at the center of Jewish liturgy, and the Feast of Purim. Ezra was considered to be as knowledgeable in the law as any and comparable to Moses in this. Nehemiah was regarded as a eunuch (rather than a cupbearer) by the Septuagint. Rabbinic literature finds fault with him in his repeated prayer to be remembered with favor, which is considered boastful, and for his disparagement of his predecessors (Neh. 5:15).

In Christianity, the patristic period produced virtually nothing on Ezra and Nehemiah. The first detailed and systematic commentary available is that of the Venerable Bede (ca. 672–735).[1] He focuses on verses that provide the best material for moral, allegorical, and typological interpretation; Bede extends this approach to virtually every text in Ezra–Nehemiah.[2] In his commentary on Ezra 7:7–10, Bede identifies Ezra as a type of Christ in terms of his name, which means "helper"; how believers are freed from tribulations and captivity as the people come back from Babylon to Jerusalem; giving money and vessels to God for the glory of his temple; and exercising authority to remove the foreigners.[3]

1. Lüthi, *Bauleute Gottes*.
2. Conti and Pilara, *1–2 Kings*, xxviii.
3. Ibid., 321.

Bede compares Nehemiah's nighttime inspection of the walls (Neh. 2:11–18) with Christian teachers who arise at night to discern the state of the church ravaged by sin and to determine how to repair and to rebuild it.[4] The ruins symbolize lives ruined by earthly desires. Those who should have been vigilant in teaching have become lazy. Referring to Nehemiah 9:3 and the act of reading from the law four times each day and four times each night, Bede comments:

> From this example, I think, a most beautiful custom has developed in the church, namely, that through each hour of daily psalmody a passage from Old or New Testament is recited by heart for all to hear, and thus strengthened by the words of the apostles or the prophets, they bend their knees to perseverance in prayer, but also at night, when people cease from the labors of doing good works, they turn willing ears to listen to divine readings. (*On Ezra and Nehemiah* 3.28)[5]

Throughout the later periods of Christian history, Nehemiah has remained a model of faith in the midst of adversity. Whether Walter Lüthi's sermons on rebuilding Jerusalem as rebuilding Europe after the destruction of World War II, Cyril Barber's model of Nehemiah as a model for management and leadership psychology, or present movements that use imagery from rebuilding the walls and Nehemiah's success in this to represent the mission of their vision for the people of God—in all these cases the text has continued to play a role in encouragement and as an example of leadership and of hope amid ruins.[6]

Higher Criticism

On the question of the relationship between Ezra–Nehemiah and 1–2 Chronicles, see "Higher Criticism" for 1–2 Chronicles. A question directly connected to Ezra and Nehemiah is the historical issue of who came first. Nehemiah appears to have arrived in Jerusalem for his first governorship in the twentieth year of the Persian king Artaxerxes I, which would be 445 BC (Neh. 1:1; 2:1; 5:14). If Ezra arrived in the seventh year of the same king, that would identify him as present before the time of Nehemiah (Ezra 7:7–8). This is a traditional understanding of the text and does not give rise to major problems. Nehemiah was present with Ezra at the reading of the law in Nehemiah 8:9. Nehemiah appears among the covenanters in 10:1 (10:2 MT). Further, Ezra leads the procession (Neh. 12:36) that forms part of a celebration organized by Nehemiah. But if Ezra arrived before Nehemiah, why does he not appear until relatively late in Nehemiah's memoirs and governorship? Perhaps after

4. Ibid., 337.
5. Ibid., 359.
6. On Lüthi, see Childs, *Old Testament Books*, 55. See Barber, *Effective Leadership*, for an example of an early attempt (1976) to connect Nehemiah with management and leadership studies. The first half of the book is the most significant.

leading the returnees back to Jerusalem (ca. 458 BC) and beginning the religious reform that the Persian king had commanded, Ezra himself moved on or returned to Babylon. Then Nehemiah arrived later and began his governorship (ca. 445–433 BC). During this time, Ezra returned and began his second visit. Although Nehemiah departed around 433 and returned to Jerusalem around 430 BC, Ezra is not mentioned then. Perhaps he again departed.

The argument for placing Ezra later, usually in the reign of Artaxerxes II (ca. 400 BC), seeks to explain the harsher reforms that Ezra undertook by banishing foreign wives. If he did this a generation later, it would be easier to explain than at a point contemporary with Nehemiah, who seems to use milder measures. The argument looks at a certain Jehohanan son of Eliashib, who appears associated with Ezra in Ezra 10:6. Nehemiah 12:10–11 identifies a certain Jonathan who is the grandson of Eliashib. Elephantine papyri from the late fifth century BC identify the high priest in Jerusalem as Johanan, and Josephus (*Ant.* 11.297–301) describes a Johanan who murdered his brother. If all of these are the same individual, then Ezra appears at the end of the fifth century (ca. 400 BC) and not in the middle of that century. However, for this to be the case, it must be shown that (1) Ezra 10:6 incorrectly identifies J(eh)ohanan as the son of Eliashib when he is the grandson; (2) Nehemiah 12:10–11 misspells the name as Jonathan instead of J(eh)ohanan; and (3) Ezra must have associated approvingly with a known murderer. Yet there is no manuscript that supports these changes, nor is it likely that Ezra would have consorted with a murderer. Further, this theory assumes that the texts mentioning Ezra and Nehemiah together must be fabricated by a later editor. This too is speculative. Finally, the name J(eh)ohanan is common throughout this period. Fourteen individuals may possess it in the Old Testament, and Josephus mentions it seventeen times.[7] Thus it is not surprising that the majority of scholars hold to the traditional sequence and place both Ezra and Nehemiah in the middle of the fifth century. The question of how the mixed marriages were handled is not decisive since even if the two men were contemporary, there could be different emphases and different measures used to deal with the issue at different times.

Beyond this, one may consider the question of sources. The book of Ezra introduces the approach of integrating existing (often archival) documents into a larger narrative with a minimum of alteration of the originals. This is especially true insofar as the official language in which many archival documents were preserved would have been Aramaic. That many chapters and texts in Ezra are in Aramaic lends an air of antiquity and authenticity to the records, letters, and other documents found here.

The first six chapters of Ezra probably use the prophecies of Haggai and Zechariah, along with a variety of documents. The author has combined these

7. Yamauchi, "Ezra and Nehemiah," 287.

with a narrative that provides the background for the second half of the book and for Nehemiah. The book of Ezra introduces Ezra's actions. This is then interrupted with "The words of Nehemiah" (Neh. 1:1), encompassed in the first six or seven chapters of Nehemiah and resumed in the final chapter (Neh. 13). Much of chapter 7 is a list of peoples of the province found also in Ezra 2, thus bringing these two literary sections together. Nehemiah 8 returns to the Ezra story of Ezra 7–10 and describes the reading of Torah. Nehemiah 9–12 includes material drawn from various sources and lists, creating in this final section a "full synchronization of Ezra and Nehemiah and a comprehensive picture of settlement and administration during this one generation under their combined leadership."[8]

In Ezra the letter of Artaxerxes (7:12–26) has been analyzed as lacking authenticity due to its sympathetic enumeration of Jewish concerns. However, such letters could well have been formulated in consultation with the people to whom they were addressed. The question of epistolary style focuses on assumptions of being able to distinguish Persian and Hellenistic styles and on the view that this might have been reedited by a Hellenistic scribe who preserved the content. Not enough is known for definitive conclusions. Changes made by an editor working with first-person accounts and adding preserved lists from archival sources could explain the switch between persons in chapters 7–10.[9]

What is known of Nehemiah is preserved largely in the book by his name. The material here could have been written to the emperor or other officials of the Persian Empire as an account and explanation (in light of criticism from Sanballat and other sources) for his actions. In its present form it appears as memoirs of the royal cupbearer, where his focus is on his achievements as a kind of offering to God, asking God to remember him for good.[10]

Literary Readings

A literary appreciation for the complex text known as Ezra–Nehemiah might well consider the critical approaches already discussed. Here it may be useful to review the major divisions of the books, the elements that compose those literary blocks, and the structural indicators used to mark significant elements in each.[11] The major literary divisions include the first six chapters of Ezra, which provide a summary of events and people who first returned to Jerusalem after Cyrus's edict, and the progress in the building of the temple and city that followed. Chapters 7–10 begin with Ezra the scribe and priest leading a new generation of returnees eighty years later and include the expulsion of foreign women as part of the reforms implemented by Ezra. The third

8. Japhet, "Periodization," 499–500.
9. Boda, "Ezra," 277–78.
10. Williamson, *Ezra and Nehemiah*, 18–19.
11. Talmon, "Ezra and Nehemiah," 358–60.

text is the Words of Nehemiah, which constitutes chapters 1:1–7:4 and 13 of the book of Nehemiah. These describe the actions of Nehemiah in returning to Jerusalem, rebuilding the walls, and completing the book with an account of his second governorship. Nehemiah 7:5–12:47 are not as easily identified. While chapters 10–12 may constitute a resumption of Nehemiah's memoirs, the provisions for the temple, along with the personnel and the people of Israel named within and around Jerusalem, are a continuation of the preaching, celebration, and prayer and fasting that Ezra led in chapters 8–9.

For this reason chapters 8–12 are connected partly to the earlier section of Ezra and partly to that of Nehemiah. They may be discerned as a fourth section of the two books, as an integration of the work of both leaders. The joining of this effort begins already in Nehemiah 7, where the list of returnees harks back to Ezra 2 and the first section of the three or four main units. In this manner all previous elements of the books are brought together and represented in this final major section. The effect is to demonstrate how the vision of the returnees (Neh. 7:5–73a) is realized through the reading and teaching of the Torah (7:73b–8:12), the celebration of the Feast of Tabernacles (8:13–18), the repentance with fasting and prayer (9:1–37), and the covenant to enforce what has been agreed on by listing the names of all involved (9:38–10:29), making provisions to continue the temple worship (10:30–39), and naming the new generation of Jerusalem in terms of residents (11:1–24), neighbors in Judah (11:25–36), and priests and Levites (12:1–26). The closing dedication of the wall and the temple service resume and summarize the themes of the earlier sections on the work of Nehemiah and Ezra, now assumed by all the people.

Within these four sections appear four major types of texts. There are the royal proclamations and documents in Hebrew (Ezra 1:1–4) and in Aramaic (Ezra 4:17–23; 6:3–5, 6–12; 7:12–26). There are letters in Aramaic by the Persians (Ezra 4:8–16; 5:6–17) and in Hebrew by Nehemiah and Sanballat (Neh. 6:2–9). A third type of texts are the lists that recur:

temple inventories (Ezra 1:9–11; 8:24–28)
returnees (Ezra 2:2–64 [= Neh. 7:7–66]; 8:1–14)
husbands of foreign wives (Ezra 10:18–44)
wall builders (Neh. 3:1–32)
covenant signatories (Neh. 10:1–27)
settlers in Jerusalem (Neh. 11:3–24)
settlers in Judah and Benjamin (Neh. 11:25–36)

A fourth type of text relates to worship and piety:

Passover celebration (Ezra 6:19–22a)
Ezra's prayer of public confession (Ezra 9:6–15)

Nehemiah's private prayer (Neh. 1:5–11)
Ezra's public reading of the Torah (Neh. 7:73b–8:12)
Levites' words (Neh. 9:5–37)
dedication of the city walls (Neh. 12:27–43)

In addition to these elements, there are certain structural features that mark the text. Perhaps the best known is Nehemiah's request to (my) God to remember either himself or others (Neh. 5:19; 6:14; 13:22, 29, and 31). There are summaries of the lists as in Nehemiah 12:26 and 47. Other summaries appear in Ezra 4:4–5a (for 3:2–4:3); 6:13–14 (for 5:1–6:12); and Nehemiah 13:29b–31a (for 10:1–13:28).

Shemaryahu Talmon also notes the use of a device in Hebrew narrative called resumptive repetition.[12] Although not always used in this way, here it betrays the insertion of an archival document or other source. So the final phrase before the inserted document is recalled immediately after the document with the resumption of the text. Ezra 4:6–24a inserts letters and accusations from neighboring leaders to the Persian king regarding those in Jerusalem. So 4:5 reads: "They hired counselors to work against them and frustrate their plans during the entire reign of Cyrus king of Persia and down to the reign of Darius king of Persia" (NIV). This is recalled in 4:24: "Thus the work on the house of God in Jerusalem came to a standstill until the second year of the reign of Darius king of Persia" (NIV). Again the list of returnees invokes a similar device in Ezra 2 and Nehemiah 7. Compare Ezra 2:1, "Now these are the people of the province who came up from the captivity of the exiles, whom Nebuchadnezzar king of Babylon had taken captive to Babylon (they returned to Jerusalem and Judah, each to their own town)" (NIV), with 2:70, "The priests, the Levites, the singers, the gatekeepers and the temple servants settled in their own towns, along with some of the other people, and the rest of the Israelites settled in their towns" (NIV). In these ways the text is made cohesive, and key themes are repeated and developed.

Gender and Ideological Criticism

The absence of specific names of women in Ezra–Nehemiah has been noted. Only the prophetess Noadiah is mentioned (Neh. 6:14), and she appears as an enemy of Nehemiah.[13] This and the emphasis on the abolition of mixed marriages, with the removal of foreign women, has led to conclusions that the author(s) and the society in general were not interested in women and that they were misogynist.

12. Ibid., 360.
13. The same name, Noadiah, is also used of a man in Ezra 8:33.

However, Tamara Eskenazi compares the society of Ezra and Nehemiah with that of contemporary Athens, in the age of Pericles.[14] She concludes that, far from a negative view toward women, the books lay out a program of citizenship rights that promotes an egalitarianism. Contrary to some interpretations, she argues that Ezra–Nehemiah and the use of the charter of Deuteronomy for restructuring the society opposed the priestly and upper-class oligarchy. Although Jerusalem resembled other groups in the period in that it built a temple that became the focus for a renewed identity, Ezra brought a concern to enhance that identity by a commitment to Israel's God and to Torah. A key to this identity was separation from other groups as opposed to intermingling with them, as Nehemiah's enemies appear to have promoted (Neh. 2:19–20). Several aspects of the reforms erode the power of the ruling class and promote an egalitarian society. Thus this review combines the concerns of both gender and ideology.

First, there is the general empowerment of the Levites, who are always mentioned with the priests, whose names are listed, and who are given responsibilities and power in reference to the temple and the walls and gates. There is a stronger interest in the Levites in these books, as seen by the frequency of references to them, than in any other biblical texts.[15] Ezra–Nehemiah does not place the Levites in a lower status. They are regularly seen as coworkers with the priests and may reflect a Persian administrative policy that, at that particular period, favored them. Even though a priest, Ezra recruits Levites to accompany him to Jerusalem (Ezra 8:15–19), assigns them sacred responsibilities alongside the priests (8:24–30), brings charges against Levitical leaders (9:2), and identifies priests (and Levites) among those who are guilty (10:18–23).

Second, there is the elimination of mixed marriages. This victimization of women who are set aside by such measures should be balanced by the protection afforded to the other women. In immigrant communities there is social pressure to marry into higher society and outward into other groups. The biblical resistance to the latter is coupled with the charge to remain faithful (cf. Mal. 2:11–16). In the discussion of Ezra 10, the only specific statement that some men will divorce their wives occurs in 10:18–19 with reference to priests. Ezra 10:44 does not explicitly state that the wives of the other men were divorced (neither in Hebrew nor in Greek). Thus the emphasis is placed on the reform of the priesthood, something that occurs not only with Ezra but also with Nehemiah (Neh. 13:29).

This activity has parallels in Pericles's law of 451 BC for the city of Athens, occurring a few years after the law enforcement of Ezra. Pericles defined a citizen as the offspring of two citizens. Both parents had to be Athenians. As Eskenazi and others observe, this was almost certainly applied exclusively

14. Eskenazi, "Missions of Ezra and Nehemiah."

15. Min, *Levitical Authorship.*

Jewish Records Preserved through the Exile

Some scholars argue that Assyrian, Babylonian, and Persian deportations and resettlements of people in Judah, beginning in the seventh century BC, produced people in and around Jerusalem who were unrelated to the pre-seventh-century inhabitants of Palestine and who developed the "myth" of an exile and return in their biblical literature to give themselves an identity. However, this runs into conflict with the known practices of Babylonia and Persia, as exemplified in the Wadi Brisa Inscription, the Cyrus Cylinder, the Neirab archive, and Herodotus's record of the Paeonians.[a] (See plate 5 in the gallery for an image of the Cyrus Cylinder.) The Wadi Brisa Inscription, from the time of Nebuchadnezzar, records how the king, on a mission to Syria, "collected and reinstalled" the inhabitants of towns that the enemy had "scattered." This indicates that new rulers were in the practice of returning those whom the disgraced dynasty had deported. The Cyrus Cylinder states that the Persian ruler returned the deported peoples to their homeland, along with their gods. The Neirab archive represents a group from about 521 BC who identified a town in Babylonia, on the Bel-aba-usr Canal, as their own. From there this ethnic group returned to their homeland in northern Syria. They brought written records (tablets) with them from their place of deportation. Deportations continued as late as Darius I, according to Herodotus (*Hist.* 5.15; 5.98), who records how the Persians exiled the Paeonians from their homeland in Thrace to elsewhere in Asia Minor. Yet they continued to live as an identifiable entity.

[a] See *ANET* 307, 316; Hoglund, *Achaemenid Imperial Administration*, 20, 27, 238.

to males who had married foreign women, and to those of the upper class. It could have been used as a weapon against the Athenian oligarchy, just as Ezra and Nehemiah's reforms could have been directed primarily against the ruling aristocracy in Jerusalem.[16]

Although he is a priest and has a royal letter to support his authority, Ezra uses actions of self-abasement and public prayer to argue his point, and he takes no further action until there is a response from the people (Ezra 9:1–10:1). Agreement with Ezra and an invitation to take charge is followed by Ezra's leadership and also by his involvement of the community (10:2–17).

The concern of foreign marriages also ties in with issues of land ownership (Ezra 9:12), something that would be a matter of dispute between those occupying the land and the returnees who now sought to possess it. If, as at the

16. See Eskenazi, "Missions of Ezra and Nehemiah," 517. For the Athenian evidence, see Ehrenberg, *From Solon to Socrates*, 225–26.

Was Judea Independent of Samaria before the Governorship of Nehemiah?

Albrecht Alt proposed the theory that before Nehemiah's governorship, Judah was a part of the satrapy of Samaria.[a] Sheshbazzar and Zerubbabel were special commissioners with restricted tasks having to do with the Jerusalem cult. Only with Nehemiah is a separate governorship introduced in Judea. The Elephantine papyri from a Jewish mercenary colony in Upper Egypt attest to a governor in Judea alongside one in Samaria by 408 BC. Alt argued that contemporary seal and coin impressions provided confirmation. However, Nahman Avigad's Aramaic bulla 14, of unknown provenance, was restored by Hugh Williamson on paleographical, linguistic, and contextual grounds as "Belonging to Shelomith, maidservant of Elnathan the governor."[b] Although the word for "governor" can be used of junior officials, (1) the wife or female subordinate of a junior officer would probably not have a seal, (2) the parallel title on Hebrew coins of the fourth century BC clearly names the provincial governor, and (3) the word for "governor" is used by a son of Sanballat on a clay seal from Wadi ed-Daliyeh concerned with a property transaction; all these points demonstrate the probability that on bulla 14 is the name of a Judean governor. Avigad dates the bullae he published to the sixth century, on paleographical grounds. Williamson follows others in associating this Shelomith with the Shelomith of 1 Chronicles 3:19, a daughter of Zerubbabel. He suggests that the title "maidservant" might be the female counterpart to "servant," which is followed by the name of a king or leader and designates the figure as an official high in that leader's administration. If Elnathan was a governor in Judea a generation after Zerubbabel, then Alt's case is disproved, and Judea was independent of Samaria and had its own governors.

[a] Alt, "Rolle Samarias."
[b] Avigad, *Bullae and Seals*; Williamson, "Governors of Judah."

Jewish colony of Elephantine four decades later, women could own land, then there would be a great concern that foreign marriages would compromise land ownership by the returnees, and it would become the possession of the other groups that had occupied the land.[17] And indeed, this may be the case. Only in Ezra (10:2, 10, 14, 17, 18) and Nehemiah (13:27) is the verb that normally means "to settle" used repeatedly for marriage.[18] Whether literally settling the women on the land or metaphorically alluding to the settlement in the land of the Israelites, in the book of Joshua the term may imply a concern for land ownership.

17. Eskenazi, "Out of the Shadows."
18. The Hiphil form of *yšb*.

Ancient Near Eastern Context

The advent of Cyrus and the Persian Empire brought no profound change in the administrative structure of the region of Judea. Even the administrative reforms of Darius in the final decades of the sixth century BC did not alter a great deal. Judea had become a separate province by the time Ezra and Nehemiah began their work in the mid-fifth century BC.

Artaxerxes I ruled in 465–424 BC.[19] He followed his father, Xerxes, who had been murdered in his bed. In 460 BC there was a revolt in Egypt. The Athenians and the Delian league joined on the side of Egypt. In 454 the Persian Megabyzus brought his army, with its Phoenician allies, into the Delta area of Egypt and scored a major victory over the Athenian navy and the Egyptian and Libyan forces. The series of battles ended in 448 BC with the Peace of Callias. The Persians agreed to avoid the Aegean, and the Athenians agreed to Persian control of the eastern Mediterranean. The same year that Ezra came to Jerusalem under the authority of Artaxerxes, the Persian king also sent Megabyzus to the Spartans, undertaking diplomacy to undermine the Athenians and the Egyptian rebellion. The mission of a priest such as Ezra, who was well versed in the law of the Jewish people, would provide them with further constitutional stability, a greater sense of identity among themselves, and a larger dependence on the Persian authority.

Likely after the Peace of Callias, Megabyzus became disenchanted with the harsh treatment of Egypt. For a while he defected from the Persians, led a revolt in the region west of the Euphrates ("Beyond the River"), and fought forces sent against him from Egypt and from Babylon. Although he was eventually reconciled, the immediate aftermath may be described in Ezra 4. The Jews appear to have begun to strengthen their Jerusalem fortress shortly after the battles of Megabyzus. This would have appeared suspicious to Artaxerxes. Those who wrote the letters in Ezra 4:7 may well have been associates of Megabyzus who saw the potential for rebellion in Jerusalem. That the building project did not succeed seems clear from Ezra 4:23. The severity of broken walls and burned gates in Nehemiah 1:3 suggests that serious actions were taken against Jerusalem.

Nehemiah's foes—Sanballat governor of Samaria, Tobiah governor of Ammon and Geshem governor of the Arabian district—are all figures attested in later texts: Sanballat's family appears in the Wadi ed-Daliyeh Papyri, Tobiah's family dynasty is known in the Hellenic period, and Geshem's son mentions him on a silver bowl found in eastern Egypt.

Kenneth Hoglund has identified a dozen forts dating from the mid-fifth century BC and located in the area of Israel.[20] Three can be dated by ceramic evidence, and the others show similar construction techniques. The forts are

19. Cf. Rainey in Rainey and Notley, *Sacred Bridge*, 288–92.
20. Hoglund, *Achaemenid Imperial Administration*, 165–205.

found throughout Israel and located away from major population centers. They overlook key roadway systems and were mostly occupied for only a generation. Hoglund argues that they represent the Persian response to the security threat posed by the Egyptian revolt. The imperial forces who occupied these forts remained until the Peloponnesian Wars (431–404 BC) eliminated any threat of attack from the Greek forces.

Commenting on the mission of Nehemiah, Hoglund argues that the citadel of the temple was a Persian garrison.[21] This and the unusual reconstruction of Jerusalem's walls may suggest that the city became a collection center for Persian revenues from the region. Nehemiah was sent, from the standpoint of Artaxerxes I, to pacify and gain the support of the local population. In this picture, Nehemiah's attempt to alleviate the economic suffering that a famine caused, and to do so by reducing the interest paid on the debts (Neh. 5), reflects an imperial concern for local cooperation without the reduction of taxes. If Ezra's earlier work reflected a similar policy, it was not nearly as successful and served only to arouse suspicion before being terminated.

The purpose of the law, then, was to provide social cohesion for the whole community. The ban on mixed marriages brings to mind Deuteronomy 7:1–4. In its imperial context, this ban provided a clear definition of the community and helped to identify the holders of community property, especially its lands. This would enhance the peace of the populace and sustain the military security that the Persians valued in a series of forts that defended against further Egyptian (and Greek) threats to imperial rule in the region. In the manner suggested here, this archaeological and historical reconstruction supplements but does not contradict the internal concerns of Ezra and Nehemiah for their people and their faith, as suggested in the preceding section, "Gender and Ideological Criticism."

Canonical Context

The connections between the first chapters of Ezra and the final chapter of 2 Chronicles have been noted in the previous chapter (see "Higher Criticism" for 1–2 Chronicles), as has the overall matter of similarities and differences in style between Chronicles and Ezra–Nehemiah as a whole. The prophets Haggai and Zechariah are mentioned in Ezra 5:1 and 6:14 as preaching to the returnees and encouraging them to complete the foundations of the temple. The prophet Jeremiah is referred to in Ezra 1:1, where he is credited with foreseeing Cyrus's edict to return the Jewish people to Jerusalem.

Nehemiah 9 records the great prayer of confession before God. Here is recalled the creation, the call of Abraham, and the covenant with him as found in Genesis (Neh. 9:6–8). The plagues against the Egyptians, the parting of

21. Ibid., 207–40.

the Red Sea, the defeat of the Egyptians, guidance through the wilderness, the law giving at Mount Sinai, the manna, and the rebellions of Israel in the wilderness—all of these are recalled as well (9:9–21). The defeat of Sihon and of Og, the gift of the land of Canaan, the expulsion of the Canaanites, and the blessings and security of the land are then remembered (9:22–25). Here the prayer turns to the sins of the people and God's patience, which finally comes to an end with judgment by the Assyrians and other armies up to the present (9:26–35). In this manner the major events of Israel's history and its most important covenants are recollected.

Neither Ezra nor Nehemiah appears in the New Testament. Only Acts 4:24 alludes to the beginning of the prayer of Nehemiah 9, and specifically to verse 6. There the creative power of God in making all things is emphasized. Beyond this it is difficult to identify distinctive connections between Ezra–Nehemiah and the New Testament.

Theological Perspectives of Ezra and Nehemiah

The book of Ezra begins with the proclamation of a foreign king (Cyrus) who acknowledges Yahweh and wishes to honor him by helping his devout people rebuild his temple and restore worship in Jerusalem. In the closest Ezra–Nehemiah connection to what might be considered the overtly miraculous, the public announcement is seen as the fulfillment of Jeremiah's prophecy of the return from exile. Thus the return of the exiles that begins the two books shows the ongoing plan of God, a plan not stopped by Nebuchadnezzar of Babylon and his destruction of Jerusalem. It also indicates that the Persian kings must serve the greater plans and purposes of the God of Israel. Likewise in Ezra 7 the second section begins with a statement by a Persian king (Artaxerxes), authorizing Ezra and other followers to return from exile to Jerusalem. Nehemiah begins in the same fashion: the cupbearer receives authorization from Artaxerxes to return to Jerusalem. The final major section, Nehemiah 7:5–12:47, does not begin with a Persian king and his proclamation. Instead, it begins with a reference to the earlier Babylonian king Nebuchadnezzar and then an inclusio where the original list of returnees in Ezra 2 is repeated. Nebuchadnezzar is mentioned five times in Ezra, always in the first section of the book (1:7; 2:1; 5:12, 14; 6:5). He is mentioned only once in Nehemiah (7:6), at the beginning of this list of returnees, repeating the mention in Ezra 2:1. Here the Babylonian king is credited with carrying off the people. That divine judgment is now reversed with the actions of the returnees. The other appearances of Nebuchadnezzar in Ezra concern his taking the vessels of the temple. That is reversed in the first section of Ezra, where the returnees bring back the vessels. This all takes place at the command of Cyrus. Thus it may appear that Cyrus has reversed the work of Nebuchadnezzar. However, the first part of Ezra 4:1–23 describes the opposition that the returnees encounter under the Persian kings Cyrus, Xerxes, and Artaxerxes. If the returnees are to complete the work of the temple, begun in Ezra 3:1–3, they must overcome the imperial opposition. It is no accident that Darius orders the completion of the temple and the project is finished with imperial support (5:3–6:18). These same verses relate that Haggai and Zechariah prophesy and promote the work (cf. Ezra 4:24–5:2). Yahweh's prophets proclaim God's message, and his word is able to guide the affairs of the mightiest empire in order to see the work completed. It is not simply the former, evil Babylon versus the later, good Persia, as the opposition of various Persian emperors demonstrates. Rather, it is the work of Yahweh that governs the affairs of the world, and it is that work that his prophets explain to his people, who hear and obey. The completion of the temple, worship, and celebration of the Passover illustrate the people of God in perfect relation to their Lord.

In the first section of Ezra–Nehemiah, the opposition comes from the empire; in Ezra 7:1–10:44 and in Nehemiah 1:1–7:4, it comes from local enemies and from the challenges within the community itself. Thus the return of Ezra brings him face-to-face with the sin of mixed marriages in the community. His decision to publicly cry to God in humiliation, fasting, and repentance does more than make a spectacle. It also proclaims God's will to the people in a prophetic manner. They must make a decision, and their choice to repent and follow God, to whatever extent that may change their lives, identifies them as true members of the community of God and therefore as forgiven and acceptable to Yahweh. Any and every reform and revival must begin with the proclamation of what is sin and the willingness of the people to repent and to act on that repentance.

The opposition of the first part of Nehemiah (1:1–7:4) comes primarily from Sanballat and regional enemies who are set on making the lives of the people difficult. The destruction of the walls had come at the instigation of such enemies. Nehemiah will not be taken in by their ruses and attempts to ambush him, whether outside Jerusalem or within the city, in decisions he makes regarding his safety. Instead, Nehemiah uses appropriate defenses against their threats issued to stop the rebuilding of the walls: he arms the populace and calls on God to remember him and his plans so that God might deliver Jerusalem. In the midst of this, Nehemiah 5 records the concern for the poor of the land, who have fallen into debt. Nehemiah reverses this by abolishing taxes and the charging of interest. The former is accomplished by the example that Nehemiah sets of not living well off the people but at the same time depending on God for provision to support the many who eat at his table. The abolition of interest is something that Nehemiah does without legislation but by appealing to the wealthy of Jerusalem to assist the poor. Their agreement to assist means that they work directly with the poor, not

The Persepolis Texts and Nehemiah

Thousands of Elamite and Aramaic Persepolis fortification texts that describe imperial receipts throughout the first half of the fifth century BC have been discovered and published. Hugh Williamson compares the practices of governors in these texts with that of their western contemporary Nehemiah.[a] He suggests that terms and ideas similar to those of Nehemiah 5:14–18 are used: "bread of the governor" with the meaning of a governor's salary; payments occurring both in kind and in cash (5:15); payments that are made to governors who maintain retainers (5:15); numbers that match and even exceed the 150 of verse 17 for those eating from the governor's table; menus of other governors that correspond to Nehemiah in quantity though superior in variety (5:18); and the mention of supplies at ten-day intervals (for wine), similar to the sort of time specifications on the records from Persepolis. Thus Nehemiah lives like other governors in providing for his officers, but without accepting the allowance or governor's salary for himself. Furthermore, Williamson found linguistic parallels between words used in the Persepolis texts and those in the Aramaic and Hebrew of Ezra and Nehemiah (e.g., "in the fortress of *x*," "dressed stone," the title "treasurer," and "a man named *x*," with the meaning of someone who is unknown to the recipient of the document). Similar details and expressions on supporting local cults in the empire match the Persian support of the worship at Jerusalem in Ezra 6:9–10 and 7:17–20.

[a] Williamson, "Ezra and Nehemiah."

through government laws. Following Nehemiah's example of feeding people at his table, the other leaders "feed" those who depend on them by removing crippling demands of interest and debt repayment. Nehemiah becomes a model leader, identifying and acting decisively toward outside threats, providing an example of one who takes less pay and fewer perks for himself, and more directly helping those in his community who are in need. From beginning to end, the story of Nehemiah poses a model of a prayer warrior who constantly turns back to God for help and support and for guidance and direction.

Just as Nehemiah models prayer, Ezra certainly models the knowledge of God's word and its proclamation. Prayer and God's word are intentionally brought together in the final major section, which begins with a list of returnees (Neh. 7:5–73a) and moves at once to the great reform, to which the previous sections all looked forward with different emphases. Here it begins with the reading and explanation of the word of God. The celebration of the Feast of Tabernacles reflects the joy in together studying God's word. Insofar as the Feast of Tabernacles, or Booths, recalls Israel's journey from Egypt to the promised land, it may provide a means for later believers to identify with that first generation and once again to rehearse a return to the promised land and to a renewed covenant. The fasting and prayer recall the need for forgiveness of sin. They also verbally affirm God's presence with his people from the beginning and in spite of their sin. Next is the agreement or covenant as it is renewed and agreed on by the community. The assignment for some to live in Jerusalem and others to live in the remaining towns held by the community provides both for security needs (Neh. 7:4) and for continued reenactment of early Israel. Having entered the land, they now allot it, as Joshua did, and possess it. The enumeration of priests and Levites (12:1–26), the dedication of the walls protecting Jerusalem (12:27–43), and the inauguration of the temple service all demonstrate the goal of the reforms: Torah study, prayer and fasting, and a renewal of the covenant, involving worship of Yahweh in his divinely ordained temple and in the manner he has determined.

Nehemiah 13:1–31 concludes the work by testifying to the harsh reality of a community engaged in the world and not yet free from sin. Reform will always be necessary: believers are not perfect, and the enemies of God's people are always present. In this manner, the text shows the reality of a people living as pilgrims in the world and looking forward to a better land. It anticipates Jesus's own proclamation of the kingdom of God, a kingdom that has begun but whose full revelation of righteousness and peace awaits the return of the king.

Key Commentaries and Studies

Allen, Leslie C., and Timothy S. Laniak. *Ezra, Nehemiah, Esther.* NIBC. Peabody, MA: Hendrickson, 2003. A valuable integration of the historical, literary, and theological elements of the text in an evangelical perspective.

Eskenazi, Tamara Cohn. "The Missions of Ezra and Nehemiah." Pages 509–29 in *Judah and the Judeans in the Persian Period*. Edited by Oded Lipschits and Manfred Oeming. Winona Lake, IN: Eisenbrauns, 2006. A key study for understanding the egalitarian nature of the reforms undertaken and their impact on the postexilic community.

Fensham, F. Charles. *The Books of Ezra and Nehemiah*. NICOT. Grand Rapids: Eerdmans, 1982. A readable evangelical presentation of the issues and exegesis of the books.

Hoglund, Kenneth G. *Achaemenid Imperial Administration in Syria-Palestine and the Missions of Ezra and Nehemiah*. SBLDS 125. Atlanta: Scholars Press, 1992. A good starting point for any study of the political, archaeological, and historical background to Ezra and Nehemiah.

Kidner, Derek. *Ezra and Nehemiah: An Introduction and Commentary.* TOTC. Leicester, UK: Inter-Varsity; Downers Grove, IL: InterVarsity, 1979. A sensitive and theologically significant work for understanding the teaching of Ezra and Nehemiah.

Williamson, Hugh G. M. *Ezra–Nehemiah*. WBC 16. Waco: Word, 1985. A large and masterful exegesis and analysis of the critical issues. It remains a starting point for any study of these books.

13

ESTHER

Who can resist the story of Esther? This Jewish woman is chosen by God and given the status of queen yet risks everything when the survival of God's people hangs in the balance.

Name, Text, and Outline

The book is named after the chief human character, Esther. Although this name has variously been identified with the Babylonian goddess Ishtar and with the Persian word for "star," it remains possible that the same meaning might be applied to this Persian name as to the Hebrew name of the same person, Hadassah (Esther 2:7).[1] If so, then it refers to the myrtle plant.

The author of the book is unknown. The tradition of the Babylonian Talmud (*B. Bat.* 15a) ascribes Esther, along with Ezekiel, Daniel, and the Minor Prophets, to the men of the Great Assembly.

While the wording of the Hebrew Masoretic Text is not disputed, it does contain some theological puzzles. Chief among these is the absence of any direct reference to God. This may have been a factor in its lack of mention in the New Testament and the lack of any manuscript referring to Esther among the Dead Sea Scrolls. One of the earliest Christian listings of the canon of the Old Testament is that of Melito of Sardis, writing around AD 170 and recorded by Eusebius, who notes that Melito journeyed to Palestine to determine the list. It matches the Protestant and Jewish canon with the exception that it omits Esther. If Esther was written in Susa, a Persian capital

1. Cf. Phillips, "Esther 6."

located in what now is modern Iran (250 miles east of Babylon), then its origins place it farther away from Jerusalem than any other biblical book. It is possible that it was first recognized as Scripture by the Jewish diaspora to the east of Israel. If so, it may have taken longer than the other books of the Hebrew Bible to achieve canonical recognition by the Jewish and Christian communities.

Two versions of Esther are preserved in Greek, the *ó* text (Old Greek) and the Alpha text (AT here; also known as the Lucianic, or L-text).[2] The *ó* text appears in the early uncials, Codex Vaticanus, Codex Sinaiticus, and so forth. The AT occurs in four manuscripts from the medieval period (tenth to thirteenth centuries). The *ó* text is the longer of the two and closer to the Masoretic Text (Heb.). The AT is shorter and either preserves a significantly different Hebrew text or is a commentary on the longer text. Both contain six additions to the Masoretic Text that are scattered throughout the book.

© Baker Publishing Group and Dr. James C. Martin
Susa archer from the Persian palace

The *ó* text with its additions is regarded as part of the canon of Scripture by the Roman Catholic and Eastern Orthodox churches. Jerome used the Hebrew text that would become the Masoretic Text for his Latin translation, the Vulgate. However, the six additions were part of the Old Latin (pre-Vulgate) form of Esther, and so he added these as an appendix, yet expressing doubt as to their value as Scripture.

Both Greek texts portray Judaism within the context of the Hellenistic world in the third century BC or later. Thus the roles of Mordecai as a loyal citizen, of the Greek world as less derisive of Judaism, and of Esther as one who swoons in the presence of her royal husband all have connections with interests and styles of the Hellenistic period, not earlier. Of the two Greek versions, the *ó* text is more religious. Even so, the *ó* text follows the Masoretic Text in Esther 4:14, where Mordecai promises Esther that aid will come "from another place" if she doesn't assist in delivering her people. In the AT, the help mentioned here is attributed directly to God. In the *ó* text Esther (2:20) holds on to her Jewish way of life. This receives no mention in the AT. The AT also

2. Cf. Jobes, "Esther 5."

emphasizes how Jews in positions of power benefit the world in general. The character of the six additions suggests that they were not original to either the ό text or the AT. Instead, they were introduced at a later date.

OUTLINE

I. Xerxes and Vashti (1:1–2:18)
  A. Vashti Rejected as Queen (1:1–22)
  B. Esther Appointed Queen (2:1–18)
II. Haman and Mordecai (2:19–7:10)
  A. Mordecai Saves the King (2:19–23)
  B. Haman Plots to Kill the Jews (3:1–15)
  C. Mordecai Challenges Esther (4:1–17)
  D. Esther Prepares a Banquet (5:1–14)
  E. Xerxes and Haman Honor Mordecai (6:1–14)
  F. Haman's Fate (7:1–10)
III. Xerxes and the Jewish People (8:1–10:3)
  A. Xerxes Exalts the Jews (8:1–17)
  B. Purim (9:1–32)
  C. Mordecai's Promotion (10:1–3)

Overview of Esther

The story begins with a description of a great banquet by King Xerxes of Persia that lasts half a year in his capital of Susa. The first chapter dwells on a weeklong party that follows the banquet and on the decorations and the king's generosity. Queen Vashti also gives a banquet. The king sends for his queen to show off her beauty to the male guests. When she refuses to appear, he consults with his sages. One of them, named Memukan, suggests that the queen's conduct will lead to widespread disaffection and social breakdown in marriages across the empire. The king follows his adviser's suggestion that Vashti be deposed from her position. He issues a proclamation that men everywhere should rule their own households.

The king determines to hold a contest to see which of the most beautiful women of the empire would please him most of all (2:1–18). The beauty treatments are described as lasting for a year for each of the women. Esther, who has been adopted by her uncle Mordecai, is one of the women chosen. She pleases both the keeper of the harem and Xerxes and wins the contest.[3] Meanwhile, Mordecai discovers a plot by two officials to kill the

3. For an important critique of the use of the term "harem" here and throughout this chapter on Esther, see Bharj and Hagerty, "A Postcolonial Feminist Critique." In this case, harem serves a heuristic role.

king (2:19–23). He informs Queen Esther, who tells the king, and the two plotters are killed.

In Esther 3, Xerxes promotes Haman the Agagite. Mordecai refuses to bow to him, despite the king's orders. Haman plots to kill Mordecai and his fellow Jews. Haman convinces Xerxes of the value of this, and Xerxes gives him authority to proceed. To determine the day on which the destruction of the Jews shall take place, the lot (*pûr*, 3:7; 9:26) is cast. It falls on the twelfth month, Adar. Haman sends orders throughout the empire that all Jews shall be killed when the time comes. When Mordecai learns of this, he dons sackcloth and ashes (Esther 4). Esther learns the reason for Mordecai's sadness and communicates with him. He tells her that she should go to Xerxes and plead for her life and the lives of the Jews. Because she has not been summoned, if she enters Xerxes's presence she risks her life. Mordecai warns her that if she does not do this, she and her family will die, but help will nevertheless come from another place. Esther asks Mordecai and the Jews of Susa to fast for three days, as she and her attendants do the same.

In Esther 5, the king receives Esther, who invites him and Haman to a banquet that same day. At the banquet Xerxes asks her to state her request. She does not do so, but instead she invites them back for another banquet, during which she will state her request. Haman is delighted, but he is also angry at Mordecai for not honoring him. When Haman tells his wife and friends, they urge him to set up a pole seventy-five feet high. In the morning Haman plans to ask Xerxes to impale Mordecai on the pole. However, that night Xerxes cannot sleep (Esther 6), so he has the archives read to him. In these records he learns that Mordecai has saved the king's life from a deadly plot but has never been rewarded. So the king seeks advice as to what to do for Mordecai. By this time it is morning, and Haman is in the courtyard, so the king asks Haman what to do for the man the king wants to honor. Thinking that Xerxes means the honor for Haman himself, he replies that a robe, a crest, and a horse should be brought. Clothed and placed on the horse, the man should be led through the streets by a herald who will proclaim that this is one whom the king delights to honor. Xerxes commands Haman to do this for Mordecai, and he does so. When Haman returns home and tells his wife, she says that Haman is doomed because his plots against Mordecai have failed. At that point Haman is taken to the banquet.

When Xerxes asks Esther what she wants, she asks for her life and the lives of her people (Esther 7). When the king asks who has dared to threaten her life and those of her people, Esther indicates that it is Haman. Infuriated, Xerxes leaves the room for a moment. Haman throws himself down before Esther to plead mercy. Upon returning, Xerxes sees Haman on Esther's couch and accuses him of attacking Esther. They cover Haman's face. A eunuch reports that gallows are standing by Haman's house and have been built by Haman for Mordecai. Xerxes orders that Haman be hanged on it, and so Haman is hanged.

Xerxes gives Haman's estate to Esther, and to Mordecai he passes along his signet ring that he has taken back from Haman (Esther 8). As Esther pleads for the salvation of her people, Xerxes authorizes Mordecai to write whatever will enable the law he has passed earlier to be nullified. So Mordecai sends throughout the empire a decree authorizing the Jews to attack and destroy any armed force assembled against them, and to plunder their property. Mordecai is given a gold crown and garments of honor. The city of Susa celebrates, as do the Jews throughout the empire. On the thirteenth day of Adar (the twelfth month), the Jews assemble and kill all of their enemies (Esther 9), including Haman's ten sons. However, they do not take any of the plunder. The fourteenth day is a time of rest and celebration throughout the empire. In Susa, though, the Jews assemble and attack their enemies on the thirteenth and fourteenth days, so they celebrate on the fifteenth day. Mordecai and Esther decree that the fourteenth and fifteenth days shall be an annual celebration, named for the *pûr*, or "lot," and so called Purim.

Esther 10:1–3 concludes the book with a note on the power of Xerxes and how all his deeds are written in the annals of the kings of Media and Persia. The final verse records that Mordecai the Jew is second in rank to Xerxes and honored by other Jews for the good he has done for them.

Reading Esther

Premodern Readings

The Greek versions of Esther and the six additional sections have already been mentioned.[4] The additions (perhaps added in the third and second centuries BC) render explicit what lies implicitly in the Hebrew text: the piety of the Jews, especially Esther and Mordecai, and God's ongoing work behind the scenes to bring about the salvation of his people. An addition addresses Esther 3:4 and gives the reason for Mordecai's refusal to bow to Haman as his refusal to perform an act of worship. The Jewish historian Josephus follows most of the Greek additions in his rendition of the Esther story and also adds his own observations. For example, Vashti's refusal to appear before Xerxes's banquet is explained as a Persian custom in which women did not appear before men in public.[5]

Among the patristic writers, there is no surviving commentary on Esther, and not much was written until the early medieval writer Rabanus Maurus

4. See "Name, Text, and Outline," above. See also Jobes, "Esther 3."

5. Josephus *Ant.* 11.184–296. See Kneebone, "Josephus' Esther."

Athanasius on Esther

The great Alexandrian bishop and defender of orthodoxy Athanasius (ca. AD 296–373) finds in the Feast of Purim an example and type of Christian deliverance and of feasts:

> When the whole nation of Israel was about to perish, blessed Esther defeated the tyrant's anger simply by fasting and praying to God. By faith she changed the ruin of her people into safety. Those days are feast days for Israel; they used to call a feast when an enemy was slain or a conspiracy against the people was broken up and Israel was delivered. That is why Moses established the Feast of the Passover: because Pharaoh was killed and the people were delivered from bondage. So then, especially when tyrants were slain, temporal feasts and holidays were established in Judea. Now, however, the devil, that tyrant against the whole world, is slain. Therefore, our feast does not relate only to time but to eternity. It is a heavenly feast! We do not announce it as a shadow or a picture or a type but as the real thing. (*Epistulae festalis* 4)[a]

[a] Conti and Pilara, *1–2 Kings*, 397.

(ca. AD 780–856). His Latin work remains extremely allegorical. From a much earlier time, Clement of Rome (ca. AD 100) writes of Esther as a heroine:

> To no less danger did Esther, who was perfect in faith, expose herself, in order to save the twelve tribes of Israel that were to be destroyed. For by fasting and humiliation, she begged the all-seeing Master of the ages, and he, seeing the meekness of her soul, rescued the people for whose sake she had faced danger. (*1 Clement* 55.5–6)[6]

One of the earliest Syrian Christian writers, Aphrahat (ca. AD 270–345), compares Mordecai and Christ in his *Demonstrations* 20.[7] Both were persecuted. Both delivered their people by prayer. Mordecai saved Esther and the Jews by clothing himself in sackcloth. Likewise, Jesus saved the church by clothing himself in a body. Because of Mordecai, Esther went before the king and pleased him instead of Vashti, who disobeyed; likewise, because of Jesus, the church pleased God and went to him in place of the community that did not obey.

Rabbinic Judaism preserves a chapter in the third-century Mishnah, and in the generally contemporary Tosefta, that describes when and how the Feast of Purim is to be celebrated.[8] The Babylonian Talmud, from the sixth

6. Conti and Pilara, *1–2 Kings*, 384.
7. Ibid., 389; Jobes, "Esther 3," 176–77.
8. See Dombrowski, "Esther 3: History of Interpretation," 177.

century, preserves a tractate that comments on this section of the Mishnah and incorporates into the Talmud the only full midrashic commentary on a book of the Bible.[9] Other midrashim further enhance the nobility of the Jewish heroes and the villainy of their enemies. The general theme is the divine deliverance of the faithful from unjust persecution. Medieval Judaism moved its interpretive methods toward more literal approaches, combined with philosophy. The absence of God and of Jewish distinctives in the Hebrew text of Esther created discussion of the meaning of the text. In one account, God protected Esther from sexual impurity by sending a female spirit to spend the night with the king in place of the Jewess.[10] Esther became an important aid for the suffering and survival of the Jews in Europe of the Middle Ages.

Although he did not write a commentary on Esther, Luther accepted the canonicity of the book but did not esteem it. Later Reformers used a literal approach to its interpretation. Roman Catholic commentators resembled their Protestant counterparts. However, they also found in Esther a type of the Virgin Mary.[11]

Higher Criticism

The major questions raised by the book of Esther have to do with its historical claims and connections. There is a general assumption and acceptance that Ahasuerus should be identified with Xerxes. If so, then the key figures who are described should find attestation in the Persian history outside the Bible. These include especially Vashti, Xerxes's queen; Esther, his second queen; and Mordecai, the second in rank to Xerxes (Esther 10:3). We should easily verify observations such as the 127 provinces (1:1) and the 180-day banquet (1:4). However, none of these people or facts occur outside the Bible. Further, if Mordecai had been one of the exiles along with Jehoiachin in 597 BC (2:5–6; 3:7), then the twelfth year of Xerxes would be about 474 BC. By that time he would be at least 123 years old.

First of all, in any consideration of the historical authenticity of a document, especially one written in a different culture for a different purpose from any of the Persian historical sources, it is important to remember that history is selective. Thus two sources describing the same time period might choose to select different people and emphases for their purposes. The result could be virtually no overlap of names of people. Indeed, for the reign of Xerxes, perhaps twenty-one royal inscriptions exist, and most of these are plagiarized from Xerxes's predecessor, Darius I. No annals have been found and preserved. Most of the history of the time comes from the writings of Herodotus and

9. *b. Meg.* 10b–17a.
10. Jobes, "Esther 3," 179.
11. Dombrowski, "Esther 3: History of Interpretation," 180.

other Greeks who were interested in the history that affected them but not the workings of the Persian court. Some later Greek writers, such as Ctesias, may preserve events from the time of Xerxes, but the sources have been preserved partially and perhaps in edited or altered forms.

So what can be said about the issues raised above? Vashti appears to be a good Persian name. However, Amestris is the only queen known to Herodotus and other Greek historians. Her character was ascribed by them as cruel. It is difficult to know whether Vashti is an alternative name, or more likely a title or nickname, for Amestris, or whether this name refers to a different person altogether. Esther is also not named in the Persian records or by the Greeks. However, if the beauty pageant and Esther's appointment as queen occurred in the twelfth year of Xerxes (Esther 3:7) or about 473 BC, then she would have been unknown until after Xerxes's wars with the Greeks had ended. It is at that point that Greek historical sources become sparse regarding Xerxes. So it may not be surprising that an additional queen is not mentioned.

The name Mordecai is a form of the Babylonian deity Marduk. This element occurs in many names contemporary with Xerxes, as attested in the Persepolis receipt tablets. A number of officials also bear this name. Mordecai's position as second in the empire does not emerge until after Xerxes's contact with the Greeks. Therefore once again there are few available sources to elaborate on this.

There were not 127 satrapies. Rather, various sources concur that the number was closer to two dozen and not more than three dozen. However, the word for "satrapy" does not occur in the Bible. The 127 provinces were represented by governors, and the far fewer satrapies had satraps over them. No doubt multiple provinces made up individual satrapies. Satraps and governors are mentioned as separate groups of leaders in Esther 3:12; 8:9; and 9:3.

A banquet lasting half a year is unusual (1:4). Yet here seems to be an event that lasts for half a year followed by an additional banquet of seven days for special residents of Susa (1:5). If this took place in the third year of Xerxes's reign (1:3), it could have been a major celebration designed to recruit the loyalty of the provinces and the leaders in order to assemble the huge army and navy that he used to invade Greece (beginning in 480 BC).

As for a 123-year-old Mordecai, this assumes that the relative particle "who" (Heb. *ʾăšer*) that begins Esther 2:6 refers to Mordecai rather than to his lineage. Yet the important emphasis that introduces Mordecai is that he is a Jew and especially that he is a descendant of Kish. This specifically connects with Saul, son of Kish (1 Sam. 10:11, 21; 1 Chron. 12:1; 26:28).[12] That ancestry is critical because Mordecai's nemesis, Haman, is identified as "the Agagite" in Esther 3:1. Not only was Agag an Amalekite; he also was the

12. Amit, "Saul Polemic," 653–55.

king whom Saul confronted in 1 Samuel 15. Indeed, there Agag proved to be Saul's undoing; now Mordecai reverses that faithlessness in the line with a triumph over the descendant of Agag, who also has plotted the destruction of Israel and the Jews.

Literary Readings

The book of Esther is first and foremost a story. Within this context it is of value to identify its genre, plot, character presentation, motifs, and structure.[13] It is most often recognized (though with different names) as a historical novella or short historical story. The degree of historicity is debated (see "Higher Criticism," above). However, Esther is set within a time and place known in history. It portrays people as participating in human decisions and interacting with known characters and events. The nature of the story, as high-quality or poor literature, and the nature of the historical value are unrelated. A well-written story may portray events that are purely fiction or extremely factual. A poorly written story may do the same. Therefore, the analysis of the elements of this historical novella does not compromise any aspect of the historicity of the account.

The plot of the story begins with a conflict between Xerxes and Vashti. This occurs because the king makes a demand that Vashti refuses. The royal counselors choose to resolve this by having the king put away the queen and search for another. Esther 2 suggests a subtle conflict between Esther and the other young virgins who all seek the king's affection. The connection with Mordecai and with the supervisor of the harem foreshadows Esther's relationship with Xerxes, where the choice of Esther as queen provides the resolution.

Chapters 3–8 reveal an ongoing conflict between Haman and Mordecai, who respectively represent the enemies of the Jews and the Jewish people in the empire. The section begins at the end of chapter 2 with Mordecai's salvation of Xerxes's life, which goes unrewarded for a time. This contrasts with Haman's promotion by the king for no clear reason. From Mordecai's refusal to bow to Haman, there emerge the anger and pride that lead Haman to devise a scheme for his rival's death and the death of his family and people. Mordecai's consultation with Esther and her resolve to assist him and her people emerge in the context of impotence. Although Esther might be expected to have much greater power and influence than Mordecai, the king's deposition of her predecessor, Vashti, has demonstrated an unpredictable aspect to his relationship with his queen.

Haman becomes so successful that the king agrees to his scheme to eliminate his enemies, the Jews, and will pay for it from the royal treasury. In an unmistakable note, as Haman glories in his large family and his success with

13. Jobes, "Esther 1."

the king and now also the queen's apparent favor, the symbol of his success is the giant wooden gallows erected next to his house. On this he plans to hang his enemy, Mordecai. Yet each of these elements will prove to be his undoing. The decision to destroy Mordecai and his people sets in motion a means to prevent this that will prove successful. Haman's perception of the queen's favor proves to be the opposite. The gallows will hang Haman, and his family will first remove their support from him and then face their own destruction. Everything hinges on the sleeplessness of the king, which leads him to the state archives (and not to his harem), and on the pride of Haman, which places him in the royal palace and encourages him to think that the king's honor is coming to him. As Haman's scheme unravels to the point where even his best actions, such as entreating the queen, only spell his doom more decisively, the plans of Esther and Mordecai to save their people cannot fail. Not only does Xerxes accede to every one of their wishes, but he also places his authority in the hands of Mordecai to accomplish that salvation in whatever way he wishes.

The identification of the Feast of Purim in the final chapters symbolizes more than the salvation of the Jewish people and God's continuing plan for them. Its name also identifies the *pûr*, a small and apparently insignificant lot or die, whose tossing was able to determine the fate of a whole people. It is a series of small and seemingly impotent decisions by the faithful Esther and Mordecai that overturn all the machinations of their enemies with the weight of the most powerful king and empire on earth. In this context the second day of fighting in Susa is less a symbol of blood vengeance and more an opportunity for Xerxes to state his last recorded words in the book, addressed to Esther, "Now what is your petition? It will be given you. What is your request? It will also be granted" (9:12 NIV). For a king who cannot make his own decisions, these final words demonstrate that he has chosen to put his trust in the right direction, that of his Jewish queen and the faith that she represents.

As seen in the overall plot just described, the four characters are well defined, despite the brevity of the account. Haman is the proud and conniving villain who has nothing good in his character. Xerxes is the king who is controlled by those around him but whose decisions ultimately determine the outcome of the story and the fate of all concerned. Mordecai is the righteous court official whose own decisions, words, and actions guide the story to its positive outcome. Esther is the one figure who may develop as a character. She has been called a "beauty queen" and a "sex slave." And so she is when she first appears. By the end, however, Xerxes is giving her the power to make the decisions, and she is acting for her people and for the empire.

The major motif that recurs throughout the story is that of the banquet or feast. This is not surprising since the work is designed to explain the Feast of Purim. Since this feast is actually two feasts, the total of ten feasts found in the book can be divided into groups of two and provide other connections. These feasts are listed by Jon Levenson:[14]

1. Xerxes's Banquet for the Nobility (1:2–4)
2. Xerxes's Banquet for the Men of Susa (1:5–8)
3. Vashti's Banquet for the Women (1:9)
4. Esther's Banquet as Queen (2:18)
5. Haman and Xerxes's Banquet after the Edict against Jews (3:15)
6. Esther's First Banquet with Xerxes and Haman (5:1–8)
7. Esther's Second Banquet with Xerxes and Haman (7:1–9)
8. Jewish Feast after the Counter-Edict for the Jews (8:17)
9. First Feast of Purim: Adar 14 (9:17, 19)
10. Second Feast of Purim: Adar 15 (9:18)

Chapter 4 is one of fasting (4:16), in contrast to all the feasting. It prepares the intended victims for their struggle and victory in the following chapters.

The book also carries a chiastic structure:[15]

- A Greatness of Xerxes (1:1)
  - B Two Persian Banquets (1:2–22)
    - C Esther Accepts Gentile Identity (2:10–20)
      - D Haman Exalted (3:1)
        - E Anti-Jewish Edict (3:12–15)
          - F Mordecai and Esther (4:1–17)
            - G First Banquet (5:6–8)
              - H Royal Procession (6:1–14)
            - G′ Second Banquet (7:1–6)
          - F′ Xerxes and Esther (7:1–6)
        - E′ Pro-Jewish Edict (8:9–14)
      - D′ Mordecai Exalted (8:15)
    - C′ Gentiles Convert to Jewish Identity (8:17)
  - B′ Two Jewish Banquets (9:20–32)
- A′ Greatness of Xerxes and of Mordecai (10:1–3)

In this manner the structure identifies Mordecai's procession at the command of Xerxes, and to the shame of Haman, as the turning point in the story. This agrees with the plot. Until this point everything seems to work in Haman's favor. However, so many things have turned against Mordecai and Esther. Even the positive events of Esther's queenship and Xerxes's agreement

14. Levenson, *Esther*, 5.
15. Ibid., 8.

to attend her banquet provide no assurance of a good outcome against the forces arrayed against them. However, the seeds behind this reversal lie not in chapter 6 but in chapter 4. There the already-mentioned fasting is accompanied by a challenge to Esther from Mordecai. Without this, there would have been no drama and no Purim. Esther's response and the fasting and prayer in which all of God's people participate for three days change the heart of Esther and prepare her for what she must do. From a canonical biblical standpoint (and from the perspective of the Greek versions of the book), it also begins the work of God to change the heart of the king and to order events toward the outcome to which the book leads.

Gender and Ideological Criticism

The figures of Vashti and Esther dominate the landscape of feminist studies of this intriguing book.[16] Vashti has been portrayed as a woman who knows her own mind and self-worth. Thus she refuses to become an object of admiration for Xerxes to display to his male guests. However, this refusal leads to an edict seeking to enforce obedience across the empire, made by Xerxes in conjunction with his male advisers. Contrast this with Mordecai, whose refusal to bow before Haman is regarded neutrally or even positively by commentators throughout history. Mordecai's action also leads to an edict, one designed to destroy Mordecai and his people. Of course, any analysis should notice that the main purpose of Vashti is to provide a role that, when vacated, will be replaced by Esther. Mordecai's refusal to bow to Haman is wrapped up in the conflict between the two men that carries the major plotline through the story.

Esther's character has been variously understood. Negatively, she becomes a woman who expresses little in the way of initiative and control of the events. Her position is obtained by beauty rather than skill, and her means of changing the mind of the king is to seduce him to come to a banquet, then ply him with wine, and then allow her enemy Haman to be caught in a compromising situation. Whereas Vashti is able to say no to the king, Esther is not, but she regularly follows the counsel of the king and his court.

There is another way to look at the character of Esther. There is growth and maturity of her character, as suggested in "Literary Readings" (above). Sidnie White observes several elements in her character that suggest positive features worthy of emulation.[17] First, there is her ability to learn from others who have seniority, wisdom, and power. This includes the royal eunuch Hegai (Esther 2:3–15), but it especially refers to Mordecai, who advises and challenges her to undertake difficult tasks and to make courageous decisions.

16. Tiemeyer, "Feminist Interpretation," 215–16.
17. S. White, "Esther."

Xerxes's Interest in Women

The fifth-century-BC Greek historian Herodotus recalls how the Persian king Xerxes became involved in romantic entanglements during the wars with the Greeks that preceded the events of Esther 2–10. Herodotus writes (*Hist.* 9.108, paraphrased here):

> While staying in Sardis, Xerxes became inflamed with desire for the wife of Masistes, who was there. However, she could not be persuaded by his entreaties, nor did he wish to use force because he had some respect to his brother Masistes. Indeed, his wife also knew that force would not be used against her. So Xerxes bent all his energy to bring about a marriage between his own son Darius and the daughter of the object of his infatuation (and the daughter of Masistes). He reasoned that if the marriage took place, he could more easily reach the mother. He arranged the betrothal and completed the customary rites before returning to Susa. Upon his arrival there, having brought the woman into his palace for Darius, Xerxes lost interest in the wife of Masistes and became inflamed with desire for the wife of his son Darius, who was daughter of Masistes. Her name was Artaÿnte, and he achieved his desire with her.

Herod goes on to describe the revenge of Xerxes's queen, Amestris, against this woman.

Second, Esther uses her position well. She does not confront or insult but chooses the right time and place to persuade, while maintaining respect for those involved. This contrasts with Mordecai, whose refusal to bow to Haman angers the latter and puts Mordecai and all the Jewish people of the empire in mortal danger. Mordecai must then rely on Esther and her style of approach to put things right. This brings to focus a third point, the manner in which Esther plans and processes matters. She moves forward only after a due time of consideration and preparation. Thus her appearance before Xerxes does not take place until she has heard and discussed the matter and its danger with her trusted relative and friend Mordecai. Even then she and her attendants, as well as Mordecai and all the Jews of Susa, fast for three days before she approaches the king. Finally, she dresses in her royal robes and only then approaches Xerxes. Her request does not come at their first meeting or even at the banquet that follows. Only at a second banquet does she reveal her concern. Even then, it is expressed as a matter of life and death and therefore worthy of the king's attention. She states that if she and her people were only to be sold into slavery, she would not bother the king. As to the success of Esther, as mentioned in "Literary Readings," the last recorded words of Xerxes are directed to Esther (9:12 NIV), "Now what is your petition? It will be given you. What is your request? It will also be granted." There may remain questions about Esther that the book can never answer and were never intended to be answered by this short story. However, it is difficult to hold that Esther was in any way ineffective in her mission to save the lives of her people.

As always, there are many places and contexts in which the resistance of God's people to others who would destroy them remains a theme in every generation. The house churches in the People's Republic of China have faced waves of discrimination and persecution. The Shouwang Church in Beijing, composed of many professionals, has sought to support the government and to find a way for it to become a legally recognized entity, but in good conscience it has refused to become part of the state church. The government has pressured the owners of the hall that the church rented to shut its doors. As they tried to meet outside in a park during the spring and summer of 2011, police forces descended on worshipers, using tactics such as house arrest for pastors, elders, and others, and holding those who do attend in police custody for up to twenty-four hours, or even twice that. Employers have been pressured to fire those who attend the church. Government church people have been enlisted to interrogate the worshipers and try to persuade them to abandon the Shouwang Church. Meanwhile, some nineteen house-church pastors from elsewhere in China have written government officials in support of Shouwang Church and asked the government to enforce its constitutional statements about freedom of religion. As in Esther, where a similar crisis has been faced, fasting has been part of the response as well as direct requests to those in power. While remaining loyal and in prayer for the government, the Shouwang Church will not bow the knee to its "Haman."

In Nazi-occupied Europe during World War II, Jews sent to the death camps wrote out the book of Esther from memory and read it in secret on Purim.[18] In such a context, resistance against genocide was recognized as a service and form of worship to God.

Ancient Near Eastern Context

This section has been addressed in a general way under "Higher Criticism" (above).[19] The historical sources for the first century of the Persian Empire in general are not numerous. There is even less for the reign of Xerxes (ca. 486–465 BC) in particular. There are fewer than two dozen royal inscriptions, many of which are taken over directly from the reigns of previous Persian monarchs. Cuneiform tablets from Persepolis (one of the capitals of the Persian Empire) and Elamite inscriptions date from the reigns of Xerxes and other monarchs in the fifth century BC. However, these are largely economic texts that deal with the payments of oil, grain, and food. These and the Daiva texts, dating

18. Gordis, "Studies in the Esther Narrative," 413–14.
19. See Briant, *From Cyrus to Alexander*, 516–68; Jobes, "Esther 2."

from the time of Xerxes, do not provide specific connections with the book of Esther. The exception to this lies in the matter of personal names. Thus the name of Mordecai, derived from the Babylonian god Marduk, is attested in a variety of forms in these records. This is not the same name bearer but attests the presence of similar names during the time in which Esther purports to originate. Various names of other officials occurring in the book of Esther also find parallels in structure and elements to those contemporary with Xerxes.

The major sources for the history of the period come from the Greek historians and writers. Some, such as the playwright Aeschylus (525–456 BC), focus on the response in Persia to the news of the Greek defeat of the Persian army. However, this and other writers seem to present their own understanding of the Persians as read through Greek lenses. Herodotus is the most important Greek source. He lived in the fifth century BC (ca. 480 to 420), a period contemporary with most of Xerxes's reign. His major interest was in the wars that Xerxes fought with the Greeks. For this reason there is little one can learn of the king's life or the history of Persia after 479 BC. Of course, it is only at this point that the story of Esther begins. The banquet of Esther 1 may be dated to about 483 BC and connected with preparations for the Greek wars that Xerxes undertook, but the events in Esther occur after those battles.

Despite the difficulty with Herodotus, his writings do provide some connections with the Esther narrative. As noted, the banquet of chapter 1, placed in the third year of Xerxes (1:3), fits with the four years of preparation for battle with the Greeks that he made. The next event, the presentation of Esther, is dated to the seventh year of the king (2:16), which would be about 479 BC, soon after Xerxes's return from his defeat at the hands of the Greeks (in 480 BC).

Xerxes's wife was Amestris, according to Herodotus. However, the name Vashti sounds like the Old Persian for "beautiful woman" and may suggest a title rather than a proper name.[20] The seven close advisers to the king in 1:14 may have been a continuation of the council of seven associated with Darius, Xerxes's father and predecessor (Herodotus, *Hist.* 3.84). Herodotus (*Hist.* 1.99; 3.77) also describes how during the reign of Darius, one could not normally reach the king except through messengers who were eunuchs. This may resemble Esther 4:1, where similar messengers could normally be used to make connection with Xerxes. The ten thousand talents of silver (Esther 3:8–9) are not extraordinary in comparison with tribute paid to Darius (Herodotus, *Hist.* 3.92–97). Lavish celebrations and the use of much wine in festivals are attested by Herodotus (*Hist.* 1.133) and found in the banquets and celebrations of Esther, especially those connected with the king (Esther 1:7–8; 3:15). It was known that benefactors of the king had their names recorded and received gifts (Herodotus, *Hist.* 8.85), as happens to Mordecai (Esther 6:1–11).

20. Jobes, "Esther 2," 173.

The traditional view is that Xerxes's defeats by the Greeks resulted in his return home and a focus on harem life. Esther certainly fits well into such a context. Yet this conclusion is uncertain since Herodotus gives less detail about the later years of Xerxes's reign. Even if Xerxes was not consumed by the harem and court matters, the events of Esther could have occupied part of those later years.

Canonical Context

There is no clear reference to Esther in the New Testament. There is almost no reference to any character or event in Esther that can be connected with another citation in the Old Testament. The exception is the connection between Mordecai as a descendant of Kish (Esther 2:5) and Saul, who is described as "son of Kish" (1 Sam. 10:11; etc.). This is to provide an intentional contrast and struggle with Haman the Agagite, who is connected with Agag, the Amalekite king whom Saul defeated but did not kill (1 Sam. 15).

While the book of Esther does not explicitly continue an earlier historical text in a manner such as Ezra 1:1–4 repeats and continues the end of 2 Chronicles (36:22–23), the final text, especially Esther 10:2, seems to intentionally connect Xerxes with the kings of Judah and Israel as found in the books of 1–2 Kings, where references to further deeds of kings—"are they not written in the annals of the kings," or something similar—appear thirty-four times. In this manner, Xerxes appears as a king who reigns over the people of God.

Theological Perspectives of Esther

Can a book that does not mention God have a theology? From the standpoint of the biblical teaching as a whole, where God is everywhere and active in all things to realize his good purposes, readers do better to ask, How does the book of Esther fit into God's great plan of creation and redemption for humanity? From this perspective, the answer is apparent. God often works, as here, behind the scenes, to bring about the salvation and preservation of his people in the face of the enemy's plans for their destruction and the end of hope and redemption on earth.

As God chooses to work through a flawed people, demonstrated so well in the Historical Books leading up to Esther, he also chooses to work through flawed persons. Of course, there is the indecisive and sometimes unpredictable King Xerxes, who can be a slave to his emotions. There is also the figure of Mordecai, who will not bow to Haman, for reasons that are never clear, and who works in the context of a morally compromised government for a greater good. And there is the figure of Esther, who is chosen "for just such a time as this" (4:14), despite the dubious manner in which she needs to act to obtain her status as queen and maintain the ongoing marriage to a pagan king. Yet in the midst of all of this, God is sovereign and at work. He continues to accomplish his purposes, and that includes keeping alive his people. As Mordecai indicates in his message to Esther, God will realize his plan, but it is up to you whether you want to participate in it. In the story of Esther, each believer finds the story of his or her own life. God's plan will be realized to bring blessing to the world through Abraham's seed and ultimately to redeem the world. People have a choice as to whether to participate in that grand plan for which humanity was created. It is such a choice that forms part of human freedom, the same freedom that Esther had and that she used to engage the hardships of a sinful world. But her sacrifices (symbolized by her fasting and that of all God's people at the critical moments in the end of chap. 4 and early in chap. 5) become the means that God uses to save the Jewish nation and the line from which would come the Messiah and Redeemer.

In a profound sense a book such as this also prefigures and foreshadows the larger plan of redemption and particularly the one found in the life and work of Jesus Christ.[21] This book shows how the smaller decisions made by Mordecai and Esther—in their actions of uncovering a plot against Xerxes, befriending the leader of the harem, and living their daily lives faithfully—lead to great challenges and opportunities of risking their lives and of addressing and counseling the king. All these elements form part of the manner in which God acts out his plan. Thus Jesus is born of lowly status in a backwater. He grows up and lives a faithful life but ultimately is rejected by his followers and dies in terrible suffering on a cross. Yet, from what by all appearances seemed to be a wasted and insignificant life, there came the power of the resurrection and the greatest turning point in history. The world would never be the same again. Such opportunity and challenge remains for the disciples of Christ who will respond in faithful lives and allow God, through them, to bear witness to his kingdom of love and mercy. Like Esther, do readers hear his call today and look beyond the circumstances and concerns of daily living to the meaning of Christ's power at work within?

Key Commentaries and Studies

Allen, Leslie C., and Timothy S. Laniak. *Ezra, Nehemiah, Esther.* NIBC. Peabody, MA: Hendrickson, 2003. A valuable integration of the historical, literary, and theological elements of the text in an evangelical perspective.

Baldwin, Joyce G. *Esther: An Introduction and Commentary.* TOTC. Leicester, UK: Inter-Varsity; Downers Grove, IL: InterVarsity, 1984. Classic evangelical exegesis by a profound and thoughtful scholar.

21. Jobes, "Esther 1."

Zev Radovan/www.BibleLandPictures.com

Plate 1. Bronze calf covered with silver on head and feet found at entrance to the eighteenth-century-BC Canaanite city of Ashkelon

Richard S. Hess

Plate 2. Shechem temple

Kathryn Hooge (via KW)

Plate 3. Tenth- or ninth-century-BC North Syrian temple of ʿAin Dara with side rooms, three parts, and other features similar to Solomon's contemporary temple

© Baker Publishing Group and Dr. James C. Martin

Plate 4. Tiglath-pileser III, ruler who attacked the northern kingdom of Israel (ca. 734–727 BC)

© Baker Publishing Group and Dr. James C. Martin

Plate 5. The Cyrus Cylinder (ca. 539 BC) records the Persian king's decree to allow exiles—such as the Judeans—to return home and rebuild their cities and temples.

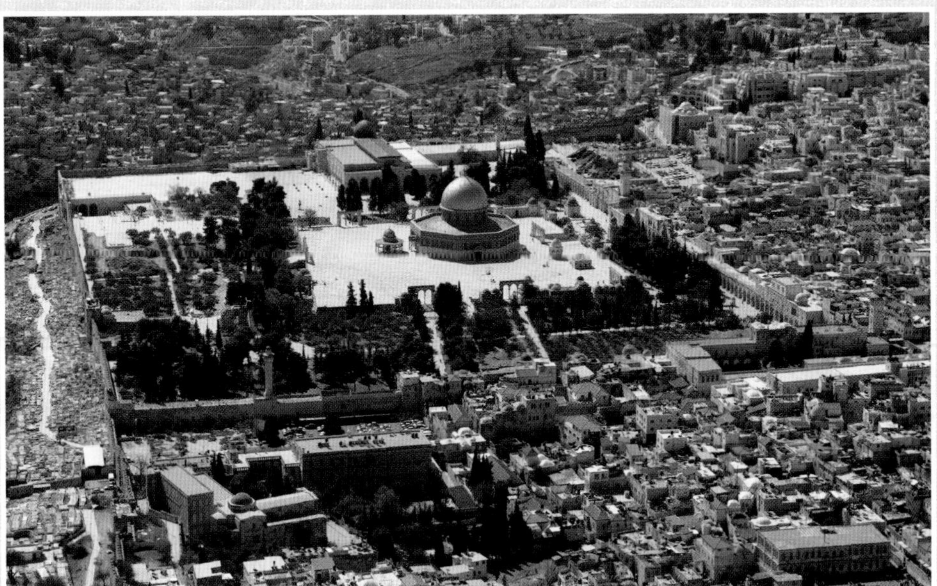

© Baker Publishing Group and Dr. James C. Martin

Plate 6. Dome of the Rock, site of Solomon's temple

© Baker Publishing Group and Dr. James C. Martin. The Israel Museum.

Plate 7. Tenth-century-BC cult stand from Taanach with images of a possible calf (like that worshiped by Israel) and sun disk (top panel), a tree (representing a goddess such as Asherah) flanked by an ibex and guarded by lions, empty space with cherubim on either side, and a female (goddess such as Asherah?) flanked by lions (bottom panel)

© Baker Publishing Group and Dr. James C. Martin

Plate 8. Ishtar gate from Babylon

Darafsh Kaviyani/Wikimedia Commons

Plate 9. King Darius I of Persia ruled when Haggai and Zechariah prophesied and the first temple was dedicated after the return from exile.

© Baker Publishing Group and Dr. James C. Martin. The British Museum.

Plate 10. Egyptian party with people wearing fine clothes and with oil on their heads

© Baker Publishing Group and Dr. James C. Martin

Plate 11. Mount of Olives

© Baker Publishing Group and Dr. James C. Martin

Plate 12. Amarna tablet from Jerusalem

Plate 13. Tel Dan inscription

© Baker Publishing Group and Dr. James C. Martin

Plate 14. The Great Isaiah Scroll

Wikimedia Commons

© Baker Publishing Group and Dr. James C. Martin

Plate 15. Cave 1 at Qumran

Zev Radovan/www.BibleLandPictures.com

Plate 16. A picture of the blessing and "Bes" figures (that some identify with Yahweh and Asherah) from the Kuntillet ʿAjrûd site in Northern Sinai

Berlin, Adele. *Esther.* JPSBC. Philadelphia: Jewish Publication Society, 2001. An excellent literary study by an accomplished scholar.

Clines, David J. A. *The Esther Scroll: The Story of the Story.* JSOTSup 30. Sheffield: JSOT Press, 1984. A good introduction to the complex issues of the Greek texts of Esther.

Fox, Michael V. *Character and Ideology in the Book of Esther*. Columbia: University of South Carolina Press, 1991. An authority in Wisdom literature examines the book in terms of the Hebrew text and its message.

Jobes, Karen H. *Esther.* NIVAC. Grand Rapids: Zondervan, 1999. Perhaps the most useful theological and exegetical work for studying the book that is available.

Levenson, Jon D. *Esther: A Commentary.* OTL. Louisville: Westminster John Knox, 1997. This slim volume is a treasury of exegesis and analysis of the work, with important questions and insights from Jewish biblical theology.

PART 3

POETIC BOOKS

The poetry of the Old Testament is found in many books and constitutes a substantial part of Old Testament literature. However, the books of this section are almost entirely poetic in their form: Job, Psalms, Proverbs, Ecclesiastes, and the Song of Songs. Rather than constituting a narrative, the poetry of the Old Testament consists of many poems and brief proverbial forms that address large and small subjects. However, each book represents a different type of literature and a distinctive approach. Job consists of a dialogue between Job and his friends. Yet the speech of God serves as the climactic point of the exchange. Psalms provides many poems that include a variety of praises to God and requests for God to assist. Proverbs consists of short, pithy observations about life and the manner in which one can live so as to honor God and find success in the world. Ecclesiastes is a lengthy reflection on the meaning of life, with attempts to appreciate the frustration of ascertaining how God works in a world where life does not turn out as one might expect and there are questions about its meaning. Finally, the Song of Songs brings together the passion and joy of romantic love in which the two lovers admire each other.

The diversity of subjects has led to the division between the Psalms as poetry and the remaining books as Wisdom literature. Although the books of Job, Proverbs, and Ecclesiastes contain the classic elements of Wisdom literature, the Song of Songs would probably not be so labeled if not for its traditional association with these other books. The Song best appears as a poem celebrating romantic and erotic love. Further, the book of Lamentations fits in these broad categories and should also be understood as part of the biblical collection of poetry. However, because of its association with Jeremiah, it naturally follows the prophet's book.

The association of many individual psalms with David and the apparent identification of Proverbs, Ecclesiastes, and Song of Songs with Solomon has led many to assume the composition of these works in the early period of Israel's history. David is indeed connected with some of the psalms, especially those in the first half of the Psalter. However, this book is best understood as Israel's hymns and prayers that may include a substantial number tracing back to David's time but also involve many later contributions. Thus Psalm 137 naturally fits the time of Judah's destruction and deportation to Babylon in 586 BC.

Proverbs may include sayings that reach back to the time of Solomon. Part of the book includes a collection that also occurs in Egyptian Wisdom literature from centuries earlier. Further, the structure of the book, with its long introduction, contains elements that fit best before the first millennium BC or at its beginning. Nevertheless, Proverbs 25:1 refers to at least some of the proverbs as having been collected by officials from the later time of Hezekiah (ca. 700 BC).

Ecclesiastes, with its apparent pessimism toward life, was once thought to reflect attitudes found only after the advent of Greek philosophy. Now scholars know that such literature existed in the West Semitic world, Israel's environment, before (and after) that nation came into existence. Thus the message and sentiments of Ecclesiastes can reach back to the time of a figure such as Solomon. The setting described in the book assumes the period of the monarchy. However, the language of Ecclesiastes points to a date of its final edition in the period after the exile, perhaps in the late sixth century BC.

Song of Songs is similar to Ecclesiastes in terms of its late language but has its setting in the time of the monarchy. However, the Song's love poetry most closely resembles the dozens of love poems from Egypt. These use language from the second millennium BC and thus suggest that the heart of the Song could have begun in the earlier period of Israel's monarchy.

Perhaps the most controversial book in terms of its origins and authorship is that of Job. The reader is referred to the following chapter for details. While there may be theological reasons why Israelite literature such as this could best be dated to the time of Abraham and his immediate family, Job himself may not be Israelite. He comes from a land outside Israel. He does not seem to follow the details of the Torah in terms of cultic laws, although his moral and ethical character represents the highest ideals of the law of Israel. His beliefs are consistent with those of a righteous gentile who believes in God's law. The poetry of the dialogues represents a dialect of Hebrew (or a closely related language) that seems distinct from the Jerusalem Hebrew of the rest of the Psalms and Wisdom literature, whether written early or late. This would be consistent with the dialect of a neighboring land and its people who are not Israelite but share many cultural features. The poetic dialogue is not necessarily identical to the language that Job and his friends would have spoken. Nevertheless, it is a clue to the different background and origin of this book in comparison with the other poetic books of the Old Testament.

Hebrew poetry and Wisdom literature have great beauty in their form and sound. They emphasize verses of two lines, where the second line enhances the first. This is true of both poems and proverbs. Because a greater emphasis is placed on the content and its parallelism than on the formal features of poetry, many of the texts can be translated with a higher degree of accuracy than some other forms of poetry in other cultures.[1] However, the more one understands the original language and its presentation of poetry, the better one will appreciate the beauty of these art forms.

1. This does not mean that texts, such as the poetry of Job, necessarily contain Hebrew that can be translated with certainty.

14

JOB

Is God evil for allowing people to suffer, especially innocent people? How should those experiencing suffering respond? Job answers these questions by pointing to something more fundamental than an explanation of why bad things happen to good people.

Name, Text, and Outline

The book of Job is named after its chief human character. The Hebrew name is *ʾîyôb*. This name occurs throughout the archives of the second-millennium-BC West Semitic population groups, at Alalakh, Mari, Ugarit, and Aštarte (a site in northern Jordan), and in additional early sources. In these cases the name carries the meaning "Where is the father?" where "father" is a term of relationship used in place of the name of a god or goddess.[1] In the case of Job, it could refer to any deity, including Yahweh.

The text of Job is notoriously difficult. Hebrew poetry by its nature presents the translator with more challenges than Hebrew prose. However, this text is especially difficult, with the presence of much vocabulary that appears only here, more syntactical issues than almost any other book, and the presence of numerous verses whose context provides few clues for a meaningful interpretation.

The presence of Aramaisms (words and expressions more often found in Aramaic than in Hebrew) has been identified in the poetic text of Job. Some have seen these as clear evidence of a late date (fifth century BC or later) for the work. For others, such as Robert Gordis, the large number of Aramaisms

1. See Hess, *Amarna Personal Names*, 23–25, and the evidence presented there.

provides evidence that the author was accustomed to think in this language.[2] Edward Greenstein suggests that the use of Aramaisms fulfilled requirements of the poetic structures and forms of the book.[3] Rather than demonstrating a particular dating for the work, they served specific purposes of the author. Robert Althann has also applied the poetry to understanding text-critical issues in the Masoretic Text.[4]

Compared to the Hebrew (MT) text of Job, the Greek (LXX) text is one-sixth shorter and has a distinctive ending. Rather than the product of an earlier and more original source than the Septuagint, the Greek text is a free translation of the Masoretic Text.[5] Attempts by Origen to interpolate the additional Greek translation connected with Theodotion into the Old Greek resulted in a mixed text rather than a more original one.[6] The freer translation of the Septuagint allowed the translator(s) to ennoble Job. For example, he withholds his thoughts from God rather than speaking without knowledge (Job 38:2; 42:3).[7] In the Greek, Job's speeches move from bitter complaints against an unjust God to assertions of the importance of personal experience with a mysterious God, who nevertheless is connected with salvation.[8]

OUTLINE

I. The Suffering of Job (1:1–2:13)
   A. Job before the Trials (1:1–5)
   B. The Loss of Job's Possessions and Family (1:6–22)
      1. God and the Satan in the Heavenly Court (1:6–12)
      2. Job Afflicted (1:13–19)
      3. Job's Response (1:20–22)
   C. The Loss of Job's Health (2:1–10)
      1. God and the Satan in the Heavenly Court (2:1–7a)
      2. Job Afflicted (2:7b–8)
      3. Job's Response (2:9–10)
   D. Three Friends Introduced (2:11–13)
II. The Dialogue of Job and His Friends (3:1–27:23)
   A. Job's Lament (3:1–26)
   B. First Round of Dialogue (4:1–14:22)
      1. Eliphaz (4:1–5:27)
      2. Job (6:1–7:21)
      3. Bildad (8:1–22)

2. Gordis, *Book of God and Man*, 162.
3. Greenstein, "Language of Job."
4. Althann, "Text of the Book of Job."
5. Dines, *Septuagint*, 20–21.
6. Gentry, *Asterisked Materials*; idem, "Text of the Old Testament," 28–29, 38.
7. Kutz, "Characterization."
8. Cimosa and Bonney, "Theology of Job."

        4. Job (9:1–10:22)
        5. Zophar (11:1–20)
        6. Job (12:1–14:22)
    C. Second Round of Dialogue (15:1–21:34)
        1. Eliphaz (15:1–35)
        2. Job (16:1–17:16)
        3. Bildad (18:1–21)
        4. Job (19:1–29)
        5. Zophar (20:1–29)
        6. Job (21:1–34)
    D. Third Round of Dialogue (22:1–27:23)
        1. Eliphaz (22:1–30)
        2. Job (23:1–24:25)
        3. Bildad (25:1–6)
        4. Job (26:1–27:23)
III. Interlude: The Inaccessibility of Wisdom (28:1–28)
IV. The Speeches of Job and Elihu (29:1–37:24)
    A. Job (29:1–31:40)
        1. Job before the Trials (29:1–25)
        2. Job's Present State (30:1–31)
        3. Job's Challenge (31:1–40)
    B. Elihu (32:1–37:24)
        1. Elihu Introduced (32:1–5)
        2. Speech 1 (32:6–33:33)
        3. Speech 2 (34:1–37)
        4. Speech 3 (35:1–16)
        5. Speech 4 (36:1–37:24)
V. The Dialogue of Yahweh and Job (38:1–42:6)
    A. First Round of Dialogue (38:1–40:5)
        1. Yahweh (38:1–40:2)
        2. Job (40:3–5)
    B. Second Round of Dialogue (40:6–42:6)
        1. Yahweh (40:6–41:34)
        2. Job (42:1–6)
VI. The Outcome (42:7–17)
    A. Yahweh (42:7–9)
    B. Job after the Trials (42:10–17)

Overview of Job

The story begins in the land of Uz, where the character of Job is described as without blame (1:1–5). His family includes seven sons and three daughters, suggesting a perfection in these ideal numbers. With his vast quantities of

The Satan

The root behind the name Satan carries the sense of hostility and here especially of accusation and faultfinding. Outside of Job 1–2, Satan is explicitly mentioned only four times in the Old Testament. He appears in 1 Chronicles 21:1 as the figure responsible for inciting David to take a census. In the parallel passage of 2 Samuel 24:1, Yahweh is the one who incites David for this purpose. There may be a similarity between Satan's role here and that of the "lying spirit" sent by God in 1 Kings 22:21–23. Elsewhere in the Old Testament "the Satan" appears only in Zechariah 3:1–2 (3×), where he seeks to accuse the good priest Joshua of wickedness and is rebuked by God. In Zechariah as in Job, the figure always appears with a definite article, indicating that this is not a personal name but a personified role. Thus this Satan may not be identical to the figure Jesus confronts in the Gospels. However, it is possible that the two figures are identical. In Job (and Zechariah), "the Satan" may focus on the role of this figure as one who accuses the righteous before God. It is remarkable how God tolerates the presence of this figure and even dialogues with him. However, it is equally of interest how God effectively uses "the Satan" for the completion of his own purposes.

livestock, he is the most important man in the east. The sons have their dinner parties in their own homes and invite their sisters to join with them. After each of these feasts, Job gets up early and offers burnt offerings for each of them. In this way he demonstrates his righteousness as a model father who cares for his children and seeks God's forgiveness for them, even if they commit a secret or inadvertent sin.

At 1:6 the scene shifts to heaven, where the sons of God present themselves to Yahweh. The Satan also appears after a journey across the earth. Yahweh invites the Satan to admire Job's righteousness. The Satan challenges Job's actions by claiming that Job does them only because of the blessings of protection and wealth that God gives him. He maintains that Job will curse God if God strikes him. Yahweh tells the Satan to do as he likes with all that Job has, but he must not touch Job.

The scene again moves back to earth (1:13), where Job receives three of his servants at once. The first two tell him how his livestock and servants have been destroyed: Sabean raiders took the oxen and donkeys, the "fire of God" destroyed the sheep, and the Chaldeans took all the camels. The worst news comes from the third messenger, who reports that a strong wind destroyed the oldest son's house where all Job's children were partying. They all died. Job goes into mourning, tearing his clothes and shaving his head. He does not charge God but instead praises Yahweh.

Job 2 begins with another divine assembly in heaven. The Satan again reports after his return from touring the earth. Again Yahweh praises Job. However, this time the Satan argues that Job will curse God if God strikes Job's body. Yahweh tells the Satan to do as he likes with Job's body, but he must not kill Job. In 2:7 the Satan afflicts Job's entire body with painful sores. Job's wife urges him to "curse" (the word is lit. "bless" but is universally recognized as a euphemism for "curse") God and die. He refuses, with the observation that summarizes his righteous attitude: "Shall we accept only good from God, and not evil as well?" (2:10 RSH).

© Baker Publishing Group and Dr. James C. Martin
Flocks captured by Assyrians

Job's three friends come to comfort him. They see his misery and empathize with him by tearing their own clothes and putting ashes on their own heads. They sit for a week with him, joining in his crying but not saying a word.

Job's introductory remarks to his friends are found in chapter 3, and this begins the poetic part of the book. Job begins by cursing the day of his birth. He wishes it had never occurred so that he would never have been born. Job compares himself to those who long for death.

Eliphaz speaks as the first of the friends (Job 4–5). He begins by reminding Job of how many people he has aided and encouraged. Then Eliphaz suggests encouragement for Job by rehearsing a vision he had at night. There a voice spoke to Eliphaz that all are unrighteous before God and that humans will die, and do so without wisdom. Job needs to recognize the problems of being foolish and rejoice in God's discipline. God will not let Job perish but will deliver him.

In chapter 6 Job recounts how his sorrows have oppressed him and rendered him weak. Job laments that his friends do not support him and instead do not believe his words. Job longs for a good night's sleep. Instead, he has nightmares and fear (Job 7). He longs for God to let him alone. In the next chapter Bildad calls Job a windbag (8:2) and states that his children have died because of their sins. If Job were truly pure before God, then God would deliver him. If one forgets God, nothing will give one security. God will not reject a blameless person.

Job says that no one can stand before God's wisdom and strength to justify oneself (Job 9). Even so, Job protests his innocence. He cannot, however, speak to God in this manner, and he longs for someone to arbitrate. Job despises his life and does not understand why God created him if only to oppress and destroy him.

Zophar's words encourage Job to turn from his supposed sin and to regain purity in his heart (Job 11). If Job does this, his life will be bright and good. However, Job mocks this wisdom (Job 12). He sees how the wicked are secure while the righteous are persecuted by God. Job will remain true to himself, even in the face of death (Job 13–14). He asks God to stop oppressing and terrifying him, so that he might be able to challenge God. Job asks God to leave people alone. Unlike a tree that, when cut down, will again sprout, humanity dies and is forgotten.

Eliphaz begins the second cycle of speeches (Job 15) by charging Job with being unwise and speaking out of turn. He should be satisfied with God's treatment. The wicked suffer torment because they defy God. They will lose their possessions and friends. Job's reply (Job 16) is to call all his friends "miserable comforters," long on speeches and short on comfort. God has attacked Job, and the wicked mock him. Job believes that there is one who intercedes for him but that such a one is in heaven. Nevertheless, Job is broken in spirit and surrounded by enemies (Job 17). His would-be comforters are without wisdom. They see darkness and call it light. Job and any hope he has are headed for the grave.

Bildad challenges Job to wise up so that he can receive the wisdom of his friends (Job 18). The evil person is the one who suffers all manner of calamity and whose name is forgotten. But Job responds that all these evils have come upon him, and he cannot respond, despite being wronged (Job 19). He is alone, and no one understands him. Yet Job trusts in his "Redeemer" (19:25), although he does not see him in this life. In the life beyond, he will see God. Job's friends are too quick to assume that his suffering is his own fault.

Zophar's final speech is in chapter 20: The delights of the wicked are fleeting. They will be forgotten, and their children will be in debt. In the end, all the enjoyment they seek will turn against them. Nature will rise against them. In chapter 21, Job counters that the wicked who reject God are prosperous and live and die in peace. The prosperous and the poor lie side by side in the grave, and both are eaten by worms. Yet the wicked have many friends and followers, and their tombs are guarded.

Eliphaz speaks in his turn (Job 22). Now he lashes out without regard for Job's feelings. Eliphaz directly accuses Job of great sin and wickedness, of taking advantage of the poor and not feeding or clothing them. Job should turn back to God, who will become his gold and silver. But Job (Job 23) will not accept this. He longs to confront God but cannot find his presence. Job asserts that he has remained faithful in all this testing, however fearful he is of what may yet lie in store for him. Then Job relates in more detail all the sins that the wicked do (Job 24). In spite of their wickedness, they prosper and oppress the poor, who have nothing and are sold into slavery. Yet God does requite the wicked: they die in their sin without mercy.

Job 25 is the shortest chapter in the book (six verses). In it Bildad praises God and his great powers. In light of this, how can any person reckon oneself as righteous before God? Man is a maggot. Chapter 26 has the hero of the story challenge Bildad with the question as to how he has assisted the poor or given counsel to those in need. Job also calls on images of God's creation power to observe how humans can understand little of what God is able to do. Although God has withheld justice from Job, Job will not speak wickedly (Job 27), nor will he accept the arguments of his friends. To do so would make Job wicked, and there is no hope for such a person in death. The children of the wicked will always be hungry. In the end, the righteous will seize what the wicked have accumulated. The wicked will know only terror and will soon be forgotten.

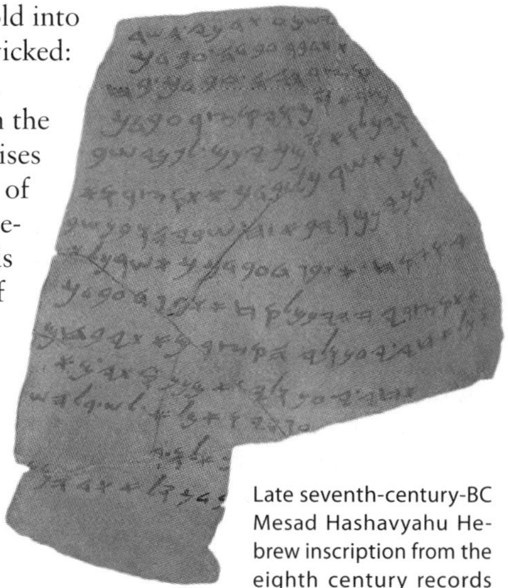

Late seventh-century-BC Mesad Hashavyahu Hebrew inscription from the eighth century records the refusal to return someone's cloak taken as a pledge

GU-theolog/Wikimedia Commons

Job 28 forms an interlude without a specific speaker identified. It is a hymn in praise of wisdom. The chapter begins with a description of how miners go deep into the earth and pierce through rock in order to find metals and precious stones. Wisdom, however, is an even more difficult commodity to obtain. Not even the most valuable metals and jewels on earth can purchase it. God alone knows how to obtain it. At creation, God decreed that the fear of Yahweh is wisdom, and it is found in avoiding evil.

Chapter 29 returns to the speech of Job. He longs for the day when God was blessing him, when he enjoyed material prosperity, when he was respected among the young and old of the city, and they spoke well of him. Then Job was known as one who assists the poor and vulnerable. He has helped the widows and the disabled, as well as those who were foreign to the land. He has attacked the wicked and assisted their victims. Job expected this to continue and to live out his days in blessing. He knew what it meant for others to listen to his counsel and for them to honor his presence.

All that has changed now (Job 30). The worthless men whom Job would not have trusted with his sheepdogs now have their sons mocking him and despising him. Now that they see how God has rendered Job powerless and vulnerable, they attack him, terrify him, and strip away his dignity. Job cries for help, but neither God nor people aid him. Job is alone and suffering.

Chapter 31 begins with Job's refusal to give in to lust. He knows that God will bring to ruin those who sin. Job claims that he is blameless and freely agrees to allow others to take his property if he is at fault. Neither adultery, nor oppressive treatment of his servants, nor refusal to be concerned about the poor and widows and orphans, nor trust in his own wealth, nor worship of the sun and moon, nor joy at his enemy's disaster, nor failure to give hospitality to the stranger, nor concealment of his sin characterizes the life of Job. With this litany of sins that he has not committed, the speeches of Job end (31:40).

Elihu, the youngest speaker, begins his indictment of Job (Job 32) in a series of speeches that try to uncover Job's sin. Elihu suggests that the three friends were unable to outsmart Job, and that it is his turn to try. Elihu will speak because he cannot remain silent, and he will speak fairly, he declares. Elihu claims his own righteousness (Job 33). Job is wrong to claim that God is silent. God speaks in dreams and in visions. If sickness drives people near to death, they can still receive counsel, confess their sin, repent, and be restored to health by God.

According to Elihu, Job claims that the righteous profit nothing from their righteousness (34:9). However, God is just, and his justice must act to uncover the evil of all. The wicked are punished. God hears the cry of the needy. One who is ready to repent will be heard by God, but Job is not ready to do that and thus speaks like the wicked. Elihu continues (Job 35) with a response to Job's complaint that God should vindicate him but does not see his righteousness. Elihu maintains that God is not affected by human wickedness or righteousness. God does not hear when the oppressed cry to him. He is beyond all of this.

God is just, Elihu says (Job 36). The wicked die, and the oppressed receive what is right for them. They are raised up like kings. Those who are bound up are invited by God to correct their ways. If they obey, they will prosper. If they don't, they will die without memory. Elihu advises Job to reflect carefully on how his wealth may have caused him to sin. God is powerful and worthy of praise (Job 37). Snow, lightning, and storm belong to God. Let all honor God so that God may look with favor on them.

At this point, Yahweh personally enters the dialogue and "answers" Job from the midst of the storm (Job 38). Yahweh exhorts Job to prepare to hear his answer. He challenges Job to respond as to where he was when God laid the foundations of the earth, when the stars began, when the sea was given its boundaries, and when the dawn first came. Has Job found the beginnings of the springs or traveled in the sea depths? Has Job seen the gates of death, traveled across all the earth, seen where the snow and hail are kept, guided the storms and rain and ice, controlled the constellations of the stars, brought rain, or provided food for the wild animals? In chapter 39, Yahweh asks questions about the natural world and exposes Job's ignorance of its operations: mountain goats, does, wild donkeys, wild oxen, ostriches, horses, hawks, and eagles. God demands an answer. Job (40:3–5) can only respond that he is unworthy and will speak no further.

© Baker Publishing Group and Dr. James C. Martin

Assyrian war horses drawing a chariot

God challenges Job to have divine strength and to crush those who are proud. The behemoth, with muscles in his stomach, a tail like a cedar, bones of bronze, and limbs of iron—this monster is the mightiest of God's creation. While God can approach him, this animal fears nothing. Chapter 41 describes the leviathan as a mighty beast who cannot be subdued by anyone. He has great teeth, and smoke pours from his nostrils. He has a powerful neck and a strong body. No weapon has any effect on him. He is stronger than any creature.

In the final chapter (Job 42), Job recognizes the great wisdom and power of God. Job knows that he has spoken beyond his knowledge. Job repents in dust and ashes. God addresses the three friends as those who have not spoken correctly of God as Job has. Therefore Job will pray for them while they offer burnt offerings for their sin. After these events, Yahweh restores Job with twice as much as before. His siblings and friends comfort him and give him gifts. He has twice as much livestock. He again has seven sons and three very beautiful daughters, all of whom receive an inheritance. Job lives 140 years and sees the fourth generation of his offspring.

Reading Job

Premodern Readings[9]

As already noted, the Septuagint's free translation of its Hebrew precursor presents the first interpretation of the book of Job.[10] There it tends to diminish

9. See Seow, *Job 1–21*, 110–248, for the most complete recent survey of the history of interpretation and *Rezeptionsgeschichte*.

10. See J. Allen, "Job 3." For the history of interpretation and Rezeptionsgeschichte, see Seow, *Job 1–21*.

any impious remarks or challenges and to magnify the piety of the sufferer. In the *Testament of Job* (first century BC or AD), Job's piety is magnified as in the Septuagint. He is virtuous, and his battle is not against God but against Satan. Job destroys Satan's image and is promised that he will suffer for doing this. Nevertheless, Job believes God will deliver him in the end. Job's chief virtue is patience or, better, endurance, as in his single mention in the New Testament (see "Canonical Context," below). The Septuagint also adds words to Job's wife as she expresses the loss of her family. She has become a wanderer and a maidservant who is frustrated by a husband who spends the night in the open.[11]

Early rabbinic traditions in the Mishnah, Talmuds, and elsewhere preserve a view of Job as the model of a righteous gentile, the only such gentile to have a major book of the Hebrew Bible written about him.[12] The same is true of the view of the early church, which took its lead from the Septuagint and saw in Job one who endured suffering in his age and was thus worthy of emulation. More important, his prefiguring of the suffering of Christ became an especially significant role that the Old Testament saint played for Christians.[13]

In light of this, an increasingly important dimension of Jewish interpretation understood Job as less than ideal. The fact that he feared God (Job 1:1)—serving out of a sense of fear rather than of devotion and love—is seen as a less-than-ideal motive for his righteousness.[14] His rewards in this life displace any hope of a life in the world to come. Among some, he is one of the pharaoh's advisers (Exod. 9:20) who suffers because he does not support the freedom of Israel and advises against the genocide of the Israelite sons.

From a different tack, some Jewish scholars understood the description of Job as "blameless and upright" (Job 1:1) to indicate that he was perfect and therefore born circumcised. Thus Job was an Israelite who was blameless. His sufferings became a model of Judaism's sufferings, and his restoration and blessing expressed Jewish hopes.

In the fourth century, Job became a key point of disagreement between the Pelagians and Augustine. The former found here the evidence of perfectibility, but the latter saw a figure who repented of his errors. Indeed, at the heart of the debate lay the question, Did Job sin? If he did, then Augustine was correct about the sin nature residing in everyone. If he did not sin, then Pelagius and his supporters were correct that the soul can be perfect apart

11. On the history of interpretation of Job's wife, which lies beyond this survey, see Low, *Bible, Gender, and Reception History*. This summary of the LXX of Job 2:9 comes from Low's introduction (6).

12. E.g., *m. Soṭah* 5:5; *b. Pesaḥ* 112a; *b. B. Bat.* 16a.

13. E.g., Augustine in *Enarrations in Psalms* 56:18; *De Symbolo ad catechumenos* 10; *De Patientia* 9.

14. *Midr. Ps.* 26:2.

from direct divine intervention. Gregory the Great agreed with Augustine. He saw in Job the foretelling of the coming of Jesus Christ.[15]

Thomas Aquinas sees Job as completely just, and the higher order of his soul remains unmoved from his belief in God's justice.[16] However, the personal experience of Job in suffering causes him to come to terms with the issues of daily living and the need to be gracious in his disputes. For Martin Luther, Job is both saint and sinner.[17] Job openly acknowledges his faults, asserting that "I fear all my works" (Job 9:8 Vulgate). However, this honest admission is what renders Job a saint, as one who is aware of his shortcomings but reliant on God's grace. For John Calvin, Job's God is an orderly Deity who maintains the cosmos but whose ways with humans, rewarding the unrighteous and punishing the just, are inscrutable.[18] It remains a matter of faith, trusting that God will execute justice at the final judgment.

Higher Criticism

The critical issues regarding the book of Job focus on the question of the origins and relation of the various elements that compose the book as now preserved. Above all, there is the matter of the prose sections that begin and end the book and the poetry in between. Related to this matter is the date of the material and the extent to which the book can be construed as reflecting authentic historical circumstances.

As to the question of the integrity of the book, there have been many challenges, especially among earlier generations of critics (and continuing presently) for whom the understanding of a work depends on identifying its diverse constituent sources. Thus the narratives that now frame the work were once thought to be the original part of the book. If the poetry was added later, it may have been added by increments. The rounds of dialogues appear to be cut short by the truncated final speech of Bildad (in Job 25) and the absence of any third speech by Zophar. Why is a wisdom poem abruptly attached in chapter 28, without identifying the speaker? Could the following speeches of Job and Elihu be later additions? Finally, might even the speeches of God have been inserted at another time?

All of these questions have been asked and form the background for the critical study of the book. However, much more is known about ancient Near Eastern and biblical literature than when these questions were first raised. Both wisdom compositions from across the ancient Near East and other biblical books include composite genres, where the texts are not limited to a single style of literature (e.g., only poetry or only prose) but include a

15. *Moralia in Job*, preface 5. See Allen, "Job 3: History of Interpretation," 369.
16. Ibid.
17. Ibid., 370. Cf. Clines, "Job and the Spirituality of the Reformation," 60–61.
18. Allen, "Job 3: History of Interpretation," 370.

variety of styles.[19] For this reason it is premature to assume that, if one can identify a variety of types of literature, there must be multiple sources behind the work. The positive argument for the coherence of Job can be found in a unified literary reading, as argued below. The contextual argument for this sort of genre can be identified in the discussion of comparative ancient Near Eastern materials (see "Ancient Near Eastern Context," below).

The question of the dating of Job proceeds from internal evidence. The description of Job's great age of 140 years, his function as a priest for his family (offering sacrifices), and the absence of a reference to the Torah have suggested to some that the book belongs in the era before Moses. This seems speculative, however. Length of years continues to be a sign of God's blessings well beyond the time of Moses. The role of Job in offering sacrifices could reflect a non-Israelite context, both ethnically and geographically. In that context there would be no law regarding such activities. This would also explain the absence of a reference to Torah.

The mention of Sabeans and Chaldeans might lead one to suppose a later first-millennium-BC context, just as the presence of Aramaisms in the text itself has led to the view that the work belongs to the latter part of the first millennium BC. However, tribal groups such as those named have no historical writings before the first millennium BC, and thus dating them based on the absence of evidence remains precarious. The issue of Aramaisms has already been addressed under "Name, Text, and Outline," above.

Traditionally, Job has been situated in one of two directions. There is the direction to the northeast of Israel, going toward Damascus and either on or east of the region of the Golan Heights of today. A second option is to the southeast of Israel, in the region of modern south Jordan and northwest Saudi Arabia. Either of these would comport well with Job's comparison with all the men of the East, with his wealth as measured pastorally in flocks and herds, and with the connection to the South Arabian tribes, the Sabeans and Chaldeans.

These locations would remove Job from the land of Israel but not from possible and indeed probable contact with Israelites and their faith. If Job represents a pious non-Israelite who has accepted the Israelite faith in a single God without converting to Judaism, he may have been seen as one who lived in the context of the covenant with Noah (Gen. 9), although doing so however many centuries later than those origins. If so, then the odd or difficult Hebrew of the poetry could reflect dialectical variations. The position east of Israel would be well suited for someone renowned for wisdom since wisdom was traditionally associated with sages from the East. Further, the absence of any awareness of a political state, or even a tribal entity to which Job could appeal

19. Walton, "Job 1," 343.

Uz

Outside Job 1:1, Uz does not appear in the book of Job. It occurs elsewhere primarily in association with genealogies, as a son of Aram (and thus an Aramaean?) in Genesis 10:23 and 1 Chronicles 1:17; as a son of Nahor (brother of Abraham) in Genesis 22:21; and as a grandson of Seir (and thus an Edomite?) in 1 Chronicles 1:42. The last identification also occurs in Lamentations 4:21, where the daughter of Edom is identified as one who lives in the land of Uz. In Jeremiah 25:20–22 the kings of the land of Uz appear alongside the kings of the Philistines and Edom, Moab, and Ammon. In Job 1:3 the people of the East are literally "the sons of Qedem" (Heb. *qedem*). This same term is found in Genesis 29:1, where it is related to Haran. Qedem is also a land mentioned in the early second-millennium-BC story of Sinuhe and his journeys around Canaan. Anson Rainey suggests the possibility of Qedem and Uz being in the Bashan/Hauran area, east or northeast of the Sea of Galilee.[a]

[a] Rainey and Notley, *Sacred Bridge*, 53–54.

for assistance against the marauders, might further the sense of someone located on the outskirts of the settled regions near the desert.

Like many of the psalms and other poetic and wisdom compositions, the dating of the story remains unclear. In part, this enables it to have application to everyone. Although in the reality behind the poem, Job and his comforters did not dialogue in poetry (any more than people do so today, especially amid pain and suffering), there is no reason to doubt that behind this tale there lies an authentic event on which the wise drew and with which they both told their tale and communicated one of the greatest literary and theological compositions of the ancient world.

Literary Readings

There are as many literary readings of the book of Job as there are readers,[20] or even more, since one reader may read the book in different ways. David J. A. Clines represents the latter as he suggests three ways to approach the book.[21] We have already seen two of these. The first is found in the outline at the beginning of this chapter. There the focus is on the speaker for each section. From this perspective the first part of each dialogue begins with some

20. See esp. Clines, *Job 1–20*, xxxiv–xxxvii. For the larger issues of the general forms of Wisdom literature, types of parallelism, etc., see "Literary Readings" for Proverbs.

21. Clines, *Job 1–20*.

vigorous interaction, but by the end of this section with the three friends, the cycle of speeches does not finish, and Job is left on his own. Chapter 28 may not be a Job speech at all. In the second half, Job reflects on his condition and then stops. Elihu keeps speaking for four deliveries but eventually stops. Yahweh then speaks, and Job responds briefly. Indeed, at the end all speaking stops, Job covers his mouth, and Yahweh acts to restore Job. In a sense all the speaking moves toward silence and does not accomplish what God does in the final few verses. Further, the speech becomes more and more oriented toward the speaker's own ideas and is less a matter of dialogue, at least among the human speakers. God restores this somewhat as Job does respond, but more in amazement than in true dialogue.

A second approach focuses on the three-part structure of the book: prose narrative, poetic speeches, prose narrative. This approach was discussed in the previous section. The problem is how to connect these different sections. Yet these sections are not so hard to relate to one another; readers have done so throughout the ages. The narrative sections set the background for the story that lies in between and serve to address two important issues that the poetry leaves unanswered but that demand some instruction. First, the narrative at the beginning explains why Job is suffering. It is not simply a whim of fate, nor is it even to test Job. According to the opening chapters, the purpose is to test God's faith in Job. Is it established and correct? Or is it merely an empty boast that God makes regarding this figure? The second purpose that the narrative frame serves is to describe the resolution to the discussion. As will be noted in the section on ancient Near Eastern comparison, most wisdom dialogues of this sort do not seek to resolve a "real" difficulty that one of the dialogue partners faces (see "Ancient Near Eastern Context," below). However, at the end of the book Job not only hears God but also receives blessing from him so that he knows old age, wealth, and a great family—all evidence of God's favor on Job.

A third approach observes the presence of the clues scattered in the prose that appear as notes throughout the poetry as well. Job's test ends not with his sinning but with his keeping quiet about God's treatment, as it is perceived (Job 2:10). However, when Job begins to speak, he curses the day of his birth (3:1) and cries out with the question as to why he is being treated in this fashion. This leads to Job's challenging God to appear and to justify his actions. Job's final statements of his innocence and unjust treatment end in chapter 31, where verse 40c makes this explicit. Job 32:1–6 begins the next major section with a series of lectures by Elihu, who carries the matter further, less in terms of new arguments and more in terms of summarizing the vanity of the whole process. Before Job has the opportunity to respond, God addresses Job and challenges the entire basis of his complaint. What right has Job to complain about the way things happen? He did not create the world, nor does he have power over it. So Job is brought to a point of repentance that causes him to withdraw his charges and to remain quiet before God (42:1–6). The effect of all of this is to provide a way for God to bless Job more than he has afflicted him.

This literary approach, as pointed out by Clines, provides less a concern for the significance of the discussion or dialogue and provides more focus on the three elements of a story: the exposition, the complication, and the resolution.[22] In the exposition of Job 1:1–2:10, readers learn of the background to the issues that follow. This backdrop occurs both on earth and in heaven. However, God is ultimately at work, setting the stage and allowing the Satan to engage in his hostilities toward Job and indirectly toward God.

The complication occupies most of the book. In this section (2:11–31:40), Job challenges God over the voices of his friends, who wish to implicate Job in a fault in which he has no part. Rather than accept some theoretical theology and search for sin (and its consequences) that is not present, Job turns to God and cries to him for justice and to defend his actions against Job. The wisdom poem (Job 28) recognizes such wisdom, but in this case the crowd (i.e., the three friends and Elihu) does not possess it. Job concludes his speeches with a reflection on his past, on his present suffering, and on the questions about where God is in all of this.

The speeches of Elihu (Job 32:1–37:24) launch the third section of Job, that of the resolution. It is not that Elihu provides resolution or even points the way. He seems to summarize the speeches of the other three friends, asserting that God is just and therefore that Job must be wrong. Job should search his heart carefully to see whether there is any part of it where he has sinned against God (perhaps in his wealth) and for which he now needs to repent. God's speeches remove the focus of Job's concerns and point to the grandeur and power of the Creator's work. Some of the mightiest beasts cannot even be understood in terms of their place in the universe. Rather, they are presented by God as created by him for his own pleasure and delight. In the conclusion, Job's repentance answers God's charges in the only fitting way possible. He humbles himself before God just as the Deity raises him up to new heights of blessing and prosperity.

Gender and Ideological Criticism

Any inquiry into the feminine and masculine elements of the book of Job cannot fail to notice the dominant masculine focus of the main human characters and that of much of the dialogue.[23] The first chapter identifies three daughters that Job has and relates them to his seven sons. They regularly are invited to feasts in the homes of the sons. They apparently do not have

22. Ibid., xxxv–xxxvi.

23. Schroer ("Ijob feministisch lesen?") tries to identify critiques of the anthropocentric worldview in the God speeches of Job 38–41.

houses of their own, but it is unclear as to why. No husbands or families are mentioned. Perhaps this was the social convention for unmarried daughters, that they presumably lived with their parents as the (also unmarried?) sons might not. Nevertheless, the picture is one of harmony.

Job's wife is the best known of the female characters. Despite their marriage and large family, she is mentioned only a few times, and never by name. In Job 2:9 she addresses Job after watching the destruction of her family, the loss of all the household fortune, and the affliction of her faithful and pious husband. She recognizes what God has witnessed earlier: Job holds on to his integrity. However, it is more than she can bear, and so she urges him to curse God and die rather than to continue to worship the one who, she believes, has brought these afflictions. In this role, Job's wife urges him to fulfill the prophecy of the Satan, that he would curse God in his troubles. In not heeding her, Job maintains a position that he will have throughout the book. Job's wife anticipates the friends of Job but also refutes their arguments. She sees what they do not. She knows Job's righteousness and realizes that it is no guarantee of well-being. Job's friends, in contrast, are forced to conclude that Job is not righteous.

Elsewhere, in 19:17, Job lists the fact that his breath is offensive to his wife as one of the examples of his loneliness and abandonment in his misery. In Job 31 the sufferer recounts his virtues. The first one is his refusal to look at another woman, in verses 1 and 9. He takes a curse on himself in verse 10 that, if he were so to abuse the marriage covenant, his wife should become a worker in another man's house and lie with that man. Although his wife is not again mentioned, Job receives back a family of seven sons and three daughters in chapter 42. There, in a departure from general convention and even from customary Israelite law (although not by any means without precedent), Job's three daughters inherit along with his sons (42:13–15). Their beauty is also mentioned in the same verse. This may be less a rationale for their inheritance and more a statement to praise them and to praise Job's family. Readers learn the names of the daughters, unlike the sons. This suggests a special honor for them.

Job appears as a righteous sufferer who, through no apparent fault of his own, faces persecution and suffering. He remains faithful and, in the end, is rewarded in this life with material blessing and with descendants. In all these ways he may be considered a masculine counterpart to Naomi, in the book of Ruth. She went through similar experiences and yet remained faithful to God.

There have been many attempts to approach the book of Job from a variety of ideological perspectives. Studies of Job have invited modern and postmodern literary approaches of deconstructionist and Marxist readings. These tend to produce conclusions more in keeping with the interests of the commentators than with any consistent and major theme in the book.[24] A consistent assumption is that God does not affirm moral retribution in the book of Job. The conclusion of the book is open ended.[25] Beyond this, several examples may be suggested here.

In one set of views, Satan is the good guy and God the bad guy. David Penchansky argues that Satan outwits God and that Job finds his integrity by blaspheming God.[26] Edwin Good concludes that Satan forces God to afflict Job and that Yahweh is evil.[27] Lowell Handy suggests that Satan is one of the lesser deities in Yahweh's pantheon, and his words and deeds demonstrate that he is completely subservient to Yahweh's instruction.[28] Therefore Yahweh, not Satan, must take the blame for Job's suffering. This argument uses Ugaritic myths to support its interpretation. However, it assumes necessarily a close correspondence between Ugaritic and Israelite mythology about the heavenly council.

Job overturns the expected wisdom script so that God shows up where the buffoon usually would, and he unexpectedly resolves the dilemma. Donald Gowan has proposed the interesting idea that there is an expected manner in which Wisdom literature would relate a story such as Job.[29] He calls this a wisdom "script." The book of Job has unexpected turns. Elihu would fill the role of the wisdom figure who resolves the problems. Instead, he appears as a buffoon. Unexpectedly, the appearance of God (theophany) and his challenges occur and move the reader beyond the expected answers of other Wisdom literature.

Katharine Dell suggests that skepticism or protest lies at the heart of Job.[30] It is a parody of wisdom and literary forms. For example, in Job 7:7–8 a traditional wish for healing becomes a wish for death. These forms build up to a dismissal of a faith that is not credible in the face of the circumstances.

Clines questions assumptions about the character of Job and the values that the book teaches:[31] (1) The book portrays poverty for Job in an unrealistic manner. The poor are concerned about the source of their next meal, not about the responses of their servants. (2) The text describes women either as a foil to contrast with Job's patience (2:9–10) or as measured by their physical beauty (42:15). (3) Everyone in the book assumes a connection between prosperity and piety. This assumption is never questioned, only how it can best

24. See, e.g., LaCocque, "Deconstruction of Job's Fundamentalism"; idem, "Job and Religion." The critique by Guillaume ("Deconstruction of Job") provides an example of some problems that need to be faced by this approach.

25. See Tsevat, "Book of Job"; and Newsom, "Cultural Politics."

26. Penchansky, *Betrayal of God*.

27. E. Good, *In Turns of Tempest*.

28. Handy, "Authorization of Divine Power."

29. Gowan, "Reading Job."

30. Dell, *Book of Job*.

31. Clines, "Deconstructing the Book of Job."

be understood and used for Job's advantage. René Girard and Leo G. Perdue argue that Job is portrayed not as a common "everyone" but as a kingly figure, or more accurately, as a royal victim.[32] Thus his responses are in accord with his position. In rebuttal, one might point out that the book never claims to represent the suffering of everyone: How could any figure accomplish that? Paul Redditt suggests that the God speeches teach Job that God is omniscient and omnipotent, and to be worshiped for these reasons alone (whether or not God is perceived as just and merciful).[33] The epilogue allows for God's mercy once Job comes to terms with who God is.

To a greater or lesser extent, all of these approaches follow the interpretation of the text. To some degree the variety of approaches supports the sense that the book is available to all on many levels. The reality of human suffering is something all persons face in their own ways. However, the diversity of approaches that have been applied to this book cannot all be accepted without question. There needs to be a consistency of reading, and words do mean something. The book does not contradict itself, and for two millennia and more, the work has fit into a corpus of the Hebrew Bible; for Christians it fits with the New Testament. Its role will be explored more in the following sections. Here believers affirm Job's consistent teaching on the importance of faith in God and endurance, even amid undeserved and inexplicable suffering.

Ancient Near Eastern Context

Wisdom literature that bemoans one's situation in life is not uncommon, especially in Mesopotamian and Egyptian sources.[34] While reflection on trials may appear as laments, and stories about them as tales, most scholars place this material under the category of speculative wisdom. Some of these compositions, expressing pessimism with a unified voice, will be reviewed under "Ancient Near Eastern Context" for Ecclesiastes. Here, special interest lies with (but is not limited to) works of dialogue.

Egyptian literature contains a number of examples of Job-like narratives.[35] Bad times and suffering in the country are reflected in the complaints of Khakheperre-Sonb, perhaps as early as the First Intermediate Period (in the late third millennium BC). From what may have been a few centuries later, the Admonitions of Ipuwer address a similar theme. While the Harper's Songs continue this theme into the late second millennium and beyond, texts such as the similarly dated Dispute of a Man with His Ba introduce the concept of a dialogue—even if the dialogue is with oneself! This character longs for death as a relief from the difficulties of life. He convinces his Ba ("soul") to

32. Girard, *Job*; Perdue, *Wisdom in Revolt*.

33. Redditt, "Reading the Speech Cycles."

34. See further Sparks, *Ancient Texts*, 61–65, 73–75, 100, 256.

35. For translations and notes, see *COS* 1.43.98–106; 2.13.64–66.

The Babylonian Theodicy

In many ways the Babylonian Theodicy resembles the book of Job. It begins with a rehearsal of the sufferer's problems. Rather than losing his children, the speaker has lost both father and mother at a young age and has no guardian to watch over him. The friend counsels that whoever is faithful in looking to his god and goddess in reverence will receive protection and prosperity. The sufferer emphasizes his physical pain, his loss of material possessions, and his lack of strength. The friend perceives his own thoughts as the best solution rather than the sufferer's experiences. Nevertheless, the sufferer insists that he has been faithful in offering and praying to his god. Like Job, he views the decision for his bad situation as coming from his god, whereas others who are unworthy receive advancement. As with Job's friends, as the discussion progresses there is a sense of frustration. Here the companion blames the sufferer for abandoning wisdom, for not following the traditional ways, and for sinning against his god by not properly worshiping him. The friend emphasizes how it is impossible to understand the purpose of the divine and refers to lies that the gods have given to humanity. However, the sufferer's circumstances have not changed as the dialogue comes to an end. Instead, it concludes with a prayer to his god for mercy and expresses hope that Shamash will treat all the faithful well.

remain with him into the afterlife, where blessings await. In all these texts, the concept of *Maʿat* ("justice, order") is questioned.

From the period of the Middle Kingdom (ca. 2030–1640 BC) there comes the Tale of the Eloquent Peasant. Khunanup is a poor man who goes in search of food and necessities for his family. His pleas for help before the local judge form the heart of the composition. After the first of nine elegant speeches by Khunanup, the judge arranges to provide food—but without telling him. After the ninth plea, the judge still officially denies the pleas but promises that they will be read before the king of Egypt. The king agrees to see to every need for the peasant. This presentation may resemble the elocution found in Job 26–31, especially the speeches of chapters 29–31.

Mesopotamian wisdom seems to be culturally closer to the sentiments and style of Job.[36] The Sumerian work Man and His God represents the earliest composition on the subject of undeserved suffering. The center of the work is a lament, a prayer to the god, who responds with healing and restoration. Unlike Job, the sufferer does admit the universal sinfulness of humanity and confesses his failings, even if done in ignorance.

36. For translations and notes to these Mesopotamian compositions, see *COS* 1.151.485, 1.152.486, 1.153.486–92, 1.154.492–95, 1.179.573–75.

The Dialogue between a Man and His God is a fragmentary Akkadian text from the Old Babylonian period. There is a conversation between a sufferer and his god. At the end the god decrees that the ailment is no longer a cause for concern and that the sufferer should remain aware of his god. Closer to the Sumerian Job is the Babylonian Job (*Ludlul Bēl Nēmeqi*), which describes how a wealthy public man lost his position, wealth, family, and health. In the midst of his intense suffering, he nevertheless honors the god Marduk and is rewarded with a restoration of what he lost. The purpose of the text, coming from about 1600–1200 BC, is to praise Marduk as chief god of Babylon.

Closer in message to the biblical Job is the Babylonian Theodicy (see the sidebar "The Babylonian Theodicy"). As its chief character this work also has a righteous sufferer who is falsely accused of sin and abandoned by friends, and yet he protests his own innocence. More than the other works, this Mesopotamian composition asserts the great power of the god and the difficulty of humans in dealing with such power. However, in this case a friend of the sufferer is persuaded that the gods allow evil people to prosper despite the divine responsibility for justice in the world. An interesting acrostic occurs in this poem, hidden in the first sign of each line. It relates the name of the author, Saggil-kinam-ubbib, a priest and scholar to Babylonian kings around 1100 BC.

From the seventh century BC is the prayer of an Assyrian king (Assurbanipal?) to the god Nabû.[37] The king is suffering. He confesses and appeals to the deity for forgiveness as well as a return to blessing and salvation from his enemies. Here as elsewhere in the Mesopotamian and Egyptian sources, there is limited discussion of divine justice. In a polytheistic context it is not possible to understand the purpose of the gods. For this reason there is no real parallel with Job. In the biblical book, the question of God's justice and righteousness forms the heart of the dialogues and later speeches by Job and his friends.[38] Indeed, behind these speeches may lie expressions of mockery and ridicule against the gods and their actions, as emerge in texts from Mesopotamian archives of the first millennium BC. See further the "Ancient Near Eastern Context" for Ecclesiastes.

Canonical Context

Job appears in Ezekiel 14:12–14 and 20, where he is listed beside Noah and Daniel as models of righteousness who altogether could not rescue the present wicked generation of Israel with their lives and prayers. In the New Testament, James 5:11 mentions Job as an example of endurance in the midst

37. See Livingstone, *Court Poetry*, 31–32, for text, translation, and notes.
38. See Bricker, "Innocent Suffering in Mesopotamia."

of undeserved suffering. The blessings that Job receives after successfully remaining faithful are presented as examples of God's certain blessing.

Job is situated in the middle of the Wisdom literature in the Bible in terms of its themes and approach. In terms of literary form, its dialogues and speeches lie between the brief and seemingly disconnected aphorisms of Proverbs and the extended treatise of Ecclesiastes. The same is true of its tone. It is neither as optimistic about the order of the world as the book of Proverbs nor as pessimistic as Ecclesiastes. Rather, the author sees problems in the apparent principles of justice that tradition has perpetuated, but the author is not ready to give up calling on God to explain and justify these ways of the world. Job may also be compared with the book of Ruth, where Naomi faces circumstances not unlike Job but also remains faithful to God and sees a divine resolution to them.

The book of Job, in its Christian canonical order, precedes the Psalms and anticipates the many psalms of lament that are found in that book. These psalms also envision problems that arise for the psalmist. As their main focus, they record the poetic cry of the psalmist for deliverance from enemies and all the difficult circumstances individually and corporately. Unlike Job, the psalms have no prose introduction that places the origin of the trials in the spiritual and heavenly world. Like Job, however, many of these psalms conclude with a note of joyful triumph, expressing praise to God for deliverance, whether realized or anticipated by divine promises.

From a Christian perspective, it is impossible not to find in the book of Job a model of endurance through persecution, especially where that persecution is related to the work and plans of Satan. Whether in texts such as Ephesians 6:10–18 or in the many passages that describe suffering in Revelation, the spiritual and cosmic reality of suffering for one's faith is a constant theme that the New Testament writers drew on in order to encourage Christians to endure. Beyond all this, however, is the powerful image of the suffering of Christ, the truly righteous one who suffers unjustly.[39] It is this suffering, without human hope or expectation of relief, this suffering unto death that fulfills the full suffering that Job began to explore. Yet it is also the physical resurrection of Christ that gives meaning to all suffering for faith and that provides new understanding to the physical and spiritual realities of what Job also finds on the other side of his own suffering.

Theological Perspectives of Job

In the book of Job, the Satan seeks in Job an instance of disinterested righteousness. This, coupled with the question of the proper manner of responding

39. Moskala ("God of Job") observes this connection and how Satan can be defeated only by weakness.

to undeserved suffering, leads each character in the poetic dialogue to emphasize elements of these issues. For Eliphaz, people are ill and suffer because they sin. While Bildad reinforces these points, Zophar adds a focus on the fate of the wicked. There is a sense in which Elihu understands suffering as pedagogic and so as designed to lead one to repentance.[40]

The book of Job represents one of the most existential works in the Bible. It describes Job's search for God's presence. In these terms, the primary purpose of the book is to bring Job into contact with God. The question of how Job experiences God becomes the key to the sufferer's search. That is realized as Job expresses and then encounters the presence of God.

Samuel Terrien describes the progression by identifying three well-known elements.[41] First, there is a presence of God that Job seeks but that lies beyond his physical ability to obtain. Although demanding an audience for his case (9:33; 13:3, 15), he is impotent to bring it about. So Job is left alone with his faith:

> If only there would be someone to bring about a decision,
> that he might lay his hand upon the two of us. (9:33 RSH)
>
> If only I could speak to the Almighty.
> I desire God to bring about a decision. (13:3 RSH)
>
> If he kills me, I will still wait for him.
> I will seek a decision from him. (13:15 RSH)

Second, the presence of God that Job seeks lies beyond the time of this world and this life, after Job's death—and notice here that his faith in God does not waver. Job believes that God truly is in control and has power over the world. He also believes, despite all that may have been wrongly done to him, that there will be a judgment, a time of confrontation with the living God.[42] Because Job has believed this all of his life, it has made a difference as to how he lives that life moment by moment. So Job believes and knows that he has a Redeemer who does live. If he does not encounter God in this life, Job certainly will meet him in the life to come.[43] So certain is he of this that he expresses it in what is called the "prophetic perfect." This is a form that often appears in the past tense. Here the past tense expresses the certainty of Job's encounter with God.

40. See Wahl, *Gerechte Schöpfer*.

41. Terrien, *Elusive Presence*.

42. See Mies, *Espérance de Job*, for the emphasis that Job's hope is God and that the book is about Job's love for God, which energizes this hope.

43. Is the "Redeemer" actually God or a member of the heavenly court? See Seow, "Job's *gōʾēl*, Again."

I know that my Redeemer lives
  and afterward he will rise upon the ground.
After they have torn my skin to pieces,
  apart from my flesh I will see God,
whom I will see for myself.
  My eyes, and not those of a stranger, have seen this.
So my innermost emotions have been satisfied. (19:25–27 RSH)

Third, there is Job's experience with God; God does appear to Job. At that point Job can only repent. According to Terrien, this constitutes presence beyond honor.[44] However, this is not so much a question of Job's honor as it is a matter of accepting the words of God. The divine perspective comes as Job is brought into the world of the divinity. Instead of offering some explanation or rational argument regarding the presence of evil and suffering, God shows his creation in its awesome power and enormity.[45] In doing so he moves the sufferer out of the center of attention. It is no longer Job and Job alone who matters. Job sees that he is one part of a much greater plan of God, a plan that he cannot always clearly understand. However, this is not what matters. It is the word of God and, through that word, the manifestation of the divine presence. So Job, before the restoration to come, voices these last words in his book:

I had certainly heard with my ears,
  but now my eyes have seen you.
Therefore I turn away,
  and I repent in dust and ashes. (42:5–6 RSH)

Job 38–39 presents another account of God as Creator. This account follows a set of topics similar to Genesis 1; Psalm 89:10–13; and Psalm 104, texts in which God creates and controls the sea (and overpowers the sea monsters), fixes the earth on its foundations, brings forth springs of waters, creates day and night, creates the sun and seasons, and creates people.[46] As with Genesis 1, so also Job 38:1–38 first reviews God as creator of the world, including the great wonders and powers of the heavens, both meteorological and astrological. As in Genesis 1, God divides and fixes boundaries, thus exerting control over these powers. At the same time he prepares the world as a background for the creation of life and populating the world with that life. Job 38:39–39:30 describes the amazing powers and abilities of various animals, beyond what people can do, yet all created by God. Genesis 1 climaxes with the creation of humanity; Job 40:15–41:34 moves forward to describe God's creation of the behemoth and the leviathan. These climax this creation story because they

44. Terrien, *Elusive Presence*, 368–71.
45. Campbell, "Book of Job."
46. M. Smith, *Priestly Vision*, 27.

demonstrate the creation of animals (though to which animals they correspond is not agreed, perhaps the crocodile and the hippopotamus) whose strength and power take on hyperbolic dimensions. For Job, the Creator's power is so far beyond what mortal minds can understand that to challenge him or to seek to understand his ways is not possible.[47]

Job 31 remains the great ethics chapter in this book and perhaps the most important summary of ethics in the Bible. It begins with Job's own refusal to allow sexual lust in his life, a key source of human temptation. This is coupled with honesty in all of his dealings with others (31:5–8). Again, resisting the sexual sin of adultery (31:9–12) is coupled with his concern to show justice and mercy (31:13–23) toward those who are dependent (slaves), poor, and vulnerable (widows and orphans). Greed for money and trust in wealth are pitfalls that Job has avoided (31:24–25), as well as worshiping the sun and moon, which are just part of God's creation and not the givers of security (31:26–28). Job does not curse or gloat over an enemy (31:29–30). Job reasserts his justice and mercy toward both his servants and the workers in his house, as well as the stranger to whom he would show hospitality (31:31–32). After a general statement of his innocence and an invitation to examine every step of his life (31:33–37), he concludes with a self-curse on his land if he has taken anything wrongfully from the tenant farmers on his land. For Job, chapter 31 combines both specific deeds and general expressions of love for neighbors.

Key Commentaries and Studies

Alden, Robert A. *Job*. NAC 11. Nashville: Broadman & Holman, 1994. Balanced, concise, evangelical exegesis.

Andersen, Francis I. *Job: An Introduction and Commentary*. TOTC. Leicester, UK: Inter-Varsity; Downers Grove, IL: InterVarsity, 1976. Strongest evangelical linguistic study.

Balentine, Samuel E. *Job*. SHBC. Macon, GA: Smyth & Helwys, 2006. Creative, theological exegesis.

Clines, David J. A. *Job 1–20*. WBC 17. Dallas: Word, 1989.

———. *Job 21–37*. WBC 18A. Nashville: Nelson, 2006.

———. *Job 38–42*. WBC 18B. Nashville: Nelson, 2011. These three volumes are the strongest of rhetorical and literary studies.

Gordis, Robert. *The Book of Job: Commentary, New Translation, and Special Studies*. New York: Jewish Theological Seminary of America, 1978. Strong linguistic approach with a sensitivity to traditional rabbinic interpretation.

Hartley, John E. *The Book of Job*. NICOT. Grand Rapids: Eerdmans, 1988. Evangelical study and linguistic analysis.

Seow, Choon-Leong. *Job 1–21: Interpretation and Commentary*. Illuminations. Grand Rapids: Eerdmans, 2013. Excellent study of the Hebrew text. Best on history of interpretation.

47. Creation is not safe, but it is divinely ordered. See Schifferdecker, *Out of the Whirlwind*. Balentine ("For No Reason") rejects an order to the universe and with respect to Job emphasizes the manner in which God is a partner for those questioning the unexplained appearance of evil.

15

PSALMS

Augustine reflected that our hearts are restless until they find rest in God. The Psalms demonstrate that rest can be found in crying to God for relief, in praising God for his blessings, and in celebrating God's great works of salvation and grace—past, present, and future.

Name, Text, and Outline

The Hebrew title, *tĕhillîm*, derives from the root *hll*, "to praise." The term thus refers to the praises that the book contains. The Greek (LXX) does not use the corresponding Greek term. Instead, from the Hebrew *mizmôr*, "song/psalm" (as in the title for Ps. 3 etc.), it derives the commonly used name (as in Luke 20:42; Acts 1:20) for "song," Greek *psalmos*, with the plural, *psalmoi*. The term "Psalter" derives from the Greek word for a stringed instrument, *psaltērion*. This first appears as the title of the book in the Septuagint Codex Alexandrinus, from the fifth century AD.

The Masoretic Text of Psalms contains some unique and difficult terms and spellings, a phenomenon not unknown elsewhere in the Bible's Hebrew poetry. However, the Septuagint does not usually reveal a clearer text at those points. It may simply be translating Greek or it may translate a different Hebrew text from that preserved by the Masoretic Text. Many scholars have found evidence of interpretation and development in comparison with the Masoretic Text, but questions about how this should be understood remain.[1]

1. Pietersma, "Septuagintal Exegesis."

What is not in doubt is that the numbering of most of the psalms differs in the two versions (see table below). The chapter numbering in most English versions follows the Hebrew Masoretic Text, rather than the Septuagint. The Septuagint adds Psalm 151, which is found in Hebrew among the Dead Sea Scrolls. The Septuagint has superscriptions that sometimes are similar to those in the Masoretic Text, yet sometimes include statements that do not occur for the Hebrew Psalms.

Numbering of the Psalms

Masoretic Text	Septuagint
Pss. 1–8	Pss. 1–8
Pss. 9–10	Ps. 9
Pss. 11–113	Pss. 10–112
Pss. 114–115	Ps. 113
Ps. 116	Pss. 114–115
Pss. 117–146	Pss. 116–145
Ps. 147	Pss. 146–147
Pss. 148–150	Pss. 148–150

Among the Dead Sea Scrolls are more fragments of the Psalms than of any other book of the Hebrew Bible. 11QPs^{a} and 11QPs^{b} attest to a distinctive order of Psalms 90–150 that is different from the Masoretic Text.[2] At least fifteen apocryphal psalms are included along with the canonical psalms. Peter Flint is persuasive that there is a distinctive tradition, preserved at Qumran, of order and contents in the second half of the Psalter.[3] It is not clear how widespread this was, or whether these texts were lectionaries or regarded with the same (or greater) status than the Psalms of the Masoretic Text.

For this reason it may be of special interest to consider the fragments of Psalms scrolls preserved at Masada. These date from the same period, first century BC and early first century AD. The two manuscripts are designated as MasPs^{a} and MasPs^{b}.[4] MasPs^{a} includes 81:1–85:6 in the Masoretic order and with no additions or deletions. MasPs^{b} includes 147:18–150:6 in the Masoretic order and with no additions or deletions. This supports the possibility that the Jewish Zealots who held Masada used scrolls in conformity with the orthodoxy that could describe the groups connected with the Jerusalem temple and with mainstream Judaism. Those at Qumran reflected sectarian concerns, and in any case the fragments and parts of scrolls may not have composed works that were intended to form a "canonical Bible." Instead, they

2. See esp. Flint, *Dead Sea Psalms Scrolls*; idem, "Book of Psalms"; and J. Sanders, *Psalms Scroll*.
3. Flint, *Dead Sea Psalms Scrolls*, 168–69.
4. Flint, "Appendix," 289.

may have served liturgical purposes. If this is the case, then it is not possible to draw conclusions about the lack of formation of the Hebrew Bible canon on the basis of these texts from Qumran. Instead, where the fragments of the Masada Psalms scrolls preserve readings, they agree with the canonical order of the Psalms in the Masoretic Bible, in the Septuagint, and in most English Bibles today.

An outline of the book of Psalms would not be useful because there is no plot or narrative to follow, nor is there an easily identifiable order or logic to the sequence of psalms. Thus one would produce a disparate listing of about 150 different subjects, in most cases with no clear relationship even between any two that are side-by-side. See the following "Overview of the Psalms" for a description of major content matters.

This is not to suggest that no outline can be produced. For example, there has long been noted a division of the entire Psalter into five sections, or books. Some have related this to the five books of the Pentateuch. However, the content does not lend itself to such a correlation. This division is based on twofold "amens" or explicit notes that appear in the last verse or two of the last psalm in each of the groups. They can be divided as follows:

I. 1–41
II. 42–72
III. 73–89
IV. 90–106
V. 107–150

Of these, Psalm 72 is the most explicit. Verse 19 ends, "Amen and Amen." The last verse of the psalm (72:20) reads, "The prayers of David son of Jesse are concluded." This not only suggests an ending to the second of the five major sections but also implies that the first two books of the Psalms contain psalms that have a special relationship to David. The verse implies that David may have composed them. He may have prayed and have sung these psalms.

There are other groupings of psalms as well. These are often identified according to the superscriptions. For example, Psalms 42–49 are attributed to the sons of Korah. According to 1 Chronicles 6:22, 37–38, Korah was a descendant of Levi (perhaps a great-grandson) and thus may have been associated with the temple service and perhaps with music and psalms. The sons of Korah could be descendants or perhaps musical groups that performed at various times for temple ceremonies.

The same may be true of the sons of Asaph. Asaph, mentioned in 1 Chronicles 15:17–19, is explicitly identified as a musician responsible for the bronze cymbals. Psalms 50 and 73–83 are connected to him or to the sons of Asaph, similar to the sons of Korah. Another grouping includes the Songs of Ascent, according to the title of Psalms 120–134. Each of these is called a song of *hamma'ălôt*, a term that can refer to steps. It is possible to think of pilgrims coming to Jerusalem and singing these songs as they climb the steps to the temple. However, this is speculative. (See plate 6 in the gallery for a view of the location of Solomon's temple.)

Overview of the Psalms

Psalm 1 opens the Psalter by encouraging the reader to delight in torah, the instruction of the law. Psalm 2 looks to God in heaven, who appoints his leader on earth to rule the nations. Psalm 3 counts on divine protection, especially during the sleeping and arising of the psalmist. Psalm 4 repeats this theme for protection against enemies, especially when going to sleep and finding peaceful rest. Psalm 5 focuses on the mourning and cries to God for help then. Psalm 6 continues this theme and speaks of crying before God all night long. Again Psalm 7 seeks salvation from one's enemies with the expectation that those who plan evil against another will fall into their own traps. Psalm 8 praises God and his creation, especially people. Psalm 9 exalts in God's triumph over the enemies and nations who attack the psalmist. Psalm 10 meditates on the schemes of the wicked who lie in wait and calls on God to give victory.

Psalm 11 describes how Yahweh is on his throne and will destroy the wicked. Psalm 12 focuses on the fate of those who speak boastfully and ignore God. With Psalm 13 the psalmist cries, "How long?" and rejoices in God's salvation. Psalm 14 touches on the fear among the wicked and considers their threat against the poor. Psalm 15 explains how one must love God and one's neighbor to worship in God's temple. Psalm 16 is filled with rejoicing as the psalmist is blessed by God's presence. Then Psalm 17 calls on God to protect the psalmist from enemies who prowl like lions. Psalm 18 describes a great theophany of God coming to aid and strengthen the psalmist. Psalm 19 celebrates God's creation and his torah. In Psalm 20 the writer pronounces a blessing on those who are faithful to God.

Psalm 21 praises God for blessing the king and promises victory over his enemies. Psalm 22 focuses on the suffering of the psalmist, who is faithful to God. The famous twenty-third Psalm describes how Yahweh is a shepherd who guides his flock and prepares blessings for them. Psalm 24 identifies those who may come to worship Yahweh and includes a ceremonial repetition, crying to God for entrance into his sanctuary. Psalm 25 calls to Yahweh and emphasizes how the psalmist waits on and hopes for him. Psalm 26 is a claim of innocence and righteousness before God. Psalm 27 is a cry to Yahweh for salvation and a confident affirmation of its realization. The twenty-eighth Psalm looks to Yahweh with a plea for mercy and praise for his strength. The voice of Yahweh as powerful and defending his people is found in Psalm 29. Psalm 30 describes a penitent psalmist, to whom Yahweh has shown mercy.

Psalm 31 seeks help from God to overcome those enemies who slander. From personal experience, the writer of Psalm 32 encourages all to confess their sin to Yahweh and to know his salvation. It is far more important to sing to Yahweh and to know his creation power and salvation than to trust in military might, according to Psalm 33. Psalm 34 counsels the righteous to seek Yahweh, fear him, watch their tongue, and know the salvation of Yahweh. The psalmist of Psalm 35 cries to Yahweh for deliverance from enemies who have betrayed him and gloated over his difficulties. Psalm 36 contrasts the sinfulness of the wicked with the faithful love of Yahweh. Psalm 37 describes the wicked and their plotting, as well as the need to wait for Yahweh's aid without worrying. The thirty-eighth Psalm reflects on how sin has brought the psalmist very low and how to wait for Yahweh. Psalm 39 reflects on human mortality and looks to Yahweh for salvation. The author of Psalm 40 rejoices in Yahweh while confessing obedience and praying for salvation.

Facing sickness and enemies who betray him, the composer of Psalm 41 takes refuge in Yahweh. Psalms 42 and 43 cry to God after disappointment, liken desire for God to a deer panting for water, and counsel hope in God. In Psalm 44 the speakers remember defeat by enemy armies and call on God to deliver them. Psalm 45 celebrates the wedding of a king and his princess bride. Psalm 46 finds Yahweh as a true refuge in the midst of life's trials. Psalm 47 praises Yahweh's universal sovereignty and the inheritance he has given those who proclaim this psalm. Psalm 48 praises Yahweh's protection of Zion (= Jerusalem) against its enemies and recommends visiting Zion and admiring its defenses. Psalm 49 describes how all die, but there is a difference between the proud, who trust in themselves, and the psalmist, whom God will redeem from the grave. Psalm 50 celebrates Yahweh's sovereignty, with no need for food (sacrifices), and warns that he will not rescue the wicked, who hate his teaching and join with thieves.

Psalm 51 is the great psalm of repentance from sin and of prayer for forgiveness. Psalm 52 contrasts the boasting wicked with the righteous, who fear God. Psalm 53 is a duplicate of Psalm 14, except for the replacement of Yahweh in the earlier psalm with Elohim ("God") in the later one. Psalm 54 includes a cry to God for salvation from enemies, followed by a promise of an offering and praise to God for his deliverance. The suffering in Psalm 55 is attributed to betrayal by a friend and his violation of a covenant. In Psalm 56, the psalmist has many enemies but trusts in God, who has delivered the supplicant. Psalm 57 moves from a cry for salvation from enemies who are like lions to verses of praise to God for his loving faithfulness. In Psalm 58 the psalmist describes the evil of the unjust and curses them, believing that the righteous are rewarded. Psalm 59 continues this description and waits for God, who laughs at them. Psalm 60 recalls a time when God rejected his people and describes how God has victory over all Israel's neighbors.

In Psalm 61 the blessings of God to the faithful are coupled with prayer for the king's life and protection. God is the psalmist's only hope in Psalm 62, for he is strong and loving. In Psalm 63 the poet promises undying love to God and receives security. In Psalm 64 God condemns those who lie in wait to ambush the innocent, with the result that all humanity will fear God. In Psalm 65 the people of God rejoice that the creator God has blessed them, forgiven them, and fed them with a bountiful harvest from his land. The power of God and his care for his people who remove sin from their lives is the theme of Psalm 66. Psalm 67 is a prayer for God's blessing, a cry for all peoples to praise God, and a promise of God's richest blessing. The psalmist of Psalm 68 combines the great power of God with his care for the poor, his destruction of the wicked, and his worthiness of praise. Psalm 69 has the psalmist crying to God for deliverance against his enemies, praising God for who he is, and confidently proclaiming God's salvation of Zion and Judah. Psalm 70 confesses how poor and needy the psalmist is and cries for deliverance.

In Psalm 71 the writer speaks of a trust in God that began at the worshiper's birth and remains into the present and forever. Psalm 72 prays to God for the universal rule and justice of the king. In Psalm 73 the writer meditates on how good the wicked seem to have it in their enjoyment of life but then visits God's sanctuary and understands that their destruction is assured, while the writer trusts in God. Psalm 74 describes the destruction of God's temple and recalls the power of the Creator over chaos, with an appeal to remember his covenant. In Psalm 75 God is portrayed as a just judge who sustains all creation and warns against boasting. In Psalm 76 God is the warrior who overcomes all rulers of the earth. In Psalm 77 the psalmist remembers God's power over all the forces of creation. Psalm 78 recalls God's salvation and provision for Israel in Egypt, the exodus, and the wilderness. It concludes with his choice of Zion for his temple and David for his shepherd. Psalm 79 reflects on the invasion of other nations and cries to Yahweh for help. Psalm 80 also reflects on this event yet reviews the earlier history of God's creation and protection of Israel as a vine.

Psalm 81 reflects on the idolatry of Israel and God's longing that they might return to him so that he could bless them again. In Psalm 82 God charges the "gods" with injustice and deposes them as mortals. In Psalm 83 the nations surrounding Israel join together to destroy God's people, and the psalmist cries to God for their defeat. Psalm 84 rejoices in Yahweh's temple and asks for divine blessing on God's chosen messiah. Psalm 85 cries to God to restore his people and promises God's faithfulness to those who fear him. Psalm 86 cries to God for mercy and deliverance. Psalm 87 celebrates Zion as at the center of the world, with all nations envying its citizens. In Psalm 88 the poet endures unremitting suffering and pain despite calling to Yahweh for help. Psalm 89 recalls God's power at creation, his selection of David and promise of an eternal line, and his rejection of his anointed one and concludes with

© Baker Publishing Group and Dr. James C. Martin. The Israel Museum.

Second-millennium-BC ivory from Megiddo with enthroned and victorious Canaanite king receiving libations, incense, music, and prisoners

a cry to God to remember his covenant. In Psalm 90 a thousand years with God are as one day, and so the psalmist cries for God's mercy.

Psalm 91 celebrates the security of the psalmist and declares confidence in Yahweh's protection against enemies. Psalm 92 continues the praise of the greatness of God and his defeat of his enemies. In Psalm 93 God's throne and statutes remain despite the powers of the seas that may attempt to destroy them. Psalm 94 describes the character of the wicked, God's judgment of them, and his salvation of the psalmist. Praise for God's power is followed by a warning not to harden one's heart in Psalm 95. Psalm 96 calls on the nations and all creation to praise Yahweh, who will judge the earth. In Psalm 97 Yahweh appears with thunder, lightning, and darkness, and those who trust in his judgments rejoice. Psalm 98 calls on all, including the seas and rivers, to praise Yahweh. Psalm 99 praises the greatness of Yahweh, recalls the early leaders of Israel, and commands further worship and praise. Psalm 100 commands all the earth to worship Yahweh and praise him in his temple.

The psalmist of Psalm 101 vows to be pure before God, to avoid the perverse, and to live among the faithful. The psalmist suffers and mourns in Psalm 102, calling on Yahweh for deliverance and for rebuilding Zion. Psalm 103 calls on the psalmist and others to praise Yahweh for his forgiveness, compassion, and faithfulness. Psalm 104 praises Yahweh as Lord of all creation and sovereign over all its powers. In Psalm 105 God's faithfulness, despite the sins of his people, is reviewed in Israel's history from Abraham through to the story of the wilderness wandering. Psalm 106 continues this theme, beginning with the exodus and tracing the later rebellions of the nation. In Psalm 107 various groups of people facing dangers cry to Yahweh, and he delivers them. The first half of Psalm 108 praises God for his love and power over all the nations; the second half repeats the song of triumph over neighboring countries, as also found at the end of Psalm 60. Much of Psalm 109 forms a set of imprecations on the poet's enemies, who seek to destroy him despite his poverty, prayer, fasting, and cries to Yahweh his God. Psalm 110 praises the messiah chosen by God as a priest after Melchizedek's order and as a world ruler.

With Psalm 111 the poet praises God for his deeds of compassion, his provision for those who fear him, his faithfulness, and his redemption. Psalm 112 blesses the righteous one who delights in Yahweh's commands and assists those in need, while the wicked are vexed at this. In Psalm 113 Yahweh is praised everywhere and always for working justice to help the poor and barren. The psalmist of Psalm 114 speaks of the departure of the sea and the "skipping" of the mountains when Israel came from Egypt and settled in the promised land, where God's temple is. Psalm 115 mocks the lifelessness of images that are worshiped and counsels all Israel to trust in Yahweh. In Psalm 116 the psalmist has faced death but calls on Yahweh, who delivers him so that he may now serve his God. Psalm 117, the shortest in the Psalter (two verses), extols the praising of Yahweh. The psalmist of Psalm 118 gives thanks to Yahweh for his eternal covenantal love and for his deliverance from nations who attacked. There is a festal procession through the gates and into the temple to worship Yahweh. Psalm 119, the longest psalm (176 verses), forms an acrostic: every line of a stanza of about eight verses begins with the same letter; the stanzas thus move through the Hebrew alphabet. Each verse extols God's word, his torah.

Psalms 120–134 comprise fifteen Psalms of Ascent: each briefly addresses a special point or subject respecting praise. Psalm 120 condemns deceit and war. The next ten psalms (121–130) look to Yahweh for protection, bless Jerusalem, seek divine mercy, praise God for deliverance just as a bird is delivered from a net, exalt Jerusalem and Yahweh's protection, seek restoration after returning to Zion from captivity, counsel that the blessing of a family comes from Yahweh, cry under the oppression of those who hate the psalmist and Zion, and extol waiting on Yahweh for redemption. In the remaining Psalms of Ascent (131–134), the singers still their hearts like a weaned child; praise Yahweh's temple in Zion, where the covenant with David's house was made; rejoice in the fellowship of believers; and exhort one another to lift their hands to the temple and praise Yahweh.

Psalm 135 returns to the theme of praising Yahweh, with recollection of his great victories for Israel in the past and meditation on the impotence of the gods of the nations. Creation and Yahweh's defeat of Egypt, Sihon, and Og form the content of Psalm 136, where each verse ends with the refrain, "for his covenantal love [Heb. *ḥesed*] lasts forever" (RSH). Psalm 137 is a psalm of the exile that condemns Babylon and its ally Edom for destroying Jerusalem. Psalm 138 recounts how the poet and all the kings of the earth should praise Yahweh. Psalm 139 recounts Yahweh's knowledge of the psalmist in every area of life, his presence with the psalmist everywhere, and the psalmist's hatred of Yahweh's enemies and request that God would search the worshiper and convict of any sin. Psalm 140 prays for salvation from the hands of the wicked and for their just punishment.

Psalm 141 distinguishes the rebukes of the righteous, which are welcome, from those of the wicked, for whom the psalmist seeks punishment. In Psalm 142 the psalmist cries to Yahweh for salvation. Psalm 143 continues this theme with requests to be delivered from divine judgment and for deliverance from

© Baker Publishing Group and Dr. James C. Martin
Assyrian musicians with stringed instruments

enemies. Beginning with a confession of Yahweh as a Rock who trains the psalmist for war and has power to set mountains smoking and send out lightning, Psalm 144 prays for deliverance from the waters and from enemies and looks forward to a time of abundant peace. In Psalm 145 the poet praises Yahweh as divine king, as compassionate, and as upholding those who fall and are in need. Psalm 146 counsels trusting and praising Yahweh, not princes. The psalm notes his special concern for the poor and vulnerable.

The last four psalms begin with "Hallelujah!" and thus command readers to praise Yah(weh). In Psalm 147 Yahweh gathers the exiles, binds the brokenhearted, and controls the stars. He provides food for all and delights in those who reverence him. Only to Israel and Jacob has he given his laws, however. Psalm 148 commands angels and the heavens and earth to praise Yahweh because he has raised a "horn" for his people. Psalm 149 counsels praise with dancing and music from Yahweh's saints, in whom he delights. They are to praise God and bind their enemies. Psalm 150 concludes the Psalter with a repeated command, "Praise him," and with lists of musical instruments and dancing to accompany the praise.

Reading the Psalms

Premodern Readings

In both Judaism and Christianity, the Psalms have been read and meditated on as a priceless means of access to a deeper spiritual life with Yahweh and with Christ.[5] So much has been written on these prayers and praises that

5. For discussion of what follows and references, see esp. Wray Beal, "Psalms 3: History of Interpretation"; Grogan, *Prayer, Praise and Prophecy*, 27–30; W. Holladay, *Psalms through Three Thousand Years*; and the essays in Gillingham, *Approaches to the Psalms*.

only a small summary can be given here. As a representative of the exegetical approach of Judaism, the midrash on the Psalms reflects early interpretive approaches. Rabbi David Ḳimḥi represents a medieval approach with profound insights. He along with Ibn Ezra and Rashi, Jewish scholars of the eleventh to thirteenth centuries, were often interested in the literal interpretation of the text.[6] Therefore they were concerned with the historical background and with the meanings of Hebrew terms. Attempts by Christian exegetes to apply the Psalms to Jesus Christ were thus rejected. For example, Rashi considers the messianic Psalm 2 to apply readily to David rather than to a later figure such as Jesus.

In early Christianity[7] the *Epistle of Barnabas* (5.13) identifies the psalmist as a prophet foretelling the passion of Christ. *First Clement* (16.15–16; 36.5) connects the Psalms (22 and 110) with messianic claims related to Jesus. The *Didache* (3.7) counsels meekness from Psalm 37:11, as Polycarp (*Philippians* 2.1) uses Psalm 2:11 to reflect on service to God. The early Christian writers made use of the Psalms as prophecies of Christ and as means of caring for the spiritual needs of their flocks.

Psalm 22 describes the suffering of Christ, according to Justin Martyr (*Dialogue with Trypho* 98–106), Irenaeus (*Adversus Haereses* 4.20, 33), and Tertullian (*Adversus Judaeos* 10). For Augustine, the Psalms of Ascent become the means by which one ascends to union with God (*Enarrationes in Psalmos*, Psalm 120). His *Enarrationes* remains one of the finest Christian theological commentaries on the book of Psalms ever written, and his *Selected Sermons* include comments on the Christian life away from sin.[8] Jerome (*Tractatus in Psalmos* 1) recognizes the first psalm as forming an introduction to the entire book. For Theodore of Mopsuestia, Psalms 1–8 are not messianic, but Psalm 45 prefigures the groom as Christ and the bride as the church.[9] The medieval period repeated many of the interpretations of the earlier times, often with emphasis on the titles of the psalms and on an allegorical interpretation.

In the Reformation, Martin Luther saw in each psalm a prophecy of Christ.[10] His study of the penitential psalms remains one of the best sources for understanding and applying the Psalms to Holy Week, especially Good Friday and Easter. John Calvin remained more in touch with an original meaning in the text.[11] However, he could also find in the psalms various types of Christ. Calvin and those who followed him used the psalms for instruction in prayer and personal devotional life. Here the Reformers found examples of holy

6. Ḳimḥi, *The Longer Commentary*; Ibn Ezra, *Abraham Ibn Ezra's Commentary on the First Book of Psalms*; Gruber, *Rashi's Commentary on the Psalms*.

7. The references follow Holmes, *The Apostolic Fathers*.

8. E.g., on Ps. 114 in Augustine, *Expositions on the Book of Psalms*, 834–46.

9. Hill, *Theodore of Mopsuestia: Commentary on Psalms 1–81*.

10. Luther, *Luther's Works*, vol. 10; idem, *Luther's Works*, vol. 11.

11. E.g., Calvin, *Commentary on the Psalms*.

and practical daily living before God. Beginning with Luther, Ulrich Zwingli, and Calvin, the Psalms were adapted to music and sung in the tunes of their period, a practice that has continued to the present (and was certainly not original to the Reformation).

Brevard Childs has recognized that some of the best Puritan exegesis was done in relation to the Psalms.[12] This includes John Owen, Richard Baker, Richard Sibbes, and Henry Ainsworth. Continuing in that tradition, Charles Spurgeon's *Treasury of David* repays study for its fine exposition.[13] John Donne's *Sermons on the Psalms and the Gospels* represents some of the finest examples of the English language put to use in interpretation.[14] It is perhaps significant to mention here the English translators of the King James Bible, whose richness of expression in the Psalms exceeds the poetic quality of the original Hebrew, in the view of some. As one moves forward in time, the Victorian appropriation of the Psalms may be found in the nineteenth-century sermons of Alexander MacLaren.[15] Of all the devotional examples of the Psalms in the last century, Dietrich Bonhoeffer's personal reflections remain an outstanding example.[16]

In 1753 Archbishop Robert Lowth, professor of poetry at Oxford University, gave lectures in which he proposed that each psalm be interpreted in its historical and cultural context.[17] His own approach set the background for modern study of the Psalms, particularly his discussion of parallelism and his division of it into three categories. In this manner he was able to provide examples of synonymous, antithetical, and synthetic parallelism, according to the manner in which the second line in a two-line verse reinforces, contrasts, or otherwise develops the first line. More on these categories of parallelism can be found in the following sections.

Higher Criticism

The development of the critical study of the Psalms was tied with identifying a *Sitz im Leben* (life setting) that could define where and how any particular psalm came into existence.[18] For most of its history, the church has interpreted the text allegorically and christologically. At the Reformation and during the subsequent Enlightenment, the psalms were seen primarily as expressions of the individual. Only beginning in the nineteenth century were serious questions raised regarding the possible connection of psalms with the cult

12. Childs, *Old Testament Books*, 63.
13. Spurgeon, *Treasury of David*.
14. Donne, *John Donne's Sermons on the Psalms and Gospels*.
15. MacLaren, *Expositions of Holy Scriptures: The Book of Psalms*.
16. Bonhoeffer, *Psalms*.
17. Lowth, *Lectures on the Sacred Poetry*.
18. See review in Day, *Psalms* (OTG).

of ancient Israel.[19] Hermann Gunkel, examining psalms texts from temple contexts elsewhere in the ancient Near East, began to look at the forms of the psalms and to link them to various aspects of the cult.[20] Thus the distinction was made between individual and communal psalms, and between laments and praises.

Sigmund Mowinckel continued the study of Psalms in the context of the cult.[21] He, and others such as Paul Volz, were instrumental in relating the Babylonian New Year's festival—the weeklong *Akitu* celebration of the coming of the New Year, which was connected with the king's participation in divine ceremonies—with a similar festival that they hypothesized in Israel.[22] Here as well, the king was enthroned as a divine figure, and the creation of the world and of the state were acknowledged through psalms of recollection and praise that found their way into the book of Psalms. Although criticized by other scholars,[23] the theory of the divine enthronement of the king as a god was taken up by the Myth and Ritual school as represented in northern Europe. For the general development and criticism of this approach, see the discussion under "Tradition History" for Genesis.

Although this theory has not remained acceptable to scholars as it was originally articulated, it did spawn attempts to connect the psalms with various festivals. From Germany, Hans-Joachim Kraus connected the psalms with a festival celebrating God's choice of Jerusalem.[24] In the same decade, that of the 1960s, Artur Weiser produced a commentary that sought to relate the psalms to an annual covenant-renewal festival in Israel.[25] This at least had some precedent with events found in texts such as Joshua 8:30–35 and Joshua 24, plus the setting presented by the book of Deuteronomy. In the end these approaches failed to endure due to their speculative and idiosyncratic nature. With the possible exception of Psalm 118:27 (which was applied to the autumn Feast of Booths in Second Temple Judaism), there is no explicit description in the Psalms that would identify an annual festival celebration. Instead, the Psalms resist an identification of each psalm with a particular *Sitz im Leben*.

In the middle of the twentieth century, Gerhard von Rad, Claus Westermann, and Weiser represented scholars who examined the theology of the Psalms and the manner in which it communicated the message of God to his

19. As noted earlier, the terms "cult" and "cult center" refer to evidence of religious activities without any pejorative implications as to the religion that may have been practiced.

20. Gunkel, *Introduction to the Psalms*.

21. Mowinckel, *Psalms in Israel's Worship*.

22. Volz, *Das neujahrsfest jahwes*.

23. See, e.g., Oesterley, *Psalms*.

24. H. Kraus, *Psalmen*.

25. Weiser, *Psalms*.

people.[26] The dialectic between theology and the connection with the cult led to a reexamination by these and other scholars in the 1960s of the matter of forms of psalms.

In the 1970s the further development of the discoveries and analysis of the poetic and other Ugaritic texts over the previous forty years led to a three-volume commentary by Mitchell Dahood.[27] His was the first intensive study to examine the research on Ugaritic, Phoenician, and other West Semitic languages and to interpret the Psalms in this context. Although his study remains groundbreaking, it went overboard in the attempt to read the Psalms almost as though written in these other languages instead of the Hebrew in which they were actually written. This interest in comparative studies also underlies Othmar Keel's emphasis on iconography (visual art), especially that found in the seals.[28]

The 1980s saw the refinement of the comparative method. Peter Craigie's application of Ugaritic and Phoenician to Psalms 1–50 was at once more restrained and more creative than his predecessors.[29] Related to this, the enduring study by Wilfred Watson, cataloging the many forms and techniques used in Hebrew and Ugaritic poetry, has proved to be invaluable for researchers and writers.[30] Michael Goulder interpreted the psalms of the sons of Korah as a collection that originated in the north, especially at Dan.[31] He suggested an imaginative re-creation of ceremonies associated with some of these psalms. From a form-critical perspective, Harry Nasuti traced the psalms of the sons of Asaph to the northern kingdom, comparing them with other putative northern documents and references in the Bible.[32] For Steven Croft, the most likely origin for many of the psalms was at the Jerusalem temple.[33] Craig Broyles represents scholars who continued the study of theology in this book, examining the faith of the psalmists.[34]

This was also the time of Robert Alter's (*Art of Biblical Poetry*) work on Hebrew poetry, which challenged Lowth's assertion of three types of parallelism.[35] He argued there was either a single form of parallelism or dozens or hundreds of variations—but not exactly three.

In the 1990s Goulder continued his speculative treatment of groups of Psalms, with those of the sons of Asaph being connected to the Bethel sanctuary, and Psalms 51–72 reckoned as a chronological treatment of David's

26. Von Rad, *Old Testament Theology*; Westermann, *Praise and Lament*; Weiser, *Psalms*.
27. Dahood, *Psalms*.
28. Keel, *Symbolism of the Biblical World*.
29. Craigie, *Psalms 1–50*.
30. W. Watson, *Classical Hebrew Poetry*.
31. Goulder, *Psalms of the Sons of Korah*.
32. Nasuti, *Tradition History*.
33. Croft, *Identity of the Individual*.
34. Broyles, *Conflict of Faith and Experience*.
35. Lowth, *Lectures on the Sacred Poetry*.

life in poetry.[36] Mark S. Smith argued for the origin and preservation of the Psalms with the Levites associated with the temple in Jerusalem.[37] J. Clinton McCann, Klaus Seybold, and Gerald Wilson each contributed to the search for a theological theme that could express the unified intent of the Psalter.[38] There seemed to be a general movement in the direction of Yahweh as king or "Yahweh reigns." In this regard, new emphasis was placed on reading the work canonically, whether with Nancy DeClaissé-Walford's emphasis on the twin themes of torah and kingship, or Walter Brueggemann's examination of the first and last psalms and of how many other psalms move from an emphasis on law and obedience at the beginning of the Psalter to one of praise and worship at the end.[39]

Incorporating theological interests with comparative ones, Marjo Korpel examined the metaphors for deity at Ugarit and in Israel, contributing to investigations of anthropomorphism in the Psalms.[40] Peter Flint's study of the Psalms scrolls from Qumran raised new questions about the date and process of canon formation (see above, "Name, Text, and Outline").[41] Carol Meyers investigated the performance of the music of the psalms and the special role of women (see "Gender and Ideological Criticism").[42]

The first decade of the twenty-first century saw further developments of previous studies as well as new areas of inquiry. Jan Fokkelman produced an important survey of Hebrew poetry, treating its nature and interpretation.[43] His work has provided both new insights and a readable presentation. In the area of theology, Gert Kwaakel and others considered various psalms and their ethical teachings.[44] John Day reexamined the question of the origins and dating of the Psalms.[45] He sees many of the psalms in the first two-thirds of the Psalter as preexilic. Day bases this on references in these psalms to preexilic beliefs (such as Zion as indestructible before the destruction of Jerusalem in 586 BC) and events (such as deeds accomplished by armies of Israelites and Judeans). Using similar criteria in the final third of the Psalter, Day finds a dominance of postexilic psalms.

An example of the variety of approaches may be found in the collection of essays edited by Peter Flint and Patrick Miller, *The Book of Psalms:*

36. Goulder, "Asaph's *History of Israel*"; idem, *Psalms of Asaph*; idem, *The Prayers of David.*

37. M. Smith, "Levitical Compilation"; idem, "Theology of the Redaction."

38. McCann, "Psalms as Instruction"; Seybold, *Psalmen*; Wilson, *Hebrew Psalter*.

39. DeClaissé-Walford, *Reading from the Beginning*; Brueggemann, "Bounded by Obedience and Praise."

40. Korpel, *Rift in the Clouds*.

41. Flint, *Dead Sea Psalms Scrolls*; idem, "Book of Psalms."

42. Meyers, "Of Drums and Damsels"; idem, "Drum-Dance-Song Ensemble"; idem, "Guilds and Gatherings."

43. Fokkelman, *Reading Biblical Poetry*.

44. Kwaakel, *According to My Righteousness*.

45. Day, "How Many Pre-exilic Psalms?"

Composition and Reception. In these a scholar such as Harry Nasuti examines psalms to find theological and other significant relations to one another and their group.[46] Goulder continues to connect groups of psalms, here the Korah psalms and Psalms 51–72, mentioned above, which he assembles in relation to the Succession Narrative of 2 Samuel and 1 Kings 1–2.[47] See also DeClaissé-Walford's relation of Psalms 22–24 to one another.[48] Erich Zenger looks at psalms with public acclamation of Yahweh as king and at psalms of private piety.[49] Seybold examines Psalms 138–145 in the light of Second Temple Judaism and judicial processes at the temple.[50] While Broyles identifies a number of psalms for entrance liturgies, J. J. M. Roberts resurrects Mowinckel's autumn "Enthronement Festival" for the interpretation of various psalms.[51] Beat Weber examines Psalm 13 and finds a transition from lament to praise, where salvation involves an understanding of God's *ḥesed*, the covenant love and faithfulness that gives the psalmist confidence.[52] Wilson suggests that the place of David's line shifts in the fourth book of the Psalms to emphasize Yahweh's kingship.[53] McCann considers the beatitudes in the first book of the Psalter.[54] There are studies on later versions and interpretations of the book of Psalms, as well as research by Dennis Pardee on where the evidence now stands for the origins of Psalm 29 in Ugaritic texts, phrases, and vocabulary.[55] Ambiguity, historical connections, ancient Near Eastern genre comparisons, and theological significance (now both unified in a dialogical relationship between God and Israel and separated into multiple theologies reflecting different social orders) all remain lively matters that find little scholarly agreement beyond the broad contours of the subject.[56]

Martin Klingbeil returned to the examination of Gunkel.[57] He concludes that the proliferation of methods that has emerged in recent years has resulted in largely ignoring the form criticism of Gunkel. Other methods of interpretation have been used. The one exception, he argues, is among evangelicals, who often retain the method despite its lack of use elsewhere. John Goldingay's major three-volume commentary that appeared in 2009 did not try to apply

46. Nasuti, "Interpretive Significance."
47. Goulder, "Social Setting."
48. DeClaissé-Walford, "Intertextual Reading."
49. Zenger, "Theophanien."
50. Seybold, "Zur Geschichte des vierten Davidpsalters"; cf. idem, *Psalmen*.
51. Broyles, "Psalms"; Roberts, "Mowinckel's Enthronement Festival."
52. Weber, "Zum sogenannten 'Stimmungsumschwung.'"
53. Wilson, "King, Messiah"; cf. idem, *Hebrew Psalter*.
54. McCann, "Shape of Book I."
55. Pardee, "On Psalm 29"; cf. idem, *Ritual and Cult at Ugarit*.
56. On the dialogical manner of God and Israel, see Brueggemann, "Psalms in Theological Use"; on different social orders, see Gerstenberger, "Theologies in the Book of Psalms."
57. M. Klingbeil, "Off the Beaten Track."

these categories systematically but provided exegesis of each psalm according to its own witness to purpose and function.[58]

Recovering the connection between the Psalms and David's life, Weber considers Psalms 2–41 and 51–72 as reflecting incidents in the king's life.[59] He notices the struggles between David and Absalom (Pss. 3–7, 63) and David and Saul (Pss. 34, 52–60) within the promise of Yahweh's salvation (so Ps. 18:1; cf. 2 Sam. 22). In *The Psalms as Christian Lament*, Waltke, Houston, and Moore look at the history of interpretation, theology, and application for Christians of ten lament Psalms.

Literary Readings

This section will focus on an attempt to understand the basics of Hebrew poetry and how to read it. At its heart Hebrew poetry has to do with lines or cola (pl. of colon). Usually the basic unit for Hebrew poetry is a verse consisting of two adjacent lines. Sometimes there can be three or more lines, but most often there are two that have a special relationship.

While the use of a two-line verse can be the foundation of many types of poetry, including English, there is an important difference in Hebrew. The connection between the two lines does not manifest itself through rhyming (as is true in many English poems), or even primarily through rhythm or meter. These last two may have existed, but their identification remains disputed. Even if they did exist, they do not serve as the main point of relationship between the lines of Hebrew poetry.

Basic to Hebrew poetry is balance of content between the two (or three) lines. In some manner, the second line develops, reinforces, or contrasts with the first line in order to reach further into the meaning and significance of the poem. Sometimes an element of syntax, such as a subject or verb or object, can appear in the first line and remain omitted in the second line because the poet assumes that the reader or listener will understand its duplication into the second line. This is called ellipsis. For example, the first line of the first verse of Psalm 1 says, "Blessed is the one who does not walk in step with the wicked" (NIV). The second and third lines assume "Blessed is the one" but do not repeat it. The reader naturally carries this phrase to the next lines: "[Blessed is the one who] does not stand in the way of sinners; [Blessed is the one who] does not sit with mockers" (RSH).

This balance of ideas, which becomes so key to Hebrew poetry, is important for another reason. It allows for the translation of Hebrew poetry into other languages without a profound loss of the central features of the poem. This has been an immense benefit for the dissemination of the book of the Psalms and for its use by so many cultures and its handling by linguists over

58. Goldingay, *Psalms*.
59. Weber, "An dem Tag."

the millennia. Of course, poetry will always lose something in the translation. However, that should not discourage the translation of the Psalms, because the major points will not be lost.

Due to ellipsis and the emphasis on content, to name but two of many features, Hebrew poetry (and many other types of poetry) is correctly characterized as "the most compact and concentrated form of speech possible."[60] Fokkelman estimates that about 35 percent of the Old Testament is written in poetry.[61] Thus understanding the nature of poetry and parallelism is essential for biblical interpretation and especially for interpreting the Psalms.

Lowth in 1753 famously identified three types of parallelism (see "Premodern Readings," above).[62] The first and best known is synonymous parallelism. This can involve similar syntax, vocabulary, ideas, or other items. An example occurs in Psalm 37:30 (RSH):

The just one's	mouth	speaks	wisdom;
his	tongue	utters	justice.

The second line conveys the same idea as the first. This is done primarily through the use of synonymous word pairs in every syntactical category: subject ("mouth," "tongue"), verb ("speaks," "utters"), and object ("wisdom," "justice"). The person identified with the subject, "The just one," is explicitly identified only in the first line, although the subject's pronominal suffix ("his") in the second line continues the idea.

A second type of parallelism, antithetical, may occur in Psalm 107:26a (RSH). Here the dangers of the sea are faced by seafarers:

They	ascend	to the sky;
they	descend	to the depths.

The lines (or here, half-lines) contain identical grammar and syntax. However, the semantics of the two phrases are different and point in opposite directions. Here the word pairs of the verbs ("ascend," "descend") and the prepositional phrases ("to the sky," "to the depths") are semantic opposites, antithetical. Notice that, while the lines express opposite directions, they actually complement each other and form what is called a merism. On the waves, the sailors are tossed from high into the heavens to deep into the ocean depths. Of course, this includes everywhere in between. The extremes are named to emphasize the peril. A merism identifies the extremes and implies everything between them as well.

60. Fokkelman, *Reading Biblical Poetry*, 15.
61. Ibid., 1.
62. Lowth, *Lectures on the Sacred Poetry*.

A third type of parallelism, which also goes back to Lowth, is synthetic parallelism. Here the relationship between lines is not always as clear. The category forms a kind of catchall for all other types of Hebrew poetic line structures. An example of this is staircase parallelism, such as found in three parallel lines in Psalm 77:17 (77:18 MT; RSH). Here the items are listed according their sequence in the Hebrew text:

First Element	Second Element	Third Element
Clouds	produced	water;
thick clouds	made	thunder;
[They] also	your arrows	sent here and there.

This description of a rainstorm adds to the picture with each line. First, there is the water that comes and can be felt. Then the same clouds bring thunder, a noise that can be heard. Finally, the "arrows" of God's storm, the lightning, can be seen. The first two lines have a parallelism of syntax, which is changed in the third line. Also, the third line does not use a word for "clouds," unlike the first two. However, the three lines are tied together and evoke the picture of a thunderstorm, with all of its threatening weather that can be felt, heard, and seen. Thus the lines build up the picture as they appeal to more senses and complete the description of the storm. The content is neither synonymous nor antithetical, but it constructs a whole picture.

The basic elements of this approach remained in place until the 1981 publication of James Kugel's *Idea of Biblical Poetry*. This work argues that these categories are artificial. Kugel maintains that they are either too narrow, in the sense that there really is one general form of parallelism, where the second line somehow restates the first line; or that they are too broad, in the sense that three types are not enough. As well recognized, parallelism can have semantic synonymy yet be antithetical when it comes to syntax, and vice versa. Many varieties of parallelism are possible, and the limitation to three types overlooks the significant differences that occur in each category (and that stretch beyond one category into another). Readers do better to speak of a hundred types of parallelism rather than just three. All of this is true. However, Lowth's divisions remain a useful starting point in order to understand the discussion.

In addition to the types of parallelism already mentioned, as well as features such as ellipsis and merism, there are other techniques to Hebrew poetry.[63] A number may be mentioned here. In these cases the name is not so important as understanding how the technique is used to add emphasis and variety. There is anaphora, in which consecutive lines begin with the same word. See Psalm 150, where nearly all the lines begin with "Praise

63. See Berlin, "Hebrew Poetry," 309–11.

him!" (Heb. *halĕlûhû*). With cataphora, consecutive lines end with the same word. An example of this occurs in Psalm 40:12, 14 (40:13, 15 MT), where the four lines (and one in v. 13 [14 MT]) end with the first-person singular suffix, "me, my," Hebrew *-î*. Anadiplosis is a phenomenon whereby the last word of one line forms the first word of the next line. An example is found in the first half of Psalm 96:13. There one line ends with "for he comes" (*kî bāʾ*), and the next line begins with the same words. See also Song 2:15, where three lines are connected, the first two with "foxes," and the second and third with "vineyards."

In side-by-side repetition the same word is repeated in the line for dramatic effect. The best-known example occurs in Isaiah 40:1, "Comfort, Comfort" (*naḥămû naḥămû*). Phrases can also be repeated. For example, the phrase "for his covenantal love lasts forever" (*kî lĕʿôlām ḥasdô*) appears as a refrain at the end of each line in Psalm 136. The line that begins Psalm 8 also concludes it, creating an inclusio that marks off the psalm and points to a major theme: "Yahweh, our Lord, how awe-inspiring is your name throughout all the earth" (RSH). Other repeated phrases or ideas occur in ABA′B′ word patterning, as in Isaiah 54:7–8:

> A For a short moment I abandoned you,
>   B but with great compassion I gather you. (NRSV)
> A′ In a blast of anger I hid myself from you for a brief time,
>   B′ but with eternal love I have compassion on you. (RSH)

This approach emphasizes both lines, but especially the contrast between them. These, as well as forms such as chiasms, occur in both poetry and prose (esp. rhetoric). They are frequent in the Psalms.

The attempt to identify meter in poetry of the Psalms remains controversial. Some feel it is impossible due to the difficulty of finding a formula that will work with every psalm. Others have convinced themselves that they have identified the meter to such an extent that they have no hesitation in changing the wording of psalms that do not fit the formula so as to make them fit. Those more flexible with their theories of meter tend to focus on either the number of syllables or the number of accented syllables in each line. For example, Fokkelman accepts the number of syllables in each line as a clue to the identification of meter.[64] He persuasively argues that each of eighty-three psalms scores a certain integer for the average number of syllables per line or colon (seven, eight, or nine; most often eight). This suggests that the authors were aware of the syllable count of their lines or cola. While it does not work

64. Fokkelman, *Reading Biblical Poetry*, 47–48.

in every case, it does demonstrate that this sort of meter can be calculated on the basis of syllable counts.[65]

Gender and Ideological Criticism

The nature of the Psalms is that they make a spiritual connection with people of all backgrounds and genders. As noted, their general cultural descriptions and their absence of specifics in terms of historical background and in the identification of specific classes allow the Psalms to speak to all peoples at all times.

Of the variety of musical instruments in ancient Israel that were used in the performance of praise and worship, there were three groups: stringed, wind, and percussion (see the sidebar "Ancient Israelite Stringed and Wind Instruments"). The percussion instruments seem to have had a particular connection with performance by women. These included the *mĕṣiltayim*, also called *ṣelṣĕlîm*. These were cymbals made of bronze.[66] They are mentioned some sixteen times in the Old Testament. The other percussion instrument that was widely used from early times was the *tōp*, a small, shallow frame with an animal skin drawn over it. It was struck with the hand. The name of the instrument may have been onomatopoetic, reflecting the sound made by striking it. In appearance it is close but not identical to the frame and skin of a tambourine. In four of the sixteen verses where the noun occurs,[67] it is specifically played by women and only by women (in Exod. 15:20 [2×]; Judg. 11:34; 1 Sam. 18:6; Jer. 31:4). Elsewhere the evidence is ambiguous as to who is doing the playing, often because the *tōp* is one of many musical instruments listed, and the attested masculine plural forms would be expected if both men and women were playing various musical instruments.[68]

In the performance of music, there was also dance. Perhaps the best known is the story of David dancing before Yahweh when the ark was brought to Jerusalem (2 Sam. 6:14, 16). However, there are many examples of different types of dancing in the Bible, with names likely related to the roots from which the verbs were taken: *rqd*, "to skip"; *krr*, "to hop"; *pzz*, "to leap"; and *ḥwl*,

65. Fokkelman (ibid., 37) breaks down a poem from the basic number of beats or stresses to the largest unit of stanzas that make up longer psalms. He suggests that most Hebrew poems have two to four stresses per colon, two or three cola per verse, two or three verses per strophe, and two or three strophes per stanza. The basic two-line, or bicolon, unit of Hebrew poetry occurs in all ancient Near Eastern poetry. The same is true of chiasm. See Kitchen, *Reliability*, 105–6.

66. See 2 Sam. 6:5; Ps. 150:5; Ezra 3:10; Neh. 12:27; 1 Chron. 13:8; 15:16, 19, 28; 16:5, 42; 25:1, 6; 2 Chron. 5:12, 13; 29:25.

67. The putative occurrence of the form in Ezek. 28:13 is likely a homonym expressing the sense of "beauty" and not related to a musical instrument.

68. See Gen. 31:27; 1 Sam. 10:5; 2 Sam. 6:5; Isa. 5:12; 24:8; 30:32; Pss. 81:2 (81:3 MT); 149:3; 150:4; Job 21:12; 1 Chron. 13:8.

Ancient Israelite Stringed and Wind Instruments

The stringed instruments included primarily two types. There was the *kinnôr*, a lyre that seems to have been composed of a rectangular sound box. It had two asymmetrical arms, an oblique yoke, and about ten strings of equal length. The box was made of almug, or red sandalwood. The second type of stringed instrument was the *nēbel*, a harp that used a skin bottle. It was composed of a waterskin-shaped sound box. Ten strings of unequal length were used. The instrument was played by plucking the strings. These two instruments are described in parallel in Psalm 33:2: "Give thanks to Yahweh with the lyre; with ten-stringed harp sing to him" (RSH).

The word for wind instrument is *ʿûgāb*, as in the last word in Psalm 150:4 (NIV, "pipe"). Often translated as "flute," the *ḥālîl* comes from the same root as the word for "round dance." It was composed of two separate metal or ivory pipes of reeds, each with a mouthpiece. The *qeren* is the general term for "horn." The less common horn was the *ḥăṣōṣĕrâ*, a trumpet or bugle made of silver or bronze. It was long and straight and used only by priests. The more frequent type of horn was the *šôpār*, a ram's horn that was the most frequent type of *qeren* and could at times be used interchangeably with it.[a]

[a] See King, "Musical Tradition of Ancient Israel."

"to whirl." The last root appears in the nouns *māḥôl* and *mĕḥôlâ*. These seem to refer to types of round dances. In addition to the performance of Miriam and other women in these dances, and throughout the Old Testament, there are examples of dancing by both men and women.

Carol Meyers has studied these occurrences in the context of ancient Near Eastern archaeology, art, and comparative literature.[69] She finds groups of female musicians who performed both in Israel and in surrounding countries of the West Semitic world and beyond. Figures of women groups playing the *tōp* and dancing are especially prominent in Cyprus, although they are also found elsewhere in the culture surrounding ancient Israel. Meyers suggests that virtually all *tōp* players in Cyprus, Phoenicia, and Israel were female, that this is one example of women's guilds or groups (prophets and domestic activities being others), and that Canaanite/Israelite orchestras (as found in 1 Sam. 10:5 and 2 Sam. 6:5) included women as well as men.

Perhaps no text has been used more to address and rectify various concerns, both personal and societal, than the book of Psalms. Dennis Sylva discusses

69. Meyers, "Of Drums and Damsels"; idem, "Drum-Dance-Song Ensemble"; idem, "Guilds and Gatherings."

the use of various psalms in the context of children and family, as a context for identifying varied means of establishing security and trust.[70] Thus Psalm 131 represents the child who trusts the mother while upon her breast. In dealing with emotional scars and with depression from the difficulties of life, the psalm also encourages secure attachment relationships. Psalm 23 represents confidence and freedom from fear, with perspectives on refreshment and peace for the child. In contrast to the lack of faithfulness among people, God models steadfast love in Psalms 92, 107, and 117.[71] Psalms 62 and 133 teach believers how to return and restore communication as well as the importance of the unity of God's people before him.

The Western appropriation of the Psalms as a counseling tool should be contrasted with a very different African perspective on the spiritual use of the Psalms. David Tuesday Adamo suggests that Africans in the African Indigenous Churches are not so interested in the traditional classifications of the Psalms (à la Gunkel).[72] Rather, they ask, "How do we use the Bible and faith as concrete and effective means to gain protection from enemies and evil spirits, to gain healing from sicknesses, and to gain successes in work, school, and business?" Africans have their own classifications for the Psalms: curative, protective, and success.

First, the curative method combines absolute faith in God's word as revealed in various psalms along with using herbal medicine, prayer, fasting, and the divine names of God. For example, in one case a vision was received. On this basis, it was determined that the reading of Psalms 1–3, along with reciting the holy name of God repeatedly and consuming water, oil, potash, salt, and an egg, would result in relief of stomach pains and irritations. Such performative use of the Psalms (in which pronouncing the words becomes effective) also occurs for a woman who is pregnant. She should read Psalm 1 daily in the morning and in the evening. With regard to birth, the recitation of Psalm 51 is associated with barrenness; Psalms 34, 59, and 60 with safe delivery; and Psalm 126 with infant mortality. Second, Psalms 1–2, 4–5, 8–14, 23, and others are recited for protection against one's enemies. Of course, this would closely resemble the original content of the Psalms. They are concerned with God providing deliverance from the enemies of the poet who seek to murder and slander. Reciting Psalm 102:14–18 may be used for protection when traveling. Third are the success psalms. For success in exams, for instance, one should

70. Sylva, *Transformation of Stress*.

71. Oddly, Sylva here criticizes some comparative work I did on Amarna letters (Hess, "Hebrew Psalms and Amarna"). He suggests that I omitted Ps. 92 from my discussion of where God has set his name and its comparison with where the pharaoh has set his name (in the letters from Jerusalem). However, I was searching for identical phrases in the Psalms and the cuneiform letters (which do not occur in Ps. 92), not for general ideas (such as God's presence expressed through his name in both the morning and the evening).

72. Adamo, "Psalms," 152.

read Psalm 4. For success in matters of love, Psalm 133 is important, as well as other texts such as the Song of Songs.

These methods appear as a danger insofar as the biblical text is made into a talisman or other means of working magic apart from faith. Even though Adamo also stresses the absolute importance of faith in the power of God's word as well as various names of God, there remains a danger of idolatry in any use of the Bible that involves its enunciation as a means to achieve something one wants.

Ancient Near Eastern Context

It is no surprise that the Bible was not alone in the ancient world in its production of music, poetry, and psalms. These elements were found throughout the ancient Near East. Readers can at least look at some of the major literatures that have often been used for comparison with the biblical psalms. Some earlier and more distant comparisons come from Mesopotamia and Egypt, and closer to Israel other sources share a common West Semitic cultural heritage.

In Mesopotamia, one of the chief sources of psalms is in materials that originate in the Sumerian psalms and laments. Although Sumer, with its major cities located in what today is southeastern Iraq, flourished a millennium before the birth of the nation of Israel, its cultural influence on Babylonian and Assyrian literature was significant. Sumerian poems to deities can be found as early as Sargon of Akkad and his daughter, who in the twenty-fourth century composed hymns to the goddess Inanna, thus being history's first-known female author.[73] One of the leading Sumerologists of the twentieth century, Samuel Noah Kramer, was unable to detect any clear signs of Sumerian influence or borrowing in the Hebrew lament psalms.[74] However, early second-millennium-BC psalm forms do demonstrate that the search for an original *Sitz im Leben* ("setting in life") of the biblical psalms is unattainable. This is because already at this point cultic hymns were used for personal purposes and personal psalms were used in the cult.[75]

Egypt was also a source of poetry and hymns to its deities. The "heretic" pharaoh Akhenaton launched a religious revolution in the mid-fourteenth

73. See Kitchen, *Reliability*, 105.

74. Kramer, "Distant Echoes." There is an ongoing discussion regarding Sumerian laments and their relationship to laments in the Psalms. The Sumerian ones fall into two groups. Some are early (twentieth century BC) and written by kings of Isin to justify their restoration work for various cities. Others were written for liturgical use and continued into the Seleucid period (called *balags* and *eršemmas*). Bouzard (*We Have Heard*) argues that Ezekiel's reference to preexilic women in Jerusalem weeping for Tammuz and the preeminent theme of the weeping goddess in the second collection of Sumerian laments suggest influence of the Sumerian laments on Psalms, especially 44, 60, 74, 79, 80, 83, and 89. However, his emphasis is on genre, themes, and motifs rather than on words and poetic structure. See O'Connor, review of *We Have Heard*.

75. See Kitchen, *Reliability*, 107.

Richard S. Hess

Tenth- or ninth-century-BC Syrian temple at ʿAin Dara

century BC. He moved his capital away from Thebes and the adjacent powerful temple and priesthood of Amon-Re. Instead, he built a new capital city (200 miles north, at a place now called Tell el-Amarna) and chose to worship only one god, the Aten or deified sun disk. Although this "monotheistic" revolution lasted only for a generation, Akhenaton left behind many distinctive art forms and literary pieces. One of these is his Hymn to the Sun.[76] While worthy of study in itself, it exhibits many lines and expressions that also appear in Psalm 104 and its praise of Yahweh as creator of beautiful and powerful aspects of nature. The similarities are too great in number and quality to be accidental. They represent evidence for common scribal traditions and a pool of literary imagery that could be applied to various deities.

From much later (second century BC) in Egypt comes a remarkable papyrus containing, among other things, an Aramaic hymn dedicated to the Egyptian god Horus and written in a demotic script.[77] The Hymn to Horus has verbal and sequential parallels to Psalm 20. This text is in Aramaic but betrays a Canaanite or Palestinian origin. Ziony Zevit considers a connection between

76. See the translation by Miriam Lichtheim in *COS* 1.28.44–46.

77. Demotic is an Egyptian cursive script, not normally used to write the Aramaic language. For a translation of this lengthy work, see Richard C. Steiner, *COS* 1.99.309–27. The papyrus is identified as Amherst 63.

Horus and Baal or Baal Shamayn.[78] Nevertheless, the close similarity with the text of Psalm 20 suggests that the elements of this psalm were known and used by scribes in the region of Egypt as they composed other psalms and hymns to their own deities.

Of all the ancient comparative literature for the study of the Psalms, the most important are the mythological poems found at Ras Shamra, ancient Ugarit. Discovered in 1928, some of the first texts found were the myths of Baal, Asherah, Anat, El, and other gods and goddesses known from the Bible, deities associated with the region of ancient Israel in the south and Ugarit in the north. The language of Ugarit was West Semitic and thus closely resembles the later Hebrew. The texts are currently thought to date to the thirteenth century BC and before the destruction of the city around 1170 BC. Although technically outside the area of ancient Canaan (150 miles north of Damascus), the culture nevertheless resembles that of Canaan.

This poetry is preserved in the form of several dozen myths. The longer ones compose several large clay tablets full of writing, and the shorter ones were found in a few fragments. These formed narratives of the lives, deaths, and adventures of the deities associated with Canaan. Unlike in the Old Testament, there are no historical accounts of work between a deity and a people or nation, virtually no praise of the deities, and, except for the single example below, little in the way of petition or prayer.

Nevertheless, the poetry preserves many remarkable similarities with texts from the Bible and especially the Psalms. For example, in Psalms 68:4 (68:5 MT) and 104:3, Yahweh rides on the clouds. In the Ugaritic myths, one of Baal's epithets is Cloudrider (*KTU* 1.1 iv, 8). Also, Psalm 92:9 (92:10 MT) reads: "For surely your enemies, O Yahweh, surely your enemies will perish; all evildoers will be scattered" (NIV). Compare the Ugaritic text praising Baal (*KTU* 1.1 iv, 9): "As for your enemy, O Baal, as for your enemy, you'll smite [him], you'll destroy your adversary." Not only do the words and phrases bear similarities, but even the syntax and meter of the poems seem to resonate with each other in translation.

As in Israel, so also Ugarit used solo, antiphonal, and unison singing. It possessed stringed, wind, and percussion instruments similar to those found in the Bible. At Ugarit there is even a Hurrian (and Hurrian Akkadian) text that preserves important information about musical notation (RS 15.30 + 15.49 + 17.389), but its meaning is unclear. Psalms and songs were used to praise gods and to bless kings.[79]

The Ugaritic text identified as *KTU* 1.119 (lines 26–36) provides the only example of a prayer to Baal that occurs at the end of a ritual tablet (RSH):

78. Zevit, *Religions of Ancient Israel*, 669–74.
79. See Koitabashi, "Music in the Texts from Ugarit."

When a foreigner assaults your gate,
A champion your walls,
Lift your eyes to Baal, [saying,]

O Baal, if you repel
The strong one from our gate,
The hero from our walls;
A bull, O Baal, we will consecrate,
A vow, O Baal, we will fulfill;
A firstborn, O Baal, we will consecrate,
A *ḥitpu*[?]-sacrifice we will fulfill;
A feast, O Baal, we will feast.
To the sanctuary of Baal we will ascend,
To the temple of Baal we will go.

And Baal has heard your prayer.
He repels the strong one from your gate,
The warrior from your walls.

The prayer includes a number of features in common with various biblical psalms. This prayer follows some patterns similar to those of the communal lament: After enemies assault the faithful, they cry to God for aid. In the conclusion is a confident statement of the Deity hearing the prayer and providing deliverance. Sacrifices are promised in response to divine salvation. There is mention of walking to the temple, as in Psalm 55:14 (55:15 MT). And, of course, there is the promise of divine support. All of these have their counterpart in various psalms. It may be argued that the quid pro quo nature of the prayer to Baal goes beyond what appears in the Psalms. Nevertheless, there are connections with the Psalms.

Here are examples of the transformation of media, in which forms found in the poetic mythologies of Ugarit are also found in the later book of Psalms. This suggests a common scribal heritage for these forms. The poets of the Psalms took this "contemporary music" and applied its style—vocabulary, meter, syntax, and parallelism—to the worship and praise of a single God, Yahweh. Rather than the mythological expressions of the Ugaritic texts, the expressions in the Psalms combine these elements and apply them to creation imagery (Ps. 74:12–15) as well as altering them into full historical contexts. Yahweh is Creator and Deliverer, but in space and time, in history—not merely in mythology.

A final point of comparison may be made between the Psalms and what at first appears to be an unrelated area: diplomatic correspondence of the fourteenth century BC between the Egyptian pharaoh as leader of the New Kingdom empire and the vassal leaders of the Canaanite city-states who belonged to that empire. These Amarna letters, as they are called, were often

Amarna Correspondence

The site of Amarna was established by the pharaoh Akhenaton to perpetuate his new religion in Egypt, the monotheistic-like worship of the Aten, the divine sun disk. It was his capital for some years until the traditional religious powers in Egyptian society took over and returned the royal family to its home in Thebes. When they were moved back, the pharaoh abandoned the city to gather dust for more than three millennia. Also left behind were more than three hundred tablets containing diplomatic correspondence belonging to Akhenaton and his father, mostly written in the Akkadian cuneiform script and language that formed the lingua franca of the fourteenth century BC. These texts include letters to and from the kings of the Hittites, the Hurrians (northern Syria), the Assyrians, the Babylonians, and Alashiya (Cyprus). They also include letters to and from regional administrators and city leaders under the control of the Egyptian New Kingdom empire in what is today Israel, Palestine, Jordan, Lebanon, and Syria. The study of these documents, since their discovery in 1887, has contributed immensely to the understanding of the culture and the geopolitics of the period and places they represent, as well as the languages, dialects, and rhetorical styles of various authors and especially the Canaanite leaders. These include important and rhetorically "rich" correspondence from Jerusalem, Shechem, and many other towns and cities in Canaan that the book of Joshua describes.[a]

[a] See Sparks, *Ancient Texts*, 46–47, and further bibliography there.

written by vassals to their pharaoh overlord and included honorifics praising the greatness of the pharaoh as a divinity, descriptions of troubles the vassals are facing, pleas for assistance from the pharaoh, and further praises. These letters thus resemble various psalms, especially psalms of lament. The same elements are present, where the psalmist corresponds to the vassal and God to the pharaoh.

Not only are general forms of the letters comparable to the psalms. The five Amarna letters from Jerusalem (EA 285–290) include expressions identical with those found in the Hebrew poetry, such as the "arm of the pharaoh" referring to strength and the act of the pharaoh setting his name on Jerusalem from the rising of the sun to its setting. Further, the various literary forms—such as synonymous parallelism, antithetic parallelism, ABA′B′ parallelism, and chiasm—all occur in the rhetoric of the leader of Jerusalem, as in the Psalms. This would seem to suggest a scribal tradition already found in fourteenth-century Jerusalem that continued in Jerusalem and perhaps the surrounding area for centuries.[80]

Canonical Context

The book of Psalms remains one of the most intertextual books in the Bible. It draws from and feeds into many themes that occur throughout the Bible. In the Old Testament the Psalms are not merely a book; they are also a genre. Psalms find their way into all of the major epochs of Israel's literature. In the Torah, beginning in Genesis, there are psalms. For example, the patriarch Jacob prophesies the future for each of his sons in a psalm in Genesis 49. Exodus 15 is a victory psalm performed by Miriam and others to celebrate the divine defeat of Egypt, which brings about the birth of the nation. In the Historical Books, set at the beginning of the monarchy, after Saul and Jonathan die in battle, David eulogizes them in a psalm (2 Sam. 1). At the other end of the monarchy, during the exile from Jerusalem, Psalm 137 commemorates the destruction of the city. Thus the psalms were in use (and probably being composed) throughout Israel's history.

While only a few psalms (e.g., Ps. 137) suggest an identifiable historical context, the titles of the individual psalms add a great deal more information to situate them in specific times and places. Many appear to be connected with David and therefore have been the subject of connections with aspects of his life. For example, Psalm 3's title indicates a composition related to the time of David's flight from Absalom. Psalm 7 identifies a psalm "of David" that was sung to "Cush, a Benjaminite." It is not clear to whom this refers. In other contexts, Cush is the name of a place, not a person. However, not all titles are equally likely. It has long been noticed that Psalm 51, the great penitential psalm, seems oddly titled as composed by David after his sin with Bathsheba. Readers point to verse 4 (6 MT), which suggests that David recognizes his sin against God and no other. Yet clearly this sin destroyed Uriah and his family. One may argue a theological point that all sin is ultimately against God alone, but this seems to strain the intensity and personal connection of both the title and the psalm itself.

There is much debate as to whether the titles were original to the psalms. Certainly, the words that occur in some of the titles were not understood by the time of the Septuagint translators. Thus many of these titles are not late. Nor do the Aramaic forms or supposed incongruities prove a late date. Nevertheless, accepting an early date for the titles is not the same as arguing that they represent authentic situations written by the original psalmist. The truth may lie in between. The titles, like the titles of the books of the

80. See Hess, "Hebrew Psalms and Amarna."

Bible, cannot be presumed to be inspired originals in the same manner as the remainder of the text.

Following the studies of others, especially Bruce Waltke, it seems reasonable to conclude that in some cases psalms possessed postscripts that have since been joined to the superscript (title) of the following psalm.[81] Superscripts contain information about composition; postscripts focus on performance. The classic example of this is found in Habakkuk 3. There the psalm ends (v. 19 RSH), "For the music director, on my stringed instruments." These terms appear at the beginning of many psalms and thus suggest that they may have been originally appended to the previous psalm. This may also help with interpreting the title of Psalm 88, which seems to contain more than one superscription.

Part of the question that Christians have regarding the psalms relates to Jesus's use of them.[82] There are many quotations of and allusions to the Psalms found in the Gospels. Sometimes they are brief summary statements, such as Psalm 6:8, cited after the teaching about doing the Father's will in order to enter heaven (Matt. 7:23; Luke 13:27). Elsewhere, Jesus applies Psalm 118:26, "Blessed is the one who comes in the name of the Lord," as he weeps at how Jerusalem will not see him again (Matt. 23:39). Yet it is also applied earlier to the triumphal entry (Matt. 21:9). From the cross Jesus recites the first line of Psalm 22 in Aramaic (Matt. 27:46; Mark 15:34). This may have been a reference to his experience of the whole psalm, including his ultimate triumph.

In the Pauline Epistles, the Psalms are used in a kind of pesher interpretation, in which the original poetry is intended to refer to something significant in Jesus's life and the gospel. The universality of sin in Romans 3:18 is based on Psalm 36:1 (36:2 MT), which forms a general introduction to the description of the wicked. The universality of the gospel message that Paul argues in Romans 10:18 uses Psalm 19:4 (19:5 MT) and creation's general proclamation honoring God. Other texts, such as the use of Psalm 68:18 (68:19 MT) in Ephesians 4:8, apply the power of Yahweh as victorious warrior to the work of Christ. In Psalm 68, God receives gifts as tribute from those he has conquered. In Ephesians 4, Christ gives gifts, a theme perhaps not self-evident in Psalms but clearly part of the actions of a victorious king (see Gen. 14; Exod. 24; 2 Sam. 6).

Elsewhere, the book of Hebrews quotes the Psalms nearly a dozen times. Hebrews 7:17 refers to Psalm 110:4 and the designation of the messiah as a priestly figure, "according to the order of Melchizedek." Hebrews 7 develops an argument from this single Old Testament verse, an argument that will continue to occupy an important place in early Christianity. Verse 4 lies at the center of Psalm 110, with three verses before it and three after it. All

81. Waltke, "Superscripts, Postscripts."

82. Bullock, *Book of Psalms*, 89–92.

the other verses emphasize the royal conquest and reign of the messiah as divinely appointed king. Of course, this is in agreement with the common use of "messiah" (lit., "anointed one") in the Old Testament to describe the Israelite king who rules from Jerusalem, and especially, after 2 Samuel 7, David and his line. However, this term is used in the Pentateuch for the priest who is "the anointed one" there. Thus there are two aspects to the messiah, and this was keenly felt in the first century AD. By that point, as many Dead Sea Scrolls scholars surmise, the Qumran community (and no doubt others as well) looked for two messiahs, a royal messiah and a priestly messiah. This was because it was deemed impossible for the royal messiah, who had to come from the tribe of Judah (i.e., David's tribe), to be identical with the priestly messiah, who had to come from the tribe of Levi.

Of course, early Christians, and especially the writer of the Epistle to the Hebrews, saw the fulfillment in Jesus as both the royal Messiah and the priestly Messiah. However, Jesus's line was traced not to the tribe of Levi but to the tribe of Judah. So how could Jesus be priestly? Here is where Psalm 110 became a key to solving this puzzle. Jesus's priesthood was traced back to Melchizedek rather than to Levi. Other than Hebrews and Psalm 110:4, in the Bible this figure appears only in Genesis 14:18. His priesthood is based not on lineage but on the declaration of the Scripture and on Abram's acknowledgment of the fact. When Abram gave Melchizedek a tithe in recognition of his role, all the descendants of Abram also gave that tithe and thereby recognized the priesthood of Melchizedek as superior to any that might come from the descendants of Abram. This included the priesthood of Aaron through the tribe of Levi. Thus Jesus's priesthood was foretold in Psalm 110 and appointed as one superior to that of the line of Aaron and the Jewish priests.

Theological Perspectives of the Psalms

The theology of the Psalms is a rich and varied topic. Every commentary, introduction, and handbook will provide a slightly different approach. Nevertheless, most seem to agree that the book is about God and his inexhaustible love for his people. God delights in both the praises and petitions of his people, whether individually or collectively. He hears those cries and regularly moves to bring aid and assistance. God's powerful torah, or instruction, and his earthly dwelling place in the temple and in Jerusalem remain as physical manifestations of his concern to guide and protect those who seek him and to provide for his people. To this must be added the pictures of God as creator of the world, as redeemer of his people in the exodus, and as the one who chose David and his line to rule over Israel.

One way to approach the question of theology is to view some selected psalms and to discuss their teaching, as already done with Psalm 110 (above).

Perhaps the best approach, which will allow the selection of a variety of psalms and theological teachings, is to examine a representative from each of the major traditional categories of Psalms.

The first type of psalm is the individual lament. This category includes the largest number of psalms in the Psalter. An example can be found in the six verses of Psalm 13. The poem begins with a cry to Yahweh for aid. The psalmist observes the triumph of the enemy. After the repeated cries of "How long?" in verses 1–2 (2–3 MT), the psalm turns to the request that Yahweh look upon the psalmist and respond to the triumph of the enemies against the poet. Indeed, as in many laments in the Bible, verse 4 (5 MT) suggests that the delight and gloating of the enemy provides as much a reason for God to intervene as the danger the psalmist faces from these opponents. In other words, as with Moses's intercession for Israel in Exodus and Numbers, the focus is on upholding God's honor by avoiding or reversing the humiliation of those who trust in him. Verses 5–6 (6 MT) have the psalmist expressing confidence in God's faithfulness and concluding with a confession of trusting divine kindness toward the psalmist. The verb forms in these verses express completed action and thus describe the faithfulness of God as already achieved. This is a common way for biblical laments to end, not on a negative note of fear or defeat, but with a positive confession of God as having given the victory. These were not added later, after the psalmist actually experienced this victory. Rather, they form an expression of the psalmist's faith that God's grace is so clear and certain that nothing can stand in the way of its accomplishment.[83] Thus these lament psalms are indeed cries to God; yet they are cries that do not remain as such. The psalmist's confession of who God is leads to joy in the salvation he has provided.

Psalm 40 provides an example of a psalm expressing praise and thanksgiving by an individual. In this case the psalm is not all joy. Rather, it expresses the difficult circumstances that the poet was in—a pit of slime and mud. Yahweh has rescued the psalmist, who uses that experience to bear testimony to others of Yahweh's mercy and salvation. The second half of the psalm continues with requests for God's ongoing mercy and deliverance from enemies. The poem concludes with the psalmist's confession of need before God and of relying on his help and salvation. In various way it resembles a lament. And psalms of lament and of thanksgiving should not be understood as two discrete categories but rather as on a continuum, reflecting the realities of people's lives.

Of special interest in this psalm is 40:6 (7 MT), where the psalmist confesses that God has pierced the poet's ears rather than letting him focus on sacrifice and offering. The verse recalls Exodus 21:6, where the Israelite slave who wishes to stay with his master as a slave must have his ear pierced at the city gate. This is a symbol of servanthood and obedience. The same is

83. See Weber, "Zum sogenannten 'Stimmungsumschwung.'"

true in Psalm 40. Verse 6 (7 MT) describes how God has made the psalmist a lifelong slave, obedient to God. This text is applied to Christ in Hebrews 10:5–7, where it defines the obedience of Jesus before God the Father. Here the clause describing the piercing of the ear is replaced with one that identifies how a body has been prepared for Christ. It is the manner in which Jesus kept his body sinless and then offered it up as a sacrifice of perfect obedience that connects this psalm text to the argument in the epistle.

Just as the psalms preserve individual laments and expressions of salvation, they also preserve communal laments. An example is Psalm 80. The first-person plural forms ("we," "us") indicate a group of people, perhaps representing the nation, who cry to God for deliverance. Yahweh is addressed as a shepherd (a common picture of a king in the ancient Near East) who leads Joseph. Joseph represents the two tribes named from his sons, Ephraim and Manasseh. They settled in the hill country and formed the center of the northern kingdom (Israel). In contrast, addressing God as the one who sits enthroned between the cherubim suggests a picture of Yahweh as dwelling in the temple of Jerusalem, where the ark (the symbol of God's special divine presence) was situated with the figures of the cherubim at either side. This would be the capital of the southern kingdom (Judah). The picture here is of the divided kingdom, which has been overrun and conquered by enemies at some point in its history. And that history is reviewed in verses 8–16 (9–17 MT), where Israel is portrayed as a vine that God plants but in later times is destroyed. The final verses cry to God for salvation. They also express confidence in "the man at your right hand" (80:17 NIV), meaning the messianic king, the son of David who reigns (or should reign) in Jerusalem. This category of lament here includes a messianic aspect in the psalms.

While there can be communal lament, there can also be communal praise. Psalm 124 is an example. Here as well the people have faced threats that are compared to a torrent of water sweeping them away. God's salvation has already taken place, and so the new image is that of a bird escaping from a trap and now free, as are the people. And in the last verse they confess that salvation comes from Yahweh.

Another type of psalm is the royal psalm. An example of this occurs in Psalm 45, which describes a royal wedding. The description of the royal bridegroom focuses on his blessing from God, his military strength, and his protection of the realm. The bride (vv. 9–17 [10–18 MT]) is portrayed as beautiful, with a gorgeous dress and surrounded by noble attendants. The final two verses turn to the couple and the promise for offspring and for perpetuation of the royal name and fame. In the midst of the wedding song is verse 6 (7 MT), which identifies the king as divine. It may be hyperbole or some attempt to connect the king with God. However, it does raise the question of the divinity of the king, something that would not be acceptable in monotheistic Israel. However, some have seen here a preexilic royal wedding song that, after the end of kingship in Judah and Jerusalem, was projected onto God so that the psalm addresses the king of heaven.

Another group of royal psalms are messianic. See here the already-discussed Psalm 110 and others, such as Psalm 2.

Psalm 24 (see also 118 and 122) is an example of a liturgical psalm that, in the first half, lists theological and ethical qualifications necessary to approach the temple of God for worship. The last four verses include refrains addressing the gates of the temple and asking that they be opened so that "the King of glory may enter" (RSH). One can imagine a psalm like this composed on the return of the ark to Jerusalem, with different choirs or groups reciting the lines and refrains. Alternatively, perhaps this would be used by a group of pilgrims climbing the Temple Mount and asking that the gates be opened.

Psalm 87 (see also 46, 48, 76, and 84) is a psalm of Zion, praising Jerusalem as the center that God has chosen for his temple and his blessing. Here the text begins with a confession of Yahweh's love for the gates of Zion, pars pro toto for the whole city. Both Rahab and Babylon acknowledge the special nature of Jerusalem (87:4). Rahab is not the woman from Jericho but a monster of the sea, as in Psalm 89:10 (89:11 MT) and Isaiah 51:9. For the association with the sea, see also Job 26:12. Babylon and Tyre represent centers of political and economic power. Philistia is a traditional enemy of Israel, while Cush is a distant and exotic land. All of these represent peoples and powers throughout the world who confess the greatness of Zion and who bless those who are born there. The confession of the final verse, "All my springs are in you," identifies springs of water that would provide for life in the climate of the Middle East. Thus Jerusalem is a source of life for all.

Several psalms contain curses against the psalmist's enemies. Perhaps the best known is Psalm 137, where Israel appears in exile in Babylon and where they are so discouraged that they cannot sing when requested to do so by their captors. Perhaps the songs of Judah were famous in Babylon. Verses 5 and 6 contain self-curses that the Judeans call down on themselves if they forget or cease to love Jerusalem. This is followed by a curse on the daughter of Babylon, who is connected with Edom. Edom was condemned by God and Israel because, despite its proximity to and ancient brotherhood with Israel (Jacob/Israel and Esau/Edom were brothers), Edom encouraged Babylon's destruction of the nation (v. 7). Although Edom would soon experience a similar fate, the calling of a curse on the people includes praising those who dash Babylon's babies against "the rock." From where does this terrible curse come? A similar curse against the children is directed to Babylon in Isaiah 13:16, to Samaria in Hosea 13:16 (14:1 MT), and to Nineveh, the capital of Assyria, in Nahum 3:10. All of these come from the mouths of prophets speaking God's word. Thus this curse is directed against enemies of God's people (in the case of Hosea, the enemies are the leaders of Israel) who sought to destroy them, and it derives from the language that the prophets used in condemning the enemies of God and his people (sometimes condemning even Israel itself). The destruction of the children would bring an end to the race or group and not allow them to continue their line and further hurt the people of God. Here it has special significance since in Obadiah 3 the capital of Edom is named *Sela'*, the same word for the "rock" that is where the children are dashed in Psalm 137:9. Thus there is an irony of justice here. The stronghold in which the Edomites trust for their security becomes the means of their own destruction.

The last category considered here is that of wisdom, especially in torah psalms. Psalm 119 is the best example of this. Its acrostic form has been recognized, as has its manner of connecting every verse with the law of Yahweh (see "Overview of the Psalms," above). However, Psalm 1 also serves as a wisdom psalm that counsels the importance of the torah. The psalm begins with a warning not to spend time with those who are wicked and scornful of the search for truth. The emphasis is not on the study of the torah but rather how one should delight in the torah through constant meditation. This delight will lead to growth, which is compared to a tree planted beside streams of water. The endurance and fruitfulness of this imagery contrasts with that of the wicked, who are compared to dead chaff that is not rooted but blows about everywhere (Ps. 1:4). Jeremiah 17:5–10 uses the same image of a tree and of a dead bush. However, there the attitude of the righteous is focused on their faith. Thus this imagery shows an interesting connection between faith in God and delight in his word. For this reason the wicked will not survive the judgment (Ps. 1:5). However, the righteous will survive because Yahweh will take care of them. The placement of this psalm at the beginning of Psalms testifies to the priority that the editor of the book gave to the torah and its pursuit. It also places the book of Psalms in the context of wisdom and the delight in the word of God. The Psalms are not so much subjugated to the torah as they become a further expression of what it means to live a life devoted to the God who has given the torah out of this faithful love for his people.

The theology of the Psalms looks to the close and continuing relationship between God and his people. It has been and always will be a key path for entering into and continuing a vital spiritual relationship with Yahweh and, for Christians, with Christ through prayer and reflection. The book is not only a personal guide to spirituality; its repeated emphasis on psalms of the community also suggests that both individual and corporate relations with God in praise and prayer are an essential part of the life of the faithful. In joy and sorrow, in pain and celebration, and in virtually every experience of life, believers are given the opportunity to identify with the psalmist and to echo the psalmist's concerns and satisfactions.

However, there is more for Christians. The frequent quotation of and numerous manuscripts of the Psalms among the Dead Sea Scrolls and the many references to the Psalms by Jesus in the Gospels attest to what the human side of Jesus encountered with the Psalms. For Jesus, as he grew and worshiped in and around Nazareth, the Psalms would have served as his prayer book, worship hymnal, and devotional guide. As the numerous references and quotations by Jesus (and his followers) attest in the New Testament, Jesus studied, prayed, and knew the Psalms. They were his means of access to the spiritual life. As disciples of Christ, believers are expected to follow Christ in his life and teaching, and also to walk with him in his relationship with his Father. The Gospels can report what Jesus said and did. This is important and key for Christians to know and to obey. However, the Psalms move readers to a deeper level. Through them, believers commune with Jesus Christ as he communes with his heavenly Father. The Psalms enable the devout to have a glimpse of what Jesus thought and felt.

Key Commentaries and Studies

Bullock, C. Hassell. *Encountering the Book of Psalms: A Literary and Theological Introduction.* Grand Rapids: Baker Academic, 2001. The best survey; evangelical.

Craigie, Peter C. *Psalms 1–50.* WBC 19. Waco: Word, 1983. Clearly written; evangelical with comparative Ugaritic studies and theological insights.

Goldingay, John. *Psalms.* Vol. 1, *1–41.* Vol. 2, *42–89.* Vol. 3, *90–150.* BCOTWP. Grand Rapids: Baker Academic, 2006–8. Postmodern exegesis with theological insight; evangelical.

Grogan, Geoffrey. *Prayer, Praise and Prophecy: A Theology of the Psalms.* Fearn, Ross-shire, UK: Christian Focus, 2001. Evangelical introduction to the Psalms.

Hossfeld, Frank-Lothar, and Erich Zenger. *Psalms 2.* Hermeneia. Minneapolis: Fortress, 2005. Explains multiple redactions in Psalms 50–100.

Kidner, Derek. *Psalms: An Introduction and Commentary.* Vol. 1, *1–72.* Vol. 2, *73–150.* TOTC. Leicester, UK: Inter-Varsity; Downers Grove, IL: InterVarsity, 1973–75. Evangelical musician and theological exegete looks at the Psalms.

Terrien, Samuel. *The Psalms: Strophic Structure and Theological Commentary.* ECC. Grand Rapids: Eerdmans, 2003. Theological and practical exegesis by a wisdom scholar.

Waltke, Bruce K., James M. Houston, and Erika Moore. *The Psalms as Christian Lament: A Historical Commentary.* Grand Rapids: Eerdmans, 2014.

Weber, Beat. "Toward a Theory of the Poetry of the Hebrew Bible: The Poetry of the Psalms as a Test Case." *BBR* 22 (2012): 157–89. Survey of major methods of interpreting the Psalms and Classical Hebrew poetry.

Wenham, Gordon J. *Psalms as Torah: Reading Biblical Song Ethically.* Studies in Theological Interpretation. Grand Rapids: Baker Academic, 2012. An excellent example of deriving the major theological concepts of the Psalms and applying them to life, whether from the imprecatory, lament, or praise psalms.

16

PROVERBS

How do you measure success in this world? Is it fame, wealth, popularity, happiness? The book of Proverbs provides a guide to success for the person devoted to God. Such a person finds success in a life lived according to principles of faithfulness to God's covenant.

Name, Text, and Outline

The Hebrew word *mišlê*, "proverbs of," forms the first word in the Hebrew text of Proverbs and thus became its name. The Septuagint uses the equivalent Greek term, *Paroimiai*, which Jerome rendered as (*Liber*) *Proverbiorum*, "(Book) of Proverbs." The Hebrew root, *māšāl*, carries the sense of a comparison. It may be used to describe a parable where something, perhaps a creature or event in nature, is compared to human action.

The Hebrew text of Proverbs, as preserved in the Masoretic tradition, is generally reliable and can be used as the basic form of the text for study.[1] Two fragments of Proverbs were found among the Dead Sea Scrolls: 4QProv[a] (4Q102) and 4QProv[b] (4Q103). Together these preserve 164 Hebrew words in whole or part. Dated to the first century BC, these fragments are closer to the Masoretic tradition than to that of the Septuagint or any other.

The Septuagint seems to preserve a text that more freely renders the Hebrew of Proverbs. Later versions sought to correct the text back to be closer to the Masoretic Text. In the latter third of the book in the later Greek versions, there are significant differences in the order of the verses in comparison with

1. See Waltke, *Book of Proverbs*, 1:1–7.

the Masoretic Text, providing for smoother transitions between sections. The versions also try to ascribe as much of the book as possible to Solomon.

The Syriac often follows the Septuagint, and the *Targum Psalms* (Aramaic) attests to readings related to the Syriac. The Vulgate follows an early Masoretic form.

OUTLINE

- I. Discourse on Wisdom (1:1–9:18)
  - A. Introduction on the Value of Wisdom (1:1–7)
  - B. Contrast of Lady Wisdom and Lady Folly (1:8–8:36)
  - C. Conclusion (9:1–18)
- II. Diverse Collection of Solomon's Proverbs (10:1–22:16)
  - A. Antitheses between the Righteous and the Wicked (10:1–15:33)
  - B. More on the Wicked and the Righteous (16:1–22:16)
- III. Thirty Sayings of the Wise (22:17–24:22)
- IV. More Sayings of the Wise (24:23–34)
- V. More Sayings of Solomon (25:1–29:27)
- VI. Sayings of Agur Son of Jakeh (30:1–33)
- VII. Sayings of King Lemuel (31:1–31)
  - A. Title (31:1)
  - B. Noble King (31:2–9)
  - C. Noble Queen (31:10–31)

Overview of Proverbs

The book of Proverbs begins by making a connection to Solomon. It identifies the purpose of the book as a matter of acquiring wisdom and locates this concern with the fear of Yahweh (1:7). The first chapter goes on to counsel avoidance of sinners due to their wickedness. Wisdom is personified as standing in the square and calling warnings to those who ignore her. However, those who listen to her will find security. Chapter 2 argues that the source of true wisdom may be found in the fear of Yahweh. This will bring success and avoidance both of those who are crooked and of the adulteress. The theme of security is repeated, now focused on living in the land. Chapter 3 endorses love and faithfulness along with the fear of Yahweh, which leads to a generous spirit but avoids the wicked who plot against others. In Proverbs 4, Wisdom (here male) recalls his youth when his father taught him the value of wisdom and to guard his heart. The fifth chapter warns the young man against the adulterous wife (married to another) who wants him. To lie with such a woman will bring destruction. Rather, Wisdom counsels that remaining faithful to one's first (and only) wife is the way of life. Chapter 6 begins with counsel to repay any debt one has as quickly as possible. It condemns pride, lying, and murder and goes on to condemn all sexual relations with prostitutes and adulteresses. Punishment is inevitable, especially from the offended husband. Proverbs 7 continues with this theme, presenting the fourth and final lecture (cf. 2:16–19; 5:1–23; 6:20–33) as an eyewitness account of a gullible young man who is seduced by the adulteress and whose end is death. Proverbs 8 returns to Lady Wisdom, standing in the public squares and calling for those who will listen and learn to fear Yahweh. Wisdom is welcome in the halls of kings and more valuable than gold, and was Yahweh's first creation, before the rest of the world, and involved in creating that world. In the last chapter (9) of this discourse, Wisdom prepares a banquet in her house and invites those who will listen. One who is wise receives rebuke and teaching. Lady Folly is portrayed as loud, undisciplined, and ignorant. Nevertheless, she sits outside her house and invites the foolish, who do not know that her house is the gateway to Sheol.

Proverbs 10 begins with a title, "The Proverbs of Solomon," for the first time since 1:1. This opening section provides general encouragements to accept the commands of Yahweh, exhibit love, learn to control one's tongue, be active, and know that the reward of the wise is success and long life. In chapter 11 the wise are exhorted to be honest with their business (i.e., scales), humble, blameless, discerning in speech, kindhearted, discreet, generous, seeking good, and trusting in God (rather than riches). Wise men and women bring honor to those around them (12:1–9) and carefulness to all life. Truth and care in speech are important, as are kind words and diligence. Honesty and hard words are themes of chapter 13. Discipline and the promise of inheritance for one's family are part of the joy of the righteous. Chapter 14 continues these themes as it also considers patience, prudence, and care for others. In chapter 15, the themes are the wisdom of rebuke and discipline, the control of one's emotions, the wisdom of seeking counsel, the rejection of bribes, the value of joy, and the importance of humility in the fear of Yahweh.

Proverbs 16 calls the wise to commit themselves to Yahweh and know that he determines the fate of everything. Wisdom possesses honesty and integrity but also knows how to appease the anger of a king. The plotting of evil, gossip, and violence all lead to death. However, old age is attained by a righteous life. Patience and self-control are better than conquest. Many previously mentioned themes continue into Proverbs 17: harmony, wisdom in poverty, God's testing, control of the tongue, the blessing of a family, the ruin from paying back evil for good, just judgment, the value of friends, the wrong of lies and bribes, and the control of the tongue. Chapter 18 looks at selfishness, justice, wisdom, hard work, gossiping and foolish words, humility, resolving issues and disputes, a good spouse, and the existence of a beloved friend who is closer than a brother. Proverbs 19 includes themes of patience, false witness, forgiveness, a prudent wife, mercy to the poor, discipline of children, faithfulness, and honoring parents.

Proverbs 20 presents a warning against drinking alcohol and encourages peacemaking, hard work, and honesty in weights. This is followed by another warning against fraud in negotiations, with advice on the importance of seeking counsel, avoidance of gossiping and cursing one's parents, staying away from oaths, and the value of discipline. Because Yahweh directs all, chapter 21 suggests that doing right by him is more important than anything else. Violence, quarrelsome wives, mocking, shutting off the cry of the poor, lack of control of the tongue, and the failure to give generously—all of these are part of the counsel of Proverbs 21. In chapter 22 the value of a good reputation is considered, as are humility and fear, seeing the warning signs of danger, avoiding the lack of discipline, the blessing of generosity and of gracious speech, the importance of truthful words and of diligence, and the need to stay away from the adulteresses, but not from discipline. Respect for both the poor and the rich are counseled.

In Proverbs 22:17 a new section of the book begins with an exhortation to listen to "words of the wise." Thirty sayings (v. 20) are introduced as wisdom. These include care for the poor, controlling one's temper, avoiding loans, and not moving a boundary stone but respecting skilled workers. Proverbs 23 continues these sayings with counsel such as to practice self-restraint, know from whom to accept gifts, avoid exploiting the weak, discipline children, put away envy and fear Yahweh, avoid the prostitute and adulteress, and know the dangers of alcoholism. Chapter 24 goes on to counsel about avoiding envy and violence, valuing the prudence of counselors, seeing the danger of theft and violence, and keeping calm amid the prosperity (as well as the downfall) of one's enemies.

Proverbs 24:23–34 continues more "sayings of the wise": Do not declare the innocent guilty and vice versa. Maintain honesty and work hard in your fields and in building your house. Neither revenge nor laziness has any benefit.

According to Proverbs 25:1, chapters 25–29 contain more "proverbs of Solomon," these having been copied by Hezekiah's servants. They begin with counsel as to how to act before a king. This leads to a set of proverbs on knowing when and how to speak and to listen. There is a section on friendship and faithfulness as well as how to respond to neighbors with love. Chapter 25 concludes with counsel on self-control, and chapter 26 considers how to regard a fool. After this come warnings about pride, laziness, deception, gossiping, and lying. Proverbs 27 begins with a theme of humility, control of one's emotions and honesty, friendship and having a good wife, and care for one's own lands and livestock. Proverbs 28 returns to themes of leadership and the maintenance of the law and justice. In addition, the reader finds the values of freedom from guilt, hard work, faithfulness, fairness, generosity, and trusting in Yahweh. Proverbs 29 begins with the fate of the stubborn and considers the result of going after prostitutes. It also develops the contrasting characters of a king practicing justice and of a flatterer. The text goes on to address caring for the poor, mockers, murderers, lack of self-control, a ruler who listens to lies, an undisciplined child, those who keep the law, one who pampers his servant, the angry, the proud, and those who trust Yahweh.

Proverbs 30 contains "the words of Agur son of Jakeh." He describes himself as ignorant but confesses that God's word is perfect. He asks only for his daily bread, and neither wealth nor poverty. He counsels humility and avoidance of envy, greed, mocking, and adultery. His proverbs conclude with two "numerical" ones: four creatures that are small but very wise, and four creatures that move in a stately manner.

Proverbs 31 concludes the book with "the sayings of King Lemuel" (NIV) as taught by his mother. In verses 2–9 she counsels for a king to avoid alcohol but to dispense it to those who are in dire circumstances. She also counsels that the king give special attention to the poor and vulnerable, who cannot speak and defend themselves. Verses 10–31 describe the *ʾēšet ḥayil*, the woman of valor or the noble woman, who is worth more than rubies. Her husband trusts her completely as she arranges for the clothing, feeding, and abundance of her family. She engages in many kinds of business, such as the purchase of property, and she is skilled in the acquisition and production of thread and textiles. She is wise, and her husband, her children, and those at the city gate praise her.

Reading Proverbs

Premodern Readings

It has already been mentioned that the Septuagint has what appears to be a free rendering of the Masoretic Text.[2] However, it remains debated as to how much of this is a matter of theological interest on the part of the translator (such as moralizing or spiritualizing tones and avoidance of sexual language), how much it reflects the influence of Hellenistic thought (as abstractions replace metaphors), and how much it is the use of a Hebrew *Vorlage* (parent text) that differed significantly from the Masoretic Text.

Although related to the Syriac Peshitta, the *Targum Proverbs* may date before or after the Syriac version. In any case, it is less expansive and more literal in its renderings of the proverbs. The midrash on Proverbs dates at the end of the first millennium AD but includes earlier sources and materials. The proverbs are interpreted through a lens of encouragement to study torah. There was also a tendency to use a midrashic type of exegesis to apply individual proverbs to biblical and other stories. At other points in the text, and also

2. See Garrett, "Proverbs 3."

among some medieval commentators (such as Rabbi Ḳimḥi), a more literal interpretation could be found.

In early and medieval Christian literature, Proverbs became the introduction to the corpus of Wisdom literature as found in the Bible and the Apocrypha. Proverbs 8 was an important text in the early church, to demonstrate Christ's presence as Wisdom. Athanasius (*Orationes contra Arianos* Ii.§18–82) identifies the figure of Wisdom as having been created by God (8:22) with the incarnation. Only then could the uncreated Son of God say, "You have created me." For Origen (*First Principles*, preface 8; 4.2.2; 4.2.4) and Jerome, the foundation of a threefold interpretation of Scripture is located in Proverbs 22:20–21. Here the Septuagint includes the phrase "Write these things in a threefold manner." For Hippolytus (in *Fragmenta in Proverbia*) and many other Christian writers, Wisdom's presentation of a table with bread and wine (Prov. 9:2–5) becomes the Eucharist. For Bede (*On Proverbs*), Proverbs 22:29, where a skilled person will "stand before kings" (KJV), becomes a means by which those who do good works will stand among the apostles, who will judge the world with Christ. Others, however, found in Proverbs instructions for practical living. Thus for Augustine (*Sermones* 36.2, 7, 11), Proverbs 13:7 serves to warn believers of the dangers of wealth.

In the second millennium of Christianity, Proverbs became a book treasured for its practical wisdom more than for any theological issues that might have divided Jews and Christians or Protestants and Roman Catholics. The eighteenth-century American theologian Jonathan Edwards used the book as a guide for righteous living.[3] However, he and others took the forms and metaphors in the text seriously as a means to understand what was said. Thus the text manifests both a guide to holiness and a beauty of form, both of which point to the holiness and beauty of Christ.

Higher Criticism

The theories regarding Proverbs can be divided into three areas: the relation of proverbs to one another, date and authorship, and formation of the collection.[4]

The question of the relationship of proverbs to one another has remained a continuing source of debate. In the center of this controversy has been the collection in 10:1–22:16. Some critics simply deny a relationship between the various proverbs and prefer to see here a random collection of wisdom sayings. Even here, however, there is an admission of at least some editorial groupings. In many cases those who hold this view direct their criticisms against scholars who try to relate the proverbs to one another. Others claim

3. Stein, "'Like Apples of Gold.'"
4. See ibid., 572–76; Heim, *Like Grapes of Gold*, 5–66.

to see an intentional arrangement in larger groupings of proverbs. In some cases the original contexts of the proverbs have disappeared due to selection and editing.

Among those who have found connections in the book of Proverbs, Steven C. Perry has examined paronomasia, or the use of similar roots and words that would tie together otherwise unrelated proverbs.[5] Perry's computer analysis of this phenomenon concludes that such links do exist. Norman Whybray identifies a common theological kernel in Proverbs 15:33–16:11.[6] Around this other proverbs gathered. Also, proverbs could be linked by similar sounds, especially where unusual words were employed. T. A. Hildebrandt identifies sixty-two pairs of proverbs bound together by similarities in sound, meaning, syntax, and so forth.[7] Using broad criteria, he seeks to connect other proverbs near to them. Duane Garrett has found groupings on the basis of parallelism, catchwords, chiasms, and similar themes or even inclusios, where two proverbs with somewhat similar words group everything between them into a unit.[8] This could also create very broad categories. Roland Murphy's commentary moves beyond previous works as he demonstrates awareness of the basic meaning of a proverb and the manner in which nearby proverbs could be connected by wordplays and could expand on these themes.[9]

David Snell's *Twice-Told Proverbs and the Composition of the Book of Proverbs* looks at variant repetitions to identify thematic connections. Ruth Scoralick's *Einzelspruch und Sammlung* also considers repeated variants in Proverbs 10–15, including those that extend across many chapters (e.g., 11:1 and 20:23; 10:1 and 15:20). The conclusions suggest a significance for these variant repetitions because they create a coherence to the book. It is this approach that has also been addressed by the commentaries of Bruce Waltke and of Michael Fox.[10] In *Like Grapes of Gold Set in Silver*, Knut M. Heim has examined the collection of Proverbs 10:1–22:16 and argues that the array of techniques used to relate various proverbs also enables readers to understand each proverb better by providing a context for their reading and interpretation. His later study, *Poetic Imagination in Proverbs:Varient Repetitions and the Nature of Poetry*, moves the reader further in identifying variant repetitions and the manner in which they shed light on one another.

A second area of study has to do with the question of date and authorship. The nineteenth century saw the development of theories in which different parts of the book of Proverbs came from different authors, with 10:1–22:16 containing the oldest parts. The book of Proverbs as now preserved finally

5. Perry, "Structural Patterns."
6. Whybray, "Yahweh-Sayings."
7. Hildebrandt, "Proverbial Pairs."
8. Garrett, *Proverbs, Ecclesiastes, Song of Songs*, 19–252.
9. Murphy, *Proverbs*.
10. Waltke, *Book of Proverbs*; Fox, *Proverbs*.

came together in the postexilic era. Thus this question became closely tied to the third issue: the origin of the book of Proverbs.

A large part of this issue has raised the question as to whether the proverbs originated as compositions of wisdom schools and of the royal court and its training of scribes and princes, or whether the wisdom sayings began in the oral context of village life and of the tribes, where early Israel began. Gerhard von Rad sees in Proverbs a close connection with international wisdom and with schools in Israel.[11] Whybray has found no necessary connection between Proverbs and a royal school or even sufficient reason to posit the existence of such a school.[12]

Some, such as André Lemaire, have argued that the existence of abecedaries (texts of the Hebrew alphabet) implies education and schooling in Israel.[13] Ronald Clements suggests that the royal court expressed the power of the elite and reflected an international context.[14] However, by the postexilic period this wisdom was made available to all. James Crenshaw suggests that the proverbs were the product of two groups: the clan and the court.[15] Clan wisdom aimed at the single goal of mastering life.

While a professional class of wisdom teachers during the Israelite monarchy may be disputed, it is clear that, in the book of Proverbs, several verses connect the wisdom sayings with kings, especially Solomon and Hezekiah (1:1; 10:1; 25:1). In professional wisdom and scribal schools of both Egypt and Mesopotamia, the teacher could be referred to as father and the students as sons. While this occurs frequently in the book of Proverbs, texts such as Proverbs 1:8 mention the mother as a source of wisdom. This betrays a connection with family wisdom, not merely with royal or school sources.

The question of authorship is answered by the book of Proverbs: along with 1 Kings 3:5–9 (2 Chron. 1:7–10) and 4:32, it attributes the proverbs to Solomon. How did this tradition regarding Solomon originate? As Kenneth Kitchen has shown, the form and structure of the book of Proverbs fit well at the end of the second millennium and beginning of the first millennium BC.[16] The Amarna correspondence of the fourteenth century attests to the sharing of international literature and scribal training. Jerusalem, and the Israelite monarchy, could well have been influenced by that tradition. It either came from the scribes of Egypt or continued in Jerusalem itself from the earlier Canaanite and Jebusite scribal tradition.[17]

11. Von Rad, *Wisdom in Israel.*

12. Whybray, *Intellectual Tradition.*

13. Lemaire, *Écoles.*

14. Clements, *Wisdom for a Changing World.*

15. Crenshaw, *Old Testament Wisdom.*

16. Kitchen, *Reliability*; see "Ancient Near Eastern Context" below.

17. This tradition was also shared with Egypt; for the connection, see Hess, "Hebrew Psalms and Amarna." For examples of connection with earlier Canaanite wisdom sources, see Albright, "Some Canaanite-Phoenician Sources." See further under "Ancient Near Eastern Context."

© Baker Publishing Group and Dr. James C. Martin. The Egyptian Ministry of Antiquities.

Egyptian scribes

Waltke proposes that the Egyptian Wisdom literature of the second millennium BC and the first half of the first millennium BC, where it can be checked, does not appear to be pseudepigraphic but rather contains authentic attributions of authorship.[18] If so, then what has been demonstrated as true for Egyptian Wisdom literature may also be true for Israelite Wisdom literature. So Solomon and Hezekiah would be responsible for originating or collecting the proverbs of most of the book. Agur of Proverbs 30:1 may have been an official in the (Solomonic?) royal administration of monarchic Israel, and Lemuel might have been an otherwise unattested non-Israelite king. The final editor may have lived as late as the Persian period, or less likely the Hellenistic period. As with other books of the Bible, however, such a person might update the language (vocabulary, spelling, and grammar) without revising the content.

Literary Readings

This section will focus on the more general topic of the meaning and world of wisdom in and around ancient Israel, the literary forms of Wisdom literature, the parallelism and significance of the proverb, and the overall structure and emphasis of the book of Proverbs. In looking at these matters with the awareness of many fine studies on Wisdom literature, I nevertheless wish to

18. Waltke, *Book of Proverbs*, 1:34–37.

Views on the Distinctives of Israelite Wisdom

Fundamentally, wisdom in ancient Israel is related to faith in God. "Happiness depends on faith in God to uphold justice. Moreover, in order that the wise may not be seduced into confounding morality with pleasure, the Lord often allows them to suffer for the sake of righteousness and thereby works patience, hope, trust, and other virtues into their character before he upholds his moral order, which includes justice."[a] Ancient Near Eastern wisdom and omen literature reflected similar concerns about living in the world. Omen literature was not predictive as much as it classified natural and unusual phenomena as either good or bad. However, these lists could contain mutually exclusive claims. This was because the form was dictated by tradition rather than by creativity, as would come with the Greek development of wisdom.[b] Biblical wisdom uses traditional forms, such as proverbs and disputation, but it has transformed them by its integrative worldview and by its ability to challenge and shatter accepted interpretations of human and divine experience.[c]

[a] Waltke and Diewert, "Wisdom Literature," 298.
[b] Machinist, "On Self-Consciousness."
[c] E.g., Job and Ecclesiastes; see Waltke and Diewert, "Wisdom Literature," 301.

single out Crenshaw's *Old Testament Wisdom: An Introduction*. Now in its third edition (2010), this work remains most useful and forms the basis for much of what is included here.

The Hebrew word for "wisdom" is the noun *ḥokmâ*. In Hebrew, feminine nouns are normally used to identify abstractions, and such is true here. The wisdom books comprise Proverbs, Ecclesiastes, and Job. Other parts of the Old Testament also may be classified as containing wisdom, especially the wisdom psalms (see "Theological Perspectives of the Psalms," in the previous chapter). In addition, wisdom books attributed to the Apocrypha include the Wisdom of Ben Sira (Sirach, Ecclesiasticus) and the Wisdom of Solomon.

The worldview of wisdom begins with people. It assumes that humans learn from experience and that this experience can be communicated in the writings of the Wisdom literature. Behind this is the idea that the world is truly a universe, a single wholeness that works together.[19] Thus what occurs on one level can be transferred to another level of existence. The proverbs make use of this worldview. If an ant gains by its industry and hard work, so humans can learn from that ant. Behind this is a fundamentally optimistic view of the universe.[20] This assumes that there is an order and it is divinely

19. Crenshaw, *Old Testament Wisdom*, 11.
20. See esp. Perdue, *Wisdom and Creation*; idem, *Wisdom Literature*.

imposed, ultimately coming from a compassionate Creator. Finally, wisdom in Israel and in the Hebrew Bible is seen through the lens of covenant faith.[21]

In Sirach 38:24–39:11 the author compares sages and those engaged in other tasks. Of course, the sages win out every time, as in similar comparisons of tasks in Egyptian Wisdom literature. The wisdom scribes were in the upper social class. They were not prophetic and did not critique a class.

Wisdom literature took a number of forms, of which proverbs were one of the most frequent. In a proverb a simple saying registers a conclusion that has arisen through observation of nature, animal behavior, or human conduct. Key to this form is the brevity of the expression. Combined with some vivid imagery, this brevity helps one to learn and memorize the proverb. A second form of wisdom is the riddle. There is no example of this form in the biblical Wisdom literature, although riddles are associated with Samson in the book of Judges (see 14:12–18). A third form is the allegory, an extended metaphor or series of word pictures related to the same theme. For example, Ecclesiastes 12:1–8 contains an allegory of old age, which is so announced in verse 1 and then portrayed in the following verses. A related form of Wisdom literature may be the hymn. This fourth form can be found in Job 28, where wisdom is praised as inaccessible, like rare gems. It also comprises the first nine chapters of Proverbs. These are all related to Lady Wisdom and the need to listen to her rather than to Lady Folly. A fifth type of Wisdom literature is the disputation or dialogue form. This is obvious in Job, where it takes the form of a narrative introduction and conclusion, between which are sandwiched the dialogue itself and the divine resolution. For ancient Near Eastern comparisons, see "Ancient Near Eastern Context" for Job. For the sixth form of wisdom, the autobiographical narrative, see the example of Ecclesiastes (see "Ancient Near Eastern Context" in that chapter). The didactic narrative is a seventh form. An example of this is found in Proverbs 7:6–23, where the seductress entices the young man to follow her.[22]

The book of Proverbs represents the basic and clearest model of Wisdom literature in the Bible. As noted above, it presupposes that there is a fundamental order to the universe, that a person's conduct either strengthens or weakens that order, and that the universe is subject to the divine will. Proverbs discovers principles in nature and can transfer them from the animal world to that of humans.

To return to the form of the proverb, its brevity betrays the long experience that many of these sayings preserved. A proverb contains a truth expressed through Hebrew poetry and its parallelism. Both the imagery and the parallel form of the two lines aid memorization and enhance appreciation of the proverb. As mentioned under "Literary Readings" for Psalms, parallelism provides

21. See Waltke and Diewert, "Wisdom Literature," 301.

22. An eighth form of wisdom, noun lists, does not appear in the Hebrew Bible.

a reinforcement of a statement. The same types occur here as are found in poetry. So Proverbs 1:8–9 provides an example of synonymous parallelism:

> Hear, my child, your father's instruction,
> and do not reject your mother's teaching;
> for they are a fair garland for your head,
> and pendants for your neck.

In the first two lines, "my son/child" appears in line 1 and by ellipsis is implied in the second line. Lines 3 and 4 also share a clearly synonymous parallelism, where "fair garland for your head" parallels "pendants for your neck."

An example of antithetical parallelism may be found in Proverbs 11:1:

> A false balance is an abomination to the LORD,
> but a just weight is his delight. (KJV)

Related to this form is the "better saying," as found in Proverbs 15:17:

> Better is a dinner of vegetables where love is
> than a fatted ox and hatred with it.

The progressive, ascending, or accumulative parallelism is illustrated by Proverbs 22:6:

> Train up a child in the way he should go,
> and when he is old he will not depart from it. (KJV)[23]

Numerical proverbs appear in Proverbs 30:29–31, where there is a listing of items that reach up to four. The text describes creatures who move stately. While the fourth item, the king, may suggest a building up to this climax, the first item, the lion, might then be expected to be the third in the sequence. The lion is surely the most stately of creatures mentioned. Why, then, are numbers two and three a rooster and a he-goat? These animals are surely less stately than a lion. They are more accurately described as silly. The lion would logically be connected with the king if the sole concern of the numerical

23. There are four possible interpretations to this well-known verse: (1) Train the child in the morally correct way. However, this ignores the "his" in "his way." (2) Train the child according to his own inclinations. However, this describes a specific way, while the proverb is general. (3) Train a child for official responsibilities so that the child can take them over at an appropriate age. However, this says nothing new or significant. (4) This is an ironic statement like 19:27: "Let a child do what he wants, and he will become self-willed and incapable of change." This seems to be the most reasonable interpretation. See Clifford, *Proverbs*, 196–97; Goldingay, *Old Testament Theology*, 2:540.

increase were sober stateliness. However, if there is something else going on, then perhaps it is not merely a collection of stately figures. The pictures of silliness suggest that a criticism of the stateliness of a king is implied. Perhaps the numerical parallelism may seek humility from the king, rather than pride, by warning that this attitude of kingship can at times be pompous, just as it can be serious. Perhaps this is also the reason for the context of the four small animals that accomplish amazing things in the preceding section, 30:24–28. By themselves, there is no apparent numerical heightening but simply a list for reflection. However, combined with what follows, they provide a background for the value of staying away from the center of attention.

Other poetic structures also occur, similar to those already discussed under "Literary Readings" for Psalms. In terms of the relation of one proverb to another, readers have already seen the difficulty with texts such as Proverbs 10:1–22:16. Yet there is logic to the connections, not unlike that seen in some of the connections between apparently disparate laws in the Deuteronomic law collection. Thus there can be association, based not on logic or similarity of theme but on the repetition of sound and sense through consonants, word roots, words, synonyms, and so forth.[24] Heim compares the arrangement of groups of proverbs with eating clusters of grapes, in which it does not matter where one begins or ends in the cluster.[25] However, the totality of the grapes or proverbs in a given group achieves an effect greater than the sum of the individual proverbs.

Gender and Ideological Criticism

The gender element has been noted insofar as, early on in Proverbs (1:8), the source of teaching for the child is the mother as well as the father. In Proverbs 1–9 wisdom is personified as a woman who has much to teach those who will listen. In chapter 8 she is with God as the first of his creation and involved in the creative process. Lady Wisdom is contrasted with Lady Folly. The assumption is that young men must choose one or the other. Although the explicit feminine connection with wisdom recedes after the initial prologue of nine chapters, it returns at the end and forms an inclusio for the entire book.[26] Thus the last chapter (Prov. 31) contains advice from a queen mother to her young son in the opening nine verses. Then follows an acrostic poem extolling

24. See Heim, *Like Grapes of Gold*, 107. Earlier attempts at systematization include Whybray's study ("Yahweh-Sayings") on the importance of the Yahweh sayings in this section for clustering groups of proverbs. Goldingay ("Arrangement of Sayings") suggests six subcollections and notices that an initial emphasis on moral sayings in Prov. 10–11 precedes the Yahweh sayings in Prov. 15–16. Heim ("Structure and Context") had already identified connections through catchwords, wordplay, theological reinterpretation, repetitions, and numerical connections (e.g., Solomon's name numbers 375, identical to the 375 single-line proverbs in this section).

25. Heim, *Like Grapes of Gold*.

26. Whybray, *Composition of the Book of Proverbs*.

the capable woman or *ʾēšet ḥayil* (see the "Overview of Proverbs"). This construction that begins and ends the book closely ties many of the aspects of wisdom with the feminine, whether the ethical and moral traits of the opening chapters or the practical business and family concerns of the final chapter. See further under "Ancient Near Eastern Context" for suggested connections with goddesses.

Elamite woman spinning

Zev Radovan/www.BibleLandPictures.com

The question of ideology raises issues about the purpose of the book. If it is a manual for kings to pass on to their heirs, and thus similar to the other ancient Near Eastern wisdom collections, does it have any value other than as a source for studying the priorities and values of the wealthy and powerful? Certainly there is the appearance of interest in preserving the status quo. For the young male ruler, the counsel of Proverbs suggests that the way of life and success is ensured by obedience to and respect of parents; discipline to be learned; self-control (the use of the tongue in eloquence, timeliness, and at times silence) and subordination of passions (Prov. 16:32 NKJV, "He who is slow to anger is better than the mighty, and he who rules his spirit than he who takes a city"); and a good wife (18:22). On the opposite end of the spectrum, death and failure come with adultery, drunkenness, laziness, gossiping, and a nagging wife.

However, as already seen, there is no absolutism to this advice. For one thing, the nature of the proverb is that it is advice, and that wisdom develops from learning when to apply it. Otherwise it is difficult to understand Proverbs 26:4 and 5. There, side by side, are the counsels not to answer a fool and to answer a fool. Further, as already recognized with the discussion about the origins of the proverbs, not all come from a royal setting. Many proverbs provide advice about mundane aspects of life and can be applied to all people. Related to this is the third point that has just been made. The totality of the book of Proverbs emphasizes the female gender in the pursuit of wisdom. Despite various male perspectives, the beginning and end of the book exalt Lady Wisdom and the woman of valor. Finally, readers notice texts such as Proverbs 16:9: "A person may plan his way, but Yahweh will direct his steps" (RSH). The future is not known to any of us. Only God knows this, and, as Proverbs reminds readers in 1:7 and throughout, all wisdom is subservient to Yahweh and the covenant relationship between God and his people. Thus the advice remains, but it is not an absolute guarantee about anything. Humans may do their best to follow this road, whatever their social and economic status, but in the end it is the will of God that is decisive.

Ancient Near Eastern Context

Wisdom literature can be found throughout the ancient Near East. John Day makes the case for influence from Ugarit and especially West Semitic literature (but also Babylonian sources), both generally regarding the idea of wisdom and more specifically as follows.[27] The first-millennium-BC Wisdom (Proverbs) of Ahiqar (*ʾăḥîqār*) includes in lines 81–82 a proverb almost certainly related to Proverbs 23:13–14. Here is Day's translation of Ahiqar:

> Spare not your son from the rod;
> otherwise, can you save him [from wickedness]?
> If I beat you, my son, you will not die;
> but if I leave you alone, [you will not live].

Both Ahiqar and the thirteenth-to-twelfth-century-BC Wisdom literature from the West Semitic city of Ugarit provide contrasts between the righteous and the wicked, ascending numerical proverbs, proverbs using pictures of animals, references to the student as "my son," the fear of a deity as a part of wisdom (if not as centrally present as in the Bible), and the personification of Wisdom as a goddess (see below).

There are also many individual proverbs that have parallels with other proverb collections. However, the largest collection of parallel materials has long been known to occur in the Egyptian Instruction of Amenemope, which is similar to Proverbs 22:17–24:22. This text was composed in the twelfth century BC and continued to be copied in Egypt well into the late dynastic period. Thus it formed a source for Proverbs 22–24, although the order of the presentations has changed.[28] There may be a shift in these instructions in contrast to earlier Egyptian works. The father motivates the son by appealing to the development of virtues rather than the promises of material rewards.

Although many would argue that the book of Proverbs should be dated late in the first millennium BC and that the parallels with Wisdom literature are of little value in addressing this question, Kenneth Kitchen does not share this

27. Day, "Foreign Semitic Influence."

28. See the table of Sparks, *Ancient Texts*, 71. For the whole question of the relationship of biblical wisdom and Egyptian wisdom, see Shupak, *Where Can Wisdom Be Found?* She notes that Egyptian wisdom differs from biblical wisdom in that the former has a stronger emphasis on the evils of greed, whereas Hebrew wisdom emphasizes much more a self-reliance in the search for wisdom. See also Maire, "Proverbs XXII 17ss." Washington (*Wealth and Poverty*) tries to argue that the whole biblical defense of the poor, rather than blaming them for their state, derives from Amenemope. However, prophetic and other sources in Israel criticized this as well (Westermann, *Roots of Wisdom*; Whybray, "Yahweh-Sayings").

Instruction of Amenemope

This text is regarded as the best example of the Egyptian instruction genre. The emphasis on achievement in the world is not so important here. Rather, the value of wealth is replaced with human character, as exemplified by humility and other qualities that are also found in Proverbs: knowing when to remain silent, kindness, humility before God, and self-control. The assignation of the text to the twelfth century BC is based on its structure. In fact, all extant copies come from a later period. The work is divided into thirty organized chapters. Some have suggested that the reference to thirty (sayings) in Proverbs 22:20 relates to the thirty chapters. There is the presentation of the ideal man, quiet and at peace with himself, and the "heated" or emotional man. A second theme warns against all types of dishonesty and repeats the theme of honesty throughout the work. In addition to the similarities with Proverbs 22–24, other parallels exist. Compare the first lines of the prologue with the beginning of Proverbs (*COS* 1.147:116):

Beginning of the teaching for life,
The instructions for well-being,
Every rule for relations with elders,
For conduct toward magistrates;
Knowing how to answer one who speaks,
To reply to one who sends a message.
So as to direct him on the paths of life,
To make him prosper upon earth.[a]

[a] See Miriam Lichtheim, "Instruction of Amenemope," *COS* 1.147:115–22.

view.[29] Kitchen reports that some forty extant works of instructional wisdom exist in the ancient world.[30] More than half of these are Egyptian. His study reveals distinctions in the structure of the wisdom collections of the second millennium BC (and possibly earlier) and those of the first millennium BC. The second-millennium-BC collections (1) have short prologues, (2) are exhortative or state an aim (the exception here is the Wisdom of Ptahhotep, because it is biographical), and (3) contain mostly verses or proverbs of two lines that function in parallelism with each other. The Egyptian collections of the first millennium BC, in contrast, (1) have long prologues, (2) are biographical in style, and (3) use single-line epigrams and short essays as their dominant forms.

29. See Weeks, *Early Israelite Wisdom*; Whybray, *Composition of the Book of Proverbs*. Washington (*Wealth and Poverty*) tries to argue for a postexilic origin of the collection based on the presence of Aramaisms, an argument used by his teacher Seow for Ecclesiastes (see "Higher Criticism" for Ecclesiastes).

30. Kitchen, *Reliability*, 135.

Proverbs 1–24 has a long prologue (chaps. 1–9) and thus resembles wisdom collections of the first millennium BC. However, it uses parallelism in two lines as its dominant mode of expression. This is closer to wisdom collections of the second millennium BC. It is exhortative in large measure, although the account of the seductress in chapter 7 could be considered biographical. Thus the first twenty-four chapters appear to be transitional and lie at the turning point between the styles of the second millennium BC and those of the first millennium BC. This would date the overall structure of the book (before Prov. 25 and the reference to Hezekiah) to approximately the tenth century BC and the age of Solomon. The second section, Proverbs 25–29, gathered by the "men of Hezekiah" (ca. 700 BC), uses parallelism less and thus fits better with the comparable wisdom collections of the first millennium BC.

In her study of the date of Wisdom literature, Katharine Dell observes the difference between the proverbial contents of Proverbs and the more abstract essays of Ecclesiastes and Job.[31] She argues for an earlier preexilic date for Proverbs by comparing a similar transition from Sumerian proverbial wisdom to the later (after 2000 BC) Old Babylonian abstract wisdom. This would be supported by her own acceptance of scribal schools during the monarchy, a belief in Yahweh at this time (also found in the Proverbs), and a generally wider presence of literacy than some would allow.

Finally, recent attempts have been made to locate ancient Near Eastern and classical goddesses behind some of the wisdom imagery in the book of Proverbs. John B. Burns sees in this text an Adonis or Melqart mythological figure who, seduced by the goddess, dies and enters the underworld.[32] The difference is the demythologization in the Proverbs text and the failure of the young man to rise again. Thus this text is a warning against involvement in such religious rituals. However, the contrast between the Proverbs text and the mythological texts is so significant that it makes the parallel difficult to maintain. Tryggve Mettinger does not even mention this text in his thorough study of the dying and rising Adonis and Melqart myths.[33]

More promising is the feminine characterization of Wisdom and her possible appearance in the tree image in Proverbs 3:18 as "a tree of life." Thus some compare this figure with the goddess Asherah.[34] Wisdom in Proverbs becomes a replacement or substitution for this deity, who was unacceptable in orthodox Israelite religion as preserved in the Hebrew Bible.[35] Here a distinction should be made between mythopoeic imagery and the importation of mythology. The former is used frequently in the Hebrew Bible. Like the Hebrew language itself,

31. Dell, "How Much Wisdom Literature?"

32. Burns, "Proverbs 7,6–27."

33. Mettinger, *Riddle of Resurrection*.

34. See esp. Hadley, "Wisdom and the Goddess"; idem, *Cult of Asherah*; M. Smith, "Mythology and Myth-Making," 327–28.

35. M. Smith, "Mythology and Myth-Making," 337.

© Baker Publishing Group and Dr. James C. Martin. The Israel Museum.

Tenth-century-BC cult stand from Taanach with tree of life surrounded by ibex and guardian lions on the outside

and other poetic features such as parallelism and word pairs, the use of this imagery was among the communicative devices available to the Hebrew poets. Their use of these word pictures to describe and develop their own understanding of their distinctive theology no more commits them to a belief in this mythology than my decision to use Thursday to designate the fifth day of the week commits me to worship the Norse god Thor.

Canonical Context

The nature of Wisdom literature is that it is removed from much of the narrative and history writing of the Bible. Nevertheless, a few connections may be observed. Proverbs 8 and its description of Wisdom's participation in creation may be compared with Job 38–39, various psalms, and the creation account of Genesis 1. All ascribe creation to God, yet the unique emphasis of Proverbs is the exaltation of Wisdom and her fundamental role in the created order of all of life and existence.

The narratives of Solomon hold the closest tie with Proverbs since the book is attributed to him, and he is mentioned several times in it. Solomon is described as the wisest of all people and as one who spoke three thousand proverbs (1 Kings 4:31–32). For this reason, when tracing his wisdom back to his encounter with God in 1 Kings 3:4–15, and the illustration of that wisdom in his judgment of the two prostitutes who each claim the baby (3:16–28), it is important to understand that for Proverbs and the other Wisdom literature, this wisdom was not limited to judicial contexts. It reached out to include all the concerns of the world, as is evident in the book of Proverbs.

Wisdom's connection with the legal elements of the Torah has been overlooked. Some study has been done on connecting many proverbs to legal formulations with the assistance of the motive clauses.[36] More homiletical, but of important theological significance, is the categorization of the Proverbs in relation to the Ten Commandments.[37] Connected with this, in several interesting ways, are the sayings of King Lemuel's mother in Proverbs 30, especially verses 1–9. Here appears the speech of a humble man near death,

36. See Chirichigno, "Motivation in Old Testament Law."
37. See Lamparter, *Buch der Weisheit*.

Solomon, Proverbs, and Wordplay

As noted in the "Overview of Proverbs," the book of Proverbs contains three occurrences of the name Solomon, always in a title, beginning either the book (1:1) or a new section (10:1; 25:1). The personal name always appears in construct with the plural noun "proverbs": *mišlê šĕlōmōh*, "proverbs of Solomon." The consistent use of this phrase, as well as its appearance as the first two words of the book of Proverbs, demonstrates its importance and priority for all the proverbs that follow. There is an intentional connection between "proverbs" and "Solomon" that is enhanced by wordplay. In both words, the same three consonants appear (here listed in sequence as in the name Solomon): *shin*, *lamed*, and *mem*. These are the only three consonants that are audible in either of the two nouns. The identical sounds of both nouns, albeit in different order, demonstrate an intentional wordplay of the same sounds that connect the two and relate Solomon to the proverbs in the book.

echoing the last words of Moses and David to express the primacy of God's revelation over wisdom.[38]

The New Testament use of the book of Proverbs includes texts that either use the same language (Matt. 16:27 and Rom. 2:6, citing Prov. 24:12) or give a literal interpretation (Prov. 3:11–12 in Heb. 12:5–6; Prov. 11:31 in 1 Pet. 4:18). Garrett notes that 2 Peter 2:22 cites Proverbs 26:11 and then also refers to a saying from Ahiqar 7.27.[39] In Proverbs the New Testament writers found primarily a source of practical guidance. Stylistically, much of the Sermon on the Mount and some of the other teachings of Jesus are couched in the form of proverbs, if not themselves borrowed from the Old Testament book of Proverbs. Among the Epistles, James remains the dominant example of the frequent use of aphorisms, like the proverbs, in order to communicate his message. Insofar as it can be connected with the earliest Jerusalem church, and the Jewish leadership there, the text of James betrays the ongoing style and influence of the book of Proverbs, something that would see its own development in the rabbinic sayings of Judaism and in the Christian tradition in various sayings, perhaps best known in the *Apophthegmata Patrum*, *Sayings of the Desert Fathers* [*and Mothers*].

Theological Perspectives of Proverbs

In spite of the polytheistic origins of the Wisdom literature in the surrounding cultures, and in spite of attempts to trace a polytheism behind the book

38. Moore, "Home for the Alien."
39. Garrett, "Proverbs 3," 569.

of Proverbs, the only conclusion that can be reached when reading the book as now extant is one of monotheism. As with the discussion of the Shema in Deuteronomy 6:4–9, the explicit confession of only one Deity moves this text out of the realm of speculation as to whether this God has the right ideas and places it squarely in the context of the loving Yahweh, who does not need to represent his selection of right and wrong as one among several possible scenarios. Yahweh's word alone is sure truth.

Tied closely to monotheism is the concern of a God who seeks to relate to his people through establishing a covenant with them. The covenant is not often mentioned in the book. However, the "fear of Yahweh" occurs eleven times, more than in all the other books of the Bible together. This fear of Yahweh is the proper attitude to have when approaching Yahweh and his covenant. With this attitude, wisdom is possible (Prov. 1:7; 9:10). This respect for God and his covenant (as well as a fear of God's wrath for flippancy) adds length to one's life (10:27; 14:27; 19:23). It is better than wealth (15:16) yet can bring one wealth and respect (22:4).

The ethical element, in its main values, has already been discussed. Certain basic concerns about humility, love, care for the poor, and prudence in speech, as well as others, are repeated many times throughout the book. This emphasizes their importance as well as an attempt to tie the whole of wisdom together by repeating the ethical values.

Many of the values, especially long life, have to do with health and healing. Healing is a theological subject in the Bible and especially in the Old Testament. The Hebrew verb "he healed" is *rāpā'*. In its noun form (Heb. *marpē'*, "healing, health") it appears more frequently in Proverbs than in any other book. As a theological subject it is key to understanding the book of Proverbs. Nevertheless, because it encompasses such a wide span of the Old Testament and Hebrew Bible, it is necessary to review some of its major ideas here.[40]

From the perspective of the ancient Near East, illness is an inability to fulfill one's role in society. Thus infertility (caused possibly due to low caloric intake) is an illness. Common illnesses, diagnosed via skeletal analyses and archaeology, include anemia, dental problems, arthritis, and ectoparasites causing skin rashes (often translated as "leprosy" in the OT). The home was the center for treatment and recovery. The main roles for the tabernacle/temple were as a place for seeking healing from God and for giving praise to God for healing. Prayer was the main treatment for healing. In some contexts various medicines or remedies were used (Gen. 30:14–16; 2 Kings 20:7). Prophets at times performed healings, especially Elijah, Elisha, and Isaiah. The Old Testament also witnesses to the treatment of mental strain and psychological ailments. Thus David played his harp to treat Saul's illness (1 Sam. 16:23).

40. For the most complete study on the subject, see Brown, *Israel's Divine Healer*.

The Hebrew word for "healer" or "doctor" is *rōpē'*, the participle form of the verb *rāpā'*. An examination of the uses of the term *rāpā'* in the Hebrew Bible leads to seven generalizations. These are summarized here with biblical quotations (NIV):

1. All healing comes from God, the only successful subject of the verb "to heal":

> See now that I myself am he!
> There is no god besides me.
> I put to death and I bring to life,
> I have wounded and I will heal,
> and no one can deliver out of my hand. (Deut 32:39)

The leaders of Israel attempt to heal but fail:

> They dress the wound of my people
> as though it were not serious.
> "Peace, peace," they say,
> when there is no peace. (Jer. 8:11)

They are false shepherds:

> You have not strengthened the weak or healed the sick or bound up the injured. You have not brought back the strays or searched for the lost. You have ruled them harshly and brutally. (Ezek. 34:4)

The only "doctors" other than God are the embalmers of Genesis 50:2.

2. Intercessory prayer occurs in matters of illness and healing. This is attested in the first occurrence of the verb "to heal" in the Bible:

> Then Abraham prayed to God, and God healed Abimelek, his wife and his female slaves so they could have children again. (Gen. 20:17)

3. Healing is part of God's blessing for obedience. This is a generalization that is true of the people of God but not individually in all circumstances. Job is the example of one who was not healed until the end of the book despite remaining faithful to God.

> He said, "If you listen carefully to the voice of the LORD your God and do what is right in his eyes, if you pay attention to his commands and keep all his decrees, I will not bring on you any of the diseases I brought on the Egyptians, for I am the LORD, who heals you." (Exod. 15:26)

> But for you who revere my name, the sun of righteousness will rise with healing in its wings. And you will go out and frolic like well-fed calves. (Mal. 4:2)

4. The lack of healing is a sign of judgment. Again, this is corporate, not necessarily individual.

> Make the heart of this people calloused;
> make their ears dull
> and close their eyes.
> Otherwise they might see with their eyes,
> hear with their ears,
> understand with their hearts,
> and turn and be healed. (Isa. 6:10)

> But they mocked God's messengers, despised his words and scoffed at his prophets until the wrath of the Lord was aroused against his people and there was no remedy (2 Chron. 36:16).

From an individual perspective, the whole book of Job confronts the charge that he has sinned and therefore must repent in order to be healed. However, Job refuses to accept that he has some unconfessed sin, and in the end he is healed.

5. Healing becomes more than physical. In the Bible it is associated with repentance. Again, this applies to the community but not necessarily to the individual.

> "Return, faithless people;
> I will cure you of backsliding."
> "Yes, we will come to you,
> for you are the Lord our God." (Jer. 3:22)

> Is there no balm in Gilead?
> Is there no physician there?
> Why then is there no healing
> for the wound of my people? (Jer. 8:22)

6. Healing can be a sign of God's love:

> I will heal their waywardness
> and love them freely,
> for my anger has turned away from them. (Hosea 14:4)

7. Healing in the Psalms is associated with God's forgiveness:

> I said, "Have mercy on me, Lord;
> heal me, for I have sinned against you." (41:4)

[The Lord] forgives all your sins
and heals all your diseases. (103:3)

Healing in the Old Testament is thus connected with God and his work with individuals and with whole nations. God is the only successful subject of the verb "to heal"; however, there is an exception. In different forms this verb occurs in Proverbs with the term "words" as something that heals:

For they [words of the teacher] are life to those who find them
and health to one's whole body. (4:22)

The words of the reckless pierce like swords,
but the tongue of the wise brings healing. (12:18)

A wicked messenger falls into trouble,
but a trustworthy envoy brings healing. (13:17)

A heart at peace gives life to the body,
but envy rots the bones. (14:30)

The soothing tongue is a tree of life,
but a perverse tongue crushes the spirit. (15:4)

Gracious words are a honeycomb,
sweet to the soul and healing to the bones. (16:24)

Key Commentaries and Studies

Crenshaw, James L. *Old Testament Wisdom: An Introduction*. 3rd ed. Louisville: Westminster John Knox, 2010. The most useful introduction to the Bible's Wisdom literature.

Fox, Michael V. *Proverbs: A New Translation with Introduction and Commentary*. Vol. 1, *1–9*. AB 18A. New York: Doubleday, 2000. Vol. 2, *10–31*. AB 18B. New Haven: Yale University Press, 2009. Mature exegesis by a master of Wisdom literature.

Heim, Knut Martin. *Like Grapes of Gold Set in Silver: An Interpretation of Proverbial Clusters in Proverbs 10:1–22:16*. BZAW 273. Berlin: de Gruyter, 2001. Study of a difficult section, with focus on how the context of each proverb enhances its teaching.

Kidner, Derek. *Proverbs: An Introduction and Commentary*. TOTC. Leicester, UK: Inter-Varsity; Downers Grove, IL: InterVarsity, 1964. A concise study sensitive to the poetry of the text.

Longman, Tremper, III. *Proverbs*. BCOTWP. Grand Rapids: Baker Academic, 2005. Most useful one-volume exegetical study.

Waltke, Bruce K. *The Book of Proverbs*. Vol. 1, *1–15*. Vol. 2, *16–31*. NICOT. Grand Rapids: Eerdmans, 2004–5. An evangelical scholar produces the best linguistic analysis of the text, with a strong introduction.

17

ECCLESIASTES

I don't see God anywhere, and I certainly don't believe in a just God." This sentiment is not new; it is something that even the author of Ecclesiastes could identify with. How does the author deal with the question of meaning in what seems to be a random world?

Name, Text, and Outline

The name Ecclesiastes comes from the identically spelled title of the Vulgate, which derives from the Septuagint's name, *Ekklēsiastēs*. This is a translation of the Hebrew title, *Qōhelet*, where it is understood as a description of one who speaks at or leads a *qāhāl*, an assembly. *Qōhelet*'s grammatical form as a feminine singular participle may seem surprising. However, such feminine singular participles may be used as titles in Historical Books of the later Old Testament period, as in Ezra 2:55; Nehemiah 7:57, 59, where Hassophereth, Sophereth, and Pokereth may all be titles of positions. The English "Preacher" (identical to Martin Luther's *der Prediger*) identifies the character, mentioned in 1:1 and the first-person speaker from 1:7–12:7. The Septuagint title, and all the tradition that has followed it, has assumed a church or ecclesiastical context. However, the concern of the speaker/writer is to teach and relate knowledge and understanding as one of the wise. Many scholars use Qoheleth as the preferred title of the book and of its main speaker.

The Masoretic Text of Ecclesiastes has few problems and may be read with the *Qere* readings as preserving an accurate and early rendering.[1] The Qumran

1. For more on *Qere* and *Kethib*, see the introduction, "Masoretic Text," under the discussion on textual criticism. In the view of some scholars, only Eccles. 5:11 (10 MT) seems to require the *Kethib* reading. See Schoors, "*Kethibh-Qere* in Ecclesiastes."

fragments largely follow the Masoretic Text. These include 4QQoh[a] (5:14–18 [5:13–17 MT]; 6:1, 3–8, 12; 7:1–10, 19–20). The other fragment, 4QQoh[b], contains parts of 1:10–14. Based on orthography (spelling)—which changes over the centuries and therefore allows for dating—the first fragment is the oldest extant manuscript of any part of Ecclesiastes, dated around 175–150 BC. The smaller fragment may date a century or so later.

Although the text is clear, the translation and interpretation are disputed in a number of places. An example is found in the earliest known translation, that of the Septuagint. The translation of Ecclesiastes into the Greek is preserved in its earliest complete form in Codex Vaticanus. The literal approach of some aspects of the Septuagint translation (e.g., translating the Heb. direct object marker with Greek *syn*) resembles that of Aquila's later work. However, the Septuagint translation of Ecclesiastes is more probably a separate version whose purpose was to aid in exegesis, as with Aquila. The variants appear to be in large measure due to (mis)translations of a Hebrew text similar to that of the Masoretic Text. The Syriac preserves a translation from the Hebrew text with occasional similarities to the Septuagint instead of the Masoretic Text. The *Targum Ecclesiastes* varies its witness between a paraphrase and a more literal translation of the Hebrew. The Vulgate seems to have followed the Masoretic Text, but it also displays awareness of Origen's Hexapla.[2]

Although the issue of canon was discussed at the beginning of this survey (see the introduction), it becomes important for understanding this book due to the unusual dispute concerning the place of Ecclesiastes, more than that for most other books of the Bible. Its appearance among the scrolls of the separatist Qumran community as early as the mid-second century BC suggests an acceptance in intertestamental Judaism. Questions arose due to some apparent contradictions in the book (cf. 2:2; 7:3; 8:15), a fatalistic view of life (1:3; 11:9), and the pessimistic nature of the work regarding belief in God.

The tradition of the Jamnia (Yavneh) Council of rabbis near the end of the first century AD, a tradition preserved in Jewish writings from a considerably later time, remembers dispute about this book and also the Song of Songs. The Mishnah, with its compilation of materials around AD 200, remembers the dispute between the school of Hillel and that of Shammai from the first century AD. Hillel, who always won these debates, argued for the authority of Ecclesiastes. The recognition of the book's canonical status (and therefore its place in the Bible) may have resulted from Jamnia or some similar consensus among rabbinic authorities. While disputes about the canonicity of this book continued in the following century in Judaism, there is no clear example of Ecclesiastes being denied canonical status among the major early Christian lists of the Old Testament canon. Even Theodore of Mopsuestia,

2. See Gentry, "Hexaplaric Materials in Ecclesiastes."

long thought to have questioned the status of the book, is now regarded as recognizing the book as authoritative and inspired.[3]

OUTLINE

I. General Thesis: Everything Is Meaningless (1:1–11)
II. Qoheleth's Biography as a Searcher (1:12–12:7)
   A. Introduction (1:12–18)
   B. Pursuit of Pleasure in Royal Deeds (2:1–11)
   C. The Wise Person Has No Lasting Value over the Foolish (2:12–26)
   D. God Chooses the Times (3:1–15)
   E. Our Fate Is No Better Than That of the Animals (3:16–22)
   F. Oppression, Laziness, Community, and Willingness to Be Taught (4:1–16)
   G. Say Little before God; Listen Much (5:1–7 [4:17–5:6 MT])
   H. Greed Is the Way of the World but Gives No Profit; Enjoy Material Things as Gifts from God (5:8–20 [5:7–19 MT])
   I. Long Life and Riches Are of No Value if They Leave No Heritage for the One Who Has Them (6:1–12)
   J. Hear the Rebuke of the Wise, Remain Patient, and Know That God's Work and Fate Cannot Be Changed (7:1–13)
   K. Seek Wisdom and Moderation (7:14–29)
   L. Follow the King but Know That the Future Is Unknown (8:1–9)
   M. No One Knows Why the Righteous Are Badly Treated While the Wicked Prosper (8:10–17)
   N. Death Comes to All, but Wisdom Can Do Much Good (9:1–18)
   O. Self-Control and Prudence (10:1–20)
   P. Generosity, Industry, and Gratitude for One's Life (11:1–10)
   Q. Remember God's Blessings before the Difficulties of Age (12:1–7)
III. Qoheleth as Wise Teacher and the Need to Fear God (12:8–14)

Overview of Ecclesiastes

The writer of Ecclesiastes begins with the thesis of much of the book. There is no real meaning behind creation, and one's effort and work contribute little or nothing because everything continues as it was. There is nothing really new, and those who have gone before are forgotten as, some day, will be everyone alive today and in the future. The primary speaker, Qoheleth, introduces himself in 1:12, where he asserts that he is a king who sought to understand the meaning of the universe but came to realize that it is all vain and that understanding only increases one's own pain in this life.

In chapter 2 Qoheleth reveals his attempt to find pleasure in life by great building projects, amassing much wealth and power, and doing all the things

3. See Jarick, "Theodore of Mopsuestia."

a great king can do. He concludes that it was all for nothing. So Qoheleth turns to observation and states how it at first appears that the wise person is so much better off than the fool. However, the fate and legacy of both are the same. Nothing enduring remains. Thus the conclusion leads to satisfying one's own needs and senses with the knowledge that what a person leaves and passes on to the next generation does not guarantee that it will be used as the departed would have used it. Chapter 3 begins by pairing opposites and observing how there is a time for each. It is all God's gift, and his acts will endure, but humans do not have control. They have no advantage over the animals in terms of origin or ultimate destination, declares Qoheleth.

Ecclesiastes 4 considers oppression, laziness, community, and the willingness to be taught. (Each of these is a theme in Wisdom literature.) All of them point toward vanity or emptiness. Only the note about community, that two are better than one, has no negative evaluation. Moving into chapter 5, the emphasis shifts to humility and saying little before God. Do not make vows to God. While oppression, greed, and conspiracy are the way of the world, in the end there is no profit to all of one's wealth. Instead, it is best to enjoy the good things God has given as gifts from him. So chapter 6 continues with this theme. Even if one lives thousands of years and has many children, this is all a matter of appetite and not of something that endures beyond this life.

Ecclesiastes 7 celebrates the house of mourning and death as that which is common to all. Nevertheless, oppression makes a wise person a fool, whereas patience is a virtue better than pride. One is to seek wisdom and moderation.

© Baker Publishing Group and Dr. James C. Martin

White blossoming almond tree

One cannot be perfect, nor can one guarantee that the righteous will live longer than the wicked. Wisdom is required to avoid the seductress, and yet hardly one in a thousand can follow the path that God made.

Chapter 8 of Ecclesiastes counsels obedience to the king, keeping in mind that no one knows the future. Further, no one can explain why some of the wicked prosper and why some of the righteous are treated like the wicked. Qoheleth counsels joy in this inexplicable world.

In the next chapter (Eccles. 9) there is an emphasis on the commonality of death. In death all is forgotten and lost. A live dog is better than a dead lion. So one is to enjoy this life: one's wife, one's work, and all one does. One doesn't know what will happen or when the end will come. A wise commoner can save a city, and still no one listens to this one. However, a sinner can create much evil.

Chapter 10 consists of a series of proverbs. Many of them address one's attitude toward power, especially the king. Qoheleth criticizes those who speak too much, who criticize the king, even when they think they are alone, and commends the powerful who rule their own appetites before trying to rule the kingdom. Because no one knows the future, chapter 11 counsels generosity toward others and industry in work. In the awareness of the judgment to come, let each one rejoice in his or her youth and in whatever long life God may give. One is to remember God, the creator, while young, and before one grows old and life is difficult.

Qoheleth ceases his speaking in Ecclesiastes 12:7. Verses 8–14 reflect on this teacher as a sage who sought out wisdom and arranged it. It concludes with an announcement of divine judgment awaiting all people and every deed, "whether good or evil." In this context, everyone should fear God and keep his commandments.

Reading Ecclesiastes

Premodern Readings

Books such as Ecclesiasticus (or Ben Sira, Sirach) and the Wisdom of Solomon appeared in the Jewish writings of the second century BC and the first century AD.[4] They represent a continuation of the style of writing as found in Ecclesiastes; yet the Wisdom of Solomon may have been written to counter some of the concerns found in Ecclesiastes. However, none of these writings directly refer to Ecclesiastes.

Before the twentieth century most commentators shared a collection of assumptions that together viewed the book of Ecclesiastes as Scripture: the author was Solomon; the *hebel*—"vanity," "meaninglessness," "fleeting," or

4. See Longman, "Ecclesiastes 3"; Bartholomew, *Ecclesiastes*, 21–34.

"enigmatic"—contrasts with the blessings of the afterlife; and tensions exist in the book. In Judaism, these difficulties led to an emphasis on midrash or allegory. In the search for justification of the canonical status of Ecclesiastes, despite the rather hedonistic sentiments that recur in it, the Babylonian Talmud (*Šabbat* 30b) argues that the book is acceptable because it begins and ends with words of the Torah. *Targum Ecclesiastes* 12:12 turns the verse on its head and argues that one should make many books to study the Torah. In the twelfth century AD, Rashbam recognized editorial additions in the opening two verses and in the final five verses. In the kabbalistic *Zohar* of the thirteenth century, the unorthodox passages are identified as quotations of unbelievers.

In the early church, Origen (*Commentarius in Canticum*, preface) believed that Solomon wrote Ecclesiastes to show the folly of human wisdom and to lead him on to the love of Christ in the Song of Songs. The third-century scholar Gregory Thaumaturgus argued that Solomon believed that earthly joys come from the Creator but that true joy comes from divine wisdom.[5] If righteousness directs the reader, then true joy can be found in creation. Some fourth-century Latin commentaries no longer survive but provide the background for Jerome's work in the fifth century. Jerome (*Commentarii in Ecclesiasten*) used Ecclesiastes to provoke Blesilla, an aristocratic woman of Rome, to despise this world. Ascetic life given to God alone is the concern of the author of the book. References to joy in eating and drinking are allegorized to express the delight of the Eucharist. The difficult sayings of doubt are understood as words uttered by the skeptics. According to Jerome, reading the text christologically, 1:1 teaches that Jesus also is believers' Ecclesiastes (Teacher), and 4:9, where two are better than one, teaches that Jesus is the second one with each Christian. In 9:13–16 the king is Satan, the city is the church, and the poor man who delivers it by his wisdom is Christ.

Jerome's interpretation of this book became the standard until the Reformation. For this reason, Theodore of Mopsuestia and his students were condemned for trying to introduce a literal form of interpretation to the book. He became known for denying the book's canonicity, although recently Syriac translations of Theodore's Greek work, discovered in the twentieth century, demonstrate that this was not his belief.[6] The rediscovery of Aristotle's *Politics* in the later medieval period led to a renewed interest in books such as Ecclesiastes that addressed this subject and ethics in general. Thus

5. Gregory Thaumaturgus, *Metaphrase on the Book of Ecclesiastes* 2. This is the earliest extant Christian commentary on Ecclesiastes.

6. For the Syriac of Theodore's commentary, see Strothmann, *Das syrische fragment*. For the conclusions regarding his original view of Ecclesiastes, see Jarick, "Theodore of Mopsuestia and the Interpretation of Ecclesiastes." For the biblical approach of this early exegete, see Zaharopoulos, *Theodore of Mopsuestia*.

the thirteenth-century churchman Bonaventura applied a more literal approach to the interpretation of the text.[7] However, he in no way disagreed with Jerome. More impressive is the work of the fourteenth-century scholar Nicholas of Lyra in the *Commentary on the Bible: Genesis to Ecclesiastes*.[8] With his knowledge of Hebrew and his appreciation for the literal interpretation of the biblical text, he stood in direct line to Luther and the other Reformers, who appeared more than a century later. The continuation of Jerome's interpretation can be found in the fifteenth-century devotional classic *The Imitation of Christ*, by Thomas à Kempis. Indeed, the ongoing popularity of this work continues that tradition and its interpretation into the present.

Luther, assisted by Philip Melanchthon and Johannes Brenz, turned the tables on Jerome.[9] They insisted on a literal interpretation. For them, Solomon promoted active involvement in community life and polity. This book challenges bad leadership and supports involvement in God's creation order. God has made a good creation, not one worthy of contempt. What, then, is *hebel*? It is not the vanity of the body and the world but the failure of the personal heart and soul.[10]

This controversy between Jerome's allegorical interpretation and Luther's literal one continued in the following centuries. In the nineteenth century, however, W. M. L. de Wette finally broke with tradition and laid the foundation for critical study by arguing that Qoheleth believed enjoyment of this life to be the only good, because there was no afterlife.[11]

Higher Criticism

Because the Wisdom literature and Ecclesiastes in particular were considered late and derivative, little attention was paid to them by the founders of modern source criticism and other critical approaches.[12] However, this was challenged by the form-critical studies of Hermann Gunkel from around 1900. He asserted that Wisdom literature represented a distinctive genre, not related to or derivative from legal or prophetic literature. A further impetus to this understanding was reached with the 1888 discovery and subsequent publication of the Egyptian Instruction of Amenemope. After World War I these trajectories coalesced into a focus on Wisdom literature in its ancient

7. Karris, *Works of St. Bonaventure*, vol. 7.

8. Based on the fourteenth-century manuscript.

9. Luther, *Luther's Works*, vol. 15.

10. In Luther's *Table Talk*, some argue that he was the first to deny Solomonic authorship to the book, ascribing it rather to disciples of the royal sage. However, Scott Jones ("Solomon's Table Talk") makes a case that Luther denied to Solomon the role as the scribe of the work, rather than the role of author.

11. De Wette, *Beiträge zue Einleitung in das Alte Testament*, §282–83.

12. See Longman, "Ecclesiastes 3," 145–49; Bartholomew, *Ecclesiastes*, 35–59.

Near Eastern context. Adolf Erman recognized much of Proverbs 22:17–23:11 in this material.[13]

Although there has been some interest in source criticism (proposing nine different sources, in one case), this has not been a focus of the critical study of Ecclesiastes. Instead, the major legacy of this approach has been to assume a separate source and later addition for the final five or six verses of the book. In the precritical tradition, this conclusion was the major guide for understanding and interpreting the entire book. As a later addition, it becomes instead a means of reinterpreting the book and thus profoundly changing its original intent. In that sense the epilogue could be understood as a redaction whose purpose is to bring the rest of the book into conformity with the canon.

As may be noted regarding the instruction texts of Egypt, of which Amenemope is the best example, this genre existed before the composition of Ecclesiastes. It existed before Solomon. However, the contrast between Ecclesiastes and the more positive expressions of many of these Egyptian works and that of Proverbs has been noted. Hartmut Gese and others have suggested that Ecclesiastes represents a crisis or revolt against the normative understanding of wisdom in Israel.[14] However, others such as Walter Brueggemann have identified in the book a royal and conservative interest.[15] Thus the nature and purpose of the book remain unresolved, a conflict that continues into the twenty-first century in traditional criticism. Some regard the book as utterly negative and hopeless (cf. James Crenshaw and Francis Watson).[16] However, others find it a positive book, where hope springs from an understanding and appreciation of God's blessing (Norman Whybray and Graham Ogden).[17] Michael Fox represents the key figure who has brought the book back into unity by reading the text as such, rather than discovering here a collection of diverse and contradictory statements.[18]

Despite the assertions of some traditionalists such as William Anderson, who finds the work written in a royal Israelite context, the linguistic features of Ecclesiastes betray a much later date, in the postexilic period (despite legitimate concerns to find in the message and form of the work evidence for much earlier traditions; see "Ancient Near Eastern Context," below).[19] Within this later context, much debate remains as to whether the work should be dated into the Persian period (539–332 BC) or in the following two centuries, when Hellenistic influence dominated. Choon-Leong Seow

13. Erman, "Eine Ägyptische Quelle der 'Sprüche Salomos.'"
14. See Gese, "Crisis of Wisdom."
15. See Brueggemann, "Trajectories in Old Testament Literature."
16. See Crenshaw, "Ecclesiastes," 277; F. Watson, *Text, Church, and World*, 283–87.
17. See Whybray, "Qoheleth"; Ogden, *Qoheleth*.
18. See Fox, "Frame-Narrative and Composition."
19. Anderson, *Pessimistic Theology*.

sees Aramaisms that occur predominantly in the Persian period and appear in Ecclesiastes.[20] He denies any clear evidence of Grecisms. However, others argue for the presence of specific Hellenistic words and context.[21] In the end the strongest case seems to remain with a Persian context for the final production of the work.

Literary Readings

There have been so many literary analyses of Ecclesiastes that it is difficult to know where to begin. It may be helpful to focus on the two major reading approaches that exist regarding the interpretation of the book, here identified as positive and negative views. This work considers each in turn yet favors the negative interpretation.

The positive interpretation has already been attributed to Whybray and to Ogden.[22] Among the many who may be added to this, one may recognize Walter Kaiser and Eunny Lee.[23]

According to Kaiser, Qoheleth was working on the problem of people's attempt to find meaning in all aspects of God's good world without coming to know the world's Creator, Sustainer, and final Judge. Central to all of a person's concerns is this problem of integrating life and truth. So Kaiser understands the work as an attempt to answer the question as to how a believer is to live in the world. What good are the possessions that anyone has?

The issue appears to focus in a text such as Ecclesiastes 3:11, where Kaiser translates and comments: "[God] has made everything beautiful in its time; he has also put eternity (*ôlām*) into man's heart so that he cannot find out what God has done from beginning to the end."[24] This is how Kaiser understands the concern of Ecclesiastes. A person has an interest and ability to want to know how all the created universe fits together but cannot know this through human efforts. Instead, it is necessary to know God the Creator, who made humanity in the divine image (Gen. 1:26–28). Only then does a person have the capacity to understand oneself, and what is the true value of things, beginning with life itself. So the expression *hebel* of *hebel*s (in 1:2, variously translated as "vanity of vanities" [NRSV], "enigma of enigmas,"[25] or "utterly meaningless" [NIV]) should be interpreted as a teaching that no single part of the universe, including any people or person, is able to unlock the mystery of its true meaning and value. Life cannot answer the fundamental questions of human existence by itself. It is not able to unravel

20. Seow, "Linguistic Evidence."
21. See the review by Bartholomew, *Ecclesiastes*, 46–54.
22. Whybray, "Qoheleth"; Ogden, *Qoheleth*.
23. Kaiser, *Ecclesiastes*; E. Lee, *Vitality of Enjoyment*.
24. Kaiser, *Ecclesiastes*, 16–17.
25. Bartholomew, *Ecclesiastes,* 105.

Hebel

The term *hebel* has been translated in various ways in the book of Ecclesiastes, from the traditional "vanity" to the more recent "futility" (James Crenshaw), "absurd" (Michael Fox), "meaningless" (Tremper Longman), and "enigmatic" (Craig Bartholomew).[a] Nearly thirty of the seventy-one biblical occurrences of the noun *hebel* are found in Ecclesiastes. However, it is of value to consider the word's appearance elsewhere. *Hebel* first appears as a personal name in Genesis 4, where it is rendered in English as "Abel." This term occurs nowhere else in the ancient world as a personal name. Here it seems to describe the nature of Abel's life as fleeting, leaving no descendants, and so of no lasting significance for future generations. It occurs elsewhere in the Pentateuch only in Deuteronomy 32:21, where it refers to the images that are worshiped in place of God. This resembles many of its usages in the Historical Books and the Prophets. In the Psalms, *hebel* often describes life as fleeting and its accomplishments as soon gone and forgotten (39:5–6 [6–7 MT]; 62:9–10 [10–11 MT]). In Job, the emphasis is on the futility of life and on empty talk (7:16; 9:29; 21:34; 27:12; 35:16). In Proverbs, *hebel* describes money and beauty (13:11; 21:6; 31:30). Thus the sense of impermanence and lack of significance or lasting value characterizes this term in a manner that is not far removed from its usage in Ecclesiastes.

[a] Crenshaw, *Ecclesiastes*, 57–58; Fox, *A Time to Tear Down*, 27–42; Longman, *The Book of Ecclesiastes*, 61–65; Bartholomew, *Ecclesiastes*, 104–7.

the true significance of ultimate purpose, value, and joy. Only in coming to know God (fear of Yahweh) are these answers provided.

The positive injunctions in Ecclesiastes include the suggestion to fear God, as found in 8:12–13 (see also 3:14; 7:18):

> Although someone sins by doing evil a hundred times over, yet I know that it will be better for those who fear God and are respectful before him. However, it will not be better for the wicked, and they will not prolong their days like the shadow. This is because they are not respectful before God. (RSH)

Instead, humans should receive all the good things of life as a gift from God, as found in 2:24–26 (see also 5:18–19; 8:15; 9:7–9):

> Nothing is better for anyone than to eat and drink and see for himself how good his work is. I see that this is also from God's hand. For who will eat and be delighted with what lies outside themselves? Indeed, to the person who is good before him, he gives wisdom, knowledge, and happiness. However, to the sinner he gives the

> hard work of gathering and storing up so that it ultimately goes to the one who is good before God. This too is meaningless and a chasing after wind. (RSH)

In the end, Lee argues, piety should be understood as the enjoyment of the activities of ordinary life, with gratitude toward God.[26] This positive approach is also supported by Douglas Miller, who understands in the book a complex rhetorical strategy in which ethos (the Preacher as trustworthy), destabilization, and restabilization occur in an interwoven fashion.[27] The result is an assertion of orthodoxy while at the same time an awareness of the fleeting nature of life and things. This is not unlike the conclusions of a different approach below.

The negative approach is already associated (above) with Gese, Brueggemann, Crenshaw, Watson, and Anderson. Crenshaw argues that "nothing proved that God looked on creatures with favor, and the entire enterprise of wisdom had become bankrupt."[28] Thus several conclusions may be reached after considering the world. First, death cancels everything, whether the good or the bad that is done. Thus Ecclesiastes 2:17 declares, "So I hated life, because the work that is done under the sun, all of it, had become meaningless to me and a chasing after the wind" (RSH).

Second, Ecclesiastes 3:11, cited earlier, is not an optimistic view about how all humans want to know the meaning of life but cannot find it unless and until God provides it. In this view it forms a pessimistic conclusion: humans cannot attain to whatever purpose for which they were created. Perhaps an even stronger indictment is that God cannot be known. So 11:5 reads: "As you have no knowledge of which direction the wind takes, or of how the bones grow in the womb, so you do not know God's work as he makes all things" (RSH). If God is inscrutable, the world is perverse (7:20): "So there is no one righteous on earth who does what is correct and does not sin" (RSH).

Second, in this negative light, readers come to the strongest indictment. Ecclesiastes 9:7–10 begins positively enough with encouragement for humans to enjoy what they have received from God. However, it turns out badly because it reminds the reader of the *hebel* of life and the common lot of death facing everyone. There is truly no room for hope:

> Go, eat your food to your heart's content. Drink your wine with a heart of joy, because for the present God favors your work. Your clothes will always be white, and on your head you will have oil. Look at life with the wife you love for your whole life that passes away. This is the life he has given you under the sun, all the days of your fleeting life. This is your fate in life, all the work

26. E. Lee, *Vitality of Enjoyment*, 128–29.
27. D. Miller, "What the Preacher Forgot."
28. Crenshaw, *Old Testament Wisdom*, 127.

> at which you labor under the sun. Do with all your might all that your hand finds to do, because there is no work, thought, knowledge, or wisdom in the grave, where you are headed. (RSH; see plate 10 in the gallery for an image of Egyptians with oil on their heads.)

Jean-Jacques Lavoie concludes that for Qoheleth the spirit of truth is found not in dogmatic revelation but in a rigorous questioning of everything.[29] No single theology is sufficient, and this book demonstrates the multiple and differing (paradoxical) theologies in the Bible.

Anderson demonstrates that, as with 9:7–10, every positive passage is set in a pessimistic context, and so an optimistic assessment of Ecclesiastes does not appreciate the full context of the work. God is a source of injustice. Life with all its good does end in death. Wisdom cannot achieve its final goal and is often thwarted by other less noble factors. Qoheleth serves as a tool for preevangelism, bringing out the problems of life and expressing them in all honesty.[30]

Gender and Ideological Criticism

The major issue in Ecclesiastes for gender studies has to do with 7:28, which the NIV renders:

> While I was still searching
> but not finding—
> I found one upright man among a thousand,
> but not one upright woman among them all.

Is this an endorsement of misogyny? It could stand as it is and be no surprise because of the general lack of orthodoxy by Qoheleth. However, it is not clear that this is what is being said. The term for "man" is *ʾādām*. However, here as elsewhere in Ecclesiastes, it may carry the more obvious sense of a person. If so, then the contrast is not between male and female but between people in general and one specific feminine figure. Craig Bartholomew believes that this is Lady Wisdom, as found in Proverbs 1–9.[31]

Again, this raises another issue, in 7:26. Here is the translation according to the NIV:

29. Lavoie, *Qohélet*.

30. Anderson (*Pessimistic Theology*) argues that Israel's wisdom tradition is not antithetical to the remainder of the teaching in the OT but serves to complement it with a diversity that allows the author to express fully the problems and concerns of life without requiring conformity to an established dogma. For the Christian, Anderson sees a canonical context in the light of the NT.

31. Bartholomew, *Ecclesiastes*, 268.

I find more bitter than death
 the woman who is a snare,
whose heart is a trap
 and whose hands are chains.
The man who pleases God will escape her,
 but the sinner she will ensnare.

Several options have been applied to this text to avoid a misogynist interpretation. Some see this as a seductress, similar to that found in Proverbs 5 and 7.[32] Others suggest that Qoheleth has a specific woman in mind, such as his wife.[33] Mitchell Dahood takes the sense of the Hebrew *mar* as "strong" rather than "bitter."[34] However, Seow understands this as a "composite image" of Lady Folly, as in Proverbs 9:13–18.[35] She seeks others and wants to ensnare them. If so, then perhaps Qoheleth here admits that he is one who has been so trapped.

Ideological approaches have abounded with Ecclesiastes. Part of the reason for this is the attraction of indeterminate meanings represented by postmodernism and applied to the most disputed and unclear book in the Hebrew Bible. Bartholomew's 2009 commentary lists half a dozen general postmodern works on the book, three queer readings of the work, and another half-dozen postcolonial readings.[36] John Prior, living in the midst of the widespread corruption of Indonesian society and the great gulf that marginalizes the majority poor, interprets the work of Ecclesiastes as a call to realistically evaluate the world, to appreciate what good can be found in God's creation, and to recognize the limitations of human experience within a rudderless postmodern world.[37]

Ancient Near Eastern Context

The sense of futility in human effort is found not only in Ecclesiastes but also earlier, in the Old Babylonian Gilgamesh epic (ca. 2100 BC), with both the hero's own reference to humanity's achievements as only "wind" (Tablet III) and the comments of the female bartender that Gilgamesh should enjoy life as much as he can because he will die (Tablet IX; see Eccles. 9:7–9).[38] As in copies from around 1600 BC, this latter point was removed from later editions of the epic.

32. The seductress view is generally found in earlier Christian writers, such as Gregory Thaumaturgos (Longman, *Book of Ecclesiastes*, 204).

33. See Spears, "Theological Hermeneutics," 159.

34. Dahood, "Qoheleth and Recent Discoveries," 308–10.

35. Seow, *Ecclesiastes*, 272.

36. Bartholomew, *Ecclesiastes*, 41–42. The queer readings include Wernik, "Will the Real Homosexual?," who argues that Qoheleth is gay.

37. See Prior, "Ecclesiastes."

38. See G. Klingbeil, "Ecclesiastes 2."

Egyptian Pessimism

Most Egyptian compositions expressing negative attitudes about life do not appear until the Hellenistic period. However, the Songs of the Harpers, which appear on tomb walls in the early second millennium BC, the time of the Middle Kingdom, exhibit an emerging transition in thought. Earlier Harper's Songs describe orthodox theology about the blessings of the afterlife. However, the tomb text of King Intef casts doubt on the afterlife and satirizes the whole tradition of tomb building. Such cynicism was accepted in tomb inscriptions and in scribal practice texts well into the period of the New Kingdom (late second millennium BC). This tradition may have influenced the Dispute of a Man with His Ba.[a]

[a] For this text, see "Ancient Near Eastern Context" for Job.

Tremper Longman's study of fictional autobiography in Akkadian texts has led him to propose that the genre of Ecclesiastes belongs in this category.[39] So it is argued that these fictional autobiographies were written long after the life of the person they purport to represent. They all have an introduction of self-identification, such as "I am . . ." Next they describe special acts of the writer. The introduction for Ecclesiastes appears in 1:12, and the special acts of the writer constitute 1:13–6:9. Then 6:10–12 overlaps both this earlier section and the following one. The last part of the fictional Akkadian autobiography style varies. However, Longman cites three examples (most completely in the Cuthaean Legend of Naram-Sin, but also in the Sin of Sargon and the Adad-guppi autobiography) where the final part consists of wisdom advice in the characteristic style of Wisdom literature. This certainly appears to be the case for Ecclesiastes 6:10–12:7. Such an interpretation seems to be persuasive, yet it remains to cite an example of one of these autobiographies that is as abstract as Ecclesiastes in terms of the person's achievements. The Akkadian texts seem to do more with specific events of construction, maintenance, battles, and so forth, and less with dwelling on the reflections that one finds in Ecclesiastes (with instructions in both major sections).

Another area of comparison has been with the pessimistic and nihilistic Wisdom literature as found in Babylonian texts, especially the Counsels of a Pessimist and the Dialogue of Pessimism. Best known is this latter dialogue, where a master and a slave take turns speaking sarcastically about the meaning of life and various things that one may do to achieve some lasting significance in this life. In the end, however, the slave advises his master that the good thing

39. See Longman, *Fictional Akkadian Autobiography*; idem, *Book of Ecclesiastes*, 15–20.

The Instructions of/for Šūpê-amēlī

Of the many wisdom compositions in the ancient Near East, this is the one text that is unique in having its second-millennium-BC origin and extant distribution limited to the West Semitic world and the Hittites. It would not be surprising to find such a wisdom composition in the cosmopolitan center of Ugarit from the fourteenth and thirteenth centuries BC. Of greater amazement is its location in thirteenth-century-BC Emar. While this site (Tell Meskene) is located along the Euphrates and long known as a stopping-over point for traders and businesses that moved along this important river, the city was not regarded as a major cultural center for international relations, at least not in the thirteenth century. However, its connection with an agrarian and tribal lifestyle at this time has been recognized; the texts of this tribal and mostly agrarian society show some unique similarities with religious texts of ancient Israel. Further, the discovery of a translation of the text into Hittite and preserved in the archives of the capital, Ḫattuša (which also preserves an Akkadian text of this work), at once bears witness to its international interest yet also testifies to the close cultural connections between the Hittites and the West Semitic world of ancient Israel. Here are the final lines of the son's response to the father (the part that is closer to Ecclesiastes, which also concludes with a discussion of death in 12:1–7) and the colophon:

> All the property and the bread and the tax—the king, it's his money—will go out.
> Many are the living beings which eat bread; many [are the living beings] who become green [from want of] drink.
> Many [of us] see the sun; many [of us] sit in the broad shadow [of the netherworld].
> In the isolated house [or: ruin] people lie down—Ereshkigal [goddess of the netherworld] is our mother, and we are her children.
> Shadows [= dividers] are placed in the gate of the isolated house [or: the ruin] so that the living will not see the dead.
> This is the word [dispute/argument] which the father and son aroused together.[a]

[a] See Hurowitz, "Wisdom of Šūpê-amēlī," 50–51. It is not clear from the preserved cuneiform whether the name Šūpê-amēlī refers to the father or the son.

is to kill both of them. This is, of course, contrary to Qoheleth, who advises appreciating the goodness of creation and fearing God.

Victor Hurowitz has studied one of the most interesting ancient Near Eastern wisdom texts yet identified, the Instructions of/for Šūpê-amēlī.[40] Unlike

40. See Hurowitz, "Wisdom of Šūpê-amēlī."

other wisdom texts in Akkadian, this one is found only in the Late Bronze Age (1550–1200 BC) West Semitic cultures of Ugarit, Emar, and the Hittite capital of Ḫattuša. The text presents a series of counsels grouped together in the form of proverbs. In contrast to other Wisdom literature outside the Bible, only here is wisdom first glorified and then criticized. The forms resemble Proverbs 22:17–24:22 and chapters 28–30. The dialogue is between the father and the son. As in the book of Proverbs, the father encourages success in life, using traditional wisdom instruction with its optimism. Akin to Ecclesiastes, the son challenges the materialistic values that he finds in his father, and he evokes a much more cynical and pessimistic view of the world. Thus this book provides a unique antecedent to Ecclesiastes (and Ps. 49) as well as Proverbs.[41] It was widespread in the West Semitic world several centuries before Solomon's traditional dates. Therefore, the basic themes in both Proverbs and especially Ecclesiastes (with its attack on traditional wisdom assumptions) cannot be considered strictly late or Greek (i.e., non-West Semitic in origin).

Canonical Context

The book of Ecclesiastes represents a departure from the norms of expected wisdom in the Bible. Unlike Proverbs, it does not provide guidance with maxims that can be used for success in this life. Instead, the book questions the enterprise of wisdom as producing any real success where it is measured in terms of what endures and creates permanent change for good in the world. Nevertheless, the connection with Solomon is established from the first verse and repeated in 1:12. His wisdom surpasses all others (1:16), and his building operations and other material activities are vast (2:4–10). In this respect the book is connected with the Solomon of the Historical Books: 1 Kings 4:29–34 (5:9–14 MT); 10:23–29; and 2 Chronicles 1:7–17.

The epilogue of the book (Eccles. 12:9–14) clearly relates it to the Wisdom literature of Job, Proverbs, various psalms, and other texts. "Qoheleth" here carries the sense of a sage and teacher. Not only is he a serious student, but also what he studies is true (12:10) and thus important for all to hear. The "Shepherd" (NASB) of verse 11 relates to the image of the shepherd throughout the Old Testament. God is a shepherd (Gen. 48:15; Ps. 23:1), but so are David (2 Sam. 5:2; Ps. 78:71–72) and rulers who faithfully follow David (Mic. 5:4). Thus this is not merely the idiosyncratic musings of one person who imagines himself to be a counselor. It is the authoritative reflection of truth that comes from one Shepherd. Verse 12 challenges further books on the subject and contrasts them with the authority of this key text. The command to fear God and the warning that nothing can be hidden from God bring the text to

41. Hess, "'Because of the Wickedness of These Nations,'" 33–35.

a conclusion that sets it within the other biblical Wisdom literature, where a similar concern exists (e.g., Job 1:9; 28:28; Pss. 19:9 [19:10 MT]; 111:10; Prov. 1:7; 2:5; 9:10; Isa. 11:2–3; 33:6).

Of all Old Testament books, Proverbs remains the closest to Ecclesiastes. While it is unlikely that Ecclesiastes 12:9–14 forms a conclusion to both books (or the entire wisdom corpus), the recently identified comparison with the full text of the Instructions of/for Šūpê-amēlī (see the previous section) suggests that Ecclesiastes does more than contradict Proverbs. It provides the necessary balance to an unrealistic assessment of human wisdom in the Old Testament by observing that the way of Ecclesiastes is also the way of life for some in this world. Not everyone is guaranteed success, no matter how hard he or she tries, and Ecclesiastes makes this point.

Direct quotations in the New Testament are rare and confined to the book of Romans. Indeed, it is in the context of the universal nature of sin that Paul, in Romans 3:20, seems to cite Ecclesiastes 7:20. The world is not a place where fullness of meaning can be found. Because of sin and the fall, all creation pays the price, and its destiny is "vanity," as is true of all who pin their hopes onto the material world. Nevertheless, redemption through Christ is coming to creation as well as to those who believe and trust in the risen Lord. This is the teaching of Romans 8:18–25, where 8:20 uses the same word for "vanity," Greek *mataiotēs*, that translates the word for "vanity, hopeless, enigmatic" in the theme word of Ecclesiastes, Hebrew *hebel*.

Brevard Childs suggests that the teaching about the ultimate foolishness of the wisdom of the world in contrast to that of God in 1 Corinthians 1:20 finds its roots in Ecclesiastes's challenge to the world's understanding of itself.[42] For the book of Proverbs, it was observed that the book of James was the closest New Testament book in form, containing wisdom sections and much in the way of aphorisms. The same may be true of Ecclesiastes, and an even closer comparison may be drawn in terms of the role of the book within the larger biblical corpus. Each in its own way balances a much larger part of the Testament to which it belongs. The teaching of James that faith cannot be excluded from "works" for it to live and grow serves to balance the large corpus of Pauline and other Epistles that repeatedly stress the importance of God's free gift of salvation, which is received by faith. In a similar manner, the small book of Ecclesiastes counterbalances the view of Proverbs and much of the Old Testament that human experience is a reliable guide to walk in God's way and to find blessing and success. However, Ecclesiastes suggests that this is not necessarily the case and that ultimately the fear of God (with the teaching of his torah) must preempt whatever good or evil humans experience in this life.

42. Childs, *Introduction*, 588.

Theological Perspectives of Ecclesiastes

The major contribution of Qoheleth lies in the philosophical underpinnings on which theology is built. Whether one begins with the modernist assumptions of building on reason and observation in a fundamentally secular world, or with the postmodernist assumptions of critiquing this as an adequate basis for any truth but providing nothing in its place other than a vague assertion of "justice," the book of Ecclesiastes concurs with the dilemmas of finding any truth or meaning in life from personal reason, observation, or experience. While appearing to commend a kind of hedonism, the book stops short of seeing this as a fulfilling or truly successful solution because of the possibility that there might be a God who judges.

The direction of the book is not nihilistic, unlike that of many forms of postmodernism. Instead, Qoheleth walks alongside the one who searches for truth and says, "I have been there. I have experienced what you have gone through." If Job considers the absence of God and lack of meaning in suffering and pain, Ecclesiastes asks where one can find God in the pursuit of everything this life has to offer. The first eleven chapters of the work end with the conclusion that everything, even the joys of youth and happiness, are *hebel*. They don't remain or have any permanence. They do not satisfy. So forlorn is this sentiment that the reader is tempted to find in references to "God" a mere cipher for *hebel* and the inexplicable nature of the world and life, their transience, and their absence of enduring value. However, the book does not end there. Chapter 12 counsels the searcher, "Remember your creator" (12:1). God is both close and personal, as "your" Deity; he is the Creator and thus the one who has infused all life and all the world with value. Rather than giving up on the search and giving in to whatever delights that youth may present, the writer counsels turning to God and, in verses 13–14, fearing God and observing his commandments.

The conclusion here does not transform what has gone before in the book. It does not suddenly make sense out of all the *hebel* of life that the author has encountered. Instead, it reaffirms that the observation of this world and the experience of any and all material things are unable to generate their own meaning and significance. Qoheleth has walked with the readers through all of their search for meaning in life. It will not be found in this world, by itself. Instead, these encouragements (and warnings) that appear at the end of the book serve as sign pointers to the true source of meaning and value: the fear of God. Qoheleth does not wish to argue some basis for this fear of God, but only to advise it to those world-weary travelers with whom he has journeyed. Thus the text of Ecclesiastes becomes first and foremost a preevangelism tract designed to "connect" with all of those (moderns, postmoderns, nihilists, etc.) who seek meaning in this life but cannot find it. It is an existential book sharing the experiences of one who has also searched for this meaning but not found it in this world. It lies in remembering one's creator and in fearing God, themes that lead to the rest of the Scriptures. Therefore, Ecclesiastes becomes for the searcher the means of access to the Bible. It is the first step to salvation, not the last gasp of one who has tried "all that" and found no value in it.

In this light, Bartholomew's foray into Jungian psychology may be of interest.[43] He observes the distinction between the selfishness of the ego and the reality of the self, which needs to recognize its dependence on others and especially on God. The problem of Qoheleth and of many in the present age is a love of self that is unable to achieve realization. The book of Ecclesiastes describes this journey and its frustration because of a lack of a correct appreciation of the self and alignment of the ego with that ill-conceived self. Perhaps Ecclesiastes 11:7 ("The light is sweet, and so it is better for the eyes to see the sun" [RSH]) is the unconscious turning point in this journey. However, 12:1, with its charge to remember one's creator, provides the reader with the full awareness of the direction to go in order to find a proper relationship between ego, self, and dependence on God, the source of value and meaning. Bartholomew goes on to find elements of this in the history of Christianity's search for union with God, especially the "dark night of the soul" as found in St. John of the Cross. Ecclesiastes stands within this tradition of spiritual literature because the search for God that the nonbeliever initiates continues in the life of the believer and allows the text to probe ever more deeply into the soul, challenging one to set aside all idols, within and without, and to recognize that all is *hebel* without the true union with God.

Key Commentaries and Studies

Bartholomew, Craig G. *Ecclesiastes*. BCOTWP. Grand Rapids: Baker Academic, 2009. The finest recent work of exegesis and (evangelical) theological reflection.

Fox, Michael V. *A Time to Tear Down and a Time to Build Up: A Rereading of Ecclesiastes*. Grand Rapids: Eerdmans, 1999. An excellent discussion of the book from the perspective of *hebel* as addressing the absurdity of life.

Krüger, Thomas. *Qoheleth: A Commentary*. Translated by O. C. Dean Jr. Edited by Klaus Baltzer. Hermeneia. Minneapolis: Fortress, 2004. A masterful study of the text.

Longman, Tremper, III. *The Book of Ecclesiastes*. NICOT. Grand Rapids: Eerdmans, 1998. An outstanding and sensitive evangelical discussion of the book, with rigorous exegesis.

Seow, Choon-Leong. *Ecclesiastes: A New Translation with Introduction and Commentary*. AB 18C. New York: Doubleday, 1997. A strong commentary on history of exegesis and the interpretive study itself.

43. Bartholomew, *Ecclesiastes*, 377–82.

18

SONG OF SONGS

From Genesis 3 onward, the Bible seems to portray sex in restrictive and judgmental ways. Does the Bible have anything good to say about the subject? The answer of the Song of Songs is yes.

Name, Text, and Outline

The name of this short work is drawn from the first two words of the first verse: in Hebrew, *šîr haššîrîm*, literally, "the Song of Songs." In Hebrew, this is the way of expressing the superlative (e.g., the holy of holies = the most holy place). So the first verse designates this poem as "the best song." The remainder of the first verse reads *ʾăšer lišlōmōh*, "which belongs to/is for Solomon." It is this latter part that the later versions picked up on and so placed Solomon in the title. This has come down through the King James Version as the Song of Solomon. While not incorrect, it loses the original point of the opening two words: to praise this song above all others.

The Hebrew text of the Song, as preserved by the Masoretes, remains an accurate and reliable rendition of the work. The earliest version, the Septuagint, provides a literal translation, not unlike that of Ecclesiastes. The Syriac Peshitta follows the Septuagint with a stylistically superior work. From Qumran, 6QCant attests to a proto-Masoretic version of the first seven verses. Other fragments, from Cave 4, may contain liturgical or other witnesses to parts of forty-one verses, including overlaps between the three fragments.

Much less certain is the means by which the work entered the canon. With the single possibility of the last part of a word in Song 8:6, which may be a shortened form of Yahweh, no name for God or the God of Israel occurs in the work. Further, its clear emphasis on erotic love may have led some to question it by the first century AD. At the traditional rabbinic meeting at Jamnia (Yavneh), it along with Ecclesiastes appears to have been discussed as to its (already existent) place in the canon. See the more detailed discussion under "Name, Text, and Outline" for Ecclesiastes. The Song was indeed affirmed as to its place in the canon. Perhaps for this reason the famous Rabbi Akiba, who lived in the first half of the second century AD (died AD 135), so highly praised its holiness and its place in the canon:

> God forbid!—no man in Israel ever disputed about the Song of Songs [that he should say] that it does not render the hands unclean, for all the ages are not worth the day on which the Song of Songs was given to Israel; for all the Writings are holy, but the Song of Songs is the Holy of Holies. (*m. Yadayim* 3.5)[1]

In the Christian church it was accepted in the early canonical lists, among others that of Bishop Melito of Sardis (ca. AD 170).

OUTLINE

I. Title (1:1)
II. Prologue: Initial Union and Intimacy (1:2–2:7)
III. Lovers Joined and Separated (2:8–3:5)
IV. Love and Marriage at the Heart of the Song (3:6–5:1)
V. Search and Reunion (5:2–6:3)
VI. Love for the Female and Lovers in the Country (6:4–8:4)
VII. Epilogue: The Power of Love (8:5–14)

Overview of Song of Songs

The book opens by praising this single song and relating it to Solomon. The female begins the prologue with a sensual expression of desire for her lover. The male responds by inviting her and praising her. The female relates her lover to an aromatic fragrance, while the male responds to her doubts by praising her beauty. Their love takes them to a bed in a strong tree, to asphodels and lotus flowers, to the apple tree with its refreshment, and to a warm embrace.

The next section begins at 2:8, where the woman spies her lover leaping toward her like a gazelle. He watches her through the lattice and invites her to come away in the springtime, with the blossoming of flowers and the songs of the doves. The woman calls to her lover again to become like a gazelle and

1. Danby, *Mishnah*, 782.

seeks him nightly on her bed. She searches the city but does not find him. She seizes him and brings him to her mother's bedchamber.

Song 3:6 begins with the man speaking as he sees a royal palanquin coming up from the desert and bearing his beloved. His imagination of a wedding day turns to consider the physical beauty of his beloved, in a poem praising her physical features (called a *waṣf* and still used in Arabic folk culture). He then turns to call her his bride and invite her to come away with him to the high mountains. He praises her lovemaking, her perfumes, and her lips and tongue. He compares her to a sealed garden with all its fruit and spices, to which he has come. This is the fourth and central section, where the beloved is called a bride and the man rejoices in lovemaking.

The fifth section begins at 5:2. Here the man comes to the woman's bedchamber at night. He thrusts his hand through the keyhole, but before the woman reaches the door, he departs. She searches the city for him, is beaten by guards, and returns without him. She calls on her friends, the daughters of Jerusalem, to search for him. She describes his physical attributes with a *waṣf* of her own, in 5:10–16. The section ends with the joy of a union between the lovers (6:2–3).

Song 6:4–10 opens the sixth section with another *waṣf* by the man for the woman. After a brief reflection by the woman on her desire for the man, and a call to her (here in 6:13 [7:1 MT] named Shulammite for the only time) to return so that the singers may gaze on her, the man launches into his third *waṣf*, or song of praise for her (7:1–9a [7:2–10a MT]; see "Literary Readings," below). The woman replies with her desire to kiss her lover in public and to bring him to her mother's house for love.

The seventh and final section, Song 8:5–14, forms an epilogue that begins with the coming and awakening of the man by his lover. She longs to be a seal on his heart and testifies to the power of love, even stronger than death. Both fire and water are images of power that are used to describe this love. And here in Song 8:6 the last word may call it a "flame of Yah[weh]." Brothers now intrude into the dialogue with a concern for their younger sister. The woman defends herself, that she does not need them to assist her. However many other places of love may be found, she has her own to give to her lover. The

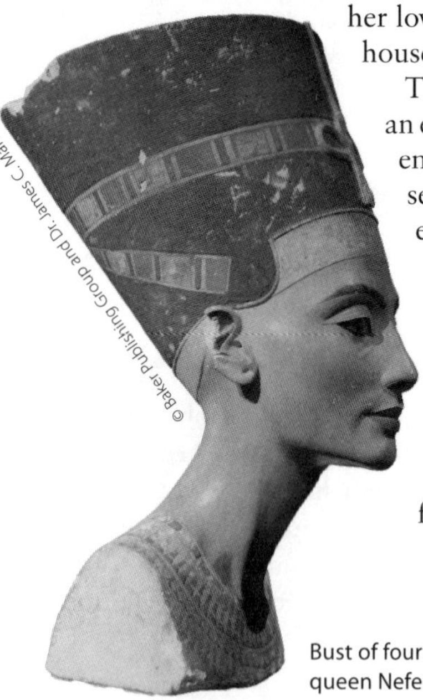

© Baker Publishing Group and Dr. James C. Martin

Bust of fourteenth-century-BC Egyptian queen Nefertiti with multilayered necklace man now listens to her voice as she calls him again to become a gazelle or a young stag and to take to the mountains.

Reading Song of Songs

Premodern Readings

Allegorical interpretations of the Song have been popular in the synagogue and the church. In the former, the male and female lovers become God and Israel. In the latter, they are Christ and the church. With a book so rich in metaphor, it is not unusual for the imagery to invite associations that have bordered on the allegorical as far back as there is evidence. In 2 Esdras (5:24–26; 7:26 NRSV mg.), Israel is pictured in images drawn from the Song (2:2; 4:15; 2:14; 4:8): lily, stream, dove, and bride. In the *Targum Song of Songs*, Judaism identifies Song 1:2–3:6 with the deliverance from Egypt and Israel's journey through the desert. With the mention of Solomon in Song 3:7–5:1, the targum relates this section to the temple and its worship. The Babylonian exile becomes the theme of Song 5:2–6:1, and Jewish independence is seen as the theme of 6:2–7:11. The targum also finds the later history of Jewish independence and Roman rule in Song 7:2–13. Finally, the expected messiah appears in Song 7:14–8:4, and the targum locates the future resurrection and end of the world in 8:5–14.

The marriage imagery in the New Testament texts[2] provided for an allegorical interpretation in early Christian approaches to the Song.[3] As early as about AD 200, Hippolytus used the Song as a means to teach asceticism.[4] Origen applied allegorical interpretation in his multivolume commentary.[5] This method continued into the Middle Ages (e.g., Ambrose, Gregory of Nyssa, and Bernard of Clairvaux). As an allegory the book became a means for teaching morals up to and beyond the time of the Reformation. Theodore of Mopsuestia, John Calvin, Edmund Spenser, and J. G. von Herder were among those who interpreted this text less allegorically and more literally.

In the earliest biblical manuscripts, such as Codex Sinaiticus (fourth century) and Codex Alexandrinus (fifth century), notes identify various speakers in the Song. The assignment of parts suggests that this text was seen as a drama played out by different parts and people. At about the same time Nilus of Ancyra also identified a dramatic theme. The Song described the

2. Cf. Matt. 9:15; 25:1–13; John 3:29; 2 Cor. 11:2; Eph. 5:22–33; Rev. 19:6–8; 21:9–11; 22:17. See Elliott, *Literary Unity of the Canticle*, 4.

3. See Pope, *Song of Songs,* 112–32, for a more comprehensive discussion of the commentators named here.

4. Smith, "Hippolytus' Commentary on the Song of Songs," 249–374, for preserved texts in Georgian, Greek, and Slavonic with translation.

5. Origen, *The Song of Songs*.

love that converted a prostitute who worshiped other gods to belief in the true God of Israel.[6] The great nineteenth-century German exegete Franz Delitzsch followed this approach.[7] The Shulammite female taught Solomon the true meaning of love. Others have followed this approach up to the present. In some cases there is the addition of a shepherd boy, who competes with Solomon for the girl's love.

Despite the popularity of the allegorical and the dramatic methods of interpretation, neither convinces. The allegorical interpretation fails because the text of the Song lacks any indication that it should be read in this way. An allegory such as Ecclesiastes 12:1–8 is identified by the way it is introduced. Never is the male character of the Song connected with God or the female with God's people. Further, Song 8:5 does not make sense if the female is God's people. How do God's people awaken God?

As to the dramatic interpretation that includes Solomon as a key actor, it seems unlikely due to the absence of Solomon as an active character in the book. He never speaks and tends to remain behind the scenes. Further, why would a Song connected positively with Solomon in the introduction proceed to portray him as a villain? In light of these observations, it is worthwhile to consider the other options that critics have suggested.

Higher Criticism

Nilus (see above) has suggested an interpretation involving the worship of false gods. More recent interpretations have suggested a liturgical origin for the Song connected with the ancient Mesopotamian story of the Sumerian Dumuzi, a shepherd and king who becomes the paramour of Inanna. Later, Akkadian forms of this account changed the names of the characters to Tammuz and Ishtar, even as the stories evolved. The actions of these characters are associated with the annual climate cycle. Several scholars working with these texts have identified various elements in the Song of Songs as connected with them. Add to this mixture the evidence of the Sumerian love songs, and there are many areas to compare. Thus Marvin Pope has connected the Song with rituals associated with a West Semitic feast known as the *marzēaḥ*.[8] These theories, however, do not persuade since they lack the sort of close connections of vocabulary, style, or form that would demonstrate dependency. Rather, Egyptian love poetry arguably forms the closest parallels with the Song on these levels. The theory of a liturgical origin in the context of foreign gods and goddesses seems most unlikely as the origin for a book that finds its way into the midst of a monotheistic canon.

6. Sovic, "De Nili Monachi Commentario."

7. Delitzsch, *Proverbs, Ecclesiastes, Song of Solomon*.

8. Pope, *Song of Songs*, 210–29. In light of additional *marzēaḥ* texts, there have been some who find funerary associations with this banquet unlikely. See McLaughlin, *Marzēaḥ*.

If the study of religious traditions and their connection with the Song has not succeeded in identifying its origin and background, neither has the search for separate literary sources fared well. In the end the problems of a form of literature and poetry so distinct from that of the other texts of the Bible have rendered an investigation into any literary sources distinct from those of the composition itself unlikely. Furthermore, the brevity of the poem, 117 verses, makes it a difficult test case for attempts to employ psychological methods (or any other methods) in analyzing the dynamics of relationship within the work.[9] Indeed, the realization of the subjective and speculative nature of the many probes into the poem has led to an ongoing body of literature arguing that the first place where one must begin is to recognize the text as a poem. Thus Othmar Keel observes: "The whole discussion has often overlooked the fact that poetry does not merely reflect reality—whether the reality of dreams or of conscious experience—but uses artistic means to create a reality of its own."[10]

Luis Stadelmann, in his *Love and Politics*, has returned to an allegorical interpretation. However, he has related his interpretation of the Song to postexilic Judean and Persian politics. While his theory is highly speculative, this view directs consideration back to the questions about the unity of the Song and its dating and authorship. As now preserved, does the Song form essentially an anthology of poetry, collecting love poems from different sources? Or does one find in it a unified work, perhaps even the work of a single author?[11] Alongside this question of unity lies the question of date and authorship.

If Solomon were the author of the Song, that would date it to the tenth century BC. Although there is reason to suggest a later date and a different author, an early date is not without its proponents. Gillis Gerleman suggests that, because this book emphasizes beauty and art, it demonstrates Egyptian influence of the sort that would have been known in the Solomonic court.[12] However, outside the Bible little is known about the reign of Solomon, and so such conclusions are not certain. One can envision the Persian period or some other later time in Israel's history as the period of such influence.

Some find geographical references such as Tirzah (Song 6:4) to be important. Tirzah was the capital of the northern kingdom (Israel) before Omri moved it to Samaria in the early ninth century. However, it is not clear that this information has anything to do with the purpose of the name in the Song. The natural beauty of Tirzah could describe any period of time during its occupation. On the one hand, as argued for other biblical books, the appearance of Ugaritic

9. On the psychological approach and that of social sciences in general, see esp. Landy, *Paradoxes of Paradise*; Krinetzki, *Hohe Lied*; Boer, "Second Coming"; and Black, "Beauty or the Beast?"

10. See Keel, *Song of Songs*, 120, discussing Song 3:1–5. However, the observation could also apply to the Song as a whole.

11. See further on this below in "Ancient Near Eastern Context."

12. See Gerleman, *Ruth*, 63–77.

cognates does not prove that these terms do not occur at a later date.[13] On the other hand, the Greek *phoreion* (loanword in 3:9 MT; cf. LXX), the Persian *pardēs* (loanword in 4:13 MT; cf. LXX, *paradeisos*), and other possibly late expressions have been used to argue a later date for the work.[14]

A single word remains a dubious basis for dating a whole text, especially if one allows for the possibility of later editors and for the word to originate from other sources.[15] The following elements in the Song itself suggest the world of the Israelite monarchy: village life, a king in the neighborhood, a fortified Jerusalem, and mention and enjoyment of the luxury products of the trade routes. While some of the language implies a postexilic date for the final composition, various themes portray an earlier time.

This is also true of the female's ability to search for her lover along the public thoroughfares of the city at nighttime (3:1–5). Commentators give different opinions but do not cite evidence to localize this picture. Only Keel notes comparative evidence in the Middle Assyrian laws (twelfth/eleventh centuries BC).[16] These require that, when women appear in public, they must be veiled unless they are slaves or prostitutes. Yet this has little direct relevance for women in ancient Israel centuries later. No respectable Israelite woman would have been found alone at night in the city streets during the intertestamental period (Sir. 42:11; 2 Macc. 3:1). However, this was not the case in earlier periods. At least for Ruth, it was possible to walk at night in the streets of Bethlehem (Ruth 3).[17]

None of this remains decisive. The environment of the Song can be situated in many times and places. As with the proverbs and the psalms, the Song addresses the subject of erotic love in a manner that reaches beyond any specific time or place. Even so, the springtime of the year is identified in various descriptions in the Song (see 6:11; 7:12–13), with new life and vegetation. This seems most likely to describe the settings of the Song. Is it for this reason that the book is traditionally read at Passover?[18]

Literary Readings

Literary and structural analysis of the poem has become the dominant means of interpreting the Song of Songs. Harold Bloom has argued that the distinction of literary and allegorical readings must be set aside for the Song

13. See Pope, *Song of Songs*; Albright, "Archaic Survivals in the Text of Canticles."

14. See the summary by Murphy, *Song of Songs*, 4n10.

15. See Goitein, "Song of Songs," 62.

16. Keel, *Song of Songs*, 122.

17. So Keel (ibid., 120), who also cites the rape law of Deut. 22:25–29.

18. See Longman, *Song of Songs*, 2, although the attribution of the reading of the Song on the eighth day is not universal. The date has varied since its association with this festival, a phenomenon at least as early as the eighth century AD (Brenner, *Song of Songs*, 20).

of Songs.[19] He advocates a variety of methods. More than anyone else, M. Timothea Elliott has identified a comprehensive structural unity to the Song.[20] Using literary, vocabulary, and phrase connections throughout the poem, she has made a compelling case for a unity to the poem and for its structure.

William Phipps rejects the interpretation that the text advocates free love and promiscuous sex.[21] The lovers may be viewed by some as unmarried. However, this is not necessarily the case, nor do the literary parallels with Egyptian love poetry prove this.[22] The term "bride" (*kallâ*) occurs only in the description of legal marriages (contrast kinship terms, such as "sister," that can describe close friendship rather than blood relationship) or as reference to a daughter-in-law.[23] In the heart of the Song, in 4:8–5:1, it appears six times. Here is described a marriage relationship, whether in fantasy or reality. A key interpretive guide for understanding this work lies in the language of commitment that pervades the whole.

If the Song is best understood as a structured whole, what is that literary structure? Elliott finds it in the repeated refrains, especially in Song 2:7; 3:5; 5:8; 8:4.[24] Because the Song is basically a dialogue between the two lovers, the recognition of this alternation of genders also becomes key for understanding its structure.[25] Thus the text can be divided according to discourse. However, at a larger level one may identify a prologue (1:2–2:7), an epilogue (8:5–14), and four parts between: I, 2:8–3:5; II, 3:6–5:1; III, 5:2–6:3; IV, 6:4–8:4. Elliott finds that, at almost every division (1:4; 2:4–7; 3:4–6; 5:1–2; 8:2–4), a collection of key terms recurs. They do not all appear at each place, but rather a cluster of many of them can be found. These include the following: "come, enter" (*bw'*); either "house" (*byt*), "room" (*ḥdr*), or "garden" (*gan*); "wine" (*yayin*); "embrace" (*ḥbq* at 2:6 and 8:3); and an adjuration to avoid "love" or "sleep." The lovers begin each section apart and then find each other and come together at the end.

Repeated images are found throughout this richly metaphoric poem, including auditory and visual pictures, as well as those concerned with taste, smell, and touch. These all enhance the picture of the relationship's intimacy.

19. Bloom, *Song of Songs*, 1.

20. Elliott, *Literary Unity of the Canticle*.

21. Phipps, "Plight of the Song," 83–84.

22. See J. White, *Language of Love*, 81–82, 91–92, 163–64. One may also conclude that Egyptian parallels do not demonstrate that the Song is a wedding song.

23. This is contrary to LaCocque, *Romance, She Wrote*, 108, who asserts that the term identifies one who is yet to be a bride. LaCocque refers to Gen. 38:24, which describes Tamar, whose main role is not that of a bride-to-be but that of a daughter-in-law with status in the family. He also cites Hosea 4:13–14, where the term is explicitly used twice in parallel with "daughters." Both passages clearly use the term in the sense of a daughter-in-law.

24. Elliott, *Literary Unity of the Canticle*.

25. See, e.g., Fokkelman, *Reading Biblical Poetry*, 189–206, 224. The young woman speaks 30 times, whereas the young man speaks 18 times (200).

Ancient Egyptian *Waṣf*?

John Foster's translation of Egyptian poetry includes a love poem that resembles the *waṣf* style as found in the Song.[a] It is located on Papyrus Chester Beatty I, on the verso:

My love is one alone, without her equal,
 beautiful above all women.
See her, like the goddess of the morning star in splendor,
 at the beginning of a happy year.
With dazzling presence and a fair complexion,
 with lovely watching eyes,
With lips that are sweet in speaking,
 and not a word too much;
Straight her neck and white her breast,
 and her tresses gleam like lapis lazuli;
Her arms are more precious than gold,
 her fingers like lotus blossoms,
With curving hips and a trim waist,
 and thighs that only heighten her beauty,
her step is pleasing as she treads upon earth;
 and she fastens my heart in her embrace.
She makes the necks of the young men
 swing round to see her.
Happy is he who can fully embrace her—
 he is the first of all the young lovers!
Look at her as she walks along,
 Like that goddess beyond, One alone!

[a] Foster, *Hymns, Prayers, and Songs*, 163–64.

Thus the woman is as secure as a locked garden (4:12). She is a vineyard (1:6; 8:12), a carriage (3:7–10), a locked room (5:5), and a walled city (8:9–10). She herself, portrayed as a private room, brings her lover into the room of her mother (3:4). Further scenes of protection are found in the context of these images: tendrils of the vineyard (7:12), sixty warriors (3:7), sixty queens (6:8), walls and guards (5:7), lattice (2:9), locks (5:5), and towers (4:4; 7:4, 8:9–10). On this important matter of the rich imagery in the Song, see further under "Gender and Ideological Criticism."

Scholars also recognize a unique literary form scattered throughout the Song. It is a poem or song that occurs in cultures of Arabic speakers. Three times the Song describes the female's body (4:1–7; 6:4–7; 7:1–7 [7:2–8 MT]) and once the male's body (5:10–16). These constitute a form known elsewhere to derive from an Arabic term for "description," that is, *waṣf*. A *waṣf* is an Arabic love song in which the lover praises the physical attributes of the partner.[26] The study of these songs in the context of a term and practice attested only in Arabic sources of a much later time is not anachronistic and therefore illegitimate. Like the Arabic language, customs such as the *waṣf* may predate their attested occurrence in the last few centuries. Furthermore, just because a literary/oral form occurs in a later period does not mean it could not have occurred earlier. Roland Murphy provides an example of a *waṣf* for Sarah as written in the *Genesis Apocryphon* (1Q20), from among the Dead Sea Scrolls.[27] Nor is this the only form in the Song that can be compared with literary forms of later Semitic cultures. Indeed, the *waṣf* form may occur in ancient Egyptian love poetry.

David Carr compares the Song with women's use of love poetry sung among themselves in Mediterranean and Middle Eastern societies.[28] He suggests that this was a means for expressing emotions of love in these cultures (hardly unique, though perhaps so in its particular form). Carr suggests that the Song may use these forms of expression and turn what is customarily said in private into a public expression.

Gender and Ideological Criticism

One may question whether the use of allegory in the interpretation of the Song assisted in the reduction of the status of the man and woman from persons to mere symbols. Of these two, the female serves as the major character. She is the first and last to speak. She speaks more than anyone else, and she commands her lover and others more than any other speakers. Thus she wants his kisses at the beginning (1:2) and commands his departure at the end (8:14). Her feelings are freely shared, unlike those of her partner.[29] She is the dominant speaker and actor (e.g., in 3:1–5 she goes out in the night to search for her lover). This leads the full impact of this Song to include an equality and independence of the female, as well as the male.

So did a female compose the Song? Athalya Brenner observes how Miriam and Deborah may have authored the poems of Exodus 15 and Judges 5, respectively.[30] She determines that the dominant female voice occupies 53

26. The nineteenth-century scholar Wetzstein ("Syrische Dreschtafel") observed local weddings in Syria and the songs that the bride and groom sang about the physical attributes of each other. Delitzsch (*Proverbs, Ecclesiastes, Song of Solomon*, 162–76) recorded them in an appendix to his commentary. See Longman, *Song of Songs*, 140–41. Thus began the study of *waṣf*s and their relation to the Song of Songs.

27. Murphy, *Song of Songs*, 158.

28. Carr, "Gender and the Shaping of Desire."

29. Walsh (*Exquisite Desire*, 106) observes how the two have a similar level of love for each other, and yet, "as desire travels through the levels of discourse, from flirtation to physical want to excitement, however, the man cannot keep up with the woman's desire."

30. Brenner, *Israelite Woman*, 46–56.

percent of the text in the Song, with the male voice accounting for 34 percent. Alongside this, consider the testimony that women could read and write, as found in 1 Kings 21:8–9; Esther 9:29. Add to this the involvement of women in composing songs for harvesttimes, laments, and victories (Judg. 11:40; 21:21; 1 Sam. 2:1–10; 18:6–7; 2 Sam. 1:20, 24; Jer. 9:17, 20), and one has a sense of women's involvement in the music and poetry of Israel and the Bible.[31] Even so, certainty about the gender of the unspecified author of the Song remains elusive.[32] Nevertheless, the Song of Songs possesses a stronger female voice in the dialogue than does any other biblical book.

Despite this, David J. A. Clines argues that the Song is a male composition of soft pornography.[33] He suggests that it was intended as male entertainment. Only late was its official interpretation allegorized in order to place it in the canon.[34] This approach runs into several difficulties. First, there is the question of the larger context of ancient Near Eastern love poetry, and especially the Egyptian love poetry. None of this appears to have been composed for the purpose that Clines suggests. Further, this approach fails to deal seriously with the delicate and nuanced metaphors that dominate the poem. These are hardly the crude descriptions as found, for example, in the Ugaritic myth of the Birth of the Gracious Gods (*KTU* 1.24). Rather, similar to the word pictures found in many of the Egyptian love poems, these descriptions portray the avoidance of an emphasis on the anatomical and an appreciation of the desire itself. Finally, the description of pornography fails to distinguish this oppressive caricature of women from the erotic literature that the Song is, with its priority on shared love and commitment.

Metaphors of vineyards and gardens dominate the Song, and these provide a special emphasis on the sexuality of the female.[35] Carey Ellen Walsh contrasts the male imagery of sexuality elsewhere in the Bible and that of the female as presented here.[36] She uses Samson's metaphor for intimacy in Judges 14:18: "plowed with my heifer." Walsh suggests that this male-oriented picture demonstrates how the farmer works the field, where the field itself is often the picture of the passive female. Thus *he* produces a harvest of dry grains. This is not the imagery of the Song. Instead, sexual metaphors of moist and succulent fruit result in a different picture, a female picture of fruitfulness and the many pleasures of touch, taste, and aroma.

31. See Bekkenkamp and van Dijk, "Old Testament and Women's Cultural Traditions"; Exum, "Developing Strategies," 226, 231.

32. Bekkenkamp and van Dijk, "Old Testament and Women's Cultural Traditions," 107–8: "The metaphorical language of women's songs seems to be: 1. more explicit as far as objects or locations from women's life are concerned; 2. more implicit regarding bodily experiences; 3. more individual."

33. Clines, "Why Is There a Song of Songs?"

34. On this subject, see Exum, "Developing Strategies," 218–19, and the bibliography there.

35. See Falk, *Love Lyrics*, 101–4; Meyers, "Gender Imagery," 201.

36. Walsh, *Exquisite Desire*, 81–94.

Marie-Lan Nguyen. The Louvre/Wikimedia Commons

Perfume makers pictured on an Egyptian tomb (ca. twenty-sixth century BC)

Marcia Falk identifies four contexts for the poetry of the Song: the wild country with its destructive natural forces; the cultivated countryside portrayed as a return to paradise; indoors within the city, where a private and supportive world is found; outdoors in the city, where there is hostility and violence.[37] There are five themes, three of which concern the beckoning of, banishment of, and search for the beloved. The remaining two concern the evaluation of self in a hostile world and the praise of love. She studies the Song's imagery within these major themes and contexts.

In Carol Meyers's observation of the architectural and military images applied to the female, there is the theme of female self-worth.[38] Song 4:1–4 portrays her neck as a tower (cf. 7:4 [7:5 MT]), her necklace as layers. Her protection is shields. Scholars do not know whether the pools of Heshbon (7:4 [7:5 MT]) served as a military defense, but it makes sense in this context. The "house of the mother" (3:4; 8:2) is surprising and contrasts with the usual term for the extended family, "the house of the father." But the latter does not appear in the Song. The reference to the house of the mother affirms the female presence and perhaps dominance.

Graceful doves (2:12; 6:9) and gazelles (4:5; 7:3 [7:4 MT]) represent images of the female and of the male (2:9, 17; 4:1; 5:12; 8:14). The female is also pictured like lions and leopards (4:8), and as a mare released among the pharaoh's

37. Falk, *Love Lyrics*. See the summary in Webb, "Song of Songs," 20–22.
38. Meyers, "Gender Imagery."

chariots (1:9). Meyers comments, "The female has a power of her own that can offset the mighty forces of a trained army."[39] The imagery depicts the female as empowered to choose the one whom she will love, just as he chooses her.

Ancient Near Eastern Context

The close connection with Egyptian love poetry has already been explored in virtually all the sections discussed above.

The Egyptian love poems from the second millennium BC portray a variety of lovers and dispositions. One of the more aggressive female lovers is attested in what Michael Fox identifies as Papyrus Harris 500, Group A: Nos. 4–5.[40] He translates:

My heart is not yet done with your lovemaking,
  my (little) wolf cub!
    Your liquor is (your) lovemaking.
I {will not} abandon it
  until blows drive (me) away
    to spend my days in the marshes,
(until blows banish me)
to the land of Syria with sticks and rods,
    to the land of Nubia with palms,
      to the highlands with switches,
    to the lowlands with cudgels.
I will not listen to their advice
    to abandon the one I desire.

Here the woman speaks with confidence regarding her desire for continued lovemaking. She speaks of beatings that alone will drive her from her lover. As with the Song, the love described is erotic, physical lovemaking. There is the beating of the female, found in Song 5, that prevents her from uniting with her lover. There is also the use of foreign lands as a means to describe the extent of the love that the couple shares (4:8; 7:4 [7:5 MT]).

However, all the examples of ancient Egyptian love poetry consist of love poems that are much shorter than the Song. For this reason, even among those who identify the Song as erotic love poetry, there has been a temptation to divide it into smaller poems and to see the work as an anthology. Some have found eight different types of poems in the Song, with multiple examples of the eight.[41] Others have found as many as thirty different poems within

39. Ibid., 207.

40. Fox, *Song of Songs*, 10.

41. See Horst, "Formen." See also Haupt, *Biblischer Liebeslieder*; Murphy, "Towards a Commentary."

the Song.[42] The appearance of modern translations of Egyptian love poems, when published as a collection, has furthered this view that the Song is an anthology.[43] This was based on the understanding that ancient love poems were much shorter compositions.[44] But because only a limited number of such love poems are available from the ancient past, it does not follow that such poetry must be of much shorter length and can never reach the length of the Song. Its 117 verses do not form a long poem, nor is it anything like an epic poem.[45] The passion of the lovers, not some predetermined view as to what the poem's length should be, determines the content and the length of the Song. Because the Song is a dialogue, it invites a greater length and provides for ongoing reflection on the object of the passion, just as the dialogues connected with Job often require a longer poem to express everything that is desired. In this manner a longer poem may heighten the passion.

Although Egyptian and other contemporary love poetry of the ancient Near East has been useful for interpreting the Song, the cited parallels do not provide much information about how significant they are. Part of this may be the common sentiments expressed across cultures regarding romantic love. John White observes:

> Not only does the Song's rustic imagery betray a close association with the ways of expressing love in Egypt, but the commonality of love-language denotes archetypal vehicles through which human, sexual love was celebrated in the ancient world. Thus, it is not surprising that specific topoi be common to both Hebrew and Egyptian love literature. The fragrances, sight of the love partners, embracing and kissing, friends and enemies of the lovers, and even specific parallels (scent of garments, the mother figure, love under the trees, gazelles, etc.) denote the Song's participation in the world of human love expression.[46]

Canonical Context

The place of erotic love poetry in the Holy Bible has always raised some eyebrows. The tendency to allegorize it has not been successful as a means to evade its message: the power of sexual love is as "strong as death" and serves as a sign pointing to understanding something of God's love (Song 8:6). Thus sex is fundamentally a gift of God to be received with joy and to be treasured. This poem balances the revelation of sex in the Bible. Some other

42. See Falk, *Love Lyrics*.

43. See Hermann, *Altägyptische Liebesdichtung*. More recent adherents of the Song as a collection include Soulen, "*Waṣfs* of the Song"; and Brenner, *Song of Songs*.

44. See J. White, *Language of Love*, 163.

45. Contrast the Ugaritic Baal Epic, many times the length of the Song.

46. J. White, *Language of Love*, 162.

biblical texts give sex a bad press. There is all the legislation in the Pentateuch and the implicitly negative evaluation of various sexual practices that these regulations forbid. The Historical Books and the Prophets are filled with vivid images condemning Israel, redeemed as God's bride, for going after other gods and goddesses as a prostitute or sexually promiscuous woman might do. The New Testament as well has little use for sexuality except to warn of practices that lie outside of God's will and to encourage celibacy. In all of this, then, there is not much to support the view of sex as something beautiful, created by God. The Song provides that balance and moves the reader of the biblical canon (Jewish or Christian) onward to a view of the world that appreciates sex as something to be enjoyed as an act of worship to the Creator.

Francis Landy argues that love and death in the Song can be identified with forces of creation and destruction.[47] These may be connected with the Eden story of the opening chapters of Genesis. Phyllis Trible maintains that Genesis 2–3 forms the source for many of the themes: all the senses are involved, plants are everywhere, harmony pervades, water is abundant, animals appear, and sexual play and work occur.[48] At Song 7:11 (7:12 MT), the conflict of wills between the man and the woman, and the domination of the man over the woman in Genesis 3:16, are both reversed.[49] The two books coincide in what must be an intentional reference to the judgment in Genesis 3:16 and the woman's desire for her husband. The opposite occurs in Song 7:10 (7:11 MT) due to the power of love. Thus the woman, according to Jill Munro,

> unties the bondage of the ancient curse, exactly as Isaiah invalidates the curse of "I [God] shall institute hostility" between man and serpent by letting a suckling play over a viper's den (Isa. 11:8). In truth, in the pages of the Song we encounter a new relationship between the two sexes, a relationship of equality and amicable mutuality.[50]

Theological Perspectives of Song of Songs

Does the Song have a central theme or point? Some take an ideological approach and emphasize the freedom of the lovers to describe and enjoy each other's bodies, as part of nature.[51] Walsh confirms this by looking at desire

47. Landy, *Paradoxes of Paradise*, 36.
48. Trible, "Love's Lyrics Redeemed."
49. See the affirming opinion of Pope, "Song of Songs and Women's Liberation."
50. See Munro, *Spikenard and Saffron*, 105–6.
51. Viviers ("Rhetoricity of the 'Body'") identifies this as the "ecstatic body," referring to Leder's (*Absent Body*) typology of rhetoric used in describing the human body.

itself.[52] Erotica here is distinguished from pornography, just as the Song is concerned with desire rather than sex. The Song does not emphasize sexual activity in the moment. Rather, it appreciates the value of waiting. The full realization of one's desire forms the expression called "love" (the Heb. verb *'āhēb* or its related noun *'ahăbâ*, already occurring 6× in Song 1:2–2:7), which understands the emotion in the context of an absolute commitment. This emphasis relates the text to Proverbs 5:15–19 (NIV):

> Drink water from your own cistern,
>   running water from your own well.
> Should your springs overflow in the streets,
>   your streams of water in the public squares?
> Let them be yours alone,
>   never to be shared with strangers.
> May your fountain be blessed,
>   and may you rejoice in the wife of your youth.
> A loving doe, a graceful deer—
>   may her breasts satisfy you always,
>   may you ever be intoxicated with her love.

Verbal images (six or seven) are found in both this passage and the Song. These assume commitment in the love poetry.[53] Such parallels suggest that the Song is Wisdom literature. In the Egyptian papyri, scribal and wisdom texts are mixed in with the love poetry.[54] The one supplements the other.

Readers may return to the key theological sense of the Song: the joys of God-given erotic love point to something beyond it, to a greater love.[55] George Knight sees the Song as a discussion of God's redemptive plan for the world.[56] Others stress the manner in which the Song places an emphasis on interpersonal relationships, and especially on the relation between God and people. This creates personal identity and gives self-worth. This love, or *'ahăbâ*, is also found in Deuteronomy and embraces commitment. The Song speaks of a similar commitment, not to God directly but to the lover. As in the Song, the *'ahăbâ* of Deuteronomy includes the emotions of a person.[57] This cannot be separated from the mind and will of the person. Love in the Song describes a love similar to that which the people of God know from God and give to him in recognition of his great sacrifice for them.

52. Walsh, *Exquisite Desire*.

53. So Webb, "Song of Songs," 29–30.

54. Specifically, J. White (*Language of Love*, 81) refers to the Harper Song between the second and third sections of love poems found on Papyrus Harris 500.

55. Cogently argued by Murphy, "History of Exegesis."

56. Knight and Golka, *Revelation of God*.

57. Lapsley, "Feeling Our Way."

Nevertheless, the Song remains concerned with physical love, and this must not be lost in any search for its theme.[58] Song 8:6–7 expresses this unbridled desire, with its exclusive commitment, as the climax of the work. Love is as strong as death. Both experiences open the door to the unknown and uncontrolled. Passion, like death, cannot be bought or sold. Rather, it expresses that which lies on the very edge of full encounter with God. More than fidelity to the covenant, love for God achieves a joy never fully realized in this life. The saints of Christianity sometimes understood this as a direct line between the passion of the Song and God's love. They both express something fundamental about the purpose of human existence. For many Christians, this side of the grave, it thus becomes the closest physical experience of the transcendent knowledge of the living God. If passion can provide a bridge to the knowledge of God in this life, death can serve as the door to that eternal knowledge.

Key Commentaries and Studies

Exum, J. Cheryl. *Song of Songs: A Commentary.* OTL. Louisville: Westminster John Knox, 2005. A thorough exegetical commentary from a feminist perspective.

Garrett, Duane A., and Paul R. House. *Song of Songs/Lamentations.* WBC 23B. Nashville: Nelson, 2004. Thoroughly researched, evenly balanced, evangelical, and reasonable application of the text.

Hess, Richard S. *Song of Songs.* BCOTWP. Grand Rapids: Baker Academic, 2005. An evangelical and exegetical study of the Song, with an integrated analysis of the Hebrew text, the poetic structure, and the theological significance for the Christian.

Keel, Othmar. *The Song of Songs.* Translated by F. J. Geiser. ConC. Minneapolis: Fortress, 1994. An authority on Israelite iconography interprets the images of the book.

Longman, Tremper, III. *Song of Songs.* NICOT. Grand Rapids: Eerdmans, 2001. Evangelical study by an expert in Wisdom literature and its literary analysis.

Murphy, Roland E. *The Song of Songs.* Hermeneia. Minneapolis: Fortress, 1990. A thorough exegetical and theological study of the Hebrew text.

Pope, Marvin H. *Song of Songs: A New Translation with Introduction and Commentary.* AB 7C. Garden City, NY: Doubleday, 1977. A large commentary with frequent digressions into comparative customs.

58. Contrast Webb ("Song of Songs," 23), who asserts that the true consummation of love is in the relationship rather than the sex. But there is no division between the two. This shortsightedness is also true of allegorical interpretations that fail to emphasize the physical side of love in the Song.

PART 4

PROPHETIC BOOKS

Prophecy is the telling of the divine word. It may or may not predict the future. It can also indict the people of the present and interpret the events of the past. Prophecy in the ancient Near East was used long before Israel appeared. In the eighteenth-century-BC texts from Mari, prophets could go into ecstatic states and give messages, ostensibly from their gods. The subjects preserved from the royal archives of Mari include concerns of when the king and his army should go to war. In the story of an Egyptian traveler named Wenamun, the Late Egyptian text (ca. 1100 BC) describes how he encounters an ecstatic prophet in the court of the king of Dor, a town along the Mediterranean coast, north of modern Tel Aviv. The Neo-Assyrian texts contain prophecies that ascribe victory and success to some of the leaders of the later period of the Neo-Assyrian Empire (eighth and seventh centuries BC).

In Numbers 22–24, Balaam, likely from north of the promised land, appears as a prophet hired by Balak to curse Israel. In a text found at Deir ʿAllā in the Jordan Valley, dating from about 800 BC, this same figure appears with a vision he supposedly had. From the Judean city of Lachish, an ostracon was found containing the message of a prophet in the form of a single word that was proclaimed in the years before the fall of Jerusalem in 586 BC. The word can be translated, "Be watchful." The Bible is replete with prophets who predate those in the prophetic books. From Lamech's prophecy of Noah (Gen. 5:28–29) onward, prophets played key roles in exhorting, warning, approving, and judging the leaders and people of Israel and of other lands.

The prophetic books include the Major Prophets and the Twelve Minor Prophets. The Major Prophets are so called due to the longer texts associated with them. Isaiah, Jeremiah (with Lamentations), Ezekiel, and Daniel number among these. The Twelve Minor Prophets, so named because of their shorter length, could have been written on a single scroll. As the discussion will suggest, there may be a reason for the order of these Twelve in terms of the relative dating of these writers, from earliest to latest. That seems to be the case with the Major Prophets. However, this is a generalization and may have been affected by related themes in some books. For example, Obadiah's prophecy against Edom naturally follows the last chapter of Amos, which also mentions this nation. The prophetic books span at least from the eighth-century-BC figures of Hosea and Amos to the fifth-century-BC prophecy of Malachi. Some would date the final chapters of Daniel to the Jewish revolts of the second century BC, but this is disputed.

Hosea and Amos prophesied primarily in the northern kingdom (Israel), as did the prophet Jonah, according to 2 Kings 14:25. Most prophets spoke to Judah during its period before the exile. These include Isaiah, Jeremiah, Joel, Micah, Habakkuk, and Zephaniah. Some of these, such as Jeremiah, survived into the exile. Others addressed specific nations: Jonah and Nahum addressed Assyria, Obadiah addressed Edom. Yet the books of other prophets also contain texts, sometimes large sections, indicting other nations. Ezekiel and Daniel prophesied during the exile and, in the case of Daniel, into the period after the exile. The postexilic prophets include Haggai and Zechariah around 522–517 BC, and Malachi in the following century. These all proclaimed their messages in Jerusalem. Daniel is different from the other prophets. Half of his book consists of narratives that take place in Babylon during the reign of Nebuchadnezzar, the fall of Babylon to Cyrus, and the following years. The second half of his book, as well as some of the dreams in the first half, includes prophecies that look forward to the rise and fall of empires as well as what some see as detailed descriptions of later events in the history of God's people. For more on this apocalyptic literature, see the chapter on Daniel.

The vivid imagery and intense language of the prophets, as well as the content of their messages, have made them the object of much study and appreciation. It is difficult to find finer examples of ancient poetry and rhetoric toward a more noble theme than what appears in the second half of the book of Isaiah (chaps. 40–66). The whole of this body of literature has much to appreciate in terms of beauty, truth, and goodness. This stands in stark contrast to the judgment and condemnation of God's people and of other nations for their sins. The placement of dark colors alongside bright ones enhances the dramatic effect of these messages. Not only is their style superior to that of the prophecies discovered from other contemporary nations; their message calling people to faith, obedience, and life in the kingdom of the one true God of Israel also towers above others. It provides insight into the ongoing relevance of these speakers for the millennia since then and even into today's world. God, his love for his people, and the human condition have not changed.

19

ISAIAH

The New Testament quotes Isaiah more than any other prophetic book. Among the Dead Sea Scrolls, no prophet is cited as much as Isaiah. Clearly, the prophet Isaiah became key for understanding the past and interpreting God's work in the future.

Name, Text, and Outline

The name of the scroll refers to the prophet Isaiah, who received the "vision" that the work records, according to 1:1. The name Isaiah is composed of two Hebrew words. The first is the root of the noun "salvation." The second is a form of the divine name of God, Yahweh. Together they form a sentence name: "Yahweh is salvation."

Along with Psalms and Deuteronomy, Isaiah is represented in a large number of references, fragments, and scrolls among the Dead Sea Scrolls from the caves at Qumran. The best known are the Great Isaiah Scroll (1QIsa[a]) and a more fragmentary second scroll (1QIsa[b]), both found in Cave 1. A comparison of the Hebrew text of these scrolls with the book of Isaiah in the Masoretic Text of Codex Leningrad (copied more than one thousand years later) reveals an amazing agreement, with only minor deviations (see the introduction). Given the unusual preservation of virtually the complete text of Isaiah in a Dead Sea Scroll manuscript and the length of time between the writing of 1QIsa[a] (ca. 100 BC) and Codex Leningrad (ca. AD 1000), the remarkable degree of agreement attests to the great care of the Masoretic copyists and their predecessors. In the age before the printing press, this forms an important witness to the reliability of the copies of the Hebrew Bible. If, where it can be attested,

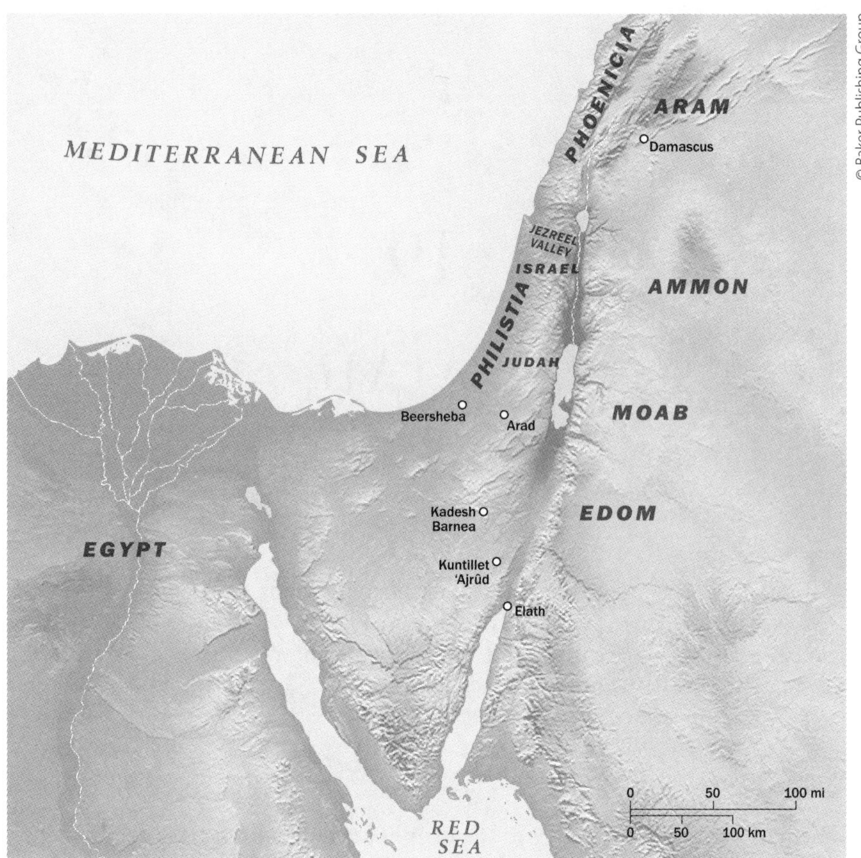

© Baker Publishing Group

The age of Isaiah

such accuracy is found, cannot a scholar extrapolate the same scribal care to the earlier periods, where no manuscripts are preserved? At least the burden of proof lies with those who would challenge the accuracy of the copying.

The Greek (LXX) text of Isaiah occasionally repositions words and phrases to what would have been other verses on the same page of the text. Otherwise, it has been used for understanding the interpretation and theology of the Greek translators and for suggesting emendations to some difficult sections of the Hebrew text.

OUTLINE

1. The Judgment at Hand (1:1–39:8)
   - A. Israel and Its Leaders Sin and Are Doomed to Judgment (1:1–5:30)
   - B. Isaiah's Vision and Mission (6:1–13)
   - C. Ahaz and the Coming Judgment from Assyria (7:1–12:6)

D. Prophecies against the Surrounding Nations (13:1–23:18)
   1. Babylon (13:1–22)
   2. Babylon's King (14:1–23)
   3. Assyria (14:24–27)
   4. Philistia (14:28–32)
   5. Moab (15:1–16:14)
   6. Damascus (17:1–14)
   7. Cush (18:1–7)
   8. Egypt (19:1–25)
   9. Isaiah's Sign of Nakedness against Assyria and the Nations (20:1–6)
   10. Wilderness of the Sea: Babylon (21:1–10)
   11. Dumah (21:11–12)
   12. Arabia (21:13–17)
   13. Valley of Vision: Jerusalem (22:1–25)
   14. Tyre (23:1–18)

E. Zion (= Jerusalem) Recognized by the Nations (24:1–27:13)
   1. God Will Reign from Jerusalem (24:1–23)
   2. God Will Exalt Jerusalem and Abase Its Enemies (25:1–12)
   3. God Will Exalt Jerusalem and Raise the Dead (26:1–21)
   4. God Will Return Israel from Its Exile to Worship Him (27:1–13)

F. Summary and Conclusion: God's Salvation of His People (28:1–33:24)
   1. God Will Judge Israel's Wicked Leaders (28:1–29)
   2. God's People Will No Longer Be Ignorant but Understand (29:1–24)
   3. God Will Judge and Then Exalt Jerusalem (30:1–33)
   4. God Will Fight Assyria and the Enemies of Jerusalem (31:1–9)
   5. The Righteous King Will Bring Fertility and Security (32:1–20)
   6. God Will Restore the Land and Bring Healing and Salvation (33:1–24)

G. God Begins to Enact His Plans for His Reign from Jerusalem (34:1–39:8)
   1. God's Destruction of Edom and All Nations Opposing Him (34:1–17)
   2. The Desert Becomes a Garden for the Faithful to Return (35:1–10)
   3. Hezekiah's Faith Stands Firm, and God Defeats Assyria (36:1–37:38)
   4. Hezekiah's Prayer for His Recovery and Its Answer (38:1–22)
   5. Hezekiah Trusts Babylon Rather than God (39:1–8)

II. The Coming Hope (40:1–66:24)

A. God Is Sovereign over Zion and the World (40:1–55:13)
   1. The Prophet Called to Comfort Israel (40:1–11)
   2. The All-Powerful Creator Has Forgiven and Will Restore His People (40:12–44:23)
   3. The Creator Commands Cyrus to Return His People to a Rebuilt Jerusalem So That the World May See and Know Him (44:24–45:25)
   4. God Humiliates Babylon and Redeems Israel So That the World May Know Him (46:1–48:22)
   5. Nature and the Nations Will Assist in Returning Israel (49:1–26)
   6. As the One Beaten and Mocked Was Assisted by God, So May Israel Trust in God's Help (50:1–11)

7. Call to Awaken by Jerusalem's Creator, Who Will Restore and Bless (51:1–23)
8. Jerusalem Honored and Its People Returned at the Announcement of Good News (52:1–12)
9. The Servant Suffers and Dies for the People's Sin, with the Promise of Life and Success after Death (52:13–53:12)
10. Continued Exaltation of Jerusalem (54:1–17)
11. The Power of God's Word to Accomplish This (55:1–13)

B. God Gives the Life of Salvation to All Who Accept It (56:1–66:24)

1. God's Expectations toward His People and a Universal Welcome (56:1–12)
2. God Has Punished Israel for Its Sins (57:1–21)
3. Fasting and Sabbath Keeping Are Useless without Obedience to and Love for One Another (58:1–14)
4. Although God's People Are Wicked, God Will Rescue Those Who Repent (59:1–21)
5. God Gives Light and Blessing to His People (60:1–22)
6. God Brings Liberty and Exalts His People (61:1–11)
7. Pictures of How God Will Bless His People (62:1–12)
8. God Fights and Wins for His People (63:1–19 [63:19a MT])
9. The People Who Rebelled against God's Blessings No Longer Have Their Sanctuary (64:1–12 [63:19b–64:11 MT])
10. The Wicked Face Destruction, but the Righteous Will Be Blessed with a New Heaven and a New Earth (65:1–25)
11. In Place of the Wicked, God Will Select Some as Priests and Levites from across the World (66:1–24)

Overview of Isaiah

Isaiah opens with a note of his vision and the period of time during which it takes place (1:1). There follows an indictment against the people and leaders of God's people, Israel. It is a time of devastation and judgment, with only a small number of people remaining. Sacrifices and offerings are meaningless when the people continue to be unfaithful to their covenant with God. Chapter 2 begins with a vision of universal peace, when all nations will stream to Jerusalem to learn about the true God of Israel (2:1–4). The pride and arrogance of the people, and their trust in their wealth and security, will lead to terrible judgment and loss of everything. Isaiah 5:1–7 pictures the vineyard Israel, which God planted and took care of only to see it produce bad fruit. Judgment is coming from God and the nations. Isaiah 6, set in the year of King Uzziah's death, describes Isaiah's call in his vision of the throne room of God, where his lips are purified by a burning coal and he accedes to God's call for a messenger to tell the people that they refuse to hear and repent. Yet a remnant, like the stump of an oak, will remain with a holy seed in it.

Chapter 7 relates how the prophet challenged the king of Judah to trust in God instead of the military power of Assyria. Ahaz's refusal to agree by asking for a sign prompts the prophecy of a virgin who gives birth to a son named Immanuel ("God with us") and the coming destruction of the nations that threaten the king, as well as Judah's close escape from the destruction of Assyria. In chapter 8, Isaiah fathers Maher-shalal-hash-baz, whose name foretells the destruction of Judah's enemies Damascus and Samaria. Isaiah is to keep God's testimony bound up and sealed among his disciples (8:16). So chapter 9 breaks forth with the promise that the first part of the Holy Land to go into exile (the far northern tribes of Zebulun and Naphtali) will also first receive the great light of hope, honor, and the coming of the one who brings worldwide peace. To bring judgment against the northern kingdom (Israel), God uses Assyria. However, they are excessively cruel, and so divine judgment will also come against Assyria.

© Baker Publishing Group and Dr. James C. Martin. The Israel Museum.

Inscription recording the later resting place of King Uzziah's bones

From the line of David will come a son who will have God's sevenfold spirit (11:2). From his judgment will come peace, an end to Judah's enemies, and a return of God's people, who will praise him. Beginning in chapter 13 are a series of prophecies and taunts against Babylon and Babylon's king, who descends into the underworld, and also against Assyria, Philistia, Moab, Damascus, Cush, and Egypt. Amid the oracles, Isaiah is commanded to walk about naked for three years to anticipate the destruction that Assyria will face (Isa. 20). The prophecies return to denounce Babylon, Dumah, Arabia, Jerusalem, and Tyre.

Chapter 24 turns to emphasize God's universal judgment on the whole planet. God will be found in Jerusalem, and his reign will go forth from there. God will bless Jerusalem and exalt it while abasing foreigners and the foreign nations around Israel (Isa. 25). In the following chapter this theme continues, with an exaltation so powerful that even the bodies of the dead will rise again (26:19) and the exiles and captives will return home to Jerusalem (Isa. 27).

As in chapter 1, in chapter 28 the religious leadership is indicted for their corruption. The people of God pass through a time of ignorance until the coming day of understanding and trust in God (Isa. 29). God will bring judgment on the present generation of Israel, but it will be followed by the exaltation of Jerusalem (Isa. 30). Egypt is no help; God himself will fight for Jerusalem and defeat Assyria and all Zion's enemies (Isa. 31). Isaiah 32 speaks of a righteous king who will arise and of an end to folly. The fearful will feel secure, and the land will become fertile. The enemies of Jerusalem will be terrified at the rising of God and his presence (Isa. 33). At the climax of this section is the promise that God will heal and forgive the sins of those who dwell in Jerusalem (33:24).

Isaiah 34 turns to consider the judgment and destruction of Edom as a symbol of all nations who oppose God and his people. In chapter 35 the desert becomes a garden and a place of healing for the redeemed of the Lord to enter Zion.

Isaiah 36 and 37 recount the taunt of the king of Assyria against a besieged Jerusalem, followed by God's promise to King Hezekiah that he will be delivered and that death will come to 185,000 of the besieging Assyrian army. Isaiah 37:38 describes how the king of Assyria's sons kill him in his temple. In chapter 38, Hezekiah suffers an illness and is dying. He appeals to Isaiah and his God, and he is given a sign and a miracle that extends his life. Yet in chapter 39, Hezekiah opens all of his secrets to the emissaries of the king of Babylon. Upon learning of this, Isaiah promises that whatever Hezekiah has shown will one day be taken to Babylon. Hezekiah's selfish satisfaction that there will be peace and security in his days ends the chapters recounting his life (39:8).

In Isaiah 40, a new theme and direction begin. Yahweh will restore Zion/Jerusalem because she has paid double for her sin (40:1–11). This message will bring comfort to those who have suffered, and the prophet is charged with its proclamation. God is creator of all and thus able to carry this plan forward (40:12–31). As all-powerful creator, God has chosen Israel as his servant. He will protect the nation so that none can oppose it any more than the useless idols can oppose God (Isa. 41). The servant of God is a person who will bring about justice just as God the warrior will decide what will come to pass (42:1–13). Despite God's promise to lead and protect the blind and lame, Israel his servant remains opposed to his will and looks to idols instead of trusting in God (42:14–25). God is Israel's redeemer and will bring them back, even though they are scattered to the ends of the earth and even though they have not worshiped him (Isa. 43). The Lord has redeemed Israel by pouring out his spirit on the people and giving the blessing of fertility to the land. Israel will identify with the living God, in contrast to the lies that are idols made from common materials such as a piece of wood, part of which is used for fuel (44:1–21). God has forgiven his people, so he commands the heavens, the earth, the mountains, and the forests to sing for joy, and he calls his people to return to him (44:22–23).

Isaiah 44:24–45:25 reaches a climax in the hymns of God's self-proclamation of his majesty. Repeatedly in this section, he is creator of everything: the world, its people, rebuilt Judah and Jerusalem, light and darkness, prosperity and disaster. In the midst of this praise, God calls the Persian emperor Cyrus by name three times. Cyrus will receive the wealth and dominion of the nations so that he can bring God's people back to a rebuilt Jerusalem and a reestablished temple (44:28; 45:4). When they see God's blessing on Israel, the nations of the world will come to know that the God of Israel alone is God (45:6, 14–15). As he saves and blesses his people, God commands all the ends of the earth to turn to him and find salvation (45:22–25).

While the Babylonian gods Bel and Nebo must be carried on carts when Babylon is captured, God has carried Israel and will deliver the nation from its captivity. God brings his "bird of prey" (i.e., Cyrus; 46:11) from the east to defeat Babylon while he saves Jerusalem and Israel (Isa. 46). God will humiliate Babylon, and it will go into darkness for its pride and sins (Isa. 47). Chapter 48 reviews Israel's sin and God's prior announcements of what would happen. As these things have come true, so now he commands Israel to flee joyfully from Babylon and to announce to the world that God has redeemed his people and brought them water in the desert.

Isaiah 49 begins with the account of the faithful servant called by God but discouraged by lack of success for all the effort invested. The text emphasizes the ways in which Israel will be a light to the nations, and how those nations will bring Israel back to its homeland. Chapter 50 emphasizes the power of God to act on behalf of Israel, despite the abuse suffered by the prophet who proclaims the words of salvation. Nevertheless, the key for the prophet and Israel is to trust God and follow him. Chapter 51 calls Jerusalem and Israel to awaken from the stupor of their sin and judgment, to remember their Creator and Redeemer, whose ancient power will restore and increase the number and prosperity of his people. Isaiah 52 includes a reversal of Jerusalem's fortunes. It rises from the dust and sits on the throne. Those who bring the good news of Jerusalem's return to honor receive encouragement and praise. The people of God must leave their place of exile and return to Zion/Jerusalem.

Isaiah 52:13–53:12 recounts how the exalted servant of the Lord faces suffering and death for the sins of God's people. Beyond his death he will again see life and provide righteousness for many, by bearing their sins willingly and without complaint. Isaiah 54 picks up from chapter 52 as the continued exaltation of Jerusalem is described. The city and people of God will prevail over all opposition. The final chapter in this section (Isa. 55) celebrates the return home, with the promise of a rich banquet. God's word will return to him and effect what he wishes. The joyful return of God's people to Jerusalem and its fruitfulness are signs to all the world that God can be trusted and that his promises will last forever.

Isaiah 56 announces key themes that will dominate the last part of the scroll. The people of God are to act with justice and keep the Sabbath. God will reach out to include those who were formerly despised and unwelcome: eunuchs and foreigners. Nevertheless, Israel has sinned and committed deeds of wickedness that God has punished (Isa. 57). Because the people rebel against God, act proudly before him, and treat one another with contempt, God will not recognize their fasting and Sabbath keeping (Isa. 58). Justice, righteousness, and honesty are missing from God's people. God girds himself with armor of righteousness, salvation, vengeance, and zeal; he will rescue those who repent (Isa. 59). The picture of Isaiah 60 is focused on the light of God, which invites his people to come to him from lands of darkness. God will bless his people with fruitfulness and riches. Chapter 61 begins with the important message of one anointed by God's spirit to proclaim the good news of liberty for prisoners and to comfort those who mourn. Others will do the work for God's people, who will all become priests. God will bless his people, and the nations will recognize this. Isaiah 62 presents images of name changing, marriage, watchers, harvest, and clearing the road of rocks. All of these describe how God will restore and bless his people. As in the ancient warrior poems, God comes from the south, such as from Edom, with his garments stained with the blood of his military victories against the nations (Isa. 63; cf. Exod. 15; Deut. 33; Judg. 5; Ps. 68; Hab. 3). Even though God helped his people, they have rebelled against him, and now enemies have again occupied God's sanctuary and destroyed it (Isa. 64). God distinguishes between some of his people who worship all sorts of images and practice idolatrous sins, and those who follow him. The former are judged and destroyed. The latter are blessed and given all good things in the new heavens and earth that God will create (Isa. 65). God is God of the heavens and earth. He will not accept the sacrifices of those who rebel but will judge them. Yet to all nations, God will extend peace and the opportunity to come and worship him. Even people from distant lands and islands will come to Jerusalem and the temple, where God will select some of them to be priests and Levites (Isa. 66).

Reading Isaiah

Premodern Readings

The book of Isaiah is one of the most widely read and used books in the Old Testament.[1] Therefore the history of its interpretation will be given

1. Cf., e.g., Wilken, Christman, and Hollerich, *Isaiah Interpreted by Early Christian and Medieval Commentators.*

more consideration than usual. In the translation of Isaiah, the Septuagint has changed declarative statements into commands, thus forming Isaiah into an instructional text.[2] *Targum Isaiah* recognizes descriptions of the messiah in Isaiah 9; 11; 52:13–53:12; and other texts. Pre-Christian writings such as Sirach (48:17–25) set Isaiah in the context of the history of Hezekiah (as in Isa. 36–39) and recognize Isaiah's role as a prophet of the future, to comfort those who have mourned. The *Martyrdom of Isaiah* recounts the story of the prophet's death when King Manasseh physically sawed the prophet apart. The Babylonian Talmud recognizes Isaiah's role as a lawgiver comparable to Moses (*Makkot* 24a).[3]

In the second century, Justin Martyr uses the prophecies of Isaiah to condemn the Jews of his own day. He intertwines both literal and typological fulfillments of Isaiah's prophecies. Thus the Suffering Servant of Isaiah 53 foretells Jesus's suffering and death and also typifies the Passover lamb, who was killed.[4] Irenaeus (late second century) is important because he places a greater emphasis on the Bible's role in salvation history. Here the Bible articulates God's single plan to bring salvation through Jesus Christ. Eschatologically, many appeals to Isaiah serve to interpret the final end of this plan. Tied to this emphasis is the importance of Jesus as fulfilling the Old Testament. Thus in Isaiah 7:14, Irenaeus recognizes the miracle of the virgin birth of Jesus while also confessing the full humanity of a child born from his mother. Clement of Alexandria, contemporary of Irenaeus, uses Isaiah 7:9 as a justification of the need to accept by faith the reality of the world around us. Origen (ca. 200) attempts to appreciate the literal meaning of the text before guiding it to the spiritual meaning that would have value for his hearers. Thus the significance of Uzziah (Isa. 6:1) is informed by the summary of his reign in 2 Chronicles 26:16–21.

Origen wrote the first-known Christian commentary on Isaiah, but Eusebius of Caesarea (writing in the early fourth century) wrote the earliest commentary on Isaiah that is extant today. For Eusebius, the primary emphasis of the book of Isaiah (indicated in 2:2–4 and traced through 66:18–23) lies in the revelation of salvation for all the world, which leads to all nations gathering to God at his temple in Jerusalem. The salvation of all peoples comes about as God considers a new plan after Israel's disobedience and rejection of his covenant. In contrast to earlier Christian writers who saw in the reference to Cyrus as the anointed one a means of addressing Jesus Christ, Eusebius understands Isaiah 44:21–45:23 as God's choice of the historical figure of Cyrus as his servant. He follows the Jewish historian Josephus in the view that the Jews showed Cyrus this prophecy in the sixth century BC.

2. Schultz, "Isaiah," 194–96.
3. Hays, "Isaiah," 404–7.
4. For this and subsequent interpreters, see Childs, *Struggle to Understand Isaiah*.

More than his predecessors, Jerome, in his early fifth-century commentary, emphasizes a close study and translation of the Hebrew text, as well as the Greek (LXX). Thus in Isaiah 7:14 the disputed translation of the Hebrew *ʿalmâ* as "virgin" should be understood as a "concealed/hidden-away virgin." Jerome studies the historical and cultural context of the book and at times faults his predecessors for shaping their interpretation to correspond to the spiritual reality they seek. At about the same time as Jerome, John Chrysostom wrote his commentary on Isaiah, of which the first eight chapters remain. For Chrysostom, God condescended to Isaiah's level of perception in Isaiah 6. While Chrysostom believed that the prophetic revelation increased in detail as time went on, he also applied the indictments of Isaiah directly to the vices of his own day.

The following generation finds Cyril of Alexandria writing with a strong appreciation of the historical background and with a sensitivity to what the Isaiah text is doing. For example, the beginning of chapter 5 forms a title or summary statement for the Song of the Vineyard. Beyond this, there is a typological application to Christ. The Suffering Servant of Isaiah 52:13–53:12 is a depiction of the passion of Christ as found in the Gospels. Yet further advanced is the Holy Spirit's gift of a vision that finds the Old Testament fulfilled in the New Testament. Theodoret of Cyrus, writing in the fifth century, also seeks to provide much historical background for texts such as Isaiah 36–39. He moves back and forth between historical contexts, such as the prophet's condemnation of Israel and the experience of Christ's condemnation. The typological interpretation of a text like Isaiah 32 comes when it cannot be applied to any earlier historical ruler from Jerusalem. Only Jesus Christ fulfills what is required.

Well into the Middle Ages, the thirteenth-century scholar Thomas Aquinas affirms the historical basis of texts found in Isaiah 7, 9, and 11. Often he presents the Jewish interpretation, the application to contemporary history, and the typological interpretation of the patristic age wherein there is an application to Christ. He opts for this latter approach and argues against the others. Thomas Aquinas possesses an ability to move back and forth between the historical approach and the application to Jesus Christ. In Isaiah 53, however, he reads the entire chapter in light of Jesus Christ's passion. Nicholas of Lyra follows in this tradition. However, he makes use of the commentary of the great Jewish scholar Rashi (1040–1105) to aid in understanding the plain sense of the biblical text. For the traditional messianic texts of Isaiah 7, 8, 9, and 11, Nicholas rejects any historical interpretation contemporary with the prophet. Rather, these all apply only to Jesus Christ.

Alongside Rashi, the other major medieval Jewish commentator on the book of Isaiah was Ibn Ezra (1089–1164). This scholar was the first to question whether Isaiah 40 and the second half of the book were tied to the first part. Ibn Ezra suggested a second author wrote this part of the book in the sixth century BC, at the time of King Cyrus of Persia.[5]

The Reformer Martin Luther sought to join the literal sense of Scripture with an application of much of Isaiah to Jesus Christ. Luther finds contrasts between the earthly and spiritual kingdoms. The first occurs in Isaiah 1, where the law brings sin and death. The second begins Isaiah 2, where the realization of the grace brought by Christ gives life and salvation. Isaiah 40 begins with the comfort that the announcement of the gospel brings. The life and salvation that Christ gives are variously portrayed in the remaining chapters. Like Luther, John Calvin (1509–64) worked with the Hebrew text. He was conscious of wordplays and literary devices known only from the original language. Yet his understanding was conditioned by context and usage as much as by the mere definition of a particular word. For Calvin, the prophecies of Isaiah address not only a single event but also the entire future work of God in human history. He finds the New Testament fulfillment of Isaiah's prophecies occurring in different ways, preserving the substance rather than the letter of the Hebrew text. Calvin constructs a biblical theology from his doctrine of salvation. These doctrines, found already in Isaiah and the remainder of the Old Testament, are gracious gifts of God that lead to the meaning of joy and contentment in life (Isa. 8:20).

In the period following the Reformation, the study of Isaiah took many turns. For example, Johannes Cocceius applied Isaiah texts to figures of his own time, implying that he recognized a recurring eschatological pattern of God's faithfulness and of human fallibility. Robert Lowth (1710–87) recognized Isaiah as a book of poetry as well as prophecy. Finally, there is Franz Delitzsch (1813–90), with four editions of his commentary. Isaiah enabled Delitzsch to combine his Christian faith, his study of Judaism and the Masoretic Text, and his appreciation of beauty and art. Thus Delitzsch produced one of the great commentaries of the period. In his fourth and final edition, he ventured to identify a second writer for chapters 40–66, yet he never changed from seeing the whole work as that of a single spirit, the original prophet Isaiah. For him, Isaiah 52:13–53:12 must describe the suffering of an individual (not a group or nation), namely, the suffering and resurrection of Jesus Christ. The goal of God's Word, including Isaiah, finds its meaning in Jesus Christ.

Higher Criticism

Of the many issues that critics have addressed regarding the work known as Isaiah, none has been more widely addressed than the division of the work into three parts, written over a period of more than 150 years. The awareness of (1) different theological emphases, (2) different vocabulary and phrasing,

5. Hays, "Isaiah," 405.

and (3) a change of addressee from those in eighth-century Judah to those in sixth-century exile led Bernhard Duhm to conclude in his 1892 commentary that much of Isaiah 1–39 (First Isaiah) was composed close to the time of the eighth century. Chapters 40–55 (given the name Second Isaiah) originated in the mid-sixth century BC, when Judah was in exile and looked to the rising star of Cyrus of Persia to change their fate. The remaining section (Isa. 56–66, called Third Isaiah) then dates from the period after the exile.[6] Some parts from the first half of the book were also written centuries later, according to Duhm. He identified chapters 24–27 as apocalyptic (see the chapter on Daniel, below) and dated their composition to the late second century BC. Although such a scenario is no longer viable, not least because the composition of the Isaiah scrolls from Qumran date close to this late date, critical scholars until the present time have accepted the basic elements of Duhm's theory.

The composition of the book has prompted a long and complex discussion, with little agreement beyond the obvious outlines.[7] Even regarding those outlines there is disagreement and ongoing discussion. On the one hand, increased skepticism regarding the historical value of texts that portray the faithfulness of Hezekiah (Isa. 36–38) has led to the view that these chapters were composed with a theological emphasis only in the time of Josiah or later, in order to confirm a belief in Jerusalem as protected by God and never to fall.[8] On the other hand, the literary connections between chapters 1–39 and 40–55 have caused others to find in Second Isaiah the editor and redactor of First Isaiah.[9]

It is not unreasonable to assume that, as with Neo-Assyrian prophetic oracles from the same period, First Isaiah recorded many of the oracles individually or in smaller collections and then combined them through editing onto a larger scroll.[10] Perhaps the Isaiah scroll was used at least as early as the Persian period in the training of Jewish scribes to understand the historical and prophetic panorama of God's dealings with his people.[11]

Thus there is little agreement about the construction of the book called Isaiah. Where a significant amount of consensus has emerged, however, is in the movement to recognize the literary construction of the book as virtually filled with interlocking themes and ideas that occur throughout the book's sixty-six chapters. The data gathered supports and at times makes use of the same evidence garnered by the precritical understanding of Isaiah's unity. Nevertheless, scholars still work on defining multiple redactional layers in Isaiah 56–66. However, others are prepared to recognize a single prophet who

6. Duhm, *Jesaia*.
7. Cf., e.g., Hayes, John, and Irvine, *Isaiah, the Eighth Century Prophet*.
8. Clements, *Isaiah and the Deliverance*.
9. Williamson, *Book Called Isaiah*.
10. Jong, *Isaiah among the Ancient Near Eastern Prophets*.
11. Van der Toorn, *Scribal Culture*, 102–3.

could have authored chapters 40–66.[12] Those who continue to divide the text do so using general criteria about the supposed concerns of later editors and redactors, and these general criteria are considered sufficient to divide verses and phrases and to assign them to different authors, editors, and periods.[13] To the observer, the element of subjectivity overwhelms "science."

A key reason (though not the only one) behind critics' decisions to recognize a later writer for Isaiah 40–55 (or 40–66) lies in the threefold naming of Cyrus, king of Persia (44:28; 45:1, 13), who overthrew the Babylonian Empire and allowed the Jews to return and rebuild Jerusalem and its temple. These events occurred in 539 BC and the following decades. The assumption that a prophet in the eighth century BC would name a king who would rule a century and a half later has been rejected by critics as fanciful. Yet perhaps even in the eighth century (or early seventh century), Judeans may have known of the name Cyrus among rulers in the east. A grandfather of the emperor also ruled in Iran under the name of Cyrus, and an earlier Cyrus ruled around 646. Still earlier Cyruses may have ruled in Iran.[14] Given these facts, it is no longer possible to assume that an early Persian leader named Cyrus was necessarily unknown to Isaiah.

Literary Readings

Few areas in the study of Isaiah have enjoyed as much attention as the emphasis on the literary form of the work and interconnections between verses. Various scholars have noticed the relationship between history and prophecy, whether viewing it as alternating, symmetrical, or chiastic.[15]

The literary connection of Isaiah 1–39 and 40–66 has long been recognized. Writing in 1993, Richard Clifford could already identify six others who were researching in this area, stressing the unity of the book of Isaiah.[16] Many of these observe the movement from the Assyrian adversary to the Babylonian ally, who will become an adversary in chapters 36–39. This ends the first part of the book with the prophecy that the Babylonians will confiscate and deport the property and descendants of Hezekiah's dynasty (39:5–8). As a natural connection to chapters 40–55 and the comfort theme, this prepares for the return from the exile (at least in part) caused by Babylon. So closely related are these concerns that some scholars place the major literary division between chapters 33 and 34, rather than chapters 39 and 40.[17] There is

12. For multiple redactions, see Stromberg, "Isaiah 61:1–3." For the unity of Second and Third Isaiah, see Hays, "Isaiah," 398.

13. See the examples cited by Schultz, "Isaiah, Isaiahs," 254–57.

14. Kitchen, *Reliability*, 380.

15. Schultz, "Isaiah," 198.

16. Clifford, "Unity of the Book of Isaiah," 1.

17. So Sweeney, *TANAK*, 270–72. This earlier division may also be supported by the three lines of empty space dividing Isa. 33 and 34 in 1QIsa[a] (*Great Isaiah Scroll*), among the Dead Sea Scrolls.

similar vocabulary bridging chapters 1–39 and chapter 40. For example, the same word for "comfort" appears in 12:1 and in 40:1. "Guilt/iniquity" in 1:4 recurs in 40:2. Clifford also suggests that the divine council of Isaiah 6 appears again in 40:1–11.

Hugh Williamson develops this connection in some detail by arguing that Second Isaiah was influenced by Isaiah of Jerusalem (author of Isa. 1–33). Williamson regards the latter's book as sealed until the day of salvation, when Second Isaiah's audience lived (Isa. 8); thus the whole chronological sequence demonstrates "earlier and continuing ways of God with Israel."[18] Williamson notices Hezekiah's observation at the end of chapter 39: "There will be peace and security in my days." It anticipates the refrain, "There is no peace, says the LORD/my God, for the wicked." This divides the whole of chapters 40–66 into three equal parts (48:22; 57:21; cf. also 66:24). Isaiah 33:7–8 provides the negative background that 40:1–11 will remedy.[19]

Clifford argues that chapters 40–55 form the center of the book and that this center develops themes about Zion: the exodus has Zion as its goal, creation language also describes the building of Zion, and Cyrus as Yahweh's king builds Zion. This develops the key theme of Zion's exaltation (e.g., 2:1–4) in the first part of Isaiah and anticipates Isaiah 55–66 (e.g., 65:17–18), where creation language is again applied to Zion.

Barry Webb, followed by Richard Schultz, finds major literary themes connecting the work of Isaiah.[20] First, the title of 1:1 emphasizes that what follows is the vision of Isaiah, given by God, and that in some sense this includes the whole of the book. Isaiah 1:1–2:4 provides a connection with the last four chapters of the book. There are complementary emphases on the heavens and earth, on the glorification of Zion, and on God's people as rebels. God's judgment on Jerusalem in chapters 1–5 contrasts with the city's exaltation in 2:1–5 and 4:2–6. The prophet's call (Isa. 6) anticipates his first mission, that of asking King Ahaz to trust not in Assyria but in God (Isa. 7–11). Ahaz's refusal anticipates the warning of trusting Egypt (Isa. 28–33) and the example of King Hezekiah's trust in God (Isa. 36–39). The oracles against the nations address first the premier political power of the ancient Near East: Babylon and its king (13:1–14:23). At the end of these prophecies, the bookend is Tyre (Isa. 23), the great economic power of the age. The mythic imagery employed to portray the downfall of Tyre's king symbolizes the opposition of human power structures to God. God's wrath against the pride of the nations continues as the literary connection with chapters 24–27. Here the theme is generalized and projected onto a universal rule of God, with judgment as well as banqueting and the end of death (25:6–8; 26:19–27:1). As noted, the

18. Williamson, *Book Called Isaiah*, 240–41.

19. Ibid., 234.

20. Webb, "Zion in Transformation"; idem, *Message of Isaiah*; Schultz, "Isaiah," 198–204.

prophecies beginning with "Woe" in Isaiah 28–33 (NIV) form a parallel to Isaiah 7–11. Here Egypt and its failure correspond to that of Assyria as an object of misplaced trust.

Isaiah 34–35 announces God's assurance of Zion's (Jerusalem's) final victory. Edom in chapter 34 serves the same role as Babylon in chapters 13–14, a symbol of human pride in opposition to God. The themes and motifs in chapter 35 virtually all recur with the same vocabulary in chapters 40–55. Thus these chapters serve to introduce the second part of the book.[21] The negative judgment of chapter 34 and the positive blessing of chapter 35 are verbally interconnected: desert and garden, streams, jackals, passing through, and journeys or their lack. The historical accounts of the life of Hezekiah in the following chapters (Isa. 36–39) provide a specific example of God's victory over proud Assyria and its ruler. The city under siege in Isaiah 1:8 is the Jerusalem of Hezekiah in Isaiah 36–37. The historical and thematic connections with chapters 40–66 have already been identified.

Beginning with the comfort of Jerusalem, the themes of chapters 40–48 are almost all found in chapter 40. These include the futility of idols, God's return of his people to Jerusalem, the transforming Word of God, and the creator God above all. The themes of God's Servant and of the call of Cyrus are introduced in the following chapters. Although the Servant is not Cyrus and will not take the path of violence (41:2, 25 vs. 42:2–3), both "are called in righteousness (41:2; 42:6), called by name (45:4; 49:1), grasped by the hand (45:1; 42:6), and will accomplish God's will (44:28; 53:10 . . .)."[22]

Isaiah 49–57 emphasizes the role of the Servant as one who will deliver the people. Three passages of the Servant's calling, suffering, and glorification (49:1–13; 50:4–11; 52:13–53:12) interweave with three that address Zion's current state and coming role and exaltation (49:14–50:3; 51:1–52:12; 54:1–17). Schultz observes that, throughout the rest of the book after Isaiah 53, the plural "servants" occurs eleven times, but the singular does not again appear.[23] The results of the vicarious suffering and death of the Suffering Servant have now passed on to the servants of God, conveying the call to live this new life. Thus chapter 54 calls on Jerusalem to rejoice. Chapter 55 invites all who are thirsty and hungry to eat and drink. Chapter 56 instructs on how to live in this new salvation, and who will live there, while chapter 57 warns against the sins of the past.

Isaiah 58–66 begins and ends with warnings against those who refuse God's plan. Yet the heart of this final section looks into the future, describing the worldwide glory of God and Zion (58:8; 59:19; 60:1–2, 13; 61:6; 62:2; 66:11–12, 18–19), the vengeance of Warrior God (59:12–20; 63:1–6), foreigners rebuilding

21. In addition to the note on Sweeney and 1QIsa[a] above, see also the two-volume commentary of John Watts, who ends vol. 1 with Isa. 33: *Isaiah 1–33*.

22. Schultz, "Isaiah," 203.

23. Ibid.

Zion (60:1–22), mourners being welcomed to the covenant (61:1–3, 8–9), and the gathering of all nations to worship God (66:18–23).[24]

Gender and Ideological Criticism

Two women play roles in the early chapters of Isaiah: the prophetess who bears Isaiah the child named Maher-shalal-hash-baz, a symbol of the judgment coming soon against Damascus and Samaria (8:1–5); and the other, famous "young woman," who appears in 7:14. There it is foretold that she will conceive and give birth to a child, to be named Immanuel. The controversy regards the Hebrew term *ʿalmâ* and whether it refers to a virgin. Of the eight other occurrences of this term in the Bible, six (1 Chron. 15:20; Ps. 46 title; Ps. 68:25 [68:26 MT]; Prov. 30:19; Song 1:3; 6:8) are unclear. In Genesis 24:43 Abraham's servant searches for an *ʿalmâ* as a wife for Isaac, presumably a virgin. The same seems to be the case in Exodus 2:8, where the sister of Moses is so identified. For the quotation of Isaiah 7:14 in Matthew 1:23, the apostle made use of the Greek (LXX), which renders Hebrew *ʿalmâ* with the Greek *parthenos*, a word that generally means "virgin."

Another important area is the feminine imagery of God that appears in the second half of the book. In Isaiah 42:14 God speaks and describes himself like a woman in childbirth, gasping and panting for what is going to happen. Isaiah 46:3–4 uses the image of the belly and womb to describe Israel's origin and how God has "upheld" and "carried" the nation. In 49:14–15 God's compassion in remembering the needs of Zion is compared to a mother not able to forget the baby at her breast, the child to whom she has given birth. In Isaiah 66:13 God compares the comfort a mother gives her child to how he will comfort Jerusalem. The picture emerges of God showing eagerness, compassion, and concern toward his people in a manner that is as strong as and stronger than a woman giving birth and caring for a child she loves.

The story of Philip's explanation to the Ethiopian eunuch who was reading from Isaiah 53 (Acts 8:26–39) nicely introduces a consideration of ideology and application of the text in Africa. Victor Zinkuratire finds many similarities between the sociopolitical world of Isaiah 1–39 and his own world of East Africa.[25] There is the dissolution of family and kinship connections and the movement toward the greater acquisition of wealth at the expense of the poor. This goes hand in hand with a retreat from the worship of Yahweh.

The devastation of Israel in Isaiah 1:5–9, perhaps set in the time of the Assyrian king Sennacherib's invasion, may be likened to war-torn Africa, a continent that is sick and bleeding from war. When Zinkuratire turns to

24. Ibid., 203–4.
25. Zinkuratire, "Isaiah 1–39."

1:10–17 and its condemnation of the rich who exploit the poor, he compares this to wealthy churchgoers who attend nice churches and give generously but do not abolish the patterns of injustice in their societies and thus where they work. The transformation of 1:18–20 and the opportunity for blessing depends on the willingness of the leaders and people of 1:16–17 to abandon their abuse of the weak and poor and to treat them with love and respect.

In Isaiah 5:1–7, the picture of Israel as a destroyed vineyard ends with the absence of justice. The consequences of the social and moral crimes are war and devastation. All this loss of food and land has occurred in countries such as Uganda, where the leaders' greed has destroyed the prosperity and lives of many.

Isaiah 2:2–5 brings the hope of international peace and prosperity, a new world order. It represents the manner in which the texts of hope interweave with those of judgment (the result of a later redactor, in Zinkuratire's opinion). The hope and rehabilitation of Zion and God's people in Isaiah 34 include both spiritual transformation and the physical blessings of providing for basic human needs. It is the promotion of this latter element that remains the greatest challenge for the church of East Africa, according to Zinkuratire.

Ancient Near Eastern Context

The book of Isaiah addresses three major historical events: the Syro-Ephraimite War of 734–731 BC, the invasion of the Assyrian king Sennacherib (705–681 BC), and the coming of Cyrus (539–530 BC) as Persian emperor.

Isaiah 7:1–11 recounts how Ahaz was then the reigning king in Jerusalem and Judah. Pekah reigned in the northern kingdom (Israel), and Rezin was king over Damascus and Aram, to the northeast. Ahaz had become king in 735 BC, and a threat arose from these northern neighbors of Ahaz, probably leading to their invasions in 736 and 735 BC.[26] Partly because of Judah's occupation of Gilead under Ahaz's father—but mainly due to Ahaz's own refusal to join Israel, Aram, and other nations in resisting the Assyrian juggernaut from the north—Ahaz's northern neighbors sought to attack Jerusalem and to replace Ahaz with the son of Tabeel, probably a relative of Ahaz who was connected with a region east of the Jordan River. Rezin and Pekah invaded Judah and besieged Jerusalem (2 Kings 16:5). Although they took many prisoners (2 Chron. 28:5–8), they could not capture Ahaz. Nevertheless, the devastation was significant. Rezin assisted the Edomites in recovering cities (Elath) and lands to the south of Judah (2 Kings 16:6). So Edom attacked Judah and carried off captives in the south, as the Philistines attacked and captured cities in the western territories of Judah (2 Chron. 28:17–18).

26. For this and the following details, see Rainey in Rainey and Notley, *Sacred Bridge*, 227–33; Richter, "Eighth-Century Issues," 337–49.

Assyrian record of King Sennacherib's campaigns, including the third campaign against city-states that included Jerusalem

At this time the king of Assyria was Tiglath-pileser III (744–727 BC).[27] After being preoccupied with other threats to his kingdom for two years, in 734 BC Tiglath-pileser III turned his attention to the eastern Mediterranean seaboard. The alliance between Israel, Aram, and Tyre was a threat that could not stand in the midst of imperial designs that sought to expand Assyrian influence southward to Egypt. By reducing Tyre and Gaza, the campaigns of that year opened the way to Egypt. In 733 and 732 BC, Tiglath-pileser III turned his attention to Israel and Damascus. Both 2 Kings 15:29 and the inscriptions of Tiglath-pileser III confirm that he conquered the territory of the Galilee, all of northern Israel. By 733 Assyria had conquered all of Rezin's territory, with only the capital of Damascus resisting. The following year Damascus itself was captured. Pekah's assassination in 732 BC led to Hoshea's possession of the throne of Israel (2 Kings 15:30). In 722 BC the Assyrian king (by that time it was Shalmaneser V) imprisoned Hoshea, captured Samaria, and deported its population. As promised by Isaiah, of the three kingdoms (Judah, Israel, Aram), only Judah would remain independent, with Ahaz and the dynasty of David continuing on the throne.

The second historical incident is the invasion of Judah by the Assyrian king Sennacherib (705–681 BC). In 701 BC Sennacherib turned to Judah and Jerusalem; under the leadership of King Hezekiah, Judah had not paid Sennacherib the tribute that he demanded. Hezekiah led a coalition of Levantine city-states that had revolted against Sennacherib. West of the kingdom of Judah lies the old Philistine city of Ekron. Ekron's king, Padi, remained loyal to Assyria, but the rest of the leadership revolted. They handed their king over to Hezekiah to be placed in chains in Jerusalem because Padi advocated loyalty to the Assyrians.

Sennacherib recorded his campaign against the Levantine coast and Jerusalem on a text written just one year after the event. Two other texts were composed ten and twelve years after the campaign. They describe how he

27. Richter, "Eighth-Century Issues," 337–49. Cf. Tadmor and Yamada, *Royal Inscriptions*, for primary sources and translations.

Siloam Tunnel and Inscription

The Siloam inscription, discovered in 1880, was positioned in an ancient water tunnel for carrying water beneath Jerusalem, which was built on a hill known today as the City of David. Although this was not the highest hill in the area, it possessed a carstic spring beneath to provide it with water. Named the Gihon (meaning "gusher"), this spring would expel water from beneath the earth at regular intervals and in such quantities to supply the city with more than enough water. The spring was located under the City of David but beyond the main city walls, which were constructed part of the way up the hill. Long before David acquired the city, large towers had been built to guard the spring. However, as a way to prepare for the Assyrian king Sennacherib's invasion in 701 BC, King Hezekiah ordered that access to the spring be blocked in the Kidron Valley and that the Siloam tunnel be constructed to channel water from the spring to where it could be accessed safely during a siege (2 Kings 20:20; 2 Chron. 32:4, 30; cf. 33:14). The inscription is on the tunnel wall about twenty feet from the Siloam pool to which the waters were directed. The scribe wrote it in a script that can be dated to about 700 BC. It describes the building of the tunnel as the diggers began at each end and approached, until they finally heard one another. Eventually they met.

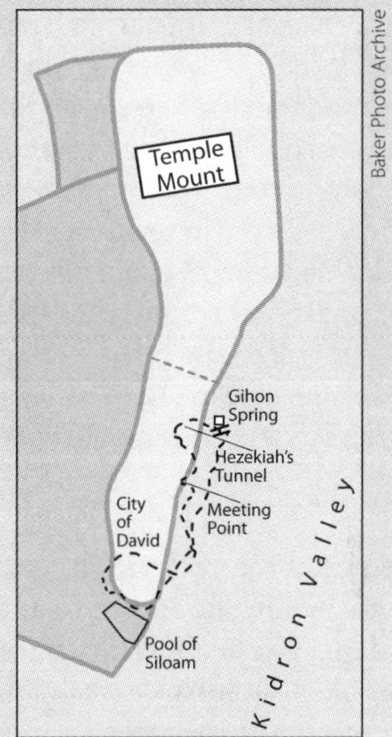

Baker Photo Archive

Jerusalem in 701 BC

© Baker Publishing Group and Dr. James C. Martin

Tunnel built by Hezekiah's servants for access to water during Assyrian siege

defeated the king of Tyre, a leading member of the rebellious coalition. With that king dead, many other city leaders in the region submitted. Sennacherib won a battle against Egyptian forces at Eltekah, a town probably near the coastal highway, west of Jerusalem. Sennacherib then took Ekron and

Hezekiah's Wine and Oil Provisions for the Siege of Jerusalem

Well over 1,700 jars to hold provisions have been identified, each containing the word *lmlk* ("belonging to the king = royal property"), dating from the period before the invasion of Sennacherib and found throughout Judah, with the largest quantity coming from Jerusalem. The inscriptions contain one of four place names: Hebron, Socoh, Ziph, and an otherwise unidentified *mmšt*. These names, representing royal vineyards (or if the jars contained olive oil, then olive groves) in these different places, identify the origin of the product. These jars were filled with provisions and stored in Jerusalem and other strategic centers in anticipation of the attack by the Assyrian king in 701 BC. In recent years some scholars have identified *lmlk* jars in use after the invasion of Sennacherib.

required that Hezekiah release Padi to be confirmed as king there. Moving into Judah, the Assyrian army destroyed all the fortified towns except Jerusalem. The second-most important city was Lachish. Sennacherib depicted his siege against Lachish and his deportation of the citizens on a major relief that adorned the central section of his palace in Nineveh. Hezekiah had prepared for the Assyrian assault on Jerusalem, making new water tunnels in the expanded city of Jerusalem and storing food and wine in the city and elsewhere. Sennacherib, 2 Kings 18, and Isaiah 36–37 all agree that the Assyrian king did not enter Jerusalem, but he did exact a heavy tribute (e.g., 2 Kings 18:14–16) after destroying virtually the whole of the country.

The third major historical event is the coming of Cyrus (539–530 BC) as Persian emperor. Most readers of Isaiah 44–45 recognize that the role of Cyrus moves readers forward in time by a century and a half to the Persian conquest of Babylon and Cyrus's release of deportees from all nations to return and rebuild their homelands and temples. See further on this in the chapter on Ezra and Nehemiah.

Canonical Context

There are numerous examples where the scroll of Isaiah influences other parts of the Bible and where it draws on Old Testament texts. Some studies have summarized the whole realm of quotations and uses of material from other Old Testament sources. Most valuable for the prophets is Schultz's *Search for Quotation*, some of which is summarized here, along with additional texts in the remainder of the Bible.[28] From Genesis, key references

28. Schultz, *Search for Quotation*, 31–42, 290–329. For the remainder of the Bible, cf. idem, "Isaiah," 204–6.

The Lachish Relief

The Lachish relief was discovered in a central room in Sennacherib's palace in Nineveh, reflecting the importance that the Assyrian king ascribed to the destruction of the Judean city. The relief was transported to the British Museum, where it can be seen today. It provides a wealth of information regarding the Assyrian army, siege and battle techniques, and the Judean people. The destruction of the city resulted in the execution of some of the Judeans, the judgment of others before the throne of the Assyrian king, and the deportation of many citizens of Lachish with their families and those items most valuable to them.

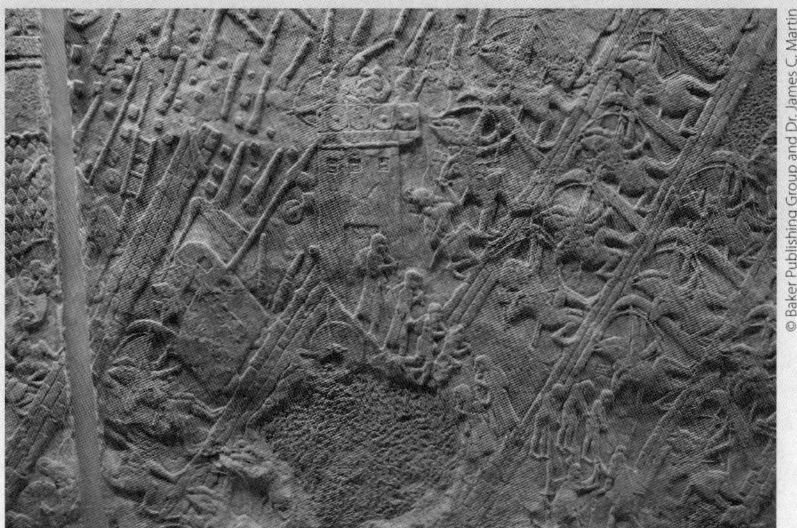

© Baker Publishing Group and Dr. James C. Martin

Assyrian army attacking Judean city of Lachish in 701 BC using siege engines, archers, etc.

to creation are found, most often in Isaiah 40–45 (40:26; 42:5; 45:7, 12, 18), which together constitute a stronger witness to "creation out of nothing" than anywhere else in the Old Testament. The judgments of the flood and of Sodom and Gomorrah (1:9–10; 3:9; 13:19; 24:18; 54:9) appear more frequently in the earlier part of Isaiah.

Isaiah 40–54 is replete with references to the exodus and wilderness journeys, where God challenges Israel to repeat this experience by returning to him in Jerusalem (48:20–21; 51:9–10; 52:11–12; 63:9–13; cf. 11:16). The figures of Joshua and the judges (9:4; 10:26; 28:21) and of David (28:21; 29:1; 37:35; 38:5; 55:3) are mentioned, as well as the division of the monarchy (7:17). Schultz observes that the covenants with Noah (54:9–10), with Abraham and

Jacob (41:8–10; 65:9), with David (9:6–7; 11:1–5, 10; 16:5; 55:3), and at Sinai (4:2–6; 56:1–8) all appear. There is also reference to the new covenant (61:8) as in Jeremiah 31.

Connections with the Historical Books are most obvious in Isaiah 36–39, which duplicates much of 2 Kings 18:13–20:19, except for the unique record of Hezekiah's prayer in Isaiah 38:9–20. See also the historical background of Isaiah 7:1 above (under "Ancient Near Eastern Context," Isa. 7:10–11), which finds a parallel in 2 Kings 16:5. A close verbal parallel is found between Isaiah 2:2–4 and Micah 4:1–3, while other allusions occur in prophets such as Jeremiah.

Some fifty-four of the sixty-six chapters of Isaiah include passages quoted in the New Testament. Whole studies have been devoted to the use of the book of Isaiah.[29] Rikki Watts's examination of Mark's Gospel and David Pao's study of Acts both use Isaiah and the teaching of the new exodus as a basis for the fundamental thematic and theological structuring of these apostolic writings.[30] Jan Fekkes has looked at the book of Revelation and found borrowing from Isaiah in four areas: visionary experience and language, christological titles and descriptions, eschatological judgment, and eschatological salvation.[31] The Suffering Servant of Isaiah 52:13–53:12 has a number of verbal parallels in the New Testament.[32] It bears repeating that the book of Isaiah influenced the New Testament more than any other book of the Old Testament.

Theological Perspectives of Isaiah

The book of Isaiah presents the grand theme of God's plan for his people and for the world. Within its pages are found all that is necessary to understand God's past, present, and future acts of grace. Much of this has been mentioned already, especially in the overview, the literary context, and the canonical context. Here it is sufficient to state the major themes that provide a masterpiece of theological reflection and justify the work's position at the head of the prophetic works as a summary of the entire enterprise. Those themes include God as Creator, God as Judge for sin, God as Redeemer, and God as bringing history to its final conclusion.

The theme of God as Creator appears most clearly in Isaiah 40–45. Creation texts abound in the Old Testament, with some of the most important occurring in Genesis 1–2; Job 38–39; and Psalm 78. However, the emphasis

29. See Moyise and Menken, *Isaiah in the New Testament*.

30. R. Watts, *Isaiah's New Exodus and Mark*; Pao, *Acts and the Isaianic New Exodus*.

31. Fekkes, *Isaiah and Prophetic Traditions*. See also Mathewson, "Isaiah in Revelation."

32. So Nestle et al., *Novum Testamentum Graece*, 860: Matt. 8:17; Luke 22:37; John 12:38; Acts 8:32–33; Rom. 10:16; 15:21; 1 Pet. 2:22, 24–25; Rev. 14:5 (cf. Rom. 4:25; Heb. 9:28; Rev. 5:6, 12; 13:8).

in Isaiah on God as Creator exceeds that in any other book. Of the fifty-four occurrences of the root "to create" (Heb. *bārā'*) in the Old Testament, twenty-one appear in Isaiah. This verb, in the basic (Qal) stem, only ever has God as its subject. Thus God creates the heavens (Isa. 40:26; 42:5; 45:18), the earth (40:28), everyone (45:12), especially God's people Israel (43:1, 7, 15), light and darkness (45:7), and the rain and its fruit (45:8). Outside these six chapters (Isa. 40–45), God has created the blacksmith to forge the weapon, and he has created the destroyer (54:16). He will create smoke and fire to act as a canopy for God's glory on Mount Zion (4:5). This is perhaps one of the new things that God will create and announce (48:7). So God will create a new Jerusalem (65:18) as part of the new heavens and new earth (65:17). As a result he will create praise on the lips of his people (57:19). God's past creation (Isa. 40–45) demonstrates his specific power over all other gods and goddesses and the nations they represent. He can do with them whatever he wants.

Israel needed to hear this message because of their dire circumstances, whether in the days of Ahaz and Hezekiah (Isa. 6–11, 36–39), when the Assyrians threatened to destroy them, or in the days of the rising of Cyrus, when their nation had been destroyed (Isa. 44–45). How could this small and insignificant people ever rise again, especially when they were scattered across the land in the Babylonian exile? Either God is the Creator or he is not. If Isaiah is correct and God did create the world, then it can be under his control, and he can bring about whatever he chooses. So the appointment of the leading conqueror and power of that age, Cyrus and Persia, remains under God's control. God will bring about a good end for his people: the return from exile, the recovery of Jerusalem, and the rebuilding of the temple.

All of this provides the background for what is anticipated in Isaiah 4:5, God's protection and leadership in Zion by the creation of a symbol of his presence resembling the fire and smoke by which he led his people in the wilderness. If God created the world and continues in power over all the nations, then no deity can oppose him, and he has the power to continue to create (48:7). The destruction of Babylon and the exaltation of Jerusalem will happen because God will create whatever is necessary for that to happen, as 57:19 suggests. The four occurrences of "create" in chapters 57 and 65 suggest that the Creator will continue to work until there is a new creation and his people praise him.

The second theme, God's judgment on sin, remains a key theme throughout Isaiah. Unlike with some churches today, where one may attend for a long time without ever hearing the preacher mention sin, Isaiah felt no such restriction to be "positive" and "upbeat." From the opening verses of chapter 1 until the conclusion of the book in 66:24, Isaiah denounces the sins and rebellion of God's people and warns them of judgment. This is most clearly seen in the first half of the book. It only makes sense that there can be no salvation unless there is the need created by sin. So Isaiah begins with iteration and reiteration of the sins of Israel and its leadership (Isa. 1–5). As if to drive the point home, the historical experience of Ahaz's unbelief, in the midst of God's signs and prophecies, illustrates how completely sin has come on the nation, and judgment is certain. Isaiah establishes the pattern for many of the biblical prophets in which the pronouncements against God's people are followed by oracles proclaiming the sin and coming judgment against many other nations of the world (Isa. 13–23). That judgment moves forward with the promised exaltation of Jerusalem (Isa. 24–27) until the prophecies return to address the sins of the people (Isa. 28–33). Even here the judgments against the nations, symbolized by Edom, continue (Isa. 34). The account of Hezekiah (Isa. 36–39) demonstrates a faithful king. However, even the best of those who followed in the dynasty of David cannot avoid pride and self-interest, as chapter 39 demonstrates.

Richard S. Hess

Midianite high place, Timna Valley in Negev, Israel

The comfort and hope of the second half of the book move away from divine judgment. Nevertheless, Babylon certainly stands under God's judgment (Isa. 48), and the Suffering Servant (Isa. 52:13–53:12) suffers and dies for the sins of others. God has punished Israel and will continue to warn them of sins in how they treat one another (Isa. 57–59). Chapter 59 also says that God fights those who oppose his people, a theme that continues in chapter 63. The final two chapters of the book interweave the identification and destruction of the wicked with the choice and blessing of the righteous, now including those of all nations of the world.

The third theme, of God as Redeemer, is a favorite one for New Testament writers. It identifies many of the classic texts from Isaiah. While Isaiah 2:1–4 and 66:1–24 frame the whole book with wonderful images of universal peace and blessing yet to come, the means of salvation is found in the redemption provided by God and especially is found in one who will come. In an early mission of Isaiah (Isa. 7), the prophet meets King Ahaz of Judah and seeks to reassure the king that he and all Jerusalem will be safe from the attacks by the northern kingdom (Israel) and by Aram (Damascus). This, however, depends on Ahaz's faith and willingness to ask for a sign from God. Ahaz refuses to ask.

Nevertheless, Isaiah gives him a sign of one to come, named Immanuel (Heb. for "God with us"). This one will be born of a virgin (KJV, NIV), and well before he grows up, Israel and Aram will be destroyed. Although some relate this to Hezekiah or another child born in Ahaz's day, the New Testament writers apply it to Jesus Christ at his birth (Matt. 1:23). There are a variety of ways in which this sort of prophetic understanding is interpreted by scholars. Many see it as fulfilled (or even "prophesied" after the event) in Isaiah's day, without any further expectation. Others emphasize a double fulfillment of some sort. Thus a child is born in Isaiah's day, and Jesus is born to Mary—both fulfill this event. Some understand the fulfillment as exclusively applied to Jesus. One way to look at the matter is that a figure from the time of Isaiah at least partially fulfills the prophecy. However, the coming of Jesus Christ brings about further fulfillment of the prophecy. Perhaps not so much in Isaiah 7, but sometimes in other prophecies that describe the universal dominion of God's chosen one, the complete fulfillment awaits the future return of Jesus to earth. This approach is sometimes referred to as typological. It establishes a type or category that may be partially fulfilled by someone in Old Testament times but is understood as completely fulfilled by Jesus Christ, in his first and second comings.

Isaiah 9:1–7 is an important thematic text that describes the salvation brought by a future child. The chapter begins by considering the most northern parts of Israel. As the Assyrians first attacked and deported the people there, so these people will be the first to experience the light of freedom and salvation. Matthew 4:15–16 applies this to Jesus's early life and ministry in the region of the Galilee. Isaiah 9:6–7 speaks of a child to come who will be part of David's dynasty and will rule over the world with justice and peace. Titles such as "Mighty God" and "Everlasting Father" suggest a divine aspect to the king, something that is difficult to apply to the Old Testament monarchy in monotheistic Israel.

Isaiah 11:1–5 looks forward to the coming of one in the lineage of David (the son of Jesse), on whom God's spirit will rest in a special way. He will receive wisdom, understanding, counsel, might, knowledge, and fear of the Lord. This describes someone who will take care of the poor and needy and will rule the earth with righteousness.

In the second half of Isaiah, the Servant Songs portray the redemptive efforts of God's chosen one. Isaiah 41:8–10 identifies Israel as God's Servant, especially those people called back from the ends of the earth in order to accomplish the mission God has given to the Servant. The Servant of Isaiah 42:1–4 receives God's spirit but does not cry out. Instead, he walks softly and brings justice to the ends of the world. In Isaiah 42:19 Israel is identified as the blind and deaf servant, despite Israel's choice by God (43:10). Isaiah 44:1–2, 21–22 reaffirms Israel's calling as God's Servant, continues the promise of divine support, and forgives the nation's sins. God calls Cyrus and gives him honor and power for the sake of God's Servant Israel (45:4). In 49:1–4 the Servant is identified as Israel with similar language as before. However, the following three verses identify a Servant distinct from the nation of Israel, as one who will gather Israel back and will restore the tribes of Jacob. Isaiah 50:10 affirms the nature of the Servant as an individual person whom others should trust and obey. The final usage of the singular term "Servant" applies to 52:13–53:12. This looks to an individual who will suffer and die for "our" sins, presumably those of the people of God. Others will cruelly punish the Servant so that his human form is hardly recognizable. The sins of God's people will be forgiven by the Servant's suffering and death. This will bring healing and justification for the people, and "the light of life" (53:11 NIV) beyond death for the Servant. This is the last occurrence of "Servant" in Isaiah. From Isaiah 54–66 the term "servants" appears eleven times to describe the faithful.

God calls forth King Cyrus, who destroys Babylon and encourages the people of God to return to Jerusalem and rebuild the temple there. The Lord designates Cyrus as his "anointed," or his "messiah." The term for "anointed" typically describes those who are designated as king. Its root appears again in Isaiah 61:1, where the figure described combines features of the chosen one of chapters 1–11, the Servant of chapters 40–55, and the messiah. Thus God's spirit anoints this one (11:1–5). He proclaims and acts on behalf of the poor and needy (42:1–4). Finally, this figure is anointed and sent by God (61:1). It is no surprise that Jesus reads from 61:1–2 (and 58:6) in the synagogue and proclaims its fulfillment in himself (Luke 4:17–21). The New Testament recognizes him as the chosen one sent by God to redeem the world.

As a fourth theme, from Isaiah 2:1–4 to the last chapter in the book of Isaiah a recurrent theme is the manner in which God will bring history to its final conclusion. In the themes already identified, God as Judge will judge the peoples of the earth, rewarding the righteous who trust in him and punishing the wicked who do not trust (Isa. 66). God has sent his Servant to accomplish this redemption, which will one day be fully realized (52:13–56:8). In all this, God as Creator will consummate the creation work that he began. The clearest sections that look forward to God accomplishing his will on earth are Isaiah 24–27; 32–33; 40:12–44:23; 49; 54:1–56:8; 60–63; and 65:1–66:23. While these sometimes envision the period of the return from exile, they interweave and blend with visions of the yet-to-come creation of a divinely ruled kingdom of life, peace, and prosperity.

Key Commentaries and Studies

Baltzer, Klaus. *Deutero-Isaiah: A Commentary on Isaiah 40–55*. Translated by Margaret Kohl. Hermeneia. Minneapolis: Fortress, 2001. Strongest on textual criticism for these chapters.

Blenkinsopp, Joseph. *Isaiah: A New Translation with Introduction and Commentary*. Vol. 1, *1–39*. Vol. 2, *40–55*. Vol. 3, *56–66*. AB 19, 19A, 20. New York: Doubleday, 2000–2003. Provides cogent analysis and interpretation of the Hebrew text.

Childs, Brevard S. *Isaiah: A Commentary*. OTL. Louisville: Westminster John Knox, 2001. A fine example of a careful reading of the Hebrew with theological insight and an appreciation of the history of interpretation.

Oswalt, John N. *The Book of Isaiah*. 2 vols. NICOT. Grand Rapids: Eerdmans, 1986–98. Evangelical and insightful in its overall exegesis and exposition of the theological message of the biblical text.

Paul, Shalom M. *Isaiah 40–66: Translation and Commentary*. ECC. Grand Rapids: Eerdmans, 2012. Strong on analysis of the Hebrew text; a good starting point for the study of any of these chapters.

Schultz, Richard L. "Isaiah, Isaiahs, and Current Scholarship." Pages 243–61 in *Do Historical Matters Matter to Faith? A Critical Appraisal of Modern and Postmodern Approaches to Scripture*. Edited by James K. Hoffmeier and Dennis R. Magary. Wheaton: Crossway, 2012. Useful for update on critical issues regarding the book.

Williamson, Hugh G. M. *Isaiah 1–5*. Vol. 1 of *A Critical and Exegetical Commentary on Isaiah 1–27*. ICC. London: T&T Clark, 2006. Strongest on textual criticism and Hebrew analysis for these chapters.

20

JEREMIAH

Have you ever felt that God has put you in a situation where, to be true to him, you need to give up friendships and loyalties that are special to you? Welcome to Jeremiah's club.

Name, Text, and Outline

As with most or all of the Major and Minor Prophets, the name of the book of Jeremiah reflects the name of its prophet. The name Jeremiah means "Yahweh founds." God's establishment of Jeremiah for his difficult mission emerges in the many texts where the prophet confesses how God has called him, despite his unwillingness (Jer. 1, 20).

The Greek (LXX) translation of Jeremiah appears to use a different text from that on which the Hebrew (MT) is based. The Septuagint is one-sixth shorter in terms of the number of words. In addition to some minor differences of word order, the Septuagint positions the prophecies against other nations (Jer. 46–51 MT) at a different place, after 25:13. Among the Dead Sea Scrolls, 4QJer[b] and 4QJer[d] provide examples of a Hebrew text that resembles the Septuagint rather than the Masoretic Text. Although the two editions agree regarding the basic elements of Jeremiah's message, the longer edition is thought by some to have been written later and to emphasize more about the guilt of the nation and the centrality of God in history.[1] However, careful study of the Septuagint finds examples of haplography, scribal errors where

1. Tov, *Textual Criticism*, 288.

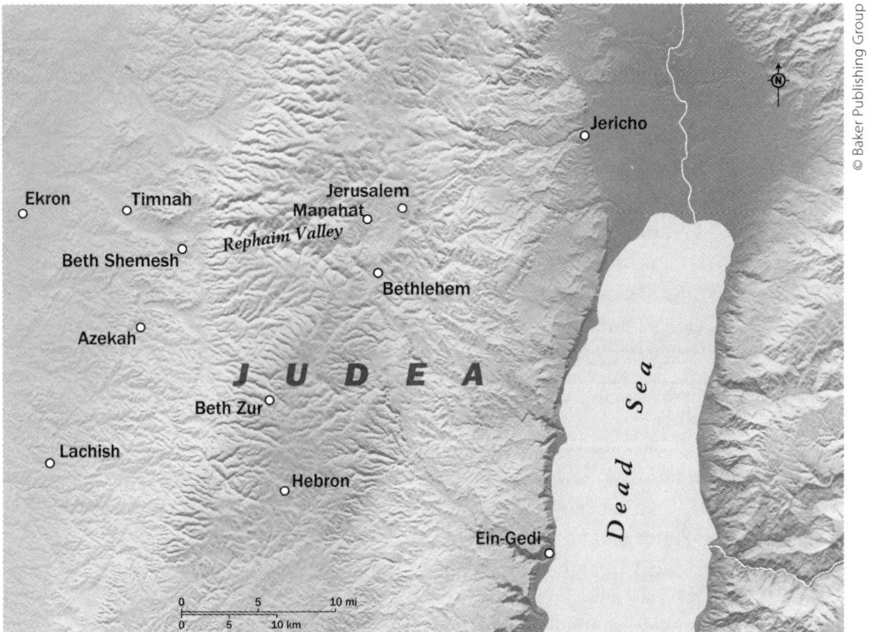

Judah in Jeremiah's day

parts of the text were missed in the copying process.[2] In other words, as the Septuagint translators were translating the Hebrew text in front of them into Greek, their eyes may have skipped some words between two identical Hebrew words. This tradition of two texts existing side by side, a shorter one and one where "many similar words were added," may find a witness in 36:32. Beyond this biblical witness, the precise process by which the two editions came into being is difficult to reconstruct.

OUTLINE

I. Jeremiah's Call as a Prophet (1:1–19)
   A. The Time of His Prophecies (1:1–3)
   B. God's Call to Jeremiah (1:4–19)
II. Prophecies against Judah (2:1–15:21)
   A. Despite Early Obedience, God's People Have Worshiped Other Gods and Acted as an Adulteress (2:1–3:5)
   B. Deported Northern Kingdom Called to Return to God as They Are More Righteous than Judah (3:6–4:4)
   C. Because of Sin, God Brings Judgment from the North (4:5–6:30)
   D. Temple Sermon: Don't Assume God Is on Your Side (7:1–8:3)
   E. Judah's Sin and God's Judgment (8:4–10:25)

2. Walser, *Jeremiah*, 16.

1. Stubbornness and Pride (8:4–12)
2. Judgment from the North (8:13–22)
3. Jeremiah Weeps for His People and Warns Them (9:1–2 [8:23–9:1 MT])
4. Deceit and Stubbornness (9:3–16 [9:2–15 MT])
5. Weeping and Death (9:17–22 [9:16–21 MT])
6. Pride, Not in Self, but in Knowing God (9:23–24 [9:22–23 MT])
7. Nations Face Punishment for Worthless Idols (9:25 [9:24 MT]–10:11)
8. Creator God Judges Judah and the Nations (10:12–25)

F. Covenant Broken (11:1–15:21)
1. Sins of God's People (11:1–23)
2. God's Punishment on Land and People (12:1–17)
3. God Will Destroy Judah's Pride Like a Ruined Loin Cloth (13:1–27)
4. Judgment and Death Are Everywhere, but There Is Redemption for Those Who Repent (14:1–15:21)

III. Response to God's Warning of Judgment (16:1–29:32)
A. Restoration Follows Judgment and Deportation (16:1–21)
B. Don't Trust in People; Show Your Trust in God with the Sabbath (17:1–27)
C. The Potter Illustrates God's Ways with Nations (18:1–17)
D. Jeremiah Threatened and a Prayer for God's Coming Judgment on His Enemies (18:18–23)
E. The Lesson of the Broken Pot (19:1–15)
F. Pashhur the Priest Persecutes Jeremiah and Will Be Judged (20:1–6)
G. Jeremiah's Message Is Not His Own but God's (20:7–18)
H. Judgment on the Kings of God's People (21:1–23:8)
1. Zedekiah (21:1–14)
2. The Remaining Kings Promised and Warned (22:1–10)
3. Shallum (Jehoahaz) (22:11–17)
4. Jehoiakim (22:18–23)
5. Jehoiachin (22:24–30)
6. The Coming King (23:1–8)

I. Judgment on the False Prophets (23:9–40)
J. Good and Bad Figs (24:1–10)
K. National and International Future (25:1–38)
L. The Priests and Leaders Seek to Kill Jeremiah (26:1–24)
M. Jeremiah's Yoke and Hananiah's False Prophecy (27:1–28:17)
N. Jeremiah's Letter to the Exiles (29:1–32)

IV. The New Covenant (30:1–33:26)
A. Sin Demands Judgment (30:1–24)
B. God Restores His People with a New Covenant (31:1–30)
C. The New Covenant (31:31–40)
D. Jeremiah Purchases Land for the Future (32:1–44)
E. God Will Restore the Fortunes of the Land (33:1–26)

V. The Last Days of Jerusalem (34:1–39:18)
A. Temporary Release of Slaves; Promises Broken (34:1–22)
B. The Rechabites; Promises Kept (35:1–19)

- C. Jehoiakim Attacks God's Word, but It Endures (36:1–32)
- D. Jeremiah Imprisoned but Still Warns Zedekiah (37:1–21)
- E. Ebed-melek Rescues Jeremiah, Who Warns Zedekiah (38:1–28)
- F. Babylonian Destruction of Jerusalem and Zedekiah (39:1–10)
- G. Salvation for Jeremiah and Ebed-melek (39:11–18)

VI. The Fate of Those Left in the Land (40:1–45:5)

- A. Jeremiah Chooses to Stay with Gedaliah at Mizpah (40:1–6)
- B. Gedaliah Becomes Governor and Gathers Those Left in the Land (40:7–16)
- C. Gedaliah Is Assassinated, and a Remnant Flees to Egypt (41:1–18)
- D. Jeremiah Is Asked and Tells the People to Remain in the Land (42:1–22)
- E. The People Disobey God's Word and Go to Egypt (43:1–7)
- F. Jeremiah Proclaims Judgment against Egypt (43:8–13)
- G. Nothing Has Changed: Despite Jeremiah's Warning, the People Practice Idolatry in Egypt (44:1–30)
- H. Jeremiah's Scribe Baruch Is Warned against Pride and Promised His Life (45:1–5)

VII. Prophecies against Other Nations (46:1–51:64)

- A. Egypt (46:1–28)
- B. Philistia (47:1–7)
- C. Moab (48:1–47)
- D. Ammon (49:1–6)
- E. Edom (49:7–22)
- F. Damascus (49:23–27)
- G. Kedar and Hazor (49:28–33)
- H. Elam (49:34–39)
- I. Babylon (50:1–51:64)

VIII. Fall of Jerusalem and Babylonian Captivity (52:1–34)

- A. King Zedekiah's Reign and Imprisonment (52:1–11)
- B. Destruction of the Temple and Deportation of the People (52:12–30)
- C. King Jehoiachin's Freedom from Prison in Babylon (52:31–34)

Overview of Jeremiah

Jeremiah first receives the word of the Lord in the thirteenth year of the reign of Josiah, about 627 BC, and continues to prophesy until after the destruction of Jerusalem and its temple (586 BC) and into the following months of the period known as the exile (Jer. 1:1–3). God calls Jeremiah, despite his protests that he is inexperienced, to uproot and destroy, but also to build and plant. Visions of an almond tree and of a boiling pot from the north enable God to describe how he will fulfill his word to bring judgment on his people (1:4–19). Following is a series of prophecies in which God remembers how Israel followed God when he led his people through the wilderness (2:1–3). However, Israel of old also worshiped idols and corrupted the land that God gave them. Using images of adultery and idolatry, God indicts Israel for its disobedience (2:4–3:5). Although God has judged the northern kingdom (Israel), they are more righteous than Judah, who has not learned its lesson (3:6–4:4). God has seen the sin of his people and their refusal to repent. Therefore he is sending upon them destruction from the north (4:5–6:30).

The Temple Sermon of Jeremiah 7:1–8:3 accuses the Judeans for trusting that God is on their side and will protect them no matter how they live or what they do. The charges continue despite Jeremiah's personal grief for his fellow citizens. Judgment is coming against faithless Judah but also will include other nations and their false idols (8:4–10:25). The prophecies turn to consider the many ways in which the Judeans are violating God's covenant: idolatries, lies, and immorality (Jer. 11). God will bring on Jerusalem and Judah punishments that will destroy the land and deport the people (Jer. 12). Like the linen belt that Jeremiah buries and finds ruined when he again digs it up, so Judah's self-centered pride will fade and disappear (Jer. 13). God will bring death and disaster on the land and its people, but there is a promise for those who truly repent (Jer. 14–15).

The following section of the book (Jer. 16–29) considers ways to deal with God's judgment. The prophecies of the coming disaster continue (16:1–21), as well as the promise that God is a refuge (17:1–18) where people who keep the Sabbath can find salvation (17:19–27). Jeremiah watches the potter at work to learn how God can choose to exalt or demean any nation, depending on its disposition toward him (18:1–17). His enemies plot to kill Jeremiah, but he prays for God's coming judgment on them (18:18–23).

In Jeremiah 16:5–9, the prophet warns of the futility of mourning because the people will be deported and die in foreign lands. Yet God predicts a time when he will return and restore his people. In chapter 19 the prophet stands at the gate from Jerusalem west to the Valley of Hinnom, where Judeans sacrificed their children to gods. He smashes a pot to warn that God's coming destruction of Jerusalem cannot be stopped, nor can things be restored to where they once were. Jeremiah 20 begins with the challenge of Pashhur, an important priest who beats and imprisons Jeremiah. Pashhur and all he loves will face deportation and death. The prophet disclaims any desire to receive credit for the message but rather sees it as wholly the product of God's initiative.

The next two and a half chapters (Jer. 21:1–23:8) deal with the four unrighteous kings of Judah who succeed their father and grandfather, the righteous Josiah. The book places the prophecy against the last king, Zedekiah (597–586 BC), first. The prophecy takes place at the assault of King Nebuchadnezzar of Babylon on Judah and Jerusalem (Jer. 21). Zedekiah asks Jeremiah to intercede so that God will show mercy. But God states that he will fight against Zedekiah and Jerusalem for their acts of injustice. At least some of the other kings (perhaps all) have received a warning from God that included words of the coming destruction but also an opportunity to repent, turn back to God, and find the mercy that Zedekiah is denied (22:1–10). Yet the king himself must show mercy and justice. Shallum, also called Jehoahaz, is deported after only a few months of reign (609/608 BC) and never returns (22:11–17; cf. 2 Kings 23:31–34). His successor and brother, Jehoiakim, reigns eleven years (609/608–598 BC), but he dies a violent death (Jer. 22:18–23). Jehoiakim's son Jehoiachin rules in Jerusalem only a few months in 597 BC before the Babylonian king deports him, with his family and other leading figures, to Babylon (cf. 2 Kings 24:8–13). This section concludes with Jeremiah's prophecy of woe on all these leaders who do not shepherd God's people, and his promise of a righteous Branch in the line of David, a future king who will reign with justice and redeem God's people from all the countries where they have been sent (Jer. 23:1–8).

Jeremiah 23:9–40 addresses the prophets of Judah who claim to be from God but are not and claim to speak the words of God but do not. God will judge and punish them. Chapter 24 presents the vision of the good and bad figs. The good figs represent those who went into exile in 597 BC with Jehoiachin. God will bless them that they might worship him. He will return their descendants to Jerusalem. The bad figs signify those who remain with Zedekiah. They will be destroyed from the land and never return. In chapter 25 God gives a vision seven years (or more) earlier than that of chapter 24. It speaks of judgment from Babylon against Judah and its neighbors so that the lands will be destroyed and the inhabitants will be enslaved by others and serve Babylon. After seventy years all of this will end, and Babylon itself will be destroyed. Nevertheless, God's anger will go out against all the nations, and they will face horror and devastation. Jeremiah 26 goes back to the early days of King Jehoiakim and describes how Jeremiah has tried to warn the people to repent. The priests and leaders seize him and put Jeremiah on trial for prophesying against the city. However, the people protest, recalling how a century earlier Micah spoke similar words. At that time King Hezekiah repented. Jeremiah is protected in this instance.

God directs Jeremiah to place a wood yoke on his neck and proclaim to all the people in Judah and the neighboring lands that God has appointed King Nebuchadnezzar to rule them and that their best course of action is to submit to him (Jer. 27). Hananiah grabs the yoke from Jeremiah and breaks it, claiming that all of those who have already been taken to Babylon will be returned, along with the items taken from the temple. Jeremiah disagrees and prophesies Hananiah's death that year—an event that occurs within a few months. Jeremiah then writes a letter to those in exile (Jer. 29). He advises them to settle there and expect to remain for many years.

© Baker Publishing Group and Dr. James C. Martin. The Israel Museum.

Lachish Letter no. 3 where the writer claims literacy and mentions the message of "the prophet": "Be on guard!"

In Jeremiah 30, the prophet proclaims that the sin of the people demands punishment from a righteous God. In chapter 31, however, there is the promise of eventual return from the land to which they have been deported. Then God will give them a new covenant that will not be disobeyed, because he will write it on the hearts of his people forever (31:31–40). In chapter 32, God commands Jeremiah to buy a field in his hometown of Anathoth, three miles northeast of Jerusalem. Thus he is to bear witness that even as the Babylonians are besieging Jerusalem, the people of God will return, and business will go on after their punishment. God will restore the land of Judah and will fulfill his covenant so that the Branch of David will not die but will rule over a repopulated land (33:1–26).

Chapter 34 turns to the historical events leading to the Babylonian destruction of Jerusalem and the end of the ruling dynasty of the house of David in Jerusalem. At first God promises King Zedekiah that the Babylonians will capture him but that he will live out his days peacefully in Babylon. Zedekiah proclaims freedom for all slaves while Babylon is attacking the remaining independent cities: Lachish and Azekah. However, Zedekiah reneges on his proclamation of freedom, and those freed become slaves again. This likely happens when the Babylonian threat is temporarily removed, as indicated in 37:5–7. At this, God tells King Zedekiah that he will no longer die peacefully but that he will die by the sword of Babylon.

Earlier, in the reign of King Jehoiakim, Jeremiah has brought the Rechabite clan to the temple and shown the people how faithful the Rechabites remain to an oath that their ancestor swore not to drink wine (Jer. 35). The faithfulness of the Rechabites will be rewarded with life, but the contrasting faithlessness of the Judeans, in their disobedience to God's covenant, will be paid back by coming disasters (35:17). Jeremiah dictates a scroll of divine judgment to Baruch, who then reads it to the people at the temple (Jer. 36). Word goes back to King Jehoiakim, who orders the scroll brought and read in his presence. As it is being read, the king cuts it apart and feeds it to the fire. Jeremiah takes another scroll and gives it to Baruch, who writes on it all the words of judgment in the first scroll, and more besides.

Returning to the days of Zedekiah, the last king of Jerusalem, and to the Babylonian siege, there comes a time when the siege is lifted as the Babylonians are called away to fight Egypt (37:1–21). The captain of the guard catches Jeremiah trying to leave the city, charges him with desertion, beats him, and puts him in prison. Zedekiah releases him and protects him, but Jeremiah continues to warn of the coming destruction of Jerusalem. He advises people to desert to the Babylonian army and thus to live (38:1–3). The royal officials take Jeremiah and put him in a pit of mud, but Ebed-melek rescues him. Jeremiah again warns Zedekiah to surrender, but the king is afraid (38:4–28). The Babylonian army sacks Jerusalem in Zedekiah's eleventh year. He is caught while trying to escape. The Judean king's sons are slain before him, and then his eyes are put out (39:1–7). All of Jerusalem is burned, its walls are broken, and its people are deported (39:8–10). However, Nebuchadnezzar orders that Jeremiah be freed. The prophet chooses to remain with those still in the land (39:11–14). Before this, Jeremiah has received God's word telling him that Ebed-melek will also live through this time (39:15–18).

The Babylonian officials allow Jeremiah to go with them to Babylon or to stay in his home country, whatever he chooses (40:1–6). He stays with Gedaliah, who has been appointed Babylonian governor and resides at Mizpah (north of Jerusalem; 40:7–16). However, Ishmael and ten accomplices assassinate Gedaliah and his officials, and the following day they kill seventy others who are going to the place of the former temple. Johanan and army officers fight Ishmael, but he and eight others escape. So Johanan leads the survivors at Mizpah on the way to Egypt (Jer. 41). They plead with Jeremiah to ask God what they should do. God's reply is to remain in the land, where they will be safe and prosper (42:1–22). However, they accuse Jeremiah of lying and go to Egypt despite his warning (43:1–7). At Tahpanhes in Egypt, God instructs Jeremiah to bury some large stones and say that this will be where the Babylonian king will set up his throne and destroy the symbols of power in Egypt (43:8–13). Chapter 44 focuses on the final word of God to the exiles in Egypt, warning them not to worship idols. However, both the men and women insist that they must worship the Queen of Heaven so that they will prosper as they did when they worshiped her in Judah. God says that most of those who have gone to Egypt will perish by the sword. Jeremiah 45:1–5 takes the reader back in time by about twenty years to when God warns Baruch, Jeremiah's scribe, not to seek personal gain but also promises him his life.

Jeremiah directs prophecies of divine judgment against all the surrounding nations, beginning with Egypt (where Jer. 44 ends) in chapter 46 and ending with the largest oracle of doom against Babylon in chapters 50–51. Between these are Philistia (Jer. 47), Moab (Jer. 48), Ammon (49:1–6), Edom (49:7–22), Damascus (49:23–27), Kedar and Hazor (49:28–33), and Elam (49:34–39).

The final chapter of Jeremiah (Jer. 52) divides into three parts. The first eleven verses describe the reign of Zedekiah as evil in God's sight, the flight and capture of the king, the death of his family, and the remaining days of

Zedekiah, blinded and in a Babylonian prison. Verses 12–30 describe the destruction of Jerusalem, the taking away of the valuable items from the temple, and the deportation of the people from Judah and Jerusalem. The final four verses conclude the book with the freedom granted to King Jehoiachin of Judah by a successor of Nebuchadnezzar and his elevation to eat at the table of the Babylonian king.

Reading Jeremiah

Premodern Readings

In addition to the distinctive Greek translation of the Septuagint, the intertestamental period also bears witness to the Epistle of Baruch, probably written long after the death of Jeremiah's secretary, perhaps in the second or first century BC. It includes instruction about a service of confession for Jerusalem, some wisdom material, and some encouragement to the city and its inhabitants. The so-called Letter of Jeremiah sometimes forms part of the Epistle of Baruch. It derives from the same general time and presents a critique of idolatry. From the early Christian centuries come the *Lives of the Prophets* and *4 Baruch*, both of which provide more stories and details on the lives of Jeremiah and others mentioned in his book. These include traditions that Jeremiah visited Babylon and that the prophet was stoned to death. Second Maccabees (2:1–8; 15:12–16) records traditions where Jeremiah provided for sacred fire to be taken by the deportees, for hiding the ark and incense altar from the Babylonians, and for a vision about Jeremiah after death, where the prophet prays for the people.[3]

Both Jewish and Christian writers found in texts from Jeremiah a rich source for sermons. In Jewish writings, Jeremiah is connected with Moses and the prophet of Deuteronomy 18:18.[4] He was a descendant of Rahab the prostitute and related to Huldah the prophetess (*b. Megillah* 14b; *Pesiqta de Rab Kahana* 13:5, 12).[5] A Rabbinic tradition placed Jeremiah before Isaiah as first among the Latter Prophets and directly following the destruction of Jerusalem as described at the end of 2 Kings (*b. B. Bat*. 14b).

From the work of Origen onward, the variety of exhortations, prophecies, and personal narratives provided Christian preachers with much to address their congregations and to leave as a heritage for the church. In early Christianity Jeremiah did not enjoy anything like the popularity of Isaiah. Jerome commented on the Hebrew text. His major enemy in the commentary was Pelagius, a Christian heretic who taught that one could

3. Dearman, "Jeremiah: History of Interpretation," 442.
4. Sharp, "Jeremiah," 428.
5. Dearman, "Jeremiah: History of Interpretation," 442.

achieve perfection in this life.[6] Jerome's strong emphasis on comparing the different texts of Jeremiah provides background to identify major literary themes.

Martin Luther used Jeremiah as a means to condemn the Jews of his day. His pamphlet, "The Jews and Their Lies," is self-descriptive of his use of the prophet's indictments, while his expectations of the future hope (Jer. 31–33) anticipate Jesus Christ. The new covenant also forms an important part of John Calvin's lectures on Jeremiah.[7]

Medieval, Renaissance, and later artists such as Donatello, Michelangelo, Rembrandt, and Chagall have visualized Jeremiah in contexts of grief and suffering. Michelangelo's early sixteenth-century portrayal on the Sistine Chapel reveals a somber and grieving prophet, as does the work of Rembrandt more than a century later. In this latter painting the artist's use of light emphasizes the Babylonian army's act of setting the city ablaze.

Higher Criticism

As the largest book in the Old Testament (in terms of Hebrew words), Jeremiah has received a correspondingly great interest through its critical study in the nineteenth and twentieth centuries. Bernhard Duhm tried to isolate the original texts of Jeremiah by distinguishing the poetry and prose parts of the book.[8] While 280 verses of poetry belong to Jeremiah, and the prose sections (as well as some poetry) could be credited to Baruch, the legalism of the redactors and their work led to a weakly structured final edition of the book. Sigmund Mowinckel separated the prose materials into sermons and narratives about the life of Jeremiah, resulting in three divisions.[9] These divisions continue to influence discussion of the book's composition.

Emphases of the last two-thirds of the twentieth century saw the development of the critical study of the book of Jeremiah in three broad areas: the personal life of Jeremiah, the Deuteronomistic emphasis of the book, and the literary role of the work. The personal emphasis could be seen in Walter Baumgartner's *Jeremiah's Poems of Lament*. He returned to earlier work in arguing that Jeremiah was building on the laments of the psalms. However, Baumgartner understood Jeremiah's use of lament as based not on the personal life of Jeremiah but rather as drawing on the style of laments as related to those of the psalms. It was A. R. Diamond who refocused the study on the individual prophet and his struggles with the message that God had given him.[10]

6. Jerome, *Commentary on Jeremiah*, xxix–l.
7. Dearman, "Jeremiah: History of Interpretation," 444.
8. Duhm, *Das Buch Jeremia*.
9. Mowinckel, *Zur Komposition des Buches Jeremia*.
10. Diamond, *Confessions of Jeremiah*.

These confessions (11:18–23; 12:1–6; 15:10–21; 17:14–18; 18:18–23; 20:7–12, 14–18) not only demonstrate how Jeremiah follows God's message despite his own inclination; they also provide evidence of the prophet's loyalty to Judah. This is not a message that Jeremiah wishes to proclaim. Rather, the weighty task of proclaiming that message was placed on him by God, and he was not given a choice. Thus Jeremiah is innocent of charges of treason. He does not want to deliver the message of doom, but God prevails.

The second area of focus has seen Jeremiah as a part of the larger picture of the Deuteronomists, who were writing during his lifetime. There can be no doubt that much of the language, such as about the new covenant of Jeremiah 31, represents the same covenantal terminology and theology that can be found in Deuteronomy and in the Deuteronomistic History of Joshua, Judges, 1–2 Samuel, and 1–2 Kings. The similarities tie the language of Jeremiah with that of Deuteronomy.[11] Thus important items, such as the centralization of the temple under Josiah, continued to be recognized as also part of the teaching of Jeremiah.[12] However, the extent to which Jeremiah's vision of a rebuilding of Judah contrasts with the Deuteronomist's assumption that God has abandoned Judah shows a significant difference between the two works.[13] Nevertheless, today the connection between the message represented by Jeremiah and that of the Deuteronomistic History continues to be recognized. While some limit the Deuteronomistic influence to the prose,[14] various commentators who consider Jeremiah a largely authentic historical character opt for a Deuteronomistic influence throughout the work.[15]

A related issue arises from the large increase in extrabiblical written evidence that appears in Judah in the seventh century BC. This can be contrasted with the fewer written materials in the earlier periods to promote the theory of a kind of revolution in reading and writing that occurred at this time.[16] While there is more evidence for reading and writing in the seventh century, increasing discoveries from the earlier periods should balance the assessment.[17]

The third area considers the literary text of Jeremiah in contrast to the existence of any historical figure by the name of Jeremiah. In this interpretation, the prophecies and narratives of the book represent metaphors for events

11. Cazelles, "Jeremiah and Deuteronomy."

12. Van der Toorn, *Scribal Culture*, 221–23.

13. Römer, *Deuteronomistic History*, 115–16. For additional differences of theological perspective, see McConville, *Judgment and Promise*.

14. Sharp, *Prophecy and Ideology*.

15. L. Allen, *Jeremiah*; Brueggemann, *Theology of the Book of Jeremiah*; W. Holladay, *Jeremiah*.

16. Van der Toorn, *Scribal Culture*; Schniedewind, *How the Bible Became a Book*; Römer, *The Invention of God*.

17. See the chapter on Amos and the sidebar, "Functional Literacy in Iron Age Israel."

taking place later in the history of the people of God.[18] Thus the book may be mined for conflicting interests of two specific but competing parties, such as the Jews in exile and those back in Judah;[19] or the work of Jeremiah may be seen as a compilation of myriad postexilic groups expressing competing interests into the fifth century BC.[20] The highly speculative nature of this enterprise has led to a wide variety of idiosyncratic approaches, but nothing that has gained the general acceptance of the second area of study (next), the Deuteronomistic characteristic of his work.

Literary Readings

In addition to the major divisions of the types of literature already noticed in the previous section, certain themes pervade Jeremiah. Foremost among these is the set of terms that are to characterize his message as described in Jeremiah's call at the beginning of the book (1:10 RSH): "Look, today I appoint you over the nations and kingdoms to uproot [13×] and to break down [7×], to destroy [6×] and to overthrow [7×], and to build [22×] and to plant [14×]." The frequency of each verb in Jeremiah is indicated within brackets.[21] All six verbs appear in 31:28 in anticipation of the announcement of the new covenant. Of these six terms, however, only "to destroy" (in the causative stem as here) occurs in the prophecies against the nations, chapters 46–51 (in 46:8; 49:38). The absence of the other relatively frequent vocabulary in these oracles may suggest a separate literary context here, or it may imply that destruction is all that remains for those outside the people of God. Otherwise, these verbs summarize the negative and positive messages, the warning and hope, of Jeremiah to his people.

The overall structure of the book is symmetrical or chiastic, in which the first and last elements correspond, as do the second and second-to-last elements, and so forth. Joel Rosenberg outlines the work as follows:[22]

A Historical headnote (1:1–3)
  B Commission (1:4)
    C "Prophet to the nations" theme introduced (1:5–10)
      D Doom for Israel; poetic oracles predominate (1:11–10:25)
        E Prophet cut off from Anathoth; focus on prophet's trials and conflicts; prose predominates (11:1–28:17)

18. Polk, *Prophetic Persona*.
19. Sharp, *Prophecy and Ideology*.
20. R. Carroll, *Jeremiah*.
21. Since the verb "to destroy" appears here in the Hiphil, I have counted only those other occurrences where it occurs in the Hiphil.
22. Rosenberg, "Jeremiah and Ezekiel," 190–91.

F Optimistic prophecies; renewal of Israel; prose brackets poetic center (29:1–31:40)
E′ Prophet returns to Anathoth; focus on prophet's trials and conflicts; prose predominates (32:1–45:5)
D′ Doom for the nations; poetic oracles predominate (46:1–49:39)
C′ "Prophet to the nations" theme culminates (50:1–51:58)
B′ Prophet's concluding message (51:59–64)
A′ Historical appendix (52:1–34)

Jeremiah's overall literary structure remains distinct from that of Isaiah, Ezekiel, and many of the other prophets. Elsewhere, the pattern is primarily one of judgment against God's people, judgment against other nations, and then the anticipation of restoration and blessing to God's people. So strongly may this have been perceived that the Septuagint order moved the prophecies against the nations after the major oracles of judgment and before the prophecies of hope in chapters 29–31. However, that is not the message of the Hebrew text. While the hope for a new covenant is present, and indeed central to the message of the prophet, the interweaving of the historical and prophetic materials demonstrates that, for each individual among the people of God, as for the whole people, there is the opportunity to repent or to continue on the road to destruction. With kings, with the prophet, with his friends, and with his enemies, opportunities are given, followed by decisions and their consequences. Chapter 52 illustrates this in its three scenes. The weak king Zedekiah remains unable to repent and sees his family destroyed before being blinded physically and led off to die in Babylon. The spiritually blind people follow their king into exile. Only hope remains for the line of King Jehoiachin, who reemerges at the very end of the book, as one shown grace by a Babylonian king and thereby anticipating a future chapter for the Branch of David (1:11; 23:5; 33:15) and the promises of hope.

Gender and Ideological Criticism

With the book of Jeremiah, significant issues arise regarding the view of women in ancient Israel, which, like all the surrounding societies, was patriarchal. The feminine role becomes evident in the pictures of a woman in labor and giving birth. The pain, fear, and vulnerability that accompany this image form part of the judgment against Judah for its sins (Jer. 4:31; 6:24; 13:21; 22:23). By the end of the book, however, this image of judgment is found only among the other nations, the enemies of God and his people: Moab (48:41), Edom (49:22), Damascus (49:24), and, of course, Babylon (50:43).

For God's people, the picture reaches a turning point in Jeremiah 30:6, where the time when God brings his people home again will be terrifying for all the strong powers that attempt to thwart them. Then even expectant women and women in labor will return (31:8), suggesting that this will become a time of prayer, joy, dancing, and prosperity for God's people (31:9–14). Even the image of Rachel bereaved of her children, which comes to pass in the deportation of the Judeans (31:15), is reversed, and those children return from the land of the enemy to their own land (31:16–17). It is in this context that Israel is called both "Virgin" and "unfaithful Daughter" (31:21–22 NIV). The people are unfaithful when they wander away from God but are recognized as "Virgin Israel" when they return, repent of their wrongdoing, and come again to their towns. In this future return, the scene culminates with a picture in which the expected gender roles of patriarchy will be reversed, and a woman will "surround" a man (31:22). Thus the assumptions of power and possession are reversed within marriage and family.

It is in this larger context that the images of Israel portrayed as a promiscuous woman in Jeremiah 3:2, 19–20 should be understood. This is indeed a negative portrayal of the feminine; yet, as Mary E. Shields observes, there is an inherent destabilization in this picture as, among other things, those who receive the warning of judgment are addressed in the masculine plural (3:20).[23] Further, the picture of male circumcision in 4:4 is not the end of the story. The whole people of God are addressed, and that includes mothers and fathers, females and males. Beyond this, as seen in chapter 31, a time is coming when the patriarchal structure itself will be challenged and refashioned.[24]

As mentioned above, some analyses of Jeremiah (such as the work by Robert Carroll) consider the book as a product of competing parties and interests.[25] Jeremiah has lent itself to such ideological analyses. One of these is the work of Christi Maier and Carolyn Sharp, titled *Prophecy and Ideology in Jeremiah: Struggles for Authority in the Deutero-Jeremianic Prose*.[26] Here an examination of chapters 7, 26, 35, and 44 of the book leads to an identification of two major parties represented: those who are taken into exile in Babylon, and those who flee to Egypt. On the one hand, the latter are tied in with the collapse of the whole state of Judah as an independent entity. They see the Judean remnants as possessing the true inheritance of the earlier nation. On the other hand, the Babylonian group seeks to remove any recognition of legitimate power from those remaining in Judah and to promise freedom from their own exile. Thus the group taken to Egypt understands their failure to emerge from their disobedience to the message of the prophets. Those in the Babylonian exile emphasize the moral corruption of the people that has caused God to abandon his temple and to transfer the authority from Jerusalem to Babylon.

23. Shields, *Circumscribing the Prostitute*.
24. Cf. Bauer, *Gender in the Book of Jeremiah*.
25. R. Carroll, *Jeremiah*; and to a lesser extent McKane, *Jeremiah*.
26. For more in this area, see the studies in Maier and Sharp, *Prophecy and Power*.

To come to these conclusions, one must divide a text such as Jeremiah 7:1–8:3 into some verses that are pro-Judean (7:1–2, 4, 7–8, 13b, 15–16, 20–29) and some that are pro-Babylonian (7:3, 5–6, 9–13a, 14, 17–19, 30–34; 8:1–3). Yet the rather arbitrary nature of this endeavor leaves remaining the point that these two views are not mutually exclusive and thus could both be held by the same individual or group, as may be suggested by the manner in which they are interwoven into this section. Indeed, the pro-Babylonian party sounds more like the position of the book of Ezekiel, especially chapters 8–11.

A larger context is the role of Babylon as the imperial oppressor and the position of Jeremiah in calling the people to deconstruct and mock the great power in its coming collapse. In the exile, the people of God are called to a process of becoming in which they are creating a new identity. This is formed under the power of their merciful God, to whom Babylon itself is ultimately subject.[27]

Ancient Near Eastern Context

Much could be discussed regarding the period that Jeremiah represents, that of the final decades and destruction of Judah. Some of the major written sources can be identified, along with possible religious artifacts from this period and remaining evidence for the destruction of Jerusalem and Judah.

First, there are the numerous written sources. In Judah itself, this includes many of the ostraca (potsherds used for writing notes and letters with ink) found on the floor in a room near the entrance to the fort at Arad in southern Judah. These include dozens of missives exchanged between Eliashib, presumably the fort's commander, and his superior, probably a figure writing from Jerusalem. There is concern for supplies for different groups of soldiers, some of whom may be Greek mercenaries. There is mention of the "house of the Lord," probably a reference to the temple in Jerusalem, but possibly used to identify the religious altars and holy place in one section of the Arad fort. Some of the personal names relate to those of Levite and priestly clans mentioned in the Bible.

A second set of ostraca was found in a similar room at the gate to the Judean city of Lachish, which guarded a key pass

© Baker Publishing Group and Dr. James C. Martin

Horned altar facsimile from Beersheba

27. Douglas, "Resistance from the Margins."

Seal Impressions of Baruch and of Gedaliah

At least ten seal impressions contain the longer form of the name of Jeremiah's scribe, Baruch, *brkyhw*. However, collectors acquired many of these through dealers rather than controlled archaeological excavations. Thus their antiquity and authenticity remain debated. These include two seals that possess the name of the father of Baruch, Neriah (Jer. 32:12, 16; 36:4, 8, 14, 32; 43:3, 6; 45:1; 51:59). Hence scholars cannot be certain that a seal or seal impression has been found whose name bearer is identical to the Baruch of Jeremiah.

At Lachish a seal impression was found with the longer form of the name of the governor Gedaliah (Jer. 40–41), *gdlyhw*. He receives the title of "one who is over the house," an important royal official for the Judean kingdom. The impression dates from about 600 BC. Could this have been an office that Gedaliah held before his appointment as the Babylonian governor of Judah?

from the coastal plain eastward into the hill country south of Jerusalem. Here there is a tone of urgency. One text mentions an unnamed prophet whose message is summarized in a single word, "Beware!" In another, an officer writes that he is able to read and thus understands the instructions given to him. More ominous is the reference to the lack of fire signals visible from the city guarding a valley to the north of Lachish, the city of Azekah. This seems to imply that the Babylonian army has succeeded in destroying this remaining outpost (Jer. 34:7).

As a third important source for reconstructing the history of the period of Jeremiah, seals and seal impressions (called bullae) have been found. Some of these were exchanged on the black market, and there is debate about their authenticity. Others were found in archaeological excavations. Most important among these were more than one hundred seal impressions found in a single room in the city of David (called the Room of the Bullae). This suggests that these clay seal impressions were used to seal papyrus documents, and thus the room may have stored official records. Each seal or seal impression from this period normally has the owner's name incised in Hebrew as well as the name of the father of the owner. Thus it served as a means of identification.

Dating from the last decades of the independent Judean kingdom are more than eight hundred clay figurines of women with prominent breasts and a pillar base for what would have been the lower part of their body. These figurines, found in private homes as much as in public places, were discovered only in the kingdom of Judah, not outside its borders. They

Zev Radovan/www.BibleLandPictures.com

Seal impression of Baruch, son of Neriah, and presumably the scribe of Jeremiah

have been variously interpreted as images of a popular goddess,[28] "prayers in clay" by women expressing their desire for successful pregnancies and healthy children, and good-luck charms. At this point it is not possible to know their significance. However, their poor quality and inexpensive material suggest they are not intended to represent deities.

Another aspect of the archaeological evidence from the time of Jeremiah's ministry is the existence of numerous destruction levels throughout Judah that date from the early decades of the sixth century. No doubt these reflect the attack and destruction by the Babylonian army. There is an important exception to this. Immediately north of Jerusalem lay the tribal territory of Benjamin, which was also part of the kingdom of Judah. Contrary to evidence elsewhere, the towns in this part of the country were not destroyed. The people and their lives seem to have continued largely as before the coming of the Babylonians. This may account for the decision to place the center of the region's Babylonian government north of Jerusalem at Mizpah. In the southern borders of Judah there is also evidence of construction and habitation. Here texts and cultural items reveal the encroachment of Edomites from the east and south. It appears that they took advantage of Judean weakness to exert control of this region. This may help to account for the negative view of Edom reflected in oracles such as Jeremiah 49:7–22; Lamentations 4:12–22; Ezekiel 25:12–14; and Obadiah.

Several texts from the Babylonian archives reveal pieces of the story as elaborated in the Old Testament. For example, Babylonian Chronicle 5 records how, in 597 BC, King Nebuchadnezzar attacked Jerusalem and took Jehoiachin (= Coniah/Jeconiah) captive, replacing him with Zedekiah (Jer. 24:1; 27:20; 29:2; 37:1). In other records, lists of rations for those who ate at the table of Babylonian king Amel-Marduk (= Evil-merodach) include the name of Jehoiachin, whom Jeremiah 52:31–34 describes as being released from prison and elevated to eat at the Babylonian king's table.

Canonical Context

The size of the book of Jeremiah and its important theological contributions invite comparisons with much of the remainder of the Old Testament.

28. Dever, *Did God Have a Wife?*

Nebo-Sarsekim

Jeremiah 39:3 mentions the important Babylonian officials who took their seats of judgment at a gate in Jerusalem after the city's defenses were destroyed by the Babylonian army. One of these officials is Nebo-Sarsekim (NIV). A small cuneiform tablet stored in London in the British Museum and dated about eight or nine years before the destruction of Jerusalem (586 BC) identifies this man's name in Babylonian. He is described as the "chief eunuch" (an important officer) of King Nebuchadnezzar, one who could afford to present almost two pounds of gold in an offering to a temple in Babylon.

Some of these comparisons note the close resemblance of a genre such as the oracles against the nations to what is found in other prophetic books. For example, specific texts against Babylon, such as may occur in Isaiah 13–14, 21, and 47, are compared with Jeremiah 50–51, and the oracle against Edom in Jeremiah 49:7–22 is compared with the book of Obadiah. Alternatively, comparison may be made with creation texts, as in Genesis 1:2, in which the formlessness of the earth is described in precisely the same language as God's judgment in Jeremiah 4:23.

However, of greater importance is the covenantal language of the book of Jeremiah that also appears in the book of Deuteronomy and the Historical Books of Joshua, Judges, 1–2 Samuel, and 1–2 Kings. Other prophets resemble Jeremiah in establishing the pattern of judgment followed by divine salvation. The renewed covenant written on the heart in Jeremiah 31:31 becomes the heart of flesh that replaces the heart of stone in Ezekiel 11:19. Deuteronomy 10:16 preserves the imagery of circumcising the heart, as in Jeremiah 4:4. Yet Deuteronomy 30:6 promises that God will circumcise the hearts of his people. Indeed, this movement in the book of Deuteronomy exemplifies the transition from judgment to promise, as Jeremiah's oracles correspondingly alternate between judgment and promise for God's people.

The historical accounts in Jeremiah relating to the last kings of Judah, the Babylonian destruction of Jerusalem, and the deportations and governorship that follow all appear in 2 Kings as well. Indeed, 2 Kings 25 closely parallels Jeremiah 52. The theological message of God's warning and judgment for the people's sin is evident in both books (Jer. 11:3–4; 2 Kings 17:19–20), building their portrayal on the covenant curses of Leviticus 26 and Deuteronomy 28. Jeremiah, more explicitly than Kings, echoes the promise of return from exile to the land (cf. Deut. 30:3–5).[29]

29. McConville, "Jeremiah," 217.

Without a doubt the new covenant of Jeremiah 31 is the most significant text from Jeremiah that Jesus refers to, in his identification of it with his blood (Matt. 26:26–28; Mark 14:22–24; John 6:54). While some ancient texts insert the adjective "new" before "covenant" in these Gospel passages, it certainly forms the understanding of Paul (Rom. 11:27; 1 Cor. 11:25) and the author of the Epistle to the Hebrews (8:8–13; 9:15; 10:16–17; 12:24). As Gordon McConville expresses, the newness of this covenant takes the old covenant and continues the resolution of God to do all that is necessary to make it effective.[30]

Elsewhere in the New Testament, Paul applies God's call on Jeremiah's life (Jer. 1:5) to his own (Gal. 1:15). God's words to Paul in helping him to understand his mission have their origin in Jeremiah 1:7–8 (Acts 18:9; 26:17). In the book of Revelation are dozens of quotations from Jeremiah. The largest number of these come from the oracles against Babylon in Jeremiah 50–51. Here in Revelation the focus on the Babylonian Empire as the destroyer of Jerusalem and on God's judgment shifts to a present and future "Babylonian" Empire of this world that tries to destroy God's people, the church. Any such empire will also face defeat and destruction.

Theological Perspectives of Jeremiah

The prophet Jeremiah was a clear and compelling preacher who was deeply attached to the people he was called on to warn. As a result we have already identified the theological themes in the overview section of this chapter. Here we will briefly examine some major points. Jeremiah addresses a people of God who feel that they have their theology all in proper order. Living in Jerusalem and the surrounding land of Judah, the people feel secure against the most powerful enemies of their day. They point to a century earlier, when God protected their ancestors from the brutal Assyrian attack, and did so miraculously. Thus they feel they have every right to trust in this "Zion theology," where God will continue to save and deliver them.

It is the unhappy calling of the prophet Jeremiah to warn the people that this confidence is false. There is no guarantee of a rescue from the Babylonians as there was a rescue from the Assyrians a century earlier. To the contrary, the rise of Nebuchadnezzar in 605 BC and his successful attack on Jerusalem, with the deportation of many and the installation of a new king in 597 BC, are portents of the greater disaster to come. Jeremiah warns that lack of faith on the part of the people and the king will lead to Jerusalem not being delivered. In the final weeks of the nation's independence, the prophet counsels the people to return to God and to seek him with acts of repentance and justice.

30. Ibid., 218.

Along with this, he recommends that all of them, from King Zedekiah on down, surrender to King Nebuchadnezzar and depend on his mercy for their survival. Their refusal to do this leads to their destruction. However, even those who survive in the land do not listen to Jeremiah but flee to Egypt when the Babylonian-appointed governor is assassinated. There they blame their loss on the worship of the God of Israel in place of the Queen of Heaven, be she Astarte or another Canaanite goddess. Thus at no time are the people of the land able to turn to God.

On the one hand, this rebellion has resulted in the condemnation of the Judeans. On the other hand, it has necessitated the development of a new or renewed covenant based on the ancient covenant. Now, however, as Jeremiah 31:31–34 makes clear, this new covenant will not depend only on words written on stone and left for the people to obey. Instead, it will depend much more on God writing the covenant on the human heart. In Old Testament times, the heart was more than the seat of emotions.[31] It included the mind, reason, and will. The heart was where the decisions that characterize each human in the world were made and put into effect. Thus the writing of the new covenant on the tablets of the heart suggests that the words will be written in a manner that enables the people of God to turn from their former stubbornness and to accept God's covenant. It will enable them to resolve to obey it and then to actually move ahead to obey it. While the concern is certainly that the entire community of God's people turn to God and live in faithfulness to his covenant, this will be accomplished one person at a time. There is never a sense here of forcing humans into accepting something that they don't want. Rather, the concern is to provide for the ability to turn from sin and to accept and follow God. So deeply has the human heart been mired in its own sin that nothing short of direct personal connection at the level of the human heart will save and deliver the individuals and the whole community of God. For this reason, it doesn't matter how strong the Babylonian Empire, its king, and its army are. What matters is that God is able to overturn the power of all the nations (Jer. 46–51) and use his own power to bring both Israel and others of this world to follow him alone.

Key Commentaries and Studies

Allen, Leslie C. *Jeremiah: A Commentary.* OTL. Louisville: Westminster John Knox, 2008. This provides the best detailed textual study of any recent commentary from an evangelical perspective.

31. See discussion of the Shema under "Theological Perspectives of Deuteronomy" in the chapter on Deuteronomy, above.

Holladay, William L. *Jeremiah*. Vol. 1, *1–25*. Hermeneia. Philadelphia: Fortress, 1986. Vol. 2, *26–52*. Minneapolis: Fortress, 1989. The best textual and Hebrew analysis of the biblical text, with historical and linguistic strengths.

King, Philip J. *Jeremiah: An Archaeological Commentary*. Philadelphia: Westminster John Knox, 1993. The best introduction to the culture and history of the period of Jeremiah.

Lundblom, Jack R. *Jeremiah: A New Translation with Introduction and Commentary*. Vol. 1, *1–20*. Vol. 2, *21–36*. Vol. 3, *37–52*. AB 21A, 21B, 22. New York: Doubleday, 1999–2004. This is the most thorough work dealing with all the issues of interpretation and providing the strongest literary analysis.

McConville, J. Gordon. *Judgment and Promise: An Interpretation of the Book of Jeremiah*. Winona Lake, IN: Eisenbrauns, 1993. Concise reflection on Jeremiah's covenantal theology.

21

LAMENTATIONS

What is the key to dealing with the loss of one's home and all that one has known? The book of Lamentations sorts through severe grief to find an answer.

Name, Text, and Outline

The name of this book is a description of the lament form that recurs throughout each of the chapters. Lament is found in individual and community forms in various psalms. Here, however, the widely recognized focus of the laments concerns the attack and destruction of Jerusalem and the effect this has on its people.

There is no evidence to suggest any fundamental problems with the Hebrew text as preserved in the Masoretic Text. The Greek text of the Septuagint is influenced by the *kaige* recension (on which, see "Name, Text, and Outline" for Judges and 1–2 Kings). The first verse of the Greek indicates the traditional understanding of the context and authorship of the book: "After Israel had been taken captive and Jerusalem destroyed, then Jeremiah sat weeping and proclaimed this lament over Jerusalem."

OUTLINE

I. Zion's Suffering and Desolation (1:1–22)
II. God's Judgment on Suffering Zion (2:1–22)
III. God's Faithfulness despite Zion's Suffering (3:1–66)
IV. Pictures of God's Judgment and Judgment against Edom (4:1–22)
V. Appeal for Restoration and Release from Suffering (5:1–22)

Overview of Lamentations

The book of Lamentations begins with a word picture of a deserted city that resembles a weeping widow and a slave. The city is Judah of Jerusalem, which has gone into exile without anyone left to attend the festivals in Zion. God has brought this punishment for the city's sins, with no one to help or comfort it. The enemy has seized the city's treasures, and now the people are hungry and despised. "Virgin Daughter Judah" (1:15 NIV) weeps without comfort. The lament cries out for God to punish Judah's enemies for their sins just as he has punished Jerusalem.

Chapter 2 laments the severe devastation that God has brought on Judah and its people. Dishonor, fire, wrath, and abandonment characterize God's judgment. Mourning, woundedness, and mockery by the enemy describe the experience of Zion. The image of eating Zion's citizens recurs: the Lord "has swallowed" Israel (2:5 NIV); Jerusalem's enemies "have swallowed" it (2:16 NIV); women eat their children for food (2:20).

Chapter 3 personalizes the experience: the poet describes himself as a man who has seen affliction. He knows darkness, death, and the taunt of his enemies. Yet there also appears the confession of God's mercy and faithfulness (3:22–33). The lament continues with a call to repentance, a confession that God does see, and a plea for returning to his enemies what they deserve.

Chapter 4 begins with a picture of gold that has lost its luster; then it turns to consider the infants and children who remain unloved and unfed

© Baker Publishing Group and Dr. James C. Martin

Judean families forced into exile from their homeland by the Assyrians in 701 BC

(4:2–5). Famine and cannibalism afflict Zion (4:8–10). Pictures of suffering and destruction continue, with a cry against Edom and a promise of its divine judgment bringing the chapter to a conclusion.

Chapter 5 concludes the laments with an appeal to God, a summary of the disgrace and suffering of Zion and its people, and a final cry to God to restore his people to himself and renew the old days.

Reading Lamentations

Premodern Readings

The earliest extant Jewish interpretations are found in *Targum Lamentations* and *Lamentations Rabbah* (both of uncertain date).[1] These texts focus on justifying God's actions in destroying Jerusalem and in subsequent judgments as originating from the sins of his people. They also describe the role of Jeremiah and his prophecies in the destruction. Lamentations has continued to be read on the Ninth Day of Ab (in July/August), which commemorates the Babylonian destruction of the temple, the destruction of the second temple, and the end of the Bar Kokhba rebellion.

In the Christian patristic tradition, Lamentations 4:20 found the most frequent reference.[2] The Greek version mentions both "spirit" and "the Lord's anointed one," taken to refer to the Holy Spirit and Jesus Christ, who would suffer so that "we shall live among the gentiles" (Irenaeus, *Demonstration of the Apostolic Preaching* 71). Other texts of Lamentations were also used with an emphasis on their relationship to Jesus Christ and the history of the church. It is only later figures, such as John Calvin, who represent a concern to position the interpretation of Lamentations in its original historical setting following Jerusalem's destruction. In some Christian traditions, portions of Lamentations are read in Holy Week (leading up to Easter) and thus associated with penitence.

Higher Criticism

These approaches have moved away from an identification of the book with the single author Jeremiah.[3] In its place they have suggested various sources for the different laments and various times and circumstances that led to their production and assembly. The laments have been compared with poems of lament in the book of Psalms. Possibly the origins of some imagery and expression in the laments can be traced back to earlier disasters in preexilic Israel or in broader ancient Near Eastern contexts. There is also the theological

1. Cf. Pickut, "Lamentations 3."
2. Ibid.
3. Pickut, "Lamentations 3," 418–19.

© Baker Publishing Group and Dr. James C. Martin

Assyrians impaling Judean prisoners of war at Lachish in 701 BC

question of breaking the covenant and of struggling with the assumption that Zion (Jerusalem and its temple) would never fall to an enemy—sometimes referred to as Zion theology.[4]

Literary Readings

The structure of the book turns on the acrostic style that chapters 1–4 have, though each in a slightly different form. The first chapter, of twenty-two verses, follows the acrostic form perfectly, according to the accepted Hebrew alphabet. In the second chapter there is a similar acrostic, but verses 16 and 17, beginning with *pe* and then *ayin*, reverse the common order. This does follow some early abecedaries and therefore is not without precedent. The third chapter represents the heart of the book. With sixty-six verses, it has three verses beginning with each letter of the alphabet. The order of the acrostic alphabet follows chapter 2. The same is true of chapter 4, but it returns to twenty-two verses, like chapter 2. Chapter 5 also has twenty-two verses but follows no acrostic pattern.

Lamentations begins with two voices, and these continue for most of the book. The first voice functions as a narrator who describes the devastation of the city, the sin of the people, and the attitude of God in judgment. The book ends with this voice directly praising God and calling for "our"

4. See under the heading "Theological Perspectives on Lamentations."

restoration (5:19–22). The final verse, "Unless you have indeed rejected us and are so very angry against us" (RSH), leaves open this cry. It suggests that ultimately forgiveness and mercy lie with God. All that the poet can do is to cry to God and wait. It also suggests that any restoration lies in the future.

A second voice comes from the city and people, who are portrayed as a woman in lament. She first speaks in 1:11b–16, describing her bereavement at the loss of her children, meaning the citizens of Jerusalem, whom the enemy has killed or deported. The sorrow and rejection by God and former allies add to the suffering. Both voices use vivid images that intensify the suffering of the people and the emotional impact of the book.

Gender and Ideological Criticism

Dirges and laments have often been sung by women mourners, and Israel was no exception (Jer. 9:17–22; 2 Chron. 35:25). It is possible that some of Lamentations (or more likely, images and poetic lines) originated with or were performed by women. However, these poems go beyond traditional mourning songs to include discussion and debate with God concerning his violence toward and punishment of his people.[5]

The imagery describing Jerusalem as a woman includes her nakedness and shame (Lam. 1:8–9, 17), her abuse and beatings from God (1:12–13), and her lost children (1:5).[6] Human suffering is a universal phenomenon. Archie Chi Chung Lee describes various poems and postings in the context of the Tiananmen Square protests of 1989.[7] In so doing, he finds many examples of laments, expressing concerns such as the loss of children, that resemble those in the book of Lamentations. Thus he reinforces the universality of tragedy and suffering, showing how mourners direct cries to heaven. Soong-Chan Rah criticizes the American church for avoiding lament. He calls on Christians to repent of their pride and, using the book of Lamentations, to learn to lament and to act out of that lament against injustice.[8]

Ancient Near Eastern Context

Lamentations finds a frequent comparison with the Sumerian laments. Some of these deal specifically with the destruction of a city brought about by warfare. The best known is the Lamentation over the Destruction of Ur, composed in the aftermath of the city's destruction around 2000 BC. Such laments might be expected to have sentiments found in the biblical book of

5. N. Lee, "Lamentations," 558.
6. Tiemeyer, "Feminist Interpretation," 214.
7. Chi Chung Lee, "Lamentations."
8. Rah, *Prophetic Lament*.

Lamentations. Various forms of Sumerian laments survive.[9] However, these do not advance understanding of the biblical poems.

Canonical Context

The important role of biblical laments in the book of Psalms has been discussed. Jeremiah, who has been associated with Lamentations (see "Name, Text, and Outline"), composed laments over the death of King Josiah (2 Chron. 35:25). References to mourning rites associated with the fall of Jerusalem appear in Jeremiah 41:4–9 and may suggest a context for the book of Lamentations.

The continuation of a penitential prayer tradition through the intertestamental period and into the time of Roman domination led to the expectation of a messiah to come who would restore God's faithfulness.[10] The Messiah of the New Testament grieves over the coming destruction of Jerusalem (Luke 13:34–35), even as he later embodies God's people and cries out in grief at his loneliness and abandonment by God: "My God, my God, why have you forsaken me?" (Matt. 27:46; Mark 15:34).

Theological Perspectives of Lamentations

Judgment and suffering characterize major themes of Lamentations.[11] The first theme comes about as a result of the loss of the covenant relationship between Yahweh and his people, a relationship created and sustained with sacrifices (2:1, 6, 7, 9). The suffering comes in order to punish and purify for sin (3:39–42), yet enemies also bring suffering (1:21–22; 2:16; 3:52–66; 4:21–22; 5:2). Ultimately it is Yahweh, Israel's God, who remains responsible for the people's suffering, and he alone can end it (5:21). If the people recognize their sin before a gracious God, then there is hope (3:19–39). Here too the key to the people's hope is found. If they abandon their sin and accept God's punishment, they can also receive his grace and restoration.

Zion is the great subject of the book. As personified, Zion experiences the devastation as Jerusalem and the people of Judah did. The cries to God have become a desire to understand how God could allow the people of Judah to see their city and the temple destroyed. This makes no sense in the light of Zion theology. Zion theology assumes that God will always protect Jerusalem and his temple: they will never be destroyed. Protection happened during the Assyrian invasion of 701 BC, when Hezekiah prayed to God, and God delivered his people (2 Kings 18–20; Isa. 36–38); many in Jerusalem believed that this

9. Ferris, "Lamentations 2."
10. Boda, "Lamentations 1."
11. Ibid., 406–7.

would happen again with the Babylonian threat. It did not. Instead, Jerusalem fell, the temple was destroyed, and the people were killed or deported. The cry of Lamentations repeatedly seeks for God to bring an end to the punishment and have mercy on the survivors. Zion now understands that sin has brought this about and that only the mercy of God remains. The survivors lament their suffering and sin, and they seek God's salvation.

Key Commentaries and Studies

Berlin, Adele. *Lamentations: A Commentary.* OTL. Louisville: Westminster John Knox, 2002. An expert in literary analysis provides a careful reading of the book.

Dearman, J. Andrew. *Jeremiah/Lamentations.* NIVAC. Grand Rapids: Zondervan, 2002. The two-part nature of this series provides for some good application in terms of responses to suffering.

Garrett, Duane A., and Paul R. House. *Song of Songs/Lamentations.* WBC 23B. Nashville: Nelson, 2004. The study provides a strong and useful emphasis on theology.

Longman, Tremper, III. *Jeremiah, Lamentations.* NIBC. Peabody, MA: Hendrickson, 2008. These valuable insights address the poetry and theology of the book.

Parry, Robin. *Lamentations.* Two Horizons OT Commentary. Grand Rapids: Eerdmans, 2010. Another good example of application and the response to suffering.

Rah, Soong-Chan. *Prophetic Lament: A Call for Justice in Troubled Times.* Resonate Series. Downers Grove, IL: InterVarsity Press, 2015. An important non-Western view of the significance of Lamentations for today.

22

EZEKIEL

At times the book of Ezekiel seems like something out of a strange fantasy or science fiction story. This unusual prophet may act surprisingly, but he paints amazing scenes of God, the present, and the future.

Name, Text, and Outline

As with the other prophetic books, the name of the book of Ezekiel corresponds to the prophet and the presumed author. The name Ezekiel consists of two parts and carries a confessional meaning, "God strengthens."

The Masoretic Text of this book is generally well preserved. The Dead Sea Scrolls of Ezekiel consist of fragments from seven scrolls, preserving only a few verses.[1] However, the Greek translation of the Septuagint, as represented in Codex Vaticanus and Chester Beatty Papyrus 967, reflects a different order in some of the material, as in Jeremiah.[2] For example, Papyrus 967 moves the vision of chapter 37 to immediately before the final vision chapters of Ezekiel 40–48. Papyrus 967 does not have the texts of 36:23c–38.[3] Overall, the Masoretic Text often includes more material than the earliest Greek versions do. Some feel that Papyrus 967 preserves the closest text to the original Greek translation and that it translates an earlier Hebrew text that predates the Masoretic Text.[4] Nevertheless, both the Masoretic Text and the early Greek

1. Lilly, *Two Books of Ezekiel*, 23.

2. Four fragments of Papyrus 967 have been published, as found in Cologne, Dublin, Madrid, and Princeton. See ibid., 1. It is dated to the late second/third century AD. For other early Greek manuscripts, see Olley, *Ezekiel*, 7–12.

3. Also missing are Ezek. 12; 26–28; 32:25–26.

4. Tov, *Textual Criticism*, 299–301; Lilly, *Two Books of Ezekiel*.

texts remain close in content. Ingrid Lilly has designated the two forms of Ezekiel as variant literary editions.[5]

OUTLINE

I. Prophecies against Israel and the World (1:1–33:33)
  A. Prophecies against Israel (1:1–24:27)
    1. Ezekiel's Call (1:1–3:27)
    2. Judgment Signs (4:1–7:27)
    3. Vision of the Temple and Judgment (8:1–11:25)
    4. Judgment Coming (12:1–14:23)
    5. Word Pictures (15:1–17:24)
    6. Personal Responsibility (18:1–32)
    7. Lament over Israel's Princes (19:1–14)
    8. Judgment and Destruction on Israel (20:1–24:27)
      a. Rebellious Israel (20:1–49 [21:5 MT])
      b. Babylon's Judgment (21:1–32 [21:6–37 MT])
      c. Judgment against Jerusalem (22:1–31)
      d. Images of God's People (23:1–24:14)
      e. Ezekiel's Wife Dies (24:15–27)
  B. Prophecies against Other Nations (25:1–32:32)
    1. Ammon (25:1–7)
    2. Moab (25:8–11)
    3. Edom (25:12–14)
    4. Philistia (25:15–17)
    5. Tyre (26:1–28:19)
    6. Sidon (28:20–26)
    7. Egypt (29:1–32:32)
  C. Ezekiel the Watchman (33:1–33)
II. Prophecies of Hope and Restoration (34:1–48:35)
  A. Proclamation of Salvation and Restoration (34:1–39:29)
    1. Yahweh's Flock (34:1–31)
    2. Yahweh's Land (35:1–36:15)
    3. Yahweh's People (36:16–38)
    4. Vision of Dry Bones as Israel Restored (37:1–14)
    5. Yahweh's Eternal Covenant with Israel (37:15–28)
    6. Gog and Magog (38:1–39:29)
  B. Vision of the Future (40:1–48:35)
    1. New Temple (40:1–43:11)
    2. New Torah (43:12–46:24)
    3. New Land (47:1–48:29)
    4. New City (48:30–35)

5. Lilly, *Two Books of Ezekiel.*

Overview of Ezekiel

Ezekiel, living in exile along the Kebar River, receives a vision when he is thirty years old (Ezek. 1). In the middle of a windstorm, a bright light reveals four humanlike creatures with faces and wings. The faces include those of a human, a lion, an ox, and an eagle. The creatures move with wheels. Above the creatures is a vault, above the vault is a throne, and above that appears a radiant figure, something resembling the glory of the Lord. God sends Ezekiel among his rebellious people Israel with the command to proclaim his message fearlessly (Ezek. 2). God gives Ezekiel a scroll and commands him to eat it (Ezek. 3). It tastes sweet as honey. God's spirit lifts Ezekiel and carries him to the exiles in Tel-abib, near the Kebar River of Babylonia. He remains seated and depressed for a week. God appoints Ezekiel as a watcher to warn the people.

God has Ezekiel draw a picture of Jerusalem on a piece of clay and then set up an iron pan to symbolize the siege of the city (Ezek. 4). Ezekiel must lie on his left side for 390 days to bear the people's sin, followed by an additional 40 days of lying on his right side. He is to be tied down during this time but have beside him a jar of grains and beans to bake bread and eat it, using human waste for his fuel. When Ezekiel objects, God allows him to use cow dung for fuel. This symbolizes the scarcity of food and water in the coming famine. God commands Ezekiel to shave his head and beard (Ezek. 5). At the end of his time of observing the siege, he must burn a third of his hair in the city, strike another third with a sword, and scatter another third to the wind. Only a few hairs are to be gathered and preserved in Ezekiel's garment. This symbolizes the terrible punishment facing Jerusalem, where a third will die by famine and disease, a third will perish by the enemy's sword, and a third will be scattered. Jerusalem's fate serves as a warning to others. God commands Ezekiel to address the mountains of Israel (Ezek. 6). He will bring a sword of judgment against the people of Jerusalem and destroy their high places, where they falsely worship other deities. (See plate 7 in the gallery for an image of a cult stand portraying images of ancient deities.) The people will also perish. A small number will remain, and God will scatter them across the nations, where they will remember God and know that he is their Lord. Israel will know this after he brings against them sword, famine, and plague (Ezek. 7). None will escape. All their precious valuables will be given to others. Nothing will save them from judgment.

Ezekiel 8 portrays a night vision in which God shows Ezekiel the temple of Jerusalem. Instead of worshiping the true God, the people are worshiping various false deities. After instructing a scribe to mark the foreheads of all of those who grieve and mourn over the detestable things in Jerusalem, God sends six armed men to kill all in Jerusalem who do not have the mark (Ezek. 9). The glory of the Lord appears above a throne and moves outward from the inner court to the threshold of the temple (Ezek. 10). This throne and the cherubim who guard it cause Ezekiel to remember the vision described in the first chapter. Ezekiel prophesies against the leaders of Jerusalem (Ezek. 11). One of them, Pelatiah, dies. God promises to bring back those whom he has deported among the nations. The glory of the Lord then departs from the city of Jerusalem and moves to the mountain east of it. Ezekiel returns to his place of exile in Babylonia.

© Baker Publishing Group and Dr. James C. Martin. The Israel Museum.

Cherubs from tenth-century-BC Taanach cult stand

God promises that his judgment—the exile of Jerusalem's leader, the fear and despair of its inhabitants—will come true. He uses Ezekiel as a sign (Ezek. 12). In chapter 13, God commands Ezekiel to prophesy against the false prophets who promise peace and those who practice magic. God speaks to Ezekiel and commands him to prophesy against the elders and others who have worshiped idols in their hearts (Ezek. 14). Even righteous figures of the past, such as Noah, Job, and Daniel (or Danel, 14:20 NRSV mg.; Ezek. 28:3 NRSV mg.), would not be able to save this generation due to its wickedness. God promises to treat the people of Jerusalem like wood that is charred and no longer useful for anything (Ezek. 15). In the longest chapter in the book (Ezek. 16), God describes Israel as one he found on the day of her birth and provided for her life. When she grew up, he married her and gave her food, clothing, and jewels. However, Israel turned against him and sought to worship other gods, described as pursuing other lovers. She paid for the lovers rather than having them pay for her. God will punish his unfaithful bride. Her sisters, Samaria and Sodom, also sinned, but Judah did much worse than the others. A parable about two eagles and a vine pictures the recent history of Israel as the country and its kings fall under the rule of Babylon's king yet seek futile alliances with Egypt (Ezek. 17). In chapter 18, God affirms that each person is personally responsible for his or her sins. A child will not be punished for the sins of the parent, nor vice versa. Chapter 19 records a poetic lament in which the kings are pictured as strong lion cubs.

Nevertheless, Egypt leads one of these kings away, and Babylon takes another captive. The prophecy warns that these word pictures are not merely words (Ezek. 20). They represent what will come to pass. In the past, Israel sinned. In the wilderness, God gave them up so that they could follow other laws, which led them to kill their firstborn (20:25–26). Israel will suffer for its sins, but God will renew and restore it in the future. The prophet announces a sword that will bring judgment against Israel and another that will destroy Ammon (Ezek. 21). The king of Babylon will bring both. God commands Ezekiel to prophesy against Jerusalem as a city that has shed blood and worshiped idols (Ezek. 22). He indicts that city for oppression of the weak, incest, and all sorts of violations of the laws of God. There is no one to build the wall where the gap was (22:30–31). Ezekiel 23 presents an allegory of two women, Oholah and Oholibah. The older sister, Oholah, is Samaria, and Oholibah is Jerusalem. They engage in prostitution with Egypt first and then continue with Assyria and Babylon. Assyria destroys Oholah, and Babylon will destroy Oholibah. Because of Jerusalem's idolatry and bloodshed, God will give her into the hands of a mob to be abused. God informs Ezekiel when the king of Babylon begins to lay siege to Jerusalem (Ezek. 24). God takes away the delight of Ezekiel's eyes but commands him not to mourn: Ezekiel's wife dies in the evening, and he does not mourn. God intends this as a sign to the people. A messenger will announce the destruction of the temple of Jerusalem, but the people should not mourn.

God turns his judgment to the other nations. Ammon and Moab have rejoiced at Israel's destruction, so they will perish at the hands of people from the east (Ezek. 25). Edom and Philistia took revenge with malice against Jerusalem and Judah. God will wipe out their people and land. Ezekiel 26 warns Tyre that, because the city rejoiced at Jerusalem's destruction, many nations will come against Tyre and destroy it. Nebuchadnezzar will bring his armies against Tyre, and the city will become a bare rock. Chapter 27 is a lament against Tyre, a city engaged in international trade, and sailors will mourn its downfall. The ruler of Tyre is full of pride and thinks he is a god, but he will be brought low and die a violent death at the hands of foreign enemies (Ezek. 28). Although the king had been in Eden and bedecked with jewels, his pride will cost him everything. The chapter ends with a judgment on Sidon and the promise that God will regather Israel. Ezekiel 29 describes the pride of the pharaoh, who claims the Nile for himself; God's judgment is coming in the form of King Nebuchadnezzar of Babylon. The following chapter (Ezek. 30) describes judgment against Egypt's allies in Africa and Arabia, and against the cities of Egypt itself. Verses 20–26 announce that the pharaoh's arm has been broken, that the Babylonian king will be strengthened in his attack against Egypt, and that the Egyptians will be deported. The prophet describes a great tree, applying it first to Assyria and then to Egypt (Ezek. 31). All die and go to the realm of the dead. Elam, Meshech, Tubal, Edom, and Sidon are among those whose kings and armies lie dead and have gone down to the pit (Ezek. 32). Pharaoh will join them.

Ezekiel 33 describes someone appointed by a city to keep watch. If he sees the enemy coming and warns the people, then he is innocent of any responsibility for what happens. If people who are sinning repent, God will have mercy. If people who are righteous begin to sin, God will judge them. In 33:21 Ezekiel is told of the fall of Jerusalem. His shock at the event contrasts with the people of Jerusalem, who have assumed it would never fall. Meanwhile Ezekiel's neighbors come to hear his prophecies, but they do not apply them.

They agree to what he says but then go their own way. In chapter 34 Ezekiel indicts Israel's leaders as shepherds who do not take care of their sheep. God will gather Israel from the nations and take care of his flock. He will give his servant David to be their one shepherd, and they will live in peace and safety.

In Ezekiel 35 God's words through the prophet indict Mount Seir, the home of Edom. Edom handed refugees from Jerusalem over to the enemy Babylonians. They rejoiced in the downfall of Israel and Judah as a means to acquire more land. God is against them and will make their land a wasteland. In contrast, chapter 36 begins with a promise that the despised land of Israel will again be fruitful. It will prepare for the return of God's people. He will take away their heart of stone and give them a heart of flesh. He will resettle them in their native land and make them fruitful, blessed, and secure. Ezekiel 37 describes this in the form of an allegory that pictures a valley of dry bones. Commanded by God, Ezekiel prophesies, and the dry bones come together, skin grows on them, and they become living creatures. God will gather Israel from the foreign lands and return them to their own land, where they will be united under God's servant David.

Ezekiel 38 and 39 turn to consider the nations and cities of the far north, the ruler Gog and the land of Magog. They will attack Israel, but God will defeat them and bring judgment on this enemy. So great will be the battle and slaughter of Gog and his armies that the nation of Israel will not need to gather wood for seven years. They will use remains from the battle for burning. The world will know that the God of Israel has punished his people for their sin but now has brought them back.

In Ezekiel 40–42 an angel shows the prophet the details of the temple and temple court that he must tell God's people. The glory of the Lord then returns from the east (43:2; where it had departed to in 11:22–23) to this temple, and an altar is to be prepared there for sacrifices (Ezek. 43). There follow instructions about the priesthood (descendants of Zadok) who will serve at the temple. Israel will allot the land as an inheritance for the tribes and will make specific sacrifices, according to the instructions (Ezek. 45–46). A river will flow from the temple, becoming deeper and broader until it reaches the Dead Sea, where it will bring life of many kinds to that place (Ezek. 47). The remainder of chapters 47 and 48 describes the division of the land in terms of what each tribe will receive. There will be three gates on each of the four sides of the city (of Jerusalem), and its new name will be "The Lord is there."

Reading Ezekiel

Premodern Readings

The earliest mention of Ezekiel outside the Old Testament may be that of Ben Sira (Sir. 49:8), where Ezekiel is one of the well-known Israelites.[6] The

6. Cf. Duguid, "Ezekiel: History of Interpretation," 229–33.

Dead Sea Scrolls community at Qumran left the *Temple Scroll*, which develops its own vision for a future temple, but one not unrelated to Ezekiel 40–46.

Rabbinic tradition appreciated the *merkabah*, the divine throne-chariot, which Ezekiel sees in a God-given vision as his book begins. This symbolizes the immanence and transcendence of God. Rabbis had problems with the legislation of Ezekiel 44–46, including how to reconcile its festivals and laws with those found in the Pentateuch.

In the early church, Irenaeus identified the four faces of the living creatures in Ezekiel 1 with the four Gospel writers and their productions.[7] These figures represent the Gospel writers throughout the history of Christian art, as illustrated magnificently in the Book of Kells (AD c. 600–1000).[8] Tertullian (*De resurrectione carnis* 30.1) used Ezekiel 37 as a proof text for the resurrection. Later sieges of the city of Rome led Jerome (AD 410, 414) and Gregory I (ca. AD 600) to preach on Ezekiel texts reflecting the captivity of the saints.[9] Nevertheless, Jerome puzzled over the prophecy of Tyre's destruction because Tyre flourished in his day. Augustine used especially Ezekiel 18, 22, and 34 in his doctrinal works.[10] In the medieval period the closed eastern gate of Ezekiel 44:1–3 became an allegory for the incarnation. Since only the Lord entered it, and then it was forever shut, it became a text to assert Mary's perpetual virginity.[11]

In the Reformation, Martin Luther identified the threat of Gog (Ezek. 38–39; cf. Rev. 20) with the Islamic Turks, who reached the gates of Vienna in 1529.[12] For Luther, Ezekiel 1 portrays Christ coming into the world. Chapters 40–48 describe the church as the temple that survives until the end of the age.[13] John Calvin followed a more historical approach and understood Ezekiel in its ancient context. Thus the vision of dry bones (Ezek. 37) becomes a picture of the scattering and restoration of Israel.[14] Its application includes passing on hope to Christianity. Among the Puritans, William Greenhill composed a commentary of five volumes on Ezekiel. While connecting the ancient historical context with current application, he nevertheless resisted many direct identifications with contemporaries. He admitted uncertainty as to who was the enemy of the church (i.e., Ezekiel's Gog), and he saw the temple vision as related to Christianity, but he did not try to resolve many issues that were puzzling to him.

7. Irenaeus, *Haer.* iii.11.7–8; Christman, "*What Did Ezekiel See?*," 14–17.

8. Meehan, *The Book of Kells*, 62–63 (plate 42).

9. Jerome, *Comm. Ezech.*, prologue; Gregory the Great, *Homilae in Ezechielem Prophetam*; Kessler, "Gregory the Great," 142–43.

10. Duguid, "Ezekiel: History of Intepretation," 231.

11. So Thomas Aquinas, *Summa Theologica* III Q.XXVII art. 3.

12. Luther, *Luther's Works*, vol. 45, 202.

13. Luther, *Luther's Works*, vol. 35, 293.

14. Duguid, "Ezekiel: History of Intepretation," 232.

Higher Criticism

In 1924 Gustav Hölscher became the first modern scholar to publish a challenge to the view of a single authorship of Ezekiel.[15] He found that only 144 of the book's 1,273 verses make up the the original text of a poet prophet. Later scribes writing in the priestly tradition added the remaining verses. Charles C. Torrey followed by assessing Ezekiel as a pseudepigraphic work written in third-century-BC Judah.[16] Views emerged that either found a lengthy redaction process or advocated a few major redactors.[17] However, some later commentators have maintained the traditional view of a single author producing the prophetic work in the Babylonian exile, during the sixth century BC. Indeed, the fourteen superscriptions with dates provide more such information than in any other prophetic book. The book opens with a date of 593 BC (1:1–3) and includes dates as late as 571 BC (29:17). Major commentaries by Moshe Greenberg and Daniel Block have challenged the assumptions about multiple layers of redaction and the likelihood of demonstrating the existence of such, as well as identifying their extent, time, and rationale of insertion.[18] Nevertheless, the search for seams and editorial layers of texts continues.[19]

Foundational to much critical discussion has been the assumption that Ezekiel represents the priestly line of thought and writing, just as Jeremiah represents that of Deuteronomy and the language of covenant. Thus Ezekiel discusses purity, holiness, and priestly manifestations such as the temple. Since the pentateuchal Priestly document has a traditional assignment to the postexilic period, the work of Ezekiel has been interpreted either as a precursor to the later priestly writings or, more often, as having its origin or significant redaction among the priestly circle of writers.[20]

Early twentieth-century scholars cited texts such as Ezekiel 18 to argue for the book propounding a radical break with Israelite corporate identity and introducing emphasis on the individual; later studies have recognized that these texts are less concerned with individual responsibilities and more concerned with each generation recognizing its own place before God, regardless of what the previous generation has done or believed.

Ezekiel has been a fruitful source for a variety of perspectives. There have been attempts to psychoanalyze the prophet in light of his strange behaviors.[21] However, such behavior is not so strange in light of prophets of the Bible, of Mari, and in other sources. Further, such analysis remains speculative given

15. Hölscher, *Hesekiel*.
16. Torrey, *Pseudo-Ezekiel*.
17. On a lengthy redaction process, see Zimmerli, *Ezekiel*; on a few major redactors, see Clements, "Ezekiel Tradition."
18. Greenberg, *Ezekiel*; Block, *Book of Ezekiel*.
19. Bowen, "Ezekiel."
20. Joyce, *Divine Initiative*.
21. Halperin, *Seeking Ezekiel*.

the huge gap in time, culture, and documentation. More productive has been the work championed by Avi Hurvitz and others to look at the language of the book.[22] This has provided a keystone for identifying late biblical Hebrew (i.e., after the exile) and comparing it to preexilic Hebrew. Those who follow this method have argued against some of the tendencies to date many self-identified preexilic texts as late in biblical Hebrew.

Literary Readings

The book of Ezekiel differs from others written by prophets, with its lengthy narratives in prose and its oracles in poetry. Like Jeremiah, Ezekiel focuses on the personal side of the prophet and his difficult circumstances in light of God's calling. Similar to both Isaiah and Jeremiah (as well as Minor Prophets such as Zephaniah), the book has three great parts: judgments against God's people, Judah (Ezek. 1–24); judgments against other nations of the known world (Ezek. 25–32); and promises of restoration and future blessing for God's people (Ezek. 33–48). The opening twenty-four chapters focus on mourning, whether consuming the scroll of mourning at the beginning (2:8) or the death of the prophet's wife at the end (24:18). The subsequent oracles against the nations, like the festive garments of 24:15–18, signify that the mourning will end with the judgment of Jerusalem's destruction. The messenger of 33:21–22 also signals that, with the judgment, the mourning has ended.

Strong word pictures appear. The stunning figure of God in his throne-chariot (Ezek. 1) gives way to a scroll of mourning that the prophet eats, which becomes part of him (Ezek. 2), and to his commission as a watcher-guardian to warn the people of death (3:16–20; also 33:1–9). Ezekiel then turns to the dramatic visuals of building a model of Jerusalem under siege and lying beside it for more than a year (4:1–8), of consuming food cooked in an unclean manner (4:9–17), and of shaving his head and burning, striking, and scattering the hair (5:1–4). There follows a twofold warning of the destructive judgment coming because of Israel's sin, a warning in prose (Ezek. 6) and in poetry (Ezek. 7).

Ezekiel becomes even more involved in the drama as he is transported to Jerusalem to see the idolatrous activities within the holy temple of Jerusalem (Ezek. 8) and the judgment that follows (Ezek. 9–11). In chapter 12 the word pictures again occur: Ezekiel must leave his home and dig through a wall as though escaping and going into exile. Israel is a useless vine (Ezek. 15), a faithless wife (Ezek. 16), and a people who follow a weak king. Nevertheless, a shoot will take root and produce a messianic figure (Ezek. 17).

A repeating indictment pattern occurs against Israel (5:7–11) and its neighbors (25:1–17). It takes the form "Because [they have sinned], . . . therefore

22. Hurvitz, *Transition Period*; idem, *Linguistic Study*.

[God will bring judgment]." In this manner God illuminates the guilt of the nations, one after the other, and provides justification for the promised punishment. The prophecy against Tyre portrays the city as a ship, laden with goods but sinking into the sea (27:1–36). A series of word pictures describes a similar fate for Egypt and its proud ruler: a sea monster hooked (29:1–6), the broken arms of the pharaoh (30:20–26), a fallen tree (31:1–18), and descent to the realm of the dead, where lie the fallen of other warrior nations (32:17–32).

One of the most powerful and enduring word pictures is that of chapter 37, where Ezekiel sees Israel as a valley of scattered dry bones that begin to take on sinew and flesh and join together to form "a vast army" (37:10 NIV). So Israel will return from the "death" of exile and unite to bear witness to God's miraculous salvation. The restored temple and land of Ezekiel 40–48 become a word picture in themselves of God's faithfulness. Chapter 47 provides a dramatic scene of water gushing from the blessed city and transforming the desert into a place of life, as the river grows deeper and wider.[23] These differing views have been used to justify or dismiss the role of the current State of Israel in God's plan.

Gender and Ideological Criticism

Ezekiel 13:17 suggests that there were women prophets before the exile (in addition to the Huldah of 2 Kings 22:14 and 2 Chron. 34:22). Such observations may balance the awful picture of Jerusalem as an adulterous wife whom the jealous husband brutally punishes in chapter 16. God found Israel as an abandoned and helpless baby, and he raised her to womanhood. At that point he married Israel. But Israel betrayed her husband. The graphic descriptions presented here have led to charges of pornography, understood as the sexually abusive portrayal of a woman. Here the prophet describes the depth and gravity of Israel's sin (not sexual but) of rebellion against the true God and the worship of other deities. The image of adultery becomes the means by which God communicates the horror and hurt that Israel's faithlessness has caused God and the terrible consequences.

A similar charge has been directed toward Ezekiel 23 and the two sisters who engage in prostitution. These represent Samaria and Judah, both of whom have committed many sins against their own people and against God. Here again, hyperbole becomes a literary means to describe the betrayal felt by God.

One of the most controversial issues has to do with the restoration of the temple and land as described in Ezekiel 40–48, and its implications for the modern State of Israel. Among evangelicals, traditional dispensationalists see a physical temple as a fulfillment of this prophecy, yet to come in the millennium. On the contrary, many amillennialists and historic premillennialists

23. Hess, "Future Written in the Past."

Tammuz and Dumuzi

Tammuz is the Semitic name of the older Sumerian figure known as Dumuzi. In a myth tradition that may have originated long before writing developed, this god negotiated with the underworld deity to arrange for the release of his beloved. However, the bargain required Dumuzi to spend six months of each year in the underworld. During this time the earth went into mourning so that there was no rain upon the land. This was the summer, when vegetation died and the end was near. Only when Dumuzi was released did the rainy season begin and the hoped-for emergence of new crops. Such a myth received popular support and worship throughout the ancient Near East, where Dumuzi became Tammuz. It also became popular in Egypt and in the Greco-Roman world, where it evolved into the myth of Adonis and Persephone. Thousands of years after its origin, Christian bishops, pastors, and theologians throughout the Mediterranean world continued to condemn practices associated with the worship of this nature cycle.

see these chapters as figurative and fulfilled in the person of Jesus Christ, or perhaps in the new Jerusalem of the final chapters of Revelation. The latter provides an explanation that does not directly create issues in terms of fulfillment. Those who accept some sort of real historical temple in Jerusalem join a variety of groups during the time of Jesus of Nazareth who also understood Ezekiel in this manner.

Ancient Near Eastern Context

The book of Ezekiel imitates the ancient laments over the downfall of a beloved city (see also Lamentations). These date more than a millennium before the time of the prophet and continue for centuries after this prophet. The most famous is the lament over the destruction of the Sumerian city of Ur, from the beginning of the second millennium BC. Ezekiel uses this form of city lament but then pours new content into it so as to benefit the community in exile with the signs and promises of a restoration.

Daniel Bodi has demonstrated structural, thematic, and linguistic parallels between the book of Ezekiel and the Babylonian poem of Erra, written about a century and a half before the fall of Jerusalem.[24] It also appears as the result of the fall of a city, in this case Babylon. Further, it describes the departure of deities from the city and their later return and the restoration of worship. It is possible that Ezekiel could have been aware of this poem.

24. Bodi, *Ezekiel and the Poem of Erra.*

Daniel in Ezekiel

Ezekiel 14:14 and 16 mention righteous heroes of the past who would not have rescued Judah despite their righteousness (for similar situations, cf. Abraham in Gen. 18:20–32 and Moses in Exod. 33:17). Noah and Job are well known in the Bible, but Danel is not attested in Scripture outside Ezekiel 14:14, 20; 28:3. The name is spelled in a manner different from that of the biblical prophet Daniel. The absence of the Hebrew *yod* is not a variant spelling of Daniel but preserves an ancient character also remembered in the myths from the thirteenth-century-BC Syrian city of Ugarit. There the mythic Danel played the role of a polytheist who offended the goddess Anat. In the Bible no such myth exists. Rather, Danel is a man who worships the true God of Israel and lives righteously.

Much of Israelite religion, both true and false, appears in Ezekiel. There are the incense burners of Ezekiel 6:4–6 that were foreign to what God commanded but part of the worship of gods throughout Canaan. The practices in the temple as outlined in chapter 8 represent the worship of other deities in God's house. The worship of animals in the sanctuary (8:9–11) may depict deities from countries such as Egypt. However, they could also identify Canaanite deities, where artists portrayed El as a bull, Baal as a calf, Astarte as a lion, and so forth. The mourning for Tammuz involved worship of the forces of nature in the annual cycle of rainy and dry seasons.

The worship of the sun was explicitly condemned in God's original covenant (Deut. 4:19; 17:3). Yet 2 Kings (23:5, 11), like Ezekiel, attests its presence in the later years of Judah's independent monarchy. The first eleven chapters of this prophetic book may be compared to the "Opening of the Mouth" rituals found in Babylonian texts.[25] In contrast to the Babylonian usage of this ritual that transformed an image into the presence of the living deity, Ezekiel has his mouth opened by God and becomes the living image of God, to proclaim his message against those who worship the false images.

Historically, the mightiest powers of Ezekiel's day, other than Babylon,[26] were Tyre and Egypt. These dominate the prophecies against the nations of chapters 25–32. Tyre represents economic wealth and pride, the desire for acquisition. It is portrayed as a sinking ship, laden with goods from trading with the world's greatest ports (Ezek. 26–27). The lament over the king of Tyre (28:1–19) incorporates imagery from ancient Canaanite mythic poetry

25. Strine, "Ezekiel's Image Problem."
26. Cf. Ganzel and Holtz, "Ezekiel's Temple in Babylonian Context."

The bronze gates of Balawat portraying the island city of Tyre

Band from the gates of the palace of Shalmaneser III, ca. 848 BC (bronze), Neo-Assyrian 9th century BC/British Museum, London, UK/De Agostini Picture Library/G. Dagli Orti/Bridgeman Images

and from the serpent (here [28:12–16] the representative of all pride and sin, often understood as Satan) in the garden of Eden (cf. Gen. 3). It applies these layers of description to the king of Tyre, who would have been Ithobaal III, according to the Jewish historian Josephus. In the first century AD, Josephus records how Nebuchadnezzar laid siege to Tyre for thirteen years and defeated it. Nevertheless, the utter destruction of the fortress island as described in Ezekiel 26 may have included, in the prophetic vision, further attacks by Alexander the Great and others. The fortress remained until the Muslims drove out the Crusaders in the thirteenth century AD. After that it was reduced to a village.

Egypt under Pharaoh Hophra remained weak and awaited Nebuchadnezzar's attack on the country, followed by the subsequent conquests by the Persians, Alexander, the Romans, and the Muslim invaders. It would never return to its power and strength as of old.

For Edom, the greatest emphasis of Ezekiel 35 is how the land will become desolate and a waste, in contrast to God's blessing on Judah. This provides an ironic twist to the archaeological evidence of Edom's encroachment over the southern border of Judah during the final decades before the fall of Jerusalem to the Babylonians. Forts, cult centers, and texts give evidence of Edom in land that belonged to Judah. Their theft of this land and its value would be reversed as Edom faced oblivion.

Canonical Context

Old Testament connections abound in Ezekiel. The indictment of the shepherds of Israel in Ezekiel 34 forms the background for Zechariah 11. The book of Daniel also shares similar themes: it is concerned with the fall of Jerusalem and a coming restoration. Both are written in a context of the authors living far from their native lands.

The new temple of Ezekiel 40–42 shares a host of architectural features with the temple of Solomon in 1 Kings 6. Although much is modeled on the earlier structure, the rooms of 42:1 and other features are not previously known. So also the various details of the offerings, priests, Levites, and diet and lifestyle have their parallels in the book of Leviticus. The priestly role to distinguish between the holy and the common, and between the clean and unclean (Ezek. 44:23), has its origins in Leviticus 10:10. Likewise, the concerns for justice, the observance of festivals, and other procedures in chapters 45–46 possess parallels in the various legal collections of the Torah. On the theme of the waters of chapter 47, see "Theological Perspectives of Ezekiel," below.

In the New Testament, Jesus identifies himself as the Son of Man (Matt. 8:20; Mark 2:28; Luke 5:24; John 1:51). No figure receives this title more frequently in the Old Testament than Ezekiel, some ninety times in this book. It appears as a common designation for Ezekiel as representative of the human race, rather than as a figure with messianic implications, such as in Daniel 7:13–14.

Ezekiel 3:17–18 (and Ezek. 22) identifies the prophet's responsibility as a watcher, a "sentinel." Along with the shepherd imagery of chapter 34, this recurs in the New Testament, as in the language in John 10:1–16 and Acts 20:28. God commands Ezekiel to eat a scroll that tastes as sweet as honey but contains laments (Ezek. 3:1–3). In like manner the angel commands John in Revelation (10:9–10) to eat the scroll that tastes as sweet as honey but contains judgments. The promise of the new life of God's spirit resurrecting the dry bones in Ezekiel 37:14 becomes a source of inspiration for the new life in Christ (John 11:25–26; Rom. 8:9–17; Col. 3:1–4; etc.).

Ezekiel 36:24–25 and the cleansing by water anticipates John 3:5. Ezekiel 36:27 and God's emphasis on "my spirit" anticipate Jesus's statements about being born of water and of the Spirit, also in the same verse in John (3:5). Jesus refers to himself as "the good shepherd" (John 10:11, 14), for which compare Ezekiel 34. The battle with Gog in Ezekiel 38–39 becomes universal in Revelation 20:8–9. Much in Ezekiel 47–48 appears in a new form in the last two chapters of Revelation. There the new Jerusalem emerges with its twelve gates and the river that flows from it, with the tree of life growing beside it. Unlike Ezekiel, there is no temple in the new Jerusalem. Instead, the entire city has become a most holy place (holy of holies).

Theological Perspectives of Ezekiel

Israel's history is one of sin and rebellion: Jerusalem has exceeded the rest of the world in wickedness (Ezek. 5:6–7) instead of being a symbol of righteousness. The 390 days when Ezekiel is to lie on his left side (4:5) symbolize 390 years from the time of Solomon's temple; it is a time of sin and corruption in worship (5:9–11), rather than the temple being a blessing for God's people to come near him. God intends that the people of Israel "will know that I the Lord have spoken in my zeal"; this phrase occurs in 5:13 (NIV) and seventy-one other times in Ezekiel. It forms the purpose of God's acts: so that his people will come to recognize him as their God. While it is true that a remnant is promised, the emphasis on the judgment of God's people and God's justice in acting as he does so dominates the first thirteen chapters with such intensity that no call to repentance appears before 14:6.

The opening chapter of the book presents a dramatic vision that highlights how different God is, thus presenting him as holy in contrast to the world he has created. Ezekiel 2:5 and the following texts present the sin of God's people, a theme that provides the background for Ezekiel's prophetic role of proclaiming the guilt of God's people. The theme of God's holiness reemerges at the end of the book, where "The Lord is there" becomes the name and thus the characteristic of restored Jerusalem (48:35). In between, the prophetic revelation seeks to answer the most vexing of questions. If God is sovereign and truly almighty, how can his temple and city fall to the Babylonians? The answer appears in the ongoing and terrible sins of God's people, even present in the temple itself (Ezek. 8). This is so great that God must judge the people. However, the sin in his holy temple cannot be tolerated. God cannot continue to live among his people. So the glory of the Lord rises from the most holy place and departs from the sanctuary, then from the temple courts, and finally from the city itself (9:3; 10:4, 18–19; 11:23). With the departure of God's presence from Jerusalem, the terrible judgment can come as the Babylonians invade, destroy, and slaughter. The city and temple fall, but not because Israel's God, Yahweh, is too weak. They fall because God is no longer there. It is this picture that is reversed in the final part of the book. God will give his people his presence again by restoring their hearts (Ezek. 34–36), re-creating their nation (Ezek. 37), granting sovereignty over their enemies (Ezek. 38–39), and then restoring the temple, the land, and the city of Jerusalem (Ezek. 40–48). The return of God's glory appears in 43:2 and the remainder of the chapter. Although it shares none of the pictorial vividness of the beginning of the book, Ezekiel compares it to his earlier vision (43:3).

The message of Ezekiel 18 and 20 stresses that sin and guilt do not pass down from parents to their children. Rather, each person remains individually responsible for his or her own sin. Further, the same is true of the righteous person. They cannot depend on their parents' righteousness but only on their own. Thus each believer bears individual responsibility before God. Such individual responsibility extends even to the monarchy: a lament is raised for the end of the rule of the Davidic dynasty (Ezek. 19). Responsibility includes decisions made in one's life. A life of righteousness that ends in sin is doomed to judgment, while a life of sin that ends with repentance and turning to follow God's will can lead to new life (33:12–16).

The indictment against Judah's leadership, the shepherds (34:1–10), follows the report of Jerusalem's fall (33:21–33, judgment for their sins) and anticipates the true divine shepherd and a coming king who will care for the sheep (34:11–24), with a covenant of peace and blessing (34:25–31). An important text is 36:24–27, where God's promise to restore Israel includes returning from exile (cf. Ezek. 37, where this is pictured as dry bones resurrecting), sprinkling with water and so cleansing from sin, heart renewal by the spirit of God, and with a new heart of flesh, the ability to live according to God's will. In 36:38 the promised abundance of God's people will be linked to the temple in Jerusalem.

As Joshua 11:23 and 14:15 describe how Israel and its land must have rest and relief from all enemies that might threaten them before the allocation of the inheritance to the tribes can begin, so Ezekiel 25–32 and especially chapters 38–39 define how the enemies of Israel must be vanquished before it can live at peace in the land and worship God unhindered (Ezek. 40–48).

The new temple, priesthood, and system of sacrifices and festivals demonstrate that the author of Ezekiel saw these not as ending but as continuing into the future. Ezekiel 47:1–12 culminates this restoration with the renewal of the land through an abundant supply of ever-increasing water flowing from the entrance of the temple and transforming the Judean desert and the Dead Sea into an Eden, with an abundance of life. The life-giving picture of water, found already in Genesis 2:10–13, recurs in Psalms (e.g., 36:8; 46:4) and in the other prophetic literature (e.g., Joel 3:18; Zech. 13:1). It reaches a climax in Revelation 22:1–2, where the New Testament fulfillment of Ezekiel's vision is presented.

Key Commentaries and Studies

Allen, Leslie C. *Ezekiel*. Vol. 1, *1–19*. Vol. 2, *20–48*. WBC 28–29. Waco: Word, 1990–94. An evangelical scholar on the Prophets addresses literary and ancient Near Eastern contexts.

Block, Daniel I. *The Book of Ezekiel*. Vol. 1, *1–24*. Vol. 2, *25–48*. NICOT. Grand Rapids: Eerdmans, 1997–98. The strongest evangelical commentary for a detailed exegesis.

Greenberg, Moshe. *Ezekiel: A New Translation with Introduction and Commentary*. Vol. 1, *1–20*. Vol. 2, *21–37*. AB 22–22A. New York: Doubleday, 1983–97. A careful commentary that traces the book as originating substantially from the author Ezekiel.

Olley, John W. *Ezekiel: A Commentary Based on Iezekiēl in Codex Vaticanus*. SCS. Leiden: Brill, 2009. An unusually strong analysis of the LXX book, with insights into the original text.

Tuell, Steven. *Ezekiel*. NIBC. Peabody, MA: Hendrickson, 2009. A recent and important guide to the theology of the book.

Zimmerli, Walther. *Ezekiel*. Vol. 1, *1–24*. Vol. 2, *25–48*. Hermeneia. Philadelphia: Fortress, 1979–83. The major critical commentary available in English, with the series's emphasis on textual criticism and analysis.

23

DANIEL

Need faith? The great stories of Daniel's faith in the face of death and destruction can teach us to hold on to God and resist the temptation to compromise, even when others are surrendering their faith.

Name, Text, and Outline

The name Daniel derives from the book's chief human character. It means "El/God is (my) judge." There are several Daniels in Israel's history (1 Chron. 3:1; Ezra 8:2; Neh. 10:6). The name of an earlier Danel, a famous wise king, is spelled slightly differently from the prophet (cf. NRSV mg. and MT's consonants: Ezek. 14:14, 20; 28:3).

The text of Daniel is preserved partly in Hebrew (1:1–2:4a; 8:1–12:13) and partly in Aramaic (2:4b–7:28). Since this is similar to Ezra, it may suggest an exilic or postexilic setting for the composition. There are two witnesses to Daniel in Greek. One is a Septuagint translation that preserves a different, more chronologically sequential (according to Daniel's own notes) order of the stories and visions: chapters 1–4, 7–8, 5–6, and 9–12. The other, which follows more closely the Hebrew and Aramaic, is Theodotion's text. According to Irenaeus (fl. ca. AD 200) and other sources, Theodotion was a convert to Judaism who lived in the second century AD. However, evidence suggests that parts of Theodotion's Daniel predate the second century. Theodotion's Daniel successfully displaced the Septuagint's Daniel so that the original Septuagint text remains in only three manuscripts from the seventh century and later. The Greek versions added four significant texts to the original (as in the Apocrypha): the Song of the Three Jews, the Prayer of Azariah (with a prose note), Susanna, and Bel and the Dragon. These remain in the Roman Catholic and Eastern Orthodox versions of Daniel.

The Dead Sea Scrolls preserve fragments of at least eight manuscripts of Daniel. Of special interest are three manuscripts from Cave 4 at Qumran that can be dated—on the basis of the style of writing (paleography)—to the second century BC.[1] Of these, Eugene Ulrich's publication of 4QDan[c] contains at least twelve verses from Daniel 11 and raises some interesting questions if the common date of composition for Daniel in the second century BC is accepted.[2] This means that at Qumran the scribes of the Dead Sea Scrolls accepted—as a document for the life, worship, and instruction of their community (as part of their sacred Scripture)—something that was written less than fifty years earlier. It is unlikely that this scroll was written by someone else in the second century BC and only acquired by the people at Qumran in, say for the sake of argument, the first century AD. This is because a community composed of many scribes would have copied their own documents rather than importing them from outside. Indeed, such a conclusion runs contrary to what is known about the Qumran community. They were conservative and unwilling to accept innovation. Therefore, it seems that they would not have readily assented to a text that could be attested by living members of their community as not existing a half a century earlier, yet purporting to come from a much earlier period. This is an unanswered question for a second-century-BC date for Daniel: How could it find its way so quickly into the "canon" of Scriptures and sacred writings at Qumran?[3]

OUTLINE

I. Stories of Faithfulness (1:1–6:28 [6:29 MT])
   A. Introduction: Daniel and Three Friends Enter the Service of the Babylonian King (1:1–21)
   B. Daniel Interprets Nebuchadnezzar's Dream about the Future (2:1–49)
   C. Daniel's Friends Refuse to Worship Nebuchadnezzar's Image and Survive the Furnace (3:1–4:3 [3:33 MT])
   D. Nebuchadnezzar's Madness, Restoration, and Praise to God (4:4–37 [4:1–34 MT])
   E. Belshazzar's Banquet, Pride, and End (5:1–30)
   F. Daniel and the Lions' Den (5:31–6:28 [6:1–29 MT])

II. Visions of the Future (7:1–12:13)
   A. The Four Beasts, the Horns, and the Ancient of Days (7:1–28)
   B. The Kingdoms of Persia and Greece and Those That Follow (8:1–27)

1. See 4QDan[c] (4Q114), 4QDan[d] (4Q115), and 4QDan[e] (4Q116).

2. Ulrich, "Daniel Manuscripts."

3. Ibid. Regarding attestations of Daniel-like statements in early intertestamental literature, that would seem to be unlikely if this book were composed in the second century BC. See R. Beckwith, "Early Traces of the Book of Daniel."

Overview of Daniel

Daniel begins with the destruction of Jerusalem and the temple by King Nebuchadnezzar of Babylon. He takes away some of the young nobles to serve in his palace. Among these are Daniel and his friends (best known by their Babylonian names): Shadrach, Meshach, and Abednego. Their preparation for royal service involves a regimen of study and diet. However, Daniel and his friends choose to forgo the richer food and wine: they request a vegetarian diet with water to drink. After ten days these four are healthier than any of their fellow students. Further, they impress King Nebuchadnezzar as being the wisest sages in his kingdom. Chapter 2 tells the story of the king's demand that his wisdom leaders not only interpret his dream but that they also identify the contents of the dream itself. When the sages are unable to satisfy this request, King Nebuchadnezzar orders them killed. However, when Daniel learns of this, he asks his friends to pray. At night God reveals the dream and its interpretation. Daniel explains to the king how the statue that he saw included a gold head, a silver chest, bronze stomach and thighs, iron legs, and feet of mixed iron and clay. The head represents Nebuchadnezzar's rule. The other parts represent future kingdoms that will be stronger but less glorious. The rock that smashes this image is a divinely established kingdom that will replace its predecessors. The king confesses Daniel's God, appoints his friends to high positions in Babylon, and establishes Daniel as ruler of the province of Babylon and as chief among the sages.

In chapter 3 Daniel's three friends refuse to worship the ninety-foot-high statue of King Nebuchadnezzar. The king is angry and orders the three thrown into a furnace so hot that it burns even those who throw them in. However, the three Jews are not burned, and the king observes a fourth figure, resembling a son of the gods, in the furnace with them. He brings them out, promotes them, and orders that nothing be said against the God of Israel. In chapter 4, Daniel interprets another dream of King Nebuchadnezzar, now one that concerns him alone. God will transform the king into a wild beast, and he will remain so for "seven times." This takes place. When King Nebuchadnezzar regains his sanity, he acknowledges and praises Daniel's God.

Chapter 5 of Daniel moves forward in time to the last day of the Babylonian kingdom. King Belshazzar gives a feast, using the holy vessels carried from the Jerusalem temple decades earlier. A hand appears and writes a message on the wall of the room where all the partyers can see it. Daniel is brought in to give an interpretation. He announces that the kingdom will end. Although the prophet is promoted to third in the kingdom, Babylon falls to the Medes and Persians on that very night. In chapter 6 the Persian king Darius is deceived into ordering that all should pray to him and not pray to anyone else. Rather than follow the king's command, Daniel prays publicly to God three times each day. The king, who likes Daniel, nevertheless must follow his own edict and cast the prophet into the den of lions. However, Daniel remains unharmed through the night. When Darius learns of Daniel's preservation, he decrees that all in his kingdom should fear and reverence the God of Daniel.

Daniel 7 returns to the time of the Babylonian king Belshazzar and describes Daniel's own dream of four hybrid animals that arise from the sea. The fourth has ten horns and a smaller horn, which boasts. This is followed by a vision of heaven in which the Ancient of Days sits in judgment until "one like a son of man" (7:13 NIV) approaches and is given authority and worship from all nations. The explanation given to Daniel involves a succession of future kingdoms. From the last kingdom will come ten kings, and then a king who will subdue three kings and speak against God. He will be destroyed, and God's kingdom will last forever.

Daniel 8 begins with a vision of a ram and a goat with horns. These are explained as the empire of Persia followed by that of Greece. In the case of the latter, four kings would follow the death of the first ruler. From these would come a king who would destroy many who are faithful to God, before this king himself is destroyed.

In chapter 9, Daniel confesses the sins of his people as he reads the prophet Jeremiah, who promises Israel's return to Jerusalem after seventy years. God sends Gabriel to explain that there are seventy sevens decreed for the atonement of Israel. Seven sevens will be followed by sixty-two sevens, at which point "the Anointed One" (9:25–26 NIV) will be put to death, and war will continue. Amid the remaining "seven," sacrifice and offering will cease, and an abomination will be erected at the temple.

In chapter 10, Daniel fasts and has a vision of one sent from God, who was detained by the prince of the Persian kingdom for three weeks and now encourages Daniel to receive the vision. Chapter 11 describes this vision as a time when the kingdom of Greece will overpower Persia. There is a detailed discussion about the king of the South and the king of the North, and their battles with each other. A successor king of the North will be evil but have victories in the South. Nevertheless, ships from the west will drive him away. This king of the North will desecrate the temple and will speak blasphemy against the true God, while exalting "the god of fortresses" (11:38). "At the time of the end" (11:40), the king of the North will fight the king of the South and invade many countries. But his end will come. At that point there will be great distress in Israel (Dan. 12), but the faithful will rise from the dead.

Daniel is commanded to seal the words of this scroll until the time of the end. He asks two others how long it will be until the end. He is told, "a time, two times, and half a time" (12:7). Daniel is to go his way "till the end," when he too will rise to receive his inheritance (12:13 NIV).

Reading Daniel

Premodern Readings

First Maccabees (2:59–60), written in the first half of the first century BC, may be the earliest to describe Daniel and his friends as models of faith and courage.[4] The additions in the Greek translation of Daniel (see "Name, Text, and Outline") demonstrate the interest in augmenting the book with related stories of faith. Among the Dead Sea Scrolls, five fragments attest additional stories related to Daniel; other texts are influenced by Daniel (*War Scroll* [1Q33]) or cite texts from the prophet (*Florilegium* [4Q174]). Jewish literature from the early Christian era develops the motif of four kingdoms (2 Baruch; 2 Esdras [*4 Ezra*]), where the last kingdom is identified with Rome. Josephus follows this approach and embellishes the historical information in Daniel 1–6. *First Enoch* 37–71 develops the Son of Man imagery.

In Judaism, the Son of Man (Dan. 7) became identified as a messianic figure, though some, such as Ibn Ezra, regarded "him" as Israel. Islam's caliphate became one of the prophesied kingdoms.

Irenaeus (fl. ca. AD 200) exemplifies early Christian thought in identifying the stone (Dan. 2:34) and the Son of Man (7:13) with Jesus. Jerome's commentary on Daniel is the best known. It attempts to answer Porphyry's critique of christological interpretations. Medieval theologians continued patristic approaches, occasionally applying the book to contemporary concerns. The Reformers sought to identify the fourth kingdom of Daniel with Roman Catholicism, although John Calvin reaffirmed the historical interpretation of pre-Christian empires. The English Puritans justified their revolution and execution of King Charles I by identifying themselves as those holy people of the Most High (Dan. 7:18, 22, 27) who would overthrow the earthly kingdoms. Sir Isaac Newton used Daniel and Revelation in his study of world chronology.

Higher Criticism

Because of the numerous later additions to the book of Daniel in the Greek text, as well as its compositions in Aramaic and Hebrew, much discussion has taken place in attempting to identify the development of the book.

4. Newsom, "Daniel," 170–71.

Modern critics look back to Porphyry, who in the third century AD challenged the prophetic nature of Daniel and argued that it was composed contemporary with the events it purports to foresee. There has been an assumption by those who eschew the possibility of foreseeing the future that the work was written in the period of the early Maccabean revolt in the early second century BC. Chapters 8–12 in particular appear to describe the rise of Hellenistic powers in Egypt and Syria, and their persecution of the Jewish people in the third and second centuries BC. Thus Daniel 11 describes in detail the activities of the Syrian Antiochus IV as he subdued Egypt, was challenged by Rome, and persecuted the Jews by attempting to force them to abandon circumcision and dietary laws, such as not eating pork. By tying verses 40–45 to this Syrian king, and noticing that they foresee a different fate for him than history records, most assume that Daniel's final composition took place late in the reign of Antiochus, but before his death (168–164 BC).

© Baker Publishing Group and Dr. James C. Martin. Karatepe Open Air Museum, Turkey.

Musicians on relief from Karatepe (eighth century BC)

This view of the book implies that the events of Daniel 1–6 are largely based on various legends that were handed down to Daniel and his companions. The repetition of the lists of officials and of musical instruments in chapter 3, as well as its unique absence of any reference to Daniel, may suggest a separate oral tradition behind the account. Chapter 4's account of Nebuchadnezzar's madness may be related to a similar account of the illness of Nabonidus (see below). Chapter 6's story of the lions' den may have given rise to the addition of Bel and the Dragon, found in the Greek text. Related doxologies in Daniel 2:20–23; 4:3 (3:33 MT); 4:34–35 (4:31–32 MT); and 6:27–28 tie these stories together.[5] The assembly and form of these chapters, in what would become the first half of Daniel, took place no earlier than the death of Alexander the Great and the division of his empire (the divided kingdom of Dan. 2:40–43).

A series of historical errors in these chapters has been suggested as evidence for their legendary character and later date. Preeminent among these are the mention of Belshazzar as son of Nebuchadnezzar and leader of Babylon at the time of its fall, the reference to Darius the Mede as the conqueror of Babylon and its first king, and the madness of Nebuchadnezzar. The difficulties arise

5. Collins, *Daniel*, 37.

insofar as Belshazzar is the son of Nabonidus, Darius the Mede is unknown outside Daniel, and there is no record of madness for Nebuchadnezzar. Rather, the latter is better applied to the already-mentioned Nabonidus and the ten years he spent in a kind of self-exile in the Arabian city of Teman. Indeed, this is seen as confirmed by the Dead Sea Scrolls fragment regarding a seven-year illness of Nabonidus, whose recovery was due to a Jewish exorcist (*Prayer of Nabonidus* [4Q242]). For the issues raised by these matters, see "Ancient Near Eastern Context."

In light of this, critical views tend to concur that the accounts of chapters 2–6 are the oldest parts of Daniel. They were gathered and the introductory first chapter was added sometime after the conquests of Alexander the Great. Chapters 7–12 were added between 167 and 164 BC.

Literary Readings

In the period following the fall of Jerusalem and the deportation of many Jews to Babylonia and other foreign lands, there arose accounts of the means by which such people retained their faith in the God of Israel. In the Old Testament, the accounts of Esther and Daniel provide early examples. Esther provides a single story, but the first half of Daniel contains six court tales about Daniel and his three friends. While the accounts are related by themes of faithfulness and worship, each of the first six chapters contains a separate narrative. Chapter 1 looks forward to the remaining five stories by explaining the origins and background of the main characters as well as their initial rise in the imperial court. The mention of King Nebuchadnezzar (1:1, 18) anticipates chapters 2–4 (cf. also 5:11), while the mention of Cyrus (1:21) looks forward to the end of this section in 6:28.

The first half of Daniel provides examples to encourage Jews to remain faithful in the midst of imperial challenges; the second half of the book provides hope for those faithful by holding out the future as a time of restoration of that which has been lost in the destruction of the Jewish homeland. The division of the future into four or more periods represented by images of beasts (Dan. 7–8) is anticipated by Nebuchadnezzar's dream and its interpretation in chapter 2. Daniel's prayer of confession for Israel (Dan. 9) reminds the reader of similar prayers, such as Nehemiah 9, where there is the hope of a new beginning for the people of God. The end of Daniel 9 and chapter 10 introduce the prophetic description of coming events (Dan. 11), with a description of the greatness of the divine messenger and his challenge in reaching Daniel with his message. As Daniel and his friends struggle with human enemies (Dan. 2–6), so the messenger from God struggles with foes in the heavens (10:12–14, 20–21; 12:1).

This form of literature, in which heavenly secrets, often about the future, are revealed to chosen figures such as Daniel, is named apocalyptic literature

Apocalyptic Literature

Apocalyptic literature is characterized by some sort of experience of revelation on the part of a human, a story about the visionary and the visionary's experience, an assistant who is a heavenly being and interprets or challenges the visionary, and the presentation of a reality in heaven or on earth that transcends the appearance of the present world.[a] There is a common use of symbols and, for some such as Daniel, the use of prophecy of the future. In addition to Daniel and Revelation, apocalyptic pieces appear in Isaiah 24–27; Ezekiel 1; 37–48; Zechariah 9–14; Joel; Matthew 25; Mark 13; Luke 21; 2 Corinthians 12:1–10; and 1 Thessalonians 4:13–18. In intertestamental Judaism the following are also often regarded as the best-known examples of apocalyptic literature: *1 Enoch*, *2 Baruch*, *3 Baruch*, *4 Ezra* (2 Esdras), and the *Apocalypse of Abraham*. Both Judaism and Christianity (as well as other groups) developed apocalypses during and after the New Testament era.[b] Drawing from social contexts where people are dissatisfied with the world as it is, the early apocalyptic literature can trace influences from Old Testament wisdom and prophetic books.

[a] Carey, "Apocalypses," 39.
[b] For most extant examples and translations, see Charlesworth, *Old Testament Pseudepigrapha*, vol. 1.

(see the sidebar "Apocalyptic Literature"). Daniel in the Old Testament and Revelation in the New Testament contain examples of apocalyptic literature. Daniel 11, for example, proceeds with the revelation of what will happen in the future. Later apocalyptic literature will involve visionary trips to heaven, as here in Daniel 7. Few, however, will match the detail of Daniel 11 in describing the events that occur in the wars of the Jewish loyalists known as the Maccabees against the brutal opposition of the Syrian king Antiochus IV.

Whether 11:40–45 continues this description in a series of events that do not fit easily into the events of that period, or whether there is an allusion (11:40, "At the time of the end") to the projection of this text into some undetermined future time, this text concludes the prophecy with the demise of opposition to the people of God. It is in the context of this victory that the resurrection of the dead will occur, and with it the final judgment (12:1–3). Then too there will be an end to sacrilege in the temple (12:8–12).

Gender and Ideological Criticism

The female presence in the book of Daniel is seen in peripheral characters such as Belshazzar's wives, who drink with him from the sacred vessels of the Jerusalem temple (5:2, 3, 23), and the wives of Daniel's accusers, who suffer the same fate as their husbands (6:24). The important female in Daniel 11:6–7 is probably Berenice, daughter of Ptolemy II of Egypt, who married Antiochus II around 250 BC. The god "desired by women" (Dan. 11:37 NIV) may be the popular Tammuz (Greek Adonis) already mentioned in Ezekiel 8:14 (see the sidebar "Tammuz and Dumuzi" in the chapter on Ezekiel). His death and return to life paralleled the annual dry and rainy seasons (summer and winter): the rain brought life, and the dryness brought death of vegetation. The one woman whose words appear is the queen (or queen mother) of Belshazzar. She counsels Belshazzar amid his terror at the writing on the wall that no one can interpret. The king accepts her counsel to call for Daniel (5:10–12), who turns out to be the only one who can do what the king wants: interpret the words.

Scholars may wonder whether, in Daniel, the absence of an Israelite woman who obeys the law influenced the inclusion of the story of Susanna in the Greek version of the book. More likely, this story resembles the accounts of Daniel as one who was ready to die rather than participate in the sinful plans of the two elders who lusted after her. This case resembles Deuteronomy 22:23–24, although the virtuous outcome for Susanna has been the subject of studies.[6]

The stories of Daniel have been a source for the encouragement of the faithful in the face of persecution, as the apocalyptic visions have assisted in the hope that believers may have. With the assurance that the powers of this world will be subordinated to "the Ancient of Days" and his "Son of Man" (Dan. 7:9–28 NASB), those who have endured persecution for their faith have looked forward to the resurrection yet to come (12:2–4).

It should then be no surprise that these promises have been read into the current events of many generations of believers. Indeed, a recent example can be found in Tokunboh Adeyemo's contribution to the *Africa Bible Commentary*.[7] The accounts of Daniel and his companions demonstrate how God has dealt with gentile empires in the past, and thus they call the people of God to remain faithful. If the little horn of Daniel 7 represents the antichrist, then the Son of Man in that chapter, like the man dressed in linen in Daniel 10, symbolizes the person of Jesus Christ. Criticism of this approach as not providing "an authentic African engagement" seems to assume that methods using historical reference and those engaging narrative are mutually contradictory.[8] Yet there is no logical basis for putting these methods at odds with each other. Rather, it seems that the question has to do with the nature of the text as inspired Scripture. If this is admitted, then both a historical and a representative component might be expected. Indeed, it is arguable that the

6. See, e.g., Jordaan, "Reading Susanna as Therapeutic Narrative"; Tkacz, "Biblical Woman's Paraphrase."

7. Adeyemo, "Daniel."

8. Van Deventer, "In Africa We Say 'His Story'!," 720.

prophecy found in this apocalyptic literature was received as just that, by the first generation of readers and all those who followed them.

Ancient Near Eastern Context

The character of Daniel is set in the days of the Babylonian Empire and the beginning of the Persian Empire. The setting for Daniel 1:1 is in 605 BC, when Daniel and other Judeans are taken to Babylon by King Nebuchadnezzar.[9] (See plate 8 in the gallery for an image of the Ishtar gate from Babylon.) Daniel 2 and Nebuchadnezzar's dream are set in 603/602 BC. Chapters 3 and 4 are not dated specifically to a year but occur sometime after the beginning of the same king's rule, one that lasted from 605 to 562 BC. The events of Daniel 4, like those of chapters 1–3, are not attested in any detail outside of the book of Daniel. Because Daniel 4:25–34 envisions a period of "seven times," often interpreted as seven years, during which Nebuchadnezzar becomes like a beast, those who date this to Nebuchadnezzar's reign assign it to the last half of his rule, for which the extant Babylonian Chronicles do not detail his exploits.

Daniel 5, 7, and 8 are dated during the years of King Belshazzar of Babylon, whose "father" is Nebuchadnezzar (5:2, 11, 13, 18) and who reigned at the end of Babylon's imperial period, when the Medes and Persians took control. Babylonian and other records list Nabonidus as the last king of the Babylonian Empire (556–539 BC). However, it is known that during the final decade of his rule he was largely absent from Babylon. He seems to have returned before the fall of Babylon. His son and coregent (during the final decade) was Belshazzar, who is named in the Babylonian Chronicle. He is not designated as "king" in Babylonian. However, the Aramaic word translated "king" (root *mlk* in Aramaic and Hebrew) can translate the Akkadian for "governor," as it does in a ninth-century-BC text written in both languages.[10] Thus it does not only translate the Akkadian for "king" but can also have a broader sense, as here in Daniel. "Father" can refer to ancestors or predecessors, as it does elsewhere in the Aramaic of Daniel (2:23) and Ezra (4:15; 5:12). The Babylonian Chronicle records that the Persian army entered Babylon without a fight and that Nabonidus was later captured in Babylon, perhaps after trying to retreat and escape outside the city.[11]

The name of Darius the Mede, as the king who succeeds Belshazzar, is unknown outside of Daniel. Who is this figure? Darius may be the Median name for Cyrus.[12] Darius is always identified as a Mede (5:31; 9:1; 11:1),

9. For a discussion of issues connected with this date, see Kelle, "Judah in the Seventh Century," 379–81.

10. Kaufman, "Reflections on the Assyrian-Aramaic Bilingual," 159. The terms occur on lines 6, 7, and 13 of the Aramaic inscription and lines 8, 9, and 19 of the Akkadian text.

11. *COS* 1.137:468.

12. See Wiseman, "Some Historical Problems."

never as a Persian. Cyrus, however, is always identified as a Persian king (1:21; 6:28; 10:1). Both names appear in 6:28, which could be translated, "during the reign of Darius, that is, the reign of Cyrus the Persian." Cyrus is known to have ruled from 550 to 530 BC.

Tetradrachma portraying profile of Antiochus IV of Syria (168–164 BC)

© Baker Publishing Group and Dr. James C. Martin. Eretz Israel Museum, Tel Aviv, Israel.

A major historical question concerns the interpretation of the figures and beasts as found in Daniel 2, 7, and 8. For the most part it appears that kingdoms or empires are being described. There is explicit identification of some of the imagery with Babylon (605–539 BC), Persia (539–331 BC), and Greece. Greece rose with the conquests of Alexander the Great, who defeated Persia in 331 BC and controlled the region from Greece across the Middle East to India by the time of his death in 323 BC. Subsequently his empire was divided into four successor states (perhaps Dan. 8:5–8, 21–22; 11:3–4). The account of the kings of the South and of the North in 11:5–39 fits nicely with the story of the struggles between the Ptolemies, who ruled Egypt, and the Seleucids, who ruled Syria in the third and second centuries BC. Although the kingdom of Judah lay between these two powers, the most difficult struggles for Judah's continued existence and faith in Israel's God occurred under the Seleucid king Antiochus IV, who declared himself a god and insisted that Judah worship him (175–164 BC). He desecrated the altar of the Jerusalem temple by offering a pig there (perhaps 8:13; 9:27; 11:31; 12:11).

Others connect the final empire on the statue (2:32–45), that of iron, with Rome. The stone that smashes this empire would be the Messiah, who comes as Jesus Christ. The toes of iron mixed with clay would then form additional rulers or states that come from the Roman Empire. If this approach is applied to the other visions of chapters 7 and 8, then the final horn (perhaps 7:8, 11, 24–28; 8:9–14, 23–27) and king of the North (11:20–45) are interpreted as an antichrist figure, who foreshadows the beast of Revelation (Rev. 13–17; 19:19–20:10).

Canonical Context

As a wise adviser and an interpreter of dreams in a foreign court, Daniel invites comparison with the figure of Joseph (Gen. 37, 39–50).[13] Both are taken out of their homeland without their consent, both remain faithful to the God of Israel, and both succeed in influencing foreign courts for the good of others, especially the people of God. The Old Testament preserves two

13. Cf., e.g., Segal, "From Joseph to Daniel."

large sections of Aramaic, found in Daniel and in Ezra. The Daniel section runs from 2:4 through 7:8. Daniel 6:5 and his prayer in 9:10–13 reference the law of God.[14] This is also found in Ezra 7:12, 14, 21, and 26. Thus an awareness of the divine revelation of God's law appears in both books. However, in Daniel 6:6–10, Daniel's enemies use this law to trap him. They find that it prohibits the worship of anyone other than the God of Israel. This is stated most clearly in Exodus 20:2–6 and in Deuteronomy 5:6–10. Although Daniel 9:10 references the prophets in general, 9:2 specifically cites Jeremiah the prophet regarding the judgment that Jerusalem is to face for its sins for seventy years. This number is found in Jeremiah 25:11–12, with the promise of a return following it in 29:10.

In the New Testament there may be hundreds of allusions to the prophecy of Daniel. However, there are a handful of quotes.[15] Matthew 13:42, 50 reverses the action in Daniel 3:6: instead of the righteous protected amid the flames, the wicked will be punished by the fire. Daniel 7:13, where one like a Son of Man appears in the clouds, is used by Jesus or about Jesus in the New Testament to refer to his divinity (Matt. 24:30; 26:64; Mark 13:26; 14:62; Luke 21:27; Rev. 1:7). Daniel 9:27; 11:31; and 12:11 refer to the abomination of desolation, whose appearance is connected with the temple and its destruction and with the appearance of Jesus (Matt. 24:15; Mark 13:14).

Theological Perspectives of Daniel

The primary concern of the book of Daniel appears to be the encouragement of the believer in Israel's God to remain faithful amid temptations and persecution. In chapter 1, Daniel and his friends refuse the practices of another culture and give credit to God. In chapter 2, Daniel interprets the king's dream but again gives all credit to God, not taking any for himself. In chapter 3, the emphasis is on the worship of God and no other, not an image or even the emperor. Chapter 4 is another dream interpretation. As in chapter 2, Daniel leads the king to understand the future and ultimately (after a period of royal difficulty) to give praise to the God of Daniel. In chapter 5, Daniel again interprets. Here, however, it is a matter of immediate judgment on the king, who does not honor God. King Belshazzar certainly does not praise God in this text, but the queen (or queen mother; 5:10–12) provides an oblique recognition by recognizing "the spirit of the holy gods" as residing in the prophet. As in chapter 3 with Shadrach, Meshach, and Abednego, so in chapter 6, jealousy of Daniel leads others to plot against him and to require him to remain faithful despite a punishment that should lead to certain death.

14. Scheetz, *Canonical Intertextuality*, 130–40.
15. Ibid., 147–59.

Daniel's active and open prayer life testifies to a faith that is not hidden but available for all. If these examples apply to those threatened under the Babylonian and Persian administrations, they also apply to those facing death at the hands of Antiochus IV, and later to the Christians of the Roman Empire. The call to faith and faithful living remains for today, when persecution of believers occurs around the world, not least among those who do so in the name of tolerance!

A related theological theme has to do with the value of human history and its role in God's plan. Daniel 2:40 and 7:23 divide history into four kingdoms, where the last is followed by additional events. Daniel 11:2 describes four kings, and the fourth is the most powerful. The tendency to divide the world into these kingdoms may be a structuring of the events between the time of the fall of Jerusalem and the defeat of Antiochus IV in the second century BC, or it may structure the remainder of human history. Daniel 9:24–27 speaks of the remaining time in terms of seventy sevens. Like the sequence of four kingdoms, whose predecessors may lie in broader world-history presentations (such as the Greek works of Hesiod or the *Sibylline Oracles* of early Judaism), so the seventy sevens of years may suggest a broad sweep of time, ranging from four to five centuries, into which the great biblical ages from the time of the flood have been divided. Thus texts such as Genesis 11:10–32; 15:13–16; and 1 Kings 6:1, and the general sweep of Judean kings from Solomon's temple dedication to Zedekiah's fall to King Nebuchadnezzar and the later return and rebuilding in the sixth century BC, all contribute to this plotting of the eras of God's work with his people.[16] Combined with the rest of the book of Daniel, these images and numbers stress the significant role of God's people. He has not abandoned them. To the contrary, despite their apparent weakness from a human standpoint, those who remain faithful can be used by God to transform the world and to advance God's kingdom and plans. They can overturn the greatest kings and their kingdoms since God's purposes will not be thwarted by any powers, whether spiritual or physical (Dan. 7–12).

Beyond this, and here introduced for the first time in the course of biblical revelation, is the promise of the resurrection of the dead in Daniel 12:1–4. This is not merely a hope for the revival and return of the Jewish nation (cf. Ezek. 37) but the expectation that those who are faithful unto death will not disappear forever. Instead, they will return, and out of the worst period of distress in human history there will emerge a resurrection of the dead to eternal physical life. Although briefly described here, it develops a trajectory already apparent in the Old Testament and thus prepares for this teaching in its fullness in the New Testament.[17]

16. Hess, "Seventy Sevens of Daniel," 328–30.
17. Parchem, "Motyw zmartwychwstania w Księdze Daniela."

Key Commentaries and Studies

Baldwin, Joyce G. *Daniel: An Introduction and Commentary.* TOTC. Leicester, UK: Inter-Varsity; Downers Grove, IL: InterVarsity, 1978. A careful and readable evangelical study with exegetical insights.

Beckwith, Carl L. *Ezekiel, Daniel.* RCSOT 12. Downers Grove, IL: IVP Academic, 2012. A compendium of quotations from the Reformers, text by text through Daniel.

Collins, John J. *Daniel.* Hermeneia. Minneapolis: Augsburg Fortress, 1993. The most complete study of the text of Daniel, with full analysis of variants.

Goldingay, John. *Daniel.* WBC 30. Waco: Word, 1989. Much exegetical detail, analyzing a symbolic approach and assuming a second-century-BC date.

Longman, Tremper, III. *Daniel.* NIVAC. Grand Rapids: Zondervan, 1999. Evangelical exegesis of the book with theological and practical applications.

Wiseman, Donald J. *Notes on Some Problems in the Book of Daniel.* Edited by Donald J. Wiseman et al. London: Tyndale, 1965. A starting point for engagement with historical-critical issues.

24

HOSEA

Those who live in a land that once worshiped God but has now abandoned him live in a world that needs to hear the message of Hosea (see the map "The age of Isaiah" in ch. 19).

Name, Text, and Outline

The name Hosea derives from the root "to save, deliver." It is shortened by omission of the divine name: "[God] saved" or "O [God,] save!" The name is common in Israel and Judah in the eighth and seventh centuries, as attested on seals and seal impressions, and as borne by the last king of the northern kingdom (Israel). Hosea was also the original name of Joshua, before Moses changed it (Num. 13:8, 16; Deut. 32:44). The name fits well in the mid-eighth century BC, as implied by the kings named in Hosea 1:1.

The text of Hosea is not always easy to interpret. It is beset by a variety of syntactical and other issues. It remains unclear whether these arise from the poetic and literary forms that saturate the book; from its northern Israelite origins, which reflect a different dialect from the one used in Jerusalem; from a lengthy and difficult textual transmission; or some other reason. The Septuagint edition of the book, like the later versions, also wrestles with the text.

OUTLINE

I. Superscription (1:1)
II. Family and Nation (1:2–3:5)
    A. Hosea, Gomer, Children, and Israel (1:2–9)
    B. Restoration of Israel and Judah (1:10–2:1 [2:1–3 MT])

   C. Indictment of Gomer and Israel (2:2–13 [2:4–15 MT])
   D. Restoration of Israel (2:14–23 [2:16–25 MT])
   E. Loving Gomer and God's People (3:1–5)

III. Indictment 1 (4:1–11:11)
   A. God's Charge against Israel (4:1–3)
   B. Sins of Priests and People (4:4–19)
   C. Sins of Rulers, Priests, and People (5:1–7)
   D. An Unhealed Sickness on the Nation (5:8–15)
   E. Superficial Repentance (6:1–7:2)
   F. Kings and People Fall (7:3–7)
   G. Israel Finds No Help in Egypt and Assyria (7:8–16)
   H. Politics and Religion without Obedience (8:1–6)
   I. False Hope in Religion and Politics (8:7–9:9)
   J. Israel in Metaphor (9:10–10:15)
      1. Grapes (9:10–17)
      2. Vine (10:1–10)
      3. Heifer (10:11–15)
   K. The Heart of God (11:1–11)

IV. Indictment 2 (11:12–14:8 [12:1–14:9 MT])
   A. Israel's Early History of Sin (11:12–12:14 [12:1–15 MT])
   B. Baal Worship and Its Consequences (13:1–16 [14:1 MT])
   C. Repentance and Restoration (14:1–8 [14:2–9 MT])

V. Wisdom Calls to Walk in God's Ways (14:9 [14:10 MT])

Overview of Hosea

The book begins by identifying the text as Yahweh's word to Hosea son of Beeri during the reigns of four Judean kings and one Israelite king, Jeroboam II. In the first chapter, God commands Hosea to marry a wife who will be unfaithful to him as Israel has been unfaithful to God. He marries Gomer. Their first child is named Jezreel, recalling the events of the ninth century when Jehu destroyed much of Israel in the Valley of Jezreel. God will bring such destruction again. The second child, a daughter named Lo-ruhamah, or "Not loved," reflects God's attitude toward Israel. The third child, named Lo-ammi, or "Not my people," identifies God's abandonment of Israel to judgment. Nevertheless, the first chapter ends and the second begins with God's promise that he will again love his children. The prophecy then plunges into a poetic recitation of the sins of Israel in forgetting all that God gave the land and chasing after other gods, a practice here portrayed as an unfaithful wife having children with other lovers. But God remembers his love for Israel in the early days and promises that he will renew this. The third chapter returns to prose. Gomer has left Hosea, and now God commands the prophet to love her

© Baker Publishing Group and Dr. James C. Martin

Jezreel

again, which means buying her back from slavery. She must remain celibate for many days, however, just as Israel will remain without king and sacrifice for many days until they return trembling to their true God and his blessings.

The fourth chapter begins with poetic verse that continues until the end of the book. God summarizes his complaint against the absence of truth or faithfulness, of covenantal love, and of the knowledge and awareness of God throughout all of Israel. The following list of Israel's sins leads to the desolation of the land and all life in it. God rejects the priests who have rejected him and his revelation. Repeated throughout this chapter is how Israel is characterized by a spirit of prostitution, of adultery, and of the worship of other gods and their rituals. Chapter 5 continues the litany of unfaithful acts. God promises that their search for salvation with Egypt and Assyria will not find success. Instead, God will become a lion and turn against his own people. In chapter 6, the people seem to misunderstand that the judgment they have seen is all that will come and that the solution lies with sacrifices to God and prayers. But God requires mercy toward one another, not murderous and thieving acts. He wants an end to their prostitution. On a community level, theft and sin take place (7:1–2), just as on a national level the rulers fail and vainly seek alliances with Egypt, Assyria, and other nations. Still Israel turns to its false gods. The northern kingdom (Israel) worships its calf images and seeks more lovers from Assyria. God will send them back to Egypt and to slavery there. This unfaithfulness will reap the whirlwind (8:7). As for those who escape, Egypt will gather and bury them (9:6). God remembers Israel as the hope for early fruit. But their sins, such as sacrificing their children, have soured the grapes. So God will not give them children to sacrifice. Israel as a fruitful vine (10:1) became addicted to idolatry. So all their symbols of false worship will perish, and their kings, leaders, and people will be destroyed. God will treat Israel like a trained heifer and place a yoke on the animal's neck. They should plow the ground and sow righteousness. Instead, they plant wickedness and reap evil. Ancient and terrible battles are remembered. They will again become Israel's experience.

© Baker Publishing Group and Dr. James C. Martin. The Israel Museum.

Tenth-century-BC cult stand from Taanach with calf (or horse) and sun disk above it

Hosea 11 reaches a high point of God's fond memories of the nation in its infancy. He led Israel with cords of human kindness and ties of love. Verses 8–9 achieve a description of God's love almost unparalleled elsewhere. Although justice demands that God destroy Israel like the cities of the plain in Genesis 19, the compassion of his heart for the nation will not allow him to treat them in this manner.

Chapter 12 interweaves the story of Jacob in Genesis with Israel's faithlessness and its worship of other gods and goddesses. The struggling of Jacob from the womb (and later with God) becomes a metaphor for Israel overcoming sin. Jacob found a wife in Haran after years of service, but Israel has become guilty and arouses divine anger. Hosea 13 begins with a detailed description of Baal worship. Although the people make their own images and kiss silver calves, God speaks of all that he has done for them. God will judge the northern kingdom, and Samaria will face terrible judgment, even to its children and pregnant women.

The final chapter ends the book with a command to repent and return to God and with a promise of restoration and divine blessings. Israel will again prosper. Let the wise realize this, and let the righteous walk in God's ways.

Reading Hosea

Premodern Readings

According to rabbinic tradition, Rabbi Johanan ben Zakkai used Hosea 6:6's message of mercy in place of sacrifice at the Council of Jamnia (Yavneh)

in the AD 70s. He argued that prayer could replace animal sacrifice.[1] The call to repentance, found in Hosea 14:1, remains in the Haftarah section on the Sabbath before Yom Kippur. Early Christianity used Hosea 14:1 in the Gospels and Epistles. Jerome wrote one of the earliest commentaries on the book, mentioning its obscurity and the difficulty of interpreting it (referring especially to the last verse of the book as an indication that Hosea himself realized this). A focus of Jerome's concern was to argue that the woman whom God commanded Hosea to marry was not a prostitute but served an allegorical purpose. God would not have ordered his servant to disobey the law. Augustine mentioned the "three days" of Hosea 6:2 and the unusual use of the first-person plural pronoun there. He concluded that it referred to the resurrection of Christ on the third day.[2]

Writing more than a thousand years later, John Calvin saw in the command to marry a prostitute a story where the prophet would assume a character and so relate to his audience.[3] On Hosea 6:2, Calvin applies the text first to the nation of Israel. Taking its historical context as a starting point, he then goes on to describe how this forms a lesson for all the people of God to remain faithful in difficult times. Believers know that the resurrection will come. From this command, Calvin finds the resurrection of Christ reflected in the lesson. In Hosea 11:8–9 the compassion of God causes him to change his mind about the destruction of people. For Calvin, this is evidence of divine accommodation to human understanding.

Higher Criticism

Traditional criticism sought to separate texts and to find justification for doing so in formal and historical criteria. Thus the prose account in Hosea 1–3 became a natural division, separating this text from the poetic oracles of the remainder of the book. Hans Walter Wolff found three groups of oracle collections that came together separately.[4] He also identified chronological "clues." Thus the mention of Judah by a prophet writing mainly to the north was thought to betray later redaction in the southern kingdom. The eighth-century prophets could express only judgment, so hope, salvation, and return also became later additions. There were and continue to be two general camps: those who trace most of the book to the eighth-century prophet Hosea, and those who see little of it as having an origin there.[5]

More recent studies have looked elsewhere for clues as to editing practices. Grace Emmerson suggests that places where restoration follows repentance

1. *'Abot de Rabbi Nathan* 4; Moughtin-Mumby, "Hosea," 375.
2. Augustine, *City of God* 18.28; Kugel, *How to Read the Bible*, 62.
3. Calvin, *Hosea*.
4. Wolff, *Hosea*.
5. Moughtin-Mumby, "Hosea," 368–69.

betray a later editor because the original prophet saw God's return of his people as purely a work of his own grace.[6] Gale Yee identifies shifts in person and repetitions as indicators of different hands.[7] However, none of this has proved compelling, and thus directions for study have moved elsewhere, to ideological and literary studies. Thus the Anchor Bible commentary of Francis Andersen and David Noel Freedman reads the text as a whole, without trying to find pieces and parts that were added.[8] Ehud Ben Zvi finds the work to have been written in its final form for the postexilic audience in Yehud.[9] Andrew Dearman stresses the distinctive literary features of the book.[10]

Literary Readings

The book of Hosea is packed with metaphors, plays on words, and allusions to Israel's earlier history. Given its size, these are found more often in this book than in any other of the prophets. The effect is to create a special poetic rhetoric that persuades the reader with form and beauty. Dearman has brought together many of the metaphors, observing that Hosea's poetry portrays Yahweh as the head of his household (much like Hosea in chaps. 1–3).[11] He is husband, father, shepherd, farmer, and king. Hosea often portrays Israel in a corresponding fashion: spouse, child, land, inheritance, and as one of several animals. A list of imagery related to Israel in the poetic sections includes mourning land (4:3), snare and net (5:1; 7:12), prostitution (5:3–4; 6:10; 9:1), bearing strange children (5:7), sickness and wound (5:13), morning dew (6:4), marauding bandits and thieves (6:9; 7:1), adulterers and heated oven (7:4–6), half-baked cake (7:8), silly dove (7:11), faulty bow (7:16), sowing wind and reaping whirlwind (8:7), swallowed (8:8a), unwanted pot (8:8b), lonely wild donkey (8:9), poisonous weeds (10:4), twig on the waters (10:7), feeding on the wind (12:1 NIV), dishonest merchant (12:7), and labor pains without birth (13:13).

Wordplay abounds throughout these texts. A few examples will suffice.[12] "Ephraim" is a "wild donkey" in 8:9 (NIV), where both terms share the *alef*, *pe*, and *resh* letters. Gilgal's altars become "piles" (*gallîm*) of stones (12:11 [12:12 MT]). In 12:3 (12:4 MT) "grasp" (NIV) shares three of its consonants (in order) with "Jacob," and "struggles" (12:3 [12:4 MT]) shares two consonants (*śin* and *resh*) with "Israel" (12:12 [12:13 MT])—wordplay also found in Genesis 25:26; 27:35; and 32:28.

6. Emmerson, *Hosea*.
7. Yee, *Hosea*.
8. Andersen and Freedman, *Hosea*.
9. Ben Zvi, *Hosea*.
10. Dearman, *Hosea*.
11. Ibid., 11–14.
12. Morris, *Prophecy, Poetry*, 148–51, has identified seventy puns in the book of Hosea.

The historical allusions begin with the naming of Jezreel for the slaughter that Jehu perpetrated a century earlier (1:4). Hosea 9:13 describes God's judgment of Israel in the form of a return to Egypt and the memories of its servitude there. Chapter 11 recalls how God led Israel out of Egypt and the loving relationship he had for his people then. Chapter 12 recalls the stories of Jacob at the beginning of Israel's existence and contrasts the faithfulness of Israel's ancestor (12:12) with Ephraim's worship of other deities and of images. Chapter 13 returns to more recent history: Jeroboam I's erection of calf images that remain in the land until Hosea's day (cf. 14:3b [14:4b MT]).

The striking images, wordplay, and historical connections tie the picture together into a complete whole. In the area of gender and ideological criticism, these poetic expressions continue to influence the message.

Gender and Ideological Criticism

Much of the imagery in Hosea relates to the depiction of Israel as an immoral woman and of the nation's worship of other gods as identical to adultery. The woman of Hosea 3, whether or not she is identical with Gomer of chapters 1–2, is explicitly adulterous, enslaved, bought back by Hosea, and compared with Israel in the eyes of Yahweh. The shocking treatment of the woman in chapter 2's poetry and the explicit sexual descriptions that recur throughout the book have formed an important part of the traditional reconstruction of Israelite religions.[13] In this view, Israel worships the chief storm-god, Baal, who brings rain on the female fertility deity in the earth. This union creates the abundant life of agriculture and aids animal as well as human reproduction. Worship takes place through the participation of Israelite males who engage in sex with female cultic officiants. Such worship, traditionally understood as sympathetic magic, in some way assists the Baal figure in his insemination of the earth through rain, thereby helping to generate crops. This traditional view has been heavily criticized as lacking evidence. Scholars do not know that anyone in ancient Israel held to this belief or participated in such a cult. This is not to deny that immoral sexual practices (from the viewpoint of the prophet) did exist. It merely leaves open the question as to whether they were the product of a Canaanite theology/ideology or more closely connected with the wild party atmosphere of later Mediterranean and other practices that intended no more than worship of pleasure. If the latter, then the prostitutes were just that and not engaged in sacred ritual.

From the traditional picture and the language used in Hosea, feminist scholars have tried to address what has been read as a justification for abusive treatment of the passive figure of female Israel.[14] More must be involved with

13. Hess, *Israelite Religions*, 332–35.
14. McConville, "Hosea," 344.

the female character(s) than only a model of sin and adultery.[15] While in some cases this has again meant dividing the text and privileging certain texts, in others it has emphasized goddess worship as a means to female autonomy and to the securing of goods for family and children.[16] Nevertheless, the text of Hosea does not support the effacement of female identity in the figure of Israel. Restored Israel retains feminine imagery and receives blessings from God. Further, much of the ideology on which the traditional picture has been based must be questioned.

More significant has been the charge of a passive role for the female, reflecting male interests and desires. Yvonne Sherwood has attempted to deconstruct Hosea and thereby retrieve a female role. Does this succeed, or does it journey too far from the text and what might have been recognized by the author?[17] Perhaps Alice Keefe is correct that one must seek neither affirming nor negating roles in the text but find a solution in the sociohistorical context of the text.[18]

Ancient Near Eastern Context

Many or perhaps most of Hosea's prophecies took place during the middle part of the eighth century BC, during the reigns of King Jeroboam II (793/792–753 BC) of Israel and of King Uzziah (also called Ahaziah; 792/791–736/735 BC) of Judah (see the chart of the kings in chap. 10). After 745 BC the rise of King Tiglath-pileser III of Assyria changed the political landscape for the northern kingdom (Israel) and for Damascus, both of whose independence came to an end by 722 BC. In the south, after a few intervening rulers, Ahaz arose, with his dependency on Assyria (see "Ancient Near Eastern Context" for Isaiah). The long reigns of Jeroboam II and his southern contemporary were a time of relative peace and prosperity. They also appear to reflect widespread worship of other gods and goddesses. The name of the king, Jeroboam, signaled a conscious imitation of his predecessor, Jeroboam I, who had erected calf images for worship at Dan and Bethel. These images were known to Hosea, and were constructed of gold and silver (8:4–6). At Beth-aven, located near Bethel, was a calf image (10:5–8) that was kissed and worshiped by citizens of the northern kingdom. The name Beth-aven could mean either "House of Strength" or "House of Iniquity." The latter creates a wordplay that Hosea 13:1–2 exploits to identify the sin. Proud Israelites may have seen Beth-aven as a symbol of strength, but Hosea found in it a sign of Israel's sin.

The death that came through Baal (13:1) reminds the reader of the sin of Baal-peor (cf. Hosea 9:10; Num. 25:1–18; Deut. 4:3–4) but may also recall

15. Moughtin-Mumby, *Sexual and Marital Metaphors*, 6.
16. Keefe, *Woman's Body*; van Dijk-Hemmes, "Imagination of Power."
17. Sherwood, *Prostitute and the Prophet*.
18. Keefe, *Woman's Body*.

Richard S. Hess

Standing stones at Gezer high place symbolizing deities

and parody myths associated with the death and resurrection of Baal.[19] As noted above ("Gender and Ideological Criticism"), the worship of Baal may not have represented a monolithic practice and philosophy. Clearly, the surprisingly large number of personal names compounded with "Baal" in the Samaria ostraca of the early or mid-eighth century BC suggest that Baal was more prominent at this time in the northern kingdom (Israel) than in the contemporary southern kingdom (Judah) as well as in the later periods of Judean history.[20] Men engaged in sexual activities with female prostitutes at the high places where Baal was worshiped (Hosea 4:10–14; 6:10).[21] Offerings were made and the names of deities (e.g., "my Baal," 2:16) invoked.[22] The extrabiblical evidence concurs with the message of the prophet Hosea that worship of other deities through the use of images and through immoral practices formed a significant part of the religions of Israelites during the time of Hosea's prophecies.

Canonical Context

Hosea stands at the beginning of the Minor Prophets in both the Masoretic Text and the Septuagint.[23] This prominent position may be justified because it is the longest of these books. It may also be the oldest book among the

19. Hess, *Israelite Religions*, 256.

20. Hess, "Aspects of Israelite Personal Names."

21. See the discussion under the heading "Gender and Ideological Criticism" as to whether this was understood as a sacred ritual or as something else.

22. Hess, *Israelite Religions*, 255.

23. Leuchter, "Another Look at the Hosea–Malachi Framework."

Twelve. It also looks back into Israel's past more than any of the other Minor Prophets. Many of the references to earlier biblical events were enumerated in the "Literary Readings" section above. This introduces and anticipates the history that the remaining Minor Prophets address. The sin of Hosea's day leads to judgment and deportation. The last group of Minor Prophets witnesses the return and beginnings of restoration. Hosea's theological connections with other Old Testament books become strongest in terms of Deuteronomy, which also emphasizes the love of God, the covenant and its conditional nature, God's gift of the land, and the dangers of entanglements with other gods and religions. As Gordon McConville observes, while Hosea says little about the inclusion of other nations (unlike, e.g., the second half of Isaiah), its emphasis on the love of God and his suffering in that love for his people Israel is without parallel.[24]

In contrast to Hosea's lack of inclusion of other nations, the New Testament reworks Hosea 2:23 (2:25 MT) as a model for the inclusion of the gentile nations (Rom. 9:25–26; 1 Pet. 2:10).[25] Jesus twice refers to Hosea 6:6 and the desire for mercy and not sacrifice (Matt. 9:13; 12:7). Perhaps most famous is the call of Israel from Egypt in Hosea 11:1, which Matthew 2:15 applies to the time of Jesus and his parents in Egypt. In Luke 23:30–31, Jesus revisits the fearful devastation of the judgment, so the people call on the hills and mountains to cover them (Hosea 10:8). In 1 Corinthians 15:54–55, Paul develops God's promised redemption of his people from death (Hosea 13:14). The grave (or Sheol) disappears from view, and death at last loses the battle.[26]

Theological Perspectives of Hosea

The theological message of Hosea is embodied in Yahweh's love for Israel, in Israel's rebellion against God, and in the judgment and restoration that God brings. The command to marry a woman (somehow) related to unfaithfulness and the unfolding story of chapters 1 and 3 become a picture of God's love for Israel, his covenantal commitment to them despite their wandering away and becoming enmeshed in sin. Hosea 2 then describes the divorce that God pronounces on Israel and the manner in which he withdraws his love from the people. Yet that is not the end of the story. God will "allure" (2:14 [2:16 MT]) his former bride to the wilderness and win Israel back. Israel will again recognize Yahweh as her husband and again know his blessing in the fruitfulness of the land.

Thus Hosea 4 begins the "indictment" against Israel for all of its sin but does so with the prophet having personally experienced something of the

24. McConville, "Hosea," 345.
25. Cf. Hosea 1:10 (2:1 MT). See also Moughtin-Mumby, "Hosea," 375–76.
26. Ibid.

sense of love, betrayal, and the cost of restoration that God experiences. Out of this experience God speaks of the absence of truth, covenantal love, and knowledge of God in the land (4:1). The "truth" (Heb. *ʾĕmet*) is the integrity that provides the connection for people to be loyal to God and to one another. Their worship of the Baals, the general abandonment of the worship of Yahweh alone, and the widespread immorality that accompanies this all serve to create a world devoid of this essential characteristic of God that he demands from his people.

The second charge in Hosea 4:1, that of an absence of covenant love (Heb. *ḥesed*), exhibits God's people's failure to hold fast to his covenant with him. The term *ḥesed* occurs an additional five times in Hosea (2:19 [2:21 MT]; 6:4, 6; 10:12; 12:6 [12:7 MT]). In 2:19 (2:21 MT) God models this characteristic for his people. He promises that Israel will return and that Yahweh will renew his marriage to his people. Despite Israel's unfaithfulness, God's covenant love will win in the end. The verse associates justice, righteousness, and compassion with this term. Israel has lost all of these because it has abandoned its covenantal love. Hosea 6:4 describes the nation's inability to remain loyal to God. Rather, its love is like morning mist and dew, which soon evaporates. Israel has pursued false lovers (2:13 [2:15 MT]; 8:9) and now is in the habit of seeking anyone (other nations and gods) other than Yahweh for aid (7:10–16). Hosea 6:6 contrasts the covenantal love that God wants from his people with sacrifices they rely on. This contrast does not eliminate the call for sacrifices. Instead, it recognizes the vanity of all cultic actions apart from this characteristic to which God calls his people. Hosea 6:7–10 goes on to illustrate the loss of covenantal love with God in terms of breaking his covenant (6:7). However, the guilt extends to those stained with the blood of innocent victims, those who lie in wait to murder and rob, and those who commit prostitution. In order for them to regain covenant love, God commands his people to "sow righteousness" (10:12). This recognizes the importance of following God's commands wholeheartedly and seeking him rather than the images and false religious practices.

Central to covenantal love, therefore, is the relationship between God and his people. This becomes evident in the opening chapters of Hosea, with the image of marriage as the key context and image that God uses to describe Israel and its sacrifices. The other aspect is the pain that Yahweh endures when his people turn to their Baals instead of him. Baal does not provide the fruits of the land, no matter how often they seek him with their offerings (4:11–13; 8:11–13; 9:4; 10:1–2). Instead, Yahweh alone has delivered and guided Israel (11:1; 12:2–6; 13:4–5) and has given them their land with its bounty, and he alone will take it away (2:8–9; 4:3) and can and will again provide the promised bounty (14:7).

The last of the three elements that Hosea 4:1 reveals has disappeared from Israel is the knowledge of God. God rejects the people and their priests (4:6) for rejecting the knowledge of God in his word. They have forgotten Yahweh (2:13; 4:6; 8:13). God ordained that the priests should teach the people this knowledge (Lev. 10:10), but the priests have neglected their role, and the people have not listened to any teaching about God. Hosea 6:3 portrays Israel as convinced that it can pursue the knowledge of Yahweh, but the superficiality of this is found in 6:6: in parallel with covenantal love, God insists that true knowledge of him is not simply a matter of performing the right sacrifices. Many of the people at this time enjoyed prosperity and had the resources to fulfill the cultic demands of the law. But while doing this, they were killing and robbing other Israelites and pursuing the worship of Baal, with the immoral gratification that it brought to them.

The promise of return and restoration after judgment forms an essential part of Israel's experience as the spouse of Yahweh. This is promised as a reversal from trouble to hope (Hosea 14:1–8 [14:2–9 MT]), from symbols of judgment to places of blessing (1:5, 11), as David again rules over a united land (3:5). In discussing this, McConville emphasizes the people's covenant with the land, which brings fruitfulness and plenty to the restoration (2:18–23).[27] If there is a time without blessing (3:4), God will nevertheless not destroy his people. Rather, his love will bring about an overthrow of his deliberate will to enact justice (11:8–9). The final three chapters of Hosea describe healing, restoration, and life (14:7 [14:8 MT]). Trees are used to create the false images and environments in which the people worship (4:12–13). Yahweh will heal his people. He will become Israel's tree to give them fruit, and they will form a strong and beautiful forest (14:4–8 [14:5–9 MT]).

Key Commentaries and Studies

Andersen, Francis I., and David Noel Freedman. *Hosea: A New Translation with Introduction and Commentary*. AB 24. Garden City, NY: Doubleday, 1980. A classic work, with strength in linguistic analysis and canonical connections in the Hebrew Bible.

Ben Zvi, Ehud. *Hosea*. FOTL 21A/1. Grand Rapids: Eerdmans, 2005. Useful for formal and literary understanding of this most literary of the Minor Prophets.

Davies, Graham I. *Hosea: Based on the Revised Standard Version*. NCB. Grand Rapids: Eerdmans, 1992. A useful resource for historical backgrounds.

Dearman, J. Andrew. *The Book of Hosea*. NICOT. Grand Rapids: Eerdmans, 2010. A study on the historical, literary, and theological aspects of the book.

House, Paul R. *The Unity of the Twelve*. JSOTSup 97. BLS 27. Sheffield: Almond, 1990. Helpful in understanding the role of Hosea in the Minor Prophets.

Macintosh, Andrew A. *A Critical and Exegetical Commentary on Hosea*. ICC. Edinburgh: T&T Clark, 1997. Important for text-critical and philological study of the book.

27. McConville, "Hosea," 347–49.

25

JOEL

Sometimes people long for God to come but don't understand what it will mean for them when God appears. The book of Joel with its discussion of the Day of the Lord provides just this sort of image.

Name, Text, and Outline

The name Joel means "El/God is Y(ahweh)" or "Y(ahweh) is El/God." This confessional name identifies the chief or only deity as Yahweh. The elements of this name are not uncommon in Israelite personal names during the monarchy. Perhaps the most common form occurs in the name Elijah, where the sequence is reversed.

The text of Joel in the Masoretic Text is good and free of many issues. Joel 1:17 is difficult to translate. Some other passages have greater clarity in the Septuagint: for example, 3:11 and 21 [4:11 and 21 MT and LXX]. Why does Joel appear after Hosea and before Amos in the sequence of the Twelve Minor Prophets? If Joel dates from the eighth century, it would fit with Hosea, Amos, and Micah as among the earliest books. In the Old Testament, Joel son of Pethuel is not mentioned outside this book in the Old Testament, and the implicit evidence of the text itself is not clear as far as dating is concerned. Its position suggests an early date, but many scholars assign a later time to the prophet, closer to the end of the monarchy in 586 BC. The Septuagint positions Hosea, Amos, and Micah before Joel, perhaps recognizing the later and other-than-northern-Israelite focus of the book.

OUTLINE

I. Superscription (1:1)
II. First Assault (1:2–20)
   A. Locust Invasion (1:2–7)
   B. Lament (1:8–20)
III. Day of the Lord (2:1–17)
   A. Warning Announced (2:1–2)
   B. Second Invasion (2:3–11)
   C. Call to Repentance (2:12–17)
IV. Response (2:18–32)
   A. God's Promise of Blessing and Security (2:18–27)
   B. Outpouring of God's Spirit (2:28–32 [3:1–5 MT])
V. Judgment against the Nations (3:1–21 [4:1–21 MT])

Overview of Joel

The prophecy of Joel begins with the announcement of an invasion of locusts against God's people. The description uses many names for the locusts. It concludes by relating this picture to an invading army (1:6–7). Next is a call to lament, both to the people in general (1:8–12) and to the priests and elders (1:8–18). The prophet sees the judgment and cries to the Lord (1:19–20). A trumpet announcement heralds the second promised invasion of 2:1–11. A call to true repentance involves the changing of hearts, of all the people from every group (2:12–17). At this point, the Lord promises a return of fruitfulness in the land, of driving away the invaders, and of abundance and security (2:18–27). He also promises the outpouring of his spirit on all peoples, with the blessing of salvation for all who call on God (2:28–32). God will then bring the nations to the valley of Jehoshaphat for judgment. The people of Tyre, Sidon, and Philistia will face severe judgment for robbing God's temple of its valuables and for selling his people into slavery. There will be great destruction of the nations (3:1–16). God will bless Zion and Jerusalem with wine and milk, while the nations of Egypt and Edom will be desolate because of what they did to Judah (3:17–21).

Reading Joel

Premodern Readings

In Judaism, the divine spirit in Joel was understood as an aspect of God's presence. *Midrash Psalms* 14 cites the promise of universal prophecy in Joel 2:28–32 as a fulfillment of Moses's desire of Numbers 11:29 that all people

Iwoelbern/Wikimedia Commons

Locust swarm from Morocco

would prophesy.[1] Christian tradition and art have most often connected Joel with the outpouring of the Holy Spirit at Pentecost. In the Eastern Orthodox Church, Joel is honored for his prophecy of the coming of the Holy Spirit.

The valley of decision and the final battles with the nations influenced early apocalyptic literature in Judaism and Christianity. Theologians and artists found in Joel a picture of the prophesied battle and the coming judgment. See, for example, Michelangelo's painting of Joel on the Sistine Chapel ceiling, where the prophet examines a scroll presumably linked to this prophecy.[2] John Calvin comments on blowing the trumpet and assembling (Joel 2:1) as the proper attitude for people to have as they approach God in a time of impending judgment: to assemble, fast and confess the sins of the people, and throw themselves on the mercy of God alone.[3]

Higher Criticism

On the question of the date of Joel, some would place it back into the period before the destruction of the northern kingdom and Samaria, and others place it even later, in the postexilic period. There is no dating formula at the beginning of the book, either for kings of Judah and Samaria in the preexilic period or for those of the Persians in the postexilic period. Thus kings are not addressed, and the mention of priests (Joel 1:9; 2:17) does not explicitly refer to any political status (as was the case after the exile) but refers

1. Linville, "Joel," 456.
2. Ibid.
3. Calvin, *A Commentary on the Prophet Joel*.

to their place and role in the religious cult. The early postexilic period does not fit since there were no walls around the city just then (cf. 2:7). As Duane Garrett notes, a catchphrase in both Joel 3:16 and Amos 1:2 may explain the book's present position preceding Amos: "The LORD roars from Zion, and utters his voice from Jerusalem."[4]

The absence of explicit references to locusts in chapters 2 and 3 of the book (other than the promise of 2:25), after their prominent role in the first chapter, has led some to argue that there are two layers to the book and that the writers of the second half inserted their work into an earlier composition. However, it is difficult to draw conclusions from a book as short as Joel regarding general matters of style and the expectation of distinct literary layers. The restoration and regathering of the exiles in Joel 3:1–2 could have relevance for preexilic or postexilic Judah and perhaps Israel. Quotations and allusions to other prophets (Joel 2:32 with Obad. 17 and Isa. 37:31–32; Joel 3:10 with Isa. 2:4 and Mic. 4:3) can go either way. Indeed, the Joel 3:10 text about beating plowshares into swords might be the original since it would make sense as an original war cry. Doing the reverse has no popular parallel in the ancient world.

Joel 3:6 mentions Greeks who buy Israelite slaves from Phoenicians and Philistines. The mention of Greeks indicates nothing about dating since they occur early and late. The references in Joel 3:11 to the heavenly warriors of Yahweh do not prove connection with late apocalyptic literature or angelology, nor does the use of other language. The book may contain protoapocalyptic materials, but that does not require a postexilic date.[5] Certainty is not possible, but a late preexilic date is by no means objectionable in view of the book's contents.

Literary Readings

The image of the locust dominates the first chapter as Joel recalls the locust plague of Egypt (Exod. 10:1–20), only now God uses it to judge his own people. As this shifts to a literary image of a military invasion in the second chapter, it demonstrates the correlation between the natural world and the human sphere. This has been noticed in the Wisdom literature, where many proverbs employ this correlation. It also occurs in the prophetic literature, as here. The dominant perfect forms of the verbs in chapter 1 indicate the completion of a past invasion of locusts, which the hearers surely remembered. The consistent imperfect forms in 2:1–11 suggest that Joel's prophesies concerning this human invasion are yet to come. Garrett provides a useful summary of the manner in which the locust plague of chapter 1 is reversed by God's blessing and restoration at the end of chapter 2:[6]

4. Garrett, "Joel," 450–52.
5. See Sweeney, *TANAK*, 350.
6. Garrett, "Joel," 454.

Tell about locusts for generations (1:2–3)	People never again ashamed (2:26–27)
Locust swarms eat (1:4)	Restoration of what has been lost from locust swarms (2:25)
Wine and oil not available (1:5, 10)	Wine and oil restored (2:24b)
Grain and granaries fail (1:10–11, 17)	Grain restored and abundant (2:24a)
Land parched (1:12, 17)	Rains come (2:23)
Trees stripped (1:12, 19)	Trees fruitful (2:22b)
Animals have no food (1:18, 20)	Animals have food (2:22a)

Gender and Ideological Criticism

The description of mourning that begins in Joel 1:8 uses the simile of a virgin who dresses in sackcloth and mourns for her lost fiancé. This picture embraces all Israel as the virgin commanded to mourn. The image of the bride and bridegroom leaving their bedroom in 2:16 implies the commitment to which all are called: they go to the sacred assembly to mourn and repent.[7]

This command to proclaim a fast and repentance in chapter 2, as well as the judgment and God's mercy and forgiveness, has provided a basis for preachers to cry for the same repentance in times of special need. In June 2014, the evangelist Anne Graham Lotz called God's people to devote seven days in July for repentance and deliverance from the sin of the world and for the Holy Spirit to fall on God's people in a special way. She based her "Urgent Call to Prayer" on Joel 2 (esp. 2:1, 13, 28–29).[8]

Ancient Near Eastern Context

The general threats of warfare and of a locust plague were common tragedies in the ancient Near East and throughout most of the history of that region. The blessing of abundance in the restoration of animals, trees, grain, wine, and oil also includes items on the staple diet of those living in and around Jerusalem. The region depends on rain for the success of the harvest; in antiquity its primary crops were barley, wheat, grapes, and olives.

Canonical Context

For connections of some of the best-known Old Testament texts, see "Higher Criticism" and "Literary Readings," above. Beyond these, the use of Joel 2:32 by Romans 10:13 promises salvation to all who call on God. The picture of

7. Wolff's (*Joel and Amos*) attempt to see in Joel 1:8 a reference to the goddess Anat's mourning for her lost lover, Baal, is misguided and without any support in terms of a name or narrative.

8. Teresa Neumann, "777."

© Baker Publishing Group and Dr. James C. Martin

Remains of wine press from Shiloh

locusts may be taken up by Revelation 9:1–11, where similar creatures appear that are also related to warhorses (cf. Joel 2:4–5). The final battles of Revelation 18–20 may have their background in the gathering of nations into the valley of decision in Joel 3:12–17.

Best known among the texts of Joel is 2:28–32. The promise of the sending of the Spirit on the Day of the Lord is declared by Peter in Acts 2:14–21 as having begun. He relates this to the miraculous manner in which the apostles preach and prophesy so that everyone who is present can hear them in their many diverse native languages (Acts 2:1–12).

Theological Perspectives of Joel

"The Day of the Lord [Yahweh]" remains the clearest and most distinctive theme in the book of the prophet Joel. If Joel wrote early, it is possible that his prophecy introduced this theme. The Day of the Lord is not seen as positive or negative by itself. It is to be a day of judgment, as summarized in 1:15 after describing the locusts that have come into the land. The promised pouring out of God's spirit on this day (2:28–32) carries with it the blessing of prophecies and dreams from God, yet also darkening of the sun and the blood-red appearance of the moon. It is a day that is both "great and dreadful" (2:31 NIV). Similar solar signs appear in 3:15, where God summons all nations to fearsome judgment in the valley of Jehoshaphat. Thus God brings both judgment and

Locust Plagues in Israel

Although recent locust plagues (such as the one in March–May of 2013) have been thwarted by the use of pesticides, such plagues earlier in the region brought devastation. Excerpts from the *New York Times* report by the American Consul at Jerusalem include the following for the summer of 1915:

> Received at Washington from the Rev. Dr. Otis A. Glazebrook, American Consul at Jerusalem, of the plague of locusts which recently devastated Palestine. He says that the oncoming of the locust was properly to be termed an invasion. As far as the eye could reach, the fields were covered by the locusts, and even the street in front of the American Consulate has the appearance, in the movement of the green and black mass, of a flowing river. . . . In the lowlands there was a complete destruction of crops. . . . In the mountain district, notably about Jerusalem and Hebron, the heaviest loss from the onslaught of the locusts has been in connection with the olive groves and vineyards.[a]

[a] American Consul at Jerusalem, "Remarkable Details from American Consul."

salvation in that day. Specific past events, such as a historic locust plague or the fall of Jerusalem, anticipate parts of the full revelation of the Day of the Lord.[9] Indeed, Peter in Acts 2 may have announced the Day of the Lord. Most likely, it was the beginning of the end, the inauguration of that day. The book of Revelation looks forward to a future time when the Day of the Lord will be revealed in all of its fullness.

Key Commentaries and Studies

Allen, Leslie C. *The Books of Joel, Obadiah, Jonah, and Micah*. NICOT. Grand Rapids: Eerdmans, 1971. A classic evangelical source for useful exegesis and insight.

Barton, John. *Joel and Obadiah: A Commentary*. OTL. Louisville: Westminster John Knox, 2001. Reads the book as a whole and provides valuable literary insights.

Garrett, Duane A. *Hosea, Joel*. NAC 19A. Nashville: Broadman & Holman, 1997. An important evangelical contribution for theological perspectives and canonical relationships.

Stewart, Douglas K. *Hosea–Jonah*. WBC 31. Waco: Word, 1987. An evangelical commentary on the Hebrew text, with detailed exegetical insights.

Wolff, Hans Walter. *Joel and Amos: A Commentary on the Books of the Prophets Joel and Amos*. Translated by W. Janzen, S. D. McBride Jr., and C. A. Munchow. Hermeneia. Philadelphia: Fortress, 1977. Strongest on the text, text-critical analysis, and form criticism.

9. Garrett, "Joel," 454.

26

AMOS

Can a nation claim special privileges with God because of its past? Amos warned Israel that, even though they thought of themselves as God's chosen people, judgment was coming for their sin.

Name, Text, and Outline

The name Amos derives from a root meaning "to carry." It occurs in longer forms with a divine name in Hebrew, Ammonite, and Phoenician personal names.[1] It also appears in its shortened biblical form in some attestations, including a bulla that designates an Amos as an official of Hezekiah.[2] The name confesses that "God has carried" or that the infant is "carried by God."

The text of Amos is fairly well preserved in the Masoretic Text, although there are places where specific words may be translated in more than one manner. The Septuagint preserves an enhanced anti-Syrian and anti-Samaritan bias with a rendering that follows the Masoretic Text but can go its own way. Edward Glenny suggests the mid-second-century-BC translator envisioned an eschatological messianic savior who would open the way for gentiles to find God.[3]

OUTLINE

1. Judgments against the Nations (1:1–2:16)
   A. Introduction (1:1–2)

1. Albertz and Schmitt, *Family and Household Religion*, 291, 598.
2. Deutsch, *Biblical Period Hebrew Bullae*, 44–47.
3. Glenny, *Amos*; idem, *Finding Meaning*.

1. Superscription (1:1)
2. Yahweh Introduced (1:2)

B. God's Indictments (1:3–2:16)
1. Damascus (1:3–5)
2. Gaza (1:6–8)
3. Tyre (1:9–10)
4. Edom (1:11–12)
5. Ammon (1:13–15)
6. Moab (2:1–3)
7. Judah (2:4–5)
8. Israel (2:6–16)

II. Judgments against Israel (3:1–6:14)
A. Word Pictures of Judgment (3:1–15)
B. Previous Judgments Ineffective (4:1–13)
C. Lament for Israel (5:1–2)
D. Call to Repent from Injustice toward Neighbors (5:3–17)
E. Day of the Lord to Be Feared (5:18–27)
F. Oppression Promised for Complacency (6:1–14)

III. Judgments and Restoration in the Future (7:1–9:15)
A. Word Pictures of Judgment (7:1–9)
B. Amos versus Amaziah (7:10–17)
C. Punishment for Those Who Cheat the Poor (8:1–14)
D. No Escape from God's Judgment (9:1–10)
E. Restoration of Israel and David (9:11–15)

© Baker Publishing Group and Dr. James C. Martin

Tekoa

Overview of Amos

Amos was a shepherd during the reigns of the kings Uzziah of Judah and Jeroboam II of Israel. He received the words of Yahweh as one whose roars dry up the pastures where Amos may have gone with his flock (1:1–2). There follow a series of indictments against the city-states and regions surrounding the northern kingdom (Israel): undue violence (Damascus), the selling of God's people as slaves (Gaza, Tyre, Edom), violence against pregnant women (Ammon), regicide (Moab), and worship of other deities (Judah). The second half of Amos 2 (vv. 6–16) zeroes in on Israel and judges it for ignoring God's word and committing immoral acts as well as selling their own poor. Chapter 3 introduces God's special love for Israel but suggests that the nation should listen to the signs of nature and of war, implying that God is bringing judgment on his people. All the false worship and all the ill-gotten wealth that Israel has will be destroyed and taken by another nation. The cows of Bashan are women being pampered at the expense of the poor among their people; God will not regard their sacrifices (4:1–6). God has withheld rain, sent mildew and plagues, and destroyed towns; yet Israel has not repented and must now meet him (4:7–13). The lament for Israel's fall (5:1–2) precedes repeated commands to seek God and find what is good, in contrast to the sins that the people act out toward one another (5:1–17). The people think that the Day of Yahweh will bring delight and good things. But God indicates that it will be just the opposite: fear, destruction, and deportation (5:18–27).

Amos 6 introduces woes for the complacent in Zion, the traditional name of Jerusalem in the southern kingdom (Judah). However, the chapter then

© Baker Publishing Group and Dr. James C. Martin. Courtesy of the British Museum, London, England.

Ivory headboard from Nimrud

considers Samaria in the same set of poetic verses. Other nations have perished, even those that were not different from Israel (6:2). The lack of concern appears in the beds of ivory on which the Israelites lie, in the harps they play, the bowls of wine they drink, and the lotions with which they pamper themselves (6:3–7). But nothing will save them from deportation. Samaria will be like a house where no one survives (6:8–11). God will no longer tolerate the pride and injustice of the northerners (6:12–14). Locusts destroy the harvest, fire devours the land, and the plumb line (or perhaps better translated, "wall of tin") announces that God will not spare his people (7:1–9). Amaziah, priest of Bethel, tells Israel's king that Amos predicts the violent death of the king and the exile of the people. He commands Amos to go back to Judah. Amos denies an official status to himself as prophet, yet he states that Yahweh has brought him to speak the divine word. He predicts humiliation and death for Amaziah's family and the loss of his patrimony (7:10–17).

God shows Amos a basket of ripe fruit to indicate that judgment is at hand (8:1–3). Israel tramples the needy and cheats its neighbors. The land will shake and tremble from all the sin and the coming judgment (8:4–8). The sun will become dark, and the festivals will become occasions for mourning and sackcloth. "The words of the Lord" will disappear from the land, and those who seek comfort in other gods and goddesses will fall and disappear (8:9–14). The altars of the northern kingdom (Israel) will be struck down, and no one will escape the sword and the deportation by their enemies (9:1–4). Yahweh is Almighty God and can control nature. He will not regard Israel as any different from its neighbors, whom he also brought into their lands, just as he brought Israel from Egypt (9:5–7). God will destroy his people for their sins (9:8–10).

After the judgment will come a time of restoration: God will restore the fallen shelter (or hut) of David, and his people, from all nations that bear his name, will possess the land of Edom (9:11–12). There will come a time of incredible abundance and fruitfulness in the land; Israel will return from exile, be restored to cities, and enjoy God's blessing of fruitfulness and security for his people (9:13–15).

Reading Amos

Premodern Readings

One of the earliest Christian references to Amos occurs in Justin Martyr (*Dialogue with Trypho* 22). He quotes at length from Amos 5:18–6:7 to demonstrate that the laws regarding sacrifices in the Old Testament came about to deal with the sins of Israel. Jerome's work (*Commentariorum in Amos libri III*) with Amos is most interesting. He accepts the Hebrew text and its proto-Masoretic tradition, in preference to the Septuagint, often using the latter only for his spiritual interpretation. Whether or not Jerome is always aware of the double meanings of the Hebrew, he appears to follow Jewish exegetical tradition. John Calvin understands Amos 9:11–12 to apply to the coming of the Messiah.[4] Edom represents the Idumaeans, who troubled the Jews in the time of Christ and whom Christ will rule over, along with the rest of the nations.

Perhaps the most famous proclamation of the book in recent times has been the use of Amos 5:24 by Martin Luther King Jr. as the climax to his "I Have a Dream" speech, given before the Lincoln Memorial in August 1963. His application of this text to his call for the full equality and acceptance of all races in the United States echoed the choice of this text by Justin Martyr and the ongoing use of the book of Amos as a source for powerful prophetic rhetoric of repentance and of justice toward other humans.

Nevertheless, rabbinic tradition held that Amos was nicknamed "the stutterer" as a symbol of contemporary rejection of his message (*Leviticus Rabbah* 10; *Ecclesiastes Rabbah* 1.1). Different traditions developed as to whether he was killed by a blow to his forehead from King Uzziah or from his priestly critic at Bethel, Amaziah. Rabbi Simlai, an Amoraite (third century), summarized the Torah with Amos 5:4, "Seek me and live!" (*b. Makkot* 23b–24a).

Higher Criticism

M. Daniel Carroll R. divides the theories of composition of the book into three overlapping groups of scholars: those who accept a series of editorial layers extending from the eighth century into the postexilic period; those who emphasize a substantial unity to the book's composition; and those who see the book as substantially a product of the postexilic period, making use of some preexilic traditions and writing the book in a manner to reflect the interested ideologies of this later period.[5] The best example of the first group may be Hans Walter Wolff, whose Hermeneia commentary identifies six layers in the production of the book, beginning with two collections of oracles from Amos, tracing through a subsequent school of Amos, moving on to redactions related to the cult site at Bethel and to the Deuteronomists of the seventh century, and finally reaching the postexilic addition of 9:11–15.[6] This latter point became a matter of critical orthodoxy. The eighth-century prophets, especially those devoted to the north, such as Hosea and Amos, did not foresee a redemptive restoration for God's people. For them, there was only judgment. Therefore, the rebuilding of David's house could not

4. Calvin, *Joel, Amos and Obadiah*.
5. Carroll R., "Amos," 26–28.
6. Wolff, *Joel and Amos*.

have been a product of the prophet himself or of his immediate school of disciples. It had to come later, often much later in the postexilic period, claim these critics.[7]

Recent study on the literary composition of the Twelve Minor Prophets has led to the recognition of some catchwords and phrases that may imply an editorial layer where such texts were inserted to relate the various books.[8] There has been a larger emphasis on the literary relationships of the text, whether explaining oracles of judgment and salvation as part of the prophet Amos's life experience or understanding the whole book as a legitimate product of eighth-century-BC geopolitical realities and comparative literary materials.[9] Shalom Paul questions even such scholarly conventions as the late dating of Amos 9:11–15. His emphasis on the literary unity and eighth-century origins provides an important corrective for the direction of many assumptions of twentieth-century critical scholarship.

An appreciation of the literary unity of the book, of course, does not require an eighth-century-BC date for most of it. To the contrary, recent directions of critical scholarship have followed wide-ranging assumptions that Amos should join the rest of the Minor Prophets and much of the rest of the Bible in a late exilic or, more likely, postexilic context. In this view the text can contain authentic kernels of earlier materials. However, the artistry of postexilic writers positioned this material so well in the texts they created that certainty regarding where their work begins and ends has become difficult, if not impossible, to achieve. Thus studies have focused on ideological reconstructions of postexilic settings in which oracles from Amos may find a home.[10] There are several questions with this approach that remain unanswered: How could the wide variety of political views and literary approaches of so many of the biblical books, including Amos, have been created in so short a period of time and with such a small population of potential writers as found in fifth/fourth-century Jerusalem and its environs? Why do texts such as Amos indict and contradict the interests of the supposed wealthy and powerful elites, who alone were responsible for their composition?[11]

Closely tied with this has been a debate over the extent of literacy among groups in Iron Age Israel and Judah. The assumption has been that no one could read and write in the eighth century BC in these countries. However, this contradicts the presence of many texts from the Iron Age. While only a

7. See a similar analysis of multiple literary stages, none of which precede the fall of the northern kingdom (Samaria), in Radine, *Book of Amos*.

8. See Jeremias, *Book of Amos*; Rottzoll, *Studien zur Redaktion*.

9. As part of Amos's life experience, see Andersen and Freedman, *Amos*; as a product of eighth-century geopolitical realities, see Paul, *Amos*.

10. See, e.g., Albertz, "Deuteronomistic History and the Heritage of the Prophets."

11. Carroll R., "Amos," 28.

Functional Literacy in Iron Age Israel

The presence of dozens of literary texts and hundreds of smaller inscriptions belies the claims that only a few elites could read or write in the period of Israel and Judah's monarchy.[a] There are the dozens of Samaria ostraca; the Siloam Tunnel Inscription; the fragmentary remains of other monumental inscriptions discovered in both Samaria and Judah; the Kuntillet ʿAjrûd, Khirbet el-Qom, En Gedi, and other tomb inscriptions from the south; the Iron Age palimpsest from among the Judean Desert discoveries; the surrounding literary texts, including the Deir ʿAllā plaster inscriptions, the Moabite Stele, the Tel Dan Stele, the Tel Miqne Dedicatory Inscription, the Amman Citadel Inscription; and hundreds of seals and bullae that attest to the widespread ability of people to read and write, however basically.[b] Recent years have seen further discoveries pushing this skill earlier. The eleventh/tenth-century-BC Khirbet Qeiyafa Inscription of five lines of text and the mid-tenth-century Tel Zayit abecedary from a village in Judah add to the eleventh-century ʿIzbet Sartah abecedary and the ninth-century Gezer poem/calendar.[c] Attempts to caricature this position as an argument for a high level of literacy among the "nonelite masses" have not been convincing.[d] To the contrary, the basic skills of reading and writing one's name are attested in Iron Age Israel and Judah by the unusually large percentage of epigraphic seals and bullae, where one's name and patronym could easily involve knowledge of half of the Hebrew alphabet, and by the increasing number of inscriptions found from this period.[e]

[a] For functional literacy, see Hess, "Writing about Writing," 345; Schniedewind, "Orality and Literacy," 331; Dever, *What Did?*, 202–21.

[b] For a convenient presentation of many of the texts, see Aḥituv, *Echoes from the Past*. For a summary of their value in this discussion, see Hess, "Writing about Writing." The seals and bullae have been published by André Lemaire ("Nouveaux sceaux"), Robert Deutsch (*Biblical Period Hebrew Bullae*), and others. See a listing of names from seals, bullae, and such, plus a study of their elements, in Albertz and Schmitt, *Family and Household Religion*.

[c] See works listed in the previous footnote; Tappy et al., "Abecedary"; Misgav, Garfinkel, and Ganor, "Ostracon"; and Yardeni, "On the Ostracon."

[d] For the caricature, see Rollston, "Scribal Education"; for analysis and response, see Hess, "Questions of Reading and Writing"; idem, review of *Writing and Literacy*. See also a response to the odd attempt to label this analysis as protective strategies, idem, "Protective Strategies Here and There."

[e] Add now a second Qeiyafa inscription from the late eleventh and early tenth centuries BC that includes the contemporary biblical name Esh-Baal (1 Chron. 8:33; 9:39; cf. Garfinkel et al., "ʾIšbaʿal Inscription"), and an inscription from Jerusalem dated to the tenth century BC. Cf. Mazar, Ben-Shlomo, and Aḥituv, "Inscribed Pithos"; Galil, "*ʾyyn ḫlqʾ*."

few people could write at the level of a prophetic book such as Amos, it is by no means impossible or unlikely that scribes and others existed in ancient Israel with the capacity to attain this level of literacy.[12]

12. Hess, "Questions of Reading and Writing."

Literary Readings

The opening two chapters of Amos repeatedly introduce each of the nations with the form, *x* . . . *x* + 1, which also occurs in Wisdom literature (cf. Prov. 30). This increases the expectation that the fourth item will be the worst example of a national sin bringing judgment. In this case only the fourth sin is mentioned. It leads to a vivid description of the terrifying judgment of God. The order of the nations begins with geographical neighbors to the north and west, and then reflects on the nations traditionally related to Israel, such as Edomites, Ammonites, and Moabites. Its closest "relative" and supposed partner in faith, Judah, is also addressed. This leads to the longest section, focused on Israel, implicitly comparing their crimes of exploitation of the poor and dependent with the war crimes of the other nations.

Following are a series of judgment oracles in Amos 3:1–15; 4:1–13; and 5:1–17. These become progressively more threatening and less punctuated by the argument of the case. Amos 3:3–8 indicts Israel with a series of rhetorical questions. Central to the book is the extended chiasm of 5:1–17, where the twin themes of justice and righteousness appear to an extent found nowhere else in the book. Here at the heart of the text lies the call to show these qualities to others and the warning that justice dictates a response from God for the failure of his people.

Much of the text is punctuated by statements indicating that Yahweh is speaking. God has entered into a dispute with his people (2:11; 3:2–8, 12; 5:18–20, 25; 9:7). These and the vivid vision reports (7:1–17; 8:1–3; 9:1–4) serve to vindicate Amos's message as authentic divine revelation. Other forms of speech include proverbs (3:3–6), comparisons and riddles (2:9; 3:12; 5:2, 7, 19, 24; 6:12; 9:9), woe sayings (5:18; 6:1), attacks on the cult (4:4–5; 5:4, 21–24), and a lament for the fall of the nation (5:1–2). Amos also uses multiple speech forms that are woven together. Perhaps best known are the oracles against the nations, which lead up to a longer oracle against Israel, with multiple forms as already noted (1:3–2:16). Certain intervention follows ineffective curses in 4:6–12. The coming judgment replaces earlier expressions of divine mercy in the visions of 7:1–9 and 8:1–3. As with his contemporary Hosea, the rhetorical forms and literary expressions of Amos surprise the reader by their sophistication and power.

Gender and Ideological Criticism

Four texts in Amos distinguish women from men. The first two occur in the oracles against other nations. In 1:11 God condemns Edom for slaughtering the women of the land. The term for "women" (NIV) derives from the root *rḥm*. This root is related to "womb" and thus may suggest a cold analysis where the concern is the loss of childbearing organisms and thus a decrease in potential population and its assumed economic prosperity. Yet it is equally possible and more likely (within the general context of these oracles about callous and brutal treatment) that the root emphasizes mercy, compassion, and love. The Edomites showed no mercy to those who might have showed them mercy. In 1:13 God condemns Ammon for ripping open those who were pregnant in Gilead, using the root *hrh*, which carries the sense of conception (cf. Isa. 7:14). Here as well the concern is for the brutality against those least able to defend themselves: both women and unborn children.

Amos 2:7 describes the young woman to whom both a man and his father go for sexual and cult-related purposes. Amos 4:1 also moves in a different direction by indicting the "cows of Bashan . . . on Mount Samaria" for their oppression of the poor and needy. They command their husbands, "Bring something to drink!" The focus on personal enjoyment contrasts with the lack of concern for the poor. The 2:7 reference forms a picture that combines the sale of fellow Israelites into slavery with false worship. God rejects this abuse of the poor, of young women, and of worship. Amos 4:1 indicts women for the abuse of their wealth and position rather than for their gender. The following two verses interchange masculine-plural forms ("You will be taken away with hooks") with feminine plurals ("the last of you with fishhooks; each woman will go out; you will be cast out" [RSH]). This suggests what the remainder of the book demonstrates: an indictment across the population of Israel, including both females and males.[13]

Given the popularity of concepts such as social justice and economic justice, it is not surprising that this work has found application in war-torn lands where economic issues have been at the forefront.[14] Carroll R. comments on his country of Guatemala after the signing of 1996 peace accords:

> For those who have lived in a country at war, the movement of language between phrases saying all will die to others suggesting the survival of some makes perfect sense. "War is hell": bodies lying everywhere (6:9–10; 8:2–3), people mourning in the fields of battle (5:1–2, 16–17), the poor scratching out a living against all odds (2:6–7; 4:6–9; 5:11–13; 8:4–6), while others in the capital city drink and dine in comfort (4:1; 6:4–6)—all these descriptions of the prophetic text of Amos are not uncommon pictures in Guatemala's recent past, where hundreds of thousands have been killed, orphaned, widowed, exiled, or displaced, whereas others seem to live as if untouched by the conflict.
>
> In such a situation of extreme loss, a few words which speak of rebuilding ruins, accompanied by general descriptions of peace and plenty, such as those of 9:11–15, are vague enough not to promise anything too specific but concrete enough to make the horror endurable. The brief hope passage, in other words,

13. On the ambiguity of the meaning for "cows" as used here, whether as fattened livestock, cultic references to calf worship, or an honored title, see King, *Amos, Hosea, Micah*, 126.

14. Carroll R., *Amos*, 69–72.

whatever the final decision on historical authenticity, ideologically coheres with a war context. Yet, and this is the point of the title of my article, we live now between the time of war and the actualization of hope. Literarily, the people live "between the lines," somewhere between 9:10 and 9:11.[15]

Ancient Near Eastern Context

The book of Amos betrays historical knowledge, not only reaching back to Israel's own exodus, but also reflecting awareness of earlier and eighth-century-BC events among the Aramaeans and Philistines (9:7).[16] Amos 1:1 describes an earthquake that has occurred only two years before Amos's oracles. Is this connected with Zechariah 14:5 or with the end of Hazor Stratum VI and Beersheba III, where the excavators found indications of an earthquake from the eighth century?[17] It may have itself become a powerful sign of God's intervention.

The oracles against the nations in Amos 1–2 also witness to a knowledge of history in Israel.[18] Thus 1:3–5 recalls the Aramaean king Hazael's conquest of Gilead in the latter part of the ninth century BC. The Philistine sale of Israelite and Judean prisoners of war to the Edomites may reflect the invasion of Judah during the reign of Joram (2 Chron. 21:16–17). Hazael destroyed Gath (2 Kings 12:17; 2 Chron. 24:23), and thus it does not appear along with the other four traditional Philistine cities (Amos 1:6–8). Does 1:9–10 recall a retaliatory act by Tyre for Jehu's murder of Jezebel, capturing Israelite towns near their border and selling the population as slaves? Ammon apparently joined Hazael in his acts of cruelty against the Israelite region of Gilead (1:13–15). Perhaps the oracle against Moab (2:1–3) also recalls events of the previous century, when the king of Moab may have captured the crown prince of Edom and burned him as a sacrifice on the walls of the besieged fortress (2 Kings 3:26–27).

Socioeconomically, both the northern kingdom (Israel) under Jeroboam II and the southern kingdom (Judah) under the reign of Uzziah (also called Azariah) found the first half of the eighth century BC to be a time of relative peace, prosperity, and expansion. However, this period did not begin with friendly relations. After an initial alliance, King Jehoash of Israel defeated King Amaziah of Judah and took him hostage (2 Kings 14:11–17; 2 Chron. 25:5–25). During the period that followed, Judah may have paid tribute to Israel. Marvin Sweeney envisions such a context as one in which Amos, a businessman of some means who was in charge of herds of sheep and the tending of sycamore trees, would have come with a group of Judeans to pay

15. Ibid., 71; cited from Carroll R., "Living between the Lines," 55.
16. Perhaps also awareness of Cush. See Strawn, "What Is Cush Doing?"
17. King, *Amos, Hosea, Micah*, 21.
18. Rainey, in Rainey and Notley, *Sacred Bridge*, 222–23.

tribute at the border sanctuary of Bethel.[19] In this context, he would identify the poor and oppressed as his fellow Judeans. Alternatively, at some point Amaziah was released, perhaps as a gesture of goodwill, and the south again prospered. In such a context, the poor and oppressed represent the indigent class of the northern kingdom. This might include those like Naboth (1 Kings 21), whose God-given patrimony was usurped by the greed of those more powerful than himself. By the eighth century it is possible that a few had acquired much land and held the many in debt servitude. This may also represent the concerns voiced in the prophet's message.

Canonical Context

Some of the historical connections with Old Testament texts have already been mentioned. In the New Testament, phrases that refer to judgment draw on the strong imagery of Amos. Jude 23 references Amos 4:11 when referring to the saving of those who are snatched from the fire of sin and judgment. Ephesians 5:16 agrees that the days are evil, a sentiment found in Amos 5:13. In his speech, Stephen condemns Israel from the days of its wilderness wandering (Acts 7:42–43). He cites Amos 5:25–27, which promises exile to those who have sinned. The picture of "the Day of the Lord" as one when the sun will go dark at noon (Amos 8:9) may be behind the descriptions of the darkness at Christ's crucifixion (Matt. 27:45; Mark 15:33; Luke 23:44–45). At the crucial Council of Jerusalem in Acts 15, the decision was made to place upon gentile Christians none of the specific obligations unique to the Jewish torah given at Sinai. Agreement was reached after James's speech, in which he quotes Amos 9:11–12 (Acts 15:16–17) and applies the restoration of David's fallen shelter to the coming of Christ, where the intent is to bring all humanity to God. It is surprising that the Epistle of James does not allude directly to Amos in his admonitions regarding the poor (e.g., 2:6–7; 5:1–6), although these contexts draw as much from the Law as from various prophetic writings.

Theological Perspectives of Amos

Yahweh roars from Jerusalem in Amos 1:2. This is the true sanctuary and center of worship for Israel's God, not the false centers in Bethel, Dan, and elsewhere in the northern kingdom. God's symbol here is the lion of Judah (who roars), not the bull-calf images in the border sanctuaries of Israel/Ephraim.[20] Thus the stage is set to emphasize the prophet's concern for natural law. Qualities of civility and of common human decency and respect for others are violated by the surrounding nations in such a manner as to bring God's wrath on them.

19. Sweeney, *TANAK*, 351–52.
20. Freedman and Welch, "Amos's Earthquake."

These derive from the universal prohibitions against violence (Gen. 9:5–6) and from the creation of all humanity in the image of God (1:26–28).

© Baker Publishing Group and Dr. James C. Martin. The Israel Museum.

Tenth-century-BC Taanach cult stand with possible representation of goddess Asherah flanked by lions

The focus on Israel highlights failures in obeying the commands to love God and to love one's neighbor. Immorality and the sale of the poor stand out here (Amos 2:6–16). Yet the call to repent of these sins does not emerge from nowhere. It comes from the heart of God's own love for his people as witnessed by their redemption from Egypt and special selection (3:1–2). If so, then how does 9:7 relate, where God appears to refuse to show favoritism? The answer lies in the rhetorical questions of chapter 2 that follow and culminate in God's choice of his prophets for his own people (3:7). Chapter 9 emphasizes the sovereignty of God as the Creator. In this context Israel's deliverance is no more difficult to accomplish than that of the other nations.

The judgment on Israel will be the destruction brought by a foreign army. This prophecy at the end of chapter 3 contrasts with the self-indulgence of the northerners that 4:1 describes. Here God refuses their offerings that they give without true repentance. His recent history with them has involved sending lesser punishments, such as lack of rain, disease, plagues, and the sword of war. But none of this has brought Israel to its knees in prayer, confession, and repentance. Thus 5:1–17 encapsulates the message of judgment with the warning that the nation is doomed and calls the people to perform acts of justice with the poor; it also focuses on the almighty God of Israel who as Creator can do anything. At the heart of the book lies the true message that God brings through Amos: "Seek me and live" (5:4). The attempt to deal with sin through seeking God at altars and religious sites that he did not command will fail. God hates these religious festivals as hypocritical and instead desires justice. Deportation is coming even though the people remain unaware. They see Amos and his message as the problem, instead of the sins he points out (7:10–17). Chapter 8's image of ripe fruit indicates that judgment is at hand and allows elaboration on how awful exile will be.

If no one can escape—including Israel, who has no special claim (9:1–10)—then all human hope is lost. Only God's own mercy and promise of restoration remain (9:11–17). It is this promise that redirects the faithful back to Jerusalem and the rulership of David, as well as to the worship of his God. Yet here at the end of his message, Amos returns to the nations he judged at the beginning of his book. While there will be punishment for those such as Edom (repeatedly mentioned in 1:6, 9, 11; 2:1), God's salvation will extend beyond the united kingdom of Israel and reach to the ends of earth. Judgment must come, but so will salvation. Both come from God. Therefore Amos counsels those who will listen to seek Yahweh and his covenant and thereby live.

Key Commentaries and Studies

Andersen, Francis I., and David Noel Freedman. *Amos: A New Translation with Introduction and Commentary.* AB 24A. New York: Doubleday, 1989. This commentary remains an important resource for linguistic analysis of the text.

Garrett, Duane A. *Amos: A Handbook on the Hebrew Text.* Baylor Handbook on the Hebrew Bible. Waco: Baylor University Press, 2008. Sensitive to the literary dimensions of the text, with theological insights.

Paul, Shalom M. *Amos: A Commentary on the Book of Amos.* Hermeneia. Minneapolis: Fortress, 1991. Strongest commentary for linguistic analysis and exegesis of the Hebrew text.

Smith, Gary V. *Amos: A Commentary.* Grand Rapids: Zondervan, 1989. A useful theological and literary study.

27

OBADIAH

Just because we choose not to believe in God does not mean that he has no business with us. Edom did not worship the Lord, but the prophet Obadiah still had a message for the Edomites, that God would deal with them.

Name, Text, and Outline

Obadiah is the name of the prophet who wrote this, the shortest book in the Old Testament. His name is best interpreted as "Servant of Yahweh." This name is composed of elements that are common in personal names throughout Israel's monarchy. The "servant" element occurs in names such as Abda, Abdi, and Abdiel. The "Yahweh" element occurs in hundreds of names, usually as the second part of the name. The text of Obadiah presents no major difficulties, and comparative examination suggests that the Masoretic Text preserves the best version. The early text of Obadiah 1–21 from Murabbaʿat (Mur 88 [XII] col. 9) preserves a variant only at verse 17b; the Qumran fragment ($4Q82^g$) also has only one significant variant.[1]

OUTLINE

I. Introduction (v. 1a)
II. Judgment against Edom Announced (vv. 1b–2)

1. Barton, *Joel and Obadiah*, 117–18. For Obad. 17b, the Murabbaʿat fragment reads (with LXX and the versions), "The house of Jacob will possess those who dispossessed them," i.e., they will possess the land of Edom, as in vv. 19–21; vs. "their [own] possessions," i.e., their own land, in v. 17 (MT, ESV).

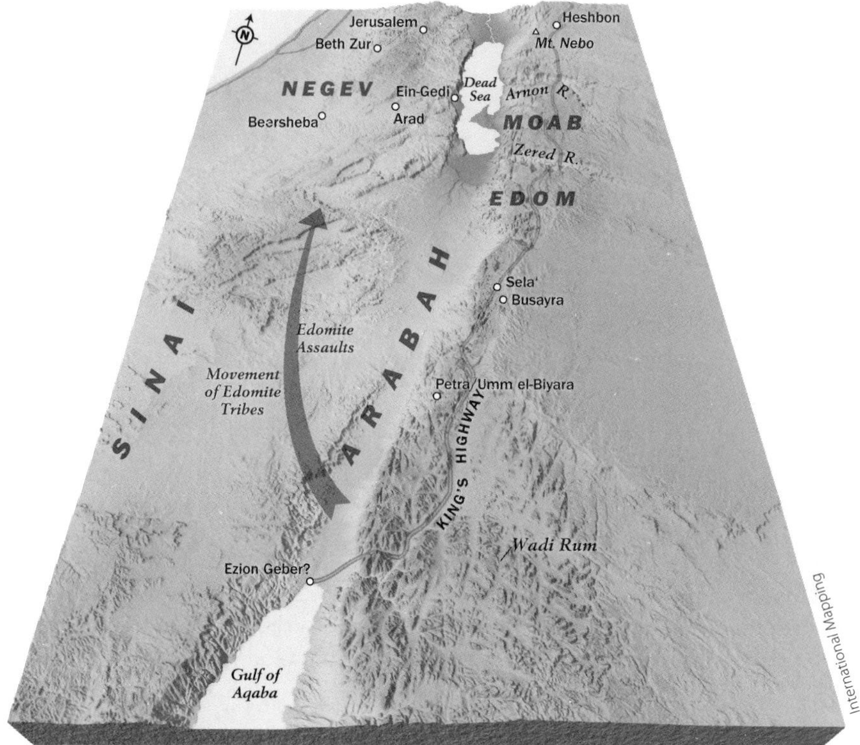

Places in Obadiah's prophecy

III. Edom's Pride (vv. 3–4)
IV. Promised Disaster (vv. 5–9)
V. Edom's Betrayal of Judah (vv. 10–14)
VI. The Day of Yahweh as a Time of Just Recompense on Edom (vv. 15–16)
VII. Salvation for Zion and Destruction for Edom and Judah's Neighbors (vv. 17–21)

Overview of Obadiah

The book begins as the vision of Obadiah. Yahweh stirs up the nations to attack the kingdom of Edom. The kingdom's location in the clefts of the rocks (v. 3) has increased its pride as an invincible enemy. But God will bring the nation to its knees (vv. 2–6). Edom will be betrayed by its closest allies (vv. 7–9). This comes due to Edom's treachery against its brother Jacob (v. 10). When Jerusalem and Judah were destroyed, Edom remained unsupportive. Indeed, Edom rejoiced, possessed Judah's cities, caught those of Judah who tried to escape, and handed them over to their enemies (vv. 11–14). The Day

© Baker Publishing Group and Dr. James C. Martin

Petra in the region of Edom, with a later edifice

of Yahweh approaches, when all nations will receive from God just what they did to God's people (vv. 15–16). Mount Zion will provide salvation, and the land that God gave to Jacob will be restored (v. 17). Jacob and the northern kingdom (Joseph) will destroy Edom (v. 18). God's people will expand their territories into Edom, Philistia, Samaria, Gilead, Zarephath (north, in the region of Tyre and Sidon), and beyond (vv. 19–20). From Zion, those who have delivered the land will govern Edom under Yahweh's sovereignty (v. 21).

Reading Obadiah

Premodern Readings

Perhaps the words of Jerome (*Commentary on Obadiah*) preserve the general feeling about interpreting the book: it is brief, and that makes it so much more difficult. Both Jerome and rabbinic interpretation connected Obadiah with the figure in 1 Kings 18. The rabbis (e.g., *b. Sanhedrin* 39b) explained that Obadiah converted to Israelite faith from Edom, where he was a descendant of Eliphaz the Temanite (see Job 2:11). Radak applies verses 10–11 to Titus's destruction of Jerusalem (AD 70). Titus and his army symbolized the Edomites. Regarding verse 15, John Calvin concludes that everyone will receive a reward and that the ungodly will receive whatever cruelty they have inflicted on others.[2] John Wesley's notes interpret the remnant that shall be delivered to the exile in such a way that the deliverer here is Cyrus, "a type of Israel's redemption by Christ." However, the deliverers of verse 21 are the leaders of the returnees such as Zerubbabel, Ezra, and Nehemiah.

Higher Criticism

Edom is Esau, the brother of Jacob/Israel (Gen. 25:24–26). The two struggled from the beginning. Obadiah contextualizes this struggle at the end of their independent kingdoms in the sixth century BC. Dating the prophecy later would lose the powerful message that this would have had for those who had experienced betrayal and loss at the hand of their southern neighbor. Dating it earlier may seem unlikely in light of a depiction of some details in verses 11–14 that correspond with Jeremiah 49, Psalm 137, and other texts that describe the events of 587/586 BC. Possible earlier conflicts with Edom might be envisioned here (2 Kings 8:21–22; 2 Chron. 20; also 2 Kings 16:6 and 2 Chron. 28:17–18). Indeed, the imperfect verb forms in this section suggest a future event is described in terms of Edom's treatment of the survivors of Jerusalem.[3]

Literary Readings

The brevity of this text does not invite a great deal of literary analysis. While most prophets devote a separate section to oracles against other nations, and it seems unusual to focus entirely on a single nation, such as Edom, it is not unknown since Jonah and Nahum do something similar with Assyria.

A significant amount of literary study has returned to traditional redaction criticism, where there are attempts to divide the text into the first part of Obadiah and a "deutero-Obadiah" consisting of verses 15a and 16–21.[4] Verse 15a follows verse 8 in introducing the "Day of Yahweh" for a second time. However, verse 15b returns to emphasis on the tit-for-tat approach, which characterizes the first part of the book. However, this requires splitting verse 15 into two parts and placing the second part of the verse with the first part of the text, and the first part of the verse with the second part of Obadiah. While such an approach is not unknown in literary criticism, it does little to respect the book's unity and its sequential presentation.

Gender and Ideological Criticism

The brevity of the book invites little in the way of original insight. It sticks to the masculine nature of war and warriors, as well as sages (vv. 8–9), and consistently portrays males in Israel's history, here as Esau and Jacob.

2. Calvin, *Joel, Amos and Obadiah*.
3. LeCureux, "Obadiah, Book of," 572–73; Ben Zvi, "Obadiah."
4. Ibid.

Ancient Near Eastern Context

In the late seventh and early sixth centuries BC, Edom enjoyed an increasing influence in the region west of the Arabah, especially the Negev of ancient Israel.[5] The evidence of Edomite culture in the region, in terms of pottery, seals, ostraca, and cultic implements, suggests Edomite presence in this area in the seventh century BC. Arad Letters 21 and 24 testify to the threat that Edomites presented to this southern region of Judah around 600 BC.

With the conquest of Jerusalem, Edom remained a vassal to Babylon and Nebuchadnezzar. The Nabonidus Chronicle recounts the Babylonian conquest and annexation of Edom in 553/552 BC. By the time of Cambyses II (530–522 BC), Arabs controlled the region of Edom (Herodotus, *Hist.* 3.88).

Canonical Context

The position of Obadiah creates no surprise. As an oracle of judgment against Edom, it naturally follows the pronouncement of Amos 9:12. The similar words of Joel 3:2 and 14 and Obadiah 15 also may explain its proximity to them: the Day of Yahweh is near for all nations (so in Joel 3:19, Edom appears). Jeremiah 49:7–22 preserves much of the same text as Obadiah, suggesting either borrowing with some editing or a common source for the two oracles.

Theological Perspectives of Obadiah

While some emphasize a vindictive streak in a prophet such as Obadiah,[6] others find here a reflection of a greater issue regarding God's covenant with his people and the manner in which he keeps his promises, despite the sin of his people.[7] In this view the prophet addresses the bewildered survivors of the Babylonian attack on Judah and Edom's encroachment into the promised land. Does this signal a new "Joshua era," in which Edom now replaces Israel, whose people are vanquished and dispossessed just as the Canaanites were in the time of Joshua? Obadiah asserts that God did not give Edom this land, but that the pride and greed of the nation drove them to acquire it and to participate and rejoice in Judah's destruction. God judges Edom and declares destruction and an end to its wanton cruelty against the brother Jacob. The Day of Yahweh ("Day of the Lord") will bring a reversal of these events. Edom will disappear as a people. Zion and Jerusalem will rise as blessed by God. In place of destruction, God's people will come to inhabit the land of Edom. The lands round about will be occupied with the people of God. All the lands will belong to Yahweh.

5. Van der Veen, "Sixth-Century Issues," 396–98.
6. Barton, *Joel and Obadiah*.
7. LeCureux, "Obadiah," 572–73.

Key Commentaries and Studies

Allen, Leslie C. *The Books of Joel, Obadiah, Jonah, and Micah*. NICOT. Grand Rapids: Eerdmans, 1971. Remains an important evangelical exegesis of Obadiah.

Barton, John. *Joel and Obadiah: A Commentary*. OTL. Louisville: Westminster John Knox, 2001. Useful insights into the message of the book from traditional critical perspectives.

Ben Zvi, Ehud. *A Historical-Critical Study of the Book of Obadiah*. BZAW 242. Berlin: de Gruyter, 1996. One of the better critical analyses of the book.

Block, Daniel I. *Obadiah: The Kingship Belongs to YHWH*. HMS. Grand Rapids: Zondervan, 2013. Strong evangelical insights on rhetorical, literary, and theological aspects of the text.

Renkema, Johan. *Obadiah*. HCOT. Leuven: Peeters, 2003. A strong emphasis on exegesis; useful for historical perspectives.

28

JONAH

Is God's love only for me and my friends, or does it include the worst enemies I can imagine? The book of Jonah deals with this challenge of extending love to people we hate.

Name, Text, and Outline

The name Jonah is the Hebrew word for "dove, pigeon." Animal names are not unknown among Hebrew and West Semitic personal names of all periods. This name appears in extrabiblical texts from Judah in the late monarchy and from Ammon.[1] The text of this prophetic book is reliable in the Masoretic Text, with no major variants.

OUTLINE

I. Jonah's Call, Flight, and Surrender (1:1–17 [2:1 MT])
II. Jonah's Prayer and God's Response (2:1–10 [2:2–11 MT])
III. Nineveh's Repentance and God's Response (3:1–10)
IV. Jonah's Response (4:1–11)

Overview of Jonah

Jonah is primarily a narrative about the prophet whom God calls to preach to Nineveh. Jonah, however, resists and runs away to Joppa, where he takes

1. Albertz and Schmitt, *Family and Household Religion*, 607–8.

Courtesy of Oriental Institute of the University of Chicago

Philistine ships call to mind the one Jonah boarded

passage on a ship bound for Tarshish (Jon. 1). Yahweh sends a powerful wind on the sea that threatens to tear apart the ship. The sailors throw the cargo overboard, but the storm does not stop. The sailors cry to their gods. They discover Jonah asleep in the hold and cast lots to see who is at fault; the lot chooses Jonah as the guilty person. He identifies himself as a Hebrew worshiper of Yahweh, who has created the sea and land. Jonah confesses that he is running away from God and tells the sailors to throw him into the sea because it is his fault that they are in peril. The sailors try to row to safety, but nothing calms the sea, so they throw him overboard. At that point the sea becomes calm; this event brings them to worship Yahweh. A big fish swallows Jonah.

The psalm of chapter 2 is a prayer to Yahweh from the realm of the dead. God has brought the sea over the prophet, but he looks forward to God's deliverance so he can again see his holy temple (2:4). The waters surround Jonah, and the earth bars him ("the earth with its prison bars closed behind me forever!" 2:6 HCSB), but God delivers him from the pit and hears his prayer (2:6–7). While the idol worshipers turn from God's love, Jonah will sacrifice and fulfill vows to God (2:8–9; just like the sailors of Jon. 1). God directs the fish, and it vomits Jonah onto dry land (2:10).

God again calls Jonah to Nineveh (3:1). He obeys and goes with the proclamation that in forty days Nineveh will be destroyed (3:4). The king proclaims a fast, and Nineveh repents in "sackcloth" and "dust"; even the animals put on sackcloth and fast (3:5–9 NIV). God hears them and relents from his destruction (3:10).

Jonah grows angry at God's mercy and complains to him (4:1–2). He prays for an end to his life, but God challenges him (4:3–4). Jonah makes a shelter east of Nineveh, and God provides a plant to shade him. But the next day God sends a worm to destroy the plant, and again Jonah wishes he could die

© Baker Publishing Group and Dr. James C. Martin

Marble sarcophagus illustrating Jonah's story (ca. AD 300)

(4:5–8). God challenges Jonah for being concerned merely about the plant that has died. Should God be any less concerned for Nineveh's more than 120,000 infants, plus youths, adults, and "many animals" (4:9–11)?

Reading Jonah

Premodern Readings

Early Christianity followed the Gospels in teaching that the story of Jonah anticipated the death and resurrection of Jesus Christ (Matt. 12:38–40; Luke 11:29–30). Whatever the character of the prophet, his psalm in chapter 2 and deliverance from death provide a typological correspondence to Christ.

In the intertestamental period, Tobit mentions Jonah. Tobit 14:4 alludes to the warning that Jonah brought of Nineveh's destruction and its imminent occurrence. Both early Judaism (*Mekilta de Rabbi Ishmael*) and Christianity (Jerome) saw in Jonah an attempt to preserve the Israelite people. So Jonah would rather die than allow himself to be used as a prophet to offer implicit salvation to Nineveh. Others such as Martin Luther and later J. D. Michaelis and Carl Friedrich Keil found a prophet who exemplified a dislike or even a hatred of other nations.[2] In contrast, the author became admired as one teaching universal toleration of peoples, by using the negative example of Jonah.[3] Meanwhile, Western art continued to focus on Jonah's experience going into and coming out of the great fish, or whale, as many took the story to mean.

2. Luther, *Luther's Works*, vol. 19 (commentary on ch. 4, Latin text); Keil, *Keil on the Twelve Minor Prophets*, 410–13. Michaelis is cited by Keil.

3. Sherwood, *Biblical Text and Its Afterlives*; idem, "Jonah," 479–80.

Higher Criticism

The questions surrounding Jonah deal with traditional critical topics: the form of literature of the narrative, the integrity of the book in the light of the psalm of chapter 2, and the historical value of the book. Jonah's story has been identified as an allegory, a midrash, a parable, a fable, and a satire. While any of these may be possible, it is difficult to establish that they are probable. Allegories such as Ezekiel 37 or Ecclesiastes 12:1–8 are normally identified as such (e.g., "these bones are Israel" or "before old age comes"). Rarely, if ever, does a reader identify a biblical allegory that is not self-identified and is as long as the book of Jonah. Further, one would expect that many elements in this account would have symbolic meanings that would be obvious. Yet such symbolism has not found agreement among interpreters. It is not obvious. A midrash should also have a text or account on which it is based and that provides an obvious connection at multiple points. Again, such identification has not found agreement, nor has an external textual source been identified. A parable is arguably the most likely of these forms[4] but also the most general. Almost any text that makes a point can be understood as a parable. Further, a parable does not by itself indicate whether the text has a historical basis. Insofar as it makes a theological point, many narratives in the Bible (and in other literature) could be interpreted as parables. Insofar as it requires an explicit interpretation alongside the narrative, Jonah is not a parable. As stated below ("Literary Readings"), the irony of Jonah has been understood as humor. This has led to identification of the book as satire. Again, the problem is the absence of identification of the individual or group being satirized.

Jonah's psalm in chapter 2 is not a lament but a thanksgiving for Jonah's deliverance from the death of drowning that he anticipates in 1:12. God's preparation of a fish to swallow Jonah in 1:17 precedes Jonah's prayer and provides the deliverance from drowning for which Jonah gives thanks, especially in 2:2, 6, and 9. The psalm's context in the book should not come as a surprise: it serves a similar role as the psalm of Hannah in 1 Samuel 2. Here as well, the psalm reaches beyond the narrative context with a realization that God's work with one person is best interpreted within the context of the cosmic plan of blessing and salvation, where God the creator of the universe works. Finally, the sacrifices and vows that Jonah promises correspond to those that the sailors give in 1:16.

The book of Jonah identifies neither the author nor the date of composition. The historical value of the book is not necessarily related to the dating of the book. Some, as early as the Babylonian Talmud (*B. Bat.* 14b–15a), have argued that a postexilic writer authored it. However, the language does not demand this dating. Identifications of Aramaic influence are not as persuasive as they were fifty years ago, before the discovery of a much more common presence

4. So L. Allen, *Joel, Obadiah, Jonah, and Micah.*

of Aramaic during the Iron Age. Nor does the expression "king of Nineveh" guarantee that the book is an anachronistic re-creation of a fictional past. Scholars now recognize that there are many gaps in their understanding of Assyria during the first half of the eighth century BC. It is possible that (1) an Assyrian monarch could have been known by this title; (2) Nineveh could have been a significant city at this time, where the king might have stayed; or (3) a writer in Israel could have interpreted the king of a region by its major city. For the latter, Sihon is called king of the Amorites (Deut. 1:4; 3:2; 4:46) and king of Heshbon (Deut. 2:24, 26, 30), and Jabin can be called king of Canaan(ites) (Judg. 4:2, 23, 24) and king of Hazor (Judg. 4:17).[5]

The grammatical form of the narrative does not differ from historical narrative as found in the books of Samuel, Kings, Ezra, Nehemiah, and elsewhere. This does not prove it should be so read. However, it does demonstrate that the text contains no special clues to suggest that the writer intended a different understanding of the text.

Literary Readings

Jonah perhaps forms the most interesting book among the Twelve Minor Prophets for the reader. With the exception of the psalm in chapter 2 and the proclamation of the king in chapter 3, the book provides nonstop "action" and forms a traditional plot, with remarkable character development of its chief human protagonist, Jonah. Whether at sea with the sailors, in the stomach of the big fish, in Nineveh pronouncing judgment, or under the leafy plant interacting with God, Jonah provides an interesting study that keeps the reader's attention with sudden shifts in scenes and events. In chapter 1, the reader has a sense that Jonah does not wish to obey God and pronounce judgment. Yet readers are not told why, only that he flees in the opposite direction, making a futile attempt to escape God's call. To the contrary, the psalm in chapter 2 establishes Jonah as a figure closely related to and trusting in God. Given this perspective, his obedience in pronouncing God's judgment in chapter 3 seems appropriate. Yet the king's command that all should repent, along with the response of universal fasting and calling on God, leads not only to God's mercy but also to Jonah's anger. So whatever Jonah has sought to avoid at the beginning now happens: the repentance of a people whom Israel regards as an enemy and whose own textual witness suggests that they committed more war crimes than any other nation in the era that they were active.

One can consider the contrasting scenes of the sea in chapter 1 and the desert in chapter 4, or of the Holy Land of God's people at the beginning of the book and the land of their enemy at the end. There are also the animals. God uses the big fish, the largest of living creatures, to protect Jonah from

5. Stuart, "Jonah," 460–61.

Key Words in Jonah

Douglas Stuart finds a key to the interpretation of the book by two frequently used Hebrew terms.[a] The first is the word "great" (*gādôl*). Nineveh is repeatedly called a great city. But there is also a great wind, a great storm, a great fear among the soldiers, great nobles of Nineveh, Jonah's great anger, and great joy in the shade of the leafy plant. The other word is "evil" (*ra*ʿ). This is the name of the "calamity" that befalls the travelers with Jonah (1:7). Jonah 3:8 and 10 describe how the Ninevites turn from their "sins." See also 4:1, where a closely related term describes how Jonah is "not pleased" with the repentance of the Ninevites.

[a] Stuart, "Jonah," 460–61.

drowning; and he uses the worm, among the smallest of animals, to give Jonah grief in chapter 4. In between, the animals of Nineveh join its king and population in fasting and wearing sackcloth. While this may seem the high point of humor, its role in the story is to place the king of Nineveh, his subjects, and their animals all on an equal level of seeking God's mercy—something like the all-inclusive Sabbath commands in the Decalogue (Exod. 20:10; Deut. 5:14). But perhaps the most important literary development comes with the human figures. Jonah, the prophet of God, disobeys God and flees to encounter sailors, Ninevites, and the king of Nineveh, who all demonstrate their loyalty and devotion to Israel's God as soon as they hear of him. The irony of the reluctant prophet—whose message everywhere brings salvation, on the stormy sea and in the condemned city—surely brings a message to Israel that earlier prophetic texts (e.g., Amos 9:7) also suggest: Yahweh desires to bless all the world that they may come to know him as their God.

Gender and Ideological Criticism

Jione Havea reflects on the story of Jonah within a postcolonial context. Here it is troubling that God would withdraw or at least delay his punishment of the Assyrians and their imperial power center.[6] In what he refers to as the philosophy of *ubuntu*, drawn from his Oceanic roots while he was growing up in Tonga (South Pacific), Havea argues that the focus on Nineveh and Assyria as a nation forces the reader to think of Israel as a nation. This transnationalizing creates a cross-cultural interpretive experience. In a world of islanders, Havea can identify with the sailors of chapter 1 to whom Jonah brings trouble. When hardship comes, the islanders assume that someone has

6. Havea, "Casting Jonah."

violated a taboo and angered the gods. The sea draws one closer to one's god. These sailors respect other deities, including that of Jonah. For Havea, the narrator has room for other gods because no condemnation is expressed of the sailors' gods. This assumes that the narrator acknowledges the existence of these deities, something the text never suggests. Nevertheless, Havea is correct in recognizing the respect that the narrator gives to these sailors and their customs. The sailors, like Jonah, find Israel's God at the heart of their dilemma.

Again, the account of the Ninevites' repentance in chapter 3 may be read from their own perspective. In such a case the aim of Nineveh is to change the mind of Jonah's God. The Ninevites transform God and make him repent. This is an important insight, but it needs to be set against the repentance, fasting, and sackcloth of Nineveh. This self-humiliation leads to God's change of mind, but first it requires that the citizens of Nineveh show sincerity in changing their own minds. Nevertheless, as Havea observes, God's repentance is an admission that Nineveh is not as wicked as he first thought. Or perhaps it is better to say that Nineveh proves itself to be repentant as God proves himself to be merciful. "Whereas Job complained that bad things (suffering) were happening to good people, Jonah complained that good things were happening to bad people (Nineveh)."[7] As Havea affirms, Jonah teaches that God gives life and refuses to give death. Even more than this, God seeks every opportunity in Jonah to encourage life and to increase it.

Ancient Near Eastern Context

The story of Jonah is normally taken as a postexilic fictional re-creation of a prophet mentioned in 2 Kings 14:25 as one devoted to predicting the expansion of Israel's territory during the first half of the eighth century BC, under the kingship of Jeroboam II. This prophet is otherwise unknown in the Old Testament texts and thus becomes an ideal "cipher" on which to superimpose the message of one who is sent to Israel's archenemy, to warn the people of judgment so that they might repent. The postexilic period held many concerns about an extreme exclusiveness that could break up marriages between the orthodox Jewish citizenry in Jerusalem and spouses from other ethnicities and religious beliefs.[8]

However, the eighth century was a period of national expansion. The northern kingdom (Israel), led by the capable leadership of Jeroboam II, might well have assumed that they were specially blessed by God and would finally surpass their enemies, above all Assyria, who would disappear into the dust of history. Israel had felt the fearful war machine that was Assyria

7. Ibid., 33.
8. See the discussion in the chapter on Ezra and Nehemiah.

in the ninth century, especially under the aggressive power of Shalmaneser III. While prophets such as Amos and Hosea might have warned them of the reemergence of Assyria within the lifetime of most who heard these speakers, the Israelites would have considered their enemy to the east as weak and perhaps ready to collapse. Assyrian leaders such as Assur-dan III (ca. 780–755 BC; sole ruler in 773–755) ruled over a weak nation, beset by strong enemies outside: Urartu to the north, Syrian states to the west, and Babylon to the south. In addition, the reality of a solar eclipse (likely June 15, 763 BC) during Assur-dan III's reign as well as civil strife would have opened such a king and a bewildered populace to consider the message of a foreign prophet and the call to repentance and worship of Yahweh, the ancient deity who had preserved his people and enabled them to expand in wealth, territory, and influence.

Canonical Context

Jonah's mention in 2 Kings 14:25 has been noticed (see the previous section). Perhaps not unexpectedly for an early prophet associated with the northern kingdom (Israel), Jonah follows in the footsteps of Elijah, who also requests death while sitting under a broom tree after fleeing from Jezebel (1 Kings 19:4).[9] Jeremiah 18:7–8 states the principle of God's willingness to reverse his judgment against a nation if they turn back to him. Does this serve as the basis for the confession of the king of Nineveh in Jonah 3:7–9, and the divine response that follows? Is this not also the reason behind the message of Isaiah in Isaiah 6?

In the New Testament, Jesus refers several times to the sign of the prophet Jonah, who was three days in the belly of a great fish before coming back to dry land and the life of his mission. Further, Jesus promises that the Ninevites who repented will arise at the judgment and condemn the Jews of Jesus's generation for their unbelief in the presence of Jesus as one with "something greater than Jonah" (Matt. 12:39–41; 16:4; Luke 11:29–32).

Theological Perspectives of Jonah

Jonah's theology proclaims the universal mission of God's people to bring his blessing to all nations of the world (Gen. 12:1–3). This is experienced by a prophet who alone is commanded to leave his homeland and to preach to an enemy, in the expectation that they might repent and find life. The key to the first chapter is the manner in which God's will for Jonah cannot be thwarted, even by the prophet himself. Nineveh's condemnation (Jon. 1:2) makes no

9. Sherwood, "Jonah," 479.

sense unless the possibility of repentance remains.[10] The sailors already believe and worship various gods, yet they come to accept Jonah's Deity as the one who delivers them from the storm and who delivers Jonah. Although Jonah has fled, his confession of his faith, his admission of his disobedience, and his advice to the sailors to escape danger by throwing him overboard all lead to his salvation inside a big fish prepared by God.

Chapter 2, the psalm of thanksgiving, praises God for his salvation of the prophet. Although it borrows imagery from the lament psalms, many of these word pictures take on new meaning with a prophet who has literally sunk into the midst of the sea and the depths of the earth. Here the reference to the futility of "worthless idols" (2:8 NIV) renders problematic the view that the book of Jonah accepts the other gods of the sailors as on a par with Yahweh.[11]

Having now experienced his own personal salvation from certain death, Jonah moves to Nineveh and proclaims judgment. Because God is "gracious and compassionate, . . . slow to anger and abounding in love" (4:2 NIV; cf. Exod. 34:6–7), the repentance of the Ninevites brings about an attitude of mercy. Unlike Jeremiah, Jonah is not perceived as inciting treason by advising the people to worship a God who is foreign to them. Instead, his message is heard. In light of the prophet's success (2 Kings 14:25) among his own people, Jonah's success with a message (these are words; Jonah does not enact any judgment on the people) among the greatest enemies of God's people invites reflection on the importance of preaching with courage in the corrupt societies of the present day and of realizing that all peoples may be brought to repentance. This should not be seen as the work of a vindictive God who will allow judgment to come upon Nineveh in later generations and who will allow this nation to bring horror on Israel itself within a generation or two. Instead, as with Joseph, whom God used to give life to the people of Canaan and Egypt (Gen. 47:13–26) and thereby became an instrument of divine life to the people (50:19–20), so Jonah is used by God to give life to Nineveh. That future generations would abuse this and face judgment for it does not change the work of God toward Israel, Egypt, Canaan, or Assyria (Jer. 18).

The final chapter of Jonah recounts the prophet's personal struggle with God. Jonah recognizes how the nationalism of Israel might see this as a betrayal and even an act of treason. He identifies with his nation more than with God's compassion. For this reason, he asks for death. The lesson of the shade plant and the worm is that God will not be any less concerned about the fate of more than 120,000 than Jonah was concerned about his own comfort. Thus

10. The "evil" (Heb. *raʿ*) of Nineveh may also be translated "troubles" (Stuart, "Jonah"; cf., e.g., Isa. 45:7), for which see the sidebar "Key Words in Jonah." As such, and given the ultimate purpose of God's plan for Nineveh, it should not be seen as "strongly condemnatory" (Sasson, *Jonah*, 25).

11. Contra Havea, "Casting Jonah."

the final question is rhetorical.[12] It leaves readers to ponder for themselves whether and how their lives may bring salvation and blessing to those around them, and whether their priorities in what they value and what they do not value reflect eternal values.

Key Commentaries and Studies

Allen, Leslie C. *The Books of Joel, Obadiah, Jonah, and Micah*. NICOT. Grand Rapids: Eerdmans, 1971. Evangelical exegesis of Jonah; accepts a postexilic date.

Sasson, Jack M. *Jonah: A New Translation with Introduction, Commentary, and Interpretation*. AB 24B. New York: Doubleday, 1990. A thorough historical-critical exegetical study.

Walton, John H. "Jonah." *ZIBBCOT* 5:100–119. The most recent review of the historical and archaeological backgrounds.

Wolff, Hans Walter. *Obadiah and Jonah*. Translated by M. Kohl. Hermeneia. Minneapolis: Augsburg, 1988. Strongest commentary in terms of textual analysis.

12. Contra Sherwood, "Jonah," 480, who finds here a genuine question as to whether God is truly concerned about any of these people. She assumes that the book was written after the fall of Assyria in 612 BC and suggests that this would demonstrate how cruel God would be to turn again and allow the capital of Assyria to perish. Thus God really doesn't care about anyone in Nineveh. Such arguments do not respect each individual and each generation. Individuals and nations can and do change, and correspondingly, God changes in his response to them. Cf. Jer. 18.

29

MICAH

Many Christians truly want to work for justice in our world. If the real concern of biblical faith is justice, what does that mean? Micah sets justice in context with covenantal love and humility before God (6:6–8).

Name, Text, and Outline

The name Micah means "Who is like [Y]ah(weh)?" The name occurs within and outside the Bible throughout ancient Israel's history.[1] The text of Micah is not without problems, although the Masoretic Text remains reliable in general. The Qumran texts include 1QpMic (1Q14) and 4QpMic (4Q168). The former interprets Micah in the context of the community's history and of its future. The latter contains one significant variant of the Masoretic Text (4:9). From about AD 135, Murabba'at 88 (XII) is virtually identical to the Masoretic Text. The Septuagint used a Hebrew text that was close, if not identical, to the Masoretic Text. The translator freely interpreted the text. The *kaige* recension, as found in the Naḥal Ḥever Scroll of the Minor Prophets, reflects a correction from the Septuagint back to the Masoretic Text. The same may be said for the later Greek translations (Aquila, Symmachus, and Theodotion).[2]

OUTLINE

I. Superscription (1:1)
II. Lament (1:2–2:13)

1. E.g., Judg. 17:8; 2 Chron. 34:20; Albertz and Schmitt, *Family and Household Religion*, 575.
2. Hillers, *Micah*, 9–10; Waltke, *Commentary on Micah*, 16–18.

- A. Yahweh Comes to Judge (1:2–7)
- B. Song of Lament for the Coming Exile (1:8–16)
- C. Funeral Lament (2:1–6)
- D. God Indicts the People for Their Sin (2:7–11)
- E. Hope in a Remnant (2:12–13)

III. Failed Leadership and Coming Salvation (3:1–5:15)
- A. Judgment against Jerusalem (3:1–12)
- B. Salvation in God's Rule and the Messiah to Come (4:1–5:15 [5:14 MT])

IV. Lawsuit, Lament, and Victory (6:1–7:20)
- A. Lawsuit against Judah (6:1–16)
- B. Lament (7:1–7)
- C. Songs of Victory and Praise (7:8–20)

Overview of Micah

Micah writes this book as "the word of the LORD" in the seventh century, a vision concerning the northern and southern kingdoms (1:1). Yahweh comes to bear witness against his people so that the earth is transformed beneath him because of the sins of Samaria and Jerusalem (1:2–5). So Samaria will be destroyed and all her images broken (1:6–7). This sin has reached Jerusalem and the towns of Judah (1:8–16). Woe to those who plan evil against their neighbors, for God is planning disaster against them (2:1–11). Yet a remnant will remain (2:12–13). Micah describes the sins of the leaders against his people (3:1–4), just as the prophets will lose their ability in contrast to Micah himself (3:5–8). Everyone is greedy for money, but disaster is coming (3:9–12). There will come a time of exaltation of Jerusalem in the last days, when the people of the world will flow to Jerusalem to learn of the peace and reign of God (4:1–5). God will gather the lame as his remnant, and Jerusalem will again be exalted (4:6–8). The cries of Jerusalem will signal the beginning of its exile (4:9–10), and yet God will give Zion the ability to destroy the nations that plot against it (4:11–13). Yet Israel now faces the striking of its ruler (5:1 [4:14 MT]). A promised ruler will come from Bethlehem (5:2 [5:1 MT]) who will bring peace and deliverance from the Assyrians (5:3–6 [5:2–5 MT]). The remnant of God's people will be victorious among other nations, and God will bring to an end all the sin of the lands (5:7–15 [5:6–14 MT]).

Kim Walton. The Israel Museum, Jerusalem.

Bronze image of deity (Baal?) from Canaanite Hazor

God reviews how he has loved his people, redeeming them from Egypt with Moses, Aaron, and Miriam (6:1–5). How should the people respond? Not with sacrifices but with acts of justice, mercy, and humility before God (6:6–8). Because the people of Jerusalem lie and steal, God will take away their food and their harvest, and he will ruin them before the nations (6:9–16). The prophet laments famine and exile, so that everyone is turned against everyone else, and even the members of one's own family prove untrustworthy (7:1–6). Only God can be trusted (7:7). Zion (not explicitly identified but generally assumed) will bear Yahweh's anger over sin, but there will come a time when Zion's enemies will be shamed and the nations of the world will come to Jerusalem (7:8–13). God's compassion will lead him to again show forgiveness and mercy to his people (7:14–20).

Reading Micah

Premodern Readings

The materials from the Dead Sea Scrolls (see above) comment on the text of Micah by applying it to struggles within the history of their community. After the New Testament, the *Epistle of Barnabas* (9.3) is the earliest Christian document (ca. AD 100) to cite Micah, referring to 1:2 and the command to hear God's word as a means of Christian circumcision. This prophetic book is cited many times in rabbinic literature.[3] In early and Reformation Christianity, interpreters and homilists often identified Zion with the church and thus applied the ethical exhortations of the book to Christians. Key texts such as Micah 5:1–9 provided a basis for Jesus as the promised Messiah and formed a useful basis for discussion of the Trinity as anticipated in the Old Testament prophets.[4]

Carolyn Sharp summarizes a collage of recent artistic ways in which the prophet has been used.[5] In Emily Dickinson's poem "'They Have Not Chosen Me,' He Said," a savior comes to a people who are not welcoming. Contrast W. B. Yeats's use of Micah 5:2 in his "The Second Coming." There the "rough beast . . . slouches toward Bethlehem to be born." The theme of Micah 4 and Isaiah 2, with its peaceful hope of beating swords into plowshares, was used by the Soviet Union's Evgeniy Vuchetich on the bronze piece given to the United Nations in 1959, with the words of the biblical text displayed outside that organization's New York City headquarters. Micah 6:8 has empowered many expressions of charity and reaching out to others as well as ecumenicity. The 2003 declaration of understanding between the Chief Rabbinate of

3. Neusner, *Micah and Joel.*
4. Ferreiro, *Twelve Prophets*; Parsons, *Calvin's Preaching on the Prophet Micah.*
5. Sharp, "Micah," 83–84.

Israel's Delegation and the Holy See's Commission for Religious Relations of the Roman Catholic Church used this text.

Higher Criticism

The major critical focus on Micah has to do with the analysis of various sections of the book as written later than the time of the prophet. While some would place the authorship of Micah into the postexilic period, most significant are those texts that have been identified as late.[6] Developing from the work of Bernhard Stade, the texts of Micah 2:12–13; 4:1–5:9; and 7:8–20 have been isolated as late and unrelated to any eighth-century context.[7] Although some of these texts have been argued as late by many scholars, there remains no absolute evidence requiring the assumptions of a later dating.[8] Bruce K. Waltke summarizes the arguments against the late dating of these texts.[9] Micah 2:12–13 can be placed within the context of the Assyrian attack on Jerusalem in 701 BC. Thus the remnant here are those who are preserved in the city while the enemies ravage the rest of the land.[10]

Micah 4:1–4 is integrated with the previous section, as the judgment of Jerusalem in rubble naturally precedes its exaltation "in the last days." So the restoration of Jerusalem (4:8) contrasts with the deportation to Babylon, that "now you must leave the city" (4:10 NIV). And the nations that flow to Jerusalem at the beginning of chapter 4 are "now" gathered against the city (4:11). The stricken ruler of God's people (5:1 [4:14 MT]) contrasts with the ruler from Bethlehem (5:2 [5:1 MT]), and the abandonment of Israel (5:3 [5:2 MT]) stands opposite the seven shepherds who will shepherd the flock and rule over Assyria (5:4–6 [5:3–5 MT]). The remnant of 2:12 reappear, no longer in Jerusalem only but also among many nations, where they triumph over enemies and no longer worship their own strength or false deities (5:7–15 [5:6–14 MT]). In this manner the prophet joins warnings and promises. These provide for an integrated literary reading.

Some have claimed that Micah 7:8–20[11] is not early or authentic to the prophet due to its role as a hymn of salvation with elements of praise and confidence. However, it is increasingly clear that, as with Amos 9:11–15, traditional "clues" and assumptions remain speculative.[12] A date from the

6. Renaud, *Michée*, 252.

7. Stade, "Bemerkungen über das Buch Micha."

8. L. Allen, *Joel, Obadiah, Jonah, and Micah*, 244, 251.

9. Waltke, *A Commentary on Micah*, 139–41.

10. Ibid., 132.

11. Micah 7:7 might also be included as a text that ties together both the preceding oracle of indictment and judgment and vv. 8–20.

12. Sharp, "Micah," 79. As an example, she notices the mention of "Abraham" (7:20), which was thought to give evidence of a postexilic date because he appears in Second Isaiah, which is postexilic. However, such arguments do not prove the case.

time of the eighth-century prophet is by no means impossible and most likely coincides with the general language of the book.[13] Shmuel Vargon has argued that the description of judgment in Micah 7:8–20 resembles the northern kingdom after the attacks of Tiglath-pileser III around 732 BC.[14]

The other issues with assumptions of a postexilic authorship concern the Hebrew language. Postexilic Hebrew has been identified in terms of some vocabulary, morphology, and syntax that are different from the preexilic language. The text of Micah lacks morphological and syntactical indicators of a later date.[15]

Literary Readings

Waltke identifies twenty-one oracles in the book of Micah, what he refers to as Micah's "sermon file." Their organization relates these through catchwords and particles.[16] Among the Minor Prophets, the norm is to collect the judgment oracles and present them first. Following that are oracles proclaiming God's salvation and restoration. In Micah, however, there are three groups of oracles in which each follows an alternating pattern of judgment and hope.[17] In addition to the verbal connections, each of the three groups includes a call to hear God's word (1:2; 3:1; 6:1), images related to shepherding (2:12; 4:8; 5:4 [5:3 MT]; 7:14), and discussion of the remnant (2:12–13; 4:6–7; 5:7–8 [5:6–7 MT]; 7:18).[18] These common elements characterize a book wherein God wishes to call the people to repentance with warnings of judgment and also with promises of salvation. The threefold repetition, a common motif on many levels in West Semitic literature, drives home the point emphatically.

Well known is the manner in which the Hebrew wordplay of similar-sounding words is related to many of the place names of Micah 1:10–15: Gath/"tell"; Ophrah/"dust" (1:10 NIV mg.); Shaphir/"live"; Zaanan/"come out"—these are some that can be identified. Literary devices also include the use of ironic reversals.[19] Thus 2:1 indicts the wealthy among God's people for planning to increase their profits by exploiting the poor, just as 2:3 promises that God will plan disaster against these schemers. Micah 3:1–3 presents vivid and terrible word pictures of how powerful leaders butcher and consume the poor. The promised one of 5:2 (5:1 MT) will shepherd his people (5:4 [5:3 MT]), and

13. So Hillers, *Micah*, 89–91, who understands the addressees as Judah.

14. Vargon, "Prayer for the Restoration of the Israelite Kingdom."

15. D. Robertson, *Dating Early Hebrew Poetry*, 154. Cf. Hurvitz, *Transition Period*; idem, "Continuity and Change."

16. Waltke, *Commentary on Micah*, 13–14.

17. See the outline, above.

18. Waltke, *Commentary on Micah*, 15–16.

19. Sharp, "Micah," 80–83.

Lachish and Horses

The kingdoms of Israel and Judah lay between great powers: Assyria and Babylon to the north, and Egypt to the southwest. In focusing on the fall of the northern kingdom and of Samaria in 722 BC, readers might overlook the long years that these kingdoms maintained relative peace and prosperity for their kings and elites, if not also for their citizenry as a whole (but see the prophetic indictments). In no small manner this is due to the horses and chariotry that provided defense for these kingdoms. It is no accident that Shalmaneser III emphasizes Ahab's chariotry in the Battle of Qarqar in 853 BC. Nor is it surprising that, a century later, Micah 1:13 and 5:10 (5:9 MT) refer to horses and chariots as symbols of military powers. Using a wordplay between Lachish and "fast horses" (1:13 NIV; Heb. *rekeš*), Micah connects this major city—which guarded a key valley from the coastal plain into the heart of Judean territory and up to Jerusalem—with the horses and chariotry that played such a significant role in defending the realm. In 701 BC, King Sennacherib of Assyria would be unable to conquer Jerusalem (2 Kings 18:14–19:37), but his assault on Lachish, the second city of the kingdom, would be celebrated in a frieze centrally located in his palace in Nineveh.[a]

[a] See the sidebar "The Lachish Relief" in the chapter on Isaiah.

seven shepherds will "shepherd" Assyria by delivering God's people from Assyria's hand (5:5–6 [5:4–5 MT]). Micah 6:3 uses sarcasm to ask Israel how God has burdened them. The book ends with the appearance of a liturgical form with three speakers: God, Jerusalem, and Micah. Thus Micah laments (7:1–7), Jerusalem confesses (7:8–10), Micah promises and intercedes (7:11–14), God accepts the prayer (7:15), and Micah ends his book: the nation's defeat is prophesied (7:16–17), God is praised (7:18), and the people of Jerusalem are promised that God will forgive their sins (7:19–20).

Gender and Ideological Criticism

Feminine imagery appears in the negative context of prostitution (Mic. 1:7) and then appears to switch with "Daughter Zion" in 1:13 (NIV). However, the context describes this in a negative light. Some later positive references to Zion do not mention "Daughter of" (4:2) while others do (4:8; contrast 4:10; 4:13). Yahweh's spirit (feminine gender in Hebrew) fills the prophet, along with justice and power (3:8). The mother gives birth to a promised son who will shepherd Israel (5:3–4 [5:2–3 MT]). As with all other deities, the feminine Asherah and her symbols are promised destruction (5:14 [5:13 MT]). Like a neighbor, so the wife (or woman) who lies with

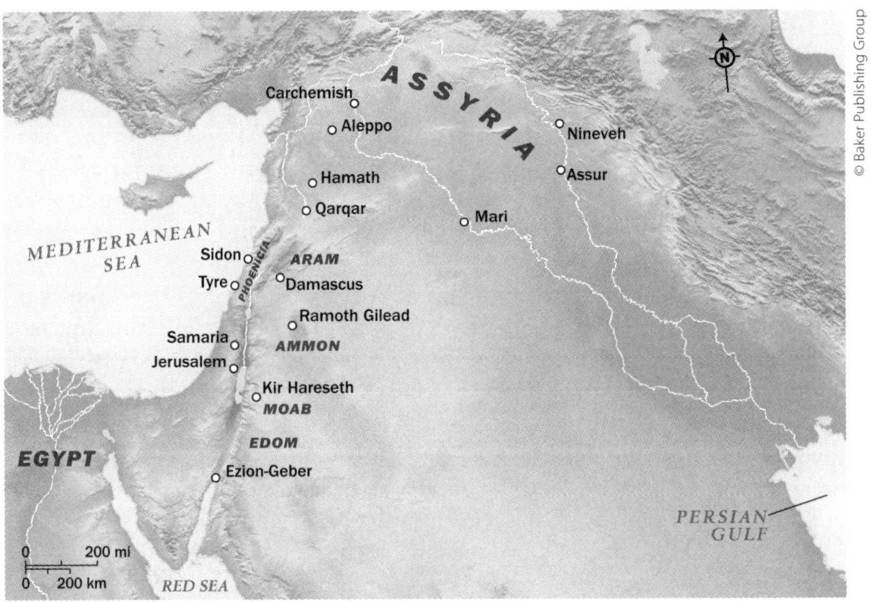

The ancient Near East in the time of Micah

you cannot be trusted in Micah's lament (7:5). Sons and daughters disgrace their parents and in-laws (7:6). In 7:10 the enemy who faces destruction is personified as a female. Although positive and negative images appear to balance one another, it is difficult to avoid noticing that sexual sin, false deities, and family strife give prominence to the female. Having said that, the divine spirit provides a unique positive image and suggests that gender focus is not the concern of Micah.[20]

Ancient Near Eastern Context

For much of the ancient Near Eastern background, see the discussions in the chapters on Isaiah, Hosea, and Amos. Micah is set in the same era, with mention of both the northern and the southern kingdoms. The prophet's hometown, Moresheth-gath (Mic. 1:1, 14), likely located on the border with Philistia, positions his origins and possibly some of his ministry farther southwest, in Judah, than any other eighth-century writing prophet. Growing up in the western Shephelah (low hill country) close to the coastal plain, the prophet would have known of Philistine Gath (1:10) and of the Judean fortress city of Lachish (1:13). Along the coastal plain lay the main land route between Egypt to the south and Babylon and Assyria to the north (4:10; 5:5–6 [5:4–5 MT]; 6:4; 7:12).

20. Cf., e.g., O'Brien, *Micah*.

Canonical Context

Jeremiah 26:17–19 provides an unusual witness of one Old Testament prophet confirming the authority of the pronouncements of another prophet. In this case, Jeremiah cites Micah and his prophecy (Mic. 3:12). Isaiah 2:2–4 and Micah 4:1–3 are nearly identical in describing the coming peace and centrality of Jerusalem in the last days. The text of Micah and the prophet himself remain firmly fixed in the greater biblical tradition of the witness of the prophets.

More than any other text in the book, Micah 5:2 (5:1 MT) becomes a resource for understanding the birth of Jesus in the hometown of his ancestor David. Matthew 2:6 (cf. John 7:42) recounts how the Jewish sages inform Herod of Jesus's birthplace in Bethlehem, based on this prophetic text.

The summary of the law in Micah 6:8 reappears in Jesus's words of Matthew 23:23, although "faithfulness" (NIV) may replace "humbly." Jesus also uses the judgment of Micah 7:6, about the breakup of households and the inability to trust anyone, to describe his mission in Matthew 10:35–36; Mark 13:12; and Luke 12:53. The promise of blessing made to Abraham and the ancestors of Genesis (Gen. 12:1–3; etc.) finds reference in Micah 7:20, and these words become the conclusion of Mary's Magnificat in Luke 1:55 (cf. also Rom. 15:8).

Theological Perspectives of Micah

Along with other literary devices, the oscillation between judgment and hope in Micah's oracles forms a dramatic appeal to the people of the land to repent. They repeatedly hear the rewards of such repentance even as they face the consequences of continuing in their present sin. This repeated change in pictures becomes a means by which the reader (and perhaps the original listeners, if the oracles were presented in the same sequence) is verbally "shocked" into hearing and responding to God's word.

As already mentioned, Micah 4:1–3 provides an oracle of hope and restoration that has enlivened the imagination of Christian reformers and others throughout human history. Its repetition in Isaiah 2:2–4 emphasizes the importance of Jerusalem's future centrality and how the word of God will bring peace and prosperity to the world in a manner not previously known.

The text of Micah 5:2 (5:1 MT) forms a promise of salvation, not only in terms of a generally better condition at some future time, but explicitly tied in with the restoration of the Davidic line. While one can imagine early readers finding here a picture of a scion in the line of David, a simple reading suggests that the birth of this promised king should occur physically in the town of Bethlehem. Other than in a passing reference in Jeremiah 41:17, this is the only prophetic reference to the town (and to Ephrathah). The central location of this text, at the beginning of an oracle of hope in the second of three cycles, focuses attention on this message as central to the restoration of God's kingdom among his people.

Micah 6:6–8 provides a valuable summary of the law, as recognized in early Judaism and quoted by Christians for two thousand years. This text does not argue the invalidity of the sacrificial system (any more than it argues for human sacrifice), but it asserts that no sacrifice or gift to God can outdo the attitude and life of justice, mercy, and humility before God and his rule. Everything else pales by significance. For Christians, the New Testament Gospels demonstrate the attitude and life of Jesus Christ in this manner and attest to his death on the cross as a means to provide access for all to the presence of God (John 3:16).

The second-to-last verse in the book (Mic. 7:19) looks forward to a time of renewal, when God will show his love and forgive his people's sins ("hurl all our iniquities into the depths of the sea" [NIV]; cf. Ps. 103:12). This picture completes the commands of Micah 6:8, where humanity fails, and it achieves the last verse's fulfillment of the promises to Abraham as part of God's great plan to bring about blessing and salvation to all peoples of the earth.

Key Commentaries and Studies

Andersen, Francis I., and David Noel Freedman. *Micah: A New Translation with Introduction and Commentary.* AB 24E. New York: Doubleday, 2000. This remains a key work for study of structure, key terms, and historical background.

Ben Zvi, Ehud. *Micah.* FOTL 21B. Grand Rapids: Eerdmans, 2000. Important analysis of the forms of prophetic oracles, key for understanding this book.

Hillers, Delbert. *Micah: A Commentary on the Book of the Prophet Micah.* Hermeneia. Philadelphia: Fortress, 1984. A key study for textual criticism of the book.

King, Philip J. *Amos, Hosea, Micah: An Archaeological Commentary.* Philadelphia: Westminster, 1988. Key for realia and background to the book.

Mays, James Luther. *Micah: A Commentary.* OTL. Philadelphia: Westminster, 1976. Useful for classic theological interpretation.

Smith, Ralph L. *Micah–Malachi.* WBC 32. Waco: Word, 1984. Helpful exegesis.

Waltke, Bruce K. *A Commentary on Micah.* Grand Rapids: Eerdmans, 2007. Best overall commentary for careful analysis of the Hebrew text.

30

NAHUM

Does God judge nations and superpowers for their brutality and injustice? The book of Nahum discusses Assyria, a great military empire that acted with impudence for more than a century.

Name, Text, and Outline

Nahum is a name meaning "comforted." It is a shortened form of a longer name, with the sense of "comforted by God." This may refer to the mother's joy at the blessing of this birth. The same element occurs in Old Testament names such as Menahem and Nehemiah. It occurs frequently in Hebrew names outside the Bible and elsewhere, especially in Aramaic, Ammonite, and Phoenician personal names.[1]

The Masoretic Text of Nahum has few textual problems and is supported, with minor exceptions, by the Qumran 4QpNah and the Wadi Murabbaʿat text of the Minor Prophets.[2] Naḥal Ḥever's Greek scroll of the Minor Prophets appears as an early revision of what will later become the Septuagint text. This Greek translation supports the Masoretic Text, with variants that can be explained as misunderstandings of the Hebrew or as interpretive glosses.

OUTLINE

I. Superscription (1:1)
II. Divine Judgment on Nineveh (1:2–14)

1. Albertz and Schmitt, *Family and Household Religion*, 599.
2. Christensen, *Nahum*, 64–66.

  - A. Yahweh's Vengeance (1:2–11)
  - B. Judah Delivered, Nineveh Forgotten (1:12–14)
- III. Nineveh's Destruction (1:15–2:13 [2:1–14 MT])
  - A. Judah Rejoices (1:15 [2:1 MT])
  - B. Nineveh Captured (2:1–7 [2:2–8 MT])
  - C. Nineveh Plundered (2:8–10 [2:9–11 MT])
  - D. Nineveh Killed as a Lion (2:11–13 [2:12–14 MT])
- IV. Taunts against Nineveh (3:1–19)
  - A. Ashamed before the Nations (3:1–7)
  - B. Sacked as Thebes (3:8–13)
  - C. Like Locusts Who Destroy and Disappear (3:14–17)
  - D. Endless Cruelty (3:18–19)

Overview of Nahum

Nahum of Elkosh sees Yahweh bringing vengeance on his enemies as he comes, drying up the sea and shaking the mountains (1:1–6). Yahweh comes to bring an end to Nineveh and its plots because God cares for those who trust him (1:8–11). Judah will have its yoke removed by God, who destroys Nineveh and its temples (1:12–14). The people of God will rejoice (1:15 [2:1 MT]). Armies advance against Nineveh while God restores Judah (2:1–3 [2:2–4 MT]). The army overruns Nineveh, which cannot defend itself. The enemy plunders the city (2:4–10 [2:5–11 MT]). Like a lion with her young, Nineveh will have no prey and perish (2:11–13 [2:12–14 MT]).

Nineveh's lust for brutality and the death it caused will bring God against it, to destroy it before all who see it (3:1–7). Thebes was sacked, with all of its inhabitants killed or enslaved. Nineveh is no better and will endure a similar fate (3:8–11). The fortresses will fall like figs while fire consumes their defensive gates (3:12–13). Prepare for a siege and increase your army like locusts, but the locusts will disappear all at once (3:14–17). Nahum addresses the king of Assyria, whose officers sleep while the army scatters. There is no healing for this city of continuing cruelty (3:18–19).

Reading Nahum

Premodern Readings

Allusions appear in the first-century-AD texts of Tobit[3] and Josephus (*Ant.* 9.11.3, though in the context of eighth-century-BC prophets), and in the

3. E.g., Tobit 1:3. For issues with this allusion, see Littman, *Tobit,* xxxiii, 2–3, 49–50.

Qumran commentary on Nahum (4QpNah), where the author relates Nahum to people and events around 100 BC.

John Huddlestun identifies two issues that emerged in rabbinic writings with regard to Nahum: the wrath of God and Nineveh's condemnation in the light of its repentance at the preaching of Jonah.[4] Regarding God's wrath, the rabbis understood that it remained entirely within his control and that in Nahum he directed this anger only against his enemies and the enemies of his people. With respect to the repentance of Assyria, the *Targum Minor Prophets* inserts sections that explain the lapse of Nineveh back into sin, a view that was followed by later Jewish interpreters such as Rashi.

In early Christianity, Tertullian (*Adversus Marcionem* 4.20.3) refers to Nahum 1:4 and God's rebuke of the waves as a prediction of Jesus walking on the Sea of Galilee. In his exhortation to celebrate Easter, Athanasius (*Epistulae festalis* 6) cites 1:15 and the command to keep the feasts.[5] Cyril of Alexandria applies 1:2–3, God's wrath against Israel's enemies, to the Jewish leaders who rejected Jesus in the Gospels.[6] Cyril compares sinful Nineveh to Jerusalem, symbolizing those who rejected Jesus. Jerome understands Nineveh to be those who oppose God and his church.

For Martin Luther, the book focuses on Judah's faith in God's promises that it will endure.[7] The "guilty" of Nahum 1:3 and the flood of 1:8 represent for Luther the papacy, its members, and its supporters. However, contra some earlier interpreters, such as Julian of Toledo, Luther does not read the text as a spiritual allegory of Christ. Only Nahum 1:15 (2:1 MT), as also found in Isaiah 52:7, can be legitimately used to identify with Christ (as in Rom. 10:15). For John Calvin, Nahum's message teaches the reader that the ungodly who oppose the church also fight with God.[8] Later commentators, especially Bishop Robert Lowth, express appreciation for the literary aesthetic of the poem.[9]

Higher Criticism

Nineteenth-century scholarship, and its preoccupation with the identification of various sources, inevitably led to arguments that Nahum should be so analyzed.[10] The identification of a partial acrostic poem in 1:2–10 by Gottlieb Frohnmeyer (in 1867) led to Gustav Bickell's 1880–81 analysis of the entire alphabet in an acrostic within these verses.[11] Hermann Gunkel challenged

4. Huddlestun, "Nahum," 106; Christensen, *Nahum*, 16–20.
5. Huddlestun, "Nahum," 107.
6. Cyril of Alexandria, *Commentary on the Twelve Prophets*, vol. 2.
7. Luther, *Luther's Works*, vol. 18.
8. Calvin, *Jonah, Micah and Nahum*.
9. Lowth, *Lectures on the Sacred Poetry*, 281.
10. Christensen, *Nahum*, 20–25.
11. Bickell, *Hebräische Metrik*.

Bickell's theory of syllable counting and replaced it with accented syllables for the determination of the poetry. In 1893 Gunkel reconstructed a full acrostic poem in 1:2–2:3.[12] Nevertheless, scholars such as Julius Wellhausen rejected these reconstructions.[13]

William Arnold's 1901 study devalued the author and redactors, arguing for the insertion of a partial acrostic with quotations from other sources and little in the way of originality.[14] In the same year Karl Budde doubted the ability to reconstruct the entire text; others, such as Paul Haupt, argued that an acrostic of half of the Hebrew alphabet (1:2–8) suited the author's purpose.[15] The absence of criticism of Judah's sin led some to find in Nahum a prophet closer to the false prophets condemned by Jeremiah. Haupt's 1907 study rejected the work as prophecy and found in it a festal liturgy from the mid-second century BC. However, the discovery of the Dead Sea Scrolls commentary on Nahum, as well as recent historical correlations with the fall of Nineveh, have cast doubt on so late a date. Some found in Nahum a liturgical expression of "cultic prophecy";[16] others rightly questioned a difference between cultic and noncultic prophecy in Israel.[17] Kevin Cathcart's 1975 study began to distinguish between the holy wars as historical phenomena reflected in the text and a greater symbolism in the prophetic speech that describes cultic events.[18] For Brevard Childs, the canonical shaping of the text affirms God's triumph over all foes.[19]

Recent discussion regarding the acrostic in chapter 1 has moved between denial and affirmation of its presence, sometimes in cryptic form.[20] Klaas Spronk and others have affirmed the literary unity of the text, drawing on expression and forms in other Hebrew literature as well as in contemporary Assyrian treaties and royal annals.[21] Duane Christensen argues for a literary unity to the text but recognizes that this approach is one of two opposing views.[22] The other dissects the text into minute literary units in the belief that the prophets spoke only the briefest of oracles, and in the scholars' own mistrust of the Masoretic Text's tradition preserved for us.[23] These conclusions

12. Gunkel, "Nahum 1."

13. Wellhausen, *Die kleinen Propheten.*

14. W. Arnold, "Composition of Nahum."

15. Budde, "Nahum"; Haupt, "Book of Nahum."

16. J. D. W. Watts, *Joel, Obadiah, Jonah, Nahum.*

17. E.g., Eaton, *Vision in Worship*, 14–21.

18. Cathcart, "War of Yahweh in Nahum."

19. Childs, *Introduction*, 440–46.

20. So Christensen, *Nahum*, 25–39. For denial of the acrostic, see Floyd, "Chimeral Acrostic"; Weigl, "Research on the Book of Nahum," 87. For affirmation, see Spronk, "Acrostics." For cryptic form, see Bliese, "Cryptic Chiastic Acrostic."

21. See Spronk, "Synchronic and Diachronic"; idem, "Acrostics in the Book of Nahum"; Machinist, "Assyria and Its Image," 733–36; Johnston, "Rhetorical Analysis," 330–98.

22. Christensen, *Nahum.*

23. So Weigl, "Research on the Book of Nahum," 88–89; cf., e.g., Lescow, "Komposition der Bücher Nahum und Habakuk."

do not appear reconcilable. However, reasonable trust in the basic antiquity and integrity of the Masoretic Text leads toward acceptance of a basic unity to the work as well as the recognition of an authentic prophetic text composed sometime after the fall of Thebes in 667 BC and before the fall of Nineveh in 612 BC. Likely the work in its present form originates close to the latter date.

Literary Readings

As noted in the previous section, there is not much agreement as to the genre of Nahum. Shifts in gender and number in the text have led to suggestions of multiple voices.[24] Marvin Sweeney identifies here a disputation speech where Nahum challenges those who doubt Yahweh's power or justice.[25] This captures a major aim of the text, though within this broad category one may identify other elements. Can these chapters serve as anti-Assyrian propaganda, or even nonviolent protest literature?[26] Are they triumph songs gloating over an enemy's defeat or a type of city lament?[27]

Vivid military images include the use of related commands that leaders might invoke to prepare a city for a siege (Nah. 2:1 [2:2 MT]; 3:14).[28] The reader finds alliteration, as in 2:2 (2:3 MT): "destroyers have destroyed them" (lit., *bĕqāqûm bōqĕqîm*). See also 2:10 (2:11 MT): "destroyed, devastated, and stripped" (lit., *bûqâ ûmĕbûqâ ûmĕbullāqâ*). One also encounters personification: Nineveh as a prostitute (3:4) and Assyria as a lion (2:11–13 [2:12–14 MT]). Fig-tree similes appear in 3:12, and those of locusts in 3:15–17. Rhetorical questions, as found in Amos and other prophetic texts, occur in Nahum 1:6, 9, 11 (NLT); 3:8, 19. Whether with more than a dozen catchwords that occur in both Micah 7 and Nahum 1 or with broader literary themes, common connections join Micah, Nahum, and Habakkuk.[29] Jonah also provides a natural connection with the subject matter of Nahum: Nineveh. Jonah 4:2 draws on the positive attributes of Exodus 34:6–7; Nahum 1:2–3 works from the same Exodus text but moves directly to the attributes of divine punishment, while retaining mention of patience.

In addition to standard literary approaches, that of Christensen should be recognized. In his large 2009 commentary, Christensen argues for complex and intricate numerical patterns that he arranges in what he terms "archaeomusicology."[30] This idiosyncratic approach has yet to find wide

24. Lanner, "*Who Will Lament Her?*," 80–86; Haldar, *Nahum*.

25. Sweeney, *TANAK*, 359.

26. The former option remains popular. For the latter, see Wessels, "Nahum."

27. For triumph songs, see Seybold, *Profane Prophetie*; for city lament, see Dobbs-Allsopp, *Weep, O Daughter of Zion*, 128–31.

28. For this paragraph, see Huddlestun, "Nahum," 103–4.

29. Nogalski, "Redactional Shaping of Nahum," 202; Christensen, *Nahum*, 4.

30. Christensen, *Nahum*, esp. 25–39.

acceptance. Using a simpler analysis, Spronk finds an acrostic in chapters 2–3, with the center lying in the repeated "'Behold, I am against you,' declares the LORD of hosts" (NASB: 2:13 [14]; 3:5).[31]

Gender and Ideological Criticism

Judith Sanderson finds in Nahum the picture of an angry male deity raping a female as punishment for her perceived wickedness.[32] Thus the book of Nahum showcases the violent God of Israel, who rapes and provides this terrible act as a model for his followers. Laurel Lanner's "*Who Will Lament Her?*" identifies a feminine element in the book as well as a negative view of the city of Nineveh, with which it is associated. She reads the text as indicating that Ishtar is the feminine goddess who is described. Earlier commentators had identified this goddess in allusions, especially 3:4–7, as a prostitute, also called "mistress of sorceries" (Heb. *baʿălat kĕšāpîm*). Alfred Haldar in particular had argued for a cultic understanding of the book, in which the political enemy becomes a religious one.[33] Further, John Eaton and John Watts identified this presence as Ishtar.[34] Lanner reads the text as fantastic literature, in which it would be impossible in reality for Judah to conquer Assyria. Yahweh directs hatred and anger against the feminine goddess and all that she and her worshipers represent. The hiding of this feminine Other behind the text (Ishtar is never named) reveals her continued presence as an ongoing threat. This contrasts with Nineveh and Assyria, which are now completely destroyed. Lanner finds this feminine Other also connected with the city of Nineveh and, before it, of Thebes. Both cities are destroyed, but Jerusalem does not rise to replace them. Rather, Jerusalem remains muted, as though the author finds problems with the urban scene and the power represented there, whether a city is foreign or domestic.

Thus Lanner is correct to conclude, "The book provides a warning against foreign alliances and against copying other nation's gods and customs."[35] Nahum's words go behind the feminine/masculine dichotomy and any values that might be assigned to those, just as they transcend the urban/rural dichotomy. These distinctions become relativized by absolute difference between the God of Israel and all other claims to divinity. Thus Nahum 3:4–7 sets the context of a prostitute who is shamed, not to condemn prostitution, but to direct this to Ishtar, the ideal deity of all prostitutes.[36] Therefore, the abuse described

31. Spronk, *Nahum*, 5.
32. Sanderson, "Nahum," 221.
33. Haldar, *Nahum*.
34. Eaton, *Vision in Worship*; J. D. W. Watts, *Joel, Obadiah, Jonah, Nahum*.
35. Lanner, "*Who Will Lament Her?*," 247.
36. Ibid., 149–50. Can one presume that, like Assur—the same name used for the city, the nation, and the deity of Assyria—so Ishtar and Nineveh were identified with each other by the prophet?

© Baker Publishing Group and Dr. James C. Martin. The British Museum.

An Assyrian king piles up severed heads of his enemy

in 3:4–7 is not something modeled for males to abuse females but represents God's abuse of all images of false deities.[37] For this reason the result in 3:7 is not some form of lust or titillation but only revulsion and abandonment of the deity and her image.

Ancient Near Eastern Context

The death of King Assurbanipal in 627 BC took away the last powerful ruler of Assyria who would be able to hold the empire together. In the years that followed, provinces withheld tribute, revolted, and began to break away. After fifteen years of ineffective Assyrian leadership, a coalition led by the Babylonians defeated the Assyrian army and destroyed their capital in 612 BC. There is not a lot of textual evidence for the destruction of Nineveh. Peter Machinist has compared the traditions of Nahum that associate water with the defense and siege of the city (2:8 [2:9 MT]; 3:8, 14) with extrabiblical sources. Especially relevant is Nahum 2:6 (2:7 MT): "The gates of the rivers are opened, and the palace/temple disintegrates" (RSH). Machinist finds a similar theme in the Greek sources and suggests that it may reflect a historical event in which the city was defeated by the use of gates that controlled the Tigris River and thereby flooded Nineveh.[38]

Driven from their homeland, the Assyrians made a final stand in the city of Harran in 609 BC. Pharaoh Neco II of Egypt brought his army north to assist

37. Cf. ibid., 133.
38. Machinist, "Fall of Assyria."

Fall of Assyria

From the Neo-Babylonian Chronicles, years 14 and 17 (612 and 609 BC; *ANET* 304–5):

> [Fourteenth year:] The king of Akkad cal[led up] his army and [Cyaxar]es . . . [the . . .]s he ferried across and they marched (upstream) on the embankment of the Tigris and . . . [pitched camp] against Nineveh. . . . From the month Simanu till the month Abu, three ba[ttles were fought, then] they made a great attack against the city. In the month Abu, [the . . . th day, the city was seized and a great defeat] he inflicted [upon the] entire [population]. On that day, Snisharish-kun, king of Assy[ria fled to] . . . , many prisoners of the city, beyond counting, they carried away. The city [they turned] into ruin-hills and hea[ps (of debris). The king] and the army of Assyria escaped (however) before the king (of Akkad) and [the army] of the king of Akkad. . . . Ashurballit . . . sat down in Harran upon the throne to become king of Assyria.
>
> <Seventeenth year:> In the month Du'uzu, Ashuruballit, king of Assyria, (and) a large [army of] E[gy]pt [who had come to his aid] crossed the river (Euphrates) and [marched on] to conquer Harran. [He laid siege to the town and] entered it, but the garrison which the king of Akkad had laid therein killed them (the assault party) and (then) he pit[ched (camp)] against the town of Harran. Till the month Ululu he made attack(s) against the town. Nothing, however, did he ac[h]ieve and they returned. . . .

the Assyrians. However, it was for nothing. King Ashur-uballit II of Assyria disappeared from the records, and the Assyrian Empire vanished with him.

The pharaoh's expansion across the Euphrates, even if only temporarily, was a sign that the downfall of Assyria had left a power vacuum. Although this would soon be filled by Nebuchadnezzar II (605–562 BC) and the rise of the Neo-Babylonian Empire, the two decades of about 625–605 BC allowed shifting geopolitical alliances and the emergence of a quasi-independent Judah under King Josiah's leadership. Although Josiah's reforms and reign were cut short by his death at Pharaoh Neco's hands in 609 BC (2 Kings 23:29), they provided a context in which a prophet such as Nahum could emerge. This prophet could support the worship of Yahweh alone as championed by Josiah's government and could join in the joy at the collapse of Judah's past oppressor, Assyria. What a contrast with his successor, Jeremiah, who might represent a similar theology but who was rejected by his fellow citizens as a traitor against the cause of Jerusalem!

Canonical Context

Already identified (above) are connections with Exodus 34, with Jonah, and with the surrounding Book of the Twelve. In the New Testament the closest relationship with Nahum occurs in the book of Revelation. There as well, great wars and terrible destructions appear. Thus the day of wrath with its earthquake appears in Nahum 1:5–6 and also in Revelation 6:12, 17. More generally the portrayals of Nineveh as a prostitute who will be abused and disgraced (Nah. 2:8–13) reappear in Revelation 17:2, 5, and 16, where it is now Babylon (i.e., Rome) that is so identified.

Theological Perspectives of Nahum

As noticed above, Nahum does not mention the sin of Judah. Nahum 1:12 does, however, recognize that God has afflicted Judah. The assumption is that this was for the sins of the people, especially in light of the manner in which God condemns Nineveh. In concert with the earlier book of Jonah, Nahum teaches that each generation remains responsible for its own sin. Thus the repentance of Jonah's day may have delivered the people, but the following generations needed to determine how they would respond to Israel's God. As both the Old Testament and the ancient Near Eastern historical sources attest, they did not continue to follow God. The violence forbidden in the first universal covenant with Noah and all of his descendants (Gen. 9:5–6) continued to be practiced against God's own people as well as against the rest of the world (Nah. 3:19). Thus there is here a natural theology, a manner in which God works that affects all people everywhere. So what Assyria did to Thebes (3:8–11) becomes a just model for what will happen to Assyria.

The God of Israel is Yahweh Almighty. The repeated use of this title separates him from all others around and establishes that it is his own decision and power that bring down destruction on Nineveh and Assyria—not the strength and plans of the army that he might choose to come against this enemy. The theophany as God comes in wrath and destruction, as found in Nahum 1:2–8, provides the background for the divine warrior bringing retribution for the cruelty of Assyria.

The promises of peace and joy to Judah (1:12–13, 15; 2:2 [2:3 MT]) provide a context that moves from destruction to restoration. Assyria will disappear, but Judah will endure, and its people will remember these events as part of a much larger picture of God at work in the world.

Key Commentaries and Studies

Christensen, Duane L. *Nahum: A New Translation with Introduction and Commentary.* AB 24F. New Haven: Yale University Press, 2009. Detailed exegesis; remarkable use of intricate number analysis of the texts and terms.

Lanner, Laurel. *"Who Will Lament Her?": The Feminine and the Fantastic in the Book of Nahum.* LHBOTS 434. New York: T&T Clark, 2006. A very good and cautionary analysis of implications for the feminine imagery in Nahum.

Roberts, J. J. M. *Nahum, Habakkuk, and Zephaniah: A Commentary.* OTL. Louisville: Westminster John Knox, 1991. An important contribution to theological observations.

Robertson, O. Palmer. *The Books of Nahum, Habakkuk, and Zephaniah.* NICOT. Grand Rapids: Eerdmans, 1990. Evangelical exegesis.

Spronk, Klaas. *Nahum.* HCOT. Kampen: Kok Pharos, 1997. Details literary and historical features of the text.

31

HABAKKUK

What is faith? What does it mean to live by faith? How are faith and works connected, or are they connected at all? In the New Testament, the Epistle of James addresses these questions. In the Old Testament, we need to begin with Habakkuk.

Name, Text, and Outline

The name Habakkuk refers to the name of a garden plant and does not otherwise appear in biblical Hebrew. Rather, the name is found in Aramaic, with cognates in Akkadian and Arabic.[1] The text of Habakkuk is complicated by problems of interpretation.[2] The scroll of the Minor Prophets from Wadi Murabbaʿat (Mur 88 [XII] cols. 18–19) preserves a reading very close to the Masoretic Text, dating from the second century AD. This is true of all three chapters that it preserves, yet it lacks Habakkuk 2:12–17. The Naḥal Ḥever Greek scroll of the Minor Prophets preserves an early form of the Septuagint, though one that is distinct from the Masoretic Text. For Habakkuk 3 there is a collection of six Greek manuscripts dated between the eighth and twelfth centuries AD. While these agree with one another, they differ from the other Septuagint manuscripts in a consistent and significant way. This distinct group is the Berberini Version. Although such manuscripts may preserve an ancient

1. Noth, *Israelitischen Personennamen*, 231; Zadok, *Pre-Hellenistic Israelite Anthroponymy*, 116.

2. Andersen, *Habakkuk*, 22–23, 264–68.

version of this Habakkuk chapter, they do not demonstrate that anyone needs to worry about the Berberini or any other manuscript tradition replacing the carefully preserved Masoretic Text. Scholars remain confident with the antiquity of the Masoretic Text, however difficult the problems with it might prove to be.

OUTLINE

I. Superscription (1:1)
II. Habakkuk and Yahweh (1:2–2:20)
  A. Habakkuk: "How Long, O Lord?" (1:2–4)
  B. Yahweh: The Rise of the Chaldeans (1:5–11)
  C. Habakkuk: Why Do You Allow the Evil to Oppress Those More Righteous? (1:12–17)
  D. Habakkuk Resolved to Stand (2:1)
  E. Yahweh: The Righteous Will Live by Faithfulness (2:2–5)
  F. Woe Oracles (2:6–20)
    1. The Thief Is Robbed (2:6–8)
    2. Let Shame Come to the Unjust (2:9–11)
    3. Woe to the Thief while the Earth Is Filled with Divine Knowledge (2:12–14)
    4. Violence Will Come to Those Who Deceive the Innocent (2:15–17)
    5. An Image Has No Power (2:18–19)
    6. Conclusion: Yahweh in His Temple (2:20)
III. Habakkuk's Victory Psalm (3:1–19)
  A. Title (3:1)
  B. Yahweh Reveals Himself (3:2)
  C. Yahweh Comes from the South (3:3–7)
  D. Yahweh's Victory over the Waters (3:8–15)
  E. Response of Fear and Praise (3:16–19a)
  F. Postscript (3:19b)

Overview of Habakkuk

The prophet begins by appealing to God for an answer. How long must the people of God suffer at the hands of their enemies, who are less righteous than they (1:2–4)? God responds that he has chosen the Babylonians and their army to attack the nations and goes on to describe their power and dread (1:5–11). Habakkuk praises God for his eternal righteousness but then wonders why this enemy, who pulls Israel into its net and then worships the net, is allowed to attack and destroy without mercy (1:12–17). Habakkuk resolves to stand watch and await God's answer (2:1). Yahweh tells him to write what

Habakkuk and the Babylonian threat

he receives but that the revelation will come when it is ready and not before. Habakkuk must wait. The enemy is proud and arrogant, "but the righteous person will live by his faithfulness" (2:2–5 NIV).

God delivers woes to the nation that plunders others and destroys people and property for its own enrichment (2:6–8). Another woe addresses those who build their houses by plotting the ruin of others (2:9–11). A third woe addresses the vanity of all the labor that other nations do. The earth will be filled with the knowledge of God (2:12–14). The fourth woe condemns the enemy for making their neighbors drunk so that they can view their nakedness; the woe now turns the table on those who have done this and acts of violence (2:15–17). Habakkuk 2:18–19 describes the skilled worker who creates an image without life, covers it with silver and gold, and worships it. Yahweh resides in his holy temple, and all the earth should become silent to honor him (2:20).

Habakkuk's psalm begins with praise and with recognition of God's power, using language of his approach in power with lightning and pestilence to bring fear to the armies of Cushan and Midian (3:1–7). The natural forces become divine weapons even as God comes to deliver his people from their enemies (3:8–15). The psalmist fears but waits for God's day of reckoning and, despite famine, will rejoice in his God of salvation (3:16–18). The psalm ends with the confident confession that God gives the psalmist sure footing, like a deer (3:19).

Reading Habakkuk

Premodern Readings

The apocryphal book Bel and the Dragon (1:33–39) portrays an angel transporting Habakkuk to Babylon in order to feed Daniel, who is in the lions' den. In 1655 Gian Lorenzo Bernini created a sculpture of this event, *Habakkuk and the Angel*, which is displayed in the Chigi Chapel, Santa Maria Del Popolo, Rome.[3]

The pesher commentary from Qumran (1QpHab) interprets the first two chapters of Habakkuk in the light of that community's history in the first century BC. The prophet thus foresaw the Roman oppression against the Jews of Palestine and the struggle between the followers of the Teacher of Righteousness and a wicked priest.[4] The Jewish *Targum Jonathan* of the Minor Prophets declares that Habakkuk's prayer (Hab. 3:1) is a response to the revelation of individual repentance. Thus even the wicked are given an extension of time, during which wholehearted repentance brings acceptance by God. Such an interpretation anticipates the Talmud (*b. Yoma* 86b).[5]

Within Eastern Orthodoxy, the victory psalm of Habakkuk 3 has been applied to Holy Saturday and Jesus Christ's "Harrowing of Hell" (the place of the dead). The most influential interpretation from the Western Christian tradition is arguably Martin Luther's rendering of Habakkuk 2:4 as found in Romans 1:17 and Galatians 3:11: "The just shall live by faith." This provided the background for the *sola fidei* ("by faith alone") principle of the Protestant Reformation. Commenting on the Habakkuk text, Luther writes: "For this is a general saying applicable to all of God's words. These must be believed, whether spoken at the beginning, middle, or end of the world."[6]

Higher Criticism

The major question here has focused on the unity of the book of Habakkuk. Critical scholars have tried to isolate independent units in the book.[7] The identification of some of the prayers and poems as cultic led to their presumed location in the context of temple worship.[8] Attempts to isolate separate literary sections led to the dissection of the book. For example, Karl Marti understood Habakkuk 1:5–10 and 14–15 as the oldest part, around

3. Vanderhooft, "Habakkuk," 356.
4. Ibid., 355–56.
5. Flesher and Chilton, *Targums*, 226–27; Cathcart and Gordon, *Targum of the Minor Prophets*, 156.
6. Vanderhooft, "Habakkuk," 356; citing Luther, *Luther's Works*, vol. 19, 394–95.
7. For a review, see Sweeney, "Structure, Genre and Intent."
8. Engnell, *Critical Essays on the Old Testament*, 597.

which later materials were added.[9] Bernhard Duhm provided one of the latest dates for the complete composition. He suggested that the author/editor wrote between 333 and 331 BC and designated the world conqueror as Alexander the Great.[10]

Nevertheless, the poem of Habakkuk 3:3–15 appears to be an ancient work. This was not always thought to be the case, as early critics assumed a later date for the psalm. William F. Albright's study was the first to apply the then-recent discoveries of Ugaritic poetry to this text. Albright saw the work as a deliberate attempt at archaizing by a poet living around 600 BC.[11] Umberto Cassuto's work established the mythopoeic background of Habakkuk 3 and its affinities to the Canaanite poetry found in the similar texts from Ugarit and dating to the thirteenth century BC.[12] Theodore Hiebert's study confirmed part of the book as an ancient poem that combined mythic and historical elements, joining them in a premonarchic composition, perhaps written during the period of the judges.[13] The prophet or a later editor incorporated this into the book of Habakkuk.

While Hiebert followed others in dating the final form of Habakkuk to the mid-sixth century or later, Francis Andersen affirmed that, although there is no sure way to guarantee that the text was not edited at a later period, there is nothing in the text that requires a date later than the beginning of the sixth century BC for the entire composition.[14] Habakkuk 1:6 identifies the Chaldeans, who are the Neo-Babylonians who came to Judah beginning in 605 BC and lived there for the next sixty-five years.

Literary Readings

The literary forms found in the book argue for a unity to the text and likely for a unity in its composition. Throughout the book two similar-sounding words often appear adjacent to each other:[15] *wĕhittammĕhû tĕmāhû* (1:5, "amaze yourselves, be amazed"), *pōʿal pōʿēl* (1:5, "doing a deed"), *hammar wĕhannimhār* (1:6, "grim and impetuous"), *lōʾ-lô* (1:6; 2:6, "not belonging to it"), *ûpāšû pārāšāyw ûpārāšāyw* (1:8, "its cavalry charge forward, and its cavalry"), *bōṣēaʿ beṣaʿ* (2:9, "one who makes a profit"), *yōṣēr yiṣrô* (2:18, "the one who forms . . . his own formation"), *ʾĕlîlîm ʾillĕmîm* (2:18, "idols that do not speak"), *ʿāmad wayĕmōded* (3:6, "he stood and shook), and *ʿeryâ tēʿôr* (3:9, "you uncovered and prepared"). Similar to this are literary forms

9. Marti, *Dodekapropheton*, 329.
10. Duhm, *Das Buch Habakuk*, 12–13.
11. Albright, "Psalm of Habakkuk."
12. Available in English as Cassuto, "Chapter III of Habakkuk and the Ras Shamra Texts."
13. Hiebert, *God of My Victory*, 118–28.
14. Andersen, *Habakkuk*, 27.
15. Vanderhooft, "Habakkuk," 353.

where a similar sound recurs in adjacent or nearby words:[16] *yābōʾû . . . yābôʾ* (1:8–9, "they come . . . come"), *miśḥāq . . . yiśḥāq* (1:10, "scoff . . . laugh"), *mibṣār . . . wayyiṣbōr* (1:10, "fort . . . and build"), *lēʾlōhô hălôʾ . . . ʾĕlōhay* (1:11–12, "belongs to its god. Is it not . . . my God"), *wĕʾetyaṣṣĕbâ ʿal-māṣôr waʾăṣappeh* (2:1, "Let me station myself on the ramparts; I will watch"), *šallôtā . . . yĕšāllûkā* (2:8, "You have plundered, . . . they will plunder you"), *qālôn mikkābôd . . . qîqālôn ʿal-kĕbôdekā* (2:16, "shame instead of glory; . . . disgrace [will come] over your glory"), *ḥămas . . . waḥămas* (2:17, "violence of . . . and violence of"), *pesel kî pĕsālô* (2:18, "an image that . . . has made it"), *bĕqereb šānîm ḥayyêhû bĕqereb šānîm tôdîaʿ* (3:2, "make them live in our years, proclaim them in our years"), *ʿôlām . . . ʿôlām* (3:6, "forever . . . forever"), and *hăbinĕhārîm . . . bannĕhārîm* (3:8, "Was it with rivers . . . against the rivers?").

Such literary connections imply that in all three chapters a similar style was at work, incorporating earlier work (Hab. 3) but also creating a final unified piece. The significance of the poem of chapter 3 has been recognized. In 2:1 the prophet describes his words as *tôkaḥtî* ("my rebuke/blame"). This suggests that his composition is a challenge to God. The response is literarily connected with the prophetic concerns.

Gender and Ideological Criticism

Innocent Himbaza speaks from the tragedy of the genocidal wars in 1994 Rwanda.[17] He writes concerning Habakkuk that the renewed movement there of churches growing and people coming to Christian faith should not lead believers to separate the concerns of the world from those of the kingdom of heaven. Habakkuk was engaged in his world and sought God for guidance. He denounced injustice. In a like manner, Bible believers should promote what is right and just in society and (like Habakkuk in 2:1–4) call on God to intervene so as to improve the world. Despite the difficult times of 3:17–19, Christians should believe that they can trust in God and not lose courage. God has not forgotten, and life remains for those who believe.

Ancient Near Eastern Context

For the destruction of Jerusalem by the Babylonians and the final years of independence with incursions in 605,[18] 597(?), and 586 BC, see the "Ancient Near Eastern Context" for 1–2 Kings and Jeremiah.

An important context can be established by examining the context of the psalm in Habakkuk 3 in the light of early pictures of Yahweh, God of

16. Ibid.
17. Himbaza, "Habakkuk."
18. Cf. Kelle, "Judah in the Seventh Century," 379–81.

The West Semitic Storm-God and the Sea

A letter from the eighteenth-century-BC West Semitic city of Mari (along the Euphrates River) attests to the role of the storm-god (here Adad) defeating the sea-god and establishing kingship and sovereignty. It applies this to the historical figure of Yahdun-Lim, king of the city. Thus Mari text A 1968: "Adad said: 'I gave all the land to Yahdun-Lim. . . . Let me put you back on your ancestral throne. I gave you the weapons with which I attacked Sea. I anointed you with my awe-inspiring brightness. No one will be able to stand against you.'"[a]

This same event is described in detail in the thirteenth-century-BC myth of Baal and Yamm (= Sea) from the city of Ugarit, near the coast of modern Syria. The poetic text of Baal's defeat of Yamm reads:

The mace leaps from the hand of Baal,
Like a bird of prey from his fingers.
It hits the skull of Prince Yamm,
Between the eyes of Judge River,
Yamm collapses and falls to the ground.
His joints buckle,
And his form breaks up.
Baal drags and sets upon Yamm,
He finishes off Judge River.[b]

[a] Hess, *Israelite Religions*, 87.
[b] Ibid., 105.

Israel, coming from the south with great power and leading his people to victory over their enemies (cf. Ps. 68; Exod. 15; Judg. 5; etc.). Teman and Mount Paran (Hab. 3:3) represent the southern desert, close to the region of Mount Sinai and the ancient home where Yahweh first met Israel (Exod. 3, 6, 19–24). "Plague" and "pestilence" in Habakkuk 3:5 are Deber and Resheph. These personifications appear in the ancient myths from Ugarit (thirteenth century BC). There they are deities feared by the people for the suffering they cause. Yahweh's control over the sea and the rivers (Hab. 3:8–15) recurs as it joins the scene where he defeats the "leader of the house of wickedness" (3:13 RSH). This may be identified with Nebuchadnezzar II, leader of Babylon in the early sixth century BC. However, the imagery draws deeply from the West Semitic picture of the chief god, the god of the storm who overcomes the threats of the sea and achieves victory. This brings order and security to the world. Such a picture is applied to Israel's divine deliverance at the Red Sea in Exodus 15 and repeatedly in the Psalms, where God sits enthroned over the seas and rivers. These themes establish God as King and

© Baker Publishing Group and Dr. James C. Martin

Reconstruction, building on Babylon's ruins

Creator (Pss. 29:10; 74:12–17; 89:9–12 [89:10–13 MT]; 93:1–4; 104:5–9; Job 38:8–11).[19]

Canonical Context

As noted, the historical context of the Chaldeans or Babylonians fits well with the final chapters of 2 Kings and the book of the prophet Jeremiah. See also the oracles against Babylon in Isaiah 13–14; 21:8–10; and 47 (and Jer. 50–51). The text of Habakkuk 3 can be compared with the divine-warrior passages of Exodus 15, Judges 5, Psalm 68, and other psalms listed in "Ancient Near Eastern Context" (above).

The most significant text for comparison with the New Testament is Habakkuk 2:3–4, which Paul quotes in Romans 1:17 and Galatians 3:11, and the author of Hebrews cites in Hebrews 10:37–38. Its key role in the Reformation has been noticed (see "Premodern Readings," above). Here readers can examine the text and its usage in the New Testament.

Contextually, Habakkuk's complaint before God against the oppressive Chaldeans climaxes in 2:1, where he awaits God's answer. Habakkuk 2:2–4 provides the answer. The key term comes at the end of the exhortation to wait for God's answer. The righteous person will live "by his faithfulness" (NIV; Heb. *beʾĕmûnātô*). What is this sense of faithfulness?[20] The faithfulness

19. Hess, *Israelite Religions*, 99–100.
20. So also Jepsen, "*ʾāman*."

is connected with the relationship or covenant between God and Israel. The vision of Habakkuk 2:3 is the future hope as found in that covenant. Faith in the covenant can be realized only through one's faithfulness to that covenant relationship in all its stipulations. Bound together with this faithfulness, the covenant contained an expectation of faith in God as its author and the personal object of the relationship. Outside the Psalms, the Septuagint translates this Hebrew noun for "faithfulness" as *pistis*. However, in Habakkuk 2:4 the Septuagint replaces the third-person suffix ("his") with a first-person pronoun, "my *pistis*." This may be taken as an objective genitive at this point, meaning "his faith in me." The life of the righteous depends on God, not on one's own strength.[21]

Paul's use of this text in his discussion of faith in Romans and Galatians is not like that of the Qumran community's (1QHab) loyalty or fidelity to the Teacher of Righteousness. Rather, Paul expands faith in the promised power and sovereignty of God, despite temporary Babylonian oppression, to include faith in the resurrection power of the crucified Christ to reconcile believers and to inaugurate God's reign among them. The personal Son of God replaces or (better) fulfills the impersonal covenant. Romans 1:17 is best understood by associating "from faith" (Greek *ek pisteōs*) with the verb: "The righteous one will live by faith." Paul here omits the suffix (Greek *mou*), perhaps to emphasize the importance of the faith.

Little needs to be added regarding Galatians 3:11, which does not differ from Romans 1:17 in wording when citing the Habakkuk quote. The Deuteronomy 27:26 quote (in Gal. 3:10) charges the legalist with failure to obey the law in every detail and emphasizes the lawbreaker's rejection of God's grace. Habakkuk 2:4 contradicts this legalism, which claims that an unjustified person can keep the law and thereby find salvation, by arguing that only the person who is already justified can please God.

The Hebrews 10:37–38 quotation (as usual in this epistle, introduced by using a word related to "speaking") of Habakkuk 2:3–4 is more of a free use of ancient prophetic language to make the point that God's will does find fulfillment, even if it seems to take a long time. Whether during the times of Isaiah, Habakkuk, the church of the New Testament era, or today, the faithful live by hope in God. Hebrews agrees with Paul on justification by faith, but Hebrews adds the sense of endurance. To Paul's definition of faith, Hebrews adds hope (10:37; cf. Rom. 8:24).[22] Faith and faithfulness become two sides of the same coin. They do not contradict each other but serve as manifestations of a single disposition toward God and the life-changing work of Jesus Christ.

21. Cf. ibid., 319.
22. Bruce, *Hebrews*, 271–75.

Theological Perspectives of Habakkuk

The question as to how God can allow terrible events to happen to his people—in which those far more evil and brutal seem to hold sway over the well-being and life of those who believe in God (and more specifically for the Christian, in Jesus Christ) and seek to follow him in faithful discipleship—remains as pertinent today as it was in Habakkuk's time. Christians in various parts of the world experience severe persecution and death. Does God not care? The answer is not easy, yet it is as true today as it was long ago. The theological discussion of Habakkuk 2:3–4 has been reviewed with its New Testament uses (see above, "Canonical Context"). Patience and faithfulness remain God's call to all who look for his return and the establishment of his kingdom forever. In the darkness of circumstances, this may seem far removed, but it continues to beckon believers to stay faithful.

The prophet does not stop here, however. He goes on to describe and praise God as one who is the divine warrior and will set all wrongs right. Habakkuk 3 demonstrates that the power of God to act in this world is not a crude tradition from Israel's barbaric past. Rather, it is a living and personal reality so that God will not forget his people, nor will he overlook those who abuse them.

Key Commentaries and Studies

Andersen, Francis I. *Habakkuk: A New Translation with Introduction and Commentary.* AB 25. New York: Doubleday, 2001. Best careful analysis and exegesis of the Hebrew text.

Baker, David W. *Nahum, Habakkuk and Zephaniah: An Introduction and Commentary.* TOTC. Downers Grove, IL: InterVarsity, 1988. Important encounter with the meaning of the text and both its OT and NT contexts.

Roberts, J. J. M. *Nahum, Habakkuk, and Zephaniah: A Commentary.* OTL. Louisville: Westminster John Knox, 1991. An important contribution to theological observations.

Robertson, O. Palmer. *The Books of Nahum, Habakkuk, and Zephaniah.* NICOT. Grand Rapids: Eerdmans, 1990. Evangelical exegesis.

Sweeney, Marvin A. *The Twelve Prophets.* 2 vols. Berit Olam. Collegeville, MN: Liturgical Press, 2000. Good theological and formal study of the text within the context of the Hebrew Bible.

32

ZEPHANIAH

To say something dramatically, sometimes it is better to use a few choice words instead of a lengthy speech. Zephaniah offers a good model of this. The book captures the major themes of many of the other prophetic writers in a brief text.

Name, Text, and Outline

The name Zephaniah is composed of two elements: the Hebrew root *ṣāpan*, which carries the sense "to protect, shelter, treasure," and a shortened form of the divine name Yahweh. So the name means "the Lord has protected," possibly referring to the child or mother at the time of birth. This name appears in extrabiblical Hebrew sources from the time of the monarchy.[1]

The text of Zephaniah as preserved in Codex Leningrad from AD 1009 and in the Masoretic Text tradition from that period (Cairo Codex of the Prophets and Aleppo Codex) does not show major differences from Judean Desert manuscripts of a thousand years earlier, specifically the early second-century-AD Scroll of the Twelve Prophets from Wadi Murabbaʿat (Mur 88 [XII]). Indeed, the earliest manuscript evidence for the Septuagint, the nearly contemporary Naḥal Ḥever Greek Scroll of the Twelve Prophets (8ḤevXIIgr), preserves much of the text of Zephaniah as a rough translation of a proto-Masoretic tradition.[2]

1. Albertz and Schmitt, *Family and Household Religion*, 553.
2. Sweeney, "Zephaniah," 472.

OUTLINE

I. Superscription (1:1)
II. Theme: "Seek the LORD" (1:2–3:20)
   A. The "Day of the LORD" Has Arrived (1:2–18)
   B. Exhortation: "Seek the LORD" (2:1–3:20)
      1. Summary of the Command (2:1–3)
      2. Yahweh's Punishment of the Nations (2:4–15)
      3. Yahweh's Restoration of Israel (3:1–20)

Overview of Zephaniah

God's word came to Zephaniah during Josiah's reign as king over Judah (1:1). God will destroy all life and humankind on earth and thereby bring an end to the worship of false deities (1:2–9). His punishment will be terrible for the complacent of all classes of people who do not worship him as they should, and it will extend to the whole earth (1:18). God calls his people together to humbly seek him (2:1–3). Philistia, Canaan, Moab, and Ammon will face divine judgment for despising God's people; meanwhile, the distant nations will worship God in their own lands (2:4–11). Cush will be slain, and Assyria, with its capital at Nineveh, will become desolate and a place where only wild beasts live (2:12–15). Zephaniah 3 turns to bring woe on the city of oppressors who do not trust God or obey him. The city's leadership is corrupt, while Yahweh, who dwells in the city, remains righteous (3:1–5). Although God has punished other nations and cities, Jerusalem has not learned from this (3:6–7). All the world will face God's wrath (3:8). God will then purify his people so that even those beyond the rivers of Cush will bring offerings (3:9–10). The humble remnant of Israel will trust in God and dwell securely in Jerusalem (3:11–13). Zion is commanded to sing for this wonderful time that is coming (3:14–17). God will bring back the exiles, and all the peoples on earth will honor and praise Jerusalem and its citizens (3:18–20).

Reading Zephaniah

Premodern Readings

Zephaniah became a book that looked forward to divine restoration after a time of judgment. Thus its inclusion in the Scrolls of the Twelve Prophets at Murabbaʿat and Naḥal Ḥever might associate this expectation with the Bar Kokhba revolt of AD 132–135. The late second-century *Apocalypse of Zephaniah* (mentioned by Clement of Alexandria) includes the prophet's witness of a sinner's punishment, followed by a journey to heaven. Rabbinic tradition attests that Zephaniah was the righteous teacher of Jeremiah (*b. Megillah* 15a). According to the rabbinic *Pesiqta Rabbati* (26), Zephaniah spoke in the synagogues of Jerusalem during Josiah's reign.[3]

Marie-Lan Nguyen/Wikimedia Commons

Mesopotamian cylinder seal showing worship of starry host and sun deity

John Calvin summarized the book: God's people are to face destruction for their sins. The Assyrians and others who mistreated Israel will also receive vengeance for their cruelty. Zephaniah describes the sins of Israel while encouraging the faithful to be patient and to remain looking to the faithfulness of the God of the covenant.[4]

Higher Criticism

Zephaniah has generally been set in the reforms of Josiah in the latter decades of the seventh century BC (cf. 1:1).[5] Josiah promoted the worship of the one God, Yahweh, at the temple of Jerusalem, and he sought to reunite the lands of the northern kingdom that Assyria had seized a century earlier. Zephaniah called the people to abandon their worship of other deities and to turn exclusively to the God of Israel as worshiped in the Jerusalem temple.

Critical scholarship has identified eschatological, universal, and remnant elements that affected the editing of the oracles in the postexilic period. This has led to a variety of views, from those who see only the later addition of the first verse, to those who add on six to twelve verses, to those who see about half of the verses added in a later phase.[6] Others, like Mark Boda, suggest that Zephaniah 3:14–20 was added when Haggai through Malachi were attached to the Minor Prophets collection.

However, Marvin Sweeney observes that none of this is definitive.[7] The eschatological pattern does not form a definitive prophetic structure in early or late Hebrew prophets. Universal perspectives with respect to Judean writings

3. Ibid., 474.

4. Calvin, *Habakkuk, Zephaniah, Haggai*.

5. Sweeney, "Zephaniah," 472–73; Boda, "Zephaniah," 899–900.

6. For the single verse, see Baker, *Nahum, Habakkuk and Zephaniah*. For the group who would understand six to twelve verses added, see W. Holladay, "Reading Zephaniah"; and Ben Zvi, *Book of Zephaniah*. For the larger addition of editorial materials, see Redditt, *Introduction to the Prophets*.

7. Sweeney, "Zephaniah," 473.

are already found in the preexilic period.[8] The nations of Zephaniah 2:8–15 characterize Judah's enemies in the late seventh century BC. Finally, the universal recognition of the God of Israel remains a constant theme from Genesis 12:1–3 onward. Jerusalem's restoration and punishment and its picture as the bride of Yahweh go back to preexilic and exilic expectation in Hosea 1–3, Jeremiah 2, and Ezekiel 16.

Literary Readings

Following Sweeney and others, the book of Zephaniah may be analyzed as basically a unity in which the prophet addresses the people of Judah and Jerusalem. He calls on them to seek Yahweh through giving support to Josiah's reform. Zephaniah 1:2–18 outlines the Day of Yahweh ("Day of the Lord") and stipulates the prophetic consequences if people do not seek Yahweh. The remainder of the book includes an actual command to seek the Lord (2:1–3), followed by the basis for this in the punishment of the nations and the specific salvation of Jerusalem and the people of God. After the core of the exhortation in 2:1–3, the identified nations in 2:4–15 are not all the earth but specific nations that opposed Josiah's plan for national restoration. Thus the focus is not worldwide judgment but Zephaniah's concern to promote the same reform as that initiated by Josiah.[9] Although it does not share in the intensity of specific literary devices that some of the Minor Prophets use, Zephaniah preserves a distinct message and is organized in a coherent manner. Nevertheless, Zephaniah 2:4 has two clear wordplays: on Gaza and "abandoned" (Heb. *ʿazzâ ʿăzûbâ*), and on Ekron and "uprooted" (*ʿeqrôn tēʿāqēr*).

Gender and Ideological Criticism

Shigeyuki Nakanose, Fernando Doren, and Enilda de Paula Pedro begin their commentary with a focus on a starving Brazilian child who is three and a half years old but has the weight of an eight-month-old baby.[10] They state that he suffers from the worst form of malnutrition and that its effects will remain with him for the rest of his life, no matter how much care he receives from this time forward. This provides a tragic human face to the more than thirty million Brazilians who, at the time of this writing, have a monthly income of less than thirty dollars. Thus it is more than understandable that the reading of Zephaniah should take place with an emphasis on God's condemnation of the wealthy and elite classes (1:8–13) who oppress the poor of

8. See the early sixth-century-BC inscription in the cave at Khirbet Beit Lei near Lachish: "Yahweh is the God of all the earth" (Aḥituv, *Echoes from the Past*, 233–35).

9. Sweeney, "Form-Critical Reassessment"; idem, "Zephaniah: A Paradigm."

10. Nakanose, Doren, and Paula Pedro, "Zephaniah."

the land (2:3, 6). It is also against the foreign oppressors of that day, such as Assyria (2:13). The son of Cushi, Zephaniah, despite his royal Judean pedigree, is the product of intermarriage with African stock (1:1).[11] He becomes the spokesperson for the poor of the land. The opulence of the wealthy contrasted with the harsh life of the poor in Zephaniah parallels Brazil. The foreign deities that the officials worship (1:4–6) contrast with the God of Israel, who champions the poor of the land who follow him. They will find God's mercy and protection when the Day of Yahweh comes as a day of fierce judgment (2:1–3). This remnant, the poor and humble, will occupy restored Jerusalem (3:12), for God is among them (3:15, 17). In Brazil, the authors suggest that this hope is present in the base communities, ecumenical groups such as the Landless Workers' Movement, and international nongovernment groups such as the Pastoral Land Commission. Surely Zephaniah emphasizes the people of God joined in worship as the focus for reform (3:14–18).

Ancient Near Eastern Context

Much of the historical background of Josiah is summarized in the chapters on 1–2 Kings and on Jeremiah (above). Zephaniah 2:4 mentions four of the traditional five cities of the Philistines, which had benefited by the Assyrian attack on Jerusalem a century earlier. Ekron especially had received much of Judah's Shephelah, a major source of its agricultural produce. This came about as the result of Padi, king of Ekron, remaining loyal to King Sennacherib of Assyria. Sennacherib recounts how, when he attacked Judah, he forced Hezekiah to release Padi from confinement in Jerusalem. Although Sennacherib retreated without capturing Jerusalem, Judah was devastated (*COS* 2.119B:302–3). Apparently Sennacherib cut the Shephelah away from Judah and passed it over to Padi. The seventh century saw great expansion of Tel Miqne, the site of ancient Ekron. Its 120 or more olive presses produced oil for export around the region and beyond.[12] This brought prosperity to Ekron and Philistia but difficult economic conditions for Judah.

Sometime near the end of the seventh century BC, an Aramaic papyrus was sent to Saqqara in Egypt from a certain Adon of Ekron. The sender recognizes the pharaoh (Neco II, connected with the death of Josiah in 609 BC) as his overlord and seeks military support. It seems that at the end of the seventh century BC, Ekron and perhaps the Philistines as a whole found alliance with Egypt to be to their advantage against the shifting political powers of the region. By 604 BC Nebuchadnezzar had come against the Philistine cities and conquered Ashkelon.[13]

11. His royal pedigree and connection with Hezekiah are established in 1:1 as well. Therefore, it is not true to state the he "was not related to the Davidic dynasty" (ibid., 313).

12. King, *Jeremiah*, 150–51.

13. Rainey and Notley, *Sacred Bridge*, 262–63; Kelle, "Judah in the Seventh Century," 379–81.

The condemnations of Moab and Ammon (Zeph. 2:8–9) may be related to the bands of these troops (and Aramaeans) coming against Judah around 600 BC (2 Kings 24:2), perhaps sent by King Nebuchadnezzar II of Babylon.[14]

Canonical Context

While Zephaniah may have some affinities with the organization and expression found in Isaiah, the role of this prophet in the Book of the Twelve is to bring an end to the preexilic period, with the warnings of terrible events to come against God's people and the nations around them, a judgment that would be experienced from the late seventh century through most of the sixth century BC.[15] The theme of the remnant emerges in the remaining three Minor Prophets as the hope and salvation of the postexilic period begins, pinned to "the Day of the Lord [Yahweh]."

In the New Testament the theme of the Day of the Lord is developed (Luke 17:30; 1 Cor. 1:8; 5:5; 2 Cor. 1:14; Phil. 1:6, 10; 1 Thess. 5:2; 2 Thess. 2:2; 2 Pet. 3:12). However, there is no specific allusion to Zephaniah in the New Testament.

Theological Perspectives of Zephaniah

Boda finds the two major theological themes of Zephaniah to be the Day of Yahweh and the remnant.[16] References to a special day occur in Zephaniah 1:7, 8, 9, 10, 14, 15, 16, 18; 2:2, 3; 3:8, 11, and 16. The initial set of occurrences in chapter 1 follows on indictments of God's people for their sins. Thus Zephaniah 1:7–10 warns that the Day of Yahweh will not be one of joy for God's people but will be one of punishment against officials, priests, and the violent. While distress and terror will come, it will be specifically directed against the wealthy. With dramatic language, those who live on earth will come to a sudden end (1:18). Zephaniah 2:2–3 identifies the Day of Yahweh as bringing Yahweh's wrath and anger. Zephaniah 3:8 speaks of the Day of the Lord as one when he will pour out his wrath on the nations. Jerusalem will not be put to shame, and Jerusalem will be encouraged not to fear (3:11, 16). Thus the day described in chapter 3 is one where God comforts Jerusalem, while that in chapter 1 brings punishment against the nations. The Day of Yahweh brings judgment to all people but also salvation and comfort in chapter 3.

The remnant appears in Zephaniah 2:7, 9; and 3:12–13. In chapter 2 it follows the judgments against Israel's neighbors. Thus in 2:7 the remnant of the people of Judah will possess the cities of the Philistines and their land.

14. Kelle, "Judah in the Seventh Century," 379–81.
15. Boda, "Zephaniah," 905.
16. Ibid., 904–5.

In verse 9 the remnant of God's people will plunder Moab and Ammon and inherit the land that God has given them. In Zephaniah 3:12–13 the remnant will remain in Jerusalem. These are the meek and humble, as opposed to the wealthy and powerful, who will trust in the name of the Lord and live in God's holy city. Thus the major theological themes balance theology with ethics as God redeems those who trust in him.

Key Commentaries and Studies

Ben Zvi, Ehud. *A Historical-Critical Study of the Book of Zephaniah*. BZAW 198. Berlin: de Gruyter, 1991. Traditional critical study of Zephaniah as a series of redactions.

Berlin, Adele. *Zephaniah: A New Translation with Introduction and Commentary*. AB 25A. New York: Doubleday, 1994. Careful analysis of poetry at the level of the cola and bicola.

Goldingay, John. "Zephaniah." Pages 93–134 in *Minor Prophets II*. Edited by J. Goldingay and P. J. Scalise. NIBC 18. Peabody, MA: Hendrickson, 2009. Useful and open evangelical study of the literary analysis of the book.

Sweeney, Marvin A. *Zephaniah*. Hermeneia. Minneapolis: Fortress, 2003. Important literary study appreciating the unity of the book.

33

HAGGAI

What can one person do that will have any impact on the world? Who are we to think that what we do makes any difference? Haggai addressed his message to a small, poor group of people living in Jerusalem who were convinced that their nation's best days had vanished. Yet the God of these people promised that he would again shake heaven and earth and use Haggai and those faithful few to change the world.

Name, Text, and Outline

The name Haggai consists of the Hebrew word for "festival," followed by an ending that suggests the name could be a shortened form of a longer expression, such as one meaning "festival of God." Given at birth, this name suggests that the child was born on a special feast day in ancient Israel. There are many examples of the name in extrabiblical Hebrew inscriptions from ancient Israel. This name also occurs in Aramaic and Phoenician inscriptions.[1]

The Masoretic Text of Haggai is reliable.[2] There is no need to rearrange the consonants or suggest emendations, beyond one or two revocalizations, which nevertheless preserve the consonantal text. The Septuagint tends to expand and harmonize in comparison to the Masoretic Text, providing two examples of revocalizations that may be correct (2:7, 16).

OUTLINE

I. Superscription (1:1)
II. Rebuild the Temple (1:2–15a)

1. Albertz and Schmitt, *Family and Household Religion*, 603.
2. Meyers and Meyers, *Haggai, Zechariah 1–8*, lxvii–lxviii.

III. Restore the Former Glory (1:15b–2:9)
IV. Purity and God's Promises (2:10–19)
V. Zerubbabel Assured (2:20–23)

Overview of Haggai

Haggai receives God's message during the second year of King Darius's rulership. (See plate 9 in the gallery for an image of King Darius.) Yahweh speaks to Zerubbabel, the governor of Judah, and to Joshua, the high priest. God's people live in paneled houses, and yet the Lord's house remains in ruins. God has brought a drought and lack of fertility on the land because the people have ignored the rebuilding of his house. Zerubbabel, Joshua, and the people respond with obedience and begin to work on the temple in Jerusalem (1:2–15a). Haggai encourages the people: God's presence that brought them from Egypt continues with them, despite the smallness in size that the temple appears to be (1:15b–2:5). God will shortly turn the world upside down, and the glory of his new temple will surpass that of the older one (2:6–9). God has destroyed the fruitfulness of the agriculture with disease, and he will again change the order of the world (2:10–19). Yahweh Almighty declares that he will take Zerubbabel and make him his signet ring (2:20–23).

Reading Haggai

Premodern Readings

The fifth-century-AD Christian Cassiodorus sees in the text of Haggai the power of God's word to soften hardened hearts and to turn people back to God. For Augustine, the temple is that "living stone" (Christ, in 1 Pet. 2:4) that, along with true conversion, brings peace to the world. Ambrose of Milan sees the divine life and its living power reflected in God's presence in the temple. For the fourth-century Gregory of Nazianzus and the sixth-century Gregory the Great, God's temple reaches beyond his people and changes the world (Hag. 2:6–9). In similar manner does his kingdom and its rule and reign extend and establish a solid worldwide foundation.[3]

Higher Criticism

The major critical question with this brief book has to do with the date formulas and their relationship to the composition of the oracles to which

3. Cook, "Haggai," 360.

they are attached.[4] Four dates appear at the beginning of the oracles, all within four months of the second year of Darius, and each specifying the day and month in chronological sequence: 1:1, 15; 2:1, 10, 18, and 20 (these last three verses all identify the same twenty-fourth day of the ninth month). The form of these dating notes is at home in the sixth century BC. There is not a consistent order of day-month-year or anything else that would imply a particular ideological tendency. Further, within and outside the Bible, oracles and Persian-era messages of various sorts had their date formulas added at the time of composition, not later. All of this suggests that the date was placed on the oracle when the oracle was written, not a century later.[5]

The oracles appear to date close to the time of the second year of Darius II, about 520 BC.[6] There is no attempt to differentiate this Darius from later Persian kings with the same name. The rededication of the temple, around 515 BC, is not mentioned. The eschatological interest of this period is found in Haggai, yet it does not occur in Ezra and Nehemiah, from the fifth century BC.

Literary Readings

The four major divisions of the book (1:2–15a; 1:15b–2:9; 2:10–19; 2:20–23) constitute oracles and responses. The opening verses (1:2–11) consist of God's challenge to the people to surrender their apathy and to turn to him and build his house. Verses 12–15a indicate a unanimous decision by the leaders and the people to respond in obedience. Haggai 1:15b–2:9 gives encouragement to the people, especially those who remembered the splendor of Solomon's temple. In 2:10–14 the priests are called on to decide a matter of uncleanness and contamination. Verses 15–19 indicate that the former absence of fertility will be changed: God will bring blessing and fruitfulness to his people. The final verses turn to address the leader, Zerubbabel, who is proclaimed as God's signet ring.

Gender and Ideological Criticism

Paul Kalluveettil, though aware of the issues regarding temples among different religious groups in his native India, challenges Christians to see themselves as living temples (1 Cor. 6:19).[7] In this process, he cites Haggai 1:13–14, where God stirs up the leadership and the people to dedicate themselves to the task of building the Jerusalem temple. So God promises to fill his rebuilt house with glory and to shake heaven and earth, turning the world upside down for the good of his people. In contrast to the fatalism of

4. Kessler, "Haggai," 302.
5. For the latter, see Ackroyd, "Studies in the Book of Haggai."
6. Kessler, "Haggai," 302.
7. Kalluveettil, "Haggai."

Hindu karma, this glorious vision can give hope and transform lives with real purpose. God's choice of Zerubbabel as his signet ring (2:23) foreshadows the promise of Jesus Christ for the Christian, as the one who enables this life-transforming vision.

Ancient Near Eastern Context

For the Persian imperial context, see the discussion (below) under "Ancient Near Eastern Context" for Zechariah. Judah itself was slowly repopulated, with little evidence of a massive return of people. Thus the community in Jerusalem was small and the workers relatively few for rebuilding the temple.

The governor of Judah, a man by the name of Zerubbabel, received the patronym of Shealtiel (Hag. 1:1, 12, 14; 2:2, 23; also Ezra 3:2, 8; 5:2; cf. Matt. 1:12; Luke 3:27). 1 Chronicles 3:17–19 identifies Shealtiel as the son of King Jehoiachin of Judah, who had been taken into Babylonian captivity, and Zerubbabel as a descendant. Thus Haggai could legitimately identify Zerubbabel as in the line of the kings of Judah and of David. The messianic expectations of Haggai 2:23 (cf. also Zechariah) were consonant with the ancient promises and with the expectation of their fulfillment that the rebuilding of the temple would bring.[8]

Canonical Context

Similar concerns about rebuilding the temple, the figures of Zerubbabel and Joshua, the narcissistic sins of the people in the holy city, and the Jerusalem of around 520–518 BC occur in Zechariah 1–8. Ezra 1–6 covers this historical context as well. Haggai is mentioned by name in Ezra 5:1 and 6:14. Imagery of God's presence bringing holiness to earth (Hag. 2:5; Exod. 29:46; Ezek. 37:14, 28), of shaking the earth (Hag. 2:21; Ezek. 38:20), of coming fruitfulness (Hag. 2:19; Ezek. 34:25–28), of nations worshiping (Hag. 2:7–8, 22; Isa. 2:2–4), and of the coming of a new ruler (Hag. 2:23; Ps. 132; Ezek. 37:24–25) echoes earlier divine appearances and prophecies.[9] Above all, there was the judgment announced by Jeremiah 25:11–12 and 29:10, which promised seventy years of desolation in Judah (586–516 BC) followed by God's great outpouring of blessings. This gave Haggai the expectation that the initial appearance of an insignificant house of worship would give way to a greater glory than ever before in Jerusalem, one that would reach worldwide proportions (Hag. 2:1–9).

In addition to mention of Zerubbabel and Shealtiel (Matt. 1:12; Luke 3:27), the New Testament attests to the promise that God will "shake the heavens and the earth" (Hag. 2:6, 21). This receives its most concrete

8. Van der Veen, "Sixth-Century Issues," 403–5.
9. Cook, "Haggai," 359.

restatement in Hebrews 12:26. This text looks back to the giving of the law at Mount Sinai and forward to the return of Jesus Christ to judge the world. Such expectation suggests that this New Testament writer did not see the fulfillment of Haggai 2:6 in the sixth century BC but at best saw the beginning realization of a prophecy whose full realization extends into the future and the coming of the true temple, the true King, and the true kingdom of God's people.

Theological Perspectives of Haggai

The first chapter of Haggai expresses how important obedience is in God's plan. The people know that the worship of God should be of first priority. Instead, they build their own houses and pursue their own interests. The result is that the concerns to which they have devoted themselves prove barren

The Signet Ring

In Haggai 2:23 God describes Zerubbabel, the governor of Judah, as the "signet ring." The Hebrew *ḥôtām* is usually best translated "seal." The common noun occurs sixteen times in the Old Testament. A seal served as a means of identification, containing either the name (Exod. 28:21; 39:6, 30) or an artistic symbol of its owner or the one it represented. Carved on a small stone or gem, it could be impressed on clay to seal a document or bear witness as a legal means of identifying the person (Job 38:14). It could be worn on a string around the neck or as a ring on one's finger (Song 8:6): the seal worn around the neck would be close to the heart, and the one worn on the finger would be part of the "arm." When God identifies Zerubbabel as his "seal" or "signet ring," he is stating that Zerubbabel serves as God's agent, leading the people of God to accomplish his divine purpose. No one should stand in his way. Note, however, that this is not a permission for the governor to do whatever he wants. God's blessing can be revoked, as it was for Zerubbabel's grandfather (Jer. 22:24). See also the sidebars "Seal Impressions of Baruch and of Gedaliah" in the chapter on Jeremiah.

Signet ring with Hebrew name of owner, Shophat

Zev Radovan/www.BibleLandPictures.com

and unproductive. The effect is the loss of produce, on which the people depend for food. Haggai's message brings repentance from the leadership and the people (1:12). God promises his presence and stirs their spirit as the people begin their work (1:13–15a). This promise of God's presence remains key to the success of any mission that God gives (Josh. 1:5–9; Matt. 28:18–20).

Haggai 1:15b–2:8 focuses on the theme of transformation, with God in control. Although the people are few in number and their work does not seem to produce results in any way similar to the original temple, God asserts that he controls all and will turn the world upside down. The glory of the temple the people build will be greater than that of Solomon's temple. God can do great things with small resources that are obedient and dedicated.

Haggai 2:10–19 begins with questions to the priests about the nature of holiness and uncleanness. On the one hand, holiness may preserve itself, but it cannot render holy what it touches. On the other hand, something that is unclean can defile others through touch. In this way God teaches that the unclean disobedience of God's people in the past (when they did not build the temple) has made everything around them unclean. So their crops have failed, and their work gives them not enough to eat. However, the obedience of the people in building the temple will now bring about blessing. This repeats the point of 1:2–11 and also warns the people not to become discouraged or give up their efforts.

In Haggai 2:20–23 the book teaches that God will work through his chosen leaders to bless his people and to enable them to serve as a blessing to all peoples of the earth. Zerubbabel, in the line of David, will be the example of the messiah for that generation. God has chosen him to lead the people and to be an instrument of blessing to all (cf. Gen. 12:1–3).

Key Commentaries and Studies

Baldwin, Joyce G. *Haggai, Zechariah, Malachi: An Introduction and Commentary*. TOTC. Leicester, UK: Inter-Varsity; Downers Grove, IL: InterVarsity, 1972. Key evangelical work for understanding the historical sense of the text.

Boda, Mark J. *Haggai, Zechariah*. NIVAC. Grand Rapids: Zondervan, 2004. Important literary analysis and application.

Hill, Andrew E. *Haggai, Zechariah, and Malachi: An Introduction and Commentary*. TOTC 28. Leicester, UK: IVP Academic, 2012. Great evangelical perspectives on background, literary aspects, and theology.

Kessler, John. *The Book of Haggai: Prophecy and Society in Early Persian Yehud*. VTSup 91. Leiden: Brill, 2002. Important for sociology of the postexilic prophets.

Meyers, Carol L., and Eric M. Meyers. *Haggai, Zechariah 1–8: A New Translation with Introduction and Commentary*. AB 25B. New Haven: Yale University Press, 2004. Best for detailed exegesis.

Petersen, David L. *Haggai and Zechariah 1–8: A Commentary*. OTL. Philadelphia: Westminster, 1984. Valuable theological exegesis.

Petterson, Anthony R. *Haggai, Zechariah and Malachi*. AOTC 25. Leicester, UK: Inter-Varsity Press, 2015. Strong literary and textual matters affecting exegesis.

Wolff, Hans Walter. *Haggai: A Commentary*. Translated by Margaret Kohl. ConC. Minneapolis: Augsburg, 1988. Important for textual criticism.

34

ZECHARIAH

What makes the difference between someone who speaks God's word and someone who speaks their own message? With his weird visions and strange predictions of the future, Zechariah must have seemed like a religious fanatic. What made Zechariah different and worth listening to?

Name, Text, and Outline

The book of Zechariah is named after its prophet. The name carries the meaning "the Lord has remembered." Zechariah is the son of Berechiah and grandson of Iddo (Ezra 5:1; 6:14; Zech. 1:7). Iddo appears in Nehemiah 12:4 as one of the priests and Levites among the first returnees from the exile. Zechariah was head of the priestly house of Iddo during the time of the high priest Joiakim (Neh. 12:16), around 500 BC and perhaps in the following decades. Situating Zechariah's initial visionary activity in the second year of Darius (520 BC) would suggest a figure who was likely a younger man, perhaps in his twenties.

The Masoretic Text of Zechariah is well preserved. The Greek (LXX) differs from the Masoretic Text at various places, but these are generally not supported by the Greek fragments from the Dead Sea Scrolls. Those follow the Masoretic Text (Heb.). Thus despite many questions of interpretation arising from obscure and difficult vocabulary and syntax (as well as poetic difficulties), for the Masoretic Text the Hebrew wording does not seem in doubt.

OUTLINE

I. Superscription (1:1)
II. The Temple (1:2–8:23)
   A. Introduction: Israel's Return to God (1:2–6)
   B. Eight Visions (1:7–6:15)
      1. Vision of the Multicolored Horses (1:7–17)
      2. Vision of Horns and Skilled Workers (1:18–21 [2:1–4 MT])
      3. Vision of the Measuring Line for Jerusalem (2:1–13 [2:5–17 MT])
      4. Vision of the High Priest Joshua in Dirty Clothes (3:1–10)
      5. Vision of the Gold Lampstand (4:1–14)
      6. Vision of a Flying Scroll (5:1–4)
      7. Vision of a Woman inside a Basket Bound for Babylonia (5:5–11)
      8. Vision of Horses and of Four Chariots (6:1–15)
   C. Fasting and Restoration (7:1–8:19)
      1. Inquiry about Fasting (7:1–3)
      2. Explanation of the Exile (7:4–14)
      3. Promise to Restore Jerusalem (8:1–8)
      4. Charge to Build the Temple and Speak Truth (8:9–17)
      5. Promise to Make Fasts Times of Rejoicing (8:18–19)
   D. Universal Search for God (8:20–23)
III. The Shepherd-King (9:1–14:21)
   A. Shepherd Rejected (9:1–11:17)
      1. Judgment of Nations (9:1–8)
      2. Judah's King Appears on a Donkey and Brings Victory (9:9–10:1)
      3. Blessing and Return for God's People (10:2–11:3)
      4. End of International Peace and Unity of God's People (11:4–14)
      5. The Foolish and Worthless Shepherd (11:15–17)
   B. Shepherd Slaughtered (12:1–14:15)
      1. Destruction for the Nations That Come against Jerusalem (12:1–9)
      2. Mourning in Jerusalem (12:10–14)
      3. Jerusalem Cleansed from Sin (13:1–9)
      4. Judgment Comes to Jerusalem (14:1–3)
      5. The Lord Defeats the Invaders (14:4–15)
   C. The Lord Is King (14:16–21)
      1. All Peoples Celebrate the Feast of Tabernacles (14:16–19)
      2. Jerusalem Becomes Dedicated to the Lord (14:20–21)

Overview of Zechariah

The book of the prophet Zechariah begins in the second year of King Darius with a call to return to the Lord, as described by the prophets (1:1–6). A few months later "the word of the LORD" comes to Zechariah in a night vision.

He sees a red horse and its rider in the midst of myrtle trees and with other multicolored horses. The horses have searched the earth and found peace. Yet God is angry because the punishment that the nations have extracted from Judah and Jerusalem was more than was deserved (1:7–17). Those who have scattered God's people will be terrified and thrown down (1:18–21 [2:1–4 MT]). The man with the measuring line in chapter 2 learns that the size of the city will not hold all of its citizens. God will bless Zion and Jerusalem with his own protection. Other nations will join as well and become God's people. In the vision of the high priest Joshua (Zech. 3), Satan's accusations are silenced, and Joshua is given clean clothes that symbolize the forgiveness of Israel's sins and the blessing of the land if the people of God obey. In chapter 4 the vision of a gold lampstand with pipes pouring out oil to two olive trees, one on each side of the lampstand, signifies the anointing of two leaders to serve the Lord. Zechariah 5:1–4 records the vision of a flying scroll, which will destroy the house of any who swear falsely. The remainder of chapter 5 portrays a basket with a lead cover and a woman, "Wickedness," inside it. Two winged women take the basket to Babylonia, where a house will be built for it. Zechariah 6:1–15 describes horses and four chariots that travel to the four directions of the earth. Those going to the north take silver and gold from the exiles in Babylon in order to construct a crown for Joshua the priest.

© Baker Publishing Group and Dr. James C. Martin

Worshipers before sun-god Shamash

In Zechariah 7:1–14 inquiries are made about fasting, and the word comes through the prophet that the people should show mercy and compassion. The people have refused to listen to God, and so he has scattered them among the nations, and the land has become desolate. This is followed by a promise to restore Jerusalem, combined with a command to build the temple of Jerusalem and to speak the truth to one another (8:1–17). The question about fasting receives an answer: fasts will become times of feasting and rejoicing (8:18–19). This will be in a time when people from all nations will desperately wish to know God (8:20–23).

The desire to know God will find an answer in the coming of the

© Baker Publishing Group and Dr. James C. Martin.

Tunnel—probably built by Hezekiah—with waters from Gihon Spring. Chief source of water for Jerusalem.

shepherd-king. Chapters 9–14 discuss this in two "burdens," or prophetic oracles. The first begins as a prophetic indictment of Damascus, Tyre, Ashkelon, Gaza, and other neighbors of Israel, whom God will judge and then incorporate the survivors into his people. In place of the conquest of Judah by foreigners, Jerusalem's king will come by riding on a donkey. Peace and prosperity will fill the land, but war will come on Israel's enemies. Chapter 10 continues the theme of blessing for his people but judgment on those who are their enemies. From powerful countries such as Egypt and Assyria, God will bring back his people. The lands of Lebanon and the Bashan are marked for devastation in 11:1–3. God removes the shepherds who take care of his people. Using the image of breaking two staffs, God removes his favor toward the nations and destroys the unity between Judah and Israel. The oracle of chapters 9–11 concludes with the promise of an evil shepherd who will not care for the flock and a curse against such a shepherd "who deserts the flock!"

Chapter 12 introduces the second "burden." The creator God promises a time when all the nations will bring their horses and instruments of war against Jerusalem, but God will protect his people. God will give Judah strength as well, so that it will subdue all of its enemies roundabout. The house of David and the citizens of Jerusalem will receive a spirit of grace and supplication to look on "me," the one they have pierced, and they will mourn. They will weep and mourn, each clan by itself and their wives by themselves.

Zechariah 13:1 promises a cleansing fountain that will remove the sins and impurities of Jerusalem and cause the idols to be forgotten. God will remove the prophets. A poem (13:7–9) calls on the sword to awake and to strike the shepherd and scatter the sheep. Only one-third of them will remain alive, and they will be so refined by fire that they will become God's people.

Zechariah returns to the theme of judgment on Jerusalem (14:1). This time the nations will invade the city and deport half of its population. Then Yahweh will fight against the invaders. He will stand on the Mount of Olives and split it. (See plate 11 in the gallery for a view of the Mount of Olives.) The Day of the Lord will be unique, and water will flow from Jerusalem to the Dead Sea and to the Mediterranean. God will be king, and Jerusalem will be exalted. All the armies and animals of war will die on their feet, but Jerusalem will remain. The survivors will make an annual pilgrimage to Jerusalem at the Feast of Tabernacles. Any who do not attend will have no rain. Every vessel in Jerusalem will be dedicated to God for use in the temple because so many visitors will come to sacrifice in Jerusalem.

Reading Zechariah

Premodern Readings

The well-known position of at least some of the literature of the Dead Sea Scrolls community was that there would be two messiahs: a political ruler and a priest (1QS 9.11; etc.).[1] The two olive trees of Zechariah 4:1–10 may have fueled this interpretation.

In the Talmud (*b. Sanh.* 93a) the red horse (Zech. 1:8) symbolizes blood, although later Jewish commentators were reluctant to find any significance in the color. The Karaites, who rejected Jewish traditions of interpretation, found the basket of Zechariah 5 to be the burdensome weights of the Talmud and Mishnah, and the winged women to be the Jewish academies that produced and taught these.[2]

The connection of God's people with his special prize ("the apple of his eye," 2:8 NIV) has provided comfort to the missionaries of ancient times, such as Saint Patrick. It also became a description of the Jews for Dietrich Bonhoeffer, who saw Hitler's Germany standing against God's people in the persecution and destruction of the Jews.[3] As a child, John Wesley escaped a fire that struck his family home. The impact of that experience caused his identification with the "brand plucked from the fire" (Zech. 3:2).[4]

In the second half of Zechariah (chaps. 9–14), early Judaism applied the royal figure of 9:9–10 to Zerubbabel, the governor who was contemporary with Zechariah. The same was true of Theodore of Mopsuestia in the Antiochene tradition of interpretation, who applied these chapters to the immediate context of Zerubbabel and to the Maccabees who would appear several centuries later.[5] Cyril of Jerusalem (*Catacheses* 15.22) represents the mainstream Christian interpretation, which finds in 12:10 and 13:7 the prophecy of the Messiah, Jesus Christ.

1. Cf. Coggins and Han, *Six Minor Prophets*, 150–85.
2. British Library MS Or.2401 fol. 174a–175b for Yefet ben 'Eli's commentary on Zech. 5:8.
3. Especially Zech. 2:12; cf. Bethge, "Dietrich Bonheoffer and the Jews," 65–67.
4. On this experience and its influence, see Hattersley, *The Life of John Wesley*.
5. Wolters, "Zechariah 14 and Biblical Theology," 264–68.

Higher Criticism

In recent times the study of Zechariah has focused on the division of the book between chapters 1–8 and 9–14. The first eight chapters have generally been assigned to the latter part of the sixth century BC, the traditional time of the prophet Zechariah. The visions encouraged the people of Jerusalem and Judah to rebuild the temple, or at least to return to this work and complete it. From the time of Julius Wellhausen in the late nineteenth century, the work was seen as promoting the leadership of the priests. Thus the political governor disappears in chapter 6, where the high priest (Joshua) alone receives one of two gold "crowns" (6:11, 14 MT), suggesting the rise of priestly power and the decline of the heir of David's throne. Others have suggested that the first half of the book tries to take advantage of suggested political upheaval as Darius established his position as Persian emperor. Perhaps some wondered whether the Judean state would regain its independence. More recent study has argued that these visions encourage the building of the temple in a time of relative calm (the early years of Darius).[6] Zechariah followed the encouragement of the Persian emperor Darius, who wished economic development and increased settlement. By addressing the building of the temple at the heart of this plan for a revitalized Judean province, Zechariah hoped to lay the groundwork for the return of God and the inauguration of his kingdom from its center in Jerusalem. In this scheme, Zerubbabel remains in office, but the point of chapter 6 is to identify a second crown as one worn by a messianic figure, "Branch," for whom the priest would wait.

The second part of Zechariah takes a different turn from that of the earlier chapters. A century ago, critics dated this material to the preexilic period, perhaps a century before the time of the prophet. In the mid-twentieth century, the mention of Greece and the apocalyptic nature of the text led some to suggest that this material should date much later, into the Hellenistic period of the third century BC. Now critics recognize the Persian struggle with Greece at the time of Xerxes and have moved toward a date perhaps seventy years after Zechariah 1–8, in the mid-fifth century. While these events remain in the tradition of Zechariah—and indeed this author is often credited with edited additions to the first half of the book—the battles with Greece and military defenses that characterized that time are identifiable (Zech. 9:13). God's people are tested, and this is reported in the context of an apocalyptic style. Nevertheless, the priestly theology of the first part of the book remains evident.[7] God now resides in the temple, where he protects the land and cleanses it. Thus many of the arguments for the mid-fifth century allow Zechariah 9–14 to be written a few decades earlier, within the possible lifetime of the prophet whose name the book bears.

6. Cook, "Zechariah," 466–67.

7. For the nature of apocalyptic literature, see the chapter on Daniel and the discussion there.

The two "burdens" or oracles of chapters 9–11 and 12–14 have also been connected with Malachi's oracle. However, significant differences in message and vocabulary suggest that Malachi should remain separate from Zechariah.

Literary Readings

Fundamental to the study of Zechariah is the identification of the type of literature and the message that it seeks to communicate. The visions of Zechariah 1–6 describe the heir of David's throne and the high priest as two leaders who benefit by the presence of God. This presence will be powerfully displayed in the temple itself, where God is represented by the lampstand, and the two human figures by olive trees (Zech. 4). God's holy presence cleanses the high priest Joshua (Zech. 3), just as it prepares Jerusalem and Judah for victory over their enemies (1:18–2:13) and over false worship (Zech. 5). At the beginning and end of these visions are heavenly visions of God's universal rule (Zech. 1 and 6).

Chapters 7–8 are the book's center and provide the message of the people's responsibility. The fasts are to become times of justice and mercy toward one another. The rebuilding of the temple and the need to speak truth to one another provide the background for God's blessing and restoration, which is here envisioned.

In the second half of the book are two sections. The first begins with the establishment of God's reign and its administration through a humble ruler (Zech. 9). There is hope for the return of Israel from exile (Zech. 10). However, the past history of sinful kings becomes the background for a future shepherd of the people who will be rejected by the people (Zech. 11).

In the second "burden," in chapters 12–14, the text begins with Israel's war and victory (12:1–9), corresponding to 10:3b–11:3. In an alternating form, the piercing of Yahweh's chosen one and the mourning and purification (12:10–13:1) correspond to the rejected shepherds of 11:4–17. The presence of idols in 10:2–3a corresponds to their suppression in 13:2–6 and frames this section. The same alternation is surrounded by a larger frame encompassing all of chapters 9–14. Thus the following appears:[8]

Ariely/Wikimedia Commons

Menorah from the Roman Period

8. Baldwin, *Haggai, Zechariah, Malachi*, 78–79; Lamarche, *Zacharie*, 112–13.

A Judgment and Salvation of Neighbors (9:1–8)
  B The King Arrives (9:9–10)
    C Israel at War, Victory from Yahweh (9:11–10:1)
      D Idols Denounced (10:2–3a)
    C′ Israel Reunited and Victorious (10:3b–11:3)
  B′ Bad Shepherds Rejected, Faithful Shepherd Called (11:4–17)
    C″ Israel at War, Victory from Yahweh (12:1–9)
  B″ Chosen One Pierced, Mourning (12:10–14)
      D′ Cleansing and Idols Removed by Yahweh (13:1–6)
  B‴ Shepherd Struck, People Tested and Purified (13:7–9)
    C‴ Israel at War, Victory from Yahweh (14:1–15)
A″ Judgment and Salvation of All Nations (14:16–21)

This formulation allows the reader to perceive the initial development of the salvation of Israel's neighbors as a precursor to the salvation of the whole world. In the process, there is a focus on the repentance of the people through the abolition of their images and a replacement of bad leadership with good.

Gender and Ideological Criticism

Along with older men and younger boys, older women and younger girls will find a good and happy life in Jerusalem after its restoration by God (Zech. 8:4–5). The process of that restoration includes a vision in which a woman named Wickedness sits in a basket with a lead cover. Nevertheless, it is two women whose wings are given power by the wind, or spirit (of God), to take this symbol away to Babylon, where a house (or temple) will provide a residence (5:5–11). The second part of Zechariah includes a poetic reference to God's restoration of Israel, which will lead to young men made attractive by grain and young women by new wine. Gazing on the one they have pierced causes both the husbands and wives of the royal, Levitical, and priestly families and clans to mourn (12:10–14). Although God's blessing on Jerusalem will come, the city will first endure an assault by all nations, which will include the raping of women (14:2; using a particularly crude word for "rape").

Paul Swarup, an Anglican priest in Delhi, brings home the message of Zechariah for his nation as he describes the greed and immorality of the Christians and their leaders, and thus the need to repent.[9] This is the key message that introduces the book in 1:1–6: "This is what the Lord Almighty says: 'Return to me,' declares the Lord Almighty, 'and I will return to you,' says the Lord Almighty" (1:2 NIV).

Many of the visions have direct application to the church in India (and elsewhere). In the vision of the red horse, God is ready to have mercy and restore (1:8–17). However, Swarup stresses the need for repentance among God's

9. Swarup, "Zechariah."

people. The four horns and smiths (1:18–21) demonstrate divine sovereignty over other nations, which Swarup applies to Christian cooperation with other organizations for assistance to those in need. The confidence of a life lived in holiness and service, rather than the wielding of power, interprets 4:6 rightly: "'Not by might, nor by power, but by my spirit,' says the LORD of hosts." For the woman in the basket (5:5–11), India knows very well of the manner in which the economic and religious sphere so readily link and bring corruption.

In reviewing the second half of the book of Zechariah, Swarup observes how many of the prophecies are fulfilled through Christ in the New Testament. Ultimately the church needs to know that God is in control within and outside the church. God will guide history to bring it where he wishes. However, all are responsible to repent of sin and to live faithful lives before one another and a watching world.

Ancient Near Eastern Context

The visions of Zechariah occur between approximately 520 and 518 BC (Zech. 1:1, 7; 7:1), set in the early years of the reign of King Darius of Persia. Darius came to power after several years of intrigue and infighting among claimants to the throne. Cambyses succeeded Cyrus, the first leader of Persia's empire who had authorized the Jewish people to return from exile around 538 BC. Cambyses gained control of Persia around 525 BC. In 522 BC, Cambyses's brother, Bardiya, claimed the throne while Cambyses was fighting in Egypt. Returning from the battle, Cambyses either committed suicide or was assassinated. Bardiya was deposed by someone who resembled him. The look-alike was himself killed, and a Median noble, Gaumata, became ruler. A Persian faction put Gaumata to death and raised Darius to his status as king in 522 BC.

The uncertainty of succession in the Persian Empire may have created uncertainty about the future in communities such as Judea (Yehud) in and around Jerusalem. The political environment could have stimulated the hope of an independent state. So in his visions, Zechariah sees the emergence of two leaders, the Davidic heir Zerubbabel and the high priest Joshua. Zechariah 4:6–10 foresees the rise of Zerubbabel, and 3:1–9 describes the emergence of Joshua. In this scenario, by the time of the vision of Zechariah 6, the reestablishment of the Persian Empire under Darius has taken place, and so there is only mention of Joshua as receiving the crown (6:11).

The problem with this theory is that it attributes too much of Zechariah's visions to the geopolitical events of the Persian Empire, and it concludes that virtually the entire visionary cycle was produced within a few months of these events. Clearly the roles of Zerubbabel and Joshua are at times emphasized. Yet some fourteen explicit references to the house or temple of the Lord suggest that its construction and future role are of far greater importance. Such a vision correlates well with the proposals of a Persian administrative system,

The Behistun Monument

The major sources for the imperial history of the late sixth century include the Behistun Inscription and the Greek historians, such as Herodotus. The Behistun Monument was carved into a cliffside. It consists of a trilingual inscription, the same text in three languages: Akkadian, Persian, and Elamite. In the nineteenth century this paralleled the Rosetta Stone (also trilingual, which enabled decipherment of Egyptian hieroglyphics) as a means for deciphering Akkadian and the two other languages. Unlike the Rosetta Stone, where one of the three languages was known (Greek), the three languages and scripts on the Behistun Monument were all undeciphered. Building on the work of earlier scholars such as Carsten Niebuhr and Georg F. Grotefend, Sir Henry Rawlinson copied the Behistun Inscription and published it (1847–51). The work of these and others led to the decipherment of Old Persian and the important language of Akkadian, with its dialects of Assyrian and Babylonian.

which took advantage of existing communities with their main temple as the center of the local economy. While recognizing a diversity in the patterns of local and regional administration, the construction of the temple, as proposed by Zechariah and Haggai, would provide a center for Persian economic and security interests in Judea. Thus the divine visions were not encouragements toward rebellion against the Persians but coincided with imperial interests.

Some of the images in the visions have a rich heritage in the iconographic traditions of the ancient world. Thus the horses in Zechariah 1:8 and 6:1–8 have a long-standing association with warfare. Compare the other references to horses in Zechariah 9:10; 10:3, 5; 12:4; 14:15, and 20. In contrast, donkeys and other beasts of burden can be used for peaceful purposes. Nevertheless, in Zechariah 9:9 the picture of a donkey ridden by a king is not without parallel. Solomon appears in such a manner as chosen by his father David to succeed him as king (1 Kings 1:33, 38, 44). The use of a donkey by a king who does not wish to prosecute war occurs already in the eighteenth-century-BC Mari texts.[10] An emphasis on lowliness and humility in Zechariah 9:9 reflects the king's humble obedience to God as a model for those loyal to him to follow.

Canonical Context

For the connection between Zechariah and Ezra and Nehemiah, see the discussion for those books (above).

10. For example, ARM 6 76:20–24; cf. Bodi, "Story of Samuel, Saul, and David," 212–14.

© Baker Publishing Group and Dr. James C. Martin
Assyrian war chariot

In the New Testament, many images in Zechariah receive significant development in Revelation. Thus Revelation 1:12 and 4:5 picture seven lampstands and a lampstand with seven lamps. The latter remains closest to the lampstand imagery of Zechariah 4:1–10, but the Revelation 1:12 image may also have borrowed from this text. Zechariah 1:7–10 and 6:1–8 clearly anticipate the four horsemen of Revelation 6.

Texts such as Zechariah 9:9–10 and 12:10 are recounted in several places in the Gospels, where they characterize Jesus's entry into Jerusalem and his death on the cross. In Matthew 21:5–7 and John 12:14–15 Jesus rides into Jerusalem on Palm Sunday on a donkey. This evokes the image of the king coming into Jerusalem.

In Zechariah 11:10–15 God's covenant of favor with the nations is broken. The result is a payment of thirty pieces of silver, given to the potter. Matthew 26:14–16 and 27:4–10 understand this text as a reference to the pay Judas receives for betraying Jesus, the return of the pay to the temple, and its use to buy the potter's field for the burial of foreigners.

Zechariah 12:10–14 describes how God's people will mourn for the one they have pierced. This finds fulfillment in the piercing of Jesus's body on the cross (John 19:34, 37). Zechariah 14:4 and the Lord's position on the Mount of Olives, where it is split apart, may be alluded to in the tearing of the temple curtain from top to bottom (Matt. 27:51). The Lord's appearance on this site is also suggested by the location of the ascension (Acts 1:9–12).

Theological Perspectives of Zechariah

As already noticed, the first six verses of the book, and especially verse 3, describe the main theological theme of the book (1:2 NIV): "This is what the Lord Almighty says: 'Return to me,' declares the Lord Almighty, 'and I will return to you,' says the Lord Almighty." Here is the urgent call to repentance, so characteristic of the writing prophets of the Old Testament. This is set within historical reflection on the disobedience of past generations and the judgment that resulted. Yet surrounding and permeating this call to repentance is the emphasis that these words come from "the Lord Almighty." This is the God who controls the fate of Israel. The local rulers and governors are not in charge. Insofar as they are chosen by God and draw their life and strength from dependence on him (Zech. 3, 4, and 6), they will be allowed to rule and even be exalted in God's plan and time. Those who reject God and practice wickedness (Zech. 5) will be removed and taken far away. Therefore the people must trust in God, not in their sense of what would be best for them at this moment.

But the threefold emphasis on the title "Lord Almighty" also teaches that God controls the whole world, both the regions around Judea (Zech. 9–11) and even Persia (Zech. 1–2) and all nations (Zech. 12–14). Thus the people should understand that their focus must be on their relationship with the Almighty, not on determining the best course of action to take advantage of the political circumstances. There is much debate about the meaning and significance of Zechariah 9–14. However, these chapters describe a kingly figure who, in the midst of judgment and blessing for Jerusalem and the people of God, does appear and is victorious. Beyond this, the messianic significance is developed and applied to Jesus Christ by the New Testament writers (see "Canonical Context," above).

In light of this, the true course of repentance will no longer come through a series of annual fasts (Zech. 7). At the center of Zechariah's prophecies are questions about fasting in the fifth month (Ab), when the first temple fell (586 BC; 2 Kings 25:8–9), and in the seventh month (Tishri), when the last righteous king, Josiah, was killed (609 BC). Instead of fasting, the people must understand that God has punished the previous generations with the exile (7:4–14) and now insists that they show mercy and compassion toward one another as a means of daily living. This is the background for the promise to restore Jerusalem and the command, anticipated time and again throughout the book, to rebuild the temple (8:1–17). If the people are able to carry this out in faithfulness, "the Lord Almighty" will bring times of rejoicing instead of fasting. And this will become the means by which Israel will both find God and be a witness to the whole world.

Key Commentaries and Studies

Baldwin, Joyce. *Haggai, Zechariah, Malachi: An Introduction and Commentary*. TOTC. Leicester, UK: Inter-Varsity; Downers Grove, IL: InterVarsity, 1972. A fine exegetical and literary interpretation of the book from an evangelical perspective.

Boda, Mark J. *The Book of Zechariah*. NICOT. Grand Rapids: Eerdmans, 2016. Best exegesis and study of the theological message.

Meyers, Carol L., and Eric M. Meyers. *Haggai, Zechariah 1–8: A New Translation with Introduction and Commentary*. AB 25B. New Haven: Yale University Press, 2004. Excellent study of the exegesis and archaeological/historical background.

———. *Zechariah 9–14: A New Translation with Introduction and Commentary*. AB 25C. New Haven: Yale University Press, 1998. Strong on analysis of the Hebrew and the archaeological background.

Wolters, Al. *Zechariah*. HCOT. Leiden: Peeters, 2014. Careful literary analysis.

35

MALACHI

No one likes to be last. But Malachi is not so much the last of the prophets as he is one who anticipates the coming of the future. The Old Testament may come to an end here, but the message of Malachi prepares the reader for the coming world and its promise of salvation.

Name, Text, and Outline

The name Malachi means "my messenger." The word for messenger (Heb. *mal'āk*) often appears as "angel" in the Old Testament. The same form as the name Malachi appears in 3:1 as "my messenger," who will appear ahead of God's own coming. The name appears on the fragment of a jug handle from Arad, dated to the late period of the monarchy.[1] It therefore serves as a bona fide personal name rather than just a common noun in the Old Testament.[2]

The text of Malachi is generally well preserved in the Masoretic Text. At Qumran, 4Q76 and fragments preserving 1:13–14 and 2:10–4:6 (3:24 MT) include variant readings closer to the Greek (LXX) than the Masoretic Text. The major difficulties with the Hebrew text occur in 2:15–16, where there may have been corruptions or changes by the scribes who copied these texts.

1. Aharoni, *Arad Inscriptions*, 109.

2. "Malachi" should be understood as referencing a person by that name, not an anonymous prophet simply called "my messenger."

OUTLINE

I. Superscription (1:1)
II. Disputes (1:2–4:3 [3:21 MT])
    A. God Loves His People (1:2–5)
    B. Judgment against the Corrupt Priests (1:6–2:9)
    C. Judgment against the Faithless People (2:10–16)
    D. God's Justice and Messenger (2:17–3:5)
    E. Repentance (3:6–12)
    F. Future Day of Judgment (3:13–4:3 [3:21 MT])
III. Epilogue (4:4–6 [3:22–24 MT])
    A. Obey God's Law (4:4 [3:22 MT])
    B. God Will Send Elijah Again (4:5–6 [3:23–24 MT])

Overview of Malachi

The text is introduced as Yahweh's word through Malachi. God declares that he loves his people (1:2–5). The people ask how this is so. God introduces the story of his love for Jacob and hatred of Esau. Esau's land of Edom is a wasteland. Edom will always stand under God's anger. Despite God's love for Israel, the people do not show their respect for God, as a child might to a parent. They present lame and diseased animals at the sacrifices. They are told to close the temple doors, because God does not accept such offerings. However, the nations across the world will honor and bring pure offerings to him (1:6–11). God curses those who vow good animals from their flocks but bring him diseased ones instead. They do not fear him as he is to be feared by the world (1:12–14).

The priests have not honored God's name, and so he will curse them with defilement. Levi was upright and dedicated to God, and so God made a covenant of life and peace (2:1–6) with him. The priest should guide people with the message of God, but these priests have caused many to stumble (2:7–9).

Malachi asks whether all the people have God as their Creator and common Father. Yet they do not treat one another as brothers. They marry outside of Israel and commit to women who worship other deities. God will cut such a person off from his community (2:10–12). The people don't understand why God withholds blessing, yet they have acted unfaithfully to the wife they first married when they were young. God condemns this and describes divorce as hating one's wife and violently abusing her (2:13–16).

God will send his messenger to prepare his way and bring the fire of purification on the priests so that God's people will bring righteous offerings. God will put on trial and testify against all sorcerers, adulterers, perjurers, and those who defraud and oppress the vulnerable (2:17–3:5).

Because God keeps his earlier promises, he does not destroy Israel altogether. He does want them to change their ways and stop robbing him. They withhold the tithes and offerings that belong to God. If they bring these, God will bless them in abundance (3:6–12).

There are two groups of people, in the opinion of those who argue arrogantly against God that serving him is futile (3:13–16). First, there are those who do evil and prosper, even when they put God to the test. Second, there are those who fear God and gain nothing for it. God then has the names of those who fear him recorded. When God acts, he will spare and bless the righteous (3:17–18). Those who do evil will face a fiery destruction. The righteous will have victory over the wicked and enjoy God's blessings (4:1–3 [3:19–21 MT]).

The command is given to remember (and thus obey) God's law given to Moses on Mount Horeb for all Israel (4:4 [3:22 MT]). Before the "great and terrible day of the Lord," God will send the prophet Elijah, who will bring reconciliation between parents and children so that God need not devote the land to destruction (4:5–6 [3:23–24 MT]).

Reading Malachi

Premodern Readings

At Qumran and with other contemporary Jewish groups, there persisted the idea of a divine record book (e.g., CD 20.18–21).[3] The Damascus Document cites Malachi 1:10 to describe their obedience to God (CD 6.13–14). Early Christians used Malachi to emphasize the need to reference God in ministry. Augustine (*ad Simplicianium* 1.2) found in Malachi evidence for God's choice or election of his people based purely on divine grace (cf. Caesarius of Arles in the sixth century AD). Malachi's vision of God's worship by the world appears in the *Didache* (14) and in the patristic period (e.g., Augustine and John Chrysostom).

Both early Jewish and Christian writers connect the reference to Elijah with the Messiah. As early as the intertestamental period Sirach (48:10) refers to Elijah's reappearance (Mal. 4:5–6 [3:23–24 MT]). Elijah's specific role of revealing the messiah was known in Judaism (*Mekilta* on Exod. 16:33) and early Christian tradition (Justin Martyr, *Dialogue with Trypho*, chaps. 49, 117). The third-century Christian writer Hippolytus (*Antichrist*) and the *Apocalypse of Elijah* both emphasize the role of Elijah as one of the two witnesses (cf. Rev. 11:6) already mentioned in Malachi. Justin Martyr may be the first to refer to Jesus Christ with Malachi's title "Sun of Righteousness" (Mal. 4:2 [3:20 MT]).

3. Cook, "Malachi," 40.

Higher Criticism

Most of this prophetic book involves the continuation and development of existing theological ideas and wording. There is general agreement on placing the date of composition in the fifth century BC. This is supported by the book's position as last (and so latest) in the Twelve Minor Prophets. There are similar social and religious concerns as found in Ezra and Nehemiah: corrupt priests (Mal. 1:6–2:9), mixed marriages and divorces (2:10–16), the lack of giving to God's work (3:8–12), and injustice (3:5).[4] However, Malachi also has similarities with Haggai and Zechariah. Thus there is the rulership of a governor (Hag. 1:1; Zech. 4, esp. v. 14, "two anointed ones";[5] Mal. 1:8), a temple in Jerusalem (Hag. 1:14; Zech. 7:1–3; Mal. 1:10–14), and general problems economically and spiritually (Hag. 1:5–6; Zech. 8:12–13; Mal. 3:8–15).[6] This context, along with the absence of a royal figure and Malachi's preoccupation with God acting to affect the whole world, fits well into the context of Persia versus the Greeks during the first quarter of the fifth century BC.

Malachi's message is directed against the religious establishment. Some suggest that he may have been a Levite who functioned in the priestly roles (see Deut. 18:1; 33:10; Jer. 33:18, 21–22) and criticized the Zadokite and Aaronite priestly leadership, using a familiar text such as Numbers 6:24–26 and inverting it to sting these elites (Mal. 1:8–9).[7] Certainly the privilege is given to Levi (Mal. 2:4–5), and the possible presumed relationship comes to children of the same father (Lev. 2:10). However, it is not so clear whether Malachi's concern for priestly systems and responsibilities (1:6–13; 2:1–4, 8–9; 3:3–4, 8–11) requires readers to count him as a Levite in the system or as a critic from the outside. While texts such as 2:7 and 11 reflect priestly responsibilities that have been ignored (e.g., Lev. 10:10), other texts such as Malachi 3:8–12 address the duties of all Israel. And 4:5–6 (3:23–24) emphasizes the prophetic tradition, not just the priestly and Levitical roles.

Literary Readings

Malachi consists of judgment speeches within which occur disputations, perhaps reminiscent of the courtroom. Scholars have also identified lawsuits that evoke appeals to God's covenant, a covenant that Israel and its religious leaders have violated. The disputation may include a claim, a hypothetical audience response, and an answer that leaves the guilty with no further recourse. For example, Malachi 1:6a accuses the priests of displaying contempt for God's name. In verse 6b they provide a response: "How have we

4. So Hill ("Malachi," 526), who compares Ezra 9:1–15; Neh. 5:1–13; 12:30, 44–47; 13:4–31.
5. Cf. "Ancient Near Eastern Context" for Zechariah, above.
6. Hill, "Malachi," 526.
7. Cook, "Malachi," 36.

shown contempt for your name?" (NIV). The text of 1:7a explains how: "by offering defiled food" on God's altar. The priestly retort ("How have we defiled you?") appears to ignore this. The following verse goes on to provide concrete evidence with respect to the offering of blind, lame, and diseased animals.

© Baker Publishing Group and Dr. James C. Martin

Winged disk, a symbol of Judean kingship (ca. 700 BC)

Malachi employs striking images and symbols in the process: "refiner's fire" and "fuller's soap" for purification (3:2), a book of remembrance for deeds and destinies (Mal. 3:16; cf. Esther 6:1), the "furnace" as a symbol of divine judgment (Mal. 4:1 NIV [3:19 MT]), and "the sun of righteousness . . . with healing in its wings" (Mal. 4:2 [3:20 MT]).[8] The last image is almost certainly borrowed from the winged sun, which plays a central role in the imperial art of Persia and may relate to preexilic winged sun discs discovered in Israel and Judah.

Gender and Ideological Criticism

The references to fathers (Mal. 1:6; 2:10; 3:7; 4:6 [3:24 MT]), brothers (1:2; 2:10), and sons (1:6; 3:3, 6, 17; 4:6 [3:24 MT]), along with the exclusive male priesthood and male Levites, largely exclude the feminine presence, certainly from direct address in the leadership.[9] Even the references to God emphasize male roles in the West Semitic world, those of Father and Creator (2:10).

The focus of 2:11–16 considers the divorce of women who are daughters "of a foreign god." The first part of verse 11 calls a feminine Judah unfaithful. However, the remainder of the verse, where Judah desecrates the sanctuary and marries the daughter of a foreign god, uses the masculine verb form. This female connection with unfaithfulness is set in the context of foreign wives, who lead their husbands away from faithfulness to God. In contrast, 2:14–16 elevates the original and presumably faithful Judean wives to a place of honor, requiring faithfulness to them. Marie-Theres Wacker notes the symbolic nature of these texts, dichotomizing women between good women and bad women.[10] This, however, is not so surprising, because all human groups (priests, officials, Judeans) are dichotomized. Indeed, in every case the question is not so much one of class, gender, or ethnicity. It is rather a question of faithfulness to God's covenant, whether for the present generation or for generations of ancestors, such as Jacob and Esau.

8. Hill, "Malachi," 531–32.

9. For Levites, however, see Wacker, "Malachi," 473–79, and her discussion of the women with bronze mirrors at the tent of meeting who may have had a Levitical function (Exod. 38:8).

10. Ibid., 480–81.

Elephantine and the Jews of the Fifth Century BC

An archive of Aramaic papyri records was discovered early in the twentieth century. It dates from the last two decades of the fifth century BC and was found in Upper Egypt on an island on the Nile known as Elephantine. Here was stationed a mercenary colony of Jews and others during that century. They and their families left behind a collection that includes records of marriages (with divorce clauses), sales, wills, and dowries. This archive forms the earliest such collection of documents detailing life in a Jewish society. The colony represents the widespread functional literacy of the era. Among 130 separate witnesses, only five could not write their own names. These Jews intermarried, and hence syncretism can be found among them. However, many preserved their faith in the God "Yaho" (Yahu/Yaho Ṣĕbāʾôt = Lord of hosts), a form of "Yahweh" found in personal names and poetry in the earlier and later Old Testament writings. These Jews had a temple that had been destroyed by their local enemies. They requested permission from the Jerusalem temple priesthood to rebuild it. The official priestly leaders in Jerusalem gave them the right to rebuild the temple but limited their sacrifices to those without blood. Their documents also preserve interest in the cultic calendar as far as rituals and feasts are concerned. These concerns reflect the same ones as found in Malachi and other biblical witnesses from the fifth century BC.[a]

[a] Lemaire, "Fifth- and Fourth-Century Issues," 411–13; Porten and Yardeni, *Aramaic Documents from Egypt*.

Ancient Near Eastern Context

The Persian rulers during the first part of the fifth century were Darius and Xerxes. For some of their history, see "Ancient Near Eastern Background" for Ezra and Nehemiah and for Esther. In the context of Jerusalem, the events of the 480s BC would have been surprising and unsettling. For centuries the center of imperial power had come from the northeast, from Assyria, Babylon, and Persia. During this decade, that focus fell under threat from the west, from the Greek states and their ability to thwart Persian advances. Xerxes succeeded his father and took power in 486 BC. In 480 BC he marched on Greece. After initial success at Thermopylae and Athens, Xerxes fought a key naval battle at Salamis in September 480 BC. Destruction of most of the Persian fleet at Salamis and the defeat of the army at Platea must have left many in the eastern Mediterranean wondering about the future. In such a world the prophet Malachi could have arisen to command purity and obedience among the people as a prelude to the next events that God had planned for them. Furthermore, if relatively small Greek city-states could defeat Persia's military might, the God of Israel could certainly alter the world according to his own purpose. This perspective provides the background for Malachi's message. He foresees the name of God as honored among the nations who worship him, fear him, and bless Israel (Mal. 1:11, 14; 3:12).

Although it is clear that at some point during the following century, Ezra brings a copy of the law and proclaims it to the people of Jerusalem, it also seems true that many of the concerns (see "Higher Criticism," above) are those of Malachi. While this may suggest a later date for this prophet, it is also possible that Malachi saw some of the same issues emerging. Although there may not have been a scribe like Ezra, the people had sufficient understanding of the law and covenantal requirements for Malachi to appeal to them. His focus on moral and ethical matters, integrated with the religious concerns, brought the people to realize their covenant before God and their calling as an organized temple community in the imperial context.[11]

Canonical Context

Malachi uses and adapts a complex variety of Old Testament texts, drawing especially from the Genesis narratives, the Covenant Code of Exodus 20:22–23:33, the Holiness Code of Leviticus 17–26, Deuteronomy, and other poetic materials in the Deuteronomistic History and in the prophets and Psalms. Karl Weyde provides a summary of the materials used.[12] Judgments against Edom (e.g., Obadiah; Jer. 49:7–22; Amos 9:12; etc.) are found in a salvation oracle for Israel (Mal. 1:3–5). Levitical laws on burnt offerings (Lev. 1; 6:9–12; 22:17–19) provide a foundation for Malachi 1:7–8 and sacrifices. The use of curses for breaking covenant (Mal. 2:2–3) occurs in Deuteronomy 28:15–68. For the one whose covenant is with God (Mal. 2:5–6), compare the Servant Songs of Isaiah 42:1–4; 49:1–4; 52:13–53:12. Malachi 2:14–16 reflects and develops the monogamous marriage commitment of Genesis 2:23–24, anticipating the stringent demands of Jesus and Paul in the New Testament (Matt. 19:11; 1 Cor. 7:1–16). God's eternal existence ensures his faithfulness (Mal. 3:6; Exod. 6:5; Lev. 26:40–42; Ps. 111:9; Jer. 31:20). In terms of the specific concerns of intermarriage, divorce, and maintaining the temple cult, the reader finds echoes in Chronicles, Ezra, and Nehemiah.

Malachi 4:4–6 (3:22–24 MT) concludes the entire collection of the prophets.[13] These verses assert the essential link between the Law of Moses and the Prophets that cannot be broken. They suggest that the prophetic word has ended until Elijah will appear again before "the Day of the Lord."

The New Testament reflects back on Malachi, such as the reference to loving Jacob and not Esau in Romans 9:13 (cf. Mal. 1:2). The book is especially

11. See "Gender and Ideological Criticism" for Ezra and Nehemiah.

12. Weyde, *Prophecy and Teaching*, 400–401.

13. Ibid., 388–92.

important in its anticipation of the messenger who prepares the way for God's own appearance (Mal. 3:1; 4:5–6 [3:23–24 MT]). Elijah is understood in part as reflected in the ministry of John the Baptist in anticipation of Jesus (Matt. 11:14), since John also preached repentance, purification, and preparation (Luke 3:4–9). Some also find Elijah in the role of one of the two witnesses of Revelation 11:3–12. More explicitly, the scroll of remembrance with the names of the righteous (Dan. 12:1; Mal. 3:16) anticipates Revelation 20:12.

Theological Perspectives of Malachi

The text of Malachi expounds the nature and character of God.[14] God, the Creator and Father of Israel (Mal. 1:6), is its master and king (1:14). He rules over the world, but Israel is his special treasure (1:2, 3–5, 11, 14; 3:17). However, God will purify his people (3:2–3). God made a covenant with his adopted child Israel (1:2, 6; 2:10). He requires Israel's obedience and readiness to repent (3:7, 16–18) in order to restore proper worship (3:3–4). God does not change (3:6): he will remain faithful to his covenant with Israel.

Israel should love God with proper worship (1:10–14) and should love its vulnerable neighbors as well (3:5). The people have sought the God of justice as one who, perhaps by bringing in the new covenant (Jer. 31:31–34), would no longer allow the wicked to prosper (Mal. 3:14–15) but would hold one another accountable for their own sins (John 9:2–3).

Marriage is a sacred covenant and a joint commitment to raise godly children (Mal. 2:14–16). This marriage covenant lies within the greater covenant of the God of Israel.[15] This covenant anticipates the call to a higher ethic by Jesus and Paul, as mentioned above.

Key Commentaries and Studies

Baldwin, Joyce G. *Haggai, Zechariah, Malachi: An Introduction and Commentary.* TOTC. Leicester, UK: Inter-Varsity; Downers Grove, IL: InterVarsity, 1972. Gems of exegetical insight.

Hill, Andrew E. *Haggai, Zechariah, and Malachi: An Introduction and Commentary.* TOTC 28. Leicester, UK: IVP Academic, 2012. Great evangelical perspectives on background, literary aspects, and theology.

———. *Malachi: A New Translation with Introduction and Commentary.* AB 25D. New York: Doubleday, 1998. Best on analysis and exegesis; written by an evangelical.

O'Brien, Julia M. *Nahum, Habakkuk, Zephaniah, Haggai, Zechariah, Malachi.* Abingdon Old Testament Commentaries. Nashville: Abingdon, 2004. Good literary analysis.

14. Hill, "Malachi," 530–31.

15. See Hugenberger, *Marriage as a Covenant*, 339–43.

Petersen, David L. *Zechariah 9–14 and Malachi: A Commentary*. OTL. Louisville: Westminster John Knox, 1995. Important for theological perspectives.

Petterson, Anthony R. *Haggai, Zechariah and Malachi*. AOTC 25. Leicester, UK: Inter-Varsity Press, 2015. Strong on literary and textual matters affecting exegesis.

Smith, Ralph L. *Micah–Malachi*. WBC 32. Waco: Word, 1984. Useful for a close study of text-critical issues.

TRANSITION

One of the Old Testament scholars who most influenced me in his spiritual life was Dr. Geoffrey Grogan, principal of the Bible Training Institute in Glasgow, where I had the privilege of teaching for six years. A few years ago Dr. Grogan was diagnosed with an illness that the medical profession referred to as "terminal." The gentle giant (as he was known for his physical and spiritual stature) responded, "It is not terminal, but transitional."

As we noted at the beginning of this book, the term "Old Testament" signifies that something more is coming. The Old Testament prepares the way. However, it does not do this so that we can discard it with the appearance of the New Testament. Instead, it provides the absolutely essential foundation for all that follows. Without the Old Testament, the New Testament would have no meaning. Its value and the value of all that flows from it would be compromised, as the words and work of Jesus Christ and his apostles would appear odd. Indeed, the name Jesus Christ would lose its significance.

But there is a further point here. It is too easy to give "lip service" to the Old Testament as foundational and not to understand how this calls us to change our perspectives on how we read and study this book as Christians. Some years ago a colleague and I interviewed a student who wished to graduate from the school where I was teaching. With regard to gender roles in ministry, my colleague was a complementarian and I was (and am) an egalitarian. The issue arose in the interview. When the two of us were together alone later, my friend challenged me regarding my position as an egalitarian. He went on for some time, while I listened and considered how I could respond. I suggested that a significant part of our differences arose from how we approached the Bible. He approached the New Testament first and read the relevant sections of the Old Testament in light of his understanding of what the Epistles were teaching. I began with the Old Testament and attempted to understand these books first. Only then would I look at the New Testament as a commentary and development of that first and prior testament. This led us in two different directions. I suspect many aspects of our beliefs and practices result in different outcomes depending on where we begin in our study of the Bible's teaching.

Perhaps more than any other unifying doctrine the Old Testament teaches us about loving God and loving one another. We looked at these two emphases in the theology of Genesis. As we moved through the books of the Old Testament these elements regularly recurred. We may love God by being faithful to him like Abraham, by studying and following his Torah, by living day by day and making the difficult decisions to follow him as illustrated in the Historical Books, by orienting our lives to contemplation, praise, lament, and thanksgiving before him as with the Psalms and Wisdom literature, and by hearing personally the indictments against our own complacencies and outright sins as in the words of the prophets. All of these are background, though necessary background, to understand and to appreciate the great lover of the Father, his son Jesus Christ.

We may love our neighors by practicing intercessory prayer for them (as Abraham and Sarah in Gen. 20), by modeling the character and values of a life lived in faithfulness to God as described in the Torah and Wisdom literature, by seeing the day-to-day examples and failures of the Old Testament people who lived out their lives as recounted in the Historical Books, and by putting into practice the concerns of the Law and the prophets to show justice and mercy toward all those who are our neighbors and share the image of God. In so doing, we understand and come to appreciate the One who loved his neighbors self-sacrificially to the point of death, Jesus Christ.

In reviewing the material covered in this introduction to the Old Testament, we can see how the name and text of each book provides an essential foundation for all teaching within the Old Testament as well as in the New Testament and later intepretation. The Outline and Overview sections build on this by identifying the essential story, sections, and instruction given in each book. Together they provide us with a window into the contents of the Old Testament and a resource for seeing its appropriation.

The Reading section for each book allows us to think through the many approaches to reading the Old Testament and to gather insights into its importance for the church and synagogue through the ages, for critics and scholars of ancient literature and history, for our global world and postmodern methods, and for the intertextual discussion within the Old and New Testaments. No longer have we studied the Old Testament when we have understood the current theories of higher criticism. No longer have we exhausted the meaning of a book when we have examined its significance elsewhere in the canon and in the history of interpretation. All of these are essential to the art of interpretation, but they are not sufficient. If this volume has served its purpose, it has demonstrated that the full exposition of the Old Testament is as rich and multifaceted as human history and thought. This is not an attempt to provide a comprehensive assessment of every view (or even every major view), but it is an argument that an introduction to the Old Testament must embrace an awareness of the many methods that now flourish.

The survey of the variety of methods prepares for the final section of each chapter, that concerning theological and ethical perspectives. By examining key texts in a verse-by-verse manner (e.g., Gen. 1) or tracing broad themes such as God's covenant, his grace, his kingdom, sin, repentance, redemption, worship, and the new creation, we consider some of the major theological themes and ethical issues that provide the basis for the New Testament story of Christ the Messiah, of salvation, and of the church.

Imbued with love and holiness, God the Father sent his Son to bring light and life into a dying world. That mission of God began with creation and the inauguration of the human story in Genesis. It continued with the formation of God's people, Israel, and it grew in the figures that God used in his mission of blessing the world and bringing it back to the full life of a relationship with him. We study and learn of God's mission as we understand the Old Testament and allow it to change us. We become like Christ as we allow God to send us into the world. Following Abram, who left his homeland to be a blessing; Moses, who left the security of royal life and then a desert family to free God's people; Deborah, who left her support role in Israel to bring victory against the nation's fiercest enemies; David, who left his sheep to shepherd God's people of his day and to become a symbol of God's present and future redemption; or the prophets, who left every type of occupation and position in society in order to follow God wherever that led and to proclaim his message fearlessly, we stand in a great host of believers and actors whom God has used to bless the world through the grace of redemption brought, above all, by the salvation that Jesus Christ earned. May we see and live out the *missio dei*, the great mission of God, that we now come to participate in and that God the Father has sent through the work of his Son and the ongoing presence and power of the Holy Spirit.

BIBLIOGRAPHY

Ackerman, James S. Review of *The Fate of King Saul: An Interpretation of a Biblical Story*, by David M. Gunn. *JBL* 101 (1982): 438–39.

Ackerman, Susan. "Digging Up Deborah: Recent Hebrew Bible Scholarship on Gender and the Contribution of Archaeology." *NEA* 66 (2003): 172–84.

Ackroyd, Peter R. "Studies in the Book of Haggai." *JJS* 2 (1951): 163–76; 3 (1952): 1–13.

Adamo, David Tuesday. "Psalms." Pages 151–62 in *Global Bible Commentary*. Edited by Daniel Patte. Nashville: Abingdon, 2004.

Adeyemo, Tokunboh. "Daniel." Pages 989–1012 in *Africa Bible Commentary*. Edited by Tokunboh Adeyemo. Nairobi: Word Alive Publishers; Grand Rapids: Zondervan, 2006.

Aharoni, Yohanan. *Arad Inscriptions*. Judean Desert Studies. Jerusalem: Israel Exploration Society, 1981.

Aḥituv, Shmuel. *Echoes from the Past: Hebrew and Cognate Inscriptions from the Biblical Period*. Translated and edited by Anson F. Rainey. A Carta Handbook. Jerusalem: Carta, 2008.

Åhlström, Gösta W. *The History of Ancient Palestine from the Palaeolithic Period to Alexander's Conquest*. Edited by D. Edelman. JSOTSup 146. Sheffield: JSOT Press, 1993.

Albertz, Rainer. "Deuteronomistic History and the Heritage of the Prophets." Pages 343–67 in *Congress Volume Helsinki 2010*. Edited by Martti Nissinen. VTSup 148. Leiden: Brill, 2012.

———. *A History of Israelite Religion in the Old Testament Period*. Translated by John Bowden. 2 vols. Louisville: Westminster John Knox, 1994.

Albertz, Rainer, and Rüdiger Schmitt. *Family and Household Religion in Ancient Israel and the Levant*. Winona Lake, IN: Eisenbrauns, 2012.

Albright, William F. "Abram the Hebrew: A New Archaeological Interpretation." *BASOR* 163 (1961): 36–54.

———. "Archaic Survivals in the Text of Canticles." Pages 1–7 in *Hebrew and Semitic Studies in the Text of Canticles*. Edited by D. Winton Thomas and W. D. McHardy. Oxford: Clarendon, 1963.

———. "The Psalm of Habakkuk." Pages 1–18 in *Studies in Old Testament Prophecy Presented to Professor Theodore H. Robinson*. Edited by H. H. Rowley. Edinburgh: T&T Clark, 1950.

———. "Some Canaanite-Phoenician Sources of Wisdom." Pages 1–15 in *Wisdom in Israel and in the Ancient Near East: Presented to Harold Henry Rowley by the Society for Old Testament Study in Association with the Editorial Board of Vetus Testamentum, in Celebration of His Sixty-Fifth Birthday, 24 March 1955*. Edited by M. Noth and D. Winton Thomas. VTSup 3. Leiden: Brill, 1969.

Alden, Robert A. *Job*. NAC 11. Nashville: Broadman & Holman, 1994.

Alexander, T. Desmond. "The Passover Sacrifice." Pages 1–24 in *Sacrifice in the Bible*. Edited by Roger T. Beckwith and Marvin J. Selman. Carlisle, UK: Paternoster; Grand Rapids: Baker, 1995.

Allen, Joel S. "Job 3: History of Interpretation." *DOTWPW* 361–71.

Allen, Leslie C. *The Books of Joel, Obadiah, Jonah, and Micah*. NICOT. Grand Rapids: Eerdmans, 1971.

———. *Ezekiel*. Vol. 1, *1–19*. Vol. 2, *20–48*. WBC 28–29. Waco: Word, 1990–94.

———. *Jeremiah: A Commentary*. OTL. Louisville: Westminster John Knox, 2008.

Allen, Leslie C., and Timothy S. Laniak. *Ezra, Nehemiah, Esther*. NIBC. Peabody, MA: Hendrickson, 2003.

Alt, Albrecht. "Die Rolle Samarias bei der Entstehung des Judentums." Pages 5–28 in *Die zehn Gebote in der christlichen Verkündigen: Festschrift Otto Procksch zum 60. Geburtstag am 9. August 1934 überreicht*. Edited by Friedrich Baumgärtel. Leipzig: Deichert, 1934. Repr. pages 316–37 in vol. 2 of Albrecht Alt, *Kleine Schriften zur Geschichte des Volkes Israel*. Munich: C. H. Beck, 1953.

———. "The God of the Fathers." Pages 1–77 in *Essays in Old Testament History and Religion*. Translated by R. A. Wilson. Sheffield: Sheffield Academic, 1989.

———. "The Origins of Israelite Law." Pages 79–132 in *Essays in Old Testament History and Religion*. Translated by R. A. Wilson. Sheffield: Sheffield Academic, 1989.

Alter, Robert. *The Art of Biblical Narrative*. New York: Basic Books, 1981.

———. *The Art of Biblical Poetry*. New York: Basic Books, 1985.

Althann, Robert. "Reflections on the Text of the Book of Job." Pages 7–13 in *Sôfer Mahîr: Essays in Honour of Adrian Schenker Offered by the Editors of "Biblia Hebraica Quinta."* Edited by Yohahan A. P. Goldman, Arie van der Kooij, and Richard D. Weis. VTSup 110. Leiden: Brill, 2006.

American Consul at Jerusalem. "Remarkable Details from American Consul, on Palestine Locust Plague." *New York Times*, November 21, 1915, http://query.nytimes.com/mem/archive-free/pdf?res=9F05E4DB153BE233A25752C2A9679D946496D6CF.

Amit, Yaira. "'Am I Not More Devoted to You Than Ten Sons?' (1 Samuel 1.8): Male and Female Interpretations." Pages 68–76 in *A Feminist Companion to Samuel and Kings*. Edited by A. Brenner. FCB 5. Sheffield: Sheffield Academic, 1994.

———. *The Book of Judges: The Art of Editing*. Translated by Jonathan Chipman. Leiden: Brill, 1999.

———. *Reading Biblical Narratives: Literary Criticism and the Hebrew Bible*. Philadelphia: Fortress, 2001.

———. "The Saul Polemic in the Persian Period." Pages 647–61 in *Judah and the Judeans in the Persian Period*. Edited by O. Lipschits and M. Oeming. Winona Lake, IN: Eisenbrauns, 2006.

Andersen, Francis I. *Habakkuk: A New Translation with Introduction and Commentary*. AB 25. New York: Doubleday, 2001.

———. *Job: An Introduction and Commentary*. TOTC. Leicester, UK: Inter-Varsity; Downers Grove, IL: InterVarsity, 1976.

Andersen, Francis I., and David Noel Freedman. *Amos: A New Translation with Introduction and Commentary*. AB 24A. New York: Doubleday, 1989.

———. *Hosea: A New Translation with Introduction and Commentary*. AB 24. Garden City, NY: Doubleday, 1980.

———. *Micah: A New Translation with Introduction and Commentary*. AB 24E. New York: Doubleday, 2000.

Anderson, William H. U. *The Pessimistic Theology of Qoheleth*. Lewiston, NY: Mellen, 1997.

Arnold, Bill T. "Deuteronomy 12 and the Law of the Central Sanctuary *noch einmal*." *VT* 64 (2014): 227–48.

———. *1 and 2 Samuel*. NIVAC. Grand Rapids: Zondervan, 2003.

———. *Genesis*. NCBC. Cambridge: Cambridge University Press, 2009.

———. "Samuel, Books of." *DOTHB* 866–77.

Arnold, William R. "The Composition of Nahum 1:2–2:3." *ZAW* 21 (1901): 225–65.

Ashley, Timothy R. *The Book of Numbers.* NICOT. Grand Rapids: Eerdmans, 1993.

Assis, Eliyahu. *Self-Interest or Communal Interest: An Ideology of Leadership in the Gideon, Abimelech and Jephthah Narratives (Judg 6–12).* VTSup 106. Leiden: Brill, 2005.

Augustine. *St. Augustin: Expositions on the Book of Psalms.* A Select Library of Nicene and Post-Nicene Fathers of the Christian Church, vol. 8. Edited by Philip Schaff. Edinburgh: T&T Clark, 1886.

Auld, A. Graeme. *Joshua: Jesus Son of Nauē in Codex Vaticanus.* SCS. Leiden: Brill, 2005.

———. *Kings without Privilege: David and Moses in the Story of the Bible's Kings.* Edinburgh: T&T Clark, 1994.

Avigad, Nahman. *Bullae and Seals from a Post-exilic Judean Archive.* Qedem 4. Jerusalem: Institute of Archaeology, Hebrew University, 1976.

Avner, Uzi. "Mazzebot Sites in the Negev and Sinai and Their Significance." Pages 166–81 in *Biblical Archaeology Today, 1990: Proceedings of the Second International Congress on Biblical Archaeology, Jerusalem, June–July 1990.* Edited by A. Biran and J. Aviram. Jerusalem: Israel Exploration Society, 1993.

Babcock, Bryan C. *Sacred Ritual: A Study of the West Semitic Ritual Calendars in Leviticus 23 and the Akkadian Text Emar 446.* BBRSup 9. Winona Lake, IN: Eisenbrauns, 2014.

Baden, Joel S. *The Composition of the Pentateuch: Renewing the Documentary Hypothesis.* New Haven: Yale University Press, 2012.

———. *J, E, and the Redaction of the Pentateuch.* FAT 68. Tübingen: Mohr Siebeck, 2009.

Baker, David W. *Nahum, Habakkuk and Zephaniah: An Introduction and Commentary.* TOTC. Downers Grove, IL: InterVarsity, 1988.

Baldwin, Joyce G. *Daniel: An Introduction and Commentary.* TOTC. Leicester, UK: Inter-Varsity; Downers Grove, IL: Inter-Varsity, 1978.

———. *Esther: An Introduction and Commentary.* TOTC. Leicester, UK: Inter-Varsity; Downers Grove, IL: InterVarsity, 1984.

———. *Haggai, Zechariah, Malachi: An Introduction and Commentary.* TOTC. Leicester, UK: Inter-Varsity; Downers Grove, IL: InterVarsity, 1972.

Balentine, Samuel E. "For No Reason." *Int* 57 (2003): 349–69.

———. *Job.* SHBC. Macon, GA: Smyth & Helwys, 2006.

Baltzer, Klaus. *Deutero-Isaiah: A Commentary on Isaiah 40–55.* Translated by Margaret Kohl. Hermeneia. Minneapolis: Fortress, 2001.

Barber, Cyril J. *Nehemiah and the Dynamics of Effective Leadership.* Neptune, NJ: Loizeaux Brothers, 1976.

Bar-Efrat, Shimon. *Narrative Art in the Bible.* BLS 17. Sheffield: Sheffield Academic, 1989.

Barkay, Gabriel. "The Priestly Benediction on Silver Plaques from Ketef Hinnom in Jerusalem." *TA* 19 (1992): 139–92.

Barkay, Gabriel, Marilyn J. Lundberg, Andrew G. Vaughn, and Bruce Zuckerman. "The Amulets from Ketef Hinnom: A New Edition and Evaluation." *BASOR* 334 (2004): 41–71.

———. "The Challenges of Ketef Hinnom: Using Advanced Technologies to Reclaim the Earliest Biblical Texts and Their Context." *NEA* 66 (2003): 162–71.

Bartholomew, Craig G. *Ecclesiastes.* BCOTWP. Grand Rapids: Baker Academic, 2009.

Barton, John. *Joel and Obadiah: A Commentary.* OTL. Louisville: Westminster John Knox, 2001.

Bauer, Angela. *Gender in the Book of Jeremiah: A Feminist-Literary Reading.* Studies in Biblical Literature 5. New York: Peter Lang, 1999.

Baumgartner, Walter. *Jeremiah's Poems of Lament.* Translated by David E. Orton. Sheffield: Sheffield Academic, 1987.

Becker, Uwe. "Endredaktionelle Kontextvernetzungen des Josua-Buches." Pages 139–59 in *Die deuteronomistischen Geschichtswerke: Redactions- und religionsgeschichtliche Perspektiven zur "Deuteronomismus"-Diskussion in Tora und Vorderen Propheten*. Edited by Markus Witte et al. Berlin: de Gruyter, 2006.

———. *Richterzeit und Königtum: Redaktionsgeschichtliche Studien zum Richterbuch*. BZAW 192. Berlin: de Gruyter, 1990.

Beckman, Gary. "Foreigners in the Ancient Near East." *JAOS* 133 (2013): 203–15.

———. *Hittite Diplomatic Texts*. Edited by Harry A. Hoffner Jr. SBLWAW 7. Atlanta: Scholars Press, 1996.

Beckwith, Carl L. *Ezekiel, Daniel*. RCSOT 12. Downers Grove, IL: IVP Academic, 2012.

Beckwith, Roger T. "Early Traces of the Book of Daniel." *TynBul* 53 (2002): 75–82.

Bekkenkamp, Jonneke, and Fokkelien van Dijk. "The Canon of the Old Testament and Women's Cultural Traditions." Pages 91–108 in *Historiography of Women's Cultural Traditions*. Edited by M. Meijer and J. Schaap. Dordrecht: Foris, 1987. Repr. pages 67–85 in *A Feminist Companion to the Song of Songs*. Edited by A. Brenner. FCB 1. Sheffield: Sheffield Academic, 1993.

Ben-Barak, Zafrira. "The Status and Right of the *Gĕbîrâ*." *JBL* 110 (1991): 23–34.

Ben Zvi, Ehud. *A Historical-Critical Study of the Book of Obadiah*. BZAW 242. Berlin: de Gruyter, 1996.

———. *A Historical-Critical Study of the Book of Zephaniah*. BZAW 198. Berlin: de Gruyter, 1991.

———. *Hosea*. FOTL 21A/1. Grand Rapids: Eerdmans, 2005.

———. *Micah*. FOTL 21B. Grand Rapids: Eerdmans, 2000.

———. "Obadiah." *OEBB* 2:123–25.

Berlin, Adele. *Esther*. JPSBC. Philadelphia: Jewish Publication Society, 2001.

———. "Introduction to Hebrew Poetry." Pages 301–15 in vol. 4 of *The New Interpreter's Bible*. Edited by Leander E. Keck. Nashville: Abingdon, 1996.

———. *Lamentations: A Commentary*. OTL. Louisville: Westminster John Knox, 2002.

———. *Zephaniah: A New Translation with Introduction and Commentary*. AB 25A. New York: Doubleday, 1994.

Berman, Joshua. "CTH 133 and the Hittite Provenance of Deuteronomy 13." *JBL* 130 (2011): 25–44.

Bethge, Eberhard. "Dietrich Bonhoeffer and the Jews." Pages 43–96 in vol. 6 of *Ethical Responsibility: Bonhoeffer's Legacy to the Churches*. Edited by John D. Godsey and Geffrey B. Kelly. Toronto Studies in Theology. New York: Edwin Mellen, 1981.

Bharj, Natasha, and Peter Hegarty. "A Postcolonial Feminist Critique of Harem Analogies in Psychological Science." *Journal of Social and Political Psychology* 3 (2015): 257–75.

Bickell, Gustav. *Die hebräische Metrik*. Leipzig: F. A. Brockhaus, 1880–81.

Biran, Avraham, and Joseph Naveh. "An Aramaic Stele Fragment from Tel Dan." *IEJ* 43 (1993): 81–98.

———. "The Tel Dan Inscription: A New Fragment." *IEJ* 45 (1995): 1–18.

Birch, Bruce C., Walter Brueggemann, Terence E. Fretheim, and David L. Petersen. *A Theological Introduction to the Old Testament*. 2nd ed. Nashville: Abingdon, 2005.

Black, Fiona C. "Beauty or the Beast? The Grotesque Body in the Song of Songs." *BibInt* 8 (2000): 302–23.

Blaikie, William G. *The Second Book of Samuel*. Vol. 2 of *The Books of Samuel*. New York: A. C. Armstrong & Son, 1888. Repr., Minneapolis: Klock & Klock, 1978.

Blenkinsopp, Joseph. *Isaiah: A New Translation with Introduction and Commentary*. Vol. 1, *1–39*. Vol. 2, *40–55*. Vol. 3, *56–66*. AB 19, 19A, 20. New York: Doubleday, 2000–2003.

———. *The Pentateuch: An Introduction to the First Five Books of the Bible*. New York: Doubleday, 1992.

Bliese, Loren F. "A Cryptic Chiastic Acrostic: Finding Meaning from Structure in the Poetry of Nahum." *JTT* 7 (1995): 48–81.

Bloch-Smith, Elizabeth. "Israelite Ethnicity in Iron I: Archaeology Preserves What Is

Remembered and What Is Forgotten in Israel's History." *JBL* 122 (2003): 401–25.

Bloch-Smith, Elizabeth, and Beth Alpert Nakhai. "A Landscape Comes to Life: The Iron Age I." *NEA* 62 (1999): 62–92, 101–27.

Block, Daniel I. *The Book of Ezekiel*. Vol. 1, *1–24*. Vol. 2, *25–48*. NICOT. Grand Rapids: Eerdmans, 1997–98.

———. *The Gods of the Nations: Studies in Ancient Near Eastern National Theology*. 2nd ed. Grand Rapids: Baker Academic, 2000.

———. "How Many Is God? An Investigation into the Meaning of Deuteronomy 6:4–5." *JETS* 47 (2004): 193–212.

———, ed. *Israel: Ancient Kingdom or Late Invention?* Nashville: B&H Academic, 2008.

———. *Judges, Ruth*. NAC 6. Nashville: Broadman & Holman, 1999.

———. *Obadiah: The Kingship Belongs to YHWH*. HMS. Grand Rapids: Zondervan, 2013.

———. "Ruth 1: Book of." *DOTWPW* 672–87.

———. "Why Deborah's Different." *BR* 71.3 (June 2001): 34–40, 49–52.

Bloom, Harold, ed. *The Song of Songs*. MCI. New York: Chelsea, 1988.

Blum, Erhard. *Studien zur Komposition des Pentateuch*. BZAW 189. Berlin: de Gruyter, 1990.

Boda, Mark J. *The Book of Zechariah*. NICOT. Grand Rapids: Eerdmans, 2016.

———. "Ezra." *DOTHB* 277–84.

———. *Haggai, Zechariah*. NIVAC. Grand Rapids: Zondervan, 2004.

———. "Lamentations 1: Book of." *DOTWPW* 399–410.

———. "Zephaniah, Book of." *DOTP* 899–907.

Bodi, Daniel. *The Book of Ezekiel and the Poem of Erra*. OBO 104. Freiburg: Universitätsverlag; Göttingen: Vandenhoeck & Ruprecht, 1991.

———. *The Demise of the Warlord: A New Look at the David Story*. Hebrew Bible Monographs 26. Sheffield: Sheffield Phoenix, 2010.

———. "The Story of Samuel, Saul, and David." Pages 190–226 in *Ancient Israel's History: An Introduction to Issues and Sources*. Edited by Bill T. Arnold and Richard S. Hess. Grand Rapids: Baker Academic, 2014.

Boer, Roland. "The Second Coming: Repetition and Insatiable Desire in the Song of Songs." *BibInt* 8 (2000): 276–301.

Bonar, Andrew. *A Commentary on the Book of Leviticus*. 3rd ed. London: James Nisbet, 1852. Repr., Grand Rapids: Baker, 1978.

Bonhoeffer, Dietrich. *Psalms: The Prayer Book of the Bible*. Minneapolis: Augsburg Fortress, 1974.

Bouzard, Walter C. *We Have Heard with Our Ears, O God: Sources of the Communal Laments in the Psalms*. SBLDS 159. Atlanta: Scholars Press, 1997.

Bowen, Nancy R. "Ezekiel." *OEBB* 1:282–300.

Brayford, Susan. *Genesis*. SCS. Leiden: Brill, 2007.

Brenner, Athalya. "Introduction." Pages 13–24 in *A Feminist Companion to Samuel and Kings*. Edited by A. Brenner. FCB 5. Sheffield: Sheffield Academic, 1994.

———. *The Israelite Woman: Social Role and Literary Type in Biblical Narrative*. Biblical Seminar 2. Sheffield: JSOT Press, 1985.

———. "Naomi and Ruth." Pages 70–84 in *A Feminist Companion to Ruth*. Edited by A. Brenner. FCB 3. Sheffield: Sheffield Academic, 1993.

———. *The Song of Songs*. OTG. Sheffield: Sheffield Academic, 1989.

Brettler, Marc. "The Book of Judges: Literature as Politics." *JBL* 108 (1989): 395–418.

Briant, Pierre. *From Cyrus to Alexander: A History of the Persian Empire*. Translated by Peter T. Daniels. Winona Lake, IN: Eisenbrauns, 2002.

Bricker, Daniel P. "Innocent Suffering in Mesopotamia." *TynBul* 51 (2000): 193–214.

Briggs, Richard S., and Joel N. Lohr. *A Theological Introduction to the Pentateuch: Interpreting the Torah as Christian Scripture*. Grand Rapids: Baker Academic, 2012.

Brooks, Simcha Shalom. "Saul and the Samson Narrative." *JSOT* 71 (1996): 19–25.

Brotzman, Ellis R. *Old Testament Textual Criticism: A Practical Introduction*. Grand Rapids: Baker, 1994.

Brown, Michael L. *Israel's Divine Healer*. SOTBT. Grand Rapids: Zondervan, 1995.

Broyles, Craig C. *The Conflict of Faith and Experience in the Psalms: A Form-Critical and Theological Study*. JSOTSup 52. Sheffield: Sheffield Academic, 1989.

———. "Psalms concerning the Liturgies of Temple Entry." Pages 248–87 in *The Book of Psalms: Composition and Reception*. Edited by Peter W. Flint and Patrick D. Miller. VTSup 99. Leiden: Brill, 2005.

Bruce, Frederick Fyvie. *The Epistle to the Hebrews*. NICNT. Grand Rapids: Eerdmans, 1964.

Brueggemann, Walter. "Bounded by Obedience and Praise: The Psalms as Canon." *JSOT* 50 (1991): 63–92.

———. *First and Second Samuel*. IBC. Louisville: Westminster John Knox, 1990.

———. "The God Who Gives Rest." Pages 565–90 in *The Book of Exodus: Composition, Reception, and Interpretation*. Edited by Thomas B. Dozeman, Craig A. Evans, and Joel N. Lohr. VTSup 164. Leiden: Brill, 2014.

———. "Pharaoh as Vassal: A Study of a Political Metaphor." *CBQ* 57 (1995): 27–51.

———. "The Psalms in Theological Use: On Incommensurability and Mutuality." Pages 581–602 in *The Book of Psalms: Composition and Reception*. Edited by Peter W. Flint and Patrick D. Miller. VTSup 99. Leiden: Brill, 2005.

———. *The Theology of the Book of Jeremiah*. Old Testament Theology. Cambridge: Cambridge University Press, 2007.

———. "Trajectories in Old Testament Literature and the Sociology of Ancient Israel." *JBL* 98 (1979): 161–85.

Budd, Philip J. *Numbers*. WBC 5. Waco: Word, 1984.

Budde, Karl. "Nahum." Pages 3259–63 in *Encyclopaedia biblica*. Edited by T. K. Cheyne et al. 2nd ed. New York: Macmillan, 1901.

Bullock, C. Hassell. *Encountering the Book of Psalms: A Literary and Theological Introduction*. Grand Rapids: Baker Academic, 2001.

Burns, John Barclay. "Proverbs 7,6–27: Vignettes from the Cycle of Astarte and Adonis." *SJOT* 9 (1995): 20–36.

Bush, Frederic W. "The Book of Esther: *Opus non gratum* in the Christian Canon." *BBR* 8 (1998): 39–54.

———. *Ruth, Esther*. WBC 9. Dallas: Word, 1996.

Butler, Trent. *Joshua 1–12*. WBC 7A. 2nd ed. Grand Rapids: Zondervan, 2014.

———. *Joshua 13–24*. WBC 7B. 2nd ed. Grand Rapids: Zondervan, 2014.

———. *Judges*. WBC 8. Grand Rapids: Zondervan, 2009.

Cahill, Jane M. "Jerusalem at the Time of the United Monarchy: The Archaeological Evidence." Pages 13–80 in *Jerusalem in Bible and Archaeology: The First Temple Period*. Edited by A. G. Vaughn and A. E. Killebrew. SBL Symposium Series. Atlanta: SBL, 2003.

———. "Jerusalem in David and Solomon's Time." *BAR* 30.6 (November/December 2004): 20–31, 62–63.

Cain, Andrew, ed. and trans. *Jerome's Epitaph on Paula: A Commentary on the* Epitaphium Sanctae Paula. Oxford Early Christian Texts. Oxford: Oxford University Press, 2013.

Callaway, Joseph A., and J. Maxwell Miller. "The Settlement in Canaan: The Period of the Judges." Pages 55–89 in *Ancient Israel: From Abraham to the Roman Destruction of the Temple*. Edited by Hershel Shanks. Rev. and expanded ed. Washington, DC: Biblical Archaeology Society, 1999.

Calvin, John. *A Commentary on the Prophet Joel*. Translated and edited by John Owen. Carlisle, UK: Banner of Truth, 1958.

———. *Commentary on the Psalms*. Edited by David C. Searle. Carlisle, UK: Banner of Truth, 2009.

———. *Habakkuk, Zephaniah, Haggai*. Vol. 4 of *Commentaries on the Twelve Minor*

Prophets. Translated by John Owen. Grand Rapids: Eerdmans, 1950.

———. *Hosea. Commentaries on the Twelve Minor Prophets*, vol 1. Translated by John Owen. Grand Rapids: Eerdmans, 1950.

———. *Joel, Amos and Obadiah. Commentaries on the Twelve Minor Prophets*, vol. 2. Translated by John Owen. Grand Rapids: Eerdmans, 1950.

———. *Jonah, Micah and Nahum. Commentaries on the Twelve Minor Prophets*, vol. 3. Translated by John Owen. Grand Rapids: Eerdmans, 1950.

Campbell, Antony F. "The Book of Job: Two Questions, One Answer." *ABR* 51 (2003): 15–25.

———. "The Storyteller's Role: Reported Story and Biblical Text." *CBQ* 64 (2002): 427–41.

Carey, Greg. "Apocalypses." *OEBB* 1:39–55.

Carr, David McClain. *The Formation of the Hebrew Bible: A New Reconstruction*. New York: Oxford University Press, 2011.

———. "Gender and the Shaping of Desire in the Song of Songs and Its Interpretations." *JBL* 119 (2000): 233–48.

———. *Reading the Fractures of Genesis: Historical and Literary Approaches*. Louisville: Westminster John Knox, 1996.

Carroll, Michael P. "One More Time: Leviticus Revisited." Pages 117–26 in *Anthropological Approaches to the Old Testament*. Edited by Bernard Lang. Philadelphia: Fortress, 1985.

Carroll, Robert P. *Jeremiah: A Commentary*. OTL. Philadelphia: Westminster, 1986.

Carroll R., M. Daniel. "Amos." *OEBB* 1:26–34.

———. *Amos: The Prophet and His Oracles*. Louisville: Westminster John Knox, 2002.

———. *Christians at the Border: Immigration, the Church, and the Bible*. Grand Rapids: Baker Academic, 2008.

———. "Living between the Lines: Reading Amos 9:11–15 in Post-War Guatemala." *Religion and Theology* 6 (1999): 50–64.

Cassuto, Umberto. "Chapter III of Habakkuk and the Ras Shamra Texts." Pages 3–15 in vol. 2 of *Biblical and Oriental Studies*. Translated by Israel Abrahams. Jerusalem: Magnes, 1975.

Cathcart, Kevin J. "The Divine Warrior and the War of Yahweh in Nahum." Pages 68–76 in *Biblical Studies in Contemporary Thought: The Tenth Anniversary Commemorative Volume of the Trinity College Biblical Institute*. Edited by M. W. Ward. Somerville, MA: Greeno, Hadden, 1975.

Cathcart, Kevin J., and Robert P. Gordon. *The Targum of the Minor Prophets*. The Aramaic Bible 14. Wilmington, DE: Michael Glazier, 1989.

Cazelles, Henri. "Jeremiah and Deuteronomy." Pages 89–111 in *A Prophet to the Nations: Essays in Jeremiah Studies*. Edited by Leo G. Perdue and Brian W. Kovacs. Winona Lake, IN: Eisenbrauns, 1984. Translated by Leo G. Perdue from "Jérémie et le Deutérome." *Recherches de science religieuse* 38 (1951): 5–36.

Charlesworth, James H. *The Old Testament Pseudepigrapha*. Vol. 1, *Apocalyptic Literature and Testaments*. Vol. 2, *Expansions of the "Old Testament" and Legends, Wisdom and Philosophical Literature, Prayers, Psalms, and Odes, Fragments of Lost Judeo-Hellenistic Works*. Garden City, NY: Doubleday, 1983–85.

Chi Chung Lee, Archie. "Lamentations." Pages 226–33 in *Global Bible Commentary*. Edited by Daniel Patte. Nashville: Abingdon, 2004.

Childs, Brevard S. *The Book of Exodus: A Critical, Theological Commentary*. OTL. Philadelphia: Westminster, 1974.

———. *Introduction to the Old Testament as Scripture*. Philadelphia: Fortress, 1979.

———. *Isaiah: A Commentary*. OTL. Louisville: Westminster John Knox, 2001.

———. *Old Testament Books for Pastor and Teacher*. Philadelphia: Westminster, 1977.

———. *The Struggle to Understand Isaiah as Christian Scripture*. Grand Rapids: Eerdmans, 2004.

Chilton, Bruce. "The Exodus Theology of the Palestinian Targumim." Pages 387–403 in *The Book of Exodus: Composition, Reception, and Interpretation*. Edited by

Thomas B. Dozeman, Craig A. Evans, and Joel N. Lohr. VTSup 164. Leiden: Brill, 2014.

Chirichigno, Greg. "A Theological Investigation of Motivation in Old Testament Law." *JETS* 24 (1981): 303–13.

Chisholm, Robert B., Jr. *A Commentary on Judges and Ruth*. Kregel Exegetical Library. Grand Rapids: Kregel, 2013.

Christensen, Duane L. *Deuteronomy*. Vol. 1, *1:1–21:9*. Rev. ed. Vol. 2, *21:10–34:12*. WBC 6A–B. Waco: Word, 2001–2.

———. *Nahum: A New Translation with Introduction and Commentary*. AB 24F. New Haven: Yale University Press, 2009.

Christman, Angela Russell. *"What Did Ezekiel See?": Christian Exegesis of Ezekiel's Vision of the Chariot from Irenaeus to Gregory the Great*. Bible in Ancient Christianity 4. Leiden: Brill, 2005.

Cimosa, Mario, and Gillian Bonney. "The Theology of Job as Revealed in His Replies to His Friends in the Septuagint Translation." Pages 55–65 in *XIII Congress of the International Organization for Septuagint and Cognate Studies: Ljublijana, 2007*. SBLSCS 55. Atlanta: SBL, 2008.

Clements, Ronald E. "The Ezekiel Tradition: Prophecy in a Time of Crisis." Pages 119–36 in *Israel's Prophetic Tradition: Essays in Honour of Peter R. Ackroyd*. Edited by R. Coggins, A. Phillips, and M. Knibb. Cambridge: Cambridge University Press, 1982.

———. *Isaiah and the Deliverance of Jerusalem: A Study of the Interpretation of Prophecy in the Old Testament*. JSOTSup 13. Sheffield: JSOT Press, 1980.

———. *Wisdom for a Changing World: Wisdom in the Old Testament*. Berkeley Lectures 2. Berkeley: BIBAL, 1990.

Clifford, Richard J. *Proverbs: A Commentary*. OTL. Louisville: Westminster John Knox, 1999.

———. "The Unity of the Book of Isaiah and Its Cosmogonic Language." *CBQ* 55 (1993): 1–17.

Clines, David J. A. "Deconstructing the Book of Job." *BR* 11.2 (April 1995): 30–35, 43–44.

———. *The Esther Scroll: The Story of the Story*. JSOTSup 30. Sheffield: JSOT Press, 1984.

———. "Job and the Spirituality of the Reformation." Pages 49–72 in *The Bible, the Reformation and the Church: Essays in Honour of James Atkinson*. Edited by W. P. Stephens. JSNTSup 105. Sheffield: Sheffield Academic Press, 1995.

———. *Job 1–20*. WBC 17. Dallas: Word, 1989.

———. *Job 21–37*. WBC 18A. Nashville: Nelson, 2006.

———. *Job 38–42*. WBC 18B. Nashville: Nelson, 2011.

———. "What Does Eve Do to Help? And Other Irredeemably Androcentric Orientations in Genesis 1–3." Pages 25–48 in *What Does Eve Do to Help? And Other Readerly Questions to the Old Testament*. Edited by David J. A. Clines. JSOTSup 94. Sheffield: Sheffield Academic, 1990.

———. "Why Is There a Song of Songs and What Does It Do to You if You Read It?" *Jian Dao* 1 (1994): 1–27.

Cogan, Mordechai. *I Kings: A New Translation with Introduction and Commentary*. AB 10. New York: Doubleday, 2000.

Cogan, Mordechai, and Hayim Tadmor. *II Kings: A New Translation with Introduction and Commentary*. AB 11. New York: Doubleday, 1988.

Coggins, Richard. "What Does 'Deuteronomistic' Mean?" Pages 135–48 in *Words Remembered, Texts Renewed: Essays in Honour of John F. A. Sawyer*. Edited by Jon Davies, Graham Harvey, and Wilfred G. E. Watson. JSOTSup 195. Sheffield: Sheffield Academic, 1995.

Coggins, Richard, and Jin H. Han. *Six Minor Prophets through the Centuries*. Chichester, UK: Wiley-Blackwell, 2011.

Cole, R. Dennis. *Numbers*. NAC 3B. Nashville: Broadman & Holman, 2000.

Collins, John J. *Daniel*. Hermeneia. Minneapolis: Augsburg Fortress, 1993.

Conti, Marco, and Gianluca Pilara, eds. *1–2 Kings, 1–2 Chronicles, Ezra, Nehe-*

miah, Esther. ACCS: Old Testament 5. Downers Grove, IL: InterVarsity, 2008.

Coogan, Michael D. "Assessing David and Solomon: From the Hypothetical to the Improbable to the Absurd." *BAR* 32.4 (July/August 2006): 56–60.

Cook, Stephen L. "Haggai." *OEBB* 1:357–361.

———. "Malachi." *OEBB* 2:34–41.

———. "Zechariah." *OEBB* 2:465–71.

Coote, Robert B., and Keith W. Whitelam. *The Emergence of Early Israel in Historical Perspective.* Sheffield: Almond, 1986.

Craigie, Peter C. *The Book of Deuteronomy.* NICOT. Grand Rapids: Eerdmans, 1976.

———. *Psalms 1–50.* WBC 19. Waco: Word, 1983.

Crawford, Sidnie White [= White, Sidnie A.]. "Exodus in the Dead Sea Scrolls." Pages 305–21 in *The Book of Exodus: Composition, Reception, and Interpretation.* Edited by Thomas B. Dozeman, Craig A. Evans, and Joel N. Lohr. VTSup 164. Leiden: Brill, 2014.

———. "The 'Rewritten' Bible at Qumran: A Look at Three Texts." *ErIsr* 26 (1999): 1–8.

Crenshaw, James L. *Ecclesiastes: A Commentary.* OTL. Philadelphia: Westminster, 1987.

———. "Ecclesiastes, Book of." *ABD* 2:271–80.

———. *Old Testament Wisdom: An Introduction.* 3rd ed. Louisville: Westminster John Knox, 2010.

Croft, Steven J. L. *The Identity of the Individual in the Psalms.* JSOTSup 44. Sheffield: Sheffield Academic, 1987.

Cross, Frank Moore. *Canaanite Myth and Hebrew Epic: Essays in the History of the Religion of Israel.* Cambridge, MA: Harvard University Press, 1973.

———. "The Priestly Tabernacle and the Temple of Solomon." Pages 84–95 in *From Epic to Canon: History and Literature in Ancient Israel.* Baltimore: Johns Hopkins University Press, 2000.

Cross, Frank Moore, Donald W. Parry, Richard J. Saley, and Eugene Ulrich. *Qumran Cave 4.* Vol. 12, *1–2 Samuel.* DJD 17. Oxford: Clarendon, 2005.

Crüsemann, Frank. *The Torah: Theology and Social History of Old Testament Law.* Translated by Allan W. Mahnke. Minneapolis: Fortress, 1996.

Culbertson, Philip, and Elaine M. Wainwright, eds. *The Bible in/and Popular Culture: A Creative Encounter.* SBL Semeia Studies. Atlanta: Society of Biblical Literature, 2010.

Currid, John D. *Ancient Egypt and the Old Testament.* Grand Rapids: Baker, 1997.

Cyril of Alexandria. *Commentary on the Twelve Prophets,* vol. 2. Translated by Robert C. Hill. Washington, DC: Catholic University of America Press, 2008.

Dahood, Mitchell. *Psalms: A New Translation with Introduction and Commentary.* Vol. 1, *1–50.* Vol. 2, *51–100.* Vol. 3, *101–150.* AB 16–17A. Garden City, NY: Doubleday, 1966–70.

———. "Qoheleth and Recent Discoveries." *Bib* 39 (1958): 302–18.

Dallaire, Hélène. "Joshua." Pages 815–1042 in *The Expositor's Bible Commentary Revised Edition 2: Numbers–Ruth.* Edited by T. Longman III and D. E. Garland. Grand Rapids: Zondervan, 2012.

Damerji, Muayad S. B., and Ahmed Kamil. *Gräber assyrischer Königinnen aus Nimrud.* Baghdad: Department of Antiquities and Heritage; Mainz: Römisch-Germanischen Zentralmuseums, 1999.

Danby, Herbert, trans. *The Mishnah.* London: Oxford University Press, 1933.

Davies, Graham I. *Hosea: Based on the Revised Standard Version.* NCB. Grand Rapids: Eerdmans, 1992.

———. "Was There an Exodus?" Pages 23–40 in *In Search of Pre-exilic Israel: Proceedings of the Oxford Old Testament Seminar.* Edited by John Day. JSOTSup 406. New York: T&T Clark, 2004.

Davies, Philip R. *In Search of "Ancient Israel."* JSOTSup 148. Sheffield: JSOT Press, 1992.

———. *Memories of Ancient Israel: An Introduction to Biblical History—Ancient and Modern.* Louisville: Westminster John Knox, 2008.

———. *The Origins of Biblical Israel*. LHBOTS 485. London: T&T Clark, 2007.

Day, John. "Foreign Semitic Influence on the Wisdom of Israel and Its Appropriation in the Book of Proverbs." Pages 55–70 in *Wisdom in Ancient Israel: Essays in Honour of J. A. Emerton*. Edited by John Day, Robert P. Gordon, and H. G. M. Williamson. Cambridge: Cambridge University Press, 1995.

———. "How Many Pre-exilic Psalms Are There?" Pages 225–50 in *In Search of Pre-exilic Israel: Proceedings of the Oxford Old Testament Seminar*. Edited by John Day. JSOTSup 406. New York: T&T Clark, 2004.

———. *Psalms*. OTG. Sheffield: Sheffield Academic, 1990.

———. "Ugarit and the Bible: Do They Presuppose the Same Canaanite Mythology and Religion?" Pages 35–52 in *Ugarit and the Bible: Proceedings of the International Symposium on Ugarit and the Bible, Manchester, September 1992*. Edited by G. J. Brooke, A. H. W. Curtis, and J. F. Healey. UBL 11. Münster: Ugarit-Verlag, 1994.

Dearman, J. Andrew. *The Book of Hosea*. NICOT. Grand Rapids: Eerdmans, 2010.

———. "Jeremiah: History of Interpretation." *DOTP* 441–49.

———. *Jeremiah/Lamentations*. NIVAC. Grand Rapids: Zondervan, 2002.

DeClaissé-Walford, Nancy L. "An Intertextual Reading of Psalms 22, 23, and 24." Pages 139–52 in *The Book of Psalms: Composition and Reception*. Edited by Peter W. Flint and Patrick D. Miller. VTSup 99. Leiden: Brill, 2005.

———. *Reading from the Beginning: The Shaping of the Hebrew Psalter*. Macon, GA: Mercer University Press, 1997.

Deist, Ferdinand E. *Witnesses to the Old Testament: Introducing Old Testament Textual Criticism*. LOT 5. Pretoria: NG Kerkboekhandel, 1988.

Delitzsch, Franz. *Proverbs, Ecclesiastes, Song of Solomon*. Translated by M. G. Easton. Vol. 6 of *Commentary on the Old Testament in Ten Volumes*. Repr., Grand Rapids: Eerdmans, 1975.

Dell, Katharine J. *The Book of Job as Skeptical Literature*. BZAW 197. Berlin: de Gruyter, 1991.

———. "How Much Wisdom Literature Has Its Roots in the Pre-exilic Period?" Pages 251–71 in *In Search of Pre-exilic Israel: Proceedings of the Oxford Old Testament Seminar*. Edited by John Day. JSOTSup 406. New York: T&T Clark, 2004.

deSilva, David A. "The Hellenistic Period." Pages 426–39 in *Ancient Israel's History: An Introduction to Issues and Sources*. Edited by Bill T. Arnold and Richard S. Hess. Grand Rapids: Baker Academic, 2014.

Deutsch, Robert. *Biblical Period Hebrew Bullae: The Josef Chaim Kaufman Collection*. Tel Aviv: Archaeological Center Publication, 2003.

Dever, William G. *Did God Have a Wife? Archaeology and Folk Religion in Ancient Israel*. Grand Rapids: Eerdmans, 2005.

———. *What Did the Biblical Writers Know and When Did They Know It?* Grand Rapids: Eerdmans, 2001.

———. *Who Were the Early Israelites and Where Did They Come From?* Grand Rapids: Eerdmans, 2003.

de Wette, Wilhelm Martin Leberecht. *Beiträge zur Einleitung in das Alte Testament*, vol. 2. Halle: Universitätsverlag, 1807.

———. *Dissertation critica qua Deuteronomium diversum a prioribus Pentateuchi libris cuisudam recentioris autoris opus esse demonstratur*. Jena: Universitätsverlag, 1805.

Diamond, A. R. Pete. *The Confessions of Jeremiah in Context: Scenes of Prophetic Drama*. JSOTSup 45. Sheffield: JSOT Press, 1987.

Dietrich, Walter. "Martin Noth and the Future of the Deuteronomistic History." Pages 153–75 in *The History of Israel's Traditions: The Heritage of Martin Noth*. JSOTSup 182. Sheffield: Sheffield Academic, 1994.

Dijk-Hemmes, Fokkelien van. "The Imagination of Power and the Power of Imagination: An Intertextual Analysis of Two Biblical Love Songs, the Song of Songs and Hosea 2." *JSOT* 44 (1989): 75–88.

Dines, Jennifer M. *The Septuagint*. Edited by Michael A. Knibb. New York: T&T Clark, 2004.

Dively Lauro, Elizabeth Ann, trans. *Origen: Homilies on Judges*. The Fathers of the Church: A New Translation, vol. 119. Washington, DC: The Catholic University of America Press, 2010.

Di Vito, Robert A. "Old Testament Anthropology and the Construction of Personal Identity." *CBQ* 61 (1999): 217–38.

Dobbs-Allsopp, Frederick W. *Weep, O Daughter of Zion: A Study of the City-Lament Genre in the Hebrew Bible*. Biblica et orientalia 44. Rome: Biblical Institute Press, 1993.

Doering, Lutz. "The Reception of the Book of Exodus in the *Book of Jubilees*." Pages 485–510 in *The Book of Exodus: Composition, Reception, and Interpretation*. Edited by Thomas B. Dozeman, Craig A. Evans, and Joel N. Lohr. VTSup 164. Leiden: Brill, 2014.

Donne, John. *John Donne's Sermons on the Psalms and Gospels with a Selection of Prayers and Meditations*. Edited by Evelyn M. Simpson. Berkeley and Los Angeles: University of California Press, 1963.

Douglas, Jerome. "Resistance from the Margins: Reading the *Book of Jeremiah* through a Postcolonial Lens." Pages 79–96 *in The Fruits of Madness: Perspectives on the Prophetic Movements in Three Traditions; Essays from the Seminar in Biblical Characters in Judaism, Christianity, Islam and in Literature*. Edited by John Tracy Greene. Newcastle upon Tyne: Cambridge Scholars Publishing, 2016.

Douglas, Mary. "The Forbidden Animals in Leviticus." *JSOT* 59 (1993): 3–23.

———. *Leviticus as Literature*. Oxford: Oxford University Press, 1999.

———. *Purity and Danger*. London: Routledge & Keegan Paul, 1966.

———. "Sacred Contagion." Pages 86–106 in *Reading Leviticus: A Conversation with Mary Douglas*. Edited by J. F. A. Sawyer. JSOTSup 227. Sheffield: Sheffield Academic, 1996.

Dozeman, Thomas B. *Joshua 1–12: A New Translation with Introduction and Commentary*. AB 6B. New Haven: Yale University Press, 2015.

Dozeman, Thomas B., Craig A. Evans, and Joel N. Lohr, eds. *The Book of Exodus: Composition, Reception, and Interpretation*. VTSup 164. Leiden: Brill, 2014.

Duguid, Iain M. "Ezekiel: History of Interpretation." *DOTP* 229–35.

Duhm, Bernhard. *Das Buch Habakuk: Text, Übersetzung und Erklärung*. Tübingen: J. C. B. Mohr, 1906.

———. *Das Buch Jeremia*. Kurzer Hand-Commentar zum Alten Testament 11. Tübingen: J. C. B. Mohr, 1901.

———. *Das Buch Jesaia*. HAT 3/1. Göttingen: Vandenhoeck & Ruprecht, 1892.

Durham, John I. *Exodus*. WBC 3. Waco: Word, 1987.

Eaton, John H. *Vision in Worship: The Relation of Prophecy and Liturgy in the Old Testament*. London: SPCK, 1981.

Edelman, Diane V. "Did Saulide-Davidide Rivalry Resurface in Early Persian Yehud?" Pages 69–91 in *The Land That I Will Show You: Essays on the History and Archaeology of the Ancient Near East in Honor of J. Maxwell Miller*. Edited by J. A. Dearman and M. P. Graham. JSOTSup 343. Sheffield: Sheffield Academic, 2001.

———. *King Saul in the Historiography of Judah*. JSOTSup 121. Sheffield: JSOT Press, 1991.

Ehrenberg, Victor. *From Solon to Socrates: Greek History and Civilization during the 6th and 5th Centuries BC*. London: Methuen, 1968.

Elliott, M. Timothea. *The Literary Unity of the Canticle*. Europäische Hochschulschriften, Series 23, Theology 371. Frankfurt am Main: Peter Lang, 1989.

Elowsky, Joel C. "Exodus in the Fathers." Pages 511–34 in *The Book of Exodus:*

Composition, Reception, and Interpretation. Edited by Thomas B. Dozeman, Craig A. Evans, and Joel N. Lohr. VTSup 164. Leiden: Brill, 2014.

Emmerson, Grace I. *Hosea: An Israelite Prophet in Judean Perspective*. JSOTSup 28. Sheffield: JSOT Press, 1984.

Engnell, Ivan. *Critical Essays on the Old Testament*. Translated by John T. Willis. London: SPCK, 1970.

Erman, Adolf. "Eine ägyptische Quelle der 'Sprüche Salomos.'" *SPAW* 15 (1924): 86–93.

Eskenazi, Tamara Cohn. "The Missions of Ezra and Nehemiah." Pages 509–29 in *Judah and the Judeans in the Persian Period*. Edited by Oded Lipschits and Manfred Oeming. Winona Lake, IN: Eisenbrauns, 2006.

———. "Out of the Shadows: Biblical Women in the Postexilic Era." *JSOT* 54 (1992): 25–43. Repr. pages 252–71 in *A Feminist Companion to Samuel and Kings*. Edited by A. Brenner. FCB 5. Sheffield: Sheffield Academic, 1994.

Evans, Craig A. "Exodus in the New Testament: Patterns of Revelation and Redemption." Pages 440–64 in *The Book of Exodus: Composition, Reception, and Interpretation*. Edited by Thomas B. Dozeman, Craig A. Evans, and Joel N. Lohr. VTSup 164. Leiden: Brill, 2014.

Everson, David L. "The *Vetus Latina* and the Vulgate of the Book of Exodus." Pages 370–86 in *The Book of Exodus: Composition, Reception, and Interpretation*. Edited by Thomas B. Dozeman, Craig A. Evans, and Joel N. Lohr. VTSup 164. Leiden: Brill, 2014.

Exum, J. Cheryl. "The Centre Cannot Hold: Thematic and Textual Instabilities in Judges." *CBQ* 52 (1990): 410–31.

———. "Developing Strategies of Feminist Criticism/Developing Strategies for Commentating on the Song of Songs." Pages 206–49 in *Auguries: The Jubilee Volume of the Sheffield Department of Biblical Studies*. Edited by D. J. A. Clines and S. D. Moore. JSOTSup 269. Sheffield: Sheffield Academic, 1998.

———. *Song of Songs: A Commentary*. OTL. Louisville: Westminster John Knox, 2005.

Falk, Marcia. *Love Lyrics from the Bible: A Translation and Literary Study of the Song of Songs*. BLS 4. Sheffield: Almond, 1982.

Faust, Avraham. "Abandonment, Urbanization, Resettlement and the Formation of the Israelite State." *NEA* 66 (2003): 147–61.

———. "Did Eilat Mazar Find David's Palace?" *BAR* 38.5 (September/October 2012): 47–52, 70.

———. "How Did Israel Become a People?" *BAR* 35.6 (November/December 2009): 62–69, 92, 94.

———. *Israel's Ethnogenesis: Settlement, Interaction, Expansion and Resistance*. London: Equinox, 2007.

———. "The Large Stone Structure in the City of David: A Reexamination." *ZDPV* 126 (2011): 116–30.

Feiler, Bruce S. *America's Prophet: Moses and the American Story*. New York: William Morrow, 2009.

Fekkes, Jan. *Isaiah and Prophetic Traditions in the Book of Revelation: Visionary Antecedents and Their Development*. JSNTSup 93. Sheffield: JSOT Press, 1994.

Fensham, F. Charles. *The Books of Ezra and Nehemiah*. NICOT. Grand Rapids: Eerdmans, 1982.

Ferreiro, Alberto, ed. *The Twelve Prophets*. ACCS: Old Testament 14. Downers Grove, IL: InterVarsity, 2003.

Ferris, Paul. "Lamentations 2: Ancient Near Eastern Background." *DOTWPW* 410–13.

Fewell, Dana N., and David M. Gunn. *Compromising Redemption: Relating Characters in the Book of Ruth*. Literary Currents in Biblical Interpretation. Louisville: Westminster John Knox, 1990.

Finkelstein, Israel. *The Archaeology of the Israelite Settlement*. Jerusalem: Israel Exploration Society, 1988.

———. "The 'Large Stone Structure' in Jerusalem: Reality versus Yearning." *ZDPV* 127 (2011): 1–10.

Finkelstein, Israel, and Neil Asher Silberman. *The Bible Unearthed: Archaeology's New*

Vision of Ancient Israel and the Origin of Its Sacred Texts. New York: Free Press, 2001.

———. *David and Solomon: In Search of the Bible's Sacred Kings and the Roots of the Western Tradition*. New York: Free Press, 2006.

Finkelstein, Israel, David Ussishkin, and Baruch Halpern. *Megiddo III: The 1992–1996 Seasons*. 2 vols. Monograph Series 18. Tel Aviv: Emery and Claire Yass Publications in Archaeology, Institute of Archaeology, Tel Aviv University, 2000.

Finkelstein, Jacob J. "Ammisaduqa's Edict and the Babylonian 'Law Codes.'" *JCS* 15 (1961): 91–104.

———. "A Late Old Babylonian Copy of the Laws of Hammurapi." *JCS* 21 (1967): 31–48.

———. "Some Recent Studies in Cuneiform Law." *JAOS* 90 (1970): 243–56.

Fitzmyer, Joseph A. *The Aramaic Inscriptions of Sefîre*. Biblica et orientalia 19. Rome: Pontifical Biblical Institute, 1967.

Fleming, Daniel. "The Biblical Tradition of Anointing Priests." *JBL* 117 (1998): 401–14.

———. "A Break in the Line: Reconsidering the Bible's Diverse Festival Calendars." *RB* 106 (1999): 161–74.

———. "From Joseph to David: Mari and Israelite Pastoral Traditions." Pages 78–96 in *Israel: Ancient Kingdom or Late Invention?* Edited by Daniel I. Block. Nashville: B&H Academic, 2008.

———. "Genesis in History and Tradition: The Syrian Background of Israel's Ancestors, Reprise." Pages 193–232 in *The Future of Biblical Archaeology: Reassessing Methodologies and Assumptions*. Edited by J. K. Hoffmeier and A. Millard. Grand Rapids: Eerdmans, 2004.

———. *The Installation of Baal's High Priestess at Emar: A Window on Ancient Syrian Religion*. HSS 42. Atlanta: Scholars Press, 1992.

———. "The Israelite Festival Calendar and Emar's Ritual Archive." *RB* 106 (1999): 8–34.

———. "Mari's Large Public Tent and the Priestly Tent Sanctuary." *VT* 50 (2000): 484–98.

———. *Time at Emar: The Cultic Calendar and the Rituals from the Diviner's Archive*. Winona Lake, IN: Eisenbrauns, 2000.

Flesher, Paul V. M., and Bruce Chilton. *The Targums: A Critical Introduction*. Waco: Baylor University Press, 2011.

Flint, Peter W. "Appendix: Psalms Scrolls from the Judaean Desert." Pages 287–90 in *Pseudepigraphic and Non-Masoretic Psalms and Prayers*. Edited by James H. Charlesworth and Henry W. L. Rietz with P. W. Flint. Vol. 4A of *The Dead Sea Scrolls: Hebrew, Aramaic, and Greek Texts with English Translation*. Tübingen: Mohr Siebeck, 1997.

———. "The Book of Psalms in the Light of the Dead Sea Scrolls." *VT* 48 (1998): 453–72.

———. *The Dead Sea Psalms Scrolls and the Book of Psalms*. STDJ 17. Leiden: Brill, 1997.

Flint, Peter W., and Patrick D. Miller Jr., eds. *The Book of Psalms: Composition and Reception*. VTSup 99. Leiden: Brill, 2005.

Floyd, Michael H. "The Chimeral Acrostic of Nahum 1–2." *JBL* 113 (1994): 421–37.

Fokkelman, Jan P. *Reading Biblical Narrative: An Introductory Guide*. Philadelphia: Westminster John Knox, 1999.

———. *Reading Biblical Poetry: An Introductory Guide*. Louisville: Westminster John Knox, 2001.

Foster, John L., trans. *Hymns, Prayers, and Songs: An Anthology of Ancient Egyptian Lyric Poetry*. Edited by Susan Tower Hollis. SBLWAW 8. Atlanta: Scholars Press, 1995.

Fox, Michael V. *Character and Ideology in the Book of Esther*. Columbia: University of South Carolina Press, 1991.

———. "Frame-Narrative and Composition in the Book of Qohelet." *HUCA* 48 (1977): 83–106.

———. *Proverbs: A New Translation with Introduction and Commentary*. Vol. 1, *1–9*. AB 18A. New York: Doubleday, 2000.

Vol. 2, *10–31*. AB 18B. New Haven: Yale University Press, 2009.

———. *The Song of Songs and Ancient Egyptian Love Songs*. Madison: University of Wisconsin Press, 1985.

———. *A Time to Tear Down and a Time to Build Up: A Rereading of Ecclesiastes*. Grand Rapids: Eerdmans, 1999.

Freedman, David Noel, and Andrew Welch. "Amos's Earthquake and Israelite Prophecy." Pages 188–98 in *Scripture and Other Artifacts: Essays on the Bible and Archaeology in Honor of Philip J. King*. Edited by Michael D. Coogan, Cheryl Exum, and Lawrence E. Stager. Louisville: Westminster John Knox, 1994.

Frei, Peter. "Zentralgewalt und Lokalautonomie im Achämenidenreich." Pages 10–26 in *Reichsidee und Reichsorganisation im Perserreich*. Edited by Peter Frei and Klaus Koch. 2nd ed. OBO 55. Freiburg: Universitätsverlag; Göttingen: Vandenhoeck & Ruprecht, 1984.

Fretheim, Terence E. *Exodus*. IBC. Louisville: John Knox, 1991.

Friedman, Richard Elliott. *Who Wrote the Bible?* New York: Summit Books, 1987.

Gal, Zvi. *Lower Galilee during the Iron Age*. ASOR Dissertation Series 8. Winona Lake, IN: Eisenbrauns, 1992.

———. "The Period of the Israelite Settlement in the Lower Galilee and the Jezreel Valley." *Ma* 7 (1991): 101–15.

Galil, Gershon. "*ʿyyn ḫlqʾ*: The Oldest Hebrew Inscription from Jerusalem." *Strata: Bulletin of the Anglo-Israel Archaeological Society* 31 (2013): 11–26.

Gane, Roy E. "Moral Evils in Leviticus 16:16, 21 and Cultic Characterization of YHWH." Paper presented at the Annual Meeting of the Rocky Mountain and Great Plains Region of the SBL. Denver, November 2001.

Ganzel, Tova, and Shalom E. Holtz. "Ezekiel's Temple in Babylonian Context." *VT* 64 (2014): 211–26.

Garfinkel, Yosef, Mitka R. Golub, Haggai Misgav, and Saar Ganor. "The ʾIšbaʿal Inscription from Khirbet Qeiyafa." *BASOR* 373 (2015): 217–33.

Garrett, Duane A. *Amos: A Handbook on the Hebrew Text*. Baylor Handbook on the Hebrew Bible. Waco: Baylor University Press, 2008.

———. *A Commentary on Exodus*. KEL. Grand Rapids: Kregel, 2014.

———. *Hosea, Joel*. NAC 19A. Nashville: Broadman & Holman, 1997.

———. "Joel, Book of." *DOTP* 449–55.

———. *Proverbs, Ecclesiastes, Song of Songs*. NAC 14. Nashville: Broadman & Holman, 1993.

———. "Proverbs 3: History of Interpretation." *DOTWPW* 566–78.

Garrett, Duane A., and Paul R. House. *Song of Songs/Lamentations*. WBC 23B. Nashville: Nelson, 2004.

Garsiel, Moshe. "Homiletic Name-Derivations as a Literary Device in the Gideon Narrative: Judges vi–viii." *VT* 43 (1993): 302–17.

Gentry, Peter J. *The Asterisked Materials in the Greek Job*. SBLSCS 38. Atlanta: Scholars Press, 1995.

———. "Hexaplaric Materials in Ecclesiastes and the Role of the Syro-Hexapla." *Aramaic Studies* 1 (2003): 5–28.

———. "The Text of the Old Testament." *JETS* 52 (2009): 19–45.

George, Mark. "Yhwh's Own Heart." *CBQ* 64 (2002): 442–59.

Gerleman, Gillis. *Ruth; Das Hohelied*. BKAT 18. Neukirchen-Vluyn: Neukirchener Verlag, 1965.

Gerstenberger, Erhard S. "Theologies in the Book of Psalms." Pages 603–25 in *The Book of Psalms: Composition and Reception*. Edited by Peter W. Flint and Patrick D. Miller. VTSup 99. Leiden: Brill, 2005.

Gese, Hartmut. "The Crisis of Wisdom in Koheleth." Pages 141–53 in *Theodicy in the Old Testament*. Edited by James Crenshaw. Philadelphia: Fortress, 1983.

Giannarelli, Elena. "The Book of Ruth." *Sidic* 23.2 (1990): 12–15.

Gillingham, Susan, ed. *Jewish and Christian Approaches to the Psalms: Conflict and Convergence*. Oxford: Oxford University Press, 2013.

Girard, René. *Job: The Victim of His People*. Stanford, CA: Stanford University Press, 1987.

Giuntoli, Frederico, and Konrad Schmid, eds. *The Post-Priestly Pentateuch: New Perspectives on Its Redactional Development and Theological Profiles*. FAT 101. Tübingen: Mohr Siebeck, 2015.

Glenny, W. Edward. *Amos: A Commentary Based on Amos in Codex Vaticanus*. SCS. Leiden: Brill, 2013.

———. *Finding Meaning in the Text: Translation Technique and Theology in the Septuagint of Amos*. VTSup 126. Leiden: Brill, 2009.

Goitein, Shlomo Dov. "The Song of Songs: A Female Composition." Pages 58–66 in *A Feminist Companion to the Song of Songs*. Edited by A. Brenner. FCB 1. Sheffield: Sheffield Academic, 1993.

Goldingay, John. "The Arrangement of Sayings in Proverbs 10–15." *JSOT* 61 (1994): 75–83.

———. *Daniel*. WBC 30. Waco: Word, 1989.

———. *Old Testament Theology*. Vol. 2, *Israel's Faith*. Downers Grove, IL: IVP Academic; Milton Keynes, UK: Paternoster, 2006.

———. *Psalms*. Vol. 1, *1–41*. Vol. 2, *42–89*. Vol. 3, *90–150*. BCOTWP. Grand Rapids: Baker Academic, 2006–8.

———. "Zephaniah." Pages 93–134 in *Minor Prophets II*. Edited by J. Goldingay and P. J. Scalise. NIBC 18. Peabody, MA: Hendrickson, 2009.

Good, Edwin M. *In Turns of Tempest: A Reading of Job, with a Translation*. Stanford, CA: Stanford University Press, 1990.

Good, Robert M. "2 Samuel 8." *TynBul* 52 (2001): 129–38.

Gordis, Robert. *The Book of God and Man: A Study of Job*. Chicago: University of Chicago Press, 1965.

———. *The Book of Job: Commentary, New Translation, and Special Studies*. New York: Jewish Theological Seminary of America, 1978.

———. "Studies in the Esther Narrative." Pages 408–23 in *Studies in the Book of Esther*. Edited by Carey A. Moore. New York: Ktav, 1982.

Gordon, Cyrus H. "Abraham of Ur." Pages 77–84 in *Hebrew and Semitic Studies Presented to Godfrey Rolles Driver*. Edited by D. Winton Thomas and W. D. McHardy. Oxford: Clarendon, 1963.

Gottwald, Norman. *The Tribes of Yahweh: A Sociology of the Religion of Liberated Israel, 1250–1050 BCE*. Maryknoll, NY: Orbis Books, 1979.

Goulder, Michael D. "Asaph's *History of Israel* (Elohist Press, Bethel, 725 BCE)." *JSOT* 65 (1995): 71–81.

———. *The Prayers of David (Psalms 51–72): Studies in the Psalter II*. JSOTSup 102. Sheffield: JSOT Press, 1990.

———. *The Psalms of Asaph and the Pentateuch: Studies in the Psalter III*. JSOTSup 233. Sheffield: JSOT Press, 1996.

———. *The Psalms of the Sons of Korah*. JSOTSup 20. Sheffield: JSOT Press, 1982.

———. "The Social Setting of Book II of the Psalter." Pages 349–67 in *The Book of Psalms: Composition and Reception*. Edited by Peter W. Flint and Patrick D. Miller. VTSup 99. Leiden: Brill, 2005.

Gowan, Donald E. "Reading Job as a 'Wisdom Script.'" *JSOT* 55 (1992): 85–96.

Grabbe, Lester. "'The Comfortable Theory,' 'Maximal Conservatism' and Neo-Fundamentalism Revisited." Pages 174–93 in *Sense and Sensitivity: Essays on Reading the Bible in Memory of Robert Carroll*. Edited by Alastair G. Hunter and Philip R. Davies. JSOTSup 348. Sheffield: Sheffield Academic, 2002.

Greenberg, Moshe. *Ezekiel: A New Translation with Introduction and Commentary*. Vol. 1, *1–20*. Vol. 2, *21–37*. AB 22–22A. New York: Doubleday, 1983–97.

Greenspahn, Frederick E. "Deuteronomy and Centralization." *VT* 64 (2014): 227–35.

———. "The Theology of the Framework of Judges." *VT* 36 (1986): 385–96.

Greenspoon, Leonard J. "The Qumran Fragments of Joshua: Which Puzzle Are They Part of and Where Do They Fit?" Pages 159–204 in *Septuagint, Scrolls and Cognate Writings: Papers Presented to the International Symposium on the Septuagint and Its Relations to the Dead Sea Scrolls and Other Writings (Manchester 1990)*. SBLSCS 33. Atlanta: Scholars Press, 1992.

———. "Textual and Translation Issues in Greek Exodus." Pages 322–48 in *The Book of Exodus: Composition, Reception, and Interpretation*. Edited by Thomas B. Dozeman, Craig A. Evans, and Joel N. Lohr. VTSup 164. Leiden: Brill, 2014.

Greenstein, Edward L. "The Language of Job and Its Poetic Function." *JBL* 122 (2003): 651–66.

Grogan, Geoffrey. *Prayer, Praise and Prophecy: A Theology of the Psalms*. Fearn, Ross-shire, UK: Christian Focus, 2001.

Gruber, Mayer I. *Rashi's Commentary on Psalms*. New York: Jewish Publication Society, 2008.

Grypeou, Emmanouela, and Helen Spurling. *The Book of Genesis in Late Antiquity: Encounters between Jewish and Christian Exegesis*. Jewish and Christian Perspectives 24. Leiden: Brill, 2013.

Guillaume, Philippe. "Dismantling the Deconstruction of Job." *JBL* 127 (2008): 491–99.

Gunkel, Hermann. *Introduction to the Psalms: The Genres of the Religious Lyric of Ancient Israel*. Mercer Library of Biblical Studies. Macon: Mercer University Press, 1998.

———. *The Legends of Genesis*. Translated by W. H. Carruth. New York: Schocken, 1901.

———. "Nahum 1." *ZAW* 13 (1893): 223–44.

Gunn, David M. *The Fate of King Saul: An Interpretation of a Biblical Story*. JSOTSup 14. Sheffield: JSOT Press, 1980.

———. "Joshua and Judges." Pages 102–21 in *The Literary Guide to the Bible*. Edited by Robert Alter and Frank Kermode. Cambridge, MA: Harvard University Press, 1987.

———. *The Story of King David: Genre and Interpretation*. JSOTSup 6. Sheffield: JSOT Press, 1978.

Gunn, David M., and Danna Nolan Fewell. *Narrative in the Hebrew Bible*. The Oxford Bible Series. Oxford: Oxford University Press, 1993.

Gurtner, Daniel M. *Exodus: A Commentary on the Greek Text of Codex Vaticanus*. SCS. Leiden: Brill, 2013.

Güterbock, Hans G., and Theo P. J. van den Hout. *The Hittite Instruction for the Royal Bodyguard*. Assyriological Studies 24. Chicago: The Oriental Institute of the University of Chicago, 1991.

Hackett, Jo Ann. *The Balaam Text from* Deir ʿAllā. HSM 31. Chico, CA: Scholars Press, 1980.

Hadley, Judith M. *The Cult of Asherah in Ancient Israel and Judah: Evidence for a Hebrew Goddess*. University of Cambridge Oriental Publications 57. Cambridge: Cambridge University Press, 2000.

———. "Wisdom and the Goddess." Pages 234–43 in *Wisdom in Ancient Israel: Essays in Honour of J. A. Emerton*. Edited by John Day, Robert P. Gordon, and H. G. M. Williamson. Cambridge: Cambridge University Press, 1995.

Haldar, Alfred. *Studies in the Book of Nahum*. Uppsala: Almqvist & Wiksell, 1947.

Halperin, David J. *Seeking Ezekiel: Text and Psychology*. State College: Pennsylvania State University Press, 1993.

Halpern, Baruch. "The Construction of the Davidic State: An Exercise in Historiography." Pages 44–75 in *The Origins of the Ancient Israelite States*. Edited by V. Fritz and P. R. Davies. JSOTSup 228. Sheffield: Sheffield Academic, 1996.

———. *The First Historians: The Hebrew Bible and History*. San Francisco: Harper & Row, 1988.

Hamori, Esther J. *Women's Divination in Biblical Literature: Prophecy, Necromancy, and Other Arts of Knowledge*. ABRL. New Haven: Yale University Press, 2015.

Handy, Lowell K. "The Authorization of Divine Power and the Guilt of God in the Book of Job: Useful Ugaritic Parallels." *JSOT* 60 (1993): 107–18.

Haran, Menahem. "The Character of the Priestly Source: Utopian and Exclusive Features." Pages 131–38 in *Proceedings of the Eighth World Congress of Jewish Studies, Jerusalem, August 16–21, 1981: Panel Sections; Bible and Hebrew Language*. Jerusalem: World Union of Jewish Studies, 1983.

Hartley, John E. *The Book of Job*. NICOT. Grand Rapids: Eerdmans, 1988.

———. *Leviticus*. WBC 4. Waco: Word, 1992.

Hattersley, Roy. *The Life of John Wesley: A Brand from the Burning*. New York: Doubleday, 2003.

Haupt, Paul. *Biblische Liebeslieder: Das sogenannte Hohelied Salomos*. Leipzig: Hinrichs, 1907.

———. "The Book of Nahum." *JBL* 26 (1907): 1–53.

Hauser, Alan Jon. "Genesis 2–3: The Theme of Intimacy and Alienation." Pages 383–98 in *"I Studied Inscriptions from before the Flood": Ancient Near Eastern, Linguistic and Literary Approaches to Genesis 1–11*. Edited by R. S. Hess and D. T. Tsumura. SBTS 4. Winona Lake, IN: Eisenbrauns, 1994.

Havea, Jione. "Casting Jonah across Seas and Tongues: A Transnationalizing Reading." Pages 25–36 in *Babel Is Everywhere! Migrant Readings from Africa, Europe and Asia*. Edited by J. Kwabena Asamoah-Gyadu, Andrea Fröchtling, and Andreas Kunz-Lübcke. Frankfurt: Peter Lang, 2013.

Hawk, L. Daniel. *Every Promise Fulfilled: Contesting Plots in Joshua*. Literary Currents in Biblical Interpretation. Louisville: Westminster John Knox, 1991.

———. *Joshua*. Berit Olam. Collegeville, MN: Liturgical Press, 2000.

Hawkins, Ralph K. *How Israel Became a People*. Nashville: Abingdon, 2013.

———. *The Iron Age I Structure on Mt. Ebal: Excavation and Interpretation*. BBRSup 6. Winona Lake: Eisenbrauns, 2012.

Hayes, John H., and Stuart A. Irvine. *Isaiah, the Eighth Century Prophet: His Times and His Preaching*. Nashville: Abingdon, 1987.

Hays, Christopher B. "Isaiah." *OEBB* 1:384–409.

Heide, Martin. "The Domestication of the Camel: Biological, Archaeological and Inscriptional Evidence from Mesopotamia, Israel and Arabia, and Literary Evidence from the Hebrew Bible." *UF* 42 (2010): 331–83.

Heim, Knut Martin. *Like Grapes of Gold Set in Silver: An Interpretation of Proverbial Clusters in Proverbs 10:1–22:16*. BZAW 273. Berlin: de Gruyter, 2001.

———. *Poetic Imagination in Proverbs: Variant Repetitions and the Nature of Poetry*. BBRSup 4. Winona Lake, IN: Eisenbrauns, 2011.

———. "Structure and Context in Proverbs 10:1–22:16." DPhil diss., University of Liverpool, 1996.

Heimpel, Wolfgang. *Letters to the King of Mari: A New Translation with Historical Introduction, Notes, and Commentary*. Mesopotamian Civilizations 12. Winona Lake, IN: Eisenbrauns, 2003.

Henry, Mathew. *Matthew Henry's Commentary in One Volume*. Grand Rapids: Zondervan, 1961.

Hermann, Alfred. *Altägyptische Liebesdichtung*. Wiesbaden: Harrassowitz, 1959.

Hess, Richard S. "Achan and Achor: Names and Wordplay in Joshua 7." *HAR* 14 (1994): 89–98.

———. "Adam, Father, He: Gender Issues in Hebrew Translation." *BT* 56.3 (July 2005): 144–53.

———. "Alalakh 1. Treaties: Abbael's Gift of Alalakh (*AT* 1) (2.127); The Agreement between Ir-addu and Niqmepa (*AT* 2) (2.128); Agreement between Pillia and Idrimi (*AT* 3) (2.129)." *COS* 2.127–129:329–32.

———. "Alalakh 5. Royal Grants: Will of Ammitaku Leader of Alalakh (*AT* 6*) (2.136); Land Grant (*AT* 456*) (2.137)." *COS* 2.136–137:368–70.

———. *Amarna Personal Names*. ASOR Dissertation Series 9. Winona Lake, IN: Eisenbrauns, 1993.

———. "Arrowheads from Iron Age I: Personal Names and Authenticity." Pages 113–29 in *Ugarit at Seventy-Five*. Edited by K. L. Younger. Winona Lake, IN: Eisenbrauns, 2007.

———. "Asking Historical Questions of Joshua 13–19: Recent Discussion concerning the Date of the Boundary Lists." Pages 191–205 in *Faith, Tradition, History: Old Testament Historiography in Its Near Eastern Context*. Edited by A. R. Millard, J. K. Hoffmeier, and D. W. Baker. Winona Lake, IN: Eisenbrauns, 1994.

———. "Aspects of Israelite Personal Names and Pre-exilic Israelite Religion." Pages 301–13 in *New Seals and Inscriptions, Hebrew, Idumean and Cuneiform*. Edited by M. Lubetski. Hebrew Bible Monographs 8. Sheffield: Sheffield Phoenix, 2007.

———. "B. Contracts 1. Alalakh. Sale Transactions: Sale of a Town (*AT* 52) (3.99B); Marriage Agreements: Marriage Customs (*AT* 92) (3.101B); Seven Years of Barrenness before a Second Wife (*AT* 93) (3.101C)." *COS* 3.99B, 101C:249–52.

———. "'Because of the Wickedness of These Nations' (Deut 9:4–5): The Canaanites—Ethical or Not?" Pp. 17–38 in *For Our Good Always: Studies on the Message and Influence of Deuteronomy in Honor of Daniel I. Block*. Edited by Jason S. DeRouchie, Jason Gile, and Kenneth J. Turner. Winona Lake, IN: Eisenbrauns, 2013.

———. "The Bible and Alalakh." Pages 209–21 in *Mesopotamia and the Bible: Comparative Explorations*. Edited by Mark W. Chavalas and K. Lawson Younger. Grand Rapids: Baker Academic; Sheffield: Sheffield Academic; New York: Continuum, 2002.

———. "The Book of Joshua as a Land Grant." *Bib* 83 (2002): 493–506.

———. "Creator of Heaven and Earth." *Touchstone: A Journal of Ecumenical Orthodoxy* 3.3 (Fall 1989): 9–10, 43. http://touchstonemag.com/archives/article.php?id=03-03-009-f.

———. "Cultural Aspects of Onomastic Distribution throughout Southern Canaan in Light of New Evidence." *UF* 38 (2006): 353–61.

———. "David and Abishag: The Purpose of 1 Kings 1:1–4." Pages 427–37 in *Homeland and Exile: Biblical and Ancient Near Eastern Studies in Honour of Bustenay Oded*. Edited by G. Galil, M. Geller, and A. Millard. VTSup 130. Leiden: Brill, 2009.

———. "E. Wills 1. Alalakh. Inheritance of a Brother and a Sister (*AT* 7) (3.129)." *COS* 3.129:283.

———. "Early Israel in Canaan: A Survey of Recent Evidence and Interpretations." Pages 492–518 in *Israel's Past in Present Research: Essays on Ancient Israelite Historiography*. Edited by V. Philips Long. SBTS 7. Winona Lake, IN: Eisenbrauns, 1999. Repr. from *PEQ* 126 (1993): 125–42.

———. "The Form and Structure of the Solomonic District List in 1 Kings 4:7–19." Pages 279–92 in *Crossing Boundaries and Linking Horizons: Studies in Honor of Michael C. Astour*. Edited by G. D. Young, M. W. Chavalas, and R. E. Averbeck. Bethesda, MD: CDL, 1997.

———. "The Future Written in the Past: The Old Testament and the Millennium." Pages 23–36 in *A Case for Historic Premillennialism: An Alternative to "Left Behind" Eschatology*. Edited by C. L. Blomberg and S. W. Chung. Grand Rapids: Baker Academic, 2009.

———. "The Genealogies of Genesis 1–11 and Comparative Literature." Pages 58–72 in *"I Studied Inscriptions from before the Flood": Ancient Near Eastern, Literary, and Linguistic Approaches to Genesis 1–11*. Edited by R. S. Hess and D. T. Tsumura. SBTS 4. Winona Lake, IN: Eisenbrauns, 1994. Repr. from *Bib* 70 (1989): 241–54.

———. "Genesis 1–2 and Recent Studies of Ancient Texts." *Science and Christian Belief* 7 (1995): 141–49.

———. "Genesis 1–2 in Its Literary Context." *TynBul* 41 (1990): 143–53.

———. "Genesis 1–3: Egalitarianism with and without Innocence." Pages 79–95 in *Discovering Biblical Equality: Complementarity without Hierarchy*. Edited by R. W. Pierce, R. M. Groothuis, and G. D. Fee. Downers Grove, IL: IVP Academic, 2004.

———. "Hebrew Psalms and Amarna Correspondence from Jerusalem: Some

Comparisons and Implications." *ZAW* 101 (1989): 249–65.

———. "Hezekiah and Sennacherib in 2 Kings 18–20." Pages 23–41 in *Zion, City of Our God*. Edited by R. S. Hess and G. J. Wenham. Grand Rapids: Eerdmans, 1999.

———. "Hurrians and Other Inhabitants of Late Bronze Age Palestine." *Levant* 29 (1997): 153–56.

———. "Introduction: Foundations for a History of Israel." Pages 1–22 in *Ancient Israel's History: An Introduction to Issues and Sources*. Edited by Bill T. Arnold and Richard S. Hess. Grand Rapids: Baker Academic, 2014.

———. "Israelite Identity and Personal Names in the Book of Judges." *HS* 44 (2003): 25–39.

———. *Israelite Religions: An Archaeological and Biblical Survey*. Grand Rapids: Baker Academic, 2007.

———. "The Jericho and Ai of the Book of Joshua." Pages 33–46 in *Critical Issues in Early Israelite History*. Edited by R. S. Hess, G. A. Klingbeil, and P. J. Ray Jr. BBRSup 3. Winona Lake, IN: Eisenbrauns, 2008.

———. "Joshua." *ZIBBCOT* 2:2–93.

———. *Joshua: An Introduction and Commentary*. TOTC. Downers Grove, IL: InterVarsity, 1996. Repr., Downers Grove, IL: IVP Academic, 2008.

———. "Joshua and Egypt." Pages 144–50 in *Visions of Life in Biblical Times: Essays in Honor of Meir Lubetski*. Edited by Claire Gottlieb, Chaim Cohen, and Mayer Gruber. Hebrew Bible Monographs 76. Sheffield: Sheffield Phoenix, 2015.

———. "Katuwas and the Masoretic Text of Kings: Cultural Connections between Carchemish and Israel." Pages 171–82 in *New Inscriptions and Seals Relating to the Biblical World*. Edited by M. Lubetski and E. Lubetski. SBL Archaeology and Biblical Studies 19. Atlanta: SBL, 2012.

———. "Kings, Books of." *DTIB* 422–25.

———. "Late Bronze Age and Biblical Boundary Descriptions of the West Semitic World." Pages 123–38 in *Ugarit and the Bible: Proceedings of the International Symposium on Ugarit and the Bible, Manchester, September 1992*. Edited by G. Brooke, A. Curtis, and J. Healey. UBL 11. Münster: Ugarit-Verlag, 1994.

———. "Leviticus." Pages 563–826 in vol. 1 of *The Expositor's Bible Commentary*. Edited by T. Longman III and D. E. Garland. Rev. ed. Grand Rapids: Zondervan, 2008.

———. "Literacy in Iron Age Israel." Pages 82–102 in *Windows into Old Testament History: Evidence, Argument, and the Crisis of "Biblical Israel."* Edited by V. P. Long, D. W. Baker, and G. J. Wenham. Grand Rapids: Eerdmans, 2002.

———. "The Mayarzana Correspondence: Rhetoric and Conquest Accounts." *UF* 30 (1998): 335–51.

———. "Multi-Month Ritual Calendars in the West Semitic World." Pages 233–53 in *The Future of Biblical Archaeology*. Edited by James Hoffmeier and Alan Millard. Grand Rapids: Eerdmans, 2004.

———. "The Name Game: Dating the Book of Judges." *BAR* 30.6 (November/December 2004): 38–41.

———. "A New Generation of Deuteronomists?" *BBR* 19 (2009): 417–24.

———. "Non-Israelite Personal Names in the Book of Joshua." *CBQ* 58 (1996): 205–14.

———. "Protective Strategies Here and There: A Review Article of Stephen L. Young, 'Protective Strategies . . .' and 'Maximizing Literacy as a Protective Strategy.'" *DJ* 18 (2015). http://www.denverseminary.edu/resources/news-and-articles/protective-strategies-here-and-there-a-review-article-of-stephen-l-young-protective-strategies-and-maximizing-literacy-as-a-protective-strategy/.

———. "Questions of Reading and Writing in Ancient Israel." *BBR* 19 (2009): 1–9.

———. "Recent Studies in Old Testament History: A Review Article." *Them* 19 (January 1994): 9–15.

———. Review of *The Bible Unearthed: Archaeology's New Vision of Ancient Israel and the Origin of Its Sacred Texts*, by Israel Finkelstein and Neil A. Silberman. *DJ* 4 (2001). http://www.denverseminary

.edu/resources/news-and-articles/the-bible-unearthed.

———. Review of *The Laws of the Hittites: A Critical Edition*, by H. A. Hoffner. *JBL* 118 (1999): 1711–72.

———. "Review of *Writing and Literacy in the World of Ancient Israel: Epigraphic Evidence from Iron Age Society*, by C. A. Rollston." *BBR* 21 (2011): 394–96.

———. "The Seventy Sevens of Daniel: A Timetable for the Future?" *BBR* 21 (2011): 315–30.

———. *Song of Songs*. BCOTWP. Grand Rapids: Baker Academic, 2005.

———. "The Southern Desert." *Archaeology and the Biblical World* 2.2 (Spring 1994): 22–33.

———. "Splitting the Adam: The Usage of ʾĀDĀM in Genesis i–v." Pages 1–15 in *Studies in the Pentateuch*. Edited by J. A. Emerton. VTSup 41. Leiden: Brill, 1990.

———. "Studies in the Book of Joshua." *Them* 20.3 (May 1995): 12–15.

———. *Studies in the Personal Names of Genesis 1–11*. AOAT 234. Kevelaer: Butzon & Bercker; Neukirchen-Vluyn: Neukirchener, 1993. Repr., Winona Lake, IN: Eisenbrauns, 2009.

———. "Textual Criticism (Old Testament)." Pages 355–56 in *Dictionary of Biblical Criticism and Interpretation*. Edited by Stanley E. Porter. London: Routledge, 2007.

———. "A Typology of West Semitic Place Name Lists with Special Reference to Joshua 13–21." *BA* 59.3 (September 1996): 160–70.

———. "War in the Hebrew Bible: An Overview." Pages 19–32 in *War in the Bible and Terrorism in the Twenty-First Century*. Edited by R. S. Hess and E. A. Martens. BBRSup 2. Winona Lake, IN: Eisenbrauns, 2008.

———. "West Semitic Texts and the Book of Joshua." *BBR* 7 (1997): 63–76.

———. "Writing about Writing: Abecedaries and Evidence for Literacy in Ancient Israel." *VT* 56 (2006): 342–46.

Hess, Richard S., Gerald A. Klingbeil, and Paul J. Ray Jr., eds. *Critical Issues in Early Israelite History*. *BBRSup* 3. Winona Lake, IN: Eisenbrauns, 2008.

Hess, Richard S., Philip Satterthwaite, and Gordon Wenham, eds. *He Swore an Oath: Biblical Themes from Genesis 12–50*. 2nd ed. Carlisle, UK: Paternoster; Grand Rapids: Baker, 1994.

Hess, Richard S., and David T. Tsumura, eds. *"I Studied Inscriptions from before the Flood": Ancient Near Eastern, Linguistic and Literary Approaches to Genesis 1–11*. SBTS 4. Winona Lake, IN: Eisenbrauns, 1994.

Hestrin, Ruth. "Understanding Asherah: Exploring Semitic Iconography." *BAR* 17.5 (September/October 1991): 50–59.

Hiebert, Theodore. *God of My Victory: The Ancient Hymn in Habakkuk 3*. HSM 38. Atlanta: Scholars Press, 1986.

Hildebrandt, T. A. "Proverbial Pairs: Compositional Units in Proverbs 10–29." *JBL* 107 (1988): 207–24.

Hill, Andrew E. *Haggai, Zechariah, and Malachi: An Introduction and Commentary*. TOTC 28. Leicester, UK: IVP Academic, 2012.

———. *Malachi: A New Translation with Introduction and Commentary*. AB 25D. New York: Doubleday, 1998.

———. "Malachi, Book of." *DOTP* 525–33.

Hill, Robert C. *Theodore of Mopsuestia: Commentary on Psalms 1-81*. Edited and Translated by Robert C. Hill. SBL Writings from the Greco-Roman World. Atlanta: Society of Biblical Literature, 2006.

Hillers, Delbert. *Micah: A Commentary on the Book of the Prophet Micah*. Hermeneia. Philadelphia: Fortress, 1984.

Himbaza, Innocent. "Habakkuk." Pages 306–9 in *Global Bible Commentary*. Edited by Daniel Patte. Nashville: Abingdon, 2004.

Hjelm, Ingrid. *Jerusalem's Rise to Sovereignty: Zion and Gerizim in Competition*. JSOTSup 404. London: T&T Clark, 2004.

Hoag, Gary G. *Wealth in Ancient Ephesus and the First Letter to Timothy: Fresh Insights from* Ephesiaca *by Xenophon of Ephesus*. BBRSup 11. Winona Lake: Eisenbrauns, 2015.

Hoffmeier, James K. *Ancient Israel in Sinai: The Evidence for the Authenticity of the Wilderness Tradition*. Oxford: Oxford University Press, 2005.

———. "The Exodus and Wilderness Narratives." Pages 46–90 in *Ancient Israel's History: An Introduction to Issues and Sources*. Edited by Bill T. Arnold and Richard S. Hess. Grand Rapids: Baker Academic, 2014.

———. *The Immigration Crisis: Immigrants, Aliens, and the Bible*. Wheaton: Crossway, 2009.

———. *Israel in Egypt: The Evidence for the Authenticity of the Exodus Tradition*. Oxford: Oxford University Press, 1997.

Hoffmeier, James K., and Alan Millard, eds. *The Future of Biblical Archaeology: Reassessing Methodologies and Assumptions*. Grand Rapids: Eerdmans, 2004.

Hoffmeier, James K., Alan R. Millard, and Gary A. Rendsburg, eds. *"Did I Not Bring Israel Out of Egypt?" Biblical, Archaeological, and Egyptological Perspectives on the Exodus Narratives*. BBRSup 13. Winona Lake, IN: Eisenbrauns, forthcoming.

Hoffner, Harry A., Jr. "A Hittite Analogy to the David and Goliath Contest of Champions." *CBQ* 30 (1968): 220–25.

———. *Hittite Myths*. SBLWAW 2. Atlanta: Scholars Press, 1990.

———. *The Laws of the Hittites: A Critical Edition*. Leiden: Brill, 1997.

Hoglund, Kenneth G. *Achaemenid Imperial Administration in Syria-Palestine and the Missions of Ezra and Nehemiah*. SBLDS 125. Atlanta: Scholars Press, 1992.

Holladay, John S., Jr. "The Kingdoms of Israel and Judah: Political and Economic Centralization in the Iron IIA–B." Pages 368–98 in *The Archaeology of Society in the Holy Land*. Edited by Thomas E. Levy. New York: Facts on File, 1995.

Holladay, William L. *Jeremiah*. Vol. 1, *1–25*. Hermeneia. Philadelphia: Fortress, 1986. Vol. 2, *26–52*. Minneapolis: Fortress, 1989.

———. *The Psalms through Three Thousand Years: Prayerbook of a Cloud of Witnesses*. Minneapolis: Fortress, 1996.

———. "Reading Zephaniah with a Concordance: Suggestions for a Redaction History." *JBL* 120 (2001): 671–84.

Holmes, Michael W. *The Apostolic Fathers: Greek Texts and English Translations*. 3rd edition. Grand Rapids: Baker Academic, 2007.

Hölscher, Gustav. *Hesekiel: Der Dichter und das Buch*. BZAW 39. Giessen: Töpelmann, 1924.

Homan, Michael M. "The Divine Warrior in His Tent." *BR* 16.6 (December 2000): 22–33, 55.

Höpfl, Harro. *Luther and Calvin on Secular Authority*. Cambridge Texts in the History of Political Thought. Cambridge: Cambridge University Press, 1991.

Horowitz, Wayne, Takayoshi Oshima, and Filip Vukosavović. "Hazor 18: Fragments of a Cuneiform Law Collection from Hazor." *IEJ* 62 (2012): 158–76.

Horst, Friedrich. "Die Formen des althebräischen Liebesliedes." Pages 43–54 in *Orientalische Studien: Enno Littmann zu seinem 60. Geburtstag am 16 September 1933*. Edited by R. Paret. Leiden: Brill, 1935.

Hort, Greta. "The Plagues of Egypt." *ZAW* 69 (1957): 84–103; 70 (1958): 48–59.

Hossfeld, Frank-Lothar, and Erich Zenger. *Psalms 2: A Commentary on Psalms 51–100*. Translated by Linda M. Maloney. Hermeneia. Minneapolis: Fortress, 2005.

House, Paul R. *The Unity of the Twelve*. JSOTSup 97. BLS 27. Sheffield: Almond, 1990.

Howard, David M., Jr. *Joshua*. NAC 5. Nashville: Broadman & Holman, 1998.

Hubbard, Robert L., Jr. *The Book of Ruth*. NICOT. Grand Rapids: Eerdmans, 1988.

Huddlestun, John R. "Nahum." *OEBB* 2:100–110.

Hudson, Don Michael. "Living in a Land of Epithets: Anonymity in Judges 19–21." *JSOT* 62 (1994): 49–66.

Hugenberger, Gordon P. *Marriage as a Covenant: Biblical Law and Ethics as Developed from Malachi*. Biblical Studies Library. Grand Rapids: Baker, 1994.

Hurowitz, Victor A. *I Have Built You an Exalted House: Temple Building in the Bible in Light of Mesopotamian and Northwest Semitic Writings*. JSOTSup 115. JSOT/ASOR Monograph 5. Sheffield: JSOT Press, 1992.

———. "Inside Solomon's Temple." *BR* 10.2 (April 1994): 24–37, 50.

———. "Solomon's Temple in Context." *BAR* 37.2 (March/April 2011): 46–57, 77–78.

———. "Wisdom of Šūpê-amēlī—A Deathbed Debate between a Father and Son." Pages 37–51 in *Wisdom Literature in Mesopotamia and Israel*. Edited by R. J. Clifford. SBL Symposium Series 36. Atlanta: SBL, 2007.

Hurvitz, Avi. "Continuity and Change in Biblical Hebrew: The Linguistic History of a Formulaic Idiom from the Realm of the Royal Court." Pages 127–33 in *Biblical Hebrew in Its Northwest Semitic Setting: Typological and Historical Perspectives*. Edited by Steven E. Fassberg and Avi Hurvitz. Publications of the Institute for Advanced Studies 1. Jerusalem: Magnes; Winona Lake, IN: Eisenbrauns, 2006.

———. "Dating the Priestly Source in Light of the Historical Study of Biblical Hebrew a Century after Wellhausen." *ZAW* 100 (1988 Supplement): 88–100.

———. *A Linguistic Study of the Relationship between the Priestly Source and the Book of Ezekiel*. CahRB 20. Paris: Gabalda, 1982.

———. *The Transition Period in Biblical Hebrew* [in Hebrew]. Jerusalem: Bialik Institute, 1972.

Ibn Ezra, Abraham. *Abraham Ibn Ezra's Commentary on the First Book of Psalms: Abraham Ibn Ezra's Commenary on the Second Book of Psalms*, vol. 1. Translated by H. Norman Strickman. Ann Arbor: Academic Studies Press, 2009.

Japhet, Sara. *I and II Chronicles: A Commentary*. OTL. Louisville: Westminster John Knox, 1993.

———. *The Ideology of the Book of Chronicles and Its Place in Biblical Thought*. Translated by Anna Barber. Jerusalem: Bialik, 1989.

———. "Periodization between History and Ideology II: Chronology and Ideology in Ezra–Nehemiah." Pages 491–529 in *Judah and Judeans in the Persian Period*. Edited by Oded Lipschits and Manfred Oeming. Winona Lake, IN: Eisenbrauns, 2006.

———. "The Supposed Common Authorship of Chronicles and Ezra–Nehemiah Investigated Anew." *VT* 18 (1968): 330–71.

Jarick, John. "Theodore of Mopsuestia and the Interpretation of Ecclesiastes." Pages 306–16 in *The Bible in Human Society: Essays in Honour of John Rogerson*. Edited by D. J. A. Clines, P. R. Davies, and M. D. Carroll R. JSOTSup 300. Sheffield: Sheffield Academic, 1995.

Jenson, Philip P. *Graded Holiness: A Key to the Priestly Conception of the World*. JSOTSup 106. Sheffield: JSOT Press, 1992.

———. "The Levitical Sacrificial System." Pages 25–40 in *Sacrifice in the Bible*. Edited by Roger T. Beckwith and Marvin J. Selman. Carlisle, UK: Paternoster; Grand Rapids: Baker, 1995.

Jepsen, Alfred. "*ʾāman*." *TDOT* 1:292–323.

Jeremias, Jörg. *The Book of Amos: A Commentary*. OTL. Louisville: Westminster John Knox, 1998.

Jerome. *Commentary on Jeremiah*. Translated by Michael Graves. Edited by Christopher Hall. Ancient Christian Texts. Downers Grove, IL: InterVarsity, 2012.

Jobes, Karen H. *Esther*. NIVAC. Grand Rapids: Zondervan, 1999.

———. "Esther 1: Book of." *DOTWPW* 160–70.

———. "Esther 2: Extrabiblical Background." *DOTWPW* 170–75.

———. "Esther 3: History of Interpretation." *DOTWPW* 175–81.

———. "Esther 5: Greek Versions." *DOTWPW* 184–88.

Jobes, Karen H., and Moisés Silva. *Invitation to the Septuagint*. 2nd ed. Grand Rapids: Baker Academic, 2015.

Johnston, Gordon H. "A Rhetorical Analysis of the Book of Nahum." PhD diss., Dallas Theological Seminary, 1992.

Jones, Scott C. "Solomon's Table Talk: Martin Luther on the Authorship of Ecclesiastes." *SJOT* 28 (2014): 81–90.

Jong, Matthijs J. de. *Isaiah among the Ancient Near Eastern Prophets: A Comparative Study of the Earliest Stages of the Isaiah Tradition and the Neo-Assyrian Prophecies.* VTSup 117. Leiden: Brill, 2007.

Jordaan, Pierre J. "Reading Susanna as Therapeutic Narrative." *JSem* 17 (2008): 114–28.

Joyce, Paul. *Divine Initiative and Human Response in Ezekiel.* JSOTSup 51. Sheffield: JSOT Press, 1989.

Kaiser, Walter C. *Ecclesiastes: Total Life.* Chicago: Moody, 1997.

Kalluveettil, Paul. "Haggai." Pages 315–17 in *Global Bible Commentary.* Edited by Daniel Patte. Nashville: Abingdon, 2004.

Karris, Robert J., ed. *Works of St. Bonaventure,* vol. 7, *Commentary on Ecclesiastes.* Edited by Robert J. Karris. St. Bonaventure, NY: Franciscan Institute Publications, 2005.

Kaufman, Stephen A. *Jacob of Sarug's Homilies on the Judgment of Solomon: Metrical Homilies of Mar Jacob of Sarug.* TCLA 18. Fascicle 4. Piscataway, NJ: Gorgias, 2008.

———. *Jacob of Sarug's Homily on Elijah.* TCLA 17. Fascicles 9–13. Piscataway, NJ: Gorgias, 2009.

———. *Jacob of Sarug's Homily on Elisha.* TCLA 28. Fascicles 23–28. Piscataway, NJ: Gorgias, 2010.

———. "Reflections on the Assyrian-Aramaic Bilingual from Tell Fakhariyeh." *Ma* 3 (1982): 137–75.

———. "The Second Table of the Decalogue and the Implicit Categories of Ancient Near Eastern Law." Pages 111–16 in *Love and Death in the Ancient Near East: Essays in Honor of Marvin H. Pope.* Edited by J. H. Marks and R. M. Good. Guilford, CT: Four Quarters, 1987.

———. "The Structure of the Deuteronomic Law." *Ma* 1 (1978–79): 105–58.

Kaufmann, Yehezkel. *The Religion of Israel: From Its Beginnings to the Babylonian Exile.* Translated and abridged by Moshe Greenberg. New York: Schocken, 1960.

Keefe, Alice A. *Woman's Body and the Social Body in Hosea.* JSOTSup 338. Sheffield: Sheffield Academic, 2001.

Keel, Othmar. *The Song of Songs.* Translated by F. J. Geiser. ConC. Minneapolis: Fortress, 1994.

———. *The Symbolism of the Biblical World: Ancient Near Eastern Iconography and the Book of Psalms.* Translated by T. J. Hallett. New York: Seabury, 1977.

Keil, Carl Friedrich. *Joshua, Judges, Ruth.* Translated by James Martin. Edinburgh: T&T Clark, 1863.

———. *Keil on the Twelve Minor Prophets: Vol. 1.* Clark's Foreign Theological Library Fourth Series. Vol. 17. Translated by James Martin. Edinburgh: T&T Clark, 1871.

———. *The Third Book of Moses.* Vol. 2 of *The Pentateuch.* Edited by C. F. Keil and F. Delitzsch. Translated by James Martin. 1862. Repr., Grand Rapids: Eerdmans, 1975.

Kelle, Brad E. "Judah in the Seventh Century: From the Aftermath of Sennacherib's Invasion to the Beginning of Jehoiakim's Rebellion." Pages 350–82 in *Ancient Israel's History: An Introduction to Issues and Sources.* Edited by Bill T. Arnold and Richard S. Hess. Grand Rapids: Baker Academic, 2014.

Kellogg, Samuel H. *The Book of Leviticus.* 3rd ed. 1899. Repr., Minneapolis: Klock & Klock, 1978.

Kelly, Brian E. *Retribution and Eschatology in Chronicles.* JSOTSup 211. Sheffield: Sheffield Academic, 1996.

Kessler, John. *The Book of Haggai: Prophecy and Society in Early Persian Yehud.* VTSup 91. Leiden: Brill, 2002.

———. "Haggai, Book of." *DOTP* 301–7.

Kessler, Stephan C. "Gregory the Great: A Figure of Tradition and Transition in Church Exegesis." Pages 135–47 in *Hebrew Bible/Old Testament: The History of Its Interpretation.* Vol. 1: *From the Beginnings to the Middle Ages (Until 1300). Part 2: The Middle Ages.* Edited by Magne Sæbø. Göttingen: Vandenhoeck & Ruprecht, 2000.

Kidner, Derek. *Ezra and Nehemiah: An Introduction and Commentary.* TOTC. Leicester, UK: Inter-Varsity; Downers Grove, IL: InterVarsity, 1979.

———. *Proverbs: An Introduction and Commentary*. TOTC. Leicester, UK: Inter-Varsity; Downers Grove, IL: InterVarsity, 1964.

———. *Psalms: An Introduction and Commentary*. Vol. 1, *1–72*. Vol. 2, *73–150*. TOTC. Leicester, UK: Inter-Varsity; Downers Grove, IL: InterVarsity, 1973–75.

Kim, Jin-Myung. *Holiness and Perfection: A Canonical Unfolding of Leviticus 19*. Das Alte Testament im Dialog. Vol. 3. Bern: Peter Lang, 2011.

Ḳimḥi, David. *The Longer Commentary of R. David Ḳimḥi on the First Book of Psalms (I–X, XV–XVII, XIX, XXII, XXIV)*. Translated by R. G. Finch. London: SPCK, 1919.

King, Philip J. *Amos, Hosea, Micah: An Archaeological Commentary*. Philadelphia: Westminster, 1988.

———. *Jeremiah: An Archaeological Commentary*. Philadelphia: Westminster John Knox, 1993.

———. "The Musical Tradition of Ancient Israel." Pages 84–99 in *Realia Dei: Essays in Archaeology and Biblical Interpretation in Honor of Edward F. Campbell, Jr. at His Retirement*. Edited by P. H. Williams Jr. and T. Hiebert. Scholars Press Homage Series 23. Atlanta: Scholars Press, 1999.

King, Philip J., and Lawrence E. Stager. *Life in Biblical Israel*. Louisville: Westminster John Knox, 2001.

Kitchen, Kenneth A. "The Controlling Role of External Evidence in Assessing the Historical Status of the Israelite Monarchy." Pages 111–30 in *Windows into Old Testament History: Evidence, Argument, and the Crisis of "Biblical Israel."* Edited by V. P. Long, D. W. Baker, and G. J. Wenham. Grand Rapids: Eerdmans, 2002.

———. "The Desert Tabernacle." *BR* 16.6 (December 2000): 14–21.

———. "How We Know When Solomon Ruled: Synchronisms with Egyptian and Assyrian Rulers Hold the Key to Dates of Israelite Kings." *BAR* 27.4 (September/October 2001): 32–37, 58.

———. *On the Reliability of the Old Testament*. Grand Rapids: Eerdmans, 2003.

———. "A Possible Mention of David in the Late Tenth Century BCE, and Deity Dod as Dead as the Dodo?" *JSOT* 76 (1997): 29–44.

Kitchen, Kenneth A., and Paul J. N. Lawrence. *Treaty, Law and Covenant in the Ancient Near East*. 3 vols. *Part 1: The Texts. Part 2: Text, Notes and Chromograms. Part 3: Overall Historical Survey.* Wiesbaden: Harrassowtiz Verlag, 2012.

Klein, Lillian R. "Hannah: Marginalized Victim and Social Redeemer." Pages 77–92 in *A Feminist Companion to Samuel and Kings*. Edited by A. Brenner. FCB 5. Sheffield: Sheffield Academic, 1994.

Klein, Ralph W. *1 Samuel*. 2nd ed. WBC 10. Nashville: Nelson, 2008.

Klingbeil, Gerald A. "Ecclesiastes 2: Ancient Near Eastern Background." *DOTWPW* 132–40.

Klingbeil, Martin G. "Off the Beaten Track: An Evangelical Reading of the Psalms without Gunkel." *BBR* 16 (2006): 25–40.

Knauf, Ernst A. "Does 'Deuteronomistic Historiography' (DtrH) Exist?" Pages 388–98 in *Israel Constructs Its History: Deuteronomistic Historiography in Recent Research*. Edited by Albert de Pury, Thomas Römer, and Jean-Daniel Macchi. JSOTSup 306. Sheffield: Sheffield Academic, 2000.

Kneebone, Emily. "Josephus' Esther and Diaspora Judaism." Pages 165–82 in *The Romance between Greece and the East*. Edited by Tim Whitmarsh and Stuart Thomson. Cambridge: Cambridge University Press, 2013.

Knight, Douglas A. *Rediscovering the Traditions of Israel*. 2nd ed. Atlanta: Scholars Press, 1975.

Knight, George A. F., and Friedemann W. Golka. *Revelation of God: A Commentary on the Song of Songs and Jonah*. International Theological Commentary. Grand Rapids: Eerdmans, 1988.

Knohl, Israel. "Nimrod, Son of Cush, King of Mesopotamia, and the Dates of P and J." Pages 45–52 in *Birkat Shalom: Studies in the Bible, Ancient Near Eastern Literature, and Postbiblical Judaism Presented to Shalom M. Paul on the Occasion of His Seventieth Birthday*. Edited by Chaim Cohen et al. 2 vols. Winona Lake, IN: Eisenbrauns, 2008.

Knoppers, Gary N. "Ancient Near Eastern Royal Grants and the Davidic Covenant: A Parallel?" *JAOS* 116 (1996): 670–97.

———. *I Chronicles: A New Translation with Introduction and Commentary*. Vol. 1, *1–9*. Vol. 2, *10–29*. AB 12–12A. New York: Doubleday, 2003–4.

———. "Jerusalem at War in Chronicles." Pages 57–76 in *Zion City of Our God*. Edited by R. S. Hess and Gordon J. Wenham. Grand Rapids: Eerdmans, 1999.

———. "The Synoptic Problem? An Old Testament Perspective." *BBR* 19 (2009): 11–34.

———. "The Vanishing Solomon: The Disappearance of the United Monarchy from Recent Histories of Ancient Israel." *JBL* 116 (1997): 19–44.

Kofoed, Jens Bruun. "Using Linguistic Differences in Relative Text Dating: Insights from Other Historical Linguistic Case Studies." *HS* 47 (2006): 93–114.

Koitabashi, Matahisa. "Music in the Texts from Ugarit." *UF* 30 (1998): 363–96.

Korpel, Marjo Christina Annette. *A Rift in the Clouds: Ugaritic and Hebrew Descriptions of the Divine*. UBL 8. Münster: Ugarit-Verlag, 1990.

Kraft, Robert A. "Para-mania: Beside, before, and beyond Biblical Studies." *JBL* 126 (2007): 5–27.

Kramer, Samuel Noah. "Distant Echoes in the Book of Psalms: Gleanings from Sumerian Literature." Pages 69–94 in vol. 1 of Tārīḫ*: A Volume of Occasional Papers in Near Eastern Studies*. Edited by Leon Nemoy and Vera B. Moreen. Philadelphia: Annenberg Research Institute, 1990–92.

Kraus, Fritz R. *Königliche Verfügungen in altbabylonischen Zeit*. Studia et documenta ad iura Orientis antiqui pertinentia 11. Leiden: Brill, 1984.

Kraus, Hans-Joachim. *Psalmen*. 2nd ed. BKAT 15. Neukirchen: Neukirchener Verlag, 1961.

Krinetzki, Leo. *Das Hohe Lied: Kommentar zu Gestalt und Kerygma eines alttestamentlichen Liebesliedes*. KBANT. Düsseldorf: Patmos, 1964.

Krüger, Thomas. *Qoheleth: A Commentary*. Edited by Klaus Baltzer. Translated by O. C. Dean Jr. Hermeneia. Minneapolis: Fortress, 2004.

Kugel, James L. *How to Read the Bible: A Guide to Scripture, Then and Now*. New York: Free Press, 2007.

———. *The Idea of Biblical Poetry: Parallelism and Its History*. New Haven: Yale University Press, 1981.

Kutscher, Raphael. *A History of the Hebrew Language*. Edited by R. Kutscher. Jerusalem: Magnes; Leiden: Brill, 1982.

Kutz, Karl V. "Characterization in the Old Greek of Job." Pages 345–55 in *Seeking Out the Wisdom of the Ancients: Essays Offered to Honor Michael V. Fox on the Occasion of His Sixty-Fifth Birthday*. Edited by Ronald L. Troxel, Kelvin G. Friebel, and Dennis R. Magary. Winona Lake, IN: Eisenbrauns, 2005.

Kwaakel, Gert. *According to My Righteousness: Upright Behaviour as Grounds for Deliverance in Psalms 7, 17, 18, 26*. OTS 46. Leiden: Brill, 2004.

Laato, Antii. "Zachariah 4,6b–10a and the Akkadian Royal Building Inscriptions." *ZAW* 106 (1994): 53–69.

LaCocque, André. "The Deconstruction of Job's Fundamentalism." *JBL* 126 (2007): 83–97.

———. "Job and Religion at Its Best." *BibInt* 4 (1996): 131–53.

———. *Romance, She Wrote: A Hermeneutical Essay on Song of Songs*. Harrisburg, PA: Trinity Press International, 1998.

Lamarche, Paul. *Zacharie IX–XIV: Structure littéraire et messianisme*. Paris: Gabalda, 1961.

Lambert, Wilfred G. "Mesopotamian Sources and Pre-exilic Israel." Pages 352–65 in *In Search of Pre-exilic Israel: Proceedings of the Oxford Old Testament Seminar*. Edited by John Day. JSOTSup 406. New York: T&T Clark, 2004.

Lamparter, Helmut. *Das Buch der Weisheit: Prediger und Sprüche, übersetzen und ausgelegt*. 2nd ed. Die Botschaft des Alten Testaments, Erläuterungen alttestamentlicher Schriften 16. Stuttgart: Calwer, 1959.

Landsberger, Benno. "Die babylonischen Termini für Gesetz und Recht." Pages 219–34 in *Symbolae ad iura orientes antiqui pertinentes Paulo Koschaker dedicatae*. Edited by J. Friedrich, J. G. Lautner, and J. Miles. Studia et documenta 2. Leiden: Brill, 1939.

Landy, Francis. *Paradoxes of Paradise: Identity and Difference in the Song of Songs*. BLS 7. Sheffield: Almond, 1983.

Lanner, Laurel. *"Who Will Lament Her?": The Feminine and the Fantastic in the Book of Nahum*. LHBOTS 434. New York: T&T Clark, 2006.

Lapsley, Jacqueline E. "Feeling Our Way: Love for God in Deuteronomy." *CBQ* 65 (2003): 350–69.

Lavoie, Jean-Jacques. *La pensée du Qohélet: Étude exégétique et intertextuelle*. Héritage et projet 49. Montreal: Fides, 1995.

LeCureux, Jason T. "Obadiah, Book of." *DOTP* 569–73.

Leder, Drew. *The Absent Body*. Chicago: University of Chicago Press, 1990.

Lee, Eunny P. *The Vitality of Enjoyment in Qohelet's Theological Rhetoric*. BZAW 353. Berlin: de Gruyter, 2005.

Lee, Nancy C. "Lamentations." *OEBB* 1:557–62.

Lemaire, André. "La dynastie davidique (*byt dwd*) dans deux inscriptions ouest-sémitiques du IXe s. av. J.-C." *SEL* 11 (1994): 17–19.

———. *Les écoles et la formation de la Bible dans l'ancien Israel*. OBO 39. Göttingen: Vandenhoeck & Ruprecht, 1981.

———. "Fifth- and Fourth-Century Issues: Governorship and Priesthood in Jerusalem." Pages 406–25 in *Ancient Israel's History: An Introduction to Issues and Sources*. Edited by Bill T. Arnold and Richard S. Hess. Grand Rapids: Baker Academic, 2014.

———. "Hebrew and West Semitic Inscriptions and Pre-exilic Israel." Pages 366–85 in *In Search of Pre-exilic Israel: Proceedings of the Oxford Old Testament Seminar*. Edited by John Day. JSOTSup 406. New York: T&T Clark, 2004.

———. "'House of David' Restored in Moabite Inscription." *BAR* 20.3 (May/June 1994): 30–37.

———. "Nouveaux sceaux nord-ouest sémitiques." *Semitica* 33 (1983): 17–31.

Lemche, Niels Peter. *Early Israel: Anthropological and Historical Studies on the Israelite Society before the Monarchy*. VTSup 37. Leiden: Brill, 1985.

———. "Israel, History of (Premonarchic Period)." *ABD* 3:526–45.

———. *The Israelites in History and Tradition*. Louisville: Westminster John Knox, 1998.

———. *Prelude to Israel's Past: Background and Beginnings of Israelite History and Identity*. Peabody, MA: Hendrickson, 1998.

Lescow, Theodor. "Die Komposition der Bücher Nahum und Habakuk." *BN* 77 (1995): 59–85.

Leuchter, Mark. "Another Look at the Hosea–Malachi Framework in The Twelve." *VT* 64 (2014): 249–65.

Leveen, Adriane. *Memory and Tradition in the Book of Numbers*. Cambridge: Cambridge University Press, 2008.

Levenson, Jon D. *Esther: A Commentary*. OTL. Louisville: Westminster John Knox, 1997.

Levine, Baruch A. "*Lpny YHWH*—Phenomenology of the Open-Air Altar in Biblical Hebrew." Pages 196–205 in *Biblical Archaeology Today, 1990: Proceedings of the Second International Congress on Biblical Archaeology, Jerusalem, June–July 1990*. Edited by A. Biran and J. Aviram. Jerusalem: Israel Exploration Society, 1993.

———. *Numbers: A New Translation with Introduction and Commentary*. Vol. 1, *1–20*. Vol. 2, *21–36*. AB 4–4A. Garden City, NY: Doubleday, 1993–2000.

Lewis, Brian. *The Sargon Legend: A Study of the Akkadian Text and of the Hero Who Was Exposed at Birth*. Cambridge, MA: ASOR, 1980.

Lewis, Jack P. "Jamnia Revisited." Pages 146–62 in *The Canon Debate*. Edited by Lee

Martin McDonald and James A. Sanders. Peabody, MA: Hendrickson, 2002.

Lewis, Theodore J. "The Identity and Function of El/Baal Berith." *JBL* 115 (1996): 401–23.

Lilly, Ingrid E. *Two Books of Ezekiel: Papyrus 967 and the Masoretic Text as Variant Literary Editions.* VTSup 150. Leiden: Brill, 2012.

Lim, Timothy H. *The Formation of the Jewish Canon.* The Anchor Yale Reference Library. New Haven: Yale University Press, 2013.

Lindars, Barnabas. *Judges 1–5: A New Translation and Commentary.* Edinburgh: T&T Clark, 1995.

Linville, James R. "Joel." *OEBB* 1:450–57.

Littman, Robert J. *Tobit: The Book of Tobit in Codex Sinaiticus.* SCS. Leiden: Brill, 2008.

Liverani, Mario. "The Ideology of the Assyrian Empire." Pages 297–317 in *Power and Propaganda: A Symposium on Ancient Empires.* Edited by M. T. Larsen. Mesopotamia: Copenhagen Studies in Assyriology 7. Copenhagen: Akademisk Forlag, 1979.

———. *Prestige and Interest: International Relations in the Near East ca. 1600–1100 BC.* History of the Ancient Near East 1. Padova: Sargon, 1990.

Livingstone, Alasdair. *Court Poetry and Literary Miscellanea.* SAA 3. Helsinki: Helsinki University Press, 1989.

Lohfink, Norbert. *Ecclesiastes.* Translated by S. E. McEvenue. ConC. Minneapolis: Fortress, 2003.

———. "Kerygmata des deuteronomistischen Geschichtswerks." Pages 125–42 in *Studien zum Deuteronomium und zur deuteronomistischen Literatur II.* SBA: Altes Testament 12. Stuttgart: Katholisches Bibelwerk, 1991.

Long, V. Philips, ed. *Israel's Past in Present Research: Essays on Ancient Israelite Historiography.* SBTS 7. Winona Lake, IN: Eisenbrauns, 1999.

Long, V. Philips, David W. Baker, and Gordon J. Wenham, eds. *Windows into Old Testament History: Evidence, Argument, and the Crisis of "Biblical Israel."* Grand Rapids: Eerdmans, 2002.

Longman, Tremper, III. *The Book of Ecclesiastes.* NICOT. Grand Rapids: Eerdmans, 1998.

———. *Daniel.* NIVAC. Grand Rapids: Zondervan, 1999.

———. "Ecclesiastes 3: History of Interpretation." *DOTWPW* 140–49.

———. *Fictional Akkadian Autobiography.* Winona Lake, IN: Eisenbrauns, 1991.

———. *Jeremiah, Lamentations.* NIBC. Peabody, MA: Hendrickson, 2008.

———. *Proverbs.* BCOTWP. Grand Rapids: Baker Academic, 2005.

———. *Song of Songs.* NICOT. Grand Rapids: Eerdmans, 2001.

Low, Katherine, ed. *The Bible, Gender, and Reception History: The Case of Job's Wife.* LHBOTS 586. Scriptural Traces: Critical Perspectives on the Reception and Influence of the Bible 1. London: Bloomsbury, 2013.

Lowth, Robert. *Lectures on the Sacred Poetry of the Hebrews.* Translated from the Latin of 1763 by G. Gregory. 2 vols. Repr., London: Routledge, 1995.

Lund, Jerome A. "Exodus in Syriac." Pages 349–69 in *The Book of Exodus: Composition, Reception, and Interpretation.* Edited by Thomas B. Dozeman, Craig A. Evans, and Joel N. Lohr. VTSup 164. Leiden: Brill, 2014.

Lundblom, Jack R. *Jeremiah: A New Translation with Introduction and Commentary.* Vol. 1, *1–20.* Vol. 2, *21–36.* Vol. 3, *37–52.* AB 21A, 21B, 22. New York: Doubleday, 1999–2004.

Luther, Martin. *Luther's Works.* Vol. 10, *First Lectures on the Psalms I: Psalms 1–75.* Edited by Hilton C. Oswald. St. Louis: Concordia, 1974.

———. *Luther's Works.* Vol. 11, *First Lectures on the Psalms II: Psalms 76–126.* Edited by Hilton C. Oswald. St. Louis: Concordia, 1976.

———. *Luther's Works.* Vol. 15, *Notes on Ecclesiastes, Lectures on the Song of Solomon, Treatise on the Last Words of David.* Edited by Hilton C. Oswald. St. Louis: Concordia, 1972.

———. *Luther's Works*. Vol. 18, *Lectures on the Minor Prophets I: Hosea, Joel, Amos, Obadiah, Micah, Nahum, Zephaniah, Haggai, Malachi*. Edited by Hilton C. Oswald. St. Louis: Concordia, 1975.

———. *Luther's Works*. Vol. 19, *Lectures on the Minor Prophets II: Jonah and Habakkuk*. Edited by Hilton C. Oswald. St. Louis: Concordia, 1974.

———. *Luther's Works*. Vol. 35, *Word and Sacrament I*. Edited by E. Theodore Bachmann. Philadelphia: Fortress, 1960.

———. *Luther's Works*. Vol. 45, *The Christian in Society*, vol. 2. Edited by Helmut T. Lehmann and James Atkinson. Philadelphia: Fortress, 1962.

———. *Ruth*. Leipzig: im Insel-Verlag, 1914.

Lüthi, Walter. *Die Bauleute Gottes: Nehemia, der Prophet im Kampf um den Bau der Stadt*. 4th ed. Basel: Friedrich Reinhardt, 1960.

Macatangay, Francis M. "Election by Allusion: Exodus Themes in the Book of Tobit." *CBQ* 76 (2014): 450–63.

Machinist, Peter B. "Assyria and Its Image in the First Isaiah." *JAOS* 103 (1983): 719–37.

———. "The Fall of Assyria in Comparative Ancient Perspective." Pages 179–95 in *Assyria 1995: Proceedings of the 10th Anniversary Symposium of the Neo-Assyrian Text Corpus Project, Helsinki, September 7–11, 1995*. Edited by Simo Parpola and Robert M. Whiting. Helsinki: The Neo-Assyrian Text Corpus Project, 1997.

———. "Literature as Politics: The Tukulti-Ninurta Epic and the Bible." *CBQ* 38 (1976): 455–82.

———. "On Self-Consciousness in Mesopotamia." Pages 183–202 in *The Origins and Diversity of Axial Age Civilizations*. Edited by S. N. Eisenstadt. Albany: State University of New York Press, 1986.

Macintosh, Andrew A. *A Critical and Exegetical Commentary on Hosea*. ICC. Edinburgh: T&T Clark, 1997.

MacLaren, Alexander. *Expositions of Holy Scripture: The Book of Psalms I to XLIX*. New York: A. C. Armstrong and Son, 1909.

Maier, Christl M., and Carolyn J. Sharp, eds. *Prophecy and Power: Jeremiah in Feminist and Postcolonial Perspective*. LHBOTS 577. London: Bloomsbury, 2013.

Maire, Thierry. "Proverbes XXII 17ss: Enseignement à Shalishôm?" *VT* 45 (1995): 227–38.

Malamat, Abraham. "A Note on the Ritual of Treaty Making in Mari and the Bible." *IEJ* 45 (1995): 226–29.

Marsman, Hennie J. *Women in Ugarit and Israel: Their Social and Religious Position in the Context of the Ancient Near East*. OTS 49. Leiden: Brill, 2003.

Marti, Karl. *Das Dodekapropheton*. KHC 13. Tübingen: Mohr, 1904.

Masenya, Madipoane (ngwana' Mphahlele). "Ruth." Pages 86–91 in *Global Bible Commentary*. Edited by Daniel Patte. Nashville: Abingdon, 2004.

Master, Daniel M. "State Formation Theory and the Kingdom of Israel." *JNES* 60 (2001): 117–31.

Mathews, Kenneth A. *Genesis*. Vol. 1, *1–11:26*. Vol. 2, *11:27–50:26*. NAC 1A–B. Nashville: Broadman & Holman, 1996–2005.

Mathewson, David. "Isaiah in Revelation." Pages 189–210 in *Isaiah in the New Testament*. Edited by Steve Moyise and Maarten J. J. Menken. London: Continuum, 2005.

Maul, Stefan M. "Gottesdienst im Sonnenheiligtum zu Sippar." Pages 285–316 in *Munuscula Mesopotamica: Festschrift für Johannes Renger*. Edited by B. Böck, E. Cancik-Kirschbaum, and T. Richter. AOAT 267. Münster: Ugarit-Verlag, 1999.

Mays, James Luther. *Micah: A Commentary*. OTL. Philadelphia: Westminster, 1976.

Mazar, Amihai. "Beth Shean in the Iron Age: Preliminary Report and Conclusions of the 1990–1991 Excavations." *IEJ* 43 (1993): 201–29.

Mazar, Benjamin. *The Early Biblical Period: Historical Studies*. Edited by Shmuel Aḥituv and Baruch A. Levine. Jerusalem: Israel Exploration Society, 1986.

Mazar, Eilat. "Did I Find King David's Palace?" *BAR* 32.1 (January/February 2006): 16–27, 70.

Mazar, Eilat, D. Ben-Shlomo, and Shmuel Aḥituv. "An Inscribed Pithos from the Ophel, Jerusalem." *IEJ* 63 (2013): 39–49.

McAffee, Matthew. "The Heart of Pharaoh in Exodus 4–15." *BBR* 20 (2010): 331–54.

McCann, J. Clinton, Jr. "The Psalms as Instruction." *Int* 46 (1992): 117–28.

———. "The Shape of Book I of the Psalter and the Shape of Human Happiness." Pages 340–48 in *The Book of Psalms: Composition and Reception*. Edited by Peter W. Flint and Patrick D. Miller. VTSup 99. Leiden: Brill, 2005.

McCarter, P. Kyle, Jr. *I and II Samuel: A New Translation with Introduction, Notes, and Commentary*. Vol. 1, *I Samuel*. Vol. 2, *II Samuel*. AB 8–9. Garden City, NY: Doubleday, 1980–84.

———. "The Origins of Israelite Religion." Pages 118–41 in *The Rise of Ancient Israel*. Edited by Hershel Shanks et al. Washington, DC: Biblical Archaeology Society, 1992.

———. "The Patriarchal Age: Abraham, Isaac, and Jacob." Pages 1–31 in *Ancient Israel: From Abraham to the Roman Destruction of the Temple*. Edited by H. Shanks. 3rd ed. Washington, DC: Biblical Archaeology Society, 2011.

McCarthy, D. J. "II Samuel 7 and the Structure of the Deuteronomic History." *JBL* 84 (1965): 131–38.

McConville, J. Gordon. *Deuteronomy*. AOTC 5. Leicester, UK: Apollos; Downers Grove, IL: InterVarsity, 2002.

———. *Grace in the End: A Study in Deuteronomistic Theology*. SBT. Carlisle, UK: Paternoster, 1993.

———. "Hosea, Book of." *DOTP* 338–50.

———. "Jeremiah." Pages 211–20 in *Theological Interpretation of the Old Testament: A Book-by-Book Survey*. Edited by Kevin J. Vanhoozer, Craig G. Bartholomew, and Daniel J. Treier. London: SPCK; Grand Rapids: Baker Academic, 2008.

———. *Judgment and Promise: An Interpretation of the Book of Jeremiah*. Winona Lake, IN: Eisenbrauns, 1993.

McDonald, Lee Martin. *The Biblical Canon: Its Origin, Transmission, and Authority*. Grand Rapids: Baker Academic, 2007.

———. *Formation of the Bible: The Story of the Church's Canon*. Peabody, MA: Hendrickson, 2012.

McDonald, Lee Martin, and James A. Sanders, eds. *The Canon Debate*. Peabody, MA: Hendrickson, 2002.

McKane, William. *Jeremiah*. Vol. 1, *I–XXV*. Vol. 2, *XXVI–LII*. ICC. Edinburgh: T&T Clark, 1986–96.

McKenzie, Steven L. *The Trouble with Kings: The Composition of the Books of Kings in the Deuteronomistic History*. VTSup 42. Leiden: Brill, 1991.

McLaughlin, John I. *The* Marzēaḥ *in the Prophetic Literature: References and Allusions in the Light of Extra-Biblical Evidence*. VTSup 86. Leiden: Brill, 2001.

Meehan, Bernard. *The Book of Kells*. London: Thames & Hudson, 2012.

Menken, Maarten J. J., and Steve Moyise, eds. *Genesis in the New Testament*. LNTS 466. New York: Bloomsbury, 2012.

Mettinger, Tryggve N. D. *The Riddle of Resurrection: "Dying and Rising Gods" in the Ancient Near East*. CB 50. Stockholm: Almqvist & Wiksell, 2001.

Meyers, Carol L. "David as Temple Builder." Pages 357–76 in *Ancient Israelite Religion: Essays in Honor of Frank Moore Cross*. Edited by Patrick D. Miller Jr., Paul D. Hanson, and S. Dean McBride. Philadelphia: Fortress, 1987.

———. *Discovering Eve: Ancient Israelite Women in Context*. Oxford: Clarendon, 1988.

———. "The Drum-Dance-Song Ensemble: Women's Performance in Biblical Israel." Pages 50–58 in *Rediscovering the Muses: Women's Musical Traditions*. Edited by K. Marshall. Boston: Northeastern University Press, 1993.

———. "Engendering Syro-Palestinian Archaeology: Reasons and Resources." *NEA* 66 (2003): 185–97.

———. *Exodus*. NCBC. Cambridge: Cambridge University Press, 2005.

———. "Gender Imagery in the Song of Songs." Pages 197–212 in *A Feminist Companion to the Song of Songs*. Edited by A. Brenner. FCB 1. Sheffield: Sheffield Academic, 1993. Repr. from *HAR* 10 (1986): 209–23.

———. "Guilds and Gatherings: Women's Groups in Ancient Israel." Pages 154–84 in *Realia Dei: Essays in Archaeology and Biblical Interpretation in Honor of Edward F. Campbell, Jr. at His Retirement*. Edited by P. H. Williams Jr. and T. Hiebert. Scholars Press Homage Series 23. Atlanta: Scholars Press, 1999.

———. "Hannah and Her Sacrifice: Reclaiming Female Agency." Pages 93–104 in *A Feminist Companion to Samuel and Kings*. Edited by A. Brenner. FCB 5. Sheffield: Sheffield Academic, 1994.

———. "Of Drums and Damsels: Women's Performance in Ancient Israel." *BA* 54 (1991): 16–27.

———. *Rediscovering Eve: Ancient Israelite Women in Context*. Oxford: Oxford University Press, 2013.

Meyers, Carol L., and Eric M. Meyers. *Haggai, Zechariah 1–8: A New Translation with Introduction and Commentary*. AB 25B. New Haven: Yale University Press, 2004.

———. *Zechariah 9–14: A New Translation with Introduction and Commentary*. AB 25C. New Haven: Yale University Press, 1998.

Mies, Françoise. *L'espérance de Job*. BETL 193. Leuven: Peeters, 2006.

Milgrom, Jacob. *Leviticus: A New Translation with Introduction and Commentary*. Vol. 1, *1–16*. Vol. 2, *17–22*. Vol. 3, *23–27*. AB 3, 3A–B. New York: Doubleday, 1991–2001.

———. *Numbers*. JPSTC. New York: Jewish Publication Society, 1990.

Millard, Alan R. "Amorites and Israelites: Invisible Invaders—Modern Expectations and Ancient Reality." Pages 148–60 in *The Future of Biblical Archeology: Reassessing Methodologies and Assumptions*. Edited by James K. Hoffmeier and Alan R. Millard. Grand Rapids: Eerdmans, 2004.

———. "The Knowledge of Writing in Iron Age Palestine." *TynBul* 46 (1995): 207–17.

———. "The Ostracon from the Days of David Found at Khirbet Qeiyafa." *TynBul* 62 (2011): 1–13.

Miller, Douglas B. "What the Preacher Forgot: The Rhetoric of Ecclesiastes." *CBQ* 62 (2000): 215–35.

Miller, Patrick D. *Deuteronomy*. IBC. Louisville: John Knox, 1990.

Miller, Robert D., II. "Deuteronomistic Theology in the Book of the Judges?" *OTE* 15 (2002): 411–16.

Min, Kyung-jin. *The Levitical Authorship of Ezra–Nehemiah*. JSOTSup 409. London: T&T Clark, 2004.

Misgav, Haggai, Yosef Garfinkel, and Saar Ganor. "The Ostracon." Pages 243–57 in *Excavation Report 2007–2008*. Vol. 1 of *Khirbet Qeiyafa*. Edited by Yosef Garfinkel and Saar Ganor. Jerusalem: Israel Exploration Society and Institute of Archaeology, Hebrew University of Jerusalem, 2009.

Mitchell, Gordon. *Together in the Land: A Reading of the Book of Joshua*. JSOTSup 134. Sheffield: JSOT Press, 1993.

Moberly, R. W. L. *At the Mountain of God: Story and Theology in Exodus 32–34*. JSOTSup 22. Sheffield: JSOT Press, 1983.

———. *Genesis 12–50*. Old Testament Study Guides. Sheffield: JSOT Press, 1992.

———. *The Old Testament of the Old Testament: Patriarchal Narratives and Mosaic Yahwism*. Minneapolis: Augsburg Fortress, 1992.

Mobley, Gregory. "Judges." *OEBB* 1:516–31.

Monson, John. "The New ʿAin Dara Temple: Closest Solomonic Parallel." *BAR* 26.3 (May/June 2000): 20–35, 67.

———. "The Temple of Solomon: Heart of Jerusalem." Pages 1–22 in *Zion, City of Our God*. Edited by R. S. Hess and Gordon J. Wenham. Grand Rapids: Eerdmans, 1999.

Moor, Johannes C. de, and Paul Sanders. "An Ugaritic Expiation Ritual and Its Old Testament Parallels." *UF* 23 (1991): 283–300.

Moore, G. F. A. *A Critical and Exegetical Commentary on Judges*. 2nd ed. ICC. Edinburgh: T&T Clark, 1908.

Moore, Rick D. "A Home for the Alien: Worldly Wisdom and Covenantal Confession in Proverbs 30, 1–9." *ZAW* 106 (1994): 96–107.

Moran, William L. "The Ancient Near Eastern Background of the Love of God in Deuteronomy." *CBQ* 25 (1963): 77–87.

Morris, Gerald. *Prophecy, Poetry and the Book of Hosea*. JSOTSup 219. Sheffield: Sheffield Academic, 1996.

Moskala, Jirí. "The God of Job and Our Adversary." *JATS* 15 (2004): 104–17.

———. *The Laws of Clean and Unclean Animals in Leviticus 11: Their Nature, Theology, and Rationale*. Berrien Springs, MI: Adventist Theological Society, 2000.

Moughtin-Mumby, Sharon Rose. "Hosea." *OEBB* 1:367–78.

———. *Sexual and Marital Metaphors in Hosea, Jeremiah, Isaiah, Ezekiel*. Oxford Theological Monographs. Oxford: Oxford University Press, 2008.

Mowinckel, Sigmund. *The Psalms in Israel's Worship*. Nashville: Abingdon, 1962.

———. *Zur Komposition des Buches Jeremia*. Oslo: Jacob Dybwad, 1914.

Moyise, Steve, and Maarten J. J. Menken, eds. *Isaiah in the New Testament*. New York: T&T Clark, 2005.

Munro, Jill M. *Spikenard and Saffron: A Study in the Poetic Language of the Song of Songs*. Sheffield: JSOT Press, 1995.

Murphy, Roland E. "History of Exegesis as a Hermeneutical Tool: The Song of Songs." *BTB* 16 (1986): 87–91.

———. *Proverbs*. WBC 22. Nashville: Nelson, 1998.

———. *The Song of Songs*. Hermeneia. Minneapolis: Fortress, 1990.

———. "Towards a Commentary on the Song of Songs." *CBQ* 39 (1977): 482–96.

Na'aman, Nadav. "The Contribution of the Amarna Letters to the Debate on Jerusalem's Political Position in the Tenth Century BCE." *BASOR* 304 (1996): 17–27.

———. "Cow Town or Royal Capital? Evidence for Iron Age Jerusalem." *BAR* 23.4 (July/August 1997): 43–47, 67.

———. "Sources and Composition in the History of David." Pages 170–86 in *The Origins of the Ancient Israelite States*. Edited by V. Fritz and P. R. Davies. JSOTSup 228. Sheffield: Sheffield Academic, 1996.

———. "The Trowel vs. the Text: How the Amarna Letters Challenge Archaeology." *BAR* 35.1 (January/February 2009): 52–56, 70–71.

Nakanose, Shigeyuki, Fernando Doren, and Enilda de Paula Pedro. "Zephaniah." Pages 310–14 in *Global Bible Commentary*. Edited by Daniel Patte. Nashville: Abingdon, 2004.

Nasuti, Harry P. "The Interpretive Significance of Sequence and Selection in the Book of Psalms." Pages 311–39 in *The Book of Psalms: Composition and Reception*. Edited by Peter W. Flint and Patrick D. Miller. VTSup 99. Leiden: Brill, 2005.

———. *Tradition History and the Psalms of Asaph*. SBLDS 88. Atlanta: Scholars Press, 1988.

Nelson, Richard D. *Deuteronomy: A Commentary*. OTL. Louisville: Westminster John Knox, 2002.

———. *The Double Redaction of the Deuteronomistic History*. JSOTSup 18. Sheffield: JSOT Press, 1981.

———. *First and Second Kings*. IBC. Louisville: John Knox, 1987.

———. *Joshua: A Commentary*. OTL. Louisville: Westminster John Knox, 1997.

———. "Josiah in the Book of Joshua." *JBL* 100 (1981): 531–40.

Nestle, Eberhard, Erwin Nestle, Barbara Aland, Kurt Aland, Johannes Karavidopoulos, Carlo M. Martini, and Bruce M. Metzger, eds. *Novum Testamentum Graece*. 28th ed. Stuttgart: Deutsche Bibelgesellschaft, 2012.

Neumann, Teresa. "777: Urgent Call to National Prayer by Anne Graham Lotz, Daughter of Billy Graham." *Breaking Christian News*, July 2, 2014, http://www.breakingchristiannews.com/articles/display_art.html?ID=14117.

Neusner, Jacob. *Micah and Joel in Talmud and Midrash: A Sourcebook*. Studies in

Judaism. Lanham, MD: University Press of America, 2007.

Neville, Richard. "Differentiation in Genesis 1: An Exegetical Creation *ex nihilo*." *JBL* 130 (2011): 209–26.

Newsom, Carol A. "Cultural Politics and the Reading of Job." *BibInt* 1 (1993): 119–38.

———. "Daniel and Additions to Daniel." *OEBB* 1:159–73.

Nicholson, Ernest W. *God and His People: Covenant and Theology in the Old Testament*. Oxford: Oxford University Press, 1986.

Niditch, Susan. *Judges: A Commentary*. OTL. Louisville: Westminster John Knox, 2008.

———. "Samson as Culture Hero, Trickster, and Bandit: The Empowerment of the Weak." *CBQ* 52 (2008): 608–24.

Niebuhr, H. Richard. *Christ and Culture*. New York: Harper, 1951.

Niedorf, Christian. *Die mittelbabylonischen Rechtsurkunden aus Alalaḫ*. AOAT 352. Münster: Ugarit-Verlag, 2008.

Nielsen, Kirsten. *Ruth: A Commentary*. OTL. Louisville: Westminster John Knox, 1997.

Nogalski, James D. "The Redactional Shaping of Nahum for the Book of the Twelve." Pages 193–202 in *Among the Prophets: Language, Image and Structure in the Prophetic Writings*. Edited by Philip R. Davies and David J. A. Clines. JSOTSup 144. Sheffield: JSOT Press, 1994.

Noth, Martin. *The Deuteronomistic History*. Translated by J. Doull et al. JSOTSup 15. Sheffield: University of Sheffield, 1981. Translation of pages 1–110 of *Überlieferungsgeschichtliche Studien*. 2nd ed. Tübingen: Niemeyer, 1957.

———. *Die israelitischen Personennamen im Rahmen der gemeinsemitischen Namengebung*. Stuttgart: W. Kohlhammer, 1928.

———. *Leviticus: A Commentary*. Translated by J. E. Anderson. 2nd ed. OTL. Philadelphia: Westminster, 1977.

———. *Überlieferungsgeschichtliche Studien*. 2nd ed. Tübingen: Niemeyer, 1957.

O'Brien, Julia M. *Micah*. Wisdom Commentary Series. Collegeville, MN: Michael Glazier, 2002.

———. *Nahum, Habakkuk, Zephaniah, Haggai, Zechariah, Malachi*. Abingdon Old Testament Commentaries. Nashville: Abingdon, 2004.

O'Connell, Robert H. *The Rhetoric of the Book of Judges*. VTSup 63. Leiden: Brill, 1996.

O'Connor, Michael P. Review of *We Have Heard with Our Ears, O God*, by Walter C. Bouzard. *CBQ* 61 (1999): 737–39.

Oesterley, William O. E. *The Psalms*. London: SPCK, 1955.

Ofer, Avi. "'At the Hill Country of Judah': From a Settlement Fringe to a Prosperous Monarchy." Pages 92–121 in *From Nomadism to Monarchy: Archaeological and Historical Aspects of Early Israel*. Edited by Israel Finkelstein and Nadav Na'aman. Jerusalem: Yad Izhak Ben Zvi, 1994.

Ogden, Graham S. *Qoheleth*. OTG. Sheffield: JSOT Press, 1987.

Olley, John W. *Ezekiel: A Commentary Based on Iezekiēl in Codex Vaticanus*. SCS. Leiden: Brill, 2009.

Origen. *The Song of Songs: Commentary and Homilies*. Edited and translated by R. P. Lawson. Ancient Christian Writers 26. Westminster, MD: Newman Press, 1957.

Oswalt, John N. *The Book of Isaiah*. 2 vols. NICOT. Grand Rapids: Eerdmans, 1986–98.

Otto, Eckhard. "Aspects of Legal Reforms and Reformulations in Ancient Cuneiform and Israelite Law." Pages 160–98 in *Theory and Method in Biblical Cuneiform Law: Revision, Interpolation and Development*. Edited by B. M. Levinson. JSOTSup 181. Sheffield: Sheffield Academic, 1991.

———. *Theologische Ethik des Alten Testaments*. Stuttgart: Kohlhammer, 1994.

———. "Die Ursprünge der Bundestheologie im Alten Testament und im Alten Orient." *ZABR* 4 (1998): 1–84.

Ottosson, Magnus. *Josuaboken: En programskrift för davidisk restauration*. Acta Universitatis Upsaliensis, Studia biblica Upsaliensia 1. Stockholm: Almqvist & Wiksell, 1991.

Pao, David W. *Acts and the Isaianic New Exodus*. Grand Rapids: Baker Academic, 2002.

Parchem, Marek. “Motyw zmartwychwstania w Księdze Daniela (Dn 12,2) [The Theme of Resurrection in the Book of Daniel].” Pages 65–77 in *Zmartwychwstał prawdziwie*. Edited by Antoni Paciorek, Antoni Tronia, and Piotr Łabuda. Scripturae lumen, Biblia I jej oddzialywanie 2. Tarnów: Wydawnictwo Biblos, 2010.

Pardee, Dennis. “On Psalm 29: Structure and Meaning.” Pages 153–83 in *The Book of Psalms: Composition and Reception*. Edited by Peter W. Flint and Patrick D. Miller. VTSup 99. Leiden: Brill, 2005.

———. *Ritual and Cult at Ugarit*. SBLWAW 10. Edited by T. J. Lewis. Atlanta: SBL, 2002.

Parpola, Simo, and Kazuko Watanabe. *Neo-Assyrian Treaties and Loyalty Oaths*. SAA 2. Helsinki: Neo-Assyrian Text Corpus Project and Helsinki University Press, 1988.

Parry, Robin. *Lamentations*. Two Horizons OT Commentary. Grand Rapids: Eerdmans, 2010.

———. *Old Testament and Christian Ethics: The Rape of Dinah as a Test Case*. Paternoster Biblical Monographs. Milton Keynes, UK: Paternoster, 2004.

Parsons, Michael. *Calvin's Preaching on the Prophet Micah: The 1550–1551 Sermons in Geneva*. Lewiston, NY: Mellen, 2006.

Paul, Shalom M. *Amos: A Commentary on the Book of Amos*. Hermeneia. Minneapolis: Fortress, 1991.

———. *Isaiah 40–66: Translation and Commentary*. ECC. Grand Rapids: Eerdmans, 2012.

Peckham, Brian. *The Composition of the Deuteronomistic History*. HSM 35. Atlanta: Scholars Press, 1985.

Penchansky, David. *The Betrayal of God: Ideological Conflict in Job*. Literary Currents in Biblical Interpretation. Louisville: Westminster John Knox, 1990.

Perdue, Leo G. *Wisdom and Creation: The Theology of Wisdom Literature*. Nashville: Abingdon, 1994.

———. *Wisdom in Revolt: Metaphorical Theology in the Book of Job*. JSOTSup 112. Sheffield: Almond, 1991.

———. *Wisdom Literature: A Theological History*. Louisville: Westminster John Knox, 2007.

Perry, Steven Cecil. “Structural Patterns in Proverbs 10:1–22:16: A Study in Biblical Hebrew Stylistics.” PhD diss., University of Texas at Austin, 1987.

Petersen, David L. *Haggai and Zechariah 1–8: A Commentary*. OTL. Philadelphia: Westminster, 1984.

———. *Zechariah 9–14 and Malachi: A Commentary*. OTL. Louisville: Westminster John Knox, 1995.

Petschow, Herbert. “Zur Systematik und Gesetzestechnik im Codex Hammurapi.” *ZA* 57 (1965): 146–72.

Petterson, Anthony R. *Haggai, Zechariah and Malachi*. AOTC 25. Leicester, UK: Inter-Varsity Press, 2015.

Phillips, Elaine A. “Esther 6: Person.” *DOTWPW* 188–93.

Phipps, William E. “The Plight of the Song of Songs.” *JAAR* 42 (1974): 82–100. Repr. pages 5–23 in *The Song of Songs*. Edited by H. Bloom. New York: Chelsea, 1988.

Pickut, William. “Lamentations 3: History of Interpretation.” *DOTWPW* 414–19.

Pietersma, Albert. “Septuagintal Exegesis and the Superscriptions of the Greek Psalter.” Pages 443–75 in *The Book of Psalms: Composition and Reception*. Edited by Peter W. Flint and Patrick D. Miller Jr. VTSup 99. Leiden: Brill, 2005.

Polk, Timothy. *The Prophetic Persona: Jeremiah and the Language of the Self*. JSOTSup 32. Sheffield: JSOT Press, 1984.

Polliack, Meira. Review of *The Book of Judges: The Art of Editing*, by Yaira Amit. *VT* 45 (1995): 392–98.

Polzin, Robert. *Deuteronomy, Joshua, Judges*. Part 1 of *Moses and the Deuteronomist: A Literary Study of the Deuteronomistic History*. New York: Seabury, 1980.

———. *1 Samuel*. Part 2 of *Moses and the Deuteronomist: A Literary Study of the Deuteronomistic History*. San Francisco: Harper & Row, 1989.

Pope, Marvin H. *Song of Songs: A New Translation with Introduction and Commentary.* AB 7C. Garden City, NY: Doubleday, 1977.

———. "The Song of Songs and Women's Liberation: An 'Outsider's Critique.'" Pages 121–28 in *A Feminist Companion to the Song of Songs.* Edited by A. Brenner. FCB 1. Sheffield: Sheffield Academic, 1993.

Porten, Bezalel, and Ada Yardeni. *Textbook of Aramaic Documents from Egypt.* 4 vols. Department of the History of the Jewish People, Hebrew University. Winona Lake, IN: Eisenbrauns, 1986–99.

Prior, John Mansford. "Ecclesiastes." Pages 175–79 in *Global Bible Commentary.* Edited by Daniel Patte. Nashville: Abingdon, 2004.

Propp, William H. *Exodus: A New Translation with Introduction and Commentary.* Vol. 1, *1–18.* Vol. 2, *19–40.* AB 2–2A. New York: Doubleday, 1999–2006.

Provan, Iain W. *1 and 2 Kings.* NIBC. Peabody, MA: Hendrickson, 1995.

———. *1 and 2 Kings.* OTG. Sheffield: Sheffield Academic, 1997.

———. *Hezekiah and the Book of Kings: A Contribution to the Debate about the Composition of the Deuteronomistic History.* BZAW 172. Berlin: de Gruyter, 1988.

———. "Ideologies, Literary and Critical: Reflections on Recent Writing on the History of Israel." *JBL* 114 (1995): 585–606.

Raban, Avner. "The Philistines in the Western Jezreel Valley." *BASOR* 284 (1991): 17–27.

Rad, Gerhard von. *Deuteronomy: A Commentary.* Translated by Dorothea Barton. OTL. Philadelphia: Westminster, 1966.

———. *Genesis: A Commentary.* Translated by John H. Marks. OTL. Philadelphia: Westminster, 1972.

———. *Old Testament Theology.* Vol. 1, *The Theology of Israel's Historical Traditions.* Vol. 2, *The Theology of Israel's Prophetic Traditions.* Translated by D. M. G. Stalker. San Francisco: Harper & Row, 1962–65. Translation of *Theologie des Alten Testaments.* Munich: Chr. Kaiser, 1957–60.

———. *Wisdom in Israel.* Translated by James D. Martin. Nashville: Abingdon, 1972.

Radine, Jason. *The Book of Amos in Emergent Judah.* FAT 2/45. Tübingen: Mohr Siebeck, 2010.

Rah, Soong-Chan. *Prophetic Lament: A Call for Justice in Troubled Times.* Resonate Series. Downers Grove, IL: InterVarsity Press, 2015.

Rainey, Anson F. "Inside, Outside: Where Did the Early Israelites Come From?" *BAR* 34.6 (November/December 2008): 45–50, 84.

———. "Manasseh, King of Judah, in the Whirlpool of the Seventh Century BCE." Pages 147–64 in *Kinattūtu ša dārâti: Raphael Kutscher Memorial Volume.* Edited by Anson F. Rainey. Tel Aviv: Institute of Archaeology at Tel Aviv University, 1993.

———. "The Order of Sacrifices in Old Testament Ritual Texts." *Bib* 51 (1970): 485–98.

———. "Shasu or Habiru: Who Were the Early Israelites?" *BAR* 34.6 (November/December 2008): 51–55.

———. "Stones for Bread: Archaeology versus History." *NEA* 64 (2001): 140–49.

———. "Whence Came the Israelites and Their Language?" *IEJ* 57 (2007): 41–64.

Rainey, Anson F., and R. Steven Notley. *The Sacred Bridge: Carta's Atlas of the Biblical World.* Jerusalem: Carta, 2006.

Rast, Walter. *Taanach I: Studies in the Iron Age Pottery.* Winona Lake, IN: Eisenbrauns, 1978.

Ratner, Robert. "Gender Problems in Biblical Hebrew." PhD diss., Hebrew Union College, 1983.

Redditt, Paul L. *Introduction to the Prophets.* Grand Rapids: Eerdmans, 2008.

———. "Reading the Speech Cycles in the Book of Job." *HAR* 14 (1995): 205–14.

Renaud, Bernard. *Michée, Sophonie, Nahum.* Paris: Gabalda, 1987.

Rendtorff, Rolf. "Chronicles and the Priestly Torah." Pages 259–66 in *Temples, Texts and Traditions: A Tribute to Menahem Haran.* Edited by Michael V. Fox, Victor Avigdor Hurowitz, Avi Hurvitz, Michael L. Klein, Baruch J. Schwartz, and Nili Shupak. Winona Lake, IN: Eisenbrauns, 1996.

Renkema, Johan. *Obadiah.* HCOT. Leuven: Peeters, 2003.

Richardson, Mervyn E. J. *Hammurabi's Laws: Text, Translation and Glossary*. The Biblical Seminar 73. Semitic Texts and Studies 2. Sheffield: Sheffield Academic, 2000.

Richter, Sandra L. "Deuteronomistic History." *DOTHB* 219–30.

———. *The Deuteronomistic History and the Name Theology:* L^e^šakkēn š^e^mô šām *in the Bible and the Ancient Near East*. Berlin: de Gruyter, 2002.

———. "Eighth-Century Issues: The World of Jeroboam II, the Fall of Samaria, and the Reign of Hezekiah." Pages 319–49 in *Ancient Israel's History: An Introduction to Issues and Sources*. Edited by Bill T. Arnold and Richard S. Hess. Grand Rapids: Baker Academic, 2014.

———. "Environmental Law in Deuteronomy: One Lens on a Biblical Theology of Creation Care." *BBR* 20 (2010): 355–76.

Riley, Jason A. "Does Yhwh Get His Hands Dirty? Reading Isaiah 63:1–6 in Light of Depictions of Divine Postbattle Purification." Pages 243–69 in *Warfare, Ritual, and Symbol in Biblical and Modern Contexts*. Edited by Brad E. Kelle, Frank Ritchel Aimes, and Jacob L. Wright. Ancient Israel and Its Literature. Atlanta: Society of Biblical Literature, 2014.

Roberts, Alexander, and W. H. Rambaut, trans. *The Writings of Irenaeus, vol. 2*. Edinburgh: T&T Clark, 1869.

Roberts, J. J. M. "In Defense of the Monarchy: The Contribution of Israelite Kingship to Biblical Theology." Pages 377–96 in *Ancient Israelite Religion: Essays in Honor of Frank Moore Cross*. Edited by P. D. Miller Jr., P. D. Hanson, and S. D. McBride. Philadelphia: Fortress, 1987.

———. "Mowinckel's Enthronement Festival: A Review." Pages 97–115 in *The Book of Psalms: Composition and Reception*. Edited by Peter W. Flint and Patrick D. Miller. VTSup 99. Leiden: Brill, 2005.

———. *Nahum, Habakkuk, and Zephaniah: A Commentary*. OTL. Louisville: Westminster John Knox, 1991.

Robertson, David A. *Linguistic Evidence in Dating Early Biblical Hebrew Poetry*. SBLDS 3. Missoula, MT: Scholars Press, 1972.

Robertson, O. Palmer. *The Books of Nahum, Habakkuk, and Zephaniah*. NICOT. Grand Rapids: Eerdmans, 1990.

Rogers, Richard. *A Commentary on Judges*. 16th–17th Century Facsimile Editions. Carlisle, UK: Banner of Truth, 1984.

Rogerson, John W. *W. M. L. de Wette: Founder of Modern Biblical Criticism: An Intellectual Biography*. JSOTSup 126. Sheffield: Sheffield Academic Press, 1992.

Rollston, Christopher A. "Scribal Education in Israel: The Old Hebrew Epigraphic Evidence." *BASOR* 344 (2006): 47–74.

Römer, Thomas. *The Invention of God*. Translated by Raymond Geuss. Cambridge, MA: Harvard University Press, 2015.

———. *The So-Called Deuteronomistic History: A Sociological, Historical and Literary Introduction*. New York: T&T Clark, 2007.

Rosenberg, Joel. "Jeremiah and Ezekiel." Pages 184–206 in *The Literary Guide to the Bible*. Edited by Robert Alter and Frank Kermode. Cambridge, MA: Harvard University Press, 1987.

Rost, Leonard. *The Succession to the Throne of David*. Translated by M. D. Rutter and D. M. Gunn. Sheffield: Almond, 1982. Translation of *Die Überlieferung von der Thronnachfolge Davids*. Stuttgart: W. Kohlhammer, 1926.

———. "Weidewechsel und altisraelitischer Festkalendar." *ZDPV* 66 (1943): 205–16.

Roth, Martha T. *Law Collections from Mesopotamia and Asia Minor*. Edited by P. Michalowski, with a contribution by H. A. Hoffner Jr. SBLWAW 6. Atlanta: Scholars Press, 1995.

Rothenberg, Benno. *Timna: Valley of the Biblical Copper Mines*. New Aspects of Antiquity. London: Thames & Hudson, 1972.

Rottzoll, Dirk U. *Studien zur Redaktion und Komposition des Amosbuchs*. BZAW 243. Berlin: de Gruyter, 1996.

Rowlett, Lori. *Joshua and the Rhetoric of Violence: A New Historicist Analysis*. JSOTSup 226. Sheffield: Sheffield Academic, 1996.

Sanders, James A. *The Psalms Scroll of Qumran Cave 11 (11QPs^a^)*. DJD 4. Oxford: Clarendon, 1965.

Sanders, Paul. "Missing Link in Hebrew Bible Formation." *BAR* 41.6 (November/December 2015): 46–52, 74.

Sanderson, Judith. "Nahum." Pages 217–21 in *The Women's Bible Commentary*. Edited by C. Newsom and S. Ringe. Louisville: Westminster John Knox, 1992.

Sarna, Nahum, and Hershel Shanks. "Israel in Egypt: The Egyptian Sojourn and the Exodus." Pages 33–54 in *Ancient Israel: From Abraham to the Roman Destruction of the Temple*. Edited by Hershel Shanks. Rev. ed. Washington, DC: Biblical Archaeology Society, 1999.

Sasson, Jack M. *From the Mari Archives: An Anthology of Old Babylonian Letters*. Winona Lake, IN: Eisenbrauns, 2012.

———. *Jonah: A New Translation with Introduction, Commentary, and Interpretation*. AB 24B. New York: Doubleday, 1990.

———. *Judges 1–12: A New Translation with Introduction and Commentary*. AB 6D. New Haven: Yale University Press, 2014.

———. *Ruth: A New Translation with a Philological Commentary and a Formalist-Folklorist Interpretation*. 2nd ed. Sheffield: Sheffield Academic, 1989.

Satlow, Michael L. *How the Bible Became Holy*. New Haven: Yale University Press, 2014.

Satterthwaite, Philip. "'No King in Israel': Narrative Criticism and Judges 17–21." *TynBul* 44 (1993): 75–89.

Schaeffer, Francis A. *Death in the City*. Chicago: Inter-Varsity, 1969.

Schäfer-Lichtenberger, C. *Josua und Salomo: Eine Studie zu Autorität und Legitimität des Nachfolgers im Alten Testament*. VTSup 58. Leiden: Brill, 1995.

Scheetz, Jordan M. *The Concept of Canonical Intertextuality and the Book of Daniel*. Eugene, OR: Pickwick, 2011.

Schenker, Adrian. *Septante et texte massorétique dans l'histoire la plus ancienne du texte de 1 Rois 2–14*. CahRB 48. Paris: Gabalda, 2000.

Schifferdecker, Kathryn. *Out of the Whirlwind: Creation Theology in the Book of Job*. HTS 61. Cambridge, MA: Harvard University Press, 2008.

Schipper, Jeremy. *Ruth: A New Translation with Introduction and Commentary*. AB 7D. New Haven: Yale University Press, 2016.

Schneider, Tammi Joy. *Judges*. Berit Olam. Collegeville, MN: Liturgical Press, 2000.

Schniedewind, William M. *How the Bible Became a Book: The Textualization of Ancient Israel*. Cambridge: Cambridge University Press, 2005.

———. "Orality and Literacy in Ancient Israel." *RSR* 26.4 (October 2000): 327–32.

———. "Tel Dan Stela: New Light on Aramaic and Jehu's Revolt." *BASOR* 302 (1996): 75–90.

Schoors, Anton. "*Kethibh-Qere* in Ecclesiastes." Pages 215–22 in *Orientalia antiqua*. Edited by J. Quaegebeur. Vol. 2 of *Studia Paulo Naster oblata*. OLA 13. Leuven: Peeters, 1982.

Schroer, Sylvia. "Das Buch Ijob feministisch lesen?" *BK* 59 (2004): 73–77.

Schultz, Richard L. "Isaiah." Pages 194–210 in *Theological Interpretation of the Old Testament: A Book-by-Book Survey*. Edited by Kevin J. Vanhoozer, Craig G. Bartholomew, and Daniel J. Treier. London: SPCK; Grand Rapids: Baker Academic, 2008.

———. "Isaiah, Isaiahs, and Current Scholarship." Pages 243–61 in *Do Historical Matters Matter to Faith? A Critical Appraisal of Modern and Postmodern Approaches to Scripture*. Edited by James K. Hoffmeier and Dennis R. Magary. Wheaton: Crossway, 2012.

———. *The Search for Quotation*. JSOTSup 180. Sheffield: Sheffield Academic, 1999.

Schwartz, Baruch J. "The Priestly Account of the Theophany and Lawgiving at Sinai." Pages 103–34 in *Texts, Temples, and Traditions: A Tribute to Menahem Haran*. Edited by Michael V. Fox et al. Winona Lake, IN: Eisenbrauns, 1996.

Scoralick, Ruth. *Einzelspruch und Sammlung*. BZAW 232. Berlin: de Gruyter, 1995.

Segal, Michael. "From Joseph to Daniel: The Literary Development of the Narrative in Daniel 2." *VT* 59 (2009): 123–49.

Selman, Martin J. *1 Chronicles: An Introduction and Commentary*. TOTC. Leicester,

UK: Inter-Varsity; Downers Grove, IL: InterVarsity, 1994.

———. *2 Chronicles: An Introduction and Commentary.* TOTC. Leicester, UK: Inter-Varsity; Downers Grove, IL: InterVarsity, 1994.

Seow, Choon-Leong. *Ecclesiastes: A New Translation with Introduction and Commentary.* AB 18C. New York: Doubleday, 1997.

———. *Job 1–21: Interpretation and Commentary.* Illuminations. Grand Rapids: Eerdmans, 2013.

———. "Job's *gō'ēl*, Again." Pages 689–709 in *Gott und Mensch im Dialog: Festschrift für Otto Kaiser zum 80. Geburtstag.* BZAW 345/1–2. Berlin: de Gruyter, 2005.

———. "Linguistic Evidence and the Dating of Qoheleth." *JBL* 115 (1996): 643–66.

Seybold, Klaus D. *Profane Prophetie: Studien zum Buch Nahum.* SBS 135. Stuttgart: Katholisches Bibelwerk, 1989.

———. *Die Psalmen.* HAT 1/15. Tübingen: Mohr Siebeck, 1996.

———. "Zur Geschichte des vierten Davidpsalters (Pss 138–145)." Pages 368–90 in *The Book of Psalms: Composition and Reception.* Edited by Peter W. Flint and Patrick D. Miller. VTSup 99. Leiden: Brill, 2005.

Sharp, Carolyn J. "Jeremiah." *OEBB* 1:414–32.

———. "Micah." *OEBB* 2:78–85.

———. *Prophecy and Ideology in Jeremiah: Struggles for Authority in the Deutero-Jeremianic Prose.* Old Testament Studies. London: T&T Clark, 2003.

Sherwood, Yvonne. *A Biblical Text and Its Afterlives: The Survival of Jonah in Western Culture.* Cambridge: Cambridge University Press, 2000.

———. "Jonah." *OEBB* 1:477–81.

———. *The Prostitute and the Prophet: Hosea's Marriage in Literary-Theological Perspective.* JSOTSup 212. Sheffield: Sheffield Academic, 1996.

Shields, Mary E. *Circumscribing the Prostitute: The Rhetoric of Intertextuality, Metaphor and Gender in Jeremiah 3.1–4.4.* JSOTSup 387. London: T&T Clark, 2004.

Shupak, Nili. *Where Can Wisdom Be Found? The Sage's Language in the Bible and in Ancient Egyptian Literature.* OBO 130. Göttingen: Vandenhoeck & Ruprecht, 1993.

Siquans, Agnethe. "Foreignness and Poverty in the Book of Ruth: A Legal Way for a Poor Foreign Woman to Be Integrated into Israel." *JBL* 128 (2009): 443–52.

Smend, Rudolf, Jr. "Das Gesetz und die Völker: Ein Beitrag zur deuteronomistischen Redaktionsgeschichte." Pages 494–509 in *Probleme biblischer Theologie.* Edited by Hans W. Wolff. Munich: Kaiser, 1971. Translated by Peter T. Daniels and reprinted as "The Law and the Nations: A Contribution to Deuteronomistic Tradition History." Pages 95–110 in *Reconsidering Israel and Judah: Recent Studies in the Deuteronomistic History.* SBTS 8. Edited by Gary N. Knoppers and J. Gordon McConville. Winona Lake, IN: Eisenbrauns, 2000.

Smith, Carol. "Biblical Perspectives on Power." *JSOT* 93 (2001): 93–110.

Smith, Gary V. *Amos: A Commentary.* Grand Rapids: Zondervan, 1989.

Smith, Lesley J. *Medieval Exegesis in Translation: Commentaries on the Book of Ruth; Translated with an Introduction and Notes.* Kalamazoo, MI: Medieval Institute Publications, 1996.

Smith, Mark S. "The Levitical Compilation of the Psalter." *ZAW* 103 (1991): 258–63.

———. "Mythology and Myth-Making in Ugaritic and Israelite Literatures." Pages 295–341 in *Ugarit and the Bible: Proceedings of the International Symposium on Ugarit and the Bible; Manchester, September 1992.* Edited by George J. Brooke, Adrian H. W. Curtis, and John F. Healey. UBL 11. Münster: Ugarit-Verlag, 1994.

———. *The Priestly Vision of Genesis 1.* Minneapolis: Fortress, 2010.

———. "The Theology of the Redaction of the Psalter: Some Observations." *ZAW* 104 (1992): 408–12.

Smith, Ralph L. *Micah–Malachi.* WBC 32. Waco: Word, 1984.

Smith, Yancy Warren. "Hippolytus' Commentary on the Song of Songs in Social and

Critical Context." PhD diss., Brite Divinity School, 2009.

Snell, David C. *Twice-Told Proverbs and the Composition of the Book of Proverbs*. Winona Lake, IN: Eisenbrauns, 1993.

Soden, Wolfram von. "Nimrod." *RGG* 4:1496–97.

Soggin, J. Alberto. *Judges: A Commentary*. Translated by John Bowden. OTL. Philadelphia: Westminster, 1981.

Soulen, Richard. "The *Waṣfs* of the Song of Songs and Hermeneutic." Pages 214–24 in *A Feminist Companion to the Song of Songs*. Edited by A. Brenner. FCB 1. Sheffield: Sheffield Academic, 1993.

Sovic, A. "De Nili Monachi Commentario in Canticum canticorum reconstruendo." *Bib* 2 (1921): 45–52.

Spanier, Ktziah. "The Queen Mother in the Judaean Royal Court: Maacah—A Case Study." Pages 186–95 in *A Feminist Companion to Samuel and Kings*. Edited by A. Brenner. FCB 5. Sheffield: Sheffield Academic, 1994.

Sparks, Kenton L. *Ancient Texts for the Study of the Hebrew Bible: A Guide to the Background Literature*. Peabody, MA: Hendrickson, 2005.

Spears, Aubrey D. "The Theological Hermeneutics of Homiletical Application and Ecclesiastes 7:23–29." DPhil diss., University of Liverpool, 2006.

Spilsbury, Paul. "Exodus in Josephus." Pages 465–84 in *The Book of Exodus: Composition, Reception, and Interpretation*. Edited by Thomas B. Dozeman, Craig A. Evans, and Joel N. Lohr. VTSup 164. Leiden: Brill, 2014.

Spronk, Klaas. "Acrostics in the Book of Nahum." *ZAW* 110 (1998): 209–22.

———. *Nahum*. Kampen: Kok Pharos, 1997.

———. "Synchronic and Diachronic: Approaches to the Book of Nahum." Pages 159–86 in *Synchronic or Diachronic: A Debate on Method in Old Testament Exegesis*. Edited by Johannes C. de Moor. OTS 34. Leiden: Brill, 1995.

Spurgeon, Charles. *Treasury of David*. 3 vols. Peabody, MA: Hendrickson, 1988.

Stade, Bernhard. "Bemerkungen über das Buch Micha." *ZAW* 1 (1881): 161–72.

Stadelmann, Luis I. J. *Love and Politics: A New Commentary on the Song of Songs*. Mahwah, NJ: Paulist Press, 1990.

Stager, Lawrence E. "The Shechem Temple Where Abimelech Massacred a Thousand." *BAR* 29.4 (July/August 2003): 26–35, 66, 68–69.

———. "The Song of Deborah: Why Some Tribes Answered the Call and Others Did Not." *BAR* 15.1 (January/February 1989): 51–64.

———. "When Canaanites and Philistines Ruled Ashkelon." *BAR* 17.2 (March/April 1991): 24–37, 40–43.

Stein, Stephen J. "'Like Apples of Gold in Pictures of Silver': The Portrait of Wisdom in Jonathan Edwards' Commentary on the Book of Proverbs." *Church History* 54 (1985): 324–37.

Steiner, Richard C. "The Aramaic Text in Demotic Script (1.99)." *COS* 1.99:309–27.

Steinkeller, Piotr. "Camels in Ur III Babylonia?" Pages 415–19 in *Exploring the* Longue Durée: *Essays in Honor of Lawrence E. Stager*. Edited by J. David Schloen. Winona Lake, IN: Eisenbrauns, 2009.

Sterling, Gregory E. "The People of the Covenant or the People of God: Exodus in Philo of Alexandria." Pages 404–39 in *The Book of Exodus: Composition, Reception, and Interpretation*. Edited by Thomas B. Dozeman, Craig A. Evans, and Joel N. Lohr. VTSup 164. Leiden: Brill, 2014.

Sternberg, Meir. *The Poetics of Biblical Narrative: Ideological Literature and the Drama of Reading*. Indianapolis: Indiana University Press, 1985.

Steymans, Hans Ulrich. *Deuteronomium 28 und die* adê *zur Thronfolgeregelung Asarhaddons: Sargon und Fluch im Alten Orient und in Israel*. OBO 145. Freiburg: Universitätsverlag; Göttingen: Vandenhoeck & Ruprecht, 1995.

Stone, Lawrence. "The Revival of Narrative: Reflections on a New Old History." *Past and Present* 85 (1979): 3–24.

Stone, Lawson G. "Early Israel and Its Appearance in Canaan." Pages 127–64 in *Ancient Israel's History: An Introduction to Issues and Sources*. Edited by Bill T. Arnold and Richard S. Hess. Grand Rapids: Baker Academic, 2014.

———. "Ethical and Apologetic Tendencies in the Redaction of the Book of Joshua." *CBQ* 53 (1991): 25–36.

Strange, John. "Theology and Politics in Architecture and Iconography." *SJOT* 1 (1991): 23–44.

Strawn, Brent A. "What Is Cush Doing in Amos 9:7? The Poetics of Exodus in Plural." *VT* 63 (2013): 99–123.

Strine, Casey A. "Ezekiel's Image Problem: The Mesopotamian Cult Statue Induction Ritual and the *Imago Dei* Anthropology in the Book of Ezekiel." *CBQ* 76 (2014): 252–72.

Stromberg, Jacob. "An Inner Isaianic Reading of Isaiah 61:1–3." Pages 261–72 in *Interpreting Isaiah: Issues and Approaches*. Edited by David Firth and H. G. M. Williamson. Downers Grove, IL: InterVarsity, 2009.

Strothmann, W. ed. *Das Syrische Fragment des Ecclesiastes-Kommentars von Theodor von Mopsuestia: Syrischer Text mit Vollständigem Wörterverzeichnis*. Göttinger Orientforschungen Reihe 1, Syriach 29. Wiesbaden: Harrassowitz, 1988.

Stuart, Douglas K. *Exodus*. NAC 2. Nashville: Broadman & Holman, 2006.

———. *Hosea–Jonah*. WBC 31. Waco: Word, 1987.

———. "Jonah, Book of." *DOTP* 455–66.

Swarup, Paul. "Zechariah." Pages 318–24 in *Global Bible Commentary*. Edited by Daniel Patte. Nashville: Abingdon, 2004.

Sweeney, Marvin A. "Davidic Polemics in the Book of Judges." *VT* 47 (1997): 517–29.

———. *I and II Kings: A Commentary*. OTL. Louisville: Westminster John Knox, 2007.

———. "A Form-Critical Reassessment of the Book of Zephaniah." *CBQ* 53 (1991): 388–408.

———. "Structure, Genre and Intent in the Book of Habakkuk." *VT* 41 (1991): 63–83.

———. *TANAK: A Theological and Critical Introduction to the Jewish Bible*. Minneapolis: Fortress, 2012.

———. *The Twelve Prophets*. 2 vols. Berit Olam. Collegeville, MN: Liturgical Press, 2000.

———. *Zephaniah*. Hermeneia. Minneapolis: Fortress, 2003.

———. "Zephaniah." *OEBB* 2:471–74.

———. "Zephaniah: A Paradigm for the Study of the Prophetic Books." *CurRes* 7 (1999): 119–45.

Sylva, Dennis. *Psalms and the Transformation of Stress: Poetic-Communal Interpretation and the Family*. Louvain Theological and Pastoral Monographs 16. Louvain: Peeters; Grand Rapids: Eerdmans, 1993.

Tadmor, Hayim. "Autobiographical Apology in the Royal Assyrian Literature." Pages 36–57 in *History, Historiography, and Interpretation: Studies in Biblical and Cuneiform Literatures*. Edited by H. Tadmor and M. Weinfeld. Jerusalem: Magnes; Leiden: Brill, 1983.

Tadmor, Hayim, and Shigeo Yamada. *The Royal Inscriptions of Tiglath-pileser III (744–727 BC) and Shalmaneser V (726–722 BC), Kings of Assyria*. The Royal Inscriptions of the Neo-Assyrian Period 1. Winona Lake, IN: Eisenbrauns, 2010.

Talmon, Shemaryahu. "Ezra and Nehemiah." Pages 357–64 in *The Literary Guide to the Bible*. Edited by Robert Alter and Frank Kermode. Cambridge, MA: Harvard University Press, 1987.

Talshir, David. "A Reinvestigation of the Linguistic Relationship between Chronicles and Ezra–Nehemiah." *VT* 38 (1988): 165–93.

Tappy, Ron E., P. Kyle McCarter, Marilyn J. Lundberg, and Bruce Zuckerman. "An Abecedary of the Mid-Tenth Century BCE from the Judean Shephelah." *BASOR* 344 (2006): 5–46.

Terrien, Samuel. *The Elusive Presence: Toward a New Biblical Theology*. San Francisco: Harper & Row, 1978.

———. *The Psalms: Strophic Structure and Theological Commentary*. ECC. Grand Rapids: Eerdmans, 2003.

Thompson, John A. *Deuteronomy: An Introduction and Commentary*. TOTC. Leicester, UK: Inter-Varsity; Downers Grove, IL: InterVarsity, 1974.

Thompson, Thomas L. *Early History of the Israelite People: From the Written and Archaeological Sources*. SHANE 4. Leiden: Brill, 1992.

———. *The Historicity of the Patriarchal Narratives: The Quest for the Historical Abraham*. BZAW 221. Berlin: de Gruyter, 1974.

———. *The Messiah Myth: The Near Eastern Roots of Jesus and David*. New York: Basic Books, 2005.

———. *The Mythic Past: Biblical Archaeology and the Myth of Israel*. London: Basic Books, 1999.

———. "A Neo-Albrightian School in History and Biblical Scholarship?" *JBL* 114 (1995): 683–98.

Throntveit, Mark A. "Chronicles." Pages 124–31 in *Theological Interpretation of the Old Testament: A Book-by-Book Survey*. Edited by Kevin J. Vanhoozer, Craig G. Bartholomew, and Daniel J. Treier. London: SPCK; Grand Rapids: Baker Academic, 2008.

Tiemeyer, Lena-Sophia. "Feminist Interpretation." *DOTWPW* 205–18.

Tkacz, Catherine Brown. "A Biblical Woman's Paraphrase of King David: Susanna's Refusal of the Elders." *DRev* 450 (2010): 39–51.

Toorn, Karel van der. *Scribal Culture and the Making of the Hebrew Bible*. Cambridge, MA: Harvard University Press, 2007.

———. *Sin and Sanction in Ancient Mesopotamia: A Comparative Study*. SSN 25. Assen: Van Gorcum, 1985.

Torrey, Charles C. *Pseudo-Ezekiel and the Original Prophecy*. New Haven: Yale University Press, 1930.

Tov, Emanuel. "4QJosh[b]." Pages 205–12 in *Intertestamental Essays in Honour of Józef Tadeusz Milik*. Edited by Z. J. Kapera. Kraków: Enigma, 1992.

———. "The History and Significance of a Standard Text of the Hebrew Bible." Pages 49–66 in vol. 1 of *Hebrew Bible/Old Testament: The History of Its Interpretation*. Edited by M. Saebø. Göttingen: Vandenhoeck & Ruprecht, 1996.

———. *The Text-Critical Use of the Septuagint in Biblical Research*. 3rd. ed. Winona Lake, IN: Eisenbrauns, 2015.

———. *Textual Criticism of the Hebrew Bible*. 3rd ed. Minneapolis: Fortress, 2012.

Trible, Phyllis. "Love's Lyrics Redeemed." Pages 100–120 in *A Feminist Companion to the Song of Songs*. Edited by A. Brenner. FCB 1. Sheffield: Sheffield Academic, 1993.

Tsevat, Matitiahu. "The Meaning of the Book of Job." *HUCA* 37 (1966): 73–106.

Tsumura, David Toshio. *Creation and Destruction: A Reappraisal of the Chaoskampf Theory in the Old Testament*. Winona Lake, IN: Eisenbrauns, 2005.

———. "The Doctrine of Creation *ex nihilo* and the Translation of *tōhû wābōhû*." Pages 3–21 in *Pentateuchal Traditions in the Late Second Temple Period: Proceedings of the International Workshop in Tokyo, August 28–31, 2007*. Edited by Akio Moriya and Gohei Hata. Supplements to the Journal for the Study of Judaism 158. Leiden: Brill, 2012.

———. *The First Book of Samuel*. NICOT. Grand Rapids: Eerdmans, 2007.

Tuell, Steven. *Ezekiel*. NIBC. Peabody, MA: Hendrickson, 2009.

Ulrich, Eugene. "Daniel Manuscripts from Qumran: Part 2, Preliminary Editions of 4QDan[b] and 4QDan[c]." *BASOR* 274 (1989): 3–26.

———. "The Text of the Hebrew Scriptures at the Time of Hillel and Jesus." Pages 85–108 in *Congress Volume Basel 2001*. Edited by A. Lemaire. VTSup 92. Leiden: Brill, 2002.

Vanderhooft, David S. "Habakkuk." *OEBB* 1:351–57.

Van der Veen, Peter. "Sixth-Century Issues." Pages 383–405 in *Ancient Israel's History: An Introduction to Issues and Sources*. Edited by Bill T. Arnold and Richard S. Hess. Grand Rapids: Baker Academic, 2014.

Van Deventer, Hans. "Did Someone Say 'History'? In Africa We Say 'His Story'! A Study of African Biblical Hermeneutics with

Reference to the Book of Daniel." *OTE* 21 (2008): 713–28.

Van Keulen, Percy S. F. *Two Versions of the Solomon Narrative: An Inquiry into the Relationship between MT 1 Kgs. 2–11 and LXX 3 Reg. 2–11*. VTSup 104. Leiden: Brill, 2005.

Van Seters, John. *Abraham in History and Tradition*. New Haven: Yale University Press, 1975.

———. "The Deuteronomist from Joshua to Samuel." Pages 204–39 in *Reconsidering Israel and Judah: Recent Studies in the Deuteronomistic History*. Edited by Gary N. Knoppers and J. Gordon McConville. SBTS 8. Winona Lake, IN: Eisenbrauns, 2000.

———. *In Search of History: Historiography in the Ancient World and the Origins of Biblical History*. New Haven: Yale University Press, 1983.

———. "The Place of the Yahwist in the History of Passover and Massot." *ZAW* (1983): 167–82.

———. "Solomon's Temple: Fact and Ideology in Biblical and Near Eastern Iconography." *CBQ* 59 (1997): 45–57.

Van Wolde, Ellen. "Texts in Dialogue with Texts: Intertextuality in the Ruth and Tamar Narratives." *BibInt* 5 (1997): 1–28. Repr. pages 426–51 in *A Feminist Companion to Reading the Bible: Approaches, Methods and Strategies*. Edited by Athalya Brenner and Carole Fontaine. Sheffield: Sheffield Academic, 1997.

———. "Yāʿēl in Judges 4." *ZAW* 107 (1995): 240–46.

Vargon, Shmuel. "The Prayer for the Restoration of the Israelite Kingdom in the Book of Micah: Literary Analysis and Historical Background." Pages 597–618 in *Homeland and Exile: Biblical and Ancient Near Eastern Studies in Honour of Bustenay Oded*. Edited by Gershon Galil, Mark Geller, and Alan Millard. VTSup 130. Leiden: Brill, 2009.

Visotzky, Burton L. "Exodus in Rabbinic Interpretation." Pages 535–62 in *The Book of Exodus: Composition, Reception, and Interpretation*. Edited by Thomas B. Dozeman, Craig A. Evans, and Joel N. Lohr. VTSup 164. Leiden: Brill, 2014.

Viviers, Hendrik. "The Rhetoricity of the 'Body' in the Song of Songs." Pages 237–54 in *Rhetorical Criticism and the Bible*. Edited by S. E. Porter and D. L. Stamps. JSNTSup 195. New York: Sheffield Academic, 2002.

Vogt, Peter. *Deuteronomic Theology and the Significance of Torah: A Reappraisal*. Winona Lake, IN: Eisenbrauns, 2006.

Volz, Paul. *Das neujahrsfest jahwes (laubhüttenfest)*. Tübingen: J. C. B. Mohr (Paul Siebeck), 1912.

Waaler, Erik. "A Revised Date for Pentateuchal Texts? Evidence from Ketef Hinnom." *TynBul* 53 (2002): 29–55.

Wacker, Marie-Theres. "Malachi: To the Glory of God, the Father?" Translated by Tina Steiner. Pages 473–82 in *Feminist Biblical Interpretation: A Compendium of Critical Commentary on the Books of the Bible and Related Literature*. Edited by Luise Schottroff, Marie-Theres Wacker, and Martin Rumscheidt. Grand Rapids: Eerdmans, 2012.

Wahl, Harald-Martin. *Der gerechte Schöpfer: Eine redaktions- und theologiegeschichtliche Untersuchung der Elihureden—Hiob 32–37*. BZAW 207. Berlin: de Gruyter, 1993.

Walser, Georg A. *Jeremiah: A Commentary Based on Ieremias in Codex Vaticanus*. SCS. Leiden: Brill, 2012.

Walsh, Carey Ellen. *Exquisite Desire: Religion, the Erotic, and the Song of Songs*. Minneapolis: Fortress, 2000.

Waltke, Bruce K. *The Book of Proverbs*. Vol. 1, *1–15*. Vol. 2, *16–31*. NICOT. Grand Rapids: Eerdmans, 2004–5.

———. *A Commentary on Micah*. Grand Rapids: Eerdmans, 2007.

———. "Superscripts, Postscripts, or Both." *JBL* 110 (1991): 583–96.

Waltke, Bruce K., and David Diewert. "Wisdom Literature." Pages 295–328 in *The Face of Old Testament Studies: A Survey of Contemporary Approaches*. Edited by

David W. Baker and Bill T. Arnold. Grand Rapids: Baker, 1999.

Waltke, Bruce K., with Cathi J. Fredricks. *Genesis: A Commentary*. Grand Rapids: Zondervan, 2001.

Waltke, Bruce K., James M. Houston, and Erika Moore. *The Psalms as Christian Lament: A Historical Commentary*. Grand Rapids: Eerdmans, 2014.

Walton, John H. "Job 1: Book of." *DOTWPW* 333–46.

———. "Jonah." *ZIBBCOT* 5:100–119.

Warning, Wilfried. *Literary Artistry in Leviticus*. Biblical Interpretation Series 35. Leiden: Brill, 1999.

Washington, Harold C. *Wealth and Poverty in the Instruction of Amenemope and the Hebrew Proverbs*. SBLDS 142. Atlanta: Scholars Press, 1994.

Watson, Francis. *Text, Church, and World: Biblical Interpretation in Theological Perspective*. Grand Rapids: Eerdmans, 1994.

Watson, Wilfred G. E. *Classical Hebrew Poetry: A Guide to Its Techniques*. JSOTSup 29. Sheffield: JSOT Press, 1986.

Watts, James W. *Reading the Law: The Rhetorical Shaping of the Pentateuch*. Biblical Seminar 59. Sheffield: Sheffield Academic, 1999.

Watts, John D. W. *Isaiah*. Vol. 1, *1–33*. Vol. 2, *34–66*. Rev. ed. WBC 24–25. Nashville: Nelson, 2005.

———. *Joel, Obadiah, Jonah, Nahum, Habakkuk, and Zephaniah*. CBC. Cambridge: Cambridge University Press, 1975.

Watts, Rikki E. *Isaiah's New Exodus and Mark*. WUNT 2/88. Tübingen: Mohr Siebeck, 1994.

Webb, Barry G. *The Book of Judges*. NICOT. Grand Rapids: Eerdmans, 2012.

———. *The Book of Judges: An Integrated Reading*. JSOTSup 46. Sheffield: JSOT Press, 1987.

———. *The Message of Isaiah*. Downers Grove, IL: InterVarsity, 1996.

———. "The Song of Songs: Garment of Love." Pages 17–35 in *Five Festal Garments: Christian Reflections on the Song of Songs, Ruth, Lamentations, Ecclesiastes and Esther*. Edited by Barry G. Webb. NSBT. Downers Grove, IL: InterVarsity, 2000.

———. "Zion in Transformation." Pages 65–84 in *The Bible in Three Dimensions: Essays in Celebration of Forty Years of Biblical Studies in the University of Sheffield*. Edited by David J. A. Clines, Stephen E. Fowl, and Stanley E. Porter. JSOTSup 87. Sheffield: JSOT Press, 1990.

Weber, Beat. "An dem Tag, als JHWH ihn rettete aus der Hand aller seinder Feinde und aus der Hand Sauls (Ps. 18,1)." *VT* 64 (2014): 284–304.

———. "Toward a Theory of the Poetry of the Hebrew Bible: The Poetry of the Psalms as a Test Case." *BBR* 22 (2012): 157–89.

———. "Zum sogenannten 'Stimmungsumschwung' in Psalm 13." Pages 116–38 in *The Book of Psalms: Composition and Reception*. Edited by Peter W. Flint and Patrick D. Miller. VTSup 99. Leiden: Brill, 2005.

Weeks, Stuart. *Early Israelite Wisdom*. Oxford Theological Monographs. Oxford: Clarendon, 1994.

Wegner, Paul D. *The Journey from Texts to Translations: The Origin and Development of the Bible*. Grand Rapids: Baker Academic, 1999.

Weigl, Michael. "Current Research on the Book of Nahum: Exegetical Methodologies in Turmoil?" *CurRes* 9 (2001): 81–130.

Weinfeld, Moshe. *Deuteronomy and the Deuteronomic School*. Oxford: Clarendon, 1972.

———. *The Place of the Law in the Religion of Ancient Israel*. VTSup 100. Formation and Interpretation of Old Testament Literature 4. Leiden: Brill, 2004.

———. *The Promise of the Land: The Inheritance of the Land of Canaan by the Israelites*. The Taubman Lectures in Jewish Studies. Berkeley: University of California Press, 1993.

Weiser, Artur. *The Psalms: A Commentary*. Translated by H. Hartwell. London: SCM, 1962.

Wellhausen, Julius. *Der Text der Bücher Samuelis untersucht*. Göttingen: Vandenhoeck & Ruprecht, 1871.

———. *Die kleinen Propheten übersetzt und erklärt*, vol. 3. Berlin: G. Reimer, 1898.

———. *Prolegomena to the History of Ancient Israel*. Translated from the 1878 German original by J. Sutherland Black and Allan Menzies. 1885. Repr., Gloucester, MA: Peter Smith, 1973.

Wells, Bruce. "The Covenant Code and Near Eastern Legal Traditions: A Response to David P. Wright." *Ma* 13 (2006): 85–118.

Wenham, Gordon J. *The Book of Leviticus*. NICOT. Grand Rapids: Eerdmans, 1979.

———. "Family in the Pentateuch." Pages 17–31 in *Family in the Bible*. Edited by R. S. Hess and M. D. Carroll R. Grand Rapids: Baker Academic, 2003.

———. *Genesis*. Vol. 1, *1–15*. Vol. 2, *16–50*. WBC 1–2. Waco: Word, 1987–94.

———. *Numbers*. OTG. Sheffield: Sheffield Academic, 1997.

———. *Numbers: An Introduction and Commentary*. TOTC. Leicester, UK: Inter-Varsity; Downers Grove, IL: InterVarsity, 1981.

———. *Psalms as Torah: Reading Biblical Song Ethically*. Studies in Theological Interpretation. Grand Rapids: Baker Academic, 2012.

———. "The Theology of Old Testament Sacrifice." Pages 75–87 in *Sacrifice in the Bible*. Edited by Roger T. Beckwith and Marvin J. Selman. Carlisle, UK: Paternoster; Grand Rapids: Baker, 1995.

Wernik, Uri. "Will the Real Homosexual in the Bible Please Stand Up?" *Theology and Sexuality* 11 (2005): 47–64.

Wesley, John. *Explanatory Notes upon the Old Testament*. 3 vols. Bristol: William Pine, 1765.

Wessels, Wilhelm J. "Nahum: An Uneasy Expression of Yahweh's Power." *OTE* 11 (1998): 615–28.

West, Gerald. "1 and 2 Samuel." Pages 92–104 in *Global Bible Commentary*. Edited by Daniel Patte. Nashville: Abingdon, 2004.

West, Martin L. *The Hesiodic Catalogue of Women: Its Nature, Structure, and Origins*. Oxford: Oxford University Press, 1985.

Westbrook, Raymond. "Adultery in Ancient Near Eastern Law." *RB* 97 (1990): 542–80.

———. "Biblical and Cuneiform Law Codes." *RB* 92 (1985): 247–64.

Westermann, Claus. *Anthropology and the Old Testament*. Philadelphia: Fortress, 1981.

———. *Praise and Lament in the Psalms*. Atlanta: John Knox, 1981.

———. *Roots of Wisdom*. Edinburgh: T&T Clark, 1995. Translation of *Wurzeln der Weisheit*. Göttingen: Vandenhoeck & Ruprecht, 1990.

Wetzstein, Johann G. "Die syrische Dreschtafel." *Zeitschrift für Ethnologie* 5 (1873): 270–302.

Weyde, Karl William. *Prophecy and Teaching: Prophetic Authority, Form Problems, and the Use of Tradition in the Book of Malachi*. BZAW 288. Berlin: de Gruyter, 2000.

White, John B. *A Study of the Language of Love in the Song of Songs and Ancient Egyptian Poetry*. SBLDS 38. Missoula, MT: Scholars Press, 1978.

White, Sidnie A. [= Crawford, Sidnie White]. "The All Souls Deuteronomy and the Decalogue." *JBL* 109 (1990): 193–206.

———. "Esther: A Feminine Model for Jewish Diaspora?" Pages 161–77 in *Gender and Difference in Ancient Israel*. Edited by P. L. Day. Minneapolis: Fortress, 1989.

Whitelam, Keith W. *The Invention of Ancient Israel: The Silencing of Palestinian History*. New York: Routledge, 1996.

Whybray, R. Norman. *The Composition of the Book of Proverbs*. JSOTSup 168. Sheffield: JSOT Press, 1994.

———. *The Intellectual Tradition of the Old Testament*. BZAW 135. Berlin: de Gruyter, 1974.

———. "Qoheleth, Preacher of Joy." *JSOT* 23 (1982): 87–98.

———. *The Succession Narrative: A Study of II Samuel 9–20 and I Kings 1 and 2*. SBT 9. Naperville, IL: Allenson, 1968.

———. "Yahweh-Sayings and Their Contexts in Proverbs 10,1–22,16." Pages 153–65 and 411–12 in *La sagesse de l'Ancien Testament*. Edited by Maurice Gilbert. Rev. ed. BETL 51. Leuven: Peeters, 1990.

Wilken, Robert Louis, Angela R. Christman, and Michael J. Hollerich. *Isaiah Interpreted by Early Christian and Medieval Commentators*. The Church's Bible. Grand Rapids: Eerdmans, 2007.

Williamson, Hugh G. M. *The Book Called Isaiah: Deutero-Isaiah's Role in Composition and Redaction*. Oxford: Clarendon, 1994.

———. *Ezra and Nehemiah*. OTG. Sheffield: JSOT Press, 1987.

———. "Ezra and Nehemiah in the Light of the Texts from Persepolis." *BBR* 1 (1991): 41–61.

———. *Ezra–Nehemiah*. WBC 16. Waco: Word, 1985.

———. *1 and 2 Chronicles*. NCB. Grand Rapids: Eerdmans, 1982.

———. "The Governors of Judah under the Persians." *TynBul* 39 (1988): 59–82.

———. *Isaiah 1–5*. Vol. 1 of *A Critical and Exegetical Commentary on Isaiah 1–27*. ICC. London: T&T Clark, 2006.

———. *Israel in the Books of Chronicles*. Cambridge: Cambridge University Press, 1977.

Wilson, Gerald Henry. *The Editing of the Hebrew Psalter*. SBLDS 76. Atlanta: Scholars Press, 1985.

———. "King, Messiah, and the Reign of God: Revisiting the Royal Psalms and the Shape of the Psalter." Pages 391–406 in *The Book of Psalms: Composition and Reception*. Edited by Peter W. Flint and Patrick D. Miller. VTSup 99. Leiden: Brill, 2005.

Winther-Nielsen, Nicolai. "Fact, Fiction, and Language Use: Can Modern Pragmatics Improve on Halpern's Case for History in Judges?" Pages 44–81 in *Windows into Old Testament History: Evidence, Argument, and the Crisis of "Biblical Israel."* Edited by V. Philips Long, David W. Baker, and Gordon J. Wenham. Grand Rapids: Eerdmans, 2002.

———. *A Functional Discourse Grammar of Joshua: A Computer-Assisted Rhetorical Structure Analysis*. CB 40. Stockholm: Almqvist & Wiksell, 1995.

Wiseman, Donald J. *Notes on Some Problems in the Book of Daniel*. Edited by Donald J. Wiseman et al. London: Tyndale, 1965.

———. "Rahab of Jericho." *TynBul* 14 (1964): 8–11.

———. "Some Historical Problems in the Book of Daniel: A. Darius the Mede." Pages 9–16 in *Notes on Some Problems in the Book of Daniel*. Edited by Donald J. Wiseman et al. London: Tyndale, 1965.

Wolf, Herbert. *The Apology of Ḫattušiliš Compared with Other Political Self-Justifications of the Ancient Near East*. Repr. of PhD diss., Brandeis University, 1967. Ann Arbor: University Microfilms, 1967.

Wolff, Hans Walter. *Haggai: A Commentary*. Translated by Margaret Kohl. ConC. Minneapolis: Augsburg, 1988.

———. *Hosea: A Commentary on the Book of the Prophet Hosea*. Translated by G. Stanstell. Hermeneia. Philadelphia: Westminster, 1974.

———. *Joel and Amos: A Commentary on the Books of the Prophets Joel and Amos*. Translated by W. Janzen, S. D. McBride Jr., and C. A. Munchow. Hermeneia. Philadelphia: Fortress, 1977.

———. "The Kerygma of the Deuteronomic Historical Work." Pages 83–100 in *The Vitality of Old Testament Traditions*. Edited and translated by W. Brueggemann and H. W. Wolff. Atlanta: John Knox, 1972.

———. *Obadiah and Jonah*. Translated by Margaret Kohl. Hermeneia. Minneapolis: Augsburg, 1988.

Wolters, Al. *Zechariah*. HCOT. Leiden: Peeters, 2014.

———. "Zechariah 14 and Biblical Theology: Patristic and Contemporary Case Studies." Pages 261–85 in *Out of Egypt: Biblical Theology and Theological Interpretation*. Edited by Craig Bartholomew, Mary Healy, Karl Möler, and Robin Parry. Scriptures and Hermeneutics Series 5. Milton Keynes, UK: Paternoster, 2004.

Wong, Fook-Kong. "1 and 2 Chronicles." Pages 119–26 in *Global Bible Commentary*. Edited by Daniel Patte. Nashville: Abingdon, 2004.

Wray Beal, Lissa. "Psalms 3: History of Interpretation." *DOTWPW* 605–13.

Wright, Christopher J. H. *Deuteronomy*. NIBC. Peabody, MA: Hendrickson, 1996.

———. *The Mission of God's People: A Biblical Theology of the Church's Mission.* Biblical Theology for Life. Grand Rapids: Zondervan, 2010.

Wright, David P. *Inventing God's Law: How the Covenant Code of the Bible Used and Revised the Laws of Hammurabi.* Oxford: Oxford University Press, 2009.

———. "The Laws of Hammurabi as a Source for the Covenant Collection (Exodus 20:23–23:19)." *Ma* 10 (2003): 11–87.

Wright, N. T. *Justification: God's Plan and Paul's Vision.* Downers Grove, IL: IVP Academic, 2009.

Würthwein, Ernst. *The Text of the Old Testament.* Revised and expanded by A. A. Fischer. Translated by E. F. Rhodes. 3rd ed. Grand Rapids: Eerdmans, 2014.

Yadin, Yigael. "The Army Reserves of David and Solomon." Pages 350–61 in *The Military History of the Land of Israel in Biblical Times.* Edited by J. Liver. Tel Aviv: Israel Defense Forces Publishing House, 1973.

Yamauchi, Edwin. "Ezra and Nehemiah, Books of." *DOTHB* 284–95.

Yardeni, Ada. "Further Observations on the Ostracon." Pages 259–60 in *Excavation Report 2007–2008*. Vol. 1 of *Khirbet Qeiyafa*. Edited by Yosef Garfinkel and Saar Ganor. Jerusalem: Israel Exploration Society and Institute of Archaeology, Hebrew University of Jerusalem, 2009.

Yee, Gale A. *Composition and Tradition in the Book of Hosea: A Redaction Critical Investigation.* SBLDS 102. Atlanta: Scholars Press, 1987.

Young, Ian, ed. *Biblical Hebrew: Studies in Chronology and Typology.* JSOTSup 369. New York: T&T Clark, 2003.

Younger, K. Lawson, Jr. *Ancient Conquest Accounts: A Study in Ancient Near Eastern and Biblical History Writing.* JSOTSup 98. Sheffield: Sheffield Academic, 1990.

———. "The Fall of Samaria in the Light of Recent Research." *CBQ* 61 (1999): 461–82.

———. *Judges and Ruth.* NIVAC. Grand Rapids: Zondervan, 2002.

———. "The Late Bronze Age/Iron Age Transition and the Origins of the Arameans." Pages 131–74 in *Ugarit at Seventy-Five.* Edited by K. Lawson Younger Jr. Winona Lake, IN: Eisenbrauns, 2007.

Zadok, Ran. *The Pre-Hellenistic Israelite Anthroponymy and Prosopography.* OLA 28. Leuven: Peeters, 1988.

Zaharopoulos, D. Z. *Theodore of Mopsuestia: A Study of His Old Testament Exegesis.* New York: Paulist Press, 1989.

Zehnder, Markus. "Building on Stone? Deuteronomy and Esarhaddon's Loyalty Oaths: I, Some Preliminary Observations." *BBR* 19 (2009): 341–74.

———. "Building on Stone? Deuteronomy and Esarhaddon's Loyalty Oaths: II, Some Additional Observations." *BBR* 19 (2009): 511–35.

Zenger, Erich. "Theophanien des Königsgottes JHWH: Transformationen von Psalm 29 in den Teilkompositionen Ps 28–30 und Ps 93–100." Pages 407–42 in *The Book of Psalms: Composition and Reception.* Edited by Peter W. Flint and Patrick D. Miller. VTSup 99. Leiden: Brill, 2005.

Zevit, Ziony. *The Religions of Ancient Israel: A Parallactic Approach.* New York: Continuum, 2001.

Zimmerli, Walther. *Ezekiel.* Vol. 1, *1–24.* Vol. 2, *25–48.* Hermeneia. Philadelphia: Fortress, 1979–83.

Zinkuratire, Victor. "Isaiah 1–39." Pages 186–94 in *Global Bible Commentary.* Edited by Daniel Patte. Nashville: Abingdon, 2004.

ANCIENT WRITINGS INDEX

SCRIPTURE INDEX

Old Testament

Genesis

Exodus

Leviticus

Numbers

Deuteronomy

2 Kings

1 Chronicles

2 Chronicles

Ezra

Nehemiah

Esther

Job

Psalms

Proverbs

Ecclesiastes

Song of Songs

Isaiah

Jeremiah

Lamentations

Ezekiel

Daniel

Hosea

Obadiah

Jonah

Micah

Nahum

Malachi

Apocrypha

Bel and the Dragon

1 Esdras

2 Esdras

1 Maccabees

2 Maccabees

Psalm 151

Sirach

Tobit

New Testament

Matthew

SUBJECT INDEX

Textbook eSources

course help for professors and study aids for students

Baker Academic

offers free online materials for this book to professors and students. These resources may include test banks, videos from the author, flash cards, or other resources.

◆ ◆ ◆

VISIT

www.bakeracademic.com/professors.